Fourth Edition

PSYCHOLOGY

Principles and Applications

Stephen Worchel

Wayne Shebilske

Texas A & M University

PRENTICE HALL, Englewood Cliffs, New Jersey 07632

Library of Congress Cataloging-in-Publication Data

Worchel, Stephen.
    Psychology : principles and applications / Stephen Worchel, Wayne
Shebilske. —4th ed.
        p. cm
    Includes bibliographical references and indexes.
    ISBN 0–13–735150—X
    1. Psychology.   2. Psychology, Applied.   I. Shebilske, Wayne.
II. Title.
BF121.W66 1992
150—dc20   91–31541
                                                        CIP

To some people whose support, understanding, and patience have
helped us appreciate and value learning about others: our parents—
Phil and Libby, Larry and Eileen; our siblings—Harvey and Jason,
Sheila, Gary, Steve, Kevin, Mark, and Mike; our wives—
Frances, Ann; and our children—Leah, Jessica, Hannah, and Elise,
Sherry, Lisa, and Laurie.

ACQUISITIONS EDITOR: Charlyce Jones Owen
DEVELOPMENT EDITOR: Susanna Lesan
PRODUCTION EDITOR: Serena Hoffman
PREPRESS BUYER: Kelly Behr
MANUFACTURING BUYER: Mary Ann Gloriande
MARKETING MANAGER: Tracy McPeake
SUPPLEMENTS EDITOR: Sharon Chambliss
COPY EDITOR: Carol Freddo
BOOK DESIGN: Lee Goldstein
PHOTO EDITOR: Lorinda Morris-Nantz
PHOTO RESEARCH: June Lundberg Whitworth
ASSOCIATE ART DIRECTOR: Florence D. Silverman
COVER DESIGN: Lee Goldstein
COVER PHOTO: Mark Tomalty/Masterfile

*Acknowledgments appear on pp. 769–770, which constitute
a continuation of the copyright page.*

 © 1992, 1989, 1986, 1983 by Prentice-Hall, Inc.
A Simon & Schuster Company
Englewood Cliffs, New Jersey 07632

Printed in the United States of America

10 9 8 7 6 5 4 3 2 1

ISBN 0-13-735150-X

Prentice-Hall International (UK) Limited, *London*
Prentice-Hall of Australia Pty. Limited, *Sydney*
Prentice-Hall Canada Inc., *Toronto*
Prentice-Hall Hispanoamericana, S.A., *Mexico*
Prentice-Hall of India Private Limited, *New Delhi*
Prentice-Hall of Japan, Inc., *Tokyo*
Simon & Schuster Asia Pte. Ltd., *Singapore*
Editora Prentice-Hall do Brasil, Ltda., *Rio de Janeiro*

Contents

3   Sensation   81

4   Perception   121

5 Alternate States of Consciousness   149

6 Learning   191

7 Memory and Cognition 227

8 Language, Thought, and Intelligence 267

12   Emotions, Stress, and Coping   429

13   Personality: Theories and Assessment   475

14   Abnormal Psychology   521

17 The Individual in Groups

Preface

We have been writing or revising this text for over a decade. In a sense, it has become almost a member of our families. This long and close relationship has made each revision an interesting experience. Given the opportunity every three years, how would you change or reshape one of your family members? In some revisions, our work was guided by significant new studies or the development of new subareas of study. Taking this approach led us to examine each broad area of psychology, asking "What's new?" in that area. Then we connected the areas by looking for common links, much like building a house, room by room.

In this revision, we have taken a somewhat different approach. We began by identifying new themes or currents that have shaped the broad field of psychology over the last decade. We wanted to take a more general look at the field and build the walls of the house before focusing on the rooms. This was an interesting exercise, but we were able to see some issues that cut across areas and charted the direction for psychology in the 90s. One such issue was an increasing sensitivity to the role of culture in influencing behavior. Psychology is taking a global view. Not only is there more cross-cultural research, but there is also greater recognition of the research and theory developed outside the United States. A second issue that crosses areas involves gender and race. Research takes these variables into account, and theory attempts to explain why they influence behavior. Third, the relationship between psychological factors and physical health is of interest to psychologists in many areas of study. While some of the linkages are obvious, others, such as the role of psychology in hearing and vision disorders, may not be so quickly recognized. Finally, psychology has become an increasingly "public" discipline. The discipline deals with topics that are of interest and importance to the general public. The popular media have been quick to recognize this fact, and psychology has become a frequent topic of discussion on radio, television, and the press.

Features of the Fourth Edition

In this edition, we have let these and other general currents drive our writing. While we have been diligent in bringing all material up-to-date (with over 500 new references), our handiwork has involved broader brush strokes. We've increased our coverage of such general themes as culture, gender, health, and application in each chapter. We've made these issues more salient through new *Highlight* sections in each chapter. At the conclusion of each chapter,

we have chosen a relevant and interesting example of the treatment of psychology in the media—articles taken from one of the more widely read U.S. newspapers, *The New York Times*. Finally, in keeping with our desire to weave general themes throughout chapters rather than chop them up into separate and isolated sections, we removed the chapter on the environment, dealing instead with environmental issues in each of the chapters. Our hope is to demonstrate that these issues are not the domain of any single area, but that they are vital to all areas of psychology.

A major renovation took place in the organization of Chapter 8 (Language, Thought, and Intelligence) to make connections between those who seek general principles and those who study individual differences by explaining how both approaches are modeling mental processes of the ways we use language, think, and act intelligently. We also expanded our coverage of other "intelligences," including those that underlie music, art, and athletics, and we explored group differences in scores on intelligence tests across gender, race, and culture.

Beyond these major changes, we included new areas of research in each chapter. For example, we examined issues of group and member development and minority influence in Chapter 17. We examined the influence of anabolic steroids on health and behavior in Chapter 2. And in Chapter 11, we expanded our coverage of violence to include the influence of pornography and a statement about global warfare.

Learning Aids

We have continued to seek ways to improve our book as a tool for learning material that is often difficult for even the most well-prepared students. Disorientation in learning from textbooks is often attributed to weak students, but we believe that even strong students benefit from well-placed "you-are-here" maps, so when our readers enter a new chapter, they are given "maps" in the form of an outline, objectives, introductory incident, and a section on history and scope. As they leave a chapter, they receive a summary to help them remember where they have been. In addition, as they go through the chapter, they are continually referred back to the introductory incident to help them keep their bearings. These introductory incidents have always been a strong point of the text; through the years we have enjoyed the feedback from students who say that the incidents made reading the text enjoyable and easier to learn from.

The chapters are clearly divided into sections, with each section focusing on a particular issue. Figures, tables, and illustrations are used to highlight important points. Key terms appear in bold type the first time they are used, and a definition is given in the margin. The terms are listed at the end of each chapter and are repeated in bold type in the summary. The glossary at the end of the book serves as a review of main terms used in the field of psychology.

Finally, we explicitly show how psychological principles can be applied to learning from textbooks. In Chapter 1, we devote a lengthy box to this topic, and in Chapter 7 we examine ways to increase reading speed without sacrificing comprehension.

Supplements

This text is the core of a *complete learning package* that includes a wide range of proven instructional aids as well as many new ones. The list of supplements has been greatly expanded in this edition to respond to the needs of students and instructors.

For the Instructor

Instructor's Resource Manual. This exceptional resource provides a detailed description of the supplements available for each chapter: chapter outlines; learning objectives; activities; questions for writing and discussion; visual, software, and audio resources; and in-class demonstrations. It is an excellent tool for organizing the psychology classroom, planning lectures, inspiring student learning, enriching classroom presentations, and preparing assignments.

The Integrator. This unique supplement is a computerized version of the *Instructor's Resource Manual*. The program allows instructors to coordinate chapter resources by computer. For IBM PCs.

Teaching Psychology: A Guide for the New Instructor. This unique guide offers a wealth of practical advice and information to help new instructors face the challenges of teaching psychology. From setting course goals, conducting the class, constructing and evaluating tests or written assignments, to advising students, many of the issues and questions related to teaching are covered. An annotated bibliography on teaching and on the various subfields of the discipline, plus actual articles on current trends in teaching in the psychology classroom, make this a useful resource for instructors of all levels of experience.

Test Item File. Available in both printed and computerized form, the test bank contains over 2000 multiple-choice and true-false questions keyed by text page reference, learning objective, type of question, and correct answer.

Core Test Item File. An additional test bank of approximately 1000 *class-tested* items is organized by major topics and accompanied by item analysis and percentage of responses to each alternative.

TestManager. This computerized test bank contains the items from the *Test Item File* and the *Core Test Item File*. It allows full editing of all questions and answers and adding instructor-generated items. Other special features include creating tests by item number or randomly, previewing tests before printing, scrambling question order, and providing content-specific help screens.

GradeManager. Our gradebook/class file program allows the professor to add an unlimited number of students and classes, include complete student information, calculate final grades based on instructor's criteria, display and print grade-point averages as either letters or numbers, curve test grades, display performance graphs for each student and/or test, and print test grades or final grades for posting.

Telephone Testing Service. Instructors using *Psychology* are eligible to use an innovative testing service when time and resources are short. Prentice Hall offers a telephone test preparation service through which instructors call a special toll-free number and select up to 200 questions from the printed test item files available with the text. The test and an alternate version (if requested) are mailed within 48 hours, ready for duplication.

Transparencies/Slides—Series II. A set of 120 one-, two-, and four-color illustrations is available in either transparency or slide format. Descriptions of and suggestions for using each illustration are included in the *Instructor's Resource Manual*.

Handout and Transparency Masters II. Over thirty additional visual resources—reproduceable as handouts, transparencies, or both—emphasize application of key topics discussed in the text.

Laserdisk for Introductory Psychology. The story of psychology will truly come alive with this exciting technology in the classroom. The two-sided disk contains approximately 500 illustrations and 60 minutes of video material supporting the concepts in the text. An accompanying manual provides bar codes for accessing the visuals and information for integrating the visuals into lectures and classroom activities.

ABC News/Prentice Hall Video Library for Introductory Psychology. Prentice Hall and ABC News bring the most innovative video ancillary available to the psychology classroom. This customized library brings to life chapter concepts by applying them to today's most interesting topics and pressing issues. The library consists of feature segments from such award-winning programs as *Nightline*, *20/20*, and *American Agenda*.

Prentice Hall Video Library. In addition to the special segments included in the customized ABC News videos, Prentice Hall is pleased to offer a wide selection of commercial videos to reinforce the text. Over 50 individual videos—in either $\frac{1}{2}''$ VHS, $\frac{1}{2}''$ BETA, or $\frac{3}{4}''$ formats—include such quality programs as *NOVA*, *The Brain* series, *The Mind* series, and *Discovering Psychology*. Up to five individual videos are available per adoption, depending on the number of texts ordered.

For the Student

Study Guide. This study manual begins with an overview of reading and study techniques that provides a foundation for effectively studying chapter content. For each chapter, the manual features learning objectives, pre- and post-tests on chapter content, a critical thinking project, and key-term review. Each chapter includes a special project, some of which are keyed to the ABC News Video for that chapter. A unique chapter discusses how to write research papers in psychology, focusing on types of papers, taking notes, library research, and documentation. A brief sample paper illustrates the APA documentation style. Saleable item to the student.

StudyManager. Our computerized study program for the student, which contains objective questions from the accompanying *Study Guide*, generates random quizzes, provides text page references, prints the corrected quiz for further study or for submission to the instructor.

A Guide to the Brain: A Graphic Workbook, 2E. This study aid reinforces text coverage of the important structures and functions of the brain and the nervous system. Using additional illustrations and figures, students can strengthen their understanding of the difficult concepts related to the brain; this new edition includes expanded figures and illustrations. Answers to exercises are included in the back of the booklet.

Forty Studies That Changed Psychology (Hock). This paperback is an ideal supplement for an introductory psychology text. It presents forty of the pivotal and influential studies in psychology that had far-reaching impact on the discipline. Each chapter focuses on a subfield of the discipline and includes two or more of the important studies pertinent to the area. The format, consistent in each chapter, includes complete background about the impetus for the study, theoretical propositions upon which the research is based, research methodology used, summary of the results, and the significance of the study to the field. In addition, a brief discussion of the enduring nature of the findings and subsequent questioning or criticism from others in the field gives students a full understanding of the past and continued influence of these studies. Saleable item to the student.

Critical Thinking Audiocassette. A 60-minute cassette shows students how developing their critical thinking and study skills will improve reading, listening, writing, note taking, test performance, job preparation, job performance. The first 50 minutes concentrate on critical thinking skills, specifically on how to ask the right questions. The final 10 minutes offer helpful tips on how to study, take notes, and be a more active, effective learner. Free to instructor.

Customized Reader. This reader, produced in association with Ginn Press Publishing, allows instructors to tailor their own special collection of supplementary readings to accompany our text. By choosing from a list of over 100 articles from journals, newspapers, and other popular sources, instructors can expose students to the results of actual research studies and to applications of psychology. The readings are made available in textbook format. Saleable item to the student.

The Contemporary View Program. A complimentary newspaper supplement containing recent articles from *The New York Times* pertinent to the field of psychology. These articles help expand students' knowledge beyond the classroom and into the world. Instructors using *Psychology* will also receive a complimentary one-semester subscription to *The New York Times*. Special reduced rates are also available for students who wish to subscribe. Free in quantity to the student.

Psychology on a Disk and Activities Software. Two computer programs provide brief and entertaining interactive experiments and activities that show how psychology works and, by using the student as the subject of the experiment, teach students about their own behavior. Most of the exercises can be completed in 15 to 20 minutes and include such topics as guilt detection, optical illusions, limits of memory, behavior modification, effects of prejudice, and more. *Psychology on a Disk* is available for IBM and Apple; *Activities Software* is available for IBM and Macintosh. Free to instructor with site licensing.

Acknowledgments

And now the newest member of our family is ready to make its debut. While the ultimate responsibility for this edition remains with us, we must acknowledge the significant and important help we had in all stages of the work. Dr. William Webb played a vital role not only in giving us suggestions for revision, but also in taking part in the actual revision of Chapters 13, 14, and 15. Our colleague and friend, Margaret Norris, was particularly gracious in helping with the sections on aging. Frances Worchel, Associate Professor in Educational Psychology, was most helpful in bringing us up to date on work in clinical, child, and psychotherapy. Several other colleagues and friends made insightful suggestions on the manuscript and brought new material to our attention. Included in this group are Dawna Coutant-Sassic, Judy Ouellette, Bill Graziano, and Kurt Riem. We'd also like to acknowledge the clerical help of Liz Stanton and Mary Ann Urbanovsky, who patiently dealt with frantic authors.

In addition, we want to thank a host of talented and patient but persistent folks at Prentice Hall who chaperoned the project from beginning to end. Charlyce Jones Owen, Editor-in-Chief, used a creative literary eye along with a gentle but firm hand to help us plan and execute the revision. Susanna Lesan, an old hand at dealing with us, was our Development Editor, confidant, friend, benign adversary, partner, and task master. Her expertise, wrapped with a wonderful coating of humor, often "saved the day." Serena Hoffman, Production Editor, worked at a furious pace to keep the book on schedule and the authors out of hot water. And Tracey McPeake, Marketing Manager, was not only in charge of getting the word out, but her suggestions also helped steer the revision. Thanks to all of you for your help and your work!

One of the most important parts of our team was the reviewers. Their efforts and help were tremendous—not only did they help shape the manuscript, but they taught us a great deal about psychology. Although they often reigned as anonymous critics, their help and guidance were much needed and greatly appreciated. The reviewers include:

Robert F. Ahlering, Central Missouri State University
Robert S. Anwyl, Director, Institute for Applied Research, Miami Dade Community College—North Campus
Gladys J. Baez-Dickreiter, St. Philips College
David J. Bailey, Community College of Allegheny County
David Barkmeier, Northeastern University
Les Beach, Hope College
Marsha K. Beauchamp, Mt. San Antonio College
Allison L. Burns, Pacific University
Dennis Carmody, St. Peter's College
D. Bruce Carter, Syracuse University
Charles Carver, University of Miami
Karen Christoff, University of Mississippi
Charles E. Clifton, University of Massachusetts—Amherst
Richard Comstock, Monroe Community College
Helen Crawford, The University of Wyoming
James Doyle, Roane State Community College

Karen Duffy, State University College of New York at
  Geneseo
William Edell, University of Massachusetts
Irene Hanson Frieze, University of Pittsburgh
Peter Gordon, Harvard University
William C. Gordon, University of New Mexico
Leonard Hamilton, Rutgers—The State University
Donald B. Helms, Mitchell College
Therese Herman-Sissons, Montclair State College
Jan Heyn, Roanoke College
William A. Johnston, University of Utah
Marilyn S. Leftwich, Fort Lewis College
Robert J. Lueger, Marquette University
David G. McDonald, University of Missouri-Columbia
Gil Meyer, Illinois Valley Community College
Richard Miller, Western Kentucky University
Peggy Nash, Broward Community College
Elaine Nocks, Furman University
Michael O'Boyle, Iowa State University
Paul Olczak, State University College of New York at
  Geneseo
Pat Patterson, DeVry Institute of Technology
Sharyl Peterson, St. Norbert College
John Pittenger, University of Arkansas at Little Rock
Antonio E. Puente, University of North Carolina at
  Wilmington
Howard Reid, State University College—Buffalo
David Richards, John Tyler Community College
Edward J. Rinalducci, University of Central Florida

Ann Marie Scheerbaum, Michigan State University
Nicholas Rohrman, Colby College
Richard Schiffman, Rutgers—The State University
Jack Shilkret, Anne Arundel Community College
R. Lance Shotland, The Pennsylvania State University
Charles Slem, California Polytechnic State University
Steven M. Smith, Texas A & M University
Anne E. Thompson, Harvard Graduate School of
  Education
Dr. Evelyn Tracy
Ishmael Stagner, Brigham Young University—Hawaii
Robert Welch, University of Kansas
Jeremy Wolfe, Massachusetts Institute of Technology

Finally, we would like to express our generally unspoken appreciation to our families. Frances and Ann not only offered constant encouragement, listened patiently to our anguished bellowing, ran the households while we frantically wrote "just one more page," and helped create a working environment; they also served as our most compassionate critics and confidants, helped gather material for the book, and offered invaluable suggestions. Our children—Leah, Jessica, Sherry, Lisa, Laurie, Hannah, and Elise—too often, but with good cheer, took a back seat to "the book." Your encouragement, your smiles, and your understanding sustained us. Thanks.

Stephen Worchel
Wayne Shebilske

Introduction

On September 28, 1976, the host of a morning radio show in Texas opened with a sad announcement:

"A bit of the twinkle in the eyes of Texas is missing today. Hondo Crouch died yesterday. Hondo was widely known as the mayor of Luckenbach, Texas. He was also the owner of Luckenbach and the chief of police and the city manager. Hondo put Luckenbach on the world's map. He held a world's fair there. Recording artists made their albums there. Chili cookoffs, tobacco-spitting contests, cow-chip throwing competitions, and no-talent shows were staged there. But mainly Hondo Crouch was there. He was the village attraction." (Patterson, 1979, p. 223)

This is an unusual eulogy about an unusual man. Nothing was really special about Hondo Crouch, yet everything seemed special to him. John Russell Crouch was born in 1915 in the obscure town of Hondo, Texas. Young John Russell lived an uneventful childhood. Most people thought that he would follow the pattern of other young men from Hondo; after high school most of the boys went to work for the railroad.

But John Russell always told people, "I'm different." And indeed, he was. As a child, he was fascinated by the way humans could propel themselves across a body of water. There was no lake or swimming hole near Hondo, so John Russell bought a swimming instruction book with cereal box tops and taught himself to swim by lying on a piano bench, kicking his feet, and moving his arms while reading the book. When it rained, John Russell would practice his swimming in the swollen creeks or in a local cattle-watering tank. When he was 18, he and a friend hitchhiked to Austin and entered the state swimming meet. John Russell won so many events that spectators and other contestants at the meet kept asking, "Who is this Hondo guy?" As a result, John Russell not only came away from the meet with a number of gold medals, he also earned a nickname that stayed with him all his life—he became known as Hondo Crouch.

Hondo's performance caught the eye of the University of Texas swimming coach, who offered him a place on the swimming team. Understandably, Hondo was a little frightened and insecure at the university, but this was concealed by his remarkable swimming ability. Hondo also hid his insecurity with his keen sense of humor; he became a renowned practical joker. Through his jokes and swimming Hondo became widely known; he was twice named All-American.

After serving in the Army, Hondo returned to the Texas ranch country that he loved so well. He married Helen Stieler, whose father owned a 22,000-acre ranch and who was known as the Goat King of the world. Helen was everything that Hondo was not. She was self-assured and refined. Helen (or Shatzie, as Hondo called her) had a serious nature that was in sharp contrast to Hondo's fun-loving spirit.

Hondo and Shatzie had four children, and Hondo delighted in teaching them everything from manners to lessons about nature. As with the rest of his life, his teaching methods were often unorthodox. In order to get his children to drink their

1

milk, Hondo would wrap a nickel in wax paper and drop it into the bottom of the glass; the children eagerly gulped their milk to get the prize.

In 1953 Hondo bought a 3,000-acre ranch. The land was hilly and rocky, dotted with sagebrush and small oak trees. Hondo loved the challenge of the harsh environment, and he was constantly experimenting to find the best breed of animal for his land.

Although his ranch prospered, it was not ranching that made Hondo Crouch the center of attraction in the Texas Hill Country. He became a writer for the Fredericksburg newspaper. Under the name Peter Cedarstacker, he used wit and humor to comment on issues of local interest. In addition to his writing, Hondo brought his humor to life on stage. He formed an acting team, and every summer the team would put on plays in the fallen-down dance hall in the ghost town of Waring, Texas.

Hondo was a grown man who never outgrew being a little boy. However, all was not happiness and jokes in Hondo's life. His favorite son, Kerry, was a talented artist and a warm, sensitive young man. He idolized his father and this admiration was returned by Hondo. When Kerry was 21 years old, Hondo received a call from a doctor in Austin. Kerry had developed a severe psychological disorder known as schizophrenia. The once-happy, playful boy now lived in a world of his own. He was unable to interact with other people, and he heard voices and saw strange figures.

Hondo was crushed. He blamed drugs and Kerry's "hippie" friends for the problem. He loved Kerry very much, but was hurt so deeply that he could not bear to visit him in the hospital. Kerry spent much of the next 8 years in hospitals and jails; despite urgings from family and friends, Hondo never visited his son.

Hondo's spirit was broken by this tragedy and his only wish after learning about his son's condition was to die soon. His will to live was restored, however, by a small advertisement in the Fredericksburg paper: "Town for sale; Luckenbach, Benno Engle, owner." The town of Luckenbach stood at the end of Hondo's ranch. Its main street (the only street in town) was 200 feet long, and the whole town consisted of a general store, which had a saloon in one section and a post office in the other. (A white line painted down the center of the floor separated the saloon from the post office.) Hondo had often admired the little town and the thought of owning it stirred his imagination. He would put Luckenbach on the map; it would be a town where anyone could feel at home. Most of all, it would give Hondo a place where he could once again be the center of everyone's attention. He bought the town and hung a sign over the general store entrance: "Everybody's Somebody in Luckenbach."

Hondo assumed his role as mayor and foreign minister of Luckenbach, and became a champion of the downtrodden. Chili contests were popular in Texas, but women were traditionally excluded. Hondo formed the "Hell Hath No Fury (Like a Woman Scorned) Society" and staged the first women's chili cookoff. In 1973 Hondo held Luckenbach's first "Great World's Fair," which attracted 10,000 people. Contests included tobacco spitting, chicken frying, cow-chip throwing, and armadillo races. Hondo encouraged aspiring entertainers to come to Luckenbach; Willie Nelson and Jerry Jeff Walker, who were unknown at the time, performed at the fair and became close friends of Hondo.

Hondo and his creative humor and insight received national attention. The Clown Prince of Texas had found his kingdom in Luckenbach. Here Hondo, the man who was really no one special, discovered a way to make all those who visited his town feel a little special. ▬

After completing this chapter, you should be able to:

Define psychology and know its main goals.

Describe the major schools of psychology and know the names of the principal individuals associated with each school.

Know the subfields of psychology and the interrelationships between them.

Describe the four methods used by psychologists to conduct scientifically based experiments.

Understand how to conduct an experiment and appreciate the ethical issues surrounding experimentation.

What Is Psychology?

Even as a young boy Hondo believed he was different from other people. Indeed, in many respects Hondo was unique. His thoughts, feelings, and actions were different from everyone else's. In fact, each of us is unique. But despite this uniqueness, we all have many things in common. We all learn (some faster than others); we all talk (some more than others); we all have goals that we are trying to reach; each of us experiences emotions such as love, hate, and happiness; and we all interact with other people and belong to groups. Most of us take our thoughts, feelings, and actions for granted. We rarely question how we see objects, learn new material, or feel emotions. We seldom wonder why we are attracted to certain people or why we have bizarre dreams. The exception to this occurs when something goes wrong. We begin to question how learning occurs if we see our child having difficulty reading or writing. We begin to question why people feel emotions when we find ourselves in a deep sadness or depression. The news that his son was suffering from schizophrenia forced Hondo to examine his relationships and struggle to explain Kerry's plight.

Psychologists are constantly asking questions and searching for answers about why and how people behave, believe, and act as they do. Psychology, like any science, has the goals of describing, predicting, and explaining events; the events at the heart of psychology are behaviors, both physical and mental. Thus psychology is a science of behavior, but it is more. Psychology has a strong applied side, in which its knowledge is used to solve problems, create a more fulfilling social and physical environment, and help people adjust to the demands of their changing world. **Psychology**, then, can be defined as the scientific study of behavior and the applications gained from that knowledge. As we will see in this book, psychology is an exciting partnership between science and application, with each opening up new directions and challenges for the other. As one student said, "Of all the fields I have studied at the university, psychology is the one that is really about *me*. In psychology I am the center of attention; its findings apply directly to me."

Having given you this relatively simple and broad definition of psychology, let's take a moment to explore some of the issues raised by this description. In order to prepare you for this discussion (and the remainder of the book), we will begin by viewing psychology as a *very* large family whose

Psychology
The scientific study of behavior and applications gained from that knowledge.

members share a common last name (psychology) but have many differences. As in most families, there is a feeling of kinship between psychologists, and there are also quarrels, some of them quite vigorous (Bevan, 1991). One area of contention concerns the very definition of the field.

We defined psychology as the study of *behavior*. What do we mean by the concept behavior? Some psychologists insist that the field should focus on *observable* behavior, actions that can be observed and directly measured (Skinner, 1990). This category includes gross actions, such as movement, and more fine actions, such as the firing of neurons (see Chapter 2). Other psychologists argue that behavior should also include actions that can be inferred, such as the processing of mental images (Fink, 1990). Although we cannot directly observe how people process and store information, we can infer these processes by observing action. As it stands, most psychologists accept the broader definition of behavior, although the debate continues.

A second bone of contention concerns whether *application* should be included in a strict definition of psychology (Fowler, 1990). The scientific study of behavior and the application of the results of this study have a long history of coexistence in the field. While there are some who believe these functions should be separated, most psychologists view the relationship between the two as mutually beneficial and believe each has a strong claim for family membership (Altman, 1987; Fowler, 1990). In fact, the breadth of psychology has been considered one of its unique strengths; few areas of study evidence the variety psychology does (Odegaard, 1987). As you read the remaining chapters in this book, you will be struck by the scope of the field, finding that some topics and methods are more like distant cousins than close family relations. Our hope is that you will find this diversity exciting and challenging rather than confusing.

The History of Psychology

Tracing the origins of psychology is somewhat like trying to find where the winds begin. At least as far back as written history goes, our ancestors wondered why people act as they do and what makes some behave differently from others. If we examine books on the history of psychology (Kendler, 1987; Leahey, 1987), we find that many of them begin with a discussion of the Greek philosophers, especially Plato (428–347 B.C.). One of the questions that interested Plato was why people are different. Why are some intelligent and others rather dull, some brave and others cowardly, some hard workers and others lazy? Plato believed these differences were largely determined at birth. The question of individual differences still excites debates today and is at the heart of the nature-nurture question. How many of our traits and behavior tendencies are inherited (nature) and how many are the products of our environment and learning (nurture)?

An issue of concern to later philosophers, including Descartes (1596–1650), was the concept of *mind*. Descartes argued that the mind and associated mental processes were located in the brain; others before him had suggested that the roots of thinking and emotions lay in various parts of the body. Descartes also believed that, like machines, human beings behaved according to laws and mechanistic principles.

While the philosophers speculated about the foundations of human behavior, the physiologists adopted a scientific approach that involved experimentation and careful observation. The early physiologists examined the nervous system and began mapping the functions of the brain. The field of psychology was created in the late 1800s when the scientific method of the physiologists was used to attack some of the basic questions of human behavior posed by the philosophers. The aim of the early psychologists was to seek understanding through observation and obtaining information in a scientific manner.

Before examining some of the specific approaches of psychology, let's first address a few ironies and patterns in the development of the field. First, although the roots of psychology are European, the field has been most strongly embraced in the United States. In fact, one psychologist observed that "most psychologists who have ever lived and who are now living can be found in the United States" (Triandis, 1980, ix). While the fact that most psychologists live in the same society has probably helped speed the exchange of ideas, it has sometimes led to ignorance of important developments in psychology in other parts of the world. Aware of this unfortunate insularity, psychologists have recently increased their efforts to create a truly world community of psychologists and to enhance communication among all psychologists (Rosenzweig, 1984).

Second, the field of psychology has developed through stages characterized by division and consolidation (Altman, 1987). Through the late 1800s and early 1900s, several diverse schools and approaches were founded. These approaches were often isolated from one another—in fact, their practitioners were often hostile toward one another. Then, from the early 1900s until 1960, the trend in psychology was consolidation. The American Psychological Association served as the organization for bringing together psychologists from different areas and with different perspectives. That trend was reversed in the 1960s, when psychologists seemed to adopt the social theme of the decade: "Do your own thing." New subareas developed, seeking independence and recognition. Now in the 1990s, psychologists are again becoming concerned that different areas in the field have drifted too far apart, and discussions of reunification are taking place. These discussions even involve the notion of developing a common curriculum of study for psychology majors during their undergraduate training (Denmark, 1989).

Finally, one other characteristic about psychology should be kept in mind as you read about the discipline. The study of behavior is an enormous field in which to roam. How do psychologists decide on what issues to tackle? Psychology has always had a close relationship with the social issues of the times (Altman, 1987), and these issues have often helped psychology identify new areas of focus. Theories and research on aggression, helping, propaganda and attitude change, and stress have flourished when war has been a social concern. When concerns about racism and sexism have

Psychologists often focus on social issues of the times. Theories and research on aggression, helping, propaganda and attitude change, and stress flourish when war is a social concern.

LEARNING FROM TEXTBOOKS IS A THREE-LETTER WORD

Many students do not learn effectively from textbooks even though they are very bright and are fluid readers of stories (Vaughan & Estes, 1985). As a result, frustrated students sometimes use four-letter words to describe learning from textbooks. We will argue that a three-letter word is more appropriate. That word is *ACE*, which stands for *A*nticipate, *C*ompare, and *E*nrich. We will describe these processes along with the features of the book that will help you use them.

This book is designed to help students by including aids and instructions that improve how well a test is learned and remembered. This design is a practical application of recent basic cognitive research that is described in chapters on perception, learning, and memory. A preview is presented here so that you can start using the aids and instructions now. They will not only help you get textbook information in your head, but they will also help you get it out when you need it on tests, in other courses, and in everyday life.

Psychologists provided a springboard for the development of modern learning aids and instructions on how to learn from textbooks. Traditional aids and instructions were based on a five-step study method called SQ3R (*S*urvey, *Q*uestion, *R*ead, *R*ecite, and *R*eview; Robinson, 1941). Psychologists still recommend these five steps. As described in Chapter 7, however, psychologists now are also able to recommend additional methods that go beyond SQ3R in explaining how each step should be done. These new methods are emerging as products of two interwoven branches of research. One branch concentrates on the textbook (Armbruster & Anderson, 1984; Baumann, 1986; Crismore, 1984; Kantor, 1983; Shebilske & Rotondo, 1981); the other focuses on the reader (Fisher & Peters, 1981; Rayner, 1983; Shebilske, 1984; Van Rossum & Schenk, 1984; Carver, 1985).

Schema theory, which is discussed in Chapters 4, 7, and 9, guides both lines of research. According to this theory, both authors and readers play an active role in the communication process. Authors write ideas in a particular structured sequence that can be represented by an outline. Readers construct an internal

representation of text that can also be represented by an outline. Cognitive psychologists have learned a great deal about the reading and learning processes by using schema theory. They specify the structure of the text, the structure of the readers' internal representation, and the relationship between these two structures (see Chapter 7). Superior readers quickly develop an internal representaton that matches the structure of the text.

Some superior readers survey the material first, ask questions about it, read it, recite it, and review it. But this SQ3R procedure alone is not what makes them successful. They succeed largely because they constantly monitor their knowledge. They ask, "Do I know what the author is saying? What can I do about it if I don't?" (Vaughan & Estes, 1985). This monitoring takes place during every part of studying, from the initial survey to the final review. Monitoring can be done by *anticipating* what the author's main points are; *comparing* your understanding of these points with what actually is written, and *enriching* your understanding with aids that will put important information at your fingertips. These are the steps you need to ACE the text.

Our goal was to include qualities in this text that would help you with these ACE procedures. The following are qualities and suggestions for how you might best take advantage of them to optimize how well you learn and remember the material:

1. We begin each chapter with a story based on real people in history or current events, and we refer back to the story throughout the chapter. Our purpose is to grab your attention and focus it effectively as you read. We hope that you will enjoy the stories and that they will put you in the mood for reading the chapters. We also hope they will help you ACE the text as follows:

Anticipate how the story will relate to the chapter. You should get some hints about the chapter by reading the outline that appears before the story and by previewing the objectives. But you should get much richer clues in the stories. The Hondo Crouch story is chock-full of them. Can you think

of one that might have enabled you to anticipate this discussion of learning from textbooks? The best way to detect them is to ask yourself questions as you read. For example, when the story mentioned that Hondo learned to swim by reading a book you might have asked how one can learn swimming or anything else from a book. You could note this question in your text simply by writing the word "how" in the margin next to the passage on the swimming instruction.

A transition section after each story will help you create expectations about what is to come. The one for this chapter directs you toward wondering about the "hows and whys" of learning, talking, goal setting, emotions, and other behaviors. It focused your attention on individual differences as well as on things that people have in common. If you haven't already done so, you might want to reread the story with an eye out for clues about these topics. Write short notes in the margin when you find one. You should have little trouble finding passages where it would be appropriate to write:

How are people similar and different? What can psychologists tell us about raising children? Why do emotions change? What causes mental illness?

Raising such questions in advance will make you a more active reader. The trick will be to learn to raise similar questions in advance when you read the remaining stories. Mastering this skill will help you anticipate what the chapter will be about.

These anticipations will help you get more out of what you read. The difference between reading with and without expectations is like the difference between being a driver or a passenger in a car. Drivers actively read signs to answer questions about speed and directions. As a result, they can usually tell you much more about speed limits and street names than can a passenger who passively looks at the same signs for no particular purpose. You will remember more about chapters if you read actively to answer questions that come to mind while reading the introductory stories.

Compare your understanding and memory with what is said as you read the chapter. The expectations you created while reading the story will be your first state of understanding.

Compare this with what is actually written. Did the text say more, less, or something different from what you thought it would? Note important differences in the margin. You might observe, for example, that the chapter does not directly answer the question of how people are similar and different. It does, however, explain methods used to answer this question and it tells what branch of psychology studies personalities and other kinds of similarities and differences.

A good way to compare your understanding with what is said is to close the book and try to summarize the material in your own words. Pay special attention to distortions or omissions.

Enrich your memory in a way that will help you recall the text. One way to improve your memory is to use the story as a framework for organizing the chapter material (see Chapter 7). You might recall behaviorism and humanistic psychology better if you relate the first to Hondo's technique for getting his kids to drink milk and relate the second to his sign "Everybody's Somebody in Luckenbach." Similarly, in the chapter on learning you can use the story about Helen Keller to help you remember the difference between classical and operant conditioning. You will avoid confusion of these two kinds of conditioning if you remember that the two kinds are related to different parts of the story. If you get an idea for using the story to help you organize your memory, write a reminder in the margin so you won't forget to use it when you review.

Compare your understanding with ours by summarizing in your own words and comparing your summary with ours. Pay special attention to distortions or omissions. The time needed to respond to these prompts will be well spent. You will learn and remember the material better. In addition, the immediate feedback on your summaries will strengthen a skill that will improve your ability to learn from all textbooks.

Enrich your understanding by writing reminders of your summary in the margin. Remember, you are writing to yourself and you will only need brief reminders of the important ideas. Use abbreviations and symbols instead of words and sentences whenever possible. For example, you

might write "ACE > SQ3R" to capture the whole discussion of the advantages of the ACE learning procedure over the traditional SQ3R method. Start each review session by testing yourself with your own reminders. Do they enable you to recall all the important information? If so, you should be in great shape for the exam. If not, add more reminders until you have enough of them to trigger your memory for all the important information. Your instructor will be happy to help you figure out the level of detail that is important for your class.

2. We also promote the ACE procedure by providing definitions of key terms in the margins. These should be used as follows:

Anticipate important ideas by previewing the key terms before you read.

Compare your understanding of key terms as explained in the text with the definitions in the margins.

Enrich your memory by writing brief reminders of main parts of the definitions. For example, your reminder for "psychology" might be "s:b:a" to indicate the scientific study of behavior and the applications of knowledge from those studies. The process of thinking of reminders will actually help you remember. During reviews, test yourself by trying to recall the definitions after looking only at the key term. Then look at your reminder and try again. Finally, look at our definition in the margin and at the text to see how the key term fits into the chapter.

3. Other aspects of the text are also designed to help you improve your memory. For instance, the relationships between ideas is clearly signaled by the way the text is physically structured and by labels. In addition, topic sentences and summaries appear before and after main ideas throughout the text. And finally, many aids such as concrete examples, thought questions, armchair experiments, and applications are included in the text. These features will work best if you deliberately use them to organize your memory as you work through the ACE process.

Anticipate the relationship between main and subordinate ideas by scanning the headings, which are organized in three levels to reflect these relationships. Topic sentences often introduce sections so that you can anticipate what will be said.

Compare your understanding of the relationships with what is said and update your understanding as you read the text. Keep your eyes open for phrases such as "note that," "in contrast," or "leads to." They signal important ideas, contrasts, and cause-effect relationships. Summary statements often conclude sections so that you can compare your understanding of the main points with ours.

Enrich your memory by thinking of ways to remember the important relationships and facts. One way is to number ideas. We often supply the enumeration in the text itself, but if we do not, you can add it yourself by making notes in the margins or in the text. The wording of topic sentences and summary statements might give you hints about the important ideas to be remembered.

We have good news for you if you are starting to worry about not having enough time for the ACE procedure. Your brief reminders in the margins about organization, summaries, and key terms should take the place of writing separate outlines, summaries, and definitions. Many students exhaust themselves writing pages for each chapter and then reviewing these pages instead of the books. Don't do it! Thinking of short reminders is far more effective than writing lengthy copies of what is in the book. You will learn why it is in Chapter 6 on Learning. You will also learn the importance of an organizational framework, which is far richer when you review in the context of the book itself.

4. Finally, we present instructions in Chapter 4 that could double your reading speed in this and other books. You will save a lot of time by doubling your reading speed but don't expect to cut your study time in half. In fact, it might be better not to cut your study time at all. Instead, plan to study more efficiently by reading faster and by using the additional time to ACE the text.

predominated, psychology has provided insight through research on issues such as intergroup relations, prejudice, self-identify, and the clinical effects of discrimination. When economic issues such as depression, recession, and international competitiveness have dominated the social scene, psychology has played its part by focusing on organizational effectiveness, burnout, and group dynamics. Today's concerns about AIDS, education, drug abuse, the environment, and the developing world community are being matched by psychological research on these issues. In other words, the field of psychology has remained attuned to the world around it, offering a scientific perspective on the prevailing social problems. This use of scientific method to study pressing social concerns is one of the reasons for psychology's immense and growing popularity.

With these points in mind, let's examine the development of psychology in more detail.

Structuralism

In 1879 Wilhelm Wundt went to Leipzig, Germany, to start the first psychological laboratory. There he developed techniques for studying the laws of the human mind. Most of his techniques involved analyzing sights, sounds, and other sensations, because Wundt believed that sensations are the "atoms" of thought. Many students came to study with Wundt; one of the most famous was Edward Bradford Titchener, who set up his own laboratory in the United States at Cornell University.

Wundt and Titchener are credited with developing an analytical approach to studying how we experience the world the way we do. This approach, which is called **structuralism,** is based on identifying the elements of human experience and finding out how those elements interact together to form thoughts and feelings. Titchener identified three categories of elements: sensations (such as sights and sounds), feelings (such as joy and sorrow), and images (such as memories and dreams). The main research tool of structuralism is the method known as **analytic introspection,** which is a way of isolating these elements of which experiences are made.

The training program to learn analytic introspection was quite rigorous. Trainees would learn to break down experiences into their most basic elements. For example, imagine yourself standing in front of a window looking at a house, trees, and sky. You would divide the window scene into separate patches of colors and brightnesses. You might notice different shades of blue and green in the sky and trees, and you might see that the light tan house looks darker in an area covered by a shadow. According to structuralists, in doing this, you would be uncovering the sensory elements used to construct your experience.

Because analytic introspection could only be used by trained observers, and because it gave different results in different laboratories, depending on how observers were trained, psychologists were not completely satisfied with this method. Thus, the first psychological laboratory sparked researchers to develop other approaches to the scientific study of behavior. Some evolved in a very different direction from structuralism. Others were motivated by the desire to study aspects of behavior for which structuralism was not well suited. Let's review some of these other approaches.

Functionalism

While structuralists' publications were still "hot off the press," an American psychologist, William James, proposed a different program of research. His new approach was called **functionalism** because it concerned the way in which mental processes (such as thinking) function to fill needs. While structuralists were asking "What is thinking?" functionalists asked "What

Structuralism
Approach to psychology based on identifying the elements of human experience and finding out how those elements are combined into thoughts and feelings.
Analytic introspection
Method used in structuralism; a way of isolating the elementary sensations of which experiences are made.
Functionalism
Approach to psychology that emphasizes the function of thought; led to important applications in education and the founding of educational psychology, a subfield of psychology.

is it for?" Specifically, they raised the question of how our mental abilities enable us to adapt to our environment. Emphasis on the function of thought led functionalists to pursue important applications in education. John Dewey, a leading functionalist, strengthened public education in America and was the founder of school psychology, which has become a major subfield. Other functionalists applied their work to a great many pressing problems. For instance, they served as advisers to the United States armed services, they contributed to the development of child psychology (see Chapter 9), and they developed tests of personalities (see Chapter 13). To this day, functionalist approaches are advocated. For example, Herek (1986) identifies roots in functionalism for current studies of how our attitudes enable us to adjust in social relationships (see Chapter 16).

Gestalt Psychology

In the 1920s, while Hondo Crouch was in grammar school, a group of German psychologists, Max Wertheimer, Kurt Koffka, and Wolfgang Köhler, established still another approach to psychology. They believed that there are experiences that cannot be broken down into separate elements. They therefore argued that structuralist "elements," or units of analysis, were unnatural. They maintained that some things have to be experienced as wholes—that they cannot be broken down any further. Thus the units of choice in the earlier example would be trees, house, and sky. These psychologists were so committed to analyzing these "whole" units that they named their approach **Gestalt,** which is a German word meaning "whole." Gestalt psychologists argued that it is the organization of elements, rather than the elements themselves, that is important. In order to understand their point of view, think of your favorite tune. Clearly, the tune is made up of musical notes, but it is not the notes themselves that give it melody. Instead, it is the *arrangement* of the notes that is important. We could take those same notes and make a different melody (or maybe just noise) if we organized them differently. Gestalt psychologists concentrated their efforts on the study of perception. We will therefore take up their contributions again in Chapter 4. For example, we will review Gestalt laws of organization and discuss modern attempts to refine those laws.

Behaviorism

When Hondo's children refused to drink their milk, Hondo found that he could quickly change their behavior by dropping a nickel into the bottom of the glass. They then quickly gulped the milk down to get the nickel. In order to understand and predict their behavior, Hondo did not have to worry about what his children were thinking or feeling; it was easy to see that "nickel in glass" resulted in "drinking the milk."

This view is characteristic of the **behaviorist approach** that developed in the 1920s. John Watson, one of the first behaviorists, argued that the science of psychology must concern itself only with *observable* events. Watson pointed out that we cannot observe events such as thinking or feeling, nor can we directly observe "the mind." He believed, therefore, that psychologists should not try to explain behavior in terms of something that cannot be observed. Further, he argued that we do not need these "fuzzy" concepts to predict behavior. In the example of Hondo's children we saw that an event could be described by referring only to what could be observed: a stimulus (nickel in the glass) and a response (drinking the milk). Watson

Wolfgang Köhler was one of the founders of Gestalt psychology.

Gestalt psychology
German school of psychology based on the premise that we experience wholes, or gestalts, rather than separate sensations.

Behaviorism
Approach to psychology based on the premise that human behavior can be described by focusing only on the observable stimulus and response.

B. F. Skinner, a well-known advocate of the behaviorist approach, is shown in the laboratory with the basic experimental apparatus named after him, the Skinner box.

WOMEN IN PSYCHOLOGY: *Setting the Record Straight*

As we read the history of early psychology, we are struck by the enormous contributions and interesting lives of many of the fathers of the field. While this history makes for interesting reading, a nagging thought occurs: Did only male scientists contribute to the creation of this exciting new field? Indeed not. From its very beginnings—even before psychology was recognized as a field of study—women made vital and significant contributions to the field.

Unlike their male counterparts, however, these women had to overcome prejudice and discrimination based on their gender rather than on the quality of their ideas. They were not allowed to study at many institutions, they found themselves barred from laboratories and professional societies, they saw their manuscripts rejected by journals for nonscientific reasons, they were denied advanced degrees even when their work warranted the awarding of these degrees, and they were unable to secure teaching and research positions at many universities and laboratories solely because of their gender (O'Connell & Russo, 1990; Stevens & Gardner, 1982; Russo & Denmark, 1987). But despite these enormous hurdles, women persisted and played a major, although sometimes overlooked, role in shaping the discipline of psychology. In order to appreciate the contribution of women in the field, consider the following selected examples.

The first edition of the misnamed *American Men of Science* (Cattell, 1906) listed 186 psychologists, 22 of whom were women. The list did not include 5 other women who were members of the newly formed American Psychological Association (APA) (Furumoto & Scarborough, 1986). Among the 50 most famous psychologists, Cattell recognized three women: Mary Whiton Calkins, Christine Ladd-Franklin, and Margaret Floy Washburn. The first five editions of *American Men of Science* starred 127 names for distinction, including 5 more women: Ethel Puffer Howes, Lillien Jane Martin, Helen Thompson Woolley, June Etta Downey, and Florence Goodenough (Bryan & Boring, 1946). The contributions of these foremothers were as follows:

Mary Whiton Calkins completed all requirements for a Harvard Ph.D. in 1895, but she and other women who studied at Harvard were denied the doctorate. Her denial was upheld by Harvard trustees even though the famous psychologist Williams James considered her his brightest student. During her distinguished career, Calkins developed a theoretical system of self psychology that influenced both psychologists and philosophers (Furumoto, 1980). She also invented the paired associate technique, which became a major research tool for studying memory (see Chapter 7). She founded the psychology laboratory at Wellesley College in 1891, and served as president of the APA in 1905.

Christine Ladd-Franklin completed all degree requirements at Johns Hopkins in 1882, but was denied a Ph.D. until 1926 because of Johns Hopkins's restrictions against granting a doctorate to women. She was a married woman and mother who never held a regular faculty appointment. Her employment record reflected the strong social sanctions against women combining a career and parenting (Furumoto & Scarborough, 1986). Despite these sanctions, however, she distinguished herself as one of America's leading scientists. She was compared to Aristotle for her contributions to logic (Stevens & Gardner, 1982). She also developed an influential theory of color vision.

Margaret Floy Washburn became the first woman to be granted a Ph.D. in psychology in 1894. The degree was conferred by Cornell, where she had studied under E. B. Titchner. Washburn taught at Wells College and Vassar for 34 years. Since these women's colleges were not research institutions, her employment limited her research activities. It also restricted her interactions with the leading researchers in psychology. Nevertheless, she made prominent contributions. One of her important works, *The Animal Mind*, was a catalyst for the development of behaviorism. She considered her most important work to be *Movement and Mental Imagery* (Washburn, 1916). This book paved the way for current work on the role of imagery in guiding our thoughts and actions (see Chapter 8). Washburn served as president of APA in 1931.

Ethel Puffer Howes completed her doctoral studies at Harvard in 1898. For the next 10 years, she held positions at Radcliffe and Simmons College. She also taught at Wellesley. During this time, she gained distinguished recognition for her book, *The Psychology of Beauty*,

Observable stimulus and response

argued that we can describe other human behavior in the same way, by focusing only on the observable stimulus and response.

In Chapter 9, we will discuss a famous experiment (Watson & Rayner, 1920). In that experiment he was able to predict and control an infant's responses, such as crying, by systematically manipulating observable aspects of the infant's environment.

The behaviorist position was well received by many psychologists because it represented an approach to understanding behavior that could be directly tested and applied in many settings. One of the well-known advocates of this approach was B. F. Skinner, who died in 1990. Skinner applied the behavioristic approach in a number of different areas, from child rearing to teaching pigeons to guide missiles (Skinner, 1960; 1990;

which was published in 1905. Over the next 12 years, Howes married and had two children. Because of the social sanctions of the time, marriage and motherhood brought her career in psychology to a halt.

Lillien Jane Martin did doctoral studies at Göttingen in 1898, but she never earned a Ph.D. Nonetheless, her career earned her a distinguished place in the history of psychology. She was the first woman to become a department head at Stanford University. Her major scientific contributions included work in sensations, esthetics, and imagery. Martin founded the first psychological clinic for "normal" preschoolers, as well as the first counseling center for senior citizens.

Helen Thompson Woolley was the first woman psychologist to receive a Ph.D. from the University of Chicago. It was granted by the department of philosophy in 1903. Woolley was also the first of the outstanding women psychologists to challenge widespread beliefs about gender differences in mental abilities. She applied her scientific skills to directly test these alleged differences (Thompson, 1903) and noted the environmental factors that might account for gifted women's frequent failure to attain eminence. In a review of research on the psychology of sex, she pointed out that "There is perhaps no field aspiring to be scientific where flagrant personal bias, logic martyred in the cause of supporting a prejudice, unfounded assertions, and even sentimental rot and drivel, have run riot to such an extent as here" (Woolley, 1910, p. 340). Her work laid a foundation for contemporary

analyses of gender differences and environmental factors (see Chapter 8). She and Helen Cleveland also developed the Merrill-Palmer Scales, which became a widely used tool for testing mental abilities in children (Rosenberg, 1982).

June Etta Downey was recognized for her study of personality traits. She appeared not only in the *American Men of Science* but also on Watson's (1974) list of eminent contributors to psychology between 1600 and 1967. This list, which was developed by an international panel, included only 228 psychologists. When Downey was appointed head of the department of psychology at the University of Wyoming in 1915, she became the first women to head a department of psychology at a state university. Her contributions to psychology included the creation of the Downey-Will Temperament Test.

Florence Goodenough was a leader in developmental psychology. She originated the Draw-a-Man Test, which is still used to test children. Her innovations also influenced research methods for observing children (Sicherman & Green, 1980). Her work gave psychology not only new methods but also new insights into children. For example, her book *Anger in Young Children* is frequently cited in developmental textbooks (Thompson, 1983).

These early contributors set the stage for many outstanding women psychologists who have had a lot to do with the course of modern psychology (Russo & Denmark, 1987). In fact, the field of psychology is proving increasingly attractive to women. Statistics indicate that out of

2,441 psychology doctorate recipients in 1989, 1,402 were women (57 percent) (American Psychological Association, 1991a). This is not to say that the field now favors women, for other statistics suggest that it does not. For example, full-time employment for 1989 psychology doctorate recipients was obtained by 85.5 percent of the males, but only 73.0 percent of the females (American Psychological Association, 1991a). Furthermore, women were significantly less likely than men to be full professors in 1988–1989 (24 percent versus 57 percent) (American Psychological Association, 1991b). However, the inflow of women is generating a trend toward balance, a trend that is evidenced by the number of assistant and associate professors who are women. In 1980–1981, 35 percent of all assistant professors and 19 percent of all associate professors were women; the corresponding figures for 1988–1989 were 46 percent and 29 percent (American Psychological Association, 1991b).

The influx of women into psychology has also opened up many new areas of research. As you will see in the remaining chapters of this text, research on gender differences is being conducted in every field of psychology. A division of the American Psychological Association (Division 35, Psychology of Women) was formed to facilitate the examination of issues of special importance to women. And women continue to exercise major influence in the development and direction of all areas of psychology.

see also Chapter 9). Throughout his career, he tirelessly advocated the position that psychology must be a science of observable behavior and avoid postulating about processes that could not be observed.

Although the behaviorist approach had many strong points, critics argued that it did not fully take into account the richness of human experience. After all, even though we cannot see a thought or a feeling, we know that people do think and experience emotions. Since these are important parts of the human experience, they should also be material for psychological investigations. Modern literature still contains debates about behaviorism. A main issue is whether it should be integrated with other approaches (e.g. Groome, 1986, Holt, 1986) or whether it should be developed as a separate discipline (e.g. Fraley & Vargas, 1986; Paniagua, 1986).

Psychoanalytic Psychology

Although many have criticized behaviorism for being too simplistic, few would accuse psychoanalytic theory of this failing. As behaviorism was being introduced in the United States, a Viennese physician named Sigmund Freud put the European scientific world in an uproar with his unorthodox views of human behavior. Freud, the founder of **psychoanalysis,** not only suggested that much of human behavior is the result of thoughts, fears, and wishes, he also suggested that people are often unaware of these motivating forces, even though they have a strong effect on their behavior. Freud argued that many, if not most, of these thoughts and wishes result from our experiences during infancy and early childhood. The greatest outcry of criticism came when he suggested that infants have sexual fantasies about their parents.

Freud's ideas had a tremendous influence on psychology. Because his early work was aimed at explaining emotional disorders, psychoanalytic theory has played a central role in understanding and treating psychological disorders. We will see this influence in Chapters 14 and 15. Psychoanalytic theory has also been used to explain differences between people. In this role, as we will see in Chapter 13, psychoanalytic theory has been the basis for important advances in understanding personality.

Although people no longer express shock and dismay at Freud's ideas, there is still a great deal of controversy about psychoanalytic theory. One of the criticisms of the approach has been that it takes a very dim view of human nature. According to Freud, the unconscious impulses that influence behavior are often destructive and antisocial. Psychoanalytic theory paints a bleak picture of the individual as being caught in a struggle to control these destructive impulses. Despite this controversy psychoanalytic theory is being applied extensively in treatments of many psychological disorders (Goldensohn, 1986) including extreme shame (O'Leary & Wright, 1986), nightmares (Cooper & Hartman, 1986), depression (Wilson, 1986), and parent-child conflicts (Ainslie & Solyom, 1986).

Humanistic Approach

If Hondo had felt inclined to adopt a school of psychology, there is little doubt he would have been comfortable with the humanistic tradition. He strongly believed in the goodness of human nature. He often said that all people need is "half a chance" and they will "do good." In Luckenbach everyone could have their "half a chance." The ragged sign over the general store proclaimed this: "Everybody's Somebody in Luckenbach."

A number of psychologists objected to Freud's view that human beings are basically destructive beasts who are constantly fighting their negative impulses. In the 1950s the *humanistic* movement began. The main theme of **humanistic psychology** is that people are basically good. We are not driven by unconscious desires to destroy; rather we have free will, and, given the proper environment, we will strive to achieve positive social goals. As we will see in Chapter 13, the humanistic psychologists argued that each person is unique, and that psychologists should examine this individuality rather than lumping people into categories. The humanists also reject the behaviorist view that psychologists should only study observable stimuli and responses. Rather, they argue, it is their thoughts, desires, and feelings that make people unique. Today, the humanistic approach is a popular training orientation in clinical psychology (Nevid, Lavi, & Primavera, 1986).

Sigmund Freud is the founder of psychoanalysis, which has played a central role in understanding and treating psychological disorders.

People are destructive

People are good natured

Psychoanalysis
Freud's technique of treating anxiety disorders by helping people recognize and deal with their repressed feelings.
Humanistic psychology
Movement formed by Carl Rogers, Abraham Maslow, and Rollo May which rejects Freudian view of people; argues that people are basically good and worthy of respect; stresses the creative aspect of people in reaching their true potential.

Subfields of Psychology

By the 1950s psychology had established itself as a major area for scientific study. The field had a rich history; it had developed methods for studying behavior; and it had a rapidly growing library of theory and research. Along with age came a wisdom that only experience can supply. Psychologists began to realize that the study of behavior was so broad that no single approach could be relied on to give the necessary answers to all the questions that were being raised. Each approach had merit, but it would take all of them to solve the puzzle of behavior. For this reason many psychologists stopped identifying with one school or approach to psychology and instead began to define areas where many approaches could be used. As a result, the branches of the psychology family tree took on a new look. They no longer bore the names of approaches to psychology in general; they took on the names of subfields of psychology (see Figure 1–1). The Directory of the American Psychological Association lists 350 subfields, and there are presently 47 divisions or societies (see Table 1–1) in the association. Let us examine some of these areas to get a better understanding of the field of psychology and anticipate its future directions.

FIGURE 1–1

This psychology family tree shows the various subfields of psychology as they are reflected in course titles in most psychology departments. If you decide to pursue your interest in psychology after the introductory course, you will have many of these courses to choose from.

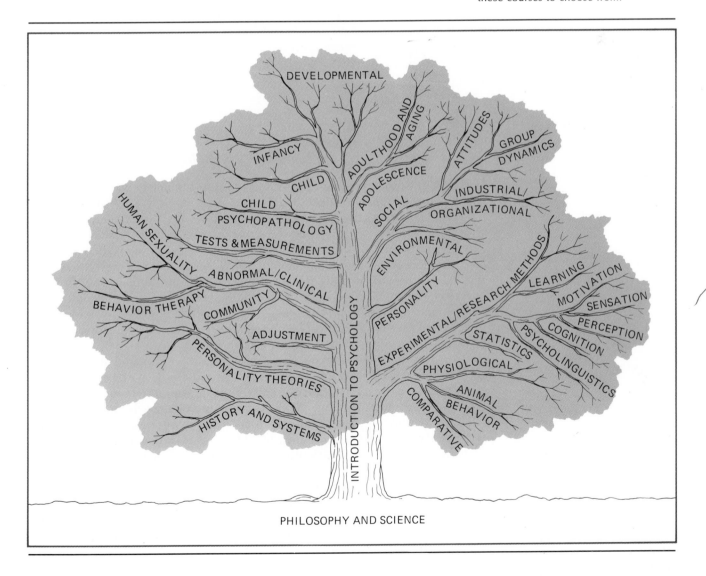

Table 1–1 Divisions of the American Psychological Association*

Division Number	Division Name	Division Number	Division Name
1	General Psychology	28	Psychopharmacology
2	Teaching of Psychology	29	Psychotherapy
3	Experimental Psychology	30	Psychological Hypnosis
5	Evaluation and Measurement	31	State Psychological Association Affairs
6	Physiological and Comparative	32	Humanistic Psychology
7	Developmental Psychology	33	Mental Retardation
8	Personality and Social	34	Population and Environmental Psychology
9	SPSSI	35	Psychology of Women
10	Psychology and the Arts	36	PIRI
12	Clinical Psychology	37	Child, Youth, and Family Services
13	Consulting Psychology	38	Health Psychology
14	Industrial and Organizational	39	Psychoanalysis
15	Educational Psychology	40	Clinical Neuropsychology
16	School Psychology	41	Psychology-Law Society
17	Counseling Psychology	42	Psychologists in Independent Practice
18	Psychologists in Public Service	43	Family Psychology
19	Military Psychology	44	Society for the Psychological Study of Lesbian and Gay Issues
20	Adult Development and Aging	45	Society for the Psychological Study of Ethnic Minority Issues
21	Applied Experimental and Engineering Psychologists	46	Media Psychology
22	Rehabilitation Psychology	47	Exercise and Sport Psychology
23	Consumer Psychology	48	Peace Psychology
24	Theoretical and Philosophical Psychology	49	Group Psychology and Group Psycho-therapy
25	Experimental Analysis of Behavior		
26	History of Psychology		
27	Community Psychology		

* There are no divisions 4 and 11.
Source: Reprinted by permission of the American Psychological Association.

Physiological and Experimental Psychology

Hondo Crouch was a great swimmer during his college days. As a young boy he spent a great deal of time teaching himself to swim. How was he able to do this and achieve such splendid results? Swimming, like many other complex behaviors, involves many steps. Swimmers must learn the best way to move their arms and legs; they must develop their muscles; they must deal with their fear of the water; and they must be able to sense where their body is in relation to the water and to the direction they wish to move in. In short, swimming involves learning, memory, perception, motivation, and emotion. The subfields of physiological and experimental psychology are concerned with the scientific examination of these areas.

Physiological psychologists examine these areas by studying the neurobiological events that underlie them. They study the eyes, ears, and other organs that we use to sense our environment. They also investigate muscles and other structures that we use to respond to our environment. Another major concern is the brain, which coordinates information coming from sense organs and going to muscles. They carefully map the brain to determine the function of various parts. In addition, physiological psychologists probe the pathways that carry information to and from the brain.

Experimental psychology examines the behaviors and cognitions (thoughts) that are related to learning, memory, perception, motivation, and emotion. The name of this subfield is more a historical accident than an identifying characteristic of the field; as you will see, all the subfields of psychology are experimental in that each uses experimental methods to investigate questions. However, experimental studies of perception and

Physiological psychology
Subfield of psychology that examines the areas of learning, memory, perception, motivation, and emotion by studying the neurobiological events that underlie them.

Experimental psychology
Subfield of psychology that examines the behaviors and cognitions (thoughts) that are related to learning, memory, perception, motivation, and emotion.

learning were some of the first in psychology, and therefore the subfield was called experimental psychology.

The areas studied by experimental psychologists are amazingly varied. Investigations examine the basic questions of how we see, hear, and feel pain. They study how people learn everything from simple tasks such as sitting upright to more complex things such as emotions and language. Experimental psychologists study both humans and animals. It is the experimental psychologists who brought to psychology the white rat, sometimes referred to as the mascot of the field. Experimental psychologists use animals to investigate a variety of issues, especially those involving learning, memory, and motivation. The use of animals in research allows psychologists to learn about animal behaviors that are important in their own right and to test new directions for human research.

The use of powerful manipulations and fine controls are two advantages of experimenting with animals even when the ultimate goal is to learn about human behavior. Psychologists can use animals to test drugs and other manipulations that might not be safe for humans. They can also control an animal's ancestry and its environment. These advantages are accompanied by the disadvantage best expressed in the question: Do the results hold true for humans? Ideally, this important question is answered in follow-up experiments on humans. In later chapters we will review many examples of animal research that have paved the way for new discoveries about human behavior.

As you can see, the subfields of physiological and experimental psychology are very large. Most psychologists in these areas are engaged in research at universities and colleges. Recently, however, more and more have been entering applied settings, where they use their knowledge to help solve a wide range of problems. As we will see later in this book, they have been involved in projects to restore sight to the partially blind and hearing to the partially deaf, they have worked on finding the best methods for teaching, and they are discovering new drugs and treatments to help people with psychological disorders.

The white rat is sometimes called the mascot of psychology because it is used in so many experiments.

Cognitive Psychology

A new branch of psychology emerged as experimental psychologists broadened their domain of inquiry. This new subfield, **cognitive psychology,** is concerned with the mental processes involved in acquiring and using knowledge. These processes are extensive even for so-called simple tasks. Consider, for example, the many processes that occurred when Hondo's son, Kerry, toddled outside to play with his pet goat. After a brief search, he saw his cute four-legged friend, heard its soft bleating, felt its fuzzy fur, and smelled its musky odor. His wobbly struggles to keep his balance were obvious. Much less apparent were his mental efforts to acquire and use information about his pet. Kerry had previously formed a mental map of his environment and a memory of what a goat is. He used this information to find his pet, and he enriched his memory with new sights, sounds, feelings, and smells. At the same time, Kerry kept his balance by processing streams of information from his legs, trunk, head, and arms. We tend to take for granted mental processes for such "simple" tasks, but cognitive psychologists have gained great respect for them (Reed, 1988; Solso, 1988). This respect grew out of attempts to apply cognitive psychology. One important application has been efforts to program computers to simulate how the mind stores, retrieves, and sees information. These efforts have been joined by cognitive psychologists, engineers, computer scientists, and others. The result has been a new branch of science called artificial intelligence (AI), which will be highlighted in Chapter 8.

Cognitive psychology
Subfield of psychology concerned with the mental events that intervene between stimuli and responses.

Developmental psychologists examine how age affects behavior. Here, a developmental psychologist checks to see if this little boy, like many other little boys his age, can perform a certain task.

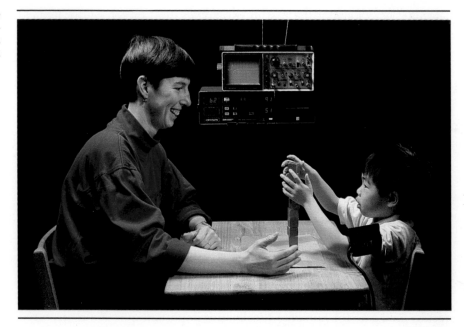

We shall see that computers are revolutionizing our world by simulating some human mental processes. We shall also see that today's computers cannot replicate many aspects of human mental abilities. They would be paralyzed, for example, by the flood of information that confronted Kerry as he searched his farmyard for his pet goat. Many of our students have become excited about learning what AI can do. This interest has led both them and us to even greater excitement about what our own mind can do. Similarly, we hope that we can share with you our ever-increasing respect for the mysteries of the human mind. Toward this end, every chapter in this book has a section related to human cognition.

Developmental Psychology

One common gift that parents receive at baby showers is the Baby Book. In this book they can record when their child first smiles, babbles, crawls, talks, and walks. Many an anxious parent has worried, "Why isn't Johnny smiling? Helen's baby smiled at 6 weeks." The subfield of **developmental psychology** examines the function of age on behavior. Developmental psychologists are not only concerned with identifying the age at which people should be performing various behaviors; they are also interested in how events that occur at various ages affect behavior. For example, they study the effects on later development of being born prematurely. They examine how family changes (such as births of siblings, divorce, or death) influence the child's development. As we will see in Chapter 10, developmental psychologists are also interested in the changes that take place in middle-aged and elderly adults. Most developmental psychologists work in universities and colleges, although many are employed in hospitals, schools, and day-care centers.

Social Psychology

In many respects Hondo was like all of us, and in other ways he was different from any of us. Hondo loved the outdoors; he enjoyed being the center of attention; he had strong attitudes about the way children should be raised; and he was always willing to help someone in distress. Most people liked Hondo, but some were irritated by his clowning.

Developmental psychology
Subfield of psychology that examines the function of age on behavior. Examines the age at which people should be performing certain behaviors and how events that occur at various ages affect behavior.

As we examine the story of Hondo's life, many of us can picture ourselves in similar situations and having similar feelings. In a sense, social psychology is concerned with similarities in people's behavior as they interact with one another. **Social psychology** is the study of the way people are affected by social situations. The field examines questions such as how people form and change attitudes; how they form impressions about themselves and each other; why they are attracted to some people and repelled by others; and how being in a group affects their behaviors and beliefs. Social psychologists develop theories that explain why people in general behave as they do in various situations. Although most social psychologists work in university settings, there are many in industry, advertising agencies, political organizations, and hospitals. The research findings from social psychology have been used by lawyers to help in choosing sympathetic juries; by advertisers to plan advertising campaigns; by politicians to design political campaigns; and by negotiators involved in planning bargaining strategies in industry as well as internationally.

Personality Psychology

Although social psychology is concerned with how most people act most of the time, investigators of **personality** are interested in individual differences. Personality psychologists focus on explaining and predicting the unique ways that people respond to their environment. They would, for example, be interested in why Hondo was always joking, while Shatzie, his wife, was serious most of the time. Personality psychologists have designed tests to measure and describe personalities, and they have developed theories to explain why people are different. Their work has been applied in business and the military to help channel the right people into the right jobs.

Clinical Psychology

When people find that you are taking courses in psychology, their first response is often, "Analyze me." Some may begin bringing their personal problems to you and asking for advice. Many people believe that all psychologists analyze and treat psychological disorders, and indeed, the subfield of clinical psychology has more psychologists than any other subfield.

Clinical psychology is dedicated to the diagnosis and treatment of emotional and behavioral disorders. Clinical psychologists are not medical doctors, but some of them work closely with *psychiatrists*, who are medical doctors specializing in psychological problems. Clinical psychologists who work closely with psychiatrists are often in private practice, in mental hospitals, or in mental health clinics. It is highly probable, for example, that clinical psychologists worked with Hondo's son, Kerry, after he was hospitalized. Clinical psychologists are also employed by probation offices, prisons, and institutions for the mentally retarded and physically handicapped. Clinical psychologists apply psychological principles, especially those related to motivation, emotions, and personality. Chapters 11, 12, and 13 set the stage for a sound introduction to clinical psychology in Chapters 14 (Abnormal Psychology) and 15 (Therapy).

Counseling and School Psychology

Counseling and school psychology are dedicated to helping people with social, educational, and job or career adjustments. Although most counseling psychologists work in schools, some assist with social and job adjustments in other settings, such as social work offices. Many psychological problems

Social psychology
Scientific study of the way in which people are affected by social situations and social relationships; the scientific study of the way most people act most of the time.
Personality
Unique set of behaviors (including thoughts and emotions) and enduring qualities that influence the way a person adjusts to the environment.
Clinical psychology
Subfield of psychology dedicated to the diagnosis and treatment of emotional and behavioral disorders.
Counseling and school psychology
Subfield of psychology that helps people with social, educational, and job or career adjustments.

reveal themselves first in schools and homes. School psychologists work with parents and teachers to help individual students before their problems become serious. Another important part of their job is administering and interpreting intelligence, achievement, and vocational tests. Seeing a school psychologist is not necessarily a sign of a problem. Many of the best college students take full advantage of school psychologists for help with vocational planning. Students who are thinking about careers in counseling and school psychology will be especially interested in the clinical and developmental chapters of this book.

Engineering and Industrial-Organizational Psychology

Hondo's world was a rather simple one. He ran his ranch on horseback or from his beloved pickup truck. He employed a ranch foreman and a few ranchmen, but each man often spent days working alone. The world in which most people live is not so simple. Many workers operate complicated machines that perform delicate and sometimes dangerous tasks. Most of us work with people, and each day we must deal with other workers and supervisors. The workplace can put a great deal of stress and strain on a person. Over the last two decades this has led psychologists to enter business and industry to help reduce many of the problems that workers face.

Engineering psychology is concerned with making human interactions with tools and machines as comfortable and error-free as possible. In other words, they work on designing machines that will "fit" people. Engineering psychologists probably played an important role in designing the car you drive; they may have even designed the chair in which you are sitting. And they are working hard to make the computers that you use maximally efficient (Paap & Roske-Hofstrand, 1986) and minimally fatiguing (Lunn & Banks, 1986). The space program employs many engineering psychologists to help design spacesuits, space capsules, and other equipment used

Engineering psychology
Subfield of psychology that is concerned with making human contact with tools and machines as comfortable and as error free as possible.

Engineering psychologists are concerned with making human interactions with tools and machines as comfortable and as error-free as possible.

Industrial-organizational psychologists study a wide range of work-related problems. For example, it is important to know how to motivate and train employees once they are in the job. An important element in job satisfaction is the employee performance evaluation, in which manager and employee review the employee's work over the last year and set goals for the future.

by astronauts. Nuclear power plants hire engineering psychologists to help design the best control panels for people who operate those plants and to lower the overall probability of human error.

Industrial-organizational psychologists are concerned with selecting, training, and managing employees. People have come to expect not only good-paying jobs but also fulfilling ones. Matching people to jobs that they will learn well and enjoy doing is not only good for people, it is also good for business. Industrial-organizational psychologists are also becoming involved in addressing specific work-related problems such as chronic pain of injured workers (Alcock, 1986), measuring performance (Pritchard, 1990), personnel decisions (Jagacinski, 1991), factors affecting job satisfaction (Rice, Gentile, & Mcfarlin, 1991), and the process of retirement (Beehr, 1986). Industrial-organizational psychologists know what Hondo proclaimed: Everyone is special in some way. An important part of their job is to make sure that a person's special talents are put to good use (e.g., Cronshaw, 1986). Today psychologists have more knowledge to offer personnel offices than ever before, thanks to intensive investigations of people across the life span (see Chapter 10).

Other Subfields

The psychology family tree continues to grow. As our world changes and new problems arise, psychologists expand their focus of study to meet these challenges. This is one of the exciting aspects of psychology; it is a dynamic science that responds to the changing issues and demands of our modern world. **Environmental psychology** analyzes how behavior is influenced by environmental factors such as architecture, weather, space, crowding, noise, and pollution. The close relationship between environment and behavior can be appreciated by trying to imagine how Hondo's life would have differed had he lived outside the Texas ranch country. **Forensic psychology** concerns behaviors that relate to our legal system. Forensic psychologists work with judges and lawyers who are trying to improve the reliability of witnesses and of jury decisions. They consult also on the mental competency of accused people and on the possibilities for rehabilitation of convicted criminals. **Health psychology** is concerned with the influence of psychological variables on physical health. The subfield not only

Industrial-organizational psychology
Subfield of psychology concerned with selecting, training, and managing employees.
Environmental psychology
Subfield of psychology that analyzes how behavior is influenced by environmental factors such as architecture, weather, space, crowding, noise, and pollution.
Forensic psychology
Subfield of psychology concerned with behaviors that relate to our legal system. Forensic psychologists work with judges and lawyers who are trying to improve the reliability of witnesses and jury decisions and are also consulted on the mental competency of accused people.
Health psychology
Concerned with the influence of psychological variables on physical health. Subfield examines not only issues such as how stress affects the possibility of developing cancer or heart disease, but also concentrates on issues such as the factors that enhance the effectiveness of the physician-patient relationship.

FIGURE 1–2

This figure shows a breakdown of the percent of psychologists engaged in work in each of the major subfields mentioned in the text.

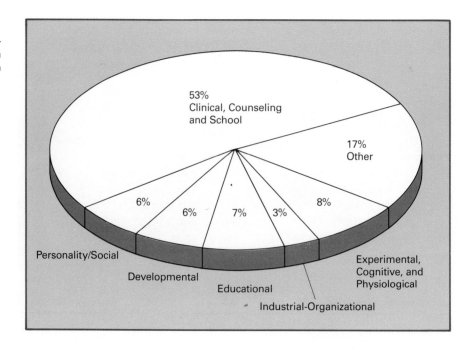

examines issues such as how stress affects the possibility of developing cancer or heart disease, but also concentrates on issues such as the factors that enhance the effectiveness of the physician-patient relationship. **Psychology of minorities** examines the behavior of people in minority groups. This subfield has emerged in response to such questions as: How important is it for minority children to have minority schoolteachers for role models? What hiring criteria will give minorities equal opportunities in the public school system? **Community psychology** is dedicated to promoting mental health at the community level. Community psychologists prevent and treat psychological problems by working to evaluate and improve community organizations. They get involved in public programs aimed at such problems as employing the handicapped, rehabilitating juvenile delinquents, and caring for the elderly. Investigators interested in **law and psychology** focus on the factors that influence jury verdicts, the way in which people determine what is just and unjust, and how the procedural aspects of a trial affect its outcome. These are just some of the new branches on the psychology family tree. We will introduce others later in the book.

The American Psychological Association (APA) Committee on Employment and Human Resources (1986) published the percentages of psychologists working in each of the major subfields (see Figure 1–2). Because of all these subfields you might get the impression that they are independent of one another. This is far from the case. In fact, the different areas of psychology are very closely related. Research and theory in any one area is important to psychologists in all the other areas. For example, an industrial psychologist must know how people learn (experimental psychology), what workers of different ages are capable of doing (developmental psychology), and the effects of job stress on an employee's emotions and behaviors (clinical psychology). Thus, in order to be a specialist, the psychologist must have a working knowledge of all areas of psychology.

One final point should be kept in mind. While we can give a definition of the field and identify its branches, psychology maintains very close relationships with many other disciplines. In fact, psychology has been identified as the "crossroads" discipline that ties together the social sciences, the humanities, and many professional areas such as medicine, law, business, and education (McGovern & Hawks, 1988). Psychologists not only conduct research on topics of concern to these fields, they also draw on the methods

Psychology of minorities
Subfield of psychology that examines behavior of people in minority groups, including women who are minorities in some contexts.
Community psychology
Subfield of psychology dedicated to promoting mental health at the community level; seeks to prevent and treat psychological problems by working to evaluate and to improve community organizations.
Law and psychology
Examines factors that influence jury verdicts, the way in which people determine what is just, and how procedural aspects of a trial affect its outcome.

and theories of these fields when examining broad issues that cut across many disciplines. For this reason, education and training in psychology should be as broad as possible (Denmark, 1989; Howard, 1991).

Careers in Psychology

You can feel at home in a psychology class or be comfortable as a psychology major even if you are not planning to become a psychologist. Students with a B.A. in psychology find themselves well received in law schools, medical schools, and business schools. Harvard Business School, for example, accepts more psychology majors than any other single major. The diversity of interests served by psychology is reflected in its popularity. It is one of the most popular college majors in America, with about 75,000 psychology majors receiving B.A. degrees in the 1983–1984 school year.

Psychology is also a popular field of graduate study. In 1984, American universities granted 3,223 doctorate degrees in psychology, which constituted 10.3 percent of all doctorate degrees granted that year (APA Committee on Employment and Human Resources, 1986). The settings in which doctoral-level APA members are employed were studied by the APA Committee on Employment and Human Resources (1986). Their findings are shown in Figure 1–3. Clearly, psychologists have many job options. Although psychologists seeking jobs in colleges and universities outnumber the available academic positions, the overall job opportunities in psychology are very good (Cantrell, 1983). Woods (1979) did a survey for the American Psychological Association that looked into where psychologists are employed outside academia. The following are some excerpts from his list of job descriptions of psychologists in innovative roles:

CONSULTANT TO A PUBLIC DEFENDER'S OFFICE

Employer description. I serve as a full-time consultant to the investigators and lawyers in the Public Defender's Office on matters relating to their clients. . . .

Job description. I am employed by the Community Mental Health Center and am placed in the Public Defender's Office. . . . My activities, which are diagnostic, evaluative, and consultative, are not innovative, but the setting in which I provide my services is a relatively new one for clinical psychologists.

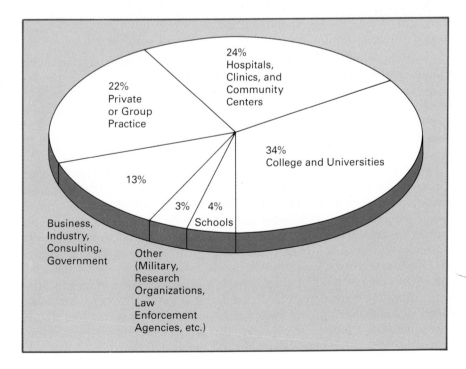

FIGURE 1–3

As can be seen here, most psychologists are engaged in research at universities and colleges, but recently more and more have been entering applied settings, where they use their knowledge to help solve a wide range of problems.

Training. I have found my training in psychological diagnostics to be essential in performing my duties. Of course, training and experience in interviewing have also been essential.

Employment prospects. It seems to me that any large Public Defender's Office could provide more efficient service and enhance the services to defendants if a behavioral scientist with clinical training and experience were added to the staff. . . .

PSYCHOLOGIST IN ACCIDENT RESEARCH

Employer description. The organization gathers and disseminates technical safety information on a nationwide basis.

Job description. The purpose of my job is to review accident literature, to design and execute original research, and to systematically evaluate accident countermeasure programs.

Training. The "traditional" degree is helpful, but I believe more of a "co-op" approach to graduate education is needed, that is, a program in which work in the real world is combined with academic coursework.

Employment prospects. There is definitely a job market for as many as 1,000 psychologists if employers could be shown the lost benefit of studying and reducing the tremendous losses caused by accidents, both on and off the job.

COMMUNICATION WORK BETWEEN PEOPLE AND COMPUTERS

Employer description. We are trying to identify design criteria to aid communication between a computer and a layperson. . . . The Office of Naval Research has partially funded our efforts, but my major employer is the research center of a large computer manufacturer.

Job description. We are trying to find ways of making it easy for people in business to tell their problems to a computer and receive some help. We do experiments to investigate features of programming languages, to study how people specify procedures in natural English, and eventually to test our ideas about how a certain set of natural-language mechanisms could be used to provide an exciting, powerful system.

Training. A person should have training in "artificial intelligence," linguistics, and computer sciences in addition to the traditional degree.

Employment prospects. This field is certainly a potentially expandable job market for psychologists. Since costs in using computers are primarily labor costs, that is, labor for translating a user's problems into computer-compatible form, we can save tremendous sums of money by solving these problems. I suggest contacting industrial companies for funding or cooperative work.

All of these jobs are held by people with a Ph.D. in psychology. Graduate training in psychology greatly expands the types of jobs available, the responsibilities associated with those jobs, and salary levels. However, people holding bachelor's degrees may be employed in many settings, including hospitals, mental health clinics, businesses, and government agencies, where their duties range from record keeping to direct-contact activities such as testing and training employees, patients, or clients.

Such diversity means opportunities, of course, but it also means complexity. After declaring psychology as a major, you face a host of career options. In response to this complexity, some universities have started special projects aimed at helping students make a smooth transition from courses to careers. One of these projects is at Virginia Commonwealth University. It links academic experience to career exploration by means of classroom activities, an alumni network, and an alumni career showcase (Brock & Yerian, 1986). A similar project is underway at Michigan State University. There the emphasis is on self-assessment, career assessment, career decision making, and placement (Overton & Forrest, 1986). If you have questions about your own career, your best bet is to contact your instructor, who will be happy to help you explore opportunities.

PSYCHOLOGY'S PUBLIC IMAGE

Considering psychology's diversity, it is no wonder that its public image has had a somewhat checkered history. The public seems to have a love-hate relationship with the field—strongly attracted to it, but also frightened by it. Psychology began as an independent field with little fanfare in the popular press. Although the first meeting of the American Psychological Association in 1892 was mentioned in the convention city newspapers, only 5 out of the next 18 annual meetings received newspaper coverage. By the 1920s, however, psychology was enjoying popularity in the press as people began to see it as a panacea for all social ills (Benjamin, 1986). In fact, one newspaper columnist advised his readers, "You cannot achieve these things [choosing careers, selecting employees, rearing and educating children, and the highest personal effectiveness and happiness] in the fullest without the new knowledge of your own mind and personality that the psychologists have given us" (Wiggam, 1928, p. 13).

The public's love affair with psychology continued until the Great Depression, when psychology's popularity dropped rapidly because the field failed to live up to the public's high expectations. On the one hand, psychology was criticized for becoming too applied, for forsaking its scientific roots (Adams, 1928). On the other hand, there was disappointment that psychology was not doing more to solve the social and economic problems of the day (Adams, 1934). It was not until World War II that the tarnished image of psychology began to take on new luster. During that era, psychology

was respected for steadfastly upholding the scientific method and appreciated for providing help in the search for solutions to problems in education, racial prejudice, clinical disorders, and business.

After the war, the field of psychology took a serious interest in its public image, and surveys of the public's knowledge and perceptions of the field were conducted. In 1948, one survey found a great deal of misunderstanding and ambivalence about psychology (Guest, 1948). Many people did not know the difference between a psychologist and a psychiatrist. And although a majority of those surveyed held a positive view of the field, psychology was most often named as the field people would *least* like to see their children enter (the other choices were architecture, engineering, chemistry, and economics).

Over the years the public image of psychology has continued to improve. One survey collected responses from 201 people in Los Angeles, Milwaukee, Houston, and Washington, D.C. (Wood, Jones, & Benjamin, 1986). Over 84 percent agreed that psychology is a science. The majority of respondents had a relatively accurate picture of the field of psychology, and most were able to distinguish between the roles of a psychologist and a psychiatrist. Also, more than 45 percent of the respondents indicated that psychology had had an impact on their lives. Still, some disturbing issues were uncovered by the survey. For instance, many people were unaware of the great diversity represented by psychology, almost 60 percent of respondents felt that psychology was incompatible with their religious

beliefs, and two-thirds believed that psychology supported liberal political positions.

It should not surprise us that there is some public confusion about psychology. For one thing, the field is very diverse; for another, psychology deals with issues of importance to almost everyone, including sexual behavior, romance, attraction, violence, drug abuse, mental health, and work behavior, and that has made it a popular topic. It is hard to pass a book rack that does not have at least one "self-help book." These books draw on psychology to tell us everything from how to be happy to how to be influential. Newspaper articles frequently cite psychological research on a host of important and interesting topics.

This popularity has been a two-edged sword for the field. On the one side, people are more aware of how much psychology has discovered about human behavior, so psychology is increasingly recognized as a "relevant" field in today's society. On the other side, many popular accounts of psychological research are misleading or incomplete, failing to identify the limitations of the research in question or to show competing and inconsistent research (McCall, 1988). In sum, the popular press is important because it excites readers to learn more about psychology, but people should be warned that these accounts are not authoritative sources for learning about the field.

We have included a selection from the popular press at the end of each chapter to give you a glimpse of how psychology is handled in press reports. Our hope is that these accounts will stimulate your interest to learn more.

Research Methods in Psychology

As you might expect, a field that is concerned with such a dazzling variety of issues has developed an equally diverse array of methods to study these issues. In general, the methods of psychology have been developed to help researchers determine what is happening and why it is happening. No single method can be crowned as the "best method"; each has its strengths and weaknesses. As we will see throughout this book, many methods may be employed to study the same problem.

There is nothing magical or mysterious about the methods of psychology. In a sense, all of us are psychologists. We watch other people, guess what they are thinking, and then test out our guesses. Hondo Crouch followed this procedure each time he went on stage. He reports looking over his audience before each show and deciding which jokes they would like. He would then test the correctness of his decisions by watching the audience's reactions to his chosen jokes.

Psychologists follow much the same procedure. They make guesses or **hypotheses** about how people will behave in certain situations. They might hypothesize, for instance, that people will remember notes in a melody better than notes in isolation. Such hypotheses are generally based on a theory. **Theories** are sets of principles that explain *why* behaviors occur. The example of remembering a melody better than isolated notes, for instance, could be based on the Gestalt theory that people respond to whole, organized patterns better than to separate elements. Psychologists test hypotheses in experiments. As we will see, there are many kinds of experiments that can be used to examine hypotheses or, in some cases, to help psychologists develop hypotheses. Regardless of the specific method, the goal is usually to help us understand why we perceive, feel, think, and act as we do.

In order to see how the research process works, let us take an example that was important to Hondo and is still an issue today. Hondo believed that the best way to raise children was to give them a lot of freedom to make their own decisions. However, he was concerned about the effects that television had on his children and he did everything he could to discourage them from watching it. Today the effect of television on behavior, especially aggressive behavior, is an issue of hot debate. Many people believe that watching violence on television causes people to engage in aggressive actions. Some parents' organizations have called for boycotts of the products of companies that sponsor violent programs on television. On the other hand, there are many people who argue that TV violence does not cause people to act violently. Who is correct? How can psychologists find evidence to resolve this debate?

In Chapter 11 we will discuss in detail the research on this issue. In this chapter, therefore, we will not be concerned as much with the question of who is right; instead, we will simply examine the ways in which an answer can be found by studying relationships between **variables,** which are factors that are allowed to vary in scientific investigations.

Case History

One approach to this question might be to examine newspaper accounts and stories about the lives of some violent criminals. We would want to determine when they started committing violent acts and what television programs they watched. If this information were not available in written sources, we might want to interview people who knew these individuals to get the information. In this way, we could learn whether these people began acting violently at the same time they began watching many violent TV programs. Another approach would be to examine people's behaviors before and after a violent program was shown. For example, we might know that a very violent movie was going to be shown on nationwide television on the night of December 14. We could examine national crime statistics for the week before and the week after that date to see if there was an increase in violent crime. Both of these approaches are examples of the **case history.**

Hypothesis
Idea that is tested experimentally; an assumption that is based on theory.
Theory
Explanation about why behavior occurs; theories generate hypotheses that can be tested experimentally.
Variable
Factor that is allowed to vary in a scientific study.
Case history
Method used in psychology that looks in depth at a few individuals or at the effects of a single event.

The method involves studying a few individuals (sometimes only one) or the effects of a single event in depth. The aim is to discover how a certain event affects behavior. The case history method has a number of advantages. It is a relatively easy way to collect a great deal of information in a short time. It examines people's behaviors in their natural surroundings. However, would you be convinced that watching television violence causes people to act aggressively if the case history studies described earlier reported a relationship between the two events?

Most people would not be convinced. One disadvantage of this method is that it uses only a few cases; thus we would not know whether the findings could be applied to everyone. For example, in the first study we looked at only a few violent criminals. Perhaps the family and economic backgrounds of these people are very different from those of most other people. If this is the case, two conclusions are possible. First, TV violence may only affect people with these backgrounds. Second, these people's violent behavior may have been due to their backgrounds and may have had nothing to do with the TV programs they watched. In the second study, it is possible that the violent TV programs caused police to become more concerned about violent crime, which, in turn, caused them to detect and report more crimes. As you can see, it is very difficult to determine the relationship between events using the case history method. Therefore, this method is generally used to help psychologists develop theories and hypotheses, and other methods are used to make clear tests of the hypotheses.

The Survey

We saw that one disadvantage of the case history method is that it focuses on only a few people; we learn a lot about a few people, but are unable

In the survey method, a questionnaire is designed and given to a large sample of people. Using this method it is possible to interview people from a number of different backgrounds and ages.

to easily apply the results to a large population. One way around this problem is to design a questionnaire and give it to a large sample of people. In this way we can choose a sample that includes people from many different family and economic backgrounds. This is the **survey** method.

If we use this method to look at the effects of television violence, we could develop questions that ask people to describe how they behaved after seeing violent TV programs. Then we could have people from all over the country respond to our questionnaire. There are many advantages to surveys. First, we can collect a great deal of information from a large number of people, and we can use people from different backgrounds and ages in our sample. Second, the survey allows for flexibility, so that we can examine a number of questions at the same time. For example, in our questionnaire, besides asking people how they *behaved* after viewing violent TV programs, we might also ask questions about how they felt and what they thought after seeing these programs. Thus, in addition to finding out how they behaved, we could determine if bad feelings or hostile thoughts were associated with violent programs.

One problem with surveys is that people often do not remember their behavior in earlier settings. For example, could you tell someone what you did after lunch last Monday? Another problem is that people may slant their answers in order to make themselves look good. In the case of our survey, people might not want to admit that they acted aggressively. A related problem is that people may be responding to the **demand characteristics.** In many cases, people want to be "good" subjects and give experimenters the "right" answers. From the subject's point of view, the right answer is the one that the experimenter is looking for. Therefore the subject may watch the experimenter for cues to the "right" answer. For example, you might express very different attitudes toward violence on television to an experimenter from the "Committee to Ban Television Violence" than you would to an experimenter from the "Let's Put Murder Back in Television Committee."

In spite of these problems, surveys have important applications. For instance, Francis Worchel (1985) developed a survey questionnaire that has shed light on how counselors can help families cope with the stresses of having a child who is dying from cancer.

Naturalistic Observation

There is an old saying that goes, "If you want to know how many teeth are in a horse's mouth, count them." If we were to apply this saying to our questions about television, the words might be changed to, "If we want to know how television affects people, go out and observe people after they have seen violent programs." **Naturalistic observation** is the research method that involves studying people's reactions to naturally occurring events in natural settings. In order to use this method to study the effects of television, we could place hidden cameras to observe children at home and in school settings to see if they behave aggressively after watching violent TV programs.

There are a number of advantages to this method of research. First, the data involve firsthand observations and do not rely on people's memories of events. Second, since people do not know they are being studied, there are few problems with people wanting to be "good" subjects and somehow doing what they believe the observer wants or expects them to do. Third, since people are being observed in their natural environment, we may feel confident that this is really the way they behave.

Survey
Method used in psychology; uses questionnaires that are given to large samples of people.
Demand characteristics
Elements in a questionnaire or experiment that communicate what behavior is expected from the subjects.
Naturalistic observation
Research method that involves studying people's reactions to naturally occurring events in natural settings.

Despite these strong points, naturalistic observation has a number of drawbacks:

1. Results are difficult to verify because natural events seldom occur in exactly the same way.

2. Naturalistic observations are difficult to analyze precisely because *the amount or degree of a variable such as TV violence may vary considerably in one example*. The same program, for instance, might have parts ranging from moderately violent to very violent.

3. Naturalistic observations cannot establish cause-and-effect relationships. They can only establish **correlations,** which are measures of the extent to which variables change together. If two variables increase or decrease at the same time, they are *positively correlated*. Watching TV violence and behaving aggressively would be positively correlated if aggressive behavior increased after people watched more TV violence. Measures are *negatively correlated* when one increases while the other decreases. Watching TV violence and behaving aggressively would be negatively correlated if aggressive behavior decreased after people watched more TV violence.

The existence of a correlation does not necessarily indicate a cause-and-effect relationship. If researchers observed a positive correlation between watching TV violence and behaving aggressively, for example, they would be faced with three possible cause-and-effect relationships: (1) TV violence causes aggression; (2) aggressive behavior causes people to watch TV programs that have many violent sequences; and (3) neither factor causes the other, but rather, an additional factor, such as grumpiness, could be causing both. That is, grumpiness could cause people to act aggressively *and* to watch more TV violence. These three possibilities are always present when one observes correlations. Despite its drawbacks, however, naturalistic observation is an important research method, especially for coming up with ideas that can be tested in experiments.

Another way to do naturalistic observation, besides using hidden cameras, is to use a special room with a one-way window through which the researcher can look out, but the people in the room cannot see the researcher. The researcher in the photo is observing the behavior of the children and parents without their being aware of it.

Correlation
A measure of the extent to which variables change together. If two variables increase and decrease at the same time, they are positively correlated; if one increases while the other decreases, they are negatively correlated. This does not necessarily indicate a cause-and-effect relationship between the variables, however.

Exposure to violent television episodes, such as the scene from a cartoon shown here, may have behavioral consequences in children and adults.

The Experiment

When we originally posed our question, we wanted to know whether or not television violence *causes* people to act aggressively. The methods that we have discussed so far may give us clues about the cause-and-effect relationship between these two variables, but we have seen that they cannot definitely establish the cause. In order to determine what events actually cause certain behaviors, psychologists use **experiments.**

An experiment is an investigation in which a researcher directly manipulates one variable while measuring the effects on some other variable. The manipulated variable is called the **independent variable;** the measured variable is called the **dependent variable.** In one experiment Liebert and Baron (1972) used TV aggression as an independent variable and play aggression as a dependent variable. Their goal was to test whether or not violent TV programs cause aggressive behavior. The subjects were boys and girls between the ages of 5 and 9 years. The experimenters assigned half the children to an experimental group in which children watched 3½ minutes of violence on TV (shooting and fighting). They assigned the other half to a control group in which children watched 3½ minutes of nonviolent television (racing and high jumping). (A **control group** is made up of subjects who are treated exactly the same as the experimental group except that they are not exposed to the independent variable and thus serve as the basis for comparison.) The experimenters used special procedures to ensure that the two groups were equivalent before they were exposed to the TV programs. After watching TV, both groups had an opportunity to "help" or "hurt" a child playing in another room. The other child was actually an actor who was aiding the experimenters. The actor played a game that required turning a handle. Children in the experiment could "help" by pressing one button that supposedly made the handle easier to turn. They could "hurt" by pressing another button that supposedly made the handle hot and difficult to turn. The actor pretended to be helped or hurt, and the experimenter recorded the length of time that children in the experiment held down each button. Children who had watched violence on TV held down the "hurt" button more and the "help" button less than children who had watched the nonviolent scenes. These

Experiment
Investigation in which a researcher directly manipulates one variable while measuring the effects on some other variable.
Independent variable
The variable that is manipulated in an experiment.
Dependent variable
The variable that is measured in an experiment.
Control group
The group of subjects in an experiment that is treated exactly the same as the experimental group(s) except that the control group is not exposed to the independent variable and thus serves as the basis for comparison.

results suggest that violent TV programs *caused* experimental subjects to act more aggressively than control subjects.

Experimental reports rarely go into detail about how an experiment can test cause-and-effect relationships. The same reasoning would be given repeatedly if they did. Once you know the logic, however, you can read it "between the lines" in every experimental report. The argument can be spelled out for Liebert and Baron's experiment as follows:

The experimental and control conditions were identical except that one group watched violent TV programs and the other watched nonviolent ones. Since there was only one difference, this difference must have caused the greater aggression in the experimental group.

Do you agree that Liebert and Baron's experimental and control conditions were identical except for the independent variable? Did the experimenters overlook any other variables that might have differed? Let's examine what Liebert and Baron did, or could have done, to control other variables.

Subject Differences and Randomization.   One thing that can differ between experimental and control conditions is the subjects. They can differ in sex, personality, intelligence, and many other variables. Liebert and Baron controlled such subject differences by using random assignments of subjects to groups. This procedure, called **randomization,** ensures that each person has an equal chance of being assigned to each group. This procedure makes it highly probable that subject differences will be equally distributed between groups. One way to make random assignments is to draw names from a list. Put all subject names in a hat; mix them up; draw them blindly, one by one; assign the first draw and all odd-numbered draws to the experimental condition; and finally, assign the second draw and all even-numbered draws to the control condition. Randomization gave Liebert and Baron a basis for saying that their two groups were the same with respect to subject differences. Randomization sometimes fails to equate subjects, which is one reason why it is important to repeat experiments.

Subject Expectations and Placebos.   We mentioned earlier that people's expectations influence their behavior. Perhaps Liebert and Baron's experimental subjects thought that they were expected to be violent, for instance. The experimenters tried to avoid such expectations. They did not tell subjects what was being tested until the experiment was completed. They gave all subjects the same instructions, and they involved all subjects in similar activities before the critical test. Still, one might argue that experimental subjects thought that they were expected to be violent since they had just viewed so much violence. A better control for expectations is possible in drug studies. Experimenters can give both groups pills that look and taste the same. That way both groups can think that they are getting the same drug, when in fact only the experimental group gets a real drug. The control group gets a **placebo,** which is a look-alike drug substitute made from inactive materials.

Experimenter Bias and Double-Blind Control.   Rosenthal (1966) showed that an experimenter's bias can influence the outcome of an experiment. **Experimenter bias** is the expectation on the part of an experimenter that a subject will behave in a certain way. Perhaps Liebert and Baron were biased toward expecting experimental subjects to be more violent. Such a bias would be especially dangerous if the dependent measure had been experimenter ratings of violent behavior. Liebert and Baron reduced this danger by having a machine time the "hurt" and "help" responses. One might argue that some danger remained. The experimenters could have unconsciously communicated their expectations to subjects. They might have done this, for example, with facial expressions, gestures, and word selection.

Randomization
Procedure used in an experiment whereby subjects are randomly assigned to either the control group or the experimental group(s). It ensures that each person has an equal chance of being assigned to each group, thus making it highly probable that subject differences will be equally distributed between groups.

Placebo
In drug studies, a drug substitute made from inactive materials that is given to the control group in drug research.

Experimenter bias
Expectations on the part of the person running an experiment that subjects will behave in a certain way—these behaviors can affect the subjects as well as the perceptions of the experimenter.

Experimenter bias is controlled best when the experimenter does not know a subject's group assignment until the experiment has been completed. This could have been done in Liebert and Baron's experiment. One experimenter could have controlled the films while another worked with the subjects. In this way, the one working with the subjects would not have to know which film was shown. Ideally, an experimenter should use a **double-blind control,** which is a procedure in which neither subject nor experimenter is aware of how the independent variable is being manipulated.

Strengths and Weaknesses of Experiments. Liebert and Baron's experiment reveals advantages and disadvantages of experiments. Several strong points are as follows:

1. Experiments can establish cause-and-effect relationships, as we already mentioned. To do so, however, researchers must be sure that they change only one variable at a time. They must guard against subject differences, subject expectations, and experimenter bias and other hidden differences between experimental and control conditions.

2. Experiments can be repeated by anyone who may wish to verify and extend them. If you examined Liebert and Baron's original report, for instance, you could get enough information to replicate the experiment in detail.

3. Experiments can be used to analyze variables precisely because researchers can control the variables. They could, for instance, make all the TV programs in one experiment moderately violent and all the programs in another experiment very violent.

Experiments also have several weak points:

1. Subjects know that they are being studied, so they may put on a false front. They may, for instance, reduce aggression when they know that they are being observed.

2. Experimental controls sometimes make independent variables unrealistic. Liebert and Baron's experiment suffers from this problem, since 3½-minute segments does not represent normal TV programming or viewing time, which currently is over 25 hours per week for children 2–17 (Nielsen, 1988).

3. Experimental controls can also make dependent variables unrealistic. Critics of Liebert and Baron's study might wonder if pushing a "hurt" button really represents aggressive behavior. We are on solid ground if we conclude that watching violent sequences on television causes children to hold down a "hurt" button longer. We are on thin ice if we try to generalize beyond the experiment to say that violence in normal TV programming causes children to be more aggressive.

4. Limited subject populations often make it difficult to determine how general research findings are. If you are now in an introductory psychology class, chances are that you will become a subject in an experiment before the semester is over, for surveys have found that most—sometimes over 90 percent—of the data collected in certain areas of psychology come from subject pools of undergraduate students (Jung, 1969; Sieber & Saks, 1989). Investigators are sometimes concerned about whether the results of research inform us about people in general or only about college students.

Some of these weaknesses can be overcome by moving experiments from laboratories to more natural settings. Liebert and Baron's study is

Double-blind control
Procedure used in an experiment in which neither subject nor experimenter is aware of how the independent variable is being manipulated.

an example of a **laboratory experiment,** which is done in a controlled environment created for the experiment. In contrast, a **field experiment** is done in a more natural setting on a broad population of subjects. Chapter 11 will discuss a field experiment on TV violence. Experimenters manipulated TV programming in a juvenile home setting, and they measured aggressive behavior in the same setting. Direct manipulations of TV programming gave more control than one gets in naturalistic observations. Doing the experiment in an everyday setting made the independent and dependent variables more realistic. Such field experiments are becoming increasingly popular. For example, Kniveton (1986) conducted a field experiment in the classroom. He found that watching aggressive models adds to the repertoire of aggressive behaviors in young boys (5–6 years old). It also adds to the time spent in aggressive behaviors.

Ethical Issues in Research

As we examine the exciting issues addressed by psychology and the methods used, it is easy to overlook an important participant in the effort to understand behavior: the *subjects* of the experiments. Whether we use observational research or laboratory or field experimentation, a common element of these methods is that all involve observing subjects, and most involve manipulating the conditions under which the subjects behave. No research project should be undertaken unless the investigator determines that the issue being studied is important for advancing our understanding of behavior.

Even if it has been determined that the issue is of importance and the results from the study will be of potential value, no investigator can ignore the rights and safety of the subjects involved in the study. The issue of ethics has long been a concern of psychologists. The ethical issues in psychology are diverse and far-reaching. Some of these issues concern the practice and application of psychology (Fremer, Diamond, & Camara, 1990; Pope, 1990), while others involve research. The overriding principle that guides psychology is that "Psychologists [should] respect the dignity and worth of the individual and strive for the preservation and protection of fundamental human rights. . . . [They should] make every effort to protect the welfare of those who seek their services and of the research participants that may be the object of study" (American Psychological Association, 1990, p. 390).

The American Psychological Association (1973, 1982) has published extensive guidelines for the conduct of research. All research that is supported by U.S. government grants must be examined by a panel of qualified experts to ensure that the investigators follow ethical guidelines. In most universities and colleges, investigators must submit all their research proposals to Institutional Review Boards (IRB) before conducting their studies. These committees evaluate the risk of the research and the safeguards, and may suggest alternative procedures. The question of ethics is clearly a difficult one.

The ethical standards for research have become more strict over the last decade, and researchers are continuing to develop new safeguards for their subjects. As you read about the studies presented in this book, you may wish to examine them in light of our discussion on ethics.

Numerous ethical issues have been identified and efforts have been instituted to deal with them. One of these issues is *invasion of privacy*. Whether we are merely observing people in their normal daily routine or taking controlled physiological measures in the laboratory, we are learning something about the subject; we are invading the privacy of that individual. In some cases, such as observing shoppers' behaviors, the invasion is mild and the behaviors that we examine are not sensitive ones. In other cases,

Laboratory experiment
Experiment performed in a controlled environment created for the experiment.
Field experiment
Experiment performed in a natural setting rather than in the controlled setting of the laboratory.

An important ethical issue is people's right to privacy. There are several ways to deal with this, including keeping a subject's responses anonymous; not making individual responses public, only the summary of the data; and getting informed consent before a subject takes part in an experiment.

however, we may be dealing with more sensitive issues (sexual behavior, prejudice) or even illegal behavior (stealing, gambling). But regardless of the content, we are intruding into areas that the individual may wish to remain private.

Given that research involves the gathering of information, how can we protect people's rights to privacy? In most studies, subjects' responses are kept *anonymous*; that is, their names or identity are not associated with their data. A second safeguard is that the data collected in studies are *not made public*. Although a summary of the results of a study may be published, the public is not given access to individual responses. Finally, a policy of *informed consent* is followed in most cases. Subjects are not forced to answer any question, and they may withdraw from the experiment at any time. Whenever possible, subjects are told about the procedures to be used in the study before they volunteer. When the subjects are children or people in institutions, the study procedures are explained to a parent or guardian, who must give consent before the subject can take part in the study.

A second ethical issue involves *deception*. In some cases, it would destroy the value of the data if subjects knew *exactly* what the experimenter was studying or what events would occur in the study. For example, if Liebert and Baron (1972) had told subjects that they were interested in studying aggressive behavior, the subjects might have changed their behavior. In this case, the subjects might have become concerned about their own aggression and tried to change their behavior to "look good" to the experimenter. If this had happened, the experiment would not have yielded valid data about the effects of TV violence on behavior. However, the point remains that the experimenter was not entirely truthful with the subjects.

The ethical rules of psychological research dictate that if deception must be used in research, the experimenter must explain this to the subject after the study is over. During this follow-up session, the experimenter reveals the true nature of the study, what issues were being investigated, and why deception was used. After subjects learn about the study, they are given the chance to demand that their data be destroyed and not be used by the experimenter.

A third ethical problem concerns the possible *harmful consequences* that people may suffer as a result of a study. In some psychological experiments people may be exposed to very stressful procedures. If we are interested in studying the effects of fear on helping behavior, we must develop severe enough experimental conditions to make subjects afraid. If our interest is to examine how well people perform under painfully noisy conditions, we must create this type of environment. In another area, we are learning today that the United States military conducted studies over 20 years ago in which soldiers were exposed to radiation. In cases like this, severe physical problems may result.

The issue of harmful consequences is a very difficult one to deal with. Sometimes it may be necessary to take some risk in order to investigate the problem at hand. When such a situation arises, the first question to be asked is whether or not the potential benefits of the study are more important than the risks the subjects are exposed to. This is clearly a hard question to answer in some cases. There is no easy formula by which to frame an answer. If the decision is made to proceed with the study despite the risks, at least two steps must be followed. First, subjects must be informed of the risks *before* they volunteer to be in the study. Second, the experimenters must follow up and examine subjects for some time after the study to see if they are suffering harmful consequences.

Another ethical problem arises from the fact that subjects may learn something about themselves in the study. For example, subjects in the Liebert and Baron study may have discovered that their behavior is influenced by TV programs. We might argue that this is a valuable lesson for

The members of this protest march for the ethical treatment of animals in research are continuing a concern for animals that dates back to the early 1800s but has become more vocal in the last few years.

them to learn. However, we must also remember that the subjects did not enter the study wishing to learn about themselves; they may not want to know this information about themselves. And some subjects may be distressed by what they learn about themselves. There is no easy way to deal with this problem. It is important that experimenters be aware of this ethical issue and evaluate their procedures with it in mind.

As we wrestle with these difficult issues, we might be tempted to solve our dilemma by turning to a different population of subjects. Why not use animals rather than people when the experiment calls for particularly severe procedures that may involve pain, stress, or surgery? For some of the issues that psychologists wish to study, such as the solving of complex reasoning problems, the use of animals in place of humans is clearly not possible. However, in other cases, it may be possible and even necessary to use animals. But simply switching from humans to animals will not solve all our ethical problems.

There has been increasing concern about the treatment of animals used in research (Cunningham, 1983; Miller, 1984). The concern over animal welfare in research dates back to 1824 (Dewsbury, 1990), when the Society for the Prevention of Cruelty to Animals (SPCA) was founded in London. This concern has centered on ensuring that the animals are housed in decent conditions and are not subjected to any unnecessary or prolonged pain or suffering. Just as committees have been set up to protect the rights of human subjects, so have they been established in many universities to oversee animal research. These committees, which often include a veterinarian, carefully review the housing and feeding of animals and the experimental procedures to be used in research. Most investigators have welcomed these committees. As one put it, "I don't believe that any of the animal rights activism has resulted in a change of investigators' attitudes toward animals because all the investigators I know are sensitive to the welfare of animals—that just makes good research sense" (Ross, 1984). As this investigator and others have pointed out, it is in the best interests of scientists to work with healthy, pain-free animals. Thus most committees established to protect animals have worked in cooperation with investigators.

Clearly, there are some tough ethical questions that must be addressed, whether the proposed research involves humans or animals as subjects. Concern for the rights of subjects is an ongoing issue that has had an important impact on research. In some cases, methods that were used 20 years ago are not allowed today. In addition, investigators are constantly searching for new ways to guard the rights and safety of their subjects.

Looking at the Numbers: Statistical Analysis

In closing this chapter, let's briefly examine one more aspect of research. Imagine that someone in your class tells you that she did a research project and found that people are more aggressive after watching a violent television show. Now she is prepared to take violent action to get violence removed from television programming, and she asks you to join her in this campaign. At first, you might be tempted to accept her invitation, but before you do, let's look at her data more closely. What did she really find? Initially, she tells you that aggression increased by 60 percent in subjects who watched an aggressive program, but only by 40 percent in those who viewed a nonaggressive program. Not bad for a start, but what more do you want to know about her data?

For one thing, you'd like to know how many subjects she used in her study. You would be less impressed with her results if you found that she used 5 subjects in each condition than if she used 100 subjects. You'd also like to know something about the variability or pattern of her results. For example, the 60 percent increase in aggression might have resulted from only a few subjects showing a dramatic increase in aggression, while the others showed no increase, or even a decrease, in aggressive behavior. Or the result could have been produced by a majority of people acting more aggressively, while a few subjects showed a dramatic drop in aggression. How do we determine what the data are telling us?

In the Appendix, we go into a more detailed discussion of **statistics,** but for now, let's just briefly see why we use statistical analyses to help interpret our data. Statistical analyses help us determine the properties of our data. For example, some statistical tests compute both the average (mean) and the amount of variability in our data. Next, the test compares these data with results obtained in other conditions of the experiment. The comparison tells us the *probability* that differences between the two sets of data could have been found by chance. Psychologists have generally adopted the rule that differences will be considered **real** if they could have occurred by chance less than 5 percent of the time. For example, we might be prepared to accept our classmate's conclusion if she told us that her statistical analyses revealed that the difference between her two conditions could have occurred by chance less than 5 percent of the time. Other types of statistics (correlation) tell us about the relationship between two variables. For example, we might want to know whether violent programs have different effects depending on the age of the viewers. In that case, we might examine the correlation between amount of aggressive behavior and age of viewer. A positive correlation would suggest that violence increased with the age of the viewer, while a negative correlation would indicate that violence decreased as the viewer's age increased. Again, we would examine the magnitude of the correlation to see whether the relationship was real (could have occurred by chance less than 5 percent of the time).

There is nothing magical or frightening about statistics. Statistical methods are simply tools that help us develop a clearer view of our results.

Statistics
Branch of mathematics used by psychologists to describe data and to draw conclusions based on the data.
Real difference
A difference that could occur by chance less than 5 percent of the time.

They also help us communicate our results to other people. We are less likely to be left wondering about a set of results if someone tells us their statistical properties than if we are only told that the responses of one group were different from those of another group. In this sense, statistics is a language that allows scientists to minimize confusion when presenting the findings of their research. Statistics do not tell us about the research project itself—in other words, whether the experimenter ran an ethical study or removed experimenter bias and demand from the study. Statistics only tell us about the relationship between the results collected from that study.

Armed with an understanding of research methods and statistics, you are now ready to enter the intriguing world of psychological research. As you read about the research we present in this text and search for the meaning of the results, keep this brief lesson in mind.

Summary

1. **Psychology** is the scientific study of behavior and the applications gained from that knowledge. Its main goals are to clearly describe, predict, and explain behavior.

2. Wundt set up the first psychological laboratory in Leipzig, Germany in 1879. Wundt and Titchener are credited with developing **structuralism,** which is concerned with identifying the elements of human experience and finding out how those elements interact to form thoughts and feelings.

3. **Functionalism** is concerned with the function of mental processes to fill needs. This emphasis led to important applications in education and to the founding of educational psychology.

4. **Gestalt psychology** was based on the assumption that many experiences cannot be broken down into separate elements—they must be experienced as wholes, or gestalts. Gestalt psychologists worked at identifying these and other organizational laws of perception.

5. Watson claimed that we did not need such unobservable events as thinking or feeling to explain behavior. He said that behavior could be explained and predicted by focusing only on observable stimuli and responses, which is the basis of the **behaviorist approach** to psychology. The debate about behaviorism still goes on.

6. Sigmund Freud was the founder of the **psychoanalytic approach** to psychology, which focuses on unconscious motivations that control human behavior. Freud thought that many of these unconscious thoughts and wishes are the result of our experiences during infancy and early childhood.

7. The **humanistic approach** to psychology is based on the idea that people are basically good and, given the proper environment, will strive to achieve positive social goals. This approach is very popular today.

8. By the 1950s psychology had established itself as a major area for scientific study. Since that time a number of subfields of psychology have developed, in which many of the approaches we have discussed are used. These subfields include the following: **physiological, experimental, cognitive, developmental, social, personality, clinical, counseling and school, engineering,** and **industrial-organizational psychology.** Some of the more recent subfields to develop are **environmental, forensic, health,** and **community psychology,** as well as the **psychology of minorities.**

9. In psychological research scientists make **hypotheses** about how people will behave in certain situations. These hypotheses, which can be tested experimentally, are based on **theories,** which are explanations about why behaviors occur. A number of different research methods were discussed, including **case history, survey, naturalistic observations,** and **experiment.**

10. An **experiment** is an investigation in which a researcher directly manipulates one variable while measuring the effects on some other **variable.** The manipulated variable is the **independent variable.** The **dependent variable** is measured to see the effects on it of the manipulation of the independent variable.

11. There are a number of other elements or variables in an experiment that must be carefully controlled. For example, **randomization** assures that subject differences will be equally distributed between the

control group and the experimental group, and **double-blind controls** assure that **experimenter bias** cannot affect subjects or the researcher's perceptions of what occurs in the experiment.

12. Ethical issues in research involve the rights and safety of subjects used in experiments.

13. Statistical methods are used to help interpret and communicate the results of research. Many statistical techniques indicate the probability that the observed results could have occured by chance.

Key Terms

analytic introspection
behaviorism
case history
clinical psychology
cognitive psychology
community psychology
control group
correlation
counseling and school psychology
demand characteristics
dependent variable
developmental psychology
double-blind control
engineering psychology
environmental psychology

experiment
experimental psychology
experimenter bias
field experiment
forensic psychology
functionalism
Gestalt psychology
health psychology
humanistic psychology
hypothesis
independent variable
industrial-organizational psychology
laboratory experiment
law and psychology
naturalistic observation

personality
physiological psychology
placebo
psychoanalysis
psychology
psychology of minorities
randomization
"real" difference
social psychology
statistics
structuralism
survey
theory
variable

PSYCHOLOGY IN THE NEWS

Despite the fact that modern technology has filled our world with an unending array of the most unusual and curious inventions, there is still one topic that continues to garner the greatest attention and fascination: human behavior. We love studying ourselves. People-watching is a favorite pastime, and when we are not actually observing humans, we spend a great deal of time speculating about or imagining human behavior.

This curiosity about ourselves has not escaped the attention of the media. Some media outlets, such as news columns and news programs, report about human behavior, while others go to great lengths to highlight the bizarre and unusual aspects of human activities. In addition, the media attempt to bring psychology to the public by reporting on psychological research or applying psychology to help us better understand our own behavior and that of other people.

In a sense, all people are consumers of psychology. Indeed, what knowledge of psychology most people have comes from accounts they have read in the popular press. We might characterize these people as "uninformed consumers" of psychology because they have little basic knowledge of the field. This situation—plus the fact that popular reports give only abbreviated accounts written for a broad audience—may result in a confusing picture of psychology.

With this in mind, we thought it would be useful to present articles about psychology from *The New York Times* at the end of each chapter. We chose articles that dealt with issues of relevance to the chapter. We hope that these selections will serve two purposes: (1) you will see examples of responsible attempts to present psychology to the public; (2) you will be reading these newspaper accounts armed with information gained from the chapter. You will not be the typical uninformed consumer. We hope you will evaluate the articles, question their conclusions, and seek additional information to gain a more in-depth understanding of the topics under consideration. We hope the articles will stimulate you to explore these matters and not accept such accounts as the "final word." And we hope you will find the topics challenging, important, and interesting.

Here is a menu of the articles:

Chapter 2: Subtle but Intriguing Differences Found in the Brain Anatomy of Men and Women.

Chapter 3: Research on Noise Disappears in the Din.

Chapter 4: New Breed of Robots Have the Human Touch.

Chapter 5: Feeling Sleepy? An Urge to Nap Is Built In.

Chapter 6: Embattled Giant of Psychology Speaks His Mind (An Interview with B. F. Skinner).

Chapter 7: Studies Offer Clues to Memory and Aging.

Chapter 8: Humor Found to Aid Problem Solving.

Chapter 9: Sensing Silent Cues Emerges as Key Skill in Childhood.

Chapter 10: Tracking the Life of the New Father: Children versus Career.

Chapter 11: Mating for Life? It's Not for the Birds or the Bees.

Chapter 12: Studies Point to Power of Nonverbal Signals.

Chapter 13: Shyness: What It Is, What to Do about It.

Chapter 14: Delusion, Benign and Bizarre, Is Recognized as Common.

Chapter 15: Cultural Differences Emerge as Key Factor in Psychotherapy.

Chapter 16: Great Altruists: Science Ponders the Soul of Goodness.

Chapter 17: As Bias Crime Seems to Rise, Scientists Study Roots of Racism.

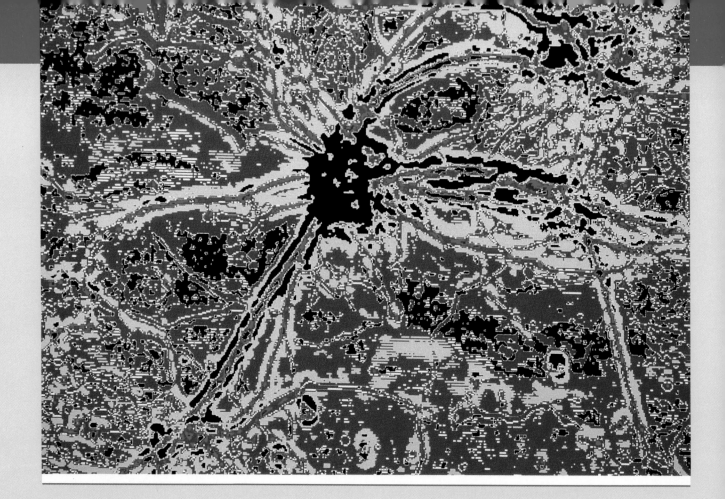

Biology and Behavior

2

Agnes de Mille had been a believer and a fighter for more than sixty years. She had believed in her own talents as a ballet dancer and choreographer. She had believed in the traditional American form of ballet and the Agnes de Mille Heritage Dance Theater, which she had founded to promote that form. More recently she had believed that she would win the fight for financial support of her theater. She was prepared for a decisive battle in that fight on May 15, 1975: A lecture-dance concert was scheduled in which she, the lecturer, and a host of supporting cast members would determine whether her theater would live or die.

That evening, however, de Mille found herself in a more critical life-or-death battle. At 5:50 P.M., a blood vessel in her brain gave way and blood gushed forth, tearing and compressing vital centers as it penetrated her brain's soft tissues. From then on, she was engaged in a battle for her own life.

What astonished de Mille most about her stroke was that it occurred without pain or any sensation that something had happened in her brain. She only became aware that something was happening to her when she tried to sign a contract with a new member of the cast and discovered that she couldn't write. "I can't write," she said quietly. "My hand won't work." She was encouraged to sit down, which she did. Her reports became more alarming. "I have no feeling in my right leg. I can't feel on the right side. Maybe we'd better have a doctor. This is very interesting. This is curious. I'm cold." It was warm in the theater, and yet she was shivering. Someone told her that she was moving her hand and foot. "But I can't feel," she said. "Am I talking funny? I seem to be talking funny."

Fortunately, Dr. George Gorham arrived within minutes. Her principal backers were no longer dancers and concert pianists. Now her supporting cast was her immediate family, close friends, and one of the world's finest medical teams, which included Dr. Gorham, Dr. Fred Plum, the neurologist-in-chief, who took charge of the case, and Dr.

Caroline McCagg, a specialist in rehabilitation medicine.

De Mille was lucky because New York Hospital was one of the three hospitals in the world that had computerized axial tomography, popularly called the CAT scanner. The availability of this X-ray device was good news because it would greatly improve the diagnosis of the extent of her stroke. But the pictures the CAT scanner produced were far from "good news." The blood that had been released took over an area as large as a walnut, and it was steadily growing. The doctors murmured, "This is speech, possibly sight." As the blot increased they said, "That is all speech and mobility." After seeing the pictures, the doctors prepared her husband, Walter Prude, for the worst: "There is blood in the spinal fluid, and that is usually fatal."

De Mille never became discouraged during the difficult days following her stroke, even though her right side was paralyzed and she could neither see nor speak clearly. She simply blocked out doubt as she had learned to do in her work. This will to live gave the doctors the edge they needed to perform a modern "medical miracle."

Her speech and sight improved quickly, but her sense of touch never returned to normal. It was as though a line had been drawn down the middle of her body and feeling had been cut off on the right side. Agnes de Mille described this condition as follows:

We always know, in normal life, where our hands and feet are. We don't think about them consciously, but we know because there is an unceasing radar playback from every part of the body telling us, "This is there," "This is near," "This is not within reach," "This is painful," "This is comfortable," "This is hot!" "This is soft." We don't have to look and we don't have to be aware, we just know. Now I was without those signals, and I didn't know.

I could feel motor impulses, and in a couple of weeks I learned how to know when I was opening and shutting my hand because I could differentiate the effort and I was generally right in my surmises. But if somebody took my hand and moved it for me and my eyes were shut, I had no idea where it was or if it had been touched at all. (de Mille, 1982, p. 57)

De Mille's physical therapy began in the hospital and continued after she returned home. As a dancer, she was accustomed to physical discipline. She was therefore able to handle the strenuous therapy. She worked especially hard after one therapist said that she would never again rise on her toes to do relevés onto full point (a ballet step). Two months later she was doing four relevés and in six months she was doing eight.

Later she persuaded Robert Joffrey to do her *Conversations about the Dance*, the lecture-dance concert that had been interrupted by the original stroke. The performance was a success. At the end, de Mille threw out both hands, extended and open, to the audience. Caroline McCagg, her rehabilitation therapist, burst into tears, for she knew that Agnes had never used her right arm since the stroke. Dr. Plum, who also attended this performance, later spoke of the example set by Agnes de Mille: "Those who can learn from and follow it will enrich their own lives as Agnes de Mille has enriched hers and, by the radiance of her spirit, mine."

After completing this chapter, you should be able to:

Review the history and influence of the early philosophers on the modern-day field of behavioral neuroscience.

Name the parts of a neuron and explain how neural messages are transmitted.

Name and explain the parts of the brain and spinal cord.

Differentiate the functional subdivisions of the nervous system: their interrelationships and their functions.

Know the glands of the endocrine system and how they regulate body chemistry.

Explain genetic inheritance.

History and Scope of Behavioral Neuroscience

Agnes de Mille's struggle for life raises important questions: How did the doctors know that her stroke threatened her speech, sight, and mobility? Why did damage on the left side of her brain affect her sense of touch on the right side of her body? Such questions are the concern of **behavioral neuroscientists,** who study the biological underpinnings of behavior.

The historical roots of these studies have been traced at least as far back as Socrates (c. 470 B.C.) and Plato (427–347 B.C.). These two Greek philosophers maintained that it is our physical body that limits our experiences of the physical environment. Aristotle (384–323 B.C.), a student of Plato, expanded this idea. He discussed the influence of body functions on three kinds of human qualities: vegetative (nutrition, growth, and reproduction), animal (movement and sensation), and rational (reason and will). Aristotle's proposal drew the attention and the criticism of religious authorities for many centuries. At issue was the relative importance of the body and the soul. A turning point in this controversy came when Thomas Aquinas (1225–1274) formulated a compromise interpretation, which made it possible for scholars to study the influence of the body on human qualities without denying the importance of the human soul. This compromise position set the stage for the French philosopher René Descartes (1596–1650) to analyze how eyes, nerves, and muscles influence human behavior (Figure 2–1).

Another milestone came around the turn of the nineteenth century. At that time, Franz Joseph Gall (1758–1829) succeeded in drawing a great deal of attention to the brain. He proposed a theory of **phrenology** that included three assumptions. First, specific areas of the brain control specific functions. Second, specific areas increase in size when they are exercised. Third, increases in the size of brain areas cause bumps on the skull. Accordingly, Gall proposed that the bumps and hollows on the skull reveal much about a person's brain functions. Although Gall was wrong about the significance of bumps on the head, his theory was important because it focused attention on the idea that specific brain areas have specific functions.

Gall's theory was the forerunner to a field that now has a respected and sophisticated research base. Today, research is conducted by **biopsychologists** to learn how the brain's biological properties correspond to the brain's physiological functions. Improved methodology has sparked a

Behavioral neuroscientists and biopsychologists
Study the biological underpinnings of behavior.
Phrenology
Determination of an individual's personality type by the examination of the bumps and contours of his or her head.

FIGURE 2–1

The seventeenth-century French philosopher René Descartes drew this figure to illustrate the function of human eyes, nerves, and muscles. Although his specific theories about how these physical parts operate were wrong, they did help to promote studies of the biological underpinnings of behavior.

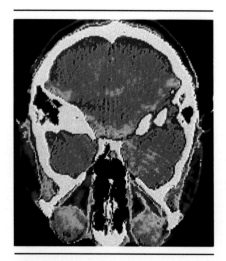

FIGURE 2–2

A CAT scan is a computer-generated representation of brain structures.

rapid expansion of knowledge about biopsychological relationships. For example, Sokolov (1987) reviewed knowledge gained through new tools for measuring electrochemical processes. Additionally, the CAT scanner, which was so rare when Agnes de Mille had her stroke in 1975, is now readily available in most communities across the nation. A CAT scan uses x-rays to detect brain structures, as shown in Figure 2–2.

We now know that the brain is part of a major coordinating mechanism, the **nervous system.** This masterful structure monitors our outside world, controls our movements, learns, remembers, and generally controls all of our behavior. It works in harmony with the *endocrine system*, glands that regulate our behavior through chemical messengers called hormones. Neuroscientists are making progress toward understanding the electrochemical code that is used to communicate messages within and between these two coordinating systems. In addition, progress toward understanding how these codes relate to psychology is being paralleled by advances in **genetics,** the study of how traits are passed from parent to child. This new knowledge is paving the way for biopsychologists to understand the genetic inheritance that determines our behavior.

Today, biopsychologists are working with other neuroscientists and geneticists to develop theories about the biological determinants of behavior and to apply these theories to improve health care. We already saw some of the applications in the medical "miracles" that saved Agnes de Mille. In this chapter, we will see other applications related to illnesses caused by poisons, popular drugs, and diseases such as epilepsy, hypertension, speech disorders, and those caused by birth defects. Other text chapters include examples of biopsychological principles and applications that relate to sensation, memory, learning, development, motivation, emotions, personality, and abnormal psychology.

Neurons: Basic Units of the Nervous System

Nervous system
Pervasive communication system in the body that monitors the outside world and manages the brain and behavior.

Genetics
The study of how traits are inherited.

Neurons
Cells in the nervous system that receive and send impuses.

Dendrites
Short fibers extending from the body of a neuron, receiving impulses from other neurons and carrying them to the cell body.

Axon
Long fiber carrying neural impulses away from the cell body to the terminal branches to be passed on to other neurons.

Myelin sheath
Fatty covering of some axons that allows neural impulses to be conducted faster.

After her triumphant lecture-dance concert, de Mille willfully extended her right arm to the audience, something she previously had been unable to do. How did her brain initiate and control this miraculous movement? We begin our search for an explanation by exploring the brain's basic components, *neuron cells*, which are specialized to send and receive information.

The brain contains between 100 and 200 billion **neurons.** As shown in Figure 2–3, neurons are similar to all other cells in that they have a *cell nucleus* within a *cell body*, surrounded by a *cell membrane.* Unlike other cells, however, neurons have tiny branchlike fibers called **dendrites** that extend from their bodies and allow them to communicate with other cells. The brain has more connections between neurons than our galaxy has stars (Hoyenga & Hoyenga, 1988). A single long extension called an **axon** carries messages away from the cell bodies toward 1,000 to 10,000 terminal branches that reach out to other cells. Most axons are one or two inches long. In contrast, some are only a fraction of an inch in length, and others are several feet long, such as the axon that reaches from the spinal cord to the toe in the giraffe. Some axons have a fatty covering called a **myelin sheath.** At intervals, the myelin sheath has gaps called *nodes of Ranvier.* Neural messages travel faster on myelinated axons because the messages skip from one node to the next. Let's look first at what neural messages are, and then discuss the way they are transmitted.

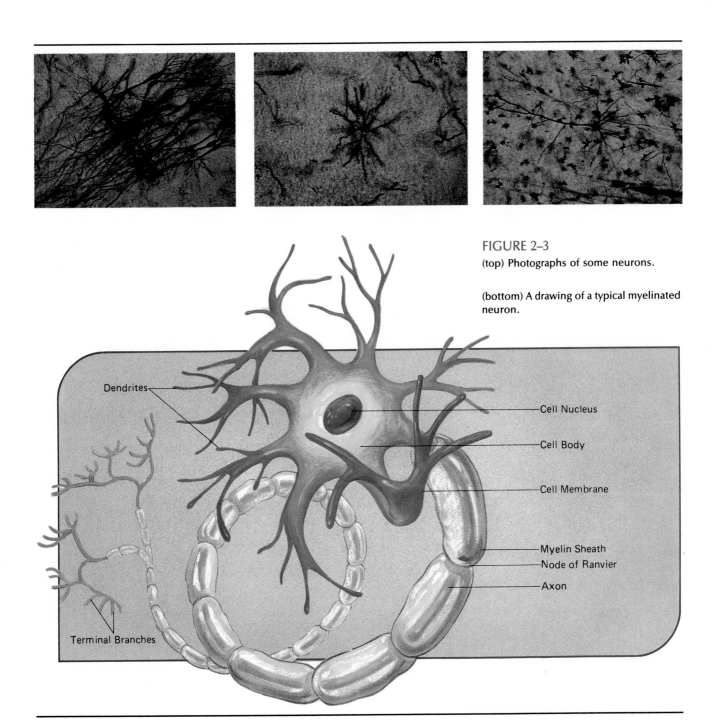

FIGURE 2–3

(top) Photographs of some neurons.

(bottom) A drawing of a typical myelinated neuron.

Dendrites

Cell Nucleus

Cell Body

Cell Membrane

Myelin Sheath

Node of Ranvier

Axon

Terminal Branches

Neural Impulses

De Mille's extension of her right arm depended on a complex communication system operating inside her nervous system. The arm movement began with activity in one or more neurons in the form of a neural impulse or message, spread methodically through a network of neurons, and ended with well-coordinated muscle movements. Understanding neural impulses is the key to understanding the language used within the nervous system.

Neurons "speak" a simple language, consisting of an "off-on" code. A neuron is "off" at all times, except during neural impulses. During the "off" or *resting state*, a neuron has an electric tension, or **membrane potential,** existing between the cell's inside and outside environments. The potential is created by an attraction that exists between negatively and positively charged particles, or *ions*. During the resting state, there are more positively

Membrane potential
An electric tension that exists in a neuron between the cell's inside and outside environment. Also called *polarization*.

HEADACHES, BRAIN, AND BEHAVIOR

Did you have a headache during the past year? If so, that puts you in the company of 75 percent of Americans, according to the National Headache Foundation. Each year, headaches cause 80 million visits to doctors' offices. Americans also spend more than $400 million on over-the-counter drugs to banish headaches (Berkeley Wellness Letter, 1990).

Types of Headaches

Some headaches are caused by serious diseases, such as strokes or brain tumors. Most, however, are not due to underlying disease; these "primary headaches" usually fall into three categories:

1. *Tension headaches,* also called *stress headaches* or *muscle-contraction headaches,* are the mildest and most common type. They are dull, steady pains throughout the head or localized in the forehead, temples, or back of the neck. They are accompanied by tightness in the muscles around the scalp and the back of the upper neck.

   Tension headaches are equally common in men and women. Most of us have one occasionally. They can occur before or after a stressful or fatiguing event; they can also be triggered by sleep deprivation or by postures that tense neck and head muscles.

2. *Migraine headaches* are pulsating pains that usually occur on one side of the head (which accounts for the name "migraine," from a Greek word meaning "half a skull"). The throbbing pain is usually intense and can be incapacitating. It may be as brief as a few minutes or as long as several days. Migraine headaches sometimes start with distorted vision such as angular bolts of light. A fully developed migraine headache can include vomiting and extreme sensitivity to light and noise.

   Migraine headaches are about four times more likely to strike women than men. The affliction tends to run in families, and a first attack often occurs before the victim is 30. Triggers include emotional factors.

3. *Cluster headaches* are steady and piercing pains often localized around one eye or temple. Each one lasts for up to several hours and they recur in groups or clusters. For instance, they might hit every day for weeks, then disappear for months before starting another round of daily attacks.

   Cluster headaches are about six to nine times more likely to afflict men than women. The first attack usually occurs in the 20s or 30s. The causes are not well understood, but triggers seem to include heavy drinking and smoking.

Brain Mechanisms Behind Headaches

Serotonin is a chemical messenger between neurons in the brain that, in addition to many other functions, controls the narrowing and widening of blood vessels in the brain. These vessels have long been implicated in headaches. Experts believe that migraines occur when a widening of the vessels permits an abnormally high blood flow. Spasms of blood vessels within the brain may also account for other migraine symptoms such as visual disturbances and nausea. Abnormal blood flow in the brain has also been linked to cluster headaches and (possibly) to tension headaches.

Drug Treatments

The link between serotonin and headaches underlies two new treatments for migraines and cluster headaches. The first is a new drug, sumatriptan, that diminishes abnormal blood flow by controlling serotonin's action in the brain. This regulation reduces headaches with

charged ions outside the cell, and more negatively charged ions inside the cell. This resting state of tension is sometimes called a state of **polarization.**

Correspondingly, the "on" state, or neural impulse, is called **depolarization.** This off-on firing process can happen spontaneously, but it is usually triggered by impulses from other neurons. During the "on" response the cell membrane momentarily opens to positive sodium ions, causing the charge inside the cell to go from negative to positive relative to the outside (Figure 2–4, top). When the charge reaches the *critical value* shown in the bottom of Figure 2–4 the membrane closes to sodium ions, and positive potassium ions are pumped out, bringing the charge back to the resting level.

As soon as the firing process is completed at one spot on a neuron, it starts at a neighboring spot, spreading the impulse down the entire length

Polarization
Electric tension that exists in a neuron between the cell's inside and outside environment. Also called *membrane potential.*
Depolarization
Occurs when a neuron is sending or receiving a neural impulse.

fewer side effects than other treatments. Sumatriptan is undergoing clinical trials in the United States and should be available in a few years.

The second new approach uses that old standby, aspirin. We have known for years that aspirin reduces ordinary headache pain. We now know that it helps to *prevent* migraines. A Harvard Physician's Health Study suggests that taking an aspirin every other day reduces the risk of migraines by about 20 percent in frequent sufferers. Aspirin is thought to start a chain of events that ends in a lower risk of migraines, and serotonin is thought to be an important link in that chain. Aspirin reduces the grouping of blood platelets, which slows the release of serotonin. This suppression of serotonin depresses the abnormal blood flow that causes migraines. Here we have an example of how a better understanding of brain mechanisms has led to the more effective use of an over-the-counter drug.

Tension headaches are also treated by pain medications sold without prescriptions. These include aspirin, ibuprofen (e.g., Advil), and acetaminophen (e.g., Tylenol). You can get these drugs on your own, but you should consult a doctor if you use them over a long period. If these drugs don't work for you, a doctor can prescribe others that may help.

Preventing and Treating Headaches Without Drugs

Some people avoid headaches by improving their posture. For example, make sure your neck is straight when you read or work at a computer terminal for long periods. Stretching exercises of the neck, back, and shoulders may also help. Muscle-contraction headaches might also respond to heat, cold, or massages around the head and neck.

Other people avoid headaches by abstaining from certain foods. Some commonly implicated foods are caffeine-rich drinks, alcoholic beverages, and cured or processed meat. Caffeine, alcohol, and the nitrites that are used in cured meats all affect blood flow.

Finally, many headaches are related to emotions and stress. Psychologists can help headache sufferers control their reactions to stressors. For example, Holroyd and colleagues (1988) used a behavioral approach with the following prevention and treatment goals: (a) coping better with stressful problems, (b) relaxing more effectively, and (c) gaining better control over stress-related physiological functions. They then compared their behavioral approach with a pharmacological treatment that required patients to take a drug when they felt a migraine coming on. Over six months, both

approaches proved very effective, but a three-year follow-up study supported the greater effectiveness of the behavioral approach (Holroyd et al., 1989). Patients in the behavioral condition were still doing very well without drugs, while all the patients receiving drug treatments had switched to a different drug. Their reasons for switching included side effects and loss of effectiveness of the original drug. These studies suggest that headache sufferers should seriously consider behavioral approaches.

Behavioral approaches are best used under the supervision of a trained professional. However, this book might help you understand the three goals of behavioral methods. The first goal, better coping, is addressed in Chapter 12, "Emotions, Stress, and Coping." The second goal, relaxing, is addressed in several places, including a section in Chapter 5 on the relaxation response, which describes a simple six-step procedure to help you relax. The final goal, physiological control, is discussed in Chapters 6 and 15. They describe biofeedback, a therapy that helps you control your physiological functions without drugs. You may want to skip directly to these chapters if you think your headaches are related to emotions and stress. We hope they help you head off your next headache.

---

of the neuron. In cells with large myelinated axons, the neural impulses travel at speeds of nearly 400 feet per second. Small axons without myelin sheaths carry impulses as slowly as 3 feet per second. When neural impulses reach the end of an axon, they are sent on to other neurons.

Synaptic Transmission

We have seen how an impulse moves down an axon of one cell; this is called axonal transmission. **Synaptic transmission** occurs as an impulse moves from one neuron to another. It is called synaptic because the junction between two neurons is called a **synapse.**

An incoming impulse must be above a minimum level or threshold

Synaptic transmission
Occurs as a neural impulse; moves from one neuron to another.
Synapse
Junction between two neurons.

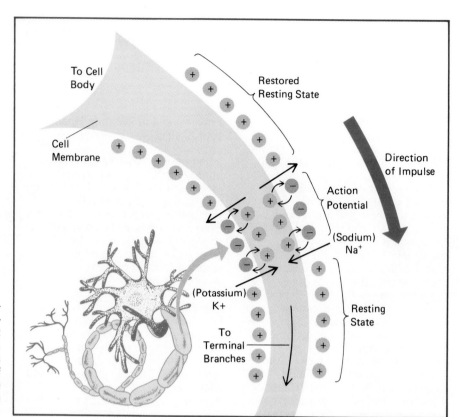

FIGURE 2–4

(top) When a point on the *neural membrane* is adequately stimulated by an incoming message, the membrane opens at that point and positively charged sodium ions flow in, depolarizing the neuron. This process is repeated along the length of the membrane, creating the neural impulse that travels down the axon, causing the neuron to fire.

(bottom) The incoming message must be above a certain threshold to cause a neuron to fire. After it fires, the cell body begins to pump potassium *ions* out of the neuron until a state of ionic equilibrium is restored. This process happens very quickly and within a few thousandths of a second the neuron is ready to fire again. The small "bump" at the lower left represents an incoming message that was too weak to cause the neuron to fire. (Adapted from Carlson, 1981)

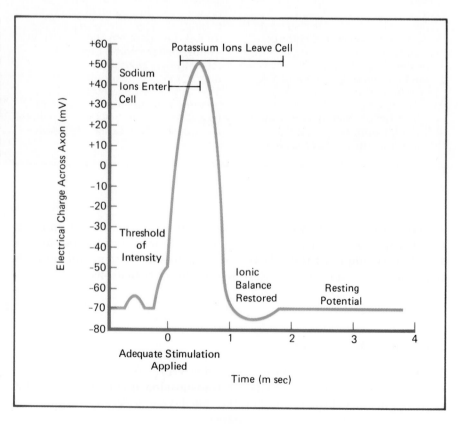

of intensity or else a cell will not fire. If the intensity is too low, the membrane will not open up to sodium. Cell thresholds are sometimes compared to triggers on a gun. You must pull a trigger hard enough or a gun won't fire. If you pull a trigger even harder, however, the bullet will not travel any faster or any farther. In the same way, cell firing is an all-or-none action. No response occurs for stimuli below the threshold level; a full response occurs for stimuli at or above the cell threshold as long as the receiving cell is ready to fire. When a cell fires once, it cannot fire again for about 1 millisecond. After this **absolute refractory period,** a cell enters a **relative refractory period** for a few milliseconds, during which time it can fire only in response to a very strong impulse. A neuron sends different messages, not by changing the strength of its response, but by changing the *rate* of its response. Stronger stimuli are indicated by faster firing rates.

As de Mille spoke her concluding lines and extended both arms to the audience, she generated messages in her nervous system that darted through millions of synapses. Let's look at just one of them to see how it works.

Each synapse has five parts: (1) the **axon terminal,** a tiny knob at the end of an axon's terminal branch; (2) the dendrite of the receiving cell; (3) the **synaptic vesicles,** tiny oval sacs on the axon terminal filled with a chemical transmitter substance; (4) the **synaptic space,** a very small gap between the axon terminal of one cell and the dendrite of the next cell; and (5) the **receptor sites** on the dendrite that receive the chemical transmitter. When an impulse reaches an axon terminal, the synaptic vesicles release a chemical that travels across the synaptic space to a dendrite on a receiving neuron (see Figure 2–5).

Chemical Transmitters.　Scientists have learned within the last sixty years that the nervous system contains many **chemical transmitters.** All carry messages between neurons, but different chemical transmitters carry different messages. Some excite neurons (that is, they cause the receiving neuron to fire); others inhibit neurons (that is, they keep the receiving neuron from firing). Some transmitters shout loudly and call for a fast response; others speak softly and influence neurons slowly but surely.

The most common transmitter is **acetylcholine (ACh).** Synapses using it are generally located on muscles. They usually transmit strong, fast-acting, excitatory messages. After the ACh delivers its message, it is broken down so that it is prevented from activating the receiving neuron again. ACh components are then transported back to the axon terminal, reassembled, and stored again in the synaptic vesicles.

Research has led to important applications, including a better understanding of such diseases as myasthenia gravis, a deadly disease in which synaptic transmission of ACh fatigues rapidly, preventing normal movement and breathing. Botulism, another deadly disease, works by blocking the release of ACh, which results in paralysis. On the other hand, if too much ACh builds up in the synaptic space, which is the effect of certain poisons (such as the venom of the black widow spider), the neuron can no longer respond to it and the muscles contract, again causing paralysis and, in extreme cases, death.

Another important kind of transmitter is a class of substances known as **catecholamines.** Synapsis using catecholamines can either transmit slow-acting, inhibitory messages or arousal messages. Unlike ACh, catecholamines are not broken down after they deliver their message. They are cleared out through a powerful transport system that returns them to synaptic vesicles. This process keeps the catecholamines from activating the receiving neuron again after their message is delivered. Although ACh and catecholamines operate differently, both have been implicated in the

Absolute refractory period
Period after a cell has fired, during which it will not fire again. Usually lasts for about 1 millisecond.
Relative refractory period
Period during which a cell will only fire in response to an extra-strong impulse; lasts for a few milliseconds.
Axon terminal
Tiny knob at the end of an axon's terminal branch.
Synaptic vesicles
Tiny oval sacs on the axon terminal filled with a chemical transmitter substance.
Synaptic space
Very small gap between the axon terminal of one cell and the dendrite of the next cell.
Receptor sites
Areas on the dendrite that receive the chemical transmitter.
Chemical transmitters (neurotransmitters)
Chemicals that carry messages between neurons; some are excitatory, some inhibitory.
Acetylcholine (ACh)
Chemical transmitter in neurons that tends to transmit fast-acting, excitatory messages.
Catecholamines
Chemical transmitters in neurons that tend to transmit slow-acting, inhibitory messages.

FIGURE 2–5

Synaptic transmission occurs when a neurotransmitter carries a neural impulse from the axon of one neuron to the dendrites of another.

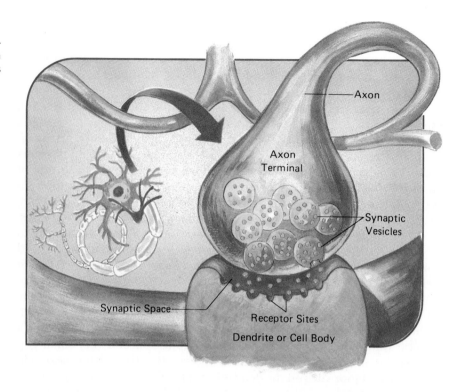

Axon

Axon
Terminal

Synaptic
Vesicles

Synaptic Space

Receptor Sites

Dendrite or Cell Body

biochemistry of memory (Chapouthier, 1989). This insight has given researchers an important lead in understanding age-related memory impairments (e.g., McEntree & Crook, 1990). Similarly, research on catecholamines is giving scientists insights into how we direct our attention (Clark, Geffen, & Geffen, 1989).

Research on catecholamines has also led to important applications, including a better understanding of commonly used drugs. We now know, for example, that when cocaine is used medically to render a local area insensitive to pain, it works by blocking the reabsorption process of catecholamines. Cocaine is also misused by some as a recreational drug. Unsupervised use of cocaine can be dangerous because it can have toxic effects, including dizziness, convulsions, and drastic drops in blood pressure.

Still another type of transmitter has a chemical structure similar to opium and its derivatives, morphine and heroin. Transmitters with this property are known as **endorphins,** a word meaning "endogenous morphine." Research on endorphins has increased our understanding of pain perception (Besson & Chasuck, 1987). This benefit is not surprising since morphine is a painkiller. But the role of "endogenous morphine" goes well beyond pain. Research on endorphins has also yielded insights into alcoholism (Gianoulakis et al., 1989) and other addictive behaviors (de Wied & Van Ree, 1989). Moreover, imbalanced endorphin levels seem to be involved in other clinical conditions—for example, in some cases of sexual impotence in men (Fabbri et al., 1989) and in a clinical syndrome that includes progressive loss of motor, cognitive, and language skills in girls (Brass, Myer, & Dewey, 1989).

Other neurotransmitters will be discussed in later chapters. For example, Chapter 13 considers the possibility that depression is related to low levels of two neurotransmitters, norepinephrine and serotonin.

Individual neurons never operate in isolation. Neurons are subsystems whose actions are integrated to form larger subsystems, which in turn are coordinated to form still larger and more complex systems.

Endorphin
Neural transmitters with chemical structures similar to opium and its derivatives, morphine and heroin.

In the next section, we will consider some of the major anatomical subdivisions of the nervous system, a major coordinating system in the body.

Anatomy of the Nervous System

Have you ever tried to place a long distance call on a holiday only to find the lines jammed for hours on end? Telephone operators cannot avoid telephone traffic jams on holidays, even with the help of computers. Yet the brain avoids neural traffic jams, even though "traffic" is much heavier in the nervous system than it is in the Bell System. Consider the neural activity taking place when de Mille threw out both hands to the audience at the end of her performance in *Conversations about the Dance*. Let's compare a single message sent between two neurons at that moment with a single phone call between two houses. De Mille's simple gesture produced more "traffic" than does the telephone system on the busiest holidays. The nervous system is more efficient because of its highly organized structure. In this section we will discuss that structure by analyzing major components of the nervous system.

We will necessarily introduce many new terms. The best way to learn them is not as a random list, but as an organized set of interrelated parts. Since the interrelationships can be hard to keep track of at first, Table 2–1 presents an overview of the contrasts between major components of these systems. We give both structural and functional characteristics, because it is useful to learn how these two aspects correspond to each other. We will begin our discussion with the brain, the master controller.

The Brain

Dr. Plum knew what patterns to expect when he looked at the CAT scan taken following de Mille's stroke because he knew the relationship between brain structures and functions. Since some of you will continue to study psychology, you will find a basic understanding of brain structures invaluable in your studies.

The human brain is about three pounds of soft, spongy, pinkish-gray nerve tissue, made up of billions of neurons. In this section we will discuss divisions and subdivisions of groups of these neurons and the ways in which they are connected. Divisions can be identified on the basis of both structure and function. First we will focus on structural divisions: the hindbrain, the midbrain, and the forebrain.

Hindbrain. The **hindbrain** is shown in Figure 2–6 along with its three main components:

1. Directly above the spinal cord, the lowest part of the hindbrain is the **medulla,** a slender tube no larger than your finger. It houses nerve centers that control breathing, heartbeat, and posture. For this reason, even slight damage to the medulla could be fatal.

2. Above the medulla is the **pons,** a broader tube formed by a massive cable of nerve fibers. It connects the medulla to the midbrain. If this cable were damaged, you might develop a sleep disorder similar to

Hindbrain
Part of the brain that develops from the bottom core in the embryonic neural tube; contains the medulla, pons, and cerebellum.
Medulla
Lowest part of the hindbrain; slender tube housing nerve centers that control breathing, heartbeat, and posture.
Pons
Part of the hindbrain; a tube formed by a massive cable of nerve fibers. Connects the medulla to the midbrain.

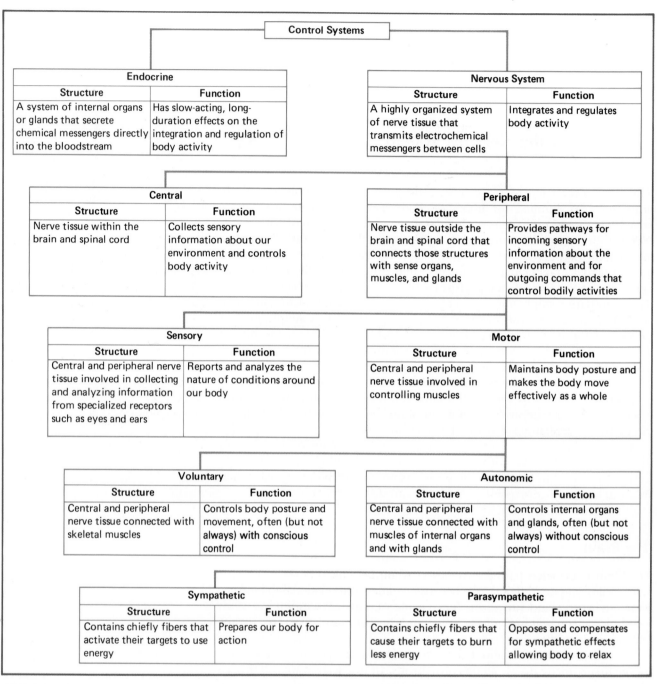

Control Systems					

Endocrine		Nervous System		
Structure	**Function**	**Structure**	**Function**	
A system of internal organs or glands that secrete chemical messengers directly into the bloodstream	Has slow-acting, long-duration effects on the integration and regulation of body activity	A highly organized system of nerve tissue that transmits electrochemical messengers between cells	Integrates and regulates body activity	

Central		Peripheral	
Structure	**Function**	**Structure**	**Function**
Nerve tissue within the brain and spinal cord	Collects sensory information about our environment and controls body activity	Nerve tissue outside the brain and spinal cord that connects those structures with sense organs, muscles, and glands	Provides pathways for incoming sensory information about the environment and for outgoing commands that control bodily activities

Sensory		Motor	
Structure	**Function**	**Structure**	**Function**
Central and peripheral nerve tissue involved in collecting and analyzing information from specialized receptors such as eyes and ears	Reports and analyzes the nature of conditions around our body	Central and peripheral nerve tissue involved in controlling muscles	Maintains body posture and makes the body move effectively as a whole

Voluntary		Autonomic	
Structure	**Function**	**Structure**	**Function**
Central and peripheral nerve tissue connected with skeletal muscles	Controls body posture and movement, often (but not always) with conscious control	Central and peripheral nerve tissue connected with muscles of internal organs and with glands	Controls internal organs and glands, often (but not always) without conscious control

Sympathetic		Parasympathetic	
Structure	**Function**	**Structure**	**Function**
Contains chiefly fibers that activate their targets to use energy	Prepares our body for action	Contains chiefly fibers that cause their targets to burn less energy	Opposes and compensates for sympathetic effects allowing body to relax

TABLE 2–1
Overview of Endocrine and Nervous Systems

the "restless-leg" syndrome, which would result in thrashing about during sleep to the point where you would repeatedly wake yourself. This effect on movement makes sense when you consider the third hindbrain component, the cerebellum.

3. The **cerebellum** looks like two wrinkled hemispheres strapped onto the back of the pons. It coordinates the force, range, and rate of body movements. If your cerebellum were injured or even destroyed, you would still enjoy all the sensations of the world around you (such as sights, sounds, and smells), but you would lose muscular tone, strength, and coordination.

Cerebellum
Part of the hindbrain; made up of two wrinkled hemispheres. Coordinates the force, range, and rate of body movements.

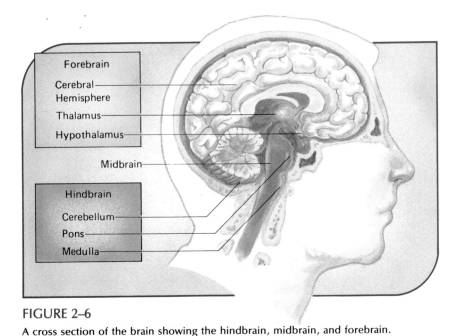

FIGURE 2–6
A cross section of the brain showing the hindbrain, midbrain, and forebrain.

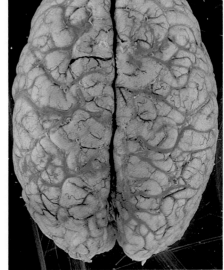

The human brain is about 3 pounds of soft, spongy, pinkish-gray nerve tissue. This incredible structure is the control center of our physical and emotional being throughout our lifetime.

Midbrain.   Above the pons and cerebellum is a still wider tube, the **midbrain.** So many vital nerve tracts run up and down it that you would face unconsciousness, if not death, if your midbrain were damaged. The core of the midbrain contains the *reticular formation*, a critical mass of neurons which is involved with alertness, arousal, and consciousness. The midbrain and hindbrain are together referred to as the **brainstem.**

Forebrain.   The rest of the brain is called the **forebrain.** In Figure 2–6 the three main components of the forebrain are highlighted.

1. Directly over the brainstem, in the central core of the forebrain, lies the **hypothalamus.** It includes several centers, some of which control body temperature and the rate at which you burn fat and carbohydrates. Damage to your hypothalamus could hinder body maintenance functions such as bowel movements, urinary output, sweating, alertness, and reaction to pleasure and pain. The hypothalamus is also the control center for our motivations and emotions. The role of the hypothalamus in eating is described in Chapter 10, "Motivation."

2. Above the hypothalamus are two egg-shaped structures called the **thalamus.** It is often called a relay station, because sensory pathways from all over the body pass through it. Brain relay stations, including the thalamus, modify incoming information by integrating it with information coming from other parts of the body. Injury to the thalamus would distort your sensations of the world around you.

3. Mushrooming out from the brainstem are two wrinkled hemispheres called the **cerebral cortex.** This is the crown jewel of our brain, accounting for about 80 percent of the brain's weight. Among other functions, it governs our most advanced human capabilities, including abstract reasoning and speech. It is more highly developed in humans than in other animals, as shown in Figure 2–7. The effects of injury to the cerebrum depend on which area is injured. De Mille's stroke affected areas related to speech. We will examine those effects when we examine the speech center in more detail. But first let's highlight some of the structures we will be discussing.

Midbrain
Part of the brain that develops from the middle core of the embryo brain; contains the reticular formation.
Brainstem
Midbrain and hindbrain combined.
Forebrain
The part of the brain that develops from the top core of the embryo brain; contains the hypothalamus, thalamus, and the cerebrum.
Hypothalamus
Part of the forebrain; controls body temperature and the rate at which we burn fat and carbohydrates, among other functions.
Thalamus
Two egg-shaped structures that are part of the forebrain. Often called a relay station because sensory pathways from all over the body pass through it.
Cerebral cortex (cerebrum)
Two wrinkled hemispheres that are part of the forebrain; governs our most advanced human capabilities, including abstract reasoning and speech.

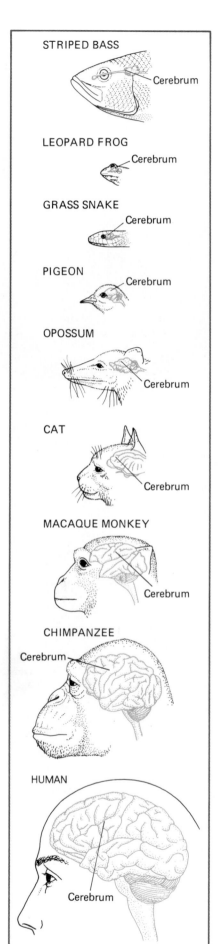

STRIPED BASS
— Cerebrum

LEOPARD FROG
— Cerebrum

GRASS SNAKE
— Cerebrum

PIGEON
— Cerebrum

OPOSSUM
— Cerebrum

CAT
— Cerebrum

MACAQUE MONKEY
— Cerebrum

CHIMPANZEE
Cerebrum —

HUMAN
— Cerebrum

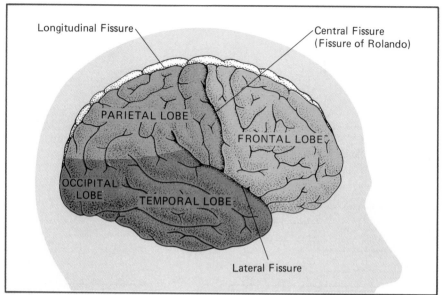

Longitudinal Fissure

Central Fissure (Fissure of Rolando)

PARIETAL LOBE

FRONTAL LOBE

OCCIPITAL LOBE

TEMPORAL LOBE

Lateral Fissure

FIGURE 2–8

Side view of a cerebral hemisphere, showing the various lobes and fissures.

The cerebrum is divided into left and right *cerebral hemispheres* which are connected by a large cable of nerve fibers called the **corpus callosum.** Figure 2–8 shows a side view of the cerebral hemispheres. Three deep grooves, or *fissures,* are labeled, as are four well-defined areas called *lobes.* The fissures are: (1) the **longitudinal fissure,** which separates the two hemispheres; (2) the *lateral fissure,* or **fissure of Sylvius,** which, if you view the figure as a boxing glove, defines the thumb of the glove; and (3) the *central fissure,* or **fissure of Rolando,** which runs across the knuckle area of our imaginary boxing glove.

These fissures separate each hemisphere into four lobes. The cortex in front of the central fissure and above the lateral fissure makes up the **frontal lobe.** It receives sensory impulses after they have been processed by other lobes, and it sends out commands to muscles to make voluntary movements. The **occipital lobe** is the hindmost lobe. This lobe receives visual impulses from the eyes. The **parietal lobe** extends back from the central fissure to the occipital lobe and responds to touch, pain, and temperature. Finally, the **temporal lobe** is below the lateral fissure and in front of the occipital lobe. (It is the thumb of our imaginary boxing glove.) The temporal lobe receives sound and smell impulses and has centers that control speech.

There is a band of cerebral cortex at the top of the head, on either side of the central fissure, which controls sensory and motor responses. The **motor cortex,** which is directly in front of the central fissure, controls motor responses of the body. The **somatosensory cortex,** which is directly behind the central fissure, controls sensory responses of the body. Figure 2–9 provides a map of the parts of the body that are affected by the motor and somatosensory cortexes.

We owe much of what we know about the motor and somatosensory cortexes to the research of Wilder Penfield, a Canadian neurosurgeon (Penfield & Rasmussen, 1950). He determined which parts of these cortexes

FIGURE 2–7 A comparison of cerebrums in a number of different species.

affect which parts of the body. Penfield did his research while surgically treating epilepsy. His technique allowed the patient to remain awake and alert during the operation. Penfield then was able to "map" areas of the cortex by stimulating a certain part of the cortex and recording the patient's response. When he stimulated the motor cortex, muscles would move; when he stimulated the somatosensory areas, people felt sensations in various parts of their body. Figure 2–9 shows the specific connections that Penfield discovered. In the figure, the body parts are drawn larger or smaller depending on how much brain surface is devoted to them. Note how much of the cortex is devoted to certain areas of the body (for example, the fingers) and how little to other areas (for example, the toes).

As we noted earlier, the effects of injury to the cerebrum depend upon which of its areas is injured. De Mille's stroke injured parts on her *left* motor and somatosensory cortexes, causing her to lose movement control and feeling on her *right* side. Why is this so? Because the left cerebral hemisphere primarily controls the right side of the body, and the right cerebral hemisphere primarily controls the left side of the body. The next section considers other functions that are localized in either the left or the right hemispheres.

FIGURE 2–9

Motor and somatosensory cortexes have regions that are associated with specific body parts. The relationships are shown by drawing body parts over the corresponding brain areas. The body parts are drawn smaller or larger to reflect the amount of brain surface devoted to each.

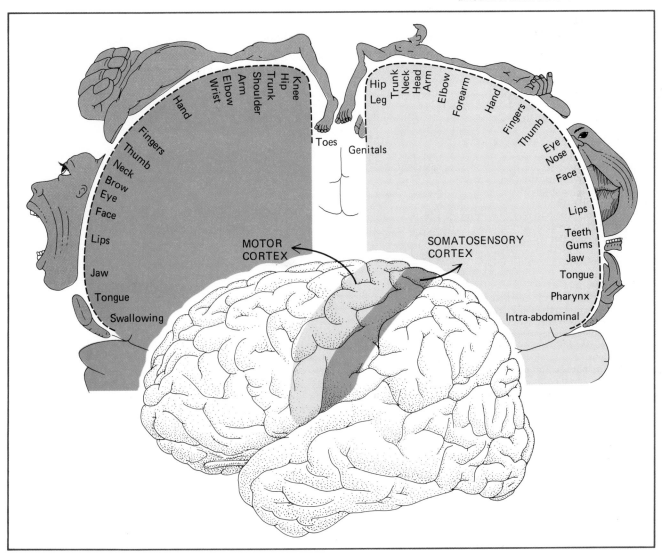

In 1981, Roger Sperry, 71, of the California Institute of Technology, won a Nobel Prize in Medicine for his pioneering brain research, which revealed the separate functions of the left and right hemispheres of the cerebral cortex. These two halves of the brain usually share information across the *corpus callosum*, a network of millions of nerve fibers. Sperry began his research in the 1950s by cutting the corpus callosum of test animals. His most revealing experiments came later when humans had the same surgery to reduce epileptic seizures. After this operation, patients are said to have a *split brain*. This surgery enables patients to function well in their everyday lives. Sperry discovered with special tests, however, that each hemisphere of split-brain patients often functions unaware of what the other is doing. Sperry studied split-brain patients to find out the way each hemisphere functions on its own (Sperry, 1970; see Figure 2–10).

Sperry's experiments took advantage of the fact that each side of the brain predominantly services the *opposite* side of the body. The right hemisphere, for example, receives touch sensations from the left hand and it moves the left hand. Therefore, when an object was placed in the left hand of a blindfolded split-brain patient, only the right hemisphere received the message telling what the object was. Sperry used familiar objects in his experiments, such as a comb, a toothbrush, a key case. After touching the objects, the patients could gesture with their left hand to show how the object was used. But they could not *say* how the objects are used and they had no idea of what their left hand was doing. The right hemisphere can apparently recognize objects, but it cannot speak. When the patients touched the same objects with their right hand, information was sent to

(Key Terms from p. 52)

Corpus callosum
Large cable of nerve fibers that connects the two cerebral hemispheres.

Longitudinal fissure
One of three fissures in the cerebral cortex; separates the two cerebral hemispheres.

Fissure of Sylvius (lateral fissure)
One of three fissures in the cerebral cortex.

Fissure of Rolando (central fissure)
One of three fissures of the cerebral cortex.

Frontal lobe
One of four lobes in the cerebral cortex; receives sensory impulses after they have been processed by other lobes and sends out commands to muscles to make voluntary movements.

Occipital lobe
One of four lobes in the cerebral cortex; receives visual impulses from the eyes.

Parietal lobe
One of four lobes in the cerebral cortex; responds to touch, pain, and temperature.

Temporal lobe
One of four lobes in the cerebral cortex; receives sound and smell impulses and has centers that control speech.

Motor cortex
Part of the cerebral cortex; located in front of the central fissure. Controls motor responses of the body.

Somatosensory cortex
Part of the cerebral cortex; located behind the central fissure. Controls sensory responses of the body.

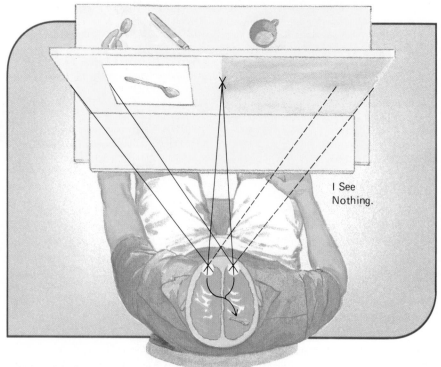

FIGURE 2–10A

When the image of the spoon is projected only on the *left* side of the screen, only the *right* hemisphere of the split-brain patient sees it. Since the image has not been received by the patient's language center, he cannot name the object. He can, however, pick it out by touch—if he uses his left hand.

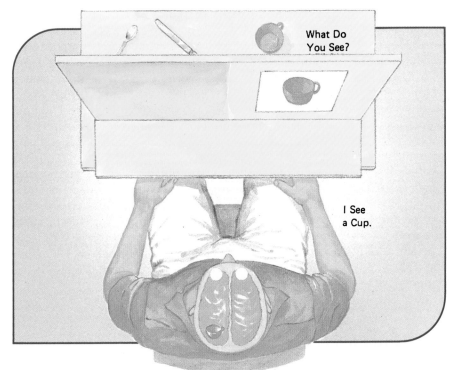

FIGURE 2–10B

Visual information on the *right* side of the screen is projected to the split-brain patient's *left* hemisphere, which controls language. When asked what he sees, the patient can reply correctly.

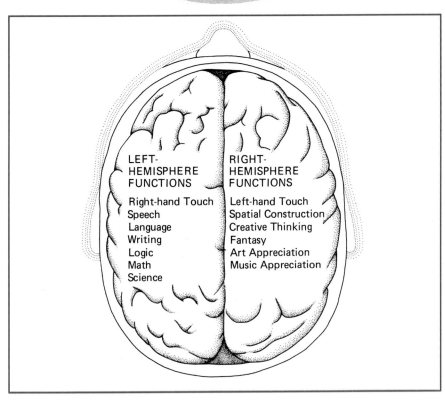

LEFT-
HEMISPHERE
FUNCTIONS

Right-hand Touch
Speech
Language
Writing
Logic
Math
Science

RIGHT-
HEMISPHERE
FUNCTIONS

Left-hand Touch
Spatial Construction
Creative Thinking
Fantasy
Art Appreciation
Music Appreciation

FIGURE 2–10C

The left and right brain hemispheres specialize in different functions. Split-brain research suggests that functions are divided as indicated in the figure.

the left hemisphere. In that case, they immediately said what the objects were, which indicated that the left hemisphere can speak.

Sperry did similar experiments with visible words and objects. He took advantage of the fact that the two hemispheres see different sides of the world. When a person looks at a point, the right hemisphere sees everything to the left of that point, and the left hemisphere sees everything to the right. Split-brain patients usually move their eyes around in order to send information to both hemispheres. Sperry prevented this strategy in his experiments, however. He flashed a stimulus on one side and then removed it before the eyes could move. Thus, only one hemisphere saw the stimulus.

Sperry found that the left hemisphere understands abstract language, enables people to speak, and performs complicated mathematical computations (Figure 2–10C). The right hemisphere understands only simple nouns and phrases. It can, for example, read the word "nut" and find a nut with the left hand in a pile of unseen objects. It can also find a match when it reads "used for lighting fires." It cannot understand abstract words such as "love" and "truth," it cannot speak, and its mathematical abilities do not go beyond adding two-digit numbers. But the right hemisphere is superior to the left in drawing, assembling blocks to match designs, and recognizing emotions in facial expressions.

Sperry's research formed a foundation for much modern brain research, which in turn guided the development of life-saving techniques of brain surgery. Today, support for different functions of the hemispheres in normal people comes from EEG and PET scans (Springer & Deutsch, 1985) and from a person's performance on recognition tasks (words versus faces). The left hemisphere does better on words (O'Boyle & Benbow, 1990) and the right hemisphere does better on faces (Moreno, Borad, Welkowitz, & Alpert, 1990).

The Spinal Cord

The structure that connects the brain with the rest of the body is the **spinal cord,** a cable of long nerve fibers running from the brainstem down through the backbone to the lower back. Fibers on the outside of the cord have myelin sheaths, which give this area a whitish color. Fibers on the inside of the cord are unmyelinated, so the color is grayish. The gray area is shaped like a bent *H* (as shown in Figure 2–11).

The neurons, or nerve tissue, of the brain and spinal cord make up the **central nervous system.** All other nerve tissue is called the **peripheral nervous system.** These two systems work together so that your mind and body function as a smooth-running machine. At the start of a race, for example, runners listen for the starting gun. Peripheral nerves in their ears respond and send impulses to the central nervous system. The brain interprets the impulses as the waited-for "go" signal, and it sends commands to peripheral nerves in muscles that launch the runner down the track.

Sometimes the spinal cord triggers responses without waiting for commands from the brain. Such responses are called **reflexes,** or automatic actions that require no conscious effort on our part. There are a number of different kinds of spinal reflexes. The gray inner area of the spinal cord plays an important role of providing interconnections as illustrated in Figure 2–11. The stretch reflex, for example, extends your arms and legs, bringing them toward a straight position. Doctors test this reflex when they tap your knee to make your leg straighten out from a crossed position. Another kind of reflex bends your arms and legs to pull them away from painful stimulation, as when you step on a tack and jerk your leg up. When your leg jerks away from that tack, another reflex extends or stiffens your other leg. The extended leg supports your weight so you don't fall.

The white mylineated outer spinal area carries impulses up and down the spinal cord. **Ascending nerve cells** carry sensory information up to specific areas of the brain; **descending nerve cells** carry commands to move muscles. Diseases and injuries that damage descending nerves can cause paralysis. Polio, for example, is a viral disease that attacks descending nerves, causing paralysis of leg and other muscles. Injury is also a common cause of paralysis. If the lower spinal cord is severed, the legs are paralyzed. If the upper spinal cord is severed, paralysis occurs in the arms and legs and in breathing. As of yet, no cure has been developed for paralysis related to these unfortunate injuries.

Spinal cord
Cable of long nerve fibers running from the brainstem down through the backbone to the lower back, through which ascending nerves carry sensory information up to the brain and descending nerves carry commands down from the brain to move muscles.

Central nervous system
Nerve tissue in the brain and spinal cord.

Peripheral nervous system
All nerve tissue that is not in the brain and spinal cord.

Reflexes
Automatic actions that require no conscious effort.

Ascending nerves
Nerves that carry sensory information up the spinal cord to specific areas of the brain.

Descending nerves
Carry commands down the spinal cord to move muscles.

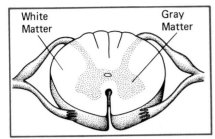

White Matter   Gray Matter

FIGURE 2-11

(Left) Cross section of the spinal cord.

(Below) Spinal cord reflexes. When a doctor taps your knee, a signal is sent through the spinal cord and back to the muscle. The signal returning from the spinal cord contracts the muscle, causing your leg to kick. When you touch something that is very hot, a signal goes through your spinal cord to a muscle that pulls your hand back. When you step on a tack, a signal goes through your spinal cord to a muscle that pulls your leg up, and at the same time another signal from the spinal cord goes to your other leg to support your weight.

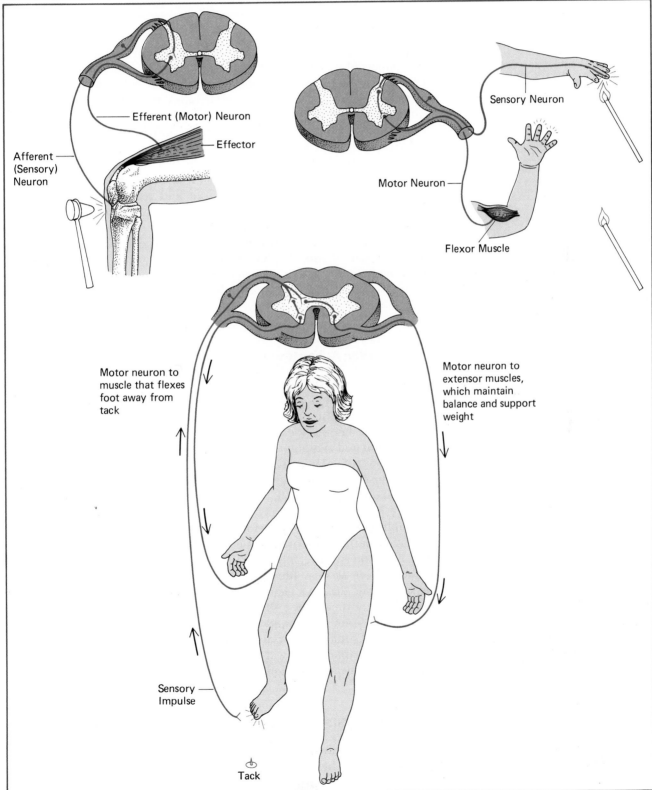

Efferent (Motor) Neuron

Effector

Afferent (Sensory) Neuron

Sensory Neuron

Motor Neuron

Flexor Muscle

Motor neuron to muscle that flexes foot away from tack

Motor neuron to extensor muscles, which maintain balance and support weight

Sensory Impulse

Tack

While an intact spinal cord is necessary for normal muscle control, it's not enough on its own. De Mille's spinal cord was in perfect condition, yet she lost a great deal of motor control after her stroke. In the next section we will learn why de Mille's brain injury affected some muscle movements and not others.

Functional Subdivisions of the Nervous System

To understand de Mille's condition, we must consider *functional subdivisions*, interconnected structures that work together to carry out certain functions in the body. The bicycle is a good example that shows us the distinction between structural or anatomical subdivisions and functional subdivisions. "Anatomical" subdivisions of a bicycle would include the front section (handlebars, brake controls, front brake, fork, and front wheel); midsection (seat, frame, and pedals); and hind section (rear wheel, rear brake, and chain assembly). A functional subdivision that includes parts from each anatomical section is the braking system. It includes brake controls, pedals, and the chain assembly, as well as front and rear brakes. Similarly, de Mille's abilities and disabilities after surgery involved coordinated efforts of many anatomical subdivisions. Parts of her forebrain, midbrain, and hindbrain work together, for example, when she performs on stage. In the remainder of this chapter we will discuss functional subdivisions of the human nervous system. We will learn the reasons for some of de Mille's handicaps and also the biological underpinnings of our own everyday experiences.

The Reticular Activating System

On the morning that she was to have an operation, de Mille was awakened at about 6 A.M. by a nurse who gave her an injection. She remembers being taken into the operating room; she remembers nothing after that. As far as she knows, she suddenly fell into a completely dreamless void beyond time and sensation. This place was created for her by a drug that blocked her **reticular activating system (RAS).** The RAS activates all of the regions of the brain for incoming sensory impulses; when it is blocked, no sensations register at all.

The RAS, shown in Figure 2–12, is a core of tissue that runs through the hindbrain, midbrain, and forebrain and joins the reticular formation with other parts of the brain to perform the function of making the brain alert. A person is awake only when the RAS is functioning. Another function of the RAS is *selective* attention. When two or more messages arrive at the same time, the RAS seems to decide which is most urgent. The system then blocks, or tones down, the irrelevant messages and prepares the upper areas of the brain to respond vigorously to the relevant message. The cry of a baby will wake you from sleep, whereas a honking horn may not be heard. (In Chapter 5 we will further explore general arousal, sleep, and ways to concentrate attention.)

Reticular activating system (RAS) Functional subdivision of the nervous system; activates all regions of the brain for incoming sensory impulses, plays an important part in alertness and selective attention.

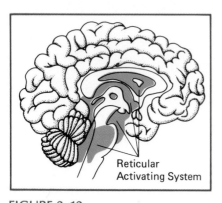

FIGURE 2–12

The reticular activating system (RAS).

The Limbic System

A functional subdivision of the brain that played a key role in de Mille's struggle to keep her spirits up was the limbic system. The structures of the limbic system, shown in Figure 2–13, play a role in emotions, memories, and goal-directed behavior. Limbic system interconnections are clearly defined, and each part seems to depend on all the other parts.

Limbic system functions are less clearly defined, however; the system does so many things that it is hard to characterize any one function. By observing the behavior of people whose limbic system is disturbed by frontal cortex injuries, we can more clearly identify the many functions. One patient laughed at sad things and cried at funny things; another was unable to plan a meal because she kept forgetting how to cook; still another urinated in public while dressed in evening clothes (Cotman & McGaugh, 1980). The ill-timed urination is one of many examples of inappropriate actions that seem to result from an inability to deal with two conflicting goals at the same time (one goal was to enjoy social interactions with companions; another was to urinate). Normally we cope with conflicting demands by responding at the right time and place. People with disturbed limbic systems often cannot deal with conflicting goals.

Another way to study the limbic system is to record cell activity in animals that are performing a task. For example, researchers have recorded cells in the hippocampus of rats while they explored for food in a radial maze. (The hippocampus is known to play an important role in memory.) This kind of maze has spokes that radiate in eight directions from a central

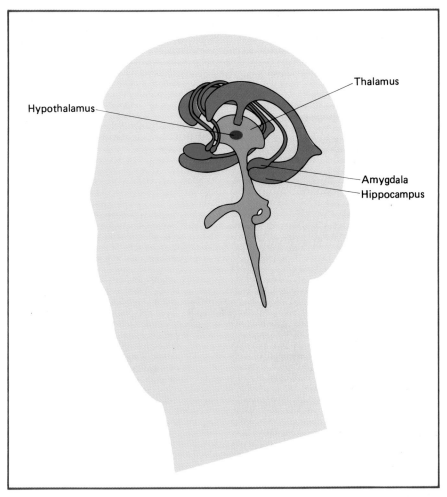

FIGURE 2–13

Components of the limbic system mediate emotions, memories, and goal-directed behavior. The components shown in this figure are located deep inside the brain. Here you can see them clearly because the rest of the brain is cut away.

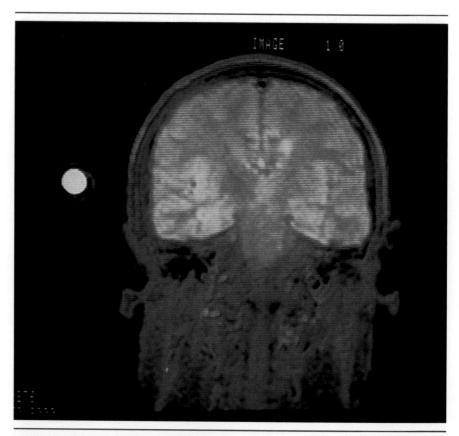

Nuclear magnetic resonance (NMR) image of a frontal section through the human head.

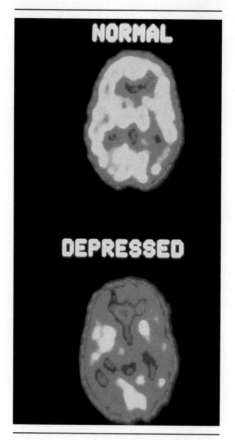

PET scans comparing normal brain (top) with that of a patient with a depressed mental disorder.

hub. A food container at the end of each spoke can be either full or empty. The researchers discovered that some cells in the hippocampus responded to the position of the spokes regardless of whether or not the spokes contained food. These cells fired maximally only when the rats entered a particular spoke and fired at a slower rate when the rats were anywhere else. They also noted that different cells fired maximally to different spokes. These results suggest that the hippocampus might provide rats with a spatial map of where they are and where they have been (Best & Thompson, 1989; Thompson & Best, 1990).

The Autonomic Nervous System

Have you ever become enraged suddenly, only to calm down after a few minutes? Such responses are governed by our **autonomic nervous system,** which regulates glands and organs. Rage is triggered by the **sympathetic division** of the autonomic system. This division prepares the body for action. The calm that follows is controlled by the **parasympathetic division,** which allows the body to relax. These two divisions, with their effects on the body, may be seen in Figure 2–14.

Sympathetic Division. Sympathetic pathways work all the time to keep our body functions stable. They are especially busy, however, during stressful situations (Wallin & Fagius, 1986). De Mille reported a stressful episode that took place during the dress rehearsal for the New York gala she was involved in following her stroke. At one point, the dancers became confused. De Mille was frustrated because she was unable to be on stage to demonstrate, and she couldn't get anyone's attention in order to help her. After a second unsuccessful attempt by the dancers, she lost her temper and yelled, "Will nobody help a cripple?!" Her complaint aroused immediate attention and the problem was solved. It wasn't long before de Mille herself was able to laugh at her comment.

Let's look at some of the body changes triggered by de Mille's sympathetic division when she lost her temper:

1. Her heart worked faster and harder to pump more blood to the muscles.
2. Her breathing rate increased, and her air passage opened to carry more air to her lungs.
3. Her sweat glands produced more sweat to help maintain normal body temperature.
4. Her digestion stopped to save energy for the other functions that were speeded up.

All of these responses prepared de Mille for action. Together they are called the *fight-or-flight* responses, because in emergencies they prepare us either to fight or to flee. Sympathetic responses are very helpful in emergencies, but they can be harmful when they are repeatedly used for minor crises. Students who have fight-or-flight reactions every time they think about exams, for example, put undue stress on their bodies. We will discuss the topic of stress again in Chapter 11.

Parasympathetic Division. Parasympathetic fibers go to all the same glands and organs as the sympathetic division, but they carry the opposite message, as if to say, "Relax." This *relaxation response* was traditionally regarded as being beyond voluntary control, as were all autonomic responses. For this reason, the autonomic nervous system is sometimes called the involuntary nervous system. Recent studies, however, show that we can

Autonomic nervous system
Functional subdivision of the nervous system; regulates glands and organs. Divided into sympathetic and parasympathetic divisions.
Sympathetic division
Part of the autonomic nervous system; functional subdivision of the nervous system; controls the fight-or-flight responses.
Parasympathetic division
Part of the autonomic nervous system; functional subdivision of the nervous system; controls the relaxation responses.

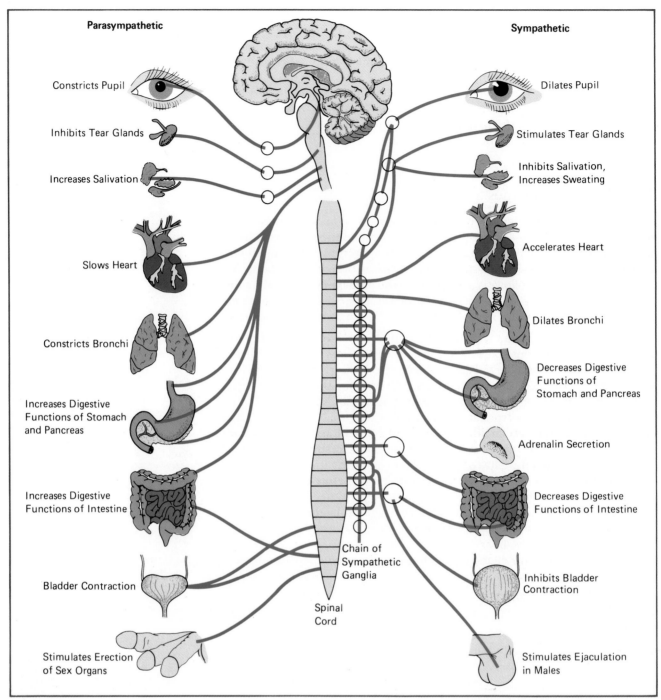

Parasympathetic

Constricts Pupil

Inhibits Tear Glands

Increases Salivation

Slows Heart

Constricts Bronchi

Increases Digestive
Functions of Stomach
and Pancreas

Increases Digestive
Functions of Intestine

Bladder Contraction

Stimulates Erection
of Sex Organs

Sympathetic

Dilates Pupil

Stimulates Tear Glands

Inhibits Salivation,
Increases Sweating

Accelerates Heart

Dilates Bronchi

Decreases Digestive
Functions of
Stomach and Pancreas

Adrenalin Secretion

Decreases Digestive
Functions of Intestine

Inhibits Bladder
Contraction

Stimulates Ejaculation
in Males

Chain of
Sympathetic
Ganglia

Spinal
Cord

FIGURE 2–14

The sympathetic and parasympathetic subdivisions of the nervous system serve many
of the same organs, but they affect them
differently.

voluntarily control our autonomic nervous system, as we will discuss in
Chapters 5 and 6. We saw an excellent example of such control when de
Mille managed to stay calm during her stroke. Even when we learn to
regulate our organs voluntarily, however, we never achieve the same sort
of precise control that we have over our skeletal muscles.

Control of Skeletal Muscles

De Mille's mobility was restricted because her ability to control her muscles
was reduced. The bones of our skeleton are rigid, but without the muscles
that move and support them we would collapse in a heap. Spinal cord
reflexes control most of the work our skeletal muscles do to maintain our

posture against the pull of gravity. We continually control our skeletal muscles, therefore, without being aware of it. At the same time we can control the same muscles deliberately and purposefully, as when de Mille performed on stage. In this section we will examine the neural processes that underlie such voluntary muscle control.

The part of the nervous system that controls muscle movements is called the **motor system.** We have already discussed the spinal reflexes; here we will consider three higher centers which are part of the motor system.

1. **Basal ganglia** are four masses of gray matter located deep in the forebrain. They have a number of functions, which are not well understood. We do know that one function is to control "background" muscle tone. In general, basal ganglia perform large, general muscle movements to set the stage for more detailed, controlled movements (Brown & Frank, 1987). When we write, for example, our basal ganglia tense muscles in the upper part of our arm to prepare for the hand movement.

2. The motor cortex (see Figure 2–9) is the place where impulses to the muscles originate. The motor cortex contains giant cells, called **pyramidal cells,** which send a long axon through the brain down to neurons in the spinal cord. From there motor impulses go directly to muscles. Most pyramidal cells in the left hemisphere send their impulses to muscles on the right side of the body, and vice versa. They tend to control precise movements such as hand movements in humans and paw movements in animals (Alstermark, Isa, Lundberg, & Peterson, 1989).

3. The cerebellum participates in controlling fine-grain muscle movements. It "puts a brake" on motor impulses to make them smoother and more coordinated.

Motor system
Functional subdivision of the nervous system; includes basal ganglia, cerebellum, and the motor cortex. Controls voluntary muscle movements.

Basal ganglia
Four masses of gray matter in the brain that control background muscle tone and large, general muscle movements—part of the motor system.

Pyramidal cells
Giant cells of the motor cortex that send a long axon through the brain down to neurons in the spinal cord. Control precise physical movements and speech.

Language Control Centers

Most of us speak, write, listen, and read with such ease that we do not appreciate the work our brain does. De Mille's stroke made her keenly aware of the brain's role in language. Her stroke temporarily caused aphasia, which is difficulty in producing and understanding language. Her case illustrates two well-known types of aphasia:

Shown here are two basic types of muscle movements. The weaver is using pyramidal cells to control precise hand movements. The javelin thrower is using basal ganglia to control general muscle tone.

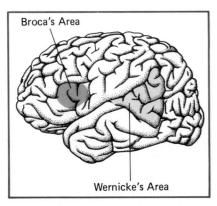

FIGURE 2–15
Broca's area and Wernicke's area of the brain.

Broca's aphasia
Speech that is slow, labored, and slightly distorted; caused by injury to Broca's area in the cortex.

Wernicke's aphasia
Speech that includes wrong words, nonsense words, and shifting from topic to topic. Caused by injury to Wernicke's area in the cortex.

1. **Broca's aphasia,** which is characterized by speech that is slow, labored, and slightly distorted. It is caused by injury to *Broca's area*, which is a part of the cortex, shown in Figure 2–15.

2. **Wernicke's aphasia,** which is characterized by speech that sounds normal until one pays attention to the meaning. The speech includes the wrong words and nonsense words, and the message seems to shift from topic to topic. Wernicke's aphasia is caused by injury to the upper area of the left temporal lobe (Figure 2–15).

De Mille's speech was halting and distorted, which is characteristic of Broca's aphasia. Also, she used wrong words and nonsense words when she spoke, which is common with Wernicke's aphasia. The day after her stroke, de Mille spoke mostly gibberish. Here is an example of an exchange with her husband: "Wa listen. Wa I groopes? Ye rideargo sutino? Rev." Her husband pretended he understood her and replied, "Yes, dear—yes. Of course I'll do it."

Two days later, it was easier to understand de Mille, but she still used words incorrectly. For instance, a close friend, Mary Green, related this conversation that she had with de Mille during this period.

De Mille:	Mary, the next time bring the Mary Janes with you.
Green:	Are they in your closet, Agnes? [Green thinks she means shoes.]
De Mille:	Of course not in my closet. My God!
Green:	Is it a person?
De Mille:	*Of course.*
Green:	Do I know her?
De Mille:	Of course you know her!
Green:	Is she a member of our company?
De Mille:	Oh, Mary!
Green:	[Now it was a game.] Is it Jane? [Nod] Jane Gilman, our lawyer?
De Mille:	Of course. I *said* Jane.
Green:	I'll have her call you, Agnes.

Broca's and Wernicke's aphasias are usually manifested separately in different individuals (Li & Williams, 1990).

The Endocrine System

De Mille's stroke injured her temporal lobe, and such injuries can influence the appetite and emotional aspects of behavior (Cotman & McGaugh, 1980). These effects occur indirectly as a result of an imbalance of the **endocrine system,** a major coordinating system that regulates body chemistry. Let's examine the structure and function of this important system.

Structure

Endocrine system
Major coordinating system that regulates body chemistry.

Hormones
Chemical messengers released by the glands into the bloodstream. Either directly change their target tissue or cause it to release other hormones that change tissues elsewhere in the body.

The endocrine system is made up of organs called endocrine glands. Located throughout the body (Figure 2–16), they touch almost every aspect of our lives. The glands release **hormones** (chemical messengers) directly into the bloodstream, and the bloodstream carries the hormones to other body tissues. When hormones reach their target, they either directly change it or they cause it to release other hormones that change tissues elsewhere in the body.

HEALTH RISKS OF ANABOLIC STEROID HORMONES

Anabolic steroids (ANSs) are the male sex hormone testosterone and its derivatives that have muscle-promoting qualities. Testosterone is produced in the testes and is sent through the bloodstream to cells throughout the body. When testosterone or its synthetic derivatives bind with receptors in cells, they modify the cells' operations, with a number of effects, including the promotion of tissue growth and the development of male characteristics such as beard growth and deepening of the voice. Synthetic derivatives of testosterone can be administered orally or by injection. ANSs are prescribed by physicians to treat certain hormonal imbalances—for example, to start puberty in adolescents who have been diagnosed as developmentally delayed (Moore, 1988).

During the 1950s and 1960s, illicit ANS use was mostly limited to highly trained athletes. They took the drug to lift more, run faster, jump higher, and generally improve any performance that benefits from the drug's ability to increase muscle size and strength. The only way they could maintain their superiority, however, was to continue taking the drug. Even rigorous weight training was not enough to maintain their strength or performance after the drug was discontinued (Taylor, 1985; 1987).

Today, however, habitual use of large doses is widespread among youths and young adults who are seeking a "shortcut to the Rambo look" (Toufexis, 1989). Experts estimate that 1 million Americans are spending $100 million on black-market ANSs. In contrast to the highly trained athletes of the past, about 25 percent of the present users are high school students (Buckley et al., 1988). Less than half of these users take the drug to improve athletic performance. They want the athletic look, but not necessarily the skill.

This trend is disturbing, because ANSs pose serious physical and psychological health risks. Physical complications include liver dysfunctions, infertility, and changes in sex characteristics, including shrinking of the testes in men and shriveling of the breasts in women

(Martini, 1989). Healthy teens are putting themselves at especially high risk of interfering with the normal endocrine functioning that occurs during adolescence. Testosterone levels rise sharply at puberty. As suggested earlier, this natural increase promotes muscle growth and development of masculine characteristics. In addition, it affects the production of skin oils, the regulation of bone length, and brain development.

The synthetic derivatives taken by ANS users upset the delicate balance needed to perform all these functions. The balance is distorted for two reasons. First, ANS users usually take 2 to 200 times the amount of testosterone produced by a healthy male per day (Wilson, 1988). This high dose sends signals to the body to reduce production of *natural* testosterone. Second, the synthetic derivatives do not carry out all the functions of the natural hormone. They enhance muscles as well or better, but they are no substitute for all the other important functions. Thus, teens can bulk up in muscles while deteriorating in other ways. For instance, ANS can cause or aggravate potentially scarring acne on the face, back, shoulders, and chest (AOASM, 1989). It can also prevent adolescent users from growing to their full height (Wilson, 1988).

Psychological effects are similar to those of other abused substances, such as cocaine. Significant psychological problems include mood swings ranging from "highs" to "lows." The high moods are characterized by increases in self-esteem, sexual interest, and energy, and sometimes by aggression, violence, and a reduced need to sleep. The low moods are characterized by depression, suicidal episodes, reduced sexual interest, irritability, impulsiveness, impaired judgment, insomnia, anxiety, panic, suspiciousness, and paranoid delusions. Withdrawal symptoms include all these problems, plus nausea, chills, headache, dizziness, profuse perspiration, increased pulse rate, and elevated blood pressure (Kashkin & Kleber, 1989). Users with these symptoms should consult a doctor.

Ben Johnson

Although urine screening and penalties are being used to deter experimentation with ANS by athletes, experience with other substance abuse disorders suggests that these strategies alone will not solve the problem (Kleber, 1988). The most publicized failure of this policy was the case of Ben Johnson, who forfeited his Olympic Gold metal in 1988 after ANS was detected during routine tests.

Kashkin and Kleber (1989) predict that present approaches will become even less effective. Clearly, they will not help the many abusers who are not athletes. Abusers of ANS need the more holistic approaches that have been developed for other kinds of drug abuse. These approaches provide professional care for withdrawal symptoms. They help patients avoid the temptations to start using again. They also help the patient achieve their life-goals without the abused drug.

Education programs should also be used to spread the word that ANSs are dangerous and that treatment is available to help break addiction to the drug.

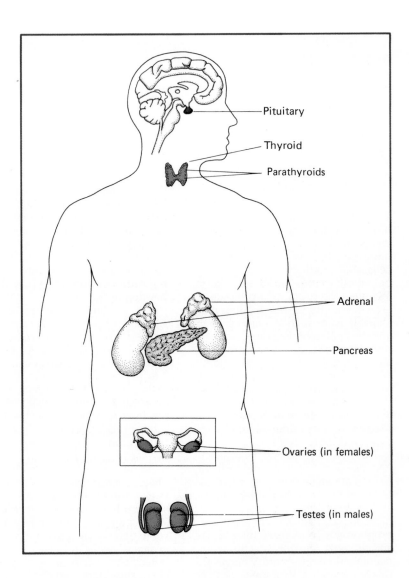

FIGURE 2–16

Glands of the endocrine system release hormones (chemical messengers) directly into the bloodstream.

Pituitary gland

Small gland that lies in a recess at the base of the brain and is connected to the hypothalamus, which controls it. Part of the endocrine system, it is often called the master gland because it has such wide-ranging effects. Secretes many different types of hormones, which control growth and sexual reproduction, among other things.

Gonads

Reproductive organs that secrete sex hormones. Called ovaries in females, testes in males. Sex hormones control ovulation, pregnancy, and the menstrual cycle in females, and the production of sperm in males, as well as regulating secondary sex characteristics in both sexes.

Function

Pituitary Gland.   The master gland of the endocrine system is the **pituitary gland.** This pea-sized gland, which has the widest-ranging effects of all the endocrine glands, lies in a small recess at the base of the brain. It is connected to, and controlled by, the hypothalamus. For example, the hypothalamus controls the level of growth hormone, which is secreted by the pituitary gland (Muller, 1987). Extreme excesses of growth hormones cause giantism; extreme deficiencies cause dwarfism. Smaller deficiencies may not impede normal growth but may be a factor in other abnormalities such as anorexia nervosa, an eating disorder (Nussbaum, Blethen, Chasalow, & Jacobson, 1990). Other pituitary hormones influence reproductive organs and sexual behavior. These effects are carried out indirectly by means of regulating another endocrine gland, the **gonads.**

Gonads.   In females gonads are called *ovaries*, and in males they are called *testes*. Hormones produced by the gonads are called *sex hormones*. Ovaries produce two hormones, *estrogen* and *progesterone*; they control ovulation, pregnancy, and the menstrual cycle. Testes manufacture *testosterone*, which stimulates production of sperm. Gonads also regulate *secondary sex characteristics*, such as the distribution of body hair, breast development, and pitch of voice. The subject of hormones and sexual behavior is discussed in Chapter 10.

Thyroid Glands. The **thyroid gland** is a large butterfly-shaped gland along the front and sides of the throat. It produces **thyroxin,** a hormone that determines the rate at which you transform food into energy. This rate, called the **metabolic rate,** determines how hungry you feel, how energetic you are, and how fast you gain weight.

If your thyroxin level is too high, you will burn food fast, which makes you hungry, gives you lots of energy, and contributes to weight loss. It also speeds up and intensifies your reactions to stress.

When your thyroxin level is too low you burn your food too slowly. Much of your food consequently turns to fat, and you feel sleepy and sluggish. In Chapter 10 we will discuss other factors that influence why we gain or lose weight. Children with extremely low thyroxin levels suffer from *cretinism*, which is characterized by arrested physical and mental development. If untreated with thyroid extract, they will become dwarfed, mentally retarded, and sterile.

Parathyroid Glands. Other glands influence general energy level. One of them is a set of four pea-shaped glands located in or behind the thyroid, called the **parathyroid glands.** The parathyroid hormone causes lethargy when its level is too high and muscle spasms when its level is too low.

Pancreas. Another gland that affects general energy level is the **pancreas,** a large gland located behind the stomach. It controls the level of sugar in the blood by secreting two hormones, *insulin* and *glucagon.* When there is too little sugar in the blood, the hormone glucagon is released in order to stimulate activity that will raise the blood sugar level. Too little sugar in the blood causes chronic fatigue. Too much sugar poisons the blood, causing *diabetes*. A person who has diabetes needs a specially controlled diet and daily injections of insulin to avoid serious complications, which include heart damage, nerve damage, and blindness.

De Mille's brush with death and her amazing recovery are both related to the organization of the body's two coordinating systems, the nervous system and the endocrine system. On the one hand, her stroke affected her in many ways, because parts of her nervous system and endocrine system depend upon one another. When one part breaks down, other dependent parts can fail in a disastrous chain reaction. On the other hand, de Mille's recovery indicates an advantage of this organization. Apparently, when one part fails, other parts can sometimes take over. In other words, within limits, parts of these systems are flexible in their ability to take on duties (Cotman & McCaugh, 1980).

Thyroid gland
Large, butterfly-shaped gland in the front and sides of the throat; part of the endocrine system. Produces thyroxin, a hormone that determines the rate at which food is transformed in the body into energy.
Thyroxin
Hormone produced by the thyroid glands; determines the rate at which food is transformed in the body into energy.
Metabolic rate
Rate at which food is transformed by the body into energy.

Genetics

De Mille's stroke serves to remind us how vulnerable we humans are, and how reliant we are upon our internal machinery. Some of us have strong, healthy bodies that give us great freedom. Others have disabilities that limit what we can do. In this next section, we will consider the origin of our bodies and the factors that determined the specific bodies that each of us inherited.

Genetics is the study of how traits are inherited, or passed on, from parent to child. The cells from which we started contain **genes,** which are the basic units of heredity. They determine our sequence of growth into a human baby instead of into a turtle, rabbit, or some other animal. Genes determine our blood type, coloration, and many other traits. In

Parathyroid glands
Four pea-shaped glands next to the thyroid in the throat; part of the endocrine system. Produce a hormone that causes lethargy when its level is too high, and muscle spasms when its level is too low.
Pancreas
Large gland located behind the stomach; as part of the endocrine system, it controls the level of sugar in the blood by secreting insulin and glucagon.
Genes
Basic units of heredity. Located on the chromosomes.

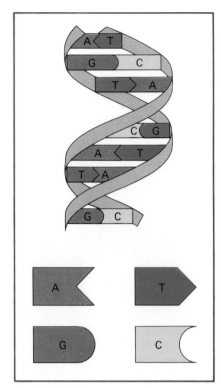

FIGURE 2–17

DNA molecules are shaped like a spiral staircase or double helix. The steps of the staircase contain a genetic code. Four chemical bases make up the steps: Adenine (A), Thymine (T), Cytosine (C), and Guanine (G). Each step contains two bases, A and T or C and G. A single gene might contain as many as 2,000 steps. The specific order of A-T and C-G pairs determines a gene's special character.

Deoxyribonucleic acid (DNA)
Controls the way in which protein chains are built, and, thus, contains the basic blueprints for life; genes are made up of DNA.

Ribonucleic acid (RNA)
Messenger molecules sent out by DNA to control how specific kinds of protein chains are made.

Chromosomes
Threadlike chains of genes; humans have 23 pairs.

Gametes
Sex cells; female gamete is an ovum, male gamete is a sperm. Each gamete has 23 chromosomes; ovum and sperm combine to form a zygote.

Zygote
Cell formed by the union of an ovum and a sperm.

Genotype
Unique set of genes that we inherit from our parents.

general, genes determine the resemblance between children and parents. People often observe that a baby "has his mother's eyes" or "has her father's chin," and so on. The resemblance becomes even more striking later on as genes continue to influence development.

The Biochemistry of Genes

Genes are located in the nucleus of every cell in the body. They are composed of **deoxyribonucleic acid (DNA),** which contains blueprints for life. Living organisms are made of protein, and DNA controls the way in which protein chains are built. Material for constructing protein surrounds cells and DNA sends out messenger molecules, **ribonucleic acid (RNA),** to control how the material is fashioned into specific kinds of protein chains. James Watson and Francis Crick (1953) made a significant breakthrough in deciphering the chemical "language" in which these genetic blueprints are written (see Figure 2–17).

Every living cell contains between 20,000 and 125,000 genes grouped together in clusters of a thousand or more. They are arranged in threadlike chains called **chromosomes.**

The Structure and Function of Chromosomes

Every plant and animal has a specific number of chromosomes, which are grouped in pairs. Garden peas have 7 pairs, fruit flies have 4 pairs, frogs have 13 pairs, chickens have 39 pairs, chimpanzees have 24 pairs, and humans have 23 pairs. Each cell in your body has 46 chromosomes, arranged in 23 pairs. You inherited one member of each pair from your mother and the other from your father. If you have children, you will pass along 23 of your chromosomes to each child; the other 23 will come from your partner.

Genes are transmitted from generation to generation by means of sex cells, which are called **gametes.** A female gamete is called an *ovum*, and a male gamete is called a *sperm*. Your gametes have 23 chromosomes each, only half the number of your other cells. Each gamete is formed by randomly choosing one member from each of your 23 pairs of chromosomes. With 23 pairs to choose from, your body can generate an incredible number of unique gametes.

Ovum and sperm combine their chromosomes when they unite, and form one cell called a **zygote.** Thus, zygotes have 46 chromosomes, half from the mother and half from the father. Each of us started from the union of one sperm and one ovum. The resulting zygote contained 46 chromosomes, which determined our **genotype,** or genetic inheritance, for the rest of our lives.

Figure 2–18 shows 23 chromosome pairs for a normal human female (left) and male (right). Scientists have classified chromosomes according to size and shape, and they have identified some pairs that carry (and pass on) specific traits. Pair 23 determines sex, for example. Notice that the male has one large X-shaped chromosome and one small, upside down, Y-shaped chromosome in pair 23. The female has two large X-shaped chromosomes in that pair. One of the important consequences of this discovery was the realization that men alone determine the sex of offspring. A female body always contributes an X chromosome to pair 23. A male can generate gametes with *either* an X or a Y chromosome. Thus, a female is conceived when a sperm carrying an X chromosome unites with an ovum, and a male is conceived when a sperm carrying a Y chromosome does so.

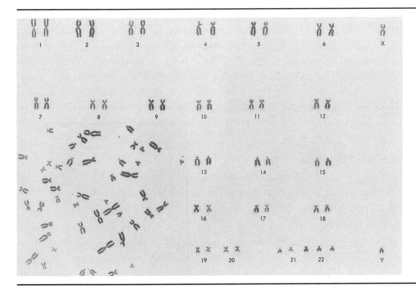
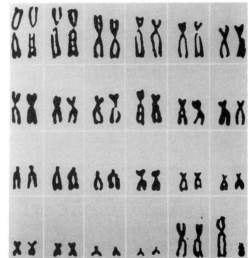

FIGURE 2-18

The numbered chromosomes are arranged according to type. Note that there are three number 21 chromosomes indicating an individual with Down syndrome. The unnumbered ones are chromosomes of a body cell before they have been arranged according to type.

Mutations. Errors are made occasionally from one generation to the next. The result is that children are sometimes born with abnormal chromosome structures, called **mutations.** Scientists have observed mutations of pair 23, as follows:

1. *Two Xs and a Y.* People with an XXY mutation (Klinefelter's Syndrome) often have characteristics of both sexes. They might have developed breasts and small testicles, for example. Some superior female Russian athletes have had XXY chromosome structures.

2. *Two Ys and an X.* Males with an extra Y chromosome (XYY) are often taller than other males. Some evidence suggests that they might also be more aggressive, but the evidence is mixed. On the one hand, XYY males are more likely than normal males to be inmates of prisons or mental hospitals. On the other hand, XYY males in the general population (about 1 in every 1,000 births) are no more aggressive than normal males (Hook, 1973; Owen, 1972).

Another kind of genetic mutation is one in which a person has 47 chromosomes because of an extra one added to pair 21. Children with this chromosome abnormality suffer from **Down syndrome,** a disorder characterized by mental retardation and a unique physical appearance, including folds on the eyelid corners, a round face, a head with a flattened back, a short neck, and a small nose. Down syndrome children are usually affectionate, calm, and cheerful. Before modern medicine, Down syndrome children did not live longer than their teen years because they were very susceptible to leukemia (blood cancer), heart disorders, and respiratory infections. Today, Down syndrome babies live longer because of better treatments for these diseases. (McGrother & Marshall, 1990).

Down syndrome can be detected before birth through **amniocentesis,** a process in which fluid is taken from a mother's womb. A fetus sloughs off cells into the fluid, enabling doctors to examine an unborn child's genetic structure, which is recorded in each cell. A mother who has already had a Down syndrome child is about three times more likely to have one again, for example, and women over age thirty-five are more likely than younger women to have a child with this disorder. Such women might consider amniocentesis, which is best done in the sixteenth week of pregnancy.

Mutation
Abnormal chromosome structure, responsible for such diseases as Down syndrome.
Down syndrome
Disorder characterized by mental retardation and altered physical appearance; caused by a genetic mutation that adds an extra chromosome to the twenty-first pair, giving the child 47 chromosomes.
Amniocentesis
Process in which fluid is taken from a mother's womb to test for Down syndrome and other genetic disorders.

Five-year-old boy with Down syndrome being held by his father.

Chapter 2: Biology and Behavior / **69**

Unfortunately, Down syndrome cannot be treated, so the only choice when amniocentesis indicates Down syndrome is whether or not to induce an abortion.

The causes of mutations are not well understood and are of great concern to modern geneticists. They have identified three causes:

1. Some people carry *mutator genes* that increase the rate of mutations in other genes.

2. High temperatures can increase mutation rate. Males generate sperm in their scrotum, a sac that is usually cooler than the rest of the body in mammals. Research has indicated that wearing tight trousers can raise scrotal temperature to a point that could almost double mutation rate (Lerner & Libby, 1976).

3. Radiation has been linked to mutation rate. X-rays are one source of radiation, and pregnant women are advised to avoid them. Radiation before pregnancy may also increase mutation rate. Recent evidence suggests that more exposure to radiation may explain the increased risk of having Down syndrome babies for older women.

Continuing research on mutations will hopefully allow geneticists to understand and treat the more than 2,000 genetic disorders that are known today.

Genetic Laws of Inheritance

Gregor Mendel started modern genetics by formulating laws of how characteristics or traits are inherited. He based his laws on years of systematic breeding of garden peas. He noticed that peas, like humans, inherit traits from both parents, and he noticed a pattern in the way these traits are passed along.

Single-Gene Traits. Modern geneticists now realize that Mendel studied a special case, known as **single-gene traits.** Some genes singlehandedly determine specific traits like hair color in humans. Such genes occur in pairs, with each member located in the same position on paired chromosomes and with each parent contributing one member to each gene pair. A single gene may occur in one of several different forms called *alleles*, which geneticists represent by means of letters. Some alleles, called *dominant*, rule over others, which are called *recessive*. Dominant alleles are represented by capital letters and recessive alleles are represented by small letters. Consider the example of inheriting red hair. This trait is carried by a recessive gene and should be labeled with a small letter (*r* = red hair). Most other hair colors are carried by dominant genes. (The exception is light blond, which is also recessive.) For the sake of this discussion, let's call hair colors other than red or light blond "normal." Because the genes for "normal" hair color are dominant, let's designate them by a capital letter (i.e., *N* = "normal" hair color). Dominant genes overtake recessive genes when the two kinds occur together. Thus, in Figure 2–19, parents with *Nr* combinations have "normal" hair color. Because both of these parents have an *r* gene, however, they can have a child with red hair. As the figure shows, this will happen when a child inherits an *r* from both parents.

Sex-Linked Traits. A complication occurs when the gene for a trait, such as color vision, is located on the chromosome that also determines one's sex. A human gene is *sex-linked* if it is located on the X chromosome in pair 23. For example, allele *C* produces normal color vision, allele *c* produces colorblindness. Either allele occurs in X chromosomes; neither one occurs in Y. Since males have only one X chromosome, which comes from their mother and which completely determines their color vision, a

Single-gene traits
Some genes determine specific traits all on their own, rather than in combination with other genes. An example is eye color.

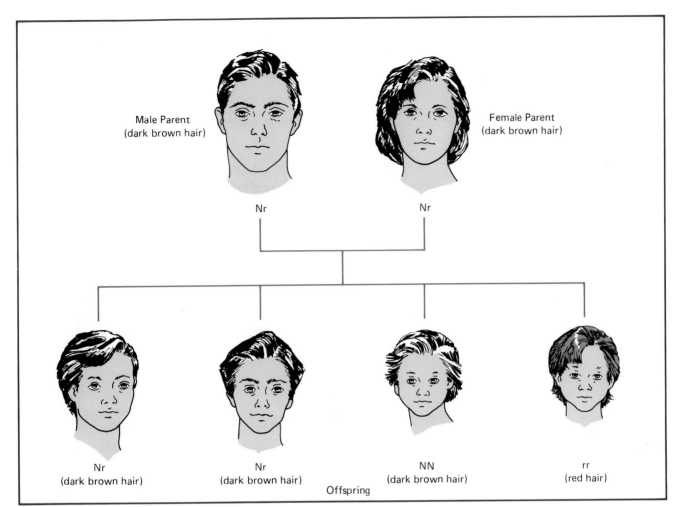

Male Parent
(dark brown hair)

Female Parent
(dark brown hair)

Nr

Nr

Nr
(dark brown hair)

Nr
(dark brown hair)

NN
(dark brown hair)

rr
(red hair)

Offspring

FIGURE 2–19

Dominant and recessive genes control hair color in humans. The gene for brown hair (N) dominates the gene for red hair (r). Offspring get one gene from each parent. An offspring will have red hair only if it gets an r from each parent, forming an rr pair.

male will have normal vision if he inherits *C* from his mother, and he will be colorblind if he inherits *c*. A female, on the other hand, has two X chromosomes and therefore has two chances for normal color vision. She will have normal color vision if either one of her X chromosomes is *C*, because the *C* allele is the dominant allele. She will be colorblind only in the event that she inherits a *c* from *both* her father *and* her mother. A female who inherits a *Cc* combination will not be color blind, but will be a carrier of the colorblind gene to the next generation (see Figure 2–20).

Codominant Genes. Some genes have many forms (alleles) even though any one person can have only two of them. *Codominant genes* occur when more than one allele is dominant. Human blood grouping is an example. There are four blood types: A, B, AB, and O. The gene that determines this grouping has three alleles: A, B, and O. Alleles *A* and *B* are both dominant; allele *O* is recessive. One interesting application of blood group genetics is for cases in which a male denies being the father of a child. To see how genetics can help resolve these cases, let's begin with the less likely situation in which neither the father nor the mother is known. Then we have to leave open the possibility that any of the three alleles could come from each parent. Table 2–2 shows the possible combinations that could be inherited and the resulting blood types. This table can also be used to identify certain impossible combinations when the blood types are known for the mother and for the alleged father. For

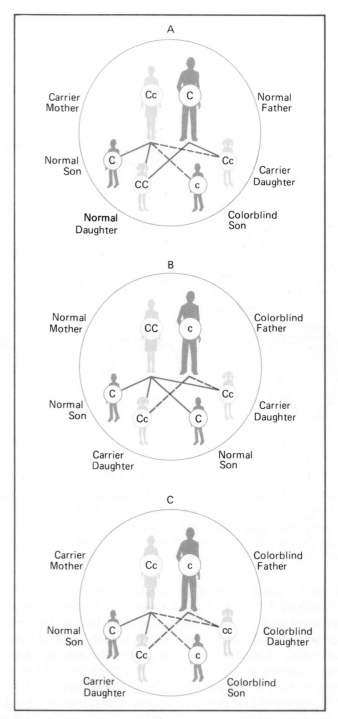

FIGURE 2–20

Color blindness displays sex-linked inheritance. Females inherit two genes for color vision. Males inherit one. There are two alleles for color vision: *C*, a dominant one that allows normal vision and *c*, a recessive one that leads to color blindness. Females can inherit the following patterns: *CC* (normal), *Cc* (carrier), or *cc* (colorblind). Males can inherit either *C* (normal) or *c* (colorblind). The circles show some common patterns of inheritance of this sex-linked gene. Solid lines indicate the transmission of the dominant allele, *C*. Broken lines indicate the transmission of the recessive allele, *c*. In Part A, a carrier mother and normal father have a 50 percent chance of producing a normal son and a 50 percent chance of producing a colorblind son. They also have a 50 percent chance of producing a normal daughter and a 50 percent chance of producing a carrier daughter. In Part B, a normal mother and a colorblind father will have sons who are normal 100 percent of the time and daughters who are carriers 100 percent of the time. In Part C, a carrier mother and a colorblind father, 50 percent of the sons will be normal and 50 percent of the sons will be colorblind. For the daughters, 50 percent will be carriers and 50 percent will be colorblind. Notice that females can be carriers without being colorblind and that, overall, females are less likely than males to be colorblind.

Alleles *A* and *B* are codominant; allele *o* is recessive. The four possible blood types are A, B, AB, and O. We only need to consider the possibility of any of the three alleles coming from each parent when neither parent is known. If the parents' blood types are known we can narrow the possibilities as follows: type A cannot transmit allele *B*; type B cannot transmit allele *A*; type AB cannot transmit allele *o*; and type O cannot transmit either allele *A* or allele *B*. As a result blood group genetics can be used for cases in which a male denies being the father of a child. The text provides examples.

		Possible Alleles from the father (assuming we do not know the blood type of the father)		
		A	B	o
Possible Alleles from the mother (assuming we do not know the blood type of the mother)	A	AA Type A	AB Type AB	Ao Type A
	B	AB Type AB	BB Type B	Bo Type B
	o	Ao Type A	Bo Type B	oo Type O

example, only the first two columns of the table apply to a type AB male because he can transmit only an *A* allele or a *B* allele. Thus, as you can see, it is impossible for him to have a type O offspring. Similarly, the last column of the table applies only to a type O male because he can transmit only an *O* allele. Clearly, he cannot have a type AB offspring. Furthermore, he cannot have offspring with type A unless the mother contributes an *A* allele, nor type O unless the mother contributes an *O* allele.

Polygenic Traits. Another complication occurs when traits are **polygenic,** which means that they are determined by the action of more than one gene pair. Most human traits are polygenic. Each human parent contributes a *set of genes*, rather than a single gene, to each chromosome pair to determine specific traits. Rules governing dominant and recessive alleles still apply for polygenic traits. As the number of genes determining a single trait increases, the task of specifying the relationship between genes and traits gets even more complicated.

Today's geneticists cannot even say how many genes go into determining complex traits like intelligence, so they are far from being able to link specific genes to intelligence. Scientists do have evidence, however, that genes influence intelligence. In one experiment, rats were separated into a "bright" group, who were good maze runners, and a "dull" group, who were poor maze runners (Tryon, 1940). "Bright" rats mated together and "dull" rats mated together for eight generations. Tryon continued to use maze-running ability as his critical measure. He found that almost every offspring of the "bright" rats was better than the average of the first generation, and almost all of the offspring of the "dull" rats were poorer maze runners than the original group. The results suggest that genetic inheritance influences intelligence, assuming, of course, that we accept maze running as a measure of rat "intelligence."

While Tryon's experiment and others like it justify further investigations into genetic influences on intelligence, other studies suggest that environment also influences intelligence. For instance, Cooper and Zubek (1958) controlled for genetic background and found that raising rats in an enriched,

Polygenic traits
Traits that are determined by the action of more than one gene pair. Most human traits are polygenic.

GENETIC ENGINEERING

On January 4, 1982, Judith and Roger Carr took their daughter, Elizabeth Jordan Carr, home from Norfolk General Hospital, where she was born a week earlier. This seemingly ordinary event was in the news because Elizabeth Carr was America's first "test-tube" baby. That is, she was conceived outside her mother's body. An egg, or ovum, was removed from her mother, placed in a test tube, and fertilized with her father's sperm. The united egg and sperm cells were then placed back in the mother, where Elizabeth developed normally.

Elizabeth Carr is the world's nineteenth test-tube baby. Dr. Daniel Petrucci was the first to successfully combine an ovum and sperm in a test tube in 1959. The first test-tube baby, Louise Brown, was born in 1978 at a clinic in England operated by Dr. Patrick Steptoe and Robert Edwards. None of the parents of test-tube babies could have conceived any other way. They and many parents in the future will forever be grateful to *genetic engineering*, the science of applied genetics. The study of how traits are passed on from parent to child led to a basic understanding of how eggs and sperm unite.

Genetic engineers are also credited with at least three other break-throughs:

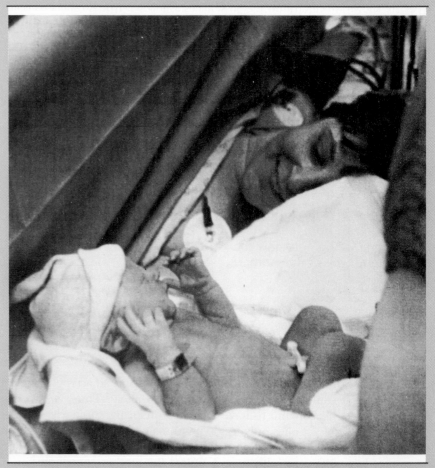

Judith Carr with her newborn daughter, Elizabeth Jordan Carr, who is America's first "test-tube" baby.

1. Dr. H. Gobind Khorana headed a team that achieved the first chemical synthesis of a gene in 1970 at the University of Wisconsin. This work opened the door for creating any gene in a test tube. A Harvard research team, for example, constructed genes that produce insulin, an important hormone discussed earlier in this chapter (Gilbert & Villa-Komaroff, 1980). More recently, researchers genetically altered mice to produce blood components that can be used by humans (*the Johns Hopkins Medical Letter*, 1989). In the future, this new technique might enable us to have blood transfusions without fear of AIDS and other diseases.

2. An Oxford team of scientists in 1971 changed the structure of defective cells in mice. They injected healthy chick chromosomes into defective mice cells. The cells used the new material to correct their own defect and to reproduce healthy cells. This research was a first step toward correcting defective human genes (see Anderson & Diacomakos, 1981).

3. J. B. Gurdon (1972) produced a frog without fertilizing an ovum with sperm. He destroyed the genes in a frog ovum and replaced them with a full set of genes from an intestinal cell of another frog. This process, which is called *cloning*, resulted in a tadpole that was genetically identical to the frog that donated the intestine cell. The tadpole is called a *clone*, which is an "identical twin" to one of its parents because of the cloning processes by which it is produced. Some researchers speculate that a day will come when scientists will be able to produce human clones.

Genetic engineering has risks. Scientists must exercise extreme caution to avoid creating a "doomsday bug," a bacteria that causes mass infections for which there is no cure. Genetic engineering also raises ethical questions. For example, who could be cloned? Despite the dangers and ethical questions, genetic engineering could obviously be a tremendous benefit to society. It will surely be in the news for a long time to come.

or challenging, environment also increases "intelligence." Traits that interest psychologists, such as intelligence, personality, and emotions, are generally influenced by both heredity and environment. Genetics sets the theoretical limits, while environment determines how an animal functions within those limits. We will therefore keep track of both factors in many of the following chapters. For example, in Chapter 8 on intelligence, language, and thought we will consider recent evidence on the relative role of heredity and environment in determining human intelligence. In Chapters 9 and 10 on human development, we will consider what studies of twins can tell us about the influences of heredity and environment. Finally, in Chapter 14 on abnormal psychology, we will review evidence about the heritability of schizophrenia, a major psychological disorder.

Summary

1. **Behavioral neuroscience** has historical roots in early Greek philosophies. Currently, this area has a scope that includes a study of both the structure and function of body parts that influence our behavior.

2. Modern day methods of studying the brain, such as PET scans, CAT scans, EEG, and NMR, are enabling **neuroscientists** to learn more about the structure and functions of the human nervous system. From this process, theories are being developed about the biological determinants of behavior in order to help improve health care.

3. **Neurons** are cells specialized to receive and transmit information. They look like other cells except that they have tiny fiber projections that allow them to communicate with other cells.

4. Neurons "speak" a simple language consisting of an "off-on" code. They go off and on at different rates to send messages that can be transmitted from neuron to neuron throughout the body.

5. Short branches, called **dendrites,** receive messages from surrounding neurons; a single long extension called an **axon** carries messages away from the cell body toward other neurons. **Synaptic transmission** occurs as the impulse moves from one neuron to another.

6. The brain's anatomical subdivisions include the **hindbrain, midbrain,** and **forebrain.**

7. The cerebrum is part of the forebrain and governs our most advanced human capabilities, including abstract reasoning and speech. The cerebrum is divided into left and right brain hemispheres, which are further separated into four lobes.

8. The **spinal cord** connects the brain with the rest of the body. It also controls important automatic responses called **reflexes.**

9. The brain's functional subdivisions include the **reticular activating system (RAS),** which controls waking and sleeping; the **limbic system,** which controls emotions; the **autonomic nervous system,** which keeps our body functions stable; the **motor system,** which controls muscles; and the language control centers, which allow us to produce and understand language.

10. Rehabilitation therapists and physicians work as teams to promote behavioral and structural recovery from brain damage.

11. The **endocrine system** consists of glands that regulate body chemistry. These glands send **hormones,** chemical messengers, through the bloodstream.

12. **Genetics** is the study of how traits are inherited, or passed on, from parent to child.

13. The basic units of heredity are the **genes** which are located in the nucleus of all cells. The chemical structure of genes contains the "blueprints for life."

14. Genes group together in structures called **chromosomes,** which are key units in the study of reproduction and in the study of errors in transmitting genes from one generation to the next.

15. Geneticists have formulated laws of how traits are inherited. These laws or principles have led to important applications in a new field called **genetic engineering.**

absolute refractory period
acetylcholine (ACh)
amniocentesis
ascending nerves
autonomic nervous system
axon
axon terminal
basal ganglia
behavioral neuroscientists and
  biopsychologists
brainstem
Broca's aphasia
catecholamines
central nervous system
cerebellum
cerebral cortex (cerebrum)
chemical transmitters
chromosomes
corpus callosum
dendrites
deoxyribonucleic acid (DNA)
depolarization
descending nerves
Down syndrome
endocrine system
endorphins
fissure of Rolando

fissure of Sylvius
forebrain
frontal lobe
gametes
genes
genetics
genotype
gonads
hindbrain
hormones
hypothalamus
longitudinal fissure
medulla
membrane potential
metabolic rate
midbrain
motor cortex
motor system
mutations
myelin sheath
nervous system
neurons
occipital lobe
pancreas
parasympathetic division
parathyroid glands
parietal lobe

peripheral nervous system
phrenology
pituitary gland
polarization
polygenic traits
pons
pyramidal cells
receptor sites
reflexes
relative refractory period
reticular activating system (RAS)
ribonucleic acid (RNA)
single-gene traits
somatosensory cortex
spinal cord
sympathetic division
synapse
synaptic space
synaptic transmission
synaptic vesicles
temporal lobe
thalamus
thyroid gland
thyroxin
Wernicke's aphasia
zygote

SUBTLE BUT INTRIGUING DIFFERENCES FOUND IN THE BRAIN ANATOMY OF MEN AND WOMEN

DAN GOLEMAN

Researchers who study the brain have discovered that it differs anatomically in men and women in ways that may underlie differences in mental abilities.

The findings, although based on small-scale studies and still very preliminary, are potentially of great significance. If there are subtle differences in anatomical structure between men's and women's brains, it would help explain why women recover more quickly and more often from certain kinds of brain damage than do men, and perhaps help guide treatment.

The findings could also aid scientists in understanding why more boys than girls have problems like dyslexia, and why women on average have superior verbal abilities to men. Researchers have not yet found anything to explain the tendency of men to do better on tasks involving spatial relationships.

The new findings are emerging from the growing field of the neuropsychology of sex differences. Specialists in the discipline met at the New York Academy of Sciences last month to present this latest data.

Research on sex differences in the brain has been a controversial topic, almost taboo for a time. Some feminists fear that any differences in brain structure found might be used against women by those who would cite the difference to explain "deficiencies" that are actually due to social bias. And some researchers argue that differences in the brain are simply due to environmental influences, such as girls being dis-couraged from taking math seriously.

The new research is producing a complex picture of the brain in which differences in anatomical structure seem to lead to advantages in performance on certain mental tasks. The researchers emphasize, however, that it is not at all clear that education or experience do not override what differences in brain structure contribute to the normal variation in abilities. Moreover, they note that the brains of men and women are far more similar than different.

Still, in the most significant new findings, researchers are reporting that parts of the corpus callosum, the fibers that connect the left and right hemispheres of the brain, are larger in women than men. The finding is surprising because, over all, male brains—including the corpus callosum as a whole—are larger than those of females, presumably because men tend to be bigger on average than women.

Because the corpus callosum ties together so many parts of the brain, a difference there suggests far more widespread disparities between men and women in the anatomical structure of other parts of the brain.

"This anatomical difference is probably just the tip of the iceberg," said Sandra Witelson, a neuropsychologist at McMaster University Medical School in Hamilton, Ontario, who did the study. "It probably reflects differences in many parts of the brain which we have not yet even gotten a glimpse of. The anatomy of men's and women's brains may be far more different than we suspect."

The part of the brain which Dr. Witelson discovered is larger in women is in the isthmus, a narrow part of the callosum toward the back. Her findings, reported in March at the New York Academy of Sciences meeting, and published in the journal *Brain*.

Dr. Witelson's findings on the isthmus are based on studies of 50 brains, 15 male and 35 female. The brains examined were of patients who had been given routine neuropsychological tests before they died.

"Witelson's findings are potentially quite important, but it's not clear what they mean," said Bruce McEwen, a neuroscientist at Rockefeller University. "In the brain, bigger doesn't always mean better."

In 1982 a different area of the corpus callosum, the splenium, was reported by researchers to be larger in women than in men. But that study was based on only 14 brains, five of which were female. Since then, some researchers, including Dr. Witelson have failed to find the reported difference while others have.

Since such differences in brain structure can be subtle and vary greatly from person to person, it can take the close examination of hundreds of brains before neuroanatomists are convinced. But other neuroscientists say the findings are convincing enough to encourage them to do tests of their own.

Both the splenium and the isthmus are located toward the rear of the corpus callosum. This part of the corpus callosum ties together the cortical areas on each side of the brain that control some aspects of speech, such as the comprehension of spoken language, and the perception of spatial relationships.

"The isthmus connects the verbal and spatial centers on the right and left hemispheres, sending information both ways—it's a two-way highway," Dr. Witelson said. The larger isthmus in women is thought to be related to women's superiority on some tests of verbal intelligence. It is unclear what, if anything, the isthmus might have to do with the advantage of men on tests of spatial relations.

The small differences in abilities between the sexes have long puzzled researchers.

On examinations like the Scholastic Aptitude Test, which measures overall verbal and mathematical abilities, sex differences in scores have been declining. But for certain specific abilities, the sex differences are still notable, researchers say.

While these differences are still the subject of intense controversy, most researchers agree that women generally show advantages over men in certain verbal abilities. For instance, on average, girls begin to speak earlier than boys and women are more fluent with words than men, and make fewer mistakes in grammar and pronunciation.

On the other hand, men, on average, tend to be better than women on certain spatial tasks, such as drawing maps of places they have been and rotating imagined geometric images in their minds' eye—a skill useful in mathematics, engineering and architecture.

Of course, the advantages for each

Detecting Differences

In the corpus callosum, millions of fibers link many parts of the brain, including a region in the left hemisphere involved in speech and a region in the right hemisphere involved in spatial perception. One study has found that the isthmus, a narrow part of the corpus callosum toward the back of the head, is larger in women than in men. Another area, the splenium, was found to be larger in women in some studies.

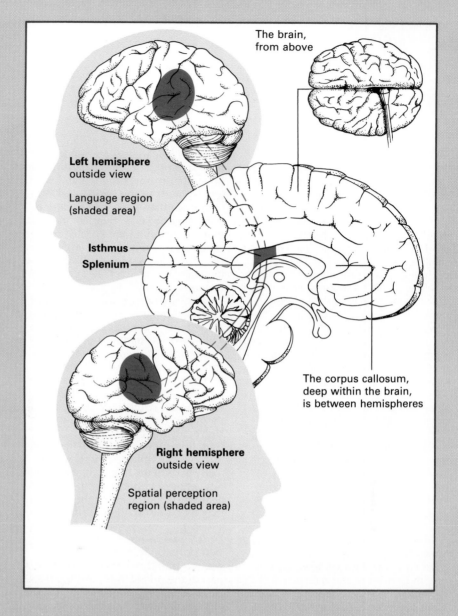

The brain, from above

Left hemisphere outside view

Language region (shaded area)

Isthmus

Splenium

The corpus callosum, deep within the brain, is between hemispheres

Right hemisphere outside view

Spatial perception region (shaded area)

sex are only on average. There are individual men who do as well as the best women on verbal tests, and women who do as well as the best men on spatial tasks.

Measuring the Brain's Anatomy

One of the first studies that directly links the relatively larger parts of women's corpus callosums to superior verbal abilities was reported at the meeting of the New York Academy of Sciences by Melissa Hines, a neuropsychologist at the University of California at Los Angeles Medical School.

Dr. Hines and her associates used magnetic resonance imaging, a method that uses electrical fields generated by the brain, to measure

the brain anatomy of 29 women. They found that the larger the splenium in the women, the better they were on tests of verbal fluency.

There was no relationship, however, between the size of their splenium and their scores on tests of spatial abilities, suggesting that differences in those abilities are related to anatomical structures in some other part of the brain or have nothing to do with anatomy.

"The size of the splenium," Dr. Hines said, "may provide an anatomical basis for increased communication between the hemispheres, and perhaps as a consequence, increased language abilities."

Researchers now speculate that the larger portions of the corpus callosum in women may allow for stronger

connections between the parts of women's brains that are involved in speech than is true for men.

"Although we are not sure what a bigger overall isthmus means in terms of microscopic brain structure, it does suggest greater interhemispheric communication in women," Dr. Witelson said. "But if it does have something to do with the cognitive differences between the sexes, it will certainly turn out to be a complex story."

Part of that complexity has to do with explaining why, despite the bigger isthmus, women tend to do less well than men in spatial abilities, even though the isthmus connects the brain's spatial centers, too.

"Bigger isn't necessarily better, but it certainly means that it's different," Dr. Witelson said.

Other Differences Detected

A variety of other differences in the brain have been detected by the researchers in their recent studies.

For instance, Dr. Witelson found in her study that left-handed men had a bigger isthmus than did right-handed men. For women, though, there was no relationship between hand preference and isthmus size.

"How our brains do the same thing, namely use the right hand, may differ between the sexes," Dr. Witelson said.

She also found that the overall size of the callosum, particularly the front part, decreases in size between 40 and 70 years of age in men, but remains the same in women.

Several converging lines of evidence from other studies suggest that the brain centers for language are more centralized in men than in women.

One study involved cerebral blood flow, which was measured while men and women listened to words that earphones directed to one ear or the other. The research, conducted by Cecile Naylor, a neuropsychologist at Bowman Gray School of Medicine in Winston-Salem, N.C., showed that the speech centers in women's brains were connected to more areas both within and between each hemisphere.

Disadvantage in Stroke

This puts men at a relative disadvantage in recovering from certain kinds of brain damage, such as strokes, when they cause lesions in the speech centers on the left side of the brain. Women with similar lesions, by contrast, are better able to recover speech abilities, perhaps because stronger connections between the hemispheres allow them to compensate more readily for damage on the left side of the brain by relying on similar speech centers on the right.

In the current issue of *the Journal of Neuroscience*, Roger Gorski, a neuroscientist at U.C.L.A., reported finding that parts of the hypothalamus are significantly bigger in male rats than in female ones, even though the size of the overall brain is the same in both sexes.

And Dr. McEwen, working with colleagues at Rockefeller University, has found a sex difference in the structure of neurons in part of the hippocampus that relays messages from areas of the cortex.

Dr. McEwen, working with rats' brains, found that females have more branches on their dendrites, which receive chemical messages to other neurons, than do males. Males, on the other hand, have more spines on their dendrites, which also receive messages from other neurons. These differences in structure may mean differing patterns of electrical activity during brain function, he said.

"We were surprised to find any difference at all, and frankly, don't understand the implications for differences in brain function," Dr. McEwen said. "But we'd expect to find the same differences in humans; across the board, findings in rodents have had corollaries in the human brain."

Sensation 3

Farley Mowat stood alone in the middle of an ice-covered arctic lake surrounded by a mountain of supplies. The decrepit ski-equipped plane that had brought him and his supplies was now climbing reluctantly into the clouds. He reached for his revolver as distant howling sounds brought to mind the hordes of bloodthirsty wolves he had been sent to study.

The Canadian Wildlife Service had sent Mowat to investigate reports that wolves were slaughtering thousands of Arctic caribou. The trappers Farley interviewed informed him that each wolf killed thousands of caribou a year just out of blood lust. He retreated under his canoe. The sound seemed deafening as the howling animals rushed toward him.

Farley then heard a loud roar followed by silence. In a state of total confusion, he peeked out from under the canoe. At first he could see only wolf feet, but then he fixed his gaze on the most welcome pair of feet he had ever seen. He poked his head out and looked upward into the

apprehensive face of a young Eskimo clad in caribou furs. The man stood next to a dog sled and team of 14 Huskies. There wasn't a wolf in sight.

Farley's 18-year-old rescuer, Mike, was a trapper of mixed Eskimo and white parentage. Mike made room in his cabin for both Farley and his supplies.

After the spring thaw several weeks later, Farley pitched a tent on a hill directly overlooking a den of wolves. This ideal arrangement for observing the study species would have been impossible if wolves were as bloodthirsty as Farley had been led to believe. Farley had found, however, not a den of killers, but a playful, friendly family of skillful providers. The family consisted of four pups, their father and mother, and another male who appeared to be their uncle. Farley named their home "Wolf House Bay," and he named each of the adults. The father, George, was about 8 feet long; the mother, Angeline, was about a third smaller; and the third adult, "Uncle Albert," was smaller than George.

Farley had not had a chance to

observe the wolves hunting, and, worse yet, he had no idea what they were eating. Ever since the caribou had migrated to some 200 or 300 miles north of Wolf House Bay, the wolves appeared to be living on air and water. This mystery weighed heavily on Farley's mind, not only because it was central to his mission, but also because he appeared to be the only suitable meal for wolves in the area.

This preoccupation about becoming a wolf snack greatly delayed his efforts to solve the mystery of the wolves' diet. The solution was under his nose all the while, but he didn't see it because he was only looking for prey worthy of the wolves' reputation. One day Angeline provided an unmistakable clue; she stood in full view of Farley's powerful telescope with the hind legs and tail of a mouse dangling from her mouth. At first Farley thought he was witnessing a between-meal snack, but when Angeline proceeded to catch and gobble 22 more mice, he realized that she had consumed a fair-sized meal. Could the Arctic's

Farley Mowat

most feared carnivores be living on a diet of mice? If the answer was yes, Farley realized that he would have a hard time persuading his superiors. He therefore designed a three-phase test. In the first phase, he did a survey of the small rodent population and determined that it was sufficiently numerous to support the wolves.

In the second phase, Farley ate little else besides mice for several weeks. He ate the whole mouse except the skin. To prepare a meal, he marinated one dozen fat mice for 2 hours in ethyl alcohol, rolled them in a mixture of flour, salt, pepper, and cloves, fried them about 5 minutes in a greased pan, and simmered them slowly for 15 minutes in alcohol. He suffered no ill effects from this diet and remained vigorous, which suggested that mice had a sufficient nutritional value to support him and, by inference, a wolf.

Farley really detested the third phase of his study: gathering and examining several months' worth of excrement from the wolf family. He found that 48 percent of the samples contained rodent remains. Other identifiable food items were fragments of caribou bones, caribou hair, and a few bird feathers. Clearly mice constituted a substantial proportion of the wolves' diet.

Ootek, an elderly Eskimo

medicine man, also told Farley an Eskimo legend about the caribou and the wolf being one because "the caribou feeds the wolf, but it is the wolf who keeps the caribou strong" (Mowat, 1963, p. 85). According to the legend, weak caribou started to outnumber strong ones because people killed the fat and the strong. Kaila, the god of the sky, therefore told wolves to "eat the sick, weak, and small caribou, so that the land will be left for the fat and the good ones" (Mowat, 1963, p. 85).

Farley was stunned to hear the theory of natural selection related in an ancient Eskimo legend. He was also skeptical because he had seen so many skeletons of what appeared to be big and healthy caribou scattered all over the tundra. He asked Mike to have Ootek explain that.

"Don't need to ask him that," Mike replied with unabashed candor. "It was me killed those deer. I got fourteen dogs to feed and it takes maybe two, three caribou a week for that. I got to feed myself, too. It's no use for me to shoot skinny caribou. What I got to have is the

big fat ones" (Mowat, 1963, pp. 85–86).

With the help of Mike and Ootek, Farley observed both trappers and wolves kill caribou. He saw for himself that trappers aimed for the biggest, fattest, and strongest, while the wolves selectively hunted the small, sick, and weak. The wolves' selection mechanism was quite simple. They pursued and killed only those they could easily catch.

Farley reported his findings in meticulous detail, pitting his first-hand scientific observations against long-established beliefs based primarily on hearsay. But his efforts were to little avail. The Canadian Wildlife Service continued its policy of wolf control, using ski-equipped aircraft to set out poison-bait stations. One of these "wolf-getters" was set up near Wolf House Bay. The officer who set it ascertained that the den was occupied when he set the trap but was unable to return to check the results because of an early onset of the spring thaw.

It is not known what the results were.

Farley Mowat lived among wild wolves gaining a great deal of respect for their life style and for their keen senses such as seeing, hearing, smelling.

After completing this chapter, you should be able to:

Define and explain the differences between sensations and perceptions.

Explain psychophysical concepts and describe methods used in their measurement.

Describe and discuss the structure and function of the parts of the eye.

Explain the neural process of light and dark adaptation and color coding.

Describe and discuss the structure and function of the parts of the ear.

Discuss the physical properties of sound and the theories of hearing.

Summarize the processes underlying the senses of taste, smell, touch, and body orientation.

History and Scope of the Study of Sensation

Farley Mowat respected his environment, and appreciated the senses that enabled him to experience it. A reader of his vivid descriptions can almost see the glistening snow, hear the howling wolves, taste his special fried mouse recipe, smell his fire, and feel its warmth. The next two chapters will introduce you to the way in which people gather and interpret information about their environment. Traditionally, these studies have been divided into two parts, *sensations and perceptions*. We have followed this tradition by devoting one chapter to sensation and the next one to perception.

From a processing point of view, sensation corresponds roughly to gathering information and perception corresponds to interpreting the information. From an experiential point of view, sensing—or detecting—"bright red," or "shiny" does not have much significance until the brain processes the information (see Chapter 2). The brain puts the information together forming perceptions—the actual experience of an apple or a sports car. Many of you have already been introduced to the sensory systems in high school biology classes. You might be surprised, therefore, to see a chapter on them in a psychology book. The reason becomes clear, however, when one looks at history. From its early days to the present, the study of sensations has involved many disciplines including psychology. Consider, for example, two of the scholars who influenced Wilhelm Wundt before he founded the first psychological laboratory in 1879 (see Chapter 1):

1. Wundt had served as an assistant to Hermann von Helmholtz (1821–1894), one of the greatest scientists of the nineteenth century. Helmholtz was a physicist and a physiologist, but his genius carried over to psychology as well. Helmholtz studied the physics of light and sound and the physiology of the eyes and ears. The belief that sensations are the elementary building blocks of all our knowledge motivated Wundt to dedicate the first psychological laboratory to the study of sensations.

2. Another influential person in the early days of psychology, Gustav Fechner (1801–1887), was a physicist and philosopher. Fechner is most famous for developing rigorous methods for studying relationships between

The experiences of "red" and "shiny" are sensations; the experiences of objects such as an apple or a sports car are perceptions.

physical stimuli and psychological responses. Although Wundt started the first psychological laboratory, Fechner is the person who laid the foundation for experimental methods in psychology. His methods for measuring sensations remain in use to this day, as we shall see in the next section.

In addition to explaining methods for measuring sensations, this chapter will review the physiology of our sensory organs, and relationships that exist between physical stimuli and sensory responses. After discussing the historical development of methods for measuring sensations, we will move forward to current applications of those methods in many branches of psychology. We will then step back in time again to consider one of the first general principles to emerge in psychology. We will then take up the physics, physiology, and psychology of each sense separately, reviewing both principles and applications.

Exploring the Limits of Our Sensations

Farley Mowat became keenly attuned to his senses as weeks passed during his vigil on the arctic tundra. Stars seemed brighter, birds louder, food more tasty, flowers more fragrant, and the sun warmer. This chapter is about these sensations of sight, hearing, taste, smell, and touch. We will begin by examining methods for measuring sensations.

Let's imagine that we take a time machine back to join Farley at Wolf House Bay. We are experimental psychologists fully equipped to measure his senses. Farley explains how much more sensitive his senses have become, and he is eager to let us study his sensory sensitivity. We agree on a good first question: How far away can Farley see a candle flame on a clear dark night? The light reaching our eye gets dimmer as the candle moves away. Therefore, our question is the same as asking: What is the dimmest light we can see?

This is a psychophysical question.

Psychophysics studies the relationship between physical energies and psychological experiences. In this example, the physical energy is light, and the psychological experience or sensation is seeing the light. Psychophysical questions can be grouped into three categories:

1. What is the **absolute threshold,** or the least amount of a certain stimulus energy, that can be detected? Asking how far we can see a candle is an example of absolute threshold.

2. What is the **difference threshold,** or the smallest difference in intensity, that can be noticed between two stimuli? For example, how far away do we have to move a candle before it is just noticeably dimmer?

3. How do the intensity and other qualities of a stimulus relate to the intensity and other qualities of our sensations and perceptions?

Psychophysics
Studies the relationship between physical energies and psychological experiences.
Absolute threshold
Least amount of a certain stimulus energy that can be detected.
Difference threshold
Smallest difference in intensity that can be noticed between two stimuli.

We could measure Farley Mowat's absolute threshold for seeing a candle in a variety of ways. Let's consider some of the methods that have played a major role in psychology. Assume that we are equipped to display an artificial candle. Two separate control panels enable us to control the brightness of this candle-like light.

The Method of Adjustment

In the method of adjustment, we would allow Farley to adjust the light's intensity. We would begin half the trials with the light off, and Farley would increase the intensity until he could just barely see the light. The other half of the trials would begin with a visible light. Farley would then decrease the intensity until he could no longer see it. We would run at least 2 trials and probably not more than 10. Each trial would end with the light on an intensity set by the subject. The average of these settings would define the absolute threshold.

The Method of Limits

In the method of limits an experimenter would control the light's intensity. Half the trials would begin with the light too dim to be seen. We would ask Farley, "Do you see the light?" He would say, "No, I don't see it." Then we would increase the intensity slightly and ask again. This would continue until Farley said, "Yes, I do see it." The other half of the trials would start with a very bright light. We would ask Farley, "Do you see the light?" He would say, "Yes, I do see it." Then we would slightly decrease the intensity and repeat the question, proceeding until he answered, "No, I don't see it." Each trial would end with the light at some intensity. As in the previous method, the average of these intensities would define the absolute threshold.

The Method of Constant Stimuli

The method of constant stimuli is sometimes used to overcome a problem presented by the other two methods. The problem is that subjects know too much about the sequencing of the intensities. Either they are controlling it themselves, or they know that the intensity is getting slightly more or slightly less on each trial. When knowledge of sequencing is a major concern, the method of constant stimuli can be used instead. We would first choose an intensity that is almost always seen and one that is almost never seen. Then we would choose seven or eight equally spaced intensities between

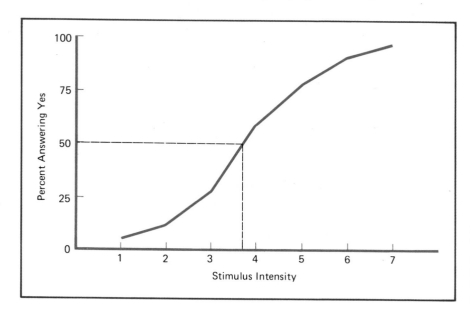

FIGURE 3–1

Typical threshold data obtained by the method of constant stimuli. The curve crosses the 50 percent *yes* point at a stimulus intensity of 3.7, which is thus considered the threshold for these data.

Table 3–1

Absolute Thresholds (These estimates of absolute thresholds indicate the incredible sensitivity of the various receptor organs.)

Sense	Absolute Threshold
Vision	A candle flame can be seen from 30 miles away on a clear, dark night.
Hearing	A watch can be heard ticking from 20 feet away in a quiet room.
Taste	A teaspoon of sugar can be tasted in 2 gallons of water.
Smell	A drop of perfume can be smelled when circulated into 6 large rooms.
Touch	A fly's wing can be felt falling onto one's cheek from a height of 1 centimeter.

After Galanter (1962).

the two extremes. On the first trial we would select one of the intensities at random, present it, and record whether or not Farley sees the light. On the next trial we would do the same thing for another intensity. This would continue until all intensities were presented 50 times (more or less, depending on the desired accuracy). Because the sequence is completely random, subjects cannot predict what intensity will be shown; thus, the method of constant stimuli eliminates knowledge of sequencing.

To calculate the absolute threshold, we would compute the percentage of times that the subject saw each stimulus. This percentage is found by dividing the total number of times the subject said "yes" by 50, which is the total number of times that each stimulus was presented. The data are then plotted on a graph, which is used to estimate the threshold, as shown in Figure 3–1. The absolute threshold is defined as the intensity that is seen 50 percent of the time.

So what would we find in our hypothetical experiment? How far could we see a candle flame on a clear dark night? The answer is 30 miles! Table 3–1 shows this and other absolute thresholds that have been measured.

Signal-Detection Theory

John A. Swets (1964) developed **signal-detection theory** to measure sensations. You will understand this method best if you imagine yourself detecting light in our hypothetical experiment. Consider the things that would influence whether or not you would say "Yes, I saw the light." According to signal-detection theory, the probability of making this response is determined both by your senses and by the processes that determine how you make decisions (see Chapter 8). Specifically, it depends in part on *sensory sensitivity*, which is the degree to which your eyes are activated by the light. It also depends on the strictness of your *decision criterion*, which is the amount of sensory activation needed to trigger a decision that a light is present. With a lax criterion, even very weak sensations would cause you to say "Yes, I see the light." With a strict criterion, you would say "yes" only for very strong sensations.

Both lax and strict criteria have disadvantages. On the one hand, lax criteria create a danger of making *false alarms*, which is saying "yes" when no stimulus is present. False alarms are possible because you can experience weak sensations even when no stimulus is present. For example, close your eyes in a dark room. You will see what appears to be flashes of light even though the room contains no light. These apparent sensations are caused by spontaneous neural activity in your visual system (see Chapter 5). With a lax criterion, you can therefore say "Yes, I see a light," even when no light is present. Thus, the strictness of your decision criterion would influence the probability of saying "yes" when there is no stimulus (a false alarm). It would also influence the probability of saying "yes" when there is a stimulus (a hit).

Signal-detection theory

Attempts to explain people's perceptual judgments by analyzing their sensitivity to sensory stimuli in addition to the criteria they use to make decisions.

The signal-detection method of collecting data is similar to the method of constant stimuli. One difference is that the stimulus is not presented on some of the trials. Not presenting a stimulus makes it possible to measure false alarms (saying "yes" when no stimulus is present). Presenting a stimulus makes it possible to measure hits (saying "yes" when a stimulus is present). Another difference with respect to the method of constant stimuli is that attempts are made to manipulate the response criterion. There are two ways that we could influence your response criterion. First, we could vary your expectations about how often stimuli would appear. Second, we could alter rewards for hits and penalties for false alarms. For example, suppose we gave you the following instructions: (1) The light will appear on almost every trial. (2) Each hit will add 10 points to your score. (3) Each false alarm will only subtract 1 point from your score. How strict would your response criterion be? You would probably use a very lax criterion because you would score high by saying "yes" on almost every trial. In contrast, suppose we gave you the following instructions: (1) The light will rarely appear. (2) Each hit will add 1 point to your score. (3) Each false alarm will subtract 10 points from your score. You would probably use a very strict criterion because you would score low by saying "yes" frequently. With either a lax criterion or a strict one, you would make some false alarms and some hits during the experiment.

After the experiment, we would use both the probability of false alarms and the probability of hits. We would use them to compute a d′ score, which indicates sensory sensitivity. We would also use them to compute a β score, which indicates strictness of the criterion.

The beauty of signal-detection theory is that these two measures are independent. That is, the measure of the sensory sensitivity and the measure of the decision criterion do not contaminate one another. Thus, two observers who have the same sensitivity will have the same d′ score even if their decision criteria are very different. In addition, they will get different β scores to indicate exactly how different their decision criteria are.

Swets's impetus for developing signal-detection theory came from the need for better tests of sensitivity in radar operators. After using the theory to test radar operators, Green and Swets (1966) promoted its use in basic research. Their book is an excellent example of how work on a practical problem can result in important theoretical advances.

Today, signal-detection theory is being used to advance principles and

Signal-detection theory emerged from efforts to develop tests for radar operators. This theory has greatly improved our ability to measure the sensitivity of sensory systems.

applications in many branches of psychology as well as in other disciplines. For example, the marketing researchers Singh and Churchill (1986) used signal-detection theory to make separate measurements of response bias and memory for advertisements. Dening and Berrios (1989) used similar procedures to separate response bias and memory in psychiatric exams. Of course, signal-detection theory is still being used to measure sensitivity of sensory systems, but even these measurements are being made in many different applied settings. Clinical psychologists have used it, for instance, to measure perception of flickering lights in depressed people. A light flickering at a fast rate appears continuous. At slower rates, the flickering can be detected. You might have noticed this effect in fluorescent lights, which flicker more slowly as they age. You don't detect the rapid flickering of a new bulb, but you often see flickering in an old bulb. Some clinical psychologists had maintained that depressed people cannot detect flickering as well as those who are not depressed. Herskovic, Kietzman, and Sutton (1986) used signal-detection theory to show that depression does not change sensory sensitivity to flickering, but it does change the response criterion. In other words, depressed people are less willing to say "flicker," even though their sensory system is every bit as sensitive to it. In another recent application, Gordon-Salant (1986) used signal-detection theory to show that the elderly have two problems when listening to speech. They are not only less able to hear speech, but also less willing to say that they don't hear. Younger people with a hearing loss are more willing to admit that they don't hear things. These admissions provide useful feedback to the speaker. In contrast, elderly listeners tend to indicate that they understand when they really don't. These indications provide false feedback and hinder communication. Gordon-Salant (1986) recommends the use of signal-detection methods in rehabilitation training to help the elderly overcome this problem. We will encounter other applications; in Chapter 7, for instance, we will review an application in which psychologists used signal-detection theory to evaluate eyewitness testimony in the courtroom.

Methods for Measuring Psychophysical Functions

Up to this point we have been discussing several different methods for measuring the least amount of stimulus energy that can be detected. For any given physical stimulus, the minimal sensitivity represents only one point on the **psychophysical function.** The whole function specifies the relationship between physical energies and perceptual experiences over a wide range of physical magnitudes. To determine Farley's psychophysical function for brightness, we would ask him to behave like a measuring instrument. In other words, we would ask him to make responses that could be translated into numbers that represent the relationship between physical energies and perceptual experiences. We might show him two lights, for instance, and ask him how bright these lights appeared in comparison to one another. A problem with such an open-ended question is that different people might give different kinds of answers. Thus psychologists have developed special methods to constrain how people respond to questions about psychophysical relationships.

Three of these methods are as follows:

1. One method is *magnitude estimation*, a procedure in which subjects are asked to assign any number they wish to match their perceptual experience. In one study on estimating brightness subjects were told:

   > Your task is to assign a number proportional to the brightness as you see it. Use any number you find necessary—fraction, whole number or decimal— but try to keep the numbers proportional to brightness. If one stimulus looks

Psychophysical function
The relationship between physical energies and perceptual experiences over a wide range of physical magnitudes.

twice as bright as another, the number you assign to one should be twice as large as the number you assign to the other (Stevens & Galanter, 1957, p. 392).

2. Another method is *category judgment*, a procedure in which subjects are asked to match their experiences to a small set of numbers. In a study on brightness the instructions might be:

   Tell me how bright each of these lights is on a scale of 1 (very dim) to 10 (very bright).

3. A third technique is *cross-modality matching*, a procedure in which subjects are asked to match one sensory quality with some other sensory quality. A typical instruction might be:

   Indicate how bright each of these lights is by adjusting the loudness of this tone to match the brightness of each light.

Modern researchers are applying these methods to practical problems such as measuring the clarity of speech (Fucci, Ellis, & Petrosina, 1990) and the quality of toilet paper (Lavenka, 1989).

Weber's Law

Scientists seek general principles to account for their observations. This pursuit takes them back and forth between observations and principles. Observations suggest general principles, and the principles in turn predict new observations. These predictions are either confirmed or disconfirmed. When a prediction is confirmed, scientists begin to test other predictions until one is discomfirmed. Then they refine the principle and start the process all over again. One of the first to propose a general psychological principle was Ernst H. Weber, a German psychophysicist who in 1846 stated the law that now bears his name.

The problem Weber worked on can be illustrated with a simple example. Suppose we held a 1-ounce weight. How much weight would have to be added before we noticed an increase in heaviness? The answer according to Teghtsoonian (1971) is that .02 ounce would have to be added. Now suppose we held a 100-ounce weight. How much would have to be added before we noticed an increase in weight? Would we notice if .02 ounce was added? That would be similar to adding a paper clip to the weight of this book. No, much more weight would have to be added: In fact, we would have to add 2 ounces or about 100 paper clips. It is also true for other kinds of stimuli, such as light, that smaller changes can more easily be detected when the original stimulus intensity is low than when it is high. For example, if you have a 100-watt reading light, you probably would not notice if someone added a 4-watt light. But you would notice if the same light was added to your darkened bedroom at night.

Weber found that a simple relationship exists between an original intensity, which he called I, and the amount that must be added to I before the intensity is just-noticeably different. He called the amount that must be added ΔI (pronounced "delta I"). Today the amount that must be added is often called a just-noticeable difference (jnd). **Weber's Law** states that for a specified stimulus, when one divides ΔI by I, one always gets the same number. This number is referred to as a constant value, K. Weber's Law often appears in the form

$$\frac{\Delta I}{I} = K$$

Teghtsoonian (1971) reported that K is equal to about .02 for heaviness, .08 for brightness, and .03 for length. Knowing these values, we can use

Weber's Law
Law stating that a just-noticeable change in a stimulus is proportional to the original stimulus magnitude.

Table 3–2
Weber Fractions
for Various Senses

Sense	Weber Fraction
Electric shock	.013
Saturation, red	.019
Heaviness	.020
Finger span	.022
Length	.029
Vibration, 60 Hz	.036
Loudness	.048
Brightness	.079
Taste, NaCl	.083

Source: Teghtsoonian, 1971.

Weber's Law to make very precise predictions. For example, suppose the only light in Farley's cabin came from 100 candles. How many more candles would we have to light before the room would become just-noticeably brighter? In this problem I equals 100 candles and K equals .08, the constant for brightness. To obtain ΔI, simply multiply I times K.

$$\frac{\Delta I}{100 \text{ candles}} = .08$$

$$\Delta I = .08 \times 100 \text{ candles} = 8 \text{ candles}$$

The answer is 8 candles. This means that 8 more candles would have to be lit before the room would appear brighter. Now, suppose the original amount of light came from 200 candles. How many more candles would we have to light before the cabin would appear brighter? Here, I equals 200, and, of course, K is still .08 because we are still talking about brightness.

$$\frac{\Delta I}{200 \text{ candles}} = .08$$

$$\Delta I = .08 \times 200 \text{ candles} = 16 \text{ candles}$$

The answer is 16 candles. With the room twice as bright to begin with, twice as many candles must be added before the room will appear brighter.

Weber's Law, or principle, stimulated a great deal of research. Scientists have found that it holds up well in all sensory modalities. The value of K is different for different modalities, as shown in Table 3–2. However, within any given modality, the value of K is constant over most stimulus intensities. It rises slightly, however, for extremely high or extremely low stimulus intensities (Gescheider, Bolanowski, Verrilla, Prpajian, 1990).

This discussion of general methods and principles sets the stage for studying specific senses. We will begin with seeing, which is perhaps our most highly developed sense.

Seeing

Farley Mowat had excellent vision, which served him well in his study of wolves and in many other adventures. Millions of people throughout the world have "seen" the Arctic through his eyes in his 25 books, which have been published in over 20 languages. Many of you also enjoy good vision. Some of you, however, see poorly without corrective lenses. And some do not see at all. The main causes of visual problems and blindness are in the eyes themselves. We will briefly study the eyes and the physiology of the visual system. We will then turn to psychophysical facts that explain some of the things that Farley saw at Wolf House Bay.

The Eyes

Figure 3–2 shows the human eye, which includes the following structures:

1. The **cornea** is the window of the eye. A healthy cornea is transparent and shaped like the side of a crystal ball. It is attached to the front of the eye. Two diseases of the cornea occur when it becomes pointed, like the end of a football, or becomes cloudy. These diseases rarely cause blindness, however, because they can be corrected by corneal transplants.

Cornea
Transparent part of the eye that is shaped like a crystal ball.

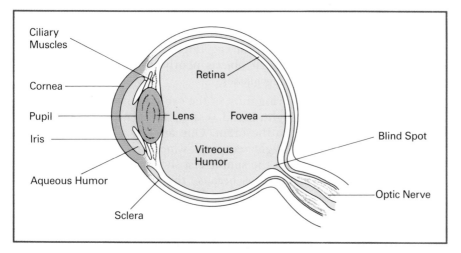

Ciliary Muscles

Cornea

Pupil

Iris

Aqueous Humor

Sclera

Retina

Lens

Fovea

Vitreous Humor

Blind Spot

Optic Nerve

2. The **aqueous humor** is a clear fluid that carries nourishment to the cornea. The aqueous humor is completely recycled every 4 hours. The most common cause of blindness is a problem with the recycling system, which causes pressure to build up inside the eye. The pressure can destroy the eye's critical structures. In America this disease, called **glaucoma,** threatens more than 1.5 million people with blindness. It can be treated with special eye drops and other methods. Early treatment is important, so it is wise to get periodic checkups.

3. The **vitreous humor** is a gel that fills the eye's main chamber and keeps it from collapsing. Have you ever seen spots that appear to hover in front of your eyes? They can be caused by impurities floating in the vitreous humor (Johns Hopkins Medical Letter, 1990).

4. When you are asked the color of your eyes, you are really being asked the color of your **iris,** which is a flat, doughnut-shaped network of muscles behind the aqueous humor. What appears to be a black spot in the center of the iris is actually an opening called the **pupil.**

Eye doctors examine the eye's internal structures with an **ophthalmoscope,** an instrument which uses mirrors or prisms to direct light through the pupil. This important instrument allows doctors to detect eye diseases as well as other diseases such as high blood pressure.

5. The **lens** is directly behind the pupil. It helps the cornea focus light onto the back of the eye. The lens does the critical fine adjustments or **accommodations** required to focus objects at various distances. It accommodates by changing its shape; it gets rounder for near objects and flatter for far ones.

The **near point of accommodation** is the nearest point at which print can be read distinctly. As we get into our 40s, we all lose some of our ability to accommodate and we accommodate more slowly. As a result, the near point of accommodation gets farther and farther away, until reading requires help from corrective lenses. In the past, the common correction for this condition was bifocals, eyeglasses that correct for near vision at the bottom of the lens and for far vision at the top. Another option today is monovision, contact lenses that correct for near vision in one eye and for far vision in the other (Schor, Carson, Peterson, & Suzuki, 1989).

The most widespread disease affecting vision is **cataracts,** a condition characterized by cloudy lenses. Blindness results if the lenses become too cloudy, but fortunately surgical procedures provide a very effective treatment (Donderi & Murphy, 1983).

6. The eye's shape is also important. It is determined by the *sclera*, which is the white, opaque, outer wall of the eye. **Nearsightedness** results when

Aqueous humor
Clear fluid that carries nourishment to the cornea of the eye

Glaucoma
Eye disease that causes pressure to build up inside the eye; most common cause of blindness.

Vitreous humor
Semiliquid gel that fills the eye's main chamber and gives it a spherical shape.

Iris
Flat doughnut-shaped network of muscles behind the aqueous humor of the eye.

Pupil
Opening in the iris of the eye; looks like a black spot in the center of the iris.

Ophthalmoscope
Uses mirrors or prisms to direct light through the pupil so that eye doctors can examine the eye's internal structures.

Lens
Part of the eye that is located directly behind the pupil; helps the cornea focus light onto the back of the eye.

Accommodation
Changes in the shape of the lens to focus objects at different distances.

Near point of accommodation
Nearest point at which print can be read distinctly.

Cataracts
Widespread disease affecting vision that is characterized by cloudy lenses and can result in blindness if lenses are not removed surgically.

Nearsightedness
Occurs when an eye is elongated like a horizontal egg; nearsighted people see near objects well, but see far objects poorly.

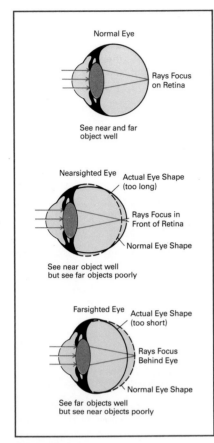

FIGURE 3–3

Nearsightedness and farsightedness are caused by abnormal eye shapes. For clear vision, light must be focused directly on the eye's back wall, as it is in the normal eye. The nearsighted eye is too long, so light focuses in front of the back wall; the farsighted eye is too short, so it focuses behind the back wall.

FIGURE 3–4

To locate your blind spot, close your left eye and stare at the X. Slowly move the book toward you and away from you at a distance of about a foot until the dot disappears.

an eye is elongated like a horizontal egg. Nearsighted people see near objects well, but see far objects poorly. **Farsightedness** is caused by an eye that is flattened, like a vertical egg (Figure 3–3). Farsighted people see far objects well, but see near objects poorly. Both of these problems are easily corrected by wearing glasses.

7. The **retina** is tissue covering most of the eye's interior wall. It contains receptors that respond to light, blood vessels, and a network of neurons that transmit information to the brain. One area of the retina is blind. This **blind spot** contains no light receptors, which are needed to see. You can find your blind spot with the simple test shown in Figure 3–4. There are no light receptors in this area because the space is taken up by the **optic nerve,** which is a bundle of nerve fibers that carry neural signals to the brain. In contrast to the blind spot, another retinal area, called the **fovea,** is especially sensitive. Most blood vessels and nerve fibers are routed around this sensitive area. In addition, the fovea is the region most densely packed with light receptors. However, this sensitive area begins to break down after fifty or sixty years. This condition causes central vision to become increasingly blurred (Johns Hopkins Medical Letter, 1990).

Light Receptors: Rods and Cones

The retina has two kinds of receptors: (1) **cones,** which are located mostly in the fovea and which are best for seeing details; and (2) **rods,** which are located mostly on the sides or periphery of the retina, and which are best for seeing in dim light.

Cones enable us to see sharp details. When you want to look at something, you move your eyes so that the image of the object you want to see is focused on your fovea. If you want to know what the world would be like without a fovea, look at a flashbulb when someone takes your picture. Almost all you will see with your fovea for the next several minutes is a bright silver spot. You will see the rest of the world only from the periphery or sides of your retina, where details are hard to make out.

When you are using only your rods you cannot see color, which is why you see shades of black and white, but not color, in dim light. Rods are located on the periphery or sides of the retina. As a result, you can see best at night if you look at something to your left or right rather than straight on. This is called **peripheral vision,** because you use the receptors on the sides or periphery of the retina. Pilots who fly at night are trained to use their peripheral vision by looking at the sides or edges of what they want to see. You can use a TV set to demonstrate that peripheral vision is better than central vision for seeing dim lights. Watch the TV set for about 10 minutes in a room with all the lights out. Then turn off the set. The screen's glow will gradually fade. Soon you won't be able to see the screen at all when you look directly at it. You will see that it still appears quite bright, however, if you direct your gaze a short distance away from the screen in any direction.

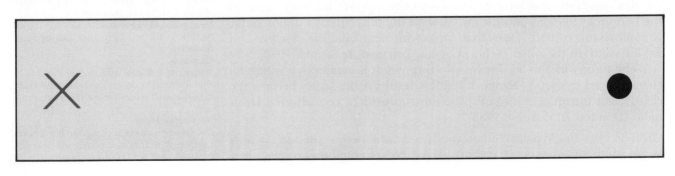

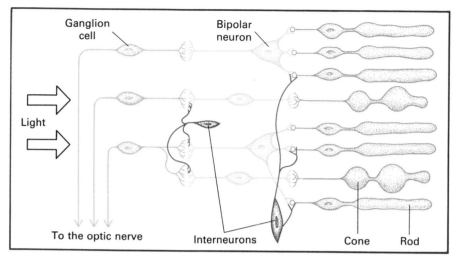

FIGURE 3–5

The visual pathways go from the retina to other brain structures. Messages first go from receptor cells to bipolar cells. Each cone sends a message to a separate bipolar cell. Many rods send messages to the same bipolar cell. Messages go from bipolar cells to ganglion cells, and then exit from the retina as part of the optic nerve.

Farsightedness
Occurs when an eye is flattened in shape like a vertical egg; farsighted people see far objects well, but see near objects poorly.

Retina
Tissue covering most of the eye's interior wall; contains rods and cones.

Blind spot
Area in the retina that is blind because it is where the optic nerve exits from the retina.

Optic nerve
Bundle of nerve fibers that carry neural signals to the brain.

Fovea
Center area of the retina where vision is best; contains most of the cones on the retina.

Cones
Light receptors in the eye; located mostly in the fovea, are best for seeing details, and are responsible for color vision.

Rods
Light receptors located on the periphery or sides of the retina; they are best for seeing in dim light.

Peripheral vision
Using the sides of one's eyes (and thus depending on the rods rather than the cones) to see something—usually occurs at night or in dim light.

Why are cones best for seeing details, while rods are best for seeing dim light? The answer is found in the neural pathways between these receptors and the brain.

Pathways to the Brain

The visual pathways connect the eyes with the brain's cortex, which we discussed in Chapter 2. These pathways are more than passive cables. They contain cells that actively participate in coding or interpreting the information contained in light. This coding process begins in the retina. Here all cones and rods are connected to bipolar cells, which are in turn connected to ganglion cells that send signals out of the retina to the brain (see Figures 3–5 and 3–6). In addition, signals travel laterally across inter-

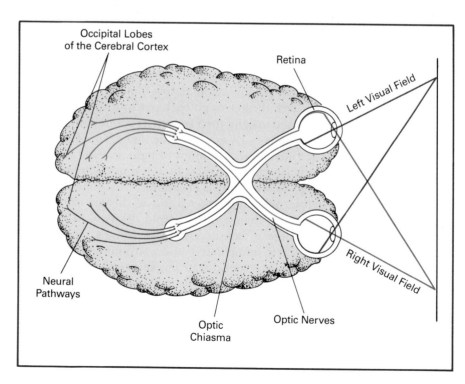

FIGURE 3–6

Messages from the left visual field travel to the right occipital lobe; messages from the right visual field of each eye go to the left occipital lobe. The place where they cross is called the optic chiasma.

FIGURE 3–7

Can you tell whose portrait this is? Block portraits have two parts: a blurred picture of a famous person and a set of sharp edges outlining the blocks. A glance will tell you that this is poor optical information. Your visual system can clear up the information, however, with a little help. Have someone jiggle the picture slightly at a viewing distance of about 8 feet while you squint your eyes to blur your vision.

Dark adaptation
Downward adjustment of sensitivity to light; occurs in the rods when one enters a dark room, for example.
Light adaptation
Upward adjustment in sensitivity to light; occurs in the cones when one suddenly goes from a dark room into bright sunlight, for example.

neurons. These lateral connections enable communication from receptor to receptor and from bipolar cell to bipolar cell. Thus, the signals originating in the receptor cells are modified before they leave the retina.

Cones and rods have different functions, in part because they are connected to bipolar cells differently. Cones are best for seeing detail because almost every cone in the fovea reports to its own bipolar cell. Consider what happens when different light patterns fall on adjacent cones. Each cone can use its own one-to-one connection to report a different message to its own bipolar cell. These separate messages enable us to discern small differences or details in what we see. Cones do not function in dim light because each cone's message gets too weak for bipolar cells to receive it.

Whereas each cone has its own bipolar cell, many rods share the same bipolar cell. These many-to-one connections allow rods to add their messages together to make a signal strong enough for a bipolar cell to receive. For this reason, rods do much better than cones in dim light. The many-to-one connection also means, however, that each rod does not really send a separate message. Rods are therefore poor at discerning details, because of the way they are connected to bipolar cells.

Most cells in the visual pathways to the brain receive messages from many other cells and send messages to many other cells. Information is thereby added and subtracted, coded and recoded, in a series of processes that determine vision. These processes somehow turn poor optical information into clear perceptions. Optical information is poor because the eye's lens creates distorted images like those you see through a cheap magnifying glass. To make matters worse, light must pass through blood vessels and nerve fibers before reaching light receptors. Cells in the visual pathway and cortex work together to "clean up" the information (Campbell, 1974; Davis, 1990). Figure 3–7 illustrates what your visual system can do with poor optical information. David Hubel and Thorsten Wiesel won the 1981 Nobel Prize in medicine for their research on how cells in the visual pathways and cortex join forces to determine what we see (Carlson, Hubel, & Wiesel, 1986; Hubel, 1982; Hubel & Wiesel, 1965, 1970).

Light and Dark Adaptation

Farley Mowat saw dim stars that sent very little light into his eyes, and he saw bright sunlight reflected from snow. In the same way, we see dimly lit faces in a movie theater and brightly lit faces on a sunny beach. But this large range of sensitivity is never available at any one moment. When we walk from sunlight into a dark theater, for example, we are almost blinded until our eyes adjust. We are again almost blinded until our eyes adjust when we leave the dark theater to go back out into the sunlight.

When the eyes are exposed to light, their sensitivity continually changes. If the amount of light remains fairly constant for about 15 minutes, the eyes will become most sensitive to that amount of light and will be unable to see lights that are about 100 times brighter or 100 times dimmer. Thus, although the overall range of sensitivity is enormous, the range *at any one moment* is relatively narrow. When we enter a movie theater on a sunny afternoon, we encounter more than a hundredfold decrease in light, far outside our momentary range of sensitivity, so we cannot see well. An adjustment in sensitivity starts immediately and continues for about 15 minutes until our eyes become as sensitive as possible to the level of light in the theater. This adjustment of sensitivity is called **dark adaptation.** The adjustment that takes place when we go from the dark theater into sunlight is called **light adaptation.**

Farley saw more stars from Wolf House Bay than he did from the city because the background level of light was lower. The dark background caused an advantageous adjustment in his momentary range of sensitivity.

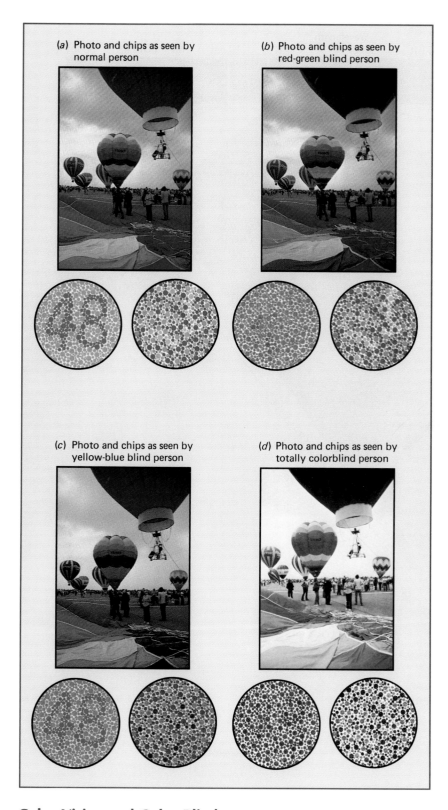

(a) Photo and chips as seen by normal person

(b) Photo and chips as seen by red-green blind person

(c) Photo and chips as seen by yellow-blue blind person

(d) Photo and chips as seen by totally colorblind person

FIGURE 3–8

These photographs of balloons and color chips are used to test for color blindness. They are shown here as they would appear to four types of people: (a) A normal person sees all the colors in the photograph and can make out the snakelike path in the chip on the right and the number 48 in the chip on the left. (b) A red-green blind person cannot distinguish red from green in the photograph and cannot see the number 48 in the left chip. (c) A yellow-blue blind person cannot distinguish yellow from blue in the photograph and cannot see the snakelike path in the right chip. (d) A totally colorblind person cannot see any colors in the photograph or the forms in the chips.

Color Vision and Color Blindness

The night-time arctic sky often treated Farley not only to billions of stars but also to a dazzling display of the many-colored flashing northern lights. The beauty of this display and many others would be greatly reduced for people who are *colorblind*; **color blindness** is the inability to distinguish between colors. Imagine walking through a grocery store and seeing yellow beefsteaks and hams, yellow cabbage, yellow radishes, and yellow spinach. Now you leave the store on a bright summer day, walk across a well-mani-

Color blindness
Inability to see or distinguish between colors. There are several types of color blindness: red-green, blue-yellow, and total color blindness.

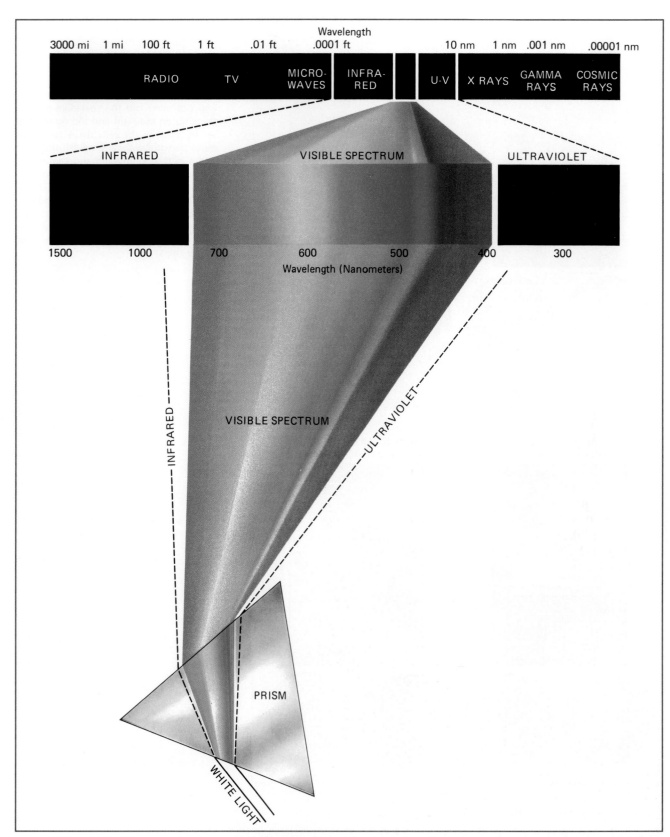

FIGURE 3–9

Sunlight, or white light, contains all the colors that we can see. A prism separates white light into its component colors. Each color in this visible spectrum corresponds to a specific wavelength. Light travels in waves, and wavelength is the distance between wave crests. The visible spectrum is only a small part of the electromagnetic spectrum which consists of energy traveling in wavelengths that are shorter or longer than the visible spectrum.

cured yellow lawn and past tall yellow pine trees, and approach a traffic signal containing three vertically arranged yellow lights. This is how the world looks to about 2 out of every 100 males and to about 2 out of every 10,000 females who have red-green color blindness. (We would have no idea how the world looks to colorblind people if it were not for a few people who had red-green blindness in one eye and normal vision in the other. Things that look red and green to the normal eye look light yellow to the colorblind eye.) There are other, less common kinds of color blindness. For example, some people have yellow-blue blindness; that is, they can't tell the difference between yellows and blues. This kind of color deficiency can be induced by tricyclic antidepressant drugs (Lagerlof, 1982). Others have total color blindness. We are not sure how their world looks, but it might be like watching black-and-white TV. Some people do not realize that they have trouble seeing colors until they are tested with the pictures such as the one shown in Figure 3–8 (Birch, 1985; Cohn, Emmerich, & Carlson, 1989).

The high value placed on color is illustrated by the popularity of color television. Today Americans buy more color than black-and-white televisions, even though color sets are more expensive. In this section we will discuss some of the research that led to the development of color television.

The first major breakthrough was Isaac Newton's (1642–1727) discovery that white light from the sun is a compound of all colors. We now know that light travels in waves, with different wavelengths for each color. Figure 3–9 shows the **electromagnetic spectrum** forming the entire range of wavelengths of electromagnetic radiation. The wavelengths corresponding to visible colors cover only a small part of the whole spectrum. For example, we do not see X-rays, which are much shorter in wavelength than light waves, and we do not see radio waves, which are much longer. Objects have particular colors because they absorb some wavelengths and reflect others. We see the reflected wavelengths; a red apple, for example, reflects red wavelengths.

The next major breakthrough occurred when Thomas Young (1773–1829) tackled the problem of how the nervous system responds to different wavelengths. He began with experiments on color mixture, which are illustrated in Figure 3–10. Three colored lights (violet, red, and green) are

Electromagnetic spectrum
Forms the entire range of wavelengths of electromagnetic radiation; wavelengths corresponding to visible colors cover only a small part of this spectrum.

FIGURE 3–10

Color mixture of three lights is shown here—red, green, and violet; they are widely spaced on the spectrum. Any color on the spectrum can be produced in the overlapping areas by adjusting the intensities of the three lights. Here we see yellow where green and red mix, and we see white where all three mix.

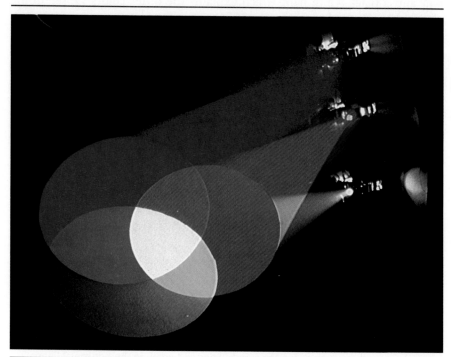

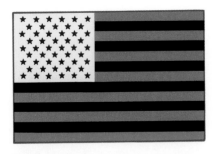

FIGURE 3–11

This green, black, and yellow flag will turn red, white, and blue in an afterimage. You can make an afterimage by staring at the lower right-hand star for about 45 seconds. You will then see the afterimage when you shift your gaze to a bright white piece of paper.

Afterimage

Visual experience that continues after the stimulus has ceased; occurs because some activity continues in the retina after seeing the stimulus. Consists of the opposite color of what was seen in the original stimulus: blue for yellow, red for green, black for white.

projected onto a screen in an otherwise dark room. The resulting pattern reminds one of an insignia on a color TV. This is no accident—experiments on color mixing led to the development of color TV. The most unusual aspect of Figure 3–10 is that white is seen where all three colors overlap, and yellow is seen where red and green overlap. Young could produce every color of the visible spectrum in the overlapping areas by varying the intensity of the lights. He theorized that the retina contains three kinds of color receptors and that the signals from these merge to produce our sensations of color. With further developments by Hermann von Helmholtz (1821–1894), this theory, called the *trichromatic receptor theory*, led physiologists to verify that the retina does indeed have three kinds of color receptors. Each kind responds differently to colors. One responds most to blue-violet, another responds most to green, and another favors yellow-red (Brown & Wald, 1964; Marks, Dobelle, & MacNichol, 1964).

This is an important fact, but it doesn't explain all aspects of color vision. For example, it does not explain what you see in Figure 3–11. If you stare at the picture for about 45 seconds and then shift your gaze to a white surface, you will see red where green had been, white where black had been, and blue where yellow had been. What you see is an **afterimage.** Figure 3–12 shows a special kind of afterimage called a *McCollough effect.* An afterimage occurs because some activity continues in the retina after you look away from the picture. The trichromatic receptor theory does not account for the colors of afterimages.

To explain this and other observations, Hering (1878) offered the *opponent-process theory*, which states that receptor cells are joined in opposing pairs. The color we see depends on whether a pair responds positively or negatively (Hovis & Guth, 1989). For example, blue is seen when a blue-yellow pair responds negatively; yellow is seen when it responds positively. This explains why afterimages appear blue when yellow is in the original. When we look at yellow, the receptor that is sensitive to yellow gets *fatigued*; that is, it responds less to the same stimulus. When cells are not fatigued, light from a white surface stimulates the blue-yellow pair equally so that neither color is seen. But when the yellow side is fatigued, it does not respond as strongly, upsetting the balance in favor of blue. As a result, we see blue. The theory also proposes the existence of a red-green opponent pair and a black-white pair, which explains the other colors we see in the afterimage (Hurvich & Jameson, 1974).

A

B

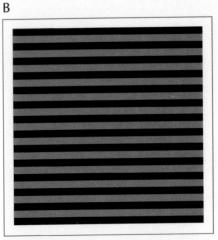

C

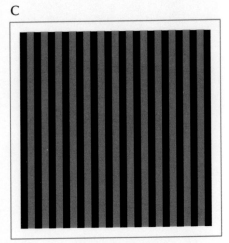

FIGURE 3–12

Look briefly at Figure A and note that it is entirely black and white. This is a pretest. For the next minute or so, look back and forth between Figures B and C, lingering about 15 seconds on each. This is an adaptation period. For a posttest, shift your gaze back to Figure A; you will now see red in the vertical lines and green in the horizontal lines.

SENSORY CHANGES, AGING, AND HEALTH

Stephen Cohen (1981) has described sensory changes in the elderly, and he has also outlined procedures that will help if you ever care for an elderly relative or some other elderly person. Some of his main points are as follows:

1. Vision is impaired in the elderly because of structural changes in the aging eye. When you assist an elderly person, you should be aware that there are reductions in abilities to see depth (for example, distance of floor from bed), to see objects located off to one side, and to see detail. Old eyes also take longer to adjust when going from dark to dim places. The elderly have trouble seeing blues, greens, and violets; they have an easier time seeing reds, oranges, and yellows. You should, therefore, select lighting, positioning, and coloring of objects carefully, especially critical objects such as stairs, handrails, doorknobs, and light switches.

2. Aging also causes hearing problems. One reason for this is a decrease in the number of nerve fibers that carry sound information. Hearing loss especially affects the ability to hear high-pitched sounds, such as high notes on a piano. Thus elderly people hear low-pitched sounds better than high-pitched sounds. You can help an aging person hear important sounds such as doorbells, smoke alarms, and telephone bells not only by increasing the volume, but also by lowering the pitch. You can help an aging person understand speech by teaching yourself and others how to modify your voice. You should speak loudly, but do not shout. Shouting conceals high-pitched speech sounds that the elderly person already finds difficult to hear. You should slow down, to space your sounds as far apart as possible. Finally, you should lower the pitch of your voice as much as possible. A deep male voice is easiest for a hard-of-hearing person to understand.

3. Other sensory impairments must be overcome. The sense of smell and taste are reduced, so that foods with intense aromas and flavors will be appreciated by the elderly. Avoid piping hot food, however, because an elderly person's ability to detect heat is dangerously reduced. For the same reason, protect the aging from hot surfaces such as faucets, radiators, pots, and pans. The sense of touch and of pain is reduced to the point where the elderly might not realize that they are cutting off blood circulation. They should be encouraged, therefore, to wear loose clothing and to change positions every so often when they are lying or sitting for long periods.

Cohen convincingly demonstrates that knowing the nature of sensory change can make life safer for elderly people. (For more details, see Eliopoulos, 1987).

Sekuler and Blake (1987) note that the normal deterioration of sight, hearing, taste, and smell are sometimes mistaken for disease or senility. They note also that this deterioration can cause a sensory "underload" that isolates the elderly from others and from their environment. This understimulation can lead to cognitive declines, which, in turn, can lead to further isolation.

By understanding normal sensory declines, we can prevent these negative consequences. We can encourage the elderly to tune in and turn on to life.

Hearing

Although Farley's hearing might have improved during his stay at Wolf House Bay, it never became as sensitive as Ootek's or the wolves', as indicated in the following incident:

> Ootek suddenly cupped his hands to his ears and began to listen intently.
>
> I could hear nothing, and I had no idea what had caught his attention until he said: "Listen, the wolves are talking!" and pointed toward a range of hills some five miles to the north of us.
>
> I listened, but if a wolf was broadcasting from those hills he was not on my wavelength. I heard nothing except the baleful buzzing of mosquitoes; but George, who had been sleeping on the crest of the esker, suddenly sat up, cocked his ears forward and pointed his long muzzle toward the north. After a minute or two he threw back his head and howled; a long, quavering howl which started low and ended on the highest note my ears would register.
>
> Ootek grabbed my arm and broke into a delighted grin.
>
> "Caribou are coming; the wolf says so!"
>
> (Mowat, 1963, p. 89)

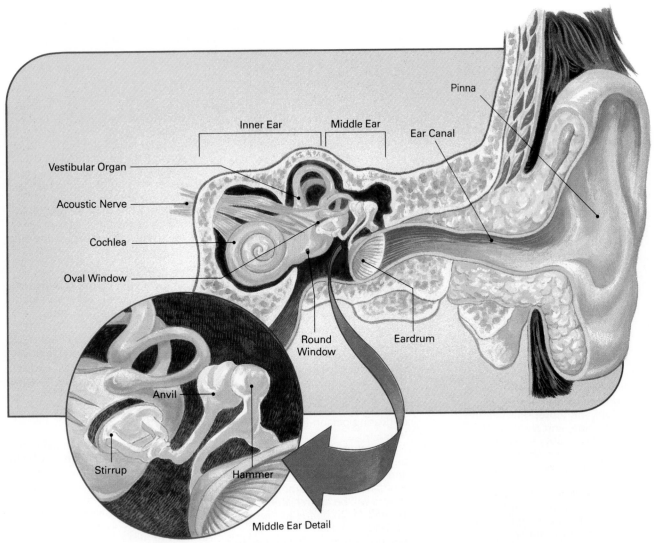

FIGURE 3–13A

The structure of the human ear.

This incident raises many interesting questions: How does sound travel for miles over the tundra? Why do people sometimes cup their hands around their ears? Why do animals turn their ears toward sounds? This section will answer these and other questions about hearing.

The Ears

Sound travels through air as waves travel through water. A stone dropped in a pond sends out ripples in all directions. Similarly, when objects vibrate in air, they create air waves. To understand hearing we must learn how these sound waves affect the ears.

The word *ears* brings to mind flaps on the sides of the head. But, as Figure 3–13 shows, these flaps are just one of three basic subdivisions of ears:

1. The *external ear* or outer ear captures sound traveling through the air. The **pinna** is the elastic flap we usually are referring to when we talk about the ear. The **ear canal** is a tubelike passage that funnels sound. The **eardrum** is a fine membrane stretched over the inner

Pinna
Outer flap of the ear.
Ear canal
Tube-like passage that funnels sound to the eardrum.
Eardrum
Fine membrane stretched over the inner end of the ear canal; vibrates when sound waves strike it.

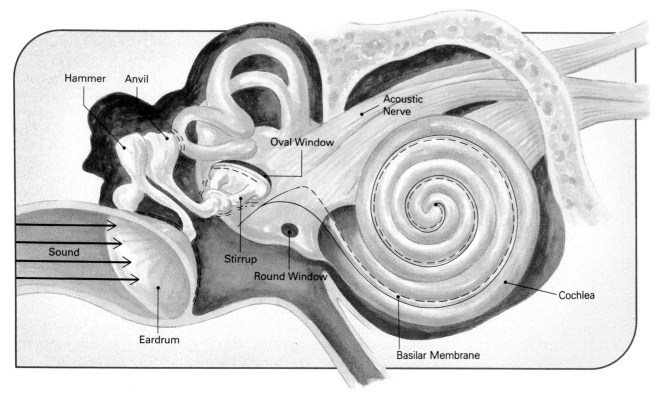

FIGURE 3–13B

A detailed drawing of the inner ear. When the eardrum transforms sound waves into mechanical vibrations, they are transmitted to the *oval window* of the cochlea. Pressure waves are then sent through the cochlear fluid in the directions indicated by the arrows.

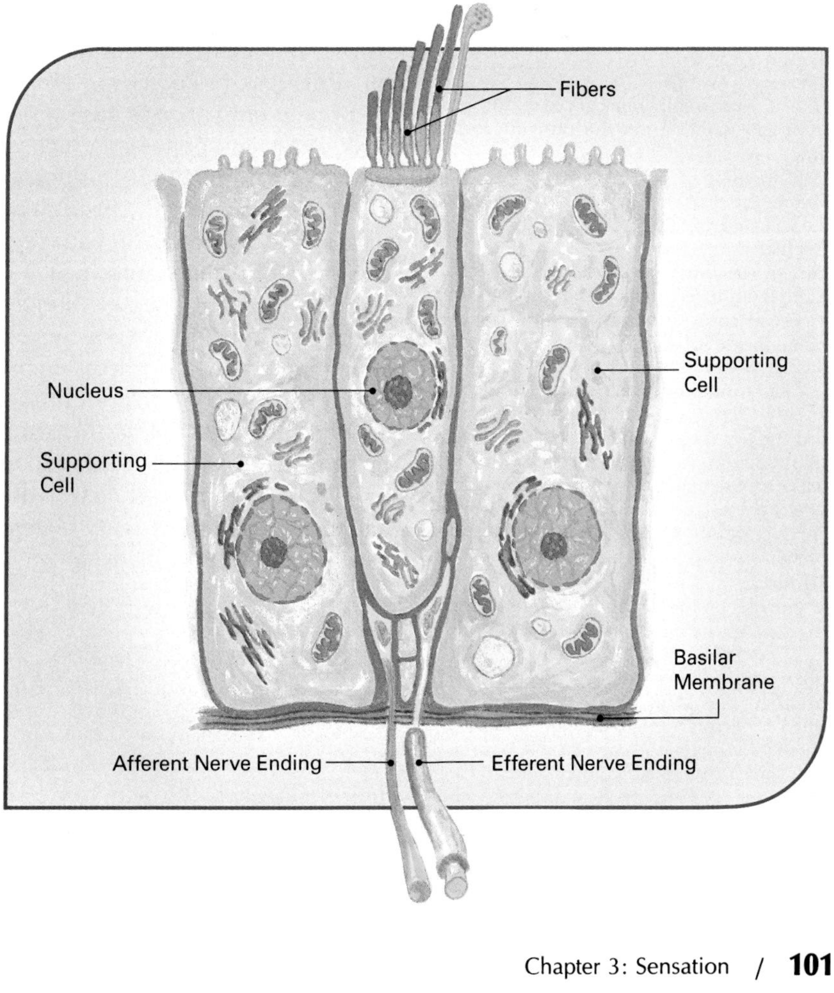

FIGURE 3–13C

A detailed drawing of a hair cell, the receptor for hearing. At the top of each hair cell are a bundle of fibers. If the fibers bend so much as 100-trillionths of a meter, the receptor cells transmit a sensory message to the brain.

end of the ear canal; it vibrates when sound waves strike it. As you might have guessed from the behavior of Ootek and George, cupping the hands around the ears and turning toward a sound source helps to funnel sound waves into the ears.

2. The *middle ear* is a small air cavity containing three small bones: the **hammer,** the **anvil,** and the **stirrup.** This delicate chain of bones transmits sounds from the eardrum to the inner ear.

3. The *inner ear* is the part of the ear that transforms sound vibrations into neural impulses, which we discussed in Chapter 2. It receives sounds through the **oval window,** which is a membrane stretched over the opening of the inner ear. Attached to the oval window is a structure that looks like a snail. It is called the **cochlea,** which is the Latin word for snail. It is a coiled tube that makes about three turns, like a spiral around a central core. Inside the cochlea is a flexible membrane, called the **basilar membrane.** It is attached to the oval window at one end and to the tip of the cochlea at the other end. Vibrations in the oval window cause hair cells on the basilar membrane to vibrate. When the hair cells are bent, they send nerve impulses along the acoustic nerve to the brain.

To sum up, the external ear collects and focuses sound, causing the eardrum to vibrate. Three delicate bones carry these vibrations to the oval window, which vibrates receptors in the cochlea, triggering nerve impulses to the brain.

Do your ears ever ring and ring? Head noises heard when there is no external source of noise are called **tinnitus.** They include low roars, high whines, buzzing, tinking, humming, popping, and clicking. About 36 million Americans hear these noises for various reasons. Some have a plug of wax in their outer ears, others have an infection in their middle ears. Most, however, have damaged nerve endings in the inner ear. Treatment varies with the cause (Berkeley Wellness Letter, 1990). (For more information about this condition, write to the American Tinnitus Association, P.O. Box 5, Portland, Oregon 97207.)

Bone conduction is another way that sound is transmitted. When you speak, your jaw bones conduct vibrations to the cochlea. Thus you hear your voice through bone-conducted sounds and air-conducted sounds. Others hear your voice only through air-conducted sounds. Your tape-recorded voice sounds strange to you because you are not used to hearing only your air-conducted sound, which is the way everyone else hears your voice.

Some hearing aids use bone conduction when the middle ear cannot conduct sound. Other hearing aids simply amplify air-conducted sound. You might have noticed the increasing popularity of the kind of hearing aid worn by former President Ronald Reagan. Recent research indicates that this kind of in-the-ear hearing aid works quite well. For mild-to-moderate hearing loss, the in-the-ear hearing aid restores speech intelligibility as well or better than the over-the-ear type (Cox & Risberg, 1986). As we shall see, this compact and effective hearing aid is just one of many applications of research on hearing.

Characteristics of Sound

Sound waves are easier to study when they are converted to visible waves. Figure 3–14 shows a way to do this with an **oscilloscope,** which is similar to a television. We can learn relationships between psychological and physical characteristics of hearing by listening to a sound while watching it on an oscilloscope. Let's imagine taking an oscilloscope to a concert.

Hammer
One of three small bones in the middle ear, transmits sounds from the eardrum to the inner ear.
Anvil
One of three small bones in the middle ear, it transmits sounds from the eardrum to the inner ear.
Stirrup
One of three small bones in the middle ear; transmits sounds from the eardrum to the inner ear.
Oval window
Membrane stretched over the opening of the inner ear.
Cochlea
Part of the inner ear; a tube coiled in on itself about three turns, like a spiral around a central core. Contains the basilar membrane inside it.
Basilar membrane
Located inside the cochlea in the inner ear, it is attached to the oval window at one end and the tip of the cochlea at the other end. Vibrations in the oval window cause hair cells on the basilar membrane to move. When these hair cells are bent, they send nerve impulses to the brain that are experienced as sound.
Tinnitus
A disorder in which one constantly hears "ringing in the ears" or noises when there is no external noise.
Bone conduction
Another way that sound is transmitted; when a person speaks, the jaw bones conduct vibrations to the cochlea. We hear our own voice through bone-conducted and air-conducted sounds; we hear others' voices only through air-conducted sounds.
Oscilloscope
Device for converting sound waves to visible waves.

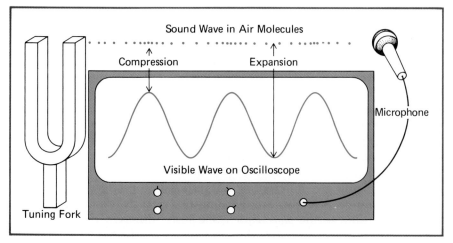

FIGURE 3–14

The device shown here, an oscilloscope, makes pictures out of sound waves. A tuning fork makes a sound wave, which, as shown here, consists of compressions and expansions of air molecules. A microphone makes an electrical response to these compressions and expansions. The oscilloscope changes the electrical response into a moving picture on a screen similar to a TV screen. The picture is a wave with high points and low points. A high point on the picture represents a compression of air molecules; a low point represents an expansion of air molecules.

Frequency and Pitch. We have all delighted in the mellow low notes of a bass singer and the trilling high notes of a soprano. But have you ever wondered how we hear the difference between low and high notes? Such differences are referred to as differences in **pitch.** In Figure 3–15A we see that changes in pitch correspond to changes in **frequency** of sound waves, which is the number of wave crests that occur in a second. The distance between two wave crests is called a *wavelength* or a **cycle,** so fre-

Pitch
Difference between low and high notes. Changes in pitch correspond to changes in frequency of sound waves.
Frequency
Number of wave crests that occur in a second; measured in cycles per second.
Cycle
The distance between wave crests in a sound wave; also called wavelength.

FIGURE 3–15

Each oscilloscope shows 1/100 of a second (.01 second) from two sound waves: (A) a low-pitched sound, with 600 cycles per second, and a higher-pitched sound, with 1,200 cycles per second; (B) a soft note and a loud note; (C) the same note played on a trumpet and on a clarinet.

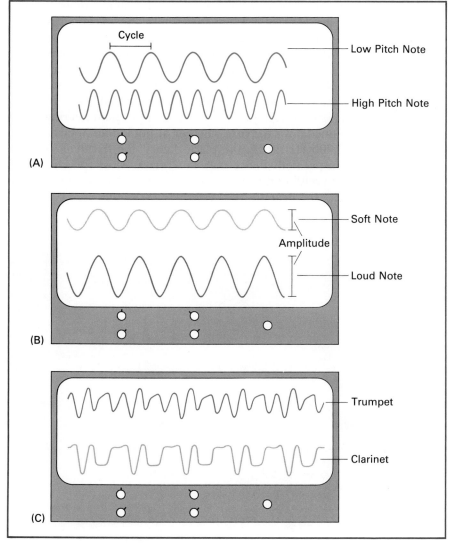

quency is measured in cycles per second. One cycle per second is called a **hertz** (Hz). As most stereo buffs know, frequency is often reported in hertz. A piano plays frequencies ranging from 27.5 Hz (low note) to 4,186 Hz (high note). A bass singer sings notes as low as 82.4 Hz, and a soprano sings notes as high as 1,046.5 Hz. You might want to consider this before buying stereo speakers. Today a good pair of speakers capable of reproducing sounds as low as 35 Hz costs about $100; a good pair of speakers capable of reproducing sounds down to about 25 Hz costs about $1500. That's an expensive 10 Hz—especially when you consider that there is very little music written in that range!

Humans hear sounds ranging from 20 to 20,000 Hz. This means that the ears somehow give different neural responses for different frequencies within this range. Scientists are debating two rival theories of how this is done. According to the *place theory*, one hears different pitches because different frequencies stimulate different places on the basilar membrane. According to the *frequency theory*, one hears different pitches because receptors send pulses up the auditory nerve at the same frequency as the sound wave.

Nobel laureate George von Békésy used a powerful microscope to show that different frequencies vibrate different parts of the basilar membrane. His work convinced most scientists that the place theory explains how people hear frequencies above 3,000 Hz. On the other hand, almost everyone agrees that the frequency theory explains how we hear frequencies below 50 Hz. Thus the debate concerns how we hear frequencies between 50 and 3,000 Hz. The major proponent of the frequency theory in this range is E. G. Wever. He realized that single nerve fibers cannot respond faster than 1,000 times per second, so he advocated the *volley principle*, which states that the combined response of different fibers corresponds to the frequency of sound waves. In other words, cells take turns firing, similar to the way Revolutionary War soldiers alternated so that one group fired a round, or a volley, while another group reloaded. With the help of the volley principle, the frequency theory could explain hearing up to 3,000 Hz. But no one knows for sure whether or not it does in fact explain it. In the 50 to 3,000 Hz range, the place theory, the frequency theory, or some as yet unspecified theory may be correct. Most speech sounds are in this range, so settling this theoretical issue will have practical consequences for helping the deaf.

Hertz
One cycle per second of a sound wave.

Carnegie Hall is designed to optimize sound quality.

Amplitude and Loudness. There is another change in sound waves that occurs as volume is increased. Figure 3–15B shows this change for the same note played softly and loudly. Notice that the frequency is the same, but the **amplitude** of the waves differs. The amplitude, which can be measured as the distance between a wave's top and bottom, gets larger as sounds get louder. The scientist's unit for measuring loudness is called the *bel*, after Alexander Graham Bell. Often scientists prefer to use a unit one-tenth as large as a bel. They call this a **decibel.** Each tenfold increase in sound level adds 10 decibels.

From what has been said so far, we would expect to hear the same pitch when we listened to the sound waves illustrated in Figure 3–15B. After all, they have the same frequency. Unfortunately hearing is not that simple. A wave's amplitude also influences the brain's interpretation of pitch. As a tone gets louder, its pitch sounds lower. Thus the higher-amplitude wave in Figure 3–15B would seem to have a slightly lower pitch than the other wave, even though the frequencies are the same. When buying a stereo system, you might ask whether or not the system electronically compensates for this distortion; better systems do.

Loud sounds can be irritating and can even cause permanent hearing loss. (This is a topic of concern to many these days, as noted in the Psychology in the News box at the end of the chapter, "Research on Noise Disappears in the Din.") For example, riveters and others who work in extremely noisy environments often suffer from **boilermaker's deafness.** This is a partial hearing loss caused by spending long periods of time amid loud noises. Experts warn that no worker should be exposed to a continuous sound level of 85 decibels (about the loudness of a vacuum cleaner) for more than 5 hours a day without using protective devices. Loud rock bands produce sound levels between 125 and 135 decibels. Thus it is not surprising that college students who frequently listen to loud rock bands suffer some hearing loss (Lipscomb, 1969). Similarly, it is not surprising that Farley, who spent several years in the noisy battles of World War II, could not hear as well as Ootek, who spent his whole life in a quiet environment. Figure 3–16 shows familiar noises that are part of our environment and how they are measured in decibels.

Waveform and Tone Quality. If we watched our oscilloscope during a trumpet solo and then during a clarinet solo, we might notice another way that sound waves change. Figure 3–15C illustrates this change for a trumpet and a clarinet playing the same note at the same sound level. Notice that the frequencies and amplitudes are the same, but the shapes are different. It is this difference in shape, or **waveform,** that allows us to distinguish between the two sounds.

Waveforms differ because most sounds contain more than one frequency. It is possible to generate **pure tones** containing a single frequency. But most musical instruments generate **complex tones** containing many frequencies. The higher ones are called *overtone frequencies*. A trumpet and clarinet sound different because they have different overtone frequencies (Agmon, 1990).

How do you feel about the sound of fingernails scraping across a blackboard? Most people rate this as a very unpleasant sound, and they report that it gives them chills. In a recent study of this chilling sound, Halpern, Blake, and Hillenbrand (1986) found that only certain frequencies contribute to the sound's obnoxious quality. They collected unpleasantness ratings with all frequencies present and with some frequencies removed. Which frequencies would you want removed? Most people think that removal of the high frequencies would help. However, the results showed that removal of low, but not high, frequencies lessened unpleasantness ratings. Even though the high pitch sounds are very noticeable, the unpleasantness seems to be signaled by lower frequencies. The different frequencies within each

Amplitude
Distance between the top and bottom of a sound wave; amplitude increases as sounds get louder.
Decibel
Unit for measuring loudness; each tenfold increase in sound level adds 10 decibels.
Boilermaker's deafness
Partial hearing loss caused by spending long periods of time around loud noises (above 85 decibels).
Waveform
Shape of a sound wave; changes in waveform allow us to distinguish between the sound of a piano and a violin, for instance.
Pure tones
Sounds containing a single frequency.
Complex tones
Sounds containing many frequencies.

FIGURE 3-16

A decibel scale for several common sounds. Prolonged exposure to sounds above 85 decibels can cause permanent damage to the ears.

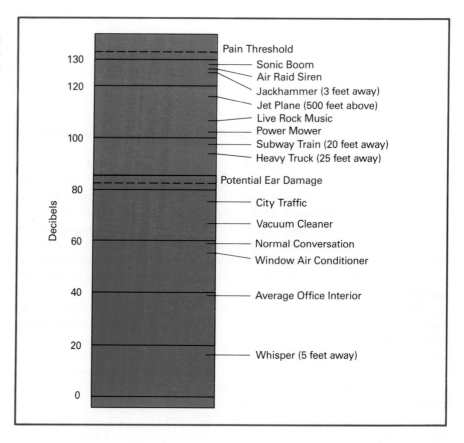

complex get combined into a single wave. But, as we see in Figure 3–15C, the resulting waves have different shapes when the sounds have different overtones.

A person's experience with music determines how such complex waves are heard. For example, Beal (1985) tested 34 musician and 34 nonmusician undergraduates in their ability to discriminate complex wave forms. He found that musicians more easily recognized the same musical chords played on different instruments than did the nonmusicians. In other words, nonmusicians were more likely to think that they had heard different chords when they had heard the same chord played by different instruments.

Locating Sounds

When Angeline hunted for mice, she listened for the rodents to reveal their location. Then she pounced on them with one swift lunge. Thus her meals depended upon her ability to localize sound. The ability to tell where a sound is coming from can also be a matter of life or death. How many times do you think our ancestors were saved, for example, by hearing a twig cracked by the foot of a stalking beast? How many lives have been saved on today's highways because a driver was able to tell where a blasting automobile horn was coming from? One way to study this important ability is by taking a mental trip to an imaginary race track. If you close your eyes at the race track, you will notice that you can locate the cars simply by listening to them. How?

The survival of these African antelopes (Impala) depends upon their keen sensory skills including their ability to localize the sound of a stalking lion.

If you listen carefully, you might notice that **loudness** plays a role in hearing a car's distance. In general, you hear louder sounds as being closer than softer ones. You might also notice that moving sounds provide more information. As the race cars roar toward you, their engines have a high-pitched, whining sound. When the cars zoom by, their engines' sounds drop sharply to a lower pitch. This is called the **Doppler shift.** It happens because sound waves bunch up as the cars approach and spread out as the cars speed away. The bunched-up waves have a shorter distance between their wave crests (higher frequency); the spread-out waves have a longer distance between their wave crests (lower frequency). You can hear both the loudness changes and the frequency changes without special instruments. But you would need to bring special equipment to the race track if you hoped to study the other ways you can localize sounds, for they depend on tiny sound differences between the two ears.

When a sound is straight ahead, it reaches both ears at the same time, it sounds equally loud in both ears, and it has the same waveform in both ears. When a sound comes from one side, all three of these things change because the sound is farther from one ear: (1) the sound arrives *later* at the farther ear; (2) the sound is *softer* in the farther ear; and (3) the *phase* is slightly different in the farther ear. That is, the wave is closer

Loudness
Measurement of sound based on the amplitude of sound waves.
Doppler shift
Occurs as cars zoom by on a racetrack; as they go by, the engine sound drops sharply to a lower pitch. Sound waves punch up as cars approach on a racetrack and spread out as cars speed away. The bunched-up waves have a shorter distance between their wave crests (higher frequency); the spread-out waves have a longer distance between their wave crests (lower frequency).

A Doppler shift in sound is demonstrated by race cars. The high-pitched whining sound of an approaching car drops to a low pitch when the car zooms by.

to its highest point when it strikes one ear before the other. Researchers have found that we are extremely sensitive to differences in time, loudness, and phase. When you close your eyes at a race track and localize the cars by sound, you are using these three sources of information, even though you are not aware of it. Humans apparently have this ability from the moment they are born (Castillo & Butterworth, 1981).

Other Senses

Earlier we mentioned that Farley tuned into all his senses. In this section we will briefly go over some of his experiences involving the senses of taste, smell, touch, and body orientation.

Taste and Food Preference

The typical arctic diet contrasts sharply with the food Americans typically eat. Eskimos mostly eat raw or only partially cooked meat. Even as a baby, Ootek ate raw caribou meat prechewed by his mother. Although Farley always insisted on cooking his meat, he did learn to eat wild game, including venison, caribou tongues, and mice, fresh from the fields. These eating habits often required spending a good part of the day hunting and preparing food. Our ancestors' diets were similar. Today, however, dinners are often prepared for us in advance and then frozen, or else all the ingredients are boxed for us in the exact quantities needed. We simply heat and eat, or stir and serve. Whether we like it or not, food preparation has become a big business. As a result, shrewd corporate executives are hiring psychologists to make sure that their company's food tastes good to as many customers as possible. In this section we will examine some of the factors that determine taste.

The primary sense organ for taste is the tongue. As shown in Figure 3–17, the tongue has small elevations called **papillae.** Our taste sensors

Papillae
Small elevations on the tongue; contain our taste sensors, called taste buds.

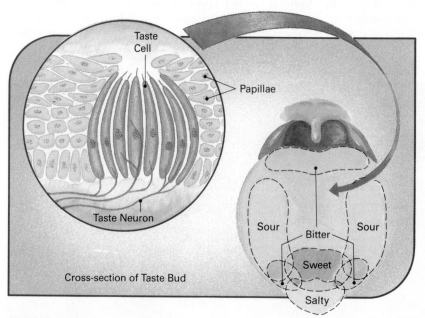

FIGURE 3–17

The tongue's taste receptors are called taste buds, which are located inside small elevations or papillae on the surface of the tongue. Different locations on the tongue are most sensitive to the four basic taste qualities: sweet, sour, salty, and bitter.

are called **taste buds.** They are located inside of papillae, away from direct contact with food. We taste solid foods by first dissolving them in saliva. The liquid solution runs down pits in the papillae and stimulates sensory cells in the taste buds. The sensory cells then send messages to the brain, giving rise to our sensation of taste. Taste cells die and are replaced about every eleven days. As people age, when their taste cells die, they are not replaced, which is why the elderly lose some of their taste sensitivity (Cowart, 1988).

There are four primary tastes: sweet, sour, salty, and bitter. Different parts of the tongue are sensitive to different tastes, as shown in Figure 3–17. Our sensitivity to all of these is greatest when the food or drink temperature is between 22° and 32°C. (about 71° to 89°F.). It is important to season food at the temperature at which you intend to eat it because the temperature of a substance changes your sensitivity to it. For example, soup salted at room temperature may need more salt when it is warmed up, and lemonade sweetened at room temperature may taste sour when it is chilled (Zellner, Stewart, Rozin, & Brown, 1988).

Smell

Can you imagine being brave enough to sample one of Farley's fried mice? You might try to make the experience more tolerable by holding your nose the way children do while taking distasteful medicine. This strategy helps because smell is important to taste (Settle, 1986; Enns & Hornung, 1988). That's why food tastes strange (or seems to have no taste at all) when you have a head cold. Also, some foods taste different to the elderly because of changes in their ability to smell (Stevens & Cain, 1987). For example, the elderly often lose their fondness for chocolate. Taste receptors register chocolate as very bitter, while smell receptors register chocolate as sweet. For this reason, chocolate may have an unpleasant, bitter taste to the elderly.

The passageway between the nose and the throat contains the odor-sensitive cells called **olfactory cells.** Gases we breathe are dissolved in a fluid covering the receptors, causing the cells to send messages to the brain. We rapidly detect a new odor, but we lose our ability to smell it after several minutes because olfactory cells respond rapidly and fatigue rapidly. In addition to fatigue of olfactory cells, the nasal passages them-

Taste buds
Taste sensors contained in papillae on the tongue.

Olfactory cells
Odor-sensitive cells contained in the passageway between the nose and the throat.

The fragrance of a flower can make us appreciate our sense of smell, about which scientists still have much to learn.

selves can become overworked. Your nose has a simple mechanism for compensating for this strain. Every few hours, your nose alternates between giving a rest to your left and right nasal passages.

A simple demonstration will illustrate this mechanism. Use your thumb to alternately block your right and left nasal passages. You will probably notice that breathing is much easier through one side than the other. The side that seems congested is being rested. Try the demonstration again in a couple of hours and you should find that the other side is being rested. If the air flow seems equal in both sides, the mechanism that rests the passages is in transition from one side to the other.

We have more to learn about the sense of smell than any other sense. One interesting research topic concerns **pheromones,** which are odorous substances that (1) emanate from animals and (2) change the behavior of other animals. For instance, a newborn rabbit's search for food is guided by a pheromone in its mother's milk (Keil, von Stralendorff, & Hudson, 1990). Pheromones influence sexual responses in most animals. Studies have shown that these responses include internal changes in hormones (see Chapter 2), and external changes in behaviors (see Chapter 11). For example, Cohen-Tannoudji, Locatelli, and Signoret (1986) studied responses of female sheep to male sheep. They found that the smell of a male sheep causes sexually related hormonal changes in female sheep. In addition, sensory cues other than smell also cause the same hormonal changes. In humans, other sensory cues seem to dominate, since no conclusive evidence has been found for the influence of pheromones on sexual responses.

Touch: Pain, Temperature, and Pressure

Our skin responds to pain, temperature, and pressure. Farley experienced all of these one day as he ran naked over rough ground after wolves who had interrupted his nude sunbathing. In this section we will review research developments on each kind of skin sensation and point out how this research has led to important theoretical and practical advances.

A better understanding of pain is being sought in order to find better ways to relieve those who have chronic pain, and to find better ways to restore pain perception to those who have lost it. You might think, "Who needs it?" But pain perception is actually quite important. Diseases that reduce or eliminate pain perception have caused people to inflict injuries inadvertently upon themselves, including serious cuts and burns. One woman, for example, even chewed off the tip of her tongue (Cohen, Kipnes, Kunkel, & Kubzansky, 1955). Most of us use "painkilling" drugs from time to time, but we may depend upon them less in the future because medical doctors are finding new ways to control pain without drugs, which we will discuss in Chapters 5 and 15.

The skin may contain specialized pain receptors, but physiologists have not identified any yet. An alternative theory is that pain results from overstimulation of the skin's temperature and pressure receptors. However, many facts argue against this. For instance, some drugs reduce pain sensations in the skin without reducing temperature or pressure sensation (Candland, 1968).

Imagine that you are sunbathing at the beach and decide to go swimming. You approach the water with confidence because it is filled with swimmers who seem to be enjoying the water as much as you were enjoying the sun. You touch the water with one toe just to make sure—*Brrr*, how can they stand it! Moments later, after much hesitation, a little coaxing,

Pheromones
Odorous chemical substances released by animals in order to communicate with other animals.

Our skin can feel comfortable in the hot sun or in a cool lake because of its ability to adjust its range of sensitivity.

and many goose bumps, you are enjoying the water as much as the others are. Thanks to our skin's ability to adjust, we can be comfortable over a wide range of temperatures. To date, no one physiological theory can explain all the known facts about temperature perception.

One popular theory is the *vascular theory*, which states that thermal receptors are actually sensory nerves that detect the contraction and dilation of blood vessels. This is a clever theory, because blood vessels contract when the skin is cooled and they dilate when the skin is warmed. However, according to the vascular theory we should be able to experience hot and cold on all regions of our body. This is a problem for the theory, because only hot is felt in some areas, called **warm spots,** and only cold is felt in other areas, called **cold spots.** The average square centimeter of skin has about six cold spots and one or two warm spots. When a warm object stimulates a cold spot, it feels cold. This is called **paradoxical cold.**

Such results lead to another popular theory, the *specific receptor theory*. According to this theory, distinct receptors exist for the sensation of hot and cold. The problem with this theory is that both hot and cold are experienced on skin areas that have few or none of one kind of receptor. For example, cold can be felt on hairy skin, where there are few if any cold receptors. Thus, for now, we have no satisfactory theory of how we experience temperature on the skin.

The blind depend heavily upon their sense of touch, and psychologists have teamed up with engineers to help the blind capitalize as much as possible on this important sense. Psychologists laid the foundation for helping the blind by doing basic research on the sense of touch. For example, they mapped the skin's sensitivity to slight amounts of pressure. They found, among other things, that the face is the most sensitive, and that females are more sensitive than males to the pressure of touch. Scientists

Warm spots
Areas on the skin where only hot is felt, even if stimulated by a cold object (when this occurs it is called *paradoxical warmth*).
Cold spots
Areas of the skin where only cold is felt, even if stimulated by a warm object (when this occurs it is called *paradoxical cold*).
Paradoxical cold
Occurs when a warm object stimulates a cold spot on the skin—cold is felt.

OTHER SENSES HELP THE BLIND "SEE"

Technological advances have led to exciting applications of sensory research, including attempts to restore sight to the blind. In a visual substitution system planned by Dr. Dobelle at Columbia University in New York, a subminiature television camera will be mounted in a glass eye. The artificial eye will be attached to eye muscles so that a blind person will point the camera as easily as we point our eyes. The camera will send optical information to the brain via a tiny computer mounted in a pair of eyeglasses. The computer will translate the information into a pattern of stimulation that will be experienced as a black-and-white picture when it is sent to the brain. Microelectrodes mounted on the surface of the visual cortex will stimulate the brain. The best Dr. Dobelle expects in the foreseeable future are low-resolution, slow-scan, black-and-white images that are like the early television transmissions sent by astronauts from the moon (Dobelle, 1977).

More recently, researchers have concentrated on substituting other senses for the eyes (National Research Council, 1986). One device, the Tactile Visual Substitution System (TVSS), was developed by Bach-Y-Rita (1982) and his colleagues at the Smith-Kettlewell Institute of Visual Science in San Francisco. A miniature television camera is mounted on spectacle frames, allowing the camera to be pointed by head movements. The camera's picture is analyzed into 400 dark or light dots, such that each dot represents a small area of the camera's field of view. Each dot's brightness depends upon the amount of light falling on the corresponding part of the visual field. Once the brightness of the dots is determined, they are translated to frequencies of vibrations on a matrix of 400 tiny skin vibrators mounted on the abdomen. When the corresponding dot is dark, the vibrator is off; when the dot is gray, the vibrator oscillates at a low frequency; and when the dot is bright, the vibrator oscillates at a high frequency. At first, it takes 5 to 8 minutes to recognize common objects such as telephones, cups, and chairs, but after only 1 hour of training, blind people can identify 25 common objects in about 5 to 20 seconds each.

After several weeks of training, blind people learn to negotiate hallways, open doors, and locate and pick up small objects with TVSS. Bach-Y-Rita and Hughes (1985) have also developed a more portable TVSS which stimulates the user's fingertip. The main advantage of the newer TVSS is that the fingertip stimulator is already available to most schools and institutes for blind persons.

Another promising sensory substitution system is the Sonicguide, a device developed by Professor Lesley Kay, an imaginative electrical engineer, at the University of Canterbury, New Zealand (see Kay, 1982; Strelow, Kay, & Kay, 1978). The Sonicguide shown in the photos here emits high-frequency sounds beyond the human hearing range. These hit objects in the environment and reflect back to the Sonicguide. Here they are converted to audible slashings, "wheeps," and rushing sounds. A user of the Sonicguide must learn to interpret this futuristic electronic "music." The sound's pitch indicates the distance of an object; it goes lower as an object moves farther away. Loudness indicates size; larger objects make louder sounds. Clarity indicates texture; when the "music" sounds like a poorly tuned radio, the object is rough; when it sounds like a well-tuned radio, the object is smooth. The time of arrival of the sounds in the two ears indicates

location; objects to the right are heard first by the right ear and objects to the left are heard first by the left ear.

Even infants who are blind can learn to interpret this code. During his first session with a Sonicguide, a 16-week-old baby boy learned to reach out and grab a small object waved in front of his face. Dr. Tom Bower (1977) swung an object by a thread toward the baby until it tapped his nose. After the third presentation, the baby moved both eyes toward his nose as the object approached, and moved both eyes away from his nose as the object receded. On the seventh presentation, the baby blocked the object by putting his hand in front of his face. The object was then moved from right to left. The baby tracked it with his head and eyes and he swiped at it with his hands, hitting it four times. The baby also learned to enjoy a game with his mother. Standing on her knee, he turned his head, bringing her in and out of the Sonicguide's sound field. The baby's smiles and giggles suggested that he enjoyed this game as much as most babies enjoy the "peek-a-boo" game.

The baby's development after the initial session was similar to a sighted baby's. He was able to identify favorite toys without touching them, and he reached for them with both hands when he was about 6 months of age. By 8 months he searched for objects that were hidden, and by 9 months

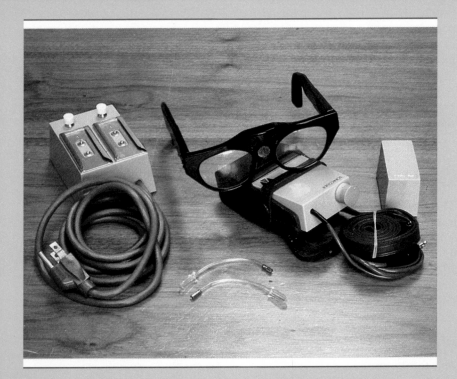

of age he reached out his hand when lowered toward a surface.

The Sonicguide also helps older children. For example, in Pennsylvania, James Newcomer (1977) is using the Sonicguide with blind children in public school. Under his direction, Dana, a 5-year-old kindergarten student, is using the device to find her way around school. Already she can locate water fountains and doorways, and she knows when to stop to reach out for objects. Gerry, an 8-year-old second-grader, uses the Sonicguide to maneuver between a maze of poles in a room without touching them. He can also find a person "hiding" in the room between the poles. Fourteen-year-old Wally is the first high-school student to own his own Sonicguide. He has learned to thread his way through congested corridors with few collisions, and he can follow other students at a distance if he chooses.

Current research efforts include attempts to identify what information is needed by blind and low vision persons and what displays are best for presenting that information (Bailey, 1984; Humphrey, Dodwell, Muir, & Humphrey, 1988; Suzuki, 1986; Warren & Strelow, 1985).

Looking into the future is always dangerous, so no predictions will be made about the course of psychological research on the senses. But after such an encouraging start, it will certainly be disappointing if in the 1990s a major effort is not made to continue basic and applied research on sensory substitution systems.

also noticed that two objects touching the skin produce two distinct sensations of pressure if the objects are far enough apart. However, if the objects are too close, they produce a single sensation of pressure. The least distance between two stimuli that can be perceived as separate is called the **two-point threshold.** You can see this for yourself through the following experiment.

Push two pins into a cork 1 centimeter apart. Push one pin into another cork. Blindfold a friend and touch his or her fingertip lightly with either cork. Have your friend say whether or not two distinct sensations of touch are felt. Repeat the experiment on the palm and the forearm. You should observe no mistakes on the fingertips, some mistakes on the palm, and many mistakes on the forearm. Such results provided important information used to develop sensory substitution systems for the blind (see Highlight: "Other Senses Help the Blind 'See' ").

Two-point threshold
The least distance between two stimuli that can be perceived as separate on the skin.

Cockpit of a 757 commercial airliner flight simulator built by Link Flight Simulation Corporation, Binghamton, NY.

Body Orientation

How do we know where we are in relation to the world around us? Basically two kinds of senses are involved here: **equilibrium,** our sense of overall body orientation (for example, the difference between standing upright or tilting backward), and **proprioception,** our sense of the position and motion of body parts. These two systems often interact in complex ways. For example, Martin (1986) studied the feasibility of using a moving seat-pan to simulate information about whole-body motion in a flight simulator. He found that seat movements did create the experience of whole body motion for experienced pilots. However, the moving seat-pan did not train new pilots to correctly interpret whole-body motion during actual flight. This failure is understandable when one considers the simulator did not reproduce the effects of gravity that are discussed in the next section.

Equilibrium.   Equilibrium is based on the body's reaction to gravity. The space program inspired a lot of research in this area, because astronauts wanted to know what to expect in outer space, where they would be free from earth's gravitational pull. In space, vision plays an important part in equilibrium; on earth, vision and gravity usually work together. Gravity affects equilibrium through the **vestibular system,** which is an inner-ear structure that detects body orientation and changes in body orientation. Figure 3–18 shows the vestibular system. The three arching structures are the **semicircular canals,** which detect changes in the position of the head. Fluids move in the canals when the head rotates in any direction. The fluid motion causes neural messages about head movements to be sent to the brain.

Semicircular canals stop responding shortly after the head stops moving. Other gravity detectors continue to report head position. They are the **otolith structures,** which are organs that signal head orientation with respect to gravity. The otolith apparatus consists of two sacs located near the junction of the semicircular canals. The inside floors of those sacs contains

FIGURE 3–18

The semicircular canals of the vestibular system are located in the inner ear. Fluids move in the canals when the head rotates in any direction, sending neural messages to the brain.

Equilibrium
Sense of overall body orientation (for example, the difference between standing upright or tilting backward).

Proprioception
The sense of where our body parts are; determined by sense organs in joints, muscles, and tendons, which connect muscles with bones.

Vestibular system
Inner-ear structure that detects body orientation and changes in body orientation.

Semicircular canals
Three arching structures in the inner ear that detect changes in head position.

Otolith structures
Organs that signal head orientation with respect to gravity.

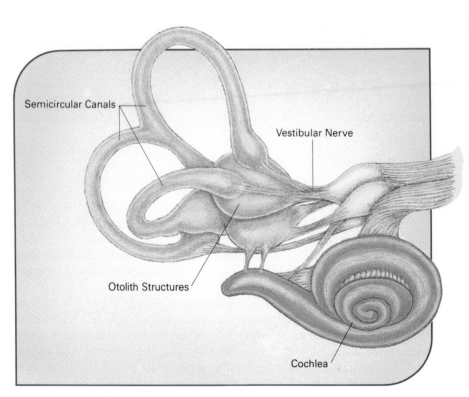

hair cells and a tissue that holds tiny stones over the hair cells. The stones change position when the head changes position. The semicircular canals and the otolith apparatus are idle in outer space, but they are continually active on earth.

Proprioception.   Equilibrium is only part of body orientation. We also need proprioception, the sense of where our body parts are. Proprioception is determined by sense organs in joints, muscles, and tendons, which connect muscles with bones (Matin, 1981; Clark, Grigg, & Chapin, 1989). An experiment by Rock and Harris (1967) illustrates proprioception. It also illustrates people's ability to adjust to an altered environment.

In this experiment subjects held their arm under a glass table top and pointed at targets that were slightly above the table (see Figure 3–19). The experiment had three parts:

1. On pretests, subjects pointed at targets with the glass covered. They pointed accurately with both arms, even though they could not see their arm or hand under the table. Proprioception is indicated by the fact that people knew where their arms were even though they could not see them.

2. During an exposure condition subjects wore goggles that displaced vision. The goggles made targets seem to be about 4 inches to the right of where they actually were. The cover was then removed from the glass table. Subjects practiced pointing at targets with one arm while they rested the other arm. They pointed off to the right at first. Within a few minutes, however, they saw and corrected their mistake.

3. The goggles were removed for posttests. The procedures for these final tests were identical to pretest procedures. Subjects pointed accurately when they used their rested arm. This result suggests that subjects still saw the targets in the correct places. It also suggests that they still knew where their rested arm was without looking at it. They pointed off to the left, however, when they pointed with their practiced hand. This result suggests that subjects had adjusted their arm's proprioception; that is, the goggle exposure caused them to feel that their arm was in a different place than it actually was. When the goggles were on, this adjustment in proprioception helped them coordinate their pointing with the displaced vision. When the goggles were removed, however, the adjustment caused errors until subjects had a chance to readjust to normal vision.

FIGURE 3–19
This is the apparatus used in the Rock and Harris experiment.

This classical experimental procedure is being used currently to study neurological disorders (Stern, Mayeuf, Hermann, & Rosen, 1988).

Recent investigations show that people can adjust to a distorted world in many ways (Kapaula, Optican, & Robinson, 1989; Ott & Eckmiller, 1989; Redding & Wallace, 1988). Scientists are not sure why we have this ability, but astronauts are glad that we do because it helped them adapt to outer space.

The ability of sensory systems to adapt also helped Farley Mowat adjust to life at Wolf House Bay. It would have been interesting to compare his pre–Wolf House Bay sensory awareness to his post–Wolf House Bay awareness. We probably would have verified that Farley's senses became more sensitive if we had actually taken the measurements that we considered at the beginning of this chapter. Furthermore, we probably would have had little trouble explaining this effect in terms of normal sensory adaptation. Farley's night vision adjusted to a more sensitive range because background levels of light were lower than what Farley experienced in city environments. Similarly, his auditory sensitivity increased because background levels of noise decreased.

This comparison of sensory adaptation in space and in the wild is an appropriate transition into the next chapter. There we will examine how modern astronauts and aviators have made good use of the precise sensory and motor skills that they inherited from ancestors who depended upon those skills for survival in the wild.

Summary

1. Our senses enable us to experience our environment. From a processing point of view **sensation** corresponds roughly to gathering information and perception corresponds to interpreting this information. From its early days, psychologists have been interested in the study of sensation.

2. **Psychophysics** studies the relationship between physical energies and perceptual experiences. This relationship can be measured by various methods, each of which has advantages and disadvantages.

3. One important psychophysical law is **Weber's Law,** which states that a just-noticeable change in a stimulus magnitude is proportional to the original stimulus magnitude.

4. The eyes convert light energy into neural responses that we experience as sight. The actual conversion is done by two kinds of receptor cells in the **retina: rods** and **cones.** They send neural messages through visual pathways to other brain structures. The pathways contain cells that participate in the interpretation of these messages.

5. The eyes can adjust their sensitivity to light. They become more sensitive in dim light through a process of **dark adaptation.** They become less sensitive in bright light through a process of **light adaptation.**

6. Light receptors are specialized so that they are more sensitive to some colors than to others. Cells in the visual pathways also participate in the coding of colors.

7. The ears convert sound waves into neural responses that we experience as hearing. The external ear collects and focuses sound, causing the **eardrum** to vibrate. Three delicate bones of the middle ear carry these vibrations to the **oval window,** which vibrates receptors in the **cochlea,** triggering nerve impulses to the brain.

8. **Pitch** (high notes versus low notes) is determined by the **frequency** of sound waves. **Loudness** is determined by the **amplitude** of sound waves. Tone quality is determined by how sound waves combine. We hear the location of sounds in part because we are sensitive to tiny sound differences between the two ears.

9. The tongue has **taste buds** that convert chemical stimulation into neural responses, which we experience as taste. Different regions of the tongue are sensitive to the four primary tastes: sweet, sour, salty, and bitter.

10. The throat and nasal passages contain **olfactory cells,** which convert the gases we breathe into neural responses that we experience as smell. Olfactory cells also influence taste.

11. The skin responds to pain, temperature, and pressure. Scientists have not yet identified all the receptor cells that underlie these sensations. The understanding that they have gained so far, however, has already helped to relieve pain for many people, and it has helped the blind to "see" with their skin.

12. There are two types of body orientation senses: equilibrium and proprioception. **Equilibrium** is our sense of overall body orientation; it is affected by gravity through the **vestibular system,** which consists of the **semicircular canals** and the **otolith structures. Proprioception** is the sense of where our other body parts are. It is determined by sense organs in joints, muscles, and tendons.

Key Terms

absolute threshold
accommodation
afterimage
amplitude
anvil
aqueous humor
basilar membrane
blind spot
boilermaker's deafness
bone conduction
cataracts
cochlea
cold spots
color blindness
complex tones
cones
cornea
cycle
dark adaptation
decibel
difference threshold
Doppler shift
ear canal

eardrum
electromagnetic spectrum
equilibrium
farsightedness
fovea
frequency
glaucoma
hammer
hertz
iris
lens
light adaptation
loudness
near point of accommodation
nearsightedness
olfactory cells
optic nerve
ophthalmoscope
oscilloscope
otolith structures
oval window
papillae
paradoxical cold

peripheral vision
pheromones
pinna
pitch
proprioception
psychophysical function
psychophysics
pupil
pure tones
retina
rods
semicircular canals
signal-detection theory
stirrup
taste buds
tinnitus
two-point threshold
vestibular system
vitreous humor
warm spots
waveform
Weber's Law

RESEARCH ON NOISE DISAPPEARS IN THE DIN

As decibels rise, stress and learning problems seem to increase.

BY MALCOLM W. BROWNE

America is noiser than ever, audiologists say, and the costs may include lost hearing, impaired health, reduced learning ability and antisocial behavior.

Noise causes stress, just as crowding and the threat of crime do, said Dr. Alice H. Suter, an audiologist at the National Institute for Occupational Safety and Health. "But unlike some of the other problems," she went on, "noise seems to be accepted by our society these days as a necessary evil."

The absence of Federal financial support for noise abatement programs in the last eight years has left the United States largely unprotected against a swelling torrent of noise, she said. A lack of research funds has prevented measurements of the overall increase in noise levels, but government and scientific experts appear to agree that they have grown steadily in the past decade.

One reason was suggested by Samuel Stempler, director of New York City's Bureau of Air Resources, a branch of the city's Department of Environmental Protection. "The trouble with noise," he said, "is that it's not visible like garbage, oil spills and other pollutants. So it seems to get less attention than the more conspicuous pollutants, despite the hazards it poses."

Dr. Ernest A. Peterson of the University of Miami School of Medicine, a leading authority on the physiological effects of noise, says noise may even be addictive. "We know that the level of sound produced by 'boom box' radios and tape players elevates blood levels of norepinephrine—adrenaline," he said. "There's evidence that some people enjoy the highs they get from adrenaline."

Government efforts to reduce the harmful effects of noise have faltered in the last decade. In 1981 the Reagan Administration ordered the termination of the Environmental Protection Agency's noise abatement program, saying the responsibility should rest with local governments, not Washington.

The decision followed a decade of what many audiologists say were significant victories. Under the Noise Control Act of 1972, the Federal Government paid for noise research, issued wide-ranging regulations and supported state and local noise abatement agencies in a variety of ways. "But since 1982, when the Federal Government's noise abatement program effectively ended, local programs have also foundered," Dr. Suter said. "At the peak of interest in noise control during the 1970's, there were 1,100 state and local anti-noise programs. Today only 15 are still active."

Most of the scientific research in the 1970's and early 80's on the effects of noise was also federally supported, and scientists say that when this support ended, research also stopped. The latest textbooks on noise and its effects are still based largely on investigations carried out as long ago as 15 years, when the Federal noise program was at its height.

All Day With a Vacuum Cleaner

Dr. Suter and other experts say more than 20 million Americans are exposed in their daily lives to persistent environmental noise loud enough to cause hearing loss—above 80 decibels, or about the level of vacuum cleaners, electric tools or heavy traffic.

Aside from loss of hearing, noise is suspected of having a variety of physiological effects. Many studies have strongly suggested a link between noise and high blood pressure. Dr. Peterson of the University of Miami established that the blood pressure of rhesus monkeys and other primates rises when the animals are exposed to noise, and blood pressure remains high even after the noise stops.

Six years after the opening of a new runway at Schipol Airport in Amsterdam, Dutch investigators found that the sale of anti-hypertensive drugs to nearby residents doubled. A Polish study showed that chronic exposure to noise between 85 and 115 decibels, about the level of a noisy factory, sharply increased the incidence of hypertension and peptic ulcers. A 1982 investigation by William Meecham of the University of California at Los Angeles found a higher rate of cardiovascular deaths, strokes, suicides and murder among 200,000 residents of a flight-path corridor near Los Angeles International Airport than in the rest of the city, although factors other than noise probably played a role. Dr. David C. Glass, provost of the State University of New York at Stony Brook, says there is evidence that noise degrades the immune response, impairing resistance to disease.

Dr. Glass, Dr. Sheldon Cohen of Carnegie-Mellon University in Pittsburgh and Dr. Jerome E. Singer of the Uniformed Services University of the Health Sciences in Bethesda, Md., investigated the effects of noise on learning ability. In the 1970's the group studied children living in a particularly noisy housing complex over the approach to George Washington Bridge in upper Manhattan. They found that children living on the lower, noisier floors did not read as well as those on the upper floors.

"Noise has to be considered as just one among many of the intrusive elements of our environment," Dr. Glass said in an interview. "But even in that context, the noise situation is simply awful. In the absence of continuing studies it's difficult to get an objective measure, but in the last year or so I've certainly experienced more irritation from noise in New York City. Among the sounds that are particularly noticeable are ambulance sirens and automobile burglar alarms."

More Noise, More Aggression

Noise may have far-reaching social effects. Studies cited by Dr. Jeffrey D. Fisher, Dr. Paul A. Bell and Dr. Andrew Baum in their book "Environmental Psychology" suggest that noise heightens aggressive tendencies and dampens helpful impulses.

In some experiments, subjects were prepared by making them angry at one experimenter. They were then seated in rooms in which noise levels were controlled, and were presented with push buttons that they were told would administer electric shocks to the experimenter.

In these tests, the subjects in noisy rooms pushed the button significantly longer and oftener than did those in quiet rooms. Noise seemed to have little effect on the button pushing of subjects who were not angry, but for those who were already aroused, noise stimulated hostile behavior.

In other studies, experimenters pretended to need help after dropping loads of books. When a nearby lawn mower or jackhammer was operating, passers-by would offer help much less often than when the environment was quiet.

Dr. Fisher, a professor of psychology at the University of Connecticut in Storrs, said many experiments show that noise modifies behavior. "There's a lot of evidence that unpredictable noise and noise that a hearer cannot control induce a sense of helplessness—a kind of giving-up—and with it, poorer performance of certain kinds of tasks," he said.

Some Federal regulations have produced lasting effects, said Dr. Kenneth Feith, the only remaining full-time employee at the E.P.A.'s noise office in Washington. Medium-sized and large trucks are significantly quieter than they were in the 1970's because of new manufacturing techniques to comply with noise regulations, he said. New jet airplanes are significantly quieter than older models. On the other hand, garbage trucks and trash compactors are still very noisy, he said, because their manufacturers regarded noise-reduction modification as too costly.

Relying on Local Action

Mr. Stempler of New York City's Department of Environmental Protection said the city gets no financial help from the state and Federal governments. "We are chronically underfunded," he went on. "Of our 42 inspectors, only 20 or 30 are qualified to investigate noise complaints, of which we get thousands each year." His office issued 700 citations in 1988 and 879 in 1989, mostly from noisy airconditioning plants, discotheques and illegal weekend construction.

New York has an anti-honking ordinance, but city noise inspectors are not uniformed and are reluctant to take action against violators, Mr. Stempler said. The police could issue tickets for honking but seldom do. "They are more concerned with drugs, violent crime and other matters," he said, "and they simply don't have time or resources to do much about noise."

One of the best-known campaigners against unnecessary siren noise is Dr. Thomas H. Fay, director of the speech and hearing department at Columbia-Presbyterian Medical Center. In the early 1970's Dr. Fay, an adviser to the city government, promoted the use of attention-getting sound patterns rather than shear volume in sirens. "The European alarm system, with alternating high and low notes, is noticeable from greater distances than the wailing sound commonly used here," he said.

"But the education program needed to use the new sirens properly was never funded," he went on, "and now the idea is to push down on the siren for all you're worth, and if that doesn't clear out the traffic congestion, lean on the air horn." Virtually every emergency vehicle in New York City consistently violates the city's noise limit for ordinary horns, he said. "I've spent a lot of time with working firemen," he said, "and I know that they keep asking for louder and louder sirens because they're half deaf themselves."

Dr. Marc B. Kramer, the consulting audiologist for New York City's Fire and Police Departments, said that only older firemen frequently complain of hearing loss.

Firefighters and police officials argue that civilian drivers are less and less willing to give way to emergency vehicles, and that in modern cars with air-conditioning, closed windows and loud radios, sirens are hard to hear.

Another anti-noise crusader is Carmine C. Santa Maria of Bensonhurst in Brooklyn. He and his allies brought so much pressure on the Metropolitan Transportation Authority that the wheels of some subway trains have been fitted with steel rings to dampen the screech caused by rounding a curve. Mr. Santa Maria's home, next to one of the noisiest elevated lines, is now spared most of the screeching.

But in a telephone interview he said: "You'll have to speak up. It's not the subway. The Fire Department's passing by, and the sirens are blotting you out."

Perception

A t 9:08 Central Standard Time on the night of Monday, April 13, 1970, an oxygen tank exploded, tearing away one side of the Apollo 13 service module. John L. Swigart, strapped to his pilot's seat in the command module, felt a shudder. Fred W. Haise, pilot of the lunar module (LM, pronounced "lem"), was in the tunnel connecting the LM and the command module when the whole tunnel violently shook up and down. Captain James A. Lovell, the commander, felt nothing—he was floating, weightless, in front of his seat. He heard a strange noise, but it didn't sound like an explosion— he thought Haise might have dropped something in the LM. Lovell's first clue to the emergency came when the master alarm sounded and Haise scrambled from the LM tunnel, slamming the hatch behind him. All three astronauts knew by then that something was fundamentally wrong, but it would be 15 minutes before they would get a rough idea of what had happened, and about an hour beyond that before they would realize that the

odds were now against their ever returning to earth.

The delay in realizing the danger was costly, because during it Apollo 13 passed the point where the spacecraft could easily have returned directly to earth, a trip of about $1\frac{1}{2}$ days. Now it would be necessary to circle the moon before returning, a trip that would take 3 or 4 days. The flight controllers began frantically calculating whether or not the astronauts could possibly last that long.

As the ground crew made their calculations, the astronauts climbed inside the LM to fly their crippled spacecraft. By Tuesday afternoon, the moon, which had looked like a small white disc at the time of the accident, now filled the spacecraft's windows. The constant chatter from mission control stopped when the astronauts circled around the moon's dark side and lost contact with earth for about 25 minutes.

As it rounded the moon, Apollo 13 was on a path that would swing it back toward earth, missing it by some 40,000 miles. To return safely, the astronauts would have to correct

their course with their manual controls, and they would have to guide their spacecraft through a narrow reentry corridor. If they went outside this narrow path, they would bounce off into space without enough power to return. Their predicament was like that of a sailor using the stars as a guide for steering a floundering vessel. Ironically, however, even though they were in the heavens, they had trouble seeing the stars. Gases coming from the spacecraft clouded their view of the sky, making it almost impossible to hold a sextant on a star long enough to get their bearings. The astronauts thus had to settle for less precise targets to steer by—the sun, the moon, and even the earth itself— which would work until they were close to the earth. Before entering the earth's atmosphere, however, they would somehow have to get a fix on a star. To further complicate matters, controlling Apollo 13 now often called for the efforts of all three astronauts—it was like driving a car with one person working the brake, another the accelerator, and the third controlling the steering wheel.

The Apollo 13 astronauts: (*left to right*) James A. Lovell, Jr., John L. Swigart, Jr., and Fred W. Haise, Jr.

A picture of the damaged spacecraft.

Although the fate of the astronauts depended on their own visual abilities and their own motor coordination, they were not alone. Dozens of mission controllers were making heroic efforts to bring Apollo 13 home safely. One of the most demanding jobs fell to mission controller John Aaron. He had to find a way to stretch the remaining power in the command module over several hours, even though it was designed to last only 45 minutes.

When the earth finally loomed in the spacecraft's windows, it was time for one last try at a star check. One of the flight controllers suggested that Swigart try to locate Altair or Vega, two stars on the side of the spacecraft facing away from the sun, where its shadow could cut the glare. When Swigart tried this, he couldn't see anything until a flight controller told him to turn off a nearby light. Meanwhile, Lovell, who could see that they were approaching the earth at an alarming

rate, shouted to Swigart to hurry up; unless the adjustments in position were made quickly, they would be too late. With the light out, Swigart found Altair easily. Moments later, the computer compared the actual position with the estimated position of Apollo 13. The astronauts could not believe their bleary eyes. There was no error! Somehow, Haise's and Lovell's rough alignment with the sun and moon had turned out to be perfect. The test was quickly repeated on Vega, and Swigart's results were the same. Suddenly the astronauts, who had been behind schedule, were now slightly ahead. They had 5 minutes to disconnect the LM from the rest of the spacecraft.

With the LM gone, the command module was flying alone. Earlier, when the service module was jettisoned, the astronauts got their only chance to see and photograph the damaged vessel. Lovell, the first to spot it, said, "O.K., I've got her. . . . And there's one whole side of

that spacecraft missing." This raised questions in everyone's minds about whether or not the ceramic heat shield on the command module, which had been near the ruptured oxygen tank, was damaged. If it was, the astronauts would burn up during reentry.

This horrible thought returned when radio contact was lost during reentry. The astronauts should have reestablished radio contact 3 minutes and 30 seconds after hitting the atmosphere, but they didn't. Everyone waited anxiously. One minute and forty seconds later, Houston called the spacecraft. There was no answer. Then, 5 seconds later, Swigart called in, "O.K., Joe."

The astronauts splashed down safely near a recovery ship at 12:07 P.M., Houston time, on Friday, April 17. It was an unsuccessful mission, but it was perhaps Apollo's greatest success story. ■

After completing this chapter, you should be able to:

Understand that sensation and perception affect one another.

Describe the role of perception in human development.

Identify and illustrate the Gestalt Laws of Organization.

Understand the role of perceptual consistencies when light, sound, and other information changes.

Define illusion and give examples of several familiar illusions.

Understand speech perception and active synthesizing processes.

History and Scope of the Study of Perception, Cognition, and Action

The preceding chapter defined *sensation* as the process of gathering information about the environment and *perception* as the process of interpreting that information. The studies of sensation and perception have been intertwined throughout history. Structuralists and Gestalt psychologists, for example, debated the pros and cons of studying them separately or together (see Chapters 1 and 3). The Structuralists tried to analyze them separately, and the Gestalt psychologists insisted on a unified analysis. The crux of this debate cannot be fully understood until you consider how sensations and perceptions are used.

Consider, for instance, the sensations and perceptions of the Apollo 13 astronauts. Advanced technology sent them to the moon, but it was their sensory, perceptual, cognitive, and motor skills that got them back to earth. Flying their spacecraft manually required a precise coordination among sensation, perception, cognition, and movement. They had to recognize and locate stars and other objects around them; they had to understand spoken and written commands that would help them guide their spacecraft safely back to earth. Every day you use perceptual and cognitive skills that are similar to the ones that enabled the astronauts to return home safely. You can demonstrate the skills of recognizing, locating, and grasping right now. Reach out and grab some object such as a can of Coca-Cola or a pencil that you recognize out of the corner of your eye while you are reading. This chapter will raise and address many questions about these skills. To what extent are they inborn? To what extent are they learned? How are sensations organized into perceptions of objects? How do perceptions represent the location, size, shape, brightness, and other qualities of objects in the environment? Or, more generally, how reliably do perceptions represent the environment? How do perceptions remain constant and stable? Can we always believe our eyes? How do we perceive and understand spoken and written language?

Our analysis of these questions will show that the processes of gathering information (sensation) and the processes of interpreting information (perception) affect one another. Again, you can consider an example now while you read. Your eyes are moving in ways that we will consider in detail later. We will see that these precise eye movement responses are determined in part by sensory properties of your eyes and in part by the way you interpret the text. This is but one example demonstrating that sensory and perceptual processes are so interwoven that we must study them together.

Perceptual Development

Before going on missions, astronauts train for years at the Johnson Space Center in Houston to extend their basic perceptual and motor skills. This process of refining basic skills raises questions that are central to this section: What perceptual skills are present during early childhood? And how are these skills modified by experience? We will address these questions with respect to seeing depth and size.

Visual Cliff Experiments

Walk and Gibson (1961) designed a clever device for studying infant depth perception. Their apparatus, which is called a **visual cliff,** consists of a special table divided into three parts (Figure 4–1). There is a center board upon which a mother places her baby at the beginning of the experiment. To either side of the center board is a checkered pattern covered by a sturdy sheet of glass. On one side of the center board the checkered pattern is just 1 inch below the glass; on the other side the pattern is about 4 feet below, making it look like a "visual cliff."

Infants between the ages of 6 and 12 months refuse to cross the visual cliff despite their mother's encouragement. In contrast, they eagerly cross the shallow side. Apparently infants see depth. However, parents should not place infants who can crawl on high beds or other high surfaces. Although babies try to avoid the visual cliff, the same experiments show that they are very clumsy—many of the 36 babies that Walk and Gibson tested would have fallen over the cliff if glass hadn't been there. A common mistake was to back off the "cliff" while looking in the other direction.

Walk and Gibson showed that chicks and lambs avoid the visual side of the cliff 1 day after birth. Experimenters cannot give humans the visual cliff test at such a young age because babies do not crawl until they are at least 4 months old, and usually older. Researchers, however, figured out a way to test younger humans. Campos, Langer, and Krowitz (1970) placed 1½-month-old babies over each side of the cliff and measured their heart rates. They found changes in heart rates when babies were placed over the visual cliff, suggesting that babies see depth long before they learn to crawl.

The visual cliff has been used recently to study how depth perception is affected by experimentally induced neural damage in animals (Burger, 1990; Hovda & Villablance, 1989).

Reaching Experiments

Another experimental approach is to study reaching behavior. In one experiment, Bruner and Koslowski (1972) observed reaching to study infant size perception.

Visual cliff
Apparatus used to test depth perception in infants.

FIGURE 4–1

This device, called a "visual cliff," is used for studying depth perception in infants.

Suppose you were asked to grasp a tennis ball with both hands. You would extend your hands, bring them closer together, and close them around the ball. Now suppose that a large beach ball were held in the same position. You would extend your arms, move them farther apart, and wrap them around the ball. Before you would begin either movement, you would know what movements were needed to grasp the ball.

What do babies do in this situation? In one study, infants (between 10 and 22 weeks old) looked at a small ball or a large ball placed within arm's reach (Bruner & Koslowski, 1972). The main finding was that babies who had not yet learned to reach and to manipulate objects nevertheless showed size discrimination. They brought their hands closer together and moved them while they were together more often when they saw the small ball. They made more forward sweeps with their arms spread apart when they saw the large ball. Apparently, then, they could see that one ball was small and the other large, and were responding to this.

The babies seemed uncoordinated because they did not order their movements in the proper sequence; they often brought their hands together and closed them before they extended their arms, for instance. This lack of coordination caused some theorists to argue that babies are confused by what they see. They cannot see size, they argued, until they add to visual information the knowledge they gain from manipulating objects (see Hochberg, 1978). Bruner and Koslowski's experiment contradicts this theory because it suggests that babies see size *before* they learn to manipulate objects. They are uncoordinated *not* because they are visually confused, but because they do not yet know how to control the order of their arm movements. More recent research is studying the development of infant motor coordination (Goldfield, 1989).

In earlier decades, limited response capabilities in infants led many to assume that babies see a "blooming, buzzing confusion." Today opinions are changing. Modern experiments suggest that babies see more than we had previously realized. These newer findings are guiding rehabilitation therapists toward the development of more effective training programs for visually impaired children (Andrew, 1989).

Psychologists study how our perceptions represent the sights, sounds, smells, and feel of objects in our environment.

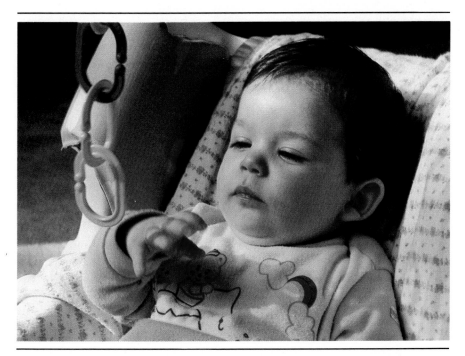

Psychologists have learned about what infants can and cannot see by studying their reaching behavior.

THE BABY AS INTERIOR DECORATOR

What would infants ask for if they could choose decorations for their room? Would pastel blues and pinks remain in vogue for nurseries if infants could choose for themselves? What about the mobiles that are found in most nurseries? Would they go or stay? Research into the perceptual world of infants suggests answers to these questions.

"Looking Box" Experiments

Infants cannot directly answer our questions about their experiences. As a result, their perceptual world remained a mystery until the mid-1950s, when Robert L. Fantz showed that psychologists can coax even newborns into answering questions about what they see (Fantz, 1963).

Fantz used a "looking box" to peek into the perceptual world of infants. The photo shows a looking box in which an infant is placed on its back. Pads beside the head keep the eyes directed upward toward two pictures on the ceiling of the box. The pictures are 2 or 3 feet from the infant. An experimenter can determine which picture the infant is looking at by peering through a peephole in the top of the box. Whatever the baby looks at is reflected in the center of its pupil.

Fantz's results with the looking box and those from other laboratories indicate the following looking preferences:

1. Infants as young as 1 week old prefer patterned pictures over unpatterned ones (Greenberg & O'Donnell, 1972).
2. Infants as young as 2 months prefer curved lines over straight ones (Ruff & Birch, 1974).
3. Infants as young as 2 months prefer bright colors to pastels (Haith & Campos, 1977; Schaller, 1975).
4. Infants as young as 4 days old prefer a human face over an equally complex pattern (Fantz, 1963).
5. Newborns and older infants prefer things that move over things that don't (Carpenter, G., 1974; Gregg, Clifton, & Haith, 1976).

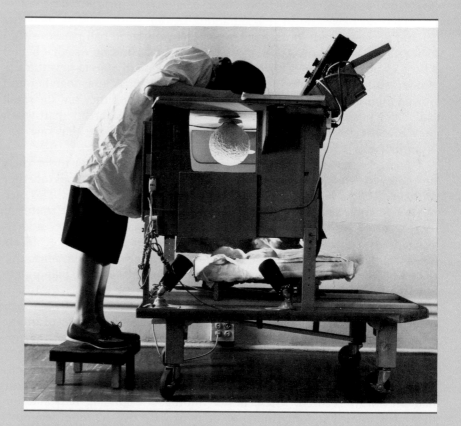

What do these looking preferences tell us about babies' decor preferences? They suggest that we might see some changes in the nursery if babies could pick their own decorations. The popular pastels would be replaced by bright colors, and pictures of faces would be all the rage. Some popular decorations would remain, however. Mobiles, for instance, would probably stay, because infants enjoy moving objects. Furthermore, since infants enjoy brightly colored curved lines, the increasing popularity of rainbow decorations would be cheered.

Parents need not wait for their own children to speak up. Representative infants have been allowed to choose in carefully controlled experiments. Although silent, the infants cast their votes decidedly with their eyes. This is one research result to which parents might want to attend before their own children are old enough to speak for themselves.

The Role of Organization in Perception

During their voyage through the heavens, the astronauts searched for familiar groups of stars to use as navagational guides. Many of us can at least recognize the Big Dipper and other familiar constellations. Just how do we organize the separate sensations of stars into groups? In the 1920s, a group of German psychologists, who were members of the Gestalt school, argued that this is far from a trivial issue. You might understand their argument better if you think for a moment about the flood of light rushing into your eyes when you stand at a window and see a house, trees, and sky. Millions of receptors are stimulated by the light stream, which contains many different wavelengths, colors, and intensities. Receptors register these separately, but you do not see separate patches of colors and brightnesses. Somehow separate sensations are organized into wholes so that you see a house, trees, and sky. You would have a hard time seeing other groupings of these stimuli. For example, you could not easily see the trees as part of the house, because you unconsciously follow a set of rules for organizing sensations into perceptions of trees and house.

Gestalt Laws of Perceptual Organization

The Gestalt psychologists attempted to describe the rules by which we organize sensations. *Gestalt* means a structure that forms a unit or a whole, and the **Gestalt laws of organization** describe the way in which we tend to group objects or stimuli according to certain characteristics that they have. For example, one such law, the **law of nearness or proximity,** says that we group elements that are close together. In Figure 4–2A we see three vertical columns of dots when the vertical dots are closer together than the horizontal ones. When the horizontal dots are closer, then we see three horizontal rows of dots.

Another law is the **law of similarity,** which states that we group elements that are similar, or look alike. In Figure 4–2B we see three vertical columns of figures when the vertical elements are similar, and three horizontal rows when the horizontal elements are similar. Other Gestalt laws of organization are illustrated and briefly described in Figure 4–2.

In addition to these traditional laws, modern researchers are continuing to discover perceptual organization effects. For example, Wong and Weisstein (1985) found that flickering regions of a visual field are seen behind nonflickering regions. This perceptual organization effect is obtained even when the flickering and nonflickering regions have the same texture and the same average brightness over time.

Rock and Palmer (1990) proposed two new laws. One is the **law of enclosure or common region.** According to this law, observers have a tendency to group elements that are located in the same perceived region. In Figure 4–2E, equally spaced dots are grouped by perceived regions. This demonstration and similar ones have been used to show that the law of enclosure holds for grouping objects.

Rock and Palmer's second proposal is the **law of connectedness.** According to this law, observers group objects that are connected. In Figure 4–2F, equally spaced dots are group according to their connections. This demonstration and similar ones show that this law holds over a wide range of stimuli.

It was also the Gestalt school that pointed out our basic tendency to divide what we see into **figure** (an object) and **ground** (the background

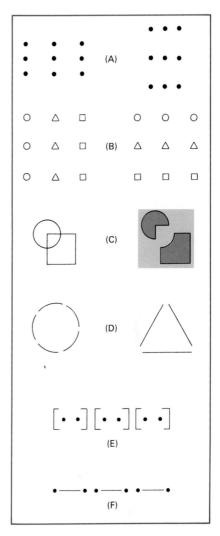

FIGURE 4–2

These drawings illustrate six Gestalt laws of organization: (A) *The law of proximity.* We group together elements that are close together. (B) *The law of similarity.* We group together elements that are alike. (C) *The law of good continuation.* We group together line segments that form straight or smoothly curving lines (thus you will see a circle and a square in the left figure rather than the two objects shown in the right figure). (D) *The law of closure.* We tend to fill in gaps in straight lines or smooth curves. (E) *The law of enclosure.* We group elements in the same perceived enclosed region. (F) *The law of connectedness.* We group connected elements.

FIGURE 4–3

The reversible goblet can be seen as a white vase against a green background or, if you reverse the figure and ground, it is seen as two green faces against a white background.

Gestalt laws of organization
Describe how we group stimulus elements according to their characteristics.
Law of nearness or proximity
One of the Gestalt laws of organization; states that we group elements that are close together.
Law of similarity
One of the Gestalt laws of organization; states that we group elements that are similar or look alike.
Law of enclosure
We group elements on the same perceived enclosed region.
Law of connectedness
We group connected elements.
Figure
Object standing out against a background or against its surroundings.
Ground
Background or surroundings against which an object stands out.
Figure-ground reversal (or multistable perception)
Occurs when figure and ground in a picture suddenly reverse; what was seen as figure is seen as background, and vice versa.

or surroundings of the object). But what happens when figure and ground suddenly reverse, as they do in Figure 4–3? When you look at this figure, you see a goblet at one moment and a pair of silhouetted faces the next. This phenomenon is called **figure-ground reversal** or **multistable perception,** since you perceive more than one image in the same figure (Attneave, 1976; Garcia & Miguel, 1989).

Organization of Moving Patterns

We also actively impose organization on moving objects. As shown in Figure 4–4A, when people view a light on the rim of a rolling wheel in an otherwise dark room, the light appears to hop along, making a series of arches. The same physical motion path looks quite different, however, if a light is added to the opposite side of the rim of the wheel. Both lights then appear to roll smoothly along, spinning around an invisible hub. The same physical motion looks different when the other light is added because viewers impose different organizations on it. Scientists are learning the rules that we use to impose organization on wheel motions, and these same rules explain how we organize more complicated motions as well, such as those made by a walking person or a waving hand, as shown in Figure 4–4B (Cutting & Proffitt, 1981; Johansson, 1976; Proffitt & Cutting, 1980).

Scientists are continually learning new things about these laws of organization (e.g., Anstis, 1986; Koenderink, 1986; Longuet-Higgins, 1986; Regan, 1986). In one recent study, Perrone (1986) found that the nature of the organization depends upon whether an object is moving toward or away from a viewer. Either kind of movement causes transformation in the retinal image. For example, if a rigid object such as an airplane approaches an observer, its retinal image will expand. If the same object moves away from an observer, the retinal image will contract (see Figure 4–6). Perrone simulated these expansions and contractions with computer-generated images. An observer of his computer displays was exposed to the same retinal transformations that would have been produced by rigid three-dimensional wire frame boxes. The displays simulated a rigid box that was moving toward or away from the eyes. The observer's task was to say whether the boxes appeared to move and/or change size. Retinal expansion patterns led to perceptions of an approaching rigid box. However, contraction patterns led to the perception of a box that was both moving away and getting smaller. Perrone concluded that humans use different organizational rules for processing expansion and contraction patterns. He hopes that a better understanding of these rules will lead to better computer simulations of motion in depth.

While some researchers are trying to improve computer displays, others are trying to improve observers. For example, Ball and Sekuler (1986)

FIGURE 4–4

This figure shows the various ways that we actively impose organization on moving objects, such as a rolling wheel, a person walking, or a hand waving.

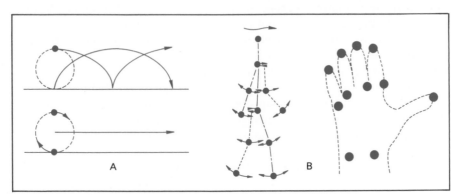

found that younger observers (ages 18–28) are better than older ones (ages 62–72) at discriminating direction of motion in moving objects. The younger observers were superior even when optical blur was equated so that the stimulus appeared equally blurry to younger and older people. This result implies that it was processing strategy rather than optics that gave an advantage to young adults. Furthermore, this result suggests the hypothesis that older observers should improve if training could help them develop more efficient processing strategies. In agreement with this hypothesis, Ball and Sekuler found that older adults could profit from perceptual training on direction discrimination. In fact, training improved performance for both groups equally. In addition, both groups fully retained their improvements for at least one month.

The Role of Constancies in Perception

If figure-ground reversals make you dizzy, you may find relief in the stability, or constancy, of our perceptual world. We depend on this constancy even to recognize a friend. For example, we may look at a friend from a number of different angles, close up and far away, in bright light or in dim light, and still recognize him or her as the same person under all these different conditions. In the same way, Apollo 13 astronauts depended on constancy as they circled the moon. They identified important land formations even though they saw them under continually changing conditions. This seems simple enough, but there really is nothing simple about it—in fact, scientists still do not understand how it is done. How can perceptions remain constant when optical information changes? Let's look at what scientists have discovered about size, shape, and other perceptual constancies.

Size Constancies

Look at the twins in Figure 4–5. The twin on the right was 4 feet away when the picture was taken, and the one on the left was 8 feet away. Their picture illustrates the **law of size constancy,** which states that we see an object's size as constant even if the object's distance from us changes.

Figure 4–6 explains how **retinal image** sizes change. Light reflects off the twins into the observer's eye. The critical light rays for this discussion are those coming from the feet and the top of the head. They are represented by two lines that cross over inside the eye's lens. The angle between these lines is called the **visual angle.** This angle gets smaller as an object moves farther away. When the visual angle gets smaller, the retinal image also gets smaller. Thus, the closer twin's visual angle is twice as big, and her retinal image is twice as big as the farther twin.

So why do we perceive the twins as being the same size? Scientists don't really know. We might suppose that the perceived size remains constant because we *know* the approximate true size. (For example, we know the twins in Figure 4–5 are the same size.) However, this explanation can be ruled out for two reasons. First, size would be perceived as constant even if unfamiliar objects were seen in place of the twins. Second, if a picture contains misleading information about distance, we will be fooled, even if we know the true size of the objects. For example, the Ames Room (see Figure 4–7A) is designed to provide misleading information about distance. As can be seen in the diagram in Figure 4–7B, the left corner of the room is actually much farther away from the right corner, yet the

Law of size constancy
Law stating that we see an object's size as constant even if the object's distance from us changes.
Retinal image
The image that the object projects on to the back wall of the eye.
Visual angle
Angle between lines formed by the top and bottom of an object one is looking at. The visual angle gets smaller as an object moves farther away, which means that the retinal image of the object also gets smaller.

FIGURE 4–5

The identical twins, Evangeline and Jacqueline Motely, look the same size in this picture, even though the image of the farther one is only half as large as that of the closer one. This illustrates the law of size constancy.

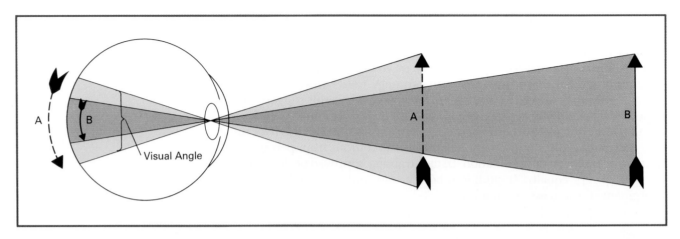

FIGURE 4–6

Retinal image size is determined by the visual angle, which is defined at the eye's lens by the angle between light rays coming from the top and bottom of an object. As an object gets closer, its visual angle and its retinal image size get larger.

Unconscious inference theory
Size constancy occurs because we unconsciously make accurate inferences about object size when we have accurate information about retinal image size and object distance.

corners of Figure 4–7A appear equally far away. People in the far corner of an Ames Room look like dwarfs, while those in the close corner look like giants. Obviously, seeing objects of familiar sizes does not guarantee accurate size perception. The Ames Room was designed to be viewed with one eye looking through a peephole. Size distortions are indeed greater under the intended viewing conditions. But they are still present when the room is viewed with both eyes and with the head moving (Gehringer & Engel, 1986).

There are two opposing theories of size constancy: the unconscious inference theory (Epstein, 1973; Rock, 1977), and the ecological theory (Gibson, 1979). **Unconscious inference theory** states that we unconsciously make accurate inferences about object size when we have accurate information about retinal image size and object distance. It follows that perceived size should be consistent with perceived distance. In the Ames Room we see distorted sizes *because* we see distorted distances. Specifically, the person on the left has a smaller image and she looks just as close as the person on the right; therefore we unconsciously infer that she is smaller.

FIGURE 4–7A

The Ames Room, shown here, distorts the apparent size of the woman. Your eye is fooled in this picture because the room looks square, but actually is not. The diagram illustrates the actual shape of the room, which causes the woman to seem to be a different size.

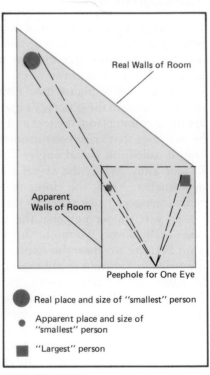

FIGURE 4–7B

In contrast, the **ecological theory** states that we see a constant size because we see some aspect of the visual scene that remains unchanged when distance changes. For example, the twins are the same size with respect to the walls near both of them. If we respond to such relationships, we would be fooled by Ames's trick room because basic relationships are distorted. Notice, for example, the size of the people with respect to the sizes of the windows. Accordingly, the trick room misleads us by distorting relationships that are critical for constancy.

Other Constancies

The issues raised about size perception also apply to other constancies. The **law of shape constancy** states that we see an object's shape as constant when the object's slant changes, or when we view it from a different angle. Figure 4–8 shows how this might occur. In the view from the top (A), the checkers are round and the board is square; in the side view (B), the checkers are shaped like footballs and the board's side edges are shorter. Because of shape constancy, however, the checkers look round and the board looks square in both views.

Unconscious inference theory says that we unconsciously infer the correct shapes when we see the correct slants (Morgan, 1989). Ecological theory states that we see a constant shape because we see some aspect of the visual scene that stays the same when the slant changes. For example, the same number of squares run along the left and right edges of the checkerboard whether it is slanted or not.

The **law of brightness constancy** states that we perceive an object's brightness as constant even when the amount of light striking it changes. For example, you see the ink on this page as black and the paper as white in dim light or in bright light. The ink reflects about 5 percent of the light that strikes it; the paper reflects about 80 percent. Thus when 100 units of light strike the page, the ink reflects 5 units and the paper reflects 80 units. When 10,000 units of light strike the page, the ink reflects

Ecological theory
Size constancy occurs because we see some aspect of the visual scene that remains unchanged when distance changes.
Law of shape constancy
Law stating that we see an object's shape as constant when the object's slant changes, or when we view it from a different angle.
Law of brightness constancy
Law stating that we see an object's brightness as constant when the amount of light striking it changes.

A   B

FIGURE 4–8
The photograph on the right here shows a very different view of the same checkerboard shown on the left, but, because of shape constancy, the checkers are perceived as round and the board as square in both photographs.

500 units and the paper reflects 8,000 units. Hans Wallach (1948) showed that the appearance of black and white remains constant because our perceptual system responds to the *ratio* of the light from an object divided by the light from what surrounds it. In our example, this ratio is the same in dim light, 5/80 = .0625, and bright light, 500/8,000 = .0625. Recent research by Burkhardt, Gottesmann, Kersten, and Legge (1984) has shown that perceptual responses to such fixed ratios remains constant over a wide range of background illumination. Furthermore, this constancy holds when a dark object is viewed against a light background (e.g., black letters on a white page) or when light objects are viewed against a dark background (e.g., car headlights at night).

How do our two theories explain this? The ecological theory says that we perceive a constant because some aspect of the visual scene remains constant. In this case, the ratio of light reflected remains constant, even though the light itself may change (Heinemann, 1989). Unconscious inference theorists, however, argue that the assumptions we make unconsciously must also play a role (Gilchrist, 1975, 1988; Gilchrist & Jacobsen, 1989). They note that changes in brightness do not always affect objects and backgrounds equally. When the sun comes out from behind a cloud, for instance, more light might shine on the ground than on a tree. We take into account such differences in lighting, according to unconscious inference theory.

Binocular disparity
Experience of seeing a different view from each of our eyes; two views are fused by the brain and produce depth perception.

Depth Perception

FIGURE 4–9

Can you trust your eyes to distinguish craters from hills in the area indicated on this photograph? Turn the book upside down and try again. Many people see a depth reversal in the two ways of looking at the photo. That is, they see hills where they had seen craters, and vice versa.

As Lovell, Swigart, and Haise rounded the back side of the moon, they were presented with a breathtaking sight. For them this was the most important part of their flight. It gave them a chance to bring back scientific data that would, in some minds, justify the expense of the mission. In order to recognize the hills and craters they were looking for, the astronauts had to be able to see the relative depth between the tops and bottoms of the land formations. Figure 4–9 shows how difficult this can be. At first glance, the craters and hills are readily distinguishable. But turn the book upside down and look again. Now what you had identified as craters are seen as hills, and vice versa. This depth reversal is related to cues provided by shadows. Although shadows have a powerful effect on depth perception, they are by no means the only source of depth information available to us.

We will discuss three kinds of depth information in this section: binocular, monocular, and kinetic. Binocular information is available through the use of both eyes. Monocular information is available even when we use only one eye. And kinetic information is available only when we move or when the environment moves.

Seeing Depth with Two Eyes

Because our eyes are separated by several centimeters, we get a different view of the world from each eye. This difference is called **binocular disparity.** You can see disparity for yourself by closing one eye while holding your right index finger about 12 inches in front of your nose, and your left index finger about 6 inches in front of your nose. Look at the far finger first with one eye and then the other. Your near finger will appear to be in different places as you look with each eye. Now look with both eyes—you will see a double image of the near finger.

When you look at distant objects, binocular disparity (the different view from each eye) is so small that you usually are not aware of it (see

Figure 4–10). Even though you see a single image, however, you notice the disparity at an unconscious level. When disparity is very large, people see double images. When disparity is small, the brain fuses or integrates the images, using the disparity as a source of information about depth. The brain can use even small disparities as a depth cue. In fact, most of us are very sensitive to disparity, and we use it to help us see depth (Stevenson, Cormack, & Schor, 1989).

Our ability to use binocular disparity to see depth is the basis for the popular View Masters that many of us played with as children (see the early model in Figure 4–11). A View Master is a stereoscope, an optical instrument that presents different images to the two eyes simultaneously. The appearance of depth in a stereoscope is created when the two images are pictures of three-dimensional objects. The pictures are taken by two cameras that are separated by about the same distance as the eyes. Thus, a stereoscope can expose you to the same binocular disparity that you would have seen if you had looked directly at the objects. That's how three-dimensional images are created in View Masters. Most of us enjoy this optical trick when the images are of spectacular scenery, such as the Matterhorn, or of our favorite cartoon character.

In addition to this entertaining application, stereoscopes have other important applications. They are used in clinics to identify people who are stereoblind, people who cannot use binocular disparity to see depth. About 2 percent of the population falls into this category. These people see depth because there are many other sources of information about depth, as we will see in the next section. Stereoblind people fail to see depth in clinical stereoscopes because these instruments control all other information about depth. This means that these people would not enjoy the optical trick of a View Master. But they would see depth quite well if they saw the real Matterhorn or other three-dimensional objects directly.

Stereoscopes also have important applications in the laboratory. They enable experimenters to control all other sources of information and to manipulate binocular disparity. Julesz (1971) introduced special computer-generated images for stereoscopes. His images are called random dot stereograms. They have two properties: (1) They are seen as random dots when they are viewed one at a time. (2) They are seen as three-dimensional objects when they are viewed in a stereoscope. A typical three-dimensional image might be a small square that appears to float in front of a larger square. These special displays have become powerful research tools for studying depth perception in humans and animals (Papathomas & Julesz, 1989). In one experiment, McFadden and Wild (1986) built a stereoscope for pigeons. They then trained the birds to peck at circles that were defined only by disparity in a random dot stereogram. They concluded that pigeons can use binocular disparity information.

Seeing Depth with One Eye

You can get a feeling for monocular depth cues by looking around with your hand over one eye. You can still see depth, but you are using different cues than you would be if you were using both eyes. **Monocular cues** are used not only to see depth (the relative distance between objects), but also to see how far away objects are from you. A number of the most common monocular cues are shown in Figure 4–12: clearness, linear perspective, and texture gradients.

One monocular cue is *clearness*. We look at objects on earth through air filled with tiny particles, which causes far objects to look blurry. This cue wouldn't have helped the astronauts on the moon, however, because in that environment there is no air or suspended particles. As a result, far objects look as sharp as near ones on the moon.

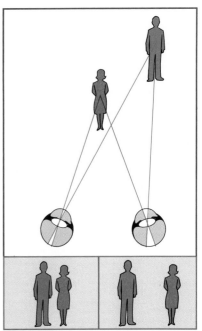

Left Eye View   Right Eye View

FIGURE 4–10

The left eye view of the man and woman is different from the right eye view. The brain uses this difference or disparity as a depth cue, in this case an indication of how far away these people are from the viewer.

Monocular cues
Cues to depth perception that operate even when only one eye is used.

FIGURE 4–11

Two young ladies viewing pictures in a stereoscope. This photograph was taken around the turn of this century when stereoscopes were a popular form of entertainment.

A

B

C

FIGURE 4–12

Monocular cues: (A) clearness, (B) linear perspective, and (C) texture gradient.

Linear perspective
Monocular cue to depth; artists use it to create the impression of depth in their paintings.
Texture gradient
Monocular cue to depth. As we look at something with texture, the nearer elements are spaced farther apart than the more distant elements.

One of the most important monocular cues is **linear perspective.** Artists use linear perspective to create the impression of depth in their paintings. Notice in Figure 4–12B, for example, how rows of crops seem to converge or come together in the distance. We often use linear perspective unconsciously to see depth in our environment.

Generally linear perspective is used in close conjunction with *texture*. Some surfaces, such as plastics and metals, have very little texture—their surfaces are smooth. But most surfaces have noticeable elements, or texture; for example, carpets, lawns, and foliage have texture, and certainly the moon's surface has texture. As we look at something with texture, the nearer elements are spaced farther apart than the more distant elements, forming what is known as a **texture gradient.** A natural example of texture gradient is shown with the field of flowers in Figure 4–12C.

Yonas, Grandud, Arterberry, and Hanson (1986) tested 5- and 7-month-old infants' ability to discriminate depth with monocular viewing. Previous results had shown that both groups can coordinate reaching with perceived distance (see Chapter 9). The question was whether or not they can do it when distance is indicated by monocular information. Their results suggest that infants are between 5 and 7 months old when they develop the ability to see depth by means of linear perspective and texture gradients. The infants viewed two objects that were placed at equal distances from them. However, these objects were presented in a display that contained false information about linear perspective and texture gradients. To an adult

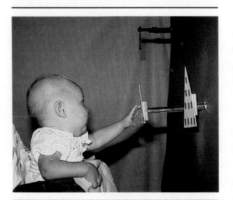

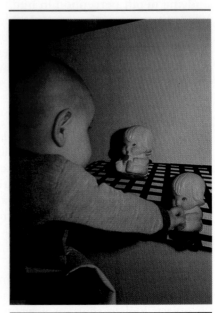

FIGURE 4–13

These two babies are taking part in experiments in depth perception. As the text explains, such experiments have suggested that infants are between 5 and 7 months old when they develop the ability to see depth by means of linear perspective and texture gradients.

observer viewing with one eye, this false information made the two objects appear to be at different distances. Seven-month-old infants showed similar results. Under monocular conditions, they seemed to respond to linear perspective and texture gradients. Specifically, they preferred to reach for the object that was made to look closer. These results suggest that 7-month olds are able to use linear perspective and texture gradients under monocular viewing conditions. In contrast, 5-month olds showed no reaching preference under monocular conditions. These results suggest that 5-month olds do not have the ability to use linear perspective and the texture gradients to see depth under monocular viewing conditions. Apparently, this ability develops between 5 and 7 months.

Seeing Depth through Motion

As the astronauts flew over the moon, their viewpoint changed continuously, giving them a powerful source of depth information. This information is called **motion parallax,** which is the apparent pattern of object motion that is seen when an observer travels past those objects. You see motion parallax, for instance, when you look out the side window of a moving vehicle. As illustrated in Figure 4–14, objects at different distances from the vehicle appear to move in different directions and at different speeds. The brain uses motion parallax as information about depth (Braunstein & Andersen, 1981; Cornilleau-Peres & Droulez, 1989).

The brain also gets information about depth when objects move (Braunstein & Andersen, 1984). This source of information is indicated by the **kinetic depth effect,** which is apparent depth that depends upon object motion. Figure 4–15 shows how you can demonstrate the kinetic depth

FIGURE 4–14

When the observer is moving, in this case a passenger riding a train, objects at different distances will appear to move at different speeds. (Speed is represented by the varying lengths of the arrows.) Further, the objects will appear to be moving in different directions depending on whether they are in front of or beyond the fixation point of your eye.

FIGURE 4–15

Kinetic Depth Effect

Bend a paper clip so that it looks like a three-dimensional figure. If you hold the clip between a piece of white paper and a lamp the shadow it casts will appear flat. If you rotate the clip in your hand, the shadow it casts will appear to be three-dimensional.

Motion parallax
Apparent motion seen when an observer moves past objects.
Kinetic depth effect
Detection of depth through movement.
Illusions
Perceptual distortions.

effect. Bend a paper clip into a three-dimensional figure. Then cast a shadow with the paper clip by holding it between a lamp and a piece of paper. You will see the shadow as flat if you hold the paper clip still. In contrast, you will see the kinetic depth effect if you rotate the clip. When the clip begins to rotate, the shadow will appear to spring into the appearance of a three-dimensional figure. This demonstration illustrates that the movement of objects provides information about depth. James Gibson and Hans Wallach were pioneers in the study of motion and depth (Gibson, 1957; Wallach & O'Connell, 1953).

Visual Illusions

The human sensory and perceptual abilities are reliable enough to bring astronauts back from the moon, but they are far from perfect. They are, in fact, very undependable in some situations. An example of this is **illusions,** which are perceptual distortions. Illusions not only endanger astronauts (Christensen & Talbot, 1986), they also threaten airplane pilots. Kraft and Elworth (1969) found evidence, for example, that visual illusions cause about 16 percent of all airplane accidents.

Boeing officials had sought scientific help after four Boeing 727s crashed within a 4-month period, without any apparent mechanical cause. Dr. Conrad Kraft, chief scientist for the Personnel Subsystem of Boeing's Commercial Aircraft Division, combined a thorough knowledge of aviation with the data and methods of experimental psychology. In their experiments Kraft and Elworth built a device to simulate night visual approaches. The simulator included a stationary cockpit and a model airport that moved in response to the cockpit controls. The device simulated distances from 34 to 4.5 miles and altitudes from 16,000 feet to *minus* 2,500 feet. Kraft asked 12 experienced pilots to make simulated visual approaches. The simulator reproduced the visual conditions faced by the pilots who had crashed in the four Boeing 727s. Had the simulated flights been real, all but one of the 12 pilots tested would have crashed short of the runway. The one successful pilot was an ex-Navy pilot who had gained his early experience landing on aircraft carriers. Kraft did not explain exactly what kind of illusion caused the others to "crash," but he did explain how the angle of approach distorted important visual information, increasing the pilots' susceptibility to visual illusions.

Psychologists studied visual illusions long before they knew that these could bring down an airplane. Let's look at some of their findings.

Geometrical Illusions

The illusions shown in Figure 4–16 are line drawings that produce perceptual errors. Look at them and then measure them. In contrast to what the drawings look like, your ruler will tell you the following: the two horizontal lines are the same length in both the Müller-Lyer illusion and the Ponzo illusion; the oblique lines are parallel in the Zollner illusion; and the inner circles are the same size in the Titchener illusion. Scientists have studied such illusions for 100 years in an attempt to gain a better understanding of perception (Gillam, 1980). In one important experiment Schiller and Wiener (1962) found that illusions are almost full strength when their parts are presented to each eye separately, indicating that the distortions are in the brain and not in the eye. Coren (1986) reviewed other studies suggesting that these illusions influence eye movements as well as percep-

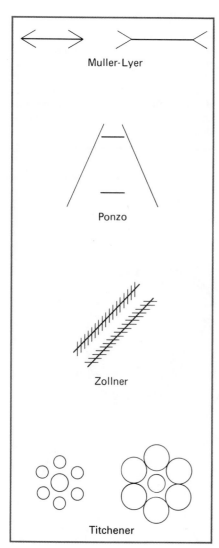

FIGURE 4–16

These drawings show several geometrical illusions, which cause a disagreement between what you see and what you can measure with a ruler.

tion. Consider, for instance, what happens when people move their eyes across the Müller-Lyer illusion. They make shorter eye movements in the "wings-in" version than they do in the "wings-out" version. This eye movement pattern corresponds to the fact that people see the "wings-out" line as being longer. More work remains to be done in this area. For example, we still are not sure whether or not there is a causal link between eye movements and illusions. Psychologists study illusions in the hope of better understanding the perceptual system. Whether or not illusions fulfill this hope, they do teach an important lesson. Those who maintain that "seeing is believing" are putting their eggs in the wrong basket. Sometimes "seeing is deceiving" (Coren & Girgus, 1978).

UFOs and Illusions: The Autokinetic Effect

The **autokinetic effect** is the tendency for a stationary light viewed against darkness to look as if it's moving. The light seems to glide, jerk, and swoop through space. The autokinetic effect could be responsible for some reports of unidentified flying objects (UFOs). Word spreads fast about UFO sightings, causing people's imaginations to run wild. This could set the stage for the autokinetic swooping of some distant house light to become a UFO in the mind of some well-intentioned witness (Geldard, 1972).

The autokinetic effect is extremely dangerous for aviators. Planes flying in formation at night have collided because pilots saw autokinetic movement of another plane's wing light. Pilots have also crashed while trying to fly next to what appeared to be another plane but that turned out to be a streetlight or marker buoy.

You can demonstrate the autokinetic effect by setting a dim penlight on a table edge in an otherwise dark room. This demonstration is fun, especially in a group. If each of you draws the motion path you see, without talking about it, you will all draw different paths. If one of you reports the light's apparent motion out loud, though, most of the rest of the group will tend to see the same path (Sherif, 1936). This shows the power of suggestion and group pressure on the illusion, which we will discuss in more detail in Chapter 17.

Psychologists have debated the cause of the autokinetic effect for over 100 years. The most popular explanation is that eye movements somehow cause the illusion. When we look at a light, our eyes seem motionless, but they actually move about randomly over a tiny area. As a result, the image of the light moves slightly over the retina. Matin and MacKinnon (1964) tested for the autokinetic effect when these small image movements were stopped by a special device. This device greatly reduced the autokinetic effect, suggesting that eye movements do play a part in the illusion. It has been suggested that eye movements produce autokinetic motion of a light because the brain fails to keep track of eye movements unless the light has a fixed relationship to other objects (Worchel & Burnham, 1967). A more conservative version of this hypothesis is that the brain makes more errors in registering eye movements when a light is viewed without a patterned background (Westall & Aslin, 1984).

Psychologists have also attempted to find practical ways to reduce the autokinetic effect. One way is to replace single lights with a cluster of several lights (Royce, Stayton, & Kinkade, 1962). Another way is to add a contour in peripheral vision (MacDuffee, Shupert, & Leibowitz, 1988). A third way is to have the light source flash or blink. A group of researchers showed that autokinetic motion is greatly reduced for lights flashing between 4 and 10 times per second (Page, Elfner, & Jarnison, 1966). No one completely understands why all of this works, but the results have practical value. Today lights on towers and aircraft blink, saving many pilots who would otherwise have fallen victim to the autokinetic illusion.

Autokinetic effect
Tendency for a stationary light viewed against darkness to look as if it is moving; the light seems to glide, jerk, and swoop through space.

PERCEPTION OF ART

Illusions underlie a 20th-century art movement called Op (for optical illusion). Arnold Schmidt, for example, created an optical illusion of pulsing light in his untitled 1965 painting shown here. Op art emphasizes that observers participate in determining what is seen. Bridget Riley provides an example in her work, "Tremor." At first, the painting looks like a slightly modified checkerboard hardly worth a second glance. But look again. You will see the elements merge to form large overlapping triangles; you will see small circles around pinwheels; you will see a grate slanted backward in depth. Once you see the grate, you will see it change its orientation. How did Bridget Riley get so much mileage from one painting? She provided us with ambiguous information and let our minds do the rest.

Another master of the kind of art that appears to change before our eyes was Maurits C. Escher, a Dutch artist. In "Fish and Fowl," for instance, we see a school of fish at one moment and a flock of birds the next. When the fish are in view, the birds lose their identity as they merge into the background. When the birds are in view, the fish merge into the background. Escher's prints were deliberately created to exemplify principles of Gestalt psychology. They illustrate that we contribute to our perceptions.

More recent examples of this can be found in the art of Bev Doolittle, a contemporary California artist who created "The Forest Has Eyes," shown on the next page. She comments, "I want to change the experience of seeing . . . to have people think when they look at my paintings. . . . When I design a painting I try to guide the viewer's eye to points within the picture that best communicate my story. The sequence in which the viewer discovers elements in a painting is planned. It is my hope that most people will experience the painting to its best possible level."

It might seem less obvious, but you are imposing organization right now, as you are reading. You also do so when you listen to someone speak, as explained in the text.

Arnold Schmidt. *Untitled* 1965. Synthetic polymer paint on canvas 4'⅛" × 8'⅛". Collection, The Museum of Modern Art, New York. Gift of Mr. and Mrs. Herbert Bernard.

Bridget Riley, "Tremor." 1962. 48 × 48".

M. C. Escher Heirs c/o Cordon Art-Baarn-Holland.

A solitary mountain man guides his mount through the shallows of a stream. Leading a pack horse, he enters the territory of hostile Indians. A feeling of apprehension, a sense of foreboding, sweep over him.

I want the viewer to share the emotions of the rider, and like him, be able to study the detail of each leaf and every branch that surrounds him. Soon, it may become apparent that the forest has eyes, and the eyes have faces.

The Forest Has Eyes, by Bev Doolittle. A limited edition print. © The Greenwich Workshop, Inc., Trumbull, CT 06611.

Illusions are caused in part by the tendency to impose organization on sensory information (see Highlight: "Perception of Art"). This tendency, which can be disastrous for pilots, can also play a highly beneficial role. For example, the astronauts' ability to understand commands from mission control depended heavily on their active organizational processes. These processes are called **active synthesizing processes.** To synthesize means to combine diverse parts to form a unified whole. The unified whole for the active synthesizing processes is perception, which is constructed out of bits of sensory and memory information. These processes play an important role in speech perception by (1) compensating for distorted speech production, (2) opening gaps where they should be, or (3) closing gaps where they should not be.

Compensation for Distorted Speech

Active synthesizing processes compensate for errors in speech production. This function is critical because slight errors in production produce major distortions of sound waves. To appreciate this function, let's consider how a speaker's actions affect speech sounds (Wilde, 1975).

Speech organs produce speech sounds as shown in Figure 4–17. The **lungs** are the source of energy for the production of sounds. This energy is a stream of breath that creates sound by vibrating **vocal cords** in the throat. The role of vocal cords in speech is similar to that of strings on a guitar. We continually change the tension on our vocal cords to alter the pitch of our voice, as when we sing low notes and high notes (see Chapter

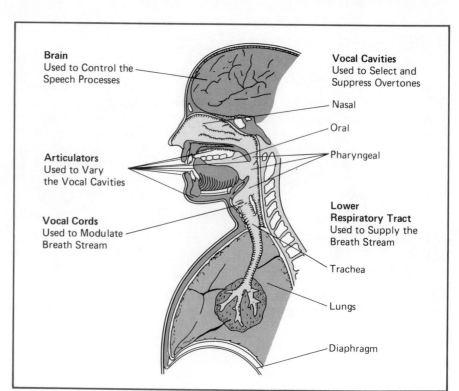

Active synthesizing processes
Mental operations that impose organization on sensory information.
Lungs
Organs of respiration lying within the chest cavity. Supply the blood with oxygen and are the source of energy for the production of speech sounds.
Vocal cords
Membranes in the throat that vibrate to make sounds during speaking.

FIGURE 4–17

Shown here are the organs of the body used to produce speech. (From Potter et al., 1966)

3). The pitch is low for low tension and high for high tension. We modify sound from the vibrating vocal cords with the **pharynx, oral cavity,** and **nasal cavity.** These structures function as resonance chambers, like the inner cavity of a guitar. Unlike the guitar, though, speech resonance chambers can be altered by the process of **articulation.** We articulate vowels, for example, by changing the location of the highest part of our tongue. The highest part can be in the front, center, or back as in saying the vowels in "eve," "up," and "boot."

Visible representations of speech are called **sound spectrograms** (see Figure 4–18). The horizontal axis represents time. The vertical axis represents the frequency of the sound wave in number of cycles per second (which is referred to as number of "hertz," abbreviated Hz; see Chapter 3). The shade of darkness of the spectrogram lines represents the intensity of the sound. Notice the dramatic difference between the spectrograms in comparison to the relatively slight difference in the articulatory movements required to produce these vowels. Similarly, when we make slight errors of articulation, we produce major changes in the sound waves.

The quality of computer-generated speech has been improving, thanks to studies of articulation and speech sound. Modern techniques generate artificial speech for female voices that are difficult to distinguish from the real thing (Klatt & Klatt, 1990).

Cole (1973) supported the idea that we use contextual information to compensate for poor articulation. Subjects listened to a passage read from Lewis Carroll's *Through the Looking Glass* and were instructed to push a button whenever they heard a mispronunciation. One mispronunciation was "gunfusion" for "confusion." Only 30 percent of the subjects noticed. In another group all heard the same mispronounced syllable clearly when it was presented out of context. We cannot be sure that the subjects actually *heard* "confusion" instead of "gunfusion," but the results suggest that we use contextual information to compensate for mispronunciations. Middelweend, Festen, and Plomp (1990) argue that clinical diagnoses of hearing can be improved by testing the accuracy of speech perception.

Opening Gaps. Active synthesizing processes also cause us to hear gaps between words when no gap exists in the speech sound. Figure 4–18 shows a sound spectrogram for the utterance "speech we may see." Notice that no gap exists in the sound between the words "we" and "may." In fact, the sound was quite intense at several frequencies during the entire interval between .7 and .8 seconds. Yet if we were to listen to a tape of the very same speech sounds that produced the spectrogram, we would "hear" a gap between the words "we" and "may." Someone who did not understand English, however, would not hear the gap. Active synthesizing processes use our knowledge of language to construct perception of discrete words even when no break between words exists in the speech sound.

Pharynx
Open space inside the throat.
Oral cavity
Open space inside the mouth.
Nasal cavity
Open space inside the nose.
Articulation
Process of altering the shape of the pharynx, oral cavity, and nasal cavity in order to change speech sounds.
Sound spectrograms
Visible representation of speech.

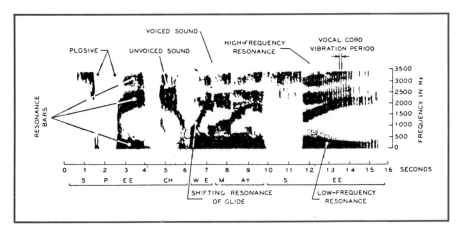

FIGURE 4–18

Sound spectrogram of the words *Speech we may see*. The panel was produced with a wide-band analyzing filter (300 Hz) to emphasize vocal resonances.

Filling Gaps.   Often when we listen to someone talk other sounds drown out parts of the conversation. For example, at a dinner party clinking glasses, loud laughs, and our own munching might muffle parts of our conversation. Warren (1970) demonstrated our incredible ability to fill in such gaps. In their experiments they used doctored tape-recorded messages. The original tape said "the state governors met with their respective legislatures convening in the capital city." The doctored tapes omitted the syllable "gis" in "legislatures" and replaced it with a cough, buzz, or tone of the same duration. When people listened to the modified tapes, they heard the missing "gis" as clearly as if it were actually on tape. The important thing here is that people actually *heard* the missing sound. Recent results suggest that this filling-in effect persists even when people receive extensive training on the location of the missing sounds (Samuel & Ressler, 1986).

This effect must be experienced to be appreciated. You can make your own tapes for this purpose. Practice saying something like "Roses are red, violets are blue, sugar is sweet, and so are you." Have an assistant cough at the moment you are saying the *v* in "violets" so that the sound of the letter is not heard on the tape. Not only will others listening to the tape hear the *v*, but you will probably hear it too even though you *know* it is not there. How can this happen? The content of the well-known verse creates an expectation for the word "violets." Active synthesizing processes act on the basis of this expectation to manufacture the missing sound. To be sure it's not there, you might want to say "iolets" instead of "violets"; you will still hear the *v*.

Our active synthesizing processes use every bit of information they can get. For instance, Massaro and Cohen (1990) combined synthetic audible and visible speech. They found that the visible speech influenced what college students heard.

We can be reasonably sure that the astronauts' active synthesizing processes played an important role in their perception of verbal messages from mission control. They also played a role in reading written messages, as we will see in the next section.

Reading

Two characteristics of vision combine to make active synthesizing processes important in reading: (1) We have a narrow range of clear vision; and (2) we move our eyes in a special way to compensate for this narrow range.

The first characteristic was illustrated by an incident during the flight of Apollo 13. A mission controller missed a sudden change in oxygen pressure readings because he was looking 3 inches to the right of the critical numbers. You will immediately see the reason for this failure if you try to identify letters that are about 45 letter positions to the right of where you are looking in this text. It's impossible because we see clearly only a short distance from where we are looking at any given moment. Bouma (1973) showed, for example, that when people look at a letter in an unpronounceable letter string, they recognize all other letters that are within about 1 or 2 letter positions. But they recognize only 75 percent of the letters that are 3 or 4 positions away, and only 50 percent of the letters that are 5 or 6 positions away. Other researchers found that the time needed to recognize letters increases when letters are viewed in peripheral vision (Jacobs, Nazir, & Keller, 1988).

We compensate for this narrow range of clear vision with eye movements. When we read, our eyes jerk from one fixation point to the next in a series of eye movements called **saccades** (Underwood, Clews, and Everett,

Saccades
Eye movements from one fixation point to the next as we read.

SPEED READING—SAVE TIME AND MONEY

This highlight can save you thousands of hours and hundreds of dollars. You can save the time by pushing your reading speed to the upper limit for actual reading of about 500 to 600 words per minute or by learning to skim at even faster rates (Hochberg, 1970). This increase will yield a substantial time saving if you are now reading at 250 to 300 words per minute, which is the average rate for college students. You can save money because you can increase your reading speed without taking courses that often cost hundreds of dollars. We have taught many students to double their reading rate by using the procedures outlined in this highlight. You will have more confidence in these procedures if you first understand why they work.

Why It Works

The key to faster reading is putting your active synthesizing processes to work for you. These processes reduce the amount of visual information you use to read because they take advantage of information from memory. They use three kinds of information from memory:

1. *Orthographic* information about how letters are combined in words
2. *Syntactic* information about how words are combined in sentences
3. *Semantic* information about the meaning of the passage.

To illustrate, suppose we see all the visual information in the following sentence except for that in the two underlined positions: "Poncho hit the I __ II." In the first underlined position, the tall vertical line indicates that the letter is a consonant. In the second underlined position, we see no visual information. In this situation, orthographic rules would provide a great deal of information. Since three of the four letters are consonants, we know the unidentified letter in the second position must be a vowel. Orthographic information thereby reduces the possible alternatives from 26 to 6. Syntactic rules also provide information. They dictate that the unidentified word must be a noun, eliminating possibilities such as *fill*, *full*, *tall*, and *tell*. In this limited context, the meaning of the sentence (semantics) provides little useful information. Poncho could have hit just about anything: a *ball*, *bell*, *bull*, *bill*, or *till*. In a richer context, semantics could help a great deal. For example, you will probably have no trouble reducing the choices to a single word in the following sentences:

To save his friend from being gored, Poncho hit the I __ II with a well-aimed rock.

With bases loaded in the bottom of the ninth, Poncho hit the I __ II out of the park.

This sample merely illustrates the meaning of the three kinds of information; it does not show how the sentence might actually be recognized. All the sources of information might be used simultaneously, or in a different order than suggested here.

The Procedure

Doing the following exercise for 15 minutes every day for a semester should activate your synthesizing processes and increase your speed. First, turn off your television. Reading with it on will lower your reading comprehension (Armstrong & Greenberg, 1990). Set a timer for 3 minutes and read at your normal speed from a section of a newspaper or magazine. When the timer sounds, stop reading and count the number of lines you've read. Multiply this by 1.20 to get the number of lines you should try to read in the next 3-minute period. The goal number of lines will be 20 percent more than you read the first time; therefore, you will have to read 20 percent faster than you normally read. It may take a little practice to reach your goal in 3 minutes but force yourself to read faster until you accomplish it. The required reading speed will be uncomfortable until your active synthesizing processes improve to meet the challenge. When you first speed up, you will not recognize all the words or understand everything you read. After your active synthesizing processes are adjusted to utilize contextual information efficiently, you will be able to read faster with no loss of comprehension. Do not expect to comprehend words that you do not "see."

The Results

Once your active synthesizing processes are working to their full capacity, you will not process all the visual information, but you will "see" all the words because the processes actually construct perceptions. As soon as you become comfortable at a speed, increase your speed by another 20 percent. Continue increasing speed until you reach about 500 words per minute. We hope that many of you will enjoy reading your assignment in half the time that it is now taking you. We also hope that faster reading will lead to higher grades. Studying involves much more than reading. Faster reading can raise your grades, however, by allowing more time for other important study processes (see Chapter 1 Highlight: "Learning from Textbooks is a Three-Letter Word").

1990). You can easily detect saccades by watching someone's eyes while that person is reading. These jerky eye movements create gaps in sensory input because the eyes are functionally blind during the saccadic movements. Active synthesizing processes fill in these gaps so well that you may have trouble believing they are there at all. To convince yourself, try the following experiment (see Shebilske, 1977; Woodworth, 1938):

FIGURE 4–19

This experiment, described in detail in the text, illustrates the fact that our eye movements or saccades create gaps in sensory input. We're not usually aware of these gaps because of our active synthesizing processes.

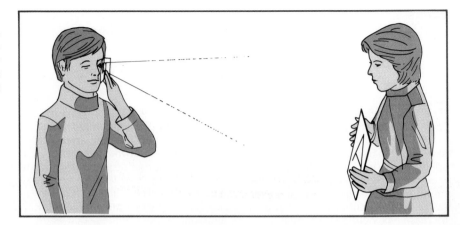

Fold a 5-by-5-inch card in half and cut a narrow slit out of the center of the fold. Open the card part way to form a wedge. Close one eye and hold the slit close to your other eye by resting it on your face. With the slit this close to your eye, you will be able to see through it when you look straight ahead, but not when you hold your gaze off to the left or right. When you move your eye from one side to the other, your line of sight is momentarily directed through the slit. If you can see while your eye is moving, you should be able to see through the slit as your line of sight goes past it. To find out, have an assistant hold up a large letter that you can easily identify when looking through the slit (see Figure 4–19). Hold your direction of gaze off to one side (at this point you should not be able to see the letter because of the wedge). Have your assistant hold up a different large letter. Now move your eye in a single movement to the other side. Can you identify the letter? Most people cannot even see the assistant, let alone the letter. If you see the letter, have your assistant watch your eyes. You are probably stopping briefly to look through the slit.

If you do this experiment correctly, it should convince you that saccades create gaps in the sensory input. McConkie (1978) conducted an experiment that might remove any remaining doubts. He used a computer to show text to people only during their saccadic eye movements. When the eyes fixated between saccades, all the letters were replaced by *X*'s. Under this condition, people could not read the text, which suggests that we are functionally blind during saccadic movements. We fill in these blind intervals just as we fill in missing speech sounds during listening.

Active synthesizing processes can also supplement information that is not seen clearly. How much this clarification function of active synthesis is needed depends on how we space fixations. According to Bouma's results, which were reviewed earlier, we see all the visual information clearly if we look at every fourth or fifth letter. For example, if we look at all the underlined letters in this sentence, we see all the letters clearly because they all fall within 1 or 2 letter positions of where we look. If, however, we look at every ninth or tenth letter, we will not see all the letters clearly.

How many letters do you usually look at? Shebilske (1975) suggested that you look at every fourth or fifth letter if you are an average college reader; that is, if you read between 250 and 300 words per minute. If you are a highly skilled college reader, you space your looks much farther apart, sometimes as much as every ninth or tenth letter. You are able to space your fixations farther apart because you allow your active synthesizing processes to supplement the visual information. This allows you to read much faster (see Highlight: "Speed Reading—Save Time and Money").

We often fail to see the mysteries in our ability to read, recognize a familiar grouping of stars, see the correct size, shape, distance, and slant of this book, or understand a lecture. In contrast, scientists realize that these are amazing abilities that are only partially understood. Scientific studies have not only increased our understanding of these abilities but have also yielded practical knowledge. This information has resulted in safer aviation and space travel, spectacular art, and many other applications. One insight gained is that we sometimes create perceptions by imposing organization on information. We will see in the next chapter that an extension of this insight has gone a long way toward explaining the mysteries of dreams during sleep and experiences during other states of consciousness, such as drug-induced states.

Summary

1. **Perception** is the process of interpreting the information that we gather from our environment through the process of sensation. Sensory and perceptual processes are interwoven.

2. In terms of perceptual development, we know that infants see depth and size and they coordinate their movements with what they see, even though their muscle control is poor. Babies also prefer to watch bright colors, faces, and moving objects.

3. We actively impose organization on what we see, according to various rules. The **Gestalt laws of organization** attempt to describe the ways in which we tend to group objects or stimuli according to certain characteristics that they have. Scientists are also beginning to understand the rules according to which we organize perceptions of moving objects.

4. We have perceptual constancies; that is, perceptions remain constant or stable when visual information changes. For instance, apparent size remains constant when we move further from an object, even though movement shrinks the retinal image of the object. **Unconscious inference theory** and **ecological theory** offer opposing explanations of constancies.

5. We respond to many sources of information about depth. **Binocular** information is available through the use of both eyes. **Monocular** information, such as clearness, linear perspective, and texture gradient, is available even when we use only one eye. **Kinetic** information is available when we move or when the environment moves.

6. Sometimes, as is the case with illusions, "seeing is deceiving." In geometric illusions (such as the Muller-Lyer, Ponzo, Zollner, and Titchener illusions) our eyes tell us one thing, but a ruler tells us something different. Other illusions, such as the **autokinetic effect,** are more serious. The study of such illusions is helping to reduce the number of airplane accidents caused by them.

7. In terms of speech perception, **active synthesizing processes** construct perceptions out of sensory and memory information. These processes compensate for distorted speech, open gaps between words, and close gaps created by extraneous noises.

8. We have a narrow range of clear vision that forces us to compensate for this by moving our eyes when we read. Our eyes jerk from one fixation point to the next in a series of eye movements called **saccades.** The eyes are functionally blind during saccades, but we "see" because the gaps are filled by synthesizing processes. These processes also supplement information that is seen clearly, and enable us to read faster.

Key Terms

active synthesizing processes
articulation
autokinetic effect
binocular disparity
ecological theory
figure
figure-ground reversal
Gestalt laws of organization
ground

illusions
kinetic depth effect
law of brightness constancy
law of connectedness
law of enclosure
law of nearness or proximity
law of shape constancy
law of similarity
law of size constancy

linear perspective
lungs
monocular cues
motion parallax
multistable perception
nasal cavity
oral cavity
pharynx
retinal image

saccades
sound spectrograms
texture gradient
unconscious inference theory
visual angle
visual cliff
vocal cords

NEW BREED OF ROBOTS HAVE THE HUMAN TOUCH

DAN GOLEMAN

Engineers are developing machines that they say will fulfill a dream of robotics: devices that can handle situations with the deftness and dexterity of humans in places too dangerous for humans. The machines are being developed for use with toxic waste, in nuclear plants, deep under the ocean, in outer space, by police bomb squads and even on the battlefield.

"The idea is being there without going there," said John D. Merritt, an experimental psychologist and consultant in Williamsburg, Mass., who is a developer of the new approach.

The designers say a person operating one of the new machines wears a helmet that receives visual and auditory signals. These signals give the operator the illusion of being in the machine and seeing and hearing precisely what it sees and hears. At the same time, the machine mimics the operator's every move. The design allows people to direct the machines at a distance with nearly the same precision they bring to tasks immediately at hand, the engineers say.

Strictly speaking, the new machines are not robots. They are called "teleoperators," referring to the fact that their operation is directed by a person at a distance. The perceptual illusion that makes the person experience the sensation of being in the same place as the distant robot is called "telepresence."

While wearing the helmet, an operator looks directly into two tiny television screens that show what the teleoperator is looking at rather than what is actually in front of the person.

"You forget where you are," Mr. Merritt said," You assume you're in the location where the machine is. If in the process you have the robot approach you, you'll see yourself as though you were someone else entirely."

One appeal of teleoperation is that it allows an expert to work in a dangerous setting while staying safe.

Mark Friedman, director of the Human-Machine Interactions Laboratory at the Rototics Institute at Carnegie-Mellon University, said, "There are certain applications where telepresence makes the most sense: where you need high levels of human judgment, inventiveness and precision, but where it's too dangerous to go.

Some of the strongest interest in teleoperators has come from the nuclear industry, where some experts see the devices as the answer to the problems of working with radioactivity.

"Since the operator can be in a safe environment while the robot goes into the dangerous area, the nuclear industry is very interested," said Lee Martin, director of Telerobotics International, in Oak Ridge, Tennessee. "The biggest growth in the use of teleoperators is going to be in nuclear cleanup and waste handling. It will grow even more as we have to dismantle and refurbish plants."

'A Better Way'

"Now many of those tasks are done by people in protective suits who can only enter a radioactive zone a fixed number of times, and then can never go there again," he said. "It's extremely expensive. Telerobotics offer a better way."

Several teleoperation systems are under development in the United States. One of the more advanced ones is at the Naval Ocean Systems Center, a Navy research site in Hawaii. Another will be designed for NASA for use in building and maintaining the planned space station. Projects are also under way in France and Germany; Japan has made teleoperators the focus of an eight-year national project based at Tsukuba Science City, a Government-sponsored research center.

Of the several versions of teleoperators now being developed, the more advanced mimic most precisely the sensory input to the brain.

"The closer you come to duplicating the human experience, the more easily your mind transposes into the zone as though you were there," said John White, president of Remotec, a concern in Oak Ridge.

Teleoperators being designed for use with the space shuttle may make it unnecessary for crew members to do any tasks themselves in space, said John Molino, president of the Tech-U-Fit Corporation in Alexandria, Virginia. "We're now testing six prototype tasks, such as locking in place the modules that will be used to build the space station."

The version being tested has a special glove that duplicates the pressures and forces on the hands of the robot. But the teleoperator need not hear, since there is no sound in space.

Overcoming Tough Problems

Such teleoperators promise to solve several problems that have stymied researchers in robotics. One is that no computer has been able to simulate the workings of the human visual and auditory system, let alone coordinate them with lifelike movement.

Thus robots that rely on computers to direct them have failed at all but the simplest perceptual tasks. Teleoperators get around the problem by having a person, rather than a computer, direct the machine. Another problem solved by the teleoperators is the relative lack of precision in three-dimensional tasks like digging a hole in which a person directs a robot's armature while viewing the task on a television screen.

Even so, the best teleoperators are not yet on par with a person's abilities in the same situation. None, for example, have a sense of smell, and their sense of touch lacks some of the sensitivity and dexterity of the human hand. Further, potential customers complain that commercial units now available lack state-of-the-art sensors.

The most advanced teleoperators use dual video cameras mounted about as far apart as a human's eyes. Each camera sends an image to one eye. That arrangement creates a crispness in depth perception that is lacking from an ordinary television picture.

In tests comparing the speed and dexterity of people using each arrangement, teleoperators were about twice as fast on simple tasks as were people operating the robot arms by watching a television screen, now the most common method. The advantage became greater the more the tasks required spatial cues, like looping a cable through rings.

A New Precision

"Where things are in three-dimensional space comes through poorly on a TV screen," Mr. Merritt said. "But it comes through with precision when you recreate the sensory inputs of someone as though they were there."

The focus in developing teleoperators is to approach ever more closely the exact combination of messages that the human brain normally receives from the senses. In seeking to duplicate the sensation and movements of the person operating the device, researchers have had to make several subtle adjustments.

One was to have the video cameras positioned about four inches ahead of the neck pivot point, simulating the relationship of the eyes to the skull's pivot point around the spine. The teleoperator duplicates the movements of the operator's torso, neck, head and arms. By mimicking human movements, the teleoperators blend cues for movement with those for sounds and sights.

Researchers are now studying the way different senses work together. For instance, they are trying to determine how distance perception is informed by sounds.

"The next generaiton of teleoperators will be based on sensory fusion, the idea that the operator gets complementary data from many senses," said Ralph C. Gonzalez, a professor of electrical and computer engineering at the University of Tennessee, and president of Perceptics, a firm in Oak Ridge.

Mr. Merritt said, "If you don't create a robotic perceptual system that mimics precisely the sensory inputs to the brain, it will make subtle differences that can be disorienting or disturbing to the person operating it. For example, an added-nuance in perception is having the microphones placed not just on the sides of the robot's "head" but also in a simulated ear.

"It's not enough just to have a microphone," he said. "You want to imitate the pattern of acoustic stimulation at the eardrum that your brain experiences as real. Ideally, each person who ran the teleoperator would have their own set of imitation ears, molded to the precise shape of their own, which their brain is used to."

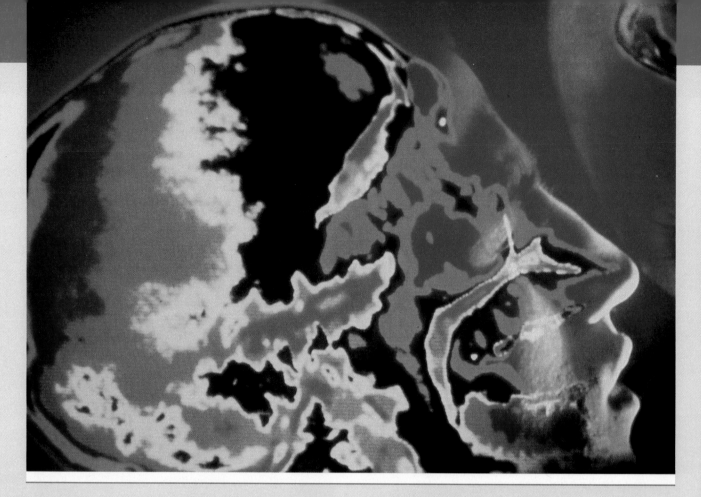

Alternate States of Consciousness

5

P rivate George Ritchie collapsed on December 20, 1943. He was trying to catch a train to take him from Army basic training at Camp Barkeley, Texas, to an Army Specialized Training Program at the Medical College of Virginia in Richmond. Instead, he was taken to a small isolation room where his condition was diagnosed as double lobar pneumonia.

Twenty-four hours later, he sat up in bed with a start. "The train—I must catch the train," he thought. He jumped out of bed and looked for his clothes. Suddenly he froze, realizing that someone was lying in the bed he had just gotten out of. That puzzled him for a moment, but then he decided it was too strange to think about. Besides, he had to hurry. Perhaps the ward boy had his clothes. Running into the hall, he was relieved to find a sergeant coming toward him carrying a cloth-covered instrument tray.

"Excuse me, Sergeant," he said. "You haven't seen the ward boy for this unit, have you?"

The sergeant didn't seem to hear or see him—he kept walking toward Ritchie.

"Look out!" Ritchie yelled, jumping out of the way.

This too was strange, but he had no time to figure it out now. He had his mind on one thing: getting to Richmond.

Before he knew what was happening, he found himself outside of the hospital on his way to Richmond, not traveling by train as originally planned, but speeding over the dark, frozen desert a hundred times faster than any train could carry him. He was flying—not in a plane or any other vehicle—he was just flying. Soon he was beyond the desert, passing over snow-covered wooded areas and an occasional town.

Suddenly he slowed down and found himself hovering about fifty feet over a red-roofed, one-story building. A blue neon "Cafe" sign was over the building's door and a "Pabst Blue Ribbon Beer" sign was propped up in the front window. The next thing he knew, he was on the sidewalk in front of the cafe, walking next to a middle-aged man wearing a topcoat.

"Can you tell me, please, what city this is?" Ritchie asked. Then he shouted, "Please sir! I'm a stranger here and I'd appreciate it if . . ." He stopped; the man obviously had heard nothing.

In desperation Ritchie tried to grab the man's shoulder, but he felt nothing, as if the man were only a mirage. Now Ritchie began to think about all the strange things that were happening to him. He remembered the young man he had seen in the hospital bed. Could it have been the material, concrete part of himself lying there? He had to find out.

In a flash, he was flying again, this time back toward Texas. Before long he was standing next to the bed from which he had started his bizarre journey, but now the person lying in the bed was covered with a sheet from head to toe. Only the arms and hands were exposed. On the left hand was a ring containing a gold owl on an oval, black onyx and the words, "University of Richmond."

149

Dr. George Ritchie

Ritchie fixed his eyes on the ring. Could this be *his* ring? How could it be? This man was obviously dead. Ritchie asked himself, "How could I be dead and still be awake?"

Suddenly the room glowed with a light that seemed too bright for mortal eyes, radiating from a man who appeared to be made of light. The man seemed to put thoughts directly into Ritchie's head. "Stand up! You are in the presence of the Son of God." Ritchie stood up and became filled with a mysterious inner certainty that this all-powerful person loved him. At the same time the room filled with a giant, three-dimensional, moving mural showing every episode of his life. It normally would have taken weeks to see so many events, but Private Ritchie seemed to be beyond any ordinary time frame.

A question filled Ritchie's head: "What have you done with your life to show me?" Ritchie knew that the all-loving being in his presence was asking, "How much have you loved with your life? Have you loved others as I am loving you?" For Ritchie, having to answer this question was like having to take a final exam for a course he had never taken. "If that is what life is all about, why didn't someone tell me?" he protested. The man who seemed to be made of light answered that he had tried to tell Ritchie and that he would show him more. With that they started to move toward a distant pinpoint of light that rapidly grew into a large city. It could have been any of several cities in the United States. The streets were crowded with living humans and many substanceless beings that were similar to Ritchie.

These nonphysical beings were unable to perform any physical acts, yet were completely and futilely absorbed in some worldly activity. One spirit constantly begged for cigarettes, while another begged for beer. Another spirit tried to manage a business as he had once done, and still another followed her middle-aged son, nagging constantly without being heard.

Ritchie realized that this was hell—a place where people were powerless to obtain those things for which they had a burning desire.

Suddenly Ritchie and the spirit guiding him were in an immense void traveling toward a seemingly endless city where everything and everyone seemed to be made of light. As he approached, Ritchie thought he might be entering heaven, the home of beings who had incorporated the man made of light and his love into their lives to such an extent that they had been transformed into his very likeness.

But a glimpse is all Ritchie got, because in a flash he was back in the room with his sheet-covered body. The man of light explained that Ritchie had to return to his body.

As Ritchie pleaded to stay with this man, his mind blurred. He was now aware of nothing except his burning throat and aching chest. He tried to move his arms, but only his hands would move. He felt his ring and began to twist it around his finger.

Just then the ward boy, preparing Ritchie for the morgue, noticed Ritchie's hands. He ran to get the doctor who had pronounced Ritchie dead about ten minutes earlier. Doctor Francy repeated his exam and again pronounced him dead.

The ward boy refused to accept this diagnosis and pleaded with the doctor to inject adrenalin directly into the heart muscle, which he did.

Today, George Ritchie is a psychiatrist at the University of Virginia Medical School. Dr. Ritchie has told many about his close encounter with death (Ritchie, 1978). Skeptics assume that he was dreaming or hallucinating. But even skeptics recognize that his experience profoundly affected his life. He is characterized by a remarkable depth of kindness, understanding, and loving concern for others.

After completing this chapter, you should be able to:

Define and differentiate between everyday consciousness and alternate states of consciousness.

List and describe the four methods for studying consciousness.

Distinguish the five stages of sleep and discuss dream patterns.

Explain the distinguishing characteristics of dreams, hypnagogic images, and daydreams.

Identify the four major classes of psychoactive drugs and describe their subjective effects.

Define hypnosis and discuss the situations in which it is used today.

Discuss the applications of sensory deprivation.

Critically review the research on extrasensory perception and psychokinesis.

History and Scope of Studying Alternate States of Consciousness

George Ritchie believes that he died for about ten minutes and then returned to life. Ritchie regained waking consciousness three days after he was revived by a shot of adrenalin. Upon waking, he never doubted for a moment that he had remained conscious of sensations, thoughts, and emotions. He also believed that he had actually walked with God in a reality that exists beyond our senses—another dimension in which our spirit lives after our body dies. His story raises questions about states of consciousness both during life and death. If he were in a state of consciousness during death, was he also in a special state of consciousness for the three days before he regained waking consciousness? What is waking consciousness, and how do we distinguish it from other states? Is it possible that what you are experiencing right now is not a waking state? Will you soon awake to find that you have been dreaming instead of reading? Students rarely have any doubt about answering this question (Tart, 1977). Sometimes dreams seem real, but we hardly ever mistake waking states for dreaming states. For consideration of some of the other questions raised by Ritchie's experience, let's turn to researchers who study states of consciousness.

The study of **consciousness** has roots and branches in common with the study of the body. Hippocrates, who was introduced in Chapter 2 as the "Father of Modern Medicine," taught in the fifth century B.C. that consciousness continues after death. This idea was not new, as you may have guessed if you have seen pictures of the fourteenth century B.C. tomb of the Egyptian boy-king Tutankhamen (King Tut). The Egyptians, who sought eternal life beyond all else, believed that King Tut's spirit would forever enjoy entombed treasures of food, water, furniture, jewelry, and tools. Obviously, then, the idea of the separateness of the body and consciousness did not originate with Hippocrates. His teachings were important, however, because they advocated careful observations of people to clarify the relationship between the body and consciousness. His work and that of later Greek philosophers, Aristotle (384–323 B.C.) and Plato (423–347 B.C.), paved the way for the study of both the body and consciousness.

Consciousness
The perception of what passes in a person's own mind (Locke's definition).

151

Egyptians filled the tomb of their boy-king Tutankhamen (King Tut) with gifts of food, water, furniture, jewelry, and tools because they believed that his spirit would live to enjoy the gifts forever.

Important milestones in these studies included a treatise by John Locke (1690) in which he defined consciousness as "the perception of what passes in a man's own mind" (p. 138). In the late nineteenth century, Wilhelm Wundt attempted to determine how we become conscious of our surroundings. Wundt, who was introduced in Chapter 1 as the founder of the first

Table 5–1   Questionnaire on Subjective Patterns of Experiences

		None	Barely Detectable							Very Vivid
1. How vivid are each of the following kinds of sensations?	Sight	0	1	2	3	4	5	6	7	8	9
	Sound	0	1	2	3	4	5	6	7	8	9
	Taste	0	1	2	3	4	5	6	7	8	9
	Smell	0	1	2	3	4	5	6	7	8	9
	Touch	0	1	2	3	4	5	6	7	8	9

	Absolutely Convinced I Am Not								Absolutely Convinced I Am
2. How sure are you that you are in an ordinary waking state of consciousness?	1	2	3	4	5	6	7	8	9

		None	Barely Detectable							Strong Feeling
3. How much are you feeling the following emotions?	Joy	0	1	2	3	4	5	6	7	8	9
	Rage	0	1	2	3	4	5	6	7	8	9
	Surprise	0	1	2	3	4	5	6	7	8	9
	Interest	0	1	2	3	4	5	6	7	8	9
	Sadness	0	1	2	3	4	5	6	7	8	9

	Events Passing by without My Control								I Am in Complete Control
4. How much are you in control of your experiences?	1	2	3	4	5	6	7	8	9

psychological laboratory, cataloged what he believed to be elements of conscious experience. Unfortunately, he and other trained scientists often failed to replicate each others' observations. These failures set the stage for the emergence of the behaviorist approach (see Chapter 1) that focused exclusively on behaviors as opposed to conscious experiences. As a result of the dominance of behaviorism, experimental psychologists did very little work on consciousness from the 1920s to the 1950s.

Between then and now, however, scientific interest in consciousness has been growing. Modern scientists have found Locke's definition of consciousness to be inadequate because it does not distinguish various states of consciousness such as waking states and dreaming states. Today, scientists refer to **alternate states of consciousness**, which they define as "a specific pattern of physiological and subjective responses" (Shapiro, 1977, p. 152). Each state is identified by a unique pattern of physiological and subjective responses. The physiological responses include brain activity, eye movements, heart rate, blood pressure, and oxygen consumption. As shown in Table 5–1, subjective patterns include sensations (Questions 1, 6, and 7), thoughts (Questions 2, 4, 5, and 8) and emotions (Question 3). The questions in Table 5–1 may help you identify subjective patterns in your own experiences. First, use a blue pen to answer the questions with respect to your present state of consciousness. Then use a red pen to answer the questions with respect to your most recent dream. The configuration of answers circled in blue represents the subjective pattern of your present state. Similarly, the configuration of answers circled in red represents the subjective pattern during your last dream state. Although this questionnaire is abbreviated, students usually find that it is adequate to reveal different subjective patterns for waking and dreaming states. For example, you probably indi-

Alternate states of consciousness
Differing mental states as measured by a specific pattern of physiological and subjective responses.

	Experiences in a Seemingly Random Order							Experiences in a Very Logical Order
5. To what extent are your experiences ordered logically?	1	2	3	4	5	6	7	8	9
	Many Strange Sensations							All Ordinary Sensations
6. To what extent are you experiencing unusual sensations?	1	2	3	4	5	6	7	8	9
	Absolutely Sure That My Experiences Are in My Mind Only							Absolutely Sure That My Experiences Are Being Caused by Something outside of Myself
7. To what extent do you believe that your experiences are being caused by something located outside of yourself?	1	2	3	4	5	6	7	8	9
	I Am Not Thinking about the Fact That I Am Experiencing Things							I Am Thinking a Great Deal about the Fact That I Am Experiencing Things
8. To what extent are you aware of your awareness?	1	2	3	4	5	6	7	8	9

Source: Zinberg (1977).

cated more control and fewer unusual sensations in your waking state. Zinberg (1977) used an extended version of this questionnaire to help people scan the contents and qualities of their experiences. He found unique response patterns associated with waking states, dreaming states, and other alternate states of consciousness, such as drug-induced states. Progress has been made in the sense that modern studies of consciousness are replicable and in the sense that we now understand sleep and other states much better. As we shall see, however, many fundamental questions remain open.

As we analyze various alternate states of consciousness in this chapter, we will (1) review methods for studying states of consciousness; (2) emphasize current efforts to distinguish the states by means of both physiological and subjective patterns; (3) critically evaluate claims that we might have hidden mental powers; (4) review evidence that others have had near-death experiences similar to Ritchie's experience; and (5) discuss whether or not common patterns run through all mental states including near-death experiences.

Methods for Studying States of Consciousness

Dr. Ritchie's book, *Return from Tomorrow*, in which he describes his out-of-body experience, is not a scientific document, nor was it intended to be. The reader learns about Ritchie's experience as it is told to a dying patient, who is at first skeptical, but who is later inspired. If Ritchie had chosen instead to objectively examine his experience, he could have used his encounter with death as a basis for a scientific inquiry. Such an investigation would be labeled the self-experience approach, the first of four methods used to study subjective patterns in various states of consciousness.

Self-Experience.　Andrew T. Wiel, a Harvard researcher, and many other scientists believe that the best way to experiment with alternate states of consciousness is for investigators to experience the states themselves. In one interesting self-experience experiment, Wiel analyzed states of consciousness induced by religious ceremonies inside a Sioux Indian Sweat Lodge. Wiel participated in this ritual several times. He found that "on coming out of sweat lodges I have felt high in many of the same ways I have felt while using some psychedelic drugs. . . . Increased awareness of one's own strength and a sense of well-being may persist for a long time" (Wiel, 1977, p. 45). He also commented on why he didn't get burned by temperatures that reached almost 212°F.: "Curiously enough, one's mental state seems to be the most important determinant of the fate of one's skin. Burning occurs only when you lose contact with the psychic energy of the group" (Wiel, 1977, p. 45). Wiel's suggestion that he was in touch with the psychic energy of the group implies the existence of a distinct source of mental energy.

Some have applied the self-experience approach to the investigation of consciousness altering drugs. They include Havelock Ellis (1902), Aldous Huxley (1952), and Carlos Castaneda (1972). Although such drug research has made important contributions, it has been extremely dangerous even for well-prepared scientists such as Timothy Leary, whose famous research on LSD resulted in tragedy (Cohen, 1976).

In this chapter we will encourage you to use the self-experience approach, but only for safe states of consciousness, such as sleep and deep relaxation. These states can be accompanied by rich and attractive experiences. In fact, we will introduce the argument that people who learn to enjoy such natural "highs" might have an advantage. Specifically, they might have less need to experiment with artificially induced states of consciousness. We will also encourage you to use questionnaires and interviews, as discussed in the next section.

Questionnaires and Interviews.   We have already seen and used a questionnaire earlier in this chapter. Similar questions could be asked in an interview. You can control exact wording better in a questionnaire, but you can often learn more in an interview by following up on a person's interesting comments.

Timing is important in the interview method. For example, say you want to interview people about their dreams. There are three ways to do this. First, you can ask people to describe the dreams they can remember having had during the past week. Second, you can ask them ahead of time to pay special attention to the dreams they have during the next week, because you plan to ask them to describe the dreams. Warning them ahead of time has an advantage—they can make a conscious attempt to remember their dreams by writing them down as soon as they wake up. But this kind of ahead-of-time warning also has a drawback. Suppose we told you to report every time you think about green flamingoes for the rest of the day. Would your reports reflect how much you usually think about green flamingoes? Probably not; you probably never thought about them until I asked you to count how many times you did. This problem can be minimized by asking open-ended questions that do not ask for specific content. The third way is to administer the questionnaire or interview during or immediately after an experience. An advantage is that the experience is more easily remembered just after it occurs. A disadvantage is that the experience usually must take place with the experimenter on hand, often in an artificial laboratory setting. Can people have normal dreams when they know scientists are observing them? Probably not, since environmental conditions affect dreams (more about these effects later).

Laboratory Experiments.   Despite the fact that they may seem artificial, laboratory experiments are valuable for studying alternate states of consciousness. In one experiment, Hilgard (1969b) induced pain by briefly submerging a person's arm in cold water. The water was held at constant temperatures of 0°C, 5°C, 10°C, or 15°C. The pain was real enough, but its consequences were different from those of the chronic pain that is treated in clinics, where patients face the prospect of life-long debilitating pain. Hilgard's subjects knew, in contrast, that their pain would terminate before the end of the experiment. Despite the contrived situation, however, Hilgard was able to validate subjective pain scales by comparing them with objective physiological measurements. The subjective and objective measures increased and decreased together as water temperature varied. Today, subjective pain scales are widely used in laboratories and clinics (Spinhoven, 1988). In another laboratory experiment, Hilgard (1967) carefully selected a group from which he could precisely compare different levels of susceptibility to hypnosis, a state induced by the words and actions of a hypnotist whose suggestions are readily accepted. He found that pain relief from hypnosis is related to susceptibility. Hilgard's experiments illustrate three important advantages of laboratory experiments: (1) They can manipulate and control factors such as water temperature and other factors that might influence states of consciousness; (2) they can supplement subjective reports with objective measures such as physiological correlates; and (3) they can carefully select subjects in order to control or study individual differences.

Clinical Case Methods.   Let us use a clinical investigation of hypnotic pain treatment as our example. (Hypnosis is defined and discussed later in this chapter.) In this study, a 58-year-old patient at Walter Reed Army Medical Center responded positively to the suggestion that he could control his severe headaches (Wain, 1980). He had a number of physical problems

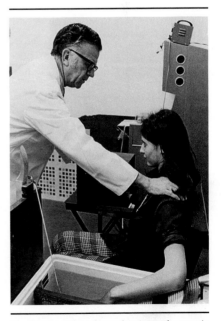

Dr. Ernest Hilgard conducting a hypnosis experiment.

that caused the headaches, including high blood pressure and a disorder of the blood vessels serving the brain. After the first hypnotic session the pain was reduced for about six hours. The patient later learned how to hypnotize himself, which he did every three hours during the days that followed. By the time he was released from the hospital, his headaches were less severe and his blood pressure had dropped, both without medication. A 6-month follow-up examination revealed that he no longer suffered from severe headaches and that his blood pressure was under control. Many other patients at Walter Reed Army Medical Center and at other clinics have also been able to control their pain through hypnosis (Davidson, 1987; Singh, 1989; Venn, 1987).

An advantage of this and other clinical case investigations is that the patients are highly motivated because they are being treated for real problems. A disadvantage is the difficulty of generalizing—the results might only be relevant for people with special conditions. This problem is minimized when investigators treat many patients, report both successes and failures, and describe cases in detail. The problem is magnified when only successes are reported and when no attempt is made to characterize those for whom the treatment succeeds or fails.

Another disadvantage is that the investigator cannot always be sure that symptoms would not have gone away without treatment. A nontreatment control group could solve this problem in principle, but this solution is often unacceptable and potentially unethical in clinical situations. One approach to establishing the extent of effectiveness is to analyze abrupt changes in symptoms when treatment is administered. Researchers can apply this strategy by taking quantitative measures of symptoms over a period of time both before and after treatment. If symptoms have remained stable for a long time, abrupt changes after treatment will signal a treatment effect. Another approach is to vary the level of treatment. Researchers can measure different levels of hypnotic susceptibility, for example, using standard scales (e.g., Hilgard & Hilgard, 1975). A treatment effect is suggested if the degree of symptom change is related to the level of treatment. Thus, although many obstacles stand in the way of definitive clinical case studies, a careful researcher can overcome them.

Scientific investigations using all four methods (self-experience, questionnaires and interviews, laboratory experiments, and clinical methods) have greatly increased our understanding of alternate states of consciousness. However, important questions remain unanswered. Scientists are still debating, for example, whether hypnosis should be classified as a special state or as part of the waking state. In the remainder of this chapter, we will review data on physiological and subjective patterns in alternate states of consciousness. You are encouraged to look for patterns that cut across several states of consciousness and to consider how these common patterns might help you to classify hypnosis as well as other states.

Sleep and Dreams

Sleep
Period of rest for the body and mind during which bodily functions are partially suspended and sensitivity to external stimuli is diminished, but readily or easily regained.

Dreams
Series of images, thoughts, and emotions that occur during sleep.

Did Ritchie dream his experience? Let's consider this question in light of the literature on sleep and dreaming. **Sleep** is defined as a period of rest for the body and mind during which bodily functions are partially suspended and sensitivity to external stimuli is diminished but can be readily or easily regained. **Dreams** are series of images, thoughts, and emotions occurring during sleep.

Scientific Studies of Sleep and Dreams

Two separate research programs sparked scientific interest in sleep and dreams. First, Sigmund Freud (1900) used special interview procedures to record dreams. The content of the dreams was varied and often bizarre. Freud, however, felt that dreams must have some function for the individual. After intensive study of dream reports, Freud concluded that there were two levels in dreams: **manifest content**, which the dreamer remembers, and **latent content**, which is the hidden meaning of the dream. For example, a patient might report that she dreamed of being chased by a big snake with a face much like her father's face (manifest content). The latent content of the dream, of which the patient was not aware, may have been the patient's wish to have a sexual relationship with her father.

Freud felt that the latent content generally involved an unacceptable desire that would create pain or anxiety if it were expressed directly. It would probably be very threatening to our dreamer if she dreamed that she was having a sexual relationship with her father. The unacceptable impulse is, therefore, disguised in the dream. Thus, Freud felt that dreams were vehicles through which individuals could express their unacceptable impulses in disguised or "acceptable" forms. Freud's work contradicted the prior notion that dreams are worthless.

Second, Eugene Aserinsky and Nathaniel Kleitman, using laboratory techniques to measure physiological responses, demonstrated that sleep is accompanied by a complex and ever-changing pattern of physiological activity (see Kleitman, 1963). In addition, they discovered that specific physiological patterns occur when a person is dreaming. This means that when such patterns occur, researchers can awaken subjects to get immediate and usually vivid recall of dreams. Aserinsky and Kleitman helped change the view that sleep and dreams cannot be studied objectively. Since then scientists have measured physiological patterns and recorded dreams of thousands of people (Dippel et al., 1987; Miyauchi et al., 1987; Wollman & Antrobus, 1987). Let's look at some of the patterns that emerged.

Physiological Patterns during Sleep

Figure 5–1 shows a volunteer sleeping with electrodes attached to her head and body. These miniature electrical conductors provide data on brain waves, eye movements, muscle tension, heart rate, and respiration. These physiological responses have characteristic patterns for resting and for the five stages of sleep (see Figure 5–2). When we relax with our eyes closed, the brain emits *alpha* rhythms, which are low-voltage, medium-frequency brain waves. Similarly, the various stages of sleep can be characterized by changes in brain waves and other physiological responses. The beginning of stage-1 sleep is indicated by the appearance of low-voltage, low-frequency brain waves called *theta waves*. In addition, the eyes often begin slow, side-to-side rolling during this stage. Stage 2 is marked by the onset of **sleep spindles**, which are medium-voltage, medium-frequency brain waves. Sleep spindles diminish in stage 3 and are replaced in stage 4 by *delta waves*, high-voltage and extremely low-frequency brain waves. During the first four stages, heart rate, respiration, and muscle tension steadily decline. After completing stage 4, people go back through stages 3 and 2 before entering the REM stage. This stage is marked by the onset of rapid eye movements (REM, pronounced "rem") and is referred to as **REM sleep**. During REM sleep, muscles can twitch in the face and limbs, and sometimes the whole body moves. However, general muscle relaxation is characteristic of this stage. Brain waves consist of fast mixed frequencies

Scientists are beginning to understand why we need to sleep.

Manifest content of dreams
Portion of the dream that the person remembers. Contrast with *latent content of dreams*, which is the hidden element determined by impulses of which the person is unaware.

Latent content of dreams
Hidden content determined by unconscious impulses. Freud says the latent content of dreams often involves an unacceptable desire that would create pain or anxiety if it were expressed directly, so it is disguised in a dream.

Sleep spindles
Medium-voltage, medium-frequency brain waves characteristic of stage-2 sleep.

REM sleep
Stage of sleep marked by rapid eye movements (REMs) and dreams.

FIGURE 5-1

This woman is sleeping in a sleep lab while her brain waves, eye movements, and muscle tension are being monitored.

FIGURE 5-2

EEG records from a male college student. For each part of the record, the top line is the EEG from one electrode on the scalp; the middle line is a record of eye movements; the bottom line is a time marker, indicating one-second units. Note the presence of slow waves in stages 2, 3, and 4. (Records provided by T. E. LeVere.)

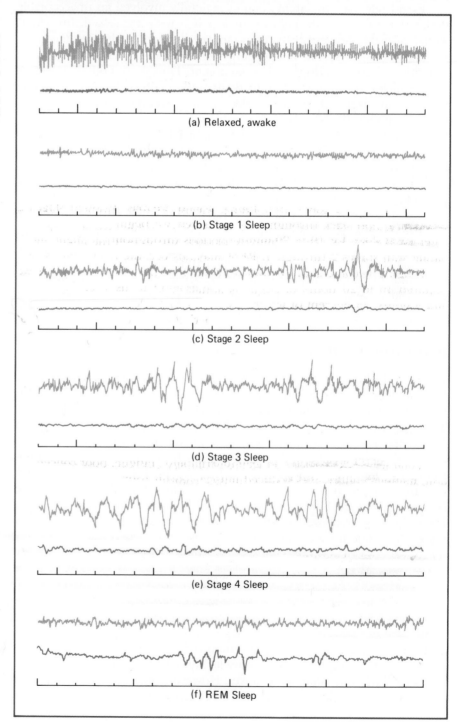

(a) Relaxed, awake

(b) Stage 1 Sleep

(c) Stage 2 Sleep

(d) Stage 3 Sleep

(e) Stage 4 Sleep

(f) REM Sleep

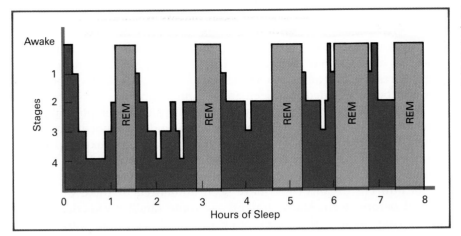

FIGURE 5–3

This graph shows the typical progression through the five stages of sleep. Note how REM intervals become longer and stages 2 through 4 become shorter toward morning. (Dement, 1974, p. 114)

with saw-toothed waves (Miyauchi et al., 1987). There is an increase in heart rate and respiration. If people are awakened during REM sleep, they almost always say they have been dreaming, and they are able to recall their dreams in vivid detail. When people are awakened during stages 2 through 4, they rarely claim to have been dreaming and they never remember many details. However, strong panic emotions with little dream imagery occur in stages 3 and 4. These emotions are called *"night terrors"* or *"sleep terrors."* They consist of labored breathing and paralysis as well as high anxiety (Koe, 1989; Kramer, 1989).

We pass repeatedly through these various stages of sleep during the night (Figure 5–3). As we approach sleep, we enter stage 1, the transition stage. Within 90 minutes after falling asleep, we pass through stages 2 through 4, and back through 2 again. Then we begin REM sleep. We enter REM sleep for 10-to-20-minute periods throughout the night, alternating with stages 2 through 4. REM intervals become longer and stages 2 through 4 become shorter toward morning. When we were infants we required 16 to 20 hours of sleep. As adults most of us sleep between 6 and 9 hours, 25 percent of which is spent in REM sleep.

When we go without sleep for long periods, the pattern of stages that occurs when we finally do sleep changes. In one case, a young man went without sleep for 264 hours in order to qualify for the *Guinness Book of Records*. When he finally gave up his quest, he went to sleep in a sleep and dream laboratory. Scientists observed that on the first night he spent much more time in stage 4, at the expense of stage 2. On the second recovery night, his REM sleep increased sharply at the expense of stages 2 through 4. The phenomenon of increased REM sleep after sleep deprivation is called **REM rebound**.

Total sleep deprivation can lead to irritability, fatigue, poor concentration, memory failure, and reduced muscle coordination. Some people behave in bizarre ways associated with mental illness, but usually these symptoms do not last after a person sleeps through a recovery period. The ill effects of total sleep deprivation can also be created in sleep and dream laboratories, where it is possible to deprive a subject only of stage 4 and REM sleep. The selective recovery of stage 4 and REM sleep along with the ill effects of such selective deprivation suggest that these stages are especially significant. It remains to be seen whether or not dreams are what make REM sleep so important.

Subjective Patterns during Dreams

As most of us know, dreaming can be an intense experience, accompanied by unusual images and extreme emotional responses such as joy and fear. The hundreds of thousands of dreams recorded immediately after subjects

REM rebound
Sharp increase of REM sleep after going through a period of sleep deprivation.

are awakened from REM sleep suggest that we dream four or five times every night, and that most of our dreams are rather ordinary. We dream about playing ball, riding buses, taking exams, and other everyday activities. Scientists have also recorded some exotic dreams, as well as some terrifying nightmares. Despite all of this, no dream as exotic as Ritchie's experiences has ever been recorded in a sleep and dream laboratory.

Failure to record similar dreams does not rule out the possibility that Ritchie was dreaming. As mentioned earlier, Freud maintained that dreams reflect memories and feelings. Accordingly, we would expect Ritchie's dreams to be unusual since his prior experiences were unusual. For instance, he had a great desire to go to Richmond—he was even willing to jeopardize his health. His dreams could have been influenced by these wishes that existed before sleep. Many students are quite familiar with daily events influencing dreams, since they often dream about exams during finals week.

Ritchie was in a strange environment and was being prepared for the morgue during the time that he might have been dreaming. These conditions could have influenced his dreams because we are not cut off from external stimuli during sleep. In one famous series of experiments, Alfred Maury arranged for an assistant to stimulate him while he slept. When the assistant tickled his lips and nose, Maury dreamed he was being tortured. When the assistant waved perfume in the air, he dreamed he was in a bazaar in Cairo. When part of the bed accidentally fell on the back of Maury's neck, he dreamed he was being beheaded (Cohen, 1976). Ritchie's experience has themes consistent with what we might expect for a dream under his unusual circumstances.

The profound effect of Ritchie's experience on the rest of his life is also consistent with the possibility that he was dreaming. Many people claim to have had their lives changed by dreams. In fact, Fritz Perls, a pioneer in Gestalt psychotherapy (see Chapter 14), tried to get his patients to use their dreams to discover ways to change their lives. Similarly, a recent study by Simmermon and Schwartz (1986) suggests that young adults (ages 17–33) can use dreams to help form and reform an adult life structure.

Dreams also can solve problems that we are unable to solve in our waking hours. A classic illustration is Friedrich August Kakule's dream of a snake eating its tail. Kakule, a German chemist, had been unsuccessfully pondering the structures of benzene. His dream suggested a ring structure that provided the correct solution. Many others have tried to utilize the creative potential of dreams without success (Baylor & Deslauriers, 1988).

George Ritchie may have been dreaming, but that doesn't reduce the importance of his experience. Dreams are much more important and far richer than many of us realize. We don't have to solve problems or have psychic powers to benefit from them. Simply by paying attention to them, we take a giant step toward understanding other forms of consciousness.

An objective scientist is free to accept or reject the possibility that Ritchie walked with God during a dream. Scientists have not *disproved* this mystical explanation, and perhaps they never will. They have, however, made a strong case for a **perceptual release theory,** which is a logical alternative to a mystical theory. Hobson and McCarley (1977) maintain, for instance, that dreams are caused by brain activity during REM sleep. Specifically, they argue that dreams are caused by the firing of giant (pyramidal) cells, which are large nerve cells in the brainstem (see Chapter 2). The firing of giant cells is associated with all the physiological patterns that are characteristic of sleep. In addition, giant cells activate parts of the brain that are associated with vision and emotions. This activation could explain the things we "see" and "feel" during our dreams, according to Hobson and McCarley. We might say that giant cells "release" perceptions that we experience as dreams. This theory is consistent with the fact that

Perceptual release theory
This theory holds that dreams and hallucinations are caused by actions and reactions in the brain.

direct electrical stimulation of the brain by means of electrodes causes people to "see" and "feel" things (see the discussion of Penfield's work in Chapter 2). In addition to studying specific brain structures, sleep researchers have begun to investigate how synaptic transmitters and hormones regulate sleep (Dugovic et al., 1989). One study found, for instance, that stimulation of acetylcholine synapsis (Chapter 2) immediately leads to REM sleep (Shiromani, Siegel, Tomaszewski, & McGinty, 1986).

Scientists are also making progress toward understanding why we sleep. One possibility is that sleep helps us repair and restore our body. For example, supplies of neural transmitters are replenished during sleep (Vertes, 1984). This result suggests that activity reduces neural transmitter levels and sleep restores the supply. Accordingly, more activity should cause more reduction in neural transmitters and create a need for more sleep (Volk, Schulz, & Yassauridis, 1990). However, sleep does not seem to be strictly controlled by the need for restoration because how long we sleep does not necessarily depend on how active we are. In one study, Horne and Minard (1985) gave young adults one of two activity levels: (1) a high activity day filled with walking, talking, sightseeing, and learning or (2) a low activity day with little to do except relax. He found that the amount of time young adults slept did not change even though there were changes in their activity level. Thus, if restoration *is* a reason for sleep, it apparently is not the only one. Another reason might be that sleep protected our prehistoric ancestors by enabling them to conserve energy at night in a safe cave when the environment was hostile outside their cave (Webb, 1974). The patterns of sleep for different animals (Figure 5–4) supports the idea that sleep varies as a function of how safe animals are from predators (Campbell & Tobler, 1984). Another interesting fact is that successive generations of people in this century are sleeping less

Much Sleep per Day			Moderate Amount of Sleep				Little Sleep, Easily Aroused			
19.9 hrs Bat	18.5 hrs Armadillo	14.5 hrs Cat	9.8 hrs Fox	9.6 hrs Rhesus Monkey	8.4 hrs Rabbit	8.0 hrs Human	3.9 hrs Cow	3.8 hrs Sheep	3.8 hrs Goat	2.9 hrs Horse

FIGURE 5–4

Animals that are in danger of attack by predators sleep only a few wary hours each day. Animals that are not often attacked sleep for many hours each day. (Adapted from Kalat, 1988, p. 245.)

(Webb, 1974). This reduction might reflect a gradual adjustment to the fact that we no longer need the protective function of sleep.

Other theoretical and practical issues are raised by comparing ourselves with our ancestors. We seem to have inherited not only a tendency to sleep, but also a tendency to get sleepy at regular intervals. Since these rhythmic intervals span about 24 hours, they are called *circadian rhythms* (*circum* = about; *dies* =day). We share with other mammals circadian rhythms in waking, sleeping, drinking, feeding, secreting, and many other activities (Tsujimoto et al., 1990a, 1990b). These rhythms are affected by cycles of light and dark (Sack et al., 1990). However, they occur even when people are in an artificial environment that is cut off from light and other external time cues (Folkard, Hume, Minors, Waterhouse, & Watson, 1985). It is as if we inherited internal biological clocks that regulate these rhythms. Our ancestors rarely, if ever, needed to reset these biological clocks. But today such adjustments are often needed by college students who study (or party) all night, shift workers who alternate between shifts (Vener, Szabo, & Moore, 1989), and travelers who cross time zones. See Highlight: "Coping with Jet Lag," which suggests ways to minimize the discomforts that often accompany these adjustments.

Sleep Disorders

The Association for the Psychophysiological Study of Sleep may be your salvation if you are one of the millions of people who suffer from a serious sleep disorder. The association's researchers have established research laboratories and clinics and have both improved the basic understanding of sleep. Their clinical contributions include spelling out dangers associated with the most common medical treatment, sleeping pills, and advancing more effective therapies. These applications grew directly out of research aimed at distinguishing the many different kinds of sleep disorders (Pressman, 1986). Two broad categories can be identified: *insomnia*, which is abnormal wakefulness, and *hypersomnia*, which is abnormal sleepiness. A sleep clinic may be your best bet if you are one of the 15 percent of all Americans who fall into one, or both, of these categories (Mayer, 1975).

The estimate of 15 percent includes only those who have serious and persistent sleep disorders. You should not count yourself among them if you cannot sleep as long as your roommates, for example. It is not unusual for one person to require six hours of sleep while another requires nine. One woman went to a sleep clinic after being treated unsuccessfully with sleeping pills. She took the pills in an effort to get a full nine hours of sleep a night like her husband. It turned out that she only needed six hours, which she could get without pills. You need not worry if you occasionally have sleeping problems associated with specific events. You might have trouble sleeping, for instance, on the night before an exciting trip. You might also have difficulty sleeping if you are experiencing stress in your coursework or on your job. These experiences are common, and they do not indicate that you should tag yourself as one of the 15 percent with sleep disorders.

One serious form of insomnia is *apnea*, an inability to breath properly during sleep. This can eventually lead to heart damage due to lack of oxygen. When breathing is interrupted, the person usually makes loud snoring sounds, wakes up momentarily, and falls immediately back to sleep. People who suffer from this problem are often unaware of it. They frequently complain of being unable to get a restful night's sleep, without knowing why. Although most sufferers of apnea are middle-aged adults (often overweight men), this disorder has also been linked to SIDS (Sudden Infant Death Syndrome). Researchers have not been able to learn why these infants stop breathing during sleep. Infants who are known to suffer

Dr. William C. Dement, a leading authority on sleep disorders, shown with equipment he used for recording brain waves, eye movements, and muscle tension during sleep.

Apnea, a tendency to stop breathing during sleep, has been linked to Sudden Infant Death Syndrome (SIDS). The mother in this photo is carrying an Apnea monitor to detect abnormal breathing patterns in her baby.

from sleep apnea are connected to a machine that monitors their breathing. If they stop breathing, an alarm sounds.

A serious form of hypersomnia is *narcolepsy*, recurrent attacks of an uncontrollable desire for sleep. This condition is indicated in the following case report of a 40-year-old businessman:

> I began to experience a sudden drop of my head and my upper arms when I laughed or was under stress. . . . Recently, I had two very frightening experiences. I took my car to go back home near 4 P.M. I remember driving out and turning on the freeway. Then I had a complete amnesia. I found myself 70 minutes later somewhere in Oakland. . . . A similar episode occurred recently . . . and when I "came back" I was once again lost, with a complete feeling of disorientation. (Guilleminault & Dement, 1977, p. 444)

Guilleminault and Dement have studied some eighty patients with similar conditions. The patients seem to have a malfunction in the brain mechanisms that control sleep. Many experts believe that the problem involves chemicals (neurotransmitters) that increase or decrease the transmission of nerve impulses (see Chapter 2).

Sleep experts are identifying and treating many kinds of insomnia and hypersomnia (Gillin & Byerley, 1990; Montplaisir, Poirier, & De Montigny, 1990). Some specialists are working toward safer and more effective drug treatment, while others are developing new approaches (e.g., Jacobsen, 1990). One new therapy involves teaching people to control their body actions. These controls include making brain waves resemble those of normal sleepers. Such control is taught through **biofeedback**, a procedure that uses instruments to inform people about the effects of their efforts to control body functions. Such applications are emerging from research that was originally aimed at understanding the psychophysiological processes that underlie sleep.

Biofeedback
Technique that provides people with feedback on their physiological functions (such as heart rate and blood pressure) so that they can learn to control these functions and achieve a more relaxed state.

COPING WITH JET LAG

*J*et lag is the discomfort that you experience after traveling across several time zones. You probably know the feeling unless you haven't traveled that far or unless you are one of the lucky 15 percent who don't experience it. Jet lag can include some or all of the following symptoms: sleepiness, weakness, depression, insomnia, irritability, confusion, and loss of memory. Changes also occur in basic body functions such as heart rate, blood pressure, and respiration. Jet lag is worst when you cross four or more time zones, when you lose time traveling west to east, and when you are over 40 years old. Recovery from jet lag occurs at the rate of about one time zone per day. This rule of thumb means that you will need about four days to recover from crossing four time zones. Obviously, jet lag can seriously hamper your fun if you are vacationing or affect your performance if you are traveling for business. Fortunately, there are steps that you can take to minimize the disruption caused by jet lag. These steps have been outlined for flight crews, athletes, executives, military personnel, and vacationers (e.g., Redfern, 1989; Chidester, 1990). We hope the following recommendations help you.

Before Your Trip

Control your mealtime so that on the day of your flight you are ready to eat at what would be appropriate times at your destination. Control your schedule of sleep and relaxation so that you are not strained or stressed at the beginning of your trip.

During Your Flight

Dress comfortably, and loosen any restrictive clothing. As soon as you get settled on the plane, set your watch to the time at your destination and start living by that time in your mind. If the destination time is the time you usually jog, then imagine jogging. You might also try some exercises in your seat. For example, you could press your head to the back of your seat for five counts to exercise your neck and upper back muscles. You could also tighten and relax your chest, stomach, and buttocks for five counts. Eat lightly and, if at all possible, eat at the appropriate times according to your destination. Avoid candy, caffeine, and alcohol. They might make you restless. Furthermore, caffeine and alcohol will increase dehydration effects of pressurized cabins. Drink lots of juice and water instead. Some experienced travellers try to drink a glass of juice or water for each hour that they fly. Finally, sleep or stay awake according to the schedule at your destination.

When You Arrive

Follow the local sleeping, eating, and activity schedules. If you must sleep during the day, keep it under two hours. Get out in the daylight as soon as you can for about two hours, if possible. Daylight will help your biological clock readjust faster. Finally, drink a glass of milk or eat some ice cream before going to bed if you are having trouble sleeping. This recommendation sounds like an old folk remedy and it is. But it is also based on scientific evidence that dairy products have several properties that induce drowsiness.

One popular sleeping pill, triazolam (marketed as Halcion), is being tested as a possible help in resetting one's biological clock (Rosenfeld, 1986). If you try it, be careful. This drug has been shown to have at least two disadvantages (Forsythe, 1986). First, you will have one or two nights of fitful sleep when you stop taking the drug. Second, you will experience memory impairments for activities that take place while the drug is in your bloodstream. One college professor learned this lesson the hard way. He took triazolam to help him sleep on a plane, and later delivered a lecture while the drug was still in his bloodstream. The next day, he was told that the lecture had gone well, but he had absolutely no recollection of having delivered it. Such memory impairments will not affect you if you are asleep. But you better make sure that the drug will be out of your system before you have to go about your business.

These recommendations probably will not enable you to completely conquer jet lag. But you should be able to minimize the discomfort of time zone changes. What works best for one person might not be best for another. You should therefore think of these recommendations as guidelines for developing your own strategies for flying right.

Visions during Drowsiness

Hallucination
Involves having a sensory experience without the external stimuli that would have caused it. Hallucinations can involve vision, hearing, taste, touch, and smell, but the most common types involve people "hearing" voices that are not there.
Hypnagogic images
Hallucinations that occur during the drowsy interval before sleep.

During the drowsy interval before sleep (stage 1 sleep), we sometimes see visions, hear voices, or feel ourselves falling without any apparent external stimuli to support these sensations. Such sensations are **hallucinations,** or false sensory perceptions in the absence of an actual external stimulus. Hallucinations may be caused by emotional factors, drugs, alcohol, or stress, and may occur in any of the senses. Hallucinations that occur during the drowsy interval before sleep are called **hypnagogic images.** (*Hypnagogic* comes from the Greek words *hypnos*, which means sleep, and *agogos*, which means causing.) We will briefly summarize the physiological patterns of stage-1 sleep and then look at its interesting cognitive patterns.

Physiological Patterns

There is an identifiable transition stage (stage 1) between waking and sleeping. Hypnagogic images occur during this drowsy transition interval, which begins with the onset of theta waves and ends with the onset of sleep spindles in EEG patterns. The interval is also characterized by the occurrence of slow, side-to-side eye movements, which are quite different from the rapid eye movements associated with REM sleep.

Subjective Patterns

Hypnagogic images occur in all senses, including smell. For example, one student smelled bacon frying before she fell asleep. When she got up to investigate, she found that she was the only one awake in her apartment. Furthermore, the smell that seemed so strong only moments earlier was gone. She had hallucinated the smell. The most common hypnagogic images, however, are those that we seem to see, hear, or feel.

Visual hypnagogic images occur in a consistent sequence of stages. In the first, we see flashes of color and light; in the second, we see geometric patterns; faces and static objects appear in the third. Finally, landscapes and more complex, prolonged scenes appear in the fourth stage (cf. Schachter, 1976). Stages 3 and 4 are the most interesting. Dreamlike faces occurring in stage 3 are notorious for their vividness, detail, and novelty. Hypnagogic faces usually are not familiar, and they often take on unusual and even grotesque qualities. Stage 3 hypnagogic images may be responsible for the popularity of night lights among children (cf. Schachter, 1976). Presleep visions of landscapes occurring in stage 4 are often beautiful and frequently contain a great deal of activity and movement. Sometimes the landscape appears as if it were being viewed from a moving car or train.

Visual images are sometimes combined with auditory hypnagogic images. We might hear imaginary faces speak or hear road noises associated with visual hypnagogic landscapes. Auditory images also occur by themselves. We might hear our name called or hear music, which can be unfamiliar and bizarre (perhaps similar to the music George Ritchie heard during his experience), or it can be familiar. In one case, a woman tried to turn off her radio after listening to several popular songs. She was amazed to discover it was already off. The music she "heard" was an auditory hypnagogic image.

The feelings of being touched and of being in motion are other possible presleep images. A rich image of riding a horse might include the sight of the landscape passing by, the sound of hooves, and the touch sensations of the reins and saddle. More typical is the sensation of falling with no associated visual or auditory images, sometimes accompanied by several involuntary jerks of the body.

Hypnagogic images are normal. Yet, Schachter (1974) found that many people are embarrassed about having them. The embarrassment presumably comes from a mistaken belief that these hallucinations are abnormal. Chapter 14, "Abnormal Psychology" will discuss various kinds of hallucinations that are indeed associated with psychological abnormalities. There might even be abnormal patterns of hypnagogic images associated with other psychiatric symptoms (Wilcox, 1986). But, the routine occurrence of hypnagogic images is *normal*, so relax and enjoy them. They can be stimulating and worthwhile. Some counselors even recommend the use of hypnagogic images to stimulate creativity (Willings & Bruce, 1984).

If you have never experienced a hypnagogic image, it may be because you pass through stage 1 too quickly. Some people go through the transition between waking and sleeping much faster than others. You might consider using procedures developed in sleep and dream laboratories to prolong the drowsy interval before sleep. You could, for example, set a "snooze alarm" on a modern alarm clock to go off every five minutes unless you push a button to stop it. Also, you might position a clock so that you must hold your forearm up to hold a button or else the alarm will go off. Either procedure will keep you awake and, if you are tired, you should slip into stage-1 sleep long enough to experience hypnagogic images.

You need not go to such extremes to experience the stage of consciousness discussed in the next section. In fact, some of you may be in it right now.

Daydreams

Imagine going to an emergency clinic with a wound on your right forearm. As the doctor sews up the cut, you wonder what she is thinking about. Most of us would like to believe that her mind is fixed on the stitches she is putting in our skin; more than likely, however, she is daydreaming. Csikszentmihalyi (1974) found that 14 out of 21 surgeons interviewed in his study reported daydreaming during routine aspects of surgery. Their daydreams were about music, food, wine, and the opposite sex, among other things. **Daydreams** can be defined as "thoughts that divert attention away from an immediately demanding task" (Singer, 1975). We all daydream, and scientists are beginning to carefully study this important aspect of our mental life.

Daydreams
Thoughts that divert attention away from an immediately demanding task.

Physiological Patterns

Unlike night dreams, daydreams are not characterized by unique physiological patterns. Physiological responses during daydreams are not very different from those of ordinary waking consciousness. One physiological response that is often characteristic of daydreaming is a blank (or unfocused) stare of the eyes, but many daydreams occur without this characteristic "staring off into space." Surely the surgeons in the study reported earlier exhibited no such blank stares. Thus, physiological responses are not useful in distinguishing daydreams from ordinary waking states.

The lack of unique physiological patterns supports Jerome Singer's claim that daydreams are an aspect of ordinary waking consciousness (Skayholt, Morgan, & Negron-Cunningham, 1989). Most of us are capable of this type of future oriented daydreaming, but females report it more than males (Goldstein & Baskin, 1988).

Subjective Patterns

Singer (1975) believes that daydreams are an extremely important part of our private mental life. He found that daydreams can be divided into three categories: *unhappy*, *uncontrollable*, and *happy*. The first category includes fantasies involving guilt, aggressive wishes, and fear of failure. The second includes fleeting, anxiety-laden fantasies that make it hard to concen-

We all daydream sometimes. One possible characteristic of a person who is daydreaming is a blank stare.

trate and to hold attention on outside events. Finally, happy daydreams are characterized by vivid visual and auditory imagery, and by fantasies used for planning future activity (Skayholt, Morgan, & Negron-Cunningham, 1989). In one study of happy daydreams, Singer (1975) reported that many women daydream during sexual intercourse. These fantasies promote arousal during the sex act, are not associated with sexual conflict, and are characteristic of women who are generally given to happy daydreaming. Each of us might engage in all three kinds of daydreams, but we are likely to experience one kind more often.

An intriguing relationship between daydreaming patterns and alcohol abuse has been observed (Singer, 1975). People prone to unhappy daydreams are more likely to drink excessively. This correlation does not mean that unhappy daydreams cause alcohol abuse (see Chapter 13). Singer speculates, however, that happy daydreams may help *prevent* it. Alcohol and other drugs induce intense, novel sensations, but they are not necessary for experiencing rich, attractive stimulation.

Since uncontrollable daydreams can disrupt your ability to perform tasks that require thought and concentration (e.g., Singer, 1985), it makes sense to strive for good attentional control. However, it is not only important to turn off daydreams when they threaten performance, but it might also be important to turn on daydreams during reflective moments of quiet. Singer (1975) maintains, for instance, that someone practiced at attending to his or her "inner" experiences can achieve a "high" while listening to music, without the use of drugs. People who learn to enjoy such natural "highs" may have no need to seek artificial ones.

Drug-Induced States

Drugs that produce subjective effects in humans and other animals are called **psychoactive drugs.** The most widely used psychoactive drugs in America are caffeine, which is found in coffee and many soft drinks, alcohol, and nicotine, which is found in tobacco. Americans use these drugs for such subjective effects as pepping up, reducing inhibitions, and relaxing. Even though the dangers of smoking are well known, many Americans continue to light up. Some also continue to abuse alcohol and caffeine even though the dangers of excessive use of these drugs are widely publicized. Why?

The Drug Abuse Council, which was established by the Ford Foundation in 1972, addressed this question along with questions about the use of illegal drugs. Although these questions have not been answered definitively, the drug council's final report suggested that illegal drug use must be considered in the context of the use and misuse of *legal* psychoactive drugs (Drug Abuse Council, 1980; also see Mehrabian & Straubinger, 1989; Grimes & Swisher, 1989). In support of this recommendation, a survey of 258 alcoholics found only 3 people who abused alcohol without using other psychoactive drugs (Zeiner, Stanitis, Spurgeon, & Nichols, 1985). Other surveys of teenagers have found a strong relationship between sensation-seeking tendencies and the use of legal and illegal drugs (Andrucci, Archer, & Pancoast, 1989; Teichman, Barnes, & Ravav, 1989). Here we will discuss the physiological and subjective responses associated with some legal and illegal psychoactive drugs. In later sections, we will show that the "high" provided by psychoactive substances can be achieved without the use of dangerous drugs.

This section should give students a chance to exercise the critical thinking required to avoid oversimplifications. Specifically, any statement about

Psychoactive drugs
Drugs that produce subjective effects: depressants, stimulants, and hallucinogens.

drugs must take several factors into consideration: dosage, an individual's tolerance for the drug, and the situation in which it is used. For example, we have already said that alcohol and caffeine can be dangerous, depending upon the amount ingested. This does not mean, however, that these are "bad" drugs. In fact, low doses may be beneficial in some situations (Drug Abuse Council, 1980). The problem is complicated further by the fact that what is an "excess" for one person might not be for another. Furthermore, subjective responses are difficult to predict because they are affected by nondrug factors. Cross-cultural comparisons illustrate this point. Psychoactive drugs are used recreationally at social events in our culture, and some of them have gained a reputation for producing heightened enjoyment of food and sexual activity. In contrast, other cultures use the same psychoactive drugs during religious ceremonies. Ancient Hindus used a **hallucinogen** called *soma* to feel at one with God, and Aztecs "became one with the Great Spirit of the Universe" by chewing the dried tips of peyote cactus (a source of a hallucinogen). Psychoactive drugs are associated with reduced sexual appetite and self-denial in these religious contexts. The same drug can increase or decrease sexual activity depending upon the culture in which it is taken, because culture influences the expectations and desires of people using drugs.

Personality also influences subjective responses. Some people have pleasant drug-induced experiences, knowing that their unusual mental state is caused by drugs. Others have terrifying experiences during which they behave as if they are mentally ill (Miller & Potter-Efron, 1989). They might, for example, become violent and be unable to distinguish between reality and drug-induced hallucinations. In some cases, mentally ill behavior persists after the drug effects have worn off. One generally cannot predict responses to drugs unless many factors are carefully controlled. One cannot even predict the effect of one hallucinogenic drug on the basis of knowing a person's reaction to another hallucinogenic drug. People who have had no adverse effects to one hallucinogen, for example, have had severe adverse reactions to others (Huba, Newcomb, & Bentler, 1986). We can nevertheless characterize typical responses.

Psychoactive drugs fall into three categories: (1) depressants, which slow body functions or calm nervous excitement; (2) stimulants, which excite body functions; and (3) hallucinogens, which cause hallucinations. A relatively new drug, PCP, or "angel dust," has been given its own category on the basis of its complicated effects. Let's take a closer look at each category.

Depressants

Three common **depressants** are *alcohol*, *nicotine*, and *heroin*. You might be surprised to see alcohol listed as a depressant. This classification seems inconsistent with the use of alcoholic drinks to "liven up" a party. The reason for the classification is clear, however, when we consider physiological patterns associated with alcohol consumption.

Physiological Patterns. Alcohol, nicotine, and heroin depress body functions. Alcohol is consumed in beer, wine, and liquor. The alcohol in three beers is enough to dilate the pupils, to slow response time, and to impair motor functions. Extreme doses can cause death. Nicotine is very poisonous, but the amount inhaled while smoking tobacco is too little to cause death. Excessive smoking, however, can cause a weak, rapid pulse, a sense of exhaustion, and a poor appetite. Nicotine is often classified as a stimulant because it initially stimulates the nervous system. We classify it as a depressant, however, because it ultimately depresses the central and autonomic nervous systems. Smoking is also associated with heart disease and lung cancer. Heroin comes from the juice of the opium poppy. It is sold illegally in the United States to users who either sniff or inject

Hallucinogens
Drugs such as LSD, STP, mescaline, and peyote, that cause people to see visions and illusions.
Depressants
Drugs that slow body functions or calm nervous excitement; examples are alcohol, nicotine, and heroin.

Scientists are beginning to study the abuse of illegal drugs in the context of the use and abuse of legal psychoactive drugs, such as alcohol, nicotine, and caffeine.

it. Heroin reduces sensitivity to pain and it depresses respiration. An overdose causes severe disruptions of the central nervous system (Kosten, 1990), which can cause death. Alcohol, nicotine, and heroin are all *physiologically addictive*, which means that body functions can become dependent upon the drug's effects and that the body can require increasingly larger doses to obtain the desired effects.

Subjective Patterns. Depressants have highly variable subjective effects. One of alcohol's main effects is to make one feel uninhibited in social situations. This release from social inhibitions explains the party effect mentioned earlier. Large doses can cause anger and aggression in some individuals, and it can cause depression and drowsiness in others. Nicotine's subjective effect is slight in comparison with other drugs. It is characterized by a subtle relaxing response. Heroin, on the other hand, has dramatic subjective effects. In some people it produces a "rush," which is an intensely pleasurable response. It causes some people to forget their troubles. They also feel no hunger, pain, or sexual urge and they often get drowsy. Heroin's dominant effect is a feeling of well-being, which is part of the lure that attracts people to this highly addictive and very dangerous drug.

Stimulants

Stimulants are quite popular in America. A common one is *caffeine*, which is available without prescription, as mentioned earlier. *Amphetamines* stimulate the central nervous system and are available in pill form by prescription under such trade names as Methedrine, Dexedrine, and Benzedrine. These pills are also sold illegally as "speed," "uppers," or "bennies." *Cocaine* is another stimulant that is sold illegally, as are its derivatives, such as crack.

Physiological Patterns. Caffeine, amphetamines, and cocaine all stimulate body functions. Caffeine increases heart rate and causes restlessness and sometimes tremors. Amphetamines increase blood pressure and breath rate. They also act as an appetite suppressant and can cause rapid and irregular heartbeats, tremors, and dryness of mouth. Cocaine also stimulates the central nervous system. It can cause dizziness, low blood pressure, and even convulsions. All three are physiologically addictive.

Subjective Patterns. Subjective effects are highly variable in stimu-

Stimulants
Drugs that excite body functions; examples are caffeine, amphetamines, and cocaine.

lants. The main effect is a feeling of energy, often accompanied by a feeling of restlessness. Caffeine can also cause irritability. The possible subjective side effects of amphetamine and cocaine use are much worse—a pleasant "rush," followed by irritability. The stimulating effect can end with a "crash," which is sleep followed by fatigue and depression. Finally, both amphetamines and cocaine can cause behaviors that are indistinguishable from certain kinds of mental illness (Estroff, Schwartz, & Hoffman, 1989).

Hallucinogens

Four common hallucinogenic drugs are *marijuana*, *mescaline*, *psilocybin*, and *LSD*. Hallucinogenic drugs are sometimes called *psychedelic*, which means "mind-manifesting." The nature of psychedelic experiences is illustrated in the following quote, which shows a partial transcript of a person who took 20 milligrams of psilocybin.

> It looks like several different whirlpools, with lots of spirals divided up into checks. It's pretty black. There's purple and green glowing areas in the middle of the spirals, kind of clouds around. These are lines going from top to bottom, kind of a grid, but the lines squiggle around. There's odd shapes, but still lots of right angles in them. Seems really bright. . . . There's like an explosion, yellow in the middle, like a volcano gushing out lava, yellow, glowing. There's a black square with yellow light coming behind it. There's a regular pattern superimposed on everything, lots of curlicues, with dots in the middle. Lots of little paisley things that fill up the spaces between the patterns of triangles, squares, or crown-shaped things. And there's a little white star that floats around the picture and sometimes goes behind what's on the screen and illuminates from behind.
>
> Now there's a kind of landscape. Very flat, flat country. The picture is very narrow. In the middle part a tree at the left and then flat with green grass and blue sky above. There are orange dots, oranges hanging all over, in the sky, on the tree, on the ground. A bicycle! Oh, my! It's headed down, not horizontal, like someone's holding it up on end. . . . There's a checkerboard superimposed on everything like the flags they wave at the races.
>
> I can see the street out there. . . . Well, it's old-golly-interesting! It's like in the forties, I guess, or maybe the fifties. . . . And there are people riding their bicycles, and there are, like, boys, in plaid vests and those funny kind of hats. . . . I was at the side walking on the sidewalk, so it wasn't like I was in the middle of the street and [laughter] you can't laugh very long in the middle of the street in the city, so that image kind of went away [laughter]. (Siegel, 1977, p. 139)

Not all drug-induced sensations are as pleasant. Sometimes people imagine that their limbs are distorting and their flesh is decaying, or they see sickly green or ugly dark reds and experience gloom and isolation. Despite the variability of drug-induced experiences, consistent patterns are present, some of which share characteristics with George Ritchie's experience, even though his was not caused by hallucinogenic drugs.

Physiological Patterns. Marijuana is the least potent of the four hallucinogenic drugs mentioned earlier. After ingesting marijuana, a person's EEG shows a higher percentage of alpha brain waves, heart rate increases, eyes redden, and the mouth goes dry, while blood pressure and respiration remain unaffected. LSD is the most potent hallucinogen. Brain waves and other physiological responses during LSD intoxication indicate intense activity similar to physiological response patterns during REM sleep. However, the most interesting effects of hallucinogenic drugs are subjective responses.

Subjective Patterns. When we suggested that Ritchie's experience may have been influenced by his background and his immediate situation, we introduced a theme that is especially important in drug research. We

Cocaine is an illegal drug that stimulates the central nervous system and is physiologically addictive. Produced from the coca plant, it is believed to be the strongest natural stimulant known. Most users inhale cocaine, but it can also be injected.

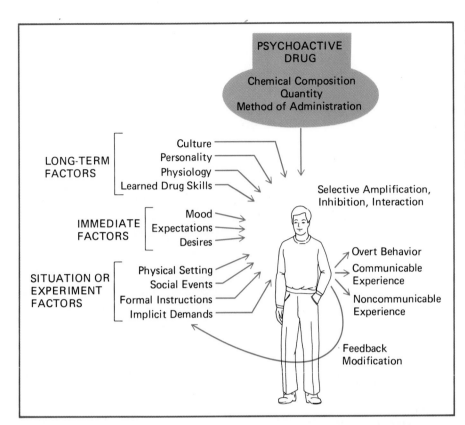

FIGURE 5–5

This model shows the many variables that should be taken into account in analyzing drug-induced states. A drug's effects are selectively modified by long-term factors (e.g., personality), immediate factors (e.g., mood) and situational factors (e.g., social events). These modified influences alter behaviors and experiences which in turn change the situational factors through feedback. (Zinberg, 1977, p. 200)

Figure contents: PSYCHOACTIVE DRUG — Chemical Composition, Quantity, Method of Administration. LONG-TERM FACTORS: Culture, Personality, Physiology, Learned Drug Skills. IMMEDIATE FACTORS: Mood, Expectations, Desires. SITUATION OR EXPERIMENT FACTORS: Physical Setting, Social Events, Formal Instructions, Implicit Demands. Selective Amplification, Inhibition, Interaction. Overt Behavior, Communicable Experience, Noncommunicable Experience. Feedback Modification.

cannot yet predict the course of psychedelic experiences because we do not understand all the factors influencing them.

Figure 5–5 shows a model used to help analyze drug-induced states (Tart, 1977). According to this model, we must know what drug a person has taken, how much of the drug was taken, and how the drug was taken, if we want to predict responses to the drug. Even more importantly, we must know many nondrug factors.

Tart's model suggests, first, that a person's mood, expectations, and desires are important short-term or immediate factors influencing drug-induced states. People who are afraid of drugs, for example, will probably have a more anxiety-laden experience than people who are comfortable with them. In addition, the situation in which the drug was taken also plays a role. People taking drugs in an unfamiliar environment surrounded by strangers are more likely to be afraid, and their fear response itself can modify the situation by making others around them more anxious. Second, Tart's model suggests that culture, personality, physiology, and learned drug-use skills are long-term factors influencing drug-induced states.

It has been found that drug-induced hallucinations have four stages in a carefully controlled laboratory setting (Siegel, 1977). The first stage is characterized by vague black-and-white forms moving about in one's visual field. You can probably see the same thing by simply closing your eyes, or by gently rubbing your closed eyelids. What you see then are **phosphenes,** visual sensations arising from spontaneous discharges of light-sensitive neurons in your eyes. Apparently, drugs make people more aware of phosphenes.

The second stage begins with the appearance of geometric forms. Siegel created a special keyboard to help people report on second-stage images. He divided the keyboard into three sections (corresponding to form, color, and movement), and put eight keys into each section. The keys offered the following options: form (random, line, curve, web, graph paper, tunnel,

Phosphenes
Visual sensations arising from spontaneous discharges of light-sensitive neurons in the eyes.

FIGURE 5–6

In the second stage of drug-induced hallucinations, the color blue dominates, along with the appearance of a spiral-shaped tunnel covered with a graph paper design.

FIGURE 5–7 (Below, left)

In this stage, images are sometimes superimposed on the spiral-shaped tunnel that is shown in Figure 5–5.

FIGURE 5–8 (Below, right)

Images in the third stage often include unusual vantage points, such as this one, showing a view from the bottom of a swimming pool.

spiral, and kaleidoscope); color (black, violet, blue, green, yellow, orange, red, and white); and movement (aimless, vertical, horizontal, oblique, explosive, concentric, rotational, and pulsating). People who were trained on the keyboard reported new images twenty times per minute. Untrained observers could only report five times per minute. Both trained and untrained subjects indicated that second-stage images are colored geometric forms that usually pulsate or rotate. All colors occur, but blue is the most frequent at first. Later, red dominates, and with the shift to red comes the appearance of a spiral-shaped tunnel covered with a graph paper design (Figure 5–6). Often a bright light seems to pulsate in the tunnel's center. The third stage usually begins after the appearance of the tunnel.

The third stage is characterized by meaningful images that sometimes appear superimposed on a spiral tunnel, as in Figure 5–7 and sometimes seem to be images drawn from memory. One student saw the backyard in which she played as a child. Images in this stage often include unusual vantage points (Figure 5–8).

If Ritchie's visual experiences can be identified by any stage, it would be the fourth. Stage-4 images seem more like moving pictures than snapshots—that is, they are more like dreams. Sometimes fourth-stage hallucinations share with Ritchie's experience a feeling that one is part of the imagery and a feeling of being dissociated from one's body.

The four stages of drug intoxication seem to be consistent across cultures. Siegel noted, for instance, that Hindu religious symbols are similar to commonly hallucinated geometric patterns. Furthermore, Huichol Indians show hallucinated patterns in their art and weaving (Figure 5–9). They also report patterns of hallucinations almost identical to those of Americans, even though Huichol Indians have been relatively isolated in Mexico since the Aztec era. Similarly, Stahl (1985) maintains that there is an hallucinogenic basis for art produced in coastal Ecuador between 3500 and 2400 B.C.

PCP or "Angel Dust"

In the early 1960s, _phencyclidine (PCP)_ was introduced as a prescription pain killer. By the late 1960s, the drug was outlawed because of many negative effects, including irrational thought processes and outbursts of violence. In spite of the law and the side effects, PCP became popular on the streets where it is often referred to as "angel dust." The drug is sold illegally in the form of pills, powder, rock crystals, or liquid. It is so easy and inexpensive to produce that it is often added to other street drugs to increase their apparent potency. Thus, one can purchase PCP directly and knowingly or indirectly and unknowingly. The latter possibility is especially scary when one considers the extreme physiological and subjective effects of the drug. The pattern of effects is so unique (e.g., Frier, 1989) that PCP has been assigned to its own special category.

Physiological Patterns. From a physiological point of view, PCP is a depressant that suppresses body functions. For high doses, this suppression can be extreme enough to cause coma and death, usually from respiratory failure. At first, it was thought that the drug is not addictive in the sense of producing physical dependence and withdrawal. Now the issue of addictiveness is unclear because monkeys will self-administer PCP. Usually, monkeys self-administer only addictive drugs. Physiological studies suggest that PCP has a strong effect on the limbic system (Ray & Ksir, 1987). This brain system is the grand moderator of emotions, memories, and goal-directed behaviors (see Chapter 2). Presumably, then, the limbic system mediates the strong subjective effects of PCP.

Subjective Patterns. From a subjective point of view, PCP is a halluci-

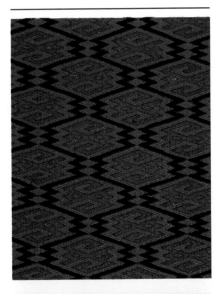

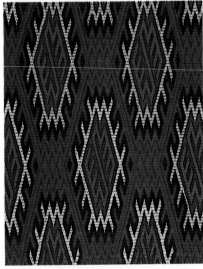

FIGURE 5–9
Huichol Indians from Mexico show hallucinated patterns such as these in their art and weaving, and report other patterns of hallucinations similar to those of Americans who use hallucinogenic drugs.

nogenic drug that produces profound alterations of thought, perception, and mood. The subjective effects of PCP resemble those of acute schizophrenia (see Chapter 14, "Abnormal Psychology"). Specifically, people under the influence of PCP can lose touch with reality and feel isolated, depressed, depersonalized, and confused. They are likely to be hostile and aggressive. They also suffer learning and memory impairment. Why then do some people intentionally take the drug? Some find the unpredictable nature of the drug fun and exhilarating. Others are hoping for the pleasant subjective effects of the drug—mood elevation, relaxation, and heightened sensitivity. Those who choose to take their chances with this drug should keep in mind that the negative effects, such as impairment of learning and memory, can be permanent (Kolb & Brody, 1982).

Issues and Applications. One could argue from a mystical or psychological point of view that drug-induced experiences and near-death experiences are closely related. People who use a drug in religious ceremonies, as Huichols do, obviously believe that it puts them in touch with a sacred external reality, presumably the same reality that Ritchie claimed to have experienced. The similarities between drug experiences and near-death episodes do not rule out the perceptual release theory. A perceptual release theorist would try to explain the similar experiences in terms of similar brain reactions. It remains for future research to determine what the common brain responses might be. A good starting point for this future research would be to replicate and extend Siegel's experiments on stages of hallucinations. Such experiments could answer important questions. For example, will scientists verify Siegel's stages and show corresponding stages of responses in brain chemistry? Scientists are already beginning to understand how hallucinogens and PCP affect brain chemistry (Buckholtz et al., 1990; Conteras, 1990; Hertzman, Reba, & Kotlyarov, 1990). Hallucinogens could create an imbalance of the chemicals that serve as central neurotransmitters. Such imbalances, according to the perceptual release hypothesis, could cause brain reactions that are experienced as hallucinations. By clarifying the relationship between brain mechanisms and drug-induced hallucinations, researchers are paving the way to a better understanding of schizophrenic disorders (Chapter 14), which produce similar hallucinations (Ingram, 1984–1985).

Hypnosis

George Ritchie took a chance with his professional reputation when he comforted his dying patient with a personal report about life after death. In the same way, Oscar N. Lucas (1975), a dentist, went out on a limb to help his hemophiliac patients, who have a tendency to bleed uncontrollably when they have a tooth pulled. At the risk of appearing unprofessional, Lucas tried to control bleeding with **hypnosis,** a state of consciousness induced by the words and actions of a hypnotist whose suggestions are readily accepted by the subject. Lucas suggested during hypnosis that his patients' mouths were filled with ice that would control bleeding. The effect was astonishing. When hemophiliacs have teeth pulled, they usually receive five pints of blood, spend six days in the hospital, and do not heal for about two weeks. With hypnosis, Lucas's patients received no blood, were not hospitalized, and healed in about four days. Such results are slowly convincing the professional community of the benefits of hypnosis in some situations.

Successful control of pain has been influential in the acceptance of hypnosis as a professional tool. In the mid-nineteenth century, England's medical society rejected as a hoax claims that hypnosis can control pain

Hypnosis
State of consciousness induced by the words and actions of a hypnotist whose suggestions are readily accepted by the subject.

during surgery. Today, medical doctors recognize many well-documented cases of pain control by means of hypnosis. Many hypnotized patients who could not use drugs as pain killers have felt little or no pain when having a tooth pulled, after being severely burned, during childbirth, and during the final stages of terminal cancer. Hypnosis has also been used to speed the recovery of heart-attack patients, to cure skin diseases, and to eliminate allergies. We have already cited some important examples of such applications in the earlier section on clinical methods.

Although hypnosis is being used more, it remains controversial as an issue. The controversy has shifted emphasis, however. Originally, it was about what hypnosis can and cannot do. Now it is about how hypnosis works. The debate is fueled by data on physiological patterns; it is calmed by data on subjective patterns.

Physiological Patterns

No consistent physiological patterns accompany hypnosis. Blood pressure, heart rate, and breathing can vary with the suggestions of the hypnotist. In some cases, EEG patterns resemble REM sleep patterns, but they are often indistinguishable from normal waking consciousness.

Subjective Patterns

Although scientists do not agree about how hypnosis works, they do agree about basic subjective and behavioral patterns associated with it. Even those who deny that hypnosis induces an alternate state of consciousness accept that hypnotists can cause the following changes:

1. Hypnosis influences judgment and suggestibility. A hypnotized subject will disregard his or her own judgment and accept a hypnotist's suggestions. A hypnotist can give suggestions to be followed during or after a hypnotic session. During a session, a subject might disregard sensory information that a paper is white and accept a suggestion that it is another color. The subject does not merely act as if the paper is another color (Orne, 1980). In fact, after accepting the suggestion, subjects will see a negative afterimage (see Chapter 3, Figure 3–11) when they look at a second sheet of white paper (Erickson, 1980). After a session, subjects might follow a **posthypnotic suggestion**. A hypnotist might suggest to a hypnotized subject that she will scratch her ear when she hears a bell ring after hypnosis has ended. A susceptible subject will scratch her ear when she hears the bell. If questioned about it, she will probably say that her ear itched.

People vary in degree of susceptibility to hypnosis. **Hypnotic susceptibility tests** are therefore used to predict the extent to which people are willing to yield to hypnotic suggestions (Barber & Glass, 1962; Horne & Powlett, 1980; Shor & Orne, 1962; Spanos et al., 1990). These tests are particularly useful when determining whether or not to use hypnosis for medical treatments. Wallace (1979) maintains that most of us could be hypnotized to some extent, particularly if we were trained to do so. He estimates, however, that only 10 percent of us could follow a hypnotist's suggestions well enough to undergo surgery without using pain-killing drugs. Researchers are addressing this limitation by developing training procedures that enhance hypnotizability (Barabasz & Barabasz, 1989).

Wallace also notes that even the most susceptible subjects retain their value judgments. Subjects will not accept a hypnotist's suggestions if doing so would require a behavior that goes against their values (Erickson, 1980; Lynn, Rhoe, & Weekes, 1990).

A solution for those worried about control is **self-hypnosis** (Pekala &

Around the turn of the 19th century, Mesmer, an Austrian physician, used hypnosis to treat patients. In this photo, the father of one of his patients, Miss Paradis, is entering Mesmer's apartment by force, while his daughter is under treatment.

Posthypnotic suggestions
Suggestions made to a subject while hypnotized which are to be carried out after hypnosis has ended.
Hypnotic susceptibility tests
Tests that are used to predict the extent to which people are willing to yield to hypnotic suggestions.
Self-hypnosis
Procedure in which people learn to hypnotize themselves so that they can more readily follow their own suggestions.

Forbes, 1990; Lombard, Kahn, & Fromm, 1990). In this procedure people learn to hypnotize themselves so that they can more readily follow their own suggestions. Following one's own suggestions is simple sometimes, but not always. You might find it easy to follow your own suggestion to stop studying right now. You might not find it so easy to follow your own suggestion to relax on the day of your next big exam. We have already seen in an earlier section on clinical methods that some patients have learned to control severe headaches and high blood pressure with self-hypnosis (Wain, 1980). Marriott (1986) reported similar positive facilitation of healing through self-hypnosis in a 17-year-old female burn patient.

2. Hypnotism influences relaxation. Light hypnosis can be induced by procedures that resemble relaxation techniques. A hypnotist might instruct subjects to tighten and then to relax muscle groups such as hands or facial muscles. Various relaxation techniques are used, for instance, in hypnotic reduction of labor pains during childbirth. In one procedure, subjects are put into a state of light relaxation. The hypnotist then gives the following instruction: "If you become uncomfortable, you may drift into a more relaxed state so that you are a bit less aware, more relaxed and with more capacity to remain free of any discomfort" (Hilgard & Hilgard, 1975). While relaxation is often associated with hypnosis, it is not necessary to the hypnotic state. Some hypnotic procedures increase tension and alertness.

3. Hypnotism influences attention. Many hypnotic procedures focus attention on some target, such as a small light or the hypnotist's voice. In addition to attention focusing, hypnotism can help subjects divide attention between two tasks. In one study, subjects performed two tasks: button pushing in a repetitive pattern and color naming. Without hypnosis, the two tasks interfered with each other; with hypnosis, they did not (Knox, Crutchfield, & Hilgard, 1975).

4. Hypnotism influences memory (Spanos, James, & de Groot, 1990). It can decrease or increase one's ability to recall facts. **Posthypnotic amnesia** is an example of how hypnosis can decrease recall. A hypnotist suggests that a hypnotized subject will not be able to recall certain experiences until an appropriate cue is given. When tested, some subjects fail to recall anything that happened during the hypnotic sessions. Others recall events, but in a distorted sequence. Still others recall facts, but they do not remember that they learned the facts during the hypnotic session (Orne, 1980).

Hypermnesia is increased recall that can result from hypnosis. One procedure for inducing this state is to suggest to subjects that they have great control over their memory. They can project their memories onto a screen. The actions on the screen can be made to go forward or backward, and they can be slowed or stopped (Kroger & Douce, 1980). Hypnosis has been used, for example, to improve the recall of witnesses of aircraft accidents (Hiland & Dzieszkowski, 1984). Hypnotically induced hypermnesia has also been a valuable tool in many criminal investigations (see Highlight: "Hypnosis and Law Enforcement"). Another procedure for improving memory through hypnosis may be to put a person into the same emotional state he or she experienced when the memory was acquired.

Issues and Applications.   The lack of distinct physiological patterns in hypnosis raises two possibilities. One is that hypnosis does not induce an alternate state of consciousness. Barber (1970) maintains, for instance, that hypnosis leaves people in a waking state, but it highly motivates them to cooperate with the hypnotist's suggestions. Accordingly, anything people can do under hypnosis, they can also do in a normal waking state, as long as they are highly motivated. Another possibility is that distinct physiological patterns do exist, but scientists have not yet found them. Those who favor the view that hypnosis induces an alternate state of consciousness

Posthypnotic amnesia
Inability of a hypnotized subject to recall certain experiences until an appropriate cue is given.
Hypermnesia
Increased recall that can result from hypnosis.

HYPNOSIS AND LAW ENFORCEMENT

Hypnosis is becoming an important law enforcement tool for refreshing the memory of witnesses and victims (Beahrs, 1989; Umakantha, 1989; Watkins, 1989). Two projects illustrate the value of investigative hypnosis. One of these projects was conducted in the Los Angeles Police Department (Reiser & Nielson, 1980). The department asked Reiser to set up a program after he had helped solve several cases. One case involved a 19-year-old woman who was kidnapped, beaten, and sexually abused by three men. She was unable to recall important details until she was hypnotized. With the aid of hypnosis, she remembered an automobile license plate number and names mentioned during the episode. She also helped the police construct accurate composite drawings. An investigation followed, and three suspects were arrested and sentenced.

An investigative hypnosis program was established for the Los Angeles Police Department in 1975. During the first phase, eleven lieutenants and two captains were trained to conduct hypnotic sessions. The trainees performed supervised practice sessions during the second phase. During the third phase, they worked on their own. Between 1975 and 1979, hundreds of volunteer witnesses and victims were interviewed by the investigators. During that time, 31.3 percent of the cases were solved, with hypnosis being valuable in 65 percent of these cases. The program is now an ongoing service within the police department (Reiser, 1986).

The second project was conducted by the Federal Bureau of Investigation (Kroger & Douce, 1980). Hypnotic investigations were conducted by a consultant in hypnosis and a special agent for the F.B.I. Independent investigations worked to confirm all evidence obtained under hypnosis. This method proved valuable in more than 60 percent of the cases investigated.

One of the cases was the Chowchilla kidnapping case. Three masked men abducted twenty-six schoolchildren and their bus driver at gunpoint. They herded them into vans, drove them to a quarry, and sealed them in an underground chamber. Luckily, the bus driver and two boys managed to dig out so that everyone could escape. The driver had seen the license plate on one of the vans, but he could not remember the number. Under hypnosis, the driver was induced to imagine himself watching the events on television. Suddenly, he called out two license plate numbers, and one of them was correct except for one digit. This information led to the arrest of the kidnappers, who were convicted and sentenced to life imprisonment.

Another case involved the kidnapping of two San Francisco area girls, ages seven and fifteen. The older girl was repeatedly raped. When the kidnapper released the girls, he warned them that he would kill their parents if they told anyone what had happened. The girls cooperated in an investigation, however, and they agreed to be hypnotized. The older girl responded to the suggestion that she would remain detached while watching the events of the kidnapping on a screen in her imagination. She recalled many details about the car and about a transaction at a gas station. In fact, she remembered that the kidnapper used a credit card to pay for repairs, and she described those in detail. This information led to a quick arrest of the kidnapper.

As a result of these and other cases, the F.B.I. regards hypnosis as a valuable investigative tool. However, the F.B.I. knows that hypnosis can produce memory distortions (e.g., Laurence & Perry, 1983; Council on Scientific Affairs, 1986).

In one case, hypnosis led to the positive identification of an accused rapist, but during the trial, the victim returned to her prehypnotic uncertainty. The judge ruled that the hypnosis had produced an error (Levitt, 1990).

Because of the possibility of errors, hypnosis is used only to gain leads on important facts of an investigation. These leads are then accepted or rejected on the basis of independent evidence. The use of hypnosis is restricted further by jury reactions. Research suggests that juries are skeptical about evidence gained under hypnosis, and this skepticism spreads to other evidence (Greene, Wilson, & Loftus, 1989).

---

point to the distinctive abilities that are possible under hypnosis, such as reduction of bleeding and severe pain (Orne, 1972).

While the debate goes on concerning the mechanisms that underlie hypnosis, new applications are being found. Applications in addition to those already mentioned include improving athletic skills (Krenz, 1986) and controlling overeating and other bad habits such as smoking (Crasilneck, 1990; Groth-Marnat & Schumaker, 1990).

Hypnosis is even finding its way onto college campuses. For example, Woods (1986) has used hypnosis to treat academic anxiety. In addition, Payne and Friedman (1986) reported that college students can learn self-hypnosis in group sessions. The students can then use this ability to reduce anxiety and to promote their own emotional and behavioral goals.

Meditation involves a series of mental and physical acts aimed at achieving an alternate state of consciousness. Some meditators encounter many of the experiences reported by George Ritchie. They feel united with God; sometimes their minds seem to leave their bodies; and they believe that they see into the future and into the past with unusual clarity. After one two-hour meditation session, Aldous Huxley reported a fantasy that brings to mind the part of Ritchie's experience in which his life "passed before his eyes." During meditation, 26-year-old Aldous Huxley found himself on a hill with himself as a 6-year-old. During the confrontation, the adult Huxley experienced in vivid detail the child's growth. As day after day passed, Huxley felt the anguish, relief, and elation of the growing boy. Huxley called his meditation procedure *deep relaxation*, which is an apt term, given recent evidence that meditation is an effective way to cope with fatigue, anxiety, and stress.

Zen and yoga are the two Eastern forms of meditation most often practiced. Zen Buddhist monks in Japan practice *Zen* meditation, in which enlightenment is obtained by thinking about paradoxical or nonlogical things such as the "sound of one hand clapping." In India, *yoga* is practiced as part of ancient Hindu efforts to give people control over their minds. Many forms of yoga exist. One emphasizes complete relaxation, another uses strenuous exercise, and still another concentrates on controlling body functions such as breathing. Yoga requires extensive training and is not easily grasped by westerners. **Transcendental meditation** (TM) is a simplified yoga technique that allows people to meditate after a short training course. The technique is simple. An instructor gives you a secret word, sound, or phrase that is called your **mantra.** You can mentally repeat your mantra over and over again while sitting in a comfortable position. If distracting thoughts enter your mind, you disregard them and return your thoughts to your mantra. You are advised to meditate for twenty minutes before breakfast and twenty minutes before dinner. TM was developed by Maharishi Mahesh Yogi, an Indian guru. In the 1960s, TM gained popularity, and over two million people now practice it.

Herbert Benson (1975), Associate Professor of Medicine at the Harvard Medical School and Director of the Hypertension Section of Boston's Beth Israel Hospital, westernized TM even further. Instead of concentrating on your own secret mantra, in Benson's procedure you are asked to keep your thoughts on the word "one." Benson's procedure has six steps:

1. Sit quietly in a comfortable position.

2. Close your eyes.

3. Deeply relax all your muscles, beginning at your feet and progressing up to your face. Keep them relaxed.

4. Breathe through your nose. Become aware of your breathing. As you breathe out, say the word "one" silently to yourself. Breathe easily and naturally.

5. Continue for ten to twenty minutes. You may open your eyes to check the time, but do not use an alarm. When you finish, sit quietly for several minutes, at first with your eyes closed and later with your eyes opened. Do not stand up for a few minutes.

6. Do not worry about whether you are successful in achieving a deep level of relaxation. Maintain a passive attitude and permit relaxation to occur at its own pace. When distracting thoughts occur, try to ignore them and return to repeating "one." With practice, the response should come with little effort. Practice the technique once or twice daily, but

Meditation
State of consciousness similar to hypnosis, except that the hypnotist's authority is transferred to the meditators themselves.
Transcendental Meditation (TM)
A simplified yoga technique that allows people to meditate after a short training course.
Mantra
Secret word, sound, or phrase used in Transcendental Meditation.

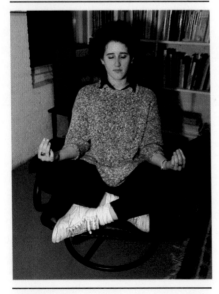

Meditation is an effective way to cope with fatigue, anxiety, and stress. Many people use the posture shown in the photo while meditating, although any comfortable posture can be used.

not within two hours after any meal, since the digestive processes seem to interfere with elicitation of the relaxation response. (Benson, 1975, pp. 114–115) In a more recent book, *Beyond the Relaxation Response: How to Harness the Healing Power of Your Own Belief*, Benson and Proctor (1984) present evidence that you will benefit by attending to your beliefs during relaxation. Simply think about whatever you believe to be important guidelines for living the kind of life you want to live.

Physiological Patterns

Herbert Benson (1975) uses the phrase **relaxation response** to refer to the physiological patterns observed during meditation. The relaxation response decreases oxygen consumption, respiratory rate, heart rate, blood pressure, and muscle tension. At the same time, it increases alpha waves to levels observed during other alternate states, including REM sleep. The relaxation response is the opposite of the **fight-or-flight response** (Cannon, 1914), which involves increased oxygen consumption, respiratory rate, heart rate, blood pressure, and muscle tension (see Chapter 2). Fight-or-flight responses seem to have evolved to prepare animals for emergencies. Perceived danger automatically triggers the response, preparing an animal to run or fight. In humans, stressful situations trigger the response, often needlessly, as when you panic before an exam. Frequent inappropriate responses may be a fundamental cause of strokes, heart attacks, and other stress-related diseases, as we discuss in Chapter 2 and Chapter 11.

Tomio Hirai (1978) has also made significant contributions to our understanding of physiological patterns during meditation. He found, for instance, that Zen meditators achieve various levels of meditation. These levels are reflected in the EEG patterns of subjects. Shallow levels are accompanied by alpha waves, which supports Benson's findings. Deeper levels are characterized by the disappearance of alpha rhythms and the appearance of theta waves. More recent studies have shown that meditation is also accompanied by changes in neural transmitters (Mills et al., 1990).

Subjective Patterns

You could encounter out-of-body experiences, hallucinations, and other psychic phenomena through meditation. You probably will not do so, however, if you limit your meditation to two 20-minute sessions per day. Cognitive patterns obtained with moderate use of the relaxation response are illustrated in the following quote, which shows a report of a woman who used Benson's procedure to treat her high blood pressure.

> The Relaxation Response has contributed to many changes in my life. Not only has it made me more relaxed physically and mentally, but it has also contributed to changes in my personality and way of life. I seem to have become calmer, and more open and receptive, especially to ideas which either have been unknown to me or are very different from my past way of life.
>
> Intellectually and spiritually, good things happen to me during the Relaxation Response. Sometimes I get insights into situations or problems which have been with me for a long time and about which I am not consciously thinking. Creative ideas come to me either during or as a direct result of the Relaxation Response. I look forward to the Relaxation Response twice and sometimes three times a day. I am hooked on it and love my addiction. (Benson, 1975, p. 119)

Swami Muktananda, and others who share his Eastern traditions, agree with Hirai's idea that deep meditation is more than relaxation. Muktananda (1980, p. 24) maintains that "we do not meditate to relax a little and experience some peace; we meditate to unfold our inner being." The goal and ultimate achievement of meditation, according to Muktananda, is to understand and honor oneself. Modern therapists are attempting to integrate

Relaxation response
Phrase used by Benson to refer to the physiological patterns observed during meditation; a decrease in oxygen consumption, respiratory rate, heart rate, blood pressure, and muscle tension.

Fight-or-flight response
Response of the sympathetic division of the autonomic nervous system that involves increased oxygen consumption, respiratory and heart rates, blood pressure, and muscle tension.

Western and Eastern views of self in therapeutic uses of meditation (Muzika, 1990; Sweet & Johnson, 1990).

Delmonte (1985a) reviewed an extensive literature of studies on the effects of meditation on drug consumption. After critically evaluating these studies, he proposed three hypotheses to show that there is a relationship between meditation and reduced drug consumption. Future research will be needed, however, to test three hypotheses about this relationship.

The first hypothesis proposes that a group conformity effect is responsible for reduced drug consumption. Ganguli (1985), for example, reviewed the effectiveness of a group meditation program on 230 white Canadians. Well over half of the participants stopped using hallucinogenic drugs within three months after joining the program. The participants also substantially reduced their use of alcohol and tobacco. Ganguli noted, however, that the group program used many ways to promote conformity to the value of reduced drug usage (see Chapter 17 on group conformity). Ganguli hypothesized that group conformity effects, as opposed to meditation, caused the reduced drug consumption.

A second hypothesis proposes that the relaxation effect of meditation is responsible for the reduction in drug consumption. Many studies document that meditation increases relaxation and lowers anxiety (Delmonte, 1985b). It is possible, therefore, that reduced drug use is an indirect consequence of reduced anxiety following regular meditation. There are many other ways to promote relaxation, however, including rocking in a chair (Van Deusen & Kiernat, 1986). It remains for future research to determine whether or not meditation reduces drug consumption more or less than other methods of relaxation.

A third hypothesis proposes that changes in neural transmitters and hormones (see Chapter 2) are responsible for the reduction in drug consumption. Research suggests that regular meditation alters levels of norepinephrine, a neural transmitter (Morrell & Hollandworth, 1986), and levels of prolactin and other hormones (Werner, 1986). Current research is focused on determining the mechanisms underlying these chemical changes. Future research will be needed to evaluate the role these mechanisms might play in reducing drug consumption.

These hypotheses are not mutually exclusive, of course. Group support and meditation could promote relaxation which in turn could lead to neural and hormonal changes that reduce the appeal of drugs. Much research remains to be done before investigators will be able to determine the possible direct and indirect effects of meditation on drug consumption. In the meantime, from a practical point of view, it is important to note that meditation is associated with reduced drug consumption.

Sensory Deprivation

The apparent psychological benefits of meditation are consistent with Peter Suedfeld's suggestion that isolation can have positive effects (Suedfeld, 1981). Meditators isolate themselves by focusing on a word or process to block out other sensory stimulation. Suedfeld studies another kind of isolation called **sensory deprivation,** a condition in which sensory stimulation is drastically reduced in quantity and intensity. Experimenters induce sensory deprivation in various ways. Some submerge people in a dark, silent tank of water that is at body temperature. The subject's only connection with stimulation outside of the tank is through an air hose (Lilly, 1956). Other experimenters use less extreme procedures, as shown in Figure 5–10. They cover people's eyes with translucent goggles, which allow them

Sensory deprivation
Absence of almost all sensory stimulation

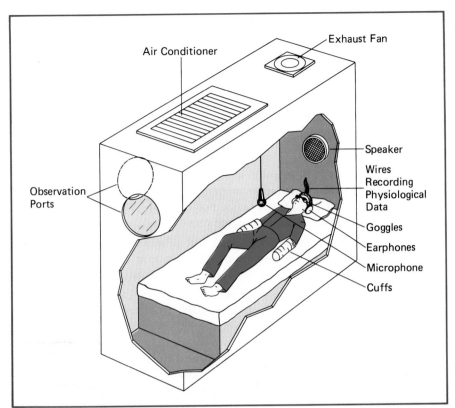

FIGURE 5–10

This shows a sensory deprivation chamber, in which goggles, earphones, and padding cover hands and arms and eliminate almost all sensory stimuli. (Heron, 1961, p. 9)

to see constant but formless light. They cover the ears with earphones that play a constant buzzing sound. Finally, they cover the hands and arms with padding to reduce touch stimulation (Heron, 1961). Research done during the early 1960s associated a long period of sensory deprivation with negative reactions such as high anxiety. Michel Siffre, for instance, remained in an isolated cave for six months as part of an experiment. Afterwards he said that he would not repeat the experiment for a million dollars. Obviously, negative reactions to sensory deprivation can be quite real. They can be avoided, however, and replaced by positive reactions (Suedfeld & Coren, 1989). Suedfeld maintains that negative reactions occur because subjects are not properly oriented to the conditions. He finds that with appropriate orientation, sensory deprivation for short periods can induce relaxation and calm. He has used sensory deprivation to treat drug addiction, hypertension, and alcoholism. Let's examine the physiological and subjective responses associated with sensory deprivation.

Physiological Patterns

Researchers have recorded many physiological responses during sensory deprivation. The measures include breath rate, heart rate, blood pressure, brain waves, eye movements, and muscle tension. The results suggest conclusions similar to those drawn for hypnosis. Sensory deprivation causes changes in physiological patterns, including changes in brain waves. But the changes do not establish a distinct pattern that can be used to identify a unique state of consciousness. Sensory-deprived subjects alternate between states of being alert, drowsy, and asleep. Physiological measures keep track of these changes.

Subjective Patterns

One of the most publicized results of sensory deprivation research is that alert subjects experience hallucinations and dreamlike episodes. Suedfeld

(1975) acknowledges these effects, noting that some subjects think they see tiny spaceships buzzing around and shooting at them. Suedfeld thinks that it is regrettable, however, that these and other negative effects have been sensationalized, while positive effects have been ignored. In the next section, we will take up his more balanced review that includes negative and positive effects.

Issues and Applications.   We can group the results that appear temporarily after sensory deprivation into perceptual, cognitive, and suggestibility effects:

1. Certain aspects of perception are distorted. For instance, people judge colors and spatial orientation incorrectly. But they do better in a wide variety of other perceptual tasks. For example, they estimate weights better, hear softer sounds, and see more detail.

2. Some cognitive abilities are dulled, but others are sharpened. People do worse on arithmetic and concept formation tasks, but they learn word lists faster and they score higher on IQ tests.

3. People are more open to suggestions. On the negative side, some fear that sensory deprivation could be used to "brainwash" subjects. In one experiment, sensory-deprived subjects were more influenced than control subjects by messages about humans having hidden mental powers, including abilities to read minds and to "see" into the future. On the positive side, people are more susceptible to suggestions about making changes that they want to make. In one experiment, sensory deprivation helped people who were eager to quit smoking. They listened to antismoking messages after sensory deprivation. Over the following two years, these people were more successful at stopping smoking than a group who heard the same message without experiencing deprivation (Figure 5–11).

Sensory deprivation not only reduces sensations, it also confines subjects and eliminates social contacts. Therefore, sensory reduction, confinement,

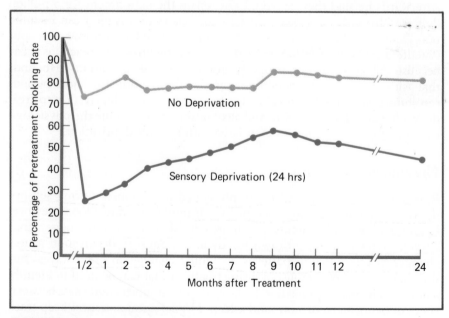

FIGURE 5–11

Sensory deprivation has been shown to have positive effects in some cases. In one experiment, subjects who were trying to stop smoking cigarettes were able to reduce their intake more after sensory deprivation than those subjects who had not experienced sensory deprivation. Suppose subjects in both groups had a pretreatment smoking rate of 20 cigarettes per day. The results show that after 2 weeks the sensory deprivation group cut to 5 per day (25 percent of pretreatment smoking rate) and the no deprivation group that had still smoked 15 cigarettes per day (75 percent of pretreatment smoking rate).

and social isolation can all contribute to effects of sensory deprivation (Zubek, Bayer, & Shepard, 1969; Zuckerman, 1969). Effects of isolation are being studied with the use of seclusion rooms in psychiatric settings and with the use of solitary confinement in prisons (Grassian & Friedman, 1986). Because of differences in the perceived intent of isolation, the former seems to be beneficial while the latter may be harmful.

Earlier, we mentioned attempts to "brainwash" people about reading minds and "seeing" into the future; in the next section we will consider such abilities.

Extrasensory perception (ESP)
Reception of information by means other than our usual senses of hearing, sight, taste, touch, and smell.
Psychokinesis (PK)
Direct mental influence over physical objects or processes.

Hidden Mental Powers

By virtue of being born human, we have a wide variety of behaviors and experiences available to us. Many of us have the potential for running a four-minute mile, for using advanced calculus, or for enjoying Beethoven's symphonies. We develop only a fraction of our human potentialities, however. Most of us never run a four-minute mile, and many of us never get beyond basic calculus. Our ability to do more remains hidden inside of us.

What are our hidden abilities and how can we discover them? It has been suggested that we might have to enter alternate states of consciousness to find some of them (Tart, 1977; Persinger & Krippner, 1989). Many of us discover, for instance, that we can create bizarre images and weird stories in our dreams that are beyond our waking imagination. If we are highly motivated, we may also find in our waking consciousness hidden abilities such as being able to control severe pain (Barber, 1970; Olshan, 1980). Here we will discuss some tests used by parapsychologists to test two kinds of mental powers. One test is for **extrasensory perception (ESP),** which is the reception of information by means other than our usual senses of hearing, sight, taste, touch, and smell. The other test is for **psychokinesis (PK),** which is direct mental influence over physical objects or processes. A person with PK could supposedly "will" dice to come to rest at desired numbers, for instance. Scientists who study ESP and PK are called *parapsychologists*.

Extrasensory Perception

Parapsychologists test ESP using a deck of Zener cards. This deck consists of twenty-five cards, five each of the five patterns shown in Figure 5–12. Imagine trying to guess what was on each of the cards: You would expect to get some correct answers by chance. In fact, wild guesses will give five correct answers about half of the time. A better test of ESP versus chance can be done by going through the deck many times. This procedure is used to test three different kinds of ESP:

1. A *test of precognition* is a test of one's ability or inability to perceive future thoughts, events, or actions. For example, a person might try to predict the order in which Zener cards will appear when the deck is shuffled and presented one at a time.

2. A *test of clairvoyance* is a test of one's ability or inability to perceive an object, action, or event without any sensory stimulation. For instance, a person might try to indicate the figure on each Zener card without looking. In this test, the deck would have already been shuffled.

3. A *test of telepathy* is a test of a person's ability or inability to perceive another's mental state or emotion by thought transference. Two people are required for this test. One looks at each card and tries to "send"

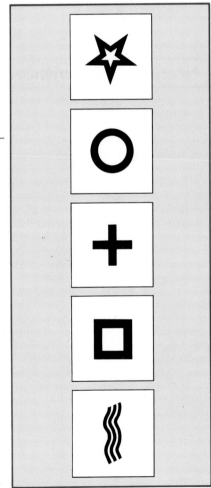

FIGURE 5–12

Zener cards, which are used to test various kinds of ESP, consist of 25 cards, 5 each of the patterns shown here.

a mental image of it. The other person tries to "receive" this message and indicate what is on the card.

Most people fail these tests when they are done carefully (Messer & Griggs, 1989). If you try them, be careful and critical when interpreting your results. But parapsychologists haven't given up (Rush, 1989). Research continues now with the assistance of computers instead of cards to present stimuli (Wolman, Dale, Schmeidler, & Ullman, 1985).

Psychokinesis

Some people claim to have psychokinetic powers. Unfortunately, we must be on the lookout for frauds when we investigate such claims. Some masters of illusion enjoy perpetrating a hoax; time after time careful investigators have exposed people as frauds who are alleged to have used psychic powers to move tables and other objects (Cohen, 1976).

Issues and Applications.   Many scientists are skeptical about ESP and PK (Diaconis, 1978; Hansel, 1980; Hyman, 1977; Clemmer, 1986). The skepticism stems from two sources. First, many ESP and PK experiments cannot be consistently replicated. Too often, scientists get different results when they attempt to repeat their own experiments or those of others. Second, the likelihood of getting ESP and PK effects is lessened when experimental controls improve. The opposite is true in most areas of research: Better controls usually yield larger and more reliable effects. Thus, scientists suspect that results were not influenced by ESP or PK in the first place if better controls reduce the effects.

Near-Death Experiences

We are now prepared to cast an analytical eye on George Ritchie's near-death experience. We can employ the same kind of analysis that we applied to other mental states and alleged mental powers. Raymond Moody (1975) interviewed George Ritchie and hundreds of other people who had had similar near-death experiences. Moody presented his results in his book *Life After Life*. Besides being catchy, his title skirts the question of whether or not his subjects had actually died. Moody plays down this issue and emphasizes instead the fact that his subjects are experts on what we all are likely to experience when we encounter death.

Physiological Patterns

Ritchie was pronounced dead because he lost his vital signs: His eyes dilated, his body temperature steadily dropped, his blood pressure became undetectable, and his heartbeat and breathing stopped for an extended period of time. Today, doctors have added a new standard by which to judge death: the absence of electrical activity in the brain as determined by EEG records. Doctors still cannot be certain, however, whether or not a person can be brought back to life in any given case. People have shown no vital signs for about a half-hour and yet have been brought back to life without any evident brain damage. Moody, a physician, suspects that some as yet unmeasurable biological activity continues to supply the brain with oxygen and nourishment for some time after vital signs are gone. He acknowledges that this hypothesis leaves open the possibility that such residual brain activity may also account for near-death experiences. Until we learn to measure this residual function, we will know little about physiological patterns that accompany near-death experiences.

In the meantime, Moody encourages us to think about the possibility that minds are released from bodies at death and that they continue to exist and to experience. Accordingly, Ritchie's mind and those of Moody's other subjects may have been released before their bodies reached the absolute point of death and rejoined when their bodies recovered. According to Moody's mystical speculation, we would not expect future research to reveal any correspondence between physiological and subjective patterns during near-death experiences, since they would be entirely *separate* during these experiences.

Subjective Patterns

Various reports of near-death experiences are so similar that Moody (1975) was able to identify fifteen elements that turn up again and again. None of Moody's subjects reported all fifteen elements, but every element was reported frequently. The elements are as follows:

1. The experience seems beyond words, leading to the feeling that descriptions are inadequate. One woman said, "That's as close as I can get it, but it's not really adequate. I can't really give you a complete picture."

2. People often hear their doctors pronounce them dead.

3. Pain and anxiety are relieved, creating a very pleasant feeling during the early part of the experience.

4. Many subjects reported hearing sounds ranging from extremely unpleasant buzzing noises to very beautiful music.

5. Upon seeming to leave their bodies, people often feel as if they are pulled through a dark space of some kind, often described as a well, a trough, an enclosure, a tunnel, a funnel, a vacuum, a void, a sewer, a valley, or a cylinder.

6. After a rapid passage through the dark tunnel, people find themselves viewing their own physical body, seeing everything going on in the room as if they were watching it from above.

7. Quite a few subjects told Moody that they saw dead friends and relatives during their experience.

8. Many also saw the being of light reported by Ritchie. Not everyone thought the being was the "Son of God," as Ritchie did, but all thought that the being was loving.

9. The being of light presents people with a panoramic review of their lives.

10. Some people report approaching a border of some kind near the end of their experience. Ritchie approached a city made of light; others have reported approaching a body of water, a gray mist, a door, a fence across a field, and a line.

11. All Moody's subjects "came back," of course. Many people resist the return and long to stay with the being of light.

12. People feel certain that their near-death experiences were real, but they are reluctant to tell others about them.

13. Their visions left Moody's subjects with new moral goals and a determination to pursue them, but with no feelings of instant or moral infallibility. Like Ritchie, many developed a deep caring for others.

14. Most of Moody's subjects were no longer afraid of death after their experience.

15. Many people have accurately reported events that occurred while they were supposedly dead. One girl believes that she went out of her body and found her sister in another room of the hospital crying. Later she told her sister where she had been sitting and exactly what she had been saying: "Oh, Kathy, please don't die, please don't die."

More recent studies have confirmed that many people do indeed have near-death experiences when they have a brush with death (Greyson & Flynn, 1984; Ring, 1980; Schnaper, 1980; Stevenson, Cook, & McClean, 1990). In a national sample of Americans, Gallup (1982) reported that 15 percent of Americans have had a close encounter with death and that one-third of these people reported near-death experiences. The people who have had these experiences include some well-known personalities such as Elizabeth Taylor and Peter Sellers. Although these experiences are important and fascinating, they are not proof of mystical theories. Mystics argue that people have similar near-death experiences because they contact the same mysterious external reality. Theorists have argued, however, that people have similar near-death experiences because they have similar brains, and that these brains remain at least minimally active for a certain amount of time after "death" (Morse, Venecia, & Milatain, 1989; Aguilar, Gomez, & Juan, 1989). Whether we prefer mystical or psychological explanations, we are faced with deciding how to categorize near-death experiences. Moody argues that they are a novel phenomenon, but we also should consider the possibility that they are closely related to other experiences (Quimby, 1989). You might have noticed, for example, that many of the fifteen elements identified by Moody also characterize other alternate states of consciousness.

A Final Comment

Did you see similarities among the various conditions of consciousness that were reviewed? A number of subjective patterns seem to cut across several states. Time distortions or feeling outside of time occur during many of the conditions that we reviewed. Several of the conditions—drug-induced states, near-death experiences, and meditation—were accompanied by a feeling of being united with the universe. Two conditions, drowsiness and drug-induced states, were characterized by hallucinations that develop in four stages. Ideally, common physiological and subjective patterns would suggest a basis for classifying alternate states of consciousness. Classification, however, is highly debatable at the present time. Scientists do not agree, for instance, about whether hypnosis is part of waking consciousness or whether it is a separate state. Unless you see some pattern that others have missed, we must conclude that the present data do not suggest a clear-cut classification system.

Similarly, the present data do not prove or disprove any one theory of alternate states. According to mysticism, alternate state experiences are caused by stimulation that originates in an external reality that is not apparent to our usual senses. According to perceptual release theory, excitations that originate in the central nervous system cause alternate state experiences when sensory input is reduced. The following generalization may have been instrumental in the development of perceptual release theory: *Whenever sensory sensitivity is extremely reduced, people experience perceptual distortions, hallucinations, or dreams.* This generalization holds when sensory sensitivity is reduced by sleep, drowsiness, drugs, meditation, sensory deprivation, near-death experiences, or hypnosis. Research aimed at articulating perceptual release theory may never disprove mystical theories, but the research has already led to important applications.

Research on perceptual release theory also may contribute to our understanding of everyday perception, learning, and memory. In the preceding chapter, we reviewed arguments that the mind plays an active role in constructing perceptions. In the next two chapters, we will consider the view that the mind also plays an important role in learning and memory.

Summary

1. Locke defined **consciousness** as "the perception of what passes in a man's own mind." Today's scientists define **alternate states of consciousness** as "specific patterns of physiological and subjective responses" that are brought about by sleep, drugs, meditation, and other causes.

2. Methods for studying consciousness include self-experience, questionnaires and interviews, laboratory experiments, and clinical case methods.

3. **Sleep,** a period of rest for the body and mind, has five stages that are distinguished by distinct patterns of brain waves and other physiological responses. An increased understanding of sleep is leading to better treatment of sleep disorders.

4. Sleep produces distinct subjective patterns that include dreams. **Dreams** are series of images, thoughts, and emotions. They occur most often during **REM sleep.**

5. **Hallucinations** or false sensory perceptions can be experienced during drowsiness (stage 1 sleep). Called **hypnagogic images,** these experiences have both physiological and subjective patterns.

6. **Daydreams** do not have physiological patterns that distinguish them from waking consciousness, but they have subjective patterns that may make an important contribution to our lives.

7. Drugs that produce subjective effects are called **psychoactive drugs.** Three major types are **depressants, stimulants,** and **hallucinogens.** Each kind produces unique physiological responses. They also produce distinct subjective patterns that can be analyzed in experiments that control the many nondrug factors that ordinarily make subjective responses highly variable. (It should be noted that PCP or "angel dust" has a pattern of effects so uniquely different that it is classified by itself.)

8. Hypnotists can control both physiological and subjective responses in susceptible subjects. Physiological measures do not distinguish **hypnosis** from waking consciousness, which leaves room for debate about whether or not hypnosis induces an alternate state of consciousness. While scientists debate this, they agree that hypnotists can influence judgment, suggestibility, relaxation, attention, and memory, both during and after hypnosis. Important applications include the reduction of pain.

9. **Meditation** is a process combining mental and physical acts to achieve an alternate state of consciousness. This process reduces oxygen consumption, respiratory rate, heart rate, blood pressure, and muscle tension. It also induces subjective responses characterized by feelings of calm and well-being. Meditation is associated with reduced drug consumption.

10. **Sensory deprivation** changes physiological responses, but not in a way that distinguishes it as a unique state of consciousness. Subjective effects include positive and negative influences on perception, cognition, and suggestibility. Important applications include helping people stop smoking.

11. **Extrasensory perception (ESP)** is the reception of information by means other than our usual senses of hearing, sight, taste, touch, and smell. **Psychokinesis (PK)** is direct mental influence over physical objects or processes. Objective evidence of such powers does not meet usual scientific standards, but many scientists are continuing to seek better evidence.

12. Many people have lost all measurable vital signs and then have been revived. Some of them report having subjective responses while they are supposedly dead. Near-death experiences are very similar, and many aspects of these experiences turn up repeatedly.

Key Terms

alternate states of consciousness
biofeedback
consciousness
daydreams
depressants
dreams
extrasensory perception (ESP)
fight-or-flight response

hallucination
hallucinogens
hypermnesia
hypnagogic images
hypnosis
hypnotic susceptibility tests
latent content of dreams
manifest content of dreams

mantra
meditation
phosphenes
posthypnotic amnesia
posthypnotic suggestion
psychoactive drugs
psychokinesis (PK)
relaxation response

REM rebound
REM sleep
self-hypnosis
sensory deprivation
sleep
sleep spindles
stimulants
transcendental meditation

FEELING SLEEPY? AN URGE TO NAP IS BUILT IN

BY DANIEL GOLEMAN

The human body was meant to have a midafternoon nap, according to a new consensus among sleep researchers who are studying the biological rhythms of sleep and alertness.

The judicious use of naps, sleep researchers now say, could be the key to maintaining alertness in people like truck drivers and hospital interns, whose urgent need for alertness must often battle with building drowsiness. Studies are also finding that an afternoon nap can significantly increase mental alertness and improve mood, particularly in the large number of people who sleep too little at night.

This interest in naps has grown almost accidentally, as researchers sought to track the cycles of sleepiness and wakefulness throughout the 24 hours of the day. To their surprise, a wide range of studies using methods ranging from brain wave recordings to sleep diaries came to the same conclusion: there is a strong biological readiness to fall asleep in the midafternoon, even in people who have had a full night's sleep.

Although many people believe that midafternoon drowsiness is caused by eating a heavy lunch, the new research shows that is not the case. The midafternoon dip in alertness and intellectual ability occurs whether or not people eat lunch, said Roger Broughton, a professor of neurology at the University of Ottawa. He said it depends purely on the time of day.

"It seems nature definitely intended that adults should nap in the middle of the day, perhaps to get out of the midday sun," said William Dement, director of the Sleep Disorders Clinic and Research Center at Stanford University. Dr. Dement made his observation in a preface to "Sleep and Alertness: Chronobiological Behavioral and Medical Aspects of Napping," the first collection of scientific studies of napping, published last month by Raven Press.

Until recently, naps were largely ignored by researchers, who routinely instructed the volunteers they observed in sleep laboratories to avoid taking naps during the day. The strongest evidence that the body has an inherent need to nap was not published until 1986. The studies were done by Scott Campbell, now at the Institute for Circadian Physiology in Boston, with other sleep researchers at the Max Planck Institute in Munich, West Germany.

In those studies, the researchers put volunteers for weeks at a time in an underground room isolated from all clocks and evidence of day and night. The volunteers were told they could sleep whenever they wanted.

Left to their own natural sleep rhythms, volunteers tended to sleep in two periods, one a long session at night, the other a shorter period of one or two hours in the afternoon. Because the body's circadian rhythms tend to move people in a time-free environment to a 25-hour day, the actual timing of the naps changed as the days went on. But on average the naps began about 12 hours after the middle of the main period of sleep.

That timing holds as well for normal afternoon naps, researchers say. For example, someone who slept from midnight to 6 A.M. would be most highly primed for a nap at around 3 P.M.

"Their study gave us the first conclusive evidence that the afternoon nap is internally generated by the brain as part of the biological clock for sleep/wake cycles," Dr. Broughton said.

It was Dr. Broughton who in 1975 first proposed the radical notion that naps were a natural part of the sleep cycle. He speculated that the body's built-in sleep rhythm included, in addition to a major period at night, a smaller period of sleep in the afternoon. Dr. Broughton's proposal challenged the conventional wisdom in the field, which saw naps as either a sign of laziness or a social artifact, irrelevant to the scientific study of sleep.

But soon evidence on napping began to mount. Dr. Broughton cites several other lines of evidence

pointing to the importance of naps. One is that babies, who begin by napping frequently through the day, usually have developed the habit of a single afternoon nap just before they give it up entirely at school age. Another is that in cultures where the siesta is a custom, its timing is always in the midafternoon.

In addition, studies of Americans who often take naps show that most do so in midafternoon. Other evidence Dr. Broughton cites is that there is a well-documented drop in people's performance at work in midafternoon, along with a simultaneous increase in accidents resulting from sleepiness.

He said he believes that a natural rise in sleepiness in midafternoon is at play in the fact that the midafternoon period is also when the highest number of deaths occur, presumably because of an increase in accidents at that time.

In more recent research, reported in the newly published collection, Peretz Lavie, a sleep researcher at the Technion Israel Institute of Technology in Haifa, found another kind of evidence for the need to nap. In Dr. Lavie's studies, volunteers are kept on a 20-minute sleep/wake cycle, where they sleep for 7 minutes and stay awake for 13 minutes for several days at a time. This allows Dr. Lavie to determine how quickly, if at all, they can fall asleep at different times throughout the day.

Dr. Lavie found that in addition to the regular night-time propensity to go right to sleep, there is a midafternoon peak in the readiness of people to sleep. That heightened sleepiness falls between peaks in alertness that occur in the morning and early evening. During these peaks it is much harder for people to sleep, even those who have been deprived of sleep the night before. But Dr. Lavie's volunteers readily fell asleep during their usual bedtime or afternoon nap time.

To be sure, naps are easily skipped. Because the urge for an afternoon nap is appreciably weaker than the need to sleep at night, naps can be suppressed when they are inconvenient, although the cost is increased drowsiness, Dr. Broughton said. While the afternoon siesta has been common in many cultures around the world, particularly in tropical climates, it seems to be waning around the globe, a victim of industrialization.

In a review of surveys of sleep habits in countries around the world, Wilse Webb, a psychologist at the University of Florida, and David Dinges, a sleep researcher at the University of Pennsylvania, found that as countries became industrialized, their governments put an end to siestas by rescheduling afternoon work hours.

Average Number of Naps

But other studies show the nap to be alive and well in America. According to Dr. Webb, surveys involving more than 10,000 people found that the average number of naps taken by Americans of all ages is one or two a week. About a quarter of people never nap, while a third nap four or more times a week.

Napping is most common in groups like college students and retired people, who have more opportunity in their daily schedules than working people. Most afternoon naps are between a half hour and an hour and a half, the studies found. Despite legendary catnappers like Thomas Edison and Winston Churchill, naps under 15 minutes are uncommon.

One reason, Dr. Dinges said, may be that naps of just a few minutes reach only the first stage of sleep. Such light sleep, unlike deeper stages of sleep, may do little to enhance mental alertness after the napper awakens, Dr. Dinges said. Such short naps have been studied far less than naps of ordinary length, which have salutary effects.

"If you didn't get enough sleep the night before, an afternoon nap will improve your alertness and give you a feeling of more energy, so you can take on more tasks," Dr. Dinges said. "After napping, people not only feel better, but do significantly better on tests of mental performance."

Among the mental abilities sharpened by naps are the capacity to pay sustained attention to a task and to make complicated decisions. These improvements are greatest in people who have had too little sleep the previous night. For those who have slept enough, the main benefit from naps is an improvement in mood rather than intellectual ability, Dr. Dinges said.

During naps, most sleep is in the deepest stages, characterized by slow, regular brain waves, Dr. Dinges said. Relatively little of a nap is spent in the phase of sleep during which most dreaming occurs. Because the sleep in an afternoon nap is so deep, people who are awakened abruptly sometimes experience "sleep inertia," an intense grogginess and confusion which, at its most severe, produces extreme disorientation.

"It normally doesn't matter, unless you're in an emergency mode like a firefighter or fighter pilot, and have to begin performing immediately," Dr. Dinges said. "It's best to awaken from a nap gradually and give yourself a few minutes before engaging in anything very important."

The longer someone has gone without sleep, the stronger is the brain's need to fall asleep suddenly, and the greater the inertia and confusion on arising, Dr. Dinges added. For that reason he recommends that people like medical interns, who may stay awake for a day or more at a time, take a nap both at night and during the afternoon, during which their duties are covered by someone else. That way there is minimal danger that they will make a mistake because of sleepiness or sleep inertia.

Cutting back the hours of medical interns from 100 to 80 hours a week, as was recently done in New York State, "Is not going to help much if they have to stay awake for a day or more at a stretch," Dr. Dinges said.

"It would make more sense to give them regular naps, instead," he said.

The New York Times, September 12, 1989. Copyright © 1989 by The New York Times. Reprinted by permission.

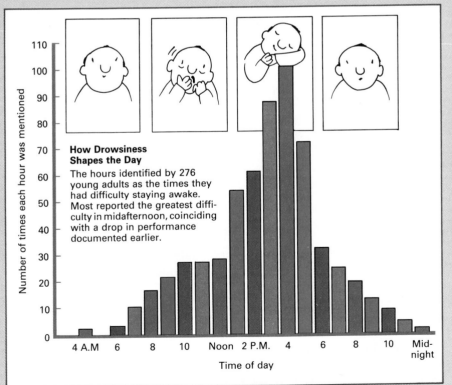

How Drowsiness Shapes the Day

The hours identified by 276 young adults as the times they had difficulty staying awake. Most reported the greatest difficulty in midafternoon, coinciding with a drop in performance documented earlier.

(y-axis: Number of times each hour was mentioned; x-axis: Time of day, 4 A.M, 6, 8, 10, Noon, 2 P.M., 4, 6, 8, 10, Midnight)

Learning  6

On April 5, 1887, 19-year-old Anne Sullivan made a dramatic breakthrough in the education of her 7-year-old deaf and blind pupil, Helen Keller. Sullivan described the event in a letter:

We went out to the pump-house, and I made Helen hold her mug under the spout while I pumped. As the cold water gushed forth, filling the mug, I spelled "w-a-t-e-r" in Helen's free hand. The word coming so close upon the sensation of cold water rushing over her hand seemed to startle her. She dropped the mug and stood as one transfixed. A new light came into her face. She spelled "water" several times. Then she dropped on the ground and asked for its name and pointed to the pump and the trellis, and suddenly turning round she asked for my name. I spelled "teacher" . . . in a few hours she had added thirty new words to her vocabulary. (Lash, 1980, p. 56)

In a moment of insight, Helen learned that the manual alphabet used to spell words in her hand was the key to release her mind from what she later called her "prison-house" of darkness and silence. This was a landmark event in what became a lifelong dedication to teaching and learning.

Helen had not always lived in her "prison-house." Born June 27, 1880, in Alabama, she was a bright child, walking at the age of 1 and beginning to speak fairly early. At the age of 19 months she was struck by a high fever that almost killed her, and she was left deaf and blind. Once a very lively baby, gay and affectionate, she now had a sad unresponsiveness of tone and look.

Helplessly the family watched her baffled attempts to deal with her world, the things she could touch, but which meant nothing to her. Nothing was a part of anything, and frequently there blazed up in her fierce anger. Helen did whatever she wanted, and the family went along with her, for though she raged and stormed, she was also a loving and lovable child. As she grew older, however, her thwarted passion to communicate produced increasingly violent tantrums, and some members of the family said she should be put in an institution. Luckily, her parents sought advice from Dr. Alexander Graham Bell, inventor of the telephone, who was deeply concerned with teaching the deaf. He suggested they contact Dr. Samuel Gridley Howe, who was director of the Perkins Institute for the Deaf and Blind.

Until the end of the eighteenth century, no special education programs existed for the deaf and blind. Most people avoided the handicapped because they were thought to have been (justly) punished by God. About 100 years before Helen Keller's birth, schools for the deaf and blind were started in France. Dr. Howe promoted this idea in America in 1831 when he became director of the Perkins Institute. However, Dr. Howe concluded after 20 years of study that the blind as a class are inferior to other persons in mental power and ability.

Anne Sullivan, a pupil at the Perkins Institute, disagreed with this conclusion. She herself had been nearly blind until she was 15, when eye surgery was performed, restoring most of her sight. Before her surgery, she was a student at the Perkins Institute, and she had learned the manual alphabet from some of the deaf students there. Sullivan doubted that blind people were mentally inferior. She believed, instead, that the blind simply faced far greater obstacles, which interfered with learning.

After she graduated from the Institute, Anne Sullivan agreed to go to Alabama to work with Helen Keller. In later years, Helen Keller always celebrated March 3, the day Anne Sullivan had arrived, as her "soul's birthday."

But things did not go smoothly between teacher and student. Although Helen quickly imitated the signs that Sullivan spelled into her hand, she made no connection between them and the objects they symbolized. Finger spelling was just a game that she soon tired of, since she couldn't see the point of it. To make matters worse, she was entirely undisciplined because of her family's indulgence of her slightest whim. Her father sided with Helen in any battle against Sullivan. Battles soon became the rule and cooperation the exception.

Then, one day the landmark breakthrough happened at the pump-house. Keller remembers it this way:

As the cool stream gushed over one hand, she (Annie) spelled into the other the word water, first slowly, then rapidly. I stood still, my whole attention fixed upon the motions of her fingers. Suddenly I felt a misty consciousness as of something forgotten—a thrill of returning thought; and somehow the mystery of language was revealed to me. I knew then that W A T E R meant the wonderful cool something that was flowing over my hand. . . . I left the well-house eager to learn. Everything had a name, and each name gave birth to a new thought. As we returned to the house every object which I touched seemed to quiver with life. (Lash, 1980, p. 55)

This was the beginning of the remarkable education of Helen Keller, who was the first blind and deaf person to pursue a higher education. She went to the Perkins

Institute and learned Braille, always accompanied and taught by Anne Sullivan. Next she prepared for and entered Radcliffe College, where she carried a full course load.

Helen Keller's academic schedule would have been challenging even for students with no handicaps. But somehow, working against all odds, she and Sullivan not only finished the schoolwork, but they also published a book, *The Story of My Life*, one of five books that this amazing woman published in her lifetime.

Keller received recognition from many sectors. Mark Twain said that "the two most interesting characters of the nineteenth century are Napoleon and Helen Keller." Keller and Sullivan were both awarded the degree of the Doctor of Humane Letters on Founder's Day at Temple University, and Keller received the degree of Doctor of Laws at the University of Glasgow in Scotland. The Glasgow *Herald* reported:

Yesterday will long be remembered as Helen Keller's day . . . [an] occasion on which honour was paid to one who, partly by her own magnificent character, partly by the help of loving friends, has achieved what is little short of a miracle.

If everyone had viewed her accomplishments as a miracle, the impact of her life would have been diminished. Fortunately, Alexander Graham Bell and others were able to persuade educators that, with the proper teaching methods, they, too, could produce similar results in other deaf and blind children. In *The Silent Educator*, June 1892, Bell wrote:

It is, then, a question of instruction we have to consider, and not a case of supernatural acquirement. Among the thousands of children in our schools for the deaf . . . there are some who are intellectually as capable of mastering the intricacies of the English language as Helen herself.

Helen Keller strongly agreed with this point of view. She did not consider herself a genius. She credited her accomplishments to the availability of education and to her willingness to take advantage of it. She expressed this best, perhaps, when she spoke to the alumnae shortly before her graduation from Radcliffe. She said: "College has breathed new life into my mind and given me new views of things, a perception of new truths and of new aspects of the old ones. I grow stronger in the conviction that there is nothing good or right which we cannot accomplish if we have the will to strive" (Lash, 1980, p. 315). ▬▬

After completing this chapter, you should be able to:

Define learning and differentiate between two types of learning; classical conditioning and operant conditioning.

Describe and apply the processes in classical conditioning.

Describe and apply the processes in operant conditioning.

Compare and contrast schedules of reinforcement.

Contrast conditioning with social learning theory and cognitive learning theory.

History and Scope of the Study of Learning

Learning is what released Helen Keller's mind from a "prison-house" of darkness and silence. The transformation that took place in her as a result of her learning experiences inspired our definition of learning. We define **learning** as the process by which experience or practice results in a relatively permanent change in what one is capable of doing. Many psychologists define learning as a permanent change in behavior through experience. The problem with this definition is that it ignores differences between what we are capable of doing and what we in fact do. If we define learning in terms of what we do, that is, in terms of our performance, we have trouble accounting for learning that is not immediately shown in behavior. Ask yourself, for example, whether or not you learned anything in the last 10 minutes of reading. You might have learned some new facts about Helen Keller, but this learning probably has not changed your behavior yet. It changed what you are capable of doing, such as answering test questions, but it probably has not changed anything that you have done so far. It might not change your behavior for weeks, or even months, and probably not until you are asked about Helen Keller, or until you act upon your knowledge for some other reason. Tolman and Honzik (1930), who were leaders in the learning field, introduced the term *latent learning* to describe learning that is not manifested until some later time. The concept of latent learning recognizes the difference between *learning* and *performance*. Our definition of learning itself makes a clear distinction between the two.

Keller's learning process was not unique; it was only more obvious because of the handicaps she had to overcome before she was able to learn. We learn from the time we are born until we die. We learn what we can and cannot eat and what we can and cannot touch. We learn to walk, talk, ride bicycles, and play games. We learn how to relate to parents, brothers, sisters, friends, and teachers. We learn how to read and write, and how to think and reason. Some of what we learn is useless, such as the infectious mannerism of saying "you know" after every sentence. Some of what we learn is even harmful, such as racial prejudice. But for the

Learning
Process by which experience or practice results in a relatively permanent change in what one is capable of doing.

193

most part, learning expands our potential as human beings every bit as much as learning expanded Keller's potential.

In this chapter we will study basic theories of learning and we will see how they apply in our everyday lives. We will find that no one theory explains every kind of learning—in fact, much remains to be discovered about learning. Some theories account well for many important kinds of learning, but no one theory explains every important type. Therefore, we will break down our discussion into separate sections on different types of learning. The first is on a simple kind of learning that was studied in the early part of this century.

In 1904, the year that Keller graduated from Radcliffe, Ivan Pavlov won the Nobel prize for his research on digestion. In some of his experiments, Pavlov (1927) measured the amount of saliva that flows when food is placed in a dog's mouth. This automatic, or *reflexive*, response to food was not surprising. But Pavlov also noticed that saliva often flowed before food was presented. It flowed at the sight of food, for example, and even at the sound of Pavlov's footsteps. His curiosity aroused, Pavlov turned to the question of why dogs salivated in response to sights and sounds. The work that followed revolutionized the study of learning.

Pavlov developed what is now called **classical conditioning,** the process by which an originally neutral stimulus (such as footsteps) comes to elicit a response (such as salivating) that was originally given to another stimulus (such as food). This learning process takes place when the neutral stimulus (footsteps) is repeatedly paired with the other stimulus (food). Classical conditioning is only one kind of learning that we will study. The other kind of learning we will discuss in this chapter is called operant learning.

A major limitation of Pavlov's work on classical conditioning is that his dogs were restrained and made to respond reflexively to external stimuli. His dogs learned to transfer responses from a stimulus that naturally elicited it (food = salivation) to other stimuli that previously did not (footsteps = salivation). When all is said and done, Pavlov's dogs were only making passive responses to stimuli that came from outside them. This limitation is serious, because many of our behaviors are internally motivated active responses. We search for food, seek companions, and ask questions. Psychologists call these actions *operant behaviors* because they actively *operate* on the environment.

Edward L. Thorndike (1898, 1913, 1932) began research on operant behaviors in cats before Pavlov had begun his classical conditioning research with dogs. In fact, Pavlov acknowledged that he was influenced, not only by previous work of his own countrymen (see Windholz & Lamal, 1986), but also by Thorndike, an American psychologist. Thorndike's work was first published in his doctoral dissertation (1898), *Animal Intelligence: An Experimental Study of the Associative Process in Animals.* Figure 6–1 shows Thorndike's apparatus, which he called a "puzzle box." The puzzle was to find out how to escape from the box. When the cat was hungry, Thorndike put it in the puzzle box with a small dish of food on the outside in open view. The cat could not get the food unless it could somehow get out of the box. Thorndike rigged the box so that it opened when the cat brushed up against a string. When the cat escaped and ate the food, Thorndike put the cat back in the box and filled the dish again. Each time the cat opened the puzzle box, Thorndike set it up again. Gradually, the cat took less and less time to open the box and escape.

Thorndike interpreted the decrease in escape time as evidence of learning. He noticed that the cat usually tried a number of actions that didn't work, such as clawing at the sides of the box before brushing up against the string. Thorndike explained his observations by proposing that animals learn according to the **law of effect.** This law states that animals tend to

Classical conditioning
The process whereby an originally neutral stimulus comes to elicit a response that was originally given to another stimulus. It takes place when the neutral stimulus is repeatedly paired with the other stimulus.

Law of effect
The law that animals tend to repeat behaviors that are followed by "good effects," and they tend to stop behaviors that are not followed by desirable results.

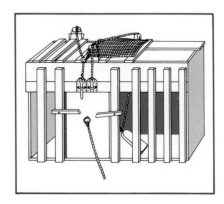

FIGURE 6–1

Thorndike's experimental apparatus, which he called a "puzzle box," is shown here. In order to escape from the box, a cat had to brush against the string inside the box, which in turn opened the door so that the cat could get out.

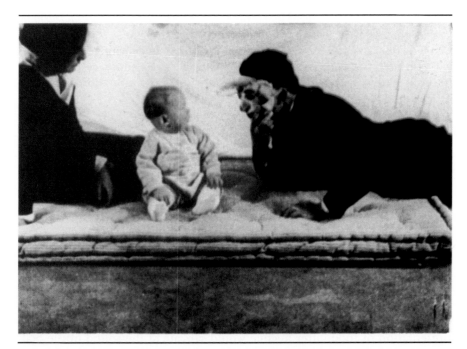

John Watson, the founder of behaviorism, is shown here with Baby Albert. Watson had conditioned the child to fear a white rat, and the fear generalized to other white, furry objects, such as the clown mask he is wearing in this photo.

repeat behaviors that are followed by "good effects" and they tend to stop behaviors that are not followed by desirable results.

The work of Pavlov and Thorndike occurred within twenty-five years of the birth of experimental psychology and had a major impact on its development. As noted in Chapter 1, philosophers as far back as Aristotle (c. 330 B.C.) had studied the phenomenon of how our experiences cause certain associations in the mind. The work of Pavlov and Thorndike gave experimental psychologists a way to study how stimuli and responses become associated, and also became the foundation upon which John B. Watson (1913) founded behaviorism. Watson maintained that the mind should not be studied because it is not observable. Instead, he argued that psychologists should study stimulus-response relationships in behavior. By 1930, Watson's approach dominated the field. A major milestone for behaviorism was achieved when B. F. Skinner (1938) expanded upon Thorndike's observations and translated the law of effect into the theory of **operant conditioning.** This theory states that operant behaviors are learned when desired responses are reinforced and undesired responses are either ignored or punished. Notice that Skinner replaced the idea of "good effects" with the notion of reinforcement, a term that has a special meaning in the theory of operant conditioning. An event is a **reinforcement** if its occurrence just after the response increases the likelihood that the response will be repeated. The theory of operant conditioning allowed Skinner to study learning without speculating about whether an animal considered an event to be "good" or "bad." Thus, Skinner avoided assumptions about these and other unobservable subjective states, placing his focus on stimulus-response relationships. Skinner hoped that this stimulus-response level of analysis would yield general principles to explain all learning in all animals from rats to humans.

The program of research that Skinner advocated did indeed yield an increased understanding of learning and many other important applications. But its generality was limited by biological predispositions and by other kinds of learning (social and cognitive) that do not depend strictly on stimulus-response relationships. We will review evidence that biological predispositions must be taken into account when comparing results across species or across different age groups within the same species. We will

Operant conditioning
Type of learning that occurs when desired responses are rewarded or reinforced and undesired responses are ignored or punished.

Reinforcement
Event whose occurrence just after a response increases the likelihood that the response will be repeated. See *positive, negative reinforcement*; compare with *punishment*.

introduce two other kinds of learning and related theories: 1) *social learning theories* that address learning by imitation, and 2) *cognitive learning theories* that address the function of thought processes in learning. Finally, we will consider two other levels of analysis that have been very productive in recent years: 1) psychobiological analyses and 2) computational analyses of learning processes (see Chapter 1).

Classical Conditioning

Pavlov knew that a dog salivates automatically in response to food. A dog doesn't have to learn this response. Pavlov figured, however, that dogs salivate in response to other stimuli because they learn to do so. He assumed, for example, that his dogs learned to respond to the sight of food and to the sound of footsteps. He decided to investigate this learning process by training dogs to salivate to some stimulus that ordinarily does not cause a dog's mouth to water. He found that a bell served his purpose. Untrained dogs did not respond to the bell; dogs who had the bell paired with the presentation of food, after a while would salivate at the sound of the bell. Presentation of food was not necessary! Figure 6–2 shows the apparatus that he used to test this.

His experiment included the four basic elements of the training procedure known as classical conditioning:

1. Food causes salivation without conditioning, so it is called the **unconditioned stimulus (US).** Food automatically or reflexively causes a dog's mouth to water.

2. The salivation response to food also happens without conditioning, so it is called the **unconditioned response (UR).** It happens automatically or reflexively in response to food, or the US.

3. The bell does not cause salivation until after conditioning, so it is called the **conditioned stimulus (CS).** It is a stimulus to which an animal learns to respond.

4. The response to a CS, such as Pavlov's bell, is called a **conditioned response (CR),** to distinguish it from a UR. One way that a CR often

Unconditioned stimulus (US)
Something that automatically or reflexively causes a response.
Unconditioned response (UR)
Automatic or reflexive reaction to a stimulus.
Conditioned stimulus (CS)
Stimulus to which a subject learns to respond through repeated pairings with an unconditioned stimulus (US).
Conditioned response (CR)
Learned response to a conditioned stimulus (CS). Usually a less strong response than an unconditioned response (UR).

FIGURE 6–2

Pavlov's basic training apparatus.

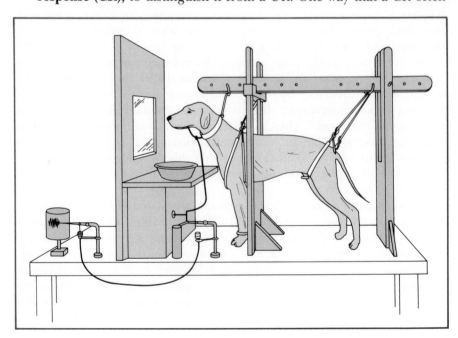

differs from a UR is in the strength of the response. In Pavlov's experiment, for instance, the CR contained fewer drops of saliva than the UR. That is, after conditioning, a dog's mouth watered less in response to a bell than it did in response to food.

Figure 6–3 summarizes Pavlov's conditioning procedure. Before classical conditioning, the CS (bell) did not cause salivation. But the US (food) did cause a UR (salivation). During the conditioning, the CS and US were paired. That is, Pavlov rang the bell and then, shortly afterward, gave food. After conditioning, the CS (bell) was presented alone and Pavlov's dogs salivated (CR). By pairing the food and the bell, Pavlov established in the dogs a salivation response to the bell.

A favorite way to test students' understanding of conditioning is to give them an example and have them identify the US, UR, CS, and CR. How would you do? Let's find out by considering a recent experiment. Jones and Davey (1990) attempted to study the worry process in a classical conditioning experiment that had three parts. The first part conditioned undergraduate subjects. Before conditioning, a mild skin shock induced a fear response, but a warning signal did not. During conditioning, the warning signal was followed by the shock. After conditioning, the warning signal elicited a fear response. In the second part of the experiment, a "worry" group thought about the feared warning signal. Control groups thought about unrelated events that were either aversive or nonaversive. In the third part of the experiment, the undergraduates were again tested by presenting the warning signal without the shock. Subjects in the "worry" condition retained the fear response, but subjects in the other conditions did not. What were the US, UR, CS, and CR? The answers are as follows: US = shock, UR = fear response to shock, CS = warning signal, CR = fear response to warning signal. The results suggest that worrying about a CS can aid in the persistence of a fear CR.

Classical conditioning is a simple kind of learning that has many important applications in its own right (see Highlight: "Applying Classical Conditioning." The applications will give you other examples in which to practice identifying the US, UR, CS, and CR). In addition, conditioning may at times provide a temporary stepping stone for more complicated learning processes, which will be discussed later in this chapter. To illustrate this, let's consider the possibility that classical conditioning paved the way for Keller's famous insight about finger spelling of the word *water*.

Recall Sullivan's description of the events leading to her student's insight: "As the cold water gushed forth, filling the mug, I spelled 'w-a-t-e-r' in Helen's free hand. The word coming so close upon the sensation of cold water rushing over her hand seemed to startle her. She dropped the mug and stood as one transfixed. A new light came into her face." Perhaps it was a coincidence that Keller's insight came at that moment. But perhaps there was something special about the pairing of cool water and finger spelling.

To relate this learning experience to conditioning, we might call water the US and finger spelling the CS. Before conditioning, the US (the water) led to a UR, which was a set of automatic responses, such as shivering. The CS (the finger spelling) led to no response. During conditioning the US and CS were paired. After conditioning the CS led to a CR, a response similar to the UR. That is, we might speculate that after the water and finger spelling were paired, finger spelling caused Keller to shiver and make other responses that she had previously made to the cold water. This new stimulus-response connection might have provided a building block for her realization that the finger spelling stood for water. After having made the connection, she repeated the finger spelling, which now had a new meaning for her. We are only speculating, of course, because

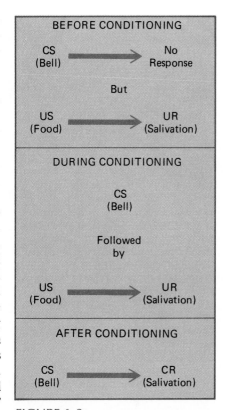

FIGURE 6–3

This is a diagram of what occurred in Pavlov's conditioning procedure.

APPLYING CLASSICAL CONDITIONING

Psychologists have used classical conditioning techniques to improve the well-being of their patients. In one case, classical conditioning was used to treat alcoholism (Davidson, 1974). Davidson paired the sight, taste, and smell of alcohol (CS) with a drug (US) that caused vomiting (UR). After many such pairings, Davidson's patients developed a nausea response (CR) to alcohol itself. This treatment is called *aversion therapy*, and it can help break other drug dependencies such as cocaine addiction (Frawley & Smith, 1990). It has also been effective in breaking bad habits such as thumb-sucking (Friman & Leibowitz, 1990).

In another case, classical conditioning was used to treat irrational fear, such as the fear of harmless bugs (Wolpe, 1962). Wolpe assumed that bugs were a CS and that fear was a CR. Working from that assumption, he experimentally extinguished the undesirable CR. He first asked patients to think about bugs. This produced a mild fear response. But the response soon extinguished, because it was never paired with a sting, bite or any other US. After the response was extinguished, Wolpe introduced pictures of bugs, which again elicited mild fear. This fear, too, was extinguished. Wolpe gradually extinguished one CR after another, until finally patients could even touch bugs without being afraid. Wolpe's procedure is called *systematic desensitization therapy*, and it has

helped many patients overcome irrational fears such as public-speaking anxiety (Longo & VomSaol, 1981).

Similar logic has been used to help cancer chemotherapy patients reduce anticipatory nausea and vomiting. Cancer chemotherapy (US) causes nausea and vomiting (UR). The treatment in a clinical setting (CS) results in pairing the US and CS. As a result, the CS begins to produce nausea and vomiting (CR) after a number of treatments. Recent research suggests that this conditioned response can be reduced by training patients to relax in the clinical setting (Andrykowski & Redd, 1987; Burish, Carey, Krozely, & Greco, 1987).

Another clinical condition that has been treated with classical conditioning is Raynaud's disease, a disorder characterized by difficulty in circulating enough blood to the hands (and sometimes the feet) to keep them warm. This failure to warm the hands and feet eventually damages the fingers and toes. Jobe, Sampson, Roberts, and Kelly (1986) found that symptoms of Raynaud's disease can be reduced through classical conditioning. They immersed the subject's hands in warm water (UCS) and simultaneously exposed the whole body to cold air (CS). Before conditioning, the warm water would warm the hands (UCR); after conditioning, cold air (CS) produced a vascular response that warmed the hands (CR). This conditioned

response helped the patients keep their hands warm on a test immediately after treatment and on a test given one year later.

Classical conditioning research has also helped save wild coyotes, an endangered species. Ranchers wanted to destroy coyotes because they prey on lamb and other livestock. Environmentalists, who wanted to save coyotes, realized that they somehow had to force coyotes to leave livestock alone. A solution emerged from classical conditioning laboratories. In one laboratory, John Garcia found that rats learned to avoid food that made them sick. In another laboratory setting, it was learned that the "Garcia effect" could be used to solve the coyote problem (Gustavson et al., 1974). The experimenters fed coyotes either poisoned lamb meat or poisoned rabbit meat. The poison (US) made the coyotes sick (UR), but it did not kill them. Afterward, the coyotes developed an aversion (CR) to the kind of food that had been poisoned (CS) even though there was no poison in the meats after the initial training session. They would eat rabbit meat if lamb had been poisoned, or lamb if rabbit had been poisoned, but they would not touch the kind of meat that had made them sick. The same procedure worked in the wild, forcing coyotes to return to their natural prey and leave livestock alone. Similar procedures are also being tested for teaching farm animals to avoid dangerous plants (Zahorik, Houpt, & Swartzman-Andert, 1990).

we cannot be sure that classical conditioning was part of Keller's learning process. One way to evaluate our speculation is to analyze factors that are necessary for establishing and extinguishing classically conditioned responses.

Important Factors in Classical Conditioning

Pavlov's work established many of the factors that are important for establishing classically conditioned responses.

Establishing a Response.   The likelihood of establishing a conditioned response depends on five factors:

1. The CS must be *strong and distinctive*. Pavlov's dogs heard his bell easily and were readily conditioned to it. Pavlov probably would have failed, however, if he had tried to condition his dogs to salivate whenever

he lightly touched their back. Helen Keller's learning experience passes this criterion, for finger spelling is strong and distinctive.

2. The *order* in which the CS and US are presented makes a difference. Conditioning is best when the CS comes slightly before the US. Pavlov, for instance, rang the bell before giving food. Conditioning is less effective when the CS and US are presented at the same time, and conditioning is weakest if the CS is presented after the US (backward conditioning). Sullivan presented water and finger spelling at the same time, which is not the most effective pairing, but it doesn't rule out classical conditioning.

3. Classical conditioning also depends on the time lapse between the CS and US. Usually, conditioning is best if the interval is between a fraction of a second and a few seconds. Pavlov's dogs did not learn to respond to his bell when Pavlov waited too long to give them food after the bell. Keller's interval was zero, which is acceptable, but not the best.

4. Most classical conditioning requires *repeated pairings* of the CS and US. Pavlov paired the bell and food several times before his dogs salivated at the sound of the bell. Once salivation occurs in response to a bell, one can measure the strength of the CR by recording the drops of saliva; the more drops, the higher the strength. One finds that strength of the CR grows gradually with each presentation, until the CR is almost as strong as the UR. Sullivan noticed a sudden response to finger spelling, but we cannot rule out the possibility that weaker responses built up gradually before that. If we want to argue that classical conditioning was involved, we must assume that a CR strengthened gradually until Sullivan noticed what only appeared to be the first response.

5. The rate at which a classically conditioned response strengthens depends upon how the experimenter *spaces* the pairings of the CS and US. Conditioning will be slower if pairings follow each other too quickly or too far apart. This factor does not help us categorize Keller's experience.

Extinguishing a Response.   Classically conditioned responses need not last forever. We find that Pavlov's dogs stopped salivating to the sound of a bell when the bell was rung many times without food being given. Figure 6–4 shows that the strength of a CR gradually decreases to no response at all if the CS is repeatedly presented alone. This falling off is called **extinction.** Once a response has been extinguished it can reappear

Extinction
In classical conditioning, the gradual falling off or decrease in a response when the conditioned stimulus (CS) is repeatedly presented alone without the unconditioned stimulus (US). In operant conditioning, a falling off of a response when it is no longer followed by a reinforcer.

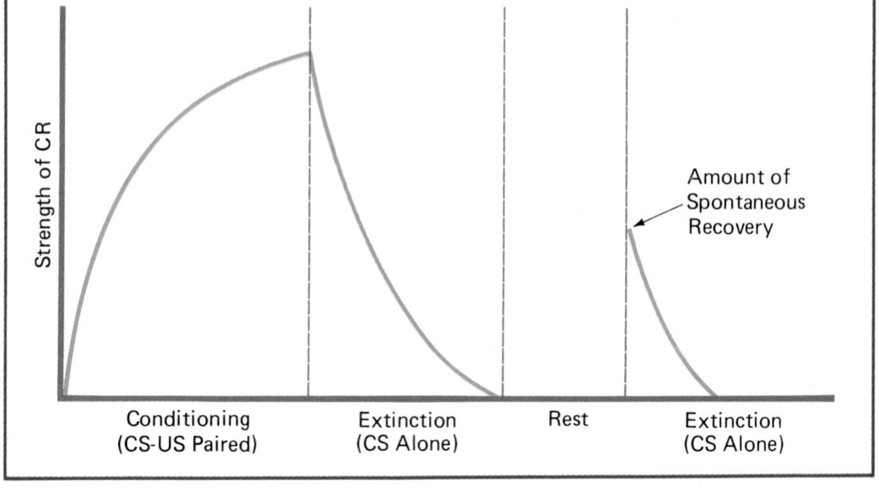

FIGURE 6–4
The strength of a CR gradually decreases if the CS is always repeated alone. This is called extinction. Spontaneous recovery occurs if the response reappears again without any further pairings of CS and US; but the response will eventually extinguish again if the CS is repeatedly presented alone.

Strength of CR

Amount of Spontaneous Recovery

| Conditioning (CS-US Paired) | Extinction (CS Alone) | Rest | Extinction (CS Alone) |

again without any further pairing of the CS and US. Pavlov called this **spontaneous recovery.** He conditioned dogs to salivate when they heard a bell, and then he extinguished the response so that his dogs' mouths did not water when they heard the bell. Several days later, Pavlov tested his dogs again. As soon as the dogs heard the bell, their mouths began to water. The response reappeared without any retraining. Figure 6–4 shows that spontaneous recovery does not bring a response back to its full strength and the response extinguishes again if the CS is repeatedly presented alone.

After the first pairing of finger spelling the water, finger spelling was undoubtedly presented alone many, many times. Thus, if conditioning played a part in Keller's learning, it was only a temporary role. Because of conditioning, Keller might have shivered in response to finger spelling, and this might have helped her learn the connection between it and water. But this was only a stepping stone to other types of learning, which supplemented and built upon the original conditioning that had taken place.

Generalizing Conditioned Responses

Staying with the idea that conditioning might have set the stage for Keller's learning, we can ask other questions about the conditioning. For example, would she have shivered only in response to Sullivan's finger spelling, or would a similar stimulus also have elicited the conditioned response? Pavlov's experiment provided an answer. After Pavlov's dogs had been conditioned to salivate to the sound of a bell, their mouths also watered when they heard a buzzer and a metronome. This reaction to similar stimuli is called **stimulus generalization.** Conditioned responses are elicited not only by the conditioned stimulus, but also by similar stimuli.

John Watson demonstrated stimulus generalization in an experiment that surely would not be allowed today (Watson & Rayner, 1920). Before the experiment, Albert, an 11-month-old boy, was not afraid of white rats. When he saw one, he crawled toward it and wanted to play with it. During conditioning, Watson and Rayner presented the white rat (CS), waited for Albert to approach, and then made a loud noise by clanging steel bars behind him (US). The earsplitting sound made Albert cry (UR). After several such pairings of the rat and noise, Albert developed a conditioned fear of the rat. When he saw it, even if there was no noise, he immediately started to cry, and he tried to crawl away. The experimenters then showed Albert a white rabbit, a fur coat, and a Santa Claus mask. All of these things terrified him; he had generalized from the white rat to the rabbit and other white furry objects.

Similarly, stimulus generalization causes long-lasting distress to rape victims. Situations that are similar to the one in which the attack occurred induce distress long after other symptoms of the rape have subsided. Using a classical conditioning model of stimulus generalization, researchers are trying to help rape victims by controlling attack-similar situations during the recovery process (Wirtz & Harrell, 1987).

Most of the traditional research on classical conditioning has concentrated on stimulus-response relationships. Few attempts were made to identify the cognitive processes that determined the observed stimulus-response patterns. Today, such attempts are being made. For example, Pearce (1987) developed a cognitive model of stimulus generalization in classical conditioning. According to the model, a memory of the stimulus is formed during conditioning. Stimulus generalization occurs after conditioning when this memory and a new stimulus have similar properties such as size, shape, color, and texture.

Spontaneous recovery
Occurs when a response reappears without any retraining after having been extinguished.
Stimulus generalization
Occurs when responses are made to stimuli that are similar to, but not the same as, the original conditioned stimulus (CS).

Discrimination

If stimulus generalization were carried too far, conditioning would not be a useful building block for learning. In finger spelling, for instance, it is necessary to discriminate between different patterns. Pavlov showed that his conditioned dogs could make **discriminations.** Pavlov presented one sound followed by food and a similar sound without food. The dogs learned to salivate to the sound that had been followed by the food, and they learned not to salivate to the other sound. In this way, they learned to discriminate between the stimuli.

Higher-Order Conditioning

Animals and humans often base new learning on old learning—for example, Keller learned new finger spellings based on old ones. If conditioning is a building block for learning, then we should expect Pavlov's dogs to be able to base new conditioned responses upon old ones. What happens is that a well-established conditioned stimulus (CS) comes to act like a US in establishing a *second* conditioned stimulus (CS). Thus a dog or a person learns conditioned responses without getting food or any other US.

To test this, Pavlov first conditioned his dogs to salivate in response to a bell (CS). He then paired a black square (CS) with the bell. He presented the square and then the bell over and over again, occasionally pairing the bell with food. The dogs learned to salivate in response to the black square, even though *it* was never paired with food. Pavlov called this a second-order conditioned response, and he went on to establish a third-order conditioned response (Kehoe, Feyer, & Moses, 1981). Pavlov speculated that all learning might be nothing more than long chains of conditioned responses.

Modern psychologists reject the notion that classical conditioning explains all learning. Instead, they see classical conditioning as one of several kinds of learning (Rescorla & Holland, 1982). They would go beyond classical conditioning, for instance, to explain all of Keller's learning. In the next section we will see, in fact, that operant conditioning played an important role in changing Keller's behavior. Interest in classical conditioning has remained high, however, despite the discovery of other kinds of learning, as we shall see when we study psychobiological models in this chapter and the next (Chapter 7).

Discrimination
Occurs when subjects learn to respond only to certain stimuli, but not to other, similar stimuli.

Operant Conditioning

Keller's education provides many examples of operant conditioning. Sullivan devoted her life to Keller's education long before psychologists formalized principles of operant conditioning, yet her ingenious instincts guided her toward operant conditioning methods.

Acquisition of Operant Behaviors

Skinner (1938, 1966) studied operant behaviors with a procedure that was similar to Thorndike's. Skinner placed a hungry rat in a small cage that contained a food cup with a bar over it (Figure 6–5). The cup was

FIGURE 6–5

Skinner's experimental apparatus, which became known as a Skinner box, is shown here. In order to get food, the rat had to press the bar inside the box, and a food pellet was delivered into a cup in the box.

empty until the rat pushed the bar, which made a small pellet of food drop into the cup. This apparatus became known as a *Skinner box*. A cat in a puzzle box had to learn to break out in order to get food; a rat in a Skinner box had to learn how to bring food into the box.

At first Skinner's rats explored the cage, making a number of ineffective responses until they happened to press the bar. The rat then ate the food pellet that was delivered and continued to explore until it again hit the bar and brought in more food. After two or three bar presses, the rat stopped most of its ineffective responses and started to push the bar repeatedly.

About 30 years earlier Sullivan had used a similar procedure to teach Keller. Teacher and student sat at a table containing familiar objects such as a cup and a doll. Sullivan placed an object in one of Keller's hands and spelled its name in the other. She then guided Keller's fingers to spell the same name. As soon as Keller finished spelling a name correctly, Sullivan gave her a small bit of cake. If the girl made a mistake, she got no cake. Gradually, Keller stopped making mistakes and started making spelling responses quickly and correctly. The parallels between Sullivan's procedure and Skinner's procedure are amazing. Skinner's rats and Keller both stopped making responses that were not reinforced and continued making responses that were.

Positive and Negative Reinforcement. There are several different kinds of reinforcement. The basic definition of reinforcement states that it is an event that increases the likelihood that a response will be repeated. In this context, psychologists distinguish between "positive" and "negative" events. A *positive event* occurs when a stimulus is added to an environment. When a positive event serves as a reinforcer, it is called **positive reinforcement.** The rat's food pellets and Keller's cake are examples of positive reinforcement. A *negative event* occurs when a stimulus is taken away. When a negative event serves as a reinforcer, it is called **negative reinforcement.**

Skinner demonstrated negative reinforcement by using an electric shock grid on the bottom of his Skinner box. He turned on the grid and put a rat in the cage. The rat received a mild shock continuously until it pushed a bar that turned off the grid. After a short time the shock grid went on again until the rat again pushed the bar. The rat soon learned to press

Positive reinforcement
Occurs when a positive stimulus is added to the environment.
Negative reinforcement
Occurs when a stimulus is taken away or stopped.

the bar to turn off the shock. Turning *off* a shock is a negative event, because it *takes away* a stimulus. It is a reinforcing event because its occurrence increases the likelihood that a rat will push the bar. Thus, it is a negative reinforcer.

Escape and Avoidance Training. Skinner used negative reinforcement in two kinds of training programs. The rat who learned to press a bar to turn off electric shock participated in **escape training.** Skinner also used **avoidance training,** in which a negative reinforcer can be avoided altogether. He placed a rat in a Skinner box, sounded a buzzer, and then turned on a shock a few seconds later. The shock did not go on if the rat pressed the bar after the buzzer sounded and before the shock started. Pressing the bar after the shock started did no good. The shock stayed on for a fixed time, and then it went off until a few seconds after the buzzer sounded again. Gradually, rats learned to press the bar to avoid being shocked.

Learned Helplessness. An avoidance training procedure is used to demonstrate another important learning phenomenon, **learned helplessness.** This type of learning occurs when exposure to unavoidable, unpleasant events leads to an inability to avoid the unpleasant event even when avoidance is possible. Maier, Seligman, and Solomon (1969) performed a classic experiment to demonstrate learned helplessness. Dogs were paired and then randomly divided into two groups. Dogs in both groups were strapped into harnesses that prevented foot movements. Then, at random intervals, shocks were delivered to the feet. Dogs in one group could turn off the shock by pushing a panel that was in front of their nose. Dogs in the other group could not control the shocks. Both dogs in a pair received the very same shocks. The only difference was that one dog could control the shocks while the other could not.

The next day, the dogs who had been able to control the shocks followed the typical avoidance training pattern. Each dog was placed in a box that was divided by a hurdle. At the beginning of each trial, a 10-second warning light flashed. Then the floor of the box was electrified for 50 seconds. At first the dogs received a shock and then jumped the hurdle to escape it—the other side of the box was not wired. Soon, however, they learned to avoid the shock by jumping the hurdle during the warning signal.

Performance on the same avoidance learning task was strikingly different for the dogs who had not been able to control the shocks they received during the first part of the experiment. They neither avoided nor escaped the shocks during ten consecutive trials (Figure 6–6). The day before they could not control their shock. They were truly helpless. During avoidance training, however, they could have helped themselves, but they did not try. They had learned to be helpless.

Scientists have begun to investigate biochemical changes that correspond with learned helplessness (Martin, Beninger, Hamon, & Puech, 1990; Martin, Massol, & Puech, 1990; Weiss et al., 1981). In experiments by Weiss et al. (1981), one group of rats was helpless—they were not given an opportunity to escape or avoid shocks in the experimental situation. In a second situation, this group of rats did not even try to avoid shocks when they were given an opportunity to do so. Another group could control shocks in one situation, and they learned to avoid shocks in another situation. Weiss found that the rats who were in control had normal levels of the neural transmitter norepinephrine in their brains (see Chapter 2). In contrast, the helpless rats had lower levels of norepinephrine in their brains. Weiss concluded that a temporary decrease of norepinephrine is responsible for the inability to learn to avoid unpleasant stimuli. This hypothesis is consistent with other research suggesting that neural transmitters are important in learning and memory (see Chapter 7).

Escape training
Through the use of negative reinforcement a subject learns to make a response to remove a stimulus (such as a shock).
Avoidance training
Occurs when a subject learns to make a response to avoid a negative reinforcer.
Learned helplessness
A response to prolonged stress; the feeling that one's actions do not affect one's environment or what happens to one. Can lead to apathy and depression.

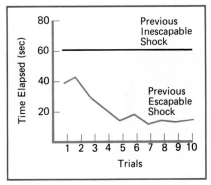

FIGURE 6–6
Learned Helplessness
The curves show the time it took two groups of dogs to escape a shock by jumping over a barrier. On each trial, one compartment of a cage became electrified after a 10-second warning signal. A trial ended if a dog did not jump the barrier to escape the shock after 60 seconds. The bottom curve is for a group of dogs who were in a similar experiment the day before. They learned to escape the shock very quickly. The upper curve is for a group of dogs who had also been in a similar experiment the day before. The difference was that they could not escape the shocks the day before. As a result, they learned to be helpless and they failed to help themselves the next day by escaping when they could have. (After Maier, Seligman, & Solomon, 1969).

Learned helplessness has also been studied in human social situations (see the discussion of Seligman's work in Chapter 11). In these situations it is related to depression. It is hoped that biochemical research on learned helplessness will lead to more effective treatment of depression (Geoffroy, Scheel-Kruger, Christensen, 1990).

Primary and Secondary Reinforcers. Besides positive and negative reinforcers, psychologists distinguish between **primary reinforcers,** which are reinforcing in and of themselves, and **secondary reinforcers,** which are reinforcing only after they have been paired with other primary reinforcers. All the examples that we considered so far (rat pellets, cake, and electric shock) are primary reinforcers. An electric shock is an effective negative reinforcer, for example, even for rats who never experienced it before. In contrast, secondary reinforcers work only after they are associated with other reinforcers. Skinner found that a rat who has had no experience in a Skinner box will not learn to press a bar if the bar turns on a light and nothing more. That is, a light is not a primary reinforcer. Skinner showed that a light can become a secondary reinforcer, however. He rigged his Skinner box to deliver food and turn on a light every time a bar was pressed. After many pairings of the food and the light, Skinner discontinued the food and continued to turn on the light whenever the rat pushed the bar. The rat continued to push the bar because the light had become a secondary reinforcer.

As a child, Keller spelled for cake, a primary reinforcer. But she probably would not have responded as well for money, because it didn't mean anything to her. Later, after money was associated with food and other rewards, Keller worked for money. In fact, she wrote her autobiography, *The Story of My Life*, primarily to earn money for her college education. Money is an effective secondary reinforcer for most of us.

Primary reinforcers
Events or objects that are reinforcing in and of themselves (such as food).

Secondary reinforcers
Events or objects that are reinforcing only after they have been paired with other primary reinforcers. Money is a good example of a secondary reinforcer.

After performing a trick, this whale accepts a primary reinforcer, food.

This new lawyer shows off his secondary reinforcer, a certificate enabling him to practice law.

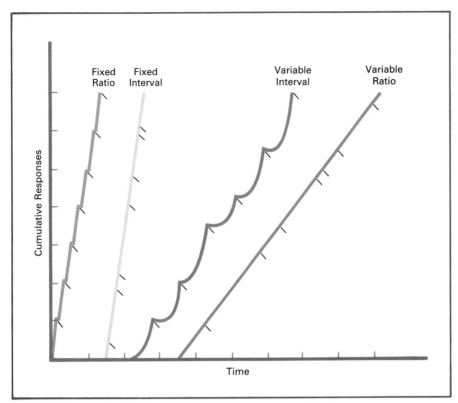

FIGURE 6–7

In a fixed-interval schedule, the scalloped line shows that the rats responded most as the end of the fixed-time interval drew closer. The variable-interval line shows more steady, constant bar presses because the animal cannot accurately judge when it will be reinforced with a food pellet. In the fixed-ratio schedule, there is a high response rate because the rats learn that the faster they press the bar, the more food pellets they receive. There is, however, a brief pause after each reinforcement. With a variable-ratio schedule, the response rate is also quite high because, again, the animal cannot judge when it will be reinforced. The pause after reinforcement is very slight.

Schedules of Reinforcement. Considering money as a reinforcer brings to mind the fact that we usually are not reinforced every time we do something. We work a certain time interval (a week or a month), and then we get our paycheck. Or we finish a fixed amount of work (mowing the lawn) and then we get paid. When Keller received cake for every correct spelling, she was on a **continuous reinforcement schedule.** Later, when she received royalty checks from the sale of her book (these came twice a year), she was on a **partial reinforcement schedule.**

Psychologists have studied schedules that are based upon time (weekly paychecks) and schedules that are based upon the amount of work done (mowing the lawn). They have also studied schedules that are fixed (e.g., a weekly allowance) and schedules that are variable (e.g., an allowance given whenever parents see fit). The following are four common schedules:

1. **Fixed-interval schedules** reinforce the first response after a predetermined constant time interval. Skinner would train the rat to press a bar for food. Then he rigged his Skinner box so that it would deliver food after a bar press, wait 5 minutes, deliver food to the next bar press, wait another 5 minutes, and so on. During the 5-minute waiting intervals, bar presses were useless; they did not deliver food. After being on this schedule for a short time, rats stopped responding immediately after food was delivered and then they resumed the response pattern at a high rate as the end of the 5-minute interval approached (Figure 6–7, top). This response pattern is similar to what students do when exams are given at fixed intervals. They rarely study immediately after exams, but they often cram like mad right before an exam.

2. **Variable-interval schedules** reinforce the first response after varying time intervals. The first time interval might be 9 minutes, the second one 2 minutes, the third one 4 minutes, and then 3 minutes, 3 minutes, 7 minutes, 5 minutes, and so on. Skinner found that rats give a slow, steady rate of response when they are reinforced on a variable-interval

Continuous reinforcement schedule
Subject receives a reinforcer for every correct response.
Partial reinforcement schedule
Subject is reinforced every few responses or every once in awhile, but not for every response.
Fixed-interval schedule
Reinforces the first response made after a certain time interval (e.g., after 5 minutes or 2 weeks). Produces a slow rate of responding immediately after a reinforcer is received, building up to a high rate of response as the end of the time interval is reached.
Variable-interval schedule
Reinforces the first response made after varying time intervals (the first interval might be 5 minutes, then 9 minutes, then 1 minute, etc.). Produces a slow, steady rate of response.

schedule (Figure 6–7, bottom). This pattern is similar to students' study habits in a course in which "pop quizzes" are given at unpredictable times. Students study at a steady rate because they have to be prepared for a quiz at any time. Scientists have recently become interested in what rats do when they are not responding during a variable-interval schedule. For example, Iverson (1986) observed activities such as grooming, exploring, and running on a wheel. He found that these activities are not ordered randomly. Lever pressing dominates short intervals, exploration dominates intermediate intervals, and wheel running or grooming dominate long intervals.

3. **Fixed-ratio schedules** reinforce the first response after a certain number of responses have been made. A fixed ratio of 1 in 10 would reinforce every tenth response. Rats on fixed-ratio schedules respond at a fast, steady rate. They have to push a bar many times to get one reinforcer, and they find that the faster they push, the more reinforcers they get. Factories sometimes pay workers on a fixed-ratio schedule. Knitting mills, for example, may pay workers for every 100 mittens finished. The more mittens workers finish, the more money they get, so they usually work at an incredibly fast rate. A job with a fixed-ratio schedule is called *piecework*; it can work out well for both the employer and the employee. Fixed-ratio reinforcement schedules have also been shown to be effective in promoting exercise. Fixed-ratio was much more effective than fixed-interval in increasing the pedaling rate of a stationary bicycle (DeLuca & Holborn, 1990).

4. **Variable-ratio schedules** reinforce the first response after a varying number of responses. A variable-ratio schedule might reinforce the tenth response, then the fourth response after that, then the seventh response after that, and so on. Animals on this kind of schedule respond at a very fast, steady rate, as do people. Experimenters control the size of the reinforcement and ratio (e.g., reinforce 1 in 10 responses on average versus 1 in 50 responses). Schlinger, Blakely, and Kaozor (1990) found that both of these factors influence the response rate.

   Slot machines are a good example of a variable-ratio schedule. They are set to pay off after varying numbers of attempts. Gamblers might win two in a row, or they might have to play a hundred times before winning. What seems to be important is that the next time *could* always bring the jackpot; one never knows. Gamblers seem to treat each attempt as if it will be the one to pay off. They respond rapidly and continue to respond over and over for a long time.

Fixed-ratio schedule
Schedules that reinforce the first response after a certain number of responses have been made. Produces a fast, steady rate of responding.

Variable-ratio schedule
Reinforces the first response made after a varying number of responses (the tenth response; the fourth response after that; the twelfth response after the previous response, etc.). Produces a rapid, steady rate of responding.

Gambling is a good example of a variable-ratio schedule of reinforcement. The best way to avoid being hooked by gambling, as Kenny Rogers warns in his song "The Gambler," may be to know when to walk away.

Kenny Rogers, in his song "The Gambler," warns us that we "have to know when to walk away and when to run." The best time to run away from slot machines may be before you deposit a single coin. That way you can avoid getting caught up in its captivating reinforcement schedule. Knowing this, some gambling casinos give customers a few complimentary coins to get them started (and hooked). This ploy is one solution to the general problem we will discuss next: How do you get someone to make that first operant response so that the behavior can be brought under the control of a reinforcement schedule?

Encouraging a First Operant Response

Once Keller started finger spelling, her teacher could reinforce her with cake. But how did Sullivan get the young girl started? Indeed, how does any parent or teacher get children to perform desirable behavior the first time? Let's look at some ways this can be done.

Hurry-Up-and-Wait.   Some responses occur without special coaxing. To bring such behaviors under the control of operant conditioning, teachers are faced with a hurry-up-and-wait routine. They must hurry up and reward a response when it occurs; then they must wait patiently for the next time it occurs. If a response is ignored, it will stop; if it is reinforced, it will recur over and over again.

Sullivan used a hurry-up-and-wait procedure to teach Keller to ask questions. Sullivan believed that "Why?" would be the door through which her student would enter the world of reason and reflection. She therefore waited watchfully for Keller to ask questions and she immediately greeted every question with warm encouragement as well as with answers. Soon Keller was asking questions all day long. "Who put chickens in eggs?" "Can flies know not to bite?" "Why is Viney black?" Her questions were not all as intelligent as these. In fact, Sullivan always insisted that Keller's mind was not superior to that of others. All children seem to crack open the "Why?" door. Parents and teachers have the power through operant conditioning either to slam the door by ignoring questions or to aid its opening by reinforcing them.

Increasing Motivation.   Another way to encourage a first response is to increase the motivation for the individual to make the response. Sullivan did this with Keller. She had been refusing to use her napkin, and Sullivan anticipated another protest. She therefore cut down on Keller's snacks, making sure that the girl was hungry before dinner. Keller's hunger increased her motivation for food, which had been paired with proper use of a napkin in earlier battles. That night Keller used her napkin properly, and she was immediately reinforced with a delicious dinner.

Verbal Instructions and Modeling.   There is, however, a limit to what one can do by increasing motivation. Even if Keller had been craving cake, she would not have started finger spelling out of the blue if Sullivan had not been "talking" to her constantly. They went for long walks during which Sullivan described in finger spelling everything that they encountered. Sullivan's finger spelling provided a model of the desired behavior. Parents and teachers often must describe and demonstrate operant behaviors in order to get them started in children. According to Huber (1986) describing and discussing specific goals is also important when using operant principles of reinforcement in personnel management. She recommends promises of pay-for-performance after a careful analysis of an individual's or group's reinforcement history. Performance should be defined with respect to specific goals and both the goals and the promises of pay-for-performance should be described and discussed in advance.

This photograph shows a scene from the movie "The Miracle Worker," which is the story of Helen Keller and Anne Sullivan. Here Anne and Helen are engaged in one of their frequent early battles at the table. Helen soon realized that Anne would not tolerate unacceptable behaviors and she gradually began to behave appropriately. Anne could then strengthen the proper responses through reinforcement.

Shaping
Procedure used in operant conditioning in which each part of a behavior is reinforced that eventually leads to the whole behavior that is desired.

Increasing Restraints on Other Possible Behaviors. Sullivan was every bit as strong willed as Keller, but the child's parents eventually gave Keller her way if she misbehaved long enough. She would grab food from her parent's plate, throw her napkin on the floor, and kick the table until she got exactly what she wanted. Sullivan figured that her war over table manners was being drawn out because Keller had too many options and too many distractions. Sullivan therefore insisted that she be allowed to spend time alone with the girl in a nearby guest house. It was in this more controlled environment that Sullivan finally gained control over Keller. At first she "kicked and screamed herself into a sort of stupor" every time she disagreed with a command (Lash, 1980, p. 51). But when Sullivan demanded a certain behavior she allowed Keller no other choice, even if it meant physically restraining her. One night they struggled for 2 hours before Keller finally stayed in bed. Eventually she realized that her tantrums were to no avail, and she started to learn rapidly in response to positive reinforcement.

Decreasing Restraints. Once Keller learned basic obedience, Sullivan removed any restraints that might have stood in the way of learning. She did not require Keller to use complete sentences or proper grammar. At first she reinforced her for using single words to express sentences. For example, she praised Keller for using "milk" to express "Give me more milk." Later she reinforced her for using poorly constructed word strings. Once Keller was trying to express "Baby cannot eat because she has no teeth." Sullivan praised her for spelling "Baby teeth-no, baby eat-no." A schoolteacher might not have praised this poorly constructed word string. But by allowing Keller more freedom than deaf children generally had in schools, Sullivan started her student down a learning path that led to much greater ease with language than any deaf child had ever had before.

Shaping. Gradually, as Keller's language skill increased, Sullivan became more discriminating with her reinforcement. Looking back, we can see that she used a procedure that is called **shaping.** That is, she realized that the child had to go through intermediate steps before she would master the whole of forming sentences. She therefore shaped the whole by reinforcing the intermediate steps.

Skinner (1938) used shaping to teach a bird to walk in a figure eight. He first reinforced the bird for turning its head in the right direction. When the bird learned that, Skinner withheld reinforcement until the bird stepped in the right direction. Gradually, Skinner demanded more and more before he gave rewards. The pigeon had to take several steps in the right direction. Next, it had to do that and also make the appropriate turn. After doing those two things, the pigeon then had to take a few more steps. Skinner continued with this procedure until the bird was making a figure eight to get its reward. More recently, Dahlquist (1990) used shaping to eliminate vomiting in a 13-year-old boy with a history of vomiting for ten days after swallowing any substance.

Benji, a lovable dog who starred in several children's movies, learned his tricks with the help of shaping. In one episode, he climbed a stack of boxes, walked a narrow plank to a roof, climbed the roof, and finally jumped through an open window into a house. Benji's trainer taught the trick by first shaping the last feat of the series, jumping through the window. He then shaped the second-to-last part, using the window as a secondary reinforcer. That is, Benji had to run across the roof in order to get to the window, which had already been paired with a reward. Benji's trainer kept working backward through the steps. Soon Benji could perform the whole behavior chain to the delight of his young audience.

Animal trainers use the technique of shaping to teach animals to perform various tricks. In shaping, they reinforce each step of a series of behaviors until eventually the animal can perform the complete behavior chain.

Extinguishing Operant Behaviors

So far, we have examined operant conditioning when it was being used to establish certain desired responses or behaviors. It can also establish undesirable behaviors. These must then be extinguished. Sullivan's war with Keller over manners was difficult, because the girl's obnoxious behavior had been firmly established by operant conditioning. Her father was the inadvertent trainer. He couldn't stand to see his daughter unhappy, so he gave her what she wanted. When she threw her napkin on the floor, he let her eat anyway. When she grabbed food from his plate, he let her have it. When she resisted going to bed, he let her stay up, and he gave her a little treat to quiet her down. Each time, he provided an immediate reward, thereby reinforcing her behavior. We can examine some of Sullivan's battles with Keller in more detail to learn general principles of wiping out or extinguishing operant behaviors.

Extinction. Operant behaviors are extinguished by withholding reinforcement. But they do not decrease immediately when reinforcement is withheld. In fact, they increase and become more forceful for a brief period after reinforcement stops. The first few times that Sullivan failed to reward Keller's tantrums, the girl unleashed fits of rage that lasted for up to 2 hours. Sullivan made sure that Keller received no rewards for such frenzies. Gradually the outbursts stopped.

Four factors affect how difficult it is to extinguish operant behaviors. Keller's behaviors made extinction difficult on all four counts:

1. The stronger the original learning, the harder it is to extinguish. Keller's tantrums had been stamped in by years of inadvertent, but effective, conditioning.

2. Behaviors are harder to extinguish when they are learned in a variety of settings. Keller's tantrums had worked for her at bedtime, mealtime, and playtime. They had worked inside or outside the house, in public or in private. In fact, they had worked at any time and in any place.

3. Complex behaviors are more difficult to extinguish. Keller's tantrums consisted of many different behaviors that had to be stopped. She cried, kicked, screamed, hit, scratched, and pinched. Each of these behaviors had to be extinguished.

4. Behaviors learned by partial reinforcement are harder to extinguish. Keller's father had unintentionally put her on a variable-ratio schedule. Sometimes he rewarded her first action; sometimes he held out until she went through ten or more actions. The girl learned not to expect a reward for every action. She learned to continue to respond until she eventually was rewarded. As a result, when Sullivan permanently withdrew rewards, Keller continued to respond for a long time.

With the deck stacked against her, Sullivan made no attempt to tiptoe around Keller's behavior. She rapidly issued one command after another, forcing the girl to comply each time. We can now see that Sullivan's instincts had taken her in the right direction again. Many experiments with animals have shown that extinction is easier when nonreinforced behaviors occur in rapid succession. Modern studies also show that responses are weaker and easier to extinguish in a new environment. Sullivan's move to the garden house was therefore another factor working in her favor.

Skinner and other behaviorists have taken the science of behavior modification well beyond the intuitions that guided Sullivan. Their many experiments have provided a solid foundation for important clinical applications of operant procedures, including extinction (Acosta, 1990).

Spontaneous Recovery. Keller moved back to the main house shortly after she started to learn names. She explored everything around her with such enthusiasm that she seemed to have no time for tantrums. One might have thought that they were extinguished for good. But when dinnertime came, she refused to use her napkin and threw it to the floor. This mild outburst was an example of *spontaneous recovery*. It occurs in animals as well as humans. Skinner extinguished bar pressing responses in rats and then he tested them again after a delay. The rats pressed the bar again with no retraining.

The spontaneous recovery of Keller's tantrums did not last long. For the most part, she left her spoiled behavior in her "prison-house." With keys provided by her teacher, she emerged from her prison of isolation a new person eager to explore every facet of her new-found world.

Punishment. A **punishment** is a stimulus that *decreases* the likelihood of a response when it is added to an environment. Spankings and scoldings are common punishments. Parents may be wise to use these when a dangerous behavior, such as running out into traffic, must be eliminated fast.

Skinner (1938) demonstrated the effectiveness of punishments in experiments on rats who had learned to press a bar for food. Bar pressing was extinguished when Skinner withheld food, but it was eliminated much faster when he shocked rats every time they pushed the bar. Again, notice that electric shock used as a punishment is quite different from electric shock used as a negative reinforcer. Punishments are imposed to eliminate responses; negative reinforcers are stopped to increase responses.

Briggs (1990) combined reinforcements and punishments to reduce absenteeism in staff caring for severely retarded young adults. Briggs rewarded staff members for reliable attendance and disciplined them when they missed work. This procedure reduced absenteeism by 27 percent over a 12-month period.

Sullivan used punishment wisely. Every time Keller hit her, she immediately slapped her hand. Studies with animals have shown that both immediacy and consistency are important. Animal studies have also shown that punishments are much more effective when they are not accompanied by rewards. Sullivan's instincts served her well with respect to this variable also. She never followed punishments with rewards. Some parents make the mistake of hugging and kissing their children immediately after a spanking. Sullivan was wise enough to avoid such mixed messages.

Thanks to her superior teaching skills, Sullivan was able to punish Keller without terrifying her. Less skilled teachers disrupt learning by frightening children with punishment. The key to Sullivan's success was her ability to provide Keller with acceptable, alternative behaviors. Keller soon learned that her teacher was as quick to reward her good behaviors as she was to punish her bad ones. Sullivan's unfailing responsiveness to Keller paid off in extremely rapid learning. Less than 2 weeks elapsed between Keller's 2-hour tantrum at bedtime and her finger spelling breakthrough at the pump house.

Implications for Parents and Teachers. Let's review what we have just discussed by looking at the implications for parents and teachers of the following operant conditioning principles:

1. *Avoid reinforcing undesirable behaviors.* Few parents reward tantrums to the extent that Mr. Keller did, but some parents inadvertently condition tantrums in public. Parents who would not dream of giving in to a tantrum at home do so in public to avoid an embarrassing scene. Such parents are soon asking why their child is an angel at home and a devil in public. The best way to avoid this Jekyll-and-Hyde behavior is to ignore or punish public tantrums right from the start. One or two uncomfortable situations in the beginning will avoid many more later on.

2. *Immediately reward desirable behaviors.* Children love attention, so a smile or a hug is often reward enough. Sullivan used lots of this kind of attention to reinforce her student. In the same way, alert parents can direct most of their attention toward positive reinforcers, which greatly reduce the need for punishment. For example, McNeill and Todd

Punishment
Stimulus that decreases the likelihood of a response when it is added to an environment. Compare with *reinforcement*.

(1986) described a case in which they designed a reinforcement schedule for a mother to use in helping her 5-year-old daughter recover from molestation. One problem was that the child frequently became emotionally upset as she talked excessively about her sexual attack. The reinforcement schedule was designed to reduce this problem by having the mother ignore the talking and reinforce other behaviors. The problem subsided after a short time and was still under control 12 months later.

Positive reinforcers are also effective in schools. In one study, Gupta, Stringer, and Meakin (1990) involved both teachers and parents. Teachers gave 24 high-school students credit cards (secondary reinforcers) for improvements at school. Their parents gave praise and other primary reinforcers for the credit cards. Teachers, parents, and students liked this approach. In addition, the students improved in attendance, motivation, and work completed.

3. *Supplement punishments with rewards of desirable responses.* Never reward and punish the *same* behavior by giving hugs and kisses immediately after a punishment, but do watch for good behaviors to reward. If Sullivan had not rewarded good behaviors, her punishments might have terrified Keller. In the same way, children may become too afraid to learn if teachers do not praise correct responses as often as they criticize wrong ones. Today, teachers' manuals include these and other principles of operant conditioning. As a result, formal applications of operant principles have found their way into the classroom.

Generalization

About 1½ months after Keller started to learn names, she demonstrated an interesting example of **stimulus generalization,** which means giving the same response to similar stimuli. One day, shortly after learning to call her little sister "baby," she ran up to Sullivan and spelled "dog-baby" over and over. She also pointed to her five fingers one after another and she sucked them. Sullivan's first thought was that a dog had bitten Keller's sister, but the girl seemed too delighted to be carrying bad news. Sullivan followed Keller to the pump-house where she found that the Keller's setter had given birth to five adorable puppies. Helen had generalized the response "baby" to include the puppies. Sullivan taught Keller the word "puppies," which she used correctly after that. Stimulus generalization is common in children and Keller's example is typical.

Children also demonstrate **response generalization,** which is giving different, but similar, responses to the same stimulus. A child who is reinforced for saying "bye-bye" may also say "gye-gye" or "pye-pye." Parents can eliminate such inappropriate response generalizations by reinforcing only the correct responses.

Discrimination

The opposite of stimulus generalization is **stimulus discrimination,** which means making different responses to different stimuli. Keller demonstrated discrimination when she gave the response "baby" to her sister and the response "puppies" to her new pets.

You are discriminating whenever you stop for a red traffic light and go for a green one. Skinner (1938) showed that even pigeons can learn simple red-green discriminations. He taught pigeons to peck at a white disc and then he presented two discs, one red and one green. He gave food every time the pigeon pecked the green disc, and he gave nothing when the pigeon pecked the red one. Soon the pigeon pecked only the

Stimulus generalization
Occurs when responses are made to stimuli that are similar to, but not the same as, the original conditioned stimulus (CS).
Response generalization
Means giving different, but similar, responses to the same stimulus.
Stimulus discrimination
Making different responses to different stimuli.

green disc. Skinner's procedure is valuable for parents to remember. When children first learn the word "mama" they often apply it to all women. Mothers can teach the appropriate discrimination by ignoring incorrect applications and by reinforcing the correct one.

Preparedness

In our previous examples, cats learned to brush up against a string, rats learned to press bars, pigeons learned to peck, and children learned names. Does it matter which animals learn which responses? Traditional theorists would have said that operant conditioning can link any stimulus with any response, and that will hold true for all animals. Modern theorists say that **preparedness** is also involved here—that animals are more prepared to make certain responses than others, and may find other responses more difficult to make (Timberlake, Wahl, & King, 1982).

Evidence favors preparedness between and within species. Rats learn to jump to avoid foot shocks faster than they learn to press a bar to avoid the same stimulus. This may be because rats are biologically predisposed to jump when they are frightened. Pigeons learn to peck a disc for food faster than rats learn to press a bar for food. One might argue that pigeons are smarter. But this explanation seems ruled out by another fact. It takes pigeons longer to learn *not* to peck than it takes rats to learn *not* to press a bar. Apparently, pigeons are more biologically predisposed to peck for food than rats are predisposed to press a bar for food. These and other results support the theory of preparedness differences between species (Wickelgren, 1977). There is also evidence for preparedness differences as a function of age within the same species. For example, Markiewicz, Kucharski, and Spear (1986) tested forgetting of classical conditioning in rats of ages 12, 16, 18, or 60 days. They found that younger rats forgot more rapidly than older ones.

Preparedness also applies to humans. We are, of course, prepared to learn speech and other behaviors that animals never learn. We are also prepared to learn different things at different times in our lives, as we will discuss in Chapter 8. Sullivan noticed, for instance, that at 15 months Keller's baby cousin could obey verbal commands such as "Go to papa," "Shut the door," and "Give me the biscuit." At the same time, the baby was not producing sentences. When she gave a command of her own, she combined single words and gestures. "Go" with a gesture meant "I want to go outside." Sullivan assumed that Keller would also be able to understand sentences long before she could produce them. Therefore she spent many hours a day spelling complete sentences into Keller's hand without requiring the girl to reproduce them. In this way, Sullivan took advantage of the fact that Keller could understand sentences before she was prepared to produce them. Today the investigation of differences in preparedness as a function of age is part of an active area of research called cognitive development. We will review this topic in Chapter 8 when we compare changes in cognitive capabilities with other aspects of development.

Another application of the concept of preparedness is in the treatment of phobias (see Chapter 15). We have already considered that systematic desensitization is a treatment based on conditioning and extinction theories. (See Highlight: "Applying Classical Conditioning.") The concept of preparedness also seems to be related to this treatment. For example, NcNally (1986) used electric shock to condition a human fear response to a flower and a snake. Acquisition of the conditioned fear was equivalent for both stimuli, but extinction of the fear of the snake was much slower. This result is consistent with the idea that snake phobias reflect a biological

Preparedness
Idea that animals are more prepared to make certain responses than others, and may find other responses more difficult to make.

predisposition to maintain a fear of objects and situations that threatened the human species throughout its evolutionary history. Other recent investigations in laboratory experiments (Merckelbach & Van den Hout, 1988) and clinical studies (Zafiropoulou & McPherson, 1986) have provided additional support for the influence of preparedness on phobias.

Cognitive Learning Theory

Conditioning results in learning by gradually strengthening responses. But we often learn things suddenly and irreversibly. Keller's learning experiences provide many examples. We have already considered her sudden understanding of finger spelling. Another example happened one day when Sullivan saw Keller trying to correct an error that she had made while trying to string beads. Noticing her concentration, Sullivan spelled "t-h-i-n-k" on Keller's forehead. In a flash, Keller realized that the word was the name of the process that was going on in her head. Her insight came suddenly, on Sullivan's first attempt to teach this abstract concept, and Keller never forgot what she learned in that moment. Since unobservable thought processes often play an important role in learning, cognitive learning theories were developed to explain the function of thought processes in learning. As mentioned in Chapter 1, cognitive theories did not become a dominant force in psychology until the 1960s. But their roots go back much further than that. Consider, for example, the early work on insights.

Insight

Wolfgang Köhler (1925), a founder of Gestalt psychology, was among the first to demonstrate the importance of insight in problem solving. An **insight** is the discovery of relationships that leads to the solution of a problem. In Köhler's experiments, chimpanzees had to solve the problem of getting bananas that were hung out of their reach. The relationship between three boxes that were also in the room was essential to the problem's solution. No one box was high enough, but all three together allowed the chimp to climb up and reach the bananas (Figure 6–8).

In another experiment the bananas were placed out of reach outside the chimp's cage. In this case it was the relationship between two sticks that formed the solution. One stick, inside the cage, was too short to reach the bananas, but it was long enough to reach a second stick outside the cage, which in turn was long enough to reach the bananas. Köhler described the behavior of one of his chimps, Sultan, in this situation:

> Sultan tries to reach the fruit with the smaller of the two sticks. Not succeeding, he tears at a piece of wire that projects from the netting of his cage, but that, too, is in vain. Then he gazes about him (there are always in the course of these tests some long pauses, during which the animals scrutinize the whole visible area). He suddenly picks up the little stick once more, goes up to the bars directly opposite to the long stick, scratches it towards him with the "auxiliary," seizes it, and goes with it to the point opposite the objective (the fruit), which he secures. From the moment that his eyes fall upon the long stick, his procedure forms one consecutive whole. . . ." (pp. 174–175)

Insight
Discovery of relationships that lead to the solution of a problem. Insight learning is the sudden and irreversible learning of a solution to a problem.

Köhler set the two-stick problem up again after that and Sultan solved it immediately.

Unlike Thorndike's cats, who *gradually*, through trial and error, learned to solve the puzzle-box problem, Köhler's chimpanzees suddenly learned

FIGURE 6–8

In one insight experiment, a chimp had to pile three boxes on top of one another in order to reach some bananas that were hung out of reach from the ceiling.

how to solve the two-stick problem all at once and irreversibly. Köhler explained that his chimpanzees had learned by insight, and that Thorndike's cats were denied the possibility of doing so. Köhler's chimps saw the relationship between the sticks, and once they did, the insight guided their behavior. Thorndike's cats could not see the relationship between the string and the door to their puzzle box, because the relationship was complex and hidden. Without the benefit of insight, the cats slowly decreased the time needed to solve their problem through many attempts. With the benefit of insight, the chimps learned to solve their problem quickly, without hesitation, time after time. The same thing happened with Keller. Once she understood what finger spelling meant, she never looked back—it was an instantaneous and irreversible insight.

Insights are common in human learning. We have all experienced the sudden emergence of solutions after the pieces of a problem fall into place in our minds. Such moments of insight are so pleasurable that they are often accompanied by an "Aha!" Cognitive psychologists consequently refer to human insights as "aha" experiences. Modern researchers are analyzing the mental processes that lead to insights in problem solving (e.g., Kaplan & Simon, 1990). Details of problem-solving research will be discussed in Chapter 7.

Learning Set

A *learning set* is the capacity to learn the solution to problems faster after having experience with similar problems. For example, in school we develop learning strategies that usually make second and third exams in a subject easier than the first. This is another mental ability that humans and animals have in common.

Harlow (1949) showed that monkeys can develop a learning set. He presented two containers, such as a cylinder and a box, and put food under one and nothing under the other. For any given monkey, the food-container pairing was always the same; for example, the food was always under the box for one monkey and always under the cylinder for another monkey. When the monkey found the food, the problem was set up again in the very same way. At first, learning was slow. The monkeys frequently looked under the wrong box even though the food was always under the other box. Eventually, however, they learned to pick up the right box immediately. At this point, Harlow changed the containers to other shapes, such as a star and a triangle, but kept the problem the same in every other way: The food was always under one shape. The monkeys demonstrated a learning set by learning to solve the problems faster. Eventually, they seemed to be operating according to a rule: Look under the same shape if food was found there the preceding time, and switch to the other shape if it wasn't. The development of this learning set is an example of cognitive learning because it requires a mental representation of the rule.

Latent Learning and Cognitive Maps

Cognitive maps are mental pictures or representations of our environment. We can study them in humans simply by asking students, for example, to draw a map of their campus from memory. But how can we study cognitive maps in animals?

Edward C. Tolman and his associates led the way in showing the importance of cognitive maps in animal learning. Figure 6–9 illustrates the apparatus that Tolman used in a classic experiment on the role of cognitive structures in animal learning (Tolman & Honzik, 1930). He placed a hungry rat in a start box and the rat had to find its way through a maze to an end box. He recorded an error every time the rat entered a blind alley in the maze. Tolman and Honzik ran three groups of rats in their experiment.

1. Group 1 ran the maze only to find an empty end box day after day for 16 days. They made about nine errors on the first day and reduced that only slightly to about seven errors by the sixteenth day.

2. Group 2 ran the maze and ate the food reward that was provided in the end box each day for 16 days. They also made about nine errors

Cognitive map
A mental picture of an area or territory.

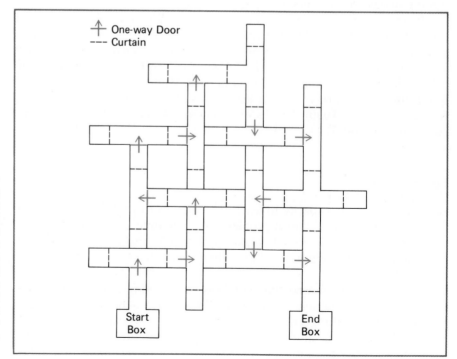

FIGURE 6–9

Tolman's experimental apparatus for testing cognitive structures in animal learning is shown here. The technique used in the experiment was to move the location of the curtains and blind alleys each time the rat ran the maze. The fact that the rats could find the food reward even though the maze had been modified strengthened the researchers' conclusion that the rats had formed a cognitive map—or a mental image—of the maze. This, even though they had not been reinforced when they completed the maze the first time. (Tolman, Honzik, 1930)

on the first day, but they greatly reduced errors to about two per day by the sixteenth day.

3. Group 3 started out like Group 1. They received no food reward for the first 10 days. Then they were treated like Group 2 rats, with food provided in the end box, for the last 6 days. They started with about ten errors per day and reduced that only slightly to about seven errors by the tenth day. Tolman and Honzik observed their critical result on the twelfth day. The number of errors dropped sharply to about two and stayed at that level until the end of the experiment. A single food reinforcement on day 11 had a powerful effect. It reduced errors to about the same number that were made by rats in Group 2, who had been reinforced every day.

Tolman and Honzik argued that conditioning theories could not explain their results. Conditioning theories hold that performance errors indicate learning strength, and that learning strength increases gradually with reinforcement. Accordingly, learning strength was very low after rats in Groups 1 and 3 ran a maze for 10 days without reinforcement. In other words, their performance suggested that rats in Groups 1 and 3 had *not* learned their way around the maze after 10 days. If that's true, why did Group 3 rats do so well on the eleventh day after receiving only a single reinforcement? Operant conditioning theory provides no satisfactory answer. Tolman and Honzik therefore broke ranks with operant conditioning theorists.

Tolman and Honzik proposed that performance does not necessarily reflect learning strength. As mentioned earlier, they introduced the term **latent learning** to refer to learning that does not show itself immediately in performance. While latent learning makes an important distinction between learning and performance, it leaves open a question: What *is* learned, if it is not *observable* responses? Tolman and Honzik answered this question with the proposal that cognitive structures are learned. Specifically, they suggested that Group 3 rats had learned a cognitive map, or mental picture, of the maze. When the rats found food in the end box on the eleventh day, they used their cognitive maps to run the maze almost without error on the twelfth day.

Tolman and Honzik's proposal of cognitive maps was out of step with conditioning theories not only because cognitive maps are unobservable mental events, but also because they are learned without reinforcement. But psychologists were slow to give up what they hoped would be a general learning theory. Almost three decades passed before a significant number of psychologists broke ranks with operant conditioning theory and turned toward cognitive learning theory.

By integrating principles of learning, memory (Chapter 7), and thinking (Chapter 8), modern cognitive psychologists are creating a training revolution (see Highlight: A Training Revolution: The Human Factor in a Computerized World).

Cognition in Classical Conditioning

As strict behaviorism declined, more studies emerged that implicated cognitive processing even for classical conditioning. One study by Leon Kamin implied that attention affects classical conditioning. Kamin (1969) discovered *blocking*, the impairment of a conditioned response between a stimulus (e.g., a light) and a US (e.g., a shock) when the light is presented with another stimulus (e.g., a tone) that was previously paired with the US. Kamin showed that if a rat is presented one stimulus (e.g., a tone) along with a US (e.g., a shock that elicits a fear response before conditioning), the tone will become a conditioned stimulus that elicits the fear response

Latent learning
Refers to learning that does not show itself immediatley in performance.

A TRAINING REVOLUTION: The Human Factor in a Computerized World

A triangle appeared at the top of the screen and dropped rapidly while Davis joggled a joystick to align a cursor with the triangle's path. Davis punched one button to "lock on" the target and a second one to select a fire mode. Then, after watching the launch indicator count down, Davis hit the ENGAGE button. He was pleased with his flawless performance, but he continued to practice, for he knew that he was a vital human element in the Patriot antiaircraft missile defense system. He also knew that the Patriot was the only thing that could stop Saddam Hussein's terror weapon, the Scud-B rocket.

Specialist John Davis, a tactical control assistant (TCA), was part of the Army's 11th Air Defense Artillery Brigade, who called themselves "Guardians of the Flame." These men and women had come halfway around the world to Saudi Arabia from Fort Bliss, Texas. Arriving several weeks before Christmas 1990, they had practiced their highly refined skills through New Year's (Dane, 1991). Then, in the middle of January, they were called to their battle stations, a condition they call "Blazing Skies." For the next several weeks, the maneuvers they had learned so well were "for real." Their training paid off. On February 27, 1991, they joined the celebration of all U.S. and allied forces, who proved that Scud missiles and Saddam's enormous army were no match for the Patriot and the world's best-equipped and best-trained troops.

Patriot equipment and crew are wholly interdependent. The equipment can perform no better than the crew operating it, and the crew can perform no better than the information provided by the equipment. Computers automatically process radar signals to localize incoming aircraft and to guide Patriot missiles after they are launched. But the system is not self-operative. Human beings are responsible for critical decision and control functions.

Most computerized military and industrial equipment have this semiautomatic characteristic.

U.S. troops celebrate victory in Kuwait City.

Computers monitor and control many functions that were previously done by people, and in this sense, there has been a computer revolution. But people still play crucial roles.

Ironically, in fact, the computer revolution has created a need for a human training revolution (Rassmussen & Rouse, 1981). People manage complexities that computers do not handle, such as the final decision about friend or foe aircraft. Their jobs are often difficult to learn. For example, Israeli crews had trained on the Patriot system for a year, but they stepped aside for more experienced operators when war broke out. Maintaining experienced crews is a continual effort because the jobs keep changing. As the computer revolution advances, crew procedures change along with the technology.

Increased computer automation has direct effects on those who interact with the computers, such as John Davis. It also has indirect effects on many others. For example, five Patriot missile launchers require a crew of 85 men and women. Those outside the ECS run and maintain the power plant, radar, launcher, missiles, communications, and trucks. For example, Sergeant 1st Class Rosa Gamboa and the mechanics under her command maintain a fleet of 30 trucks that must be ready to roll at a moment's notice. Gomboa and her mechanics also maintain 14 diesel generators, which run the power plant. If they go down, the whole system goes down. As the system becomes more complex, so does their job. Consequently, even the old-timers need continual training.

These soldiers are typical of the many military and industrial personnel whose jobs are shaped by computer advances. The need for a training revolution is therefore a widespread problem throughout our society.

Computers, which created the problem, are also part of the solution.

Computers, when combined with principles of learning, are powerful teaching tools. Many principles of learning suggest that students tutored one-on-one do better than students taught in groups. For example, one-on-one tutoring makes it much more likely that an individual's desirable responses will be reinforced immediately. We experience the delayed reinforcement of group learning when we are one of the first to understand a problem, but have to wait until most of the class gets it. Tutoring also reduces the chances of reinforcing an individual's undesirable responses. We experience inappropriate reinforcement in a group when our misunderstanding goes unnoticed because most of the class understands. Indeed, research shows that the average student who receives one-on-one tutoring learns better than 98 percent of students who receive group instruction (Bloom, 1984). Before the development of powerful computers, the advantages of one-on-one tutoring could rarely be realized because it is usually impossible to provide one teacher for every student. A powerful computer, however, can respond to the individual learning needs of many students at one time.

Modern computer-based teaching systems are called *intelligent tutors*. They apply the principles of operant conditioning, which are discussed in this chapter, as well as principles of memory and thinking, which are presented in the next two chapters. Intelligent tutors use all these principles to formulate rules on how students learn and teachers teach, and they combine these rules with a detailed knowledge of the facts that need to be taught. To complete the system, they add a means to communicate with each student individually. One intelligent tutor knows all the facts needed to engage enemy aircraft and to select appropriate firing modes on a Patriot missile system. It teaches that knowledge through realistic simulations of air warfare. TCAs, such as Specialist John Davis, learn through hands-on experience with the kinds of maneuvers and decisions they have to make during actual battles. Other intelligent tutors know all the facts needed to maintain the Patriot equipment. One of the most interesting ways of teaching trouble-shooting skills is by simulating equipment problems on a computer monitor. Sergeant 1st Class Rosa Gamboa and other Patriot mechanics learn by working with animated televisionlike pictures of their equipment. The intelligent tutor enables students to work at their own pace. It also lets them repeatedly practice procedures that would be too dangerous to try on real equipment. The intelligent tutor can immediately reinforce correct responses to an "emergency" and punish "dangerous" responses without ever putting the student at risk.

In short, the intelligent tutor combines principles of learning, memory, and thinking with sophisticated technology to bring humans up to speed in the computer revolution. It is creating a training revolution, without which most of the advanced computer systems in our society would be useless. Intelligent tutors played an important role in training the crews that operate the Patriot missile system. The success of the Patriot is due largely to their superb training.

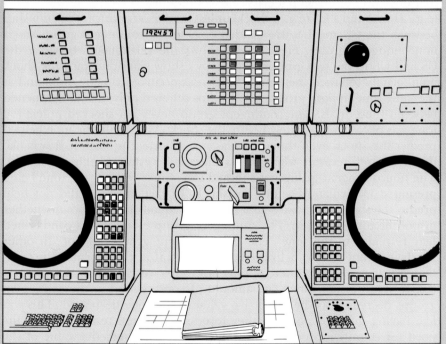

An Engagement Control Station (ECS) houses the two control panels shown. A tactical control assistant (TCA) operates the one on the left, and a tactical control officer (TCO) works the one on the right. A third crew member maintains communication with commanders and other crew members outside the ECS. The radar screens show everything in the sky. The TCO's job is to identify a potential target as friend or foe. Airplanes can be difficult to identify, but Scud missiles are easy because of their simple up-and-down flight path. When a foe target is identified, the TCA takes over to aim and fire. The training of TCAs and TCOs relies heavily on realistic computer-generated simulations.

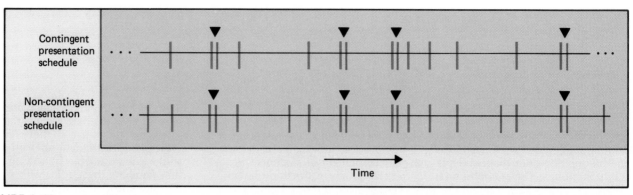

FIGURE 6–10

A contingent presentation schedule always pairs tones (blue lines) and shocks (red lines), and animals learn to use the tone as a warning. A noncontingent schedule pairs the tones and shocks equally, often at the times marked by the black triangles, but it also presents shocks just as often without tones. Thus, tones carry no information about the shock, and animals do not learn to respond to the tone.

when presented alone after conditioning. Later, if both the tone and a second stimulus (e.g., a light) are presented with the US, the light does not become a conditioned stimulus—that is, it does not elicit fear when presented alone. Conditioning to the second stimulus is impaired, or blocked. This result suggests that attention—a cognitive process—plays a role in classical conditioning. It can be explained by proposing that the rat attended to the first stimulus, the tone, because it carried information about the shock, but did not attend to the second stimulus, the light, because it carried no new information about the shock.

Robert Rescorla (1967) used a different procedure to arrive at a similar conclusion about cognitive effects during classical conditioning. He studied *stimulus contingency,* the dependence of one stimulus on another. He showed that dogs do not develop a classically conditioned response between a CS (e.g., a tone) and a US (e.g., a shock) unless there is a contingent relationship between the CS and US. He divided dogs into a contingent group and a noncontingent group. Figure 6–10 shows the relationship between the CS and US in the two groups. The arrows show trials on which the shock immediately followed the tone. These trials occurred equally often and at the same time in both groups; the groups differed only in what happened between these trials. The contingent group never got shocked unless the tone was played immediately before the shock. As a result, the tone helped predict the shock even though it was not a perfect predictor. It was like the weather forecaster who tells us there is a certain likelihood of rain. The noncontingent group got shocked sometimes without the tone being presented immediately before the shock. In fact, the tone did not help predict the shock in any way—the shock was equally likely to occur whether or not the tone occurred. The contingent group established a conditioned fear response to the tone. The noncontingent group did not. In other words, the tone had to help predict the shock if it was to acquire a conditioned fear response. Other contingent groups were used to vary the predictive value of the tone. The amount of conditioning in the contingent groups decreased as the predictive value of the tone decreased. This was like having good or poor weather forecasters. These results suggest the need for cognitive processes to keep track of the predictive value of the tone.

These results have been replicated (e.g., Rescorla, 1972, 1978; Fontino & Logan, 1979). Various specific interpretations are possible (e.g., Wagner & Rescorla, 1972; Gluck & Bower, 1988; Martin & Levey, 1989). Clearly, however, the results indicate that the informational value of a stimulus is important in classical conditioning.

Cognition in Operant Conditioning

Rescorla and his colleagues have also demonstrated the importance of contingencies in operant conditioning (Rescorla, 1990; Colwill & Rescorla,

1990). While the important issue for classical conditioning is whether one stimulus will follow another, the important issue for operant conditioning is whether reinforcement will follow a response. We have already seen that reinforcement schedules have a dramatic effect on operant conditioning. Resorla argues that schedule effects happen because animals and humans learn cognitive rules about how likely it is that reinforcements will follow responses. Accordingly, our responses are determined by cognitive processes concerning expectations about their consequences.

Later, in the chapter on intelligence, language, and thought (Chapter 8), we will discuss how animal cognition includes the learning of complex concepts and the use of abstract symbols. For now, however, let's return to simpler learning to consider its biological basis.

Psychobiological Analyses of Learning: Issues and Applications

Pavlov believed that conditioning formed connections in the brain as illustrated in Figure 6–11. Accordingly, a part of the brain that processes a US (food) is connected to a part that controls a UR (salivation in response to food). Conditioning then establishes a connection between the part that processes the US and the part that processes the CS (bell). Thus, the old and new connections establish a pathway from the CS to the CR (salivation in response to bell). Pavlov's psychobiological model seemed reasonable to many scientists even though it had not been tested. Lashley (1929, 1950) was the first to test it. He described his test as a search for **engrams,** physical representations of learning, similar to the connections inferred by Pavlov. One method of search was to cut the cortex of rats in order to sever the connections from the CS to the CR and thereby eliminate the learned response. First he trained the rats to run mazes and then made numerous cuts in the cortex. Unlike Pavlov's model, Lashley's procedure did not eliminate the learned response even though he made numerous cuts. Lashley concluded that learning does not depend upon connections across the cortex. Suddenly, Pavlov's psychobiological model lost credibility.

In other experiments Lashley removed large portions of cerebral cortex of the rats both before and after training them to run a maze. The brain-damaged rats learned more slowly, which was not surprising. The astonishing part of the results was that the magnitude of the learning deficit depended more on the amount of brain damage than on the location of the damage to the brain. These results suggested to Lashley that the brain somehow works as a whole in forming a physical representation of learning. Similar results have been observed in humans. For example, Grafman, Salazar, Weingartner, Vance, and Amin (1986) studied Vietnam soldiers who survived bullet wounds to the head. They found a decrease in IQ

Engram
Name assigned by Karl Lashley to the elusive physical representation of learning and memory in the brain.

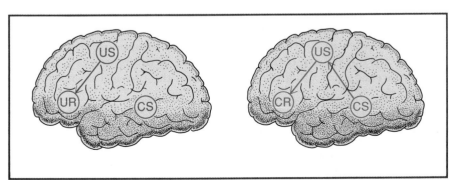

FIGURE 6–11

Pavlov believed that classical conditioning changes connections in the brain. Before conditioning, a connection exists between a stimulus such as food (US) and a response such as salivation (UR). However, no connection exists between the food (US) and a bell (CS) until conditioning establishes the connection. After conditioning, the newly established connection between the bell (CS) and the food (US) provides an indirect pathway to the CR (salivation in response to the bell).

scores of these soldiers, and in agreement with Lashley, the magnitude of the decrease depended upon the *amount* of brain damage.

To this day there is no generally agreed upon model of the physical representation of learning. But, with the help of modern technology, scientists are gaining ground in their search for engrams. For example, Richard Thompson (1986) and his colleagues recorded activity from brain cells in different parts of the brain during classical conditioning of an eye-blink response in rabbits. Before conditioning, a puff of air (US) caused an eye-blink response (UR) but a tone (CS) did not. After conditioning, the tone also caused an eye-blink response (CR). Their recordings suggested that parts of the hippocampus and cerebellum were critical to learning in this situation. When they destroyed the critical part of the cerebellum after conditioning had occurred, they eliminated the conditioned response. Apparently, the search for engrams is zeroing in on specific brain structures that play important roles in certain kinds of learning.

Although specific brain structures are critical, recent research suggests that many other areas of the brain are also involved in learning. For example, John, Tang, Brill, Young, and Ono (1986) took advantage of the fact that carefully placed visual targets can stimulate the two hemispheres of the brain separately (see Chapter 2). They trained cats to approach a visual target. Then they presented the learned stimulus to one hemisphere and an unlearned stimulus to the other hemisphere. Their final step was to use a radioactive labeling technique to measure brain activity in response to each target. They reasoned that any area that participated in the brain's reaction to learning would respond more on the side of the brain stimulated by the learned target. Their results suggested that nearly all areas of the brain participate in learning and that some areas are more active than others. Specifically, more activity was found in certain areas of the cortex, the hippocampus, and the cerebellum. These results are consistent with Thompson's suggestion that parts of the hippocampus and cerebellum are critical, but they also suggest that the physical representation of learning is distributed throughout the brain.

Other recent research has shed light on the nature of engrams in simple neural structures. A popular subject in these experiments is *Aplysia*, an invertebrate related to the common slug. The advantages of studying this little creature were advocated by Eric Kandel, the director of the Center for Neurobiology and Behavior at Columbia University College of Physicians and Surgeons. Kandel found that Aplysia has a simple nervous system that can be studied during learning. In one series of studies, Kandel and his colleagues measured the release of neural transmitters during classical conditioning (Hawkins & Kandel, 1984; Kandel & Schwartz, 1982). Before conditioning, an electric shock to the tail of an Aplysia (US) causes a vigorous withdrawal response (UR), but lightly touching the siphon (CS) does not. During conditioning, the US and CS are paired. After conditioning, lightly touching the siphon produces a vigorous withdrawal response (CR). The neural observations suggested that the engram for this learned response was related to the release of a specific neural transmitter (see discussion of serotonin, Chapter 2) in a specific synapse. In addition, Kandel and his co-workers were able to propose detailed models of the neural representation of learning in Aplysia. These models call attention to the fact that synapses are not passive connections between neurons. Instead, they are active processing units that play a key role in the physical representation of learning.

The active role of synapses is also supported by other studies of neural transmitters. Scientists use drugs to manipulate neural transmitters in animals. Then they observe the effect of these manipulations on conditioning and extinction. The results suggest that neural transmitters are involved in the learning process (e.g., Asin & Wirtshafter, 1990).

Summary

1. The definition of learning has changed over time depending upon the focus of research at the time. For us, **learning** is a process by which experience or practice results in a relatively permanent change in what one is capable of doing.

2. One type of learning is **classical conditioning** which occurs when an originally neutral stimulus comes to elicit a response that was originally given to another stimulus. It takes place when the neutral stimulus (CS) is repeatedly paired with the other stimulus (US).

3. Another type of learning is called **operant conditioning.** The animal or individual is actively operating on the environment with **operant** behaviors. Operant conditioning occurs when desired responses are rewarded or reinforced and undesired responses are ignored or punished.

4. In classical conditioning, a number of factors help in establishing **conditioned responses (CR).** The **conditioned stimulus (CS)** must be strong and distinctive; the CS should be presented shortly before the **unconditioned stimulus (US);** the time lapse between the CS and the US should be brief; there should be many pairings of CS and US; and the pairings of CS and US must be spaced properly.

5. **Extinction** occurs if the CS is repeatedly presented alone, without the US. But in **spontaneous recovery,** the conditioning effect appears again without any further pairings of CS and US.

6. **Stimulus generalization** occurs when responses are made to stimuli that are similar to, but not the same as, the original CS. **Discrimination,** on the other hand, occurs when subjects learn to respond only to certain stimuli, but not to other, similar stimuli.

7. In operant conditioning, **reinforcement** is an event whose occurrence just after a response increases the likelihood that the response will be repeated. **Positive reinforcement** is the presentation of a stimulus, **negative reinforcement** is the removal of a stimulus.

8. A subject who learns to make a response to remove a stimulus, through the use of negative reinforcement, has participated in **escape training.** In **avoidance training,** a negative reinforcer can be avoided altogether. **Learned helplessness** occurs when exposure to unavoidable, unpleasant events leads to an inability to avoid the unpleasant event even when it is possible.

9. Schedules of reinforcement can be either continuous (rewarding every response) or partial (rewarding only some responses), based on reinforcement of a certain number of responses or reinforcement after a certain interval of time. There are four basic schedules: **fixed interval, variable-interval, fixed ratio,** and **variable ratio** schedules of reinforcement. Each type affects the rate of responding in different ways.

10. **Shaping** is a procedure used in operant conditioning in which each part of a behavior is reinforced, eventually leading to the whole behavior that is desired.

11. **Extinction** and **spontaneous recovery** occur in operant as well as in classical conditioning (extinction in operant conditioning occurs through the withholding of reinforcement). **Punishment** is a stimulus that decreases the likelihood of a response when it is added to an environment. **Generalization** and **discrimination** also occur in operant as well as classical conditioning.

12. **Preparedness** is the idea that animals and humans may be more prepared to make certain responses easily while finding others difficult. Preparedness varies between and among species.

13. **Cognitive learning theory** attempts to explain the function of thought processes in learning. It includes such concepts as **insight, learning sets, latent learning,** and **cognitive maps.**

Key Terms

avoidance training	extinction	partial reinforcement	spontaneous recovery
classical conditioning	fixed-interval schedule	schedule	stimulus discrimination
cognitive map	fixed-ratio schedule	positive reinforcement	stimulus generalization
conditioned response (CR)	insight	preparedness	unconditioned
conditioned stimulus (CS)	latent learning	primary reinforcers	response (UR)
continuous reinforcement	law of effect	punishment	unconditioned
schedule	learned helplessness	reinforcement	stimulus (US)
discrimination	learning	response generalization	variable-interval schedule
engram	negative reinforcement	secondary reinforcers	variable-ratio schedule
escape training	operant conditioning	shaping	

EMBATTLED GIANT OF PSYCHOLOGY SPEAKS HIS MIND

BY DANIEL GOLEMAN

Cambridge, Mass.—B. F. Skinner is a creature of carefully shaped habit. At the age of 83, he has fashioned a schedule and environment for himself that is in perfect keeping with his theories of behavioral reinforcement.

Dr. Skinner's personal Skinner box—his own self-contained environment of positive reinforcements—is his basement office in his home here, a 1950s flat-top set among charming New England-style saltboxes.

"I spent a lot of time creating the environment where I work," Dr. Skinner said as he recently led a visitor through the home where he and his wife, Yvonne, live. "I believe people should design a world where they will be as happy as possible in old age."

Burrhus Frederic Skinner, the chief architect of behaviorism, uses the office to marshal a crusade against what he sees as grave mistakes in psychology that have left his own once preeminent theories in decline.

Behaviorism holds that people act as they do because of the rewards and punishments—positive and negative reinforcements—they have received. The mind and such things as memory and perception cannot be directly observed, and so, in Dr. Skinner's view, are unworthy of scientific study.

Much of Dr. Skinner's efforts now aim at meeting two major challenges to behaviorism: brain science, the study of links between brain and behavior, and cognitive psychology, the study of how the mind perceives, thinks, and remembers and how goals and plans influence behavior.

During the recent visit, Dr. Skinner, known to colleagues as Fred, was in the midst of preparing a talk for psychology's major annual convention.

It is to maximize his productivity in such writing, and to conserve energy in his later years, that Dr. Skinner has designed this environment. He sleeps in the office, in a bright yellow plastic tank just large enough for the mattress it contains, a small television, and some narrow shelves and controls. The bed unit, which bears some resemblance to a sleeper on a train, is one of those used by the Japanese in stacks in tiny hotel rooms, Dr. Skinner explained.

The office-bedroom suits Dr. Skinner's habits well: He goes to bed each night at 10 P.M., sleeps three hours, then rolls out of bed to his nearby desk, where he works for one hour. Then he goes back to bed for another three hours, getting up to begin his day at 5 A.M.

Positive Reinforcement: Music

In these early morning hours, Dr. Skinner puts in about three hours of writing, which he considers to be his main work. After his writing, he walks a mile or so to his office at Harvard University, where he answers mail and attends to other business. And then, for reinforcement, he spends the afternoon listening to music—which he loves—on the quadrophonic tape deck in his office.

This schedule, with its work output and rewards, allows Dr. Skinner to continue to act as the undisputed leader of modern behaviorism. As such, he fights a continuing battle for his ideas on many fronts, many of which he touched on in the wide ranging interview.

"I think cognitive psychology is a great hoax and a fraud, and that goes for brain science, too," Dr. Skinner said. "They are nowhere near answering the important questions about behavior."

Dr. Skinner is still vigorous in arguing his cause. In addition to the speech opposing cognitive psychology he is giving at the annual meeting of the American Psychological Association, next month he will publish in the *American Psychologist* an article attacking not only cognitive psychology, but also other enemies of his brand of behaviorism: humanistic psychology and other nonbehaviorist psychotherapies.

Humanists, Dr. Skinner writes in his article, have attacked behaviorism as undermining people's sense of freedom and have denounced its claims that the environment determines what people achieve. And, he writes, psychotherapists— apart from those who practice a behaviorist approach—rely too much on inferences they make about what is supposedly going on inside their patients, and too little on direct observation of what they do.

The use of punishment is another issue Dr. Skinner stills feels impassioned about. He is an ardent opponent of the use of punishment, such as spanking, or using "aversives"—such as pinches and shocks—with autistic children.

"What's wrong with punishments is that they work immediately, but give no long-term results," Dr. Skinner said. "The responses to punishment are either the urge to escape, to counterattack, or a stubborn apathy. These are the bad effects you get in prisons or schools, or wherever punishments are used."

One of the ways Dr. Skinner feels behaviorist techniques have been underappreciated is in the failure of teaching machines to find wide acceptance in the schools. The machines, which can be computerized, break a topic like division or Russian history into small, manageable concepts, and methodically teach each so a student gets the reinforcement of knowing he has mastered it before moving on to the next.

The learning devices had a great advantage over the classroom teacher, according to Dr. Skinner. "Schools were invented to extend a tutor to more than one student at once," Dr. Skinner said. "That's O.K. with 3 or 4, but when you have 30 or more in a classroom, the teacher is no longer able to give the student the reinforcement of a 'right' before moving on to the next task."

Such machines are widely used now in industrial education, but are not widely used in schools.

Rewards of Work

Dr. Skinner continues to act as a social philosopher, a role he played most prominently with his 1948 book *Walden Two*, which described a behaviorist utopia. In an article last year in the *American Psychologist* in which he examined "What Is Wrong with Daily Life in the Western World," Dr. Skinner charged that common practices had eroded that natural relationship between what people do and pleasing effects that would reinforce their activities.

For instance, in Dr. Skinner's view, fixed salaries do not reinforce workers because they are paid whether or not they do more than the minimum job. If workers were paid on a commission or by the piece, their pay would be a direct reinforcer for their labors, and they would work with more effort and pleasure, according to behaviorist principles.

Another aspect of modern life Dr. Skinner criticizes, in all seriousness, is labor-saving devices, such as dishwashers or frozen dinners, which he sees as depriving people of the small satisfactions that accomplishing something brings. "We've destroyed all the reinforcers in daily life," said Dr. Skinner. "For example, if you wash a dish, you've accomplished something, done something that gives you a pleasing result. That is far more reinforcing than putting the dishes in with some powder and then taking them out again."

The device for which Dr. Skinner may be most famous, the original "Skinner box," was a large, glass-enclosed, climate-controlled baby crib with equipment to keep infants amused and well-exercised. Dr. Skinner is still pained by the rumors that his daughters, who used the box, became psychotic or suicidal as a result. Today one daughter is an artist and writer living in London, and the other is a professor of educational psychology at Indiana University; both are married.

When Dr. Skinner first began in the 1930s and 1940s to develop the principles of what he calls "radical behaviorism"—to distinguish it from the earlier theories of Pavlov and Watson—he argued that a scientific psychology could only study behavior that can be directly observed. For that reason, Skinnerian behaviorists have studied the laws of learning through observing responses such as the pecking of a pigeon, and avoided the "black box" of the inner workings of the mind.

In recent decades, though, advances in devices for monitoring faculties such as attention have spurred studies linking the brain and mental activity. If he were starting his research today, Dr. Skinner was asked, would he avail himself of these techniques?

"If I had it all to do again, I would still call the mind a black box," Dr. Skinner said. "I would not use any of the new techniques for measuring information processing and the like. My point has always been that

psychology should not look at the nervous system or so-called mind—just at behavior."

For Dr. Skinner, the mind is irrelevant to understanding why people behave as they do. In his view, most assumptions about mental life made by laymen and psychologists alike are based on fallacies. In his address next week before the American Psychological Association, he will argue that all the words that describe mental activities actually refer to some behavior.

"No one invented a word for mental experience that comes from the mind," Dr. Skinner said. "They all have their roots in a reference to action.

"To contemplate, for instance, means to look at a template, or picture. 'Consider' comes from roots meaning to look at the stars until you see a pattern. 'Compare' means to put things side by side to see if they match."

"All the words for mental experience go back to what people do," Dr. Skinner continued. "Over thousands of years, people have used these terms to express something that goes on in their bodies. But these are action terms; they do not mean that these things are going on inside the mind."

"The cognitive revolution is a search inside the mind for something that is not there," Dr. Skinner said. "You can't see yourself process information; information-processing is an inference from behavor—and a bad one, at that. If you look carefully at what people mean when they talk about the mind, you find it just refers to how they behave."

One of the major disputes between the cognitive and behaviorist viewpoints is whether a person's actions are guided by goals and plans, or whether they are a result of that person's history of rewards and punishments. For Dr. Skinner, there is no question. "Behavior is always reinforced behavior," he said.

Despite their differences with other points of view, behaviorists are influential in many psychology departments, and the school of thought remains prominent, particularly among those who are trying to apply its principles in areas like psychotherapy, industrial

motivation, and remedial education. From the 1930s through the 1960s, behaviorism dominated academic psychology; in the 1960s the so-called cognitive revolution began and would go on to sweep psychology.

There is no precise estimate of the numbers of behaviorists, although there are 1,228 members of the division of the psychological association that is devoted to behaviorist research and applications. The strongholds of behaviorism tend to be in colleges in the South and Midwest, according to Kurt Salzinger, a psychologist at Polytechnic University in Brooklyn who is the new president of the behaviorist division.

Dr. Skinner concedes that behavorism is on the decline while the cognitive school of thought is increasingly popular among psychologists. There is now a move afoot to reconcile the two approaches.

"Behaviorism was right in saying the task of psychology is to account for what people do, but wrong in ruling out talking about what's going on in the head that generates what people do," said Stephan Harnad, one of the editors of a collection of Dr. Skinner's major papers, along with more than 150 comments by leading scholars. The book is scheduled to be published this winter by the Cambridge University Press.

"That left behaviorists only able to talk about a person's history of rewards and punishments," Dr. Harnad said. "But that accounts for almost nothing of what we can do—our perception, our being able to remember something and our speech. This calls for a cognitive theory."

As the field evolves, an increasing number of behaviorists are violating Dr. Skinner's tenets by studying mental activity. "My major research now is a collaborative project with a cognitive scientist," said Richard Herrnstein, a psychologist who is a former colleague of Dr. Skinner at Harvard University. "We're studying how organisms perceive shapes; we're doing studies of pigeons, humans, and computers. I'm pretty comfortable with much of the cognitive school, and I consider myself a behaviorist."

Memory and Cognition

7

O n December 24, 1919, three bandits attacked a payroll truck in broad daylight, firing at it as it skidded down an icy street in Bridgewater, Massachusetts. The bandits, unsuccessful in their robbery attempt, drove off in a getaway car. No one was injured.

Several months later, there was a similar crime in the neighboring town of South Braintree. At about 3 o'clock on the afternoon of April 15, 1920, armed robbers ambushed and shot two guards in a truck that was carrying the payroll of a local shoe company. The gunmen grabbed the cash box containing $15,000 from the dying guards and jumped into a car that had pulled up while the shooting was going on. Two days later the getaway car was found abandoned in some nearby woods, with the tracks of a smaller car leading away from it. During the investigation that followed, the police theorized that the tracks of the smaller car might have been made by the vehicle used in the earlier crime at Bridgewater. This

theory would later form the net that snared Sacco and Vanzetti.

To understand how these two rather ordinary men (one a factory worker, the other a fish peddler) came to the center of national and international attention, one must consider the historical backdrop as well as the details of the case itself.

The two crimes and the Sacco-Vanzetti trial took place during a period of acute social unrest and upheaval in America. Labor strikes had shocked the nation in 1919, and prominent figures in government and business were targets of radical assassination attempts. Americans blamed their troubles on the strangers (the immigrants) in their midst.

Neither Sacco nor Vanzetti had a background of crime or violence. But they had two strikes against them. Both were Italian immigrants; both had spoken rebelliously about the lot of immigrant laborers; and both took a small car into a Braintree garage for repairs.

They roughly fit the description of the bandits, and they were

carrying guns when they were stopped for questioning, so they were arrested. Only Sacco had an alibi for the day of the unsuccessful Bridgewater holdup. Neither Sacco nor Vanzetti had an airtight alibi for the day of the Braintree murders. Thus Vanzetti was charged with the Bridgewater attempt, and both men were charged with the killings in Braintree.

Vanzetti stood trial from June until August of 1920, charged with assault as one of the gunmen who shot at the payroll truck in Bridgewater. The testimony of witnesses for the prosecution was riddled with contradictions and inconsistencies.

The three key witnesses gave three reports of the incident: the first on the day of the crime (December 24); the second at a preliminary hearing on May 18; and a third at the trial in late June. The first reports were as follows:

1. Alfred Cox (a passenger in the payroll truck):
   "The man with the shotgun was

227

a Russian, Pole, or Austrian, 5'8", 150 lbs., dark complexion, 40 years of age, was without a hat and wore a long, dark overcoat with the collar up. He had a closely cropped moustache which might have been slightly gray."

2. Benjamin Bowles (an armed guard who returned the fire from the truck):
"I can positively identify two of the bandits. The man with the shotgun was 5'7", 35 or 36 years, 150 lbs., had a black, closely cropped moustache, red cheeks, slim face, black hair and was an Italian or Portuguese. He had no hat on and had a black overcoat with collar up."

3. Frank Harding (a bystander):
"The man with the shotgun was slim, 5'10", wore a long black overcoat and derby hat. I did not get much of a look at his face but I think he was a Pole."

Vanzetti, who was accused of being the shotgun bandit at Bridgewater, had a distinctively full, long, and droopy mustache, and he had always worn it so. The moustache originally seen on the shotgun bandit was apparently smaller than Vanzetti's, but as time passed and the witnesses had the chance to see Vanzetti, the moustache "grew to fit the man." Other details changed also. For example, Cox changed his description from "dark" complexion to "medium" complexion—closer to Vanzetti's coloring. Bowles added at the trial that the gumman had a "high forehead," moving closer to a description of Vanzetti.

Other confusions were apparent. Under cross-examination, Bowles (the armed guard) revealed that he was unsure of whom he shot at, and was therefore unsure of whom he got a "good look" at. He also was unsure about which of the gunmen had fired first. Inconsistencies in his testimony suggested that he had altered his story (possibly unconsciously) to please his questioners. Despite its defects, the

testimony persuaded the jury, for they found Vanzetti guilty.

The joint trial of Sacco and Vanzetti began a year later, on May 31, 1921, in Dedham, Massachusetts. It lasted nearly 7 weeks. Only one question was relevant: Were Sacco and Vanzetti the assailants of the two men at Braintree? There was a mass of conflicting evidence regarding this question. The discord in the testimony was summed up by Francis Russell (1962) in his book *Tragedy in Dedham*:

Scarcely a minute had elapsed from the first shot until the getaway car vanished, but with its disappearance the actuality faded and the myth took over. All in all there were more than fifty witnesses of the holdup in its various stages, yet each impression now began to work in the yeast of individual preconceptions. The car was black, it was green, it was shiny, it was mud-streaked. There were two cars. The men who did the shooting were dark, were pale, and had blue suits, had gray suits, wore caps, were bareheaded. Only one had a gun, both had guns. The third man had been behind the brick pile with a shotgun all the time. Anywhere between eight and thirty shots had been fired. (pp. 41–42)

Apparently, the witnesses at Braintree could do no better than those at Bridgewater. But again it was good enough for the jury. On July 14, 1921, Sacco and Vanzetti were found guilty of murder in the first degree.

Many who studied the trial carefully were unconvinced. Because of the inconsistencies in the testimony and other irregularities, many thought (and many still think) that Sacco and Vanzetti did not get a fair trial. Six long years passed, taken up with appeals for a new trial. All this was to no avail, however—on August 22, 1927, Sacco and Vanzetti were executed. ■

Sacco (right) and Vanzetti (left) were accused of participating in a robbery in which guards were killed. Despite inconsistencies in witness testimony they were convicted and executed. Their trial raises many questions about the reliability of human memory and testimony.

After completing this chapter, you should be able to:

Describe and differentiate between the two major theories of memory: multiple memories and levels of processing.

Describe how memory can be divided into three types: sensory store, short-term store and long-term store.

Discuss encoding and retrieval in terms of capacity and forgetting in each type of memory.

Understand the neurological basis of memory processes.

Apply several techniques of improving memory through better study habits.

History and Scope of the Study of Memory

Why did the witnesses in the Sacco and Vanzetti case remember some facts and forget others? Are witnesses usually as unreliable as the ones in that case? Is there any way to improve witness reliability? Why do you remember answers to some test questions and not others? Is there any way to improve your test-taking ability? These are questions for those who study **memory,** the system that allows us to retain information over time. The Greeks and Roman were the first people to study memory. They studied it as an art, not as a scientific subject. While Greek and Roman orators sharpened their skills as public speakers, they also developed techniques for improving memory because all their speeches were delivered "from memory." As a result, techniques for improving memory were developed long before the scientific method was applied to the study of memory.

Memory
System that allows people to retain information over time.

College grades often depend upon how much students can remember from lectures and textbooks. The present theoretical analysis of memory will be combined with practical suggestions on ways to improve your memory.

Herman Ebbinghaus conducted the first scientific studies of memory.

This tradition was so firmly rooted by the 17th and 18th centuries that memory remained an art rather than a subject for scientific investigation even after the scientific method was well established (Yates, 1966).

The first scientific investigations of memory were conducted in 1885 by a German scholar, Herman Ebbinghaus (1850–1909). His countrymen, who had established the first psychology laboratory six years earlier (see Chapter 1), influenced him to use experimental methods. The British associationists, who, like their Greek predecessors believed that things experienced together become associated in memory, influenced him to study how associations are formed and remembered. Using himself as the subject, Ebbinghaus devised memory experiments with unrelated three-letter *nonsense syllables* (e.g., DAC, JEK, TUZ). He randomly drew anywhere from 7 to 36 of these syllables to memorize in a predetermined order. In one procedure, he started with the syllables facing down, turning them over one at a time, pacing himself with a metronome. He then repeated the procedure except that he tried to recall each syllable before he looked at it. He kept at it until he could recall the whole list perfectly. Sometimes he waited up to 48 hours and tried to recall the list again. This enabled him to measure the rate of memorizing and forgetting. As we shall see, some of his findings led to the discovery of general principles of memory.

Other researchers took Ebbinghaus's experiments a step further by having subjects learn and remember lists of paired verbal items. For the most part, however, the focus of memory research remained on verbal material that was unrelated before the experiment (e.g., dog–light; stone–tree). Behaviorists fostered the belief that this narrow focus would lead to the discovery of general principles of memory and explain why our ability to remember is so far ranging.

Behaviorists were sometimes called stimulus-response psychologists because they limited their investigations to objective, observable stimuli and responses. They promoted the methods used by Ebbinghaus and his followers because each item in Ebbinghaus's serial list could be easily identified as a response for the previous item and as a stimulus for the next item. Similarly, pairs of verbal items can be viewed as stimulus-response pairs. Researchers give one member of the pair as a stimulus; subjects give the other member as a response. This stimulus-response approach gave us the foundation for understanding memory.

By the 1960s, scientists were ready to test whether the principles of memory for lists could be generalized. They began to study a person's memory for a range of meaningful verbal material such as sentences, paragraphs, stories, and passages from textbooks. At the same time, cognitive psychologists began to study mental events (see Chapter 1). Although Skinner (1957), a leading behaviorist, argued that a stimulus-response approach should be applied to all verbal behavior, many psychologists began to see the value of studying mental operations as they related to the learning and remembering of complex lessons.

This chapter will review principles that emerged from both the stimulus-response approach and the cognitive approach. We have organized this chapter around cognitive models of memory processes. Your memory will be tested several times by asking what you read earlier in the chapter, so stay alert! The first test will show how good your memory can be; some others will probably reveal weaknesses in your memory. We will end the chapter with suggestions for improving memory. Some of the suggestions will date back to ancient Greece before the study of memory became a science. Most of the suggestions, however, will be based on modern principles that are presented in the first part of the chapter.

The best way to analyze the relationship between memory research and eyewitness testimony, such as the eyewitness testimony we saw in the Sacco and Vanzetti case, is to take part in a memory experiment. We will test your memory in several different ways. We will then compare these tests with school tests and with interrogations of witnesses in the Sacco and Vanzetti case.

Test Yourself

Miller, Galanter, and Pribram (1960) outlined an experiment that is fun to experience firsthand. You must first learn the following verse: "One is a bun, two is a shoe, three is a tree, four is a door, five is a hive, six are sticks, seven is heaven, eight is a gate, nine is a line, and ten is a hen." This verse provides a mental framework for learning a study list. Psychologists call such mental frameworks *schemata* (e.g., Bonanno, 1990). Study the following list of numbers and words, using the verse to help you learn which word goes with each number. You already know that "bun" goes with the number 1. Now you must learn that "ashtray" goes with 1. Try learning this new relationship by forming a bizarre image in your mind of a bun with an ashtray—you might imagine a pipe spilling ashes into a bun, for example. Follow the same procedure for every number until you have formed an image relating the right verse word to every word on the study list.

STUDY LIST

1 ashtray
2 firewood
3 picture
4 cigarette
5 table
6 matchbook
7 glass
8 lamp
9 shoe
10 phonograph

When you finish going through the list once, take the following test. Next to each number write the word that was next to it on the study list.

3 ——————
8 ——————
6 ——————
4 ——————
9 ——————
1 ——————
7 ——————
2 ——————
10 ——————
5 ——————

How many did you get correct? People often get all the words correct after one time through the list (Miller et al., 1960).

Elliot and Gentile (1986) showed that this procedure (which is often called the peg word method) also works well in a high school setting. After learning the "one is a bun" rhyme, adolescents outperformed others who tried to learn paired associate lists in whatever way they chose. This memory advantage was obtained immediately after learning, 1 week later, and 5 months later. We will discuss other ways to improve memory at the end of this chapter.

Methods of Testing Memory

Some students like to recall things in their own words on essay tests. Others prefer to pick answers from a list on multiple choice tests. Do you think that one is a better indicator of what you remember about a lesson? Why? You should be able to answer these questions better after we consider the various methods that psychologists use to measure memory.

Recall Tests. **Recall tests** measure a person's ability to reproduce material. The test you just took gave a number as a cue, and you had to reproduce the rest of the number word pair. When part of an item is provided as a cue for the other part, the test is called *cued recall*. Teachers use cued recall tests when they ask fill-in-the-blank questions, such as "Mental frameworks are also called _____."

Another kind of recall test is *free recall*, in which no cues are provided and any order of recall is allowed. A teacher might say, "List three technical terms used in last night's homework assignment." Similarly, police asked Cox, Bowles, and Harding to give free recalls of what they had witnessed during the attempted payroll robbery at Bridgewater.

Recognition Tests. **Recognition tests** measure a person's ability to pick the correct answer when several answers are given. Teachers use recognition tests in the form of multiple-choice questions, such as "Mental frameworks are also called: (a) conditioned stimuli, (b) schemata, (c) operant responses, or (d) primary reinforcers." Recognition is usually, but not always, easier than recall. The difficulty depends on the answers you have to choose from (Hall, 1983). You might have had more trouble, for example, if the answers had been: "(a) schematics, (b) schemata, (c) schemes, or (d) schemas."

You would be taking a recognition test if you tried to select the word that goes with 7 on the earlier study list: Is it firewood, lamp, glass, or table? Witnesses at the Slater and Morrill holdup took recognition tests when they tried to identify the shotgun bandit from a number of pictures of suspects.

Savings Tests. **Savings tests** measure people's ability to take advantage of what they have learned before in order to relearn material faster. You rely on **savings** every time final exams roll around. By the time you get to the end of a course you have probably forgotten some of the facts you learned in the beginning, so you must relearn them for the final exam. You might not recall the name of one of the founders of structuralism, for example, even though you learned it in Chapter 1 of this book. You might not even recognize the correct name from the following list: Skinner, Watson, Wundt, James. But if you learned it earlier, you will probably learn very quickly that Wundt is the correct answer. Savings is better than recall and recognition for pictures as well as words. For example, MacLeod (1988) found that subjects relearn both pictures and words faster after failing to recognize or to recall them. The fact that you relearn old material faster than you learned it the first time shows that you remember something about it even if you cannot recall or recognize the information. To measure your savings in the earlier list you would have to record how long it took

Recall tests
Measure a person's ability to reproduce material. *Cued recall* is when part of the material is provided as a cue for the rest; *free recall* is when no cues are provided and any order of recall is allowed.

Recognition tests
Measure a person's ability to pick the correct answer when several answers are given; often occur in the form of multiple-choice questions on tests.

Savings tests
Measure people's ability to take advantage of what they have learned before in order to relearn material faster.

Savings
Difference between one's original learning time and the relearning time; measured by a savings test.

you to learn the list the first time and how long it took you to relearn the list at a later time. The difference between your original learning time and your relearning time is your savings. (If you waited long enough, you would probably find a time at which you could neither recall nor recognize the list, but you would still show savings.)

Notice that all three tests—recall, recognition, and savings—measure memory indirectly, through performance. Inferring memory from performance is no simple matter. Lawyers know full well that performance is not a perfect indicator of memory. A good question will often bring forth key evidence that a witness failed to produce on earlier occasions. Students also know that tests do not always reflect what they learned in a course. As our analysis of memory research unfolds in this chapter, we will learn many reasons why performance does not perfectly reflect memory.

Types of Memory

There are basically two different theories about memory. One theory, called the *multiple memory theory* (Atkinson & Shiffrin, 1971, 1977), states that there are three kinds of memory (see Figure 7–1): sensory memory, which holds sensory impressions for only 1 or 2 seconds; short-term memory, which holds information for less than 30 seconds; and long-term memory, which holds information for long periods of time (perhaps permanently).

Another theory, the *levels of processing theory*, agrees about the existence of sensory memory. But it disagrees about the distinction between short-term and long-term memory. It maintains that both are part of the same system. We forget some things rapidly because we process them minimally. We remember other things longer because we process them more extensively or deeply (Craik & Lockhart, 1972). According to this theory, we recode information into more and more abstract forms as we process it at deeper levels. At a surface level, we code the letters we read. At a deeper level, we recode letters and words into word meanings. At a still more abstract level we recode word meanings into concepts that are expressed in sentences. As we process more deeply, the level of information we get becomes more meaningful and is remembered longer. For example, undergraduates studied either the rhyming sounds or the meanings of words in an experiment by Duchek and Heely (1989). Later the students reviewed a list containing words they had studied and new words. The students

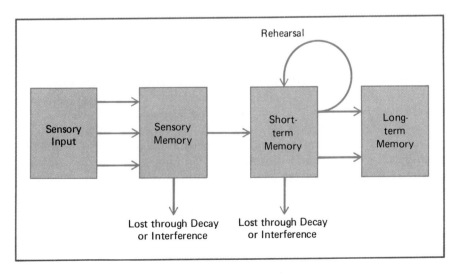

FIGURE 7–1

Atkinson and Shiffrin's multiprocess view of human memory is shown in this model. Sensory information is briefly retained in some type of sensory memory system; some of it is then recoded into short-term memory, where it may be retained through rehearsal. The longer it remains in short-term memory, the more likely it is to be transferred into long-term memory. While information can be lost from sensory and short-term memories through decay or interference, retention in long-term memory is assumed to be virtually permanent.

attempted to recognize the words that they had studied. Recognition was better when meaning had been studied. This advantage was obtained even though rhyming was studied for the same amount of time. According to the levels of processing theory, the advantage for meaningful study was obtained because rhyming involves a surface-level processing while meaning engages deeper-level processes.

We'll come back to these theories throughout this chapter. First let's look at what the multiple memory theorists call sensory, short-term, and long-term memory. These three types of memory would have come into play if you had been a witness at the Sacco and Vanzetti trial. Let's see how they would have operated, for example, if you had had a very brief glimpse of the license plate on the getaway car during the Braintree armed robbery. Suppose you saw the plate for a fraction of a second and then you closed your eyes to concentrate on what you saw.

Sensory Memory

Sensory memory holds visual sensations for up to 1 or 2 seconds, allowing enough time for the recognition processes to operate. Sensory memory would have held the visual sensation of the license plate about 1 or 2 seconds after you closed your eyes. Sensory memory even holds visual information *through* disruptions such as eye blinks so that recognition processes can operate without interruption. Try waving a pencil in front of your eyes. The shadowy image that trails behind the pencil means that your sensory representation of the pencil in one position stays on after the pencil moves to a new position. This information fades or decays from sensory memory within 1 or 2 seconds.

Sperling (1960) used an interesting method to study visual sensory memory. In his experiment, he presented 12 letters in three rows with 4 letters in each row (Figure 7–2). He flashed the letters for 50 milliseconds, then asked subjects to name as many letters as they could. They were able to name only 4 or 5 letters, even though they claimed that they had seen more than that. Sperling concluded that subjects did not see all the letters because the flash was too brief. They saw more letters than they could report because they forgot some before they could say them.

Sperling ran a second experiment to test his hypothesis. This time he directed his subjects to view only a portion of the 12-letter display. He did this by using various tones as stimuli, sounding the tones after the letters were presented: A high-pitched tone meant that they should name the letters in the top row; a medium tone cued the middle row; and a low tone indicated that the subjects should concentrate on the bottom row. Sperling called this a *partial report procedure*, because subjects only report part of the display that is shown to them. The procedure is based on the same logic that teachers use to determine course grades. Teachers sample only part of a course's material on exams. They then use the percentage correct on the exam to estimate what percentage you know of all the material in the course. If you get 90 percent correct on the exam, the teacher assumes that you know 90 percent of all the material. Sperling found that subjects knew 75 percent of the letters in his display (3 out of 4) when they were cued immediately after the display went blank.

In other conditions, Sperling delayed the cue 150 milliseconds, 300 milliseconds, or 1,000 milliseconds after the letters were presented. This forced subjects to remember all the letters until they got the cue. As Figure 7–2 shows, the percent correct gradually dropped. In fact with a 1,000 millisecond delay, the cue was useless, since subjects did no better than when they received no cue at all. From this Sperling concluded that sensory memory held visual information for a short time after the display went blank, and that the memory gradually faded.

Sensory memory
Holds sensations briefly so that they can be identified; lasts from 1 to 2 seconds.

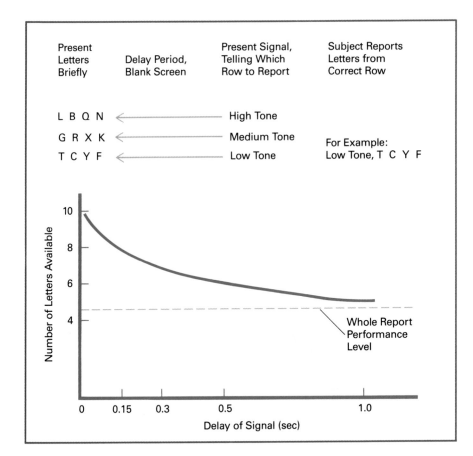

FIGURE 7–2
Sperling's partial report technique is shown in the upper part of the figure. Below it is a graph of the results: The number of letters recalled decreases as the signal to report is delayed. The dashed line represents the results of the subjects' ability to recall all 12 letters in the report (Sperling, 1960).

Sperling determined these important properties of sensory memory in related experiments:

1. Visual properties of a stimulus, such as brightness, determine the length of sensory memory. The brighter the stimulus, the longer sensory memory lasts. Usually sensory memory lasts less than 1 or 2 seconds.

2. Sensory memory for one stimulus is wiped out when another stimulus is presented after the first one is out of sight. The ability of a stimulus to wipe out the sensory memory of a preceding stimulus is called **backward masking.**

3. Sensory memory contains visual information that has not yet been recognized or named. Based on physiological evidence reviewed in Chapter 2, we can assume that sensory memory contains information represented in terms of visual features such as angles, curves, and straight lines.

Massaro (1970) showed that auditory sensory memory has similar properties. Since then, many studies have revealed auditory sensory memory. For example, Kallman, Beckstead, and Cameron (1988) asked 16 college students to judge the duration of test tones. In one condition, the experimenters presented a test tone, a silent interval, and a masking tone. The results suggested that subjects heard an auditory sensory image during the silent interval and combined this image with the actual test tone. As a result, they judged the test tone to be longer as the duration of the silent interval increased.

Tests of sensory memory have proved to be useful with special populations. For example, a study by Hornstein and Mosley (1987) suggests that mildly mentally retarded individuals seem to be deficient in using visual

Backward masking
Ability of a stimulus to wipe out the sensory memory of a preceding stimulus.

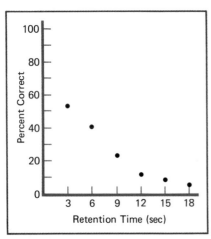

FIGURE 7–3

Research has shown that people rapidly forget isolated facts if they do not rehearse them. In the graph here we see a rapid decline in the amount of correct recall of trigrams. (Peterson & Peterson, 1959)

sensory memory. The experimenters used backward masking to wipe out sensory memory. The masks occurred after short delays that minimized the usefulness of sensory memory or after long delays that maximized the utility of sensory memory. The task was to recognize polygons or two-letter words. In comparison with normal control subjects, mentally retarded individuals were comparable at short delays. However, the retarded subjects were much worse at long delays when performance depended most on sensory memory. This result suggests that retarded individuals are deficient in using sensory memory. Similarly, schizophrenic patients are also worse than normal subjects on visual backward masking tasks (Braff, 1989; Schuck & Lee, 1989).

Short-Term Memory

Short-term memory holds information that has been transferred out of sensory memory. Transfer of information from sensory memory to short-term memory usually involves a considerable loss of information. Suppose the license plate number on the getaway car had been SMT-253, and you only had time to recognize the letters. The numbers would have been lost, in addition to many other details that you did not have time to identify. The part you did recognize, however, would be saved. Specifically, it would be transferred to short-term memory for further processing. Information will last only about 30 seconds in short-term memory if it is not repeated. The process of repeating information in order to retain it in short-term memory is a process called **rehearsal.** If we do not rehearse the information, the memory decays or fades rapidly. A good example of this is the way you repeat or rehearse a phone number that you have just looked up. If you do not repeat it, or if someone interrupts you before you can make the call, you will probably forget the number almost immediately.

Peterson and Peterson (1959) developed a way to measure how long information is held in short-term memory when it is not rehearsed. They divided their procedure into three intervals: presentation, retention, and recall. During presentation, subjects looked at a three-letter unit called a trigram, such as XNT. During retention, subjects did a math problem that was designed to keep them from rehearsing the trigram. During recall, subjects simply attempted to say the trigram that had been presented. Figure 7–3 shows the results. Subjects recalled trigrams correctly about 50 percent of the time after 3 seconds, about 25 percent of the time after 9 seconds, and about 8 percent of the time after 18 seconds. This and many other experiments show that we forget new, isolated facts (such as trigrams) in less than 30 seconds if we do not rehearse them.

More recent studies have shown that there are important individual differences in this forgetting rate. For instance, Cariglia-Bull and Pressley (1990) found that short-term memory differences affect sentence comprehension. After testing short-term memory, the experimenters read sentences to 165 fourth- and fifth-graders. In one condition, the students were told to form images to help them remember the sentences. These imagery instructions helped students who were good on the short-term memory test, but did not help students who were poor on the short-term memory test.

Multiple memory theory supports Peterson & Peterson's results because it says that we retain isolated facts in short-term memory until we transfer them to long-term memory. Transfer is impossible without rehearsal, so we quickly forget facts that we do not rehearse. Levels-of-processing theorists offer a different explanation for the same results. They assume that facts are remembered longer when they are processed more deeply, not because they are transferred to a different type of memory. Peterson and

Short-term memory
Holds information that has been transferred out of sensory memory; lasts about 30 seconds unless information is repeated or rehearsed.
Rehearsal
Process of repeating information in order to retain it in short-term memory or transfer it to long-term memory.

The probability that you will remember faces is not determined exclusively by how long you see them. Memory for faces is affected also by how deeply the face is processed—for example, you will remember faces better if you judge them on certain qualities, such as likeableness, friendliness, honesty, intelligence, and so on. This finding is of special interest in matters of eyewitness testimony.

Peterson's subjects only had time to do surface-level processing of trigrams, so they forgot them quickly. Both multiple memory theories and levels-of-processing theories pass the test of being able to explain the Peterson and Peterson results.

Long-Term Memory

Long-term memory holds information that is transferred from short-term memory through rehearsal or some other process. As you repeated the letters you had just seen on the license plate of the getaway car, you might have tried to think of ways to remember them. You might have noticed, for instance, that they are the first letters of the first three days of the week. Repetition and additional processing would transfer the information to long-term memory. The longer information stays in short-term memory, the more likely it is to be transferred to long-term memory. Some researchers assume that our long-term memory is virtually permanent—that is, we lose nothing from long-term memory, although we may sometimes fail to retrieve information from it (Atkinson & Shiffrin, 1971, 1977).

Types of Long-Term Memory. We store concrete information about sensory aspects of our experiences in long-term memory. We remember the sound of voices over long periods, as when an old friend calls and we immediately recognize his or her voice. We remember body movements. If you drive a car with a bright-light switch on the floor, for instance, you will probably hit the switch rapidly on your first try, even if you haven't used it for some time. Keele and Ells (1972) showed that we remember both the switch's position and how far we have to reach to step on it.

We also remember smells extremely well. In one experiment, people recognized smells as accurately after 30 days as they did after 30 seconds, and they forgot very few smells over a period of one full year (Engen, 1980).

As mentioned earlier, levels of processing can also explain long-term retention as well as multiple memory theory. Let's look at some support for the levels-of-processing theory.

Deeper Processing Means Longer Memory. Many experiments

Long-term memory
Holds information that is transferred from short-term memory; it can last a lifetime.

show that memory depends upon levels of processing—the deeper the level, the better the memory (cf. Wickelgren, 1979). There is one experiment that is of particular interest with respect to eyewitness testimony (Bower & Karlin, 1974). The experimenters showed pictures of faces and manipulated the levels of processing that people engaged in while looking at the pictures. Sometimes subjects used surface levels of processing to make judgments about simple things, such as the sex of the person in the picture. Other times subjects used deeper levels of processing to make more difficult judgments, such as likeableness or honesty. Subjects recognized pictures better on a later test when they had processed the pictures more deeply, even though they looked at all pictures for the *same* amount of time. This and other experiments suggest that theories of memory must take into account levels of processing.

We will continue to review evidence for multiple memory theory and levels-of-processing theory as we go on to discuss the processes of encoding, retention, and retrieval in short-term and long-term memory.

Encoding

Encoding is the process of selecting incoming stimulus information and coding it so it can be stored in memory. Video and audio tape recorders passively take in, or encode, everything that is bright enough or loud enough to record. A lawyer's job would be much easier if human witnesses did the same. But, of course, people don't; they decide what to take in and how to represent it. For instance, you used a special plan to encode, or represent, the study list at the beginning of this chapter. Cognitive psychologists include analyses of encoding as a major part of their research on memory. They find that encoding comes into play in short-term memory and long-term memory. Let's discuss each of these in turn.

Encoding in Short-Term Memory

Encoding
To select and represent information in a specific form (verbally or visually) in memory.

In traffic, our senses are often flooded with more information than our minds can handle at one time. We manage in this sort of situation because we pay attention only to important stimuli, which, in the case here, might be the road sign.

We have already said that much information is lost between sensory memory and short-term memory. Let's take a closer look at the selective way in which most of us encode information.

Attention.   Put yourself in the place of Benjamin Bowles on Christmas Eve in 1919. You are riding shotgun in a payroll truck when suddenly it comes under fire. Your first instinct is to hit the floor, but you have committed yourself to defending the money, so you return the fire. Moments later the truck swerves out of control and hits a telephone pole. Think about the rush of stimuli you would experience—the gunmen, the smoke from their guns, the smoke from your gun, bystanders running, the background spinning by, the smell of the truck's heater and of rubber burning, the bumps against your body as you and the other passengers are bounced around, the bangs, the squeals of tires, the shouts. You would not experience all of these to the same extent. Your mind would zero in on some and ignore others. Just by imagining the situation you probably have a good idea about which stimuli would get your attention.

The process by which we notice important stimuli and ignore irrelevant stimuli is called **attention.** Without it, our minds would surely drown in a churning, muddled ocean of stimuli. In traffic, on disco floors, at cocktail parties, and even on a tranquil stroll through the woods our senses are flooded with more information than our minds can handle at one time. We manage in these situations because we attend selectively to important information.

Figure 7–4 illustrates one of the artificial laboratory settings used to study attention. The procedure is known as **dichotic listening.** Each earphone carries a separate message. The subject is asked to ignore one message and to *shadow* the other, that is, to repeat it aloud as it is heard, staying as "close behind" the speaker as possible. This procedure allows the experimenter to examine two questions: What happens to the message that the subject is asked to ignore? When does this irrelevant message interfere with perception of the relevant one?

Before looking at the answers, try to guess. What do you think happened to the irrelevant smells, sounds, and bumps that rushed in on Bowles when his truck was attacked? Do you think they were noticed in the first place? Surely these irrelevant stimuli excited his sensory receptors, but perhaps the signals from the receptors were filtered out before his brain recorded them. If they did reach the brain, and if they were noticed, perhaps they were remembered for only a very short time.

One way to find out what happens to the message the subject is asked to ignore is to give subjects a surprise test on their ability to recall the irrelevant message in a shadowing experiment. Research has shown that 30 seconds after the material is presented, the content of the irrelevant message is forgotten (Moray, 1959). In some experiments the irrelevant message was alternately presented in English and an unfamiliar foreign language, or in English and gibberish; 30 seconds later subjects had no recollection that these changes occurred.

Attention
Focusing on important stimuli and ignoring irrelevant ones; a selective process in memory.
Dichotic listening
The subject hears different messages in each ear and is asked to repeat only one of them.

FIGURE 7–4

This is the apparatus used in a typical shadowing experiment. Separate messages are played through earphones to each ear of a subject, who tries to ignore one message and to repeat the other.

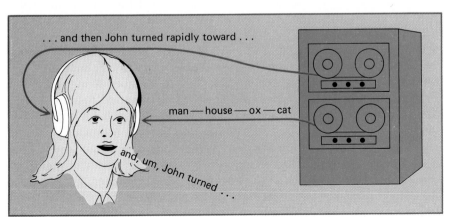

. . . and then John turned rapidly toward . . .

man — house — ox — cat

and, um, John turned . . .

It is interesting to note that the physical characteristics of the irrelevant message *are* remembered. For example, people remember whether it was a man's voice or a woman's voice they heard, whether or not it stopped completely, and whether or not it was replaced by some other sound. Apparently people attend to an irrelevant message enough to determine its physical characteristics, but not enough to determine its meaning, or at least not enough to remember the meaning 30 seconds later.

The question of when the irrelevant message interferes with perception of the relevant one also deserves some thought before we look at the answers regarding the shadowing experiment. We all know that irrelevant stimuli sometimes interfere. For example, try listening to a lecture while someone next to you cracks his or her knuckles. Sometimes, however, irrelevant stimuli don't seem to matter. The hum of an air conditioner, for instance, probably does not take your mind away from a lecture.

As you might have guessed, the content, or meaning, of an irrelevant message can make a difference. For example, if a subject's name is mentioned, shadowing of the relevant message is disrupted. This is similar to losing track of your own conversation when hearing your name mentioned in a nearby discussion. Hearing one's name mentioned is distracting because people are somehow predisposed to hear their names. A researcher found that other words also become distracting when we are inclined to hear them (Treisman, 1960). For example, one sentence in the relevant message started with the words "Poor Aunt . . ." Consequently, subjects expected to hear a woman's name. A woman's name (Jane) was then played in the irrevelant message and something else was played in the relevant message. Subjects suddenly started shadowing the irrelevant message and said "Jane." This mistake was often noticed and subjects stopped to apologize. These subjects had a hard time ignoring the distracting message when they were predisposed to hear it.

Encoding, of course, is more than selecting certain information; it is also representing it in a certain form. If you had seen the license plate number on the getaway car at the Braintree armed robbery, would you have tried to form a mental picture of the license plate, using a visual code, or would you have repeated the number to yourself? How would you have tried to remember the bandit's face? Would you have repeated facial features to yourself—black hair, red cheeks, slim face—or would you have formed a mental picture of it? Evidence suggests that you would have used both kinds of codes.

Verbal Codes.   Many experiments have shown that we prefer to use verbal codes for verbal materials such as digits, letters, and words. In one study, Conrad (1964) found evidence for verbal codes in the errors that people make. He briefly exposed six consonants and then asked people to write down all six letters in order. When people made mistakes, the incorrect letters were usually ones that *sounded* like the correct ones. For the list R L T K S J, a subject might substitute a B for a T, recalling R L B K S J. It is hard to imagine that subjects would have made this mistake if they had remembered the letters by means of a visual image. After all, a B does not *look* like a T. The mistake makes good sense, however, if people are using verbal codes, because B does *sound* like T. Such mistakes, therefore, support people's claims that they remember strings of letters by repeating the letter names to themselves. If we tried to remember a license plate number on a getaway car, we would probably repeat it to ourselves several times until we had a chance to write it down.

Visual Codes.   While we *prefer* verbal codes for verbal material, we don't always use them. For example, we used visual codes to memorize the words in the study list at the beginning of this chapter. For example, we tried to visualize a bun being used as an ashtray. Similarly, we seem to prefer visual codes for memorizing stimuli that are difficult to describe. Kosslyn, Ball, and Reiser (1978) found evidence suggesting that people use visual codes when they are asked to memorize maps (see Chapter 8). This and other evidence (Kosslyn, 1981, 1984; Wickelgren, 1977) suggest that we use visual codes. We could certainly use them to remember a robber's face if we happened to witness a crime.

Our choice of codes depends to some extent on how long we must remember something. So far we have only talked about experiments on memory for short intervals. Experiments on memory over longer intervals suggest that we *recode* information for long-term memory.

Encoding in Long-Term Memory

Which of the following sentences was the second sentence in this section on encoding?

1. Video and audio tape recorders actively decide what bright or loud information should be recorded.
2. Audio and video tape recorders automatically record everything that is bright enough or loud enough to take in.
3. Video and audio tape recorders passively take in, or encode, everything that is bright enough or loud enough to record.

Sentence 1 is easy to eliminate because its meaning is different from the first sentence in this section. You may have had more trouble, however, deciding between sentences 2 and 3. Sachs (1967) read sentences to subjects such as "The author sent a long letter to the committee." Two minutes later subjects remembered sentence meanings, but they did not remember exact words. They could not choose between the actual sentence and a different one that had the same meaning: "A letter that was long was sent to the committee by the author." In the same way, you may be representing the meaning of sentences that you are reading here, but you probably are not representing the exact words in long-term memory. Will you remember the meaning at test time? That will depend on many factors, which we discuss in the next section.

Retaining and Recoding

Tape recorders are passive instruments. They retain whatever information they pick up, and they play it back in the same form in which they have recorded it. Retention in humans is quite another matter. Humans alter some memories and forget others during retention. Testimonies by Cox, Harding, and Bowles during the Vanzetti trial illustrated the changeable nature of human memory. Over time their descriptions of the bandit changed in many ways; they altered their statements about characteristics such as moustache length, complexion color, and forehead shape. Here we will review experiments that shed light on what might have caused these changes.

We have already discussed the kind of coding that takes place when information is transferred from sensory memory to short-term memory. In this section, we will more closely follow the path of information to explore how it is *retained* after it is encoded in short-term memory and in long-term memory.

Capacity of Short-Term Memory

Memory theorists try to distinguish short-term and long-term memory on the basis of how much each holds or *retains*. Try to dial the following

We have a short-term memory span of 5 to 9 items. This means that looking up a phone number and trying to remember it while you dial it works better with local numbers (7 digits) than with long distance numbers (10 digits).

Memory span
The number of items that we can read through at one time and then recall in sequence with no mistakes.

Chunking
Process of grouping elements such as letters or words into units (or chunks) that function as wholes. Memory span consists of 7 ± 2 chunks.

number without looking back at it: 924–3401–5732–816. Most of us can't do it. We're used to handling 7 digits without much trouble, but we find 14 almost impossible. Why? Multiple memory theorists say that we have trouble dialing 14 digits because our short-term memory has a limited capacity, or a limit to how much information it can hold. While long-term memory can hold almost any amount, short-term memory can only hold a limited number of digits. Fourteen is well beyond that limit.

Our short-term **memory span** is the number of items that we can read through once and then recall in sequence with no mistakes. Experiments have shown that seven-digit numbers seem to mark the limit of our short-term memory span. Ebbinghaus (1885) was one of the first to estimate his own memory span at seven items. Many years later, George Miller (1956) saw the estimate of seven coming up so often in experiments that he wrote a paper entitled "The Magical Number Seven, Plus or Minus Two." While people differ greatly in their ability to remember facts for exams or lines for plays, virtually all normal adults have a short-term memory span that falls between 5 and 9 items.

Multiple memory theorists explain this "magical number" with the assumption that short-term memory has a limited storage capacity of 7 ± 2 items. It is as if short-term memory is a small filing box with only 7 ± 2 slots. When all the slots are filled the only way we can get new information into short-term memory is by displacing some item that is already there (see Waugh & Norman, 1965).

Levels-of-processing theorists explain limited memory span not in terms of *limited storage capacity*, but in terms of *limited processing capacity*. They assume that we are limited in the rate at which we can perform the processes of holding items and of repeating them. Since storage limitations and processing limitations are both plausible, the existence of memory span limitations does not help us choose between multiple memory theories and levels-of-processing theories.

Chunking.   **Chunking** is the process of grouping stimuli into meaningful units. We can say that memory span is limited to 7 ± 2 items, but what exactly is an item? Experiments have shown that our short-term memory span can correspond to 7 ± 2 digits, letters, syllables, words, or even sentences. The letters NOTTER UOL YRAM formed this way each represent one chunk of information. If we see the letters in reverse order, MARY LOU RETTON, the entire string of letters becomes one information chunk. In fact, we could manage five or six more names in our memory. When we process information, we group elements together to form units that function as wholes. We group visual features into letters, letters into words, and words into sentences. Miller (1956) labeled the units *chunks* and concluded that memory span corresponds to 7 ± 2 chunks.

Given the economy of chunks, it is not surprising that individuals who chunk better also remember better. For example, glance at the chessboard in Figure 7–5 for 5 seconds and then cover it. This figure reproduces a board during an actual game. Suppose that the board and pieces were real instead of a picture. Suppose also that you were given an empty board and asked to put the pieces back where you saw them. How many would you get right? The answer depends upon how well you know familiar groupings (chunks) in chess. DeGroot (1966) as well as Chase and Simon (1973) found that master chess players could recall the positions of pieces much better than weak players, but only if the pieces were seen in familiar positions that resulted from actual games. Saariluoma (1985) replicated the finding that master chess players recall specific chessboard plays better than novices. Without seeing the board, however, masters guessed positions only slightly better than novices. When the board was seen with pieces in random positions, masters recalled the positions no better than novices. Further, the same masters could not perform better on simple perceptual tasks such as counting specific pieces. These results suggest that memory for chess pieces improves when they can be chunked into familiar groups. An expert chess player recognizes familiar chunks in real games better than a novice does, so the expert remembers better. This effect of expertise on chunking and memory is not limited to chess. Allard and Bennett (1985) observed similar effects in basketball, for instance. They found that varsity basketball players do better than less experienced subjects at remembering the positions of players in snapshots of basketball games. Here again, the experts remember better because they can chunk stimuli into familiar groups.

Most of the time, we try to remember things for a fairly long period of time, as when we study for exams. Let's look now at the special characteristics of retention in long-term memory.

Retention in Long-Term Memory

The eyewitness testimony at the Sacco and Vanzetti trial illustrates two principles of retention in long-term memory: *organization* and *reconstruction*. People organize the information that they store in long-term memory, and they continue to work on or reconstruct that organization as time passes. Initial organization was revealed in reports by Cox, Bowles, and Harding to police at Bridgewater. These descriptions of the "shotgun bandit," which we quoted earlier, depended upon long-term memory, because the police did not arrive immediately. The free recall reports were highly organized even though the questions did not impose an organization. Specifically, all three witnesses used organizations that grouped together facts into four categories: body build, facial features, clothing, and nationality. As time passed, all three witnesses changed their testimony in a way that might have indicated a reconstruction of their original memory. Let's take up this example in more detail and relate it to research on principles of organization and reconstruction.

Organization in Long-Term Memory. People store a wealth of general knowledge, and they use this background knowledge to organize memories for episodes that they witness. Cox, Bowles, and Harding, for instance, already knew the categories that they used to organize their memories of the "shotgun bandit." Tulving (1972) formalized the distinction between the long-term retention of background knowledge and specific episodes as follows:

1. **Semantic memory** refers to a person's general background knowledge about words, symbols, concepts, and rules.

2. **Episodic memory** refers to a person's memories about events, including the time and place they occurred.

We will use this distinction in the following discussion, even though researchers are still debating its value for theories of memory (McCloskey & Santee, 1981).

The extent to which semantic memory can impose itself on episodic memory is illustrated by Harding's testimony. He did well, remembering details such as a black overcoat, but he got one fact wrong. He reported that the "shotgun bandit" wore a derby hat, when he actually wore no hat at all. Overcoats and derby hats were probably closely associated in Harding's semantic memory, and he may have mixed up his semantic memory with his episodic memory of the event he witnessed. We are, of course, just speculating about the reason for Harding's error. For better evidence of the interaction between semantic and episodic memories, we should turn to the research in this area.

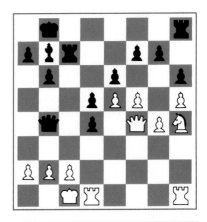

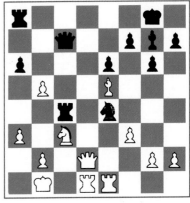

FIGURE 7–5

Examples of experimental positions used in the guessing and reproduction experiments. (Reed, S. K., 1988)

Semantic memory
A person's general background knowledge about words, symbols, concepts, and rules.
Episodic memory
A person's memories about events, including the time and place they occurred.

All three witnesses in the Sacco and Vanzetti case changed their testimony from the time they first talked to the police to the time they actually testified at the trial. Their memories of the body build, facial features, clothing, and even nationality of the "bandits" may have been affected by the process of reconstruction in long-term memory.

Galton (1879) studied semantic memory with a **free association test,** which is a procedure in which a person looks at, or listens to, a target word and then reports other words that come immediately to mind. Deese (1959) combined free association tests with free recall tests to show that we use semantic memory to organize episodic memory. Free association tests measure semantic memory, because they reflect the way our general knowledge about words is organized. Free recall tests measure episodic memory in that they reflect the organization of memory for a list learned at a specific time and place. Deese first measured free association in one group. He then gave a list of words in random order to another group. The second group was allowed to recall the words in any order. The subjects recalled the list not in its original order, but in an order that grouped together things that were related in earlier associations. Apparently, associations that were present in semantic memory imposed themselves on episodic memory.

Other researchers used a clever procedure to study semantic memory (Collins & Quillian, 1969). They measured how long it took people to answer simple true-false questions. Consider one of their questions: A canary can fly, true or false? The question asks about general knowledge; it doesn't ask about a specific piece of information (that is, you can answer it without saying when or where you saw a canary fly, or without ever having seen a canary fly). They used such questions to test a model of how people organize semantic memory. Figure 7–6 shows an example of their model. Information about canaries is stored in different places, according to the model. Some is stored under a high-level category, "animal"; some is under a lower level or subordinate category, "bird"; and some is under a still lower category, "canary." This organization, which is called a **hierarchy,** arranges information into levels of categories and subordinate categories. Collins and Quillian assumed that it would take time to move

Free association test
Procedure in which a person looks at or listens to, a target word, and then reports other words that come to mind.
Hierarchy
An organization that arranges information into levels of categories and subordinate categories.

between categories. They found, in agreement with this prediction, that it takes longer to decide "A canary can fly" than it does to decide "A canary can sing." It takes even longer to decide "A canary has skin." Today many models of semantic structure include similar structures (Anderson & Bower, 1973). Other studies show that we use our knowledge of categories and hierarchies to organize and, thereby, to improve our episodic memory (Bower, Clark, Winzenz, & Lesgold, 1969; Horton & Turnage, 1976). That is, subjects in laboratory experiments act like the witnesses in the Sacco and Vanzetti trial. They use familiar categories and associations to add new information to their memories. Laboratory experiments have also answered interesting questions about old and new memories. For example, do you think it is easier to learn a new word or to add a new association between words you already know? Dagenbach, Horst, and Carr (1990) found that new associations take much longer than new words. Accordingly, it will take extensive study to add a new association to your semantic memory, such as a new association between memory and chunk. It will be much easier to learn a new word, such as "episodic."

Reconstruction in Long-Term Memory. We start organizing material when we first encounter it, and we continue to organize and reorganize as time passes. We are often unaware of our efforts to reorganize, or recode, material in long-term memory. Such unconscious reconstruction of memory is a major source of unreliability in eyewitness testimony.

After witnesses saw Vanzetti during his trial, their description of the shotgun bandit moved closer to a representation of Vanzetti. We might think that the witnesses were deliberately trying to frame Vanzetti. But research suggests another possibility: Witnesses may have unconsciously distorted their memories.

In one experiment, Elizabeth Loftus found that exposure to new information can distort a witness's memory (Loftus, 1975, 1981; Loftus & Palmer, 1974). Subjects were shown a film of a traffic accident, and they then answered one of five questionnaires. The questionnaires were all the same except for the wording of a question about speed. One questionnaire asked, "About how fast were the cars going when they smashed into each other?" The other questionnaires substituted the verbs "collided," "bumped," "con-

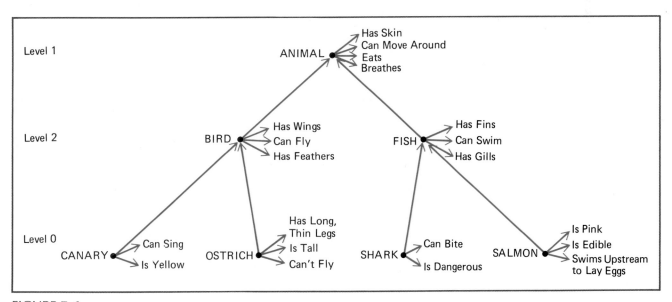

FIGURE 7–6

This is a model of semantic memory. This type of organization of ideas is called a hierarchy. (Collins & Quillian, 1969)

tacted," or "hit" in place of "smashed." Loftus had two ways to measure the influence of the verbs. One measure, the estimate of speed, showed that the verb "smashed" drew higher speed estimates than the other verbs. A second measure came a week later, when Loftus asked, "Did you see any broken glass?" Subjects who had the questionnaire with the verb "smashed" in it were more likely to say yes, even though there had been no broken glass. Apparently, memory was altered to include details that did not actually exist, but which were consistent with an accident at higher speeds.

In courtrooms, questions that "lead" a witness to a particular answer are not permitted. However, the rules against them may be inadequate. Leading questions asked well in advance of a trial seem to alter memory for an event. Consequently, answers to "fair questions" during the trial might be unreliable.

What exactly is a leading question? To get at a precise, unambiguous definition, researchers must show exactly how and when people can be led by questions. Loftus has begun to explore the kinds of questions that cause memory distortions. For instance, she conducted an experiment similar to the one above, except she used a different leading question. Immediately after showing a film of a fast-moving event, she asked a question that presupposed the existence of an object that was not in the film. For example, in a film showing no barns, the leading question was "How fast was the white sports car going when it passed the barn while traveling along the country road?" One week later, nearly one-fifth of the students who heard this question "remembered" a barn being in the film. In a later study, Bekerian and Bowers (1983) suggested that people can recall their original memories better if they have good retrieval cues. Specifically, subjects do poorly when test questions are given in a random order. But they do much better when the question sequence matches the order of the original event. Thus, good retrieval cues might help offset the effects of leading questions.

Your memory for this traffic scene can be distorted by how questions are asked. Without looking back, try to answer the following questions: How many cars were in front of the flag pole? Can you visualize the flag that you saw? If so, your memory was distorted by the first question. Many people recall seeing objects that are mentioned in previous questions even though they are not in the picture.

Push a button and mechanical recorders play back information exactly as they have recorded it. Human **retrival,** the process of getting information out of memory, is not as reliable. We sometimes fail to retrieve, or get back, information that is stored in our memory. You might be unable to recall a date on a history exam, for example, but then it comes to mind right after the exam. This suggests that the date was in your memory all along, but you failed to retrieve it during the exam. In the same way, witnesses sometimes fail to recall details until a hypnotist helps them remember (see Chapter 5). Such retrieval failures increase unreliability stemming from inattentiveness during encoding and from memory distortions during retention.

Memory researchers would have a fairly easy time studying retrieval if all of our retrieval efforts were open to conscious inspection, but they are not. We often search through our memory without being aware of it, which makes memory research both more difficult and more interesting. Let's turn to some of the special techniques used to study conscious and unconscious retrieval processes.

Retrieval from Short-Term Memory

Saul Sternberg (1966) conducted an experiment that shed light on retrieval from short-term memory. You can get a feeling for his experiment easily enough with the following test. Memorize the numbers 2, 3, and 8, and then cover them. Now, ask yourself whether or not the following numbers were on the list: 3, 7, 1, 2, 9, and 8. The answers "yes, no, no, yes, no, yes" come to mind so quickly and effortlessly that it is hard to realize that we have to search our short-term memory at all. Sternberg found evidence, however, that we do, in fact, search our short-term memory for such information.

He recorded how long it takes people to respond "yes" or "no" in a task like the one that you just tried. He had subjects memorize numbers, ranging from one to six items on a list. He tested a list only once, then asked subjects to memorize another list. On each test he presented a digit, and subjects pushed a "yes" button if the digit was on the memorized list and a "no" button if it was not.

Sternberg found that response time depends on the length of the original list (Figure 7–7). It takes about 440 milliseconds with one item, about 480 milliseconds with two items, about 520 milliseconds with three items, and so on, with each additional item taking about 40 additional milliseconds. Sternberg concluded that we retrieve the test digits one at a time, with each comparison taking about 40 milliseconds.

Sternberg's procedure has been used to reveal interesting individual differences. A recent experiment by Mosley (1985), for example, suggests that memory-search rate is slower in retarded individuals even though encoding, decision, and response times are not slower. Similarly, grade-school children with language disorders have a per-item scanning speed that is about four times slower than normal children's (Sinenger, Klotzky, & Kirchner, 1989). In comparison with normals, however, paranoid schizophrenics (see Chapter 14) seem to have comparable memory-search times, but slower encoding times (Highgate & Neufeld, 1986). Finally, people with Type A (coronary prone) personalities (see Chapter 13) have faster

Retrieval
Process of getting information out of memory.

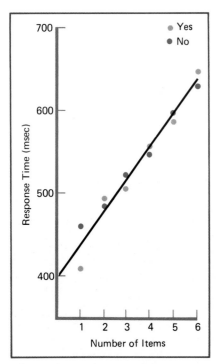

FIGURE 7–7

The time it takes to decide if an item is in one's memory increases as the number of items in short-term memory increases. This result shows that it takes time to search through items in short-term memory. (Sternberg, 1966)

memory-search rates than people with Type B (noncoronary prone) personalities (Damos & Sloem, 1985).

Retrival is not open to conscious inspection in Sternberg's experiment. Yet he was able to make a strong case that retrieval from short-term memory involves a search process. His experiment and those of others (Glass, 1984) go beyond our intuitions about retrieval from short-term memory. Similarly, cognitive psychologists have been able to go beyond what introspection reveals about retrieval from long-term memory.

Retrieval from Long-Term Memory

We are often unaware of our efforts to search long-term memory (Raaijmakers & Shiffrin, 1981). Sometimes, however, we are aware of our attempts to retrieve information from long-term memory and we deliberately control our search (see Norman, 1973). Suppose you are questioned in connection with a crime because it was committed by someone fitting your description. All you have to do to put a end to this unfortunate case of mistaken identity is account for your whereabouts any time between 3:00 and 5:00 P.M. on the first day of last month. Can you do it? If you try, you will probably find yourself consciously reconstructing the events of that day. You might say to yourself, "I get paid on the first of the month and I usually deposit my check shortly before the bank closes. Oh, yes, I remember now. I deposited my check at about 4:30 on the first of last month. In fact, that was the day I complained to the service manager about an unexplained service charge on my account. I hope she has a record specifying the time of my complaint." But maybe you are not so lucky. Perhaps you can remember classes you attended in the morning and the play you saw that night, but you cannot remember what you did that afternoon. The point is that you are sometimes aware of your efforts to search your memory.

We are not always aware of our retrieval processes, however. Researchers, therefore, cannot rely entirely on people's direct reports of efforts to search memory. One way that researchers investigate retrieval processes that are not always open to consciousness is by manipulating cues that are designed to aid retrieval.

Organization and Retrieval Cues.   Tulving and Pearlstone (1966) argue that we can take advantage of organization when we retrieve information from episodic memory (see also Masson & McDaniel, 1981). They showed subjects long lists containing words from common categories such as animals, colors, and professions. The words were presented in random order, and then subjects attempted to recall the lists. Half the subjects were told the category names at the time of recall; the other half were not. Subjects who were given category names did much better than the other subjects. Both groups were given category names in a later test, and they both recalled the same number of words. Both groups must have had the words in memory, but subjects could not retrieve as many without the help of category names. The category names served as aids to retrieval, or what psychologists call **retrieval cues.** We apparently use retrieval cues to organize our search through memory.

Tip-of-the-Tongue Phenomenon.   We reveal other aspects of our retrieval processes when we come close to information in our memory without actually finding it. This uncomfortable state of being on the verge of recalling something is called the **tip-of-the-tongue (TOT) phenomenon.** For example, what word means "lying on one's back, with the face upward" (Hint: the word starts with "s"). If you think you know it, but you can't recall it you are in a TOT state. (The word we are looking for is "supine.") Brown and McNeill (1966) produced over 200 TOT states in students who were asked to recall particular word definitions they were given. When

Retrieval cues
Aids to retrieval that are often encoded with the information to be remembered; an example would be category names.

Tip-of-the-tongue (TOT) phenomenon
State of being on the verge of recalling something; often subjects say that the word or whatever they are trying to record is "on the tip of the tongue."

students indicated that a word was on the tip of their tongue, Brown and McNeill asked them questions about the word. Students knew the number of syllables in the word over 60 percent of the time; they knew the word's first letter over 50 percent of the time; and they could give words that sounded like the words being defined (for example, *secant* instead of *sextant*). Brown and McNeill suggested that we retrieve information by sound as well as by meaning.

In a similar study, Brennen, Baguley, Bright, and Bruce (1990) induced TOT states by asking college students to name famous people—for instance, who was the first women to run for the vice presidency? Brennen and colleagues found that such questions could induce a TOT state. They also found that some hints were more helpful than others. Which do you think would be more helpful, a picture of the first female vice presidential candidate or her initials? Brennen and co-workers found that initials were much more helpful. In our example, the picture is shown at the right and the initials are *G.F.* Did either of these hints help you recall the correct answer, Geraldine Ferraro?

Does this photo help you remember the name of the first female vice-presidential candidate? (See text on this page.)

Anxiety and Retrieval. Most of us have panicked on an exam at one time or another. Panic is especially likely when there is a lot at stake. Consider a particularly crucial exam that you have taken. Passing means that you finally reach a long sought after goal; failure prevents you from getting something you really want. Suddenly you become overwhelmed by a fear of failure, even though you know the material. Your anxiety level rises as each difficult question is reviewed until finally you are so panicked that you cannot remember a thing. Anxiety does not wipe out your memory, but it does make memories harder to recall (Richards & Whittaker, 1990). Things you couldn't remember during the exam often start coming to mind when you calm down after the exam.

Holmes (1974) argues that anxiety does not in itself prevent retrieval. Anxiety produces extraneous thoughts, such as, "I'll never be able to face my dad," or "This is unfair because I've worked so hard." Holmes argues that these thoughts are what stand in the way of retrieving answers to exam questions. You might try to control such distracting thoughts. This should help, but it will not completely solve the problem. Hedl and Bartlett (1989) found, for instance, that anxiety reduces recognition memory for sentences even when the need for retrieval is minimized. It is important, therefore, to control your anxiety level directly. Chapter 5 outlines procedures that you can use to relax before taking exams. Chapter 5 also reviews evidence that to most easily recall memories, you should be in the same state during study and test periods. Therefore, maintaining lower anxiety levels during both study periods *and* tests may improve your performance.

Decision Factors. Tape recorders report everything that has been recorded. With human retrieval, however, we *decide* what we want to say before we report anything. This intermediate decision allows us time to edit what we report.

Imagine yourself on a television game show. You are asked to name the children in the Walton's television family. How would you answer? That would depend upon the *cost* of wrong answers and the *rewards* for correct answers. If you had everything to gain for correct answers and nothing to lose for errors, you would probably include some guesses. You might say "John Boy, Jim Bob, Mary Ellen, I think there was a Jason, maybe an Aaron, how about a Beth?" If, on the other hand, your winnings were taken away for each error, you might be more cautious. For example, you might say, "John Boy, Jim Bob, and Mary Ellen—that's all I can remember."

Costs and rewards also influence the testimony of witnesses in a trial. The cost in such a situation might be guilt associated with identifying the

COURTROOM TESTIMONY BY PSYCHOLOGISTS ON EYEWITNESS RELIABILITY

William Jackson spent 5 years in prison, convicted of rape even though he had not committed any crime. He was released in 1982 after police arrested the real rapist, a man whom Jackson strongly resembled. Can psychologists help prevent such miscarriages of justice?

Robert Buckhout (1986) and Elizabeth Loftus (1986) have spoken out strongly in favor of the use of psychological evidence in criminal proceedings. Most of you know that psychologists contribute to the insanity defense and lie detector tests (Graham & Kabacy, 1990; Ogloff, 1990; Heilbrun, 1990). You might not know, however, that they also offer testimony on eyewitness reliability. For more than ten years, Buckhout, Loftus, as well as other psychologists, have been applying their research by providing expert testimony on eyewitness reliability. In a special issue of *Law and Human Behavior* (1986) a group of psychologists took time out to debate the ethics of expert testimony. Buckhout and Loftus took the side of the debate that favored expert testimony; others took the opposition side (e.g., Knoecni & Ebbesen, 1986; Pachella, 1986), and still others made a balanced presentation of both sides of the issue (e.g., Hastie, 1986; Yarmey, 1986). To fully appreciate the strong undercurrents of this debate, one must realize that there is money involved—lots of money. A first-time expert witness can easily command $1000 a day plus expenses for providing testimony, and the pay jumps substantially for more experienced experts. There is no argument about money being paid for services that have been provided. The question is whether the judicial process is receiving enough benefit to justify the cost of the service.

The controversial issue of whether psychologists should give expert testimony in court is complex. As Wells (1986, p. 83) points out, it involves "not only the effects on the verdicts but also the effects of expert testimony on the process by which verdicts are reached, the practices of police in subsequent investigations, the public's view of psychology, the practices of judges in subsequent

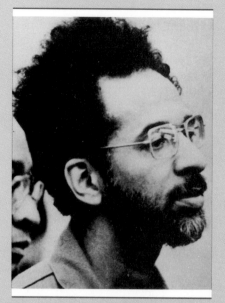 

The wrong man: William Jackson, right, was imprisoned for five years for two rapes actually committed by Dr. Edward Jackson, Jr., left.

cases, and the interaction between expert testimony and research activities." We cannot address these many facets of the issue here, but we can focus on a central question in the debate: *Is there an adequate scientific foundation to support expert testimony of psychologists on eyewitness reliability?*

On one hand, a case can be made for there being a solid foundation of laboratory research. For example, we have already considered Loftus's research indicating that a witness's memory can be distorted by the way he or she is questioned. Loftus's basic laboratory observations have been replicated many times (e.g., MacLeod & Ellis, 1986). Psychologists have also been able to document several other important findings. For instance, there is growing evidence that high confidence of a witness does not relate to high accuracy of testimony, that juries are greatly influenced by the confidence of a witness, and that expert testimony can reduce the impact of witness confidence (e.g., Fox & Walters, 1986; Lindsay, 1986). There is also growing evidence that young children as eyewitnesses (3- and 4-year-olds) are less accurate than adults and are more influenced by leading questions (Ceci, Ross, & Toglia, 1987; Goodman & Reed, 1986).

On the other hand, one can question the extent to which laboratory research can be generalized to cases outside the laboratory setting. Both Konecni and Ebbesen (1986) and Pachella (1986) maintain that psychologists who routinely offer expert testimony have unwarranted faith in the ability to generalize laboratory results. Their skepticism was supported by a recent field study reported by Yuille and Cutshall (1986). They investigated a case in which 21 witnesses had observed an actual shooting in which one person was killed and a second was seriously wounded. The witnesses were highly accurate in their accounts and, contrary to laboratory evidence, they were very resistant to leading questions. Clearly, there is a need for more field research to evaluate the generalizability of laboratory research. Let's also remember that field studies have their limitations, too (see Chapter 1). It would be misleading for us, therefore, to decide this issue solely on the bases of field studies, laboratory studies, or case studies (such as Sacco and Vanzetti). Future research should include coordinated efforts to conduct both laboratory and field research to supplement the growing empirical foundation for continuing to evaluate eyewitness testimony. It should also continue developing ways to educate expert witnesses in courtroom procedures. Such education can improve the effectiveness of expert testimony (La Forge & Henderson, 1990).

While the debating goes on, let us look at yet another side to this issue: How have the courts reacted to more than 10 years of expert psychological testimony? Woocher (1986, p. 47) commented on this reaction as follows: "A comprehensive review of the judicial decisions in this area reveals that there has recently been a significant shift in the courts' receptivity toward such testimony. Many courts now believe that psychological research on human perception and memory has progressed to the point that the expert's testimony is considered both reliable and helpful enough to the jury to justify its admission in the appropriate case." This evaluation suggests that psychologists are making a valuable contribution even though debate among psychologists is likely to continue as long as questions remain under investigation. This debate is a sign not of weakness but of strength. Public debate is a hallmark of good science, both basic and applied. Valuable applications of psychological principles are often developed at the same time that experiments are improving our understanding of those principles.

wrong person; the reward might be the satisfaction of seeing justice done. Buckhout (1974) maintains that two witnesses with the same memory might decide to say quite different things, and he developed a test to identify good witnesses. He based his test on **signal detection theory,** which makes it possible to measure memory and decision factors separately (Green & Swets, 1966). To give the test he shows a film of a staged "crime" and then presents 20 true statements about the incident and 20 false statements. Witnesses score a *hit* whenever they say "yes" to a true statement, and they score a *false alarm* whenever they say "yes" to a false statement. The percentage of hits and false alarms is used to calculate the witnesses' measure of sensitivity. If witnesses say "yes" as many times to true statements as they do to false statements, they obviously have no sensitivity about the truth of the statements, and their score is 0. If, on the other hand, witnesses almost always say "yes" to true statements and almost never say "yes" to false statements, they are very sensitive and they get a high score. Generally, observers who score high on Buckhout's test prove to be the best witnesses in other situations. For example, they do better at picking suspects from a lineup. For about 80 years, psychologists have warned about the unreliability of witness testimony. Now they are taking positive steps toward identifying reliable witnesses. (See Highlight: "Courtroom Testimony by Psychologists on Eyewitness Reliability.")

Forgetting

Forgetting is defined as an inability to remember. Chapter 12 will discuss situations in which we try to forget. Here, we will analyze forgetting that occurs even though we are trying to remember. Let's consider some examples. What was the name of your third-grade teacher? Can you name five students who were in your fourth-grade class? What is the formula for figuring the area of a circle? What is your social security number? Can you name five glands in the endocrine system along with the hormones they secrete (see Chapter 2)?

If you answered all these questions correctly, you should be pleased. If you answered some of these questions incorrectly, you might ask yourself why your memory failed you. If you knew why, you might be able to improve your memory. With that in mind, let's review the possibilities.

Signal detection theory
Attempts to explain people's perceptual judgments by analyzing their sensitivity to sensory stimuli in addition to the criteria they use to make decisions.

Forgetting
Inability to remember or retrieve information from memory.

Trace Decay

One of the earliest theories of forgetting, **trace decay theory,** holds that memory traces fade away in time. The theory's appeal to early theorists is apparent. Memories are natural, and things of nature change. Trees grow leaves only to lose them again; grass turns green only to fade back to a tawny brown; the sun rises and sets; we wake up fresh only to get tired again.

In the same way, according to trace decay theory, memory traces start out strong, and their strength is maintained through use. But traces gradually weaken and fade away if they are not used. Trace decay theory would explain a failure to recall the name of your third-grade teacher as follows: You once had a strong memory trace for the name and you refreshed the trace regularly by using it. Your trace gradually lost strength, however, when you stopped using it, and it became so weak that you could no longer recall the name.

Wickelgren (1977) argues that trace decay may contribute to forgetting, but other factors are also involved. For example, you learned many names since the third grade, and these may have interfered with your ability to remember your third-grade teacher's name. The next section presents an interference theory of forgetting.

Interference

When we learn different things, we create the possibility that learning one thing will cause us to forget something else. A popular theory of forgetting, **interference theory,** holds that we forget information because other information gets in the way. Two kinds of interference are as follows:

1. **Proactive inhibition** means that something that has already been learned interferes with our ability to commit something new to memory. Suppose historians suddenly discovered that Columbus really discovered America in 1534. Our previous memory of Columbus discovering America in 1492 would hinder our learning of the new date. Researchers study proactive interference with experiments similar to the one illustrated in Table 7–1. The experiment has three steps and two groups of subjects.

    In the first step, the experimental group learns a list of words, List A; the control group does some unrelated activity. In step two, both groups learn a list, List B. In the third step, both groups recall List B. Proactive inhibition is shown by lower recall of List B for the experimental group, who had previously learned List A.

2. **Retroactive inhibition** means that new learning interferes with the memory of what you learned earlier. Suppose you went away for 6 months and you did not use your phone number during that time. You might have trouble recalling your number, but you would probably have even more trouble if you had acquired a new phone number in the meantime. The interference of the new number with your memory

Trace-decay theory
Memory traces fade away in time if their strength is not maintained through use.
Interference theory
Theory that we forget information because other information gets in the way. See also *proactive inhibition; retroactive inhibition.*
Proactive inhibition
Interference of previous learning with memory for new learning.
Retroactive inhibition
Interference of new learning with memory for previous learning.

Table 7–1 Proactive Inhibition	Experimental Group	Control Group
Step 1	Learn List A	Rest or engage in unrelated activity
Step 2	Learn List B	Learn List B
Step 3	Recall List B	Recall List B

	Experimental Group	Control Group
Step 1	Learn List A	Learn List A
Step 2	Learn List B	Rest or engage in unrelated activity
Step 3	Learn List A	Recall List A

Table 7–2
Retroactive Inhibition

for the old one is retroactive inhibition. An experiment for studying retroactive inhibition is outlined in Table 7–2. It has three steps and two groups.

In the first step, both groups learn List A. In the second step, the experimental group learns List B, and the control group does some unrelated activity. In the third step, both groups recall List A. Retroactive inhibition is reflected in lower recall of List A by the experimental group, who learned List B after learning List A.

Old and new material do not always interfere with each other in our memory, of course (see Shebilske & Ebenholtz, 1971). Sometimes old memories help us learn new material, as in the "one is a bun" experiment cited in the beginning of this chapter. Similarly, new learning sometimes helps us remember things that gave us trouble in the past. Isolated dates in history are often difficult to remember until we learn enough facts about a period to provide a frame of reference. Determining when memories will help or hinder the recall of other memories is one of the major challenges facing memory researchers today (Smith, 1988).

Another challenge is explaining how one memory interferes with another. Some theorists argue that a memory can be erased or dissolved by other memories. Other theorists claim that interfering memories do not destroy other memories; they only make them harder to locate during recall.

In the next section we will discuss the rapidly developing work of neuroscientists. They have taken up the difficult task of specifying the neurobiological basis of learning and memory.

The Neurobiological Basis of Learning and Memory

We have seen that a brief glimpse at a getaway car can trigger a complex sequence of learning and memory processes. We can assume that all of these processes have a neurobiological basis (see Chapter 2). Similarly, as you are reading at this very moment, billions of neurobiological changes are taking place in your brain (see Chapter 4). These physical changes will ultimately determine whether or not you will recall this material at test time. They are the basis of all our cognitive operations—they determine selective encoding, retention, and retrieval processes operating over short-term and long-term periods. Scientists are therefore eager to understand the neurobiological basis of learning and memory.

We will briefly review three approaches used in this important area of investigation:

1. Determining whether damage to specific brain structures produces loss of retention of learned responses

2. Examining changes in the brain that correlate with learning

3. Stimulating brain structures electrically or chemically in order to increase or decrease memories

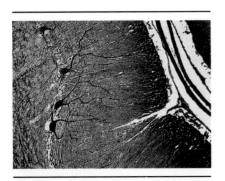

Scientists are beginning to understand how learning and memory change neurons.

Neurobiological Correlates of Memory

Learning and memory produce many neurobiological changes. For example, learning produces alterations in the following:

1. EEG activity (Landfield, 1976)
2. Firing pattern of single cells (Olds, 1973)
3. RNA and protein synthesis (Glassman, 1974; Shashoua, 1967)
4. Biochemical excitability of cell membranes (Alkon, 1983)
5. The number of connections between neurons (Greenough, 1984)

Greenough (1984) compared and contrasted the neurobiological changes that underlie short-term and long-term effects of learning and memory. Any given stimulus will cause some cells to "turn on" and others to "turn off." After learning and storing items in memory, the pattern of these "on" and "off" responses changes. One way to change firing patterns is to change the excitability of cell membranes in existing pathways between cells. The cell membrane acts as a gate. Thus, a message might not go from one cell to another even though the cells are physically connected. The more excited the cell membranes become, the more likely it is that messages will go between cells (see Chapter 2). Another way to change firing patterns is to change the physical links between cells. That is, cells can grow new branches to reach more cells (see Chapter 2). Greenough (1984) hypothesized that (1) the basis for short-term effects is change in the excitability of cell membranes, and (2) the basis for long-term effects is the establishment of new connections between neurons. Testing this hypothesis will be an exciting task for future researchers (C. F. Hoyenga & Hoyenga, 1988).

Effects of Brain Damage or Disease on Retention

Researchers have sought the location of **memory traces** by observing the effects of brain damage on memory retention (Herbert, 1983; Mayes, 1986; Weingartner, Grafman, Boutelle, Kaye, & Martin, 1983). In Chapter 2 we discussed the possibility that the hippocampus plays an important role in learning and memory. This idea has been supported in animal laboratory experiments in which researchers damage the hippocampus before or after learning (Olton, Becker, & Handelmann, 1980). The importance of the hippocampus in human memory processes is also suggested by clinical research.

In 1957, a 28-year-old man had part of his brain removed in an attempt to ease his violent epileptic seizures. The patient, who is referred to as H.M., developed a severe memory disorder following the removal of the hippocampus and related structures (see Chapter 2). As a result, this procedure has never been repeated. A clinical report describes some of his problems as follows:

> Ten months after the operation, the family moved to a new house which was situated only a few blocks from their old one, on the same street. When examined . . . nearly a year later, H.M. had not yet learned the new address, nor could he be trusted to find his way home alone, because he would go to the old house. Six years ago, the family moved again, and H.M. is still unsure of his present address, although he does seem to know that he has moved. [He] will do the same jigsaw puzzles day after day without showing any practice effect, and read the same magazines over and over again without finding their contents familiar.
>
> On one occasion, he was asked to remember the number 584 and was then allowed to sit quietly with no interruption for 15 minutes, at which point

Memory trace
Change that occurs as as result of memorizing.

he was able to recall the number correctly without hesitation. When asked how he had been able to do this, he replied, 'It's easy. You just remember 8. You see 5, 8, and 4 add to 17. You remember 8, subtract it from 17 and it leaves 9. Divide 9 in half and you get 5 and 4, and there you are: 584. Easy.'

In spite of H.M.'s elaborate . . . scheme he was unable, a minute or so later, to remember either the number 584 or any of the associated complex train of thought; in fact, he did not know that he had been given a number to remember. (Milner, 1970)

Such loss of memory is called **amnesia.** It can occur because of injury (Levin, 1990) or surgery, as in the case of H.M., or it can stem from psychological problems, which are discussed in Chapter 13. There are two kinds of amnesia brought on by physical injury: **retrograde amnesia,** which is partial loss of memory for events that occurred before the injury, and **antrograde amnesia** which is difficulty in remembering events that take place after an injury. Although H.M. had some retrograde amnesia for events that occurred 1 to 3 years before his surgery, he had good recall of his earlier life. He generally experienced antrograde amnesia; he had difficulty remembering events that took place after he had the brain surgery.

We can get some clue as to the role the hippocampus plays in memory by considering H.M.'s history. First, since he had good recall of his earlier life, we know that the hippocampus does not play a critical role in maintaining or recalling "old" long-term memories. Second, since H.M. had a severe impairment in his ability to form new memories, the hippocampus must be essential for storing "new" long-term memories.

These conclusions are supported by another case study in which a patient suffered a stroke that destroyed part of the hippocampus on both sides of the brain. The patient lived for five years after the stroke, and he experienced memory deficits similar to H.M.'s. That is, he could remember events that happened before the stroke, but he had severe difficulty storing new memories (Zola-Morgan, Squire, & Amarai, 1986).

There are two other diseases that cause people to forget specific new information while they can remember generalities that they learned before the disease: One is *Korsakoff's syndrome*, which is brain damage caused by severe thiamine (vitamin B-1) deficiency and is characterized by apathy, confusion, and memory impairment. This disease is rarely observed except in alcoholics who go days or weeks without eating. A second is *Alzheimer's disease*, a condition associated with degeneration of neurons that manufacture the neurotransmitter acetylcholine, and characterized by memory loss, confusion, depression, hallucinations, and an inability to complete an action or maintain a train of thought. Occasionally the disease starts in middle age, but generally is evidenced in people over sixty. Recently, St. George-

Amnesia
Partial forgetting of past events. Some forms of amnesia are caused by physical injuries, such as a blow to the head. *Psychogenic amnesia* means that the cause of the memory loss is stress rather than physical injury.

Retrograde amnesia
Partial loss of memory for events that occurred before an injury.

Antrograde amnesia
Difficulty in remembering events that happen after an injury.

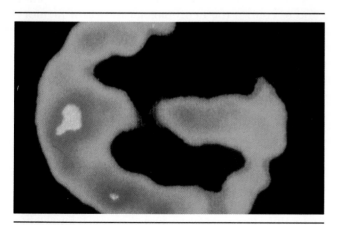

PET scan of Alzheimer's diseased brain.

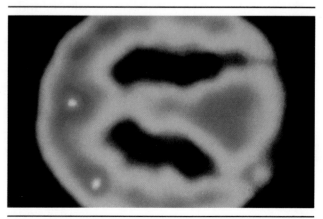

PET scan of normal brain.

Hyslop et al. (1987) reported that Alzheimer's disease may be inherited through a genetic defect carried in the same chromosome that is linked with Down Syndrome (see Chapter 9).

Barbizet (1970) reported a case study of a 59-year-old Korsakoff's patient who could easily recall events from his youth but had trouble remembering recent events. For example, if a person left the patient's room for a few minutes after a long conversation, the patient would forget that he had the conversation. The patient also forgot that he read certain newspaper articles and read the same ones over as if he were reading them for the first time. When he sat at a dinner table with an empty plate in front of him, he did not know if he had finished eating or if he hadn't started yet.

Schachter (1983) observed similar memory deficits in an elderly Alzheimer's patient. While playing golf, the patient remembered the rules and the jargon, but he could not keep track of his game. He teed off five times from the same hole because each time he forgot that he had already teed off. When he did remember that he had teed off, he couldn't remember where he hit the ball, and he couldn't recall the label on his ball.

These examples illustrate three kinds of brain damage that disrupt short-term memory and the formation of new long-term memories. Other kinds of brain damage can impair previously well-established episodic and semantic long-term memories (Mayes, 1986). Scientists have not yet identified specific kinds of memory loss with specific sites of damage in the cortex, but they have determined that damage to certain subcortical structures, such as the hippocampus, produces specific kinds of short-term memory loss (Kalat, 1988).

Electrical and Chemical Regulators of Memory

Scientists have discovered neurobiological manipulations that alter memories. Electronic stimulation of the brain can either increase or decrease memory depending upon a variety of conditions (Gold & McGaugh, 1975). The chemicals that have been shown to influence memory include the neural transmitters dicussed in Chapter 2 and the stimulants discussed in Chapter 5. These chemicals influence memory and some can either improve or impair memory depending on the dose (Gold & McGaugh, 1977). The effects of both electrical and chemical stimulation are greatest if they occur shortly before or after training. This time period is when one would expect memory storage processes to be operating. This suggests that electrical and chemical stimulation might affect memory storage.

Will this line of research lead to improved memory through an electronic thinking cap or a memory pill? Probably not in the near future. Although progress has been made, neuroscientists have a long way to go. Their goal is to understand and to control the neurobiological basis of memory. They still have much to learn about the relationship between cognitive processes and neurobiological changes before they will be able to exercise precise control. Therefore, the best way to improve your memory at this time is to concentrate on learning, review, and recall procedures, as described in the next section.

Improving Your Memory

"You can remember all the things that make the vital difference in your everyday existence, eliminating the unnecessary loss of so much knowledge and information that should be yours to keep and use forever" (Lorayne

& Lucas, 1974, p. 1). So begins *The Memory Book*, which is filled with ways to improve your memory for things you do in school, such as giving speeches and taking exams. It also helps you remember people's names, shopping lists, playing cards, and important numbers such as telephone numbers. The book promotes a general understanding of how memory works and it gives hints on how to apply this insight to your own ability to memorize. We have already discussed how our memory operates. Now let's see how we can make that understanding work to our advantage in our everyday lives.

You can take steps to improve your memory when you first encounter new material, when you review and rehearse, and when you try to recall. These three actions correspond to the three basic processes of memory: encoding, retention, and retrieval.

Encoding Efficiently: Putting Memories Where You Can Find Them

A key to encoding is attention. You must pay attention to important material if you want to remember it. We have all had experiences that help drive home the importance of attention. Perhaps you have failed to pay attention during a social introduction. Then you realized immediately afterward that you did not catch the name of the person to whom you were introduced. Or perhaps you have found yourself at the bottom of a page without any idea of what you have just read. You can take steps to overcome these common problems of not paying attention.

You can ask yourself two questions during an introduction that will heighten your attention:

1. Is there anything unusual about the name?
2. Does the name go with the face?

The first question is easy to answer for some names that have obvious peculiarities, such as Mr. Katz Meow. Finding unusual aspects will be harder for other names. What's unusual about the name Shebilske? Different people will notice different things, of course. Did you notice, for example,

A simple, but important, habit is to study in a quiet location without many distractions.

that if you allow for misspelling, the name can be broken down into three common words—*she, bill,* and *ski*? With practice you will get good at finding something unique about any name. The second question is also easy to answer for some names. Mr. Katz Meow might have a moustache that looks like cat whiskers. You will have to be more imaginative to link other names with faces. You might notice, when being introduced to Mr. Shebilske, that his "bill" (nose) looks like a ski slope. Get in the habit of asking yourself these questions during every introduction. They will sharpen your attention to details, even if you don't have time to answer them right away.

You might also get in the habit of using the person's name immediately after hearing it. "It's a pleasure to meet you, Mr. Shebilske." You will force yourself to pay attention if you hold yourself responsible for saying the name. Be careful not to get these two habits mixed up. You don't want to find yourself saying, "It's a pleasure to meet you, Mr. Ski Face."

You can also develop special study habits that will help you overcome inattentiveness during reading. First of all, admit that you do not have a will of iron. Certain things are going to capture your attention despite your best efforts to ignore them. You will be distracted by radios, televisions, and nearby conversations when you read. You may do well at first if you try to read in the presence of these distractors. Sooner or later, however, something will capture your attention, and your mind will be taken away from your reading. You will improve your memory if you get in the habit of reading in a quiet place.

The next step is to develop the habit of focusing your attention on important parts of your reading. Your memory will increase significantly if you identify important ideas and concentrate on them (Shebilske & Rotondo, 1981).

There are certain steps that will help you put your attention in the right places. These steps are as follows:

1. Survey material before reading it carefully. You can determine important ideas better after you see a whole passage. You should therefore go over a passage quickly, keeping an eye out for the main ideas. Topic headings often identify main points. Chapter objectives are also helpful. Read them before you read whole passages.

2. Ask yourself, "What are the main points?" Come up with a temporary list that can be refined as you read more carefully. Also, ask yourself questions that you think the text will answer.

3. Read the text carefully, noting the main points and answering your self-generated questions.

4. Recite the text in your own words after you finish reading. Note the main points that you do and do not know.

5. Review, firming up what you do know and learning main points that you may have missed the first time.

Organization is another key to efficient encoding. You find information better in an organized memory, just as you find things better in an organized home. Disorganized people spend more time looking through their homes for things they have misplaced than organized people spend returning things to their proper places after each use. In the same way, organizing your memory will take time during encoding, but it will save time during retrieval. It will also save time because you won't need to relearn forgotten material.

The trick in organizing is to relate new material to things that you already know. You can organize shopping lists, for example, according to familiar categories. Consider this shopping list: milk, bananas, spinach, oranges, cheese, lettuce, radishes, apples, and butter. You will have an easier time remembering it if you reorganize it according to categories: milk, cheese, butter, bananas, oranges, apples, spinach, lettuce, radishes (see Bower et al., 1969).

You can reduce organization time by using one of many preestablished systems. Memory-aiding systems are called **mnemonic systems.** The "one is a bun" experiment at the beginning of this chapter taught you an effective mnemonic system. You can use the whole system to learn other lists, or you might simply use the image-forming part of the system. To remember that B. F. Skinner did experiments on operant conditioning, for example, you might visualize a hunter skinning wild game on top of a rat cage. Wallace, Turner, and Perkins (1957) found that people can learn to form images for most word pairs in less than 5 seconds and they can remember about 95 percent of 700 pairs after a single exposure to each. Obviously, imagery can be a quick and effective organizing system.

Imagery is used in the **key-word method** of learning foreign vocabulary. Let's use this method to learn that *muleta* means *crutch* in Spanish. We first look for part of the foreign word that sounds like an English word. "Mule" is an obvious choice, so it becomes our key word. We then form an image between the key word and the English equivalent of muleta. We might visualize a mule hobbling along with its front leg propped up on a crutch. Figure 7–8 illustrates this image. You should find that the key-word method will help you with any foreign language you try to learn (Atkinson, 1975).

In addition to helping college students remember foreign words, the key-word method also helps learning-disabled children remember word meanings in their own language. Condus, Marshall, and Miller (1986) found that the key-word method is an effective way to teach vocabulary words to learning-disabled students. They taught 50 words to 12-year-old students over a 5-week period. Students taught by the key-word method remembered more word meanings than students who were taught by other methods. This memory enhancement was revealed on tests taken during training and on tests taken 10 weeks later. In a similar study, Veit, Scruggs, and Mastropieri (1986) combined the key-word method with the peg word ("one is a bun") that you learned at the beginning of this chapter. They found that the combination of these two methods helped learning-disabled 6th, 7th, and 8th graders remember vocabulary words in lessons about dinosaurs. Apparently, these methods are versatile mnemonics that can help advanced college students and learning-disabled grade schoolers.

Many medical students have learned the twelve cranial nerves by remembering, "On old Olympus' towering top, a fat armed German viewed some hops." The first letter of each word reminds them of the first letter in each nerve: olfactory, optic, oculomotor, trochlear, trigeminal, abducens, facial, auditory vestibular, glossopharyngeal, vagus, spinal accessory, hypoglossal.

Using a memory aid called **verbal mediation,** students have learned the Greak Lakes by remembering HOMES: Huron, Ontario, Michigan, Erie, Superior. They relate new material to *verbal mediators,* which are words that have easy-to-remember structures. Mediators are extremely powerful. In one study, Bower and Clark (1969) asked 84 subjects to use mediators to learn 12 lists of 10 words each. Subjects made up 12 short stories to connect the words in each list. Afterward they recalled 90 percent of the words. You can make up mediators to improve your memory for facts.

Many other easy-to-use memory aids have been described in the literature on memory (e.g., Bellezza, 1983). In addition, try making up your own memory aids. Anything you do to organize your memory at the time of encoding will be to your benefit. No matter how good your encoding procedures are, however, you will often find it necessary to review. It is therefore also important to learn special review procedures.

Spanish — Muleta   Key Word — Mule   English — Crutch

Spanish — Pato   Key Word — Pot   English — Duck

Figure 7–8

Imagery is used in the key-word method of learning foreign vocabulary. Forming an image like the one shown here will help you remember that *muleta* means *crutch* in Spanish, or *pato* means *duck.*

Mnemonic systems
Systems created to aid memory; examples are the key-word method and verbal mediation.
Key-word method
Mnemonic system of using imagery to learn foreign vocabulary; consists of forming an image that will act as a link between the key word and the other word we want to remember.
Verbal mediation
Mnemonic system in which one relates new material to verbal mediators, which are words that are easy to remember.

Better Retention through Better Review

How do you review for exams? Reviewing for some people is characterized by repetition. They reread material, paying special attention to parts that they highlighted or underlined the first time. Such selective rereadings are better than no review at all. But if your reviewing tends to be selective repetition, you are not getting as much out of your reviewing hours as you could be. Effective reviewing is characterized by *organization* and *depth of processing*. You should approach your reviewing with a two-part plan.

The first part of your review plan should serve to improve upon the organization you started during encoding. But it is not essential to finish all your organizing during your first study session. You can use review time to put lists in order, to form verbal mediators, and so on. The techniques used during reviews are identical to those used during encoding, except that you can spend more time on them.

The second part of your review plan should serve to increase your depth of processing. Earlier we learned that the more deeply we process material, the better we remember it. You can increase your depth of processing of textbooks in three ways:

1. First, outline the topics. List all the main topics (for example, theories, encoding, retention, retrieval, forgetting, applications). Under each topic, write as many subheadings as you can remember. If you don't remember some, look them up. Under each subheading write as many facts as you can remember. Again, look up facts you don't remember. Make sure you see how the facts, subheadings, and main topics relate to one another.

2. After you know what is in a passage, think up good test questions for the material and then write out answers. Your questions should cover the material as thoroughly as possible. Your answers should be short notes on key ideas related to each question. You will be able to process more deeply because you will be forcing yourself to think about relationships that exist in the text material.

3. Another way to think about relationships is to criticize the text. Do you think it makes sense to compare human memory with computer memory? What are the strengths and weaknesses of this approach? Does it make sense to distinguish between multiple memory theories and levels-of-processing theories? Can you think of an experiment that would test the two theories? Does the text contain gaps? Have you learned things in other books that fill in gaps in the present text? Perhaps this chapter failed to mention your favorite memory-aid system. How does your favorite memory aid relate to the ones reviewed here? Critical thinking of this sort will increase your depth of processing and thereby improve your retention.

Reviewing is important outside of school as well. You might be introduced to several people at once during your first day on a new job. You would do well to review their names before going to work the next morning. If you memorized a shopping list, you would do well to review it on the way to the store. Follow the same principles outlined in this section. Your review should improve your organization and your depth of processing. Reviewing also plays an important role in remembering emotionally charged events (see Highlight: Flashbulb Memories). If, for some reason, you don't have time to organize or to process deeply during encoding and retention intervals, don't panic. There are things you can do during retrieval to improve your memory.

FLASHBULB MEMORIES

Many people have *flashbulb memories*, which are vivid memories of unexpected and emotionally important events. Let's try to tap some of your flashbulb memories with the following questions: (a) What were you doing when you learned that war had broken out with Iraq? (b) Do you remember where you were and what you were doing when you learned that the space shuttle *Challenger* had exploded? Many of us can answer these questions in vivid detail. For example, I heard a TV bulletin announcing that the bombing had started in Baghdad. At that moment, I was taking an apple from my refrigerator. I dropped the apple and ran to the living room. My wife was standing in front of the TV. She was pale and shaking when she turned to me and said, "This is it."

Roger Brown and James Kulik (1982) found that most Americans over 40 can recall exactly what they were doing when they learned about President Kennedy's assassination. I am no exception. I remember clearly the moment the announcement came over my school's PA system.

According to Brown and Kulik, this moment was set in my memory like a photograph taken with a mental flash camera.

Do you have vivid memories of sudden, emotionally charged events? If you do, you may be surprised to learn what recent research has shown about them. First, *vivid* is not necessarily *accurate*. Flashbulb memories are both vivid and accurate a week or two after events such as the *Challenger* explosion. They remain vivid, but they lose accuracy as time passes (Neisser, 1982, 1986; Thompson & Cowan, 1986; McCloskey, Wible, & Cohen, 1988). Second, much of what is remembered is rehearsed in conversation. If it is not rehearsed, it will not be remembered accurately eight months after the event (Bohannon, 1988). Special memory mechanisms are therefore not necessary to explain flashbulb memories. The memories are important, however. They are, according to Neisser (1982), the "places where we line up our own lives with the course of history itself and say 'I was there.'"

Retrieving Effectively: Knowing How to Look for Memories

We learned earlier that retrieval cues aid recall. People remember lists better, for example, when they are given category names during retrieval. We set up retrieval cues in advance when we form images, key words, and mediators during encoding. The payoff for the extra work comes during retrieval, when all we have to do is use our preestablished memory aids. Planning is recommended but you still can use retrieval cues even if you did not develop memory aids in advance.

What do you do when a memory demand catches you completely off guard? This might happen, for example, if you lost a shopping list which you had not committed to memory. There are two things that would improve your recall in this situation.

1. First, search your memory systematically. Try to think of categories. If you recall one vegetable, try to think of others.

2. Second, try to reestablish the context in which you wrote the list. Lawyers sometimes return witnesses to the scene of a crime because the original context helps them remember details (see Norman, 1973). You might mentally retrace the steps you made when you searched your cupboard to see what you needed.

You can follow these two procedures on exams, too. If a question seems to come out of the blue, search your memory systematically and try to remember the context in which you might have studied the relevant information. Suppose you draw a blank when you are asked to define *mnemonics*. You should try to figure out which main section might have included this word. If you can correctly place it in the section on improving your memory, you will greatly increase your chance of coming up with the definition. Try to remember as much as you can about the session in which you studied the material. What was the first thing you reviewed? What questions did you ask? You still might not remember, but you will at least be improving your chances if you use these strategies, which are based on current theories of memory. In fact, the use of similar memory-guidance techniques in police interviews significantly enhanced eyewitness memory in a recent experiment (Geiselman, Fisher, & MacKinnon, 1985). The experiment also showed that the memory enhancement was as good as that obtained through hypnosis (see Chapter 5).

Based on the overwhelming success of *The Memory Book*, we can assume that it has helped people. Hopefully, this is one application that you will be able to put to use immediately. Someday you may be able to strengthen your memory further with the help of computers. Computerized memory aids are already available on a limited basis.

Has your memory ever failed you during a social introduction? You realize immediately afterward that you do not remember the person's name. The text explains how you can overcome this problem.

Summary

1. The Greeks and Romans studied the art of memory. Ebbinghaus pioneered the scientific study of memory with memory experiments. The behaviorists believed that Ebbinghaus' methods would lead to a general principle of memory. By the 1960s scientists began to test these theories. At the same time, cognitive psychologists became involved in the study of mental operations as they relate to learning and remembering complex lessons.

2. **Memory** is a system that allows people to retain information over time. Researchers often study memory by testing subjects. The most frequently used methods of testing memory are with **recall tests, recognition tests,** and **savings tests.**

3. Multiple memory theorists distinguish three kinds of memory: sensory memory, which lasts 1 or 2 seconds; short-term memory, which lasts less than 30 seconds; and long-term memory, which may be permanent. Levels-of-processing theorists reject the distinction between short- and long-term memories as separate memories. They believe that all information is processed in the same memory, but that we process this information to various levels of abstraction.

4. **Sensory memory** represents, or **encodes,** information in a form, or code, that is similar to sensations. **Short-term memory** uses verbal codes and other abstract codes to represent only a small part of the original information. **Long-term memory** uses even more abstract codes to represent meaning.

5. People recode, or change the representation of, memories during retention intervals. They group or **chunk** information in short-term memory. They organize long-term memories according to preexisting categories. They sometimes reconstruct these organizations, including new things that were not part of the original memory.

6. People sometimes fail to recall, or to **retrieve,** information that is present in memory. Retrieval from short-term memory involves a search that takes additional time for each item in memory. Retrieval from long-term memory also involves a search that is often very organized. **Retrieval cues** aid in this organization.

7. **Forgetting,** the inability to remember, may be caused by **trace decay** and/or by **interference.** There are two kinds of interference: **proactive inhibition,** the interference of things learned earlier; and **retroactive inhibition,** the interference of things learned later.

8. Neurobiological changes in the brain are the basis of all our cognitive operations. Evidence that the hippocampus is important in memory retention has been supported by clinical evidence.

9. You can improve your memory by improving your **attention** and organization when you first encounter new material. You will remember textbook material better, for example, if you identify important ideas and concentrate on them when you read. You should also organize new material by relating it to things you already know.

10. You can improve your memory through effective reviewing. Do not just repeat what you have learned—organize it, test yourself, and criticize it.

11. Memory also can be improved during **retrieval.** At this stage it is important to search your memory systematically and also to try to recall the context in which something was learned.

Key Terms

amnesia
antrograde amnesia
attention
backward masking
chunking
dichotic listening
encoding
episodic memory
forgetting
free association test
hierarchy
interference theory

key-word method
long-term memory
memory
memory span
memory trace
mnemonic systems
proactive inhibition
recall tests
recognition tests
rehearsal
retrieval
retrieval cues

retroactive inhibition
retrograde amnesia
savings
savings tests
semantic memory
sensory memory
short-term memory
signal-detection theory
tip-of-the-tongue (TOT) phenomenon
trace decay theory
verbal mediation

STUDIES OFFER FRESH CLUES TO MEMORY

BY DANIEL GOLEMAN

Forget the old maxim that memory deteriorates with age. The new wisdom, emerging from recent studies, is that there are several kinds of memory, only one of which worsens in old age.

Though psychologists still dispute precisely how many kinds of memory there are, most agree that there are at least three major kinds: "episodic," for specific events; "semantic," for knowledge and facts; and "implicit," for skills one exercises automatically, like speaking grammatically or hitting a golf ball. Semantic and implicit memory do not decline with age, the new studies show. And declines in episodic memory may be due to factors like retirement rather than aging itself and may be reversible, psychologists say.

These encouraging findings, and the framework they support, are gaining wide acceptance among memory researchers. For scientists trying to understand the workings of memory, the findings offer important clues to fresh avenues of research and to new models of how the mind stores and retrieves information.

For example, it has long been known that elderly people who forget recent events can still recall memories from the distant past. But the new findings suggest that even this memory loss is not inevitable except in those with an illness that affects the brain.

"The idea that memory inevitably deteriorates as you age came from studies that only tested one kind of memory," said David Mitchell, a psychologist at Southern Methodist University. "Now we see that there are multiple memory systems, and they each hold up differently as you age."

The type of memory that declines substantially in old age is "episodic" memory, which deals with specific events like what happened at yesterday's meeting, the name of someone you have just met, or where the keys to the car were left.

Peter Graf, a psychologist at the University of British Columbia, said, "The scientific literature shows that episodic memory is stable through the mid-60s, with a slight drop but no real problems for most people. But there is a pronounced drop in the 70s for most people. The drop may be largely due to retirement, and the way that changes how you use your memory; people usually don't exercise their mental faculties as much after work demands stop."

Memory researchers point out that many people develop strategies that compensate for the decline, like writing notes to themselves. Mulling events over or talking or thinking about them later also seems to help store the memory in the "semantic memory," the overall store of information and experience people accumulate over a lifetime. "Semantic memory does not decline with age," Dr. Mitchell said. "It grows."

Data suggesting that people continue to accumulate information comes from older studies reported by Dr. Robert Katzman, chairman of the department of neurosciences at the University of California Medical School at San Diego. A group of men and women in their 60s were tested on the same vocabulatory list that Dr. Mitchell used, and then tested again ten years later.

In Some Cases, Memory Improved

During the intervening decade of life, the men and women improved their scores by an average of six or seven words, which Dr. Mitchell called a substantial increase. The studies, done at the National Institute of Mental Health in 1956 and 1967, were first published in the 1970s but were largely overlooked by memory researchers. Only when they were republished in 1983 in a book on the neurology of aging did they catch the attention of researchers, Dr. Mitchell said.

The data were particularly important, he said, because almost all research on memory and aging involves comparing a younger group with an older group. Longitudinal data, in which the same people are tested years later, are able to establish more strongly that any differences seen are a result of aging itself.

The findings make sense of the long-observed fact that the elderly seem better able to retrieve memories from the distant past than from last week or the last hour. It is only within the past five years that data on memory in the elderly showed clearly "that it was semantic memory that the elderly rely on for distant memories, while it is a failing episodic memory that interferes with remembering recent events," said Dr. Mitchell.

"The memories from long ago are for stories or emotional moments that people have thought about over and over, storing them in semantic memory. Recent memory lapses that plague the elderly are for more everyday events, such as where you put your glasses. Those are part of episodic memory."

Robust Forms of Memory

The findings about other kinds of memory are also positive. In a paper to be published this spring in *The Bulletin of the Psychonomic Society*. Dr. Graf shows that although most people experience a strong drop in episodic memory in their 70s, other kinds of memory remain robust.

For example, researchers say that among healthy adults there is generally minimal decline with age in "implicit memory," which deals with the large variety of mental activities that occur spontaneously, without having to make an intentional effort, like driving a car.

The recognition that implicit memory is distinct from other kinds of remembering came in large part from observations of people with amnesia. In a paper published in 1983, Dr. Daniel Schacter, a psychologist at the University of Arizona, described a golf game with an amnesiac patient who had been an avid golfer before suffering a brain lesion that led to his memory problem. During the game, the patient forgot having played each hole or making each stroke within minutes of having done so.

Even so, he played the game as though he knew exactly what had just happened; for example, he reached for the right club for his next stroke. And over a series of days, his game improved steadily from practice, even though he did not recall having played the day before.

Facts and Amnesiacs

In later studies, Dr. Schacter found that if he taught amnesiac patients made-up facts, such as that "Jane Fonda's favorite food is oatmeal," they would later answer the question "What food does Jane Fonda love?" about as well as people with intact memory. But if he asked where they had learned that fact, the amnesia patients would have no idea, a phenomenon called *source amnesia*.

Dr. Schacter observed the same split in memory in studies with the elderly. Like the amnesiacs, people in their 60s and 70s were able to answer the questions as well as young people, but they were worse at remembering exactly when and where the new knowledge came from.

One implication is that the elderly can learn from experience just as younger people can, but may not remember exactly when and where the new knowledge or skill came from.

Problems in the Frontal Lobes

Brain studies of memory suggest that the decline in episodic memory, such as for the list of words, is related to a degeneration of the frontal lobes. Using a blood flow measure, Endel Tulvig, a psychologist at the University of Toronto, found that while people were engaged in episodic memory tasks like remembering words they had just memorized, the frontal lobes were more active.

Other data also point to the frontal lobes as the source of memory problems in the elderly. Larry Squire, a neuropsychologist at the University of California Medical School at San Diego, found that the greater the damage to the frontal lobes in amnesia patients, the greater was the loss of episodic memory.

"The frontal lobes decay more quickly in aging than do other parts of the brain," Dr. Craik said.

But Dr. Schacter has recent evidence that there are strategies older people can use to compensate for their memory deterioration in some situations.

"Part of the problem in the elderly may be in switching attention," he said. "If things come too quickly or in a confusing fashion, it may not register as well. But if older people are able to focus on what is happening without distractions, their memory may be just as good as ever."

Language, Thought, and Intelligence

8

Twenty-four-year-old James Watson felt knots in his stomach as he anticipated the contents of a manuscript by Linus Pauling, one of the world's leading chemists. Pauling had already discovered that the structure of protein is a single helix, or spiral. Now Pauling was proposing a three-chain helix as the structure of deoxyribonucleic acid (DNA). This molecule is especially important because it is the genetic key to the transmission of hereditary traits. Watson became interested in DNA when he studied biology as an undergraduate at the University of Chicago and again as a graduate student at Indiana University. Now he was on a postdoctoral fellowship to study the chemistry of DNA at Cambridge University. He and a Ph.D. candidate, Francis Crick, were working with Maurice Wilkins and Rosalind Franklin at nearby King's College in London. Wilkins and Franklin were learning a great deal about the structure of DNA by X-raying the molecule. And they were generously sharing their data with Watson and Crick.

Suddenly, Watson's mood skyrocketed. After studying Pauling's manuscript for a few minutes he could see that the structure proposed was wrong. After convincing his co-workers that the puzzle had not been solved and that they were back in the race, Watson hurried to the machine shop to order more model parts.

Both Pauling and Watson and Crick worked by constructing models from pieces of metal shaped like the molecules known to be present in DNA. Three groups of molecules—sugars, phosphates, and bases—were thought to be especially important. The bases were further divided into four kinds: adenine (A), thymine (T), guanine (G), and cytosine (C). Model builders had to answer the question of how these parts are arranged.

Rosalind Franklin had collected what were perhaps the best X-ray data on DNA. These data had convinced her that the sugar and phosphate backbone of the molecule was on the outside and the bases were on the inside. However, she was not yet convinced that the

structure was a helix. Her reluctance to accept a helix structure not only created doubts about her conclusions regarding bases, but also created friction between her and the rest of the group.

Watson's mind was open to Franklin's suggestion of a base-in (base on inside of the molecule) model, but he wanted a closer look at the new evidence. He visited Wilkins and Franklin at King's College. During this visit Watson acquired some data that were to prove critical. Specifically, Wilkins showed him a new kind of X-ray photo of DNA. Thanks to Franklin's superior X-ray work, it had become possible to sort out two forms of pictures—one with which they had already been working and a new form. The instant Watson saw the X-ray of the new form, he realized that it was a veritable treasure map of guidelines for model building.

Watson resumed his model building but, despite Franklin's idea about the position of the bases, he worked with base-out models. He finally decided that no harm could come from trying base-in models for a couple of days. Once he did so, he and Crick had no trouble structuring a beautiful double helix external framework from sugars and phosphates. This success suggested that Franklin was right about the bases being on the inside of the molecule and that the rest of the group was right about the helix structure. Any conclusions were premature, however, since a frightful problem remained. Nobody had a clue about how the bases might fit inside the double helix structure.

The next four days yielded endless doodles of bases but no useful ideas. On the fifth day, however, while drawing a base, Watson suddenly realized that pairs of identical bases (A-A, T-T, G-G, C-C) might fit together to form connections between the two chains like the steps in a spiral staircase. This idea seemed promising at first, but it did not hold with his co-workers' detailed analyses.

By the next morning, Watson was ready to consider other base combinations. He arrived at his office before anyone else and started shifting bases. In a flash, Watson realized that A-T and C-G pairs might work as stair steps in his model. Watson became ecstatic and he made no effort to hide his enthusiasm from his colleagues.

Crick was skeptical when he entered the office and heard Watson shout that the puzzle was solved. But then he quickly saw that major puzzle pieces were indeed in place. Being an expert in the mathematics of helical structures, he also saw other pieces fall into place. Both he and Watson knew that many detailed analyses remained before they could be sure that this model correctly represented the structure of DNA. Yet, by lunchtime, Crick could not contain his enthusiasm. He announced for the whole lunchroom to hear that the secret of life had just been discovered.

For those who could appreciate the model's beauty, it was love at first sight. The model had this effect on Wilkins and even on Franklin, who had resisted the helix structure.

Both immediately agreed that it was too pretty not to be true. They began to check the model against details of X-ray data. As more and more facts were studied, support for the model mounted. Pauling himself, upon hearing about the double helix, wanted to see this evidence from King's College. When he saw it, he was genuinely thrilled. He knew that this discovery would cause a tremendous surge forward in the field of biochemistry. Indeed it did, and for this accomplishment Watson and Crick were awarded a Nobel Prize in medicine and physiology.

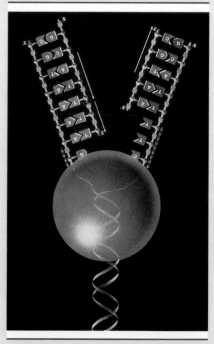

Artwork illustrating the DNA double helix.

James D. Watson (left) and Francis Crick (right) are shown studying a model of the molecular structure of DNA, one of biology's great riddles.

After completing this chapter, you should be able to:

Discuss the evolution of and interrelationships between language, thought, and intelligence.

Identify and discuss the three properties that make human language unique.

Compare and contrast the major theories of language development.

Understand what a concept is and how it is formed.

Define and give examples of imaginal thought and propositional thought.

Discuss the various strategies to approach problem solving and apply the three steps used to solve problems.

Define two major types of IQ testing and understand the controversies in IQ testing.

Scope and History

The traditionally separate fields of biology, chemistry, and physics were united to solve the mystery of DNA. Similarly, the traditionally separate areas of language, thought, and intelligence are being drawn together to solve the mystery of artificial intelligence (AI). For Marvin Minsky, a leader in this quest, the heart of the mystery is "figuring out how minds work and how computers work, and finding ways to get machines to do the things that people do, many of which are considered to be 'intelligent'" (Lipkin, 1988, p. 16). As intelligent human beings, we use language and thought processes to learn and to solve problems. Attempts to make computers do the same are pulling together the areas of language, thought, and intelligence.

Each of these areas has its own focal questions, though there are overlaps. Many studies of language concentrate on how we learn language. Others ask how our language differs from animal languages. A question that overlaps with the area of thought is how language affects the way we think. Other questions about thought include how we use mental images, form concepts, and solve problems. Many scientists are seeking general answers to these questions. At the same time, scientists in the field of intelligence are concentrating on individual differences. Their aim is to develop practical guidelines for predicting what can be expected of individuals. The field explores individual differences in many of our abilities, including music, art, and athletics. Its main focus, however, is on language and thought.

The convergence of language, thought, and intelligence was foreshadowed around the turn of this century by linguists and anthropologists who compared the languages of many different cultures. This work led to a proposal by Benjamin Whorf (1956) that people who speak different languages think and perceive the world differently. Whorf's proposal stimulated a great deal of research by psychologists and others. Researchers looked not only at whether language influences thought and perception, but also at whether thinking is guided by language or images. It was found that language guides thought sometimes but not always. In this way, for example, we can say that Watson used language to guide his thinking when he decided upon two-chain models because "important" biological

Tests of intelligence quotient, or IQ, are used to predict school performance.

objects come in pairs" (Watson, 1968, p. 108). He also used visual images, however, when he "watched images of DNA models dance behind his closed eyelids" (Watson, 1968, p. 118). Modern psychologists study the impact of both language and imagery on thinking.

The study of problem solving—or thought directed at reaching a goal—has become an important area of investigation in its own right. It has been found that people use various approaches in problem solving. Consider, for example, some of the approaches used by Watson and his colleagues. One approach was clearly the trial-and-error method, in which work proceeds step by step, fact by fact. Many scholars have developed ideas about trial-and-error learning. In the 17th century, for instance, John Locke maintained that thoughts are chains of associated ideas. Accordingly, each idea in a chain is triggered by an association with the preceding idea. This philosophy, which had originated with Aristotle, was the foundation for the development of the 20th-century school of psychology called stimulus-response psychology (see Chapters 1 and 6). Psychologists from this school offered a good account of the trial-and-error approach to problem solving. They could not do as well, however, with other approaches.

Yet, as demonstrated by Watson and his co-workers' research—or, for that matter, by our own more mundane experiences in problem solving—humans don't just approach problems by trial and error. We make and test educated guesses about possible solutions. We think of strategies and employ other abstract thought processes and approaches. Many 20th-century scholars have based their analyses of these approaches on Plato's view that abstract ideas guide the sequencing of thoughts. Two such analyses were by Lashley (1950) and by Miller, Galanter, and Pribram (1960). They argued that abstract mental plans guide many of our thoughts and behaviors. Today, psychologists who study problem solving look at the use of trial-and-error *and* these more abstract thought processes.

The challenge of understanding individual differences in problem solving and other intelligent behavior was taken up in the late nineteenth century by Sir Francis Galton. He developed the first intelligence tests and administered them to 9,000 people in London in 1884. Many of Galton's tests were invalid, since they did not do what they were designed to do. Specifically, they did not distinguish eminent British scientists from ordinary citizens on the basis of their intelligence. In 1905, Alfred Binet, a French psychologist, published the first useful intelligence test. He based his test on the idea that mental ability increases with age. He tested many children on mentally demanding tasks, recording each child's **chronological age** (the age in years and months) and then defining **mental age** as the average performance of children at a specific chronological age. A mental age of 10, for example, is the *average* performance of 10-year-olds. He converted each child's performance score into a mental age. Average children received a mental age that was the same as their chronological age. Below-average children received lower mental ages, and above-average children received higher mental ages. Binet recommended that children should get special educational attention when their mental age tested at 2 years below their chronological age.

In 1916, Lewis Terman introduced a modified version of Binet's test in the United States under the name of the Stanford-Binet test. Terman also popularized the concept of **intelligence quotient,** or **IQ,** which is determined by a formula that divides mental age by chronological age and then multiplies the resulting sum by 100. For example, a child with a mental age of 12 and a chronological age of 10 would have an IQ of 120:

$$IQ = \frac{\text{Mental Age}}{\text{Chronological Age}} \times 100 = \frac{12}{10} \times 100 = 120$$

Chronological age
A person's age in years and months.
Mental age
Average performance of children at a specific chronological age.
Intelligence quotient (IQ)
Mental age divided by chronological age and multiplied by 100.

Binet assumed that his test measured general intelligence, which he defined as the ability to judge, to comprehend, and to reason. Charles Spearman (1927) also argued that intelligence test items measure general mental capacity, which he called g. But he said that test items also measure some specific abilities, s. Later on, Louis Thurstone (1946) concluded that intelligence test items measure seven independent factors. The seven were verbal comprehension, word fluency, number, space, memory, perceptual speed, and reasoning. J. P. Guilford (1967) stated more recently that intelligence includes at least 120 separate abilities. We will expand on these efforts to identify separate mental skills in a later section on group-factor theories. Despite these efforts, however, the most popular tests remain those that yield a general IQ score. Such tests predict school performance as well as or better than tests yielding multiple scores.

In 1958, David Wechsler greatly advanced intelligence testing by introducing the Wechsler Adult Intelligence scale. As shown in Table 8–1, Wechsler included both verbal and performance scales on his test.

Current work in the areas of language, thought, and intelligence is linked to these historical roots. Computers, however, have added the new goal of developing artifical intelligence. The quest for this goal is infused with the same excitement and import as the quest to crack the genetic code.

This chapter reviews central topics in each area. It emphasizes overlapping topics and highlights the real world of artificial intelligence.

Table 8–1
Sample Questions from the Wechsler Adult Intelligence Test

Verbal Scale

Information	What is steam made of? What is pepper?
Comprehension	Why is copper often used in electrical wires? What is the advantage of keeping money in a bank?
Arithmetic	Sam had three pieces of candy and Joe gave him four more. How many pieces of candy did Sam have altogether?
	Three women divided eighteen golf balls equally among themselves. How many golf balls did each person receive?
Similarities	In what way are a lion and a tiger alike? In what way are a saw and a hammer alike? In what way are an hour and a week alike? In what way are a circle and a triangle alike?
Vocabulary	This test consists simply of asking, "What is a _____?" or "What does _____ mean?" The words cover a wide range of difficulty.

Performance Scale

Picture Arrangement	A story is told in three or more cartoon panels placed in the incorrect order; put them together to tell the story.
Picture Completion	Point out what's missing from each picture.
Block Design	After looking at a pattern or design, try to arrange small cubes in the same pattern.
Object Assembly	Given pieces with part of a picture on each, put them together to form various objects.
Digit Symbol	Learn a different symbol for each number and then fill in the blank under the number with the correct symbol. (This test is timed.)

A central component of human intelligence is language. **Human language** is a systematic means of communicating by use of vocal sounds (spoken language), marks (written language), or gestures (sign language). There are some 5,000 languages in use today. This section will take its examples from the English language. But the properties it will review are common to all human languages.

Language Development

Children move in a few years from absence of speech to exhibiting an amazing mastery of language. Before starting school at the age of 5, children understand and say thousands of words. They also can combine words to express thoughts in well-formed sentences. Some landmarks in language development are as follows:

1. About 2 months old: Children make cooing sounds, which are pleasant sounds made in response to pleasant stimuli. During their second month many babies also start to express happy feelings by smiling.

2. About 6 months old: Children start making babbling sounds, which are nonsense sounds containing many different speech sounds. At first, babbling contains speech sounds from many languages that babies have not heard as part of their environment (for example, they will make the French "eu" sound, or the German "u," even though their parents or those around them have never made those sounds). Within several months, however, babbling includes mostly sounds from only those languages that babies hear spoken.

3. About 10 months old: Children distinguish between a few adult words. They might, for instance, give different responses to the words "cookie" and "bed." Thus, comprehension of words seems to start before production of words. The ability to understand speech stays far ahead of the ability to produce it throughout a child's development.

4. About 12 months old: Children utter single words to name people and objects around them. They might, for example, say "dada" and "block."

5. About 15 months old: Single words begin to be used in a new way. They are used in what is called **holophrastic speech,** which is the use of single words to express whole phrases. For example, a child might say "out," meaning "I want to go outside."

6. About 24 months old: Children combine words into two-word statements. Table 8–2 gives examples of some two-word statements and their function.

7. During second year: Children rapidly learn to expand two-word statements into longer, grammatically correct sentences. To illustrate, Limber (1973) reported the following sentence spoken by a 34-month-old child: "When I was a little girl I could go 'geek-geek,' like that; but now I can go, 'This is a chair.'"

Theories of Language Development. How do children learn to speak sentences? Psychologists have considered three possible answers. First, social-learning theory suggests that children might learn to speak by imitating adults. Indeed, some children do learn some *words* by imitating elders (Bloom, Hood, & Lightbown, 1974). However, children apparently do not learn *sentences* by imitating. If they did, they would say word combinations that are similar to sentences used by adults. But children constantly say

Human language
Systematic means of communicating verbally, with the written word, or with a sign language.

Holophrastic speech
Use of single words to express phrases. For example, "out" might mean "I want to go out."

things that adults never say. Table 8–2 gives examples of primitive sentences uttered by 2-year-olds. These observations seem contrary to the idea that children learn sentences by imitating adult utterances.

Second, operant conditioning suggests that parents might teach children to speak by reinforcing correct utterances and by ignoring or punishing incorrect ones. B. F. Skinner (1957), in his book *Verbal Behavior*, tried to explain language acquisition strictly in terms of such stimuli and response patterns, without reference to cognitive representations. Skinner argued that science has no room for speculations about mental processes, because scientists cannot actually observe them. Most psychologists agreed with Skinner at that time. Gradually, however, evidence was gathered in opposition to this view. Scientists found, for example, that parents rarely pay attention to grammar when children are learning to form sentences (Brown, Cazden, & Bellugi, 1969). Parents do not ignore or punish grammatically incorrect statements. Yet incorrect sentences usually stop anyway, and they are replaced by correct ones.

Third, Chomsky, who was a leading critic of Skinner's views and an advocate of cognitive theories, had his own views regarding language development (Chomsky, 1975). He pointed out that operant conditioning cannot explain the fact that we speak and understand sentences that are novel in the sense that we have had no prior experience with them (Chomsky, 1975). He argued further that scientists must postulate cognitive representations to explain language acquisition. He proposed that children learn cognitive representations that include units of thought and rules for combining those units. For instance, one rule is that "-ed" is added to verbs to change them from present tense to past tense (look-looked). Children give evidence of having formed a rule when they overgeneralize it, producing utterances that they have never seen or heard. They might say, "I goed outside," or "I taked the cookie." Later on, they learn that irregular verbs are exceptions to the rule, and they learn the correct past tense form of these verbs. Cognitive psychologists must observe children's speech to infer the rules that children learn (Bates, et al., 1984). It does no good to ask children what rules they use, because they cannot say. Children learn to verbalize the rule about "-ed" endings, for example, only after the rule is taught in grammar school. By that time, of course, children have been using it for years.

Lenneberg (1967) proposed that human brain development passes through a critical period between 2 years and about 13 years. During this period children learn language "from mere exposure" to it. The "critical period" theory has two versions. One version suggests that people cannot acquire language from mere exposure before or after the critical period; the second version states that people cannot acquire *normal* language from mere exposure before or after the critical period. Evidence is contrary to the first version and supports the second. Some evidence comes from the case of a girl who was locked away and deprived of exposure to language through most of her childhood (see Highlight: "Genie, a Modern 'Wolf' Child").

The question of how humans learn language brings to mind a related question of whether animals can learn a human language. Before we can address this question directly, we must consider what makes human language unique.

Properties of Human Language

What is it that makes human language unique? To answer this question we must consider three properties of human languages. All human languages are (1) structured to enable creative usage (2) interpersonal and (3) meaningful or referential. Let's examine each of these properties in turn.

Table 8–2
Two-Word Sentences In Children's Speech

Function	Two-Word Sentence
Locate, Name	there book that car see doggie
Demand, Desire	more milk give candy want gum
Negate	no wet no wash no hungry allgone milk
Describe Event or Situation	Bambi go mail come hit ball block fall baby high-chair
Show Possession	my shoe mama dress
Modify, Qualify	pretty dress big boat
Question	where ball

Source: Slobin (1971).

GENIE, A MODERN "WOLF" CHILD

Children raised with little or no contact with other humans are sometimes called "wolf" children. The name was first used to describe children who had been lost or abandoned in a forest and supposedly reared by wolves (Brown, 1958). It is now also used to designate children raised by humans under extremely deprived conditions. Genie fits into this second category.

In the winter of 1970 Genie was admitted to a hospital suffering from extreme malnutrition. At the age of 13 years, 7 months, she weighed 59 pounds and was 54 inches long. She could not straighten her arms or legs and she could not walk more than about 10 feet. She could not chew and she swallowed with difficulty. She could not control her feces or urine. She would look at people with interest, but she would not speak. In fact, she suppressed almost all vocalizations.

Genie was a victim of child abuse. At the age of 20 months, her father confined her to a small room. He harnessed her to an infant's potty seat during the day. At night, when he didn't forget, he would put her in a sleeping bag in a crib. He beat her whenever she was noisy, and he never spoke to her. Instead, he barked and growled at her like a dog. He fed her cereals, baby food, and an occasional soft-boiled egg. When Genie was almost 14 years old, her mother finally took action and escaped with her.

After regaining her strength in the hospital, Genie was transferred to a rehabilitation center, where she had greater opportunity to interact with a warm, loving staff. She developed affectionate relationships with several adults, including her mother, who visited her twice a week, and Dr. James Kent, who supervised her activities. Gradually, Genie internalized the caring she experienced from others. On one occasion, a teacher asked a child how many balloons he had. Although the boy held only two balloons, he answered, "Three." Genie looked startled and quickly gave him one of her balloons. This act of sharing revealed not only her social development, but also her language development.

Genie learned to understand sentences long before she produced them. When she did finally string words together, she produced grammatically primitive and ill-formed strings. Here are some examples, recorded when she was between the ages of 14 and 16 years: "Cow tongue meat," meaning "A cow's tongue is meat"; and "Graduation to buy presents," meaning "At my graduation, people will buy me presents." On the one hand, Genie's progress in language acquisition suggests that people can learn a language merely from exposure after the age of 13. On the other hand, Genie's unusual language habits suggest that people might not be able to acquire *normal* language after that age.

Genie's language is marked by characteristics that are found in people with brain damage. She rarely makes use of rules that she knows, such as forming plurals. And she never learned certain aspects of language, such as asking WH- questions (who, what, where, etc.). Genie may never speak normally, because her brain may have matured past a critical period for normal language development (see Lenneberg, 1967).

Genie's cognitive development was also quite abnormal. Standard tests suggested that 20-year-old Genie was in Piaget's concrete operational stage, which usually extends from about 7 to 12 years of age. Genie did make progress, however, after she was free to experience the world. In 1977, Susan Curtiss summarized the progress as follows: "My work with Genie continues, and Genie continues to change, becoming a fuller person, realizing more of her human potential. . . . [My hope is] that I will not be able to keep up with her, that she will have the last word" (Curtiss, 1977, p. 42).

Human Language Is Structured to Enable Creative Usage.   Humans continually create new ways of saying things. For example, try to think of ten ways that Watson could have told Crick that the DNA puzzle was solved. Your examples could include rather ordinary expressions such as "We did it!" The examples could also include much more unusual expressions such as "Look stellar—you're a Nobeler." If you're having problems thinking of new ways to announce Watson's discovery, try saying something about a green salami instead. The chances are that you'll be making a statement that you have never heard or read before. The point is that we can use language creatively. That is, we can use and interpret sentences that we have not experienced before. We can therefore generate and understand an unlimited number of expressions. In contrast, animals communicate with one another by using relatively few vocalizations or gestures.

How can we generate and interpret entirely new sentences? You can get a clue by examining the sentences that you made up about Watson's discovery or about the green salami. The clue is that your sentences are well formed according to *rules of grammar*, which are principles for structuring language. There are general rules, which apply to all languages. In addition, each language has its own set of rules. Therefore, although you might have said "We did it," you probably did not say "Did it we." This second sentence violates rules for word order in English.

It can't be the case that you produced the sentences you did because you recalled them word for word from memory; after all, you had probably not experienced most of these sentences before. What you did recall were rules of grammar, and you used them to construct your sentences. The use of rules is the key to generating and interpreting new sentences. Anyone who knows a language knows its rules and can understand sentences generated according to those rules. In this way rules make language creativity possible: We're not limited to the small set of sentences we could store in memory, but, knowing the rules, we can produce any number of sentences.

Rules can act on units to produce structures. Languages have units and structure at many levels. Figure 8–1 illustrates the structure of a simple sentence. Notice that the structure has several levels. The lowest level has the smallest units, which are combined to form larger units at the next level. The larger units are then combined to form the next larger units, and so on until a sentence is formed.

The smallest units differ for written and spoken language. **Letters** are the smallest meaningful units of written language. **Orthographic rules** specify legal and illegal letter combinations. For example, *ck* is a legal letter combination at the end of a word. But it is an illegal letter combination at the beginning of a word. In contrast, **phonemes** are the smallest speech sounds that can change meaning. For example, the sounds at the beginning

Letters
The smallest meaningful units of written language.
Orthographic rules
Law that specifies legal and illegal letter combinations in a word.
Phonemes
Smallest meaningful unit of speech sound.

Scientists have identified the properties of human language that make it so much more sophisticated than animal communication systems.

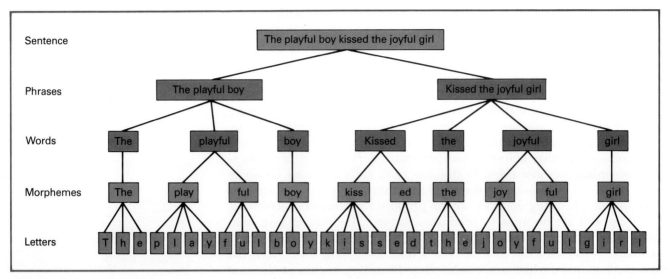

FIGURE 8–1

A sentence has a structure that can be creatively constructed by combining small building blocks (letters) to form larger building blocks (morphemes), which in turn are combined to form larger building blocks (words) and so on.

of "bat" and "cat" are phonemes because they change the meaning of the word. **Phonological rules** specify legal and illegal phoneme combinations. For example, *tl* is a legal phoneme combination near the end of an English word (e.g., in "little") but not at the beginning of one.

The larger units in Figure 8–1 are the same for written and spoken language. Letters or phonemes are combined to form **morphemes,** which are the smallest word parts that have meaning—prefixes, suffixes, roots, and stems. Morphemes are combined to form words, which in turn are grouped into phrases. Finally, phrases are used as building blocks for sentences. You need look no further than the text you are reading to see that sentences are also subunits in larger language structures. Here, the larger units include paragraphs, chapters, and a book. Sentences are also used, of course, to form many other structures, such as speeches or stories. Each of these different structures is formed according to different rules.

As an example, let's consider the rules for structuring stories. The sentences in Table 8–3 can help demonstrate your knowledge of such rules. The sentences can be unscrambled to form a short story about a farmer and a donkey. Try it, and your story will probably be almost identical to the original. How did you know the correct order? You knew because of your memory, which contains rules for structuring stories (Black, 1984). Most of us started learning these rules as young children by listening to stories our parents told. We can use those rules to make a story out of a scrambled list of sentences (Kintsch, Mandel, & Koziminsky, 1977; Shebilske & Reid, 1979).

Researchers have developed formal grammars for diagramming text structures (Deese, 1984; Kintsch & Van Dijk, 1978). The result of this diagramming resembles a hierarchical tree structure, with general ideas near the top and specific details near the bottom. These same tree structures are used when people try to summarize a story from memory. Psychologists generate tree structures and predict rank orders of sentences according to specific rules. The fact that recalls fit the predicted rank orders suggests that we unconsciously follow similar rules for remembering stories.

Human Language Is Interpersonal.   Language is interpersonal in that speakers or writers use language to communicate their thoughts to others. The goal is to create similar thoughts in listeners or readers.

Because language is interpersonal, the meaning of spoken and written utterances may depend not only on their formal structure, but also on the context in which they occur. Language users must be aware of the effects of context, including social context. For example, suppose a speaker

Phonological rule
Rule that specifies legal and illegal phoneme combinations.
Morphemes
Smallest sounds that can change the meaning of words.

Table 8–3
Scrambled Sentence Test
(Unscramble these sentences and put them in the proper order to form a story about a farmer and a donkey)

But the cat replied, "I would gladly scratch the dog if only you would get me some milk."

Thus, the farmer went to the haystack and got some hay.

The barking so frightened the donkey that it jumped immediately into its shed.

So, then, the farmer asked his cat to scratch the dog so the dog would bark loudly and thereby frighten the donkey into the shed.

Then the farmer pushed the donkey, but still the donkey wouldn't move.

As soon as he gave the hay to the cow, the cow gave the farmer some milk.

As soon as the cat got the milk, it began to scratch the dog.

But the cow replied, "I would gladly give you some milk if only you would give me some hay."

Finally, the farmer asked his dog to bark loudly at the donkey and thereby frighten him into the shed.

But the dog refused.

First, the farmer pulled the donkey, but the donkey wouldn't move.

So the farmer went to his cow and asked for some milk to give to the cat.

There once was an old farmer who owned a very stubborn donkey.

As soon as the cat scratched the dog, the dog began to bark loudly.

Then the farmer went to the cat and gave the milk to the cat.

One evening the farmer was trying to put his donkey into its shed.

said "My feet hurt." The language used in this statement does not in itself suggest that a request is being made. But a listener might interpret the statement as a request in certain situations. In a doctor's office, the statement might be used to request treatment. In a parking lot, the statement might be used to request a ride. At a dance, it might be used to request a rest. A cooperative hearer will try to figure out the speaker's intention by considering both the language and the context (Grice, 1975). Cooperativeness, an important consequence of the interpersonality of language, is also manifested in many other ways. When people take turns in conversations, for example, speakers will signal their readiness to end their turn not only by finishing their statements, but also by stopping their hand gestures or by turning their head toward the listener (Walker & Trimboli, 1984).

Human Language Is Meaningful and Referential. The story about Watson and Crick can be used to illustrate the fact that language is meaningful and referential in the sense that it is used to express meaning by referring to objects, events, or thoughts. Try to answer the following questions in your own words: How did Watson feel when he heard about Linus Pauling's manuscript on DNA? How did he feel when he read the manuscript? If you can't remember, review the first paragraph that describes the incident and try again. The events that you are trying to report actually happened. Watson used language to tell about them in his book. You read about them in our words. Now you are being asked to tell about them in your words. You need not use the same words, but you should express the same meaning.

Our language typically expresses what we are thinking about. Sometimes those thoughts are about things that actually happened, as when Watson expressed his thoughts about his research. Other times our thoughts are about things that are made up, as they were for the story about the farmer and the donkey. Even in fiction, however, meaning and reference are essential. You were able to unscramble the story partly because you know story structures. But you were also helped by the fact that you know a lot about animals. Imagine how much more difficult the task would have been if the story had been about unfamiliar things. The story might have said, for example, that a mite was the vector for rickettsiae. Many of you probably would not have understood. In contrast, microbiologists would have understood. They know that mites are similar to tiny spiders. Mites are carriers, or vectors, for rickettsiae, which are microbes that cause certain diseases. The point is that language is meaningful by referring to the world. Thus, a person's knowledge about the world will partially determine what that person understands.

Now we are ready to return to the question of animals learning a human language.

Uniqueness of Human Language Abilities

We can raise two questions about animals and human language: (1) Do any naturally occurring animal communication systems have the properties of human language? (2) Can scientists teach animals to use a language that has the properties of human language? Let's take up each of these questions in turn.

Animals communicate in nature, but their communication systems are simple in comparison to human language. Consider, for instance the language of honey bees. They do a dance to tell other bees in the hive the distance and direction of nectar that they have just found (von Frisch, 1974). Their dance is quite involved, but it has only some of the properties of human language. It has the equivalent of the interpersonal property because messages are sent from one bee to another. It also has the property of being meaningful and referential since it indicates the location of nectar. But honey bee language is not structured in a way that allows creative usage. It is structured according to a grammar that does not enable flexible usage of symbols. For example, a honey bee cannot vary symbol order to change meaning. Such flexibility is, of course, a key feature of human language, as when we say "The allied forces defeated Saddam Hussein's army" versus "Saddam Hussein's army defeated the allied forces." To date, scientists have not found a naturally occurring animal language that is structured to enable creative usage. For now, therefore, the answer to the first question seems to be a tentative "no." The naturally occurring animal languages that have been decoded do not have all the powerful properties of human language. Some scientists believe, however, that further investigations of naturally occurring animal communication will reveal far more sophisticated systems than have been observed so far (e.g. Seyfarth, Cheney, & Marler, 1980; Gouzoules, Gouzoules, & Marler, 1984).

What about the second question? Can scientists teach animals to use a language that has the properties of human language? Early attempts failed. For example, Keith Hayes and Cathy Hayes (1951) tried, without success, to teach a chimpanzee to speak English. The results of later attempts are far more interesting.

Researchers hypothesized that chimps might lack human vocal abilities without lacking human language abilities (Gardner & Gardner, 1975). To test their ideas, they tried to teach a chimp, Washoe, the American Sign Language, which is a human language used by many deaf people. It is based on hand gestures, which Washoe was able to learn. Once she learned the gestures, Washoe used them in a way that shared some of the properties of human language. She answered questions with simple statements like "Me Washoe." She also made simple requests such as "Gimme flowers."

Other scientists achieved similar results. In one study, a female chimp named Sarah was taught to read and write using plastic symbols (Premack

& Premack, 1972). In another, Lana, also a female chimp, was taught to read and write on a special plastic keyboard (Rumbaugh, 1977). Gorillas also got into the act. Francine Patterson (1978) taught Koko, a female gorilla, to use American Sign Language. One day Koko broke a sink by jumping on it. When asked about it, she seemed to blame the damage on a researcher (Kate). She signed, "Kate there bad." This simple communication seemed to have all the properties of human language. It was interpersonal, meaningful, and referential. It also seemed to be creative. However, scientists demanded more rigorous evidence that animals can really demonstrate all the properties of human language (Limber, 1977; Terrance et al., 1979).

This challenge is being addressed, and so far the results have been exciting enough to make national news (e.g., Cowley, 1988). With the help of two chimps named Sherman and Austin, Duane Rumbaugh and Sue Savage-Rumbaugh removed any doubt that animals can use language referentially and interpersonally (Savage-Rumbaugh, 1986a). Sherman and Austin first learned to use symbols on a special plastic keyboard. They then performed tasks that would have been impossible without meaningful and referential use of the symbols. In one task, the animals look at a symbol and then go to another room to retrieve the object represented by the symbol. They pick the correct object from a room filled with many different kinds of objects. Furthermore, they come back empty handed if the requested object is not among the others. Clearly, the chimps understand that the symbols represent specific objects in the environment. In another study, Sherman and Austin used the symbols interpersonally to place orders with each other. One would use a symbol to request a specific food and the other would locate and share the food. In a separate project, Savage-Rumbaugh et al. (1986b) trained a mother chimp while her baby was at her side. Although the baby received no formal training, it watched its mother and learned. After a year and a half, the baby, Kanzi, started to show interest in the symbols. After another year, Kanzi demonstrated interpersonal and referential use of the symbols.

Primates are not the only animals that have dazzled language researchers. Dolphins and sea lions have also learned to use communication systems with the properties of human language (Herman, Richards, & Wolz 1984;

Rocky with trainer; chimp using the Savage-Rumbaugh keyboard.

Schusterman & Krieger, 1984, 1986). Rocky is one of Schusterman's sea lions. Cowley (1988, p. 55) described a session with Rocky as follows: "After a dozen or so water toys have been scattered in a pool, graduate student Becky Hardenberg dons a blindfold (to keep the animal from reading any unwitting glances she might make) and takes a seat at the edge of the pool. Then, with Rocky's chin resting on her foot, she flashes two hand signals—one for ball and one for over. When she withdraws her foot, Rocky takes off like an underwater missile, whizzing past pipes, cones, cubes, discs and bottles and breaking the surface just in time to sail gracefully over her target. She returns with equal gusto to collect payment in the form of a fish." This much is kid's stuff. The really difficult commands are the ones that designate a relationship between one object and another. According to the system Rocky has learned, "Ball disc fetch" means "Take the *disc* to the *ball*," but "Disc ball fetch" means "Take the *ball* to the *disc*." A ball is not just a ball; it may serve as what Schusterman calls a "goal item" or a "transport item," depending on its position within the command string. To make sure Rocky is using the rule, and not just memorizing responses, Schusterman and his colleagues constantly hit her with new combinations. Rather than drill her on "Take the ball to the disc," they jump directly to "Take the small black cube to the Clorox bottle" or "Take the football to the large white ring." Because the signs can be combined in thousands of different ways, each sequence is in effect a new one." Rocky clearly demonstrates comprehension of symbols that are used flexibly and creatively.

Taken as a whole, these studies suggest that the answer to our second question is "yes." Animals can be taught languages that have the properties of human language. The same kind of persistence that led Watson and Crick to crack the genetic code has led psychologists to discover that animals are capable of more advanced uses of language than we had thought possible. Some people might feel humbled by this discovery. Such people should take heart in the next section, which discusses the incredible power of human thought.

Thought

Watson could hardly keep his mind off DNA for several weeks before his important discovery. He even hoped for sudden insights when he played tennis, watched films, or daydreamed. At night he lay awake, images of DNA whirling before his closed eyes. In terms of our everyday language, we could say that Watson spent a lot of time thinking about DNA. Similarly, in the last twenty years, psychologists have spent a lot of time thinking about thinking. They have analyzed how people think in a wide variety of situations, ranging from students solving simple puzzles to physicians diagnosing patients. This section and the next will review progress that has been made in this important area of research.

We use the word *think* in many different ways. "I think I understand what you mean." "I think you should go now." "I'll think about it." To avoid confusing these various meanings, we should agree in advance on how the word will be used here. Let's define **thought** as the mental activity of manipulating symbols. Words are symbols, and we sometimes almost hear ourselves use them as we think. We would therefore expect language and thought to be related. The next section reviews studies of this relationship.

Thought
Mental activity of manipulating symbols.

Propositional Thought and Linguistic Relativity

Does language influence the way we think? Research on this question has focused on **propositional thought,** which is the conscious and unconscious manipulation of abstract symbol structures that can be true or false. English sentences are examples of propositions that can be true or false. You manipulate these linguistic propositions when you use "inner speech" while you think. But propositional thought does not necessarily require linguistic propositions. It can also involve unconscious manipulations of abstract propositions that are not in a natural language form. It is possible, therefore, that people who speak very different languages could think in very similar propositional structures. It is also possible, however, that people who speak different languages think differently. The latter possibility is known as **linguistic relativity,** which was more precisely defined by Au (1983) as follows: "Structural differences between languages will generally be paralleled by non-linguistic cognitive differences in the native speakers of the two languages" (p. 156). Sapir (1949) and Whorf (1956) advocated this idea, which is sometimes called the *Sapir-Whorf hypothesis*. They inspired many experimental tests, most of which failed to support their hypothesis. Let's review some of the tests.

Most of the tests were aimed at the relationship between vocabulary differences and perceptual distinctions. For example, languages may differ in the number of words that they use to describe different kinds of snow or different colors. The Sapir-Whorf hypothesis predicts that if a language had fewer words for snows or colors, speakers of the language will make fewer distinctions. Conversely, if a language has more terms, speakers will make more distinctions. English speakers, for instance, who have few words for snow should be able to make few distinctions. In contrast, Eskimos, who have many words for snow, should be able to distinguish many kinds of snow.

Berlin and Kay (1969), two anthropologists, tested the Whorfian hypothesis by investigating color perception. They showed 320 different shades of colors to people who used diverse color terms. First, they discovered the existence of **focal colors,** eleven colors that are seen as being more salient than other colors. English has a term for each of these focal colors: black, white, red, green, yellow, blue, brown, purple, pink, orange, and gray. Speakers of Ibibio in Nigeria have terms for only the first four of these colors, and they associate terms with the same shades of colors that English speakers do. In addition, speakers of Ibibio choose the same shades as English speakers to represent the other focal colors—even though they do not have a term for them. These results suggest that existence of universals of color distinctions and argue against linguistic relativity (see Figure 8–2).

Psychologists have added further support for universal characteristics of color distinctions. For example, Rosch (1974) found that the Dani, a New Guinea people, have only two color terms, *mili* for black and *mala* for white. Yet, the Dani can distinguish the same focal colors as other people. In other words, people who have terms for only two of the focal colors seem to see color variations the same way as people who have terms for all eleven focal colors. Furthermore, developmental psychologists have found that infants who haven't yet learned any color terms nonetheless see the same color variations as adults (Bornstein, Kessen, & Weiskopf, 1976). Thus, evidence concerning relationships between vocabulary differences and perceptual distinctions is stacked heavily against linguistic relativity.

Bloom (1981) started another line of research by suggesting that language may exert its strongest effects on higher levels of abstract thought.

Propositional thought
Conscious or unconscious manipulation of symbols that can be true or false.
Linguistic relativity
Sapir-Whorf's hypothesis that language influences the way we perceive things and the way we think.
Focal Colors
Eleven colors that are seen as being more distinct than other colors.

FIGURE 8–2

Three ways to categorize the colors of the rainbow. English, as compared to the two African languages shown, has more and different distinctions for these colors. This probably reflects the different needs of these cultures.

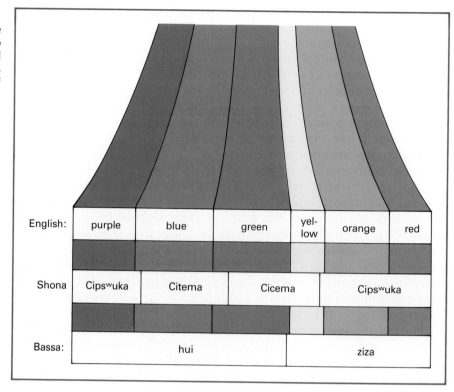

English:	purple	blue	green	yel-low	orange	red
Shona	Cipsʷuka	Citema	Cicema		Cipsʷuka	
Bassa:	hui			ziza		

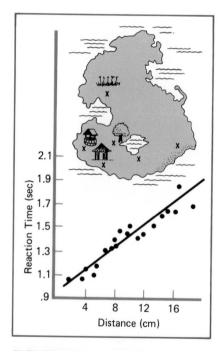

FIGURE 8–3

People can use visual images to memorize maps. They can also imagine a dot moving from one object to another on the map's image. As the lower portion of the figure indicates, the reaction time from the beginning to the end of the imagined movement increases as objects on the map are shown farther apart. (Kosslyn et al., 1978)

Consider, for example, the abstract thought expressed by the following statement: "If Mrs. Wong knew English, she would be able to read the New York *Times*." The statement is counterfactual in the sense that Mrs. Wong does not know English. The same idea can be expressed in Chinese, but not in one sentence. The English equivalent of the Chinese statement is as follows: "Mrs. Wong not know English. If Mrs. Wong know English, then can read the New York *Times*." Bloom (1981) maintained that such differences in language cause differences in understanding. Specifically, he argued that Chinese speakers are less likely than English speakers to give counterfactual interpretations to a counterfactual story. More recently, however, Au (1983) found convincing evidence that Chinese speakers are not less likely than English speakers to give counterfactual interpretations to counterfactual stories. Thus, evidence concerning the relationship between abstract language structures and abstract thoughts stacks up against linguistic relativity.

Some researchers are persisting in the quest to find support for linguistic relativity. For example, Chaika (1984) suggested that negative attitudes toward women are fostered by language that is sexist and biased against them. In addition, Garro (1986) suggested that memory for focal colors might be influenced by how accurately one can describe colors. It is too early to tell whether or not these suggestions will open up new lines of research that will finally clarify the relationship between language and propositional thought. While some scientists have been trying to solve this mystery, others have been trying to understand another kind of thought that is discussed in the next section.

Imaginal Thought

Albert Einstein reported that he usually thought in terms of visual images rather than words. In order to solve a problem, he would manipulate and combine images. Then, after solving the problem, he would translate the solution into words. You don't have to be a scientist, however, to use images. People often engage in **imaginal thought.**

Try answering the following questions: How many windows are there in your parents' living room? What new letter is formed when an upper case *N* is rotated 90 degrees? What shape are a German shepherd's ears? Ask yourself whether or not you used images in trying to think of the answers to these questions. Most people report that they form visual images and then use those images to answer the questions (Kosslyn, 1983; Shepard & Cooper, 1982). That is, they not only form images, but also, if necessary, scan and manipulate them.

A number of studies provide more specific support for the idea that people can scan mental images (e.g., Kosslyn, 1981, 1984; Wickelgren, 1977). For example, Kosslyn, Ball, and Reiser (1978) worked with subjects who had been asked to memorize maps. After subjects memorized a map similar to the one in Figure 8–3, they seemed to have a mental image of it. They could use their image to visualize a dot moving from one object (the hut) to another (the pond). The farther the dot had to move, the longer it took to visualize the movement, suggesting that subjects were "seeing" the dot move across the remembered image of the map.

Manipulating Mental Image Size. Can you manipulate the size of your mental images? Try it. Form a mental image of the cover of this book. (You might want to refresh your memory by looking at the cover first.) If you can form an image of the cover, you probably can also change the size of the image. For instance, try forming a small, medium, and large image of the cover. Kosslyn (1980) found that most people have the impression that they can follow instructions to form different image sizes. Kosslyn also thought of a way to test this ability. He reasoned that people should be able to see details more readily in larger images, just as they can see details better in larger pictures. He therefore asked people to report details from small, medium, or large images. He found that they could report details faster in larger images. You might want to try this yourself. Form a small, medium, and large image of the book cover and scan each one to answer the following questions: Where are the authors' names located? Are the authors' middle initials given? What edition is this book, and where is that information given on the cover? If you are like the students tested in Kosslyn's experiment, you can answer these questions faster when you scan the larger image.

Mental Rotation of Images. Thousands of students across the nation have participated in experiments on mental rotation. If you are like most of them, you can rotate your mental images (see Figure 8–4). Imagine, for example, the cover of this book as a hand on a clock. Form a mental image of the book being upright when the clock hand points to twelve. Now watch the book rotate in your "mind's eye" as the hand sweeps around the face of the clock. Studies of mental rotation suggest that people can use this skill to identify objects. Figure 8–5 shows a stimulus that was used in one experiment by Cooper and Shepard (1973). Students had to decide if an uppercase *R* was normal or a mirror image. Students were able to perform this task regardless of whether the *R* was upright or rotated to some other orientation such as upside down. The important result was that the more the letters were rotated from the upright position, the longer identification took. This result suggested that subjects mentally rotated the letter to a vertical orientation before responding. Similar results in other experiments have suggested that people can also mentally rotate more complicated geometric figures, such as those shown in Figure 8–6 (Cooper & Shepard, 1984; Shepard & Farrell, 1985).

Categorizing an *R* as normal or backwards is easy for most of us. We are more challenged by other categories. Let's turn to more challenging categories, such as deciding whether a penguin is a bird.

FIGURE 8-4

You are probably already familiar with the front view of Leonardo Da Vinci's *Mona Lisa*. Close your eyes and try to visualize what Mona Lisa would look like if she turned her head so that you could see her profile. Such manipulations of mental images are being studied to learn more about how we use images in our thinking.

Imaginal thought
The conscious or unconscious manipulation of "mental images."

FIGURE 8–5

Students presented with these figures in random order were asked to say as quickly as possible whether each figure was a normal R or a mirror image. The more the figure was rotated from a vertical orientation, the longer the reaction time. (After Shepard & Cooper, 1982)

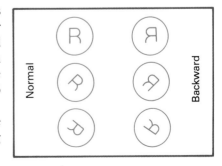

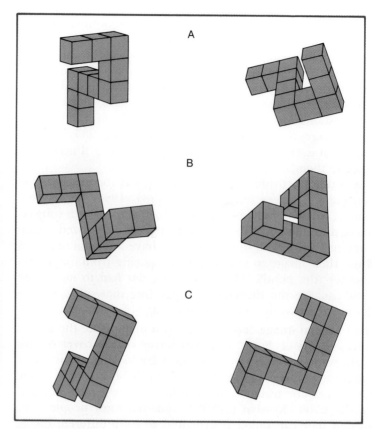

FIGURE 8–6

Examples of pairs of perspective drawings used by Shepard and Metzler (1971) to demonstrate mental rotation of visual images: A is a "same" pair, which differ by an 80° rotation in the picture plane; B is also a "same" pair, which differ by an 80° rotation in depth; and C is a "different" pair, which cannot be brought into alignment by rotation.

Concept Formation

Some words, such as your name, refer to one person, place, or thing. However, most words refer to **concepts**, which are mental groups of objects (e.g., minerals), events (e.g., exams), states (e.g., cold), or ideas (e.g., justice). Such groups are based on similarity. We seem to have a natural ability to form concepts, that is, to group similar things together into categories. This section reviews theories, research, and current trends in the study of concept formation.

Psychologists have applied theories of operant conditioning to concept formation. You might recall from Chapter 6 that operant conditioning is based on the idea that learning occurs when desired responses are reinforced. Conditioning theorists suggest that concepts are gradually learned on the basis of repeated encounters with instances of the concept. They focus on three aspects of these encounters. First, certain responses identify concepts. For instance, the response "square" identifies the concept of a plane figure having four equal sides and four right angles. Second, all positive instances of a concept have common elements. All squares, for example, have four equal sides and four right angles. Third, responses to the positive instances are reinforced and responses to the negative ones are not. In other words, the response "square" is reinforced when it is correctly used to identify actual squares and is not reinforced when it is wrongly used to identify other figures. As a result, the responses that identify the concept become conditioned to the common element (Bourne & Restle, 1959).

Concepts
Mental or cognitive groups of similar objects, events, states, or ideas.

Jerome Bruner and his colleagues proposed an alternative to conditioning theories (Bruner, Goodnow, & Austin, 1956). Their alternative has been called a cognitive learning theory because it focuses on mental strategies that people use to form concepts. Accordingly, when people encounter instances of a concept, they form a *best guess*, or hypothesis, about what the concept might be. On later encounters they test this hypothesis and form a new one if it is wrong. Evidence favors the cognitive learning theory.

Figure 8–7 illustrates the type of materials and concepts used in early investigations of concepts. The dimensions in the stimulus set are size, color, and shape. The values in these dimensions are large or small, blue or red, and square or circle. Six concepts are possible in a single attribute identification task. They are large forms, small forms, blue forms, red forms, square forms, and circular forms. Each concept would have four positive instances and four negative instances, as illustrated in Figure 8–7.

In a typical experiment you would be told the names of stimulus dimensions (size, color, shape) and the attribute values (large/small, blue/red, square/circular) of those dimensions. You would then be shown one of the eight forms for each concept, and you would be asked if it was a positive instance of the correct concept. After you responded "yes" or "no" the experimenter would tell you if you were right or wrong. This procedure would continue until you could verbalize the concept or until you reached some criterion of consecutive correct response.

Figure 8–7 shows a hypothetical sequence of trials. In this sequence, you are shown a large red circle on the first trial. You hypothesize that the concept might be a circle so you say "yes." The experimenter informs

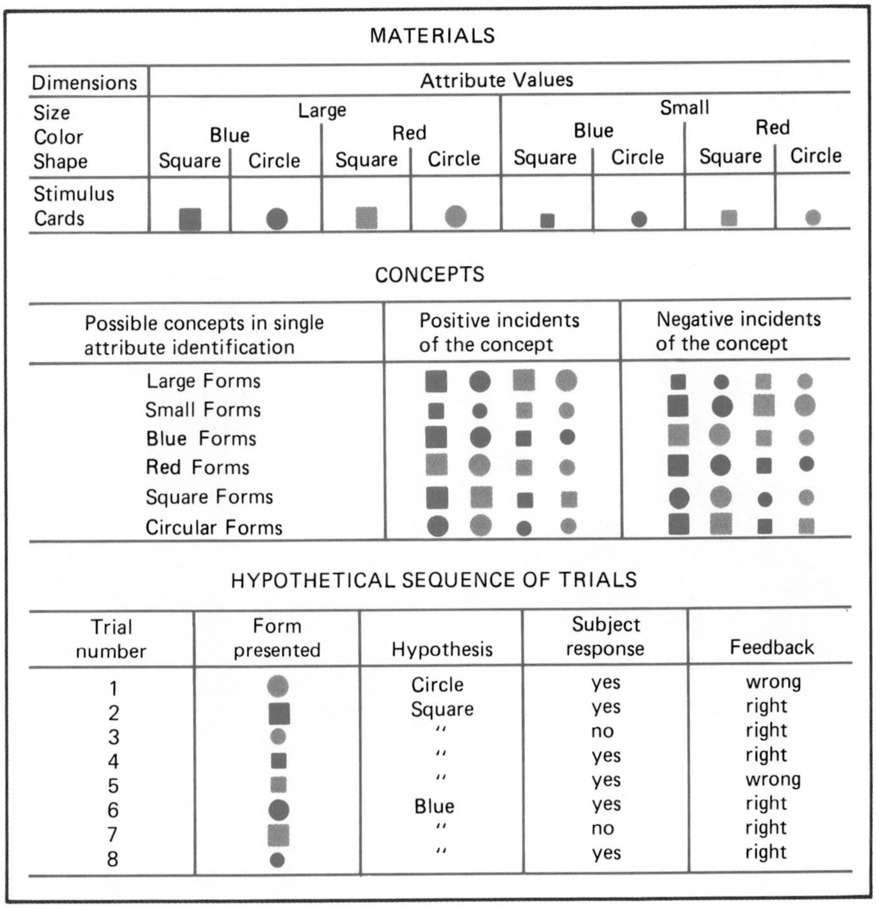

FIGURE 8–7

A concept formation experiment can seem quite difficult until you work through a simple concrete example. Try it.

you that you are wrong. You therefore shift your hypothesis. This time you try square as your best guess. Since the large, blue square on the second trial fits this hypothesis, you say "yes." The experimenter indicates that you are correct, so you stay with your hypothesis. You also stay with it on trials 3 and 4 because you are correct. However, your hypothesis of square forms leads to a mistake on trial 5, so you shift to a new hypothesis—blue forms. This hypothesis leads to correct responses on the next three trials and you decide that blue forms is the correct concept.

This hypothetical experiment is simplified, but it does illustrate a strategy that people use in actual experiments with more dimensions and more attribute values. That is, people generate hypotheses and they follow a "win-stay, lose-shift" strategy. As long as a hypothesis generates correct responses, they stay with it. As soon as the hypothesis leads to an incorrect response they shift to a new hypothesis (Bower & Trabasso, 1964; Levine, 1975; Restle, 1962).

The concepts in this hypothetical example are defined with certainty by specific attribute values. Many actual experiments have used categories defined in this way. Today, however, interest has shifted to studying **family-resemblance concepts,** in which members of a category share more attribute values with one another than they do with members of other categories (Rosch & Mervis, 1975). Such categories are often represented by a **prototype,** a typical or standard example. Nature provides many examples of family-resemblance categories and prototypes. Consider the concept *birds*. No specific attribute or attributes precisely define this category. Not only do we identify animals as birds by means of combinations of attributes that they share, but we also recognize some members of the category as more typical than others. Thus, robins are seen as the most typical birds by most Americans (Rosch & Mervis, 1975). We can decide very quickly that a robin is a bird. We are slower when it comes to penguins and other less typical birds that do not fit our mental image of the prototype (see Figure 8–8).

Family-resemblance categories might be learned in a different way than the categories in our hypothetical example of concept formation. Subjects learn the categories by analyzing one attribute after another. Researchers seem to agree that we sometimes use a more holistic approach

Family-resemblance concepts
Categories where members share more attribute values with members of their own group than they do with members of other groups and no particular attributes define a category.
Prototype
Typical, or standard example.

FIGURE 8–8

Most Americans identify robins as the most typical bird. Americans also answer quickly when they are asked if a robin is a bird. They are slower if asked about pictures of an ostrich, a penquin, and other less typical birds.

to learn family-resemblance categories. That is, we sometimes learn such concepts according to overall appearance (Kemler Nelson, 1984). Researchers have also shown, however, that we sometimes learn family-resemblance categories by means of an attribute-by-attribute analysis (Ward & Scott, 1987). Current research is aimed at determining when holistic approaches are used (Kemler Nelson, 1988; Ward, 1988).

There is also a growing interest in the ability of animals to form concepts (Roitblat, Bever, & Terrance, 1984). Many studies have shown that animals can categorize simple geometric forms and more complicated stimuli (Herrnstein, 1984). In one experiment, pigeons showed evidence of making a discrimination between groups of slides in that they pecked for food more often for one group than for another (Herrnstein, 1979). By means of similar studies it has also been shown that pigeons can discriminate fish from other sea creatures such as turtles (Herrnstein & de Villiers, 1980); white oak leaves from other tree leaves (Cerella, 1979); Charlie Brown from other *Peanuts* characters (Cerella, 1982); and the letter *A* from the numeral *2*, each one being presented in many different type-faces (Blough, 1982; Morgan, Fitch, Holman, & Lea, 1976).

These results are impressive for pigeons; classifying oak leaves can be difficult even for those of us who have more than a bird brain. But we still haven't considered some of the more challenging problems that humans face in our complex world. Let's turn to some of those now.

Problem Solving: Creativity, Planning, and Decision Making

From a cognitive point of view, we can define **problem solving** as thinking aimed at overcoming obstacles that stand in the way of a goal. Your main goals might be to graduate from college and begin a productive career. You see many hurdles between you and those goals, but you are determined to overcome them. Doing so will require you to solve many problems along the way. Some problems require endless efforts. Many people, especially scientists and artists, seek out unsolved problems and work on them for years. Like persistent detectives, Watson and his co-workers never quit, although time after time the solution to one problem revealed the existence of an even more challenging problem. Why did they do it? Metcalfe (1986) suggests that people are often spurred on by feelings of getting closer and closer to a solution. Furthermore, the "discovery experience" that occurs when the solution is achieved is highly rewarding. Other problems require split-second decisions. On July 3, 1988, for example, Will O. Rogers 3d, the captain of the *Vincennes* warship in the Persian Gulf, had only minutes to make a life-or-death decision. At 10:47 A.M. the ship's radar detected a nearby plane (Figure 8–9 shows the position of the warship and the plane as these events occurred). The problem was to decide whether or not the plane was a threat that required defensive action. At 10:49 A.M., the plane failed to respond to repeated radio warnings. The plane was declared hostile at 10:51 A.M. and shot down at 10:54 A.M. The plane was actually an Iranian passenger jetliner carrying 290 people, all of whom were killed. Despite this tragic reminder of fallibility, we shall see that scientists are making rapid progress toward understanding and improving problem-solving skills. This section reviews typical steps in problem solving within the context of Watson's quest and within the context of everyday applications. You will be given a chance to have "discover experiences"

Problem solving
Thinking aimed at overcoming obstacles that stand in the way of a goal.

FIGURE 8–9

Scientists have come a long way in improving our ability to solve problems. However, the downing of an Iranian passenger jetliner by an American warship in 1988 is a tragic reminder that there is still a long way to go in understanding and enhancing our ability to solve problems.

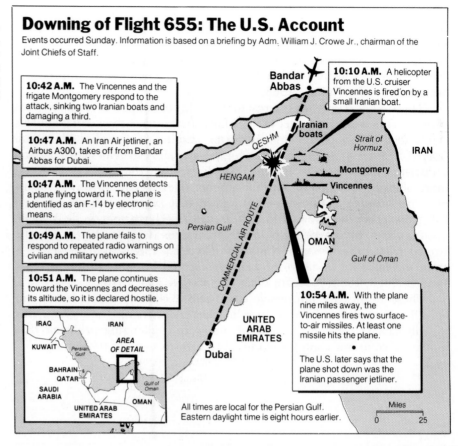

Downing of Flight 655: The U.S. Account

Events occurred Sunday. Information is based on a briefing by Adm. William J. Crowe Jr., chairman of the Joint Chiefs of Staff.

10:42 A.M. The Vincennes and the frigate Montgomery respond to the attack, sinking two Iranian boats and damaging a third.

10:47 A.M. An Iran Air jetliner, an Airbus A300, takes off from Bandar Abbas for Dubai.

10:47 A.M. The Vincennes detects a plane flying toward it. The plane is identified as an F-14 by electronic means.

10:49 A.M. The plane fails to respond to repeated radio warnings on civilian and military networks.

10:51 A.M. The plane continues toward the Vincennes and decreases its altitude, so it is declared hostile.

10:10 A.M. A helicopter from the U.S. cruiser Vincennes is fired on by a small Iranian boat.

10:54 A.M. With the plane nine miles away, the Vincennes fires two surface-to-air missiles. At least one missile hits the plane.

The U.S. later says that the plane shot down was the Iranian passenger jetliner.

All times are local for the Persian Gulf. Eastern daylight time is eight hours earlier.

yourself by solving problems and puzzles that illustrate problem-solving components. Three major steps in solving problems will serve as an organizational framework. These steps are (1) defining the problem, (2) making plans that include subgoals (intermediate goals that are steps toward the ultimate goal), and (3) choosing and evaluating approaches to each subgoal.

Defining a Problem

The problem confronting Watson and other model builders was whether DNA had two or three chains. Without a solution to this problem, scientists were faced with an overwhelming number of interpretations of the X-ray data. Watson thought about this problem many times in terms of structural laws of chemistry. But a solution eluded him until one day he thought of the problem in terms of biology instead of chemistry. When he defined the problem from a biological point of view, he realized that "important biological objects come in pairs" (Watson, 1968, p. 108). He had made a major breakthrough by deciding to work on two-chain models.

Is it unusual for Watson to have used ideas from biology to solve problems in chemistry? Or, more generally, is it unusual for people to use familiar ideas in new ways? This ability is an important part of **creative thinking,** which is the capacity to think up new and useful ways to solve problems. Figure 8–10 shows examples of creative solutions to problems. Don't let these examples mislead you into believing that creative thinking is commonplace. It is far from ordinary, according to experts on thinking. Robert Sternberg noted, for instance, that "academic smarts are easy to find, but creativity is rare and precious" (Trotter, 1987). Tests exist for identifying creative individuals. Although the tests do help identify individuals who can use ideas in novel ways, Sternberg and other researchers are

Creative thinking
Capacity to think up new and useful ways of solving problems.

FIGURE 8–10

Some creative solutions to problems serve useful functions. Shown here are Henry Ford and his first car, the 1941 Lincoln Continental Cabriolet, and the Ford Probe IV concept car.

committed to developing better tests to assess practical intelligence (Sternberg, 1985, 1986; Sternberg & Davidson, 1986; Sternberg & Wagner, 1986).

People generally have difficulty using familiar information in new ways. This difficulty has been illustrated in experiments where people are slow to use familiar objects in unusual ways to solve problems. In one such experiment, Dunker (1945) asked people to place three candles at eye level on a door. Dunker supplied a box of candles, a box of matches, and a box of tacks (Figure 8–11A). How would you solve the problem? Dunker's subjects were slow to see that the boxes could be tacked to the door to serve as platforms for the candles (Figure 8–11B). These subjects did much better, however, when Dunker gave them empty boxes. In other words, people were less likely to see that boxes could serve as platforms when the boxes were serving as containers. Dunker called this effect **functional fixedness,** which is the tendency of people to see an object only in terms of its most familiar use. In Dunker's experiment, subjects had trouble classifying boxes as platforms when they had already classified them as containers. People must overcome functional fixedness in order to produce creative solutions to problems.

Watson's performance stands in sharp contrast to that of subjects in experiments on functional fixedness. Watson went to Cambridge to work on a chemistry problem. Because he did not limit his scope of thinking, he was able to recognize, however, that the problem could also be classified as a problem in biology. Thus, he was able to use familiar biological ideas in new ways.

Choosing the right definition or classification of a problem is also important in the classroom. For example, you might have noticed the importance of problem classification on math exams. Usually an exam will cover a

Functional fixedness
Tendency of people to see an object only in terms of its most familiar use.

FIGURE 8–11A
The Candle Problem

Using only the materials on the table, how can the candle be mounted on the wall? The solution is shown on the next page. (Glucksberg & Weisberg, 1966)

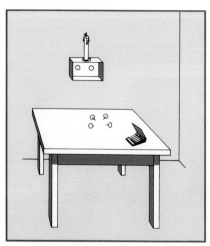

FIGURE 8–11B

In order to solve the candle problem, the subjects had to figure out that the container holding the tacks could also be used as a platform on which the candle could be placed. Because we tend to see things as they are most commonly used, we need to allow our minds to think creatively in order to serve certain problems.

limited number of principles, and you can do much better if you can figure out which problems go with which principles. Silver (1981) analyzed this effect in an experiment with seventh graders. He tested four mathematical procedures by giving four problems on each procedure. He asked the students to classify and solve each problem. The results showed the importance of defining math problems correctly. Students who classified the problems well also solved them well. Conversely, students who classified poorly solved the problems poorly.

You might be able to experience the power of defining a problem correctly by trying to solve the problem in Figure 8–12. One morning, exactly at sunrise, a monk began to climb a mountain. A narrow path, a foot or two wide, spiraled around the mountain to a temple at the summit. The monk ascended at varying rates, stopping many times along the way to rest. He reached the temple shortly before sunset. After several days at the temple, he began his journey back along the same path, starting at sunrise and again walking at variable speeds with many pauses along the way. His average speed descending was, of course, greater than his average climbing speed. Prove that there exists a particular spot along the path that the monk will occupy on both trips at precisely the same time of day (Adams, 1976, p. 4).

If you tried the problem in Figure 8–12, you saw that a difficult problem about a monk walking became obvious when it was defined as being equivalent to a simpler problem. Now imagine how easy it would be to solve a problem that was identical to the monk walking except that it was about a ship sailing. We save a lot of time and energy when we can define problems as being equivalent to ones that we already know how to solve.

Making Plans and Forming Subgoals

An important difference between an expert and a novice solving a problem is that the expert usually spends more time planning. The plans often divide the problem of reaching some ultimate goal into a series of steps for reaching subgoals. Watson and Crick, for example, divided their problem of determining the structure of DNA into subgoals. The subgoals included resolving the following issues: two chains versus three chains, helix structure versus some other structure, bases in versus bases out. Watson and Crick pondered all the evidence that they could find on these issues before they started building models.

Planning also seems to be a key factor in solving classroom physics problems. In one study, Larkin and Reif (1979) compared the performance of a physics professor, the "expert," with that of an excellent student, the "novice." Both the professor and the student generated equations to help them solve the problems. The difference was that the professor made a plan and then generated all his equations within a short time span. In contrast, the student generated equations from beginning to end. This pattern of results has also been observed in comparisons of novices and experts solving classroom math problems (Heller & Greeno, 1979).

Choosing and Evaluating Approaches to Subgoals

After Watson and his co-workers had divided their problem into subgoals, they had to choose and evaluate approaches to each. Let's take a closer look at the approaches that they used.

Trial and Error. **Trial and error** is an approach to solving problems that involves trying different possibilities until something works. The process might start with an arbitrary choice of possibilities to test, but later choices

Trial and error
Approach to problem solving that involves trying different possibilities until something works.

are often guided by the results of earlier tests. For example, Thomas Edison used trial and error to test thousands of substances for a light bulb filament (Hunt, 1982). He had no way of knowing in advance what would work. But after his initial trials he could choose substances that were most like the ones that had worked best so far. Similarly, trial and error played an important role in Wilkins and Franklin's X-ray studies of DNA.

Hypothesis Testing. **Hypothesis** testing is an approach to solving problems that involves testing an educated guess, or hypothesis, on the basis of the evidence available. This approach also proved important to the DNA research. The models were in a sense hypotheses, tested against the X-ray and other data. In one case, it took Wilkins and Franklin only minutes to reject one of the three-chain models of DNA. And the X-ray data itself served as a basis for hypotheses.

Earlier, we considered some simple hypothesis testing in an easy concept formation task. Figure 8–13 gives you a chance to try a more challenging hypothesis-testing task. The figure shows four cards, each of which has one of the letters or numbers *D*, *3*, *B*, and *7*. You are told that if a card has a letter on one side it has a number on the other side. Your task is to test a hypothesis about these four cards. The hypothesis is that if there is a *D* on one side of any card, there must be a *3* on the other side. Most people turn over the *D* first and that's fine. What would you do next, however, if the hypothesis passed that test? Many people turn over the *3*, but that doesn't help because the hypothesis could be correct regardless of what is on the other side of the card. The correct test is to turn over the *7*. This is a good test because if a *D* is on the other side, the hypothesis is wrong. Watson and Johnson-Laird (1972) found that people generally were slow to make an observation that might disconfirm a hypothesis. People preferred to make an observation that might confirm a hypothesis even though that observation could not provide a conclusive test of it. These results suggest that people have a **confirmation bias.** This bias is a tendency in hypothesis testing for people to avoid observations that might be disconfirming instances in favor of ones that might be confirming instances.

Watson and Johnson-Laird related the confirmation bias to the more general tendency for people to want to verify their own beliefs. This tendency can be a serious pitfall in hypothesis testing. Even Watson, a skilled scientist, was not immune to it. He got very excited about his idea that identical base pairs could serve as stair steps in a double helix. He even dashed off a letter to one of Pauling's colleagues saying that he had constructed a beautiful DNA structure that was different than Pauling's. The letter was in the mail less than an hour when Watson encountered disconfirming evidence. He spent a good part of that day trying to find a gimmick that would save his idea, and he persisted even though strong arguments had been advanced against it. Fortunately, by the next day, Watson was ready to consider new ideas, and he thought of the correct solution, complementary base pairs in the stair steps.

The lesson to be learned is clear. We should form hypotheses to guide

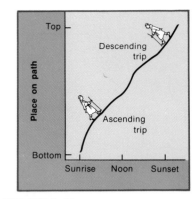

FIGURE 8–12

The Monk and the Mountain Problem

This problem seems very difficult until you realize that it is equivalent to a much simpler problem. The simpler problem involves two people who start a trip at the same time. They start on opposite ends of the same path and go to the other end. Obviously, each has to pass the other. When they pass, they will be at the same place on the path at the same time. It doesn't matter that the monk in the original problem traveled on different days. The important point is that he left at the same time on those two days and walked to the opposite end of the path. Imagine superimposed videotapes of the downward journey and of the upward one, both starting at sunrise. The videotaped travelers would cross on the path regardless of whether they had started at sunrise on the same day or on different days.

Hypothesis
Idea that is tested experimentally; an assumption that is based on theory.
Confirmation bias
Tendency in hypothesis testing to avoid observations that might be disconfirming in favor of those that offer confirmation.

FIGURE 8–13

The text explains how these stimuli are used to test the confirmation bias, which is the tendency to test hypotheses by looking for confirming instances.

FIGURE 8–14

Luchins conducted an experiment in which subjects were asked to measure water using any or all three jars. All of the first problems could be solved by filling the largest jar and then pouring from that jar into the smaller ones as indicated in the upper drawing. The water remaining in the largest jar was the correct amount. This solution also worked for later problems but so did the simpler solution indicated in the lower drawings. The discovery of the simple solution was greatly delayed for people who had experience with the other solution.

Algorithm
Step-by-step procedure, that, if used properly, guarantees a correct response to a specific problem.
Mental set
Readiness to view a problem in a particular way and see certain relationships.
Heuristic
Rule-of-thumb strategy that is used because it has been successful in the past. Sometimes used when solving a problem backward—from the goal to the beginning.

our thinking about problems, but we should not cling to them. To be successful problem solvers, we must overcome the confirmation bias. Solutions will emerge from constructive responses to disconfirming evidence.

Algorithms. Another approach to solving a problem is to use an **algorithm.** This is a step-by-step procedure that guarantees a solution to a specific problem if it is used properly. All mathematical formulas are algorithms. They guarantee a correct solution as long as you choose the right formula and make no mistakes in using it. For example, suppose a problem you were working on had a subgoal of computing the hypotenuse of a right triangle. Let us assume that you recall from your high school geometry course that the square of the hypotenuse is equal to the sum of the squares of the other two sides. You could then use this formula, or algorithm, to get a solution. And the solution would be correct as long as you hadn't made any arithmetic errors.

Although all mathematical formulas are algorithms, not all algorithms are mathematical formulas. Suppose you wanted to make a great tasting bowl of chili like your mother used to make. Your best bet would be to get your mother's recipe and follow it step by step. In that case, your mother's recipe would be the algorithm.

Figure 8–14 presents problems that illustrate one of the potential dangers of using algorithms. The problems require you to measure certain quantities of water using jars of various sizes. Most people develop an algorithm that uses three jars to solve each problem. This approach is fine. Unfortunately, many people also develop a **mental set,** which is a tendency to repeat fixed patterns of thinking that worked in the past. These people continue to use a three-jar solution on problems for which a much easier two-jar solution would work. Their mental set for using a three-jar solution also makes it difficult for them to discover the two-jar solution on problems for which only a two-jar solution will work.

Again, the lesson is clear. We should use algorithms in solving problems, but we should not cling to them. We should avoid developing a mental set in which we blindly apply algorithms without considering other possible solutions.

Heuristics. A **heuristic** can be defined as a rule-of-thumb problem-solving strategy that often works but does not guarantee success. An example is the strategy of solving a maze problem by starting at the goal and working backward to the start (see Figure 8–15). Compare the use of a mathematical algorithm to compute a hypotenuse with the use of a working backward heuristic to solve a maze. Once you select an appropriate algorithm, you have no other choices to make; you just follow the step-by-step procedure. Anyone who can do arithmetic correctly will get the correct solution. Once you select an appropriate heuristic, however, you still have many choices to make. The heuristic doesn't tell you what to do at each choice point, so you might not find the solution.

The use of heuristics is common in science. Watson used what might be called a simplicity heuristic. He believed that the key to successful modeling is reliance on simple laws of structural chemistry. He held that it would be foolish to build in complications before ruling out the possibility that the answer is simple. This heuristic of first looking for the simple way to do things is characteristic of successful problem solvers.

Heuristics are also quite helpful in everyday life. We can save ourselves a lot of time, for instance, by looking for simple solutions first. Rather than breaking a window when locked out of the house, it might be simpler to visit a neighbor until someone comes home with a key. But, like other approaches that we have considered, heuristics have pitfalls. Let's look at some examples.

We often estimate probabilities before we make decisions. We try, for instance, to figure out the probability of rain before we plan a picnic or the probability of getting a better price before we make a purchase. In other words, we try to estimate whether a day will be in the rainy or sunny category and whether a purchase is in a good buy or bad buy category. Several heuristics help us make these important estimates. One is the **representativeness heuristic,** according to which we estimate the probability that an event fits a category by determining to what extent the event is representative of that category. This heuristic often works well. Suppose you are driving to a party and you catch the last part of a news report about a woman who won a literary award. You hear that she lives in a dorm, carries a heavy course load, and works part time as a research assistant. Later, her name comes up at the party and someone asks if she is a college student or a professor. What would you answer? Using the representativeness heuristic, you would answer "student" because you know things about the woman that are representative of college students. It's hard to imagine how you could go wrong by applying the representativeness heuristic in this case.

However, let's consider another example. You are driving to a party and you catch the last part of a news report about an article written by a man. You hear that the man has written many other articles and that he's an avid reader of mystery novels. Later, his name comes up at the party and someone asks if he is an Ivy League classics professor or a truck driver. What would you answer? Using the representativeness heuristic, you would probably answer "Ivy League classics professor" because you know many things about him that are representative of that category. You would be going strictly by representativeness and would be ignoring the relative size of the two categories (professor and truck driver). Kahneman and Tversky (1972) found that in fact people do go strictly by representativeness even though it is a serious mistake to ignore category size. Think about the implication of category size in our example. There are probably about 40 Ivy League classics professors (10 Ivy League schools × 4 classics professors per school) and about 400,000 truck drivers. Suppose, as an extreme case, that all classics professors wrote articles and read mystery novels and that only 1 in 1,000 truck drivers did these things. Accordingly, the total number of writers and mystery readers would be 40 for Ivy League professors and 400 for truck drivers. The chances are therefore greater that the person in the news was a truck driver. Researchers, using similar examples, have generally supported Kahneman and Tversky's claims regarding both the power and the dangers of the representativeness heuristic (Nisbett & Ross, 1980).

Kahneman and Tversky (1973) also found that we use an **availability heuristic,** according to which we assume that more probable events are recalled more easily. This heuristic often works well because the most frequent events are often the most memorable. For example, the availability heuristic will serve you well in judging whether your grocery store sells more yellow or more purple fruits. Yellow fruits are easy to recall: bananas, pears, peaches, golden delicious apples. In contrast, it's hard to get beyond

Representativeness heuristic
Strategy whereby we estimate the probability that an event or object belongs to a category because of its similarity to that category.
Availability heuristic
Assessment of the probability of an event by how many similar events can be recalled easily.

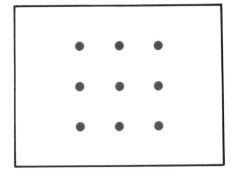
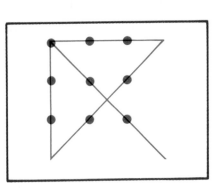

FIGURE 8–15
The Nine-Dot Problem
Without lifting your pencil from the page, connect all nine dots by drawing four straight lines.

grapes and plums when trying to recall purple fruits. The availability heuristic would therefore guide you to judge that the grocery store sells more yellow fruit, and you would be right.

The availability heuristic can also lead to errors, however, because the most frequent events are not always the most memorable. For example, it is easier to recall words that begin with *k* than it is to recall words that have *k* as their third letter. Try it by seeing how many of each category you can recall in one minute. If you are like most people, you will recall many more words that start with *k*. The availability heuristic would therefore lead you to judge that there are more words in this category. But you would be wrong. There are about three times more words with *k* in the third position than there are words with *k* in the first position. This example illustrates that frequency of exposure is not always the dominant factor in recall. We are often exposed to words with *k* in the third position, but it is hard to search our memory for letters that are tucked away inside words. Other researchers have used similar examples to show that most of us use the availability heuristic even though it sometimes gets us into trouble (Williams & Durso, 1986).

Psychologists have learned a great deal about problem solving by attempting to program computers to solve problems. Simon and Newell at Carnegie Mellon University were pioneers in this approach (Newell, Shaw, & Simon, 1958; Newell & Simon, 1972; Simon & Newell, 1971). They collected verbal reports from people who were attempting to solve problems. These verbal reports contained enough detail for Simon and Newell to write computer programs that would solve problems the same way humans do. As mentioned earlier, **artificial intelligence (AI)** is a new field of research that combines computer science and cognitive psychology. It is concerned with programming computers to simulate human thought processes and/or to act "intelligently" in the sense of adapting to changing conditions. Work in AI has emphasized the importance of plans and subgoals in problem solving (Figure 8–16).

Don't let the simple example shown in Figure 8–16 fool you. AI is already being employed in complex applications. It is used to help automobiles run more efficiently, to control automatic pilots on aircraft, to assist astronauts during space flights, and to help doctors diagnose and treat patients (see Highlight: "The Real World of Artificial Intelligence").

Psychologists are also exploring thought by studying individual differences in human intelligence. Let's take a look at what they are finding.

Artificial intelligence (AI)
Field where computers are programmed to simulate human thought processes and to act intelligently.

FIGURE 8–16

AI researchers have used this simple problem to study formation of plans and subgoals. The problem is to get a robot to push Box 1 next to Box 2 and then to put the robot in Room A. You could solve this problem easily without giving much thought to plans or subgoals. But if you think about it a minute you will realize that you do use them. For example, a subgoal is getting the robot next to Box 1 and a subgoal of that is getting the robot into the same room as Box 1. Sacerdoti (1974, 1977) has been a leader in programming computers to use plans and subgoals to solve such problems.

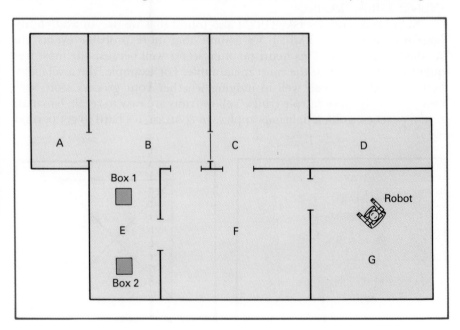

THE REAL WORLD OF ARTIFICIAL INTELLIGENCE (AI)

At Campbell Soup Company, workers are stalled because one of their "cookers" for sterilizing cans is down, and Aldo Cimino, the expert who usually solves such problems, is nowhere to be found. They turn instead to Cooker, their computerized adviser. Cooker asks a series of questions about the broken-down sterilizer and within a matter of minutes diagnoses the malfunction. Cooker is an *expert system*, a computer program that knows lots of facts about its area of expertise and lots of rules for applying those facts to solve problems. Expert systems are among the most marketable applications of AI. They are becoming increasingly commonplace in medicine, law, aerodynamics, education, and businesses that make things from computers to soup (Lipkin, 1988).

The father of expert systems, Edward Feigenbaum, was trained in cognitive psychology. He became interested in AI when he studied with Herbert Simon, and he developed the world's first expert system, Dendral, to analyze complex organic molecules of the kind decoded by Watson and Crick. He did this work with Joshua Lederberg, who is a Nobel laureate in organic chemistry.

By the mid-1970s, Douglas Lenat had developed a general self-programming AI problem solver, Eurisko. After winning the 1981 and 1982 naval war games tournament, Eurisko was banned from future tournaments and put to work solving real military problems. In 1974, Roger Schank and his students created Sam, a story-analyzing program with inferencing abilities. One of Sam's offspring, Cyrus, learned all it could about Secretary of State Cyrus Vance. Then it began to flex its AI muscles by correctly inferring facts before they were reported in the news. According to Schank, the head of Yale University's artificial intelligence laboratory, his view of AI has been shaped by psychology, his main interest.

Lipkin (1988) reviewed expert systems and other applications of AI. The Pentagon, for example, has developed a driverless Autonomous

FIGURE A
The Autonomous Land Vehicle (ALV) requires no driver in or outside of the vehicle. Computers aboard the ALV use artificial intelligence to interpret signals from television cameras and to drive the AVL along a safe path.

FIGURE B
Computers aboard spacecrafts use artificial intelligence to assist astronauts. Rapid progress in replacing and improving equipment seems to be the point of the "For Sale" sign that astronauts jokingly hold over an "old" communications spacecraft.

Land Vehicle (Figure A). Coming soon from the Air Force will be jets with "smart skins" that detect surface damage and adjust controls accordingly and "super cockpits" in which video displays, gauges, meters, and voice controls replace switches and buttons. As impressive as all these applications are, they all seem down to earth in comparison to current NASA plans, which call for AI in space. NASA is developing a number of expert systems for the U.S. space station expected to orbit the earth before the end of this century: Les will control liquid oxygen supplies; Kate will troubleshoot equipment problems; and Imis will answer the crew's questions about the space station. In addition, NASA hopes to

develop AI robots to assist astronauts in space (Figure B).

Optimists who see the existing applications hope that AI systems will someday learn and solve problems on a par with humans. Pessimists view these applications with a jaundiced eye. They argue that intelligence is "a human trait, rooted in human life and human experience. No machine could ever match, perceive or appreciate that" (Lipkin, 1988, p. 11). We are bound to hear debates for years to come about how similar artificial intelligence is to the real thing. In the meantime, it seems obvious that there is nothing artificial about the applications of AI. They are real, and they are revolutionizing our world.

Intelligence is the capacity to learn and use information. People have different levels of intelligence. At one extreme are people who are totally dependent on others for basic care. At the other extreme are individuals who excel extraordinarily, such as Aristotle and Plato. Through intelligence testing, psychologists attempt to measure individual differences in capacity to learn and use information. These measurements are difficult because individuals differ in their opportunities to learn and use information.

Psychologists formally recognize the problem of different opportunities by distinguishing between two kinds of tests: (1) **achievement tests,** which are designed to measure a person's current knowledge and skills, and (2) **aptitude tests,** which try to predict capacity for future performance. Some achievement tests are **standardized;** that is, they have been given to many people so that one person's score can be evaluated with respect to a large population. Many achievement tests are not standardized, however. Examples are the tests and quizzes used in most college courses. They enable teachers to evaluate a class, but they do not enable comparisons with a general population.

Most aptitude tests are standardized. You may take standardized aptitude tests on many specific skills, including artistic, musical, mechanical, physical, foreign language, and mathematical skills. Your score in each case would be compared with those of people who are successful in that specific area. You may also take standardized aptitude tests to measure a broad range of aptitudes. An example is the General Aptitude Test Battery (GATB), which measures 10 aptitudes, including verbal, numerical, clerical, and motor speed. Finally, you may take, and probably have taken, intelligence tests, which are broad-range aptitude tests that are designed to measure IQ. Lets look at how IQ varies with age.

IQ and Age

Binet introduced the concept of mental age because his research showed that mental abilities increase with age. His investigations were limited to children, however. Modern researchers are only beginning to understand what happens to intelligence in adulthood and old age. Early studies used *cross-sectional* designs that measured different people at different ages; for example, one group at age 15, another at age 30, another at age 60, etc. (Jones & Conrad, 1933). These studies were contaminated by the fact that different age groups had different educational experiences, and thus researchers could not say whether differences between groups were due to differences in age or to differences in education. Later studies used *longitudinal* designs, which measured the same people as they grew older. Overall IQ scores showed gain to age 32, little or no change until age 60, and significant decline thereafter. The decline after age 60 did not include declines in important subtests such as verbal meaning and reasoning (Schaie & Labouvie-Vier, 1974).

However, the use of one overall IQ score to represent intellectual changes with age has been criticized (Horn, 1978). Horn argues that the declining scores for older adults represent only one aspect of intelligence. He calls this aspect **fluid intelligence,** which we can roughly define as general mental skills, such as the ability to make inferences. Horn and Donaldson (1980) state that fluid intelligence starts to decline at age 40 primarily because of a decline in physical and neurological functioning (see Chapter 10). They also feel that part of the decline is due to reduced practice of certain mental skills. Horn's main point, however, is that there is another aspect of intelligence that steadily increases with age. He calls

Intelligence
The capacity to learn and use information.
Achievement tests
Designed to measure a person's current knowledge and skills and reflect what has been learned in the past.
Aptitude tests
Tests used to predict capacity for future performance
Standardized tests
Tests that have been given to many people so that one person's score can be evaluated with respect to a large population.
Fluid intelligence
General mental skills, such as the ability to make inferences or deductive reasoning.

this ever-improving aspect **crystallized intelligence,** which we can define as specific mental skills, such as one's vocabulary, or the ability to define words. Figure 8–17 helps clarify the distinction between general and specific skills by showing test questions that tap either fluid or crystallized intelligence. Crystallized knowledge is specific, in the sense that it depends upon exposure to a specific environment. People in different cultures would learn to define different words, for instance. Horn and Donaldson (1980) imply that such culturally specific knowledge "crystallizes in the mind," so that it is less affected by physical and neurological deterioration. People thus retain culturally based knowledge through the years, and they continually learn new specific facts. Figure 8–18 shows the end result. Although fluid intelligence first increases and then decreases with age, crystallized intelligence steadily increases. The most widely used IQ tests, which predate the discovery of this distinction, primarily measure crystallized intelligence.

Crystallized intelligence
Specific mental skills, such as one's vocabulary.

FIGURE 8–17
These are sample test items used to measure fluid intelligence and crystallized intelligence. Answers to the items are given below. (Horn & Donaldson, 1908).

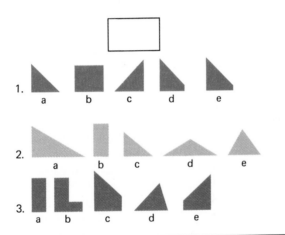

SAMPLE TEST ITEM: FLUID INTELLIGENCE

Below is a geometric figure. Beneath the figure are several problems. Each problem consists of a row of five shaded pieces. Your task is to decide which of the five shaded pieces will make the complete figure when put together. Any number of shaded pieces from two to five may be used to make the complete figure. Each piece may be turned around to any position, but it cannot be turned over.

1. a   b   c   d   e

2. a   b   c   d   e

3. a   b   c   d   e

SAMPLE TEST ITEM: CRYSTALLIZED INTELLIGENCE

Choose one of the four words in the right-hand box which has the same meaning as the word in the left-hand box.

1.	bizarre	market imaginative	conventional odd
2.	pecuniary	involving money trifling	esthetic unusual
3.	germane	microbe relevant	contagious different

Answer:
Fluid intelligence item: (1) a, c, d, e; (2) a, d, e; (3) b, c, e

Crystallized intelligence item: (1) odd; (2) involving money; (3) relevant

FIGURE 8–18
The graph shows how fluid intelligence first increases and then decreases with age, while crystalized intelligence steadily increases. (Horn & Donaldson, 1980)

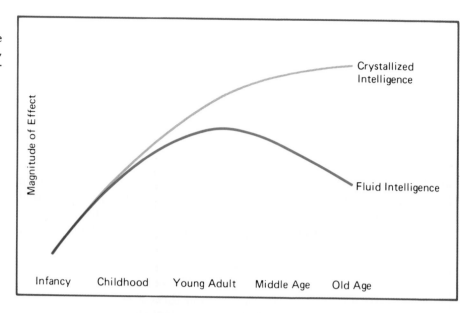

IQ: The Extremes

Intelligence tests have been most successful at identifying the extremes of intelligence (Isaacson, 1970). At one extreme, people with IQs below 70 are labeled **mentally retarded.** There are degrees of mental retardation. People with IQs below 30 are totally dependent. About 1 out of every 1,000 people fall in this category. Those with IQs between 30 and 50 are trainable; that is, they can learn to take care of their daily needs in a sheltered environment. About 3 out of every 1,000 people are in this category. People with IQs between 50 and 70 are educable; that is, with special training, they can learn to support themselves in the community (Zucker & Altman, 1973).

At the other extreme, people with IQs of 140 or above are classified as mentally gifted. In 1921, Terman and his associates started a longitudinal study that followed mentally gifted people from early childhood through adulthood (see Sears, 1977; Sears & Barbee, 1977). The results supported two conclusions. On the one hand, high IQ scores are associated with good health, outstanding school performance, and leadership. On the other hand, a high IQ is not a perfect predictor of success, because other factors are also important. Some of the mentally gifted people in the study, for example, failed in college and in their careers. Many factors are important in determining differences between the least and most successful mentally gifted individuals, including motivation, perseverance, and creativity (Crockenburg, 1972).

IQ: The Controversies

Classifying people at the low and high extremes of intelligence is an important contribution, for it helps educators provide programs that are best suited for individual needs. Few would deny that people and society are well served when educable individuals and mentally gifted individuals receive different education programs. Yet tests are also used to group people who are in between these extremes. The usefulness of IQ tests in these mid ranges is not as clear. Not surprisingly, several controversies have

Mentally retarded
Significant subaverage intellectual functioning; specifically an IQ of 70 or lower.

arisen. These include the question of whether or not IQ tests are fair to minority groups. Let's consider this controversy.

Culture Fairness. Those who question the validity of IQ tests for minorities argue that the tests are not fair to blacks, Hispanics, poor whites, and other cultural subgroups. As indicated earlier, differences in performance on IQ tests could be caused by differences in opportunity to learn the tested material or by differences in capacity to learn. If everyone has the same opportunity, then differences can safely be attributed to capacity. If a cultural subgroup has had less of an opportunity to learn the tested material, then the IQ test is an invalid test of capacity for that group.

Test-makers have tried to develop "culture-fair" tests. Most often this has meant cutting down on the use of verbal materials, since there are obvious language differences between subcultures. Nonverbal tests usually involve geometric relationships of some kind. The tasks on such tests include fitting pegs into holes, judging relationships between geometric forms, making designs with blocks, and completing drawings (Cattell, 1949; Raven, 1947). Unfortunately, test-makers have too little data to back up their assumption that everyone has an equal opportunity to learn even the skills required for these tasks. Developmental psychologists are only beginning to understand the effects of experience on cognitive development. What they have learned so far suggests that environments during infancy and childhood do make a difference, but many questions remain unanswered: At what age do children learn aspects of geometric relationships? What elements of the environment are essential for providing an opportunity to learn geometry and other skills that are examined on IQ tests? If there are critical environmental factors, how are they influenced by the complex and subtle differences between subcultures? Until these and other questions about opportunities to learn are answered, it will be impossible to establish the validity of culture-fair IQ tests for cultural subgroups. A related controversy concerns the role of heredity and environment in determining IQ.

Nature and Nurture. What is the relative contribution of heredity and environment to IQ? In the study of genetics one estimates the heritability of traits in plants and animals by controlling environment while manipulating the proportion of genes held in common. Such experiments cannot be done with humans, of course. Although members of human families vary systematically in the extent to which they share genetic makeup, they also vary systematically—and in much the same way—in their environments. Specifically, those who have the more similar genes (parents and children) also have the more similar environments. Those who have less similar genes (grandparents and grandchildren) also, for the most part, have less similar environments. Some authorities argue, in fact, that genetic similarity is so interwoven with environmental similarity that scientists cannot make meaningful heritability estimates for humans (Feldman & Lewontin, 1975).

Many investigators have nevertheless studied genetic relatedness in humans. They have used three procedures:

One way to separate effects of heredity and environment is to study identical twins who have been raised in different environments.

1. *Studies of identical twins who are raised apart.* These have often failed to separate effects of heredity from effects of environment (e.g., Shields, 1962). The twins were reared in separate but similar environments and often had contact with each other. One study that claimed to avoid this problem (Burt, 1966) is now regarded as fraudulent. Burt apparently invented much of this data (Kamin, 1973).

2. *Studies comparing identical and fraternal twins.* As we discussed in Chapter 2, identical twins come from the same egg, and thus their genes are exactly the same. Fraternal twins, on the other hand, come from two

It is difficult to interpret differences between group averages on IQ scores. We sometimes understand the difficulty better when we look at several groups. The text discusses differences between blacks and whites. Let's consider other groups: females versus males and Asian versus American children. Then let's compare differences between average scores with differences between individual scores.

Psychologists have traditionally maintained that females surpass males in verbal skills, and males exceed females in spatial and math abilities. However, Janet Hyde and Marcia Linn (1988) found no meaningful gender differences on verbal abilities when they analyzed thousands of test scores, though evidence still supports some developmental differences. For example, males outnumber females three to one in remedial reading classes (Finucci & Childs, 1981). But average differences between males and females in verbal abilities may be less than once thought. In contrast, evidence continues to suggest that average spatial and math test scores are higher for males (Maccoby & Jacklin, 1974, 1980; Halpern, 1986). Before interpreting these differences, let's consider similar differences between Asian and American children.

Harold Stevenson (1983, 1988) compared children in similar cities: Sendai, Japan; Taipei, Taiwan; and Minneapolis, USA. He found higher math test scores for the Japanese and Taiwanese grade-school children than for the American children. Figure A shows the average math scores that Stevenson observed in kindergarten, first grade, and fifth grade. In kindergarten, the Japanese averages were well above those of both the Americans and Taiwanese. In the first and fifth grades, the Japanese averages remained high. At the same time, the Taiwanese averages moved up to Japanese levels and the American averages steadily fell. Only one American was among the top 100 fifth-graders, while 67 Americans were among the bottom 100 fifth-graders.

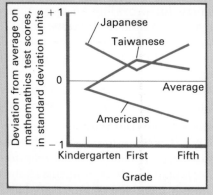

FIGURE A

Math test scores as a function of grade for Japanese, Taiwanese, and American children. (Adapted from Stevenson, 1987).

Clearly, the Asian children prevailed.

Similar results have been seen within America. Asian-Americans make up only 2 percent of the population of the United States, yet their representation is much higher among students receiving math and science awards. For example, Asian-Americans won 25 percent of the top 120 places in the Westinghouse Talent Search between 1983 and 1985 (Doerner, 1985).

Americans are quick to look for—and find—possible environmental causes of these differences. For instance, children in Sendai and Taipei have 30 percent more elementary school days per year than children in Minneapolis, they spend more school time on math, and they do more homework. They also value hard work. Similarly, Asian-American students place a high value on hard work, educational achievement, and family cohesiveness (Caplan, Whitemore, Bui, & Traupmann, 1985).

Could environmental differences also cause the superiority of males over females in math and spatial ability scores? These differences occur on SAT scores even for males and females who have taken the same math courses and have the same expressed interest in math (Benbow, 1988). However, other environmental factors could favor males. Students know that males hold most of the jobs related to math and spatial abilities. For instance, 96 percent of American

---

separate eggs, and thus their genetic makeup differs. If correlations of IQs were higher with identical twins than with fraternal twins, this would say something about the heritability of IQ (Plomin, DeFries, & McClearn, 1980). Such studies, however, are also inconclusive. That is, although correlations between IQs are higher for identical twins (Bouchard & McGue, 1981; Erlenmeyer-Kimling & Jarvik, 1963), it has also been found that identical twins are more likely than fraternal twins to share a highly similar environment—to play together and to have the same friends and teachers (Loehlin & Nichols, 1976).

3. *Studies of adopted children, which compare their IQs to those of both their biological parents and their adopted parents.* Such studies suggest that IQ heritability is low to moderate (Horn, Loehlin, & Willerman, 1979; Scarr & Weinberg, 1977). This conclusion is further supported by the fact that the IQ correlation between parent and biological child is not consistently higher than that between parent and adopted child. In addition, IQ correlation between genetically related brothers and sisters

architects are men. Gilbert (1986) argues that this high percentage reflects an environmental bias. Many women who score as high or higher than male architects on math and spatial ability tests do not become architects because the architectural field is biased against them. Bias might affect motivation so that women who are interested in math still might not be motivated to perform at their best on SAT tests because they think they will not get a math-related job. We know that lower motivation yields lower test scores (Bradley-Johnson et al., 1984), so environmental biases could cause the advantage of males over females in the average math and spatial ability scores.

An illustration of the influence of environment on outcome is the fate of flower seeds planted in poor and fertile soil. Figure B shows four pairs of seeds, pairs A, B, C, and D. The seeds in each pair are identical, but the A seeds are better than the B seeds, which are better than the C seeds, which are better than the D seeds. One seed from each pair is planted in fertile soil and the other seed from the pair is planted in poor soil. In both soils the better seeds produce taller flowers. In addition, the average height is higher in the fertile soil. Specifically, flowers A, B, C, and D are 8, 6, 4, and 2 inches tall in the fertile soil, but only 7, 5, 3, and 1 inch tall in the poor soil. The average height in the fertile soil is 5

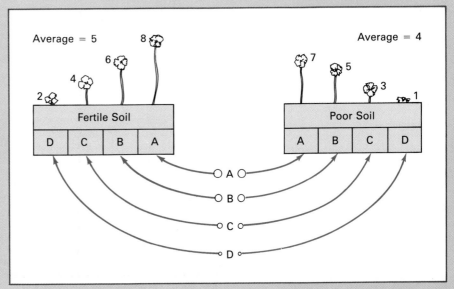

FIGURE B

Flower seeds planted in fertile or poor soil illustrate environmental influences on average scores (see the text for an explanation).

inches; the average in the poor soil is 4 inches. This example shows that average differences between groups may be caused entirely by the environment. This possibility exists even when individual differences *within* environments are caused by qualities of the seeds themselves.

The same example shows that average differences tell us nothing about individuals. Plants in poor soil are shorter on the average. However, knowing a flower's soil does not tell us its height. For example, flower A in the poor soil is taller than three of the flowers in the fertile soil. So do not judge your own math potential according to your group. You could have great math potential even if your group has a lower average. The way to find out is to give it your best shot.

Studying group differences helps us understand how heredity and environment interact to determine our abilities.

is not consistently higher than that between brothers and sisters who are only related by adoption.

The controversy is far from settled. Jensen (1969) reviewed the literature on genetic relatedness and concluded that heredity is about four times as important as environment in determining IQ. More recent reviews maintain that heredity is no more important than environment, or that it is perhaps not even as important as environment (Kamin, 1979; Plomin & DeFries, 1980).

Race and IQ. The most heated debate about intelligence concerns the fact that in the United States black people average 10 to 15 points lower on IQ tests than white people. A number of researchers (Eysenck, 1971; Herrnstein, 1973; Jensen, 1969, 1973; Shockley, 1972) have used this and other selected results to argue that blacks are innately less intelligent than whites. Other scientists (Kagan, 1973; Kamin, 1976, 1979; Scarr-Sala-patek, 1971) rebut this conclusion with one or more of the following arguments:

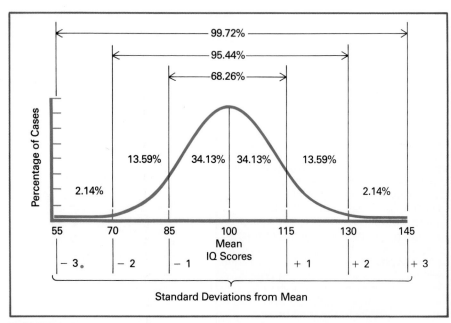

FIGURE 8–19

Most people fall in the middle range of IQ scores. The average IQ is 100. About 68% of people fall between ± 15 of the average, about 95% fall between ± 30 of the average. Extremely high and extremely low scores are rare. About 2% of people have scores above 130; about 2% have scores below 70.

1. Even if IQ has a hereditary element, that refers only to heredity within the group being studied—it does not say anything about differences *between* groups, such as blacks and whites.
2. IQ tests are biased against black people and other minorities.
3. Average IQ differences can be attributed entirely to environmental differences.
4. Differences in heredity and environment are so interwoven that IQ differences cannot be attributed to one or the other at this time (see Highlight: "IQ, Gender, and Culture").

IQ and You

You probably know your IQ or your scores on scholastic aptitude tests (SAT), which also are used to predict school performance. Figure 8–19 gives you a chance to compare your score with the norms. Don't let a high IQ score give you a false sense of security. Remember that a number of Terman's mentally gifted subjects failed in college. On the other hand, remember that you don't have to have a genius IQ to do ingenious things. For example, James Watson, the Nobel Prize winner who you read about at the beginning of this chapter, reported that his IQ was in the middle range (about 115).

Beyond IQ

The discrepancy between Watson's lukewarm IQ score and his hot intellectual achievements suggests that intelligence goes beyond IQ. Traditional IQ tests measure some important components of intelligence, such as word fluency and perceptual speed. But some psychologists believe that traditional IQ tests fail to measure other important aspects of intelligence.

Multiple Component Theories

We saw the historical roots of these objections when we reviewed Thurstone's and Guilford's work on multiple components of intelligence. We now take a closer look at their work. Both men were responding to Spearman's

(1927) claim that intelligence tests measure a general ability, *g*, and specific abilities, *s*. Spearman based his claims on *factor analysis*, a statistical procedure that analyzes correlations between subtest scores to extract common factors shared by all the tests. He developed this procedure and used it to support the *g* factor. Thurstone (1946) argued that intelligence test data were better explained by multiple factors. He refined statistical techniques for analyzing correlations among subtest scores and identified the seven factors mentioned in our earlier review (verbal comprehension, word fluency, number, space, memory, perceptual speed, and reasoning). Later researchers have continued to refine statistical analyses and group factors. The example given earlier of Guilford's 120-factor system is the most famous (Guilford, 1967). It includes social abilities and creativity, which were untapped in previous works.

Howard Gardner also argues for abilities that are disregarded by traditional intelligence tests. He has proposed that there are six independent "intelligences": linguistic, logic-mathematical, spatial, musical, bodily-kinesthetic, and personal (Gardner, 1983). Most IQ tests measure the first three, but ignore the last three. The last two of Gardner's intelligences might need some explanation. *Bodily-kinesthetic intelligence* is the ability to learn and create complex body movements. Outstanding dancers and athletes are high in this intelligence. *Personal intelligence* is the ability to understand oneself and others. Sensitive parents and teachers are high in this intelligence.

Gardner claims that the effects of brain damage support his theory. Brain damage often seems to affect independent abilities. It can degrade language skills without affecting math abilities, it can make the recognition of drawings impossible without reducing word recognition, and so on (see Chapter 2). Gardner interprets these results as effects on independent abilities.

Gardner also argues for multiple intelligences on the basis of so-called *idiot savants*. These are individuals who have low general intelligence but high mental abilities in some area. For example, Nadia, an autistic child (see Chapter 9), had remarkable drawing ability even though her mental abilities were very poor (Selfe, 1977). (See Figure 8–20.) Others with very low general intelligence have extraordinary mechanical or numerical abilities (Hill, 1978). In the movie *Rainman*, for instance, Dustin Hoffman plays a character who dazzles everyone by keeping track of all the cards in a casino blackjack game. He does this and other feats of numerical wizardry even though he cannot care for himself without the help of others. This character is based on real cases, which supports Gardner's theory of independent intelligences. The *idiot savant* is extremely rare, however. Only 1 or 2 are found among every 1,000 institutionalized retardates (Hill, 1978). This low frequency is hard to explain from Gardner's point of view.

Gardner's strongest point is that our mental abilities include more than those that enable us to succeed in school. Many theories of intelligence put language and mathematical abilities on a pedestal. Gardner, in contrast, draws attention to a wider range of abilities.

A similar view was advanced by Sternberg (1984, 1985). He suggests that a comprehensive theory must cover three aspects of intelligence: componential, experiential, and contextual. He is now developing an intelligence test based on his three-part theory (Trotter, 1987).

Sternberg's componential aspect of intelligence includes the components of analytic thinking that are covered by traditional IQ tests along with other components such as planning and evaluating strategies. The experiential aspect refers to the ability to combine experiences in insightful ways. And the contextual aspect emphasizes adaptation to the environment. Watson's story illustrates the importance of such adaptation. It was not just a matter of luck that he was in the right place at the right time to

FIGURE 8–20

This is one of many drawings by Nadia, an autistic child. Her drawings reveal a high artistic ability even though her other mental abilities are very low.

discover the structure of DNA. His original fellowship specified that he should study biochemistry at another lab in Europe. He moved to Cambridge after he discovered the opportunities that he would have there. Furthermore, he demonstrated his commitment to pursuing those opportunities by moving before he knew if he would continue to be paid by his fellowship or any other source.

Sternberg (1985) argued that students with high IQ scores as well as those with moderate ones will benefit by trying to reach their full potential. And that means expanding their componential, experiential, and contextual aspects of intelligence. We are called on to use the various aspects of intelligence in our daily lives. For example, one way that you can adapt as a student is by choosing a major that capitalizes on your strengths and minimizes your weaknesses.

An Information-Processing Analysis of Intelligence

Sternberg and other cognitive psychologists are also trying to understand the processes that underlie intelligence. They have already revealed simple cognitive components that are related to IQ scores (Sternberg & Gardner, 1983). For example, high scores relate to faster decision times on simple tasks. One simple task is deciding whether or not strings of letters are words. Try some. Is "board" a word? Is "biost" a word? College students with higher verbal intelligence scores respond faster to these simple questions (Jackson & McClelland, 1979).

Unique problem-solving strategies also relate to high IQs. Sternberg studied the strategies people use when answering multiple-choice analogies. An example is "Indian is to tepee as Eskimo is to _____." Choices might include: (a) Native American, and (b) igloo. Such questions are on many intelligence tests. Some are as easy as this one, in which the correct answer is *igloo*. Others are more difficult. Sternberg presented the question, and subjects signaled when they understood it. He then presented the multiple-choice answers, and subjects made their choice. Sternberg measured correctness as well as time taken on each part. He found that people with high IQs spend more time than those with lower IQs analyzing the question on the first part. Then they choose the correct answer faster in the second part. The strategy of spending more time on the questions is one of several hints that high IQ is associated with unique problem-solving strategies (Sternberg, 1984, 1985; Pellegrino, 1985).

These information-processing analyses of intelligence clearly indicate that the once-separate areas of language, thought, and intelligence are converging.

A Final Comment

Scientists have come a long way in their thinking about intelligence, language, and thought. In 1884, Galton was stymied by the now manageable task of using intelligence tests to distinguish extreme differences in abilities to learn and to solve problems. Similarly, in comparison to modern AI researchers, later 19th-century scientists had only vague, isolated pockets of knowledge about language and thought processes. Today there is a quest to develop better tests of real intelligence and better systems of artificial intelligence. This quest is revolutionizing the study of intelligence, language, and thought, drawing together psychologists, neuroscientists, computer scientists, engineers, and others. We will continue to explore these mysteries in the next two chapters, which discuss development through the life span.

Summary

1. Historically, the study of intelligence, language, and thought has moved from isolated areas of inquiry toward unified efforts to understand language and thought as mental processes that underlie intelligence. This unification has resulted in the emergence of a new area, **artificial intelligence (AI),** which is aimed at getting computers to behave intelligently.

2. Steps are being taken to study how language and thought processes determine our intelligent behavior. These studies have concentrated on three properties that make **human language** unique. Specifically, all human languages are structured to enable creative usage, interpersonal, and meaningful or referential. Most words refer to concepts, which are mental groups of objects. Thus, many studies have also investigated the formation of **concepts.** Some of these studies have shown that animals also form concepts, and other studies have explored the potential for animals to use language.

3. **Thought,** the mental activity of manipulating symbols, is related to language. This relationship is especially close for **propositional thought,** which is manipulation of "mental sentences." The relationship is looser for **imaginal thought,** which is manipulation of "mental images." In addition to considering the relationship between language and thought, scientists have debated the extent to which language influences the way we see the world.

4. Special attention has also been dedicated to **problem solving,** which is thinking aimed at overcoming obstacles that stand in the way of a goal. Three steps in problem solving are defining the problem, making plans, and deciding on the best solution. Defining a problem often requires creative thinking, which is the ability to think of new and useful ways to solve problems. Planning often involves the formation of subgoals. Decision making often involves choosing and evaluating the best approach to subgoals. The approaches include **trial and error,** hypothesis testing, and **algorithms,** which are step by step procedures that guarantee a solution. A **heuristic** is a rule of thumb problem-solving approach that often works but does not guarantee success.

5. Scientists in AI are debating whether or not **artificial intelligence** will ever think and solve problems as well as real human intelligence does. There is no debate, however, about the reality and importance of AI applications. They are revolutionizing our world.

6. **Intelligence,** the capacity to learn and use information, was initially studied from the point of view of individual differences. Psychologists developed **achievement tests** to measure a person's current knowledge and **aptitude tests** to predict one's capacity for future learning and use of information. The best known of the latter type are IQ tests, which do well at distinguishing the low and high extremes of intelligence. Distinguishing between people in the mid-range of intelligence is hampered by difficulties in creating a test that is fair to everyone. New approaches to intelligence testing take into account the components of thought processes, skills of learning from experience, and abilities to adapt to one's environment. Information-processing analyses of intelligence are revealing language and thought skills related to high IQ scores. These findings are unifying the fields of language, thought, and intelligence.

Key Terms

achievement tests	family-resemblance concepts	intelligence quotient (IQ)	phonological rule
aptitude tests	fluid intelligence	letters	problem solving
algorithm	focal colors	linguistic relativity (Sapir-Whorf	propositional thought
artificial intelligence	functional fixedness	hypothesis)	prototype
availability heuristic	heuristic	mentally retarded	representativeness heuristic
chronological age	holophrastic speech	mental age	standarized tests
concepts	human language	mental set	thought
confirmation bias	hypothesis	morphemes	trial and error
creative thinking	imaginal thought	orthographic rules	
crystallized intelligence	intelligence	phonemes	

HUMOR FOUND TO AID PROBLEM-SOLVING

BY DANIEL GOLEMAN

"In America, everything is permitted that's not forbidden," a European joke has it. "In Germany, everything is forbidden that's not permitted. In France, everything is permitted, even if it's forbidden. And in Russia, everything is forbidden, even if it's permitted."

Such jokes suit the notion that much humor veils aggression, permitting the joke-teller, in Freud's words, "to be malicious with dignity." But Freud's longstanding analysis of humor as the release of repressed feelings is receding as a growing group of social scientists, for whom humor is no joke, make it the focus of serious research. In the new work, humor is seen less as disguised hostility and more as a stimulant to problem-solving and productivity, as an aid to education and as the stuff of social bonds.

Humor and its uses have been a subject of conjecture since Aristotle, and a large body of psychoanalytic literature deals with jokes. But "humor has been a neglected topic among researchers," said Donna Cooper, a psychologist at the University of Connecticut who is a consultant on the uses of humor in organizations. "Most psychologists are preoccupied with grim topics and problems; humor and the positive emotions get little interest or funding."

Of late, though, that has begun to change. Some of the more visible new research, inspired by Norman Cousins' account of how watching Marx Brothers movies and other comedy films helped him recover from a debilitating illness, deals with links between positive feelings and healing.

Less well known is recent research suggesting that putting people in a good mood by telling them jokes makes them think through problems with more ingenuity. Casual joking at work may thus improve people's effectiveness in their tasks.

"Any joke that makes you feel good is likely to help you think more broadly and creatively," said Alice M. Isen, a psychologist at the University of Maryland in Baltimore. The elation that comes from hearing a good joke, Dr. Isen has found, is similar to that which people feel when they receive a small, unexpected gift. Such elation, her research shows, facilitates innovation.

In the research, reported in a recent issue of *The Journal of Personality and Social Psychology*, Dr. Isen found that people who had just watched a short comedy film of television "bloopers" were better able to find a creative solution to a puzzling problem than were people who had watched a film about math or who had exercised.

The problem posed was one frequently used in such research: People were given a candle, matches and a box of tacks and asked to attach the candle to a corkboard wall so that the candle would burn without dripping wax on the floor.

Most people who try to solve this problem fall prey to "functional fixedness," the tendency to see the objects presented them only in terms of their conventional uses. Those who were in a good mood from watching the funny film, however, were generally able to solve the problem by seeing another use for the box holding the tacks: They tacked the box to the wall and used it as a candleholder.

In other studies, Dr. Isen found that the comedy film increased people's ability to think more broadly, seeing relationships that otherwise eluded them. This is a mental skill that is important in finding creative solutions to problems and in foreseeing the consequences of a given decision. The ability to recognize complex relationships and far-flung implications has also been found, in other research, to mark the most successful business executives.

"The mind associates more broadly when people are feeling good after hearing a joke," said Dr. Isen. "They think of things they ordinarily would not and have access to a broader range of mental material. And the more ideas present in your mind, the more ways you see to connect things; you're able to see more solutions."

Beyond Satisfaction

In light of this and other research, joking at work is being appreciated as more than mere diversion. Research reported recently at the annual meeting of the American Psychological Association showed that the feeling of having fun at work is more important than overall job satisfaction in workers' effectiveness.

In a survey of 382 people from a wide variety of work places, David Abramis, a psychologist in the School of Business Administration at California State University at Long Beach, found that those who felt their work was fun performed better and got along better with co-workers than did those who were satisfied with their jobs but did not see them as fun.

Traditionally, psychologists have focused on people's sense of satisfaction with their jobs as a measure of their psychological adjustment to work. Dr. Abramis, though, believes that the feeling that one's work is fun is of equal importance and that job satisfaction and having fun at work are independent considerations.

A major source of fun at work, the study showed, is joking with fellow workers, according to Dr. Abramis. "If you are trying to improve people's performance at work, it is not enough to improve job satisfaction," he said. "Increasing their sense of having a good time at work improves their performance over and above satisfaction."

Joking also has its dangers, particularly carelessness, according to Dr. Isen. "If you want a jocular environment at work, you need to make sure people keep in mind the importance of their work," she said. "If you don't, feeling good may make people sloppy where they should be plodding. But if you tell people who are feeling good that they have made a mistake, they are especially thorough in correcting their errors."

Implications for Children

Although it is a relatively new idea that joking may enhance productivity at work, humor has long been used to make learning more palatable for children, as "Sesame Street" demonstrated. At first, some educators argued that such humor was detrimental to learning, because it drew children's attention away from the serious parts of the material presented. More recently, though, interspersing humor among the serious has been shown to improve children's learning, provided the humor is of the right sort.

New research on which sorts of humor aid learning and which hinder it shows that when the humor distorts the information, it often confuses children. According to findings by Dolf Zillman, a psychologist at Indiana University, irony is particularly confusing to young children, who do not yet have the basic knowledge that would allow them to see what is true and what a distortion. Dr. Zillman cites as an example of distortion a "Sesame Street" depiction of seat belts on an airplane; when the plane turns upside down the seat-belted characters hang from the cockpit as if the belts were rubber.

Children up to fourth grade, and perhaps beyond, are often confused by such distortions, Dr. Zillman reported in the "Handbook of Humor Research" (Springer-Verlag). On the other hand, he has found that humor that does not distort generally enhances children's ability to master new material. The solution he recommends is to use jokes that are unrelated to the topic at hand, rather than jokes about the information itself.

The Maturing Process

By the time students reach college age, though, humor that is unrelated to the educational topic can backfire, Dr. Zillman warns. A lecturer who habitually tells such jokes may be viewed as digressing, according to Dr. Zillman, and the joking asides seem to interfere with the students' grasp of the material presented. On the other hand, lecturers who weave into their material humor about the topic seem to be more effective.

Exactly what people find funny changes as they age, according to a survey of 40 stand-up comedians performed by Lucille Nahemow, a psychologist at the University of Connecticut. "Adults of all ages respond to sexual humor," she said, "while younger audiences like aggressive humor, such as put-down jokes, and older audiences like jokes about family life."

Jokes serve an important social function in strengthening the bonds between people, researchers are finding. By laughing at the same things, people let one another know that they have a similar outlook, without having to say so. This makes jokes especially important in communicating about discomforting topics.

"Many jokes are a way to talk about troubling topics like sex and racism," according to Alan Dundes, a folklorist at the University of California at Berkeley, who in "Cracking Jokes" (Ten Speed Press) analyzes the hidden meanings of humor. By laughing at a joke, the listener tacitly signals that he shares the attitude implicit in it, Dr. Dundes argues.

"Wherever there is anxiety in a culture, you find humor," Dr. Dundes said. "In Eastern Europe, for example, you find many more jokes about politics and Russians than you do in the West, where these concerns are not so overriding."

Indeed, Dr. Dundes takes the popular jokes of a people as a barometer of their hidden concerns. Of particular significance, he finds, are "joke cycles," jokes on a single topic that spring up suddenly, have many variations and are extremely popular. Thus, in his view, "Jewish American princess" jokes of the late 1970's were a reaction to feminism.

"All jokes are serious, and anything funny is at someone's expense," Dr. Dundes said. "It is hard to find a truly harmless joke, one without a serious overtone."

Infancy and Childhood

9

A perfect specimen," the nurse said, as newborn Raun Kahlil Kaufman began to breathe and cry at the same time. Raun's parents, Suzi and Barry Kaufman, experienced the birth of their third child and first son with pride and joy. And he soon won the hearts of his older sisters. At 1 year, Raun seemed on track for normal and healthy development. The only exception was that he did not put out his arms to be picked up. This peculiarity was of only minor concern until his second year, when he started to show other signs of aloofness. Raun became less responsive to his name, even though he would sometimes attend to a soft and distant sound. When his sisters or parents tried to hold or hug him, he often pushed their hands away, and when someone picked him up, he let his arms dangle at his side. Although his family wanted desperately to play with him, he preferred to sit alone and to stare blankly into space. As an experienced and sensitive father, Barry Kaufman knew that these

behaviors were unusual. As a former graduate student in psychology, he also knew that many of his son's abnormal behaviors fit dreaded patterns corresponding either to infantile autism or childhood schizophrenia, the most irreversible conditions of profoundly disturbed children.

Besides the aloofness and blank stares, other behaviors fit the patterns. For example, Raun spent long periods rocking back and forth while sitting on the floor. Sometimes he would sit on the floor and spin plates, seeming to be completely absorbed with the spinning objects. However, Raun was unlike autistic children in that he seemed at peace. Autistic children often engage in violent, self-destructive behaviors— for example, some will bang their heads against walls. Raun never did these things. But Raun's parents knew that something was seriously wrong.

They consulted with experts in New York, Philadelphia, and California who confirmed that Raun was autistic. They also expressed the

widely held belief that autism is irreversible and incurable. Although some treatment programs existed, they were aimed at older children. The Kaufmans were therefore urged to wait a year before starting any type of treatment.

But waiting was impossible; they could not stand by and watch their son slip further and further away. After reading everything that they could find about autism and carefully observing Raun, they devised a plan based upon three beliefs about Raun:

1. They believed that Raun's processing of perceptions and utilization of memories were disorganized. A "hidden cookie test" helped reveal this problem. Raun would look at a cookie and follow it as one parent moved it in the boy's field of vision. The parent would then hide the cookie behind a sheet of paper. Raun would then stare and turn away. The average 8-month-old has the ability to retain the hidden object in his or her mind and to look for it, but Raun, at 20 months,

could not. For him, out of sight seemed to be out of mind. Similarly, each time his own hands came into view he acted as if he were seeing them for the first time. From these observations, the Kaufmans decided to simplify events as much as possible for Raun. For example, the task of inserting a puzzle piece was divided into four parts. They first taught him to pick up the piece, then to move the piece to the puzzle, to find the right place, and finally to insert the piece.

2. The Kaufmans believed that Raun needed extra motivation because his perceptual and memory problems made interactions very difficult for him. They tried to show Raun that the extra effort was worth it because the outside world is beautiful and exciting.

3. They strongly believed that their son deserved their acceptance and approval. They tried to motivate him to accept attractive alternative behaviors, but did not disapprove of his preferred behaviors. They did not try to stop him from rocking or from spinning plates. Instead, they joined in these activities with him. Most importantly, no matter how much time they spent, they were willing to accept no progress. They considered any contact with Raun its own reward.

Since the program called for long, one-on-one sessions in an environment with few distractions, Suzi spent many hours alone with Raun on a bathroom floor in their home. At first, 9 hours were planned. But gradually the time increased until Suzi was spending 75 hours per week working with her son. In addition, Barry spent whatever time he could on evenings and weekends. Two volunteers, trained by the Kaufmans, assisted Suzi so she could have more breaks while Raun could continue one-on-one sessions for about 75 hours per week. In the eleventh week, Barry received a special treat

when he returned from work. Raun gave him his typical casual look. But then he raised his arm as if he were taking an oath of office and he flopped his fingers against his palm. He was waving hello.

Feeling so elated because of Raun's response, Barry decided to give Raun the cookie test. With Suzi at his side, he presented a cookie as he had done on each previous night of the program. On previous nights Raun had seemed interested at first, but not after the cookie disappeared behind a paper. This night was different. It was Raun's night for triumph. He pushed the paper aside, grabbed the cookie, and ate it. Barry and Suzi repeated the test again and again. Each time, Raun snatched the cookie with more enthusiasm than the time before. The cookie test had been conquered.

Suzi called Barry at work the next day to tell him about Raun's progress.

This morning when I gave him the puzzle, mixed up all the pieces and scrambled everything, he worked it out. Completely. Without any help or guidance. It's like he can retain more, use more. He's switched on like a thousand-watt bulb!

The whole family celebrated as Raun joined in their activities over the next 4 months. He started talking, using a small vocabulary: "wa" (water), "down," "more," "ba" (bottle), "Mommy," "Da-da," and

"hot." He also started to play with them. One morning he joined his mother at the piano. He soon learned to mimic the notes of "Three Blind Mice." Mother and child were equally pleased, smiling repeatedly at each other.

His vocabulary expanded from 7 to 75 words. He started using small phrases and sentences, and he learned to sing songs such as "Three Blind Mice," "Over There, Over There." " 'A'—You're Adorable," and "Splish Splash." Raun developed a morning ritual that contrasted sharply with his earlier withdrawal activities. When he was greeted at his crib, he would clap and shout "Mommy" and "Daddy." Then he would turn toward each and request a big "Hugga Hugga."

Suzi and Barry took Raun to an outpatient clinic for a development workup at the age of 20 months and again at 24 months. Raun's language and socialization at 20 months old were on a level appropriate for an 8 month old. At 24 months old, the same tests showed that Raun was functioning at or above his age level in every way. Raun's level on over half of the tests was 30 to 36 months. In four months, he had made an incredible developmental surge of 16 to 26 months.

Raun continued to soar at the age of two-and-a-half when his father recorded the successful effort to reach an "unreachable" child in a book, *Son-Rise*. It ends not with the usual phrase, "The End," but with a more appropriate one, "The Beginning."

At age 15 (1988), Raun has developed into an extroverted, extraordinarily articulate, loving, and playful youngster who demonstrates a near genius IQ and maintains a straight "A" scholastic average at a neighborhood school.

Raun's triumph was also a new beginning for Suzi and Barry. They have now achieved similar results with other autistic children and with rebellious teenagers (Kaufman, 1982; 1984).

Identify and discuss the major themes and approaches to the study of development.

Compare and contrast the methods used to study development.

Describe the important developmental landmarks in the three stages of prenatal development.

Review the significant cognitive, physical, and social developmental landmarks through infancy and childhood.

Discuss Piaget's theory of cognitive development.

Identify and discuss the four major disorders that can occur during childhood.

History and Scope of the Study of Human Development

Human development is a process by which the genes that we inherit from our parents (see Chapter 2) come to be expressed as specific physical and behavioral characteristics. The goals of developmental psychology are to describe and explain that process in terms of general principles that can be employed in education, medicine, and parenting, just to mention a few practical applications. Raun's rise from self-destructive isolation to self-fulfilling interactions with others illustrates four themes that have been important in the study of human development.

The first one concerns the relative roles of *heredity* and *environment* in shaping development. Heredity alone determined the color of Raun's hair and eyes. But heredity and environment both influenced Raun's learning of music. He inherited genes that gave him the potential to learn music, and his mother helped him realize his potential by providing an environment that included lessons and encouragement. Many modern developmental psychologists believe that important aspects of development are determined by a continuous interaction between heredity and environment (e.g., Kagan, 1986).

In the 17th and 18th centuries, this conclusion would have been at odds with two extreme theories of development. One theory, called *nativism*, emphasizes the role of heredity in the development of mind and behavior. Nativism says that infants are born with innate capacities to experience the world pretty much as adults do. Extreme nativism holds that development is nothing more than **maturation,** which is the unfolding of genetically determined abilities. Another theory, called *empiricism*, holds that experience is the source of all knowledge. This theory states that newborns experience the world as very confusing until they learn to perceive as adults do. Extreme empiricism holds that all development is determined by learning through experience. Leading philosophers in the debate were Plato (ca. 427–347 B.C.), Descartes (1596–1650), and Kant (1724–1804) on the side of nativism, and Aristotle (384–347), Hobbes (1588–1679), Locke (1632–1700), and Hume (1711–1776) on the side of empiricism. By clearly stating the extreme positions, these philosophers set the stage for scientific inquiry to test both

Human development
Process by which the genes inherited from parents come to be expressed as specific physical and behavioral characteristics.
Maturation
Unfolding of genetically determined abilities.

sides. These tests disproved both extremes and established a balanced approach that included parts of each.

The second theme concerns the *continuity* or *discontinuity* of development. On the one hand, Raun's physical growth during his first two years was normal, which means that it was relatively continuous. On the other hand, Raun's rapid surge forward after passing the hidden cookie test could indicate a discontinuity in development. In other words, it could mean that he had made a transition from one stage of development to a more advanced stage. Later in this chapter, we will review other examples of discontinuities in psychological and physical development.

The third theme concerns the importance of *early* and *later* experience. That Raun's positive response to his parent's acceptance and encouragement occurred within his first two years illustrates the importance of early experience. However, his parents' current work with older children indicates that later experiences are also important. In this chapter and the next, we will discuss the impact of experiences throughout the life span.

The fourth theme concerns *unidirectional pressures* and *reciprocal interactions*. Until recently, research has been on a one-way street examining agents that affect a child's development without studying the other side of the coin, the effects of the child on the agents. For example at four weeks old Raun developed an ear infection that almost turned into a crisis. This ear infection is an example of a unidirectional pressure. It changed Raun, but Raun did not change it. In contrast, Raun's relationship with his parents is a reciprocal interaction. Raun's autistic condition changed the way Raun's parents treated him; Raun responded to their special treatment, which again changed the way they treated him, and so on. In this reciprocal process, Raun and his parents dramatically changed the course of each other's lives. In this chapter, we will review recent research efforts to capture the reciprocal nature of many interactions during development. Today, many developmental psychologists see that each theme and the various theoretical approaches can be complementary.

Table 9.1 shows which themes have been adopted by the advocates of five theoretical approaches. The first three, functional, psychodynamic, and behavioristic, were introduced in Chapter 1 as dominant schools of thought in the history of psychology. The fourth, ethological/organismic, originated in biology and was adopted by leading psychologists whose work we will discuss in detail. The fifth, lifespan, is a current approach that we have drawn upon heavily in organizing this chapter and the next. We will employ these themes as a schematic framework for comparing and contrasting the various approaches.

Table 9–1   Major Themes and Approaches to Developmental Psychology

Theme	Approach				
	Functionalism	Psychodynamic	Behavioristic	Ethological/ Organismic	Life-span
Heredity vs. Environment	Interaction of both	Interaction of both	Environment	Interaction of both	Interaction of both
Continuity vs. Discontinuity	Discontinuous	Discontinuous	Continuous	Discontinuous	Discontinuous
Early vs. Late Experience	Both	Early	Both (Search for principles that transcend age)	Limited by stage (emphasis on early)	Both
Unidirectional vs. Reciprocal	Reciprocal	Unidirectional	Both	Reciprocal	Reciprocal

We mentioned in Chapter 1 that the functionalists William James and John Dewey promoted both the study of children and the application of those studies. In 1900 Dewey delivered a presidential address to the American Psychological Association entitled "Psychology and Social Practice." His speech emphasized the need for a formal program of research on the education of children. Stanley Hall and many women psychologists were instrumental in turning the proposed program into a reality. Some of the outstanding foremothers in this area were Lillien Jane Martin, Helen Thompson Woolley, and Florence Goodenough (see Highlight in Chapter 1: "Women in Psychology: Setting the Record Straight").

In addition to publishing many papers on developmental issues concerning children, adolescence, and adults, Hall published *Pedagogical Summary*, a journal aimed at applying psychological research to education. Hall was the first Ph.D. student of William James and was a functionalist. Table 9.1 suggests that the functionalist's views anticipated the current synthesis of our schematic themes. On one hand, this impression is accurate. The functionalists did recognize the interaction of heredity and environment, the existence of discontinuities in development, the importance of early and later experiences, as well as the reciprocal nature of developmental interactions. On the other hand, we do not want to leave you with the impression that the contributions of later psychologists were little more than "reinventing the wheel." Although functionalists anticipated some of the current ideas, their research methods were far too inadequate to develop those ideas empirically. Hall's methods, for example, relied heavily on questionnaires distributed to uncontrolled samples. He mostly studied adults who were asked to recall things about their childhood. Today, far more precise methods are helping to establish a strong scientific foundation.

The psychodynamic approach also suffered from weak research methodology. Beginning with Sigmund Freud, psychodynamic psychologists have emphasized the importance of childhood in the development of personality (see Chapter 13). Freud recognized the interaction of heredity and environment, which he believed took place in discontinuous stages of development during childhood. However, his extreme emphasis on early life experiences made his approach unidirectional. For example, his theory had much to say about how early interactions between children and parents might affect the child, but it had nothing to say about how those interactions might affect the parent. Erik H. Erikson (1963), a contemporary advocate of the psychodynamic approach, has advanced a theory with stages that take place throughout life (see Table 10–2). Until recently, these theories were not developed using rigorous research methods.

A giant step forward in the use of scientific methods was taken by John Watson and other behaviorists such as B. F. Skinner. During the 1920s, Watson studied infants at Johns Hopkins Hospital from a behavioristic point of view, which he subsequently applied to all psychological research. He and other behaviorists took extreme positions on several of our schematic themes. They dedicated themselves to establishing principles of environmental influences that could be generalized across ages and even across species. These principles were expressed in terms of theories of classical and operant conditioning (see Chapter 7). Accordingly, in contrast to the modern synthesis, behaviorists focused on environmental and continuity theories to the exclusion of theories of heredity and discontinuity. In accordance with the current life-span theory, they did recognize the importance of environmental influences throughout life. Furthermore, although their research was mostly unidirectional, they did see that parents and children can condition each other in reciprocal relationships. Behaviorists stated their faith in the power of conditioning with great force. For example, Watson stirred the interest of many scholars and lay persons when he claimed: "Give me a dozen healthy infants, well-formed, and my own speci-

Parents provide both the genetic inheritance that determines a child's potential and the environment that enables a child to realize its potential.

fied world to bring them up in and I'll guarantee to take any one at random and train him to become any type of specialist I might select—doctor, lawyer, merchant, chief, and yes, even beggarman and thief, regardless of his talents, penchants, abilities, vocations, and the race of his ancestors (1913)." More recent claims of the general applicability of behaviorism can be found in several books by B. F. Skinner: *Walden Two* (1948), *Science and Human Behavior* (1953), *Verbal Behavior* (1957), and *Beyond Freedom and Dignity* (1971). Although the eloquence of these leaders helped to promote their views, the true power of behaviorism was in its rigorous research methodology. Behaviorism dominated psychology from the 1930s through the 1950s because principles of conditioning were firmly grounded in scientific observation. Balance was not restored to the issues of heredity versus environment and continuity versus discontinuity until psychologists developed equally powerful scientific methods to document the impact of heredity and discontinuities.

We want to place the emphasis on balance. We favor the view that rigorous methods should be used in order to prove or disprove hypotheses. However, balance between seemingly opposing theories can be achieved as long as there is agreement that different theories apply to different aspects of development. Chapter 7 indicated that behavioristic principles of conditioning are still an important approach to learning. They provide the best account to date for many important aspects of behavior, and they are an integral part of important applications in education, medicine, and parenting. Today, however, behaviorists share the limelight with advocates of other approaches that will be introduced in this and the next chapters.

The ethological/organismic approach is one that has moved into the spotlight. "Ethological" reflects the fact that the approach relies heavily on methods of natural observation that are often used by ethologists. "Organismic" refers to the approach's theoretical emphasis on inherited biological predispositions that change systematically during the course of development. When Charles Darwin (1859) published *Origin of Species*, he maintained that animals and humans are governed by the same natural laws. Soon he and other scholars began to look for parallels between the evolution of a species and the development of an individual child. In 1877, for example, Darwin published a book in which he maintained that his son's inborn reflexes echoed early stages of evolution. These conclusions were based on detailed observations of his son's sneezing, hiccuping, yawning, stretching, sucking, screaming, and other behaviors. In the 1920s, Watson and other behaviorists joined the search for common threads between animal and human behavior. At the same time, Arnold Gesell, a psychologist and physician, set up a laboratory to observe children at Yale University. In contrast to behaviorists, Gesell believed that the influence of learning and experience were minor compared to inherited tendencies. He documented through systematic observations that all healthy children, regardless of training, go through similar stages in mastering skills. They grasp, sit, stand, and walk at about the same time and in the same order, regardless of efforts to speed up the stages or to change their order through conditioning or other forms of training. He used hidden observers and motion picture cameras to record these schedules of development, which he published in meticulous detail. Some of his publications, such as *Infant and Child in the Culture of Today* (1943), became standard references and are still used by physicians and parents to evaluate the developmental progress of children. Despite this popularity among physicians and parents, Gesell's work was either ignored or scorned by American psychologists during their heyday of behaviorism.

Outside of America, however, other research was adding evidence in favor of the ethological/organismic approach. In 1925, the Swiss psychologist, Jean Piaget, married one of his students, Valentine Chatney. Piaget's

"At about fifteen months of age the American baby becomes something more than a 'mere' infant. He is discarding his nursing bottle. . . . He says 'ta-ta' on more or less suitable occasions; by gesture language he calls attention to wetted pants; he makes an imitative stroke with a crayon; he helps to turn the pages of a picture book, albeit several leaves at one swift swoop" (Gesell, 1943, p. 131).

Jean Piaget (center) observes children who are working with a research assistant (right). Piaget advanced our understanding of how children think by observing how they answer questions and how they perform simple tasks.

training in biology and ethology probably played a role in the systematic observations he and his wife made of their son and two daughters. Piaget's major contribution, which we review in this chapter, was the proposal of a theory of development. His theory states that a child's cognitive development unfolds in discrete stages that determine how the child views and copes with his or her world. Elsewhere in Europe, other scientists were also advancing the ethological/organismic point of view. Konrad Lorenz (1937), an Austrian ethologist, discovered a special kind of stage in young goslings. He observed that baby geese will become attached to, or **imprint** on, the first moving object they see, including Lorenz himself, during their first 24 hours. They express this attachment by following the moving object everywhere and by running to it for comfort in stressful situations. We will return to this work later when we consider related research that stemmed from the work of Mary Ainsworth (1973) and John Bowlby (1973), who promoted an ethological theory of attachment and loss in children (Sroufe, 1986). We shall see that European influences found their way to America where they helped to restore balance to the themes that are summarized in Table 9.1.

The life-span approach is also a balanced approach, as indicated in the table, but its emphasis is unique. "Life-span" psychology is the study of continuity and change throughout life.

Today, developmental psychology is a major branch of science. To understand how this area expanded, one must consider not only the scientific themes but also the social and cultural ones (see Highlight: "Socioeconomic Reforms, You, and Developmental Psychology").

Methods of Studying Development

The doctors who observed Raun's rapid developmental surge were both surprised and impressed. They videotaped one of Suzi's sessions with Raun, hoping to gain insights that would help them with other autistic children. They were cautious, however, about generalizing from observations of

Imprinting
Process whereby a young fowl or bird attaches itself to the first object it sees.

SOCIOECONOMIC REFORMS, YOU, AND DEVELOPMENTAL PSYCHOLOGY

Many college freshmen are still on the child side in parent-child relationships, the student side in education, and the minor side in the legal system. You were born in the mid-1970s. You have passed at least 12 years of formal education, and now you are attending college. How do socioeconomic reforms affect you? To find out, let's consider what your life would have been like if you had been born in an earlier time.

Suppose you had been born at the turn of this century. Your chances of surviving your first year would have been ten times less than they are today. About 140 out of 1,000 American infants died in their first year, compared to 14 out of 1,000 today (Uhlenberg, 1980). If your parents were laborers in Europe or America, you probably would have become a laborer. Chances are good that before you were 10 years old, you would have been doing hard and dangerous labor 10–12 hours a day in the fields, in a mine, or in a factory (Kessen,1965; Baumeister & Tice,1986).

You would have avoided this fate if your parents had the money for higher education, but your education still would have been an uphill battle if you are a woman. Then you would have had to overcome strong social sanctions against higher education for women. These restrictions stemmed from the belief that "developing one's intellectual capabilities was incompatible with the female qualities needed to fulfill the obligations of the 'woman's sphere' and attain 'true womanhood'" (Russo & Denmark, 1987, p. 289). Helen Thompson Woolley and Leta Stetter Hollingworth were among the first psychologists to lead the fight against these obstacles (see Highlight in Chapter 1: "Women in Psychology: Setting the Record Straight").

If you had been born 25 years later, in 1925, you would have benefited from increasing pressure against child labor. Pioneers in child psychology were leaders in mounting this pressure. Chances are good that you would have started school, but you might have had to quit to earn money during the Great Depression of the 1930s. Not too many years later, if you are a male, you would have been drafted to fight in World War II.

Research suggests that children raised in poverty benefit most from day care experience.

If your birth date was 25 years later, in 1950, you would have found a greatly improved situation. Your health, education, and general well-being would have benefitted from many more social reforms for children. After the shock of the Soviet launch of Sputnik I in 1957, millions of dollars were pumped into the American school system in an attempt to keep America technologically competitive with the Soviets. In the 1960s President Lyndon Johnson made preschool health and education a priority of his war on poverty program. But the reforms also brought restrictions. Laws were created to establish how long a child had to remain in school, when working full time was legal; a minimum age for marriage, driving, buying liquor, voting, running for public office, entering into contracts, retiring and receiving social security.

The 1960s were also a turning point for blacks and other minorities. The nation's schools were desegregated by the United States Supreme Court. In addition, the 1965 Civil Rights Act prohibited discrimination against minorities in employment. Thus, in principle, minorities could achieve equal opportunities in education and employment.

Adding yet another 25 years brings us close to the actual birth date of many of you. Your generation has

benefited more than any other so far from the socioeconomic reforms that have taken place in this century. But much remains to be done. Minorities still are not receiving the equal opportunities they have been promised. More than 10 million American children are poor. They are better off than poor children of a century ago, but many are not receiving adequate health and education services (Edelman, 1981). Achievement scores are declining in our schools. Minimum age laws for drinking have been enacted, but not to the satisfaction of everyone.

Would you like to promote the best possible developmental environment for the next generation, the one that will include your children? If so, you will find much of relevance in this chapter and the next. To get the most out of what you are about to read, you might want to ask yourself about how the information can be applied. For example, are middle-school and high-school students being challenged at, above, or below their cognitive competence? Are they being challenged at, above, or below their social competence? If the level of challenge is not appropriate, what can be done? Are social reforms influenced by developmental psychologists? Are developmental psychologists influenced by social reforms?

one child. Surely there are problems with doing so, especially when circumstances are as unusual as Raun's. But are any methods used to study development completely trustworthy?

Longitudinal versus Cross-Sectional Research. In **longitudinal research** investigators periodically test the same person or group of people over a period of time. In **cross-sectional research** investigators compare the responses of people of different ages, education, ethnic background and economic status; all studied at the same time. Each method has both advantages and disadvantages:

1. *Measuring stability of behavior* is a main advantage of longitudinal research. For example, Schaie & Geiwitz (1982) reviewed studies on verbal abilities. The question was whether or not a person's verbal abilities remain stable with age. Figure 9–1 shows that the answer depended on the study method. Cross-sectional methods suggested that verbal abilities decline with age, but longitudinal methods indicated that they remain stable or even improve. Which answer should we accept? We cannot accept the cross-sectional answer about this or any other question about stability. The cross-sectional method should not be used to measure stability over time because it does not measure the same people at different ages. The longitudinal method measures the same people repeatedly and can therefore determine whether their performance changes.

2. *Control of cultural and historical experiences* is a closely related advantage of longitudinal methods. Each person accumulates his or her own experiences as he or she moves through a longitudinal study. In contrast, cross-sectional studies compare people who may have had very different experiences. The people are different, therefore, not only in age, but also in experiences. In the cross-sectional studies of verbal abilities, for instance, the different age groups were different in education. The

Longitudinal research
Research in which the same person or group of people is tested over a period of time. An example would be studying the same group of people from their birth until they were in their twenties. Compare with *cross-sectional research*, in which a number of people of different ages are tested at one time.

Cross-sectional research
Research in which people of all different ages are tested in various ways; compare with *longitudinal research*, in which one group is tested continually over a period of time, at different ages.

FIGURE 9–1

Verbal intelligence scores drop with age in cross-sectional studies but not in longitudinal studies. (Schaie & Strother, 1968)

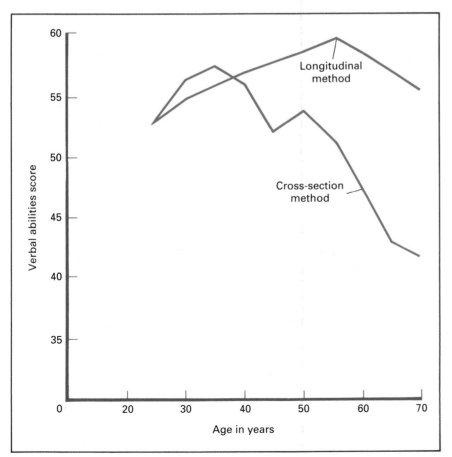

older subjects had lower verbal abilities because they had had less education. Longitudinal studies provide better answers about stability because they have better control over experience.

3. *Loss of subjects*, however, is a disadvantage of longitudinal methods. People die, move away, or quit. These losses restrict generality. For example, the longitudinal studies on verbal abilities can only be generalized to people who live as long as those who completed the studies. Those who die younger might have less stable cognitive abilities (Botwinick, 1977). Cross-sectional studies reduce this problem by collecting data over a shorter time period.

4. *Lack of practicality* is another disadvantage of longitudinal studies. The designers of the longitudinal studies on verbal abilities had to answer some difficult practical questions: Can we wait 45 years for our answer? Do we have the time and resources to keep track of the same people for that long? The cross-sectional methods studied the same age range in about a month for much less money.

5. *Flexibility* is another consideration that weighs against longitudinal studies. They are inflexible because they have to hold everything constant over many years. For instance, the longitudinal studies of verbal ability had to use the same tests over 45 years. Verbal ability tests had improved during that period, but the studies had to use their original tests because the design demanded that the same people take comparable tests over time, and the newer tests were not comparable to the older ones. In contrast, the cross-sectional studies were free to use the most up-do-date measures.

No single design is best for every purpose; researchers must select the right design for studying the problem at hand. Ideally, researchers strive to apply both longitudinal and cross-sectional designs to the same problems. They can be more certain that they are on the right track when results from both designs agree. A recent study by Stack and Muir (1990) illustrates the use of both cross-sectional and longitudinal studies to investigate the same problem. These researchers tested how 3- to 9-month-old babies respond to adult touching when the adult's face remains neutral. Both methods agreed that the infants smiled more, grimaced less, and were more content when they were touched. Notice that the disadvantages of the longitudinal method were reduced because of the short time period involved. Notice also that both methods had advantages. The cross-sectional method immediately suggested that these positive effects apply over the entire age range. Six months later, the longitudinal study indicated that the effect is stable for the same individuals. In general, both designs have been valuable in testing theories of development.

Prenatal Development

Prenatal refers to the 9-month period of development before birth. Mothers carry the developing organisms in a hollow muscular organ called the **uterus** or **womb.** In this section we will outline stages of normal prenatal development and discuss environmental forces that affect that development.

Stages of Prenatal Development

Uterus (womb)
Hollow, muscular organ in which a mother carries a fetus in the 9 months before birth.

We can assume from Raun's healthy condition at birth that his prenatal development was normal. He grew from a microscopic cell through a natu-

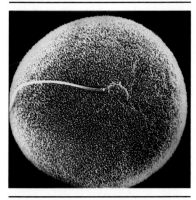

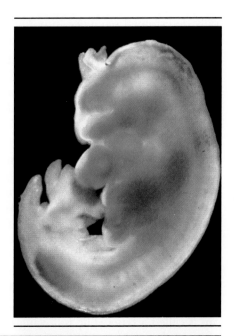

These photos show a fertilized ovum (top, left); an embryo at 4 weeks (top, right), 6 weeks (middle, left), and 8 weeks (middle, right), and a fetus at 4½ months (bottom).

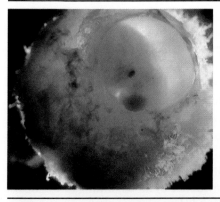

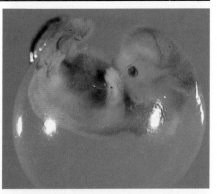

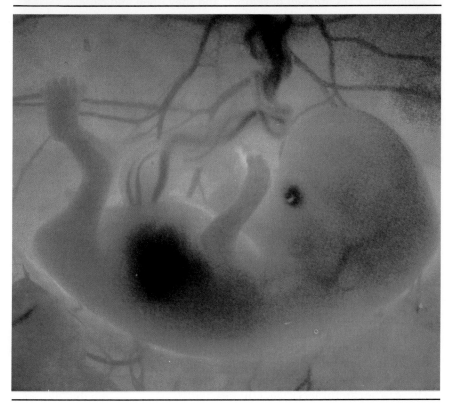

rally determined sequence into a beautiful baby. Let's look at some of the highlights of this stage of development.

Period of the Ovum.   An **ovum** is a mature female sex cell which after fertilization develops into a zygote (see Chapter 2). The first 2-week period of development after fertilization is called the period of the ovum. A fertilized ovum immediately divides, forming new cells that cluster together in a ball, which grows to about the size of a poppy seed, travels down the Fallopian tube, and implants itself in the wall of the uterus.

Period of the Embryo.   From the third week through the eighth week the organism is called an **embryo.** This period is characterized by extremely rapid growth, in which the embryo grows to a weight of about 1 ounce and is about 1 inch long. By that time, the embryo is dependent on the **placenta,** which is a mass of tissue that acts as a special filter to allow for the exchange of food and waste with the mother. The embryo develops internal organs, limbs and separate fingers and toes, a face with a prominent nose, and external sex organs (although it is difficult to distinguish males from females at the end of the second month).

Period of the Fetus.   From the third month through birth the organism is called a **fetus.** The following is a breakdown of this period.

1. By the end of the third month, the heart starts pumping blood through the fetus, and its beat can be heard by a stethoscope. Teeth begin to develop, and males can be distinguished from females.

2. A mother often feels fetal movement during the fourth month. Weight increases to nearly half a pound, and the fetus is about 8 inches long. He or she develops eyebrows, eyelashes, fingerprints, and footprints.

3. During the fifth month the fetus gains another half-pound and grows about 4 inches longer; sucking, swallowing, and hiccuping reflexes develop. It sleeps and wakes.

4. The sixth month adds 1 additional pound and about 2 inches in length. The skin is wrinkled with the first evidence of fat beginning just beneath the skin. Eyes are well developed and they open and close.

5. After 7 months, the fetus reaches the *age of viability*, a time at which the fetus might survive if born prematurely. At this important point, the fetus is about 16 inches long and weighs about 3 pounds, with more fat under his or her skin.

6. Fat continues to develop during the eighth month and the skin loses some of its wrinkles. The fetus gains about 2 pounds and grows another 2 inches longer. The arms and legs move about strenuously, often kicking, or punching the uterine wall. Mothers feel this movement inside them, and others can feel it by placing a hand over the uterus. The fetus will probably survive if it is born after the eighth month.

7. The fetus is fully prepared for birth after the ninth month. Even its behaviors are similar to those of a newborn. Mary Pillai and David James (1990) found similar frequencies of eye, limb, and body movements before and after birth. They used ultrasound recordings to make their observations before birth. This device is similar to a submarine's sonar. It generates moving images of a fetus and stores them on videotape. In addition to being powerful diagnostic and research tools, these tapes are becoming a popular supplement to baby books for proud parents.

Average birth weight is about 7 pounds, and average length is about 20 inches. Genes determine birth size, for the most part. Mothers who eat more because they are "eating for two" find that the extra food is not used by the baby, but is stored in the mother's body as fat. Mothers, however, do have to be careful about what they eat and drink (see Highlight: "Prenatal Environment and Health").

Ovum
Mature female sex cell which after fertilization develops into an offspring. The first two-week period of development after fertilization is called the period of the ovum.
Embryo
Term for a human organism from the third week through the eighth week in the uterus.
Placenta
Special filter used to exchange food and wastes between an embryo and his or her mother.
Fetus
Human organism from the third month through to the time of birth.

Raun started withdrawing shortly after his first birthday. What was unusual about his first year? What factors contributed to his condition? We will analyze normal patterns of development in detail in order to establish a standard for comparison with Raun. We will also discuss the extent to which heredity and environment influence each aspect of development.

Physical Growth

Was Raun's condition related to abnormalities in his physical growth? This question is not easy to answer. We do know that his rate of growth was normal for his age. That is, it followed two simple rules:

1. An infant grows about 1 inch per month in the first 6 months and about ½ inch per month for the rest of the year.

2. An infant should gain about 5 to 7 ounces a week during the first 6 months and 3 to 5 ounces a week during the second 6 months.

Pediatricians and parents routinely measure gains in height and weight because abnormal growth rates can warn of health problems. Some aspects of physical growth such as the development of the nervous system cannot be detected during a routine observation.

The physical growth of the nervous system follows a more complex pattern. Infants are born with an incomplete nervous system. It develops rapidly after birth, slowing down between the second and fourth year. Therefore, the first years are vital to normal neural development. The nervous system at birth is "unfinished" in three ways:

1. The brain we are born with is smaller than it will be later in life. The brain is much nearer to its final size, however, than are muscles and other structures.

2. A newborn's cortex is very underdeveloped. During the first year, new cortical cells are formed, cells become larger, and new interconnections are formed between cells. Parts of the cortex develop at different rates. Areas that control hearing and seeing develop within 6 months, as do areas that control movement of the head, upper trunk, arms, and hands. Areas that control movement of the lower trunk and legs develop slowly over almost a 2-year period. Rosenzweig (1966) found that raising rats in enriched environments (with "toys"—wheels, ladders, platforms, and so on) greatly increases cortical development.

3. Newborns lack some important nerve coverings called *myelin sheaths*, which we discussed in Chapter 2. Development of myelin sheaths, a process called **myelinization,** determines control over body parts. For instance, a child has poor control over lower body parts until spinal cord myelinization reaches a critical stage at about 2 years of age.

The nervous system is most vulnerable to diseases, malnutrition, and other environmental influences while it is developing. Thus, we might wonder whether the development of Raun's nervous system was disturbed, perhaps by the severe dehydration he experienced in early infancy. We cannot, however, rule out other possibilities. For example, Raun might have inherited his condition. Instead of speculating about causal factors, let's continue to compare Raun's condition with normal trends.

Myelinization
Development of myelin sheaths during infancy, childhood, and adolescence.

At the age of 12 months, the average height for an infant is 30 inches and the average weight is 22 pounds (girls tend to weigh slightly less than boys in the first year).

PRENATAL ENVIRONMENT AND HEALTH

Heredity and environment start interacting long before birth. A host of environmental influences can prevent an unborn infant from achieving its full inherited potential. Mothers who take the time to learn some fundamental precautions can provide an optimal prenatal environment for their baby. Let's go over some of the major environmental influences.

Nutrition

A good diet is essential for healthy fetal development, including brain development. A baby's brain can be 60 percent smaller than normal at birth if he or she is seriously malnourished (Wyden, 1971). Doctors emphasize adequate amounts of protein in a pregnant woman's diet, and they prescribe iron and vitamin supplements, being cautious to avoid too much or too little (Truss, 1981). Not much evidence is available on the long-term effects of this kind of program. A study by Barret, Radke-Yarrow, and Klein (1982) suggests, however, that diet supplements given to severely malnourished pregnant women are related to better activity levels, social responsiveness, and expression of emotions of the children at school age. These effects were much greater when the diet supplements were also given to the children for two years after birth.

Diseases

Many diseases, including heart disease, diabetes, and hypertension, hamper fetal development. Mothers are warned to avoid exposure to German measles during early pregnancy; it can cause many birth defects, including impaired vision and hearing, heart malformation, and mental retardation. *Venereal diseases*, which are contagious diseases that are transmitted by sexual intercourse, also have tragic effects (Truss, 1981, see Chapter 10).

Drugs

Drugs taken by the mother during pregnancy can have disastrous effects on fetal development. Those that cause abnormal fetal development are called **teratogens** (from the Greek word for monster). A well-known example is *thalidomide*, a drug once prescribed to calm nervousness (it has been taken off the market). Its use during pregnancy caused serious developmental deformities of the baby's limbs. Many other drugs are dangerous during pregnancy. For example, drugs used in the treatment of epilepsy cause growth and mental deficiencies as well as major deformities (Adams, Vorhees, & Middaugh, 1990).

Mothers can also harm their fetus with "street drugs" such as marijuana, cocaine, and heroin. These drugs impede physical, behavioral, and cognitive development. Physical symptoms include growth deficiencies and abnormal brain development (Hutchings, 1990). Behavioral differences occur during simple movements and during interactions with adults, according to some researchers (Rodning, Beckwith, & Howard, 1989). Researchers have also observed poor cognitive performance during play that required abstract representations. In addition, Fried and Watkinson (1990) found lower verbal and memory scores for 2-year-olds who had been exposed to marijuana prenatally. Other recent findings concern the various kinds of "street drugs." Using multiple drugs is more injurious than using one, and "crack" seems to have worse effects than other forms of cocaine (Kaye, Elkind, Goldberg, & Tytun, 1989). Marijuana delivered through a mother's milk can slow a baby's development (Astley & Little, 1990).

Cigarettes and Alcohol

Prenatal exposure to cigarette smoking and alcohol are also associated with cognitive, physical, and behavioral deficits. Poorer language and cognitive abilities have been observed at 36 and 48 months for infants exposed to cigarettes prenatally. Similar deficits have been observed at 24 and 36 months for infants exposed to moderate alcohol consumption prenatally (Fried & Watkinson, 1990), although these deficits were no longer detectable at 48 months. Physical and behavioral symptoms have been analyzed through careful comparisons of

animals and humans (Driscoll, Streissguth, & Riley, 1990). Animal studies indicate that moderate prenatal alcohol consumption causes brain damage, which is worse when the alcohol is consumed in binges (Bonthius & West, 1990). Thus, a mother's moderate alcohol drinking is unhealthy for a developing fetus. Occasionally pulling the stops out at parties is probably even worse.

Heavy drinking can lead to **fetal alcohol syndrome,** which includes low birth weight, retarded mental and motor development, and physical abnormalities in the heart, face, and joints (Richardson & Day, 1986; Becker, Warr-Leeper, & Leeper, 1990). Learning and attention deficits have been observed in both animals and humans (Driscoll, Streissguth, & Riley, 1990). In addition, Becker and associates observed language disorders in children with fetal alcohol syndrome aged 4½ years to 9½ years. Problems were seen in grammatical, semantic, and memory abilities as well as in articulation.

Radiation

The effects of exposure to X-rays during pregnancy can also be very serious. For example, it can cause mental retardation. Both animal and human studies have indicated that radiation exposure is especially dangerous during fetal brain development (Schull, Norton, & Jensh, 1990). The developing human brain is most vulnerable 15 to 25 days into prenatal development, but brain damage can also occur in the last month of pregnancy. These dangers are well known and precautions are taken. For instance, fertile women are advised to avoid exposure to X-rays except during the first 10 days following the onset of menstruation. The aim is to protect the early prenatal days when a mother may not know that she is pregnant.

Delivery Complications

Most births (over 90 percent) occur without serious complications, but sometimes infants are injured during the birth process. The most serious injuries involve too much pressure on the brain and too little oxygen being supplied to the brain (Blackman,

1989). These disorders occur during stressful deliveries where the head is squeezed too hard or when the baby is cut off from the placenta's nourishment too soon. Both of these factors can cause neurological damage leading to mental deficiencies (Pasamanick & Lilienfeld, 1955). Such injuries can be detected shortly after birth, and deficiencies can still be detected up to about school age, at which time they tend not to be evident (Sameroff & Chandler, 1975).

Assessing a Newborn's Health

Many hospitals assess the condition of newborns with the **Apgar scoring system,** which is shown and described in the table. Low Apgar scores indicate possible neurological damage. Raun had a high Apgar score, suggesting that he did not suffer neurological damage during birth.

Another test given to newborns is the *Brazelton Neonatal Behavioral Assessment Scale,* or the Brazelton Scale for short. It is given every 2 or 3 days, starting with the third day after birth. The Brazelton Scale observes twenty reflexes, as well as reactions to people and other stimuli such as rattles. Fast responding indicates a healthy infant; extreme unresponsiveness suggests brain damage; slow responding suggests the need for rehabilitation training. Brazelton has developed a training procedure in which parents increase their infant's alertness by stimulating them. Brazelton (1987) showed that such training often improves an infant's interactions with its parents and others.

This discussion of risk factors may create a misleading impression that the odds are against a normal birth. In fact, the odds are overwhelmingly in favor of a normal birth. Our species would not have survived if we were unlikely to produce healthy offspring, so the odds have been in our favor for some time. The odds are even greater today, because doctors are continually improving their ability to prevent, detect, and correct prenatal problems. Most parents who enter hospitals to have babies leave for home a few days later to assume full care of a healthy infant. The text examines some of the many developmental changes that take place during the first year of the infant's life.

Sign	0	1	2
Heart Rate	Absent	Below 100	Over 100
Respiratory Effort	Absent	Minimal; Weak Cry	Good; Strong Cry
Muscle Tone	Limp	Some Flexion of Extremities	Active Motion; Extremities Well Flexed
Reflex Irritability (response to stimulation on sole of foot)	No Response	Grimace	Cry
Color	Blue or Pale	Body Pink; Extremities Blue	Pink

The infant is tested at one minute after birth and again five minutes later for the signs listed in the table. The infant's response to each item is scored 0–2. A total score of 7 or better signifies a healthy baby. A score of 4 or less signifies that the baby has a serious physical problem.

Source: Apgar (1953).

Motor Development

Motor development refers to a baby's increasing ability to control muscles in order to move around and to manipulate objects. Raun's motor development did not follow normal patterns. He began on schedule, but he fell behind in areas such as controlling his jaw and tongue. Let's examine the normal pattern and the meaning of deviations from it.

Reflexive Movements. Infants are born with many reflexes, which are movements that are made automatically in response to stimuli (Sheppard & Mysak, 1984). The presence or absence of reflexes can indicate normal or abnormal development. Raun's later abnormal development, however, could not have been anticipated by his early reflexive movements, which were normal.

Some reflexes are protective, such as *coughing* and *sneezing*, which clear the respiratory tract. Other reflexes are involved with eating such as swallowing. The **rooting reflex** causes infants to turn their head toward anything that touches their cheeks. It helps in feeding because it moves the mouth closer to a nipple. The **sucking reflex** causes sucking when anything touches the lips. It is, of course, essential for getting milk from a breast or bottle. Four other common reflexes are:

Teratogens
Drugs taken by the mother during pregnancy that cause abnormal fetal development.

Fetal Alcohol Syndrome
Postnatal birth complications caused by a mother drinking heavily during pregnancy. The condition is identified by low birth weight and developmental abnormalities.

Apgar scoring system
Scale used to assess the condition of newborns; low scores show possible neurological damage.

Rooting reflex
Causes infants to turn their head toward anything that touches their cheek.

Sucking reflex
Causing sucking in infants when anything touches the lips.

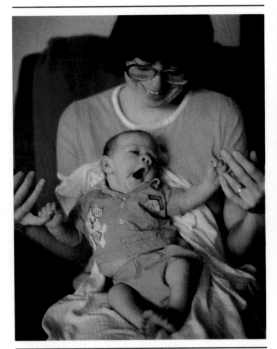

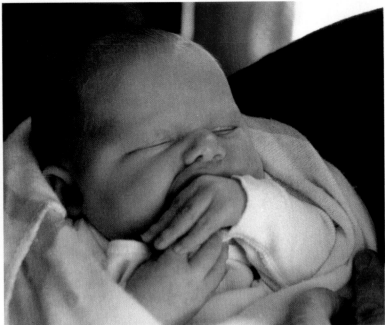

(Top, left) The grasp reflex causes infants to close their fingers tightly around anything that touches their palm.

(Top, right) The sucking reflex causes the baby to suck when anything touches the lips.

(Bottom) In the tonic neck reflex, when the head is turned to one side, infants who are lying on their back move their arms and legs into a "fencing" position.

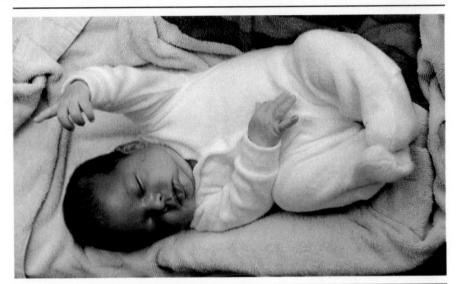

Grasp reflex
Causes infants to close their fingers tightly around an object that touches the palm.
Dancing reflex
Causes infants to prance with their legs in a "tip-toe" stepping motion when they are held upright with feet touching a surface.
Moro reflex (also called the **startle reflex**)
Causes a motor reaction of infant's arms, legs, and trunk in response to a sudden loud noise or loss of support.

1. The **grasp reflex,** which causes infants to close their fingers tightly around an object that touches their palm (thumbs do not respond in this reflex). An infant's grip is so strong that you can insert your index fingers into a newborn's palms and then lift the baby into a standing position. The reflex is present at birth, but disappears at about 6 months after conscious control takes over grasping.

2. The **dancing reflex,** which causes babies to prance with their legs in a "tip-toe" stepping motion when they are held upright with feet touching a surface. (Perhaps there is some truth to the saying that we are "born to boogie.") This reflex is usually no longer seen by the seventh or eighth month.

3. The **Moro reflex** or **startle reflex,** which causes a motor reaction of infants' legs, arms, and trunk in response to a sudden loud noise or loss of support. You can observe it best by suddenly slapping a baby's

mattress. The newborn will draw up his or her legs with the soles of the feet turned toward each other. The arms will stretch out into an embracing position, and the back will arch. This reflex disappears by the fifth month.

4. The **tonic neck reflex,** which causes infants who are on their back to move their arms and legs into a "fencing" position when the head is turned to one side. Newborns extend the arm and leg on the side that they are facing and draw up the other arm and leg into a flexed position. This reflex disappears by the fourth month.

The lack of any of these reflexes at birth can mean that there is an abnormality in the nervous system. Continuation of these reflexes for too long after they should have disappeared can also be a sign of abnormal neural development.

Voluntary Movements. A major accomplishment in the first year of life is the replacement of motor reflexes with voluntary motor control. This achievement greatly increases an infant's ability to explore its environment. A baby begins to successfully reach for and grasp objects at about 4 or 5 months of age. One-year-olds like to feed themselves with their fingers, and they are able to scribble with a crayon.

Figure 9–2 summarizes landmark achievements in infant mobility. Some infants reach each stage ahead of others but all infants go through all these stages in the same order. Most babies learn to roll over sometime between the second and fifth month, and many walk alone by the end of their first year. Raun showed no significant deviations from this schedule.

Tonic neck reflex
Causes infants who are on their back to move their arms and legs into a "fencing" position when the head is turned to one side.

FIGURE 9–2
This diagram shows some landmarks in an infant's ability to move around. Each line shows the age range, and the "X" shows the average age, at which the achievement occurs. (Frankenburg & Dodds, 1967)

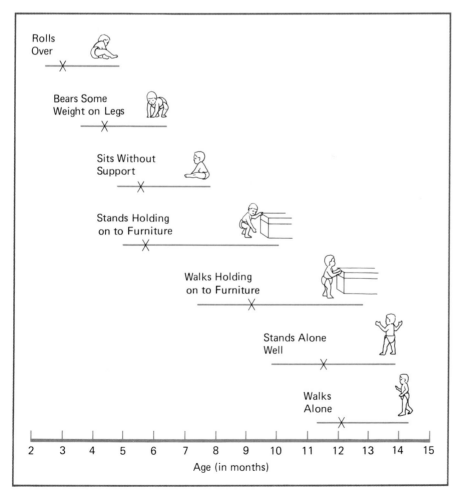

Self-produced locomotion changes an infant's sensorimotor world as he or she struggles to maintain balance against the pull of gravity (Bertenthal & Bai, 1989). It also gives babies new freedoms and restrictions. They are freer to explore new people and places that grab their attention. Every parent and older brother or sister knows that newly mobile babies love to get into things. As they do, they discover that their exciting explorations are regulated by disappointing restrictions. Therefore, self-locomotion changes more than a baby's sensorimotor world. It also changes the baby's attention, as well as his or her social and emotional worlds (Bertenthal & Campos, 1990).

A baby's first year is also important for perceptual development, which was discussed in Chapter 4, and cognitive development, which will be discussed in the next section on childhood.

Childhood

The rapid growth rate of the first year continues through the second year. Then it slows down until the end of childhood, when it increases again. Children usually grow about 3 inches and gain about 5 pounds per year between their third birthday and the beginning of adolescence. In addition to growing physically, children between the ages of 2 and 13 make important gains in cognitive development, as well as in social and personality development. We will consider normal development in these areas and then examine Raun's patterns.

Cognitive Development

Cognitive development involves changes in how children understand and think about their world as they grow older. This section will review evidence that children understand and think about their world in qualitatively different ways as they pass through various stages of cognitive development. The data on normal development provide a frame of reference for evaluating abnormalities. Studies have found, for instance, that a delay in mastering cognitive skills, such as Raun experienced, is characteristic of autistic children (e.g., Waterhouse & Fein, 1984).

Piaget's Approach. As we discussed earlier, American behaviorists in the early years limited their research to discovering relationships between stimuli and observable responses. Their theories held that learning at all ages can be explained without considering what goes on in a person's mind. In contrast, Jean Piaget made observations precisely in order to figure out what goes on in a child's mind. He argued that (1) we cannot understand learning without understanding thinking, and (2) that children think differently from adults. We will cover his methods and theories in detail, because they had a tremendous impact on modern psychology.

Piaget used open questioning sessions with his own three children and with other children to find out how they interpreted objects and events in the world around them. He concluded that children of the same age make similar incorrect responses, which are different from errors made by both older and younger children. This pattern of errors suggested that children develop qualitatively different ways of organizing and responding to experiences. He used the term **schema** to refer to a mental structure that organizes responses to experience. He proposed that newborns inherit *schemas*, which are simple reaction patterns and reflexes, such as a sucking

Schema (plural, **schemata**)
Term used by Piaget to refer to a mental structure that organizes responses to experiences.

schema and a grasping schema. Gradually, these independent schemas become integrated through the process of *organization,* an inherited predisposition to organize simple schema into higher-order ones. A higher-order schema would control a response pattern for grasping a bottle, bringing it to the mouth, and drinking it, for example.

A child also inherits two other processes: (1) **assimilation,** which is the process of responding in a way that fits existing schemas; and (2) **accommodation,** which is the process of adjusting a schema to fit environmental demands. Consider a baby with a schema to control bringing a bottle to his or her mouth. Suppose a bottle was placed behind a plexiglass barrier. The barrier allowed the baby to see the bottle, but did not allow the baby to reach the bottle directly. Assimilation would be shown if the baby responded according to its existing schema, that is, if the baby tried to reach directly for the bottle. Accommodation would be shown if the baby changed its schema by reaching around the barrier.

Piaget (1960) is perhaps most famous for his assertion that the sequence of cognitive development is divided into a series of stages. He assumed that stages are organized around a dominant theme and that each stage contains qualitatively different behaviors. He did not claim that all children go through stages at exactly the same ages, but he did state that all children go through the same stages in the same *order,* and he identified four stages.

1. The **sensorimotor stage** extends from birth to about 2 years. Its main theme is discovering relationships between sensations and motor behavior. As we mentioned earlier, children replace reflexes with voluntary actions during the first 2 years. At first, reflexes supply the means for infants to gain nourishment by sucking. Later they learn that they can grasp a bottle and bring it to their mouth at will. They learn that they can cause other sensations as well, such as sucking, banging, or shaking a rattle.

   You could easily modify the cookie test devised by Raun's father to use with an infant who is in the first 4 months of the sensorimotor stage. Simply place a favorite toy in front of the infant. He or she will express interest by looking, moving both arms, and so on. Now, drop a screen in front of the toy, hiding it from view. The infant will act as if the toy no longer exists! He or she will not search for it visually or manually (out of sight, out of mind). Piaget claims that infants act this way because they lack the concept of **object permanence,**

Assimilation
Term used by Piaget to refer to the process of interpreting events in a way that fits existing ideas (or schema). Compare with *accommodation.*

Accommodation
Term used by Piaget to refer to the process of adjusting one's schema to fit environmental demands. Compare with *assimilation.*

Sensorimotor stage
One of Piaget's stages of cognitive development, extends from birth to about 2 years of age. Main theme is discovering relationships between sensations and motor behavior.

Object permanence
Knowledge that objects continue to exist even when they can no longer be experienced.

If a screen is put in front of a toy, blocking it from view, infants in the first 4 months will act as if the toy no longer exists, and will not try to find it behind the screen. Piaget says infants do this because they do not yet have the concept of object permanence.

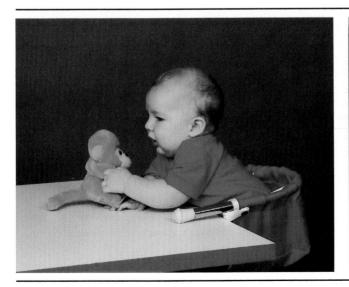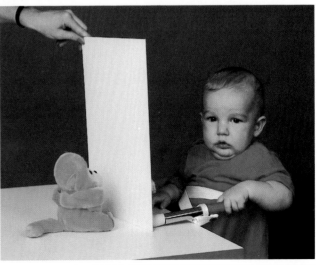

which is knowledge that objects continue to exist even when they can no longer be experienced.

An alternative explanation is that infants know that hidden objects exist but don't know how to search for them. This view is supported by experiments with tasks that do not require a search. In one study, Baillargeon (1987) inferred knowledge of a hidden box from the time that 4½-month-olds spent looking at two events. Both events started with a drawbridge lying on a stage between the infant and the box. The infant could see the box when the drawbridge was in this flat position. The drawbridge then rotated up until it stood vertically on the stage. At this point, the drawbridge hid the box. During one event, it continued to rotate back until it hit the box. Then it reversed direction and rotated until it was down again. During a second event, the box was secretly removed so the drawbridge could rotate through the space where it had been. It rotated all the way to the stage floor, reversed direction, and returned to its original position. When the drawbridge was vertical for the second time, the box was secretly returned. Infants, therefore, saw the box when the drawbridge returned to its original position. The first event is possible and the second one is impossible if one assumes that the box remains in place. Baillargeon inferred that infants make this assumption because they spend more time looking at the second event. This experiment and similar ones (Haith & McCarty, 1990) suggest that infants know the existence of hidden objects long before they know how to search for them.

Infants usually start searching for concealed objects somewhere between 8 and 12 months of age. In contrast, Raun did not start reaching for a hidden cookie until he was about 21½ months old. Apparently his development of object permanence was delayed until then.

2. The **preoperational stage** extends from about 2 to 7 years of age. Its dominant theme is discovering *operations*, which are plans, strategies, and rules for solving problems and for classifying information. Preoperational children have the basic mental abilities for doing mental operations: They can form mental images and they can represent things symbolically with words. Judy DeLoache (1987) showed, for example, that 3-year-olds can use words and symbols to find a hidden toy. She hid the toy in a room and in a model of the room. She showed the children the model and told them to go find the toy in the same place in the real room. The 3-year-olds went right to the toy. In contrast, 2½-year-olds searched all over the real room even though they had been shown the hiding place in the model. Thus, sometime between 2½ and 3 years of age, preoperational children learn how to use words and models as symbols. But preoperational children are only beginning to discover the logical mental operations that will characterize their later thinking.

Their immature thinking leads to unique responses, which you might observe during an interview. Striking up a conversation about the sun might reveal two characteristics of preoperational thought: *animism*, which is the tendency to attribute life to inanimate objects, and *egocentrism*, which is the belief that everything is centered around one's self. The following conversation between Piaget and a child illustrates both characteristics (Piaget, 1960, p. 215):

Piaget: Does the sun move?
Child: Yes, when one walks it follows. When one turns around it turns around too. Doesn't it ever follow you too?
Piaget: Why does it move?
Child: Because when one walks, it goes too.
Piaget: Why does it go?

Preoperational stage
One of Piaget's stages of cognitive development; lasts from 2 to 7 years of age. Main theme is discovering mental operations, which are plans, strategies, and rules for solving problems and for classifying.

Child: To hear what we say.

Piaget: Is it alive?

Child: Of course, otherwise it wouldn't follow us, it couldn't shine.

Another characteristic of preoperational thought is lack of *conservation*—a lack of the understanding that amounts do not change when shapes change (e.g. Madden, 1986). For example, if you rolled out a ball of clay into a log shape, the preoperational child would say that the log has more clay than the ball. If you spread out a row of five chocolate candies next to a bunched-up row of five pieces, this same child would say that the longer row had more candy, and he or she would be much happier to get it as a prize (Halford & Boyle, 1985). If you poured orange juice from a short wide glass into a tall, narrow one, the child would say that the taller glass has more juice in it. Again, he or she would be much happier to have the taller glass, even after watching you pour the liquid from one glass to the other without adding a drop.

3. The **concrete operational stage** extends from about ages 7 to 11. Its main theme is extending mental operations from concrete objects to purely symbolic terms. Concrete operational children have learned most of the principles of conservation, which means that they correctly use mental operations about concrete objects. They also use operations to form mental maps of their environment. Although preoperational children can find their way to a friend's house by learning a specific place to turn, they do not have an overall picture of their surroundings. Concrete operational children, on the other hand, can draw maps of their environment. They are only beginning to form operations about abstract concepts, however, so their reasoning process differs from those of older children and adults.

For example, concrete operational children would have much more trouble than an adult with the following problem:

Andy, Bob, Charles, and Doug are close friends. How many groups of two, three, or four of these friends can be formed with Andy in each group? In a few minutes, you would be able to figure out that the answer is 7, as follows:

1. Andy, Bob
2. Andy, Charles
3. Andy, Doug
4. Andy, Bob, Charles
5. Andy, Bob, Doug
6. Andy, Charles, Doug
7. Andy, Bob, Charles, Doug

Concrete operational children would probably find this problem to be very difficult for two reasons. First, they have trouble thinking about hypothetical examples. They might wonder why Andy gets to be in every group, for instance, even though that is irrelevant to solving the problem. Second, they have trouble thinking of all the possible combinations of things. Furthermore, cognitive limitations would reduce concrete operational children's ability to benefit from feedback in trying to learn how to do tasks (Gruen, Offenbach, & Keane, 1986). The ability to consider many possibilities readily and to benefit from feedback doesn't come until the last stage of cognitive development.

4. The **formal operational stage**, Piaget's last stage, extends from about 13 years of age on into adulthood. Its main theme is the ability to consider many possible solutions to a problem and the ability to systematically test those possibilities. Formal operations are required to under-

One characteristic of preoperational thought is lack of conservation—a lack of the understanding that amounts do not change when shapes change. To test this, Piaget poured water from a short wide glass into a tall narrow glass and asked if the amount of water was the same. Preoperational children tend to say that there is more water in the taller glass.

Concrete operational stage
One of Piaget's stages of cognitive development; lasts from 7 years to 12 years of age. Main theme is extending mental operations from concrete objects to purely symbolic terms.

Formal operational stage
One of Piaget's stages of cognitive development; lasts from about 13 years of age through adulthood. Main theme is the ability to consider many possible solutions to a problem and the ability to systematically test those possibilities.

stand many of the concepts introduced in this text. They are also required to understand many concepts introduced in our everyday lives. For example, TV, radio, and other media have tried to help us understand acquired immune deficiency syndrome (AIDS). How well do teens grasp AIDS-related concepts? It depends on their operational reasoning ability. Candia Peterson and Lisa Murphy (1990) tested Piagetian operational reasoning in 163 Australians aged 12–17. The teens then completed a questionnaire that measured their AIDS knowledge, AIDS fears, and sexual knowledge. Reasoning level was significantly related to all these measures. Advanced reasoning was linked to better knowledge and realistic fear.

Critical Periods.   Piaget's stages suggest that cognitive development unfolds during interactions with the environment according to a genetically determined plan. Even better evidence that heredity and environment interact comes from a phenomenon called **critical period,** which is a stage of development during which an organism must have certain experiences or it will not develop normally. One clear demonstration of critical periods was done in studies of vision in kittens. In one study, Hubel and Wiesel (1970) sutured closed the eyelids of kittens to deprive them of visual stimulation for controlled periods of time.

They varied the age of the kittens at the beginning of deprivation and they manipulated the length of deprivation. The kittens learned to get along quite well while they were deprived. But, depending on the timing, deprivation sometimes caused permanent damage to the kitten's visual system. Hubel and Wiesel tested development of the visual cortex by placing tiny electrodes in cells of anesthetized kittens (see Chapter 2). Deprivation damaged cortical cells only if it came between the fourth and twelfth week of life. Deprivation in kittens younger than 4 weeks caused no noticeable damage, nor did deprivation in kittens older than 12 weeks, even if it lasted for months. In contrast, 3 to 4 days of deprivation during the fourth and fifth week of life caused irreversible damage. Weeks 4 through 12 bound a critical period during which kittens must have visual experience or else their visual system will not develop normally.

We cannot explain critical periods without assuming that heredity

Critical period
Stage of development during which the organism must have certain experiences or it will not develop normally.

Smiling is an often studied social response. Social smiles begin to appear between 3 and 8 weeks of age.

(maturation) and environment (learning) interact. Genes regulate a time-table that determines the critical period for developing cortical cells. The environment must then provide certain experiences, or development will be knocked off track. Traits that interest psychologists, such as intelligence, personality, emotions, and disorders, are generally influenced by both heredity and environment. We will therefore pay attention to both factors when we follow the course of human development in this and the next chapter.

Personality and Social Development

Raun's withdrawal demonstrated that personality and social development include many other behaviors such as smiling and hugging. We will discuss some of these other behaviors in this section.

Smiling: An Early Social Response.   Both heredity and environment influence smiling, an often studied social response. Evidence suggests that genetic factors influence the age at which infants start social smiles. Not all smiles are social responses. Infants sometimes smile, for instance, as a reflex when someone strokes their lips (Gewirtz, 1965). Smiles are not considered to be social responses until they are elicited by social stimuli, such as faces and voices. Social smiles start between 3 and 8 weeks of age. Fraternal twins, who have different genotypes, start smiling at different ages; identical twins, however, who have the same genotype, start smiling at similar ages. The higher correlation of starting age for identical twins suggests that genes influence the onset of social responses. Environmental conditions also influence early social responses. Institutionalized infants decrease their smiling rate when they receive little social stimulation. They smile more again when caregivers play with them regularly (Brackbill, 1958; Dennis, 1973). There are probably many aspects of the interactions that make a difference. Seeing smiling faces might be one factor, since blind babies who interact with their mother smile less than sighted babies (Fraiberg, 1980).

Attachment.   Heredity and environment also interact to determine other social behaviors. An important one is **attachment,** which is the tendency of youngsters to seek closeness to certain people. In our historical overview, we already discussed the work of Konrad Lorenz, who found that goslings become attached to the first moving object that they see during their first 24 hours. Other animal research suggests that this might be a critical period for the development of attachments. Hess (1958) showed, for example, that ducklings are most likely to form attachments during their first 14 hours of life; after 2 days, attachment will probably not occur. A critical period in the formation of human attachment is not easy to identify, if it exists at all (Stendler, 1952). Human attachments normally develop in a series of three steps during the first 6 months of life: (1) infants first begin to show a preference for any human over any object; (2) they then show a preference for familiar people over unfamiliar ones; and (3) finally, they become attached to certain people, usually their mother or other primary caregiver. These attachments provide a foundation for social and personality development. Raun's development in this area was disrupted when he withdrew into his own world. At that point, his parents turned to the psychological literature to determine how to reach him. We will review some of these important works on attachment.

Cross-Cultural Comparisons.   The three-step pattern of developing attachments is found not only in Western society (Schaffer & Emerson, 1964), but also in cultures with greatly different child-rearing practices, such as Africa (Ainsworth, 1963; Kermoian & Leiderman, 1986), a Hopi Indian reservation (Dennis, 1940), and Japan (Takahashi, 1986). This devel-

Dr. Konrad Lorenz discovered that goslings become attached or imprinted on the first moving thing that they see after they hatch. Usually that's their mother, who is then followed wherever she goes. But in this case it was Dr. Lorenz himself who was the imprinting figure.

Attachment
Tendency of youngsters to seek closeness to certain people.

In Dr. Harry Harlow's studies, infant monkeys became attached to a terrycloth "mother" and their typical response when frightened was to cling to it. This occurred even if the infants had only been fed by a less cuddly wire "mother." Harlow concluded that contact comfort rather than feeding determines attachment.

opmental consistency across different cultures suggests that genes play a role in developing attachments (Bowlby, 1973). Environmental factors are also important, especially in determining the choice of attachment figures and the quality of attachment.

Determining Factors.   Early theories on attachment held that a mother's presence becomes satisfying because it is associated with food. Accordingly, attachments should develop only to those who provide nourishment. This prediction was challenged in famous experiments on attachment in monkeys. Harlow and Zimmerman (1959) raised monkeys in the presence of two artificial mothers. One substitute "mother" had a bare wire body and the other had a cuddly terrycloth body. Either one could supply milk from a bottle attached to the "chest." No matter which one provided food, infant monkeys became attached to the terrycloth "mother." They clung to the cloth substitute, for example, in strange environments or in other stressful situations. Harlow and Suomi (1970) showed that infant monkeys also prefer artificial mothers that rock over ones that don't move, and they prefer warm substitute mothers over cold ones. The fact that the mother provides food is neither necessary nor enough to establish attachment.

This conclusion also applies to human infants. Although attachments usually form between infants and their primary caregiver, it is not the giving of routine care, as such, that determines choice of attachment figures. A father who responds appropriately to his child in play is more likely to be an attachment figure than a mother who limits her interactions to mechanical feeding and cleaning (Schaffer & Emerson, 1964). You are more likely to become an infant's attachment figure if you provide appropriate visual, auditory, and tactual stimulation, and if you are responsive to smiles and to other social signals (Gewirtz, 1965; Kiser, Bates, Maslin, & Bayles, 1986).

Mary Ainsworth and her colleagues emphasize the importance of responsiveness of the mother to the infant's needs. Ainsworth (1973) analyzed mother's responsiveness to their babies in several situations, including face-to-face play and feeding. Responsive mothers continually adjust their actions to maintain their baby's attention in play. They also respond to their baby's hunger, allowing the baby to influence when feeding begins, its pacing, and when it ends. One study periodically observed the same infants from birth to about 1 year old (Ainsworth, 1967). The experiment used a method called the *strange situation procedure*, in which researchers unobtrusively observe an infant in the presence or absence of several combinations of the child, mother, and a stranger. This procedure has played a central role in studies of infant-caregiver relationships (Sroufe, 1985). In the original study, attachments were divided into two categories:

1. Some infants were characterized as *securely attached*. They sought closeness and contact with their mother, but they did not whine and cling. They were not too disturbed by brief separations, and they enthusiastically greeted their mother's return with hugs and affection.

2. Other infants were characterized as *anxiously attached*. If they had any interest in contact with their mother at all, it was often ambivalent. They would seek her contact, and then reject and push her away, especially after she returned from a brief separation. These babies were often upset in the presence of a stranger, whether their mother was present or not.

The infants were observed for a year, during which time it was clearly indicated that responsive mothers tend to have securely attached babies, and unresponsive mothers tend to have anxiously attached babies. A more recent study suggests that intermediate levels of responsiveness are best. Over- and understimulation can lead to less secure attachments (Belsky, Rovine, & Taylor, 1984). Another recent study videotaped facial expressions of 28 13-month-old middle-class children to determine their emotions during a 3-minute separation in the strange situation procedure. Securely attached and anxiously attached children both showed anger as their dominant emotion to the same extent, but securely attached children expressed more interest and less sadness (Shiller, Izard, & Hembree, 1986).

Early attachments influence a child's later development. Sroufe (1978) argues that "securely attached" infants are more likely to enjoy problem solving at the age of 2 and 3 years; they get more involved in problems and they work on them longer. Lieberman (1977) found that "secure" mother-infant attachments are associated with better relationships with other children. Securely attached children show more sharing or giving and less crying or fighting in social relationships with other children at the age of 3 years. These positive behavior patterns might explain why securely attached children are perceived as more attractive playmates by other children (Jacobson & Wille, 1986). Finally, Slade (1987) found that securely attached 20- to 28-month-old children engage in more symbolic play (make-believe). This is significant because make-believe play during this age period is associated with higher levels of cognitive development (Skolnick, 1986). Apparently, a healthy attachment to parents encourages both curiosity in problem solving and generosity in social relationships with others. We can't be sure whether these are lasting effects of the early attachment or a reflection of continued responsive parenting (Lamb, 1987).

Caregivers who provide stimulation and responsiveness become attachment figures and they can influence later development. Raun's parents carefully controlled the stimulation that Raun received and their responsiveness to him. This approach helped them to reestablish attachments before his second birthday. The parents also significantly influenced Raun's development in other areas by reestablishing other processes as well. We will now discuss some of these other processes.

Identification, Imitation, and Reinforcement. **Identification** is the

Identification
Process of acquiring personality and social behaviors by taking on characteristics of others.

Preschool children often imitate their parents and other family members, as well as TV characters; once they enter school they find other important models in their friends and teachers.

Imitation
Acquisition of knowledge and behavior by watching other people act and then doing the same thing ourselves.
Reinforcement
Event whose occurrence just after a response increases the likelihood that the response will be repeated. See *positive, negative reinforcement*; compare with *punishment*.

process of acquiring personality and social behaviors by taking on characteristics of others. Sigmund Freud felt that identification involves more than just copying. He proposed that when children identify with their parents they unconsciously respond as if they *were* their parents. You might, for example, remember feeling proud when your father or mother received an award, as if you yourself had been honored.

Modern psychologists recognize the importance of copying the behavior of others, but they do not necessarily agree with all that the term "identification" stands for in the Freudian sense. They therefore often use the term **imitation** to refer to the process of copying other people's behavior (Hay et al., 1985). Preschool children in our society often imitate their parents and other family members. They also imitate TV characters. Once children enter school, at the age of 5 or 6, they find other important models in their friends and teachers. A child's tendency to imitate is often reflected in games, as when children dress up in their parents' clothes. Raun's older sister Bryn took the game a step further. She often delighted and amused others by acting out expert imitations of family and friends. Psychologists agree that infants have the capacity to imitate no later than about the end of the first year. Some have claimed that the capacity develops much earlier, but more research is needed to verify this claim (Abravanel & Sigafoos, 1984).

Family members, friends, and teachers influence children not only by modeling behaviors, but also by *reinforcing* them. Praise is often an effective reinforcer. If you praise children for a job well done, you will increase the probability that they will repeat their efforts. **Reinforcement,** then, is another important mechanism for shaping personality and social development.

Now that we know the processes by which people influence development, let's look at some of the important effects these people have on children.

Parents. Mothers and fathers influence almost every aspect of their children's personality and social development. Children adopt their parents' values and standards and try to live up to them even when their parents aren't watching. One area of parental influence that has received much attention concerns the development of **gender roles,** which are a society's approved ways for men and women to behave (see Chapter 10). Societies assign distinctive roles to males and females. Traditionally, American men were expected to be self-sufficient, powerful, and tough, whereas American women were supposed to be dependent, weak, and tender. Those expectations are changing. Today, for example, more and more women are becoming equal wage earners in families, and, in general, men and women are exchanging or sharing many responsibilities. Behavior standards still differ for males and females, however, and parents help transmit those standards.

Parents treat boys and girls differently long before the children realize the difference between sexes. Most children cannot use the labels "boy" and "girl" correctly until about the age of 3 years. The labels are first used on the basis of external differences in dress and hair styles. Children are usually 5 or 6 before they relate their concept of boys and girls to genital differences. Parents, however, start treating boys and girls differently at birth. They describe newborn daughters as *delicate*, *beautiful*, and *weak*. But they describe newborn sons of the same height and weight as *robust*, *coordinated*, and *strong* (Rubin, Provenzano, & Luria, 1974). The descriptions apparently reflect parents' expectations. Parents express their expectancies in other ways as their children grow. Mothers and fathers handle their sons more roughly, protect them less from physical harm, and punish them physically more than they do their daughters (Maccoby & Jacklin, 1974). In addition, both mothers and fathers of firstborn children (11 to 17 month olds) are "more likely to discourage aggression and encourage prosocial behavior in their girls and to encourage household responsibilities and turn-taking games in their boys" (Power & Parke, 1986, p. 331). Parents also model gender roles, of course, and by the age of 6 years children prefer to imitate the parent of the same sex. Parents therefore transmit gender roles both through differential treatment of their sons and daughters and through modeling (Perry, White, & Perry, 1984).

Teachers. Personality and social development are also shaped by teachers who transmit personal attitudes and beliefs in addition to academic lessons (Walter & Ashton, 1980). Teachers shape development both through modeling and through reinforcement (Ringness, 1975). In fact, the roles of reinforcer and model seem to be interrelated. In one study, Portuges and Feshbach (1972) demonstrated that children are more likely to imitate teachers who reward successes as opposed to teachers who punish failures. Both reinforcement and modeling may be responsible for the fact that students of warm and friendly teachers tend to be less aggressive, and to be more conscientious in their attitudes toward school (Cronbach & Snow, 1977). Because it is easier for students to imitate teachers who are similar to them, many think that having more black teachers will cause black students to develop a more positive attitude toward school.

Peers. In the normal course of development between the ages of 1 and 11 years, children steadily decrease their contact with adults and increase their contact with other children, as shown in Figure 9–3 (Wright, 1967). They prefer friends of the same sex, especially between the ages of 8 and 11. "Fitting in" with their friends becomes very important. Children want to conform to the trends established by their peers. They try to be

Gender roles
Society's approved ways for men and women to behave.

Mothers and fathers influence almost every aspect of their children's personality and social development.

WORKING MOTHERS, DAY CARE, AND CHILD DEVELOPMENT

Today, about half of the nation's mothers who have young children work outside the home while their children stay with substitute caregivers. Many of these children stay in day-care centers in which groups of children are cared for by groups of caregivers. The demand for day-care is expected to increase. It is predicted, for instance, that by 1995, 34 million American children will have mothers working outside the home (Hofferth & Phillips, 1987). This trend is also evident in other countries, such as the Soviet Union, China, and Israel. These countries encourage mothers to work full time outside the home while child-care professionals care for their children.

It is important that we determine what effects substitute caregivers will have on our children. Recent literature suggests answers to several important questions.

1. Does day-care experience damage the basic trust and security engendered by the attachment bond between mother and child?

In her book *Mother Care/Other Care*, Sandra Scarr (1986), a leading developmental psychologist, argues that children are biologically pedisposed to cope with a wide variety of life situations. She is very optimistic, therefore, about the effects of good day care. Research supports her optimism, though a few studies have suggested that the day-care experience can reduce the quality of the mother-child relationship (e.g., Belsky & Rovine, 1988). Most studies, however, have found no reduction in quality. For example, one group of researchers compared infants enrolled in day-care centers with infants reared at home (Kagan, Kearsley, & Zelanzo, 1977). They found that day-care did not weaken attachments to mothers. Similarly, Farran and Ramey (1977) observed that although children prefer their day-care teachers over strangers, they still prefer their mothers over their teachers. Further, a mother's satisfaction with her maternal role must be taken into account. High role satisfaction is one of the best predictors of high quality mother-child interactions regardless of a mother's employment status (Lerner & Galambos, 1986).

2. How do multiple attachments to day-care staff and mother affect social development?

On the one hand, some researchers have suggested that children in day-care may be less cooperative with adults (e.g., Schwartz, Strickland, & Krolick, 1974). However, other researchers have found that infants with day-care experience play more with other children and adapt more quickly to new environments (Kagan et al., 1977, Belsky, 1985). It seems to be the quality, not the number, of attachments that makes the difference. Furthermore, a study by Moore (1975) suggests that the positive influence of day-care on peer relationships carries over to the teen years.

3. How does day-care experience influence cognitive development?

A recent review of studies on child care has addressed this question (Scarr, 1984). It seems that cognitive development is determined by a child's background. Children from advantaged backgrounds perform well in school whether they are reared at home or in day-care centers. Children from disadvantaged backgrounds, however, seem to do better in school if they have had experience in day-care centers that provide structured educational programs (McCartney et al., (1985).

4. Does employment status affect the nature of the time parents spend with their children?

Research answers to this question are mixed. One national survey examined the amount of time spent in child-centered activities on weekdays (Timmer, Eccles, & O'Brien, 1985–1986), including reading, conversing, and playing with children. The average amount of time spent daily on these child-centered activities was 8 minutes for fathers, 11 minutes for employed mothers, and 30 minutes for mothers at home full time. Other studies have suggested that employed mothers set aside more uninterrupted time with their children (Pederson, Cain, Zaslow, & Anderson, 1983). Furthermore, when they are with their children, they pay more attention to them and talk more with them (Hoffman, 1984). The surprising thing is how little quality time parents spend with their children, whether or not the mother is employed. This issue will surely generate more research in the future. Quality is also becoming a central issue for day-care centers.

5. What features of day-care will optimize healthy child development?

Most of the research on day care has evaluated high quality day-care centers associated with universities. Little is known about day-care programs in under-privileged areas.

Psychologists have offered a number of suggestions about how to optimize the day-care experience: (1) To avoid severe separation distress, children should be enrolled in day-care either between 1 and 7 months of age or after they are about 18 months old; (2) each caregiver should be responsible for no more than three infants or toddlers; (3) class sizes for older preschoolers should not exceed 12 for 2 and 3 year olds or 16 for 3 to 6 year olds; (4) teachers should be trained in early childhood education; (5) the physical space should be safe and attractive, indoors and out; (6) a variety of play materials should be available; and (7) the children enrolled in the program should be happy and involved (Kagan et al., 1977).

as similar as possible in dress, hair styles, language, and mannerisms. Peers gradually take over more and more both as models and reinforcers.

Suzi Kaufman caught a glimpse of what might have been the start of this process in Raun. Some time after passing the cookie test, Raun hugged a little boy that he met in a park. The boy was startled and cried. Raun mimicked the boy's sad face, and waited for him to stop crying. Raun then reached out and softly stroked the little boy's arm. At about the same time, Raun started playing with his sisters again, as he had done during his first year. These interactions with his sisters also influenced his personality and social development, as we will discuss in the next section.

Brothers and Sisters.   Effects of birth order on personality and social behavior suggest that brothers and sisters (*siblings*) influence development. Firstborn children or only children tend to be more cooperative, conscientious, and cautious than later-born children (Altus, 1966). They also score higher on intelligence tests, go farther in school, and obtain more honors. The sex of older siblings seems to make a difference: For example, boys with older sisters tend to be less aggressive than boys with older brothers (Longstreth, Longstreth, Ramirez, & Fernandez, 1975). Direct interactions between children probably cause some of the effects. Younger siblings, for example, are notorious for being pests to older brothers and sisters. Older children often control their younger siblings through acts of aggression. The aggressive acts reduce an annoyance and are therefore reinforced (Patterson, 1979). Dunn and Kendrick (1982) have found that older children get along with their younger siblings better when they (1) are the same sex, (2) have a positive response when the young sibling is first brought home, and (3) participate in infant care.

Parents also contribute to birth-order effects by treating siblings differently. In one study, researchers found that parents spend more time with firstborn infants and talk to them more (Thoman, Liederman, & Olson, 1972). Parents also exert more pressure on firstborn children to achieve (Rothbart, 1971). Birth order does not affect everyone in the same way, of course. Family situations are different, as are individuals. Consequently, children with older brothers and sisters often have qualities that are associated with a firstborn, and many later-born children have achieved great accomplishments. One example is Georgia O'Keeffe, a famous American artist, whose life story will be told in the next chapter.

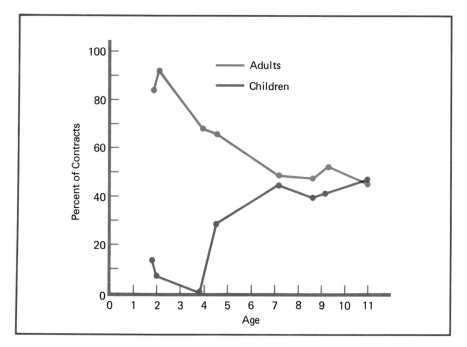

FIGURE 9–3

The graph shows how, between the ages of 1 and 11, children have more and more contact with other children, and less and less contact with adults. (Wright, 1967)

Psychologists have identified a wide variety of severe psychological disorders that occur during childhood. Although the nature of these disorders varies, they tend to show an interesting pattern: Childhood disorders occur with greatest frequency during two rather distinct age periods (Rutter, 1974). The first period is between 6 months and 3 years of age, and the second is during early adolescence (12–14 years of age). These two "high-risk" periods are not confined to American children; research done in Great Britain, Japan, and the U.S.S.R. has also found a strong tendency for childhood disorders to begin during these two periods.

There are many childhood disorders that extend from early childhood through adolescence. We have already considered mental retardation, which can be detected at birth (see Chapter 2 and Chapter 8). We will also discuss eating disorders that occur during the teen years (see Chapter 11). Here we will analyze the characteristics, frequency, causes, and treatments of four disorders that occur during early childhood: (1) infantile autism, (2) childhood schizophrenia, (3) gender identity disorders, and (4) attention deficit disorder with hyperactivity.

Infantile Autism. In 1943, Leo Kanner, a child psychiatrist, observed that some very young infants seemed to live in a world of their own. These infants were suffering from **infantile autism.** They showed no interest in social stimulation. They would not hold eye contact with others and showed no reaction to noise or to people who talked to them. By the age of 18 months or 2 years, when most children begin increasing their vocabulary and interacting with others, these autistic children would not talk and became preoccupied with inanimate objects. They were particularly fascinated with spinning objects and formed attachments to them much as normal children form attachments to other people. These autistic children spent hours on end touching objects or engaging in other motor activities such as rocking back and forth. They developed very rigid schedules and showed strong resistance to change; they refused new foods and new activities.

One of the most serious symptoms of this disorder is self-destructive behavior: Autistic children will often bang their heads on floors and walls with such force that they suffer severe concussions. Because of their failure to develop speech, these children have often been diagnosed as mentally retarded. However, it has been found that although autistic children do show retardation on some skills, they generally do not have subnormal intelligence (DeMeyer, 1976). Because a number of disturbances are involved in autism there has been some disagreement as to the type of disturbance that is most central. Most investigators believe that perceptual or cognitive disturbances make up the core of autism (Wicks-Nelson & Israel, 1984). This conclusion is consistent with Raun's case. Raun was delayed in the development of object permanence as indicated by a hidden cookie test. When he did master this test of object permanence, he developed rapidly.

Autism usually begins during the first year, and certainly by age 3. It is relatively rare, occurring in about 4.5 per 10,000 children. It is four times more likely to be found in boys than in girls, and it is most common in firstborn children. The parents of autistic children are generally in the higher social classes and have above-average intelligence.

What could cause such an unfortunate condition in infants? Most current theories focus on damage to the central nervous system (see Chapter 2 and Cohen & Shaywitz, 1982). Organic diseases that can cause damage to the central nervous system have been associated with autism. For example,

Infantile autism
Infants who from a very early age are withdrawn, do not react to others, and become attached to inanimate objects rather than to people.

This photograph is an artistic interpretation of perceptual disorganization experienced by autistic children. In addition to experiencing perceptual confusion, autistic children live in a world of their own. They are not responsive to other people and they will often spend hours on end engaged in various actions, such as rocking back and forth. One of the most serious symptoms is self-destructive behavior such as banging one's head into a wall.

a child who has encephalitis or meningitis during infancy is more likely to become autistic than a child who has not had these diseases. Other research has found that women who have rubella during their first trimester of pregnancy have a greater chance of giving birth to an autistic child than women who do not contract this illness (Chess, 1971). Present research efforts are aimed at determining how the social environment influences the probability of autism and identifying exactly what nervous system damage leads to autism (Minshew, Payton, & Sclabassi, 1986). Autism is not associated with gross brain damage according to computerized brain scans (see Chapter 2 and Creasey et. al., 1986). Autistic children do, however, seem to have abnormally high levels of endorphins, which are neural transmitters (see Chapter 2 and Gillberg, Terenius, & Lonnecholm, 1985).

The treatment of autism is still in the experimental stage. Drugs have been used with some success (Herman et al, 1986), and behavior-modification programs have been applied to increase the child's language and social skills (Nedelman & Sulzbacker, 1972). Such behavior modifications are long-lasting (Lovaas, 1987). However, the autistic child rarely improves enough to be placed in regular schools. In fact, Stafford-Clark and Smith (1978) report that most autistic children stay in institutions, with only about 10 percent making some social adjustment to life outside the institution.

It was this poor prognosis for autistic children that motivated the Kaufmans to develop a new treatment approach. Success with their son, Raun, brought new hope to the Kaufman family. Their more recent success with other autistic children has extended that hope beyond their family (Kaufman, 1982).

Childhood Schizophrenia. The term *schizophrenia* is applied to a range of disorders that are characterized by disorganization in thoughts, perceptions, communication, emotions, and motor activity (see Chapter 14, "Abnormal Psychology"). Schizophrenic children are sometimes difficult to distinguish from those with infantile autism. A main difference is that schizophrenic children are more socially responsive and emotionally dependent. They also experience hallucinations. The onset of childhood schizophrenia occurs between 2½ and 12 years of age, which is later than the usual onset age for infantile autism. Childhood schizophrenia affects about 6.5 per 10,000 children. The causes and treatments are discussed in Chapter 14, "Abnormal Psychology," and Chapter 15, "Therapy" in relation to adult schizophrenia. The chances of a child or an adult being cured are poor.

Gender Identity Disorders.   Imagine parents' reaction as their rugged young son strides into the living room sporting a dress and hugging a doll. Equally upsetting to some parents is a little daughter who insists on dressing like a cowboy and beating up the little boy next door. We discussed the development of gender roles earlier in this chapter and pointed out that at a certain age these cross-gender behaviors are indeed normal. In fact, it is now recognized that sex-typing children and forcing rigid gender-role behavior on them is inadvisable. But although a rigid view of the role prescribed for one's sex may have undesired consequences, the problems created when people rigidly adopt the role of the opposite sex are even greater. This relatively rare childhood **gender identity disorder** is more often found in males than in females. Boys who suffer this disorder often shun playing with other boys, develop female gestures, and engage solely in female play activities. Girls with a gender disorder join male groups and engage in male play activities. Although it is often difficult to distinguish between a gender disorder and a healthy ability to avoid stereotyped gender-role behavior, the gender disorder is characterized by an exclusive or near-exclusive attraction for the opposite-sex role.

People who have a gender disorder are likely to be ridiculed and rejected by their peers and punished by their parents. These responses often lower the individual's self-esteem and create a great deal of unhappiness. There is disagreement about the cause of the disorder. Some investigators believe that hormone disturbance is responsible. Others argue that the root of the problem lies in the family. Boys who develop the disorder often have mothers who are overly protective, and fathers who are absent or very submissive. In this case, the boy identifies with the mother and begins to model her behaviors. Girls with gender disturbances come from families in which the mother is either absent or cold. Their fathers, on the other hand, are affectionate and serve as their role model. It is likely that future research may show that the disorder results from a combination of hormonal disturbances and family patterns. Gender identity disorders often disappear at an early age. However, in some cases, the disorder persists into adulthood and the individual gains the label of *transsexual* (see Chapter 14).

Attention Deficit Disorder with Hyperactivity.   The ability to concentrate on a task or activity usually increases with age. An **attention deficit disorder** is indicated when children seriously lag behind others their age in this ability. Such children are often described as *hyperactive*, which means that they find it difficult or impossible to reduce their physical activity level. They therefore have great difficulty concentrating on any work or play that requires them to sit still (Lambert, 1988). Their behavior often exhausts and annoys caregivers and teachers. In elementary schools about 3 percent of females and 9 percent of males are hyperactive.

The causes of attention deficit disorders and hyperactivity are not well understood. Possibilities include "allergies, family conflicts, head injuries, complications during prenatal development and birth, malnutrition, early exposure to toxins, viral infections, delayed brain maturation, or genetics"

Gender identity disorder
Disorder that can occur in childhood, when a child rigidly adopts the role and outlook of the opposite sex.
Attention deficit disorder
Inability of a child to concentrate on a task for the same length of time as another child of the same age.

(Kalat, 1988). Researchers have not yet determined how these factors operate individually or in combinations.

Stimulant drugs are the most common treatment for attention deficit disorder with hyperactivity (Solanto, 1984). Many children with this disorder are subdued by these drugs. This effect is unusual, since the same drugs usually increase arousal and activity in normal adults. Current research is aimed at testing how neural transmitters might be involved in these effects (Zometkin, Rapoport, Murphy, Linnoila, & Ismond, 1985). Recent research also suggests that a small minority of hyperactive children (10 percent or lower) are helped by a diet free from artificial food additives such as colorings and flavorings (Weiss, 1982).

The diagnosis of childhood disorders can be very difficult because of natural differences in the maturation process (Gibbs, 1982). However, the proper and early diagnosis of such disorders is very important for two reasons. First, early diagnosis can lead to early treatment, which will improve the child's chances of making a satisfactory adjustment. Second, a correct diagnosis can have long-term consequences for the child. In many cases, the diagnosis influences how people react to the child, and these reactions, in turn, encourage certain patterns of behavior from the child. Raun, for instance, was encouraged to practice cognitive skills and to warmly embrace the people and world around him. Today, Raun is a talented and caring teenager, working with his parents to help other autistic children. His victory is a reminder that children can conquer childhood disorders and go on to lead happy, productive lives.

Summary

1. **Human development** is a process by which the genes that we inherit from our parents come to be expressed as specific physical and behavioral characteristics. The goals of developmental psychology are to describe and explain that process in terms of general principles that can be applied to such areas as education, medicine, and parenting.

2. There are four major themes which are important in the study of human development. The first concerns the relative roles of **heredity** and **environment** in shaping development (most modern psychologists recognize that a continuous interaction between heredity and environment determines the important aspects of development). The second theme concerns **continuity** and **discontinuity** of development. The third involves the importance of *early* and *later* experience. The fourth theme concerns **unidirectional pressures** and **reciprocal interactions.**

3. Five theoretical approaches to the study of human development are presented, including functionalism, behavioristic, and psychodynamic. The ethological/organismic approach originated in biology. The lifespan approach is the main approach used in this chapter. Today developmental psychology is a major branch of science.

4. There are two major methods of studying development. **Longitudinal research** involves periodically testing the same person or group of people over a significant period of time. In **cross-sectional research** investigators compare the responses of people of different ages, education, ethnic background and/or economic status, all studied at the same time. Each method has both advantages and disadvantages.

5. Prenatal development refers to the approximately 9-month period of development before birth and is divided into the periods of the **ovum,** the **embryo,** and the **fetus.** A number of factors can influence prenatal development, including nutrition, disease, drug use by the mother, and delivery complications.

6. The next stage of development, from birth to 1 year, is marked by the development of the nervous system, including **myelinization,** which determines control over body parts. Motor development is marked by the disappearance of various **reflexes** that the body is born with, and the development of voluntary movement, such as sitting up, crawling, and standing.

7. Childhood is most notably marked by increases in cognitive development. Piaget studied two processes in children that account for much of this

development: **assimilation** and **accommodation.** As a result of his years of observation and research on children, he divided cognitive development into a series of stages: **sensorimotor** (birth to 2 years), **preoperational** (2 to 7 years), **concrete operational** (7 to 11 years), and **formal operational** (about 13 years and older).

8. A **critical period** is a stage of development during which an organism must have certain experience or it will not develop normally. Critical periods support the belief that heredity (maturation) and environment (learning) interact.

9. An important part of personality and social development in infancy is **attachment,** the tendency to seek closeness to certain people. Attachment normally develops in a series of three steps during the first 6 months of life; the quality of attachment, usually between infant and mother, affects later personality and social development in children.

10. Another important element in personality and social development in childhood is **identification,** which is the process of acquiring personality and social behaviors by **imitating** those around them. Family members, friends, and teachers influence children not only by modeling behaviors, but also by **reinforcing** them.

11. Parents transmit **gender roles** to their children both by treating boys and girls differently from an early age, and by modeling different behaviors for each sex.

12. Psychologists have identified a wide variety of severe disorders that occur during early childhood. The characteristics, frequency, causes, and treatments of four childhood disorders were analyzed including: (1) **infantile autism,** (2) **childhood schizophrenia,** (3) **gender identity disorder,** and (4) **attention deficit disorder** with **hyperactivity.**

Key Terms

accommodation
Apgar scoring system
assimilation
attachment
attention deficit disorder
concrete operational stage
critical period
cross-sectional research
dancing reflex
embryo
fetal alcohol syndrome
fetus
formal operational stage

gender identity disorder
gender roles
grasp reflex
human development
identification
imitation
imprinting
infantile autism
longitudinal research
maturation
Moro reflex (startle reflex)
myelinization
object permanence

ovum
placenta
preoperational stage
reinforcement
rooting reflex
schema
sensorimotor stage
sucking reflex
teratogens
tonic neck reflex
uterus (womb)

SENSING SILENT CUES EMERGES AS KEY SKILL

BY DANIEL GOLEMAN

Unpopularity, poor grades and a host of other problems that afflict schoolchildren may derive from an inability to read the nonverbal messages of teachers and peers, new findings show.

The results are based on a new test that measures nonverbal skills: reading the emotions revealed in tone of voice, for instance, and sensing how close to stand while talking to someone. It is the first such test designed specifically for use with children.

The test assesses a child's ability to read nonverbal messages in several ways. For instance, a child watches 40 slides of children and adults, rating their expressions as happy, sad, angry and so on. The same is done with slides showing various postures and gestures, and with audiotapes of various tones of voice.

The child's ability with nonverbal messages is also measured more actively. In one test, he or she is videotaped while making an expression to communicate the emotion for a hypothetical situation like receiving a long-wanted birthday present. In other tests, the child is told to use only hands and arms to communicate a particular emotion or to read a sentence in ways that express a variety of emotions from happiness to anger.

Studies of more than 1,000 children aged 9 to 11 showed that those who scored lowest on the test tended to be among the least popular in their class. They also tended to do less well academically than other children, even though their intelligence was just as high on average.

The studies found that as many as 10 percent of all children may have problems with nonverbal communication severe enough to impair their social or academic functioning. When trying to make friends, they are typically unable to approach other children without putting them off, and they often unwittingly respond to teachers in ways that get them in trouble.

The test will allow psychologists and school counselors to screen children and identify such deficiencies. Psychologists believe that helping the children improve those skills may save them from serious setbacks in their later social, academic and working life.

Since most of the emotional messages sent between people are communicated nonverbally—by a gesture or tone of voice, say—the inability to read or send such messages adeptly is a major social handicap, said Dr. Stephen Nowicki, a psychologist at Emory University in Atlanta, who developed the scale.

"Because they are unaware of the messages they are sending, or misinterpret how other children are feeling," he said, "unpopular children may not even realize that they are initiating many of the negative reactions they receive from their peers."

For instance, unpopular children may inadvertently communicate overeagerness that their peers misinterpret as aggression, according to a study published by Dr. Nowicki and Carolyn Oxenford this year in The Journal of Genetic Psychology.

Among the problems common in children lacking nonverbal skills, Dr. Nowicki said, is a continual sense of frustration that can lead to depression or apathy.

Result: A Defeatist Attitude

"They get rebuffed and don't know why," Dr. Nowicki said. "In essence, they just don't understand what's going on. They may think they're acting happy but actually appear to others too excited or even angry. They are mystified when other kids are angry in return."

Such children develop a sense that they have little or no control over how people treat them, Dr. Nowicki found. By extension, they feel they lack control over their fate in general. Other research has shown that this attitude leads to a defeatism that undermines children emotionally.

"The look emotionally disturbed, anxious, depressed, angry," said Dr. Nowicki. "But something else is going on. The anger and such don't come from family conflict or other typical sources of emotional disturbance in children. It's an effect of being poor at reading nonverbal messages. If you

teach them to do it correctly, the signs of emotional disturbance appear."

Dr. Nowicki believes that the problem is a leading disability, akin to reading problems. "If a child makes consistent errors in using nonverbal language, such as standing too close when talking to someone or talking too loud or soft," said Dr. Nowicki, "other children will see them as strange and to be avoided." He and his colleagues are using the new test to identify the deficiencies so the children can be tutored in overcoming them.

In one approach, children are trained to read facial expressions. They begin by watching videotapes of expressions and try to tell if the faces are expressing different feelings. Once they are able to distinguish expressions, something many of them cannot do at first, they try to express those same feelings themselves. In this stage, the children are videotaped, then shown what they are doing right or wrong.

Finally, the children try out what they have learned in a controlled situation, showing what they would do, for example, if they met another child they would like to make friends with.

"We've tried the training with 150 children so far, and the results have been quite positive," said Dr. Nowicki, adding that some children have become markedly better at making friends and getting along with their teachers.

The 9- to 11-year-olds Dr. Nowicki has been studying are in an age period that developmental psychologists consider crucial for learning the basic skills of friendship. At this age most children enter an intense relationship with a chum of the same sex. The psychiatrist Harry Stack Sullivan wrote that chums experiment with intimacy and learn patterns that will shape their later intimate relationships. In the same way, Dr. Nowicki says, an inability to read nonverbal messages in these years can lead to failures in mastering basic social skills that will mar later relationships.

Adolescence, Adulthood, and Aging

10

On November 15, 1887, in Sun Prairie, Wisconsin, Ida and Francis O'Keeffe gave birth to their second child and their first daughter, Georgia. Ida and Francis had no way of knowing that their daughter was to become one of the world's outstanding artists. Nobody would have guessed that for many years—nobody, that is, except Georgia herself. At the age of 12, after less than a year of private art lessons, she announced to a friend that she was going to be an artist. In 1976, Georgia reflected back on that statement and wrote in her autobiography that it was inspired in part by a small illustration of a beautiful Grecian maiden in one of her mother's books. She wrote, "I believe that picture started something moving in me that kept on going and has had to do with the everlasting urge that makes me keep on painting."

In March, 1903, Ida and Francis sold their Wisconsin farm and moved to Williamsburg, Virginia. Georgia went to Chatham Episcopal Institute, a girl's boarding school about 200 miles from Williamsburg. There she was lucky to have a sensitive art teacher, Elizabeth May Willis, who let Georgia work at her own pace. Sometimes Georgia worked intensely; at other times she refused to work for days. When others complained about Georgia not working, Willis would reply, "When the spirit moves Georgia, she can do more in a day than you can do in a week" (Lisle, 1980, p. 34).

During the next few years Georgia attended various art schools, and then, when her parents could no longer afford the tuition, she began to earn her own living. She worked first as a freelance illustrator in Chicago (one of the images she created, a bonneted Dutch girl chasing dirt with an upraised broom, is still used today to sell a cleanser); later she taught art and resumed painting.

After one year of studying at Columbia Teacher's College in New York, Georgia accepted a teaching position in South Carolina. During that time, her own dissatisfaction with her art led her to begin to learn all over again. She spent time working only in charcoal. She also corresponded with a friend in New York, Anita Pollitzer, to whom she sent her new work. Pollitzer brought the work to the photographer, Alfred Stieglitz, who, after looking at the charcoals, knew that he had to show them in his gallery. A month later Georgia came to New York and met Stieglitz. That meeting sparked a continuing correspondence which developed into a romance. O'Keeffe finally returned to New York where she became the favorite subject for Stieglitz's photographs. Many critics recognize his photographs of her as the height of his artistic achievement (Lisle, 1980). The couple married on December 11, 1924.

Several years later, at the age of 41, O'Keeffe returned to the West to seek inspiration. She found what she was looking for in Taos, New Mexico. She returned to New York after a few months with enough paintings to put on an exhibition in February, 1930. O'Keeffe returned to New Mexico during the next two summers, each time returning with paintings that amazed New York art critics. They were especially fascinated by paintings of white animal skeletons. Friends worried that the paintings indicated depression and a morbid concern with death. Their concerns proved valid. O'Keeffe suffered a nervous breakdown and was admitted to a hospital on February 1, 1933, at the age of 45.

She left the hospital 7 weeks later, spent a quiet winter with Stieglitz, and then once again headed West. Gradually, O'Keeffe started painting again. Although friends saw in her work signs of a triumphant convalescence, she suffered a brief relapse in 1939. Some attributed her rapid recovery after that to Stieglitz's unwavering support and to the fact that she was now widely recognized as America's most successful female painter.

A combination of factors slowed O'Keeffe down considerably in the 1950s. First, Stieglitz died in 1946 at the age of 82. Even though O'Keeffe had spent many months away from her husband each year, she missed him intensely after his death. Furthermore, his passing put new demands on her time. She put long hours into settling his estate, and she took on the business end of selling her paintings, which Stieglitz had always handled for her.

O'Keeffe made an incredible comeback in the 1960s after taking an around-the-world trip. Her paintings of this period captured her fascination with the extraordinary spectacle of earth and clouds from jet airplanes. At the age of 77 she completed the largest painting of her life, *Sky Above Clouds IV*, a 24' × 8' "chunk of heaven" depicting clouds viewed from above floating off into infinity. She exhibited her new painting in 1966 along with 96 other paintings at the biggest exhibition of her lifetime in Fort Worth. The reviews of her exhibition indicated that, at the age of 78, O'Keeffe had captured the hearts and imaginations of yet another generation of Americans.

O'Keeffe's productivity was slowed once again late in 1971 when she lost her central vision because of an irreversible degenerative eye disease found among the elderly. Her blurred vision stopped her from painting between the ages of 84 and 88. But by 1976, at the age of 89, she again started painting. She proudly stated that her shadowy vision gave her an interesting new way of seeing light and it gave her new painting ideas. By 1980 her paintings were back in the news. Georgia O'Keeffe died in 1986 at the age of 99. Her paintings, however, live on as a testimony to her invincible spirit. ▬▬

After completing this chapter, you should be able to:

Explain the life-span developmental approach to human development.

Review the significant cognitive, social, and physical developments in adolescence.

Discuss Erikson's theory of development and Kohlberg's theory of moral development.

Discuss the commitments and accomplishments that generally occur during adulthood.

Understand the physical and mental changes that occur during late adulthood and the process of adjusting to death.

History and Scope of a Life-Span Approach to Development

Georgia O'Keeffe's career as an artist puzzles those who attempt to classify artists and their works. She joked that critics had tried to place her "in every movement that came along—expressionism, precisionism, regionalism, surrealism, and all the rest—until pop art came along, and then they gave up" (Lisle, 1980, p. 392). She fits no ready niche. In the same way, her incredibly fluid and dynamic life clashes with traditional development theories, which assume that development moves in one direction until maturity, at which point a person remains basically the same until old age causes a decline (Harris, 1957). Such theories do not seem to explain O'Keeffe's life very well. They offer little or no framework for explaining her adaptive responses to life in places as varied as New York City and the desert of New Mexico. They have little to say about the adjustments she made to her husband's death, or about the comeback she made in her career late in life.

A defender of traditional developmental theories might argue that O'Keefe's life is too exceptional to be captured by theories about ordinary people. It is indeed unusual to find so much dynamism in one lifetime. But when we observe people throughout their life span, we find that change is the rule, not the exception. Thus a developmental framework is needed to integrate changes that occur within an individual over time and the differences in such changes between individuals. That need may be met by a **life-span development approach,** which is concerned with the description and explanation of changes in behavior within an individual and differences between individuals from conception to death (Hultsch & Deutsch, 1981, p. 15).

This chapter adopts the life-span approach to development in adolescence, young adulthood, middle age, and old age. If you do not already identify with Georgia O'Keeffe, you may come to feel a bond with her by virtue of being a developing individual. In fact, the life-span perspective on physical, social, and cognitive changes may show you the common themes as well as individual differences running through the lives of all people (see Chapter 9 for a discussion of scientific and social trends that led to this approach).

Life-span development approach
Concerned with the description and explanation of changes in behavior within an individual and differences between individuals from conception to death.

Adolescence, which extends from about age 12 to the late teens, is a time of passage from childhood to adulthood. Georgia's favorite childhood toy was a dollhouse, but she set it aside at about the age of 12. She announced her desire to be an artist at about the same time, marking the beginning of her transition from a dollhouse world to the real world beyond her home. Let's follow some of the many significant events that happened to Georgia during this period and that happen to each of us during adolescence.

Physical Changes

At 12 O'Keeffe looked like a little girl. By the time she was 16, however, she was the very image of herself as a woman. Such a rapid physical transformation is characteristic of adolescence.

Height and Weight. The accelerated growth rate during adolescence (often referred to as a "growth spurt") is apparent in Figure 10–1, which shows average heights and weights for girls and boys from birth to 17 years of age. Girls' growth rate increases earlier than boys, so that most girls are larger than boys between the ages of 11 and 13. Once boys start their growth spurt, however, they rapidly overtake girls. By the age of 17, boys are, on the average, about 4 inches taller and about 17 pounds heavier than girls (Elkind, 1984). Boys and girls also differ in the extent to which their muscles and strength change during adolescence. At the age of 10, girls and boys are generally of equal strength. But, while girls stay about the same strength, boys almost double their strength during their teen years. At the end of the "adolescent growth spurt," at about age 15 for boys, and age 13 for girls, adolescents have adult body proportions.

Puberty and Sexual Characteristics. Adolescence is also associated with **puberty,** the time when sexual reproduction becomes possible. Development occurs in all **primary sexual characteristics,** which are traits directly concerned with reproduction. For instance, girls begin to produce ova and boys start manufacturing sperm. Puberty starts between 11 and 13 for most girls and between 13 and 15 for most boys. (Chumlea, 1982) The timing, however, varies considerably among individuals. **Secondary sexual characteristics** are those traits typical of a sex, but not directly concerned with reproduction. The development of secondary sexual characteristics provides external signs of the approach of puberty.

The first visible sign of puberty for girls is usually breast development, followed by the appearance of pubic hair. The onset of puberty is often assumed to be **menarche,** the beginning of *menstruation*, which is the periodic discharge of blood and tissue from a nonpregnant uterus. However, the ability to reproduce is often not present for 1 or 2 years after menarche. Using menarche as a dividing line is therefore only an approximation.

The first external indicator for boys is growth of the scrotum and appearance of pubic hair. Beard growth is another sign, but this is often delayed for several years. Growth rate and muscular development is the most obvious visible evidence of puberty in boys.

Complex changes in hormones (see Chapter 2) cause both the adolescent growth spurt and the development of sexual characteristics. They also cause behavioral changes, such as interest in the opposite sex (Nottelman and Susman, 1985). In addition to behavioral changes, there are important psychological and social changes that take place during adolescence.

Adolescence
Passage of time from childhood to adulthood that extends from about age 12 to the late teens.

Puberty
The time in adolescence when sexual reproduction becomes possible.

Primary sexual characteristics
Traits directly concerned with sexual reproduction; the production of live ovum by girls and live sperm by boys.

Secondary sexual characteristics
Traits typical of a sex, but not directly concerned with reproduction; for girls, the development of breasts and pubic hair; for boys, growth of the scrotum, pubic hair, and a beard.

Menarche
Beginning of menstruation, which marks the onset of puberty for girls.

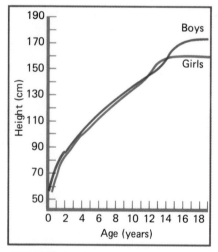

FIGURE 10–1

The graph here shows average heights and weights for girls and boys from birth to 17 years. Note that on the average the adolescent growth spurt occurs earlier for girls than for boys. (To convert cm to inches, use 2.54 cm per inch. 110 cm equals 3.6 ft; 150 cm equals 4.9 ft and 170 cm equals 5.6 ft.) (Tanner, 1978)

The timing of the adolescent growth spurt, as well as the onset of puberty, varies among individuals.

Cognitive and Moral Development

Moral development refers to principles of right and wrong in behavior. Societies have rules about the rightness and wrongness of behaviors, and various authorities enforce a society's rules through rewards and punishments. Parents rely heavily on such external controls to maintain appropriate behaviors in children. Teenagers require less supervision because part of

Most teenagers know the principles of right and wrong, but their development of moral reasoning does not guarantee moral behavior.

their moral development involves **internalization,** which is the process of bringing behavior under the control of inner, personal standards that make people obey rules even if there are no external restraints. The development of moral reasoning and moral behavior is the focus of research that we will review in this section.

Jean Piaget (1932) and Lawrence Kohlberg (1963, 1978) have done a great deal of research on the development of internalization and moral reasoning. Both investigators asked children to comment on stories containing moral dilemmas; both proposed theories that related moral development to cognitive development. In Chapter 9, we reviewed Piaget's theory including adolescent cognitive development which is characterized by the beginning of the formal operations stage. Adolescents who enter this last stage in Piaget's theory acquire the abilities of hypothesis testing and problem solving that are discussed in Chapter 8. Here we will concentrate on Kohlberg's theory of moral reasoning.

Moral Reasoning. One of Kohlberg's stories was about a man, Heinz, who stole drugs in order to save his wife's life. Kohlberg asked children of various ages, "Should Heinz have done that? Was it actually wrong or right? Why?" The "why" question was the important one. Answers to this question suggested three levels in the development of moral reasoning, with two stages in each level (Table 10–1). A typical answer in the first level (preconventional) might be, "The man was wrong because he could be sent to jail for stealing." Or it might be, "The man was right because he would get in trouble for letting his wife die." Both answers characterize the preconventional level, because right or wrong is decided in terms of possible punishment. Children often give this kind of answer, but teenagers rarely do. A typical answer in the second level (conventional) might be, "The man was wrong because people don't like thieves." Or it might be, "The man was right because his friends wouldn't like him if he let his wife die." Both answers characterize the conventional level, because right or wrong is decided in terms of being liked or disliked for one's actions. Teenagers often give this kind of response. A typical answer in the third level (postconventional) might be, "The man was wrong according to social law, but he was right according to divine law, which holds that human life is sacred." This answer characterizes Kohlberg's highest level, because it is based upon abstract principles. Exposure to other cultures and value systems encourages the development of this level, which few people reach before their twenties (Keniston, 1969; Stevens-Long & Cobb, 1983).

Some investigators have suggested that Kohlberg's scale reflects several

Internalization
Process of bringing behavior under the control of inner, personal standards that make people obey rules even if there are no external restraints.

Table 10–1   Stages and Levels of Kohlberg's Theory of Moral Development

	Names of Levels and Stages	Aims of Morality in Each Stage (Something Is Moral if It Serves to:)
Level I	Preconventional morality	avoid punishment
Stage 1	Obedience and punishment orientation	gain concrete rewards
Stage 2	Naive hedonistic and instrumental orientation	
Level II	Conventional level: Morality of conventional rules and conformity	gain approval/avoid disapproval
Stage 3	"Good boy/Good girl" morality	avoid dishonor or guilt
Stage 4	Authority and social order morality	
Level III	Postconventional level: Morality of self-accepted moral principles	uphold widely agreed-upon rights and responsibilities
Stage 5	Morality of contract, individual rights, and democratically accepted law	uphold own ethical principles
Stage 6	Morality of individual principles and conscience	

kinds of bias (Hoffman, 1979; Kurtines & Grief, 1974; Simpson, 1974). First, one could argue that the scale is politically biased because the lower levels seem to display political conservativeness. Second, the scale may be culturally biased. Kohlberg compared people in different cultures, but these comparisons might not have been fair. This criticism stems from the fact that the theory focuses on American values. The classification of levels might not be appropriate, therefore, in cultures with different values. Third, the scale might be biased according to gender because females do not show the expected pattern of movement through the stages (Gilligan, 1976).

A final criticism concerns the distinction between moral issues and social conventions. Kohlberg's theory states that people do not make this distinction until they reach the postconventional reasoning level. Accordingly, children would rarely make the distinction. But Turiel (1978) found that most children distinguish between moral rules, such as "Do not steal," and game rules, such as "Do not pass go." They also distinguish between behaviors that harm others and those that create disorder (Smetana, 1985).

These critiques do not make the theory less important. Kohlberg intentionally provided a framework that invites further research and enables others to focus on meaningful issues. For example, Thorkildsen (1989) is using Kohlberg's methods to study moral reasoning in the classroom. Kohlberg provided a theory that will be continually evaluated and revised as we learn more about development. See if you can find implications for moral development in the next sections reviewing other psychological and social changes.

Personality Development

Personality influences the unique way that we adjust and respond to our environment (see Chapter 13). This section will deal with questions about the development of personality: Does personality develop throughout the life span? Does it ever stop developing?

O'Keeffe's noncomforming nature illustrates that some personality traits can remain stable throughout a person's lifetime. O'Keeffe recalled evidence from her childhood: "From the time I was a little girl, if my sisters wore their hair braided, I wouldn't wear mine braided. If they wore ribbons, I wouldn't. I'd think they'd look better without it, too" (Lisle, 1980, p. 11). As an adult, Georgia O'Keeffe continued to be a nonconformist. This strong personality trait may have been responsible for launching her career, since she achieved her first widely acclaimed work by consciously breaking with the traditions in which she had been trained. Her popularity survived the coming and going of many different trends in the art world, perhaps because she always had a style of her own. The survival of one personality trait in a person does not mean, of course, that our personality remains the same throughout life, or even that certain traits will stay with us throughout life. In fact, modern theories assume that our personalities continue to develop and change as long as we live.

Erik Erikson's Theory.   As we will discuss in Chapter 13, Freud and his followers argued that our personality is determined by the time we are 6 or 7 years old. The rest of life is spent following the script written during these "formative years." Erik Erikson, who studied with Freud, acknowledged that early childhood is an important period for personality development. He believed, however, that our personality goes through stages throughout our lifetime. Each stage has a crisis. You have probably heard of some of them, such as the teenage "identity crisis." That popular expression comes from Erikson's theory. Each crisis shapes our personality and determines how we resolve the crisis we encounter at the next stage.

As you can see in Table 10–2, Erikson listed eight stages of life. The first four occur before puberty (about 12), and the other four occur after

Table 10–2   Erikson's Psychosocial Stages

Approximate Age	Crisis	Adequate Resolution	Inadequate Resolution
First year of life	Trust vs. mistrust	Sense of security	Feelings of anxiety
1–3	Autonomy vs. self-doubt	Sense of self as capable of making things happen	Feelings of inadequacy to control events
3–6	Initiative vs. guilt	Confidence in oneself as an originator	Feelings of low self-worth
6–12	Competence vs. inferiority	Sense of capability in basic social and intellectual skills	Lack of self-confidence, feelings of unskillfullness
Adolescent	Identity vs. role confusion	Assured sense of self as a person	Fragmented sense of self
Early adulthood	Intimacy vs. isolation	Capability of closeness and commitment to another	Feeling of loneliness and aloofness
Middle adulthood	Generativity vs. stagnation	Expansion of concern beyond oneself to family, society, future generations	Self-centered concerns without future orientation
Later adulthood	Ego-integrity vs. despair	Sense of completeness and satisfaction with life	Feelings of hopelessness and disenchantment

Source: Based on Erikson, 1963.

puberty. Each stage is defined by a major crisis over issues that are either adequately or inadequately resolved. Thereafter, the adequacy of the resolution determines how well a person copes with the issues related to the crisis. The first stage and probably most critical crisis involves issues of trust and mistrust. The way in which this crisis is resolved will determine whether a person approaches the world in a trusting, open way or with a suspicious, cautious outlook. According to Erikson, social trust will develop to the degree that infants have an inner sense of security that their mother will love and take care of their basic needs.

An important stage in Erikson's theory is the **identity crisis,** which occurs during puberty. Identity is an understanding of one's own uniqueness and an appreciation of what one has in common with others (Marcia, 1980). The search for an identity is particularly difficult in our complex Western culture. The sheer number of choices facing the adolescent is bewildering, and, to complicate matters even further, there are few guides to help someone make these choices. During adolescence, people begin to confront issues concerning career, education, marriage, and place of residence. The decision about each of these issues will influence how people view themselves. In earlier, more traditional societies, the search for an identity was not so difficult. People rarely moved away from the area in which they were raised; male children were generally expected to adopt the occupation of their fathers; and females "naturally" got married, raised a family, and kept house. The difficulty of the identity crisis in our present-day society is reflected in the fact that this period is characterized by a great deal of trying out and testing of different roles as adolescents struggle to "discover" themselves. College students may change their major a number of times as they attempt to discover "their niche." Even by graduation, many college students have not settled on an identity, and many choose to "take a year off" to travel, work at different jobs, and learn about themselves.

Thus, Erikson argues that our personality changes throughout our lifetime. Erikson's theory also includes a certain amount of continuity in personality, however, since the way one crisis is resolved affects later stages.

Identity crisis
Term used by Erikson to describe the search for an identity during adolescence that involves trying out and testing different roles.

Logan (1986) argues, in fact, that the stages from identity to integrity are a replay of the basic trust to identity cycle. We will end our discussion of the developing teenage personality by considering how physical changes affect the identity crisis.

Influence of Physical Changes. A teenager's search for identity is influenced by the adolescent growth spurt, which we discussed earlier. Late maturing boys and girls have an especially difficult time. Researchers found that boys who mature late often feel inadequate, and this feeling persists into adulthood (Mussen & Jones, 1957; Livson & Peskin, 1980). Early maturers take over as leaders, especially in sports, because of their greater strength. Later maturers try to compensate with immature, attention-seeking behaviors such as bossiness. Reactions of others to these annoying behaviors tend to reinforce the low self-image of the late maturers. These researchers also found that late-maturing girls face similar adjustment problems, but to a lesser extent. High-school girls who are physically mature early on tend to be leaders among girls and popular with guys, but they tend to perform poorly in school (Simmons, Blyth, & McKinney, 1983). Late-maturing girls tend to be less self-confident and less relaxed in social relationships. These effects carry over into adulthood, but they are small in comparison to the influence of late maturing on boys.

One effect these physical changes have is on the way parents, teachers, and friends treat teenagers. The less teenagers *look* like adults, the less they are treated like adults, which could contribute to low self-esteem in late maturers. In addition, many other social variables change dramatically during adolescence.

Physical Change, Culture, and Race. Recent research indicates that the timing of physical maturation has similar effects across culture and race. One study of Swedish males suggests that early and late maturers have different drinking habits as adults (Andersson & Magnusson, 1990). The longitudinal study investigated drinking habits of 88 males born in 1955. The same individuals were questioned during their teen years (at 14 years 5 months and 15 years 10 months) and during young adulthood (18 to 24 years). The most dramatic differences were observed after adolescence. In young adulthood, the percentage registered for alcohol abuse was 36 percent for late maturers, 14 percent for normal maturers, and 8 percent for early maturers. These results support the notion that effects of late and early maturation carry over into adulthood.

A study of Turkish adolescents indicated that they also are influenced by early and late maturation. Cok (1990) measured body image satisfaction in Turkish students aged 11 to 18 years. Both males and females were affected, but the effects were different. Higher levels of body image satisfaction were associated with early-maturing males and late-maturing females. The reversal for females suggests that the early-maturing girls might be uncomfortable with the differences between themselves and their peers.

A third study compared black and nonblack females in America (Phinney, Jensen, Olsen, & Cundick, 1990). There were differences between the groups. For example, the blacks matured earlier on average than the nonblacks. For both groups, however, early maturation was associated with earlier dating and earlier sexual intercourse. It was also associated with earlier marriage for nonblacks. The point we want to emphasize is that the effects of maturation are strong enough to show up across diverse socialization patterns and cultural expectations.

Social Changes

Think back to the interpersonal, or social, relationships that you had as a 12-year-old. In all likelihood you lived at home, and your parents kept a fairly close eye on your activities. If you got into trouble at school, they found out almost immediately; they decided when, where, and whom you could date; and they were close at hand when you needed encouragement. Contrast that to your social situation at the age of 19. Many 19-year-olds move away from home and enter college or begin working. Most make their own decisions about school, dating, and careers. Parents care as much as ever, but their involvement is generally limited. O'Keeffe followed this pattern, assuming more freedom and responsibility during adolescence. At the age of 12 she lived in a sheltered home environment, but by the time she was 19 she was living alone while attending the Art Students League in New York City. Much research has been done on various aspects of the movement toward independence during adolescence.

Peer Groups. As children approach their teen years, contact with other children, that is, their peers, becomes more and more important. Adolescent peer groups often take on highly organized structure. Dunphy (1963) observed, for instance, that peer-group structures of urban teenagers develop through five stages. Boys and girls remain separate in the first stage; they form small groups with members of their own sex. These groups, which are called *cliques*, contain members that share common interests and emotional attachments. Boy and girl cliques start interacting as groups in the second stage. Dating starts in the third stage, causing boy and girl cliques to merge. The isolated sex groups often maintain their identity as well during this stage. The fourth stage is characterized by larger groups, called *crowds*, which are made up of several merged boy-girl cliques closely interacting. These crowds dissolve in the fifth stage, and fully mixed boy-girl cliques reappear. The cliques during this last stage consist of loosely associated couples.

Middleton, Zollinger, and Keene (1986) found a way to use peer pressure constructively. They recruited popular middle-school students to promote the acceptance of socially neglected classmates. The popular students were trained as social skill facilitators and assigned to work with a target student in their classroom. This program was successful in that the target students increased in peer acceptance. This result is encouraging, since self-esteem in middle school and high school is closely associated with group acceptance (Brown & Lohr, 1987).

Peer-group structures of teenagers seem to develop through several stages. In an early stage, separate cliques of boys and girls start interacting as groups.

Some social scientists have expressed concern about age segregation in American adolescent peer groups. Almost all American teens attend age-grouped schools. As a result, they spend most of their time with people of their own age even when they participate in extracurricular activities (Medrich et al., 1982). This grouping has a dramatic effect on friendship patterns, since the vast majority of teen friends come from the same grade in school (Blyth, Hill, & Thiel, 1982). This age segregation is also promoted in suburbs where teens get together after school before their parents return home from work (Langway, Abramson, & Foote, 1981). Some educators believe that efforts should be made to increase contact between adolescents and adults (e.g., National Commission on Youth, 1980). One way to achieve this goal would be to offer teens a well-designed work-experience program in the community (Hamilton, 1981).

Intimacy and Sexuality

The word "intimacy" as used by Erikson has a psychological meaning as opposed to a physical one. An *intimate relationship* is characterized by concern for each other's well-being, willingness to disclose private or sensitive information, and sharing of interests and activities. People can therefore have an intimate relationship without having a sexual one. They can also have a sexual relationship without being especially intimate. As indicated by Erikson's theory, intimacy is an important psychological need. Hunter and Youniss (1982) have found that friends become increasingly important in fulfilling this need during adolescence. At the same time, parents do not become any less important. At the age of 9, children rate their intimacy with parents and friends to be about the same. Adolescents, on the other hand, report being more intimate with their friends. This reversal happens for two reasons. First, intimacy among friends increases steadily through ages 9, 12, 15, and 19. Second, intimacy with parents remains about the same during this time period (see Figure 10–2). Blyth, Hill, and Theil

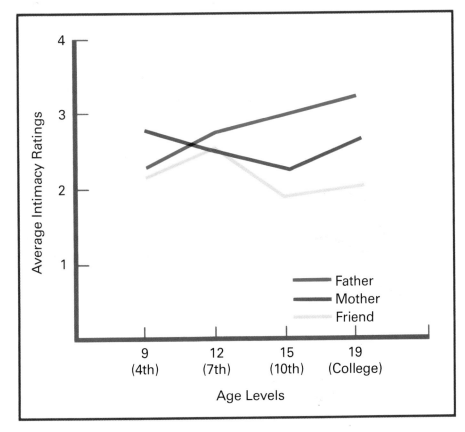

FIGURE 10–2

As the Hunter and Youniss study shows, intimacy relationships with peers increase as we go from childhood to adolescence. It is important to note that the intimacy relationship with a parent does not decline; rather it stays about the same over time. (Adapted from Hunter & Youniss 1982)

(1982) found a similar pattern of results. They asked adolescents to list the important people in their lives. Older adolescents listed peers more often than did younger adolescents. Yet older and younger teens both listed their parents about 93 percent of the time.

Teenagers also increase sexual behaviors ranging from kissing and petting to sexual intercourse. Almost all American teenagers participate in kissing and petting. Slightly more than half experience sexual intercourse according to Gordon and Scales (1977).

It is interesting to compare these results with more recent surveys. In 1988, the proportion of sexually active females was estimated to be 38 percent for ages 15–17 and 75 percent for unmarried 19-year-olds. The proportions for males in the same year were 33 percent at 15, 50 percent at 16, 67 percent at 17, and 86 percent at 19 (Hersch, 1991). We contacted the Planned Parenthood Federation of America to obtain statistics on teen pregnancy for the same year, 1988. They reported that 20 percent of white women and 40 percent of black women became pregnant before they reached 18. Over 1 million teenagers became pregnant that year alone.

Conventional wisdom once said that fear of AIDS would greatly suppress teen sex. Clearly, however, teens are still having lots of sex despite AIDS and other health risks that will be discussed in the next section.

Sex and Health.   Sexual activity puts teenagers at high risk of unwanted pregnancy and disease. The causes and consequences of these problems are both psychological and physical. Let's look at both aspects and then consider the role of psychologists in helping teenagers lower the risks.

The psychological turmoil of teen pregnancy contributes to the fact that those who do get married often get divorced later on (Presser, 1977; Stark, 1986). Not only do teenage pregnancies cause considerable emotional trauma, they also increase the risk of physical complications for both mother and child (Moore, 1978; Stark, 1986).

The full impact of the risks of pregnancy becomes most apparent when one adds teen premarital pregnancies to other pregnancy before marriage. The result is that 30 percent of all American girls who are not virgins

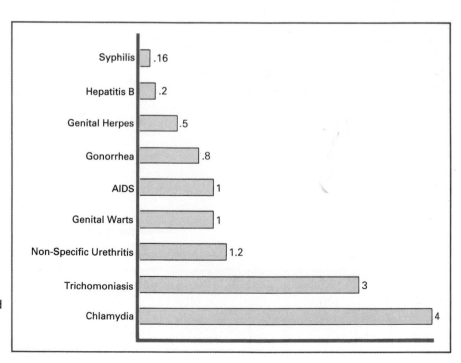

FIGURE 10–3

About 33,000 new sexually transmitted diseases (STDs) occur each day in America. This bar chart shows the most common kinds in 1990.

get pregnant at least once before they are married (Zelnick, Kantner, & Ford, 1981).

Sexually active teenagers are also putting themselves at risk of contracting a **sexually transmitted disease (STD),** which is any infectious disease transmitted by sexual intercourse. Each year in America, 8 to 12 million cases of STD are reported, and 75 percent of those occur among 15- to 24-year-olds (USDHHS, 1980).

Initial symptoms of syphilis include sores on the genitals. Early treatment is effective and important because untreated syphilis can lead to blindness, sterility, brain damage, heart disease, and death. A mother can transmit syphilis to infants before or during birth. Survival rate is poor for infants born with syphilis.

About 1 million cases of gonorrhea, or "clap," as it is called on the street, and 3 to 5 million cases of chlamydia strike Americans each year. Symptoms of gonorrhea and chlamydia include discomfort in urinating and/or a discharge from the urinary tract. Women might also experience a discharge and irritation in the vagina. Both of these can be treated with drugs, and early treatment is important. A possible complication of both of these diseases for women is pelvic inflammatory disease (PID), an abdominal infection. About 25 percent of PID cases require hospitalization. Consequences of PID include possible scarring of the uterus and fallopian tubes (see Chapter 2). This scarring can cause infertility or pregnancies occurring outside of the uterus. The latter problem can cause death. Possible complications for men include inflammation of the sperm ducts that can cause sterility. Chlamydia's greatest threat is that a person can have it without any symptoms until serious complications set in. This makes it the "silent menace" that can be spread without people knowing that they are spreading it. In fact, about 75 percent of women with chlamydia have no symptoms (Fuerst, 1991). Many of them will not discover their STD until they try to get pregnant and discover they cannot. Chlamydia affects the rich as well as the poor. For example, studies have found the disease in 5 percent of female college students (Fuerst, 1991). Infants exposed to these diseases by their mother before or during birth often develop complications such as eye infections.

Herpes simplex is a highly contagious STD that is increasing at the rate of between 400,000 and 600,000 new cases a year. About 20 million people have yearly recurrences. The worst aspect of herpes simplex is that it is not curable. Victims suffer for their lifetime from recurring, painful sores on the genitals. Mothers can transmit the disease to their newborn infants during delivery. Effects on the infant can include life-threatening disorders of the central nervous system.

Another incurable STD is genital warts. They are like other warts except that they occur in the vaginal area, on the penis or cervix, and near the anus. They are caused by a human papilloma virus (HPV) and are spread by sexual contact. There are over 60 different kinds of HPV. Most of them only cause itching and discomfort. However, some are associated with cancer of the cervix, vagina, penis, and anus. Those associated with cancer are the least common, but they are also the most difficult to detect. Genital warts can be removed, but the HPV often remains. Thus, recurrence is common.

Although these diseases are serious and prevalent, they have been overshadowed by an uncurable and deadly SDT, acquired immune deficiency syndrome (AIDS). The U.S. Department of Health & Human Services (1988) warned that "AIDS is one of the most serious health problems that has ever faced the American public." Not long ago, people thought that only homosexuals were at high risk. Today, however, 30% of AIDS victims are heterosexuals. The truth was stated plainly by the U.S. Department of Health & Human Services (1988): *Who you are has nothing to do*

Sexually transmitted disease (STD)
Any infectious disease transmitted by sexual intercourse.

with whether you are in danger of being infected with the AIDS virus. What matters is what you do." There are four ways to get the AIDS virus: (1) by having sex—oral, anal, or vaginal—with someone who is infected with the virus; (2) by sharing needles and syringes with a person infected by the virus; (3) by receiving blood that is contaminated by the AIDS virus; and (4) by contracting it before or during birth from a mother who has the AIDS virus. Let's concentrate on the first two ways which are risky behaviors that are completely under an individual's control. A main reason for the spread of AIDS is that a person can be infected with the AIDS virus without showing any symptoms at all for years. As a result, a person can acquire and transmit the disease for years without knowing it. For example, in one case reported by the U.S. Department of Health & Human Services (1988), Carmen Reyes didn't know that she had AIDS until her newborn son was diagnosed as having it. People can be infected for five years or more without knowing it because they look fine and feel fine. In other words, a sexual partner or a needle sharer who looks and feels fine can give you the disease. They could have contracted it from any person with whom they have had sex or shared a needle within the last five years or more. Once symptoms appear, health declines rapidly because AIDS prevents the body's natural defenses from operating correctly. Before symptoms appear, the only way that a victim can find out if he or she has the disease is to have a test for the AIDS virus. The U.S. Department of Health & Human Services (1988) recommends that you have a test done if any of the following risk factors pertain to you:

1. You have had any sexually transmitted disease.
2. You have shared needles.
3. You are a man who has had sex with another man.
4. You have had sex with a prostitute, male or female.
5. You have had sex with someone to whom any of the first four risk factors apply.

No single approach will solve the problems of unwanted pregnancies and STDs among teenagers. Psychologists will have to join forces with other health scientists who are working on physical factors. In addition, understanding and controlling the psychological factors will require team efforts of psychologists specializing in many of the areas that are reviewed in the chapters of this book: biology, learning, thought, problem solving, development, motivation, emotion, stress, personality, abnormal psychology, therapy, interpersonal relations, individuals in groups, environment, behavior and health. It is easy enough to see how each of these topics are relevant. It is less easy to see how research in all these areas can be integrated into practical solutions. It is a good bet that effective solutions will have at their foundation a comprehensive, data-based, theoretical framework.

We hinted about a step toward a theoretical framework in our earlier discussion of the relationship between intimacy and sexuality. We noted that people can be intimate without being sexually active and vice versa according to Erikson's theory of development. Our discussion brings to mind a recommendation of the U.S. Department of Health & Human Services (1988, p. 4):

> You are going to have to be careful about the person you become sexually involved with, making your own decision based on your own best judgment. That can be difficult.
>
> Has this person had any sexually transmitted diseases? How many people have they been to bed with? Have they experimented with drugs? All these are sensitive, but important, questions. But you have a personal responsibility to ask.

Think of it this way. If you know someone well enough to have sex, then you should be able to talk about AIDS. If someone is unwilling to talk, you shouldn't have sex.

The theme is clear—*GET INTIMATE BEFORE GETTING PHYSICAL*. Perhaps psychologists and other health scientists will be able to develop this theme into empirically and theoretically based practical solutions.

Young Adulthood

O'Keeffe's life is a valuable reminder that adults do not necessarily experience the same life events in the same order. Many adults marry and have a first child between the ages of 20 and 25. O'Keeffe's parents followed this pattern, but O'Keeffe herself did not marry until she was 37, and she never had children. She did, however, dedicate herself at about this time to what became her lifework, her career in art. This became the most important commitment of her life.

Lowenthal (1977) unified the study of young adulthood by focusing on commitments. Specifically, she directed attention to three particularly important commitments: moral, interpersonal, and mastery. *Moral commitments* relate to development in Kohlberg's highest stage of moral development, the postconventional stage. *Interpersonal commitments* relate to Erikson's sixth stage of development, "intimacy versus isolation." Most young adults at this point commit themselves to intimate relationships that are characterized by deep caring and mutual respect. Avoiding this type of commitment may lead to a deep sense of isolation from other people. To illustrate this stage we will discuss marriage and child rearing, which are the most common ways for adults to develop intimate relationships. *Mastery commitments* refer to occupational commitments, such as the one O'Keeffe made to her career in art.

Family Commitments

O'Keeffe's mother, Ida, moved away from her parents' home at the age of 20. She married and had her first child within the next 2 years, and her last of five children was born before she was 30. Much of her young adulthood was therefore committed to starting and raising her own family. Most modern U.S. citizens are still making marriage and family commitments. The Bureau of the Census (1987) reported that 95 percent of U.S. citizens get married before they reach 40. Although there is a trend toward having fewer children, 90 percent of U.S. women do have children during young adulthood. Alternatives to marriage are more popular today, however. One option is **cohabitation,** a relationship between two unmarried people who live together. The range of possibilities for this choice is quite wide, including relationships between heterosexuals and relationships between gay or lesbian couples (Kurdek, 1989). Despite the increasing popularity of alternatives, we will concentrate on marriage, because it affects the vast majority of young adults.

Marriage and the Family Cycle.   Marriage and child rearing create a *family cycle*, which is a sequence of family events that repeat themselves generation after generation. Major events in the family cycle are: (1) leave parental home; (2) marry; (3) have first child; (4) bear last child; (5) first child leaves home; (6) last child leaves home; (7) children marry; (8) grandchildren are born. These events are among the important influences that interact to produce unique patterns of adult development. Researchers therefore observe the timing, duration, and clustering of family-cycle events.

Cohabitation
Relationship between two unmarried people who live together.

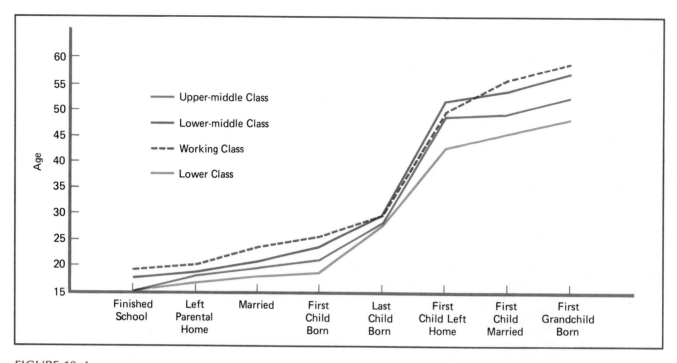

FIGURE 10–4

These are the results of a study that compared the average age at which certain family events had occurred in the lives of women of different social classes. (Olsen, 1969)

There is considerable variability in the age at which family events occur. Your own informal comparisons of family histories will varify this variability. Psychologists have nevertheless found interesting trends by observing average ages for these events. Figure 10–4 shows the results of one study that compared averages for women of different social classes (Olsen, 1969).

Upper-middle-class women were 4 to 8 years older than lower-class women for each event, with lower-middle-class and working-class women falling in between. A notable difference between groups was the time span between first and last child. The average age for upper-middle-class mothers at the time their first child was born was 26, and it was 29 for the last. The comparable averages for lower-class mothers were 18 and 27. Beyond those differences, the sequencing of events was similar between classes. The average woman left her parents' home 1 to 2 years after finishing her formal education; she got married 1 to 3 years later; and she had her first child 1 to 3 years after that.

Some evidence suggests that timing of family events may be related to marital and parental satisfaction. For instance, middle-class women who marry between 20 and 30 years of age report happier marriages than those who marry earlier or later (Nydegger & Mitteness, 1979). Being "off-schedule" is not always associated with dissatisfaction, however. Most men become fathers before they are 40, but those who wait longer tend to be happier with their parental role. Nydegger and Mitteness suggested that men who wait to have children may experience less conflict between family life and career demands. Schlesinger & Schlesinger (1989) agree that career tensions are important. They note, however, that satisfaction with delayed parenthood for men and women also depends on support from family, friends, and physicians.

Career pressures may also play a role in increasing the average age at first marriage. In 1985, the averages were 25.7 years for males and 23.8 years for females (Schmid, 1987)—more than two years higher than they were in 1970. Compared to their counterparts in the 1970s, young adults of the 1980s were also more concerned about their careers and financial security (Astin, Green, Korn, 1987). Astin et al. (1987) argue that these two trends are connected and that the link between them is college. Marriage is delayed because more young adults, especially more women, are pursuing a college education in order to establish a career.

Occupational Commitments

O'Keeffe launched her career as an artist with her first showing in Stieglitz's gallery at the age of 28. By the time she reached middle age she was recognized as "the greatest woman painter in America" (Lisle, 1980). Not everyone can become the greatest in their field, of course, but many young adults achieve high levels in their chosen occupation before they enter middle age. Young adults usually dedicate themselves to the mastery of knowledge and skills, and sometimes will have several different jobs that can advance them in a chosen occupation.

Mastery of specific knowledge and job-related skills is not the only developmental change necessary for a successful career commitment. White (1975) outlines four aspects of personality and social development that are also associated with careers. Young adults must learn to (1) respond to people warmly and respectfully without anxiety; (2) base decisions upon their own beliefs; (3) respect cultural values; and (4) care about society and the people in it. Accordingly, career commitments depend upon cognitive, social, and personality development during young adulthood.

Becoming One's Own Man. Daniel J. Levinson (1978; 1986) and four colleagues at Yale University conducted one of the most comprehensive studies of development in young male adults. The research team studied 49 men who were either executives, biologists, novelists, or hourly wage earners. The team interviewed the men for a total of 10 to 20 hours, in sessions that were spread over about 1½ years. All men were between 35 and 40 years of age at the first interview; 2 years later the team conducted follow-up interviews. During the sessions the men were asked to recall the events of their young adulthood. The results suggested that males go through three periods during young adulthood: Men go through a phase Levinson called *entering the adult world* between their early and late twenties. In this phase they seek a balance between keeping options open and establishing a stable life structure. Most men experience an *age 30 transition* within several years of their thirtieth birthday. They think then that it will soon be too late to make changes, so they carefully evaluate their commitments. Between the early thirties and about age 40, men go through an important period that Levinson called *settling down*. They emphasize stability and security now, often fixing on some key goal, such as a promotion. The end phase of *settling down* is called *becoming one's own man*. As men grow out of early adulthood, they urgently strive to advance as far as possible in their careers, to gain greater authority, and to be independent. Some men experience a severe crisis during this phase. They try to drastically alter their existing life structure through divorce or career changes. The phase of becoming one's own man, whether smooth or rocky, usually ends at about 40 years of age, as new developmental demands usher in middle age.

Levinson's work gave psychologists not only an important theory, but also a useful procedure. For example, Cary Cherniss (1989) used Levinson's interview procedure to study why people stay in or leave public service. She studied 25 professionals who had entered public service 12 years earlier. People left to seek financial independence and/or greater work satisfaction. People stayed for many reasons. A main one was to minimize stress. These personal reasons were often shaped by family obligations and encouragement from friends. It remains a challenge for future researchers to determine how all these influences combine to determine career changes and adult development.

Becoming One's Own Woman. Suzyn Ornstein and Lynn Isabella (1990) found that Levinson's model also applies to professional women. Specifically, 204 female managers between the ages of 24 and 64 years reported their career experiences. These experiences changed with age, supporting Levinson's model.

Increasingly more women are finding it possible to enjoy the pleasures of both a career and a family.

These results confirm and extend earlier findings by Henning and Jardin (1976). They identified characteristics of 25 women who had established themselves as successful executives by the end of young adulthood. These women tended to be the firstborn children in their families and they tended to excel in college. Their fathers were extremely supportive of their careers, encouraged them to develop their abilities, reinforced them for breaking away from sex-role stereotypes, and financially assisted the launching of their careers. The women accepted assistance from senior male executives in the beginning, but they became independent by the time they reached middle-management positions. This profile of the successful career woman is sketchy in comparison to the more detailed observations that are available on the successful career man.

Middle Adulthood

O'Keeffe seemed to "begin" over and over again throughout her life. Since one of her fresh starts came at about the age of 40, the adage "Life begins at 40" certainly applies in her case. "Having abandoned the idea of having a child, and approaching her fortieth birthday, Georgia began planning precisely every detail of her daily existence to eliminate anything unnecessary to art. . . . She set new goals for herself and became absorbed in solving various technical problems after the critics had given her high praise for her technical virtuosity" (Lisle, 1980, pp. 182–184). Her experiences between 40 and 60 years of age provide an interesting frame of reference for our discussion of middle adulthood.

Sequence of Development in Middle Years

Erikson's Generativity versus Stagnation. Erikson (1959, 1963) maintains that one of two feelings dominate during middle adulthood: (1) *generativity*, a sense of producing and contributing to the world, or (2) *stagnation*, a sense of not fulfilling expectations. Sense of generativity can be gained through family, job, or community involvement. O'Keeffe clearly gained a sense of generativity through her career; her mother gained it by rearing children. People who feel no sense of worthwhile accomplishment form an impression of being bogged down in a life without meaning. People can get beyond this sense of stagnation, however, and doing so can make them more compassionate about the weaknesses and suffering of others.

Levinson's Periods of Middle Adulthood. Levinson (1978) proposed a universal sequence of periods during middle adulthood. Although more data are needed on possible gender differences before this can be confirmed, we will assume for now that the stages apply to both men and women (Cherniss, 1989). The stages are as follows: Men and women experience a *midlife transition* between the ages of 40 and 45. This is the period of the so-called midlife crisis, a time of conflict and stress. Forty-five- to 50-year-old middle-agers settle into a new life structure during a period called *entering middle adulthood*. Those who created a satisfactory structure during the previous transitional period enjoy one of the happiest times of their lives. (Levinson's conclusions about life after 45 are more speculative because they are based on biographies instead of interviews.) *Age 50 transition* occurs between 50 and 55. It is analogous to the *age 30 transition*, in which middle-agers reevaluate previous commitments. A stable period, *culmination of middle adulthood*, is enjoyed between 55 and 60. Levinson has very little

GENDER ROLES AND DUAL-CAREER FAMILIES

Gender roles are behavior patterns that a given culture associates with being male or female. At one time these were called *sex roles*. It has become customary, however, to reserve the term *sex* for female-male differences related to reproductive functions. Gender roles go far beyond those functions. The traditional gender roles in Western cultures are based on the expectation that men are logical, competitive, aggressive, ambitious, and domineering. Women, in the traditional view, are sensitive, emotional, dependent, and talkative (Morrison, White, & Van Velsor, 1987; Bozzi, 1987; Benderly, 1987).

Sandra Bem (1987) reviews a variety of theories about how we acquire our concept of gender roles. A common thread running through the theories is that homes and schools teach gender roles in subtle ways. The lessons include encouraging children to play gender-appropriate games, giving instructions about who can express what emotions, and supplying models for gender-related behavior. Direct lessons from parents and teachers are supplemented by television and textbooks. Stories in textbooks, for instance, show males as strong, active, and adventurous. In contrast, females are depicted as gentle and dependent (Wirtenburg & Nakamura, 1976). Children learn these concepts and use them as a looking glass in which they view themselves and others. As a result, children become their own teachers, organizing their world into gender-role categories.

Despite these self-sustaining mechanisms, gender roles are changing. In traditional gender roles,

the male is expected to be head of the family: "A man's home is his castle." The male is also expected to rule the world outside the home. The female is expected to be a full-time homemaker. Her traditional role includes maintaining the house and caring for the children. Many of today's men and women are reevaluating these roles. Women are moving into traditional male roles in the workplace (Stark, 1987b), and in the community (Kimmel, 1988). We have already considered the impact of these changes on child rearing (see Highlight in Chapter 9: Working Mothers, Day Care, and Child Development). Now let's take a broader look at how they are affecting family obligations and careers.

Family obligations influence both male and female careers (Cherniss, 1989). Societal biases, however, put extra pressures on female homemakers employed outside the home. Women in dual-career families do housework equivalent to an extra month's work per year, according to Arlie Hochschild (1989). The men in Hochschild's sample "help out," but they do much less. Obviously, women would like more help. Recent research also suggests more subtle effects. Men who pitch in more at home are happier with their dual-earner families and with their careers (Parasuraman, Greenhaus, Rabinowitz, & Bedeian, 1989). Furthermore, when family demands are equal, men and women enjoy equal levels of mental health (Rosenfield, 1989).

Under these conditions, homemakers employed outside the home are happier than full-time homemakers (Rosenfield, 1989). However, we should be careful not

to overgeneralize this result. It is quite likely that lower happiness only applies to a subset of full-time homemakers. For example, full-time homemakers who have children are especially depressed when they would prefer to be employed outside the home (Hock & DeMeis, 1990). Other homemakers are neither conflicted about working at home full time nor less happy than homemakers who are employed outside the home (Baruch & Barnett, 1980; Wright, 1978). There is no single path to happiness. On one path, many career women and men get a sense of pride and power from their work outside the home. These feelings are especially strong for high-prestige occupations (Baruch, Barnett, & Rivers, 1983; Stark, 1987a). On another path, many women and men find parenthood to be the major source of satisfaction. On a third path, women and men derive fulfillment from both family and career (Gerson, 1986; Stark, 1987b). A challenge for future research is to identify the many complex factors that work together to create satisfaction or dissatisfaction with both family and career roles (Gerson, 1986).

The challenge is to find a path that works for you. This is not a once-in-a-lifetime challenge. When you read the later sections of this chapter on "persisters" and "shifters" and on retirement, you should note that this challenge will be with you throughout your life span. Most people have a looking glass of gender roles, which changes as a function of age (Kite, Deaux, & Miele, 1991). It will influence what feels best, but it need not blind you to other possibilities that might work better in today's world.

data on this period, but he suspects it is similar to the settling down period discussed earlier.

Clausen (1986) has proposed an alternative to Levinson's theory. Specifically, he rejects the idea that all people go through the same sequence of stages. He argues instead that people are unique and that there are different social and economic forces that act on them. As a result, some individuals go through more transitions than do others.

Levinson is the first to acknowledge that it is too early to tell if he is correct in postulating a universal sequence. You might judge the appropriateness of his periods for yourself as we consider physical, family, and occupational events during middle adulthood.

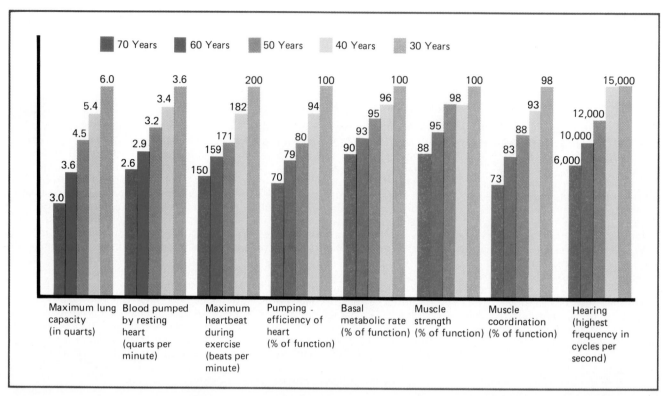

FIGURE 10–5

Lung capacity, cardiac output, muscle strength, and other functions decline with age.

Studies of these patterns have practical applications. For example, they might help clinicians work with people having adjustment problems.

Physical Changes

O'Keeffe's appearance during the middle years portrayed years of joy, laughter, pain, and sorrow, which, together with the harsh southwestern sun, etched character into her face. Physical alterations in middle age call attention to the aging process. Baldness, wrinkles, and weight gain affect physical appearance. As indicated in Figure 10–5, physiological capacities, such as muscle strength, lung capacity, cardiac output, and other functions decline (de Vries, 1970; Maranto, 1984). There is also a slight increase in the time it takes to make simple responses, such as braking a car in an emergency (Hodgkins, 1962). Middle-aged people may also notice visual loss caused by changes in the eye (Sekuler, Kline, & Dismukes, 1982). The lens becomes yellower, cloudier, and less able to focus light for close work such as reading (Fozard et al., 1977). All these biological changes remind people that their life span is limited (Levinson, 1978).

Physical decline causes professional athletes and others with physically demanding jobs to make radical career adjustments during middle age. Biological changes have little effect, however, on the everyday lives of most middle-agers. Yet most middle-aged adults, especially men, express considerable concern about their decreased physical efficiency (Neugarten, 1968).

Some changes must be accepted, of course, but currently many more middle-aged men and women are taking steps to stay in shape than in previous years. Exercise programs including calisthenics, running, and swimming can be very effective (de Vries, 1970). Physicians highly recommend such rigorous programs for those who can pass a careful physical examination (de Vries, 1975; Woodruff, 1977). Less strenuous programs are suggested for people of varying capabilities. People can, for instance, take short brisk walks that will help them stay in good physical condition.

Family Commitments

O'Keeffe's family commitments were unusual, as mentioned before. She had only been married 8 years on her forty-fifth birthday, and she had no children. Most middle-aged people have about 20 years of marriage behind them at this age, and they find themselves sandwiched between the needs of two generations (Pearlin, 1980). Their children, generally teenagers, have special needs as they seek greater independence (Troll, 1982), while their aging parents have special needs as they become more dependent (Cicirelli, 1982).

Many middle-aged people have a special relationship with their own parents. Much as parents value independence, aging parents gradually become more and more dependent upon their offspring (Blenker, 1965). People meet their aging parents' needs in many ways. They visit, do household tasks, run errands, and give physical care (Sussman & Burchinal, 1962). Some even take their parents into their homes (Spark & Brody, 1970). Research has indicated that 80 to 90 percent of parents studied have children living within an hour's driving distance. Of these, 80 percent had seen their children within the past week (Riley, Johnson, & Foner, 1972). Such interactions are best when elderly parents are allowed to preserve their personal dignity and when middle-aged sons and daughters are allowed to pursue their other commitments (Blenker, 1965).

Occupational Commitments

O'Keeffe made stronger commitments to her career, and she became more successful during her middle years. Many people follow this pattern. An increasing number, however, change careers at this age. Clapton (1973) calls those who stay with the same career *persisters*, and he calls those who change careers *shifters*. Let's look at the developmental patterns of men and women who fall into these two categories.

People at this age are truly the "middle" generation—they are parents themselves, and they usually have their own parents living within visiting distance. As their children grow and become independent, their aging parents often begin to become more dependent.

Career Men. Evidence indicates that there is a strong positive side to midlife career shifts. Researchers found, for instance, that such shifts can be satisfying, productive, and orderly (Murray, Powers, & Havighurst, 1971). This positive pattern is more likely evidenced in white-collar workers than in blue-collar workers (Schein, 1975).

Males who persist in a career are not always highly successful. In one study, Bray and Howard (1980) found considerable variability in success of managers who had stayed with the Bell Telephone System for over 20 years. The successful managers were more intelligent, more motivated, and more aggressive than less successful ones. They were also happier with their jobs, but they were not necessarily happier in their overall life situations. The most and the least successful managers found happiness through different life patterns.

Career Women. We have already identified various career patterns:

Although we all age, we do not all do so at the same rate. Some people, such as the woman shown in the photos on these two pages, go through life with great energy and enthusiasm, as much in their fifth decade as in their first.

women who stay with the same company through young adulthood and middle adulthood, women who remain full-time homemakers, and women who interrupt their outside-the-home careers to raise children. We might call the first two groups *persisters* and the third one *shifters*.

The shifters are especially interesting. Full-time homemakers are more likely to reenter the labor force during middle age when they are better educated and when they experience a change in marital status because of death or divorce (Moen, Downey, & Bolger, 1990). Many women return to school during their middle years for a wide range of reasons. At one extreme, some women merely brush up on previously held skills before resuming a career. At the other extreme, some women complete graduate degrees in order to become full-time professionals. Middle-aged women tend to enter graduate school with fire in their eyes. Their confidence often diminishes midway through the program, as both school and family pressures mount. The original determination usually wins out, however, and the women emerge with increased self-esteem and assertiveness (Lefevre, 1972; Rubin, 1979). These shifters tend to be happy despite unfortunate discrimination against them in wages and job opportunities (Blau, 1975; Ritzer, 1977). In fact, shifters seem to be as happy as persisters, which is consistent with an important theme that emerges from life-span research: There are many ways to be happy.

One recent trend concerns a woman's ability to combine a work life and a family life. Baruch, Barnett, and Rivers (1983) administered questionnaires to 298 women between the ages of 35 and 55. Their sample was selected randomly from six categories: (1) employed women who never married, (2) employed married women with children, (3) employed married women without children, (4) employed divorced women with children, (5) married homemakers with children, and (6) married homemakers without children. On the average, these women had two years education beyond high school, and they had an annual income range from $4,500 to over $50,000. The women reported the degree of control that they felt over their life and the pleasure they got from this control. The lowest scores came from married homemakers without children. The highest ratings on control and pleasure came from employed married women with children. The latter result suggests that middle-aged women can be happy in multiple roles.

The Census Bureau predicts a drastic increase in the number of senior citizens in this country (Ubell, 1984). In 1900, 1 American in 25 was over 65; today, that figure is 1 in 9. The prediction for the middle of the next century is that 1 American in 4 will be 65 years of age or older. This dramatic increase in the elderly is expected to include a sixfold increase in those over the age of 85.

O'Keeffe's elderly years, like her younger ones, are typical in some respects and unusual in others. Like many elderly people, she struggled to cope with the death of her spouse. Overcoming this loss seemed to be as hard, or harder, than overcoming her own physical hardships. She virtually retired from her career during her first 10 years of widowhood. Her elderly years were also hampered by declining vision, which is a common problem for the aged. Her uncommon spirit, however, enabled her to rekindle her career. Her persistence in the same career is unusual, as is the mental and physical agility that characterized her later years. However, more active senior citizens are staying spry and alert today than ever before. This is one of several current trends that we will review in this section.

Physical and Mental Abilities

O'Keeffe always took an active part in maintaining her good health. She had an organic garden that formed the basis of her carefully planned diet. A typical day began with a big breakfast that included beef butchered to her specification, a morning snack of homemade yogurt, a lunch consisting of an organic salad, and a light dinner of little more than fruit and cheese. She especially loved the strong flavors of garlic, raw onion, and chili peppers. She maintained her weight at 127 pounds, and she was very healthy for her age.

We all understand the qualifier "for her age" to some extent because of our experiences with older adults. We know that our health will decline. Physical changes will eventually touch every aspect of our lives, including our mental abilities. We may have to give up things that we now enjoy; we may have to slow down. But we can follow O'Keeffe's example in taking steps to maximize our health as we age. We can stack the deck in our favor by doing the right things now.

Biological Theories of Aging. Many researchers believe that the maximum life span, which is now about 110 to 120 years, will increase as they discover the basic mechanisms of the aging process (Medvedev, 1975). Cell malfunctions in elderly people are caused in part by mutations that damage genes, according to Sinex (1974). (See the discussion of genetics in Chapter 2.) Abnormal cell functioning interferes with the normal operation of physiological systems such as the endocrine system. This in turn leads to the physical changes we know as aging.

Lifestyle and Longevity. You can ignore the present realities of aging in the hope that scientists will discover a biological fountain of youth before you reach old age. Or you can take steps to maximize your well-being as you age. In her book, *Can You Live to Be 100?*, Diana Woodruff (1977) estimated the extent to which heredity factors, personal factors, and health factors extend or shorten a person's life. There's nothing you can do about the heredity factors, but there's a lot you can do *now* about the personal and health factors (see Table 10–3).

Individual and social variations will determine what you can and cannot do to remain vigorous as you age. Not everyone can look forward to being as hearty as former President Reagan in his seventies. Some of us would

HABITS IN EARLY YEARS AND HEALTH IN LATER YEARS

If we practice a few simple habits while we are young, we will lower our risk of disease as we age. (Here we will consider exercise and diet. You can refer to Chapters 12 and 13 to find other vital habits related to stress and personality.)

Research suggests that people change their health habits when they understand their vulnerability and believe in their ability to change (Wurtele, 1988). Your authors are continually reminded of their own vulnerability. We see it in the mirror and feel it in our bones. Most of you, however, are going to need other reminders because Father Time and Mother Nature won't be giving you the natural ones for many years to come.

We have some bad and some good news for you. The bad news is that *everyone* is vulnerable eventually. Some statistics are fairly hard to disregard. For instance, the primary cause of death in the United States is arteriosclerosis (Martini, 1989). This age-related disease is a thickening and toughening of the walls of vessels that carry blood away from the heart. It damages the heart and the brain. A considerable degree of age-related mental decline is associated with arteriosclerosis (Rinn, 1988). In fact, there is very little mental decline in disease-free aging (see Highlight: Disease-Free Aging versus Senile Dementia).

The good news is that acquiring a few health habits will greatly reduce your vulnerability. For example, three simple habits will lower your risk of arteriosclerosis. They are: Don't smoke, exercise regularly, and restrict your dietary intake of salt, fat, and calories. Let's call these controls of smoking, exercise, and eating the SEE Controls. They will go a long way toward keeping your blood vessels healthy if you start them before significant damage has occurred. Acquiring all three is best, but taking up any one will certainly help. If you smoke and can't quit or cut down, at least try some exercise and diet routines. Simple habits do help. A brisk half-hour walk several times a week will make a difference. Substituting cereal with skim milk for eggs with sausage at breakfast will help immensely. While corn flakes and skim milk have about 3 grams of fat and 150 calories, eggs and sausage have about 73 grams of fat and 1,080 calories. The *American Heart Association* has a cookbook that will give you many other delicious ideas. Even fast-food restaurants are providing more selections low in salt, fat, and calories. Clearly, it should not be difficult for you to exercise and eat your way around the nation's number-one killer. Start the SEE Controls today and see the results tomorrow.

The SEE Controls will also avert many other diseases related to aging. They are the core of many recommendations for maintaining a fit body and mind. For example, many articles have been written about health habits acquired during youth that will protect against *osteoporosis* in old age. This condition makes bones thin and weak. The recommended health habits are the SEE Controls plus adequate calcium intake. Most current articles on osteoporosis are about women because they are at higher risk for the condition than men. But the recommendations apply to both genders, so young men should tune in. Between the ages of 45 and 79, about 29 percent of American women and 18 percent of American men suffer from osteoporosis (Martini, 1989). One sign of the condition is a stooped posture from the waist up, caused by fractured vertebrae in the backbone. The stoop is often severe enough to reduce the person's height by 4 inches or more. Normal function is greatly compromised by the curved backbone, other weak bones, and pain that characterize osteoporosis.

We've already discussed the SEE Controls, so here we will concentrate on calcium. The Recommended Daily Allowance (RDA) for both genders between the ages of 11 and 24 is 1,200 mg. This is also the RDA for women of any age who are pregnant, nursing a child, or have entered *menopause* (the end of menstruation and the ability to bear children). Otherwise, the RDA drops to 800 mg. after the age of 24 for both genders. Current estimates suggest that many of you will have to change your eating habits to get the recommended amount of calcium (Lerch, 1991). The changes should be easy, however, because there are many delicious sources of calcium. One cup of skim milk has 302 mg; 1 ounce of mozzarella cheese (pizza cheese) has 73 mg; 1 ounce of swiss cheese has 275 mg; 3 ounces of sardines canned in oil with bones has 326 mg; $\frac{1}{2}$ cup of baked beans has 64 mg; 1 cup of fresh or boiled broccoli has 178 mg; one orange has 52 mg; $\frac{1}{4}$ cup of dried figs has 72 mg; and 1 ounce of almonds has 75 mg. Sharon Lerch (1991) provides a more complete calcium source book, along with mouth-watering recipes for calcium-rich treats.

Risk factors for osteoporosis include genetics, a small frame, and hormonal changes—none of which you can do anything about. However, you can do something about other risk factors. The SEE Controls and adequate calcium intake are your best insurance policies.

have trouble keeping up with a man of his vitality now, let alone when we reach his age. Nevertheless, we can start now to maximize our potential. You won't have to wait as long as you might think for the payoff. The things that are recommended as being good for you in the long run will make you feel great now.

Cognitive Changes. Elderly people are often the first to admit a decline in their cognitive abilities. Those who work with the elderly also notice declining mental abilities in their patients. Experimenters, however,

Table 10–3
Family, Personal, and Health Factors Affecting Longevity

Family Factors

Grandparents lived to 80—add 1 year for each

Mother lived to 80—add 4 years

Father lived to 80—add 2 years

Grandparent, parent, or sibling died of cardiovascular disease before age of 50—subtract 4 years for each incidence; before age of 60—subtract 2 years

Grandparent, parent, or sibling died of diabetes or peptic ulcers before age of 60—subtract 3 years for each incidence; if died of stomach cancer—subtract 2 years

Mother under 18 or over 35 when born—subtract 1 year

Personal Factors

Work as a professional—add 1.5 years; as a manager, administrator, or agricultural worker—add 1 year

Active job—add 2 years

Live most of life in urban area—subtract 1 year

Live most of life in rural area—add 1 year

Married and living with spouse—add 1 year

Male separated or divorced and living alone—subtract 9 years

Male separated or divorced not living alone—subtract 4 years

Male who never marries—subtract 2 years for every 10 years beyond the age of 25

Female separated or divorced and living alone—subtract 4 years

Female separated or divorced not living alone—subtract 2 years

Female who never marries—subtract 1 year for every 10 years beyond the age of 25

Aggressive personality—subtract up to 5 years

Health Factors

More than 30 percent overweight—subtract 5 years

More than 10 to 30 percent overweight—subtract 2 to 4 years

Eat plenty of vegetables and fruits, stop eating before full—add 1 year

Smoke two or more packs of cigarettes a day—subtract 12 years

Smoke between one and two packs of cigarettes a day—subtract 7 years

Smoke less than a pack of cigarettes a day—subtract 2 years

Heavy drinker—subtract 8 years

Moderate or light consumption of alcohol—add 2 years

Exercise regularly at least 3 times a week—add 3 years

Regular physical checkups—add 2 years

Based on a Metropolitan Life Insurance Company chart.

have had trouble analyzing cognitive changes because of certain methodological pitfalls.

A study by Jerome (1959) illustrates some of the snags. He tested problem-solving abilities with a logical analysis device. People had to gather information piece by piece and then integrate it to solve problems. A group of subjects who were about 66 years old did much worse than a group of subjects who were about 23 years old. The older people tended to ask for the same information over and over again. Jerome tried to cut down on the need to remember information by allowing subjects to write notes. Younger people made good use of the notes, but older people did not. Jerome's experiment left no doubt that the older subjects had greater difficulty solving problems because they approached the problems haphazardly. However, we cannot be sure that age caused the difference that was observed between young and old subjects. The two groups might have differed in motivation. Perhaps older people considered the problems meaningless and irrelevant and therefore may have exerted themselves less. Furthermore, the two groups might have had different educational experiences. Schools for the younger subjects may have put greater emphasis on problem solving. As a result, the younger subjects may have been better problem solvers than the older people were at *any* point in their lives. For these reasons, Jerome's experiment does not prove that age causes a decline in problem-solving ability.

Whenever researchers compare different age groups, age is not the only difference. Motivation, education, and health are three other factors that often differ. Researchers do not agree on how to define motivation or on how to measure it. Until they agree on these issues, there will be little hope of controlling motivation in studies of aging (Botwinick, 1977). Motivational changes could cause changes in performance even when researchers study the same people at different ages. Education is also difficult to control because the educational system keeps changing. Finally, health is another factor that is difficult to control. For example, it is difficult to assess the effects of stroke and Alzheimer's disease for three reasons. First, as discussed in Chapters 2 and 7, these diseases are known to impair cognitive functioning. Second, the risk of these diseases increases with age. Third, these diseases often go undetected. In fact, the only sure diagnosis of Alzheimer's disease is by examination of the brain at autopsy (Kokmen, 1984). Despite these methodological problems, however, researchers have gathered important data on cognitive changes.

Botwinick (1977) tentatively suggests six cognitive changes that occur with age and aids to counteract them:

Georgia O'Keeffe is shown here at age 75, shortly after her rigorous raft trip down the Colorado River. When this photograph was taken, she had just been elected a member of the American Academy of Arts and Letters, the nation's highest honor society of the arts.

1. Older people need more time to respond in learning situations (Canestrari, 1963). The pacing of learning tasks should be slowed to allow for this.

2. Older people are prone to have high anxiety, which limits responses in learning tasks (Eisdorfer, 1968). Researchers should take steps to reduce anxiety as much as possible in learning and testing situations.

3. Elderly people tend to resist learning things that seem to them to be irrelevant and meaningless (Hulicka & Grossman, 1967). It's a good idea to make sure an elderly person wants to learn something or understands why it is important before teaching is begun.

4. The elderly often fail to take advantage of organizational strategies that could help them learn. We learned in Chapter 7, for instance, that list learning is easier when similar items are grouped together. Elderly learners do not try such groupings on their own (Denney, 1974). They may improve considerably if they are helped to organize in this way (Hultsch, 1971).

5. Elderly people tend to be insecure. They will therefore respond much better if they are praised rather than criticized.

6. Elderly people's short-term memory (Chapter 7) is better for things they hear than it is for things they see (Arenberg, 1967). If you want to help an aging person remember a phone number long enough for a single dialing, say it for them.

Most of you will not personally experience sensory or cognitive declines for many years. You may, however, be able to help aging relatives counteract such sensory and cognitive changes. We mentioned earlier, for instance, that aging parents often depend upon support from their sons and daughters (Spark & Brody, 1970). In the next section, we will reexamine this important phase of the family cycle from the aging parents' perspective.

Family Commitments

O'Keeffe's decision not to have children meant that she had few family commitments during late adulthood, especially after her husband died. She made up for this, however, by becoming a "foster grandparent" to children in her village. These children visited her regularly. They ate with her, colored with crayons in her studio, and sometimes they even helped her prepare canvases. She took some of her favorites camping with her, and she sent several to private schools. She supplied a Little League team with uniforms, balls, and bats. She provided funds to bring educational programs to local television stations, and she supported the construction of a local recreational center with a donation of about $60,000. She may have been motivated by the fond memories she had of her own grandmothers. Psychologists are only beginning to gather data on grandparenting. They are finding that this important role enriches the lives of grandchildren *and* grandparents. The enrichments are plentiful in situations ranging from "foster grandparenting" (Haber & Short-DeGraff, 1990) to live-in grandparenting (Pearson, Hunter, Ensminger, & Kellam, 1990).

Being a Grandparent. Grandparents and grandchildren mutually enrich each others' lives. Ninety-two percent of grandchildren in one study thought that grandparents contribute much to growing up (Robertson, 1976). Children like doing things with their grandparents, and they value the love and gifts they receive from them (Kahana & Kahana, 1971). In return, they give their grandparents great satisfaction. The majority derived pleasure from a feeling of renewal, from meaningful companionship, and from being able to contribute to the development of their grandchildren. Grandparents also enjoy seeing their grandchildren accomplish things that neither the grandparent nor their children were able to do. They enjoy these experiences even more after taking classes that have been designed to increase the benefits of grandparenting (Strom & Strom, 1990). Grandmothers and grandfathers agree that the gender of the grandchild does not affect the pleasure they derive from grandparenting (Thomas, 1989). Grandparenting can become especially important when death of a spouse

Grandparents and grandchildren mutually enrich each others' lives.

DISEASE-FREE AGING VERSUS SENILE DEMENTIA

Many people fear that becoming "senile" is an inevitable part of aging. In correct medical usage, the term *senile* means "related to old age." So, yes—you will get old when you get old. But in shirtsleeve English, the term is incorrectly used to refer to the extreme memory loss and mental confusion often associated with old age. This usage reinforces the fear that severe mental deterioration is inescapable. Both the usage and the fear are inappropriate. Drastic declines in memory and cognition are not a *normal* part of the aging process. So, no—you will not inevitably lose your memory and cognitive abilities in old age. Your mental functions will remain relatively clear unless you acquire a disease that affects them. (See Chapter 8, "Language, Thought, and Intelligence.")

General mental decline caused by an organic disease is called *dementia*. When a disease causes a mental decline during old age, it is called *senile dementia*. The syndrome of dementia is defined by the American Psychiatric Association (1987) as having the following symptoms, which interfere with social and occupational functioning: (1) impaired short-term memory (inability to learn new information) and long-term memory (inability to remember past personal information); (2) impaired abstract reasoning—for example, difficulty in understanding the meaning of a proverb; (3) impaired judgment—for example, making unreasonable plans to deal with interpersonal or job-related problems; (4) disturbances of other mental abilities, such as language and visual-spatial skills; and (5) personality change, such as going from conscientious to compulsive.

Would you fear that something is inevitable if it occurred 15 percent of the time? Of course not! Then you shouldn't fear that senile dementia is inevitable because it is estimated that only 15 percent of people over 65 suffer from senile dementia (Katzman, 1976).

The pattern of physical and cognitive changes associated with senile dementia and disease-free aging are different (Albert & Moss, 1988). Here we will concentrate on differences in cognitive changes. Specifically, we will compare memory changes. An interesting comparison is between normal memory changes and those associated with Alzheimer's disease. This disease is the most common cause of senile dementia; it accounts for 50 to 70 percent of all cases of dementia in the elderly (Mortimer, 1983). The causes of Alzheimer's disease are not yet known, nor has a successful treatment been identified. Like many other causes of dementia, Alzheimer's disease is progressive, with symptoms steadily worsening until the person is completely dependent on others.

In contrast to the case with senile dementia, the cognitive changes associated with disease-free aging are *not* pervasive, severe, and progressive. Occasional lapses in memory occur in healthy elderly people, but they need not interfere with everyday functioning and they do not progress to general intellectual impairment (Kral, 1962). Smith (1977) has noted that some laboratory experiments overestimate the memory differences between young and old adults. In order to gauge age-related decline with respect to everyday memory demands, we must study tasks that are representative of those demands.

This point was driven home recently by Norris and West (1990). They analyzed age differences in the recall of subject-performed tasks (SPTs). Recall of SPTs requires a person to perform a list of discrete actions such as "lift the cup" and "stretch the rubber band." These actions provide auditory, visual, motor, and tactual cues similar to everyday memory demands. They also can be grouped into natural categories, such as actions performed in the office, kitchen, and garage. Norris and West (1990) found that healthy older adults recalled SPTs as well as young adults. In contrast, Alzheimer's patients had very poor recall of SPTs. These results illustrate the importance of simulating everyday memory demands when comparing the memories of young and old. They also exemplify the importance of distinguishing between the effects of disease-free aging and senile dementia.

Alzheimer's disease is far from inevitable. The odds of acquiring it are relatively low, and researchers are looking for ways to make them even lower. In the meantime, researchers have found relatively simple things that you can do now to reduce the risk of other forms of dementia (see Highlight: Habits in Early Years and Health in Later Years).

deprives an elderly person of one of his or her most important sources of life satisfaction. These many sources of satisfaction help explain why 75 percent of today's grandparents in America see their grandchildren at least once a week (Troll, 1983).

Elderly Husbands and Wives. Marital satisfaction is very high for elderly couples. In fact, it may reach its highest level during late adulthood (Miller, 1976). Older husbands and wives find happiness in companionship, mutual expression of true feelings, and economic security, among other things (Stinnett, Carter, & Montgomery, 1972). Unless health problems dictate otherwise, older couples can enjoy sexual relations to the age of 80 years and beyond (Rubin, 1966). Reduced occupational commitments enable elderly couples to spend more time together. In the best situations, husbands help more around the house and women become more loving

Many retired people stay active in volunteer activities and sports.

and understanding (Troll, 1971). If all these research results seem too obvious to you, consider this one: Older adults' marital satisfaction seems to be related to perceived physical attractiveness of the elder husband, but not the wife (Webb, Delaney, & Young, 1989).

Occupational Commitments

O'Keeffe widely exhibited new paintings as she advanced in years through her eighties and into her nineties. She remained in the mainstream of art when others her age had long since retired. Many people cannot stay engaged in their careers as she did. But most people can make up for career retirement by increasing involvement in other activities (Neugarten & Hagestad, 1976). Retirement, from this point of view, can be as fulfilling as O'Keeffe's late-life career. In this section, we will consider how people plan for retirement, how they adjust to it, and how satisfied they are with it.

Planning for Retirement. Retirement in the United States is usually mandatory at the age of 65 or 70 years. The mandatory versus voluntary retirement issue will probably be debated for some time to come. On the one hand, mandatory retirement seems to discriminate against older people who are ready and able to continue to work. On the other hand, Botwinick (1977) argues in favor of mandatory retirement on several grounds, one of which is that a fixed age limit will better enable people to plan for retirement.

To what extent do people actually plan under the present mandatory system? There is no simple answer, because many variables influence the extent of planning. However, one good sign is that today 9 out of 10 Americans are registered for a pension plan (Crystal, 1982). A tendency for men to plan is positively associated with high socioeconomic status, leisure-time interests, financial security, and good health (McPherson & Guppy, 1979).

Adjusting to Retirement. Lowenthal (1972) suggests that the trick to a successful retirement is substituting activities for the time previously spent on an occupation. Career women are often better prepared to make this adjustment because the role of homemaker is a traditionally acceptable substitution. Men also adjust better when they share in household tasks. Some men, however, especially working-class men, consider "women's work" demeaning. As a result, adjusting to retirement can be more problematic for this group (Troll, 1971). A second popular substitution is another job. Streif and Schneider (1971) observed that 73 percent of people who consider work to be a major source of satisfaction find another job after retirement. A third substitution is well-planned leisure activity, which can be especially fulfilling for those who have a history of sharing recreational interests with their spouses. Whatever the substitution is, a redistribution of energy seems to be basic to a satisfying adjustment. Activity after retirement sustains physical health and cognitive skills (Rogers, Meyer, & Mortel, 1990).

Retirement and Life Satisfaction. The impact of retirement is often not as negative as people anticipated, according to Streif and Schneider (1971). They measured attitudes of 4,000 people before and after retirement. Their sample included people from many walks of life, ranging from unskilled laborers to professionals. The results indicated that about 33 percent found retirement to be better than they had anticipated. Only about 5 percent found it to be worse. Most people in the sample adjusted well to retirement and were satisfied with life.

Streib and Schneider's study raises the question of why so many people are overly pessimistic about retirement. One reason may be that some of the negative feelings are not actually related to retirement itself. A worker inevitably associates retirement with old age, and that may be associated with death. Older people have had a chance to come to grips with aging and they are less fearful of death (Kalish & Reynolds, 1976). After retirement we would therefore expect a reduction in some of the pessimism that was associated with the fear of aging and death.

Death and Dying

O'Keeffe was almost 60 when her husband died. Many friends and relatives also died as she advanced through her sixties. These deaths forced her to realize that she must make plans for her estate in the event of her own death. She assigned some paintings to be left to several museums and universities. She wanted most of her art to be displayed, however, in an O'Keeffe art museum in New Mexico. In terms of Erikson's (1963) theory, O'Keeffe faced the last stage of development, the crisis of *integrity versus despair*. Resolution of this crisis determines whether one faces the end of life with a feeling that a full and meaningful life has been led or with a feeling that life has been wasted (Antonovsky & Sagy, 1990). O'Keeffe emerged with wisdom that is related to integrity. She achieved the wisdom to be pleased with her accomplishments and to be accepting of her death. We will conclude our life-span investigations with a discussion of the processes of accepting the deaths of others and accepting one's own death.

Adjusting to the Death of Loved Ones

O'Keeffe grieved over the deaths of her parents, other relatives, and friends. But the death of her husband seemed to be the most devastating. Death of a spouse requires more than an emotional adjustment. It also requires the adoption of new roles and responsibilities (see Chapter 12). Life-satisfaction ratings of widows and widowers correlate highly with having skills necessary for making these adaptations (Rux, 1976). Another important factor is the extent of involvement in a spouse's life. Lopata (1973a, b) observed, for instance, that widows report more life disruption when they identified strongly with their husband's activities. Widows and widowers experience severe loneliness and grief, however, whether or not they are forced to make drastic lifestyle changes.

Psychologists are only beginning to learn about the grief process (e.g., Parkes & Brown, 1972). Glick, Weiss, and Parkes (1974) outlined distinct phases of grieving:

1. The *initial response* is a phase characterized first by shock and then by an overwhelming sorrow.

2. The second phase, *coping with anxiety and fear*, is characterized by worry of a nervous breakdown. Some people depend upon tranquilizers during this period.

3. The third phase, the *intermediate* phase, consists of obsessional review of how the death might have been prevented and a review of old memories of times with the loved one.

4. *Recovery* is the last phase, which usually begins after one year. People become proud that they survived an extreme trauma, and they begin to develop a positive outlook once again.

Recent research casts a different light on the first phase. It suggests that the first task is to accept the reality of the death. Furthermore, this task can be facilitated by working in advance with spouses of terminally ill patients (Huber & Gibson, 1990).

Some widows and widowers experience panic disorders, generalized anxiety disorders (see Chapter 14), and other symptoms of pathological grief (Raphael & Middleton, 1990). In one study, Jacobs and Kim (1990) investigated psychiatric complications in widows and widowers during the first year after the loss of their spouse. In their sample of 102 grieving spouses, about 10 percent had panic disorders and about 30 percent had generalized anxiety disorders. Acute grief is common during the first year. Children can be an important source of support (O'Bryant & Morgan, 1990), as can clergy (Hovey & Berkram, 1990). However, grieving spouses with serious complications should be referred to a trained therapist (see Chapter 15).

Accepting One's Own Death

How often do you think about your own death? Can you face it without fear or despair? Your answers probably depend upon your age. Young people think about death much less than old people, and they are more fearful of it (Kalish & Reynolds, 1976). The question of accepting one's own death becomes especially relevant to those who are told that they have a terminal illness. In her book, *On Death and Dying*, Elisabeth Kübler-Ross (1969) summarized results of interviews with over 200 people in this situation. She identified five stages in the adjustment process:

1. *Denial and isolation* is first. A common initial statement is "No, not me, it cannot be true." Some denials are long lasting and are accompanied by conviction that the doctors are wrong. Other denials are soon replaced by isolation, which is the ability to talk about one's own death as if it were happening to someone else.

2. The second stage is *anger*, which typically stems from resentment and from concern about being cast aside. One patient reported wondering, "Why couldn't it have been old George instead of me?" Another patient cried out "I am alive, don't forget that. You can hear my voice, I am not dead yet!"

3. Anger is often replaced by *bargaining*. This third stage usually involves private promises with God. For "a little more time," patients promise "a life dedicated to God" or "a life in the service of the church."

4. Most people move quickly from bargaining to *depression*, the fourth stage. Kübler-Ross distinguishes two kinds of depression: *Reactive depression* is feeling downcast because of people and things that need to be taken care of. A mother will be depressed, for instance, until she knows the kind of care that will be provided for her children. *Preparatory depression* is a sense of impending loss of everything and everybody one loves. Patients at this time are grateful to those who can sit with them in silence.

5. People who work through their depression reach the final stage, *acceptance*. It is not a happy stage, but it is a time of peace. Most patients in the Kübler-Ross study died in this stage without fear or despair.

Kübler-Ross (1974) warns that her "stages" are not invariant or universal. She was not trying to prescribe a "best way" to prepare for death. She is disturbed that some health caretakers are trying to manipulate patients through her stages. It is far better to accept an individual's response pattern (Butler & Lewis, 1982; Franke & Durlak, 1990).

If you were told that you had a terminal disease and had 6 months to live, how would you want to spend your time? One study obtained answers to this question from people in three age groups: 20 to 39 years old, 40 to 59 years old, and over 60 years old (Kalish & Reynolds, 1976). More younger respondents thought that they would change their lifestyles, and more older people thought that they would reflect on spiritual needs.

Such reflection may be adaptive since people with strong religious beliefs have less fear of death (Nelson & Nelson, 1973; Templar, 1972; Peterson & Greil, 1990).

Georgia O'Keeffe revealed that she reflected on spiritual beliefs. In fact one wonders if her desire to display her art in New Mexico was related to a view she once expressed about death: "When I think of death, I only regret that I will not be able to see this beautiful country [the New Mexico countryside] anymore, unless the Indians are right and my spirit will walk here after I'm gone" (Lisle, 1980).

Summary

1. The **life-span development approach** studies human development from conception to death. It is concerned about changes that occur within an individual over time as well as the differences in such changes among individuals.

2. In **adolescence** the physical changes include the adolescent "growth spurt," **puberty,** and the development of **primary** and **secondary sex characteristics.** Morally, teenagers generally progress through Kohlberg's conventional level of moral reasoning. Moral development may be related to cognitive development. An important stage in the personality development of the adolescent, according to Erikson, is the **identity crisis.** Identity is an assured sense of self as a person. Peer groups become very important and early sexual activity seems to have become more common. Consequently, **sexually transmitted disease (STD)** and teenage pregnancy are growing social problems.

3. One way of looking at development in young adulthood is in terms of commitments that are made at this time: moral commitments (Kohlberg's postconventional stage is usually reached at this point); interpersonal commitments (Erikson's stage of intimacy versus isolation, in which marriage and family commitments are a major theme); and mastery commitments (the establishment of and mastery in a career or occupation).

4. Levinson's framework for development in young adulthood contains several stages, including a transition stage at about age 30, and a settling down stage, in which in terms of occupation the person seeks a certain amount of independence.

5. Middle age is concerned first with Erikson's generativity versus stagnation stage, in which one's involvement in family, job, or community work can either be fulfilling or leave one with a sense of being meaningless. In the same way, Levinson's framework at this age includes a kind of midlife transition (often called a midlife crisis, but not necessarily so). In terms of family commitments, for many this is a time when children begin leaving the home, while, at the same time, middle-aged people often become more involved in caring for their elderly parents.

6. Late adulthood involves many physical changes, which affect sensory abilities as well as general health and mobility. There are also changes at this age in cognitive abilities, but only of a certain type. Family commitments at this point include being a grandparent, and there is often an increase in marital satisfaction for elderly couples. In terms of occupation, one of the major themes is planning for and adjusting to retirement. The elderly face Erikson's final crisis, the stage of integrity versus despair, which determines one's final outlook on life.

7. It may be possible to maximize our potential for being hearty in our older years by controlling diet, smoking, exercise, and stress during our life span. The benefits can start immediately.

8. Just as there are stages that we go through adjusting to life, there seem to be stages in adjusting to death—the death of those close to us and our own death. Kübler-Ross has outlined what seem to be five distinct stages in this adjustment process: denial and isolation, anger, bargaining, depression, and, finally, acceptance.

Key Terms

adolescence
cohabitation
identity crisis
internalization

life-span development approach
menarche
primary sexual characteristics
puberty

secondary sexual characteristics
sexually transmitted disease (STD)

TRACKING THE LIFE OF THE NEW FATHER

BY CAROL LAWSON

Princeton, N.J.

For the 16 people seated around a horseshoe-shaped mahogany table in their company's conference room here, lunch was sandwiches and parkbench talk. As they ate, they shared worries about a deep concern in their lives: how to pursue a demanding career yet be an involved parent.

Here is what some of them had to say:

"I have so little time with my child. I feel so guilty."

"The stress factor is astronomical. There is so much pressure on my time at work and at home."

"I feel like I'm stretching myself as far as I can. I fear it's going to take a toll on my health."

These were not mothers talking. All the speakers were fathers.

"Fathers are beginning to talk about the same issues that working mothers are struggling with," James A. Levine told the group. "Men feel torn between juggling their jobs and a commitment to being a father. They feel pulled in both directions."

Mr. Levine, who studies and writes about the behavior of the man he calls "the new father," was leading one of the fatherhood seminars he conducts in the offices of major corporations around the nation. This one was at an office of Merrill Lynch, Pierce, Fenner & Smith, and it drew a diverse group of men from marketing, accounting, international banking and other departments in the company.

To a previous generation, the new father was a bleary-eyed male who struggled to survive his baby's 2 A.M. feedings and get a few hours of sleep before shuffling off to work. Today the term has taken on new meaning: the new father is perceived as a man who has thrown himself into the total world of child care: the good, the bad and the messy.

Mr. Levine, a former vice president of the Bank Street College of Education, defined the new father for his audience as a man who "attempts to make child rearing an important part of his life."

"It does not mean that a man gives up a career or the drive to succeed," said the 43-year-old speaker, who began studying changing patterns of fatherhood in the early 1970's with a Ford Foundation grant. "It means trying to achieve more balance."

As evidence of the emergence of a new father, Mr. Levine listed a number of trends: an increase in men who take time off from work following the birth of a child; an increase in men who drop off children and pick them up at day-care centers; the growing visibility of men in pediatricians' offices and parenting classes; the installation of diaper-changing tables in men's rooms in airports and train stations; the high visibility of fathers with babies in advertisements and an increase in the number of men who attend the birth of their children.

"Thirty years ago it was virtually unheard of for men to attend childbirth," Mr. Levine said, "Twenty years ago, less than 10 percent of men did. Today, the number is over 90 percent."

He also mentioned the small but growing examples of men who turn down employers' requests to relocate because they do not want to uproot their families, or who switch to less demanding jobs so they can spend more time with their children.

Still, Mr. Levine was careful to say he did not want to overstate his case.

"There is a tendency today to hype fatherhood, to say that everything has changed dramatically," said the speaker, who has interviewed hundreds of men nationwide. "We are seeing an evolution, not a revolution. It is a mistake to overdramatize the new fatherhood, but it is also a mistake to say that men are acting the way they always have."

Others who have studied contemporary fathers also take a cautionary view. "Fatherhood is changing more in the media than in reality, but there is some real behavioral change out there," said Joseph H. Pleck, Luce professor of family studies at Wheaton College in Norton, Mass.

In the opinion of Dr. Kyle D. Pruett, clinical professor of psychiatry at the Yale Child Study Center, the emergence of today's father "is not like discovering a new moon around Neptune."

"Still, there are subtle shifts," said

Dr. Pruett, author of "The Nurturing Father" (Warner Books, 1988). "We are raising a generation of children who expect their fathers to be more than baby sitters in their lives."

Mr. Levine said he agreed with the assessment of the sociologist Arlie Hochschild that probably no more than 20 percent of men fully share with their wives the responsibilities and chores of fatherhood. Ms. Hochschild made that statement in her book "The Second Shift" (Viking, 1989), which argued that "most women work one shift at the office or factory and a 'second shift' at home."

Mr. Levine, who is married to his high school sweetheart and is the father of two children, told the Merrill Lynch audience that changes in fatherhood can best be seen "in a very long-term perspective." He recalled that when he began writing his 1976 book "Who Will Raise the Children: New Options for Fathers (and Mothers)," (J. B. Lippincott) no state allowed joint custody of children in divorce cases. "Now over half the states have legislation allowing it," he said.

Paternity leave did not have much support at that time, either, Mr. Levine said. At a 1974 hearing in California, a public official called it "completely ridiculous" for a father to take time off from work to care for a new baby, he said.

That kind of thinking had deep support, according to his book, which presented stories of pioneering men who had chosen to take on major responsibility for the care of their young children. Many people believed, as Dr. Bruno Bettelheim wrote in 1956, that "the male physiology and that part of his psychology based on it are not geared to infant care."

Another expert, Dr. Haim Ginott, is quoted as saying in his best-selling 1975 book, "Between Parent and Child," that if a father engages in activities like feeding, diapering and bathing a baby, "there is the danger that the baby may end up with two mothers, rather than a mother and a father."

Mr. Levine became interested in the role of fathers in 1968, when he taught pre-school in Oakland, Calif. "I was constantly being asked, 'What do you *really* do?'" he said. "That question never would have been asked of women. I began to realize that people had different expectations for men, that men weren't supposed to connect with young children."

In 1973, he received the Ford Foundation grant to study fathers who were caring for young children. His research became the basis for "Who Will Raise the Children."

As he began his study, he found that little had been written from the point of view of fathers. It was the norm for studies of parents to be based solely on interviews with mothers, even a 1969 study titled "Father Participation in Infancy."

In 1981 Mr. Levine began the Fatherhood Project, which conducts research and acts as a national clearinghouse on issues related to fatherhood. He operated the project out of Bank Street until last year, when he moved it to the new Families and Work Institute, a nonprofit research organization in New York. He also runs James Levine Communications Inc., a consulting and literary agency that specializes in developing projects related to childhood education and family life.

The project's current research, financed by the Ford Foundation, is a study of how corporate policy and culture support or inhibit men in balancing their commitments to work and family. The study centers on samplings of men who work at Apple Computer, Ortho Pharmaceutical Corporation and the New York law firm of Milbank, Tweed, Hadley & McCloy.

"We are slowly bringing fathers into focus as part of the family picture," Mr. Levine said. "It is almost like we have discovered there are fathers out there. The question for the 90's is, how do we allow them to be full participants in family life?"

The New York Times, April 12, 1990.

Motivation 11

As dawn broke, the airport in Uruguay was filled with the excited chatter of the forty passengers who waited to board the plane for the four-hour trip to Santiago, Chile. Fifteen of the passengers, ages eighteen to twenty-six, were members of the Old Christians Club rugby team, which had organized the trip and chartered the airplane. They were going to Chile to play against the tough Chilean national teams. At 8:05 A.M., on October 12, 1972, the plane taxied down the runway and took off for the 900-mile trip. The flight plan took them through Argentina and over the snow-covered peaks of the Andes.

The plane bounced savagely in the light air as it tried to climb above the clouds. Among the passengers there was a holiday atmosphere; the young men joked at each lurch of their tiny aircraft. The atmosphere in the cockpit, however, was not so jovial. The pilot was fighting to maintain control of the plane and searching desperately for landmarks.

Suddenly the plane swooped out of the clouds just in time for everyone to see a massive rock not more than ten feet from the wing tip. The wing slammed into the mountain, ripped off, and sliced into the tail section. The torn body of the plane hurtled down the snowy mountainside like a toboggan. Finally it came to rest in a snowbank. For a moment, there was utter silence, and then the moans of the injured filled the air. One by one, those who were not hurt climbed out of the plane and sat bewildered in the snow.

Soon the survivors began a gruesome search through what was left of the plane. Five people, including the pilot and copilot, were dead, and many of the others were so badly injured it was clear that they, too, would soon die. Mustering all of their strength, the survivors untangled the injured and dead from the wreckage; the dead were dragged out of the plane and the injured were carefully laid inside.

The subzero cold of the Andes quickly made the survivors realize that their first task must be to clear an area inside the wreck for shelter.

Seats were dragged out and a makeshift wall was built over the gaping hole in the tail area. No one was prepared for the cold; many of the passengers wore only short-sleeved shirts. As the sun began to set, they huddled together inside the shelter.

By morning, more of the injured had died, leaving twenty-eight survivors to share a cramped twenty-foot section of the plane. The morning also brought another problem; many of the survivors began to complain of thirst. This problem was especially acute for those who had lost a lot of blood. A careful search uncovered an odd assortment of food and drink, including some bottles of wine, brandy, whiskey, and creme de menthe; eight chocolate bars; three jars of jam; and two cans of mussels. With all the snow around, they felt that water would not be a problem, but they were wrong. They soon found that it was hard to melt the snow, and eating snow did little to quench their thirst. Finally they found they could get water by putting a little snow in some pans and placing the pans in the sun.

The survivors organized themselves into three teams. Some of the men were in charge of melting snow to provide water. A second team, which included three medical students, was responsible for the injured. A third team had the duty of clearing more space in the wrecked plane. It was impossible to stretch out in the area they had—each time someone moved, he intruded on the others around him. One of the men found a transistor radio; on it they were excited to hear that search parties had been sent out to find them. But no help came that day, and the survivors trudged into the plane as night came and temperatures again plunged below zero.

The expected rescue did not come the next day, or the day after that. As time wore on, many of the survivors became more and more irritable; the slightest frustration was met with a stream of curses, and conflicts between survivors led to violent confrontations. During the day, they could not stray far from the plane because the snow was soft and they would sink into it above their waists. They spent the time exploring the area immediately around the plane and talking about their families.

The days passed and they realized that no help was coming. By the ninth day, another realization sank in, one that was even more frightening than the diminished prospects for a speedy rescue. As the survivors looked at one another they became aware of wrinkled skin, protruding bones, and sunken eyes; they were all slowly starving to death. Their meager food supply was nearly gone. Their strength had so dwindled that a walk around the plane left even the strongest survivors panting and exhausted. At this point a few of the men cautiously mentioned the possibility of eating the bodies preserved in the frozen snow outside the plane.

This idea was met with shock and disgust. But since their situation had now become desperate, a meeting of the twenty-eight survivors was called. Most of them realized that, however repugnant the thought, only by eating human flesh could they survive. One of the rugby players argued, "I know that if my dead body could help you stay alive, then I would want you to use it. In fact, if I do die and you don't eat me, then I'll come back from wherever I am and give you a good kick in the ass" (Read, 1974, p. 84). Another of the men argued that it was like Holy Communion: "When Christ died he gave his body to us so we could have spiritual life. My friend has given us his body so that we can have physical life" (Read, 1974, p. 91).

One by one, over the next few days, the starved survivors forced themselves to eat human flesh. Only

an older couple refused to eat. But finally, on the verge of starvation, they, too, gave in and ate the flesh. A group was chosen to find the rest of the bodies and prepare the meat and fat for eating.

Then disaster struck again: Without warning, a wall of snow broke through the barrier at the back and swept through the plane. Nine more people died in this avalanche. When the nineteen survivors had regrouped, all agreed they could wait no longer for rescue; they must send out a search party of their own. The four most physically able young men were chosen to make up the search party. In the weeks that followed the avalanche, this group began to explore the area around the plane in order to find a way out of the mountains.

On the fifty-sixth day after the crash, the survivors saw their first signs of outside life; two giant birds circled lazily over the wreck. That same day a bee flew into the plane. These signs brought the realization that the snow was melting as summer came to the Andes. The melting snow meant that the bodies of the dead would thaw and rot, and then the only source of life for the survivors would be gone. The search party had to set out immediately, or it would be too late.

Three of the men left, dressed in many layers of clothing and carrying socks full of meat. After struggling through the mountains for nine days, they saw a peasant tending his cattle. The young men wept with joy; they had been saved.

The other survivors were soon picked up and taken to Santiago. The world buzzed with excitement as news spread that the young men had survived for seventy days in the subzero temperatures of the Andes. The excitement gave way to horror when pictures of human bones scattered around the wreckage were published and it became known that the survivors ate human flesh to stay alive. Their survival was truly remarkable, but the moral questions raised by their methods of survival were debated for many years. ▪▪▪

After completing this chapter, you should be able to:

Explain what is meant by the word ''motive'' and differentiate between primary motives and social motives.

Compare and contrast the theories of motivation.

Review the factors that influence when, how much, and what we eat.

Identify the factors associated with obesity and discuss eating disorders.

Differentiate between osmometric and volumetric thirst.

Describe the biological basis of sexual behavior and human sexual responses.

Identify the arousal theories that may explain our stimulus-seeking motives.

Differentiate social motives from biological motives and give examples.

Explain how achievement motivation is defined and the developmental factors that may influence achievement motivation.

Explain Maslow's hierarchy of needs and the probable order of motives in a hierarchy.

Motivation: Scope and History

As you read the story of the survivors, you probably found yourself asking: "What would I do in their situation? Would I eat human flesh rather than starve to death? Would I be encouraging the group about the hope of survival, or would I myself give up?" Each of us has the ability and knowledge to behave in any of these ways. But given a particular set of circumstances, how would we actually behave?

It is on this question of how people behave and why that we now focus our attention. We have already examined the human being much as we would a machine. In Chapter 2 we discussed the physical makeup of the human machine. In Chapter 3 we looked at how these parts work together, and in other chapters we have seen how humans learn to behave. Now we will examine what energizes this complex machine and guides its actions.

As an analogy, we might consider a jukebox. It has the necessary physical parts to play music, and it also has a wide selection of tunes. The biological and physiological components of the individual are like the physical parts of the jukebox; they define the capacity of the machine (the human) to act. A jukebox does not have the physical components to think, and the human body is not endowed with the components necessary for flying. Learning, along with a limited range of innate behaviors, determines the specific behaviors that can occur at any time. These learned behaviors are similar to the records in the jukebox. Together, the biological structure and learning form the enduring capability of the individual to perform certain behaviors. In order for the jukebox to play, someone has to plug it in (that is, give it energy) and select a tune. In a similar way, the human machine has a wonderful variety of behaviors it can perform, but it needs energy and some selection device to determine which behaviors it will perform in a particular situation. The energy source/selection device temporarily translates the capabilities into actions; it is temporary in the sense that it determines why the individual acted in a specific way at a specific time, given the wide range of capabilities that existed.

Primary motives such as hunger and thirst involve our biological needs and are usually unlearned. Social motives such as affiliation, aggression, and achievement usually involve social interaction and learning.

Psychologists have used the term **motive** to describe the condition that energizes and directs the behavior of organisms. **Motivation** explains why an organism acts in a certain way at a certain time—it provides the bridge between learning and performance. For example, we may ask why on the ninth day did some of the survivors turn to eating human flesh? The bodies of the dead were there right after the crash, and those who survived could have eaten them at any time. To answer this question we talk about motivation using such concepts as hunger and conflict.

When we speak of motives, we can loosely place them in one of two groups. On one hand, we have **primary motives,** which concern our biological needs. These motives are usually unlearned, common to all animals, and vital for the survival of the organism or the species. Motives such as hunger, thirst, the need for air and rest, and sexual desire fall in this category. The second group consists of **social motives.** These motives come from learning and social interaction. They include the needs for affiliation, aggression, and achievement.

Possibly no question about the human being has raised such violent disagreement as the issue of the basis for motivation. Since the time of the early Greeks, debates have been flavored with religion, philosophy, and science. Gods, demons, and even tiny creatures (homunculi) have been said to guide and energize human behavior. People have been burned, poked, stabbed, whipped, and otherwise tortured to rid them of these influences on their behavior and to change their motivation. The nature of the human organism has been questioned and debated. According to the doctrine of *determinism*, the human is like a machine. An extreme view of this doctrine holds that humans, like all other living creatures, react automatically to internal and external forces; there is no planning or control exercised over behavior. The doctrine of *rationalism* or *free will* holds that people make free choices about how they will behave; in other words, their actions are controlled by reasoning and planning. Implicit in the free will position is a desire to distinguish humans from animals (Beck, 1990; Petri, 1991).

Instinct Theories. Psychologists began trying to explain motivation around the turn of the century. The early views invoked the concept of **instinct:** an innate or inborn predisposition to act in a specific way. William James (1890) and later William McDougall (1908) argued that nature sup-

Motive
Condition that energizes and directs the behavior of an organism.
Motivation
Why an organism acts in a certain way at a certain time.
Primary motives
Motives such as hunger, thirst, and the need for air and rest. These motives are usually unlearned, common to all animals, and vital for the survival of the organism or the species.
Social motives
Motives that come from learning and social interaction rather than based on biological needs (see *primary motives*). These motives include affiliation, aggression, and achievement.
Instincts
Innate or inborn predispositions to act in specific ways.

plies us with both the energy and the pattern of behavior. They suggested that although certain external cues or events might release specific instincts, our actions are guided by internal forces. The early instinct theorists spent considerable effort developing lengthy lists of human instincts, including rivalry, sympathy, hunting, fear, jealousy, secretiveness, repulsion, and combat.

The early instinct theories met with several obvious criticisms. One criticism was that they involved circular reasoning. For example, we might argue that people are aggressive because they have the instinct to be aggressive. We know that the instinct exists because we see people behave aggressively. Used in this way, the concept explains nothing. A second criticism was that the instinct theories did not explain the wide variety of human behavior. For example, some people are very aggressive whereas others are not. Some people use guns and knives as their weapons and others use words.

Although the list-making approach to instincts has disappeared, the concept itself has not. Rather it has evolved and been incorporated into the areas of ethology, sociobiology, and developmental psychobiology (Carins, 1987). Briefly, these areas involve the search for common behaviors within and between species. Investigators look for biological bases for these behaviors and attempt to explain how these behaviors evolved. For example, researchers have examined genetic, hormonal, and biological sources to explain gender and age differences in aggressive behavior (Carins, 1987).

Drive Theories. While one line of investigation used instinct to develop a comparative approach to motivation, most other motivation theories turned away from the concept of instinct all together. However, they did not forsake the position that motivation comes from inside us. Sigmund Freud (1933; see Chapter 13), who based much of his theory on instincts, actually laid the groundwork for the development of drive theories. Freud believed that psychic energy is created when an organism has needs. This energy is the moving force or **drive** behind the organism's motivation. Freud argued that the aim of behavior is to reduce the tension created by the existence of a need.

In the 1940s Clark Hull (1943, 1951) incorporated the drive-reduction perspective with the behaviorist perspective to develop a comprehensive drive theory of motivation. The theory was based on the principle of **homeostasis.** According to this principle, the body tries to keep a constant internal state. When changes occur, the homeostatic mechanism stimulates the organism to act in ways that will return the internal state to what it was. This mechanism works much like the thermostat in your home. The thermostat is set to maintain a certain temperature. When the temperature in the home goes too high, the thermostat will turn on the air conditioner; when it drops too low, the thermostat will turn on the heater. In this way, the temperature in your house can be kept at a certain level. The human body works in a similar fashion. When your body temperature drops, the homeostatic mechanism may cause your body to shiver and constrict your blood vessels. If these actions do not make you warm enough, you may be motivated to seek shelter. On the other hand, if you become too hot, the homeostatic mechanism may stimulate your body to sweat, which causes cooling. If this fails to reduce your body temperature, you may find yourself seeking out a cool swimming pool.

According to Hull, **needs** result when the homeostatic balance within the organism is upset. The existence of a need provokes the organism to satisfy the need. In other words, the need sets up a drive. The specific way in which the need is satisfied and the drive reduced is determined in large part by learning: Behaviors that are better learned than others are more likely to be performed. Hull argued that the likelihood of a behavior depends both on strength of learning (habit) and strength of motivation

Drive
Tension or state that results when a need is not met; it compels the organism to satisfy the need.
Homeostasis
Attempt by the body to maintain a constant internal state.
Need
Internal or homeostatic imbalance that must be satisfied in order to keep the body performing at a consistent level.

Such behaviors as thrill-seeking cannot be clearly explained by a drive-reduction theory. The goal of these behaviors seems to be the increase in drive and stimulation.

(drive). To see how this works, consider the rugby players after the crash. When the food supply was depleted and the players had nothing to eat, the resulting starvation set up the need for food. This need drove the players to search for food. The search focused first on familiar items such as chocolate that they had learned to eat. Only much later did they see the dead bodies as objects to satisfy their drive to eat.

Drive theory clearly makes a great deal of sense. We get hungry when we don't have enough food in our body, and we then search for food. Hundreds of other examples seem to fit this model. But does drive theory cover the whole picture of motivation? As you might suspect, it does not. First, consider the time you paid to have the life scared out of you on a roller coaster. Here is a case where drive reduction did not guide your behavior. In fact the aim of this experience and similar ones (e.g., skydiving, horror movies) is to increase drive, not reduce it. Hence, not all behaviors are motivated by drive reduction, contrary to Hull and other drive theorists. A second problem with the theory is that it suggests that reinforcement, and consequently learning, result from stimuli that reduce drive. Yet research has shown that rats will learn new behaviors for a saccharin reward (Flaherty, 1982) which, having no food value, cannot reduce drive. Finally, the theory suggests that behavior is always internally motivated. But how many times have you attacked a chocolate sundae after a large meal? In all likelihood it was not the internal motivation of hunger that drove you to the sundae, but, rather, the mouth-watering allure of the thick chocolate running down the mountain of ice cream. The bottom line is that we do not live by drive reduction alone; the theory explains many aspects of motivation, but not all.

Incentive Theories. Realizing that not all behavior is motivated by internal needs, a number of investigators looked outside the organism for an explanation. The basic position of these incentive theories is that external events control and determine behavior. An **incentive** is an external stimulus that has the capacity to motivate behavior even if a drive is not apparently present. Incentives can be positive or negative, motivating the organism to move toward or away from a situation. The incentive "pulls" behavior as opposed to the drive that "pushes" behavior. For example, in the previous section, we cited the experiment in which rats worked to obtain a saccharin solution. The solution did not reduce any drive; rather, it was the sweetness of the solution that pulled the behavior. Another example that is closer to home is the rescue of my indignant cat from the depths of an uncovered well. Cuddles was happily sleeping until the well cover was removed, and then he just couldn't resist the call of the open hole.

Cognitive Theories. As we have discussed the motivation theories, you may have begun to experience a vague discomfort. Although each of the previous theories makes sense, they all seem to view us as a being pushed by inner forces or pulled by external forces. Certainly, there is more to our behavior than that! The rugby players survived because they planned and anticipated, and did not simply react to immediate needs or situations. Although theorists such as Kurt Lewin recognized the role of cognitions in the 1930s, cognitive theories of motivation didn't appear until the late 1950s. And by the 1980s, investigators of social behavior rarely referred to the term *motivation*. Instead, their attention focused on the role of cognition as a guide of behavior (Geen, 1991). Their emphasis was on thinking, judging, and information processing.

One early cognitive theory (Miller, Galanter, & Pribram, 1960) argued that behavior is influenced by plans and goals. A goal is an end point that an individual desires to reach. With a goal in mind, the individual develops a plan (or program) about how to reach that goal. The ultimate

Incentive
External stimulus that has the capacity to motivate behavior even if a drive is not apparently present.

goal of the rugby players was to be rescued from the mountain. In order to reach that goal, they developed plans that included setting signal fires, building a shelter, finding food, and sending out a search party. Their goal was influenced by their needs, but it was the goal and plans that directed their behavior.

Another early theory that focused on cognitions was cognitive dissonance theory (Festinger, 1957; see Chapter 16). This theory argues that people strive for consistency between their cognitions (beliefs, attitudes, knowledge about their behaviors). Discomfort results when inconsistency (dissonance) exists between cognitions. This discomfort motivates the organism to restore consistency. For example, it would be dissonant for you to smoke while believing that smoking will kill you. This dissonance should motivate you to change either your behavior (stop smoking) or your belief.

Cognitive theories have focused on how people seek and process information, and how this information affects their choice of behaviors. Recently, however, cognitive theorists have realized that the most complete explanation of human behavior must combine cognition and motivation. The theorists now struggle with the problem of relating cognition and motivation (Geen, 1991; Berkowitz, 1990, Brehm & Self, 1989).

We have examined the general approaches to motivation. Now we will turn our attention to specific motives. As you will see, no single theory explains all these motives. Hence, our aim is not to determine which theory is right, but to see how each approach adds to our explanation. We will begin by examining biological motives that are necessary for survival of the individual or species (hunger, thirst, and sex). We will then turn our attention to social motives that influence development and social relationships (exploration, affiliation, aggression, and achievement).

Hunger and Eating

As time passed and hunger gripped the survivors, they began to look for food. Their first efforts turned up a meager assortment of candies, jam, and canned fish. Soon, however, this supply began running out, and their search intensified. By the ninth day, the once husky rugby players became aware of their deteriorating physical condition (one of them lost eighty pounds during the ordeal). Their gnawing hunger drove them to consider eating the flesh of their dead companions. After much discussion they overcame their initial revulsion and ate the flesh.

Clearly, hunger was a motivating force behind many of the survivors' behaviors. They were desperate people driven to desperate acts. However, much of our own behavior is also aimed at satisfying our hunger and our desire for food. In order to prove this, make a note of the amount of time you spend in food-related activities: eating, shopping for food, talking about food, worrying about your weight, and so on. *Hunger*, then, is a motive common to us all.

When we first consider the issue of eating and hunger, we might think that it should be easy to develop a theory on these topics. We get hungry when we haven't eaten, we search for food, eat, and then feel full and stop eating. How simple and straightforward can you get? But the issues surrounding eating and hunger are more complex than you would ever have dreamed, and attempts to explain them rival the best "whodunit" mystery on the market today. To begin our discussion, consider just a few of the questions faced by investigators. How do you know when you are hungry? You don't consult your diary to determine the last time you ate and conclude, "It has been six hours since I last ate, so I must be hungry." Why do you choose to eat certain foods and avoid others? Is

Hunger is a motive common to us all. It influences our thoughts, our buying activities, and even our social interactions, as well as our eating behavior.

hunger the only reason you eat? Once you start eating, why do you stop? Although your eating behavior may vary a great deal from day to day, why doesn't your weight vary in similar fashion?

The Experience of Hunger

The Gut Reaction.   When most of us think about hunger we think of cramping and pangs coming from an empty stomach. This was, in fact, the position accepted over 200 years ago when one scientist wrote that hunger arises when "the naked villi of nerves on one side (of the stomach) grate against those on the other (side) . . ." (Cofer & Apley, 1964). Cannon and Washburn (1912) set out to demonstrate that contractions of the stomach cause people to feel hungry. Washburn swallowed a balloon, which, when it reached his stomach, was inflated and hooked to an amplifying device (see Figure 11–1) to record the contractions of his stomach. He sat with this balloon in his stomach and pressed a key each time he felt hungry. The results showed that feelings of hunger often occurred at the same time as strong contractions of the stomach.

This experiment seemed strong support for the internal cause of hunger. However, later experiments cast doubt on the role of stomach contractions. For example, researchers (Penick et al., 1963; Tsang, 1938) found that rats whose stomachs had been removed and whose esophagi were connected to their small intestines searched for food and ate as much as those with normal stomachs. The only difference was that the former group of rats ate less food at any one time; however, they ate more often. In the same way, human patients whose stomachs have been removed report feeling hungry (Janowitz, 1967).

The most recent conclusion is that stomach contractions play a minor role in signaling hunger. There is evidence, however, that a full stomach plays a large part in getting us to *stop* eating (Mook, 1987). Interestingly, this "stop" signal is conveyed to the brain by both stretch receptors and nutrient receptors in the stomach (Carlson, 1991).

Blood-Sugar Level.   If we can't blame our stomachs for making us eat, what can we blame? One answer may be the glucose (blood-sugar) level in the blood. When we eat, enzymes in the saliva, stomach, and small intestine break down the food into sugars, amino acids, and fats (Petri, 1986). Sugars and amino acids are absorbed into the bloodstream, where they travel to the liver and later to the brain. Investigators began to focus on the role of glucose (sugar) when it was found that a hungry animal (one that had not eaten for a period of time) would not eat at all or would eat less food when it was injected with the blood of another animal that had been well fed (Davis et al., 1967, 1971).

FIGURE 11–1

In this experiment, Washburn swallowed a balloon, which was inflated once it reached his stomach. The balloon was attached to an amplifying device to record contractions. Washburn pressed a key every time he felt hungry. The results showed that Washburn's feelings of hunger often occurred at the same time as strong contractions of the stomach. (Cannon & Washburn, 1912)

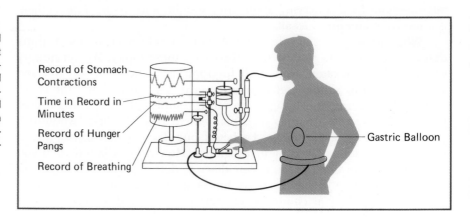

Record of Stomach Contractions

Time in Record in Minutes

Record of Hunger Pangs

Record of Breathing

Gastric Balloon

But how is the glucose level monitored? A simple theory would be that some area of the brain that is rich in blood vessels has **glucoreceptors,** receptors that detect the level of glucose in the blood. When the blood is low in glucose, this area signals that it is time to start eating and when to stop eating.

Two types of experiments have suggested that the ventromedial hypothalamus and the lateral hypothalamus (see Chapter 2) might be the location of such glucoreceptors. In one type, areas of the hypothalamus are stimulated with electrical current. When these "eating centers" are stimulated, even an animal that has been well fed starts to eat (Hoebel & Teitelbaum, 1962). Such studies have also shown that there are areas of the hypothalamus that, when stimulated, will cause the animal to stop eating, even if it is hungry. The other type of experiment involves destroying cells in the hypothalamus. Results from these studies have shown that destruction of certain areas will cause the animal to refuse food. Destruction of other areas will result in the animal eating continuously. In some cases the animal will eat until it has doubled or even tripled its body weight. In other words, we may have different "on" and "off" centers that monitor the level of glucose in our blood and regulate our eating.

These findings suggest a rather simple end to our story on hunger, but alas, they are not the last word. Further research found that the glucoreceptors in the lateral hypothalamus were sensitive only to drastic changes in glucose level. Hence, they could signal hunger under rather extreme starvation conditions such as those experienced by the rugby players, but they couldn't control our everyday eating under normal circumstances. Further, it takes some time for food to be broken down into glucose and the glucose-rich blood to find its way into the brain. If we waited for this process to tell us when to stop eating, we might be well on our way through our fourth steak or second gallon of ice cream! Thus, there must be other areas where the monitoring occurs more quickly and the receptors are more sensitive (Campfield & Smith, 1986).

The search for these elusive receptors moved closer to the sites where the food is broken down and absorbed into the blood. One area that contains glucoreceptors and seems to play a role in signaling hunger and satiation is the upper part of the small intestine, called the *duodenum.* A second site of the receptors is the *liver.* After food is broken down in our stomachs and small intestines, nutrients are absorbed into the blood. The blood then flows to the liver before going to other parts of our body, including the brain. Research has shown that there are indeed centers in the duodenum and liver that monitor the blood-sugar level of the blood and transmit signals to the brain (Tordoff & Friedman, 1986; 1988). The receptors in the duodenum and liver are very sensitive to changes in glucose levels and can quickly signal hunger and satiation.

Petri (1991) has compared our body's hunger system to a NASA rocket in which several systems become active when change occurs. The glucoreceptors at different sites back each other up to signal hunger and satiation, to start and stop eating. These receptors work in concert with signals from the stomach and other sites (see below) to form a wonderfully complex system. The next time you bite into that hamburger, you might consider the cast of characters in your body that are in action or will move into action as the burger makes its way through your body!

The Role of Taste.   Although important, glucoreceptors cannot be the whole story. Recall that on the ninth day after the crash, some, but not all, of the survivors ate the flesh of the dead. Some of those who did not eat actually put the flesh to their mouths, only to become violently sick. Their eating behavior was not simply determined by the level of glucose in their blood. On the other hand, you might recall a time when you went to a party shortly after eating a large meal. You were stuffed,

Investigators are still trying to determine how the brain affects our eating behavior. Two methods of research on this issue involve stimulating parts of the brain and destruction of areas or pathways in the brain. After lesions in the ventromedial nucleus of the hypothalamus, the rat pictured above ate until it weighed three times its normal weight.

Glucoreceptors
Cells in the hypothalamus that monitor the glucose content of the blood. If the blood is low in glucose, the glucoreceptors send out signals that cause hunger and motivate us to eat.

but when the host or hostess placed a tantalizing tidbit in your hand, you quickly devoured it and spent much of the night munching away. At a party where there are many different foods to eat, we tend to eat more than we need to satisfy our hunger because there are a variety of tastes available to us (Rolls, 1985). One possible reason for the behaviors described here is learning; we learn what (and what not) to eat and when to eat. Recalling our earlier discussion of motivation theories, certain tastes may become incentives for eating behavior.

Another explanation for why and what we eat centers on *taste*. Indeed, if the glucoreceptor mechanism completely controlled our eating, we would expect organisms to eat the same amount of food whether they took food through the mouth or directly into the stomach. One investigator compared the eating behavior of rats who ate normally with those who pressed a bar to have food delivered directly to their stomachs through a tube (Snowden, 1969). There were some interesting differences. First, although rats fed through a tube maintained their original body weight, they did not grow as fast as rats normally do. Second, while it is generally easy to teach rats to press a bar to get food that can be eaten, it is difficult to teach them to press a bar to get food delivered directly into their stomachs.

Other studies have shown that taste is also important for the cessation of eating behavior. For example, the esophagi of rats have been cut so that when the rats eat, the food never reaches their stomachs. If blood-sugar levels alone regulate eating, we might expect these rats to eat continuously because food never gets into their stomach or bloodstream. However, the rats do not eat continuously; although they eat larger than normal meals, they do pause before eating again (Janowitz & Grossman, 1949).

Sweet taste seems to play an important role in stimulating eating. Rats who were given saccharin to drink ate 10–15 percent more food than rats who did not have this sweet drink (Tordoff, 1988). This finding prompted one investigator to note that diet drinks may actually make dieting more difficult even though they do not contribute calories (Carlson, 1991).

Body Weight and Long-Term Eating.   Thus far we have focused on short-term mechanisms of hunger; they are short-term in the sense that they control our behavior from meal to meal. There is another interesting phenomenon of eating behavior, however, that cannot easily be explained by these short-term mechanisms. Most animals, including humans, tend to keep a stable body weight for long periods of time even though the availability of food may change over this time. If you think about your own weight, you will probably find that it varies by less than 5 percent annually. You may also notice how difficult it is to gain or lose weight. Few people can sustain weight loss for one year, regardless of the weight loss program they follow (Grinker, 1982).

Our bodies require a certain energy level to keep going. The exact amount of energy (measured in the form of **calories**) varies from one person to another and is dependent on such factors as size, level of activity, and metabolism. When we take in more calories than our bodies need, these calories are converted to fat and the fat is stored in our body tissues.

These fat deposits or fat cells play a role in determining our weight and our long-term eating behavior. According to *set-point theory*, the number of fat cells in the body is established during early childhood. Receptors, probably located in the hypothalamus, monitor the condition and size of these cells. Based on the information it receives from these cells, the hypothalamus regulates eating and body metabolism to maintain the body's weight in a normal range (Keesey et al., 1976; Nisbett, 1972).

The important issue here is that there may be two general mechanisms controlling our eating behavior. The short-term mechanism seems to center on the nutritional requirements of the body, whereas the long-term mechanism seems most sensitive to body weight.

Calories
Units of energy produced when food is oxidized or burned by the body.

What We Eat: Specific Hungers and Learning

Thus far we have been discussing why we eat. Our focus has mainly been on how deprivation causes us to become hungry and to search for food. It is also believed that the types of foods we choose to eat are, to some degree, controlled by our needs. In support of this position, Davis (1928) allowed newly weaned infants to choose their diet over a period of months from a cafeteria-like selection of foods. On any given day the infants might choose a "bad diet," but over a long period of time they selected foods that met their nutritional needs. In one case, a child who had rickets chose foods that had high concentrations of cod-liver oil and in doing so helped cure the rickets. In another study, rats were fed a diet that did not provide enough calcium (Rozin & Kalat, 1971). When these rats were later given a choice of things to eat, they chose high-calcium foods. Taking another approach, investigators have shown taste plays an important role as a cue teaching us to avoid poisons and eat "good" foods (Sclafani & Nissenbaum, 1988). The survivors of the plane crash also seemed to select what to eat according to their needs. At first they ate only the flesh of the victims. After a time, however, many began eating kidneys and livers, which were high in necessary vitamin and mineral content. Experiments like those discussed earlier led one investigator to suggest, "Perhaps, rather than a hunger system per se, we have separate systems controlling hunger for *this*, and hunger for *that*" (Mook, 1987, p. 73).

It seems logical to conclude that people eat because they are hungry and that they eat the foods needed to nourish their bodies. Unfortunately, this is not always the case. Animals and humans, even at early ages, learn to prefer certain foods, and they even learn when to be hungry. Often these learned preferences go against the body's needs. For example, Harriman (1955) found that rats learned to prefer sugar over salt. Even when these rats had their adrenal glands removed and needed to eat salt to survive, they continued choosing the sugar diet. Some of them died as a result of this choice. Thus, when we eat and what we eat are influenced by our bodily state *and* by our learned habits and preferences.

The research on specific hungers has taken on new importance recently as numerous psychologists report that our mood and performance are affected by the food we eat (Spring, Chiodo, & Bowen, 1987; Chollar, 1988). For example, the results of research and observation suggest that excessive amounts of carbohydrates can calm and fatigue us and slow our

Learning plays an important role in determining our eating behavior. It affects what we eat, when we eat, and where we eat. The role of learning helps explain differences in eating behavior between people.

The food we eat influences our mood. Research suggests that excessive amounts of carbohydrates can calm and fatigue us and slow our reaction times.

reaction times. In one case a psychologist (Christensen et. al., 1985) was able to reduce a client's frequency of headaches and physical exhaustion by eliminating sugar in her diet.

Obesity

Although our bodies may have natural selection processes that help ensure our nourishment, those of us who have struggled with diets know that our eating patterns can present major problems for our body weight.

The incidence of obesity has reached an extremely high level in the Western world; over half the people in the United States can be classified as being significantly overweight. In humans, **obesity** is defined as more than 15 percent over the weight that's "ideal," given a person's height and overall body build. Obesity is a major factor in many physical and psychological disorders. It has been found to increase the likelihood of cardiovascular disease and diabetes (Geen, Beatty, & Arkin, 1984). Men who weigh 20 percent or more above the average for their height have a 25 percent higher mortality rate than men of average weight. Obesity also can reduce job advancement opportunities (Jeffrey & Katz, 1977) and feelings of self-esteem (Leon & Roth, 1977).

Adding to our concern about obesity is the fact that people literally seem to keep growing; the typical adult in the 1970s was 10 pounds heavier than the average adult in 1912 (Scala, 1978). Obesity also becomes a more common problem with age. As we get older, our metabolism rate decreases so that our body burns up less fat. If we maintain a constant caloric intake as we grow older, we will store more fat. In addition, as we grow older, the composition of our body changes; the mass of muscle and bones decreases, and the percentage of fat increases. And maybe the most depressing fact of all is that fat begets fat. Many obese people have a high insulin level. Insulin reduces blood glucose levels, and as we saw earlier, low levels of blood glucose cause us to experience hunger and eat. Eating leads to more fat, which in turn further decreases blood glucose, which leads to more eating, and so on. On this cheery note, let us turn our attention to theories about the cause of obesity.

Obesity
In humans, being more than 15 percent over the "ideal" weight, given the person's height and overall body build.

Set-Point Theory.   As you struggle to tighten your belt, it may interest you to know that the bulge you are capturing can probably be blamed on two sources—the *number* and the *size* of fat cells in your body. Many obese people suffer the double whammy of having both many fat cells and large fat cells. Fat cells store excess fat not used by our bodies. Investigators believe that the number of fat cells we have is determined partly by genetics and partly by our diet during the first two years of our lives (Nisbett, 1972). Once the number of fat cells is set, it cannot be altered to any great degree. The size of these fat cells, however, is determined by our eating habits during adolescence and adulthood. Someone who has a high number of fat cells will be predisposed to being obese, and poor eating habits will ensure obesity by increasing the size of the fat cells.

As we suggested earlier, **set-point theory** argues that our bodies develop a weight based on the size and number of fat cells. Once the set point is established, the homeostatic mechanism works to maintain this weight. If our weight falls below this set point, we become hungry and our metabolism slows to push us toward the set weight. Similarly, if we begin to gain weight, our appetite may decrease and our metabolism increases to burn off fat and get us back to the set weight. Thus, while our minds may goad us to diet (or add weight), our bodies are working to maintain a fixed weight. This battle of the bulge is so difficult because, no matter what we do, we cannot change the number of fat cells in our body; we can only influence their size.

The Influence of External Cues.   Set point theory emphasizes the role of *internal* mechanisms in obesity: Our bodies push us to maintain a certain weight, and presumably the bodies of obese people are pushing them to maintain or regain a high set point weight. There is, however, another approach that suggests that the eating behavior of obese people is more controlled by external events than is the eating behavior of normal-weight people (Rodin, 1975, 1977). In other words, obese people are not only pushed to eat by the internal cue of hunger, but they are also pulled to eating by external cues such as the attractiveness of food or the ringing of the dinner bell.

For example, Schachter and Gross (1968) suggested that obese people are more likely than normal-weight people to "eat by the clock"; that is, obese people will eat because the clock says it's dinner time. In order to show this, the investigators had normal-weight and overweight subjects arrive at the laboratory at 5:00 P.M. The subjects were told that their physiological responses would be measured while they worked on tasks. Their watches were removed and electrodes were strapped on their arms; then the experimenter left the room so that they could work. There was a large clock in front of the subjects, which, unknown to them, was controlled by the experimenter. The experimenter returned to the room thirty minutes later (5:30) eating crackers. However, in some cases, the clock in front of the subjects had been slowed to read only 5:20, while in other cases it had been moved forward to read 6:05. The experimenter asked the subjects to complete questionnaires and left the box of crackers with them so that they could munch while they worked. The number of crackers eaten by the subjects was counted. Obese subjects ate more crackers than did normal-weight subjects when the clock read 6:05 (dinner time), but they ate fewer crackers than the others when the clock read 5:20.

There are a number of external cues other than time that may affect the eating behaviors of obese people. Nisbett (1968) found that obese subjects ate more than thin subjects if the food tasted good, but less than the thin subjects if it had an unpleasant taste. Overweight subjects will also increase their food intake if the food looks attractive (Hashim & Van Itallie, 1965) and is easily available (Schachter & Friedman, 1974). Obese

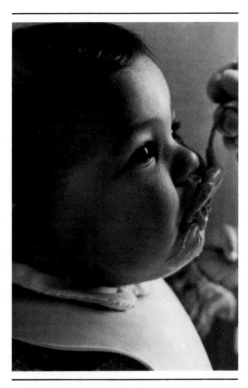

Fat babies often grow up to be obese people. According to set-point theory, the number of fat cells we have is partly due to genetics and partly due to our diet during the first two years of life.

Set-point theory
Suggests that the number of fat cells in the body is established during early childhood and does not change later in the life span.

Set-point theory helps explain why dieting is so difficult and unsuccessful. According to this theory, the number of fat cells is set at a young age. When the body falls below a certain weight, metabolism slows and "pushes" the person to eat.

people will actually eat less than normal-weight subjects if the food is difficult to obtain.

Although this theory is interesting, it has been criticized and now appears to be of limited value. There are many situations in which normal-weight people are not less sensitive than obese people to external cues such as time (Nail et al., 1981; Rodin, 1981). Another question that has not been addressed adequately is why obese people might be so sensitive to external food cues. Does obesity lead to increased sensitivity or does increased sensitivity lead to obesity?

Arousal and Eating.   Who can resist the lure of munchies while watching (or after) an exciting movie? In an interesting study, White (1977) had normal-weight and obese subjects watch four different movies; three of the movies were arousing and one was a nonarousing travelogue. After each session, the subjects were allowed to sample crackers under the guise of consumer-preference research. Although normal-weight individuals ate about the same amount no matter which film they had seen, obese subjects ate a lot more after seeing the arousing films than after the travelogue.

An interesting follow-up to this work subjected normal-weight and obese people to either physical threats (shock) or threats to their self-esteem (failure) (Heatherton, Herman, & Polivy, 1991). The physical threat reduced the amount that normal subjects ate but did not suppress eating by obese subjects. The threat to self-esteem resulted in increased eating by obese people but did not influence the amount normal subjects ate.

These results suggest that obese people are not insensitive to their internal cues. Rather, they may have a hard time figuring out or understanding what cues their bodies are sending them. Obese people may be misinterpreting the threats to self-esteem as hunger rather than as anxiety or anger. This type of misinterpretation appears to be far less common in thin or normal-weight people.

Anorexia Nervosa and Bulimia

Before leaving our discussion of eating behavior, we focus on two eating disorders that have received a great deal of attention. One of the disorders is **anorexia nervosa,** a condition in which a person refuses to eat enough food to maintain a minimum normal weight for age and height and slowly

Anorexia nervosa
Condition in which a person loses his or her appetite, eats little, and slowly begins to starve.

WEIGHT LOSS PROGRAMS: Are They Effective?

As I launch into my fourth attempt in two months to rid myself of unwanted pounds, writing this section is excruciatingly painful. Our discussion of theories of obesity suggests that both internal forces (set point) and external forces (taste, attractiveness of food, arousing events) work against my losing weight. Our metabolism and our body weight are largely determined by heredity and are, therefore, very difficult to change (Bouchard, 1990). In fact, one study found that fewer than 3 percent of the people who participated in a 15-week weight-loss program were able to maintain their weight loss after four to five years (Kramer, Jeffrey, Forster, & Snell, 1989). The failures of weight loss programs are caused not so much by the frailty of our will and resolve as by the wonderful (and in this case, infuriating) adaptability of our bodies. It seems that once our set point weight is reached, reducing our food intake leads to many internal changes. It's true that fat will be drawn out of our fat cells and burned. But at the same time our metabolism rate will begin to slow. That is, we won't be burning the fat at the same rate as before; our bodies are trying to "save" the fat that has been stored. The reduced metabolism rate will make us feel less energetic, and we will be tempted to reduce our activity. With the lower metabolism rate, if we go back to eating normally, we will store more fat than we were storing before we started our diet. Before long we may have to rush back to our diet and begin the painful process again. However, successive diets have the strongest depressing effect on our metabolism, so that people who "alternate chronically between dieting and regular eating actually increase their chances of becoming obese" (Taylor, 1986, p. 114). With this thought in mind, let us quickly examine some of the ways people attempt to reduce weight. Note that more Americans are treated for obesity than for all other health habits and conditions *combined* (Stunkard, 1979).

1. *Dieting*. Dieting involves restricting calories. Because the body needs certain types of nutrients, a diet must be planned carefully. Weight loss through dieting alone is generally slow and often not long lasting. Hence, effective weight loss programs combine dieting with other treatments.

2. *Fasting*. Fasting involves severely curtailing food intake over a period of a few days. The diet is often restricted to low-calorie liquids. In some extreme cases, individuals may have their jaws wired shut to prevent them from eating. It is important to point out that fasting never involves altogether eliminating food and liquid and that fasting requires medical supervision. Fasting may produce quick and dramatic weight loss, but because it can only be used on a short-term basis, eating often returns to normal and weight is quickly regained (Wadden, Stunkard, & Brownell, 1983).

3. *Appetite-suppressing drugs*. These drugs, both prescription and over-the-counter, act to reduce appetite and facilitate dieting. The drugs work for some people but not others. Appetite-suppressing drugs may have side effects and are not recommended for long-term weight loss.

4. *Behavior modification*. This approach draws on behavioral learning theories. People are retrained in eating habits. They are taught to eat at certain times and not to eat while engaged in other pleasurable activities such as watching television. People begin by removing high-calorie foods from their kitchens, and they are reinforced for eating low-calorie foods and staying on a schedule. In some cases, behavior modification techniques have produced long-term success.

5. *Multidimensional approaches*. These approaches combine techniques based on a number of psychological theories. Participants are encouraged to keep records of what and how often they eat. This self-monitoring approach helps them define the behavior to be modified. People are often surprised by their eating habits. An important part of multidimensional programs is to develop participants' concept of control. Thus, participants are taught to eat foods that are low in calories and to confine eating to certain places. People are placed on regular exercise programs to help take off weight and maintain weight loss. This exercise is made interesting and enjoyable, so that participants will continue it (Brownell, Stunkard, & Keon, 1985). Social support is also emphasized, and participants use support groups to talk about feelings and problems and to receive help from others in similar situations. Programs like these that rely on changing *behavior* and *cognitions* have proven successful for some people, especially for those needing to lose 20–30 pounds. Many participants are able to maintain this weight loss, but we caution you that like the other approaches, these programs will not work for everyone.

6. *Commercial weight loss programs*. As many as 400,000 people each week participate in programs like Weight Watchers and TOPS (Take Off Pounds Sensibly) (Taylor, 1986). These commercial programs are based on many of the techniques discussed earlier. In particular, behavior modification techniques are used to change people's eating habits. Some programs require that participants purchase their food from the program. Participants attend lectures about eating and nutrition, and they belong to a social support group. Although the success of these programs is difficult to evaluate precisely, they have proved effective for some people.

Taking pounds off is always difficult and often costly. For this reason, some investigators (Brownell, Kelman, and Stunkard, 1983; Taylor, 1986) argue that we should focus our attention on prevention instead of treatment, by educating families about nutrition and obesity, to establish lifelong patterns.

Anorexics may starve themselves to death because they are unhappy with their physical appearance. Anorexics generally have a low self-esteem and an intense fear that eating will make them very fat. Anorexia is a serious eating disorder most common in adolescent females.

Bulimia
Eating disorder in which the individual goes through cycles of dieting for a period of time and then gorging with food (binging). After binging, the person will purge the food by vomiting or using laxatives.

"wastes away." A weight loss of 25 percent is one of the main criteria for diagnosing anorexics. Bachrach, Erwin, and Mohr (1965) report a case where their patient's weight fell from 118 to 47 pounds.

At first anorexia was thought to be relatively uncommon, but more recent estimates are that between 5 to 15 percent of adolescent females suffer the disorder (Nagelman, Hale, & Ware, 1983). The condition is most commonly found in white adolescent females from middle- or upper-middle class families, although males in early adolescence make up about 10 percent of the cases. For unknown reasons, anorexia is very rare in black women. About 15 percent of the cases actually end in death (Van Buskirk, 1977). Death often results from complications associated with depleting the body of needed energy or with the stress of rapid weight loss or later weight gain.

Anorexics starve themselves because they are unhappy with their physical appearance. Casper and Davis (1977) identified three phases of anorexia. In the first phase, people develop a low self-esteem and an increasing concern for their physical appearance. The second phase is characterized by an intense fear that eating will make them very fat. They adopt a very restricted diet and begin to lose weight. When hunger pains occur, anorexics exhaust themselves through strenuous exercise. The severe loss of weight is accompanied by constipation, cessation of menstruation, and a slowing of the pulse and respiration. Interestingly enough, no matter how thin they are, anorexics still feel fat (Gomez & Dally, 1980). In the third phase, anorexics admit that they have a problem and they increase food intake. However, at the first sign of weight gain, they begin to fear that they will become fat, and the slow starvation process may begin again.

Bulimia, a related eating disorder, is most common among females in their late teens and early twenties. Like anorexics, people suffering from bulimia have a distorted image of their body and are obsessed with weight. However, the bulimic is seldom grossly underweight like the anorexic. Rather, bulimics go through cycles of dieting and then "binging," or gorging themselves with food. At the time of binging, the bulimic may consume over 20,000 calories! After binging, the bulimic will purge the food by vomiting, or by using laxatives or diuretics. One study reported that vomiting occurred more often during the cycle than did binge eating; 56 percent of the sample reported vomiting at least once a day. The average duration of the bulimic symptoms is over six years (Herzog, 1982). In December 1984, actress Jane Fonda shocked her fans by revealing that she had suffered from bulimia from the age of twelve to thirty-five. She reported that she often vomited fifteen to twenty times a day. She stated, "It's an addiction like drugs or alcohol."

There are many theories about the causes of anorexia and bulimia. Some researchers think the cause may be a hormone disorder or a malfunctioning of the hypothalamus. Women with anorexia have abnormally low levels of reproductive hormones released by the hypothalamus and the pituitary (Beumont et al., 1982). Other researchers (e.g., Minuchin, Rosman, & Baker, 1978) suggest that the problem may be the result of family conflict. Many anorexics report feeling intense pressure from their parents to meet high standards, in areas including physical appearance. Their cessation of eating may be an attempt to rebel against these felt demands; they adopt the "I'll show you" attitude. Still other researchers argue that anorexia and bulimia result as a means of coping with depression and feelings of helplessness (Sugarman, Quinlan, & Devenis, 1981). According to this point of view, anorexics and bulimics attempt to demonstrate control over the environment by showing that they have mastered their own bodies.

Most recently, efforts to understand the causes of anorexia and bulimia focus on the fact that the disorders generally occur among white middle-class adolescent females. What is it about this group that puts its members at risk? Our society emphasizes thinness and "appropriate" eating behavior for women but not men. For example, in one study (Chaiken & Piliner, 1986) subjects watched videotapes of a male or a female eating either a large meal or small meal. The subjects were then asked to rate these people on a number of dimensions. The size of the meal consumed by the male made no difference to how he was rated. However, the female who ate the small meal was rated as more feminine, better looking, and more concerned about her appearance than the female who ate the large meal. The catch was that the female on the two videotapes was the same person. Only her eating behavior was different!

Rodin and her colleagues (Striegel-Moore, McAvay, & Rodin, 1987; Striegel-Moore, Silberstein, & Rodin, 1985) argue that females who internalize society's norms for thinness and attractiveness are most in danger of developing eating disorders. The disorders are particularly common in adolescence because women at this age tend to focus more on developing social relationships. Adolescent males focus more on gaining independence. Further, women have a clearer view of what they want their bodies to look like than do men, and women are more prone to overestimate their body size. We can add to this volatile situation the fact that females at puberty tend to gain their weight in the form of fat tissue, whereas males' weight gain at this time is largely in the form of muscle tissue. Thus, pressures from society, an exaggerated estimate of body size, and physiological changes place enormous demands on adolescent women to "do something" about their weight. In fact, studies show that 80 percent of girls, as opposed to 10 percent of boys, report having been on a diet before the age of 13. But as we saw earlier, periodic dieting often has the cruel result of increasing weight over the long run. Given this set of events, some young women may feel driven to more drastic measures to control their weight. Although adolescence is a particularly vulnerable time, more recent research indicates that *regardless of age* women are more concerned about eating, body weight, and physical appearance than men (Pliner, Chaiken, & Flett, 1990). However, older women may deal with this concern in different ways than younger women.

Thirst

The morning after the crash, the dazed survivors were awakened by the cries of the injured begging for water. Those who had lost blood made the most agonizing appeals. In a short time, the survivors realized that they might be able to live for days on very little food but that they had to have a supply of drinking water. Why do people become thirsty? How do we know when our bodies require fluids?

Early researchers argued that thirst results when our mouths feel dry (Cannon, 1929). However, other studies have shown that this is not the case (Fitzsimons, 1973). People who experience frequent dryness of the mouth (common with the use of certain drugs or because of other physical conditions) may drink more often than others, but they do not drink more. As with hunger, our search for the cause of thirst will take us to many regions of the body. Most of the theories involve a need-drive approach.

Two-thirds of the water in our bodies is located within our cells (*intracellular*), and about 26 percent of the water is located in the spaces around these cells (*extracellular*). The remaining 7 percent of the water is contained in the blood. The water within and outside our cells is not pure; it normally contains .9 percent salt (sodium chloride). Whereas water can pass in and out of the cells by a process called osmosis, the salt cannot. We will now use this information to examine how the body experiences thirst.

Osmometric Thirst.　If the concentration of salt in the extracellular fluid increases, water seeps out of the cells to restore the original concentration. Water moving from the cells puts the extracellular fluid in proper balance, but the intracellular water level becomes depleted. Investigators believe that there are cells called **osmoreceptors** in the hypothalamus that are sensitive to the intracellular water levels (Bass, 1968). When they detect that water is being depleted from the cells, they send "thirst" signals to other areas of the brain and motivate the person to drink liquids. Thus, drinking motivated by **osmometric thirst** restores intracellular fluid levels.

The hypothalamus also stimulates the pituitary gland to release the antidiuretic hormone (*ADH*), which causes the kidneys to reabsorb more water. Normally our kidneys filter about forty-five gallons of water a day. Most of this water is reabsorbed back into the system, but some of it is excreted in the form of urine. The increase in ADH causes the kidneys to reabsorb more water than usual to combat the decrease in intracellular water level.

Volumetric Thirst.　Why were the injured survivors so thirsty? People who experience blood loss, diarrhea, or vomiting generally become thirsty, even though the salt content of their extracellular fluid has not changed. In all these cases, fluid is lost directly from the extracellular areas while intracellular fluid is not depleted. Exactly what mechanism is at work?

When the volume of extracellular fluid decreases, there is an accompanying decrease in blood pressure. As a result, the blood supply to the kidneys and heart is reduced. Investigators have suggested that there are volumetric receptors in both these locations which detect this drop in blood pressure (Carlson, 1991). When a change is detected, these receptors stimulate thirst (called **volumetric thirst**) and trigger the pituitary gland to release ADH. As in the case of osmometric thirst, the ADH, along with hormones secreted by the kidneys, causes the kidneys to reabsorb more water than usual. The intake of additional fluids restores the extracellular fluid level.

As you can see, the thirst mechanisms are wonderfully adaptive. They motivate drinking behavior by signaling thirst *and* they start immediate adjustments within our bodies to conserve the liquids that are available.

Osmoreceptors
Cells in the hypothalamus that are sensitive to intracellular water levels; they send "thirst" signals to other areas of the brain when they detect that water is being depleted from the cells.

Osmometric thirst
Thirst motivated by osmoreceptors in the hypothalamus that detect the depletion of intracellular water cells.

Volumetric thirst
Thirst motivated by a drop in blood pressure caused by a depletion of extracellular fluid.

Thirst results when either intracellular or extracellular is decreased. Thirst not only motivates drinking, but it also initiates internal activities such the kidneys reasorbing water. These internal activities are aimed at conserving fluids.

The Effect of Eating on Drinking. An interesting feature of drinking that is often overlooked is its relationship to eating. If we consider our own behavior, we will find that much, if not most, of our drinking occurs during mealtimes. A similar pattern is found in other mammals. Rats, for example, take 70–90 percent of their liquids between ten minutes before meals and thirty minutes after meals (Kissileff, 1969). This observation has prompted many investigators to suggest a link between eating and drinking. One theory is that predigested food stimulates cells in the mucus membranes of our mouths and esophogi to release a substance (histamine). This substance stimulates other receptors, which motivate drinking (Kraly, 1984). Another theory is that the predigested food stimulates the release of insulin in the digestive tract, which in turn motivates drinking (Kraly, Miller, & Hecht, 1983). Although these theories must await further testing, they do point out the need to examine drinking behavior in light of related behaviors and to study naturally occurring patterns of drinking.

Sexual Behavior

As you can see, hunger and thirst are powerful drives. Sexual desire, too, can be a powerful motivator. However, unlike food and drink, sex is not necessary for the survival of the individual. And sexual desire is less tied to deprivation alone; as we will see, hormone levels and external stimuli may be more important factors. Finally, sexual behavior uses up energy, whereas eating and drinking restore energy.

Another interesting difference that sets sex apart from most other motives involves its history of study. Motives such as hunger and thirst have been carefully studied in both animals and humans and have been widely discussed in textbooks for nearly a century. The study of sexual desire and behavior, however, was avoided until the late 1940s when a few investigators dared to study the topic.

The Biological Basis of Sex

Let's begin our examination of sexual behavior by focusing on its biological foundations. We should point out that the sexual behavior of humans is far less under the control of hormones and innate patterns than is the sexual behavior of animals. We might state that biology supplies the tools for human sexual behavior, but it doesn't build the house. In short, biology sets the limits and may influence when sexual behavior is most likely to occur (especially in animals), but opportunity, environmental stimuli, and learning (especially in humans) are major factors in guiding sexual behavior.

Male Biological Sexual Behavior. When the male reaches sexual maturity, the pituitary gland (as discussed in Chapter 2) located at the base of the brain stimulates the **testes** (the male reproductive gland) to secrete **androgens** into the bloodstream. These androgens, or male sex hormones, increase the sex drive in men. In humans, androgens also influence the development of **secondary sex characteristics,** such as the growth of pubic hair and the deepening of the voice. Androgen levels remain fairly consistent through a man's life. Thus there are no definite biological cycles for male sexual behavior; given the proper stimuli, sexual behavior from both animal and human males can be elicited at almost any time. Although androgens are necessary for the development of sexual behavior, they do not control the sex drive after maturity.

Testes
Male reproductive gland, which secretes androgens into the bloodstream.
Androgens
Male hormones secreted by the testes that increase male sex drive and influence the development of secondary sex characteristics.
Secondary sexual characteristics
Traits typical of a sex, but not directly concerned with reproduction; for girls, the development of breasts and pubic hair; for boys, growth of the scrotum, pubic hair, and a beard.

In most animals, both hormone levels and external stimuli control mating behavior. Human sexual behavior is neither as dependent on hormones nor as stereotyped as animal sexual behavior.

Ovaries
Female reproductive glands that secrete estrogen into the bloodstream.
Estrogen
Female sex hormone. The level of estrogen is at its highest during the period of ovulation, and determines the onset of menstruation and the period of fertility. Estrogen also influences the development of secondary sex characteristics.
Ovulation
In women, the time when the egg is available to be fertilized and secretion of estrogen is at its highest; occurs once a month.
Releasing stimulus
In animals, an event that causes a predetermined response. For example, some female mammals release pheromones, a chemical substance signaling the male that the female is sexually receptive.
Pheromones
Odorous chemicals released by one animal that directly affect the arousal of another animal.

Female Biological Sexual Behavior. Female sexual behavior has a more complicated biological basis. When the female reaches sexual maturity, the pituitary gland stimulates the **ovaries,** which are the female reproductive glands, to secrete **estrogen** (the female sex hormone). However, unlike androgens in males, the rate of secretion of estrogen rises and falls in a cyclical way. The secretion of estrogen is at its highest level during **ovulation,** the time when the egg is available to be fertilized. In most animals, it is only during this period of estrus or "heat" that the female animal is receptive to sexual advances. Therefore, the level of hormones controls the animal's sexual response patterns. Removal of the ovaries eliminates sexual behavior for these animals (Carlson, 1977). This, however, is not the case for humans. Many women who have had their ovaries removed or who have reached menopause still have strong sex drives and are sexually active. Thus, although the level of estrogen determines the onset of menstruation and the period of fertility, it does not control the human female's sex drive. The human female may engage in sex at any time. It may, nevertheless, be the case that the female human's sex drive is influenced by hormonal levels (Bancroft, 1984). Females are evidently more likely to engage in sexual behavior at some times during their cycle, but there is disagreement about what these times are and whether they are influenced directly by hormones.

The Importance of External Cues. Even in animals, the hormones only prime the organism to act; it generally takes an external stimulus to release the behavior. Such a stimulus is known as a **releasing stimulus.** You may remember the discussion of instinct theory, which suggested that fixed action patterns are built into the organism and that external stimuli and events simply release this predetermined behavior. In some animals, sexual behavior seems to fit the instinct model although in the higher species of animals, and particularly in humans, it does not, and learning plays a significant role.

For those animals that respond to a releasing stimulus, the most common stimulus is a receptive partner. In some mammals, the receptive female releases **pheromones,** odorous chemical substances that attract mature males. For some animals, then, the nose may be a vital sex organ! If you have a female cat, you may blame pheromones for inviting every male cat in your neighborhood to your home when your cat is in heat. In other animals, the releasing stimulus is visual, for example, swollen areas around the genitals or changes in color. Humans are not programmed to respond to a releasing stimulus (Mook, 1987), but learning determines what stimuli will arouse us, and, therefore, each of us may respond to a different set of stimuli.

The Human Sexual Response

The Role of Learning. As already indicated, human sexual behavior is neither as dependent on hormones nor as stereotyped as animal sexual behavior. Because of this, humans have to learn the "when and how" of sexual behavior. This seemingly simple fact of life has many important consequences. One consequence is that human sexual behavior is widely varied, being limited only by a person's physical capabilities, imagination, and ideas as to what's acceptable, rather than by a predetermined plan set by nature. A second consequence is that humans can learn to be sexually aroused by an almost inconceivable range of stimuli.

Although these points add to the excitement and variety of human sexual behavior, the important role of learning adds a third consequence: if the proper learning situations do not occur, normal sexual behavior will fail to develop; early childhood experiences influence the development of later sexual behavior (Rosen & Rosen, 1981).

Phases of Sexual Response.   It was not until the late 1950s, when William Masters and Virginia Johnson began their studies, that much of the mystery of the human sexual response was lifted. Masters and Johnson carefully monitored the responses of a large number of subjects engaged in both intercourse and masturbation. They found that male and female sexual responses were alike in a number of ways.

These researchers found that it was possible to roughly categorize the human (male or female) response into four phases (Masters & Johnson, 1966, 1975). The first phase is the *excitement phase*. During this phase heart rate increases and breathing becomes deeper and faster. In males the penis becomes erect, and in females vaginal lubrication occurs. This lubrication not only makes penetration easier, but it also neutralizes the vagina's natural acidity, which would kill sperm (Hyde, 1986). In the second stage, the *plateau phase*, swelling of the penis and secretion in the vagina increase. The clitoris retracts under a fold of skin so that it cannot receive further direct stimulation, because it is so sensitive that such stimulation would be painful. The testes increase in size, sometimes as much as 100 percent, and move up in the scrotum. The *orgasm phase* is accompanied by a release of tension and intense pleasure. In men there are rhythmic contractions of muscles in the penis and ejaculation of semen. In women, there are muscular contractions in the vagina and uterus. During orgasm the heart rate may double and muscles may go into intense spasms. In the *resolution phase* the body returns to normal. At this point males enter a refractory period, which may last from a few minutes to several hours, during which they are incapable of sexual arousal or orgasm. Recent evidence suggests that this refractory period may be produced by prolactin, a hormone that stimulates milk production in females (Carlson, 1991; Oaknin et al., 1989). Prolactin is released by male rats after ejaculation and inhibits male sexual behavior.

Comparing Male and Female Sexual Response.   Males and females show similar changes in breathing, muscle tension, and heart rate during the phases. Enlargement of genitals occurs in both sexes (Maier, 1984). Further, there is an indication that males and females experience orgasm in a similar way. In one study, investigators asked male and female subjects to write descriptions of their orgasms (Vance & Wagner, 1976). These descriptions were then shown to a group of judges (clinical psychologists, medical students, and gynecologists) who were asked to decide which descriptions were written by males and which by females. The results showed that these judges could not correctly match the description with the sex of the author.

Although there are many similarities in the sexual responses of males and females, there are also some important differences. Males generally have only one orgasm; females show more variability. Some women have no orgasm whereas others experience multiple orgasms during intercourse. Yet others experience several small orgasmic peaks without reaching an orgasmic climax. A second difference is that males generally become sexually aroused more quickly than females (Hite, 1976). In an interesting study highlighting similarities and differences between male and female sexual behavior, investigators found men and women generally agreed on the sequence of foreplay behaviors leading up to actual intercourse (Geer & Broussard, 1990). Males, however, reported experiencing increasing arousal with each successive behavior. Females, on the other hand, gave high arousal values to actions that involved males stimulating them. They gave low arousal values to activities in which they stimulated males (touching the penis or orally stimulating the penis). Finally, women report considerable variation in the strength and duration of orgasm from one intercourse experience to the next. The orgasm for the male is generally very similar on these dimensions across sexual encounters.

Human Sexual Behaviors

Throughout much of time, many parents resorted to the "ultimate threat" to control their child's sexual behavior: "Nice girls (boys) don't do that" (e.g., masturbate or engage in premarital sexual intercourse). This type of statement could hardly be challenged before 1948 because we had little idea of the type or frequency of sexual activities of humans in general, let alone that of "nice girls and boys." In the late 1940s, however, Kinsey and his colleagues (1948, 1953) interviewed a large sample of American males and females on a wide range of topics regarding their sexual habits. Because of this study and those that followed (e.g., Hite, 1976, 1988; Hunt, 1974), we now have a clearer picture of the nature of human sexual activities. Now that we've made this statement, we must raise the cautionary note that these surveys give us only a general picture of sexual patterns. There are many reasons for exercising care when interpreting survey results. Most important is that it is difficult to determine the representativeness of the survey sample to the general population. Most surveys are printed in magazines or mailed to large numbers of individuals. Only a small percentage of people who receive surveys actually fill them out and return them. Given the sensitive nature of sex surveys, the majority of respondents may be unusual types; for example, they may be people who are generally open about discussing their behavior, sexual or otherwise. Surveys in magazines involve only those people who read the particular magazine. A second issue concerns how truthful people are in their answers. We could go on listing concerns with surveys, but the point should be clear: While not dismissing the results, we should embrace them with caution. With this in mind, let's review what the surveys tell us about human sexual behavior.

Autosexual Behavior. The first and most common sexual experience for most people is **masturbation,** or autosexual behavior, the self-manipulation of one's genitals. Masturbation is common among both children and adults; Kinsey found that more than 90 percent of males and more than 60 percent of females masturbate. A later survey by Hunt (1974) supported these findings. Hunt also found that 72 percent of married men over age thirty and 68 percent of married women over age thirty masturbate.

For a long time, masturbation was thought to be not only shameful, but dangerous as well. Children have been told that masturbation leads to blindness and, for males, the eventual separation of the penis from the body. Kinsey (1948) summed up such feelings about masturbation: "Every conceivable ill, from pimples to insanity, including stooped shoulders, loss of weight, fatigue, insomnia, general weakness, neurasthenia, loss of manly-mindedness, genital cancer, and the rest, was ascribed to masturbation" (p. 513). In the early part of the century, the U.S. Patent Office issued a patent for a device that would ring a bell in the parent's room if the child's bed moved in a pattern suggesting masturbation (LoPiccolo & Heiman, 1977)! Hyde (1986) has proposed that the taboos against masturbation can be traced back to the Old Testament, which had a positive view of sexuality but stressed intimacy and procreation. When the Old Testament was written, the Jews were a nomadic people whose survival depended on close relationships and reproduction. Masturbation fostered neither of these goals. Today we know that masturbation is not physically harmful; in fact, the most damaging results come from the emotional trauma and guilt instilled in children to prevent masturbation. In some cases, masturbation is recommended by therapists treating sexual disorders (McMullen & Rosen, 1979).

Heterosexual Behavior. The Kinsey report also shed light on heterosexual behavior, the sexual desire for people of the opposite sex. Despite

Masturbation
Self-manipulation of one's genitals.

religious and social taboos and the fear of pregnancy, 27 percent of college-educated women and 49 percent of college-educated men said that they had engaged in premarital sex. This was considered by many at the time to be a high figure. The last few decades have seen vast changes in social attitudes toward premarital sexual behavior, along with the introduction of "the Pill" and other safe and easy means of birth control. These attitudinal and technological changes have been accompanied by changes in sexual practice. In one study, an investigator interviewed married people and found that of those under age twenty-five, 95 percent of the males and 81 percent of the females had engaged in premarital intercourse (Hunt, 1974).

Simply looking at the numbers gives the impression that the sexual experience of males and females is becoming a great deal more alike than was the case thirty years ago. To a degree this is true; however, there are still some important differences between male and female views of sexual behavior. Women who engage in premarital sexual intercourse tend to do so with more emotional involvement and with fewer partners than do men; Hunt reports that men averaged six premarital partners, women only two. The recent fear of AIDS, however, has affected sexual behavior and there are indications that the number of sexual partners for both men and women may be declining (Masters, Johnson, & Kolodny, 1988). Further, male and female attitudes toward sex are different. Females voice concerns about pleasing their partner, while males are often more concerned about their own pleasure (Bardwick, 1971; Tavris & Offir, 1977).

In addition to studying when people engage in sexual intercourse, investigators have examined how often people engage in it. According to one survey, the median frequency of sexual intercourse for married couples in the United States is three times a week; median frequency means that half of all married couples had sex more often than this and half had sex less often (Hunt, 1974). This same survey found great individual differences: Some couples reported having intercourse more than once a day, whereas others reported averaging less than once a year. As shown in Table 11–1, frequency has changed over time.

The table also shows that frequency of sexual intercourse declines as people get older. But, although the frequency declines, older men and women often continue to enjoy active sex lives. Although older men require longer periods of stimulation to achieve an erection, they are typically able to maintain an erection longer than younger men (Schulz, 1984). Women experience **menopause**, the cessation of menstruation, in their late forties or early fifties. Menopause marks the end of a woman's ability to bear children and is accompanied by physical and hormonal changes. This period does not signal the end of a woman's sexual drive. In fact,

Menopause
Cessation of menstruation, marking the end of a woman's ability to bear children; accompanied by physical and hormonal changes.

1938–1949		1972	
Age	Median	Age	Median
16–25	2.45	18–24	3.25
26–35	1.95	25–34	2.55
36–45	1.40	35–44	2.00
46–55	0.85	45–54	1.00
56–60	0.50	55 and over	1.00

Source: Hunt (1974), p. 196.

Table 11–1
Weekly Frequency of Marital Coitus in the United States, 1938–1949 and 1972

some women become more interested in sex because they are no longer concerned with the possibility of pregnancy or cyclical hormonal changes. The physical changes that sometimes accompany menopause, such as liver spots on the back of the hands, lack of vaginal lubrication, and "hot flashes," can be inhibited or reversed with hormone treatment.

While the frequency of marital sexual intercourse has increased over the years, so too has the frequency of extramarital sexual relationships. Kinsey and colleagues (1948; 1953) reported that 50 percent of married males and 26 percent of married females reported having had extramarital relationships. More recent surveys (Hite, 1981, 1988; Wolfe, 1980) have found that about two-thirds of married males and females report having had extramarital relationships. These findings are particularly startling given that a majority of people feel that extramarital relationships are "always wrong" (Hite, 1988).

Homosexual Behavior.   Over the last few years the gay rights movement and the incidence of AIDS have combined to put homosexuals and homosexuality in the news. It might be easy to think that homosexuality is a product of modern times. This is far from true. In fact, homosexual relationships were common among ancient Greeks; both Plato and Socrates wrote about homosexuality and may have practiced homosexual behavior. Homosexuality was widely accepted by the ancient Romans; Julius Caesar has been described as "every woman's man and every man's woman." The advent of Christianity, however, was accompanied by a condemnation of homosexual behavior. St. Augustine (354–430 A.D.), for example, declared homosexuality a crime against nature, and homosexuals were burned at the stake.

Even today there is a great deal of misunderstanding about **homosexuality,** sexual desire for those of the same sex as oneself. In terms of percentages, the number of people who engage exclusively in homosexual behavior is rather low; perhaps about 4 percent of men and 2 percent of women in the United States are exclusively homosexual (Gebhard, 1972). However, Kinsey and others have estimated that possibly as many as 45 percent of all people in the United States have had some homosexual encounter during their lives, often during childhood. Further, most people who are labeled

Homosexuality
Sexual desire for those of the same sex as oneself.

Theories about the cause of homosexual behavior focus on hormones, early family relationships, and physiological and social development. Although there is a tendency to focus on the sexual behavior in homosexual relationships, many of these relationships, like heterosexual relationships, are based on love, intimacy, and the desire for an enduring partnership.

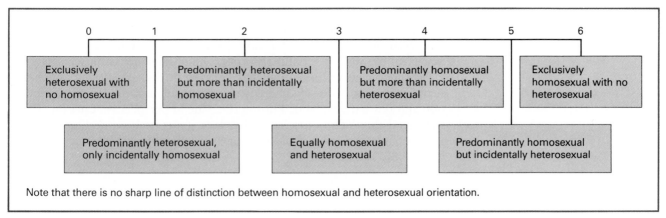

0	1	2	3	4	5	6

Exclusively heterosexual with no homosexual

Predominantly heterosexual, only incidentally homosexual

Predominantly heterosexual but more than incidentally homosexual

Equally homosexual and heterosexual

Predominantly homosexual but more than incidentally heterosexual

Predominantly homosexual but incidentally heterosexual

Exclusively homosexual with no heterosexual

Note that there is no sharp line of distinction between homosexual and heterosexual orientation.

FIGURE 11–2

Sexual Orientation. (Adapted from Kinsey et al., 1948, p. 638.)

homosexuals are not exclusively homosexual; rather, they are bisexual and are attracted to members of both sexes. The Center for Disease Control estimates that 2.5 million males in the United States are exclusively homosexual while another 2.5 to 7.5 million males have occasional liaisons (Booth, 1988). In fact, Kinsey suggested that there is no clear line dividing homosexuals from heterosexuals. Sexual orientation should instead be viewed on a continuum running from exclusive homosexual to exclusive heterosexual (Figure 11–2). Some people believe that homosexual relationships are based solely on sexual behavior and that all homosexuals are promiscuous. In fact, many homosexuals enter relationships in search of mutual love and intimacy, with sexual gratification being of secondary importance (Hyde, 1986). Like heterosexual relationships, homosexual relationships are often long lasting and exclusive.

Nonetheless, homosexual relationships are atypical in our society, and there are many theories about the cause of homosexual behavior. It is possible that a hormonal imbalance is involved. Some studies found lower levels of the male sex hormone in males who were exclusively homosexual than in males who practiced only heterosexual behavior (Kolodny et al., 1971). However, this finding does not necessarily demonstrate that the level of hormones *causes* homosexual behavior. It is possible that the stress and anxiety associated with a homosexual lifestyle cause the reduction in hormone level. Other researchers have reported no notable differences in hormone levels when comparing homosexuals and heterosexuals (Maier, 1984).

Some investigators have suggested a link between early family experiences and homosexuality. For example, Bieber (1976) found that homosexuals tended to have dominant mothers and passive fathers. Other research shows that **lesbians,** female homosexuals, often had lost one or both parents before the age of ten or had poor relations with their mothers (Saghir & Robins, 1973). However, these results have not been confirmed (Siegelman, 1974). In addition, these studies rely on people's memories of their family relationships, and memories are sometimes distorted.

Another theory links physiological changes and social development with homosexuality (Storms, 1981). According to this theory, a homosexual orientation may develop if an individual's sex drive develops during a period when most friends are of the same sex. This period is generally during childhood and before adolescence. Thus, Storms argues that the sex drive in homosexuals may have developed at an earlier age than that of heterosexuals. The theories about the causes of homosexual behavior go beyond simply explaining the behavior. It has been reported that heterosexuals who view the cause of homosexuality to be beyond one's control hold more favorable attitudes toward lesbians and gay men than those heterosexuals who view the cause of homosexuality as being under a person's control (e.g., free choice or learning) (Whitley, 1990).

Lesbians
Female homosexuals.

Although the causes of homosexuality still remain a mystery, it has become clear that homosexuality is not a mental disease or disorder. In fact, according to the most recent edition (1988) of the Diagnostic and Statistical Manual of Mental Disorders, homosexuality is only considered a disorder when an individual has "persistent distress" about his or her sexual orientation. Clearly, there is a lot of speculation about sexual orientation and few hard answers. Putting the issue in perspective, Carlson (1991) suggested that "The question 'Why does someone become homosexual?' will probably be answered when we find out why someone becomes *heterosexual*" (p. 337).

Coercive Sex: Aggression, Not Sexual Behavior

We debated whether this section should be included under the topic of sex or aggression, and as you will see, the section could well have been placed under aggression. Traditionally, **rape** is the term used to describe coercive sexual intercourse, but more recently terms such as "sexual assault" and "sexual aggression" are used to emphasize the violent nature of these acts (*Options for Health*, 1987). If we look only at the published figures on rape, we come away with the idea that although deplorable, rape is a relatively infrequent behavior. In 1982, for example, 77,763 cases of rape were reported. However, the Federal Bureau of Investigation (1983) estimates that 80 percent of rapes go unreported and that there is a 26 percent chance that a woman will be a rape victim at some time in her life. We can add to this alarming picture cases of **date rape,** which involve coercive sex that occurs in dating relationships. In one survey (Muehlenhard, Linton, Felts, and Andrews, 1985), 16 percent of the women and 9 percent of the men reported being on dates in which the female was forced to have intercourse against her wishes.

Many of us hold the belief that rapes are initiated by some sex-crazed maniac who preys on unsuspecting women. In fact, research suggests that in over 50 percent of the cases the victim knew her attacker (Russell, 1984). And in the majority of cases the motivation of the rapist was not sex, but dominance. Males use coercive sex to "prove" their masculinity, self-worth, and sexuality (Worchel & Goethals, 1981; Groth & Birnbaum, 1979). Rape, especially date rape, may also be motivated by misperceptions and miscommunication. Some common misperceptions include the "Token No" (women say no even when they mean yes), "Leading on Justifies Force" (women who tease deserve what they get), and "Women Like to Be Dominated" (Muehlenhard et al., 1985). Hence, in most cases, rape is more an outlet for aggression than an act motivated by a desire for sexual contact.

Motivation and Sexual Behavior. As we conclude our examination of sexual behavior, let's recall our earlier discussion of motivation theories. Human sexual behavior offers an excellent example of how each theory adds to our understanding of motivated behavior. On one hand, a combination of biological, hormonal, and need-drive factors influence our sexual activity. But clearly, this is not the whole picture. Hite (1988) reports that a majority of women felt that the existence of a loving and trusting relationship motivated their sexual behavior; not an internal need for sex. Learning influences every aspect of our sexual behavior, including what arouses us and the way in which we engage in sexual activities. And our cognitions play an equally important role in determining the when, where, and how aspects of sexual behavior. Cultural, moral, and religious beliefs shape and guide our actions. Our goals and plans for sexual behavior are designed not only to satisfy sexual desires, but they also include relationships and health issues. Most recently, the threat of AIDS has been on the minds

Rape
Coercive sexual assault on an individual.
Date rape
Coercive sex that occurs in dating relationships.

PORNOGRAPHY: Violence Against Women, Not Sex

One of the more heated and long-lasting debates raging in our society involves the public display of pornographic materials. This debate pits the Bill of Rights against religious and moral doctrines, and researchers who argue that few, if any, negative effects result from viewing pornography against investigators offering data that there are broad and pervasive negative effects. Our interest is not to present the final word in this debate but to help clarify some of the issues involved.

One of the core issues involves definitions. *Pornography* is material that is sexually arousing. *Obscenity* is pornography that offends and is degrading to the individuals involved (Hyde, 1986). Obscene material often goes well beyond sexual acts, depicting instead violence and rape. While many people would agree that some pornography should be protected under the First Amendment, they do not feel that this protection extends to obscene material. A problem arises here, however, because material that one person considers obscene my be merely pornographic to another person.

Beyond the concern with definitions is the concern about the behavioral effects of viewing pornography. This is an important issue because of the increasing availability of pornography in our society. One study, for example, found that 81 percent of all males surveyed had recently viewed pornographic material (Demare, Brier, & Lips, 1988). In the United States, local laws regulate the availability of pornographic material and, in many cases, define what is obscene. Other countries have eliminated most or all laws regulating pornography. When Denmark took these steps in 1969, many people predicted there would be a rapid increase in sex-related crimes. In fact, there was no increase in such crimes (Geen, 1987). When West Germany legalized pornography in 1972, there was actually a slight decrease in the rate of sex-related crimes. Even with regard to sexual behavior, one investigator found that although two-thirds of male adolescents and half of female adolescents expressed a desire to imitate the sexual behavior they observed in their first encounter with pornography, less than 25 percent of the males and 15 percent of the females acted on this desire (Bryant, 1985). There is, however, evidence that pornography does increase the likelihood that men will view women merely as sex objects and become more sexist in their behavior toward women (McKenzie-Mohr & Zanna, 1990).

Given these results, we might be tempted to conclude that the concern about pornography is much ado about nothing. Recent laboratory research on pornography suggests otherwise. Concern has shifted from the pornography-sexual behavior link to the pornography-violence link, especially violence against women. Much pornography depicts violence against women and rape. Men who view this type of pornography have more fantasies about rape (Malamuth, 1984), have reduced sensitivity to the plight of victims of rape (Malamuth, 1987), and harbor greater feelings that they, too, could commit rape (Malamuth, Haber, & Feshbach, 1980). In addition, males who have viewed violent pornography are subsequently more aggressive toward females (administer higher levels of shock) than males who have viewed either nonviolent pornography or violent films devoid of sexual content (Linz, Donnerstein, & Adams, 1989). This increased violence is especially likely to occur if there is any indication that the woman being victimized in aggressive pornography is experiencing any pleasure (Donnerstein & Linz, 1986).

You may feel that this finding is of little relevance, for how could anyone believe that the victim of assault or rape is enjoying the experience? Yet this is precisely what is often depicted in pornography. In one survey of the material in "adult" books, less than 3 percent of the rapists suffered negative consequences, and their victims were seldom shown to have regrets about being raped (Smith, 1976).

These results, taken together, indicate that violent pornography may desensitize people to the plight of victims of sex crimes, give the perception that aggressive violence is normative and acceptable, associate sexual violence with sexual pleasure, and increase aggression against the kind of victims portrayed in violent pornography. This is clearly a situation that deserves the greatest degree of concern. Does it suggest that we should outlaw violent pornography? Maybe. But as we pointed out, how can we determine what pornography should be outlawed? Who should make that determination? At what point would censorship infringe upon the rights of free speech and creative expression? These are, indeed, difficult issues, and they are the reason that there is no end in sight to the debate over pornography.

and in the hearts of people contemplating sexual activity. Once thought to be a disease confined to intravenous drug users and people engaged in homosexual activity, AIDS is becoming an issue in heterosexual activity. Masters, Johnson, and Kolodny (1988) created a furor by suggesting that AIDS is likely to be transmitted through heterosexual intercourse. They also suggest that the incidence of AIDS among exclusively heterosexual people is rapidly increasing. The credibility of their position is still in question, but the concern raised by such statements is likely to influence the sexual behavior of many people. Hence, our sexual activities are pulled, pushed, guided, and shaped by a multitude of motivational forces.

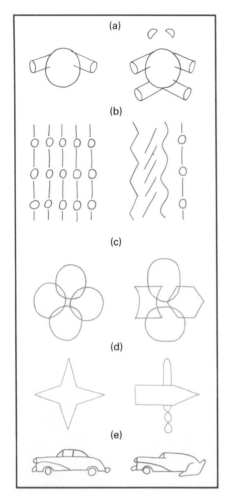

FIGURE 11–3

In this study, Berlyne found that most people, when presented with the figure pairs shown here, preferred the more complex figures on the right to those on the left in each pair. Subjects showed their preference by focusing more quickly and for a longer period on the right-hand figures. (Berlyne, 1958)

After dealing with the immediate perils of the crash, many of the survivors began to get restless; they wanted something to do while they waited for rescue. As a result, despite the bitter cold, some of them spent their daytime hours searching the area around the plane, and several set out to explore the larger area around the crash site. Others spent time wandering through the plane. When a new object was found, such as a broken piece of radio, the discoverer spent hours examining and fingering it.

Many animals have this same desire to explore and manipulate new objects, which is also referred to as a **stimulus-seeking motive.** When rats, cats, or dogs are put in a new environment, their immediate response is to explore the area. Dember (1965) found that rats given a choice between a familiar area and a new one will choose the new environment. It also has been observed that monkeys will spend hours opening and closing locks and other mechanical devices (Harlow, Harlow, & Meyer, 1950).

What is behind this common and seemingly insatiable behavior? Two important elements are novelty and complexity. Researchers have found that infants spend more time looking at complex figures than at simpler figures (Berlyne, 1957, 1958, 1960). Adults, too, focus their attention more on complex and novel pictures (see Figure 11–3).

The motive to explore and manipulate is important for our survival. It is through searching new areas and feeling, touching, and manipulating objects that we learn about our environment and how it works. In addition, exploration and manipulation help us learn how to control our environment. As already discussed, the motives to explore and manipulate do not easily fit the drive-reduction model of motivation. First, they do not seem to be caused by some internal state or lack. Rather, it is new and complex stimuli that elicit these responses. Second, the aim of these motives is to increase arousal or tension, not to reduce it. For this reason, the stimulus-seeking motive is better explained by incentive theory.

Similarly, some investigators have suggested that there may be a particular motive for arousal, or a **sensation-seeking motive** (Franklin, 1982). Some people take risks or perform behaviors designed to arouse them. They are actively drawn to horror movies and scary amusement park rides, for example, while others find thrills in parachuting from an airplane. Once a task is mastered, people often are quick to search out one of even greater risk. For example, the rugby players were able to beat the teams in Uruguay, and the Chilean teams represented a greater challenge. These activities are also intriguing because other research has found that we are attracted to and most comfortable with familiar objects and people (Moreland & Zajonc, 1982). Hence, we seem to be both attracted to and repelled by the novel, the new, and the exciting.

For these reasons, certain activities have captured our attention, and many arousal theories have been advanced to explain them. One position is that people seek high levels of arousal because the reduction of these high arousal levels is more rewarding than the reduction of lower arousal levels. This position tends to stretch the limits of credibility; it suggests that we might seek out painful experiences because the elimination of pain is so satisfying. Further, this theory does not explain why people increase their level of risk over time. A second position suggests that high arousal releases the drug norepinephrine into our systems (Zuckerman, 1979). According to this theory we seek arousal so our bodies will release norepinephrine into our systems because it makes us feel good. Risk-taking is kept within reason, however, because there are negative costs associated with higher risks.

Stimulus-seeking motive
Motive to explore and manipulate new objects to increase stimulation and arousal.
Sensation-seeking motive
A motive for arousal.

Affiliation

The crash caused many drastic changes in the lives of the survivors. No longer did they have a familiar environment and a routine daily schedule. Their lives were filled with fear: fear of the cold, fear of going hungry, fear that they would never be found, and fear that each day might be their last. Their response to this situation was to seek comfort in one another. The survivors sat together, talked together, slept together, and ate together.

The **affiliation motive,** the desire to be with others, does not only occur in the cold isolation of the Andes. If you look around your own environment, most of the people you see will be in pairs, trios, or other small groups. And if you talk to those people, you are likely to find that most of them spend a great deal of their time with other people.

We can think of a number of obvious reasons for wanting to affiliate with others. We need other people to achieve certain goals, for example building a house or moving a heavy object. There is safety in numbers; other people can protect us. We can gain knowledge and learn new activities from other people. In addition to these and other obvious reasons for affiliation (see Chapter 17), there have been some intriguing findings that suggest additional reasons for our motivation to be with others.

Although it may seem that humans have a natural drive to affiliate, research suggests that learning and early experiences strongly affect our desire to be with others. Harry Harlow (1971) studied infant monkeys who were raised in social isolation. Although they were well fed, they lacked the comfort of a mother and the opportunity to play with peers. When these isolated monkeys were one year old, Harlow placed them in a cage with other young monkeys who had been raised in a normal environment. Instead of joining the others in play, the isolated monkeys avoided social contact and cringed in a corner of the cage. If one of the other monkeys approached, the previously isolated monkey would react viciously. Somewhat related to this work are studies that show that we develop tendencies to trust or distrust others based on experiences during infancy (Ainsworth, 1979; Webb & Worchel, 1986). Caretakers who are sensitive and responsive to infants' needs foster feelings of trust and comfortableness with others. In contrast, individuals, who as infants had unresponsive caretakers, develop distrust and experience anxiety in interpersonal relationships. Thus, it seems that early experience of social comfort and interaction is crucial to the development of the desire to affiliate. (Also see Chapter 9 for a discussion of attachment.)

In addition to childhood experiences, our emotional state also appears to influence our desire to be with other people. Think about all the emotions the rugby players must have experienced after the crash. It is likely that fear was a primary emotion that drew them together. This idea is supported by research on affiliation. One of the early studies on fear and affiliation was conducted by Stanley Schachter (1959). Subjects in the "high fear" condition were led to believe that they would soon receive some painful electric shocks. Subjects in the "low fear" condition, in contrast, were told that they would receive only mild shocks that would "resemble more a tickle than anything unpleasant" (p. 14). After this fear manipulation, all subjects were told that there would be a ten-minute wait before the shocks, and they were given the choice of waiting alone, waiting with other people, or expressing no preference. As Table 11–2 shows, subjects in the high fear condition had stronger preferences for being with others than did subjects in the low fear condition.

Affiliation motive
Motive or desire to associate with and be around other people.

Table 11–2
Effect of Fear on Affiliation

Group	Number Choosing		
	Waiting Together	Didn't Care	Waiting Alone
High fear	20	9	3
Low fear	10	18	2

Source: Adapted from Schachter (1959).

In addition, subjects preferred to wait with other people who were also waiting to be shocked as opposed to others who were not waiting to be in the fear-arousing situation. In other words, they wanted to be with similar others rather than with people in dissimilar circumstances. The fear-affiliation relationship was found for subjects who were firstborn or only children. Fear did not motivate later-born subjects to affiliate with others.

Schachter suggested that the fearful situation was rather ambiguous for subjects; they didn't know what to expect or what they should be feeling. Their desire to be with others resulted because they wanted to reduce the ambiguity. They could observe the response of others, especially others who were in the same situation, and adjust their own actions and feelings accordingly. In childhood, Schachter speculated, only children and firstborn children received more attention from their mothers than later-born children. As a result they had learned to seek their mother's companionship in fearful situations and to rely on her response to reduce ambiguity in a way that later-born children had not. For this reason, fear motivated affiliation primarily in first or only children.

Although Schachter's theory is an interesting one, another explanation has also been suggested to explain affiliation (Rofe, 1984). According to the *utility affiliation theory*, people will seek out others who they think can help them reduce anxiety or fear. Further, they will avoid people who may increase fear or anxiety. In support of this position, one study found that severely ill patients (suffering from cancer, diabetes, and hypertension) preferred to be with healthy people rather than with other patients who had similar diseases (Rofe & Lewin, 1983). Further, they preferred to talk about things other than their disease. This position suggests we are motivated by our desire to get something from others. The opposite position has been offered by Batson (1990), who argues that we often interact with others because we "feel empathy for others in need, we are capable of caring for them for their sakes and not our own" (p. 336). This certainly puts affiliation in a positive light!

A third factor that may affect our desire to be with other people is our own traits. Beginning with Murray (1938) investigators have developed a number of tests to measure people's need for affiliation. Significant differences among individuals have been found. Exactly why such differences exist is not clear, but differences in early interactions with people seem to play a role. People high in affiliation motivation tend to interact more with others, form more stable friendships, and know more about their friends than people lower in affiliation motivation (McAdams & Losoff, 1984).

Aggression and Violence

In addition to hunger, thirst, and cold, the plane-crash survivors were forced to deal with one another's reactions to the crisis. From the very beginning there were fights. Many a night's calm was suddenly shattered by angry shouts and fighting. Some of the men fought often and with little provocation, whereas others rarely, if ever, participated in a fight.

Examples of violence and aggression aren't limited to extreme situations; they surround us. Nearly every page of a newspaper carries a story of violence; even the comics are liberally sprinkled with it. As a case in point, count the number of aggressive incidents or stories of aggression that you witness or hear about in one day. It seems, then, that although humans have a desire to affiliate, many of their social encounters are characterized by aggression.

The attempt to identify the basis for aggression is somewhat complicated by the likelihood that there are many types of aggression. For example, Moyer (1968) suggested a number of categories including maternal aggression (protecting the young), fear-induced aggression, territorial defense, predatory aggression, and instrumental aggression (aimed at obtaining a goal such as material or power). It is likely that no one theory of aggression can explain all types of aggression and that some theories deal more clearly with some types of aggression. For example, the instinct approach may be less applicable to instrumental aggression than to maternal or territorial aggression. With this point in mind, let's briefly examine some of the theories of aggression.

Instinct Theories. One of the earliest views was that aggression is an instinct. Influenced by the human destructiveness that he witnessed in World War I, Sigmund Freud held that humans have a basic instinct to aggress. To Freud, the motivation to aggress arises within the person.

The instinct position was further developed by those who argued that although an organism may be naturally endowed with the readiness to aggress, an external cue is necessary to release the response. According to these theorists, only certain stimuli are capable of releasing aggression. This external trigger is viewed as a key that opens the door for aggression; just as only the proper key can open a lock, so it is that only certain predetermined stimuli can trigger aggression.

Although such theories are of value in explaining aggression in some animals, it is hard to apply them directly to human behavior. Human aggression varies from culture to culture. For example, in a recent year there were 213 homicides in Tokyo, a city with a population of 11 million, as compared to 1,117 in New York City, with a population of 8 million. Individuals also vary greatly in levels of aggressiveness. Such cultural and individual differences make it difficult to argue that humans are instinctively aggressive.

Biological Theories. Genetic or biological factors could conceivably determine our aggression. Many biological theories have focused on hormones (Maccoby & Jacklin, 1974). In most species the male is more aggressive than the female. Further, it has been shown that injections of the male sex hormone, **testosterone,** can increase aggressiveness, especially in lower animals, and that drugs that reduce the level of this hormone can reduce violent aggression in males (Moyer, 1983). A number of investigators have shown that individuals with high testosterone levels are most likely to engage in antisocial behaviors and react with aggression when threatened (Dabbs & Morris, 1990; Olweus, Mattesson, Schialling, & Low, 1988). In addition, testosterone increases before competitive encounters and decreases after defeat (Booth et al., 1989). While the level of testosterone may be related to aggression in some cases, it is unclear whether this hormone actually *causes* people to aggress or what role it plays in aggression. Increased presence of the hormone may prepare people to aggress, but other factors may trigger aggression.

Testosterone
Male sex hormone.

Other researchers have attempted to identify "seats of aggression" in the brain (Geen, 1990). The notion here is that aggression results from stimulation of an area of the brain. For example, one study reported that injecting the hypothalamus of rats with stimulating drugs made them behave in an aggressive manner. Other investigators have argued for a role for the limbic system (see Chapter 2).

Although this line of research is interesting, it raises many questions. First, does stimulation of these parts of the brain motivate aggression, or does it cause pain, which leads to increased aggression? It may also be that such stimulation leads to a heightened state of arousal; as we will see, people are often more likely to aggress when they are aroused. Finally, even if we find some physiological basis for aggression, it is clear that no human or animal is constantly aggressive. We would therefore have to identify the conditions that are likely to lead to stimulation of this area.

Frustration-Aggression Theory. Despite attempts to show that the motivation for aggression arises from within the individual, most investigators believe aggression is set off by external events. One of the most widely studied theories was developed by a group of psychologists at Yale. John Dollard and his colleagues (1939) stated, "aggression is always a consequence of frustration," and "frustration always leads to some form of aggression" (p. 1). **Frustration** results when people are blocked from getting what they want when they want it. This **frustration-aggression theory** fits many of the incidents of aggression that occurred among the survivors in the Andes. For example, a survivor's desire to sleep was clearly being thwarted when he was stepped on or kicked in the face by a neighbor. In many cases, the result of this frustration was aggression against the neighbor.

But certain instances of aggression among the survivors don't seem at first glance to fully fit the frustration-aggression model. Canessa, one of the strongest survivors, tended to bully the smaller men. Although there were some direct attacks on him, his actions more often set off a chain reaction; he attacked one person, who, in turn, took out his anger on someone else. In other words, aggression resulted from frustration and anger but was not directed at the person who provoked these feelings. Such behavior has been labeled **displaced aggression.** Dollard and his colleagues argue that when we are frustrated, our first tendency is to attack the person responsible. However, if that person is either unavailable or feared (as in our example), we will displace our aggression onto another target. In Chapter 17 we will discuss how displaced aggression may be at the root of some cases of prejudice.

Another important but controversial part of the theory deals with reducing the urge to aggress. According to the theory, as we face various frustrations in our daily lives, tension builds up inside us. This tension must be released in some way. One of the quickest ways to do this is through aggression. Dollard and his colleagues suggest that if people behave aggressively they will release the tension and thus be less likely to aggress in the near future. **Catharsis** is the term used to describe this release of tension. This is a very important concept, because it argues that aggressive behavior can have a good effect on people and, in some cases, should be encouraged. However, although catharsis may occur after some acts of aggression, surveys and research indicate that the effect is, at best, limited to a very narrow range of conditions (Geen & Quanty, 1977; Konecni & Doob, 1972). In many cases, the expression of aggression not only fails to reduce future aggression, but actually increases the probability of it.

The frustration-aggression theory overall has received both support and criticism. It has been generally accepted that frustration often sets off aggression. However, frustration is not the only source of aggression,

Frustration
Basically, the result of being blocked from getting what you want when you want it.
Frustration-aggression theory
Theory that aggression is always a consequence of frustration and that frustration always leads to some form of aggression.
Displaced aggression
Taking out one's anger and/or frustration on someone or something other than the actual cause of one's anger.
Catharsis
Release of tension through aggression.

According to frustration-aggression theory, frustration is at the root of all aggression. The catharsis hypothesis argues that the expression of aggression reduces the likelihood of future aggression.

nor does it always lead to aggression. Further, the theory does not adequately explain the wide variety of human aggressive behavior. For example, why did some of the plane-crash survivors respond aggressively to their frustrations whereas others did not? Why did some of the young men use physical violence as a response to frustration while others resorted to verbal forms of aggression?

Social-Learning Theory. Despite the wide appeal of frustration-aggression theory, it is clear that not all aggression is the result of frustration. It has been argued that aggression, like most other behaviors, is the result of learning, rather than some natural link with frustration (Bandura, 1973, 1977; Bandura & Walters, 1963). The **social-learning theory** suggests that we learn both when and how to aggress. The theory focuses on two major mechanisms for the learning of aggression: *reinforcement* and *imitation*.

As discussed in Chapter 6, we tend to repeat behaviors that bring positive rewards. According to Bandura and Walters, children in our society are often rewarded for behaving aggressively; the rewards come in many forms. The rewards may be direct (e.g., Johnny beats up Jim and gets his football) or indirect (e.g., Suzy pinches Robert and gets the attention of her teacher and principal).

A second important way to learn aggression is through the imitation of models. On television, children see such stars as Magnum P.I. achieve fame through strength and aggression. Even at home, children see their parents use strength and aggression (spankings) to control their offspring. All these models broadcast the lesson that successful people use aggression to achieve their success.

In order to demonstrate the effectiveness of models, Bandura, Ross, and Ross (1961, 1963a) had nursery school children observe an adult model aggressively playing with an inflated doll ("Bobo doll"); the model kicked, hit, and beat the doll with a hammer (see Figure 11–4). When the children were later allowed to play with the doll, they too kicked, hit, and beat the doll with a hammer, just as the model had done. Bandura and his associates (1963b) also found that children imitated an aggressive model even when the model was seen on film or in a cartoon. Although learning occurs through imitation, research suggests that people mainly express aggression when they feel they will be rewarded for their behavior (Bandura, 1965a).

Recently Leonard Eron (1987) reported the results of a 22-year study that sheds some light on the causes of aggression. Investigators examined the behavior of a group of 7–9-year-olds and identified aggressive and nonagressive children. As would be predicted by social learning theory, aggressive children were often physically punished at home and they tended to watch a great deal of aggressive television programs; both these situations supplied them with aggressive models. In addition, the aggressive children often came from environments with a high degree of frustration, in that their parents tended to be less nurturant and accepting. Two follow-ups were conducted, 10 and 22 years after the initial study. The investigators reexamined the subjects, looked at how others rated the subjects, and went through records for hospital admissions, violent behavior, violent crimes, and even traffic violations. They found that those subjects who had been identified as aggressive when they were children also showed the highest number of aggressive behaviors as adolescents and adults.

Data from this study and others suggest not only that children learn aggressive behavior from models, but also that they learn to interpret events as threatening or to be particularly sensitive to threatening events (Dodge & Crick, 1990; Boldizar, Perry, & Perry, 1989). In addition, these aggressive children do not internalize norms against aggressing. For example, if someone steps on your toe, you may interpret this as an attack or simply an accident. If you see the event as an attack, you are more likely to respond with aggressive behavior than if you see it as an accident. Thus, early

Social learning theory
Learning by imitation.

FIGURE 11–4

These photos were taken during Bandura's study of modeling and aggression. After watching an adult model kick and beat up the Bobo doll, boys and girls repeated these actions when they were allowed to play with the doll. (Bandura et al., 1963)

experience and models can have wide-ranging and long-lasting effects on our behavior and perceptions.

Social-learning theory helps us understand why different people respond to the same situation in different ways. For example, Canessa, the most aggressive rugby player, may have learned that physical aggression was an effective way for him to deal with people who annoyed him. Thus, when people bothered him or got in his way during the mountain ordeal, his response was a violent one. Other survivors may have had very different experiences and models and, as a result, learned to approach problems with reason and calm.

In addition to explaining why people aggress, social-learning theory can also be used to develop ways of preventing or reducing aggression. If parents who use physical violence to punish their children are providing them with aggressive models, it follows that parents should instead use other methods of punishment, such as withholding rewards. Social-learning theory also argues strongly against the catharsis notion: If people learn aggression, then allowing them to participate in aggressive activities will increase their future aggression, not reduce it, as suggested by the catharsis hypothesis. In the next section, we will see yet another implication of social-learning theory for the control of aggression.

Media Violence and Aggression. It is interesting to examine frustration-aggression theory and social-learning theory in light of a major controversy that still rages today: What are the effects of media violence on aggression? An act of violence is shown on television every fifteen minutes, and a murder is shown every half-hour. If you grew up in the average family, you probably saw about 13,000 murders on television by the time you were sixteen years old (Waters & Malamud, 1975). Even shows specifically designed for young audiences are filled with examples of aggression: Nine out of ten characters in weekend children's programs are involved in some type of violence (Comstock et al., 1979).

What is the effect of watching such violence? Social-learning theory suggests that we learn aggression through modeling. According to this theory, we learn to aggress from watching these violent models. The majority of the evidence supports social-learning theory, although the link between media violence and aggression has still not been *proved*. Evidence for a relationship between the two comes from studies showing that aggressiveness increases in isolated communities after television is introduced (NIMH, 1982). Other evidence comes from more controlled studies. For example, researchers divided juvenile delinquents in minimum custody units into two groups: One group watched aggressive movies every night for a week, while the other group saw only nonaggressive movies during the week (Parke et al., 1977). The effect of the aggressive movies was to increase aggressive behavior—those who saw the violent films behaved more violently than those who had seen the nonviolent films. Taking this issue into the computer age, several investigators have shown that children become more aggressive after playing or watching video games (Cooper & Mackie, 1986; Silvern & Williamson, 1987). If you recall your own experience with these games, you will realize that in many of them the characters hit, kick, eat, beat, or destroy "the enemy."

In addition to affecting our behavior, the regular viewing of aggression on TV may affect our *reactions* to violence (Thomas et al., 1977). In one study, children watched either an aggressive episode of a TV program or a nonviolent film showing a game of volleyball. After this they were all shown a scene of "real-life" aggression. Those who had seen the aggressive film were less affected by the "real" violence than those who had seen the nonviolent film. Such results suggest that viewing aggression on TV may make us less sensitive to aggression in our own lives.

In 1969 the National Commission on the Causes and Prevention of Violence stated: "It is reasonable to conclude that a steady diet of violent behavior on television has an adverse effect on human character and attitudes. Violent behavior fosters moral and social values about violence in daily life that are unacceptable in a civilized society." More recent research (Eron, 1982) suggests that not everyone is affected the same by television violence. Overall, boys are more affected by violence than girls. And boys who are low achievers and unpopular at school are more likely than other boys to imitate aggression they see on television. It must also be remembered that in the real world our behavior is influenced by many factors; some, like media violence, may increase the likelihood of aggression, but there are also many factors that motivate us to inhibit aggression (Oskamp, 1988).

Desire for Control. The plane-crash survivors often engaged in aggression that seemed unprovoked. At times, one of the players would push or threaten another seemingly without reason and without reward. In a sense, vandalism follows a similar script. An individual or group may explode with violence aimed at destruction. It all seems senseless, since the aggressors get nothing for their actions. However, some investigators (Allen & Greenberger, 1980) argue that some people use violence to demonstrate their control. Being able to hurt an individual or destroy an object offers the ultimate sense of control; the aggressor derives a feeling of success and mastery over the environment. These investigators suggest that people who feel that they are losing control over their environment may turn to aggression to demonstrate to themselves that they are still in control.

The Role of Arousal and Aggression Cues. The survivors were in a constant state of tension during their mountain ordeal due to fear and

IS WAR INEVITABLE?

If we look at the history of humans, either recent history or far in the past, a number of points stand out. Certainly one issue that is quickly recognized is how difficult it is to find a period of time when there was *not a war somewhere in the world*. Even when our weapons were spears, knives, and rocks, the suffering and destruction caused by war were of great concern. But now that we possess weapons that can destroy our own species, the terror of war is much greater. As we read the research on aggression, we may conclude that the human is a naturally aggressive animal, and war is the inevitable consequence of this tendency.

In 1986, however, twenty internationally known scholars from around the world met in Seville, Spain, at the Sixth International Colloquium on Brain and Aggression to examine the question of whether humans are disposed to war by innate, biological characteristics. As you will see from their statement, they concluded that humans are not so predisposed.

This statement was adopted by UNESCO in 1989 and endorsed by the Council of Representatives of the American Psychological Association in 1987. It does not deal with specific inherited traits, but it is designed to present the social position that we, as humans, can control our destiny as it relates to war.

. . . we, the undersigned scholars from around the world and from relevant sciences, have met and arrived at the following Statement on Violence. In it, we challenge a number of alleged biological findings that have been used, even by some in our disciplines, to justify violence and war. Because the alleged findings have contributed to an atmosphere of pessimism in our time, we submit that the open, considered rejection of these misstatements can contribute significantly to the International Year of Peace.

Misuse of scientific theories and data to justify violence and war is not new but has been made since the advent of modern science. For example, the theory of evolution has been used to justify not only war, but also genocide, colonialism, and suppression of the weak.

We state our position in the form of five propositions. We are aware that there are many other issues about violence and war that could be fruitfully addressed from the standpoint of our disciplines, but we restrict ourselves here to what we consider a most important first step.

It is scientifically incorrect to say that we have inherited a tendency to make war from our animal ancestors. Although fighting occurs widely throughout animal species, only a few cases of destructive intra-species fighting between organized groups have ever been reported among naturally living species, and none of these involve the use of tools designed to be weapons. Normal predatory feeding upon other species cannot be equated with intra-species violence. Warfare is a peculiarly human phenomenon and does not occur in other animals.

The fact that warfare has changed so radically over time indicates that it is a product of culture. Its biological connection is primarily through language, which makes possible the coordination of groups, the transmission of technology, and the use of tools. War is biologically possible, but it is not inevitable, as evidenced by its variation in occurrence and nature over time and space. There are cultures which have not engaged in war for centuries, and there are cultures which have engaged in war frequently at some times and not at others.

It is scientifically incorrect to say that war or any other violent behavior is genetically programmed into our human nature. While genes are involved at all

anxiety about staying alive and about being rescued. Outside of the airplane nearly every step taken was a major ordeal as they sank into snow up to their waists. Is it possible that these added sources of arousal increased the aggressiveness of the survivors?

Researchers have suggested that arousal of any type can cause people to act more aggressively when they are frustrated or angered (Zillman, 1983). In one study, Zillman (1971) showed subjects either an aggressive film, a sexually arousing film, or a nonarousing film. The subjects were then either angered or not angered by an experimental confederate. Finally, they were given the chance to shock the confederate under the guise of a learning task. The results showed that subjects who were sexually aroused and later angered were the most aggressive (delivered the highest amount of shock) and subjects who watched the nonarousing film were least aggressive. Researchers also found that watching arousing but displeasing sexual films increased later aggression (Zillman et al., 1981). The results of this study highlight one of the main concerns with pornography.

Other research has shown that arousing exercise (Zillman et al., 1974),

levels of nervous system function, they provide a developmental potential that can be actualized only in conjunction with the ecological and social environment. While individuals vary in their predispositions to be affected by their experience, it is the interaction between their genetic endowment and conditions of nurturance that determines their personalities. Except for rare pathologies, the genes do not produce individuals necessarily predisposed to violence. Neither do they determine the opposite. While genes are co-involved in establishing our behavioral capacities, they do not by themselves specify the outcome.

It is scientifically incorrect to say that in the course of human evolution there has been a selection for aggressive behavior more than for other kinds of behavior. In all well-studied species, status within the group is achieved by the ability to cooperate and to fulfil social functions relevant to the structure of that group. "Dominance" involves social bondings and affiliations; it is not simply a matter of the possession and use of superior physical power, although it does involve aggressive behaviors. Where genetic selection for aggressive behavior has been artificially instituted in animals, it has rapidly succeeded in producing hyper-aggressive individuals; this indicates that aggression was not maximally selected under natural conditions. When such experimentally-created hyper-aggressive animals are present in a social group, they either disrupt its social structure or are driven out. Violence is neither in our evolutionary legacy nor in our genes.

It is scientifically incorrect to say that humans have a "violent brain." While we do have the neural apparatus to act violently, it is not automatically activated by internal or external stimuli. Like higher primates and unlike other animals, our higher neural processes filter such stimuli before they can be acted upon. *How we act is shaped by how we have been conditioned and socialized.* There is nothing in our neurophysiology that compels us to react violently.

It is scientifically incorrect to say that war is caused by "instinct" or any single motivation. The emergence of modern warfare has been a journey from the primacy of emotional and motivational factors, sometimes called "instincts," to the primacy of cognitive factors. Modern war involves institutional use of personal characteristics such as obedience, suggestibility, and idealism; social skills such as language; and rational considerations such as cost-calculation, planning, and information processing. The technology of modern war has exaggerated traits associated with violence both in the training of actual combatants and in the preparation of support for war in the general population. As a result of this exaggeration, such traits are often mistaken to be the causes rather than the consequences of the process.

We conclude that biology does not condemn humanity to war, and that humanity can be freed from the bondage of biological pessimism and empowered with confidence to undertake the transformative tasks needed in this International Year of Peace and in the years to come. Although these tasks are mainly institutional and collective, they also rest upon the consciousness of individual participants for whom pessimism and optimism are crucial factors. Just as "wars begin in the minds of men," peace also begins in our minds. The same species who invented war is capable of inventing peace. The responsibility lies with each of us.

Seville, May 16, 1986

UNESCO General Conference, 1989
(Document 25C/20)

humor (Mueller & Donnerstein, 1977), and noise (Donnerstein & Wilson, 1976) can also increase aggression when subjects are frustrated. There are two possible explanations for this effect. First, the heightened state of arousal may serve to energize people's responses. A second explanation is that people may misinterpret the cause of their arousal, as we shall discuss in Chapter 12. That is, the person who is first sexually aroused and then made frustrated and angry may feel that all the arousal is a result of anger.

This line of reasoning has been extended by several investigators. They argue that negative feelings, regardless of their source, may activate ideas, memories, and expressive behavior associated with anger and aggression (Berkowitz, 1990). The person will most likely respond with aggression if he or she views the source of the arousal as having threatening intentions (Geen, 1990) and if **aggression cues** are present in the environment (Berkowitz, 1965; Carlson, Marcus-Newhall, & Miller, 1990). An aggression cue can be any object or other stimulus that the person has learned to associate with aggression. For example, a weapon or even a name (Rambo) may be an aggression cue.

Aggression cues
Any stimuli that an individual has learned to associate with aggressive behavior.

Many years ago, Henry Murray (1938) suggested that some people are driven by the motive "to do things as rapidly and/or as well as possible." Later, McClelland (1958) argued that people can be categorized by the strength of their **achievement motive (nAch).** People with high nAch are driven by the general desire to set and achieve high standards of excellence. These people seek out challenging tasks and do their best to perform well even if the task holds no special interest for them. They have an internal standard of excellence that they strive to meet. More recently, it has been shown that people with a high need for achievement want a leader who will show them how to "get the job done" rather than one who is mostly concerned with the feelings of group members (Mathieu, 1990).

Atkinson and Birch (1978) suggested that to understand the achievement motive we must look at two dimensions: *hope for success* and *fear of failure*. The need for achievement will be highest in people who have a high hope for success and a low fear of failure. People dominated by a high hope for success should seek out tasks that will challenge their abilities yet not be unattainable. In contrast, people who are dominated by a fear of failure should be attracted to either very easy goals or very difficult ones. They can be certain to achieve the simple goals, whereas failing to meet a very difficult goal cannot be too upsetting because failure would be expected from the start. In an interesting study designed to test this theory, subjects who had been identified as either very hopeful for success or highly fearful of failure were given some practice trials in a ring-toss game (Hamilton, 1974). After seeing their ability at the game, the subjects were given the opportunity to choose their own distance for the next set of trials. Subjects identified as hopeful of success chose distances where the probability of success was moderate. Subjects fearful of failure chose distances where success was very unlikely. Thus, the theory was supported on two points but not on the third: None of those who feared failure set themselves a very easy goal. Either the theory is wrong in this respect or a short distance would have been so easy that subjects were reluctant to choose it.

Recently, cognitive psychologists have reexamined the concept of achievement motivation (Dweck, 1986; Nicholls, 1986). They suggest that the tasks people choose may reflect not "high" versus "low" achievement motivation, but rather, an orientation to learning versus performance goals. The basis of a *learning goal* is to gain new knowledge, develop strategies for overcoming obstacles, and increase our abilities. People whose motivation focuses on learning goals should therefore prefer tasks of moderate difficulty. If they fail at this type of task, their attention will be focused on increasing their effort or developing new ways to tackle the problem. The basis of a *performance goal* is to gain favorable judgments from others. People who have such goals should choose simple tasks, on which they can do well and gain praise. Or they choose very difficult tasks, where failure will not bring criticism—who could criticize you for failing at a task where nobody has succeeded? The focus on performance goals heightens concern with self-concept and ability. In a sense, the basis for this goal is a fear of being rejected by others (Geen, 1991). As you might suspect, the learning goal is more adaptive, because it leads us to improve and to develop new skills. The rugby team exemplifies the orientation to learning goals, such as acquiring new skills. Had their aim been performance and winning praise, the team could have chosen an easy opponent at home.

Achievement motive (nAch)
Motive to do things as rapidly and/or as well as possible.
Extrinsic motivation
Motivated behavior that results from external factors, such as a promotion or other type of reward.
Intrinsic motivation
Motivated behavior that derives from the enjoyment of performing the task rather than from an expected reward.

INTRINSIC AND EXTRINSIC MOTIVATION

An important and central question in the study of motivation can be examined by focusing on your present behavior: reading this book. What is it that motivates you to read and learn the material in this book? That may seem like an unnecessary question. Certainly you are reading so you can do well on your tests and earn a good grade in the course. Although this answer may reflect reality, it is not the response that we, as textbook writers and teachers, would like to hear. Our hope is that students will be "turned on" to their texts because of the pride and satisfaction they feel in knowing more about themselves and their world. These two answers represent the basic reasons why people work or perform almost any task. The first response (reading to pass a test) is an example of **extrinsic motivation.** This type of motivation comes from factors external to the individuals; it can be based on a desire for pay, status, grades, promotion, or any similar types of rewards. The second response is an example of **intrinsic motivation,** which involves deriving enjoyment and satisfaction from performing the task itself, not from the expected rewards. There are two bases for intrinsic motivation. First, people have a need to see themselves as controlling their own behavior. Second, people also want to see themselves as capable and competent (Deci, 1971). Intrinsic rewards such as intellectual challenge or pride make us feel that we are in control. On the other hand, when we work only for an external reward such as money, it is the reward that is controlling our behavior.

The concept of extrinsic versus intrinsic rewards gives rise to some interesting and important predictions regarding work behavior. One prediction is that people who are extrinsically motivated will stop working when that extrinsic reward is no longer available. On the other hand, people who are intrinsically motivated will continue to work regardless of external conditions. In

a series of studies, subjects were either paid money (extrinsic motivation) or given no reward to work on puzzles (Calder & Staw, 1975; Deci, 1972). When they completed the experiment, subjects were given free time to engage in a number of activities such as reading magazines or working on more puzzles. The results showed that subjects who had been paid to work on the puzzles spent less free (and unpaid) time working on the puzzles and reported enjoying the puzzles less than subjects who had never been paid to work on the puzzles. Likewise, if you are reading this book only to pass the course (extrinsic motivation), it is unlikely that you would continue to read it after the course is over.

This does not mean that rewards are always bad. For one thing, rewards can have two very different functions (Pittman & Heller, 1987). On one hand, they can have a *controlling* function, that is, they tell us that we were performing in order to obtain the reward. In this case, rewards shape and determine our behavior and will have the negative effects of extrinsic motivation. On the other hand, rewards can have an *informational* function; they indicate how well we did and give us information about our competence. In this case, rewards will not dampen intrinsic motivation, because they were not the goal of our behavior. Hence, the reward itself is not so bad; often, it's the way in which the reward is presented that determines its effect on our motivation.

Furthermore, research indicates that if a task is dull and uninteresting, rewards will increase our performance (Lepper & Greene, 1978). But the story is different when we consider tasks that are interesting and can be intrinsically motivating. In this case, giving people a reward for performing a task that they enjoy performing may change their perception of their own behavior; they may see themselves as working only for the reward, and consequently reduce performance when the reward is no longer

available. This effect can be seen clearly in the old Jewish fable offered here.

In a little Southern town where the Klan was riding again, a Jewish tailor had the temerity to open his little shop on the main street. To drive him out of the town the Kleagle of the Klan sent a gang of little ragamuffins to annoy him. Day after day they stood at the entrance of his shop. "Jew! Jew!" they hooted at him. The situation looked serious for the tailor. He took the matter so much to heart that he began to brood and spent sleepless nights over it. Finally out of desperation he evolved a plan.

The following day, when the little hoodlums came to jeer at him, he came to the door and said to them, "From today on anybody who calls me 'Jew' will get a dime from me." Then he put his hand in his pocket and gave each boy a dime.

Delighted with their booty, the boys came back the following day and began to shrill, "Jew! Jew!" The tailor came out smiling. He put his hand in his pocket and gave each of the boys a nickel, saying, "A dime is too much—I can only afford a nickel today." The boys went away satisfied, because, after all, a nickel was money, too.

However, when they returned the next day to hoot at him, the tailor gave them only a penny each.

"Why do we get only a penny today?" they yelled.

"That's all I can afford."

"But two days ago you gave us a dime, and yesterday we got a nickel. It's not fair, mister."

"Take it or leave it. That's all you're going to get!"

"Do you think we're going to call you 'Jew' for one lousy penny?"

"So don't!"

And they didn't.

(Taken from *A Treasury of Jewish Fables* by Nathan Ausubel. Copyright 1948, © 1976 by Crown Publishers, Inc. Used by permission of Crown Publishers, Inc.)

Basis for the Achievement Motive. The fact that people have achievement motives of different strengths, or have different goals for tasks they undertake, raises the question of where these motives come from. As with so many things in life, it seems that much of the blame (or praise) rests with our parents. Family characteristics and lifestyle influence the development of the achievement motive. Winterbottom (1953) found that individuals high in nAch had been raised by their mothers to act independently. They had been allowed to make decisions on their own and had been rewarded with affection for independent actions. Other researchers found that both the opportunity for independence and the reward for independent behavior were necessary for developing high nAch (Teevan & McGhee, 1972). Children who are forced to act independently but are not rewarded for these behaviors do not develop high achievement motives; they may learn to act on their own, but they do not strive for excellence.

People with high nAch outperform those who have similar IQ scores but are low in achievement motivation. People with high achievement motive tend to get better grades in school (Raynor, 1970) and be more successful in business (Andrew, 1967) than those who have a low need to achieve.

Research has shown that the strength of a person's motive to achieve is related to the type of occupation he or she chooses. McClelland (1955) found that people scoring low on the need to achieve chose jobs that involved few risks and few opportunities for independent decision making. However, people scoring high in nAch chose entrepreneurial positions such as sales or were self-employed; in either case they had to make decisions and their salary and success were dependent on their own actions.

The reason for these differences are not entirely clear. However, it seems that people scoring low in nAch tend to be most concerned with either succeeding or having an excuse for not succeeding. In contrast, those higher in nAch desire a challenge that they can work and succeed at, with success measured by their ability and work.

Although having a high need to achieve has many positive consequences, it does have its drawbacks. Recent evidence suggests that people scoring high in nAch take everything as a challenge. In their drive for perfection, they run the risk of becoming "workaholics." In some cases, they have difficulty "letting go" and relaxing and are prone to getting

People with high achievement motivation tend to choose occupations that require decision making and involve high risks. Based on this finding, we might speculate about the level of achievement motivation of people who choose political careers!

ulcers (as we will discuss in Chapter 12). While it has not yet been shown whether these same distinctions characterize people with learning goals versus those with performance goals, we might anticipate that many of them do.

Fear of Success. The strong desire to achieve and be successful in school and work is encouraged for males, but what about females? Researchers point out that the traditional view of women in our society discourages success and striving for achievement (Frieze et al., 1978). Women often are not encouraged to seek independent careers, and when they do so, they may be the object of social scorn and discrimination. As a result of these traditional values, Horner (1968) argued, women learn to avoid and fear success.

In order to demonstrate this position, Horner asked male and female subjects to write a story about the following situation: "After first-term finals, Anne (John) finds herself (himself) at the top of her (his) medical school class." As can be seen in Table 11–3, when males wrote about John, they described him in positive terms and predicted that he would have a happy future. However, when females wrote about Anne, their descriptions were far from flattering and they expressed concern about her future.

Although Horner's conclusions are provocative, they have been criticized. Later studies suggested the findings might have some other explanation, rather than reflecting women's fear of success. For example, one study had men write about Anne's outcome and women write about John's outcome (Monaham et al., 1979). The results showed that men wrote less successful outcomes for Anne than women wrote about John. Another study found that women wrote successful outcomes about a female in a more "typically female role" such as nursing (Feather, 1975). Two explanations can be offered for these responses and Horner's. One is that the stories written about Anne and John simply reflected prevailing expectations and sex stereotypes. In other words, the writers were indicating that Anne might meet social rejection if she succeeded, whereas John would not. A second explanation focuses on the importance of succeeding in a particular task (Eccles, 1983). That is, the situations involved in the stories may have been ones where males felt it was important to succeed while females did not. Still other investigator's criticize the concept of fear of success (Walsh, 1987; Palvdi, 1987). They argue that the research shows a cultural stereotype about women's success and not a motive. They also point out that there is no strong evidence linking responses on the measures with the actual behavior of women in achievement situations.

Sample Male Response	Sample Female Response
John is a conscientious young man who worked hard. He is pleased with himself. John has always wanted to go into medicine and is very dedicated. His hard work paid off. He is thinking that he must not let up now, but must work even harder than he did before. His goods marks have encouraged him. . . . He eventually graduates at the top of his class.	Anne has a boyfriend in the same class and they are quite serious. Anne met Carl at college and they started dating. . . . Anne is rather upset and so is Carl. She wants him to be higher in school than she is. Anne will deliberately lower her academic standing next term, while she does all she subtly can to help Carl. His grades come up and Anne soon drops out of medical school. They marry and he goes on in school while she raises their family.

Table 11–3
Sex Differences and the Achievement Motive

Source: Horner (1968).

Early views on achievement motivation identified two dimensions: hope for success and fear of failure. Recently cognitive psychologists have suggested that achievement involves two different goals: learning versus performance. People with a learning goal choose moderately difficult tasks that give them new information, increase their abilities, and challenge them to develop strategies for overcoming obstacles.

A Hierarchy of Motives?

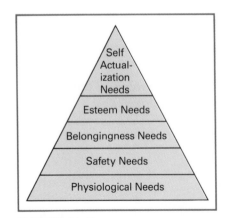

FIGURE 11–5

Maslow's Hierarchy of Needs

Maslow believed that motives at each level must be satisfied before motives at the next higher level will direct behavior.

We have examined a number of different motives. Looking back over these motives, we ask whether some are more important or basic than others. Immediately after the crash, the survivors turned their attention to clearing out what was left of the plane and trying to warm themselves. After doing this, they worried about finding a water supply and seeing what food was available. The survivors seemed to care very little about what others thought of them during these early days. Some openly wept, some reverted to childish behavior, and others performed such socially disapproved behaviors as wetting their pants. After their hunger and thirst had been satisfied, the survivors began organizing themselves into groups. Leaders emerged, and people who broke loosely defined rules were reprimanded. The young men began thinking about their families and sweethearts, and a few even wrote letters expressing their feelings for their loved ones.

As we look over this sequence of behaviors, we can ask why the survivors did particular things in a certain order. Why did it take them time to begin thinking about their families? Why didn't they organize into effective working groups right after the crash?

It has been suggested that our motives are organized into a hierarchy, with the stronger biological motives at the bottom and the more complex psychological motives at the top (Maslow, 1954, 1970). Maslow further believed that the motives at the lower level must first be satisfied before the motives at the next higher level will influence or direct one's behavior. For example, if you look at Maslow's hierarchy (Figure 11–5), you can see that hunger and thirst must be satisfied before you will begin to direct behavior at satisfying security or social order needs. You may have had your own experiences with this hierarchy of motives if you have ever tried to study when you were hungry. It is likely that this was a difficult, if not hopeless, undertaking. You probably interrupted your studies frequently to search your room for food. If you didn't find any, you probably found yourself staring at the pages of your books while your mind wandered to thick, juicy steaks, steaming baked potatoes, and chocolate ice cream. The behaviors of the survivors fit nicely into Maslow's scheme. Their first actions were aimed at satisfying their physical needs (warmth, liquid, and food), whereas later actions seemed to be directed by desires for social order, thoughts of their families, and the need for respect from their companions.

Research findings do not support Maslow's theory, however. Much of the research on the hierarchy has been conducted in work settings. For example, in one study managers and other white-collar workers were asked to rank a list of needs in order of importance (Wahba & Bridwell, 1976). These rankings did not fit Maslow's hierarchy. Other investigators (e.g., Alderfer, 1972) have suggested that there are three types of needs: existence (physiological and safety), relatedness (belongingness needs), and growth (esteem and self-actualization). In contrast to Maslow's model, this theory suggests that the needs are not hierarchical and that more than one need may be operating at any given time. That is, a person may be striving to satisfy both existence and growth needs. This newer theory seems to more closely fit the results obtained in a variety of settings and may more accurately reflect the way in which our motives are interrelated (Geen et al., 1984).

Summary

1. The study of **motivation** is concerned with how and why people behave as they do—what energizes and directs their behavior.

2. A distinction is made in the chapter between **primary motives** (such as hunger, thirst, the need for air and rest, and sex) and **social motives** (such as affiliation, aggression, and achievement).

3. The basic theories of motivation are instinct theory, drive theory, incentive theory, and cognition theory. Instinct theory argues that behavior is preprogrammed and guided by internal forces. Drive theory suggests that needs result when homeostasis is upset and that behavior is directed toward restoring homeostasis. Incentive theory suggests that behavior is determined by external conditions such as reinforcement. Cognitive theory emphasizes the role of thinking, judging, and information processing.

4. Hunger is one of the most basic primary motives. In looking for what controls eating and hunger, researchers have studied contractions of the stomach, the level of glucose in the bloodstream (as monitored by the hypothalamus, duodenum, and liver), the role of taste, and the influence of body weight. The research suggests that we have different systems that control short-term eating and long-term eating. While glucoreceptors influence short-term eating, other receptors, which monitor fat deposits, control eating over longer periods of time and ensure weight stability.

5. There are a number of factors associated with **obesity** and overeating. **Set-point theory** argues that our weight is determined by the number and size of the fat cells in our body. The number of fat cells is determined by genetics and eating patterns during the first few years of our lives. Our body weight gets set at a certain level, and our eating behavior is motivated to maintain this level. Eating, especially in obese people, may also be affected by external cues and arousal not related to hunger. **Anorexia nervosa** is an eating disorder in which a person loses appetite, eats very little, and loses at least 25 percent of his or her normal body weight. **Bulimia** is an eating disorder involving binging and purging cycles.

6. **Osmometric thirst** is motivated by a reduction of intracellular fluid levels—the hypothalamus is believed to signal the need for fluids when the intracellular fluid levels are changing. **Volumetric thirst** is a reaction to changes in blood pressure.

7. Unlike hunger, sex is not necessary for the survival of the individual; but it is necessary for the survival of the species. The biological basis of male and female sexual behavior is hormonal (**androgen**

in the male, **estrogen** in the female). However, human sexual behavior is neither as dependent on hormones nor as stereotyped as animal sexual behavior. Because of this, learning, external cues, and other motivational forces play an important role in human sexual response.

8. Masters and Johnson have categorized the human sexual response into four phases: the excitement phase, the plateau phase, the orgasm phase, and the resolution phase. Males then usually enter a refractory period, which may last from a few minutes to several hours, during which time they are incapable of sexual arousal or orgasm. Women, on the other hand, are capable of multiple orgasms in quick succession.

9. The desire to explore and manipulate new objects is called a **stimulus-seeking motive.** It is important for our survival, because it causes us to learn about our environment, how it works, and how to control it. The **sensation-seeking motive** is based on the desire to be aroused.

10. The **affiliation motive,** the desire to be with others, is a social motive. It may differ from person to person and may vary in strength depending upon circumstances. Fear often increases one's desire to affiliate with others.

11. Human aggression has long intrigued psychologists. There are many types of aggression. There-fore, no one theory of aggression yet developed can clearly explain all of them. Among the theories considered here are: instinct theories, biological theories, frustration-aggression theory, and social-learning theory.

12. Factors that are thought to influence aggressive behavior are early experiences, imitation of models, viewing media violence, desire for control, and arousal.

13. The **achievement motive (nAch)** can be defined as the general desire to set and achieve high standards of excellence. The cognitive approach to achievement motivation suggests that the tasks people choose may reflect an orientation to learning versus performance goals. The learning goal motivates people to choose moderately difficult tasks from which they can learn new skills; while the performance goal leads to the choice of either very difficult or very easy tasks to gain praise or avoid criticism.

14. Maslow has suggested that our motives are organized into a hierarchy, with the stronger primary motives at the bottom and the more complex social motives at the top. Motives at any given level come into play only when motives at lower levels have been satisfied. Another theory suggests that there are three types of needs and that more than one need may be operating at the same time.

Key Terms

achievement motive (nAch)	glucoreceptors	ovaries
affiliation motive	homeostasis	ovulation
aggression cue	homosexuality	pheromones
androgens	incentive	primary motives
anorexia nervosa	instincts	rape
bulimia	intrinsic motivation	releasing stimulus
calories	lesbian	secondary sexual characteristics
catharsis	masturbation	sensation-seeking motive
date rape	menopause	set-point theory
displaced aggression	motivation	social-learning theory
drive	motive	social motives
estrogen	need	stimulus-seeking motive
extrinsic motivation	obesity	testes
frustration	osmometric thirst	testosterone
frustration-aggression theory	osmoreceptors	volumetric thirst

MATING FOR LIFE?
IT'S NOT FOR THE BIRDS OR THE BEES

BY NATALIE ANGIER

Ah, romance. Can any sight be as sweet as a pair of mallard ducks gliding gracefully across a pond, male by female, seemingly inseparable? Or better yet, two cygnet swans, which, as biologists have always told us, remain coupled for life, their necks and fates lovingly intertwined.

Coupled for life, with just a bit of adultery, cuckoldry and gang rape on the side.

Alas for sentiment and the greeting card industry, biologists lately have discovered that, in the animal kingdom, there is almost no such thing as monogamy. In a burst of new studies that are destroying many of the most deeply cherished notions about animal mating habits, researchers report that even among species assumed to have faithful tendencies and to need a strong pair bond to rear their young, infidelity is rampant.

Biologists long believed, for example, that up to 94 percent of bird species were monogamous, with one mother and one father sharing the burden of raising their chicks. Now, using advanced techniques to determine the paternity of offspring, biologists are finding that, on average, 30 percent or more of the baby birds in any nest were sired by someone other than the resident male. Indeed, researchers are having trouble finding bird species that are not prone to such evident philandering.

Faithless Females

"This is an extremely hot topic," said Dr. Paul W. Sherman, a biologist at Cornell University in Ithaca, New York. "You can hardly pick up a current issue of an ornithology journal without seeing a report of another supposedly monogamous species that isn't. It's causing a revolution in bird biology."

In related studies of creatures already known to be polygamous, researchers are finding their subjects to be even more craftily faithless than previously believed. And to the astonishment, perhaps disgruntlement, of many traditional animal behaviorists, much of that debauchery is committed by females.

Tracking rabbits, elk and ground squirrels through the fields, researchers have learned that the females of these species will copulate with numerous males in a single day, each time expelling the bulk of any partner's semen to make room for the next mating. Experts theorize that the female is storing up a variety of semen, perhaps so that different sperm will fertilize different eggs and thus assure genetic diversity in her offspring.

Males Retaliate

Most efficiently energetic of all may be the queen bee, who on her sole outing from her hive mates with as many as 25 accommodating, but doomed, dromes.

Scientists also have gathered evidence of many remarkable instances of attempts by males to counteract philandering by females. Among Idaho ground squirrels, a male will stick unerringly by a female's side whenever she is fertile, sometimes chasing her down a hole and sitting on top of it to prevent her from cavorting with his competitors. Other squirrels simply use a rodent's version of a chastity belt, topping an ejaculation with a rubber-like emission that acts as a plug.

The new research, say scientists, gives the lie to the old stereotype that only males are promiscuous. "It's all baloney," said Dr. Sherman. "Both males and females seek extra-pair copulations. And what we've found lately is probably just the tip of the iceberg."

Even mammals, which have never been paragons of virtue, are proving to be worse than expected, and experts are revising downward the already pathetic figure of 2 percent to 4 percent that represented, they thought, the number of faithful mammal species.

"It was believed that field mice, certain wolflike animals, and a few South American primates, like marmosets and tamarins, were monogamous," said Dr. David J. Gubernick, a psychologist at the University of Wisconsin in Madison who studies monogamy in mammals. "But new data indicate that they, too, engage in extra-pair copulations."

Scientists say their new insights into mating and the near-universality of infidelity are reshaping their ideals about animal behavior and the dynamics of different animal social systems.

"It's been a bandwagon," said Dr. Susan M. Smith, a biologist at Mt. Holyoke College in South Hadley, Mass. "Nobody can take monogamy for granted anymore, in any species they look at, so we're all trying to rewrite the rules we once thought applied."

Old Assumptions:
Darwin's Misconceptions

Biologists say their new research suggests that many animal social systems might have developed as much to allow animals to selectively cheat as they did out of a need for animals to divide into happy couples. They propose that pair bonds among animals might be mere marriages of convenience, allowing both partners enough stability to raise their young while leaving a bit of slack for the occasional dalliance.

More than anything else, say biologists, they are increasingly impressed by the complexity of animal sexuality.

"It seems that all our old assumptions are incorrect, and that there's a big difference between who's hanging out with whom and who's actually mating with whom," said Dr. Patricia Adair Gowaty, a biologist at Clemson University in South Carolina and one of the first to question the existence of fidelity among animals. "For those of us in the field, this is a tremendously exciting time."

Researchers say that many of the misconceptions about monogamy and infidelity began in Darwin's day, when he and other naturalists made presumptions, perhaps understandable, about mating based on field observations of coupled animals. Nearly all birds form pairs during the breeding season, and biologists assumed that the pair bond was necessary for the survival of the young. Without the contributions of both males and females to feed and protect the young, experts thought, few offspring would make it to the fledgling stage. And that demand for stability, biologists assumed, likely included monogamy as well.

But as field researchers became more sophisticated in their observation techniques, they began spotting instances in which one member of a supposedly monogamous avian couple would flit off for a tête-à-tête with a paramour.

"Extra-pair copulations are called sneakers, and they really are," said Dr. Robert Montgomerie, a biologist at Queens University in Kingston, Ontario. "They're not easy to observe because the birds are very surreptitious about such behavior."

Such sightings inspired biologists to apply DNA fingerprinting and other techniques used in paternity suits to help determine the parentage of chicks. They discovered that between 10 percent and 70 percent of the offspring in a nest did not belong to the male caring for them.

Explanations: Females Look Up

Redoubling their efforts in the field, biologists began to seek explanations for the infidelities. In some cases, the female clearly was the one seeking outside liaisons.

Dr. Smith has studied the familiar black-capped chickadee of North America. She had found that, during winter, a flock of chickadees forms a dominance hierarchy in which every bird knows its position relative to its fellows, as well as the ranking of other birds.

In the spring breeding season, says Dr. Smith, the flock breaks up into pairs, with each pair defending a territorial niche and breeding in it. Though she has determined that infidelity is rare among the chickadees, it does occur "and in a very interesting way," she said. On occasion, a female mated to a low-ranking male will leave the nest and sneak into the territory of a higher-ranking male nearby.

"In every single case of extra-pair copulations, the female wasn't moving randomly, but very selectively," said Dr. Smith. "she was mating with a bird ranked above her own mate."

Dr. Smith suggests that the cheating chickadee may have the best of both worlds: a stable mate at home to help rear the young, along with the chance to bestow on at least one or two of her offspring the superior

genes of a dominant male. "This fits into the idea that the female is actively attempting to seek the best-quality genes," she said.

Selectivity of Barn Swallows

In similar studies, Dr. Anders Moller, a biologist at the University of Uppsala in Sweden, has found that female barn swallows likewise are very finicky about their adulterous encounters. When cheating, he said, the females invariably copulate with males endowed with slightly longer tails than those of their mates. Dr. Moller has learned that, among barn swallows, a lengthy tail appears to be evidence that the birds are resistant to parasites; this trait would be beneficial to a female's young. "Females mated to very short-tailed males engage in these extra-marital affairs the most," he said. "Short-tailed males attempt to have affairs themselves, but they're rarely successful."

Some females that mate promiscuously may be gaining not so much the best genes as enough genetic diversity to assure that at least some of their offspring thrive. Biologists studying honeybees have found that the queen bee will leave her hive only once, to mate with as many as 25 drones patrolling nearby. Tabulating her wantonness is easy: to complete intercourse, the poor drone must explode his genitals onto the queen's body, dying but leaving behind irrefutable evidence of an encounter.

And while the queen bee does have considerable reproductive demands, needing enough sperm to fertilize about four million eggs, researchers have determined that any one of the drones could provide enough sperm to accommodate her. They, therefore, suspect that her profligate behavior is intended to insure genetic diversity in her brood.

The Devious Males: Strategies For Success

But biologists say there are evolutionary counterbalances that can keep cheating in check. Females that actively seek outside affairs might risk losing the devotion of their own mates. Researchers have found that among barn swallows, a male that observes his mate copulating with other males responds by reducing his attention to her babies. Of course, males themselves are always

attempting to philander, say biologists, whether or not they are paired to a steady mate at home. In an effort to spread their seed as widely as possible, some males go to exquisitely complicated lengths.

A Kind of Betrayal

Studying the purple martin, the world's largest species of swallow, Dr. Gene S. Morton, a research zoologist at the National Zoo in Washington, has found that older males will happily betray their younger counterparts. An older martin will first establish his nest, attract a mate, and then quickly reproduce, both parents again being needed for the survival of the young.

His straightforward business tended to, the older bird will start singing songs designed to lure a younger male to his neighborhood. That inexperienced yearling moves in and croons a song to attract his own mate, who is promptly ravished by the elder martin. A result is that a yearling male manages to fertilize less than 30 percent of his mate's eggs, although he is the one who ends up caring for the brood.

"The only way for the older males to get the younger females is to attract the young males first," said Dr. Morton. "The yearlings end up being cuckolded."

Older males often try to appropriate a younger male's partner. Studying mallards and related ducks. Dr. Frank McKinney, curator of ethology at the Bell Museum of Natural History at the University of Minnesota in Minneapolis, has found that males often try to force sex on females paired to other males. The females struggle mightily to avoid these copulations, he said, by flying away, diving underwater or fighting back.

"Our finding is that it's usually the older, experienced males that are successful in engaging in forced copulation," he said. They have more skills, and capturing females is a skillful business."

Guarding the Females

Driven by evolutionary pressures, males have developed an impressive array of strategies to fend off competitors and keep their females in line as well. "In almost any animal you look at, males do things in order to be certain of paternity," said Dr. David F. Westneat, a biologist at the University of Kentucky in Lexington.

Mate-guarding is one widespread strategy, he said, with males staying beside females during her fertile times. But other strategies result in what biologists have called "sperm wars," a battle by males to give their sperm the best chance of success.

Among many species of rodents, the last male's sperm is the sperm likeliest to inseminate the female, for reasons that remain mysterious. Hence, several males may engage in an exhausting round robin, as each tries, repeatedly, to be the last one to copulate with the female.

In studies of the damselfly, Dr. Jonathan Waage, a biologist at Brown University in Providence, Rhode Island, has learned that the male has a scoop at the end of his genitals that can be used before copulating to deftly remove the semen of a previous mate.

In other species, natural selection seems to have favored males with the most generous ejaculation. Over evolutionary time, researchers say, this has resulted in the development of some formidable testicles. The more likely a female is to mate with more than one male, they say, the bigger the sperm-producing organs will be.

Comparing the dimensions of testes relative to body size among several species of primates, biologists have found that gorillas have the smallest. Among the great apes, a dominant silverback male manages to control a harem of females with little interference from other males, biologists say.

Chimpanzees have the largest testes of the primates relative to body size. They are the ones that live in troupes with multiple males, multiple females, and considerable mating by all.

Human beings have mid-sized testicles, further evidence, biologists say, that our species is basically monogamous, but that there are no guarantees.

One Exception:
A Paragon Of Fidelity

But lest everybody cynically conclude that nothing and nobody can be trusted, a study has unearthed at least one example of an irrefutably monogamous animal: *Peromyscus Californicus*, or the California mouse, found in the foothills of the Sierra Nevada.

Dr. David Ribble, of the University of California at Berkeley, and Dr. Gubernick of the University of Wisconsin have performed extensive tests to prove the rodent's fidelity. DNA analysis has shown that, in 100 percent of the time, the pups are fathered by a female's lifelong mate.

The scientists also have coated the female in fluorescent pigment powders to see with whom the female has contact. "The powder only shows-up on her mate and offspring," said Dr. Gubernick. Mother and father split child-rearing duties 50–50 he says.

"This is an extremely unusual animal," said Dr. Gubernick, "It may be one of the only truly monogamous species in the world."

The New York Times, August 21, 1990.

Emotions, Stress, and Coping

12

Have you ever wondered what people in the United States did for entertainment before television? During the first part of this century and for much of the last century the circus brought joy and excitement to residents of large cities such as New York and Boston and to small towns such as Cabool, Missouri, and Old Dime Box, Texas. Some of these circuses were so small that they traveled on makeshift horse-drawn wagons, while others, such as the Ringling Brothers and Barnum & Bailey Circus, needed over a hundred railway cars to transport the show.

Emmett Kelly became a part of the circus tradition in the early part of the twentieth century, and his name quickly became a household word. He had a rather usual and uneventful childhood. One of his earliest recollections was his first spanking. At the age of five, he climbed a tall telegraph pole and sat surveying the world from the crossbeam. Suddenly the serenity of this world was broken by the shrieking of his terrified mother and neighbors. Seeing their fear caused Emmett to reassess his own situation; his own exhilaration quickly changed to fear.

Kelly, like other children in his Kansas farming community, was fascinated by the circus, and he looked forward to the arrival of the traveling companies. However, his main interest lay in art; he wanted to draw cartoons.

In 1917 he headed for Kansas City with $20 in his pocket and visions of earning a fortune as an artist. He soon found that realizing his ambitions as an artist would be more difficult than he expected. His first "art job" was painting letters on signs. His next job involved painting faces on plaster kewpie dolls that were given as prizes in circus sideshows. Then he painted horses for circus merry-go-rounds. Kelly's work thus brought him into contact with the circuses that traveled through Kansas City. He became intrigued with the work of the aerial trapeze acts, and he began practicing on the trapeze in his spare time.

The persistent Kelly finally got a job as a trapeze artist with Howe's Great London Circus. He was delighted with his job until he was told that he would also have to do a clown act. He had no desire to be a clown, but he reluctantly accepted the part.

The typical clown act of the time was called "whiteface." The clown painted his face white with a mixture of zinc oxide and lard. Next, grease paint was used to outline the eyes and exaggerate the nose and mouth. The goal of a clown was to capture and exaggerate an emotion such as joy, surprise, or sadness, and portray it in situations that made it funny. For example, a favorite act of the time was a sad-faced clown who searched for his dog, who secretly trailed along behind the clown during the search.

Although Kelly loved the circus, he was not happy being a clown. When the chance arose he took a job with a new circus, where he only performed as a trapeze artist. There he met Eva Moore, a tiny, slim blond who excited the circus patrons with

429

her daring acts high above the big top. He proposed to Eva at the top of the Ferris wheel at a carnival, and they were married a few days later.

About this time the Depression began to grip the Western world. A number of circuses were forced to close, including the one Kelly worked for. After searching desperately for a job, Kelly reluctantly accepted an offer to be a clown, but he decided that he would do a different kind of act.

He wanted to do something that would turn people's attention away from their own sadness and depression and cause them to laugh as they watched someone less fortunate deal with hard times. He wanted to show people that there was both humor and hope in their situation. So, "Weary Willie" was born. In Kelly's own words, Willie was "a sad and ragged little guy who is serious about everything he attempts—no matter how futile or how foolish it appears to be" (Kelly, 1954, pp. 125–126). Willie was a tramp with a dirty face, exaggerated frown, and ragged clothes who delighted circus fans when he tried to crack a peanut with a sledgehammer or sweep away light rays with an old broom.

Kelly (or Willie, as he became known throughout the United States) won the hearts of thousands even though he never spoke a word in his act. He found that he could get his greatest laughs when he performed after the most dangerous circus acts, such as the lion-taming or trapeze acts. He also found that no matter what language circus patrons spoke, they all understood

Using exaggerated facial expressions in humorous situations, "Weary Willie" won the hearts of thousands of people without speaking a word. He made them forget their own sadness as they watched Willie deal with hard times.

the silent antics and sad face of Willie.

Emmett Kelly continued his act until the 1960s. He was a featured performer in the Ringling Brothers and Barnum & Bailey Circus, the world's largest circus. He brought his clown act to Broadway and found his way into the hearts of millions in the movie *The Greatest Show on Earth*. Even in the complicated world of the 1990s, clowns who imitate many of Willie's antics bring laughter and tears of joy to circus audiences.

After completing this chapter, you should be able to:

Define the term "emotions" and compare and contrast the theories of emotion.

Debate whether some emotions are innate or learned and whether they are universal across cultures.

Explain and give an example of Selye's General Adaptation Syndrome (GAS).

Identify the causes of stress and discuss our physiological and psychological reactions to stressful situations.

Describe the mechanisms that people use to cope effectively with stress.

The Study of Emotions: History and Scope

A Search for a Definition

Emmett Kelly spent his life influencing people's emotions. As Willie, the little tramp, Kelly could make the audience feel sad when he smashed a peanut into an inedible pulp with a sledgehammer. And just as quickly, Willie could make the audience laugh and feel happy as he frantically chased the light beams with his frayed old broom. All of us are familiar with emotions; we talk about emotions and we experience them many times a day. We seek out situations that arouse certain emotions and avoid other situations because they will arouse unwanted emotions. In a sense, we might regard much of the material we have examined in earlier chapters (learning, perception, physiological processes, and motivation) as the meat and potatoes of life; they guide us through the daily events of life. In this light, *emotions* can be viewed as the spice of life; they give our lives character and pizazz.

Despite this tantalizing picture of emotions, we will see that the concept has spawned, and continues to spawn, a host of definitions, categorizations, theories, and debates. Let's begin our brief overview with a look at attempts to define and categorize emotion and related concepts.

One of the continuing debates about emotions involves what they are (Russell, 1991; Clore & Ortony, 1991). Some people have argued that emotion is simply another term for motivation. Most investigators, however, take the position that although the two concepts may be related, they are not the same thing (Buck, 1985). As we discussed earlier, motivation is generally seen as arousal or energy that directs behavior. Emotions, on the other hand, are viewed as the blending of arousal, behavior, cognition, *and* feeling. We *are* hungry, thirsty, or tired, but we *feel* happy, sad, or afraid. Hence, **emotions** are affective states (or feelings) accompanied by physiological changes that often influence behavior.

Before you breath a sigh of relief at the rather painless journey for developing a definition, there are a few other points to consider. No member of the American Kennel Society would be happy with the generic definition of "dog," and similarly, investigators have not rested with a simple definition

Emotions
Affective states or feelings accompanied by physiological changes that often influence behavior.

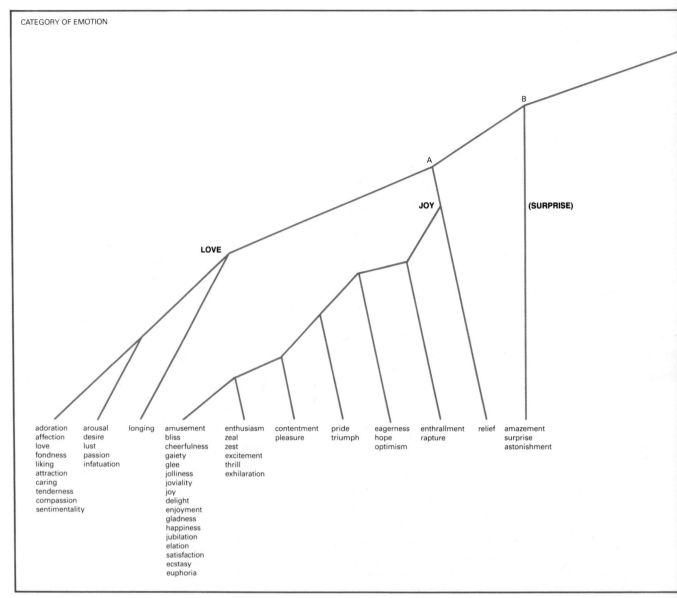

CATEGORY OF EMOTION

LOVE   JOY   (SURPRISE)

A   B

adoration	arousal	longing	amusement	enthusiasm	contentment	pride	eagerness	enthrallment	relief	amazement
affection	desire		bliss	zeal	pleasure	triumph	hope	rapture		surprise
love	lust		cheerfulness	zest			optimism			astonishment
fondness	passion		gaiety	excitement						
liking	infatuation		glee	thrill						
attraction			jolliness	exhilaration						
caring			joviality							
tenderness			joy							
compassion			delight							
sentimentality			enjoyment							
			gladness							
			happiness							
			jubilation							
			elation							
			satisfaction							
			ecstasy							
			euphoria							

FIGURE 12–1

Categories of Emotion

This figure represents an attempt by one group of investigators to identify the relationship between emotions. The higher-order or basic emotions are in bold-face type. (After Shaver, Schwartz, Kirson, & O'Connor, 1987.)

of emotions. Recently, emotions have been distinguished from moods. **Moods** are viewed as general feeling states that are less intense, less specific, and more long-lasting than emotions. Also included in discussions of mood are behaviors aimed at managing the mood state (Mayer, Salorey, Gomberg-Kaufman, & Blainey, 1991). These management behaviors include thoughts of actions that might be taken to prolong the feeling, suppression of the mood, or denial of the mood. For example, you may have had some days where nothing seemed to go right. These events left you in a generally negative state, a bad mood, that dampened your enthusiasm and motivated you to avoid others.

Within the concept of emotions, investigators have attempted to make distinctions. Some investigators have argued that certain emotions are pure or basic, whereas others are hybrids or combinations of the basic emotions (Shaver, Schwartz, Kirson, & O'Connor, 1987). Figure 12–1 gives one example of an attempt to categorize and relate emotions. Development of these types of classifications have led investigators to question whether emotions can be divided along some basic dimensions. Most researchers agree that emotions can be classified along *pleasantness* and *arousal* dimensions, although other dimensions such as control, anticipated effort, and attention

Moods
General diffuse feeling states that are often long-lasting and low-intensity.

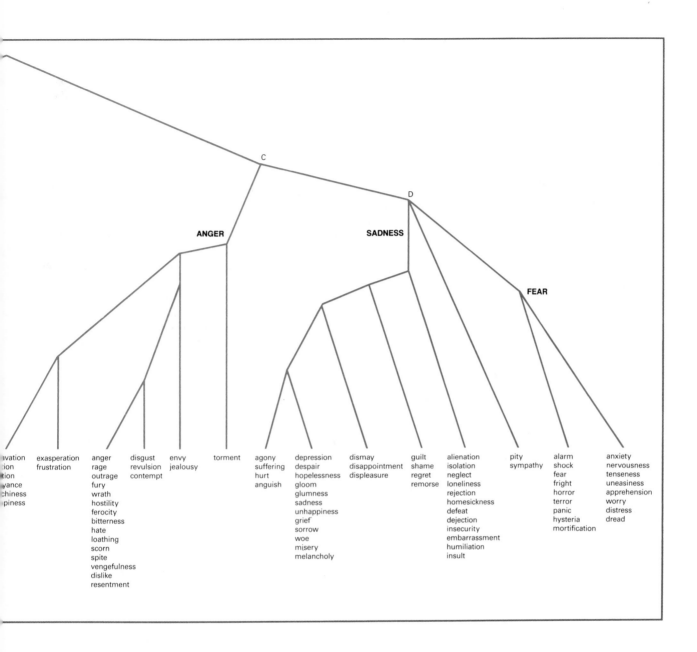

avation	exasperation	anger	disgust	envy	torment	agony	depression	dismay	guilt	alienation	pity	alarm	anxiety
ion	frustration	rage	revulsion	jealousy		suffering	despair	disappointment	shame	isolation	sympathy	shock	nervousness
tion		outrage	contempt			hurt	hopelessness	displeasure	regret	neglect		fear	tenseness
yance		fury				anguish	gloom		remorse	loneliness		fright	uneasiness
chiness		wrath					glumness			rejection		horror	apprehension
piness		hostility					sadness			homesickness		terror	worry
		ferocity					unhappiness			defeat		panic	distress
		bitterness					grief			dejection		hysteria	dread
		hate					sorrow			insecurity		mortification	
		loathing					woe			embarrassment			
		scorn					misery			humiliation			
		spite					melancholy			insult			
		vengefulness											
		dislike											
		resentment											

may also separate groups of emotions (Smith & Ellsworth, 1987). Despite these impressive classification schemes, other researchers have concluded that there are no "basic emotions" from which all other emotions are built (Ortony & Turner, 1990). These investigators also point out that even those psychologists who believe in the "basic emotion" concept fail to agree on which particular emotions are "basic." At this point, we can only say that there is disagreement about the existence of basic emotions, but that considerable effort is still being devoted to studying this topic.

Emotions: An Historical Overview

Although emotions have been discussed as far back as Aristotle, a careful examination of emotions can be traced back to Charles Darwin (1859, 1872). Darwin was more interested in identifying the functions of emotions than in developing a theory about their structure or their experience. Darwin argued that emotions have an adaptive significance for both humans and animals. The adaptive role is not so much tied up with the experience of emotions as it is with the expression of emotions. The expression of emotion helps humans and animals survive because it both acts as a signal

Charles Darwin argued that the expression of emotions has adaptive significance for humans and animals. This inquisitve dog would do well to recognize the emotional message being given by his unwilling playmate!

of intended action and a preparation for that action. For example, I once had a cat that terrorized every dog in the neighborhood. When a dog approached the yard, Cuddles (the inappropriate name of the demon feline) would arch his back, lay his ears back, bare the most terrible set of incisors in the species, raise the hair on his back, and let out a blood-curdling hiss. (I would swear that these actions somehow doubled Cuddles's size.) The smart dog would heed this signal of anger and put as much distance as possible between Cuddles and himself. But if the signal didn't work, these expressive activities prepared Cuddles to spring into battle. Darwin argued that many, but not all, emotions and the expression of emotions did not require learning, and he believed that recognizing emotions was also largely innate. We will examine Darwin's important work in more detail later in the chapter, but for now, it is sufficient to identify Darwin as one of the first investigators to carefully examine emotions.

The study of emotions in the 20th century has focused more directly on understanding how we experience emotions, and like waves on the beach, a new approach seems to emerge almost every 20 years. The early theories focused on the psychophysiology of emotions; these investigators were most concerned with specific bodily changes associated with specific emotions. The second wave of theories developed out of learning and drive theories (see Chapters 6 and 11); these theories focused on how emotions were learned and their relationship to motivation. A third wave has focused on the role of cognition in the experience of emotions. We now seem to be in the midst of the fourth wave of the century, and although its form is a bit difficult to identify, its focus seems to be a kin of the earliest views of emotion. Once again there is an attempt to identify the functional nature of emotions and to link the experience of emotion with bodily change. However, instead of examining visceral responses, such as heart rate or blood pressure, this work has uncovered a fascinating relationship between changes in facial expression and the experience of different emotions (Izard, 1977; Plutchik, 1980).

With this brief history as a background, let's focus our attention on some of the specific theories.

Getting That Feeling: Theories of Emotion

On the afternoon of July 6, 1944, Kelly was busy getting into his costume for the first performance of the day in Hartford, Connecticut. The show had started and the big top was packed. Suddenly someone ran past Kelly's tent and shouted "Fire!" Kelly ran outside and saw a column of black smoke billowing from the main tent. His heartbeat quickened and fear gripped him as he ran to the big top. A sickening sight greeted Kelly; hundreds of people ran screaming from the tent, circus animals stampeded in wild panic through the smoke, and the stench of burning flesh settled over all.

Kelly experienced a wide variety of emotions in a short period of time during that tragic day. He reported feeling fear when he heard about the fire and saw the smoke, hope that the fire was not in the main tent, anger as he grabbed a bucket of water to fight the fire, and sadness as he cried when he saw some charred little shoes and part of a clown doll lying in the smoldering ashes. Why did Kelly experience these particular emotions in this situation? The story of how we experience emotions reads much like a detective novel with investigators following leads, running into dead ends, and developing new theories.

James-Lange Theory

Kelly vividly described his feelings of fear and sadness on the day of the Hartford fire. The common-sense view of emotions suggests that feeling caused Kelly to react in certain ways. For example, we might argue that when Kelly saw the charred shoes and doll he felt sad, and because of this feeling he began to cry. This sequence of events makes sense to most of us, but it did not to William James, writing in the 1880s. James argued that it is difficult to imagine feeling an emotion without experiencing a bodily change at the same time. He also pointed out that people often feel emotions without knowing exactly what has caused the emotion. For example, you may be suddenly overcome with feelings of sadness while you are sitting quietly in your room. You may not know why you feel sad, but you can clearly identify your feelings.

Because of these and other considerations, James (1884) argued that events cause bodily and behavioral changes in people, and the emotion lies in the *perception* of these physiological and behavioral changes. According to this investigator: "Common sense says that we lose our fortune, are sorry, and weep; . . . (My) hypothesis . . . is that we feel sorry because we cry, angry because we strike, afraid because we tremble . . ." (James, 1890). The Danish psychologist Carl Lange arrived at the same conclusion, which has become known as the James-Lange theory of emotion (see Figure 12–2). An example of this theory that is familiar to many of us occurs during "near miss" automobile accidents. In such cases, when you are confronted with the possibility of an accident, you respond almost without thinking: you swerve and brake your automobile. After the danger has passed, you notice yourself trembling or sweating. Only then do you feel overcome with fear. It was not the emotion that guided your actions or affected your physiological responses. It was your perception of these responses (physiological and behavioral) that caused you to feel fear. One assumption of the James-Lange theory is that we have different physiological arousal patterns for each emotion. Supposedly the perception of these arousal patterns "tells" us what emotion we are feeling. (Izard, 1990).

Cannon-Bard Theory

Walter B. Cannon (1929) criticized the James-Lange theory and offered another point of view. Cannon argued that physiological changes on body organs occur too slowly to be the basis of emotions. He pointed out that body organs such as the stomach, the intestines, and the heart (visceral organs) are relatively insensitive because they don't have many nerves. Thus, people are not normally aware of changes in these organs, for example, stomach contractions or relaxations. Cannon performed experiments in which he severed the sympathetic nervous system tract in cats so that it was no longer connected to the brain. As a result of this operation, even when presented with the appropriate stimuli the heart rate of the cat did not increase, body hairs could not be erected, and the liver was unable to release sugar into the blood. However, Cannon found that these animals continued to show typical behavioral reactions of fear, anger, and pleasure in the appropriate situations. Given these criticisms, Cannon argued that emotions could not be simply the perception of physiological changes.

Cannon proposed a theory (see Figure 12–3) that was later extended by Bard (1938). According to this theory, stimulus events activate the thalamus (see Chapter 2), which sends messages to the cerebral cortex and to organs such as the heart and the stomach. The stimulation of the cerebral cortex leads to the emotional experience, while the excitation of the organ

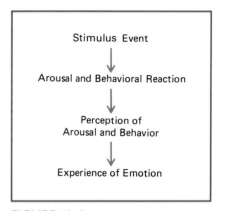

FIGURE 12–2

James-Lange Theory of Emotion

According to the James-Lange theory, emotion is the result of perceiving our arousal and behavior.

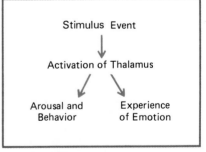

FIGURE 12–3

Cannon-Bard Theory of Emotion

The Cannon-Bard theory states that events activate the thalamus, which in turn leads to simultaneous arousal of organs and the experience of emotion.

TRUTH IN EMOTIONS: Lie Detection

As we have seen, emotions are reflected in physiological arousal. This fact has long intrigued researchers who wanted to find a way to tell when a person is lying. The basic assumption in the search for the perfect lie detector is that people experience a twinge of guilt or stress when they tell a lie. This "twinge" should be reflected in their physiology, which, unlike verbal behavior, is not under their control. Thus, all that is needed to detect lying is some way to measure a person's physiological responses.

Like so many of our "modern" inventions, a search of history reveals that the concept of the lie detector was conceived hundreds of years ago. The ancient Chinese had a suspect chew rice powder while being questioned (Rice, 1978). After the questioning period the wad of powder was carefully examined. If it was found to be dry, the suspect was found guilty. The Chinese reasoned that lying would create tension, which would slow or block the flow of saliva. Thus the dry mouth resulted in dry rice powder, which, in turn, resulted in a guilty verdict. Interestingly enough, the basic theory behind this test was quite sound; strong emotions are associated with less secretion of saliva.

The modern lie detector, called a **polygraph,** does not use rice powder. Instead, it records changes in heart rate, blood pressure, respiration, and galvanic skin response (GSR). Suspects are hooked up to the polygraph, and the operator asks them a number of questions (see Figure A). Theoretically, if a person is lying, the polygraph will record a *change* in the baseline response. The operator generally avoids asking the "did you do it" question, since this question may cause even innocent suspects to feel stress. Rather, the operator asks questions that are related to the crime but would create stress only in someone who was familiar with the crime. For example, Lykken (1959) had subjects act out a crime that involved stealing an object from an office and hiding it in a locker in the hallway. The subject in each case was then given a polygraph test in which the operator asked questions about where the object was hidden.

"Was it (a) in the men's room, (b) on the coat rack, (c) in the office, (d) on the window sill, or (e) in the locker?" (p. 386). The mention of the locker would have meaning only for someone who was familiar with the crime. Thus, if the suspect showed a change in physiological response at the mention of the locker, the operator could detect his or her guilt.

Unfortunately, determining innocence or guilt is not this simple. The polygraph only charts physiological arousal; it does not identify lies. It is important to understand that people respond differently to lying and that the polygraph may not identify these differences. Further, a guilty person may be able to fake responses and "fool" the lie detector. A person may intentionally make him- or herself tense during the neutral questions so that a baseline cannot be established. One investigator reports a case where a prison inmate coached twenty-seven other inmates on how to lie successfully when attached to the polygraph machine (Lykken, 1981). All twenty-seven had admitted their guilt, yet after a 20-minute coaching session, twenty-three of the twenty-seven passed the lie detector test.

The role of the operator is also important because that person must read and interpret the charts. Some studies have shown high agreement (80 to 90 percent) between operators reading the same chart, yet other studies have found that agreement is not much greater than would occur by chance (Kleinmuntz & Szucko, 1984a). Not only may agreement be low between operators, but the accuracy of detecting lies may also be low. In one study, polygraph operators were shown 100 charts—50 from guilty persons and 50 from innocent persons (Kleinmuntz & Szucko, 1984b). They were asked to identify the guilty and innocent by analyzing the records. On the average, 37 percent of the innocent people were classified as guilty! This number of incorrect interpretations is frightening, particularly if your freedom, or perhaps your life, is to be based on the results of the test.

FIGURE A

The polygraph records heart rate, blood pressure, respiration, and galvanic skin response (GSR). The basic assumption is that people's physiological functioning changes when they tell a lie. There are still many questions about the accuracy of the polygraph in detecting lies and about the ethics of forcing people to submit to a lie detection test.

Clearly there is still a great deal of debate about the reliability and accuracy of lie detectors. Because of these issues the lie detector cannot be used as the basis to convict people of crimes in the courts in most states. However, some businesses are more willing to accept "false positions" and they use lie detectors in deciding who to hire and who to keep on the job. However, in November 1987, the U.S. House of Representatives passed a bill to outlaw the use of polygraphs by employers (Bales, 1987).

Recently, a new method of lie detection has been introduced. During the Vietnam War, the Army searched for a simpler, more covert way to detect lies, one that could be used during the interrogation of prisoners (Rice, 1978). They turned to voice analysis. The theory behind this method is that the muscles controlling voice tremor are affected by stress. The voice can be recorded and a visual picture of voice tremor can be made on graph paper, as shown in Figure B, by a machine called a **voice stress analyzer**. Subjects can be asked questions similar to those used in the polygraph test. A lie can be detected when the voice stress analyzer indicates tension in the individual's

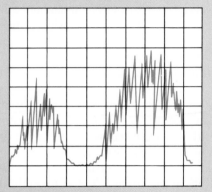 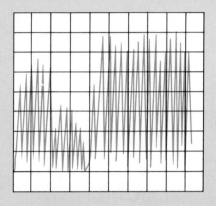

FIGURE B

The voice stress analyzer measures voice tremor. It has been found that the arousal produced by telling a lie changes the voice tremors. The graph on the left is the voice tremor of a relaxed speaker. The graph on the right shows the voice tremor of a speaker under stress. (After Holden, 1975)

voice in response to the critical questions.

The beauty, and the frightening feature, of this method is that it can be used to analyze any voice that can be recorded. This includes personal conversations, telephone conversations, and even speeches by politicians. And people can have their voices recorded without their

knowledge or consent. This raises an important ethical question about the use of lie detection. In addition to the question of ethics, there is also the question of how accurate the voice stress analyzer method is. There have only been a few carefully controlled studies and the results are often contradictory. Hence, there is at present no perfect way to detect lying.

leads to the accompanying physiological arousal. Thus, Cannon argued that emotional experience and arousal occur at the same time, rather than one after the other, as proposed by James.

More recent research has shown that Cannon's theory was not entirely correct (Plutchik, 1980). This research proposes that the hypothalamus and limbic system, and not the thalamus, play central roles in the experience of emotion. Also, emotions are not simply events that we experience only for the moment; emotions can last long after the event has passed.

Cognitive Theories

Many investigators over the last three decades have turned their attention to the role of cognitions or interpretations in the experience of emotion. Although they have still been concerned with the raw materials of emotions such as physiological arousal and behavior, they have also been interested in how the mind processes these data to yield a specific emotion. In fact, the question of the role of cognition in emotion has become one of the most hotly debated topics of recent research and theory (Buck, 1990). The debate revolves around such issues as whether or not we can experience emotion without cognition and whether emotion or cognition is the primary guide of our responses to the environment.

Schachter and Singer Theory. As early as 1927, Gregorio Marañon argued that there is more to emotion than simply the perception of bodily

Polygraph
Also called a lie detector. Machine that records changes in heart rate, blood pressure, respiration, and galvanic skin response. Lies are identified when there is a change from baseline responses to neutral questions to a heightened response to questions about critical events.
Voice stress analyzer
Records amount of voice tremor, which may be affected by stress. A decrease in voice tremor indicates tension, and, presumably, the fact that the person is lying.

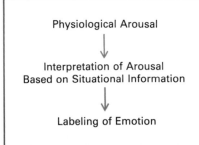

FIGURE 12–4

Schachter-Singer Cognitive Theory of Emotion

According to Schachter and Singer, unexplained arousal leads people to search their environment to find a label for the arousal. The interpretation of the arousal leads to a specific emotion.

changes (Cornelius, 1991). He contended that some consideration of the framework in which the change occurs must precede the experience of emotion. In other words, cognition has a role in emotional experience. Nearly 40 years later, Schachter and Singer (1962) extended this line of reasoning. They agreed with James's position that emotions occur after physiological arousal. But they argued that specific arousal patterns are not associated with specific emotions. They suggested that the arousal accompanying emotions is diffuse and that the same pattern of arousal could be found with many emotions. According to Schachter and Singer, people become aware that they are aroused and then they seek the reason for it (see Figure 12–4). People may use their actions, the actions of others, and/or events occurring in the environment to explain their arousal and label their emotion.

In order to illustrate this theory, let us take the example of Emmett Kelly at the circus fire. Kelly fought the fire and helped people and animals escape from the burning tent. Surely all these activities caused a heightened arousal state. Kelly was probably not completely aware of how aroused he was until it was over and he had time to look back on the situation. At this point Kelly saw the charred shoes and the doll. According to the Schachter and Singer theory, Kelly may have used the sight of these pitiful remains to label his emotional state as sadness. If, on the other hand, Kelly had seen a happy scene such as a little girl being reunited with her family, he might have interpreted his arousal state to be happiness or relief.

In an effort to support their theory, Schachter and Singer (1962) told subjects who volunteered for a study that this research project was aimed at examining the effects of a vitamin supplement. The subjects were then given an injection that they believed was the vitamin supplement being studied. Unknown to them, some of the subjects were actually injected with epinephrine, a hormone that increases heart rate, raises blood pressure, and increases breathing rate. Subjects were then given one of the following explanations:

1. Informed: These subjects were accurately informed; they were told that the injection would increase arousal.

2. Misinformed: These subjects were given incorrect information; they were told that the injection would cause some numbness, itching, and headaches.

3. No information: This group was told nothing about the effects of the injection.

A final group—the control group—was given an injection of a saline solution that did not have any physiological side effects, and they were told nothing about the injection.

After the injections, subjects were led to a waiting room. In the room was another subject, who was actually working for the experimenter. When the experimenter left the room, this confederate began to act either wildly happy and euphoric or very angry. Soon the experimenter reentered the room and asked subjects to complete a questionnaire describing how they felt.

The interesting situations are the no-information and misinformed conditions where subjects experienced unexplained arousal. The results suggested that these subjects used environmental cues (confederate's behavior) to label their arousal in these conditions. Subjects with the happy confederate reported "feeling" happy and those with the angry confederate reported feeling angry. This difference in emotional label occurred despite the fact that both groups of subjects had received the same injection and should have been experiencing the same arousal. Subjects in the informed condition who knew what caused their arousal and subjects in the control condition who were not aroused were not influenced by the confederate's behavior.

Although the Schachter and Singer approach offered an interesting way to view emotions, later research uncovered a number of problems with the theory. One problem is that some researchers have not been able to replicate the Schachter and Singer findings (Hogan & Schroeder, 1981; Rogers & Decker, 1975). Another investigator found that unexplained arousal caused subjects to feel uncomfortable and negative; they did not simply search the environment for an explanation, as suggested by Schachter and Singer (Maslach, 1979). It has been proposed that high arousal is necessary for some emotions, such as fear, anger, and love, but not for others, such as happiness or sadness (Laird & Bresler, 1990). In other words, Schachter's theory may be much more limited than first thought. Finally, some people have forcefully argued that emotions and cognitions are separate and that cognitions cannot determine emotions (Zajonc 1980, 1985). This position suggests that emotions are more basic than cognitions, and that we cannot change our emotions by voluntary thoughts. You may be able to relate to this position if you've ever tried to change your mood when you were feeling depressed; no matter what you do or think about, you can't change your feeling.

The Role of Appraisal.   Imagine how Emmett Kelly felt when he saw smoke coming from the big top. His heart rate probably increased tremendously, his muscles tensed, and he may have felt like running from the scene as the fear of fire and the thoughts of the potential tragedy gripped him. However, would Kelly's emotions and his actions have been the same if he had known that this was all part of another clown's act (for example, a clown performing an act that involved a little dog jumping out of a smoking house into a firefighter's net)? If he had thought this, it is unlikely that he would have become tense and fearful when he saw the smoke and heard a few screams. He may even have been amused by the screams as he imagined the success of the act in thrilling the spectators.

This example shows that the way we evaluate a situation affects not only our response but also our emotions related to it. It has been suggested that the first step in experiencing emotions is appraising (judging or interpreting) the situation (Arnold, 1960; Lazarus, 1968, 1981). The **appraisal** may simply determine if the situation is threatening or nonthreatening. Or it can be a much broader type of appraisal, considering the likelihood of certain outcomes of the situation, how desired these outcomes are, and how much power and control the individual has over the situation and its outcomes (Roseman, Spindel, & Jose, 1990). The appraisal takes place immediately after the event is perceived, and is intuitive and automatic. Our emotion surfaces as we examine both our appraisal of the situation and our responses to it. Sometimes, the emotional label may guide our behavior. Figure 12–5 illustrates the sequence of events in the appraisal theory. As you can see, this position gives cognition a broader role than it has in the Schachter and Singer theory that we just discussed. In the appraisal theory, cognition not only influences the label of the emotion, but also affects the level of arousal and reaction to the situation.

In an effort to demonstrate this effect, Speisman and his colleagues (1964) showed subjects a film of the gory and painful circumcision rites practiced by an aboriginal Australian tribe to initiate boys into adulthood. Although all subjects saw the film, Speisman varied the sound track that went with the picture. In one track (stress), the narration emphasized the pain associated with the rites. In the second (intellectual), the ceremony was described in a detached, clinical manner. A third track (denial) glossed

Appraisal
Automatic evaluation of a situation as threatening or nonthreatening. Appraisal influences both arousal (emotions) and behavior (response).

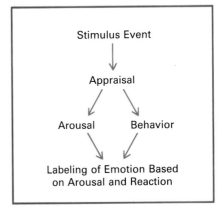

FIGURE 12–5

The Appraisal Theory

This theory suggests that people automatically appraise events as threatening or nonthreatening. This appraisal influences arousal and behavior. The experience of emotion is the result of interpreting the arousal and reactions. In some cases, behavior may follow the labeling of emotion.

FIGURE 12–6

In this experiment, all subjects saw the same film, but were divided into groups that heard one of four different sound tracks to accompany the film. As measured by their GSR, arousal was higher in the group that heard the sound tract emphasizing the pain of what was being seen in the film. (Speisman et al., 1964)

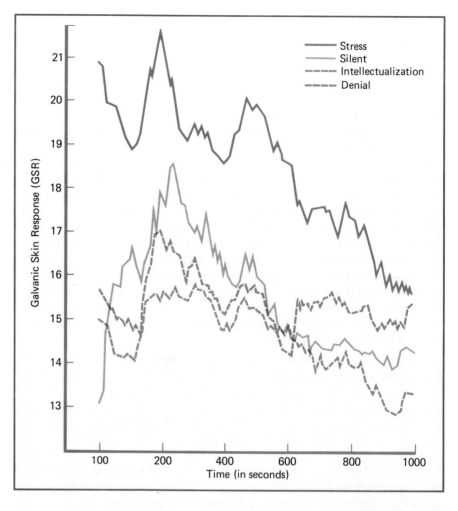

over the pain and focused on the boy's happiness at becoming a man. Finally, in a control condition, subjects saw the film with no sound track. The experimenters recorded subjects' arousal (heart rate and GSR, or galvanic skin response) while they watched the film. As can be seen in Figure 12–6 subjects who watched the film with the sound track emphasizing pain were significantly more aroused than the other subjects. The investigators reasoned that the sound track influenced the subjects' judgment of the event, and so influenced their emotional response to it. The appraisal theory may explain the popular saying, "If you expect something to make you feel bad, chances are it will."

Somatic Theory of Emotions

Kelly made an interesting observation about his own feelings that leads us to another theory of emotions. He reported that no matter how he felt before a show, his feelings changed when he painted on the face of "Willie" and did his act. When he acted sad, he felt sad; when he acted and looked embarrassed, he felt embarrassed.

The other theories we have discussed focus on how arousal (such as rapid heartbeat, sweating, or fluttering stomach) affects emotions. This type of arousal involves the autonomic nervous system (see Chapter 2). Some investigators have argued that another nervous system plays a central role in the experience of emotion; this system is the *somatic nervous system* (Izard, 1977, 1982). The somatic nervous system controls many of our muscles, including the muscles of our face. These muscles not only receive messages

FIGURE 12–7

Somatic Theory of Emotions

The Somatic theory argues that events lead to reactions of the facial muscles and possibly behavior. The emotion label is the result of interpreting these reactions. The theory also holds that the autonomic nervous system can respond either before or after the labeling of emotion.

about when and how to respond, they also feed messages back to the brain when they are activated. These facial muscles may also play another role by affecting the blood vessels in the face, thereby influencing the blood supply to the brain.

According to the somatic theory, it is this feedback that is vital to our emotional experience (see Figure 12–7). Most of the research on this theory has focused on the facial muscles. The theory argues that there are distinct facial expressions that accompany a number of emotions, including fear, excitement, joy, surprise, anger, scorn, and sadness. When an event occurs, our facial muscles react with an emotional expression. The message of how the face is responding is transmitted to the brain, which uses this information to label a specific emotional state. Thus autonomic arousal may occur either before or after the labeling of an emotion. If the arousal occurs before, it may be incorporated in the label, influencing the interpretation about the magnitude of the emotion (Izard, 1990).

When we experience emotions, our facial expressions are usually dramatically altered. Somatic theory argues that these changes in expression help us determine and label our own emotions.

As you can see, the somatic theories of emotion incorporate many of the positions advanced in earlier theories by Charles Darwin and William James. They suggest that emotions have an adaptive function and they include an emphasis on the expression of emotion. They also accept that there are specific responses associated with specific emotions; these responses are facial rather than visceral. The somatic theories differ somewhat on the role of cognitions in the experience of emotions; some argue that emotion and cognition are separate systems, whereas others allow a role for cognition and interpretation of emotions.

There have been scores of experiments testing the somatic theory of emotions. One study found that people reported being happier after they were instructed to smile (Kleinke & Walton, 1982). Another found that subjects reported feeling fearful and showed physiological responses associated with fear when asked to make a face that showed fear, even in the absence of fear-provoking stimuli (Lanzetta & Orr, 1986). On the other side of the issue, one study found that emotion and physiological arousal were reduced if subjects were told not to change their facial expression during arousing events, such as watching a funny movie or experiencing pain (Orr & Lanzetta, 1984). You might, in fact, try your own experiment on this theory by changing your facial expression and determining if your own mood is affected. As you might expect, there have been some studies that are not entirely supportive of the theory. There is some controversy as to whether facial feedback influences emotions at a broad level (pleasant/unpleasant) or if it actually determines specific emotions (grief, agony, sadness) (Winston, 1986).

Opponent-Process Theory

Before leaving our discussion of theories of emotion, let us briefly examine one additional theory that has received recent attention. As the name of the theory implies, this theory is more a theory of process than of specific emotions. In order to understand the theory, let's recall a point made by Emmett Kelly; he observed that he was able to create the greatest happiness and enjoyment for his audience just after they had watched a fear-arousing act such as the liontamer or the trapeze act. Why should this be the case?

On one hand, we could argue that these daredevil acts aroused the audience and they then labeled their arousal as happiness when they saw Kelly. Richard Solomon and his associates (1980; Solomon & Corbit, 1974) developed the **opponent-process theory of emotion,** which offers another explanation for this effect. The theory suggests that each state or emotion that we experience triggers a force to experience the opposite state. For example, happiness generates its opposite, unhappiness; fear generates its opposite, elation, and so on. The effect of these opponents is to dampen the intensity and length of time that we experience any emotional state, and to increase the likelihood that we will experience the opposite emotional state. Mook (1987) argues that this is very adaptive because it is potentially dangerous for us to be in any emotional state (elation or depression) for too long a time.

Returning to our example, we might argue that after experiencing the high state of fear, the audience was naturally primed to experience elation and joy when Kelly appeared. The opponent-process theory goes on to suggest that repeated experiences of an emotion lead us to anticipate and consequently experience even greater levels of the opposite state. This theory, which has also been used to explain drug addiction and tolerance, offers a provocative picture of how our various emotions may be linked to each other and how emotions are regulated.

Opponent-process theory of emotion
Theory suggesting that each emotion or state that we experience triggers an opposite emotion or state.

Theories of Emotion: An Overview

It may seem odd that although performers such as Emmett Kelly can so easily cause people to feel certain emotions, it is very difficult to explain why people experience those emotions. However, if we take another look at the theories we can see how this happens. The differences in the theories are important because they indicate the true complexity of emotions. But there are also important similarities in the theories.

All the theories show that events do not automatically lead to specific emotions. They also propose that no single factor is responsible for emotions. Instead, a picture emerges that shows emotions to be a combination of arousal, facial expressions, behavior, environmental events, and cognitive interpretation. Changes in any of these factors may alter the emotion that is experienced. Thus, although there is some question as to what components are most central and how these components are combined, we can see that emotions represent a unique combination of the mind and body.

Nonverbal Communication: Saying It Silently

Kelly had the opportunity to take his clown act to Cuba. He wondered whether the Cubans would be able to understand his act; would they recognize sadness in Willie's drooping eyes and turned-down mouth? Since Willie never spoke a word, it was very important that the audience respond to his actions and facial expression. On opening night Kelly walked into the ring and began sweeping at the little white puddle that the spotlight threw at his feet. He heard some laughs and his spirits rose. Soon he heard the crowd hissing and waving him away. Kelly turned and ran off the stage, feeling that for the first time in his life he had found a group of people he couldn't communicate with (or who didn't like his act).

Once off the stage, Kelly sought out a clown who spoke Spanish and told him what had happened. The other clown laughed and explained, "In Cuba, that waving means they want you to come closer." He also said, "That isn't hissing as we know it in America; that's part of the handwaving—to get your attention, just as we do when we yell 'Hey' " (p. 238).

Kelly's adventures in Cuba tell us two things about nonverbal communication. First, it is possible to communicate without words and to communicate across national boundaries—the Cuban audience understood immediately what Willie was all about. The second thing is that the style of nonverbal communication used in some cultures may be misunderstood in others. How much of nonverbal communication is universal and how much is learned as part of one's culture?

The Face

The most important part of a clown costume is the face. Kelly would spend hours getting his face ready for a show; he worked on accentuating his mouth and eyes, building up his nose, and emphasizing the wrinkles in his brow. Research indicates that this concern with the face may be well placed.

Children as young as 3 years old can identify emotions (happiness, sadness, and anger) by looking at someone's face (Stifter & Fox, 1986). In an attempt to identify the critical features of facial expression, investigators cut photographs of faces into three partial pictures: brow-forehead, eyes, and mouth (Boucher & Ekman, 1975). These partial photos were

The face shows others the emotion we are feeling, and may also help us to determine our own emotions.

then shown to judges who were asked to guess which of six emotions (surprise, anger, fear, disgust, sadness, or happiness) were being illustrated. The researchers discovered that different parts of the face are important for communicating different emotions. For example, the eyes are most important in communicating sadness, while the mouth best communicates happiness and disgust, and the forehead sends signals of surprise. All three parts of the face, however, are necessary to clearly communicate anger.

In a revealing set of studies, individuals in pictures that gave prominence to the face (high in face-ism) were seen as more dominant than were individuals in pictures giving more prominence to the person's body (low in face-ism) (Zuckerman, 1986). Even more interesting was the finding that traditional publications such as *Time* and *Newsweek* tend to print pictures of males that are higher in face-ism than are pictures of females. However, magazines geared for women, such as *Ms.* and *Working Women,* print pictures relatively equal in face-ism for males and females. Indeed, this subtle difference in the pictures in traditional magazines may perpetuate sex role stereotypes of dominance. You may want to replicate this experiment by looking at pictures portraying a single individual in a publication of your choice. Do you notice that pictures of males show more of the face and less of the body than pictures of females?

Body Language

Not only does our face speak, but according to one researcher, our bodies are also expressive (Birdwhistell, 1967). Birdwhistell used the term **kinesis** to mean the study of body language. He argued that no body movement is accidental or meaningless and that something is communicated in even the slightest movement. For example, Beier (1974) studied fifty newlywed couples and found that conflict and insecurity were expressed by frequent self-touching, sitting with arms and legs crossed, and avoiding eye contact.

One of the more carefully studied areas of body language is **personal space,** the distance we place between ourselves and others. Edward Hall (1959, 1966) observed people interacting in a variety of circumstances and noticed that the space between them was often a function of the nature of their interaction. *Intimate distances* (touching to 18 inches) are used for comforting, protecting, loving, and telling secrets. The *personal distance*

Kinesis
Study of body language, or communication through body movement.
Personal space
The area around the body that people feel "belongs" to them. When interacting with others, people maintain a distance to protect their personal space.

(18 inches to 48 inches) is used by close friends when conversing or by strangers in light social settings when discussing personal matters. *Social distance* (4 feet to 12 feet) is used when conducting personal business or in more formal business and social settings. Finally, *public distance* (12 feet and more) is the space set around important public figures. When our personal space is violated by others moving too close, we become uncomfortable and physically aroused, and we often move away to regain "proper" spacing (Worchel, Cooper, & Goethals, 1991).

Besides the nature of the interaction, many other factors influence the personal space we use. For example, people in Western cultures such as the United States, Canada, and Western Europe tend to maintain greater personal distances than do Latin Americans, Arabs, or Eastern Europeans (Hall, 1966). Males keep greater distances when interacting with other males than do females in same-sex interactions (Aiello, 1987). Children have closer personal spaces than do adolescents or adults (Aiello & Aiello, 1974).

Personal space has many functions for us. One is that we can communicate attraction through distance; we move closer to people we like and away from those we dislike. A second important function, and the one of most interest here, is that spacing influences the channels we can use to communicate our feelings. For example, when you are very close to people, you can determine if they are looking at you, if their brow is furrowed, and if they are perspiring. You cannot see their hands or determine their posture. At farther distances you can observe their gestures and posture, but you cannot see distinct aspects of their face. Therefore, personal distance is not only used to communicate, it also influences other types of body language that can be used in communicating emotions.

While personal space has received the closest attention, there are several other aspects of body language that communicate emotion. For example, we are more likely to maintain eye contact with people we like than with people we dislike (Rubin, 1970). We also hold eye contact with others we wish to dominate (Exline, Ellison, & Long, 1975). Overall, a high degree of eye contact can be used to itensify feelings, either positive or negative (Ellsworth & Carlsmith, 1968). We show openness, attraction, and interest by turning our bodies toward others and leaning forward (Brown, 1986).

An interesting feature of body language is that we are often unaware of it. We usually do not consciously decide that we will smile, dilate our pupils, and move closer to someone to show our attraction. Because of this lack of awareness, people may give themselves away through nonverbal cues when they are lying. Such betrayal of feelings has been referred to as **nonverbal leakage.** Mehrabian (1971) asked subjects to tell a lie while he studied their body language. He found that people who are telling a lie show less frequent body movement, smile more, keep a greater distance from the listener, and lean backward more than people telling the truth.

Emotional Expression: Innate or Learned?

Clearly, we all use our face and bodies to express our emotions. But an interesting question is whether this expression is a natural innate tendency or whether it is learned. Almost 100 years before Kelly's experience in Cuba, Charles Darwin studied how humans express emotions. Darwin believed that the human expression of emotion is inborn and has definite survival value. He pointed out that many animals bare their teeth and the hair on their neck becomes erect when they are angry and ready to attack (recall Cuddles). This has survival value because other animals of the same species can readily interpret it and avoid the angered animal. Darwin pointed out, too, that humans also grit their teeth and the hair on their neck becomes erect when they are angry.

Nonverbal leakage
Betrayal through nonverbal cues of emotions people are attempting to hide.

In 1986 Vice President George Bush shared a quiet moment with Soviet leader Mikhail Gorbachev in Washington. Although we don't know what these two men were discussing, their body language suggests they are not intimate friends; it looks more like a "stand-off" on all accounts.

At the base of Darwin's evolutionary theory of emotion is the hypothesis that some, but not all, of the ways in which humans express emotions are inborn. In order to support this position Darwin needed to show two things: (1) emotions are expressed the same way by all people regardless of their background, and (2) people inherit rather than learn the tendency to express emotions in these patterned ways.

Darwin made careful observations of the people he met on his voyages around the world. He found many similarities in the way people from different cultures expressed specific emotions. For example, he reported that Australian aborigines, African Kafirs, Malays, "Hindoos," and South American Guaranies frown when they are puzzled, and they express grief using similar facial signs. Darwin's observations were supported by Ekman, Sorenson, and Friesen (1969), who showed pictures of faces expressing various emotions to subjects in the United States, Brazil, Japan, New Guinea, and Borneo. The subjects were asked to identify the emotion expressed in each photo, and there was relatively high agreement in their judgments of the pictures. In a follow-up study, Ekman and Friesen (1971) found that even members of the Fore tribe, a preliterate group who led an isolated, almost Stone Age existence in New Guinea, were able to judge the facial expressions correctly. Finally, a group of investigators (Arnoff, Barclay, & Stevenson, 1988) found striking similarities in the expression of masks picturing threatening faces in many cultures. For example, threatening masks used lines on the forehead, eyes oriented downward and the mouth open and showing teeth. The high degree of agreement found in these studies suggests that there is some universality in the way people in different cultures express emotions. However, none of the cross-cultural studies found complete agreement. Kelly learned when he interpreted the waving hands of the Cuban audience to be signs of anger or disapproval, that culture and background also influence the way emotions are expressed.

Although these cross-cultural studies demonstrate some degree of universality in emotional expression, they do not prove that this expression is inborn. It is possible that people in the various societies simply learn to express themselves in similar ways. How would you go about demonstrating that the nonverbal expression of emotions is innate rather than learned?

 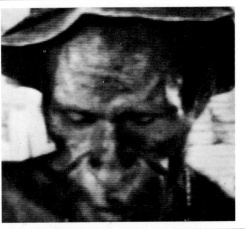 

Darwin answered this question by observing children who had been blind from birth. He reasoned that it would be impossible for these children to have learned the intricacies of nonverbal expression of emotions, since they could not observe others. His observations and those that followed showed that the emotional expression of both blind and blind-and-deaf children was similar to that of sighted children for a number of emotions (Eibl-Eibesfeldt, 1970; Thompson, 1941). For example, the blind children cried when unhappy, laughed and smiled when happy, frowned and stamped their feet in defiance, and shook their heads as a gesture of refusal. These observations support Darwin's position, but they cannot be taken as absolute proof; it is still possible that the children learned some of their responses by receiving rewards for "proper" expressions. These rewards could have been in the form of touching or hugging.

Still a different approach to the question of how expression is linked to feelings concerns whether or not we can "fake" emotional expression. If there is no direct link between feeling and expression, we should be able to control our expression, regardless of our feeling. This, however, has not proven to be the case. Paul Ekman and his associates (Ekman, Friesen, & O'Sullivan, 1988) asked subjects to convince an interviewer that they were experiencing happy feelings after they had watched either a pleasant or an unpleasant film. Observations of the subjects' smiles in both conditions revealed striking differences in the happy smile and deceptive smile (see Figure 12–8). These data add further support to the position that there may be a direct, possibly innate link between feelings and expression.

Although nature may have a hand in our expression of emotions, there are, indeed, a number of findings to suggest that learning also plays a role in emotional expression. One study found that some families are

FIGURE 12–8

Which is a happy smile? Research suggests that it is difficult to truly fake the expression of emotion. Only one smile (a) was elicited under happy circumstances. The others show traces of disgust and sadness. (Ekman, Friesen, & O'Sullivan, 1988)

A   B   C

very expressive whereas emotional expression is very reserved in others (Halberstadt, 1986). The interesting effect is that expressive families tend to produce members who are good at sending emotional cues but poor at identifying emotions in others (poor receivers). On the other hand, members of reserved families tend to be poor senders but good receivers, especially in the case of negative emotions. You might imagine that if you grew up in a family where people showed few outward signs of emotion, you would learn to read what little information was displayed. Based on our earlier discussion of somatic theories of emotion, we may wonder how learning emotional expression affects our feelings. A related question is whether members of nonexpressive families actually feel fewer or less intense emotions than members in the more expressive families.

The bottom line of this discussion is that evidence suggests that some of our emotional expression may be innately determined. However, learning affects both our expression and ability to interpret emotional cues.

The Influence of Emotions

We have now examined how people experience and express emotions. It is clear that emotions influence how we feel; happiness and joy make us feel good, whereas sadness and anger are associated with bad feelings. Recent research has shown, however, that the experience of emotion has a much wider effect on our lives.

Persuasibility

Spend an evening watching television commercials or leaf through a magazine and note the many advertisements. You will quickly become aware of the commercials or ads that are designed to arouse an emotion in you. Some will be aimed at getting you sexually aroused; others will try to excite you by portraying an exciting sports game; still others will try to make you happy by picturing a cuddly kitten or a happy event. These attempts to arouse you are not accidents—research has found that people are more easily persuaded when they are emotionally aroused. This effect has been found for both positive emotions (Biggers & Pryor, 1982) and negative emotional states such as fear (Leventhal & Niles, 1965).

There are a number of possible reasons for the influence of emotions on persuasion. We may pay closer attention to messages that arouse us. As we will see in the next section, we may remember more of a message that we hear when aroused. Finally, we may use our emotions to determine the quality of the message: If we feel happy listening to a certain message, that message must be a positive one (Petty & Cucioppo, 1990). However, as we will discuss in Chapter 16, high emotional arousal may increase attitude change only for simple or weak messages where attention and reasoning are not important (Bless, Bohner, Schwarz, & Strack, 1990).

Judgment and Memory

There is evidence that our emotions affect our judgment and memory (Forgas, Burnham, & Trimbali, 1988). In one study, subjects who were either happy, angry, or sad were asked to describe what was happening in a rather ambiguous picture (Clark, 1982). Subjects described the pictures to fit their own emotions; happy people saw happy events, sad people described sad events, and so on. Leventhal (1982) found that emotions affect how people respond to illness. For example, depressed cancer patients focused on their pain and the futility of life, whereas angry patients focused on coping and ways to combat their illness. In another case, subjects placed in either a happy or unhappy mood tended to recall early life experiences in line with their mood (Rholes, Riskin, & Lane, 1987). Summing up these effects, one investigator noted that "when we are feeling good, the evidence indicates that we tend to view others more positively, to give more favorable reports about products we have purchased, to rate ambiguous slides more pleasant, to have more positive expectations about the future, and to give more positive associations to situations in which we imagine ourselves" (Clark, 1982, p. 264).

An interesting new twist has been added to this picture. Investigators have found that when some people find themselves experiencing a negative emotion such as sadness, they will recall happy events (Parrott & Sobini, 1990). It seems they do this to help them change their mood from negative to positive. Thus, emotion affects recall, but the influence can work in a number of ways.

People's attention becomes more narrow and restricted when they are emotionally aroused. Because they are so wrapped up in each other, this couple is unaware of the pickpocket behind them.

Behavior

We have already discussed theories of emotion which suggest that our actions may influence the label we place on our emotions. There is also evidence that our emotions affect our performance and behavior along a variety of dimensions. For example, Kelly stated that he performed best when he was in an excited, happy state. He often "psyched" himself up before a show so that his creativity would shine. In a more controlled setting Alice Isen and her colleagues (Isen, Daubman, & Nowicki, 1987) found that students who were placed in a positive mood by watching a comedy or receiving a candy bar turned in their best performance on tasks requiring creativity. Negative moods, on the other hand, did not increase creativity. Another example of the effect of emotion on behavior was a study showing that subjects who were placed in a positive mood and made to concentrate on their mood were more likely to help a person in need than subjects not in a positive mood (Berkowitz, 1987). All of this taken together suggests that positive moods may be good medicine; they lead us to see the world as a better place, recall happy events, intensify our enjoyment of situations, become more creative, and increase our willingness to help others. On the down side, these moods, like any other highly emotional state, may make us more vulnerable to persuasion.

Specific Emotions

We have examined the basic theories of emotions and learned how people express emotions. Now we will illustrate these points by examining some specific emotions. Rather than making comments on an endless list of emotions, we will look at two: fear and love. These two emotions represent extremes on many levels. Fear is considered to be negative, whereas love is viewed as positive, and many of us will go to great lengths to experience this positive emotion. Also, fear has been studied a great deal, whereas love has, until recently, been seen as the domain of only poets and playwrights.

FIGURE 12–9
A Prototype of Fear

Fear is aroused by many situations (I) and associated with a variety of responses (II). This figure lists some of the preconditions and behaviors associated with fear. (After Shaver, Schwartz, Kirson, & O'Connor, 1987.)

I Conditions that lead to fear

> *Threat of social rejection
> *Possibility of loss or failure
> *Loss of control or competence
>
> *Threat of harm or death
>
> *Being in a novel, unfamiliar situation
> *Being alone (walking alone, etc.)
> *Being in the dark

II Responses to fear

> *Sweating, perspiring
> *Feeling nervous, jittery, jumpy
> *Shaking, quivering, trembling
> *Eyes darting, looking quickly around
>
> *Nervous, fearful talk
> *Shaky, trembling voice
>
> *Crying, whimpering
> *Screaming, yelling
> *Pleading, crying for help
>
> *Fleeing, running, walking hurriedly
>
> *Picturing a disastrous conclusion to events in progress
> *Losing the ability to focus; disoriented, dazed, out of control
>
> *Hiding from the threat, trying not to move
> *Talking less, being speechless
>
> *Acting unafraid, hiding the fear from others
> *Comforting oneself, telling oneself everything is all right, trying to keep calm

Fear and Anxiety

Fear is one of the most carefully studied emotions, along with the related concept of anxiety. **Fear** is the emotional state that results when we interpret events as potentially harmful or threatening to the self; it most commonly involves the anticipation of physical harm, loss, rejection, or failure (Shaver, Schwartz, Kirson, & O'Connor, 1987). As can be seen from Figure 12–9, there are a number of conditions that can lead to fear and a variety of responses associated with the emotion. Although fear and anxiety can be caused by a variety of situations, there is also evidence that personality may also influence how much and how often we experience these conditions; that is, anxiety may be a trait as well as a situational state (Taylor, 1951). *Anxiety* is a very close cousin of fear although it is somewhat more commonly experienced and often lasts longer than fear (Wicker, Payne, Roberson, & Garcia-Falcon, 1985). Because of this close relationship, we will use the concepts interchangeably in this book.

Although we can develop new fears at almost any time in our lives, some fears are age related. For example, infants between 6 and 9 months of age develop a fear of strangers (Stroufe & Waters, 1976). The fear of noises tends to decrease between the ages of 1 to 6 years, whereas the fear of animals increases until the age of 4 and then levels off. One fear that does seem to increase with age is the fear of imagined situations. An example of this age-related fear can be seen in the reaction of Emmett Kelly's mother upon seeing her 5-year-old son sitting atop the telegraph pole. She was overcome by fear because she imagined the numerous disas-

Fear
Reaction to a specific danger in the environment.

Many fears are age related. The fear of strangers develops in infants between the ages of 6 and 9 months.

trous consequences that could result from the situation. However, the brave 5-year-old showed no fear because his imagery process had not developed to the extent that he could conjure up these consequences.

The Functions of Fear. Imagine a life without fear. You could go into an exam for which you had not studied feeling confident. You could walk through the most wicked neighborhood on the darkest night feeling secure and safe. Sound nice? As hard as it may be to believe, a life without fear could be far more dangerous than Kelly's trapeze act. Fear is important in our lives; it leads us to avoid objects and situations that are dangerous. For example, people who cannot swim may fear jumping into deep water. This fear leads them to refrain from this life-threatening activity.

Fear also prepares the body for action. The heart rate increases, muscles tense, digestive functions slow, and epinephrine pours into the bloodstream when we face the object of our fear. These physiological changes enable us to act quickly and decisively. In addition, fear often leads to the strengthening of social bonds (Suomi & Harlow, 1976). Children seek out their parents when they are fearful and fear leads adults to affiliate with others.

Thus, although the experience of anxiety may be unpleasant, it can play a constructive role in our lives. Of course, fear can become destructive. Problems occur when we develop irrational fears of objects that are not real dangers (see Chapter 14). Fear can also be destructive when we are consumed by it and are unable to direct our behavior to deal with the object of our fear.

Reactions to Fear and Anxiety. Research has shown that fear influences our perceptions, our performance, and our social behavior. With regard to our perceptions, Izard (1977) states that fear is the most limiting emotion. It leads to "tunnel vision," where people block out all stimuli except the object of their fear. Thinking becomes rigid and concentrated on the objects related to fear. This rigidity may lead to tragic results.

Anxiety also affects performance, but not in the way many people might expect. As we have shown, anxiety is accompanied by physiological

FIGURE 12–10

The Yerkes-Dodson Principle

The graph shows the relationship between arousal and performance. A certain amount of arousal is necessary to function, but a very high degree of arousal, such as that caused by excess anxiety, makes it difficult to perform at all. The most effective level of arousal for performance depends on the difficulty level of the task. (After Hebb, 1955)

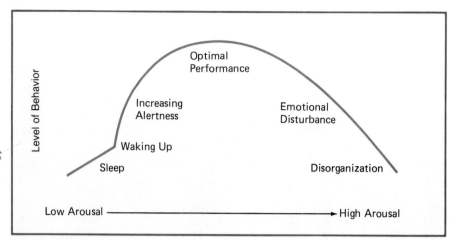

arousal. According to the **Yerkes-Dodson principle,** the most effective level of arousal for performance depends on the difficulty of the task. Some degree of arousal is necessary to perform well on any task. However, although high levels of arousal will aid work on an easy task, they will hinder work on difficult tasks (see Figure 12–10).

In addition to perception and performance, social interaction is influenced by fear. In Chapter 11 we discussed in some detail an experiment which demonstrated that fear causes people to want to be with others.

A negative aspect of anxiety is that it can lead to symptoms such as insomnia, depression, inactivity, forgetfulness, and dread (Gatchel & Baum, 1983). These problems generally result when people feel helpless and are unable to cope with a situation and their feelings. In extreme cases, the end result can be a severe emotional disorder (see Chapter 14).

Love

In 1923 sisters Eva and Mitzie Moore brought their trapeze act to John Robinson's Circus. Emmett Kelly watched with a pounding heart as Eva Moore hurled her tiny, slim body through the air. This young woman had talent and courage. There was only one problem: She also had a protective father. Mr. Moore did not want his children to get married and break up their circus act. Kelly fell in love, however, and soon he and Eva were arranging secret meetings. The romance progressed quickly despite the interferences, and when the circus set up in Charlottesville, Virginia, the couple sneaked off to the home of a preacher and got married. Although love is a common theme in our history, our literature, and even in our own daily lives, it has generally eluded the careful eye of the scientific researcher. Only recently have investigators begun to study love.

Have you ever tried to define love? This is a difficult task partly because there are many types of love. Consider the romantic love you feel for your boyfriend or girlfriend, the love that a parent feels for a child, and the less passionate but intense feeling that characterizes long-term relationships such as those of your grandparents. Overall, love relationships are characterized as a personalized form of joy; they are viewed as joy caused by the presence of the love object (Shaver, Schwartz, Kirson, & O'Connor, 1987). Love is made up of various components including intimacy (feeling of closeness), passion (arousal), and commitment (Sternberg, 1986). Drawing on these three components, Sternberg developed a *triangular* theory of love. As you can see in Figure 12–11, the theory suggests six types of love in addition to simple liking. Each type of love has different mixtures of these components. Another component of love that is often overlooked is sacrifice (Brickman, 1987). Love grows out of a sense of sacrifice; the

Yerkes-Dodson principle
Theory that the most effective level of arousal for performance depends on the difficulty of the task.

Love involves various components including intimacy, passion, and commitment. There are many types of love including romantic love, mature love, and the love between parents and children.

sacrifice may involve time, material goods, or the forsaking of others for the object of our love. In our discussion of cognitive dissonance theory in Chapter 16, we will see that we come to value those things and people for whom we suffer or give up things, and the more we give up the more we value the person for whom we have sacrificed.

Although we can identify some of the components of love, we often have a difficult time determining why we love someone. In a recent class discussion on love, I posed a fiendish question to a student who had just described her feelings of love for her boyfriend. I asked, "Why do you love him?" The student stammered, offered a few platitudes (he's nice, kind, and easygoing), and then she sat down. I was reminded of the following statement by Moreno (1977):

> There are essentially two ways of explaining why we have the special feelings we call love. The first one is by asserting that those whom we claim to love are objectively deserving of special consideration: "If you knew her as well as I do, you would realize how wonderful she really is." The problem with this type of explanation is that the special qualities we see in those we say we love are seldom, and never to the same degree, seen by anyone else not equally

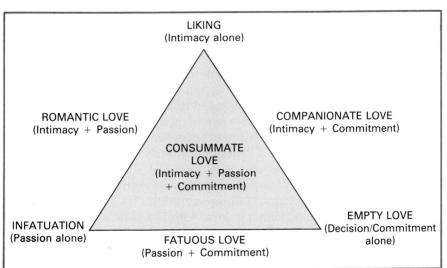

FIGURE 12–11

Sternberg (1988) proposed that love is made up of three different components, called intimacy, passion, and commitment. Using these three components, he defined six types of love (in addition to liking), which are shown here in this diagram. (From Sternberg, 1988)

in love with the person in question. So sooner or later we resort to the other type of explanation: "I love her because I love her." We abandon the pretension that our loved ones are really special or we try to make ourselves believe that others are unable to see their true qualities, and we explain how, regardless of whether or not they are endowed with special qualities, and regardless of whether other people can detect these qualities, they are special to us by the mere fact that we feel deeply about them. This second explanation, which is the more common one and which is always put forward when the first is challenged, is of course no explanation at all. (pp. 36–37)

Another interesting (and sometimes troublesome) aspect of love is that it seems to have many faces over time. If you have been in a long-term loving relationship, you might recall that it began with passion, consideration, and excitement. As the relationship progressed, you began to have feelings of being "taken for granted"; you no longer received flowers or love notes, yet you still felt deeply committed to your partner. Then something happened that interrupted your harmony; a competitor arrived on the scene or you went away for a vacation by yourself. This interruption seemed to ignite the old spark of passion; you again received (or sent) flowers, notes, and so on. Ellen Berscheid (1983) suggests that romantic love lasts for a relatively short time. Soon it is replaced by predictability and coordination that makes for a comfortable albeit emotionless relationship. Interruptions may rekindle passion to the relationship. This may also be why you suddenly feel longing and love for an ex-partner after a relationship has broken up. Hence, predictability may be very important for a smooth relationship, but it may also reduce the level of emotion in the relationship.

Learning to Love.   Love is an emotion that most of us regard as positive and desirable, and many people spend much of their lives in search of it. An interesting but sad feature of love is the fact that some of these "searchers" have a very difficult time experiencing love. This is not because they do not have the opportunity to form a loving relationship, however. Many researchers believe that people must learn to love (Fromm, 1956, Harlow, 1971). The ability to experience love and form loving relationships is strongly influenced by past experience. Harlow (1971) demonstrated this by removing infant monkeys from their mothers shortly after birth. These monkeys received adequate care and feeding, but because they were reared in isolation they were deprived of maternal love. At 3 months, 6 months, and 2 years of age these monkeys were introduced to other monkeys their own age, and their interactions were observed. The isolated monkeys could not form friendships or play with their own age-mates. Nor were they receptive to sexual advances from other monkeys. Harlow impregnated some of the isolated female monkeys in order to study whether or not they could develop maternal love for their own offspring; the results were startling. The isolated mothers failed to feed or care for their young, and in many cases the mothers treated them so brutally that the infants would have been killed had the experimenter not removed them.

More recently, research has suggested that the attachment process also affects love in humans; people who experienced close, secure attachments form love relationships characterized by trust, friendship, and positive emotions (Hazan & Shaver, 1987). These individuals seem more able to "let themselves go" to experience love. Because of this, they not only get strong positive feelings from a love relationship, they also suffer emotional distress when the relationship collapses (Simpson, 1990).

Emmett Kelly recalls "falling in love" with Eva as he watched her flying through the air on the trapeze. His story is reminiscent of romantic cases of "Love at first sight." This "instant love" phenomenon, however, seems to be found more frequently in novels and poems than in actual life. In one study, 226 engaged couples were interviewed, with only 8 percent of the men and 5 percent of the women revealing that they felt "strong physical attraction" for their partners during the two days following their first meeting (Wallin, 1953). Thus, love does seem to be an emotion that takes some time to develop.

Effects of Arousal. While a loving relationship clearly takes time to form, the passion side of love follows the same course as any other emotion. That is, people experience arousal when they are together, and they attribute this arousal to love. This hypothesis leads to an interesting prediction that was tested by Dutton and Aron (1974). An attractive female experimenter approached men as they walked across a bridge. In half the cases, subjects walked on an old wooden bridge that swayed above a 230-foot precipice. All other subjects used a solid bridge that crossed a small stream 10 feet below. The experimenter showed the men a picture of a woman covering her face with her hand and asked the subjects to make up a story about the picture. After they finished, she gave the subjects her name and telephone number and said they could call her if they had any questions. Two differences were found in the responses of the two groups. First, the subjects who had just crossed the rickety bridge told more sex-related stories about the picture than subjects who had crossed the sturdy bridge. Second, subjects who had walked across the old wooden bridge were more likely to call the interviewer after the study than were subjects who had used the sturdy bridge. How can we explain these results? Dutton and Aron argued that crossing the swaying bridge aroused subjects. In most circumstances individuals would interpret this arousal as fear. However, when the subjects met the attractive female, they attributed their arousal as attraction or sexual arousal. On the other hand, individuals crossing the sturdy bridge would not be aroused and, hence, they were less likely to experience attraction when met by the female experimenter. Although this explanation is consistent with the Schachter and Singer theory of emotion, an alternative explanation is that the attractive female reduced the men's fears on the rickety bridge. As a result of this fear reduction, the men became attracted to the experimenter (Kenrick & Cialdini, 1977).

The possibility that passionate love may result from the misidentity of arousal has some intriguing applications. Often, young lovers are faced with interference and disapproval from their parents. These interferences and frustrations may arouse the lovers, who may incorrectly identify the cause of the arousal as love. Thus, the attempts by parents to break up a love relationship may unwittingly increase the feelings of love between the thwarted adolescents. We can see this effect in Kelly's case; Eva's father attempted to keep Eva and Emmett away from each other. This interference led them to have secret meetings and eventually they were married . . . and divorced. Another intriguing possibility derivable from the cognitive theory of passionate love was suggested by the Roman author and philosopher Ovid in his first century Roman handbook on romantic conquest. Ovid suggested that an excellent time to arouse passion in a woman was while she was engrossed in watching gladiators attack each other. The modern interpretation of this advice would be that the exciting gladitorial event arouses the woman, and the task of the amorous-minded male is to have the woman interpret the arousal as love or sexual excitement. It is, in fact, interesting that Kelly's love for Eva bloomed while he watched her perform dangerous and exciting feats on the trapeze.

Certainly, love is a complex emotion. Social scientists are just scratching the surface in understanding the pathways to love. It is, however, important to notice that a familiarity with the basic theories of emotion may help in understanding the more complicated emotions such as love.

People involved in exciting situations may misinterpret their arousal as being love. This effect may be one of the causes for the high number of wartime instant romances.

When Emmett Kelly was 19 years old he decided he had had enough of life on the farm; he wanted the excitement and fortune offered by the city. He packed his bag and off he went to Kansas City. However, life in the city was not what Kelly had imagined it would be. Everything about the city was different from his Kansas farm life, and Kelly spent the first few days exploring his surroundings. His introduction to Kansas City involved changing jobs frequently. He made sign frames, he painted the inside of steel tanks, he tried to drive a lumber truck, and he painted kewpie dolls. Kelly rarely had much money, and at times he went to bed hungry because he couldn't afford to buy food. The fast life of the city and the numerous changes in job and lifestyle most certainly created a great deal of stress for this young man from the farm.

The concept of stress is one that we are all familiar with. Many of us use the term *stress* to describe a feeling or emotion. **Stress,** however, is not an emotion; rather, it is the process by which the individual responds to environmental and psychological events that are perceived as threatening or challenging (Gatchel & Baum, 1983; Selye, 1976). As we will see, stress does not necessarily involve negative events. Positive situations can also lead to stress. The events that give rise to stress are called *stressors.* Such events are *perceived* as threatening or challenging; this emphasis on perception means that an event may be a stressor for one person, but not for another person. Recalling our earlier discussion of the role of appraisal in emotions, it has been suggested that appraisal plays a major role in determining stress (Lazarus & Folkman, 1987). In this case, appraisal takes place in two steps. First, we appraise the event as being harmful, threatening, or challenging. Next we assess our ability to cope with the event. As you might expect, the greatest stress results when we interpret an event as harmful or challenging and determine that we have little ability or resources to deal with the situation. Kelly's move to Kansas City was a stressor because he worried about how he would support himself and whether he would make friends. This same move for a person who had ample resources and knew people in the city would not be perceived as threatening.

Hans Selye, a Canadian physician, spent years examining the body's response to stressors. He found that the stress response, which he called *general adaptation syndrome* (Figure 12–12) was very systematic and could be charted in three phases (Selye, 1976). During the first phase (*alarm reaction*) the body prepares to meet the stressor. Adrenal hormones such as epinephrine, or adrenalin, (see Chapter 2) are released into the bloodstream causing an increase in heart rate and breathing rate. Because the major body effort is focused on preparing to meet this stressor, the body's resistance is temporarily lowered elsewhere. If the stressor persists, the body enters the *stage of resistance.* In this stage, the body attempts to bring its emergency resources to a more normal level. However, as you can see in Figure 12–12, if the stressor continues, the body will function at a somewhat higher-than-normal level. If the stressor disappears during this stage, the body returns to a normal functioning level. On the other hand, if the stress-producing situation continues, the *stage of exhaustion* begins. This is the point where the body begins to wear down, and many of the symptoms of the alarm reaction reappear. If the stress is extreme and the stressor is not removed quickly, the person may even collapse and die.

Accordingly to Selye, the general adaptation syndrome occurs regardless of the stressor. The stressor may be external (such as a loud noise or adverse climate), internal (such as disease or physical injury), or emotional (such as conflict, fear, or anger).

Stress
Process by which the individual responds to events that disrupt or threaten to disrupt his or her equilibrium.

Stress is the process by which individuals respond to threatening and challenging events in their environment. According to the general adaptation syndrome theory, the immediate response to stress (alarm stage) involves the mobilization of most body systems to meet the challenge. However, if the stress continues, the body wears down and death may result (stage of exhaustion).

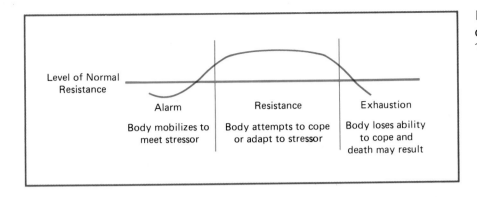

FIGURE 12–12
General Adaptation Syndrome (Selye, 1956).

Level of Normal
Resistance

Alarm | Resistance | Exhaustion

Body mobilizes to meet stressor | Body attempts to cope or adapt to stressor | Body loses ability to cope and death may result

The Causes of Stress

The range of events that give rise to stress is almost unlimited. Although the list of potential stressors is almost inconceivably long, there are certain characteristics that increase the degree of stress arising from a situation. We will quickly examine four of these factors: change, unpredictability, lack of control, and conflict.

Change.   There are many ways to describe Kelly's life in the city, but it clearly involved a great deal of change. He changed his home, his lifestyle, and his diet; his friends changed; and he changed jobs many times. Kelly enjoyed some of these changes, but some were not as pleasant as others. All of us experience a great deal of change in our lives; we look forward to some of the changes, and we would prefer to avoid others. It may, however, come as somewhat of a surprise to learn that change itself, whether positive or negative, is a stressor.

Thomas Holmes and his colleagues (Holmes & Masuda, 1974; Holmes & Rahe, 1967) studied thousands of medical histories and interviews and then questioned over 400 men and women in an effort to identify stressful events. Based on their research, the investigators developed the Life Events Scale (see Table 12–1), which attempts to give stress values to life events. As can be seen from the list, the common thread is that each event involves some *change* in an individual's life. Although many of the events are negative (death of a spouse, being fired from a job), some are clearly positive changes (outstanding personal achievement, vacation). Holmes argued that stress is directly related to major illness, and he suggested that the scale could be used to predict when an individual is most likely to suffer a severe illness. Specifically, he predicted that individuals who score over 300 points during a 1-year period run a high risk of being struck down by a major illness during the following year.

Although there has been some evidence linking major life events to stress and illness, there have also been a number of criticisms about the approach. Many of the criticisms center on features of the Life Events Scale (e.g., values given to events and use of recall). Other criticisms question the focus on *major* life events. These major events are relatively rare occurrences and we often have a great deal of social support when they happen. For example, after the recent birth of my twins, I received so many calls and visits congratulating (and in some cases consoling) me, that it was over a month before I had time to consider the impact on my life that these bundles of joy would have.

Although major events are relatively rare and far between, minor hassles seem to be our constant companion. These hassles might include the car that won't start, the coffee that is spilled on our term paper, or the roommate who always wears our clothes. Few people rush to our side when we face these minor hassles. Could these events, however, be more stressful than the major events identified by Holmes and Rahe?

Table 12–1
Life Event Scale

Life Event	Stress Value	Life Event	Stress Value
Death of spouse	100	Son or daughter leaving home	29
Divorce	73	Trouble with in-laws	29
Marital separation	65	Outstanding personal achievement	28
Jail term	63	Wife begins or stops work	26
Death of close family member	63	Begin or end school	26
Personal injury or illness	53	Change in living conditions	25
Marriage	50	Revision of personal habits	24
Fired at work	47	Trouble with boss	23
Marital reconciliation	45	Change in work hours or conditions	20
Retirement	45	Change in residence	20
Change in health of family member	44	Change in schools	20
Pregnancy	40	Change in recreation	19
Sex difficulties	39	Change in church activities	19
Gain of new family member	39	Change in social activities	18
Business readjustment	39	Mortgage or loan less than $10,000	17
Change in financial state	38	Change in sleeping habits	16
Death of close friend	37	Change in number of family get-togethers	15
Change to different line of work	36	Change in eating habits	15
Change in number of arguments with spouse	35	Vacation	13
Mortgage over $10,000	31	Christmas	12
Foreclosure of mortgage or loan	30	Minor violations of the law	11
Change in responsibilities at work	29		

Source: Holmes & Rahe (1967).

Richard Lazarus and his colleagues examined the effects of minor but frequent daily events on illness (Lazarus, 1981; Lazarus & Delongis, 1983). Lazarus identified two types of daily events involving change. On the negative side are **hassles,** which are the "irritating, frustrating, or distressing incidents that occur in our everyday transactions with the environment" (p. 58). Common hassles include misplacing or losing things, having too many things to do, and being concerned about physical appearance. On the positive side are *uplifts*, which include such pleasures as completing a task, visiting or phoning a friend, and feeling healthy.

Lazarus selected a sample of 100 people (48 men, 52 women) who were mainly middle-aged, middle-class, and white. At the beginning and at the end of the year-long study, the subjects filled out the Holmes and Rahe Life Events Scale. Each month during the study the subjects indicated the hassles and the uplifts that had occurred during the month. Lazarus also collected information on the subjects' physical health and mood during the study.

A number of interesting findings came out of this study. First, Lazarus found that hassles "turned out to be much better predictors of psychological and physical health than life events" (1981, p. 62). People who suffered frequent and intense hassles had the poorest health, whereas the link between major life events and health was weak. Lazarus also found that uplifts did not offset the negative impact of hassles. In fact, the study found that, for women, uplifts had a temporary negative effect on emotions and mental health.

Although this study supports the position that change itself can be stressful and contributes to physical and mental alertness, Lazarus concludes, "It is not the large, dramatic events that make the difference, but what happens day in and day out, whether provoked by major events or

Hassles
Minor, but daily annoying events.

not" (1981, p. 62). Recently, an intriguing finding suggests that Lazarus's statement might not be completely correct (Caspi, Bolger, & Eckenrode, 1987). This study looked at the effects of both major and minor life events on stress levels. These researchers found that the stress levels were highest when accompanied by chronic ecological stress such as high neighborhood crime, noise, poor housing, and high density. Most interesting, however, from the standpoint of our present discussion was that the female subjects in the study who had experienced major life events over the previous year were *less* bothered by minor life hassles. The investigators suggest that minor hassles are seen as even more minor and less bothersome when we compare them to a major life event we have recently experienced. Also, once we learn to cope with major life events, we are better prepared to cope with hassles. These are interesting ideas, but more research is needed before we prescribe major life events as inoculations against daily hassles!

Finally, before we label change as a villain, we should realize that a lack of change can also be stressful. We saw in Chapter 5 that sensory deprivation and social isolation, which was characterized by a lack of stimulation, can be very stressful. Similarly, boredom and monotony can distress people. In fact, Kelly writes that he was becoming depressed and restless with his dull life on the farm. It was this boredom that led him to seek change and move to Kansas City. Taking another perspective, one researcher reported that if a person expects change, no change may actually be more stressful than the expected change (Graham, 1974). You can understand this if you have ever spent time preparing for an exam only to find out that it has been postponed, or if you have had an expected vacation canceled.

Despite these qualifications it is clear that change in many situations can create a great deal of stress. Change, whether positive or negative, requires the individual to make psychological and physical adjustments. These adjustments place certain demands on the body and each demand is experienced as stress. Also, change often makes our lives less predictable and reduces our feelings of control. As we will soon see, both of these factors are stressors.

Unpredictability. Although all change is stressful, we are able to predict and prepare for some events. Others are unpredictable. For example, you know that you will graduate from college on a certain date, and if you are planning a wedding, you probably will know many months in advance the date on which you will get married. Many other events, however, happen in a very unpredictable fashion.

Unpredictability is stressful because you cannot plan for these random events—you have to be constantly "on your toes." One of the most vivid examples of unpredictability occurs in the job of air-traffic controllers. Imagine yourself as a controller at Chicago's O'Hare Airport, where an airplane lands or takes off on the average of every 20 seconds. Although some of the flights are scheduled, many others are not. Martindale (1976) compared the medical records of 4,000 air-traffic controllers with those of second-class Air Force airmen who generally have regular and predictable jobs. The controllers were significantly more likely to suffer from high blood pressure, anxiety attacks, peptic ulcers, and depression.

Lack of Control. After overcoming his early fears, Kelly loved the city life. He could choose where and what he ate because of the wide variety of restaurants. He could decide what type of entertainment would fill his evenings. He had a wide variety of people from which to choose his friends. And he found that if he became bored with one job, he could always find other types of work. In short, Kelly found that the variety of the city offered him a chance to control his own destiny and life. These opportunities for control may well have reduced the stress that Kelly might otherwise have experienced in the city.

Change, even positive change, leads to stress.

HEALTH PSYCHOLOGY: The Field and an Application to Women's Health

As we begin our examination of stress, we are treading into one of the domains of a new and rapidly growing area of psychology: health psychology. **Health psychology,** as the name implies, studies the links between psychology and illness. The field draws on all areas of psychology, including clinical, industrial/organizational, social, cognitive, personality, community, and physiological psychology. In fact, we have discussed research in health psychology in almost every chapter in this book. We cannot hope to cover the field in this short section, so let's briefly review some of the areas and relate the approach to an important issue, women's health.

One area of health psychology examines the social and psychological factors that lead to illness (Rodin & Salovey, 1989; Taylor, 1990). We know that many diseases have a physical basis such as bacteria and virus. But why are some people more likely to be ill than others, and why are some people likely to contract one disease while other people are likely to fall prey to another disease? In tackling these and related questions, much research has focused on the role of stress. What is stress? How does it influence the body's physical functioning? Health psychologists also examine how social and

personality factors relate to illness. For example, how do poverty, education, and culture affect illness? Are people with some types of personality more likely to become ill than people with other types of personality? Cognitive factors such as the way people perceive illness have been found to affect health (Bishop, 1987). For example, some people believe that illness is solely due to physical causes and there is little they can do to avoid getting sick. Others feel that behavior and emotions influence health and that therefore they have some control over their own health.

Another focus of health psychology is on coping with illness. Research in this area examines whether people view illness as harmful, threatening, or challenging, and how these different appraisals affect their recovery (Stone & Neale, 1984). Other questions concern what factors influence whether or not people will follow their physician's orders about how to treat their illness and what factors determine whether they will take their prescribed medicine or follow suggestions about resting and getting exercise. Another important issue is social support (Cutrona & Russell, 1990). How does having the support of others affect an ill person's recovery? Who is most likely to seek the support of others when ill?

A third major area concerns intervention and health policy. What is the most effective way to teach people about such illnesses as AIDS and heart disease? How can we convince people to get regular medical checkups? Health psychologists are also interested in national health policy. How much effort should be devoted to prevention compared to treatment?

Health psychology is clearly a broad, important, and timely area of study. We have only touched on its issues of concern here. In order to demonstrate the importance of the field, we will briefly focus on one issue, women's health.

In some ways, women seem to be healthier than men. "At any age across the life-span, from conception to death, girls and women are on the average biologically more advantaged and live longer than boys and men" (Strickland, 1988, p. 381). At every age more men than women die, and five times as many women as men celebrate their hundredth birthday. While these figures may give women something to cheer about, there is another side to the story that is more sobering. As Table 1 indicates, women are more frequently ill, more likely to suffer a serious illness, and more likely to visit a physician than men are (Verbrugge, 1989). And even women's advantage in life expectancy

Table 1
Morbidity Indicators by Sex and Sex Ratios in the United States in 1987

Indicator	Females	Males	Sex ratio (Female/male)
Restricted activity days			
Total days of disability (millions)	1,984	1,464	1.35
Days/person	16.1	12.7	1.28
Bed disability days			
Total days of disability (millions)	879	595	1.48
Days/person	7.1	5.2	1.36
Work loss days			
Total (millions)	304	299	1.02
Days/person	6.1	4.8	1.27
Hospital utilization rates			
Patients discharged per 1,000 persons	159	116	1.37
Days of care per 1,000 persons	968	860	1.20
Average stay (days)	6.1	6.9	0.88
Physician visits			
Total (millions)	765	523	1.46
Visits/person	6.2	4.5	1.38

Source: U.S. Bureau of the Census, *Statistical Abstract of the United States: 1990.*

Health psychology
Branch of psychology that examines the relationship between psychological factors and illness, including intervention to reduce illness and policy formation.

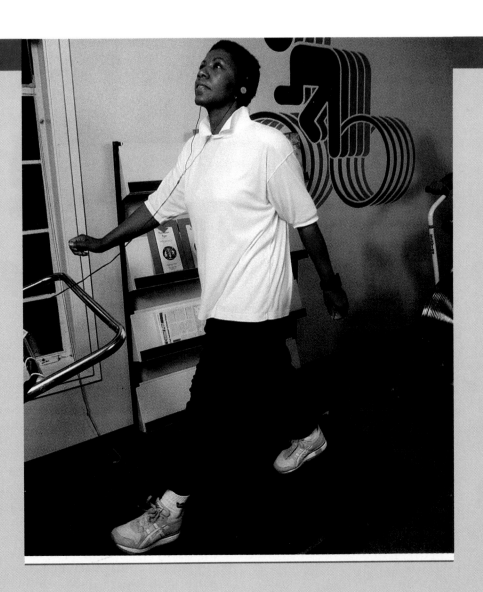

is declining, especially for people over 45 years of age.

How can we explain these sex differences and the decline in some differences that once existed? Investigators have laid much of the blame on the psychological and behavioral effects of major social trends (Rodin & Ickovics, 1990). To begin with, it is suggested that as much as 50 percent of the mortality from the ten leading causes of death in the United States can be traced to aspects of lifestyle, including cigarette smoking, substance abuse, harmful dietary habits, maladaptive responses to social pressures, and reckless driving (Hamburg, Elliot, & Parron, 1982). Women's lifestyles have changed dramatically over the last few decades as social norms changed. Their smoking rates have increased, while men's smoking rates have declined. The number of women using alcohol has also gone up. Women have been entering the

workforce in rapidly increasing numbers. Not only do they now hold jobs that pose high health risks, but their roles at home have not changed to accommodate their new work roles. So women must often deal with the stress of performing the multiple roles of worker, mother and homemaker.

At first glance, then, we might conclude that our more open and equal society is a negative factor in women's health. However, research shows that employed women are generally healthier than nonemployed women (LaCroix & Haynes, 1987). It is not *equality* that is associated with harmful behaviors such as increased smoking. Rather, these behaviors increase for women who adopt masculine roles rather than more egalitarian androgynous roles. In other words, strict adherence to either masculine or feminine sex roles may lead to unhealthy behavior.

The important task for health psychologists is to identify the factors that place women at a higher health risk in today's changing society, to make women more aware of these risks, and to help develop conditions that promote both change and health. For example, it has been found that social support networks in the workplace are especially beneficial to women (Waldron & Jacobs, 1989). Other research has focused on how family systems can be altered to support the new roles for women without weakening the family structure (Rodin & Ickovics, 1990). And investigators have pointed out the importance of focusing research on women rather than simply drawing conclusions about them from previous research involving men.

Such issues are important, but a sensitive and careful research program will have immeasurable benefits for all aspects of our society.

Lack of predictability leads to stress. One reason that air-traffic controllers are stressed is that they often cannot predict when an airplane will request landing or take-off permission, and they cannot anticipate when trouble may develop.

In order to study the effects of control, a group of elderly residents in a nursing home were given more control over their day-to-day lives (Langer & Rodin, 1976). These residents were able to do such things as choose their own meals, care for plants in their rooms, and decide how to arrange the furniture in the rooms. A second group of residents were treated according to the standard nursing home routine where staff members make all decisions on these issues. The results of the study showed that residents given control over their own lives became more alert and more involved in activities than residents who did not have this control. The residents given control also showed significantly greater improvement in their health than residents who did not have control. In fact, during the 18 months of the study, only 15 percent of the patients with control over their daily lives died; 30 percent of the comparison group died.

Many events in our environment may be particularly stressful because they emphasize our vulnerability and lack of control. For example, natural disasters such as earthquakes or nuclear accidents such as Three Mile Island and Chernobyl cause stress for many people long after they have passed. A similar effect is seen in victims of crime (Normoyle & Lavrokes, 1984). People who are robbed, raped, or assaulted are not only burdened with the immediate injury; they must also struggle with the fact that these incidents show that they are not in control of their environment and their own bodies. Because of this, the aftereffects of these acts can be equally or more devastating.

It is not entirely clear why control reduces stress. One view is that having control increases the predictability of events and allows people to feel more prepared to deal with their environment (Pervin, 1963). Whatever the reason, we do know that the degree of control people have over their lives influences the amount of stress that they experience.

Conflict.   Kelly had an important choice to make when he found that he would have to be a clown in the circus: Would he do a white-face act like other clowns, or would he develop a whole new character? Although there were strong points in favor of each of the acts, Kelly had to choose one—he couldn't do both. This is an example of **conflict,** which is a state that occurs when a person is motivated to choose between two or more mutually exclusive goals or courses of action. Events are mutually exclusive when choosing one automatically eliminates the other.

Conflict
State that occurs when a person is motivated to choose between two or more mutually exclusive goals or courses of action.

Some conflict occurs almost every time you make a choice; the degree of conflict is influenced by the attractiveness of each choice and by how equally they are matched in attractiveness.

Conflict has been found to be one of the conditions that causes stress for people. Although there are many situations in which a person experiences conflict, investigators have identified four major types of categories of conflict (Lewin, 1931; Miller, 1944). In defining these types, they have focused on people's tendencies to either approach or avoid a goal.

1. **Approach-Approach Conflict.** After Kelly had become famous as the clown Willie, he was offered a chance to act in the movies. This excited him, because it meant that millions of people could see Willie, and it also offered him financial rewards. However, becoming an actor would force Kelly to give up the circus for a certain amount of time. He loved working with circus people and dealing with live audiences. Thus, Kelly was faced with making a choice between two very attractive alternatives.

This is an example of an approach-approach conflict, which involves a choice between two attractive goals. In theory, this conflict should be easy to resolve, because it is a "no lose" situation—either choice brings rewards. However, anyone who has had to make the choice between two good job offers or two attractive dates knows that this type of conflict can be stressful.

2. **Avoidance-Avoidance Conflict.** This type of conflict results when people must choose between two unattractive goals. This type of conflict is difficult to resolve. For this reason, people faced with this situation often try to delay making a decision. They sometimes hope that if they delay long enough, they can either escape the situation or something will happen that will make the decision for them.

3. **Approach-Avoidance Conflict.** Kelly's first job offer in the circus involved being a clown. This created a great deal of conflict for him. On the positive side, he would be with the circus, and he would be earning a regular salary. On the negative side, however, Kelly knew nothing about clowning and he really wanted to be a trapeze artist. The approach-avoidance conflict involves only one goal which has both attractive and unattractive qualities. People's desire to both obtain the goal and avoid it traps them in conflict.

4. **Double Approach-Avoidance Conflict.** This type of conflict results when a person has to choose between two goals, each of which has both positive and negative qualities. For example, as a teenager, Kelly had to choose between staying on the farm or going to the city. Kelly had many friends (+) and security (+) at home on the farm, but he was bored (−). On the other hand, Kansas City offered excitement (+) and jobs (+), but he had no friends there (−). The double approach-avoidance conflict is the most common of the four types we have discussed, because it is rare that people are faced with goals that are completely positive or negative. In fact, many conflicts that appear to be simple approach-approach conflicts can actually be viewed as double approach-avoidance conflicts, because choosing one goal (+) means giving up the other (−).

As we all know, conflicts can be hard to resolve. Unfortunately, the longer we delay in resolving a conflict, the more stress and anxiety may increase. An interesting point about most conflicts is that the closer we get to a goal, the stronger the approach and avoidance forces become. As can be seen in Figure 12–13, the strength of the avoidance tendencies increases at a faster rate than the strength of the approach tendencies. In other words, the closer you get to making a decision, the more you will be disturbed by the negative qualities of the choice. You may have experienced this in choosing what college to go to: When you first learned that you had been accepted at your two top choices, you were very happy

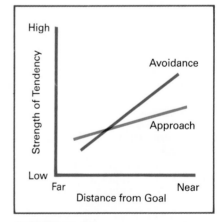

FIGURE 12–13

The graph shows approach and avoidance tendencies as one nears a goal. Both approach and avoidance tendencies increase the closer one gets to the goal, but the avoidance tendency increases more rapidly than the approach tendency.

WORK STRESS AND BURNOUT

*A*ll students who complain about their tough life have probably heard their parents or professors warn, "You think you have it bad now, wait until you get a *real* job!" Over the last few years, psychologists have begun to focus more attention on work-related stress. If we review the work environment, we find that it has each of the stress-producing ingredients we just discussed and a few we didn't discuss! *Work overload* has been identified as a chief factor producing job stress (Taylor, 1986). A related problem of *work pressure* (the perceived demand to achieve more and work harder) has also been found to increase stress. Another important job stressor that is often overlooked is the number of people a person works for; the more people, the greater the stress (Spector, Dwyer, & Jex, 1988). All of these factors lead workers to feel that they have little control over their lives on the job.

The increase in technology has forced many workers to make major changes in their work habits. The computer, for example, has made many jobs more efficient, but it has also drastically changed the nature of those jobs.

The list of job stressors could go on, but the point is that there are many such stressors in the workplace. The effect of job stress is far-reaching. For one, there are many illnesses associated with job stress. One study reported that the death rate from coronary heart disease was twice as high for industrial workers who spent 48 hours a week or more on the job than it was for workers on the same job who worked less than 40 hours a week (Breslow & Buell, 1960). Burnout seems to be particularly common where the job involves work with needy people (nurses, physicians, psychologists); **burnout** involves emotional exhaustion, depersonalization of the client, and a reduced feeling of accomplishment. As a result of burnout, people lose interest in their jobs and confidence in themselves. Burnout has been identified as a major factor creating staff turnover and the ironically high rates of health and personal problems suffered by people in the health care professions (Bloom, 1988). And job stress has been linked to a host of

Burnout is especially common in professions involving work with needy people. Burnout includes emotional exhaustion, depersonalization of the client, and a reduced feeling of accomplishment.

maladaptive behaviors such as drug and alcohol abuse, psychophysiological disorders and anxiety disorders.

Many businesses have taken a series of steps to combat job stress. These include reducing environmental stressors such as noise, crowding, and harsh lighting. Efforts have been made to reduce the unpredictability and ambiguity associated with job tasks. Workers are given more control over their jobs and increased opportunity to have their points of view heard by employers. Many businesses have attempted to adopt more flexible schedules in order to reduce role conflict. Many employers arrange social events in order to help develop positive social relationships and social support networks in the workplace. And supervisors have been trained to spot signs of stress in workers so that it can be dealt with before it becomes devastating. Some companies have drawn on the procedures used by Japanese firms to reduce stress. These include daily exercise classes and routines designed to build up a feeling of "team spirit." Recognition for outstanding performance is given to both the worker and his or her team.

Still another approach suggests that individuals would be able to adapt to job stress if they were made aware of the stressors associated with their work and taught to monitor their reactions. However, self-monitoring alone has proved to be ineffective in reducing job stress. In fact, for many workers, being aware of their reactions to stress actually increases their level of stress (Matheny et al., 1986). On the other hand, programs that encourage workers to monitor their stress *and* teach them how to actively cope with their stress have proved effective in helping people adjust to their jobs (Frone & McFarlin, 1989).

Women who are homemakers face many, if not more, of the stressors than women who work outside the home (Baruch, Biener, & Barnett, 1987). The roles of mother, wife, and homemaker are often conflicting. There is a lack of structure and reward for many of the jobs faced by a homemaker. In addition, being isolated at home gives one few opportunities to develop social relationships and networks. Perhaps efforts to reduce stress in the workplace may also be applied to the home with very positive benefits.

and felt the decision would be easy. However, as the decision deadline approached, you found the choice increasingly hard to make. This fact not only increases the stress associated with conflict, but, as we will see in Chapter 16, it increases how hard we must work to justify our final decision.

(Key Term from previous page)
Burnout
Job-related emotional exhaustion that includes a depersonalized feeling and a reduced sense of accomplishment.

The Reactions to Stress

All of us experience stress many times each day. In fact, some of us seek out stress-producing situations by engaging in sports such as sky diving or going to scary movies. In most cases, the level of stress is not particularly high, and if it becomes too uncomfortable, we take the necessary steps to reduce the stressor. However, some people are subjected to such high levels of stress or to such long periods of stress that they develop severe physical or psychological symptoms. Let us examine some of these symptoms. First, we will take a quick look at bodily reactions and then examine some behavioral reactions.

Psychological Factors Affecting Physical Condition. Few college students need to be told that stress can make people physically sick. Anyone who has had to prepare for a big exam knows that stress can lead to a loss of appetite, insomnia (the inability to fall asleep), and tension headaches. These are real physical illnesses in which stress is a contributing factor. The list of disorders is long and includes a surprising range of illnesses.

One of the most common disorders associated with stress is the *peptic ulcer*. Ulcers are lesions or holes that develop in the stomach or upper part of the small intestine. These holes are caused by the oversecretion of stomach acid, which literally eats through the lining of the digestive tract. Ulcers are often referred to as the "executive's disease," and it was once thought that the stress associated with making decisions was responsible for the oversecretion of the acid. However, further research indicates that control and decision making are not responsible for ulcers (Weiss, 1972). Rather, it is the pressure arising from the need to respond quickly over an extended period of time, and the uncertainty associated with choosing an effective response, that cause ulcers.

Other disorders include asthma, hypertension (high blood pressure), headaches, and heart disease. For example, one group of researchers found that widowed people are more likely than others to die of heart disease; this is especially true within 6 months of the spouse's death (Stroebe & Stroebe, 1983). Stress has even been related to cancer and the rate of tumor growth (Sklar & Anisman, 1981).

Stress contributes to getting sick in a number of ways. First, because the body must mobilize to deal with the stress, the resistance to diseases is lowered. Second, people may become so preoccupied with or depressed about the stress that they fail to notice or deal with symptoms of impending illness. We do not know exactly what factors determine the specific illness a person will suffer. That is, why does one person get colds when distressed while another suffers from ulcers? Part of the answer may involve constitutional weakness. That is, people may be born with or develop a weak spot in their stomach. When these people encounter stress, the symptoms find expression in the already weak stomach and an ulcer appears. Others may have a high susceptibility to colds, and, when stress lowers their immunity, they catch colds. Another factor may be the environment or culture in which we live. Certain bacteria or viruses are more common in some environments than in others, and lowered immunity will allow these more common bacteria to take control of our systems, giving rise to specific diseases.

Coronary-Prone Behavior Pattern. Stress not only causes changes within our bodies, it also may move us to action. Some people seek to "get away from it all" when they feel the pressure building. These people may take a relaxing drive or engage in a hobby to relieve the pressure. Others may turn to alcohol or drugs when they feel pressured. However, some people may respond to stress by becoming competitive and hostile. These people often feel increasing time pressures to "get the job done" and they feel overwhelmed by external demands. Their desires for achievement increase and their actions and speech patterns become more animated and abrupt. These individuals give the impression of someone running on "nervous energy" with the single goal of achievement (Friedman & Rosenman, 1974). This constellation of behaviors was labeled **Type A behavior** or *coronary-prone behavior pattern* because it was believed that people who behaved this way were more likely to become the victims of heart attacks than those who did not respond to stress in this manner.

Initial research tended to support this position (Matthews & Carra, 1982). However, more recent research failed to find a direct relationship between Type A behavior and coronary heart disease. Instead, the research found that certain Type A behaviors may yield positive outcomes, while other Type A behaviors are related to illness. One approach has identified two components of Type A behavior (Spence, Pred, & Helmreich, 1989; Bluen, Barling, & Burns, 1990). One component, labeled Achievement Strivings (AS), involves taking one's work seriously, being active, and working hard. High scores on the AS dimension are associated with positive performance. For example, students who scored high on AS tended to have higher grade point averages than those who scored low (Spence, Helmreich, & Pred, 1987). And AS was significantly related to academic performance by social psychologists; those who scored high on AS had a higher number of publications in professional journals than those who scored low (Helmreich, Spence, & Pred, 1988). AS behavior was not associated with illness.

However, the second component of Type A behavior was related to illness. Impatience-Irritability (II) reflects intolerance, anger, hostility, and an obsession with time. People who score high on II tend to experience illness and depression (Bluen, Barling, & Burns, 1990). One study involving salespersons also found that people high on the II scale were more dissatisfied with their jobs and did not perform better than other salespersons.

It seems, therefore, that illness may be related to certain Type A behavior, those involving anger and impatience, but not to a strong desire to perform well.

Learned Helplessness. The issue of control has been linked to another type of behavior that can have negative health consequences. In this case, however, the response involves "giving up" and *not* attempting to control the environment.

If people make repeated attempts to control stressful events in their environment and fail, they may give up trying to gain control, even in situations where control is possible. In a sense, these people have learned to respond as if they were helpless pawns; they have developed a state of learned helplessness (see Chapter 6, Seligman, 1975). Apathy, depression, reduced intellectual abilities, and negative emotions are associated with learned helplessness.

The effects of learned helplessness have been illustrated by one researcher (Hiroto, 1974). In this experiment, subjects in one condition were forced to listen to noise, and they were unable to escape it. In another condition, the subjects could stop the loud noise by pushing a button, and in a third condition, the subjects were not exposed to any noise. In the next phase of the study, all subjects were given a finger shuttle box. The box was designed so that loud noise was played when the subject's finger was on one side of the box. A subject could stop the noise by moving

Type A behavior
Coronary-prone behavior pattern; a response to stress that involves becoming more active, more competitive, more "driven."

Faced with an environment that is unpredictable and uncontrollable, people may learn helplessness and simply give up trying to influence events. Large confusing airports with unpredictable flight schedules may make some people feel helpless.

one finger to the other side of the box. Subjects who had been in the escapable or no-noise conditions in the first phase of the study quickly learned to control the noise. However, subjects who could not escape noise in the first phase of the experiment did not learn to control it in the second phase.

An unfortunate aspect of learned helplessness is that it tends to feed upon itself; that is, people who stop trying because they feel they can't control their stressful environment may never learn to exercise control in situations where control is possible. In addition, the learned helplessness response may generalize from one situation to another (see Chapter 1). For example, one group of investigators found that students who were unable to control social interactions in their dormitories showed a pattern of learned helplessness in a laboratory setting (Baum & Valins, 1977).

Coping Effectively with Stress

Emmett Kelly longed to do the trapeze act in the circus. He thought his chance had come when he was offered a job in Howe's Great London Circus. Unfortunately he found that the job involved being a clown, not swinging from the high trapeze. The situation created a great deal of stress for Kelly. How could he effectively cope with the disappointment?

Cognitive Responses

Reappraisal.   Not getting the job that he wanted was disappointing and stressful, but the degree of stress would have increased greatly if Kelly interpreted this failure to mean that he would never do the trapeze act. As we pointed out earlier, the amount of stress experienced is as much a function of the way we interpret the event as it is due to the event itself. Thus, Kelly could have reduced his stress by reexamining the situation and identifying the positive aspects of it. For example, he would not be

Stress may be reduced by increasing people's feelings of self-efficacy, their judgment of their ability to cope. Training in ways to deal with stress may increase self-efficacy.

doing a trapeze act, but he would be working with the circus. Being a clown would offer him the chance to be the center of the audience's attention, and he could dazzle them in a different way. By viewing his situation in this manner he could turn defeat into a minor victory and reduce the sting of his disappointment. Note that reappraisal does not involve denying the situation or the disappointment; it does involve looking at the good as well as the bad. Taking this a step further, investigators report that maintaining a sense of humor and perceiving the lighter side of stressful situations reduces the negative reactions to stress (Nezu, Nezu, & Blissett, 1988).

The effectiveness of reappraisal was demonstrated in a study of patients undergoing surgery (Langer et al., 1975). In many cases, patients tend to look at the gloomy side of surgery; they think of the pain, the risks, and the inconvenience of a hospital stay. One group of patients was trained to look at the good and bad aspects of surgery. They acknowledged the pain and risk, but they focused also on how the operation would improve their health and give them the opportunity to participate in new activities. In addition, the patients were trained to consider that the hospital stay would give them the opportunity to rest and get away from daily stress. Patients who were taught this approach experienced less pain and requested less pain medication than patients who did not go through the reappraisal technique.

Belief in Self-Efficacy. Reappraisal involves the way we interpret a situation. In addition, the way we view ourselves and our self-esteem have been identified as influencing how well we cope with stress (Hobfoll & Lieberman, 1987). Feeling that we are not in control and cannot handle the situation is very stressful in itself. Bandura (1982) focused on this aspect of stress and suggested that stress could be reduced by increasing people's **belief in their self-efficacy,** their judgment of their ability to cope with situations (see Chapter 15). Bandura suggests that people's reaction to stressful situations and, indeed, the amount of stress they experience is directly related to their beliefs about the effectiveness of their actions. Extending this theory, Litt (1988) found that people high in self-efficacy were better able to use control than people low in self-efficacy. It seems that if we have self-confidence in our ability, we will exercise control over our environment; however, if we have low self-confidence, we will not attempt to control our fate, even when control is available.

According to this theory, we develop beliefs in our self-efficacy through our experiences. Hence, people can be trained to handle situations that were once out of their control. There are many ways that this training can occur. Bandura found that he could reduce people's fear of snakes by having them successfully perform a number of unrelated tasks. Other research suggests that regular exercise may be beneficial in reducing stress (Davidson & Schwartz, 1977). There are a number of possible reasons, both physiological and psychological, for this effect. One possibility is that exercise may allow us to gain mastery over our environment and increase our belief in our self-efficacy.

Informational Responses

Kelly's job offer to be a clown was stressful not only because it was not the position he wanted, but also because he knew nothing about being a clown. The uncertainty caused by his lack of information contributed to the stress of the situation. In a similar way, uncertainty may contribute to the stress people experience upon learning that they have a physical ailment such as cancer (Taylor et al., 1984). Imagine that you have just been told that you have cancer; a million thoughts probably run through your mind including the gruesome stories that you have heard about the treatment

Self-efficacy belief
Belief that the individual can cope well with stress and change, based on personal abilities and available resources.

OPTIMAL SUPPORT: Matching Type of Social Support to Type of Stress

Social support, or a network of people upon whom you can rely in time of crisis, plays a major role in coping with stress. Psychologists recognize that all stressors are not the same, and that social support comes in many types. It seems only logical, then, that certain types of support are most effective for dealing with certain types of stress. In fact, the research suggests that this is true.

In order to understand this effect, let's begin by examining stress more closely. We can identify four dimensions of stress. Stress may vary along a *desirability* dimension; it can be either positive (i.e., job promotion) or negative (i.e., illness). Stress can be *controllable* or uncontrollable. The *duration* of stress may vary. And finally, stress may affect different *life domains*, such as relationships, achievements, personal assets, or social roles (Cutrona & Russell, 1990).

Now let's consider the types of social support that would be most beneficial to people suffering these different types of stress. Cutrona (1990) suggests that support involving material resources or information will be most valuable to people dealing with controllable stress. On the other hand, emotional support will be most helpful to those facing uncontrollable stress. Looking at life domain, individuals suffering the loss of assets

will be most benefited by tangible support, while those suffering stress related to their achievement (job promotion or demotion) will benefit from emotional support that bolsters their self-worth. When the stress involves the loss of a relationship, support that offers attachment or intimate interaction will be most welcome. Finally, when the stress involves a change in social roles, support networks that allow social participation in a group will be most helpful. According to this approach, the duration and desirability of stress influence the amount and duration of support that are needed. As you can see, there is nothing particularly startling about this view of social support. However, it does make the important point that we should attempt to match our support to the needs of others.

How does social support help people cope? In some cases, the answer to this question is clear. A person who loses his or her job may get direct benefits from money, clothing, or other tangible aid. However, in many other cases, the support works by building the individual's feelings of self-efficacy. One study that examined women's responses after undergoing an abortion found that emotional support helped build up their self-esteem and gave them the feeling that

they could cope with the stress they were suffering (Major et al., 1990). This, in turn, enhanced their adjustment. Social support may also work directly on the immune system. One study found that social support of spouses of cancer patients resulted in increased functioning of the immune system, making these spouses less prone to illness themselves (Baron et al., 1990). Thus, social support seems to affect a variety of psychological and physical systems that aid people in coping with stress.

We cannot conclude this discussion without acknowledging the social support available from pets, especially dogs. An interesting study of Medicare enrollees found that people with pets made fewer visits to their doctor and felt less stressed than people without pets (Siegel, 1990). Many of these subjects reported that their pet provided them with companionship, gave them a sense of being needed, and increased their feelings of control. But it was dogs who provided strong social support; other pets did not. Other health-related benefits from dog ownership were that people reported spending more time outdoors with their dog, and they talked to their pet more frequently than did owners of other pets. Indeed, social support can come in different forms, and from a variety of sources.

of cancer and the fear that you may soon die. These thoughts, which may well be based on your ignorance of cancer, will greatly increase your stress and may actually interfere with effective treatment of your condition. One study found that patients who believed their condition was incurable delayed treatment two and a half times longer than people with the same disease who believed it was curable (Safer et al., 1979).

Seeking out information and gaining a better understanding of the stressful situation can be an important step in coping with stress. Seeking out information not only helps people make an accurate appraisal of the situation, but it also can help them develop an effective response to cope with their stress.

Behavioral Responses

Exercise, rest, and good diet are behavioral responses that help the body cope with stressors. Relaxation techniques such as meditation or yoga are aimed at counteracting the body's physiological reaction to stress. In Chapter

Social support
Network of people upon whom you can rely in time of crisis.

15 we will discuss biofeedback, which teaches people to relax by giving them feedback about the arousal levels of their bodies. The assumption is that we are generally unaware of such physiological activities as our heart rate and blood pressure. In order to learn to reduce the levels of these activities we must first be able to monitor them. Biofeedback equipment does just this; it monitors our physiological activity and gives us feedback about it. Many businesses have introduced stress management programs to help their employees cope with stress. These seminars first teach participants what stress is and how to identify stressors. Next, participants are taught behavioral techniques for coping with stress. Finally, they practice these techniques under controlled conditions until they become adept at coping with stress (Taylor, 1986).

On a broader level, being part of a social network and knowing that we can rely on others to help us in time of crisis plays a major role in coping with stress. Interestingly, social support helps us deal with stress in two ways. Knowing that we have the support of others reduces the range of situations under which we will experience stress and the amount of stress we suffer; in other words, support acts as a stress buffer. Second, others can provide aid when we experience stress; this tends to reduce the duration of stress (Sarason & Sarason, 1987). For example, after a natural disaster such as a flood or tornado, friends may feed, clothe, and give shelter to people whose homes have been destroyed.

Social support can take many forms including (1) physical assistance; (2) material aid; (3) intimate interactions; (4) guidance or providing information; (5) feedback, such as helping one understand problems; and (6) social participation, such as cheering someone up. One individual may offer a number of types of social support, or a person may seek different types of social support from different people. For example, a person may rely on his or her parents for material aid, a doctor for guidance, and a friend for feedback and social participation. In a recent study, it was found that the companionship component of support was most important in helping people cope with minor life stress (Rook, 1987). The material and emotional aspects of support only played a role in helping people deal with major life stress.

Summary

1. **Emotions** are affective states (or feelings) that are accompanied by physiological changes that often influence behavior. **Moods** are general feeling states that are less intense and less specific than emotions but are longer lasting.

2. Charles Darwin was one of the first investigators to carefully examine emotions. He believed that emotions have an adaptive function and that the expression of emotion signaled an intent to act and prepared the individual or animal to act. Since Darwin, theories of emotion have taken a different focus almost every 20 years. Early theories were concerned with the physical effects accompanying emotions. Next, theories focused on the relationship between emotions and drive. The next wave found cognition theories of emotion, and more recently theories have focused on the relationship between emotional expression (especially facial expression) and the experience of emotions.

3. Several viewpoints have contributed to the present theories of emotions. James and Lange argue that external events cause physiological changes in people and that it is the perception of these changes that leads to emotions.

4. Cannon, however, showed that emotions can occur in the absence of physiological responses. Cannon and Bard propose that emotions and physiological changes occur together.

5. Schachter and Singer introduced cognitions as most important in labeling emotions. They suggest that once people are physiologically aroused, they will search for environmental cues to explain their arousal and label their emotion.

6. Another theory assumes that the way we interpret a situation influences the emotion we experience. In other words, interpretation or **appraisal** comes before emotion.

7. According to the somatic theory, the somatic nervous system, which controls many of our muscles, sends messages to the brain when muscles respond to an event. Thus, emotions are the result of how we interpret our responses. This theory pays particular attention to the role of facial muscles in determining our emotions.

8. The **opponent-process theory of emotion** suggests that each state or emotion that we experience triggers a force to experience the opposite state. The effect is to dampen the intensity and length of time that we experience any emotional state, which may be very adaptive.

9. Emotions can be expressed without words. Facial expressions and body language are effective methods of communicating emotions. **Personal space** behavior not only communicates feelings but also determines the other nonverbal channels that can be used to communicate feelings. It has been suggested that facial expression communicates the quality of emotion, whereas body language communicates the strength of the emotion.

10. Darwin argued that the expression of emotion is innate and has survival value by communicating feeling and preparing a person to act. While there is evidence suggesting that some of our emotional expression may be innately determined, findings also suggest that learning effects both our expression and ability to interpret emotional cues.

11. Emotions affect how easily persuaded we are. They also affect judgment, memory, and behavior.

12. Two specific emotions have been examined in this chapter. The first, **fear,** which may be either inborn or learned, serves two important functions. Fear causes us to avoid objects and situations that may be dangerous and, when danger is encountered, prepares the body for action.

13. Investigators have only recently begun to study love. Overall, **love** is characterized as a personalized joy that involves intimacy, passion, commitment, and sacrifice. The quality and intensity of emotion that one experiences in love varies over time. It has been suggested that people must learn to love and that our ability to love is affected by our past experiences.

14. **Stress** is not an emotion but is the process by which the individual responds to environmental and psychological events that are perceived as threatening or challenging. **Stressors** are the events that cause stress. Several factors that affect the amount of stress experienced in a situation are change, unpredictability, and lack of control. Change, whether positive or negative, may be stressful; however, the stress is lessened if we are able to predict and control the situation. **Health psychology** examines the role of psychological factors in influencing illness and the implications of this relationship for health policy.

15. Another element of stress is **conflict,** which is a state that occurs when a person is motivated to choose between two or more mutually exclusive goals or courses of action. Some of the various types of conflict are approach-approach, avoidance-avoidance, approach-avoidance, and double approach-avoidance.

16. When people are exposed to a great deal of stress, they may develop real physical disorders, ranging from insomnia and headaches to ulcers and heart attacks.

17. When people repeatedly find themselves unable to control a stressful situation, they may develop a state of **learned helplessness** in which they become apathetic, depressed, and do not make any effort to control their environment.

18. There are three major categories of coping responses: cognitive, informational, and behavioral. Cognitive coping involves reappraisal, raising self-esteem, and developing a belief in self-efficacy. Seeking out information and gaining a better understanding of the stressful situation can be an important step in coping with stress. Behavioral techniques include exercise, rest, good diet, relaxation efforts, and **social support.** To achieve maximum benefit from the support, it is important that the type of social support be matched to the type of stess the individual in suffering.

KEY TERMS

appraisal theory	hassles	opponent-process theory of emotion	stress
burnout	health psychology	personal space	Type A behavior
conflict	kinesis	polygraph	voice stress analyzer
emotions	moods	self-efficacy belief	Yerkes-Dodson principle
fear	nonverbal leakage	social support	

STUDIES POINT TO POWER OF NONVERBAL SIGNALS

The nonverbal messages people send, with a look, a gesture, a tone of voice, are far more pervasive and important in the workaday world than have been generally realized, researchers are finding. But they are concluding too, that these messages are more complex and subtle than the popular accounts of "body language" that have appeared in recent years have indicated.

Such covert cues, the new data show, have a strong impact in key relationships such as those between judge and jury, physician and patient, or teacher and student.

Indeed, the tacit communication of expectations between one person and another are found, in many cases, to make all the difference between success or failure in various kinds of endeavors.

How a judge gives his instructions to a jury was perceived to double the likelihood that the jury would deliver a verdict of guilty or not guilty—even when on the surface the judge's demeanor seemed perfectly impartial. A doctor's attitude affected the course of a patient's disease; a teacher's attitude influenced the intellectual progress of students.

And findings of the new research are likely to have repercussions in areas of life where it is crucial to avoid bias, even the most subtle. For example, according to some legal experts, one consequence of the study of research on judges, if it is borne out by further research, may be to provide a more precise basis for showing when a judge may have silently biased a trial.

The judicial study, reported in the November 1986 issue of *The Stanford Law Review*, is believed to be one of the first scientific tests of the courtroom lore that the judge's attitudes, even if never openly expressed, are often crucial to a trial's outcome. One striking finding concerned trials in which the judge knew that the defendant had a record of previous felonies, a fact that a jury, by law, is not allowed to know unless the defendant takes the stand. When the judges were aware of past felonies, the Stanford study found, their final instructions to juries were lacking in warmth, tolerance, patience and competence.

The juries in these cases said they were unaware of any bias on the part of the judges, yet their verdicts were twice as likely to be "guilty" than in cases in which the charges were as serious but defendants had no record of felonies.

When videotapes were analyzed by independent raters, they found that the judges' tone of voice, rather than anything in their words or body movements, communicated the strongest, most negative messages.

"Judges can't come out and say, 'This defendant is guilty,'" said Peter Blanck, who did the study. "But they may say it subtly, nonverbally—even if that message is inadvertent."

A judge's charge to a jury is, by law, supposed to be free of such bias, and Dr. Blanck, a social psychologist who is a Stanford law student, said he believed that most of the biasing elements he found in his research were unintended. He sees his study as a first step in helping judges to neutralize their hidden messages, as well as, one day, providing lawyers with a new basis for challenging verdicts.

"If judges became sensitized to the problem, they could learn to be more impartial in their demeanor," Dr. Blanck said.

Dr. Blanck's research is one of a wave of studies assessing the subtle influence. The whole line of research owes much to the work of Robert Rosenthal of Harvard University, with whom Dr. Blanck did graduate studies before going to Stanford Law School, where he became head of The Law Review.

"Rosenthal is the pioneer in the field," said Randolph Lee, a clinical psychologist at Trinity College in Hartford, who edits *The Journal of Nonverbal Behavior*. "He was the first to find a way to measure how people send and receive nonverbal messages."

A physician's rapport with his patients, for instance, depends to a great extent on his body language, according to Dr. Rosenthal's recent studies, done with Jinni Harrigan, a psychologist at the University of Cincinnati Medical School. The research is described in *Nonverbal Communication in the Clinical Context*, published in 1986 by the Pennsylvania State Press.

The studies found that physicians who were rated as having the best rapport sat leaning toward the patient, with arms and legs uncrossed, and nodding as they talked to patients. Another sign of rapport was looking the patient in the eye from time to time, but not staring. The net effect seemed to communicate a desire to be attentive and intimate.

The meaning of a given posture or movement, Dr. Rosenthal cautions, is highly specific to a given situation. Thus, a physician who leaned back in his chair, which in many social settings would be a sign of feeling relaxed, could be seen by a patient as signaling a lack of interest.

Dr. Rosenthal, like many other researchers, is cautious in attempting to derive anything like a vocabulary of nonverbal messages from the research results. The field, he says, has suffered from popularizers who presumed to tell people exactly which movement or posture would communicate what message—a precision that the scientific data do not yet allow and may never, since much of what is communicated nonverbally means one thing within a given context and quite another in different situations.

"It's too simplisitic to say that, for example, a physician is sending a message of rapport when he nods or tilts forward," said Dr. Rosenthal, "When you freeze the moment and extract one part of what is going on from it, you lose the richness of the phenomenon. When people try to equate a specific cue with a given message, it gets too mechanical."

Nonetheless, it is clearly important for everyone to know that, in one way or another, they are in almost constant nonverbal communication with others.

Tone of voice was a potentially damaging covert bias found in one study of psychotherapists with their patients. When the therapists talked to resident patients at a large private hospital, their tone was much more hostile and anxious than when they spoke with patients who lived outside the hospital.

The message received by the inpatients was comparatively pessimistic. Often it was something like, "You don't think I'm going to get that well, because I'm an inpatient," in the view of Dr. Blanck, who was one of the researchers. Moreover, when the psychotherapists talked to their supervisors about their patients, the tone of voice they used reflected the tones used with the patients.

"The nonverbal messages during therapy can be more important than what is said," Dr. Lee said.

In another setting, a study of job interviews found that the more often an interviewer touched his foot, the more likely that his hiring decision was favorable. While at first glance that result may seem curious, an explanation is provided by Dr. Rosenthal and Shelly Goldberg, a student at Harvard with whom he did the study.

When people are feeling ill at ease, as is often the case during such interviews, they tend to sit stiffly and shift very little. One possibility, according to Dr. Rosenthal and Miss Goldberg, is that once an interviewer makes a favorable hiring decision, he becomes more relaxed and shifts position more, making it more likely that he will touch his foot, which is otherwise difficult to reach if he is sitting in a more formal position. The study is published in *The Journal of Nonverbal Behavior*.

In the 1950's, while doing dissertation research, Dr. Rosenthal discovered that, somehow, he had influenced the volunteers in his study to show the effect he expected even before he performed his experiment.

Dismayed, Dr. Rosenthal began to investigate the possibility that psychologists running experiments were on the power of their expectations alone, inadvertently leading the volunteers in their studies to show the predicted results. When, for example, Dr. Rosenthal told half of a group of testers that they were to duplicate a "well-established"

result that people would judge photographs of faces positively, those experimenters found exactly that. But when the other half of the testers were told that the "well-established" result was that the judgments would be negative, that was what they found. In short, the testers' expectations swayed the results.

The same effect, Dr. Rosenthal discovered, even held when the testers were measuring how quickly rats were able to learn to find their way through a maze. Those testers who were told their rats were quick learners proved to have rats that learned the maze quicker than rats whose testers expected them to be slow. The rats in both groups were identical at the outset, but the smart ones were handled with greater care. Taking the principle that expectations become self-fulfilling one step further, in 1964 Dr. Rosenthal performed his famous "Pygmalion" experiment, in which teachers were given the names of children in their school who, supposedly, had been identified by a new test as being on the verge of blooming intellectually. The children had actually been chosen randomly.

At the end of the school year, though, the selected children showed gains in intellectual abilities compared with the other children. Moreover, teachers perceived the children in the "bloomer" group as more appealing, adjusted and affectionate than the others.

The Pygmalion study evoked heated objections from many educational psychologists. But by 1978 Dr. Rosenthal was able to review 345 studies showing the power of the Pygmalion effect.

Many of the Pygmalion studies, he found, pointed to subtle factors. Teachers, for example, became especially warm toward the "special"

students, gave more specific reactions to how ther performed, taught them more difficult material and gave them greater opportunities to respond than with the other students.

"The same factors operate with bosses and their employees, therapists and their clients, or parents and children," said Dr. Rosenthal. "The more warmth and the more positive the expectations that are communicated, the better the person who receives those messages will do."

To better understand the nuances of how such messages are sent and received, Dr. Rosenthal and his colleagues designed a special videotape test, called the PONS, or Profile of Nonverbal Sensitivity. The test portrays people in a range of scenes, including nagging a child, seducing someone, and praying. The test allows the analysis of the different aspects of nonverbal messages, including facial expressions, body movements and tone of voice.

The PONS test has been used now in hundreds of studies, with thousands of people in twenty countries. The data show that women, by and large, are better than men at reading nonverbal cues and at expressing their feelings nonverbally, reports Judith Hall, a psychologist at Harvard Medical School.

One implication of the new research, Dr. Rosenthal and others believe, is for physicians' behavior with their patients. "When a physician gives up on a patient, that patient gets the most negative of nonverbal messages—too bad you're dying—which makes the patient give up hope," said Dr. Rosenthal.

Personality: Theories and Assessment

13

J ust as David and Goliath dueled before anxious onlookers on the field, every four years in the United States two or more warriors march out from the ranks of their political parties to fight the battle for the presidency. The candidates typically hurl challenges and charges at each other as they try to convince voters that they are the best choice and that their opponent is unfit for office. This ritual battle took place in 1984 when Ronald Reagan and Walter Mondale sparred to gain the voter's favor. The campaign was like most that had preceded it, with one rather frightening exception. Faintly hidden in many lines of the campaign rhetoric was the portrayal of President Reagan as a man who not only might lead the nation into war, but who might order the use of nuclear weapons. Most voters obviously dismissed this portrayal; Reagan was elected by a landslide, and in December 1987, he signed a treaty with the Soviet Union aimed at reducing the number of nuclear warheads deployed by the U.S. and the Soviet Union.

Although the voters in the 1984 election reassured themselves about the utter folly of the use of nuclear weapons, they would only have had to turn back the pages of the history book thirty-nine years to find the one person who did order the use of nuclear weapons. Who was this person who added a terrible note of reality to our present day concern about nuclear war? This man had just sat down to eat lunch with a group of officers on the presidential yacht in 1945 when he was handed a telegram informing him that his order to drop an atomic bomb on Hiroshima had been completed. The man nodded in deep thought as he carefully read and reread the telegram. And, three days later, President Harry S. Truman would make the decision to drop a second atomic bomb on Nagasaki. The destruction caused by the two bombs was tremendous; over 100,000 people died immediately, and countless others were afflicted with radiation sickness that would slowly and painfully end their lives.

Was the use of the atomic bomb necessary? This question is still debated today. Truman, however, never took part in these debates. He felt that he had made the best decision possible based on the facts available at the time. He would not labor over a past decision or become involved in second guessing.

Truman held a similar attitude about the other decisions he made during his eight years as president. Although his other decisions were not as momentous as the one involving "the bomb," many of them still play a dramatic role in our lives today. Truman's decisions divided Europe into democratic and communist blocs, entered the United States into the Korean War, and made the United States a charter member of the United Nations.

Many historians rate Truman among the greatest presidents of the United States. Ironically, Truman probably never would have been president except for the death of Franklin D. Roosevelt; Truman was a rather obscure politician before being named Roosevelt's vice president. He had one of the most humble and least glamorous backgrounds of all our modern presidents. In fact, only four years before Truman became president, the banks foreclosed on his mother's farm because there was no money to make the mortgage payments.

Harry S. Truman was born on a small farm outside of Independence, Missouri, in 1876. His parents could not agree on a middle name for their first child, so they simply gave him the initial "S." Harry's father was a farmer who had the reputation of being the most honest man in Jackson County. The elder Truman, a small, neatly dressed man, was a fighter: ". . . he could whip anybody up to two hundred [pounds] if they got in his way" (Miller, 1973, p. 66). Harry's mother was a strong woman who paid close attention to her children's education. She was very strict and insisted on obedience and honesty.

As a child, Truman received a great deal of warmth and affection from his parents. At the age when other boys were becoming interested in sports, Harry developed a fondness for books. He read the Bible twice before he began school. Truman states, "I guess I read the Bible because the type was large, but then it developed about the time I was six years old, it was then that we first noticed it, that I had flat eyeballs" (Miller, 1973, p. 52). Harry's eyesight was so bad that he had to be fitted with thick eyeglasses.

The glasses were a major influence on his life. They set him apart from the other kids, and they restricted his activities. His poor eyesight also brought him closer to his mother. She encouraged his reading and, later, his interest in the piano. "Harry was a sort of mamma's boy, oddly more like a little old woman than a sissy child. He helped in the kitchen with neither reluctance nor boyish clumsiness" (Daniels, 1950, p. 50).

Although he dreamed of becoming a concert pianist, economic considerations forced him to change his plans. After he graduated from high school, Truman took a job as timekeeper for a railroad construction crew. This job presented quite a picture of contrast as the small, owlish-looking young man worked with the burly construction workers. After working at the railroad, Truman went to Kansas City, where he worked as a bank clerk and joined a field artillery unit. He became a captain and was sent to France to command Battery D during World War I. The battery, known as "Dizzy D," had gone through four commanding officers, none of whom could control the outfit. Truman took charge of the unit and won the trust of his men.

On his return from the war, Truman married his childhood sweetheart, Bess. He had known her since he was 4 years old. Truman had always been painfully shy around women; this shyness, combined with the feeling that Bess deserved more, kept him from proposing until he was 35 years old. Bess was much the opposite of her new husband. She came from a well-to-do family and was outgoing.

After the war, Truman opened a clothing store with a war buddy, but the business went bankrupt. Soon after the store closed, Mike Pendergast persuaded Truman to run for a county judge post. The Pendergast family headed a strong political machine in Missouri; with their help Truman was elected county judge. One of his major jobs

was to oversee the county road system. The previous judges had been corrupt, taken bribes, and given contracts to political friends. Truman attacked the job with a zeal and honesty that surprised even the Pendergasts.

In 1934 the Missouri Democratic party, headed by the Pendergasts, ran Truman for United States senator. He won the election and went to Washington, D.C. He was very self conscious about not having a college education and became a champion of the "common man." He gave a stirring criticism of big business on the floor of the Senate in 1937. "One of the difficulties as I see it is that we worship money instead of honor. A billionaire in our estimation is much greater in the eyes of the people than the public servant who works for the public interest. It makes no difference if the billionaire rode to wealth on the sweat of little children and the blood of unpaid labor . . ." (Miller, 1973, p. 152). Truman's work earned him the reputation of being an honest politician. However, he was a modest man who never boasted of his power and accomplishments. Therefore, Truman was surprised to learn that he had been chosen to be Franklin D. Roosevelt's running mate in 1944. Eighty-two days after Roosevelt was elected to his fourth term, he died, and Truman became the thirty-third president of the United States. It has often been argued that power has a way of corrupting those who hold it, but Truman proved to be an exception to this rule.

The debates about what type of president Truman was will probably rage on for many years to come. Eric Sevareid, the news broadcaster, expressed the opinion of many. "A man's character is his fate, said the ancient Greeks. Chance, in good part, took Harry Truman to the presidency, but it was his character that kept him there and determined his historical fate. He is, without any doubt, destined to live in the books as one of the strongest and most decisive of the American Presidents."

After completing this chapter, you should be able to:

Define the term "personality" and list the various approaches to the study of personality.

Discuss Freud's psychoanalytic theory; distinguish between the id, ego and superego, and describe Freud's stages of personality development.

Explain the focus of humanistic theory with particular attention to the theories of Maslow and Rogers.

Contrast the learning theories of personality.

Compare and contrast the psychoanalytic, humanistic, and learning theories of personality.

Contrast type and trait approaches to personality and discuss the advantages and disadvantages of each approach.

Define personality assessment and discuss the requirements for a good personality test.

Describe the tests used to assess personality.

Personality Defined

". . . but it was his *character* that kept him there and determined his historical fate." With this statement Eric Sevareid echoed a sentiment of the ancient Greeks that character is destiny. While many of us may feel that such a claim is too bold, it does seem reasonable to believe that one's character or personality determines, if not one's destiny, then at least one's day-to-day behavior. What could be more obvious? Honest people behave in honest ways. Extroverts are outgoing. Pessimists always expect the worst. Surely knowing someone's personality *can* help us explain and maybe even predict that person's behavior. Or can it? This question is at the heart of the psychologist's interest in personality. For as we will see, not all psychologists believe that knowing someone's personality gives an advantage in knowing how that person will behave.

We will return to this issue later in the chapter, but first things first. What do we mean when we refer to someone's character or personality? Think for a minute how you would define your own personality. If you are like most students, your first thought will be that your personality is what makes you different from other people. And if you were asked to describe your personality, you might say that you are friendly, intelligent, somewhat shy, caring, determined, and so forth. Is this what psychologists mean by personality? Well, partly. Personality does consist of traits and dispositions, even thoughts and emotions, that are combined in a way that makes the person unique. But a list of traits is not enough to define personality. Unless that unique set of traits remains stable within the individual over time and across different situations, it makes little sense to suppose that they are a defining aspect of that person's character.

With that in mind, we will define **personality** as the unique set of enduring characteristics and patterns of behavior (including thoughts and emotions) that influence the way a person adjusts to his or her environment. The goal, then, of personality psychologists (sometimes called *personologists*)

Personality
Unique set of enduring characteristics and patterns of behavior (including thoughts and emotions) that influence the way a person adjusts to his or her environment.

is not only to identify the commonalities shared by all human beings, but also to explain the differences among them.

The goal of personality psychology is an ambitious one because it addresses the kinds of questions that are most central to an understanding of human behavior. What are people like? How did they get that way? How is one's personality reflected in one's behavior? It should be noted that no single theory of personality has emerged as the "right" approach. You probably should fight the temptation to try to choose the "best" one because each theory offers new insights into human behavior.

Freud's Psychoanalytic Theory

At the beginning of the twentieth century, Sigmund Freud shocked the sensitivities of Victorian society and aroused the interest of the intellectually curious with his *psychoanalytic theory of personality*. This theory is one of the most comprehensive and ambitious theories in psychology, and also one of the most controversial. In fact, there is perhaps no greater testament to the impact of Freud's theory than that even today, nearly 100 years after he introduced it, scholars are still engaged in critical analyses of both the theory and its author.

Sigmund Freud

Sigmund Freud was born in 1856 in Freiburg, Moravia (Czechoslovakia). He studied medicine at the University of Vienna. He was interested in the scientific approach used to study medical problems, and while attending the university, he worked as a laboratory assistant examining the nervous system of animals.

Freud would have been content to continue research in the laboratory, but his plans to marry demanded that he find a position that offered financial security. He therefore began a private medical practice. The turning point in Freud's career came when he was awarded a fellowship to study the treatment of nervous disorders with the famous French neurologist, Jean Charcot. Charcot used hypnosis to treat patients classified as hysterics. These patients suffered from paralysis of limbs or from partial or total loss of sight or hearing. The cause of these symptoms was not physical; the paralysis was the result of psychological stress. Charcot discovered that he could relieve the physical symptoms through hypnotic suggestion.

Free association
Freud's method of having patients express every thought (no matter how unimportant or irrelevant) that came into their minds during the therapy session.

Freud became dissatisfied with hypnosis as a tool because not everyone could be hypnotized. He found, however, that he could uncover the events that were related to the hysterical symptoms by having patients express every thought (no matter how unimportant or irrelevant) that came into their minds during the therapy session. Freud used this method of **free association** to discover the traumatic (painful, emotional, shocking) events that were the root of his patients' problems.

Most of Freud's patients were women from middle- and upper-class Victorian society. As Freud listened to them talk, he noticed a striking similarity in their stories. Many of his patients talked about upsetting events related to sexual experiences in early childhood. The patients talked about strong sexual urges and fantasies that they had experienced as children.

His discussions with patients led Freud to draw two conclusions. First, early childhood is a critical time for the formation of personality. Second, children, indeed even infants, have sexual urges, and much of their behavior is motivated by these urges. This second idea was especially shocking to

Sigmund Freud, founder of psychoanalytic theory.

FREUD'S THEORY OF CHILDHOOD SEXUALITY SHOCKED VICTORIAN SOCIETY

Freud's assertion that repressed sexual desires lay at the core of many of his patients' neurotic behaviors shocked and outraged prudish, straight-laced Victorian society, for which even the word *sex* was dirty and taboo. Freud received his most severe criticism for this aspect of his theory.

It is true that Freud put greater emphasis on the biological motive of sex than on the life instinct or the death instinct (the other two important sources of instinctual demands in his theory). But given the cultural climate, it is easy to see why he felt compelled to stress the role of repressed sexual desires.

Freud saw personality as being shaped by conflict. On the one hand, the individual is driven by self-centered biological wants and needs. On the other hand, the individual feels compelled to follow internalized standards of behavior, standards that reflect society's rules for proper conduct. Clearly, then, the more severe the societal restrictions against expressing one's biological desires, the greater the potential for conflict experienced as anxiety.

Just how severe were Victorian attitudes toward sexual matters, particularly childhood sexual behavior? To answer that question, consider the following excerpt from a book written in 1901 by a noted expert on child-rearing practices (Melendy, 1901):

Teach him that these [sexual] organs are given as a sacred trust, that in maturer years he may be the means of giving life to those who shall live forever. . . .

If the sexual organs are handled it brings too much blood to these parts, and this produces a diseased condition; it also causes disease in other organs of the body, because they are left with a less amount of blood than they ought to have. The sexual organs, too, are very closely connected with the spine and the brain by means of the nerves, and if they are handled, or if you keep thinking about them, these nerves get excited and become exhausted, and this makes the back ache, the brain heavy and the whole body weak.

It lays the foundation for consumption, paralysis and heart disease. It weakens the memory, makes a boy careless, negligent and listless.

It even makes many lose their minds; others, when grown, commit suicide.

How often mothers see their little boys handling themselves, and let it pass, because they think the boy will outgrow the habit, and do not realize the strong hold it has upon them! I say to you, who love your boys—"Watch!"

Right here I want to relate a fact that came under my observation. In our immediate neighborhood lived an intelligent, good and sensible couple. They had a boy about five years of age who was growing fretful, pale and puny. After trying all other remedies to restore him to vigor of body and mind, they journeyed from place to place hoping to leave the offending cause behind.

I had often suggested to the mother that "self-abuse" might be the cause, but no, she would not have it so, and said, "You must be mistaken, as he has inherited no such tendencies nor has he been taught it by playmates—we have guarded him carefully."

Finally, however, she took up a medical book and made a study of it and, after much thought, said, "I cannot believe it, yet it describes Charlie's case exactly. I will watch."

To her surprise, she found, notwithstanding all her convictions to the contrary, that Charlie was a victim to this loathsome habit.

On going to his bed, after he had gone to sleep, she found his hands still upon the organ, just as they were when he fell asleep. She watched this carefully for a few days, then took him in her confidence and told him of the dreadful evil effects. Finding the habit so firmly fixed, she feared that telling him, at his age, what effect it would have upon his future would not eradicate the evil as soon as she hoped so, after studying the case for a time, she hit upon the following remedy. Although unscientific, literally speaking, it had the desired effect. Feeling that something must be done to stop, and stop at once, the awful habit, she said, "Did you know, Charlie, that if you keep up this habit of 'self-abuse' that a brown spot will come on your abdomen, light brown at first, and grow darker each week until it eats a sore right into your system, and if it keeps on, will eventually kill you?"

After Charlie had gone to sleep, and finding his hands again on the sexual organs, to prove to him the truth of her argument, she took a bottle of "Iodine" and, with the cork, put on the abdomen a quantity sufficient to give it a light brown color, and about the size of a pea. Next night, in bathing him, she discovered the spot, and said, "Look! Already it has come!" The boy cried out in very fear, and promised not to repeat it again.

The next night the mother put on a second application, which made the spot still darker and a trifle sore. Charlie watched the spot as he would a reptile that was lurking about to do his deadly work—and the mother was never again obliged to use the "Iodine." (p. 304).

Such was the punitive, oppressive counsel of one of the leading authorities on child-rearing practices at the time that Freud was formulating his theory of childhood repression. Perhaps Freud did overemphasize the importance of childhood sexuality. But given the Victorian attitudes and sanctions against the natural expression of childhood sexual pleasure we glimpsed in the above excerpt, we can see why Freud felt that sexuality was a primary contributor to psychic conflict.

Victorian sensibilities, and Freud was accused of overemphasizing sexual matters. (See Highlight: "Freud's Theory of Childhood Sexuality Shocked Victorian Society.")

Unconscious Motivation and Defense Mechanisms. In addition to having his patients free-associate, Freud had them report their dreams.

He was convinced that free associations and dreams were vehicles through which people expressed their unacceptable impulses in disguised or altered form. In fact, for Freud, the dreams that his patients actually reported to him were rarely as significant as the underlying, hidden meanings of those dreams. The remembered and reported dream was referred to by Freud as the *manifest content,* and the hidden, underlying meaning of the dream as the *latent content.* The task, then, for the psychoanalyst is to go beyond the manifest content of the dream and interpret the latent content, for it is there that one will get a glimpse of the true desires of the patient. In addition to dreams, hidden desires and impulses can be expressed in altered form through humor, slips of the tongue, and even accidents.

Freud's observations of these phenomena reinforced his belief that much of our behavior is motivated by unconscious desires. He distinguished this unconscious aspect of the mind from two other aspects—conscious and preconscious. What are the contents of these three aspects of mind?

The **conscious mind** consists simply of those things of which we are immediately aware, what we are thinking and perceiving at the moment. The **preconscious mind** includes thoughts and feelings that we are not aware of at the moment, but could bring to awareness if we chose to retrieve them from memory. It is the unconscious aspect of mind, however, that held the greatest fascination for Freud.

The **unconscious** is the "storehouse of unacceptable images, including past events, current impulses, and desires of which one is not aware" (Byrne & Kelley, 1981). The unconscious makes up the largest part of our personality. Impulses are "filed" in the unconscious because people find them painful or threatening. Examples of these impulses might be the sexual desire to possess one's mother or an intense hatred of one's brother or sister. Once these images are *repressed,* or forced into the unconscious, they are removed from our awareness. However, the fact that we are not aware of these images and desires does not mean that they do not influence our behavior. According to Freud, these desires "push" for expression.

The possibility that these unacceptable impulses might find their way into the conscious causes us to experience fear and anxiety (see Chapter 12). The anxiety leads us to use **defense mechanisms** to keep these impulses out of the conscious mind or to disguise the form of their expression. Freud's daughter, Anna, was herself a noted psychoanalyst, and much of what we know about defense mechanisms comes from her work (Freud, 1936/1946).

Conscious mind
According to Freud, this includes whatever the person is perceiving or thinking at the moment.
Preconscious mind
According to Freud, the preconscious is essentially one's memory, including thoughts that people may not be aware of but that they can retrieve from memory.
Unconscious
According to Freud, a storehouse of unacceptable images, including past events, current impulses, and desires of which one is not aware.
Defense mechanisms
Ways of coping with anxiety; an unconscious distortion of reality in order to defend against anxiety. See *displacement; projection; rationalization; reaction formation; repression; sublimation;* and *suppression.*

"Freudian slips" are one way that people express unconscious feelings.

Repression.   Repression has been referred to as the fundamental defense mechanism because it is primarily responsible for keeping the contents of that "storehouse of unacceptable impulses and desires," the unconscious, from breaking into conscious awareness. But repression also refers to the process of motivated forgetting—that is, pushing painful or unpleasant thoughts or memories out of conscious awareness. For example, someone who was sexually abused as a child may have no awareness of that event.

It is possible, however, for repressed thoughts and desires to escape from the unconscious. When this happens, the result is, again, the experience of anxiety. The anxiety calls into play other defense mechanisms, which, rather than push the unacceptable thoughts, emotions, and desires back into the unconscious, function to distort or transform them in order to make them more acceptable. In this way, partial satisfaction of the unconscious desire can be gained while the anxiety is avoided. The defense mechanisms that follow are of this sort.

Rationalization.   This defense mechanism is a widely used strategy that involves the invention of logical or rational reasons to justify unacceptable or embarrassing behavior. For example, a student who fails a psychology course may say that it doesn't matter because psychology isn't an important subject.

Projection.   Projection involves attributing to others the unacceptable wishes, feelings, and impulses that we ourselves are experiencing. An example of this defense mechanism might be the person who avoids hard work as much as possible by viewing his or her co-workers as lazy.

Denial.   Denial seems similar to repression in that it involves a lack of awareness of unacceptable feelings and impulses. There is a subtle difference between these two defense mechanisms, however. Repression keeps our internally motivated, unacceptable thoughts and feelings out of awareness by banishing them to the unconscious. There are occasions, however, when people, events, or circumstances in the external world arouse anxiety by provoking unacceptable or painful feelings or impulses. Denial allows us to avoid this sort of anxiety by simply ignoring the reality of the circumstance. An example of denial would be the devoted mother who ignores the many obvious indications that her son is a drug abuser. Through her "blindness" the mother avoids the anxiety-provoking awareness of her son's unacceptable behavior. If repression can be described as motivated forgetting, then denial can be described as motivated misperceiving.

Reaction Formation.   Reaction formation is a way of distorting and concealing unacceptable feelings by expressing the opposite feeling. This defense mechanism is exemplified by the person who conceals from himself his hatred of his parents by treating them with excessive kindness.

Displacement.   This defense mechanism involves discharging pent-up feelings, often hostility, on a safer target than the one who aroused the emotion. An example of this defense mechanism is the husband who verbally abuses his wife after being frustrated by his boss.

Sublimation.   One final defense mechanism that we will mention is sublimation. Freud was clear that the pervasiveness of unacceptable impulses made the use of defense mechanisms unavoidable. We all use them to one degree or another. The best that we can hope for is that our defense mechanisms will not distort reality too severely or disrupt our social relationships. For Freud, sublimation is the least distorting defense mechanism available to us. Sublimation involves transforming our unacceptable urges into socially acceptable forms of behavior. For example, unacceptable sexual impulses can be sublimated into artistic endeavors, or unacceptable aggressive urges can be sublimated into high-level athletic performances.

As you can see, there are a wide variety of defense mechanisms. It is important to remember that defense mechanisms are not used to hide our true impulses from other people, but rather to hide them from ourselves. Therefore, we are not aware that we are using these defenses, but the particular defenses we use become an enduring part of our personality.

The Structure of Personality

Freud believed that the individual's personality is the scene of a never-ending battle: On one hand there are primitive and unacceptable drives striving for expression, while on the other hand there are forces trying to deny or disguise these impulses. Freud not only viewed the personality as a battlefield, but he also identified the participants in this battle: the id, the ego, and the superego (see Table 13–1).

The Id. Freud believed that each of us has a savage quality at the root of our personality. He labeled this part of the personality the **id.** According to Freud, people are born with two instinctual drives that serve as the basic motivation for all behavior. One, called *Eros*, is the drive for survival. Included in this drive are the needs to eat and drink, to be warm, and above all to engage in sexual activity. The energy force that propels the person to satisfy these drives is called **libido.** The second innate drive, *Thanatos*, is a destructive drive. The aim is to destroy others, but there is also a self-destructive aspect to it. In fact, Freud took the grim position that "the aim of all life is death." This self-destructive impulse is seen not only in suicide, but in the harmful excesses in which so many people engage, such as drinking alcohol, smoking, and overeating. According to Freud, it is the unconscious desire for self-destruction that leads us to drive our automobiles at dangerously fast speeds, to get drunk at parties, and to smoke cigarettes.

The id, like the savage, wants to satisfy these primitive drives in the most direct and immediate way. It is not concerned with reality, logic, or manners. It functions on the **pleasure principle,** which dictates the immediate satisfaction of drives. We are not aware of these drives because the id operates at the unconscious level of our personality.

The Ego. Although each of us may have these primitive desires, it is clear that we could not function long in our social world if we gave free expression to the savage within ourselves. Thus, Freud suggested that at around the age of 6 months the **ego** develops to control the impulses

Id
According to Freud, part of the personality made up of instinctual drives that serve as the basic motivation for all our behavior.
Libido
Energy force that propels people to satisfy the drive for survival (includes eating, drinking, and sexual activity).
Pleasure principle
Immediate satisfaction of drives without regard to reality, logic, or manners; guides the id.
Ego
According to Freud, a second dimension of personality that works to control the impulses of the id; tries to satisfy the desires of the id by dealing with the environment.

Table 13–1
Mental Structure According to Freud

Structure	Consciousness	Contents and Function
Id	Unconscious	Basic impulses (sex and aggression); seeks immediate gratification regardless of consequences; impervious to reason and logic; immediate, irrational, impulsive
Ego	Predominantly conscious	Executive mediating between id impulses and superego inhibitions; tests reality; seeks safety and survival; rational, logical taking account of space and time
Superego	Both conscious and unconscious	Ideals and morals; strives for perfection; observes, dictates, criticizes, and prohibits; imposes limitations on satisfactions; becomes the conscience of the individual

Source: Mischel (1986).

of the id. The ego is the person's view of physical and social reality. It tries to satisfy the id impulses by taking into account the possibilities of reward and punishment that exist in a situation. In other words, it works on the **reality principle.** For example, suppose you are very thirsty and see a nice cold beer sitting on a table in a restaurant. Your id impulses would tell you to grab the beer and drink it. The ego, however, would calculate the possible results of this action, the worst thing being that the 200-pound man at the table will punch you and the bartender will call the police. Thus, the ego would direct you to order and pay for your own beer.

The Superego.   We can view the id as operating on the signal "I want it now." The ego answers this demand by saying, "Let's be realistic and get it in a way that won't cause trouble." These two forces, however, must also deal with the **superego,** which says, "Think. Is it right to want it?" The superego represents our conscience. It includes the moral values of right and wrong that are largely instilled in us by our parents. The superego makes us feel guilty when we have done the wrong thing. As you might imagine, people who are dominated by the superego will be very uptight and self-conscious; they must constantly ask themselves, "Is it right to feel or act this way?" It is also the superego that motivates us to better ourselves and to live up to our ideals. This aspect of the superego is sometimes referred to as the *ego ideal.*

Orally fixated people orient much of their life around their mouth. They may be heavy smokers, constant eaters, or excessive talkers.

The Emergence of Personality

We have set the stage (unconscious, preconscious, and conscious) and introduced the cast of characters (id, ego, and superego). Now we must turn our attention to the play itself. What determines the specific personality that someone will have? Freud believed that the major "battles" of the personality are fought during childhood. Events that occur during childhood mold and form the personality, which then remains basically stable throughout the rest of the person's life. Freud argued that there are certain critical events during childhood; these events occur in a fixed order and in distinct time periods or stages. Because he focused on the expression of the libido, or sexual energy, these became known as *psychosexual stages.* At each stage, the libido seeks an outlet through a different part of the body. According to Freud, if people suffer a traumatic experience or are overprotected in a particular stage, they may become fixated at that stage. The personality will then take on the characteristics of the stage in which the fixation occurred. Let us examine Freud's view of how the personality develops.

Oral Stage.   According to Freud, the infant is born with the general desire for physical pleasure, which quickly becomes focused on the mouth region. This is known as the **oral stage.** The infant satisfies these impulses by eating, sucking, and biting. In addition to satisfying the need for food, these behaviors are also a source of sexual pleasure.

Fixation at this stage can occur in two ways. First, a mother may overindulge her infant's sucking desire, feeding on demand and catering to all his or her wishes. This overindulgence will result in the development of an oral personality characterized by excessive trust, unreasonable optimism, and a strong dependence on others. Second, fixation can also occur at the oral stage if the mother is underindulgent and abruptly weans the infant. The underindulged infant may develop into an aggressive, sadistic person who exploits others for his or her own benefit. Orally fixated people also orient much of their later life around the mouth, engaging in such activities as smoking, excessive eating, talking, or singing.

Reality principle
This is what guides the ego; it tries to satisfy the desires of the id by taking into account the possibilities of reward and punishment that exist in the situation.
Superego
According to Freud, the superego represents our conscience, including the moral values of right and wrong instilled in us by our parents.
Oral stage
Infant is born with general desire for physical pleasure, which is focused in the mouth region; these impulses are satisfied by eating, sucking, and biting. This is a stage of total dependency on the parents.

According to Freud, people's personalities are generally developed by the time they enter the latency stage (around six years old). For this reason, examination of early childhood is most important for determining events that shape personality.

Anal Stage.   During the second and third years, the child enters the **anal stage.** The main focus of pleasure shifts from the mouth to the anal area. During this period children are faced with the trauma of toilet training. A major battle between the child and parents occurs during this stage; the parents try to force the child to control his or her bowels, and the child resists and strives to be independent. The child takes a negative attitude toward the parents and is determined to do just the opposite of what the parents want. Two types of anal personalities can result from fixation during this stage. The *anal retentive* is compulsively neat, stingy, and orderly. The *anal expulsive* is rebellious and very messy.

Phallic Stage.   The **phallic stage** begins around the age of 4. During this stage the child discovers his or her genital organs and delights in masturbation. The trauma of this stage is different for males than it is for females. According to Freud, boys desire a sexual relationship with their mother. This desire, however, is thwarted by the realization that the father already possesses the mother. The little boy becomes fearful that the father will discover his lust and castrate him as punishment. In order to get rid of these fears, the child identifies with and tries to be like his father. This identification with the father helps form the superego, because the child internalizes the father's values. Freud called events occurring to males during the phallic stage the **Oedipus complex,** since they reminded Freud of the Greek play *Oedipus Rex*, in which the hero, Oedipus, kills his father and marries his mother.

If you find it difficult to understand the Oedipus complex, Freud's view of the female's conflict during this stage will stretch your powers of imagination even further. During the phallic stage girls discover that they are biologically inferior to males; to their horror, they find out that they lack a penis. Although girls were sexually attracted to their mothers, they now blame her for this "anatomical inferiority." They envy their father's penis and become attracted to him. The little girl now begins to fantasize about having a male baby by her father; in this way she can deliver an individual into the world who possesses the desired penis. Freud delivered the crowning blow by concluding that because females never experience castration anxiety, they must have inadequate superegos and, hence, cannot

Anal stage
During the second and third years of life, the main focus of pleasure shifts from the mouth to the anal area. A major battle between child and parents occurs during this stage over the issue of toilet training.

Phallic stage
According to psychoanalytic theory begins at the age of four; focus on pleasure is the genital organs. Trauma at this stage is called Oedipus complex for boys, Electra complex for girls.

Oedipus complex
According to Freud, boy desires sexual relationship with mother, but is afraid father will find out and castrate him as punishment. In order to get rid of these fears, boy identifies with and tries to be like father. Identification with father helps form the superego because boy internalizes the father's values.

be as morally strong as males. Some of Freud's followers refer to this situation as the **Electra complex** after a story in Greek mythology in which Electra feels love for her father and induces her brother to kill her mother.

An inadequate resolution of the Oedipus complex leads to a personality that is reckless and self-assured. The phallic-type male overvalues his penis and seeks to prove that he is a "real man"; he has a constant need to sexually conquer women. This individual is also likely to be vain and boastful. The female who becomes fixated at this stage will develop the "castrating female" syndrome. She will strive for superiority over males and may seek out "typically male professions." The castrating female will delight in criticizing and dominating males. As we will see later in this chapter, the Oedipus and Electra complexes are among the most criticized and least empirically supported of Freud's ideas.

Latency Period.   The **latency period** begins during the child's sixth year and lasts until puberty. Freud felt that the individual's personality is generally determined by this time. During this period children lose interest in sex-related activities and focus their energy on other things, such as schoolwork and hobbies. There is also a tendency for children to confine themselves to all-male or all-female groups at this age.

Genital Stage.   The **genital stage** begins at puberty, when sexual tension erupts. If the person has successfully weathered the earlier stages, sexual feelings reemerge, this time focused on seeking a mutually gratifying relationship. However, people who have become fixated at one of the earlier stages will have a great deal of difficulty adjusting to puberty.

Psychoanalytic Theory: An Evaluation

We have covered a lot of ground with psychoanalytic theory. Before evaluating it, let's quickly review how we might use the theory to better understand Truman. As we've seen, Truman was a modest and very honest man. He was excessively neat and paid close attention to even the smallest detail. He did not like people in authority, especially the military. He described generals and admirals as being "like horses with blinders on. They can't see beyond the ends of their noses, most of them" (Miller, 1973, p. 220). Following psychoanalytic theory, we would examine Truman's early childhood to better understand his personality. We would pay particular attention to his relationship with his parents, noting with interest the indulgence of his mother and the strict discipline of his father. We would also look for traumatic events that might have led him to become fixated in one of the stages. We would explain many of Truman's adult characteristics as the result of unconscious desires and fears that were repressed during childhood. We would also argue that Truman was unaware of many of the forces that influenced his behavior.

Does this approach help us to better understand Truman or give us insights into why he developed his particular personality? More generally, we might ask whether or not psychoanalytic theory is useful in understanding human behavior and personality. The theory is so broad and covers so many areas that a definite answer cannot be given. Psychoanalytic theory has greatly influenced the study of human behavior. In fact, Freud is generally identified as the person who has had the greatest impact on psychology. Freud's influence also can be seen in art, in poetry, and in literature. Freud was most influential in the areas of infancy and early childhood concerning the formation of the personality. Freud's emphasis revived the study of early childhood, and in a very real sense, his work served as a foundation for the emergence of developmental psychology (see Chapters 9 and 10). Freud also pointed out that our behavior can be

Electra complex
During the phallic stage, according to Freud, girls discover that they are biologically inferior to boys because they lack a penis. They envy their father's penis and become attracted to him, fantasizing about having a male baby by their father.
Latency period
Lasts from sixth year to puberty. Children lose interest in sex-related activities and focus energy on schoolwork and hobbies, among other things.
Genital stage
Begins at puberty with the start of sexual tension. Basic goals are to marry, raise a family, and become involved in a life's work.

influenced by motives of which we are unaware. Although there is still a great deal of disagreement about how the unconscious works, research has shown that hidden motives can influence us.

Although Freud is clearly a major figure in the study of modern psychology, his theory has been criticized on a number of levels. The broadest criticism concerns whether or not Freud's work is really a theory in the scientific sense. It is difficult, if not impossible, to test many parts of psychoanalytic theory (Balay & Shevrin, 1988). For example, could we test a speculation that Truman's dislike of military officers was motivated by his unconscious hatred for his father? A second criticism is that psychoanalytic theory places too much emphasis on early childhood. It largely ignores the effects of events occurring during adulthood, and it deemphasizes the likelihood of personality change during adulthood. Another broad criticism was raised by some of Freud's very close followers (Alfred Adler, Carl Jung, and Karen Horney). They argued that Freud overemphasized the role of sex in the development of personality. Although guilt and conflict about sexual matters may be an issue that influences the formation of personality, there are many issues that have at least as much, if not more, influence.

In addition to the broad criticisms, a number of questions have been raised about specific parts of the psychoanalytic theory. For example, Freud's view that women are biologically inferior to men and, therefore, doomed to have inadequate superegos was first attacked by Karen Horney (1937). She pointed out that Freud's argument was typical of the male point of view. She argued that women may envy the status that society has given men, but not the penis that men are born with. She also attacked the position that penis envy is the basis for the "castrating female" personality, saying that the drive for power is at least as common in men as it is in women. Cross-cultural research (Malinowski, 1927; Mead, 1928) has produced results that question Freud's idea that the Oedipus complex is universal and based on sexual dynamics. Finally, research has not found strong support for Freud's identification of specific stages of personality development (Kline, 1972).

The inaccuracies of his developmental work may, in part, be explained by the fact that Freud never actually worked with children. Freud's major therapy work involved women with a variety of "neurotic" disorders. In his one classic case which involved a child—the Case of Little Hans—Freud worked with the child's father to cure Hans's fear of horses!

Thus, although the psychoanalytic position is creative, radical, and rich in ideas, many of the specific hypotheses have not been supported.

A Change of Focus: Revisions from Psychoanalytic Theory

In 1902 Freud formed the Vienna Psycho-Analytic Society, which consisted of a small group of scholars who met to discuss and advance psychoanalytic theory. However, it was not long before some of the members began to find fault with traditional psychoanalytic theory. In some cases these disagreements gave way to bitter disputes that led to defections. Some of the scholars who rebelled went on to make notable revisions in psychoanalytic theory and others developed their own theories that represented significant departures from Freud's position. Two of the best-known figures in this latter group, those who developed their own theories, are Carl Jung and Alfred Adler.

Carl Jung: Analytical Psychology. Jung broke with Freud over the interpretation of libido. As you will recall, Freud viewed libido as being the sexual energy that directs personality. Jung (1928) felt that the libido was a force resulting from the desire to be creative; it resulted from spiritual needs rather than biological needs. From this foundation, Jung went on to develop a complex, almost mystical theory of personality, generally referred to as **analytical psychology.**

Jung suggested that the personality has three components (Stein, 1982). The *ego* includes everything that we are conscious of. Its main function is to see that our everyday activities are carried out. In this sense, it is similar to Freud's concept of the ego. The second component is the *personal unconscious*, which is similar to Freud's preconscious. The personal unconscious contains experiences that were once conscious but have been repressed or forgotten.

The most unusual and controversial component is the *collective unconscious*. According to Jung, this component holds memory traces of experiences from our ancestral past. It includes material not only from human history—it holds experiences from our prehuman and animal ancestors as well. The contents of the collective unconscious are similar for all people, since they share roughly the same common history. The ancestral experiences are stored in the collective unconscious in the form of *archetypes*, which are inherited predispositions to respond to certain concepts. For example, throughout history, and specifically in the early cave drawings, there has been a tendency to view the sun with awe and wonder. Other archetypes include such common concepts as God; heroes; sun; moon; fire; water; the wise old man; Mother Earth; and the Shadow, which contains inherited animal instincts such as aggression and unchecked passion. In order to show the existence of these archetypes, Jung studied myths and art throughout human history. He tried to show that there were common themes and symbols that have been expressed throughout time in these mediums.

To Jung, like Freud, the personality was the result of an inner struggle. Although Freud viewed this struggle as resulting from the person's efforts to keep unacceptable biological urges in check, Jung saw the struggle resulting from opposing tendencies fighting for expression. Jung believed that for every force, there is a counterforce; the goal in life is to achieve a good balance between these opposing forces. For example, he believed that every person has both masculine and feminine tendencies within their

Karen Horney argued convincingly against the male bias in Freud's theory. Her views laid the early framework for studying sex differences in light of social variables such as status and power rather than biological differences.

Analytical psychology
Jung's complex, almost mystical theory of personality; includes his belief that the libido was a force resulting from the desire to be creative.

Jung attempted to support his hypothesis about the existence of a collective unconscious by showing the similarities in the themes of drawings, songs, and stories between cultures and over time. These themes occur in the form of archetypes.

personality. If one tendency is emphasized, it is at the expense of the other. The unexpressed tendency will often occur in the form of dreams or fantasies. Therefore, Jung believed that dreams function to compensate for neglected parts of the personality. A man who overemphasizes the masculine tendencies of his personality may find himself having dreams centering on feminine themes or symbols. Therefore, analyzing dreams is one method of identifying the neglected aspects of one's personality.

In addition to the struggle between male and female tendencies, Jung believed there were other pairs of opposites affecting our personalities. The introvert is quiet, withdrawn, and interested in ideas rather than people. The extrovert is outgoing and socially oriented. Other opposites struggling for expression cited by Jung include the conscious and the unconscious; rational and irrational impulses; and the archetypes involving one's public self and private self. We achieve a healthy personality to the extent that we realize these opposite tendencies within ourselves and can express each.

Jung, in contrast with Freud, held an optimistic view of human nature. Despite the struggles within, Jung believed that people strive to achieve a balanced and integrated personality. This positive view anticipated the humanistic emphasis on personal fulfillment and self-actualization. Also, although Jung acknowledged the importance of childhood on the development of personality, he viewed later life as an important period for the synthesis of personality. Jung felt that we are able to achieve the insight and integration of personality only in our middle and later years.

As you might expect, there have been many criticisms of Jung's theory. Some find his views too mystical, too spiritual, and "too far out" to represent a true theory of personality. His ideas tend to be scattered, unclear, and hard to draw together. Finally, it is difficult to test many of his central concepts such as archetypes.

Alfred Adler: Individual Psychology. Alfred Adler, like Jung, felt Freud placed too much emphasis on sexual instincts. Instead, Adler believed that we are influenced by our social environments and genetic makeup. However, he did propose that we have the freedom to shape our own personalities. Adler termed his approach **individual psychology** because he believed that each person is unique and adjusts differently to social influences. He stressed the positive nature of humans.

Adler's (1927, 1939) theory evolved over a period of years. The foundation of the theory is that people develop as they strive to overcome or compensate for inferiorities. His first focus was on physical problems or *organ inferiorities*. He noted that people who have a physical ailment or bodily defect often devote much of their life to compensating for this defect (see Highlight: "Organ Inferiority"). In doing so, the weakness becomes a strength. We could suggest that Truman's fascination with reading was influenced by his very poor eyesight—an organ inferiority.

Adler soon realized that a personality theory could not be based solely on the concept of organ inferiority. He turned his focus to the psychological feelings of inferiority. He argued that all people begin life feeling inferior: Children see themselves as helpless in the face of powerful adults. Just as people attempt to compensate for organ inferiority, Adler felt that the feeling of inferiority leads people to compensate by striving for power and perfection—the *striving for superiority*. An *inferiority complex* results when people are overwhelmed by feelings of inferiority. In this case the inferiority acts as a barrier to positive adjustment.

In the final version of his theory, Adler stated that the striving for superiority was aimed not at individual superiority but at building a superior society. He suggested that people have an innate *social interest* that motivates them to seek perfection in their society and interpersonal relationships. Whether or not people have a well-developed social interest is largely depen-

Individual psychology
Adler's approach to personality development, based on his belief that each person is unique and adjusts differently to social influences.

ORGAN INFERIORITY

An interesting concept developed by Adler was organ inferiority. Adler felt that people who are born with organ defects have feelings of inferiority centering on these deficiencies. He felt that it was likely that they would develop a lifestyle to compensate for these defects.

In fact, the history of sports is filled with athletes who overcame organ inferiorities to become stars. For example, Wilma Rudolph had polio as a child, but she went on to become one of the greatest women runners of all times, winning three gold medals in the 1960 Olympic games. As a young boy, Johnny Weissmuller was frail and sickly. Many childhood diseases sapped him of his strength, and it was feared that he would be bedridden for the rest of his life, even if he managed to survive childhood. Weissmuller was determined to prove the doctors wrong. This frail boy went on to set 67 world swimming records, and he led the United States team in the 1924 and 1928 Olympics. After his amazing swimming career, Weissmuller became an actor, and, as the first actor to play Tarzan in the movies, he became a universal symbol of health and strength.

At the age of 8, Walt Davis was stricken with infantile paralysis that left both legs and one arm paralyzed. Learning to walk would have been an unbelievable accomplishment for someone with this condition. Davis not only learned to walk, but he became a world class high jumper, winning a gold medal at the 1952 Olympics and setting five world records. After his career as a high jumper, Davis became a professional basketball player.

The list of famous people who were motivated to overcome organ inferiorities is long. Recently, the media reported the heart-rending story of someone whose accomplishments were equally as great as those found in the history books. Terry Fox was a 22-year-old student in Canada when his right leg

was amputated below the knee to stop the spread of bone cancer. After a long recuperation period spent learning how to walk with an artificial leg, Terry learned that his cancer was spreading. At that point, he set out to raise money for cancer research. On April 12, 1977, he dipped his artificial leg in the Atlantic Ocean off Newfoundland and began jogging across Canada. For 4½ months he did what he called his "Fox trot," averaging almost 30 miles a day. Terry ran 3,339 miles before lung cancer made him too weak to continue and eventually took his life. His heroic efforts raised 20 million dollars for the Canadian Cancer Society.

When Jeff Keith completed his cross-country run across America on February 18, 1985, he said he "wanted to get my message across to the world that I'm not physically handicapped. I was physically challenged."

Stories such as these make Adler's ideas about organ inferiority seem more believable. It must be remembered, however, that there are many other cases in which people become overwhelmed by their defect. It remains an interesting research question: Why do defects motivate some people to strive for accomplishment, while they have the opposite effect on others?

dent on the relationship they have had with their mothers. A positive nurturant relationship will encourage the development of this social interest; an overprotective mother will foster low social interest.

Whereas striving for superiority is the energy behind personality, the

In the final version of his theory, Adler suggested that people have an innate social interest that motivates them to seek perfection in their society and relationships. It is this social interest that leads people to such prosocial acts as community volunteer service.

style of life represents the form of the personality. A person's style of life determines how he or she will solve problems, get along with others, and work for superiority. One's style of life is essentially formed by the age of 5. It is affected by relationships within the family, including such variables as family size, relations between siblings, and birth order.

Adler had important impacts in many areas of personality psychology. He stressed the importance of social interaction in influencing the personality. He argued for the role of free will in the forming of the personality. Adler, even more so than Jung, anticipated the position of the humanistic movement. In addition, his theory stimulated some important research in such areas as the effect of birth order on personality and behavior (Schachter, 1959; Zajonc, 1976). Despite his contributions, Adler's theory has been criticized because it lacks precision and integration. Unlike Freud, Adler did not develop a structure of personality; it is unclear, for example, how Adler views the roles of the conscious and unconscious. Overall, the theory lacks the systematic nature characteristic of Freud's psychoanalytic theory.

Humanistic Theories

With its emphasis on the evil in us and the self-centered drive to satisfy the pleasure principle, examining psychoanalytic theories gives us the feeling of traveling through the dark side. With this theory in mind, we probably wouldn't be too surprised with Truman's order to use nuclear weapons. However, before we get carried away with these negatives, we must remember the caring and concern Truman showed in so much of his behavior. On a grand scale, Truman turned the United States on a course aimed at rebuilding Europe and Japan after the war; certainly an evil person would have opted for punishment and retribution. Truman spent his life trying to help and protect the poor. At a more individual level, Truman demonstrated his caring for his men during World War I. A soldier who served with Truman said, "He used to get a lot of letters from the old Irish mothers of the boys in the outfit, and most battery commanders, company commanders, wouldn't pay attention, but not Harry. I don't think he ever went to bed at night before he answered every one of those letters." (Miller, 1973, p. 97).

The fact that so much of human behavior has a positive, caring overtone led a number of personality theorists, such as Abraham Maslow, Carl Rogers, and Rollo May, to form the humanistic movement, which rejected Freud's position that humans are inherently evil savages who must be controlled by society. Instead, the humanists argued that people are basically good and worthy of respect. **Humanistic psychology** stresses the creative aspect of people and argues that they are driven by the desire to reach their true potential. These differing views of personality can probably be traced to the different segments of the population studied by each group of investigators. Freud and others in the psychoanalytic tradition worked with clinical patients. Rogers, Maslow, and many of the other humanists worked with a more healthy population on university campuses and in counseling centers.

The humanists argue that the study of personality should include human virtues: love, humor, creativity, joy, and personal growth (Maslow, 1968). In light of the gloomy outlook projected by psychoanalytic theories, the humanistic approach stands as an optimistic testimony to human personality. Let us briefly examine two of the more widely known humanistic theories of personality.

Abraham Maslow

Abraham Maslow believed that humans have a natural motivation to be creative and reach their highest potential. Maslow (1970) argued that people cannot begin to achieve their highest potential until their more basic needs have been met. As we pointed out in Chapter 11, Maslow suggested that human needs are arranged in a hierarchy like the rungs on a ladder. The bottom rungs are the basic or lower-order needs, while the top rungs include the growth needs. Once these basic needs are satisfied, a person can focus on the desire to belong to groups and experience love, the wish to be competent and develop a positive self-esteem, and the need to be creative and become self-actualized. The role of society should be to create an environment that will encourage these natural tendencies. The concept of **self-actualization** is a bit fuzzy, but it is conceived of as the process by which people strive to learn, create, and work to the best of their ability. Such a process is indeed an important element in the psychological life of the individual. Many theorists and researchers continue to add to our understanding of this process through theoretical papers, empirical research, and refinements of the measurement of self-actualization (Jones & Crandall, 1991).

As people move toward self-actualization, they will experience periods of increased insight and feelings of completeness and of being in harmony with their surroundings. These feelings, which Maslow called **peak experiences,** are fleeting moments in people's lives when they feel truly spontaneous and unconcerned with time or other physical constraints. You may have had such a peak experience while walking in a peaceful forest or viewing a beautiful picture; the feeling is one of being totally absorbed in the situation, in the moment, without cares from the past or concern for the future.

Maslow, unlike many personality theorists, felt that research in personality should focus on healthy individuals. He criticized theories that were based on studying people with psychological disorders; ". . . the study of crippled, stunted, immature, and unhealthy specimens can yield only a cripple psychology and a cripple philosophy" (Maslow, 1970, p. 80). He identified a group of historical figures whom he considered self-actualized

Humanistic psychology
Movement formed by Carl Rogers, Abraham Maslow, and Rollo May which rejects Freudian view of people; argues that people are basically good and worthy of respect; stresses the creative aspect of people in reaching their true potential.

Self-actualization
Process whereby a person strives to learn, create, and work to the best of his or her ability.

Peak experiences
Fleeting moments in people's lives where they feel truly spontaneous and unconcerned with time or other physical constraints. A feeling of being totally absorbed in the situation, in the moment, without cares from the past or concern for the future.

(Maslow, 1954). Included in his list were Abraham Lincoln, Thomas Jefferson, Eleanor Roosevelt, Ludwig von Beethoven, and Albert Einstein. Table 13–2 lists the characteristics that Maslow felt these self-actualized people possessed. He later extended his research to college students and concluded that less than 1 percent of all people are truly self-actualized. Thus, the state of self-actualization is one to which we all aspire, but few of us ever reach it.

Carl Rogers

While Maslow focused on the importance of satisfying needs, Carl Rogers identified another hurdle that had to be overcome before people could reach their full potential. Rogers believed that people must accept themselves (their feelings and behaviors) before they can begin to reach their potential. This may sound simple, but according to Rogers, most people hide or deny parts of their own personality and behavior. This is because there are rules or norms in society that outline a wide range of behaviors and thoughts that are "permissible." When people do not act "in the right way," they are scorned by those around them. According to Rogers, all of us have a need for *positive regard* from others; that is, we want other people to like and value us.

We develop our self-concept by accepting certain values and behaviors and rejecting others. **Self-concept** consists of our judgments and attitudes about our behavior, ability, and even our appearance; it is our answer to the question, "Who am I?" The self-concept is very important, because it determines how we act and how we perceive our world. For example, people with positive self-concepts also tend to be high in achievement (Green, Miller, & Gerard, 1975). Because our self-image is so vital to the way we behave, it is crucial that it include an honest representation of our feelings, values, and experiences, not just those that society or the people around us find "acceptable." In fact, Rogers believes that people can become *self-actualized* (reach one's highest potential) only to the extent that they can accept all of their personal experiences as part of their self-concept. A cornerstone in Rogers's approach is the belief that people have the freedom to chart their destiny and determine their self-concept.

Sound complicated? Let's take an example from Truman's life to demonstrate these points. As a young boy, he enjoyed domestic activities, such as reading, cooking, and playing the piano. His father and peers pressured him to engage in more "manly" activities such as sports and farming. These

Self-concept
Consists of our judgments and attitudes about our behavior, abilities, and even our appearance; it is our answer to the question, "Who am I?"

Table 13–2	
Characteristics of Self-Actualizing People	1. They perceive reality accurately and fully.
	2. They demonstrate a greater acceptance of themselves, others, and/or nature in general.
	3. They exhibit spontaneity, simplicity, and naturalness.
	4. They tend to be concerned with problems rather than with themselves.
	5. They have a quality of detachment and a need for privacy.
	6. They are autonomous and therefore tend to be independent of their environment and culture.
	7. They exhibit a continued freshness of appreciation.
	8. They have periodic mystic or peak experiences.
	9. They tend to identify with all of mankind.
	10. They develop deep interpersonal relations with only a few individuals.
	11. They tend to accept democratic values.
	12. They have a strong ethical sense.
	13. They have a well-developed, unhostile sense of humor.
	14. They are creative.
	15. They resist enculturation.

Source: Maslow (1970).

pressures conflicted with Truman's true feelings and experience and could have made him deny his own desires. Fortunately, Truman did receive support from his mother and some other friends, and he was able to adopt his love for reading, cooking, and playing the piano in his self-concept.

Truman was fortunate compared to many other people. According to Rogers, many people react to similar pressures by denying parts of their experience in an effort to gain positive regard from others. They try instead to adopt the values and attitudes of others and, as a result, they lose touch with themselves. They become defensive, depressed, tense, and unable to form close relationships with others. Rogers believed that this damaging situation could be reversed by getting people to recognize and accept a broader range of their own experience. In order to do this, a different social environment must be created; this environment must include **unconditional positive regard** from others. People must be made to feel accepted and liked regardless of their behavior.

In an interesting study, a group of investigators tested Rogers's position that creativity will develop in an environment that provides psychological safety (the social world accepts the individual as having unconditional worth) and psychological freedom (granting the individual permission to engage in unrestrained symbolic expression). The investigators (Harrington, Block, & Block, 1987) believed that early childhood experiences would set the stage for later creativity. They interviewed parents of preschool children about their child-rearing practices, and they observed how the parents worked with their children on specific tasks. Table 13–3 shows the behaviors they felt created psychological safety and freedom and those that worked against these conditions. The investigators followed the children through their school years and had sixth- and ninth-grade teachers describe their performance. The results shows that the students who experienced psychological safety and freedom as children tended to show more signs of creativity during the sixth and ninth grades than did students who experienced less psychological safety and freedom during childhood.

Unconditional positive regard
Part of client-centered therapy, in which the therapist tries to create a condition of unconditional positive regard by accepting and caring for clients no matter what feelings or behaviors are revealed in the session.

Items Consensually Judged Most Typical of Rogers's Creativity-Fostering Environment

Parent encouraged the child.
Parent was warm and supportive.
Parent reacted to the child in an ego-enhancing manner.
Child appeared to enjoy the situation.
Adult derived pleasure from being with the child.
Parent was supportive and encouraging of the child.
Parent praised the child.
Parent was able to establish a good working relationship with the child.
Parent encouraged child to proceed independently.

Items Consensually Judged Least Typical of Rogers's Creativity-Fostering Environment

Parent tended to overstructure the tasks.
Parent tended to control the tasks.
Parent tended to provide specific solutions in the tasks.
Parent was hostile in the situation.
Parent was critical of child; rejected child's ideas and suggestions.
Parent appeared ashamed of child, lacked pride in child.
Parent got into power struggle with child; parent and child competed.
Parent gave up and retreated from difficulties; failed to cope.
Parent pressured child to work at the tasks.
Parent was impatient with the child.

Source: Harrington, Block, & Block (1987).

Table 13–3
Behaviors that Build (or Inhibit) a Creativity-Fostering Environment

Humanistic Theories: An Evaluation

Compared to the gloomy positions taken by other personality theories such as psychoanalytic theory, the humanistic theories are like a bright light on a dark night. In a broad sense, the humanistic concern with people's integrity and uniqueness has influenced research in many areas. Research on the self has ranged from interest in how self-concept develops (Baumeister, 1987) to people's perception and awareness of the self (McGuire, 1984). This focus on the self and self-concept helped lay the foundation for cognitive theories of personality that are currently at the heart of work on personality (Singer & Kolligan, 1987).

The humanistic values have been adopted in applied settings such as clinical therapy (person-centered therapy) and in the T-group or encounter group movement, which is aimed at providing environments to aid personal growth. We will discuss these in detail in Chapter 15.

There have also been criticisms of the humanistic approach. The humanists have failed to clearly define the important terms of their theories. For example, what is self-actualization and how can we measure it (Hall & Lindzey, 1978)? This kind of vagueness makes their theories difficult to test. A second criticism is that the humanistic approach is mostly concerned with human nature. In doing this, it takes such a broad view that it is impossible to make predictions about behavior in specific situations. Finally, Rykman (1979) argues that humanistic theories rely on too few concepts to explain the complexity of human behavior. The theories fail to take into account situational variables that can affect behavior. Thus, although the humanistic position is appealing, more attention must be given to making the theories more testable and more applicable to specific situations and behaviors.

Learning Theories

Although each of the theories we have discussed so far explains behavior in a different way, they all have one point in common: They propose the existence of an internal drive or need. In all of them, people are seen as acting because of a motivation arising from inside of them. As we have pointed out, it is difficult if not impossible to measure these internal forces. We are placed in the position of guessing that these internal drives exist because we see the results in the person's behavior. The learning approaches to personality were developed to avoid this problem. Learning theorists argue that much, if not all, human behavior can be explained by looking at environmental conditions, and by examining the rewards or punishments the person receives or expects to receive for certain behaviors.

Initially, the focus of learning theories was solely on behaviors. Behaviorists took the position that people learn behaviors and perform these behaviors when there are rewards for doing so. More recently, however, there has been increasing attention given to what may be called *cognitive learning theories of personality*. These theories take the position that we learn ways of perceiving and interpreting situations, expectations, and schemas (or representations) of ourselves, other people, and situations. It is these cognitions, in conjunction with environmental demands and reinforcers, that determine behavior. Let's now sample a variety of approaches that take the learning approach to explain individual differences in behavior.

According to behaviorism, our actions are determined by the system of rewards and punishments in our environment. A person will continue to perform a behavior if he or she is rewarded for that behavior.

Behaviorism

It is somewhat ironic for us to examine the work of B. F. Skinner in a section devoted to personality theories. As Phares (1988) suggests, it is like "inviting a wolf to a party of lambs" (p. 297). Skinner rejects personality theories altogether. He argues that we do not need to use such concepts as traits, psychodynamics, or free will to explain human behavior. Behavior for Skinner is not something directed by the individual; behavior is determined by the environment. Behavior is the result of rewards and punishments in the environment. For example, Skinner would propose that Truman acted decisively and honestly because he was rewarded for such behavior. Further, if the reinforcement contingencies (see Chapter 6) changed so that Truman was rewarded by being indecisive and dishonest, his behavior would soon change toward these directions.

With a masterful touch, Skinner (1953, 1974, 1987) presents an intriguing case for explaining behavior in terms of operant conditioning. As you will recall from Chapter 6, the operant principle suggests that behaviors are learned and continue to be displayed when they are positively reinforced or rewarded. Behaviors that are not reinforced or those that are punished are extinguished. Another rule of operant conditioning is that behaviors reinforced on a partial reinforcement schedule will resist extinction longer than behaviors that have been reinforced on a continuous schedule. Complex behaviors can be taught through the process of shaping, which involves rewarding each small part of the larger behavior. According to the behavioristic approach, we need merely examine a person's past schedule of reinforcement and punishment to predict how he or she will respond in the present situation. If we all grew up in and existed in the same environment, we would all behave the same way; there would be no individual differences. However, we are not reared in the same environment and we do not have the same reinforcement schedules. Therefore, there are individual differences in behavior.

Skinner drew on these behavioristic principles in his fascinating book *Walden Two* (1948). In the book a character named Frazier designed the ideal community where people lived together in harmony, enjoyed art, music, and literature, consumed only the resources they needed, and bore no more children than they could comfortably raise and support. This wonderland was not the result of reason or choice. Rather, people's behavior was controlled by immediate and positive rewards for desirable actions. This book echoes the behavioral principle that the person who controls the reinforcers controls people's behaviors. Although we might take comfort that Frazier used the reinforcers to build a Utopian society, we might take note that if Skinner's view was correct, Frazier could have used those same reinforcers to turn the inhabitants of Walden Two into murderous selfish monsters!

As you can see, Skinner's model is a radical departure from most personality theories. According to Skinner's view, a person is little more than a lump of clay in the hands of the environment, which can shape and reshape it by varying rewards and punishments. It is hard to decide whether Skinner's view of the person as lacking will or freedom is much more flattering than Freud's view of the individual as driven by primitive instincts of lust and aggression! As you might imagine, Skinner has been strongly criticized by humanists, who attack the position that people have no free will. Skinner's description of a society of people totally controlled by rewards and punishments has also pricked the sensitivity of many who view this possibility as dangerous and as having fascist overtones. However, operant principles have been used successfully to treat a wide range of behavior disorders (see Chapter 15). There can be little argument that reinforcement schedules can influence people's behavior. The real question is whether or not the behaviorist position can explain the rich range of human behaviors, thoughts, and feelings.

Social-Learning Theory

As we have seen, Skinner believes that the environment controls people's behavior, whereas the psychoanalytic theorists argue that internal forces guide behavior. The social-learning theorists suggest that both these approaches are too narrow (Bandura, 1977; Rotter, 1982). They take a position of *reciprocal interaction*, which states that the person and the environment affect each other. For example, recall how Truman answered each of the letters he received from his men's parents during World War I. This behavior impressed his unruly troops, who became more loyal and willing to obey Truman. This new loyalty may further have motivated Truman to do other things for his men. Hence, Truman's initial behavior affected his environment (his troop's behavior), which, in turn, influenced Truman's behavior.

Social-learning theorists also expand the scope of what can be learned. Skinner focused strictly on behavior because only overt behavior can be observed. Originally, social theory, too, was concerned only with observable behavior. However, investigators felt that this limitation did not allow the theory to recognize that people plan their activities, hold expectations about events, and interpret situations. In fact, the actions of individuals are often determined by their interpretation of the situation, not necessarily by the actual characteristics of the situation. Due to these added factors, social-learning theory has expanded to include cognitions (Ross, 1987). Individual differences in behavior can be explained by the different cognitions people hold. The expansion of the theory also allows for the view that we can determine our own behavior rather than being completely controlled by our environment.

Learning.   The social-learning theorists divide behavior into two processes, learning and performance (Bandura, 1977; Bandura & Walters, 1963). We *acquire* knowledge and behavior in many ways—one of the most important is **imitation.** We learn by watching other people act and by observing what happens to them. We can then copy their behavior. For example, we discussed research in Chapter 11 that showed that children could learn how to aggress by observing a model. When given the opportunity, they imitated this behavior. We can also learn behavior that we read about or that has been explained to us. This type of learning is called **observational learning;** it occurs without external reinforcement or without even performing the behavior.

Reinforcement and Performance.   Does this mean that external reinforcement has only a slight effect on human behavior? Obviously not. According to the social-learning approach, reinforcement may not be necessary for learning, but it does determine the actual performance of what has been learned. For example, you certainly know how to yell loudly. It is, however, unlikely that you will demonstrate your talents during a psychology lecture or in the library; you would be punished for yelling in these situations. On the other hand, you would probably yell until you were exhausted if you entered the annual hollerin' contest at Spivy's Corner, North Carolina; your loud yell in this situation could bring you a trophy, fame, and a reward.

Cognitive Social-Learning Theories

Social-learning theories have their roots in the behavioral approach to personality because they acknowledge the importance of our life experiences in shaping our characteristic ways of behaving. The cognitive theorists recognize, however, that we not only learn characteristic ways of behaving from our life experiences but also characteristic ways of thinking. These characteristic cognitive styles influence the way we interpret the things that happen to us. (See Highlight: "The Importance of Optimism.") Moreover, our cognitive style determines, in part, the kinds of activities we will choose to engage in. For example, if you believe (beliefs are cognitions) that you are socially awkward and rarely make a good first impression, you will probably avoid parties and other activities that require you to socialize with others. Of course, your choice to shy away from social functions will likely reinforce your belief that you are socially inept. This, in turn, will make it even less likely that you will attend social gatherings unless absolutely required to. This example shows how the reciprocal interaction of the person and the environment is extended to include the person's cognitions.

Our cognitions influence our interpretation of the situation, which influences our behavior, which further influences our cognitions. This cycle of reciprocal influences can establish styles of behaving that are so pervasive and enduring that they can be said to reflect one's personality. But in contrast to the psychodynamic theories, in which personality change is nearly impossible because of the internal, often hidden, motivations that shape personality, cognitive social-learning theories hold out the possibility that personality can be changed—not, indeed, by changing one's behaviors, but rather by changing one's cognitions.

Theorists who hold this view of personality have attempted to identify certain characteristic cognitive styles that influence behavior and explain individual differences in actions. One such theorist is Julian Rotter (1966, 1978), who focused on the cognitive variable of expectancies.

Locus of Control.   Rotter believed that people learn to expect certain outcomes from their behaviors. The probability that a certain behavior will occur is determined by what the person expects as a reward for that

According to social learning theory, we learn new behaviors by observing others. We will be most likely to perform those behaviors when rewarded for doing so. Children provide wonderful examples of social learning because many of their new behaviors are modeled after their parents' behaviors.

Imitation
Acquisition of knowledge and behavior by watching other people act and then doing the same thing ourselves.
Observational learning
Learning by watching other people and observing the consequences of their actions. This type of learning occurs without external reinforcement or without even performing the behavior.

behavior, and what the reward means to the person. Rotter worked with the premise that our general expectancies lead us to act in consistent ways. (These expectancies are like traits, but they are viewed as *learned*, and thus can be influenced by the environment.) Let us briefly examine one of the more widely researched expectancies, **locus of control,** to see how it can affect our behavior.

When Truman became president, he placed a sign on his desk that read "The Buck Stops Here." One of his favorite sayings was, "Things don't just happen, you have to *make* them happen" (Ferrell, 1980). Truman was a man of action and he believed that his actions had consequences. Truman's attitude is characteristic of an internal locus of control position. According to Rotter (1966), individuals learn generalized expectancies to view reinforcing events either as being directly dependent on their own actions or as being beyond their control. In other words, people develop expectancies about the locus of control of reinforcements. At one extreme are *internals,* who believe that they control their own fate. Internals feel that they can have an effect on the environment through their actions, and they feel responsible for the results of their behavior. One investigator found that internals grew up in families where the parents were warm and supportive and gave praise for accomplishments (Crandall, 1973). At the other extreme are *externals,* who believe that what happens to them is the result of luck and chance; they believe that they can do little to directly influence their own surroundings. Rotter (1966) developed the I-E Scale (see Table 13–4) to measure people's perceptions of locus of control.

An individual's perception of locus of control not only influences the way he or she interprets situations, it also affects behavior. For example, Seeman and his associates found that internals are more likely to seek out information to help them cope with problems than are externals (Seeman & Evans, 1962). In one study, the investigators found that tuberculosis patients described as internals were more likely than external patients to ask their doctor for information about their disease. Locus of control also influences the *attribution* one makes about the reasons for success and failure. It was found that internals believed that their failures were due to their own lack of ability or effort (Phares, 1976). Externals, though, felt that their failures were due to task difficulty or bad luck. As a result of these attribution differences, internals felt more shame for their failures than did the externals. These attribution differences extend beyond explaining the individual's own behavior. Phares (1976) also found that internals felt that other people are in control of their own outcomes. As a result,

Locus of control
According to Rotter, people learn general expectancies about whether the source of control of what happens to them is outside or inside them. Internals believe they control their own fate; externals believe luck and chance control their fate.

Table 13–4
Sample Items from Rotter's
Internal/External (I-E) Scale

1A. Many of the unhappy things in people's lives are partly due to back luck.
*1B. People's misfortunes result from the mistakes they make.
2A. No matter how hard you try, some people just don't like you.
*2B. People who can't get others to like them don't understand how to get along with others.
*3A. In the case of the well-prepared student, there is rarely if ever such a thing as an unfair test.
3B. Many times exam questions tend to be so unrelated to course work that studying is really useless.
*4A. Becoming a success is a matter of hard work; luck has little or nothing to do with it.
4B. Getting a good job depends mainly on being in the right place at the right time.
*5A. The average citizen can have an influence in government decisions.
5B. This world is run by the few people in power, and there is not much the little guy can do about it.

* These items represent an internal locus of control outlook; the others reflect an external locus of control view. Rotter developed the I-E scale to identify people's orientation about locus of control. On the scale, people are asked to indicate which of two statements most nearly reflects their feelings.
Source: Rotter (1966), p. 11.

THE IMPORTANCE OF OPTIMISM

Some people seem to lead charmed lives. Nearly everyone knows someone whose life appears to be a succession of positive events. Good luck just seems to follow these folks. And in those rare instances when misfortune or adversity does find them, things seem to turn out well in the end. You watch in amazement as this type of individual turns a lost job into a better employment opportunity or remains the happy-go-lucky model of good health while the stress of final exams is turning you into the perfect host for cold germs and flu viruses. And how could your roommate be so lucky as to find that wonderful guy she's now dating after having been "dumped" by her previous boyfriend only a month ago? Some people have all the luck!

According to psychologist Martin Seligman (1991), luck has very little to do with it. Over the course of our lives, we all have our share of ups and downs. So it's not simply life circumstances that determine whether we will be happy and successful, but rather how we explain those circumstances, both good and bad, *to ourselves*.

Seligman and his colleagues believe they have found two very different "explanatory styles" that determine how people respond to success and failure experiences in their lives. One style of explanation is optimistic and enhances the feeling that we have personal control over the circumstances of our lives. The other style is pessimistic and diminishes the feeling of personal control. Although optimists and pessimists differ in the way they explain their successes, the differences in their explanatory styles have the most serious behavioral consequences when explaining failures. Take the loss of one's job. Certainly few people would feel positive about losing their job. But the inner dialogue that you have with yourself about this disappointing turn of events can make all the difference in determining whether you grow beyond this disappointment or stagnate in limbo, immobilized by the hurt and frustration it has caused you.

According to Seligman, the optimist sees failures and setbacks as temporary and specific. Faced with the loss of her job, the optimist tells herself, "This unemployment won't last long." (The setback is temporary.) She opens herself to new opportunities by thinking, "Another job will come along soon. And besides, this is just one part of my life. I still have my friends, my family, my church; I can still paint and go to exercise class." (The disappointment is specific to her job.) Such an explanatory style is optimistic because it holds out hope and restores a feeling that your life is still under your control.

The pessimist responds to that same situation with a different explanatory style. Pessimists tend to see setbacks and failures as permanent and universal. "This is the best job I'll ever have. I'll never get another job like this one." (The setback is permanent.) "What am I going to do now that I don't have a job? My family and friends won't have anything to do with me now. I might as well drop that exercise class." (The disappointment has become universal, generalizing to every aspect of the person's life.) This type of explanatory style is pessimistic because it withdraws hope and engenders a feeling that you might as well give up because no matter what you try to do, it won't make a difference.

Besides explaining their failures as permanent and universal, Seligman also shows how pessimists tend to personalize failure—that is, to see it as occurring because of some personal limitation or inadequacy. ("I'm really incompetent. Why else would I have lost my job?") Optimists, on the other hand, tend to externalize their failures. ("If the company had better personnel managers, this would never have happened to me.") By adopting this explanatory style, optimists are able to maintain higher levels of self-esteem than pessimists.

These different explanatory styles can have a dramatic impact on the quality and successfulness of one's life.

Hundreds of studies show that pessimists give up more easily and get depressed more often. These experiments also show that optimists do much better in school and college, at work and on the playing field. They regularly exceed the predictions of aptitude tests. When optimists run for office, they are more apt to be elected than pessimists are. Their health is unusually good. They age well, much freer than most of us from the usual physical ills of middle age. Evidence suggests that they may even live longer. (Seligman, 1991).

This may sound pretty bleak to a person who has a pessimistic explanatory style. But Seligman believes that since our explanatory style is learned, it can also be unlearned. The key is to learn to recognize the self-defeating statements we make to ourselves, and then to challenge those statements, much as we would challenge derogatory statements directed at us by someone whose opinion we don't trust or respect.

Changing our style of thinking can be a very difficult enterprise, but Seligman's research strongly suggests that the success and happiness that come from learning the optimistic explanatory style is well worth the effort.

internals judged others more severely than did externals, and they were more likely to deliver harsh punishment for failures or rule violations.

A second important factor that influences whether or not a behavior will be performed is *self-efficacy* (Bandura, 1982). Self-efficacy involves our beliefs about what we can or cannot do (see Chapter 11). In general, it is the degree of confidence we have in ourselves. For specific behaviors, it concerns the belief that we can or cannot successfully execute that behavior.

People with a high degree of self-efficacy will attempt to do things that people with low self-efficacy will not. For example, a person who believes that he or she could not pass college courses would not choose to enter college.

Mischel (1973, 1981), building on the work of Rotter and Bandura, has identified five categories of cognitive factors that can influence the way an individual interprets and responds to certain situations. Because these cognitions determine the individual's contribution to the reciprocal interaction between the person and the environment, Mischel calls these cognitive factors *person variables*.

1. *Competencies*. The individual's social skills, task accomplishments, and abilities. (Self-efficacy involves the person's perceptions of his or her competencies.)
2. *Encoding strategies*. The way the individual categorizes and interprets events and the features of the environment to which the individual attends.
3. *Expectancies*. What the individual expects will happen in different situations and the rewards or punishment he or she will receive for certain behaviors.
4. *Subjective values*. The value or importance the individual attaches to various outcomes.
5. *Self-regulatory systems and plans*. The rules that guide the individual's behavior, his or her goals, and the self-imposed standards for behavior.

These person variables help explain why different people respond differently to the same situation. How many times have you heard two people give totally different accounts of the same situation? Sometimes their stories are so at odds that it is hard to believe they were at the same place at the same time. When that happens, it is a good bet that they approached that situation with differences in one or more of these person variables.

But remember, according to the cognitive-social learning perspective, the individual's behavior is a function of the interaction of person variables and the situation. In order to understand the impact of person variables, then, we need to know something about the situation. Situations differ in their power to elicit certain behaviors. Sometimes the situational demands are so strong that they overwhelm the person variables. For instance, consider people's behavior in church. In that situation, the social roles and behavioral expectations are quite explicit. Thus, there is not much variability in people's behavior in church. It is a different matter, of course, when people are attending a party. In that setting, there is more ambiguity regarding the situational demands. Mischel argues that person variables have the greatest impact when situational demands are ambiguous.

Learning Theories: An Evaluation

As we suggested, the main strength of Skinner's theory of behaviorism is its clarity. It offers numerous testable hypotheses, and, for the most part, its concepts are precise and clear. It deals with observable behavior and can make a wide range of predictions without resorting to events that may be going on within the person. In a real sense, behaviorism's strength is also its weakness. Because it avoids activities within the individual, it cannot capture the richness of human thought, feelings, and plans. Opponents argue that behaviorism cannot explain the complex and complicated nature of human behaviors.

Social-learning theory, on the other hand, stresses the importance of language, information processing, and planning. The theory attempts to integrate environmental variables with cognitive functioning to explain human behavior. Social-learning theory emphasizes the importance of the present and the future for predicting behavior. Like behaviorism, the theory suggests that behavior can change as environmental factors change; it does not accept the psychoanalytic position that personality is largely determined by the time a person is 5 or 6 years old. By focusing on the present and future, social-learning theory offers an optimistic outlook for humans. The theory suggests that even some of the most dysfunctional behavior patterns can be changed through observational learning and the proper reinforcements in the environment. Finally, social-learning theory, like behaviorism, has initiated a tremendous amount of research, and, as we will see in Chapter 15, the theory has served as the foundation for some very successful therapy techniques.

Social-learning theory has been criticized because it lacks the integration found in psychoanalytic theory. Social-learning theory is constantly changing, and it stands as a number of interesting concepts and observations without neat ribbons to tie it all together. A second criticism is that the theory fails to take into account the importance of developmental change in personality formation. As children grow, they experience dramatic physical, biological, and psychological changes that should affect their behavior and perceptions of their environment. Although much of the social-learning research involves children, the theory does not address how maturational changes influence behavior. Third, the addition of the cognitive focus greatly enhances the ability of the theory to predict and explain behaviors. However, cognitions, unlike behaviors, are not observable. We can only infer their existence. Thus, the theory is not as directly testable as is the behavioristic theory. Finally, some critics feel that learning theories are theories of specific behaviors, not of people. In other words, we might be able to explain why a person behaves in a certain way in a certain situation, but we do not get a picture of the person as a whole; we cannot see how all these behaviors "fit together" to make up the total personality.

Types and Traits

Some researchers in the area of personality are less interested in *explaining* personality than *describing* it. For these theorists, the question of *how* people differ is more interesting than *why* they differ. This approach to personality has been called the *trait approach*. Actually, this approach is two approaches, one focusing on distinct global categories and the other viewing personality as varying degrees of a combination of specific characteristics.

In order to illustrate the global or *type* approach, consider our friend Susan. She's a bright engaging person who has one annoying habit; whenever we ask her to describe someone, she responds by telling us signs of the zodiac. ("He's a perfect Pisces" or "She's a Libra.") In doing this, Susan feels that she is not only telling us when the person was born, but also what type of person he or she is. Types are discrete categories that describe an individual (Figure 13–1). Because they are discrete, people can be placed into only one category: you're either a Libra or you are something else. Further, all people in a category or type are similar, and they are different from people in another category or type.

There is a seductive simplicity to the type approach. If we can type people like we type blood (A, B, AB, O) we can quickly and neatly communicate a great deal about them. But, people's personalities do not fit cleanly into a small set of distinct categories. Rather, people are similar on some dimensions, and different on others. And we can best describe people in

FIGURE 13–1

Sheldon's Somatotypes

One of the early type theories related personality to body type. Sheldon argued that body type determines personality. According to him, endomorphs love food and comfort and need social approval and affection; mesomorphs are assertive, physical, aggressive, and active; and ectomorphs are restrained, socially inhibited, artistic, and oriented toward intellectual activity. As with other type theories, a person could fit in only one category.

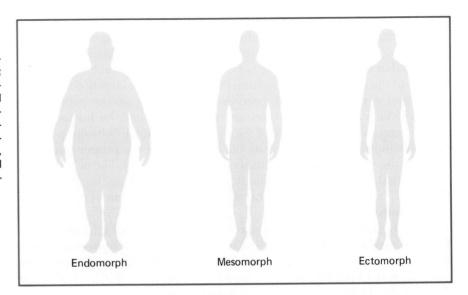

Endomorph   Mesomorph   Ectomorph

terms of degrees rather than "either-or" categories. For example, rarely do we find a completely friendly (or unfriendly) person; instead people tend to be friendly to various degrees.

Taking these issues into consideration, some personality psychologists adopted the *trait approach*. Gordon Allport (1937), one of the early advocates of the trait approach, stated that traits are "the building blocks of personality." **Traits** represent an organization of a person's experience. We can think of them *as a readiness to think, perceive, or act in a particular way across a variety of different situations*. People possess varying degrees of traits. For example, we would say that Truman had a high degree of honesty whereas some of our other presidents had less of this trait. It would be inaccurate to describe Truman as honest and another president as dishonest.

According to Allport, all traits are not equal; some are more important and more likely to influence behavior than others. The most influential are the *cardinal traits*. These are traits around which an individual's life will revolve. For example, if a person's life is dominated by blind ambition and the desire for power, then power would be that person's cardinal trait. Fortunately, Allport suggested that few people are dominated by cardinal traits. More common are *central traits*, which play a major role in guiding a person's behavior, but the person is not consumed by them. We might conclude that honesty and modesty were central traits for Truman. *Secondary traits* are the least influential characteristics; they involve specific situations or events. We might consider these traits as preferences or attitudes. For example, Truman preferred small towns over large cities. What makes people unique is the degree to which they possess traits, and which of those traits are central to them.

One of the major issues faced by trait theorists is the identification of traits. Researchers have pointed out the size of this problem by drawing up a list of 17,953 English words that could be used to indicate personal traits (Allport & Odbert, 1936). Imagine having to describe Truman by showing where he falls on 17,953 dimensions! Raymond Cattell (1973) set out to reduce this unmanageable number and to identify the "basic traits." He spent a number of years collecting data on the personality and behavior of thousands of subjects. Cattell identified 16 basic traits that could be used to describe people. He also developed a questionnaire, the "Sixteen Personality Factor Questionnaire," to find out where an individual was located on these 16 dimensions (see Figure 13–2).

More recently, theorists have developed a model of personality that includes higher order traits and lower order traits (Buss & Finn, 1988;

Traits
Fairly permanent qualities that cause people to respond similarly across a variety of situations.

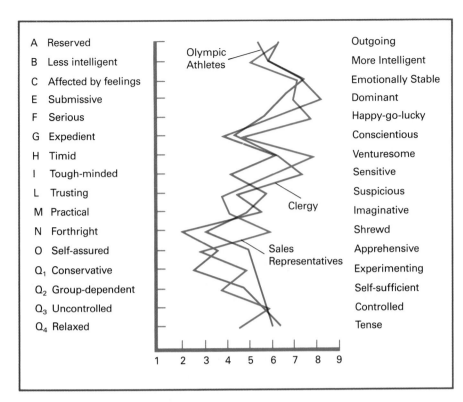

A	Reserved		Outgoing
B	Less intelligent		More Intelligent
C	Affected by feelings		Emotionally Stable
E	Submissive		Dominant
F	Serious		Happy-go-lucky
G	Expedient		Conscientious
H	Timid		Venturesome
I	Tough-minded		Sensitive
L	Trusting		Suspicious
M	Practical		Imaginative
N	Forthright		Shrewd
O	Self-assured		Apprehensive
Q_1	Conservative		Experimenting
Q_2	Group-dependent		Self-sufficient
Q_3	Uncontrolled		Controlled
Q_4	Relaxed		Tense

1 2 3 4 5 6 7 8 9

FIGURE 13–2

Cattell's 16-Factor Questionnaire

Shown here are scores from three quite different groups: Olympic athletes, clergymen, and sales representatives. Cattell tried to identify the 16 basic traits that describe personality. (Cattell, 1965, pp. 242, 347)

Norman, 1963). As can be seen from Table 13–5, the higher order traits are broad dispositions, whereas the lower order traits tend to be more narrow, often involving a specific behavior (e.g., talkative-silent). This model has stimulated a great deal of research aimed at determining if it really represents the way people view personality, whether the "Big Five" traits adequately describe personality, and how the higher and lower order traits are related (McCrae & Costa, 1987; Peabody, 1987). In general, using both self and observer ratings, the research supports the position that we view personality on two levels, and that the adjectives we use to describe

Higher Order Factor	Lower Order Traits
Extraversion or surgency	Talkative–silent Frank, open–secretive Adventurous–cautious Sociable–reclusive
Agreeableness	Good-natured–irritable Not jealous–jealous Mild, gentle–headstrong Cooperative–negativistic
Conscientiousness	Fussy, tidy–careless Responsible–undependable Scrupulous–unscrupulous Persevering–quitting, fickle
Emotional stability	Poised–nervous, tense Calm–anxious Composed–excitable Not hypochondriacal–hypochondriacal
Culture	Artistically sensitive–artistically insensitive Intellectual–unreflective, narrow Polished, refined–crude, boorish Imaginative–simple, direct

Source: Buss & Finn (1988).

Table 13–5

A Model of Higher Order and Lower Order Traits

ourselves and others can be roughly combined into five major dimensions. Interestingly, the research also suggests that we use traits to explain other people's behaviors, but we tend to see our own actions as caused by situations, rather than personal traits (Jones, 1976). (See the discussion of attribution theory in Chapter 16.) An illustration of this finding recently occurred when I interviewed two students who were caught cheating on an exam. In private, one student confessed to the cheating, explaining that he "was forced to cheat" because he had a fight with his girlfriend and couldn't study for the test, and he had lost his notes (situation). However, he hung his friend out to dry, saying that the friend cheated because he was dishonest (trait).

The Trait Approach: An Evaluation

The trait approach is popular for a number of reasons. First, it suggests that personality can be measured. Indeed, a number of scales have been developed to measure specific traits. Second, the view that a person can be described with these traits seems logical. Finally, the trait approach has stimulated a great deal of interesting research aimed at identifying and measuring traits. This research has shown that in many cases we can make more accurate predictions about a person's behavior by identifying his or her traits (Eysenck, 1986).

Despite the appealing nature of the trait approach, there have been some important criticisms. First, the use of traits to explain behavior can lead to circular reasoning. Traits are not something that we can see. Rather, we must infer them from behavior or answers to personality tests. Thus, we may infer that Bill is aggressive because we see him hit other people or verbally abuse them. This may, indeed, be a reasonable conclusion to draw from his behavior. However, we then get into trouble if we conclude that Bill acted aggressively because he is an aggressive person. In essence, we would be saying that Bill is aggressive because he acts aggressively and he acts aggressively because he is aggressive.

A second problem is that many trait theories do not pay enough attention to the influence of the situation on behavior. For example, we might conclude that Truman was a shy and modest person. However, in 1948, Truman was in danger of losing his bid for reelection. He chartered a train and went across the country giving speeches about his accomplishments and shaking hands with thousands of people. In these situations he acted neither shy nor modest. Clearly, then, situations play a large role in determining behavior.

Finally, trait theories are criticized because they are designed to identify traits and measure them, but they are not involved with how personality develops or changes. In this sense, they are not really theories of personality; instead, they are models. Trait theorists feel this is an unfair criticism saying ". . . description must proceed explanation. We must know what is to be explained before we can proceed to frame causal hypotheses (Eysenck, 1986, p. 104)." Despite these problems, the identification and measuring of traits represents an important area of personality psychology.

Personality Theories: A Concluding Remark

This brief introduction to personality theories may have left your head spinning, wondering which one is right. As we have pointed out, each of the theories has its strengths and weaknesses. The answer to the question of what makes people act differently is found in all the theories together

Table 13–6   Theories of Personality

Theory and Major Figure(s)	Important Period(s)	View of Basic Human Nature	Guiding Force of Personality	Important Concepts
Psychoanalytic Freud	early childhood	evil	internal (libido)	id, ego, superego, conscious, pre-conscious, un-conscious
Analytical Psychology Jung	early childhood, middle years, and later years	positive—strive to achieve balance among opposites	internal	ego, personal conscious, collective uncon-scious, arche-types, opposites
Individual Psychology Adler	childhood	positive	internal, but influenced by social environment	social interest, or-ganization in family, inferior-ity complex, style of life
Humanistic Theory Rogers, Maslow	childhood, later adulthood	very positive	internal—basic needs and striving for self-actualization	basic needs, self-actualization, self-concept, unconditional positive regard
Behaviorism Skinner	present	no reference to basic human nature	external environment	operant behavior, schedules of re-inforcement, shaping
Social-Learning Theory	present	no reference to basic human nature	external (reinforce-ment and models)	response, obser-vational learn-ing, model
Cognitive Learning Theory Bandura, Rotter, Mischel	present (past and expected future situations also in-fluential)	no reference to basic human nature	external factors and cognitions—thoughts, expec-tancies, plans inter-pretations, view of self	cognitions, plus expectancies, locus of control, self-efficacy

and in none of them on its own. Research is even now going on to define and redefine the theories. Few investigators are willing to adopt one theory and exclude the others.

The human personality is wonderfully complex, and the various theories offer different perspectives in the effort to understand it (see Table 13–6). Psychoanalytic theory suggests that we can best understand human behavior by identifying internal forces that are set into action during infancy and childhood. Humanistic theories argue that we can best understand personality by looking at the "good side" of people and examining how the desire for self-fulfillment guides behavior. Learning theories add that our quest to understand personality must take into account external events; these theories also suggest that personality changes throughout life, as well as present situations, are at least as important as past events in directing behavior.

These different theories influence the direction of research. For example, an investigator guided by psychoanalytic theory will focus his or her attention on early childhood experiences, whereas a researcher who adopts a learning perspective will study external variables that occur in the person's present environment. Although the different methods of study uncover different characteristics of the personality, we cannot conclude that one method is more correct than the others; each has a purpose and helps us understand personality. And each theory offers insight into the nature of psychological disorders and helps chart treatment programs for those disorders (see Chapters 14 and 15).

How Consistent Is Behavior?

At the beginning of this chapter we posed a question that seems to be at the center of personality theorizing and research. Specifically, we asked whether knowing someone's personality can help us predict that person's behavior. In other words, what is the relationship between personality and behavior? In order to understand this issue, consider the following example from Truman's life.

At the end of his speeches, Truman would hold question-and-answer sessions. During one of these sessions a small, red-haired boy meekly asked him, "Mr. President, was you popular when you was a boy?" Truman smiled and slowly replied, "Why no, I was never popular. The popular boys were the ones who were good at games and had big, tight fists. I was never like that. Without my glasses I was blind as a bat, and to tell the truth, I was kind of a sissy. If there was any danger of getting into a fight, I always ran. I guess that's why I'm here today" (Miller, 1973, p. 32). Truman's answer shows a modesty that characterized him throughout his life. He rarely boasted about his accomplishments. He was always willing to praise others, but slow to take credit himself.

From this example we get a picture of Truman as a modest man who acted modestly in a variety of situations. This view is compatible with most theories that view personality as a relatively stable part of the person that serves as a constant guide of behavior. But is behavior really consistent across situations? If we look more closely at Truman's life, we can find many examples where he boasted of his accomplishments. This was particularly true during the election campaigns when he wanted to convince the public that he was the best person for the presidency. Just how consistent is behavior across time and situations? This is a central question for personality theories because if we find little or no behavioral consistency from one setting to the next, it would be difficult to support the position that personality influences behavior. Indeed, there would be little reason to postulate the existence of a stable personality!

The issue of consistency has sparked a lively debate that continues to rage (Conley, 1984; Peake & Mischel, 1984). The argument centers on how much consistency there is; in other words, how much do personal dispositions influence behavior?

One group of investigators has amassed an impressive collection of data suggesting that behavior is largely determined by the situation (Mischel & Peake, 1982). They argue that accurately predicting how a person will act in one situation based on knowledge about his or her behavior in a previous situation is improbable. For example, in a classic study, children's moral behavior was examined in a wide variety of situations (Hartshorne & May, 1928). Each child was given the opportunity to commit dishonest behavior (lying or cheating) in a number of settings (home, classroom, party, and athletic contest). If we believe that behavior is consistent across situations, we would predict that a child who acted dishonestly in one setting would do so in other settings. However, the results of the study did not strongly support this position. There was only a slight tendency for children who were dishonest in one setting to be dishonest in other settings.

Other investigators dispute the conclusion that there is little consistency in behavior (Epstein, 1983; Rushton, Bainerd, & Pressley, 1983). They argue that the scope of the studies must be broadened. Instead of looking at one situation and trying to predict behavior in another situation, they say that we must examine behaviors across a wide variety of situations to predict future behavior. We can see general tendencies of stability and consistency over a broad range of time and situations, but cannot make accurate predictions from one specific situation to the next.

Additional research has identified other factors that influence behavioral consistency. One factor involves the clarity and intensity of situational cues (Mischel, 1981). When situational cues are very clear, the demands of the situation may dominate behavior. On the other hand, when the requirements of the situation are more ambiguous, a person's dispositions or unique characteristics will influence behavior. For example, Truman may have been a modest person in many situations, but when his future as president demanded that he convince others of his ability, all modesty was set aside.

Another factor is the individual. Some people pay close attention to situational cues, and their behavior varies considerably from situation to situation. Other people have been found to pay less attention to the external environment, focusing instead on their inner states. These people show more behavioral consistency across situations. A scale called the Self-Monitoring Scale has been developed to differentiate between people whose main focus is on situational cues versus those most concerned with inner states (Snyder, 1987).

Still another group of investigators (Bem & Allen, 1974) have found that consistency is affected by the specific trait and how important that trait is for the individual. For example, modesty may have been a very important trait to Truman, and consequently he behaved modestly across a variety of situations. Although you might consider yourself to be a modest person, this trait may not be as central or important to you. Hence, you

The question of how consistent behavior is across situations has become a central one for personality theorists. Truman was a modest person in many situations, but he was a fierce campaigner who rallied to the cry, "Give 'em hell, Harry." When situational cues are clear and strong, they can override the effects of personality characteristics.

wouldn't show the same degree of consistency in modest behavior as did Harry Truman.

Clearly, both situational demands and personal dispositions influence our behavior, and a number of factors affect how strong the influence from each will be. The richness and diversity of the personality theories presented in this chapter should challenge you to think and, in some cases, test the limits of your imagination. Remember, however, that each theory was developed to better understand people and make more precise predictions about their behavior across time and situations.

Personality Assessment

We began this chapter asking the question, "What was Harry Truman really like?" How was he different from other people and why was he different? Our discussion of personality theories focused on the *why* issues. We used the various theories to explain why Truman chose to enter politics or why he became a modest, studious individual. We will now turn our attention away from the issue of *why* Truman was the way he was and focus on identifying what Truman was like.

Personality assessment is the description and measurement of individual characteristics. Most *assessment techniques* are aimed at identifying the typical or most common characteristics displayed by a person. For example, we would predict that a person who scored high on internal locus of control would generally feel responsible for the outcomes of his or her actions. Recently, some investigators have suggested that we may also want to assess the maximum limits of a personality dimension in addition to the most typical level (Paulhus & Martin, 1987). For example, it may be of some comfort for you to know that your new roommate scores very low on a test of aggressiveness. However, your comfort may erode if you find out that he or she is capable of having extremely violent, albeit infrequent, outbursts of aggression.

We all make personality assessments. On the first day of class, for example, you might anxiously assess the personality of your professor. Is she rigid and a tough grader, or is she a rather easygoing, vague type who will generally assign good grades? There are many ways you can make your assessment. You can concentrate on what the professor says: "There will be no curves, and I am willing to fail half the class." Or, you can review the professor's behavior: Last semester she failed 72 percent of the class. A third way of learning about the professor is to see how she interprets some rather ambiguous information about grading at your university or college. For example, does she think that grading has become too easy because last semester over half the students at the school had an A average? If so, you had better plan on spending a lot of time preparing for the course.

Each of these methods (looking at behavior, examining verbal or written responses, and studying the interpretations given to ambiguous information) is used to assess personality. The method a researcher will use often depends on the particular theory or approach to personality that he or she holds. Also, just as there are strengths and weaknesses associated with each theory, the different personality tests, too, have strengths and weaknesses.

Before discussing the specific methods of assessment, let us look at some requirements for any test, whether it is measuring personality characteristics or what you learned in class last week.

Personality assessment
Description and measurement of individual characteristics.

Requirements of a Test

Any test that measures stable dimensions, whether it be personality or one's academic abilities, must have two qualities before it can be considered a good test. First, the test must have **reliability**—it must yield consistent results. There are many types of consistency that a test must have. There must be *inter-rater reliability* so that a test scored by one person yields the same results as when the test is scored by another rater. There must also be *test-retest reliability* so that the results on the test are similar each time the same person takes the test. Consider this example. You took the college entrance examination twice in a 2-month period. The first time you took it, you scored 1200, the second time you scored 650. Since it is unlikely that your ability to do college work changed that much over time, you could rightfully argue that the test was not reliable. In this case, the test-retest reliability was low.

On the other hand, suppose you took the test and scored 640 the first time and 650 the second time. In this case, you could not criticize the test's reliability. However, before you decide not to go to college, you could evaluate the test—what is the test estimating? Does it really measure one's ability to do well in college? In other words, does the test have **validity**—does it measure what it is designed to measure? Like reliability, there are many types of validity that concern us. One of the most popular ways to determine the validity of a test is to see if it is a good predictor of the behaviors it was designed to test; in other words, does the test have *predictive validity*? Consider the college entrance examination. We could examine the college performance of students who had scored high or low on the test. If we found that the high scorers did better in college than the low scorers, we could argue that our entrance examination was a valid test; it proved to have predictive validity. In the same way, if we design a personality test to measure aggressiveness, we could determine validity by examining the behaviors of people who had received different scores on the test.

Another common type of validity is *concurrent validity*—does a test of a trait yield the same score as another test measuring that same trait? For example, suppose someone developed a new test measuring musical ability and compared it to an already established test of musical ability. If the new test had concurrent validity, then it would be expected that students taking either test would receive similar scores. Thus, a useful measure of personality must be both reliable and valid. The test must give consistent scores and it must measure what it is designed to measure.

Behavioral Assessment

Since one of the aims of personality tests is to predict behavior, a number of investigators have examined an individual's present behavior to predict future actions, which is known as **behavioral assessment.** This type of assessment focuses on how behavior is affected by various situations (O'Leary & Wilson, 1987). It provides an account not only about the consistency of behavior, but also how the behavior changes from one situation to another. Behavioral assessment can also be used to assign traits to individuals. There are a number of techniques of behavioral assessment. One involves observing an individual's behavior in natural settings. For example, if we wanted to determine how modest or friendly Harry Truman was, we could carefully watch him in a number of settings. We could note his verbal behavior (how often he talked about himself, praised others, asked for help) and his nonverbal behavior (how often he smiled, touched other people, moved away from crowds). It is important that we make our observations in a number of different settings to ensure that we are not simply seeing how Truman is affected by one specific situation.

Reliability of a test
Means that you get the same results on the test every time you administer it.
Validity of a test
Means that the test actually measures what you say it measures; best way to tell this is to see if the results of the test successfully predict the type of behavior in which you are interested.
Behavioral assessment
Assessment that consists of examining a person's present behavior to predict future actions. Can also be used to assign traits to people.

Behavioral assessment involves observing a person's behavior in a number of situations to predict how he or she will act in other settings. Most behavioral assessments are unobtrusive because the person is observed in a natural setting without being aware that he or she is being observed.

This **naturalistic observation** method has many advantages. It is unobtrusive in the sense that people do not know they are being studied. There is a great deal of research showing that people are likely not to behave typically if they are aware that they are being studied (Orne, 1962). The naturalistic observation method may also offer a high degree of predictive validity because it offers a sample of behavior in a number of real settings.

Despite these important strengths, there are also problems with the naturalistic observation method (Kent & Foster, 1977). First, it takes a great deal of time. In many cases, the researcher may have to observe a single individual for many days in many settings. One way to deal with this problem is to use self-researching where the person keeps a diary about his or her behavior over a period of time (Table 13–7). Another approach involves arranging for the individual to be observed in a laboratory or other controlled environments. For example, in order to determine how aggressive you are, a researcher could set you up in a laboratory and observe how you deal with several frustrating tasks. Second, it may be hard to get a high degree of interjudge reliability. For example, the acts that one judge rates as "friendly" may not be rated the same by another judge. One might categorize a person's behavior as friendly when he or she smiles and says hello to a professor; another person might score this behavior as manipulative.

The Interview

There is an old story about two philosophers who wanted to know how many teeth were in a horse's mouth. These two learned individuals spent days arguing about such issues as how many teeth the horse needed, the optimal arrangement of teeth in the horse's mouth, and the probable size of the horse's teeth. In the middle of their heated argument, a small child walked up to the horse, forced its mouth open, and counted the teeth. This solution was so simple that it had not occurred to the two philosophers. We might apply the same type of reasoning to the measurement of personality; if we want to know what people are like, why not ask them? Psychologists do use the "asking" method, in the form of the **interview.** Two main types of interviews have been used.

Naturalistic observation
Research method that involves studying people's reactions to naturally occurring events in natural settings.
Interview
Assessment technique that involves direct questioning of a person. Unstructured interview consists of planned questions to start, but interviewer is free to develop the conversation as he or she wishes. Structured interview consists of a set of specific questions asked according to a set plan.

In the *unstructured interview*, the interviewer has a particular area in which he or she is interested, and the interview begins with some planned questions. However, the later questions are determined by the subject's responses. The unstructured interview is often used in clinical settings or in other situations where the interviewer is interested in getting a broad picture of what the person is like.

In the *structured interview*, the interviewer asks specific questions following a set plan. Employers often use this method when they are interviewing prospective employees in order to get specific information from them. Some personality tests use structured interviews. For many years, interviews have been conducted using a format called the Mental Status Exam. With this technique, both direct questions and observations about the subject are combined under such categories as general appearance (dress, posture), speech (incoherency, use of strange words), mood (happy, fearful, suspicious), orientation (time, day of the week), memory (for both recent and past events). More recently, a number of structured interviews have been developed which gave specific guidelines for assessing both overall functioning, as well as specific disorders such as schizophrenia or depression (Siassi, 1984). The advantage of asking all the people the same questions is that responses can then be directly compared.

The interview is being used more frequently by universities to select graduate students. The feeling is that although we can learn some things about a person by examining test scores, school records, and responses on an application, we can gain a good deal more information by adding an interview to this information. In the interview we can determine how the person responds in a social setting, how clear the person is about his or her goals, and how inquisitive the individual is.

The interview is a direct method of obtaining information and is very useful. It does, however, have drawbacks. In some cases it may have little validity because respondents are reluctant to present themselves in a bad light. For example, imagine how you might respond if an interviewer asked you to discuss your sex life. Reliability may also be low, because people's responses can be affected by their feelings about the interviewer. An interviewer who seems cold and critical may get very different responses than

Preceding Events	Feelings	Consequent Events
Monday Got a 65 on chemistry exam.	Had no energy. Didn't want to talk to anyone.	My boyfriend said I was a bore.
Tuesday Had a good night's sleep.	Good day!	Caught up on Bio homework.
Wednesday Saw my boyfriend eating lunch with another girl.	Felt angry and jealous.	Cut class and took a nap.
Thursday Couldn't do Chem lab assignment.	Just can't learn Chemistry.	Called teaching assistant to ask about tutoring.
Friday Roommate got a permanent—looked great.	I'm ugly! (cried a lot)	She said she would cut my hair tomorrow.
Saturday My parents called.	Lonely—nothing to do here.	Listened to records and went to bed early.

Table 13–7
Example of a Diary of Behavior and Feelings

Source: O'Leary & Wilson (1987).

Interviews are used to assess personality. In the unstructured interview, the examiner's questions are influenced by the subjects' responses. In the structured interview, the examiner has a set of predetermined questions that the subject answers.

would a warm and understanding interviewer. Finally, interviews are very time consuming. Generally only one person can be interviewed at a time, and someone must spend time reviewing and scoring the responses.

Interviews with children present special problems since children are not as articulate or cognitively sophisticated as adults. In many cases, the interview of the child involves observing what the child does as much as listening to what he or she says (Hughes & Baker, 1991). For example, the interview might include playing with the child and watching what toys the child selects, what themes are acted out in the play (aggression, fear of rejection), and how the child relates socially to the interviewer.

Thus, assessing personality is not as simple as counting the teeth in a horse's mouth; the most direct method may not always give us the most useful information. However, valuable information can be obtained from an interview. The interview can also be used to make someone feel more at ease before taking some other personality test. Because of this, interviews, like behavioral assessments, are often used along with other tests.

The Questionnaire.   In order to get around some of the problems associated with behavioral assessment and interviews, many personality tests in the form of questionnaires have been developed. The **questionnaire** involves a standard set of questions; often people respond by indicating their answers on computer forms. The questions are often true/false or multiple choice. The strengths of the questionnaire are (1) They can be given to many people at one time; (2) all people answer the same questions under the same conditions; and (3) the tests usually can be scored quickly. A number of questionnaires have been administered and scored by computer (Butcher & Owen, 1978; Korchin & Shuldberg, 1981). In some cases, a person can read the questions on a monitor and type a response on the computer keyboard. The computer can then immediately score the test.

There are, however, potential problems with questionnaires. The first problem concerns understanding. Because people may fill out the questionnaire either alone or in groups, we can't be sure that they understand

Questionnaire
Standard set of questions used to assess behavior that can be given to many people at one time and usually can be scored quickly.

each question or even interpret the questions in the same way. A second problem is that we can only assume that people answer honestly. In some cases, people may be motivated to give the answer that makes them look good or the answer that they feel the examiner wants. It would be difficult for some people to answer "true" to the following question, even if it honestly reflected their feelings: "Sometimes I feel intense hatred toward my mother." The third problem of this test is *response bias*. Some people have a tendency to agree (or disagree) to almost any position presented.

Let us examine one questionnaire.

Minnesota Multiphasic Personality Inventory (MMPI). One of the most popular personality questionnaires used by clinicians in diagnosis is the **Minnesota Multiphasic Personality Inventory (MMPI)** (Hathaway & McKinley, 1942, 1943). The MMPI was designed to identify specific psychological disorders. Hathaway and McKinley developed the scale by preparing a number of one-line statements to which the individual could respond "true," "false," or "cannot say." The items concerned a wide range of issues such as attitudes, past experiences, emotions, and psychological symptoms. For example, the following statements were offered to people: "I tire easily," "I believe there is a God," "My mother often made me obey even when I thought it was unreasonable." The investigators then presented these items to patients in mental hospitals who had been diagnosed as suffering from specific psychological disorders (e.g., depression, hysteria, paranoia). They also had a control group of nonpatients answer the questions. Their next step was to choose the items that distinguished patients from nonpatients. For example, they would look for an item that most depressed patients answered in the same way, but that was answered differently by the control group. This item would be included in the test as one that could identify depression.

Using this procedure, Hathaway and McKinley eventually chose 550 questions to be included in the MMPI. The MMPI has sets of items or scales aimed at identifying ten different disorders (e.g., hysteria, depression, or schizophrenia). The investigators also added some items to determine the validity of responses. For example, the Lie Scale included an item, "I do not always tell the truth." It is, indeed, a rare individual who never tells a falsehood; thus, a "false" response to this question would cast some doubt on the validity of the individual's responses to other items in the questionnaire.

The MMPI was revised in 1989. Many awkward or obsolete items were dropped, repeated items were deleted, and new content areas were added. The MMPI is most effective in separating those suffering from mild disorders from those suffering from more serious personality disturbances. Subscales of the MMPI have also been developed to predict alcohol and drug abuse (Zager & Megargee, 1981). Because of the large number of scales available on the MMPI, it has been used in research with a wide variety of subject groups. For example, recent research has examined characteristics of such diverse groups as Vietnam veterans suffering from Post-Traumatic Stress Disorder (McCormack, Patterson, Ohlde, Garfiedl, & Schauer, 1990) and professional prostitutes (De Schampheleire, 1990). Because the MMPI was designed to detect psychological disorders, it is of little use for identifying personality traits in a "normal" population. The California Psychological Inventory (CPI) was designed to incorporate many of the strengths of the MMPI in a test that could be used to measure more normal traits such as poise, dominance, self-assurance, sociability, maturity, achievement, and aptitude. The CPI is similar in form to the MMPI; in fact, half of the CPI items are taken from the MMPI. The test has been used widely in personality research.

Minnesota Multiphasic Personality Inventory (MMPI)
One of the most popular personality questionnaires used by clinicians. Designed to identify specific psychological disorders. Consists of 550 statements to which people can respond true, false, or cannot say. Aimed at identifying 10 different disorders.

Projective Tests

As we discussed earlier, Freud believed that people have unconscious drives that motivate their behavior. Some of these drives are very threatening and, consequently, they are repressed or disguised. In fact, people may not be aware of these drives even though they affect their behavior. One of the disguised ways in which these drives are expressed is through projection; people see others as having these forbidden drives and desires. According to this position, we might have difficulty learning about an individual's personality by asking direct questions about his or her personal feelings and desires. However, these unconscious drives will be expressed if we ask the individual questions about others or about ambiguous events. In these cases the individual will project these unconscious desires onto the ambiguous and unthreatening stimulus.

This is the reasoning behind **projective tests.** In these projective measures of personality, the individual is asked to discuss an ambiguous or vague stimulus. The individual's responses are analyzed to determine what they tell about him or her. An advantage of projective tests is that there are no correct or incorrect answers. Thus, it is unlikely that a person will give the answer that he or she assumes the examiner wants. And, unlike many of the questionnaires, projective tests can be used with people who do not read or write.

There are, however, problems with projective tests. First, they are often difficult to interpret or score; the same response may be interpreted differently by different judges. Second, responses to projective tests have not proven to be good predictors of specific behaviors. For example, we might find that certain people have a strong unconscious aggressive drive. However, they may rarely act aggressively. Finally, because most projective tests are given individually, the administering and scoring is very time consuming.

Despite these problems, projective tests are used by many clinicians to aid them in diagnosis. Let us examine two of the most widely used projective techniques.

Rorschach Inkblot Tests.   Have you ever become absorbed in watching clouds floating lazily through the sky and suddenly realized that you "saw" pictures in the clouds? In one cloud you might have seen a fat woman sitting on a broken chair, while in another cloud you noted the outline of a lion attacking a small lamb. Yet another person may see completely different scenes in the same formations. These "pictures" are projections that are being made onto ambiguous stimuli.

Hermann Rorschach, a Swiss psychiatrist, was aware that people "see things" in ambiguous stimuli, and he felt that much could be learned about individual personalities from the things that people "saw." In 1911, Rorschach began showing cards containing inkblots to his patients. He asked them to describe what they saw in the blots. After using many different inkblots for over a decade, he chose the 10 blots that brought out the most vivid and emotional responses. These blots make up the **Rorschach inkblot test.**

Each blot has a different shape; some are colored and others are black-and-white (Figure 13–3). The blots are printed on cards and presented to subjects in a set order. The individual is asked what each blot "might be."

Controversies about the Rorschach test do not so much center on the gathering of responses as they do on the scoring or interpretation of these responses. There are a number of techniques used for scoring the Rorschach test; however, the most comprehensive is Exner's system (Exner, 1986a). This very complex system allows for 90 possible scores per response, divided into seven major categories. The scorer examines such details as whether the response was concerned with the whole blot or only part of it; the

Projective tests
Based on Freud's theory that people will project unconscious desires onto ambiguous and nonthreatening stimuli. The stimuli can be an incomplete sentence or a picture. People's responses are analyzed to see what they tell about them.

Rorschach inkblot test
Projective test that measures personality by having subjects describe what they see in ten different inkblots.

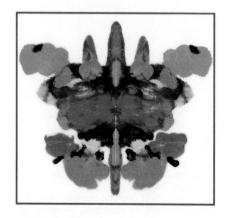

FIGURE 13–3

The Rorschach inkblot test involves subjects stating what they see in ambiguous inkblots such as this one. It is assumed that subjects will project their feelings in their responses.

shape, color, and amount of activity present; and the subject of the response (human figure, animal, plant, or inanimate object).

Revisions to the Exner scoring system (Exner, 1990) have distinguished between Level 1 and Level 2 responses in an attempt to evaluate the degree of distorted thinking present in a response. Other new additions have been the development of groups of scores that identify the presence of suicidal thinking, schizophrenia, depression, and personalities with obsessive or paranoid styles.

Recent work has used the Rorschach test to identify characteristics of opiate addicts (Blutt & Berman, 1984), mothers of incest victims (Wald, Archer, & Windstead, 1990), and individuals who have suffered traumatic loss in childhood (Cerny, 1990).

As you might imagine, it takes a great deal of training to interpret the Rorshach test. This test has been used almost exclusively for the diagnosis of personality and emotional disturbances.

Thematic Apperception Test (TAT).   Although the Rorschach test was developed to identify psychological disorders, the **Thematic Apperception Test (TAT)** was originally designed, not as a test, but to help in the process of therapy. It was expected that with the aid of TAT cards, the therapy client would reveal personality characteristics which would otherwise take months to uncover (Worchel & Dupree, 1990). The TAT quickly came to be used almost exclusively as a personality test, in which clients made up stories about ambiguous scenes (see Figure 13–4). Subjects are asked to tell what is happening in the picture, what led up to it, what the characters might be thinking or feeling, and what might happen in the end. Numerous scoring systems have been developed for the TAT. The first, developed in 1935 (Morgan & Murray, 1935), analyzed stories in terms of the hero (main character), the motives of the hero (such as achievement, aggression, need for nurturance), forces in the environment, and themes elicited across one or more stories. Another scoring system (Dana, 1986) looked at five major focal points in the TAT story—ego strength, needs, sex roles, control, and story content.

Recent work with the TAT continues to find problems with the test. Worchel, Aaron, and Yates (1990) examined the TAT for possible gender

Thematic Apperception Test (TAT)
Projective test that measures personality by showing the subject an ambiguous scene and asking him or her to tell a story about it.

FIGURE 13–4

The Thematic Apperception Test (TAT) is a projective test. Subjects are asked to describe what is happening in the picture. This picture was used in Vietnam to examine the affiliation needs and personal needs of villagers.

bias. Since males are typically shown a different set of cards than females, a potential bias could exist in that the different sets of cards might elicit certain types of responses. The research confirmed that the female cards produced more evidence of emotional distress than the male cards in a number of areas. Kaiser and Prather (1990) reviewed ten years of TAT research and concluded that there is a lack of consistency both in terms of the cards used and in instructions given.

Despite these problems, the TAT continues to enjoy widespread use. Like the Rorschach, the TAT remains among the top ten most frequently used personality tests (Lubin, Larsen, & Matarazzo, 1984). Many variations have been developed for use with other cultural groups. For example, as can be seen in Figure 13–4, it may be necessary to redraw the pictures to make them more suitable to the culture being examined. Other TAT-type tests have been developed, for use with Hispanic children—the Tell-Me-A-Story (Costantino, Malgady, & Rogler, 1988) and for use with black children—Themes Concerning Blacks (Williams, 1972).

Choosing an Assessment Technique

As you can see, there are a number of ways to measure an individual's personality. Given the wide range of methods, how do you decide which ones to use? One of the major factors that will determine your decision is the personality theory in which you most strongly believe. For example, if you adopt the psychoanalytic theory, you will be interested in measuring unconscious drives that influence people's behavior. Given this approach, you will most likely choose projective tests as the basis for your assessment. However, if you are a learning theorist, you will use behavioral assessment. As you will recall, learning theories argue against the importance of internal drives; instead they focus on observable events such as behavior. If you adopt the humanistic point of view, one of your main interests will be to identify goals; you will want to learn what type of person the individual desires to be. The most direct way to determine these goals is to ask the person. Therefore, you will use the questionnaire method.

In addition to theoretical considerations, you must also take into account the characteristics of the people who make up your sample. Can they read or write? If they cannot, you will not use a questionnaire.

Clearly there are many factors that will influence your choice of an assessment technique. It should, however, be remembered that in almost all cases, the psychologist will not rely on only one method. Rather, a battery of techniques will be used. This battery will often include an interview, behavioral assessment, and questionnaire or projective test. Just as no single theory can account for the complexity of human personality, no single assessment method can adequately measure personality.

Summary

1. **Personality** is defined as a unique set of enduring characteristics and patterns of behavior that influence the way a person adjusts to his or her environment. The study of personality focuses on examining individual differences and explaining why people act differently in similar situations.

2. **Psychoanalytic theory** was developed by Sigmund Freud. It focuses on the internal, often unconscious forces that cause people to act in certain ways. Freud described personality as the result of a constant struggle between the **id, ego,** and **superego.** Freud identified specific stages of personality development and argued that an individual's personality is formed during the first 6 years of life.

3. Some scholars, such as Carl Jung and Alfred Adler, accepted much of Freud's psychoanalytic theory but argued that Freud focused too heavily

on sex. They suggested other motives, such as power and the social environment, that influence personality.

4. **Humanistic theories** stress the creative aspect of people and suggest that they desire to become **self-actualized**. Humanists encourage people to learn about and accept themselves rather than try to live up to standards set by others.

5. Behaviorism argues that outside environmental events determine human behavior. According to learning theories, people act only to obtain rewards and avoid punishment. Their personality is dependent on the rewards available in their environment, and because of this personality is formed and changed throughout people's lives.

6. **Social-learning theory** suggests that people learn new behaviors by **imitating** others. Whether or not they perform these behaviors will be determined by the reinforcement contingencies available in the environment.

7. Cognitive social-learning theories suggest that thoughts can influence behavior. These theories have identified a variety of cognitions that affect behavior and explain individual differences including expectancies, interpretation of the situation, locus of control, self-efficacy and a host of person-cognitive variables.

8. Many personality theories assume that people tend to act the same way in many different situations. Research, however, has shown that situational variables may determine a person's behavior. It therefore seems that personality factors predispose the individual to act in a certain way, but this predisposition may be overridden by situational factors. Further, consistency in behavior is most likely to be seen over an extended time period and over a broad range of situations; we cannot accurately predict behavior from one specific situation to another.

9. Some of the earliest theories of personality were type theories, which tried to place people into "either/or" personality categories. A related approach occurs in **trait** theories. People possess traits to varying degrees. These theorists try to determine the structure of personality by identifying and measuring relatively permanent qualities that people may possess.

10. **Personality assessment** is the description and measurement of individual characteristics. While there are many techniques used to assess personality, a good measure must be both **reliable** (give consistent results) and **valid** (measure what it is designed to measure).

11. One of the most common assessment techniques is **behavioral assessment.** This method involves observing how people act and determining what their actions indicate about their personality.

12. Both structured and unstructured **interviews** are used to obtain information about an individual.

13. A number of **questionnaires** have been developed to examine specific parts of the personality. For example, the **Minnesota Multiphasic Personality Inventory (MMPI)** includes 550 questions aimed at identifying personality disorders.

14. **Projective tests** are based on the psychoanalytic theory that unconscious motives influence behavior. These tests attempt to identify these unconscious motives by allowing people to project their feelings onto ambiguous stimuli. The **Rorschach inkblot test** involves having people describe what they see in inkblots. With the **Thematic Apperception Test (TAT),** people tell stories about what is happening in a series of pictures.

15. Most **personality assessment**s involve using many assessment techniques together. However, the main focus of the assessment is often based on the examiner's preference of personality theories and on the characteristics of the subject. For example, an examiner who was strongly influenced by psychoanalytic theory may rely on projective tests, while one who agreed with learning theory would emphasize behavioral assessment.

Key Terms

anal stage
analytical psychology
behavioral assessment
conscious mind
defense mechanisms
ego
Electra complex
free association
genital stage
humanistic psychology
id

imitation
individual psychology
interview
latency period
libido
locus of control
Minnesota Multiphasic Personality Inventory (MMPI)
naturalistic observation
observational learning
Oedipus complex

oral stage
peak experiences
personality
personality assessment
phallic stage
pleasure principle
preconscious mind
projective tests
questionnaire
reality principle
reliability of a test

Rorschach inkblot test
self-actualization
self-concept
superego
Thematic Apperception Test (TAT)
traits
unconditional positive regard
unconscious
validity of a test

NEW TECHNIQUES HELP MILLIONS OF WALLFLOWERS OVERCOME THEIR FEARS

BY JANE BRODY

Perhaps you dread being among people you don't know or seek the security of a quiet corner at parties. Or maybe you can speak your mind among people you know well but cannot defend your rights or express your feelings to strangers or authority figures.

You may be adept at one-on-one conversations with friends but become tongue-tied and terrified when having to address a group. Or maybe only certain groups frighten you. And who does not feel shy when discussing personal problems with a health professional?

So if shyness is a character flaw, it is one that nearly everyone shares. Indeed, about 40 percent of adults describe shyness as one of their persistent personality traits, according to a survey of 10,000 American adults by researchers at Stanford University.

The findings suggest that for two million adults, shyness is a serious problem that inhibits their social and professional growth. In its most extreme form, shyness can become a crippling fear called agoraphobia that turns people into emotional prisoners, afraid to leave their homes.

Recent research has not only delved into the origins and facets of shyness, but therapists have also developed techniques for overcoming it, even in its most severe forms.

Shyness is an anxiety reaction in social situations, a failure of confidence and extreme discomfort when interacting with or confronting other people. Shy people are overly concerned with themselves, how they look, how they sound, how others view them. They are afraid they will be regarded as foolish, unattractive, unintelligent or unworthy.

But they are not uncommon. The Stanford survey found that only one person in 20 reports never having suffered attacks of shyness.

Of those questioned, 40 percent said they used to be shy but overcame their reticence. And 15 percent said they are shy under certain situations, like being at a party with strangers, delivering a speech or when asked personal questions in public.

Hallmarks of Shyness

Dr. Philip G. Zimbardo, a psychologist at Stanford University who has spent two decades studying shyness, says the all-too-familiar symptoms of shyness may include blushing, cold clammy hands, dry mouth, excessive perspiration, trembling hands and legs, pounding heart, queasy stomach, a sinking feeling or even a sudden need to go to the bathroom.

The person experiencing such anxiety may describe feelings of embarrassment, self-consciousness, inadequacy or inferiority and a desperate desire to get out of the situation.

Among the characteristics typical of shy people are an inability to make eye contact when talking to others, an avoidance of social gatherings and a tendency to speak in a voice almost too low to be heard.

Shy people may never volunteer or complain about poor service or go back to a store to return an unwanted item or rectify an error. They may suffer in silence about inequities at work, have difficulty describing symptoms to a physician and be unable to convey their desires to their sex partners. Shy people are unable to "sell" themselves to others. They tend to have few, if any, friends, they avoid intimate contact and they fail to seek promotions, raises and other rewards for jobs well done.

Origins of Shyness

Lacking the skills for righting a wrong, a shy person may overreact to a distressing situation by becoming belligerent, Dr. Zimbardo reported. The resulting confrontation merely reinforces the shy person's belief that he or she is socially inadequate or lacks personal control.

Various studies in recent years have identified three potential sources of shyness: heredity, lack of social skills and improper social programming that fosters poor self-esteem instead of self-confidence.

One study, conducted by psychologists at Yale and Harvard, found that 10 to 15 percent of children are born with a propensity to become shy. We have all seen infants who turn away from strangers and toddlers who hide behind a parent when spoken to, even by an adult they know.

Dr. Jerome Kagan of Harvard reports that shy infants and toddlers develop a rapid heart rate and become wary, withdrawn, reserved and silent when faced with unfamiliar people or new situations. Even a new toy may not draw them out of themselves.

Such children seem to have nervous systems that are too easily aroused. Their hypersensitivity makes them uncomfortable, self-conscious, even panicky in social settings.

Of course, circumstances play a role in determining whether an inherited tendency to become shy is expressed. The Yale-Harvard study revealed that two-thirds of shy children had older siblings who perhaps bullied or belittled them, shaking their self-confidence.

Parents can also seriously undermine a child's self-esteem through repeated negative comments about the child's ability or appearance or by failing to praise the child's accomplishments, however limited.

Dr. Kagan found that children who were not shy as infants and toddlers did not become shy when reaching school age. And about one-third of those who started out shy were less so by the age of 5 or 6. He said this group had been encouraged by their parents to be more assertive and to think more highly of themselves.

Dr. Zimbardo says most shyness represents a learned pattern of reactions, either from social experiences in which the person was degraded or ridiculed or from the lack of a competent role model.

Overcoming Shyness

Contrary to popular belief, people can change. Even a lifelong shyness can be overcome, and many professionals now conduct clinics and workshops to help people gain the self-confidence and social skills that will enable them to assert themselves in most situations. Even agoraphobia can now be successfully treated in programs that gradually expose people to social situations they fear while they are in a state of deep relaxation.

Even without a clinic, there is much that shy people can do for themselves. These are some tips from psychologists who treat shyness:

¶ Rehearse what you want to say. Write down your questions, complaints, desires, medical symptoms or whatever. Read them out loud, first by yourself, then in front of a mirror, then on the telephone and finally face-to-face with a friend.

¶ Build self-esteem by focusing on your strong points and praising yourself for good deeds or a good performance. Avoid putting yourself down. Focus only on the positive. Never dwell on what you or others perceive as failures or weak points.

Concentrate on turning stumbling blocks into stepping stones, rather than making them impenetrable barriers.

¶ Practice smiling and making eye contact. Start with a mirror, progress to a good friend, then try it with acquaintances and finally with strangers.

¶ Work to improve your speaking voice and volume by talking into a tape recorder. Make successive tapes and compare them to see how much better you are getting.

¶ Observe and copy the behavior patterns of people who are assertive, who can get what they want without being obnoxious. See how others laugh at themselves when things go wrong, rather than launching into a self-depreciating tirade.

¶ Remember that you are not alone. At least two of every five people are probably as uncomfortable as you are. In fact, find someone else who seems shy and try to help them by initiating a conversation.

¶ Do not try to hide your "true self." Accept who you are. Think of your peculiarities as special traits that make you distinctive, rather than odd or unattractive.

¶ When with other people, focus your attention on them and what they are saying. Ignore the inner voice that is trying to draw your attention to your own words, actions and appearance.

¶ Use imagery to enact a mental scenario of social success. Do not dwell on negative outcomes.

¶ Practice relaxation techniques, like deep breathing, meditation, yoga and other means of reducing stress.

In addition, avoid using alcohol or drugs to relax. These can reduce, not enhance, your self-control and increase the chance that you will make a fool of yourself.

The New York Times, November 16, 1989, p. B19. Copyright © 1989 by The New York Times. Reprinted by permission.

Abnormal Psychology  14

When Debbie Spungen learned she was pregnant, she was in her senior year at the University of Pennsylvania. She and Frank had planned to wait until they were more financially secure before starting their family, but things did not turn out as planned, and they were determined to make the best of it. At least Debbie would almost be through her last semester before the baby was born.

However, a setback occurred when Nancy decided to arrive more than five weeks premature. Nancy's introduction to the world was a rough one. She was born with the umbilical cord wrapped around her neck, which cut off her supply of oxygen. She had to be given stimulants to bring her to life. In addition, she was jaundiced and had a blood disorder that required her to have a complete transfusion.

After a hectic few weeks in the hospital, Nancy came home and seemed to do very well. She was a quick learner and by her first birthday she had a twelve-word vocabulary. Debbie was concerned, however, because Nancy cried a lot and had violent temper tantrums. Because

this was Debbie's first child and she didn't know what to expect, she coped with the problem the best she could. The child's tantrums soon turned into aggression, however. One morning, Debbie heard the telephone repairman who had come to fix their telephone screaming, "Lady, get her the hell off me!" She rushed into the room to find two-year-old Nancy wrapped around the man's legs, pounding him with her fists.

Nancy's aggressive behavior continued and Frank and Debbie decided to take her to a clinic for testing. The tests indicated that Nancy had superior intelligence, an IQ of 134, but that her motor-visual development was behind her age level. The social worker suggested that her aggression resulted from the frustration of being bright but not being physically developed enough to carry out her thoughts.

The first and second grades went reasonably well for Nancy. In fact, her classwork was so good that she skipped the third grade. Socially, however, Nancy made little progress. She couldn't form lasting relationships; she'd have a friend for

a week and the next week that friend would be her bitter enemy. Her teacher remarked that Nancy seemed to retreat into her own world at times. "She's tuned in to her own private TV show and just starts giggling" (Spungen, 1983, p. 56). At home, Nancy would experience lapses in memory. She couldn't stick with one task and her mind seemed to wander. But most disturbing was her violence. The slightest irritation would set her off. Once she walked into the television room where her younger brother and sister were watching TV, changed the program, and when her siblings complained, Nancy yelled and began to beat them. When she was eleven years old, she tried to stab her babysitter with a pair of scissors. Another time, Debbie told Nancy that they could not go to the science museum because it was closed. Nancy screamed, grabbed a hammer from a table, and attacked Debbie. Sometimes the violence was turned on herself; Nancy often threatened to commit suicide.

These continuing episodes prompted Frank and Debbie to take Nancy to a child guidance clinic.

Although the psychologist did not share his thoughts with Debbie and Frank, he wrote in his clinic notes, "My diagnostic impression of Nancy is that she is a schizophrenic girl . . . (Spungen, 1983, p. 108)." Therapy did not help Nancy and her social problems increased. She ran away from school. One morning Debbie received a call from the school counselor. "Mrs. Spungen, I don't think Nancy belongs in school. At least not in this school."

Now the Spungens were faced with an 11 year old whose behavior had gotten her expelled from public schools and who was ruining the Spungen's home. Frank and Debbie were in a constant state of tension, waiting for the next outburst, and their other two children were afraid of their sister. Something had to be done.

After an exhaustive search, they located a residential school in Connecticut designed to handle children with emotional problems. Nancy's first year at the school went very well. She wrote warm and happy letters to her parents and she received very positive evaluations from her teachers and her therapist. The family had a good summer together and Debbie thought their troubles were behind them.

However, when Nancy went back to the school for her second year, problems began almost immediately. She called home constantly, begging Debbie to let her come home. When she was home at Christmas, she was suspicious of everything and everyone, making wild and unfounded accusations. For example, at a family gathering, Nancy suddenly screamed at one of her cousin's friends sitting across the table, "What are you looking at?" She then yelled at Debbie, "He was staring at me! I saw him!" The startled man protested that he had not been looking at Nancy. In a fit of anger, Nancy grabbed her coat and ran out the door.

The next year, at age 13, Nancy went to a new residential school. Her behavioral problems continued and were made worse when she started

using drugs. In addition to her antisocial behavior she engaged in self-mutilation. Yet she did well in school, and at age 15, when she took the SAT test she scored 1030. The residential school, only too happy to get rid of Nancy, suggested that she apply to colleges and find "a more challenging environment." She applied to the University of Colorado because she liked to ski, and to her delight, she was accepted.

At age 16 Nancy enrolled in summer school at the University of Colorado and did well. She loved college and when she saw Debbie at the end of the summer, she beamed, "You know what, Mom? I'm happy for the first time in my life. Really happy. I'm not a sickie anymore. For sure" (Spungen, 1983, p. 187).

But in the fall things went sour. Nancy got mixed up with drugs and was charged with receiving stolen property. She was forced to withdraw from school and return home. Despite therapy, she remained a constant disruption at home, even encouraging her brother and sister to experiment with drugs. Nancy spent a great deal of time sitting in her room listening to hard rock music and retreating further into her own world.

It was soon clear that Nancy could not live at home. It was decided that she should move to New York City, get a job, and try making it on her own. She had great plans about getting into the music business and her first few months in New York found a happy and excited Nancy. Soon, however, she was back

into drugs. Her job "in music" was as a go-go dancer in a night club, which also involved her in prostitution. She alternated between being happy and hopeful and depressed and violently angry.

Still dreaming of the music world, Nancy saved some money and went to London with a friend. There she met a tall taciturn musician who was a member of a hot new British punk rock group, the Sex Pistols. Nancy fell in love with Sid Vicious and began traveling with the band. She wrote home: "Now, I have two best friends that I love—you, and Sid. I hope you're happy your daughter finally found a guy and settled down" (Spungen, 1983, p. 307). Although Debbie was shocked at what she learned about punk rock and the Sex Pistols, she again had hope that her daughter would finally be happy.

However, when the punk rock craze cooled, Sid and Nancy came back to the United States. After visiting Debbie, they took a room at the Chelsea Hotel while Sid looked for work. On October 12, 1978, Debbie received a call from Lieutenant Hunter of the NYPD. "Mrs. Spungen, I'm sorry to tell you that your daughter is dead." Nancy had been found stabbed in her hotel room, and Sid was charged with murder. Nancy was 20 years old. ▬

After completing this chapter, you should be able to:

Understand that there are different ways to define abnormal behavior, and know that the DSM III-R is the most commonly used system of classifying psychological disorders.

Know that "insanity" is a legal term not a psychological term, and understand the dangers of assigning labels to people.

Describe the models used to identify the causes of maladaptive behavior.

Describe the various anxiety disorders and their symptoms.

Explain how people with somatoform disorders do "feel" their symptoms, and differentiate between a hypochondriac and a person with a conversion disorder.

Describe the various dissociative disorders and the circumstances of their onset.

Discuss the theories of depression.

Identify and differentiate the two categories of sexual disorders.

Describe the various types of schizophrenia and discuss the theories about its cause.

Abnormal Behavior: History and Scope

Almost from the time Debbie brought Nancy home from the hospital, she began to suspect that Nancy was unusual or abnormal. As an infant, Nancy seemed to cry all the time. As a young child, Nancy had trouble keeping friends, and she was moody and aggressive. As Nancy grew older, her problems increased; she couldn't stay in school, she was suspicious of other people, she began using drugs, and she attempted suicide. When she was a teenager, Nancy dyed her hair different colors, dressed in strange clothes, got into violent fights, and increased her involvement with drugs. Debbie watched Nancy's development in disbelief, confusion, and pain. She constantly asked, Is Nancy's unusual behavior simply different from that of other people or is it a serious problem? What is causing her to behave in these ways? What can and should be done about her behavior?

These questions are not new or confined only to Nancy Spungen. People have been perplexed, awed, frightened, amused, and enraged by the strange behaviors of their fellows for thousands of years. They have struggled with trying to define what actions should be defined as harmlessly different and unusual and what actions are problematic and abnormal. They have searched for and debated the causes of behaviors they defined as "abnormal." And through the ages they have attempted to use almost every conceivable means to treat, cure, or change these abnormal behaviors. The area of clinical psychology is devoted to identifying, understanding, and treating maladaptive behaviors. In this chapter, we will examine some of the definitions and classifications of abnormal behavior and review the explanations for them. In the following chapter, we will focus on the efforts to treat or change these behaviors. In this section on history and scope, let's look separately for a moment at the issues of definition and classification and then at explanations for abnormal behavior.

What do Christopher Columbus and sky divers have in common? If we use the statistical definition of abnormality, we would have to classify any behavior that deviated from the average as abnormal. Consequently both Columbus and the sky divers would fall in the abnormal category.

Defining Abnormality

As we read Nancy's tragic story, we can identify a variety of striking behaviors. She acted aggressively, she had wild swings in mood, she couldn't form close relationships, she used drugs, she wore wild clothes and weird hair styles, she had hallucinations, and she attempted suicide. Many of her behaviors were different and unusual, but at what point, if any, do we define her actions with the more value-laden term **abnormal?** Many of us have acted aggressively, experienced wild swings in mood, dressed in ways that sent our parents screaming in horror, used drugs, and so on. Are we abnormal? Where do we draw the line? This is a tough question, but it has important implications. If we define the behaviors as different or unusual, there is little cause for concern and we may even wish to encourage them if we determine they are signs of creativity or individualism. On the other hand, if we define the behaviors as abnormal, they may need treatment or change, and the earlier disorders are identified, the more likely treatment will be successful.

One of the definitions of the word abnormal in the Random House Dictionary is "not average, typical, or usual." This is a *statistical definition*, describing as normal what most people do, and as abnormal any deviation from the average. According to this position, college students who sleep during the day and study all night are abnormal, because most people do not follow this pattern. At first glance, you may accept the statistical definition of abnormality. However, you may begin to feel uneasy when you find yourself having to label Christopher Columbus abnormal because he believed the earth was round when others "knew" that it was flat. The uneasiness may persist when you find that the abnormal "night-owl" students we mentioned are earning straight A's.

A second way to define abnormality is in light of what the *culture* defines as acceptable and normal behavior. Under this definition, an act that is abnormal in one culture may not be abnormal in another. For example, if we examine the Zhun/twa of Zambia, we find that killing a twin is standard practice. It is not done out of cruelty; practice has taught the Zhun/twa people that there is not enough food to keep two newborns alive. Thus while killing a twin would be abnormal in our culture, it is considered normal in the Zhun/twa culture.

Another way to define abnormality is to examine whether the individual's action or thoughts enable him or her to successfully adapt to the situa-

Abnormal behavior
Behavior may be so labeled when it is unusual, causes distress to others, and makes it difficult for a person to adjust to his or her environment.

One of the criticisms with DSMIII-R and other classification systems is that they do not take into account cultural variations in accepted behavior patterns. Probably no single system could be expected to do so, but we must keep this issue in mind when using the systems.

tion. Under this definition, abnormality is equated with *maladjustment* and/ or *personal distress*. Using this definition, we view Nancy's repeated aggressive behavior as abnormal because it kept her from making friends and from being accepted by her family. It also distressed her and placed her in danger. On the other hand, Nancy's punk outfits and hair styles would not be defined as abnormal because Nancy was happy with this style and it helped her to be accepted by friends she had chosen. Taking this approach further, some investigators (Baker & Butler, 1987) have suggested that the issue of *control* be incorporated into the definition of abnormal behavior. They argue that behaviors over which we feel no control are most likely to interfere with our adjustment and cause us distress.

As you can see, there are many ways to define abnormal. Most psychologists take into account all of the definitions, but many give special attention to the maladjustment and personal distress dimensions.

Classifying Disorders

As we read the account of Nancy Spungen's life, we can identify many bizarre behaviors. But if someone were to ask you to describe Nancy, it would be inconvenient for you to recite a long list of specific behaviors. This list becomes even more cumbersome if you are interested in comparing Nancy to other people who might display a similar pattern of behaviors. It would be a great deal simpler if you could use a single word or phrase to classify her behavior; this classification would serve as a shorthand summary of a number of behaviors or traits.

Almost every field of science and even our own everyday language make use of classification systems. If someone asks you how you are feeling, it is unlikely that you will reply that you have been sneezing, your nose has been "running," you have a slight fever, and your head feels stuffy. You are more likely to reply that you have a cold. The classification *cold* is a short way to summarize your symptoms.

Modern attempts to classify psychological disorders date back a hundred years to the German psychiatrist Emil Kraepelin. Although he believed that psychological disorders could be traced to specific organic causes, Kraepelin's focus on symptoms is still used in today's classification systems.

Reprinted with special permission of North America Syndicate.

The most commonly employed system is the ***Diagnostic and Statistical Manual of Mental Disorders*** (*DSM*), which was developed by the American Psychiatric Association. Psychologists and psychiatrists are continually refining the classification system and shaping it to bring it into line with current views and research on psychological disorders. The latest edition of the manual (DSM III-R) was published in 1987.

DSM III-R describes the symptoms of disorders rather than interpreting them or speculating about their causes. Rather than placing people in a single category, it classifies them along five axes or dimensions. The first axis is *current clinical syndromes*, such as major depression or schizophrenia. Axis II lists *personality disorders* and developmental disorders. These disorders share the common feature of having onset in childhood or adolescence and persisting in a stable form into adult life. Axis III is concerned with *physical and medical disorders* that may be relevant to the psychological problem. This would include, for example, information about a person's history of heart disease. The fourth axis focuses on the severity of *psychosocial stressors*, such as divorce, that may be contributing to the person's condition. Not only is the stressor noted, but it is determined whether it is acute (short duration and/or episodic) or chronic (an enduring, long-lasting stressor). On Axis V, the individual is rated on the *highest level of adaptive functioning*. Ratings are made for both the current functioning and the highest level of functioning during the past year. The ratings are based on psychological functioning, social relationships, and occupational activities. Taking the whole system together, we might see a person classified as alcohol dependence (Axis I), antisocial personality (Axis II), diabetes (Axis III), widowed (Axis IV), good level of functioning (Axis V).

DSM III-R is a complex and involved classification system. Its complexity is both a curse and a blessing. On the negative side, the system is difficult to grasp and much training is necessary to use it correctly. In addition, DSM III-R says little about the causes of disorders.

Some investigators (Quay, Routh, & Shapiro, 1987) have argued that causes are as important as symptoms in classifying disorders. But others (Sarason & Sarason, 1987) point out that given the disagreement about the causes of some disorders, including causes would complicate the classification system further. On the positive side, because of its complexity and breadth, DSM III-R allows professionals to draw from many avenues to achieve greater validity in their diagnoses. As we will see, psychological disorders are composed of a number of symptoms; it is difficult to capture this variability under a single classification. Also, more precision can be gained by using the multiple axes.

There are several points to remember about classification. First, a classification system is only an attempt to arrive at a shorthand method for communicating and keeping records on psychological disorders; it does not dictate the treatment of these disorders. Another point is that people

DSM-R III
Stands for Diagnostic and Statistical Manual, revised third edition, which was published in 1987. It is one of the most commonly used systems for classifying abnormal behavior, and was developed by the American Psychiatric Association.

often suffer from symptoms associated with a number of disorders. There are few "pure" obsessive-compulsives or paranoid schizophrenics. People are placed in the categories that are most nearly represented by their symptoms. In order to arrive at a useful classification, clinicians carefully review the individual's life history, examine test results, interview the individual and his or her acquaintances, and consider the individual's environment, culture, and language (Malgady, Rogler, & Constantino, 1987).

Insanity: A Legal Label, Not a Psychological Term

Sid Vicious was charged with Nancy's murder, but he died of a drug overdose before he could be tried. Debbie's feelings about Sid ranged from rage to pity. She recalled that Sid had written her of his devotion to Nancy. "Nancy once asked if I would pour petrol over myself and set it on fire—if she told me to. I said I would, and I meant it (Spungen, 1983, p. 397)." Debbie wondered if Sid knew what he was doing when he killed Nancy. Was he sane or insane?

Insanity is a legal term, not a psychological one. It was used in English law as early as the thirteenth century; the prevailing feeling was that a person who was "mad" was not responsible for his or her actions and therefore could not be held accountable. In 1843 Daniel M'Naghten, a Scottish wood turner, was found not guilty by reason of insanity of assassinating the secretary to the prime minister of England. The judges stated that M'Naghten "did not know he was doing what was wrong." The *M'Naghten rule* became the Anglo-American legal standard for defining insanity; it argued that an individual must be able to determine right from wrong at the time of the crime before he or she can be judged responsible and therefore guilty.

The M'Naghten rule has undergone numerous revisions in the United States. The public and professional outrage that followed John Hinckley's acquittal on grounds of insanity for shooting President Reagan and his press secretary James Brady prompted a careful review of the definition of **insanity** (Rogers, 1987), and in 1984 Congress passed the Insanity Reform Act. The present position is that a person cannot be held responsible for an act committed if, "as a result of a mental disease or defect, he lacks substantial capacity to appreciate the wrongfulness of his conduct to the requirements of the law." As you might imagine, it is exceedingly difficult to "prove" insanity, and court trials sometimes result in a battle between the conflicting testimony of experts. Because of this problem, many judges, including former Chief Justice of the Supreme Court Warren Burger, have suggested that the insanity ruling be abolished or drastically restricted. Despite recent publicity, however, the insanity plea is rarely used; in less than 3 percent of homicide trials is the plea invoked (Lunde, 1975).

There are many reasons why defendants avoid the insanity plea. The label "mentally ill" or "insane" often carries a worse social stigma than the ruling "guilty" of a crime. Further, a person who is judged "insane" under the law can be sentenced to a mental institution until he or she has "recovered sanity." In some cases, this sentence keeps a person institutionalized for a longer period than the ordinary prison sentence for the crime. In other cases, the person may be kept in a mental hospital only a short time and then be set free. Both alternatives present dangers to the individual and to society. Finally, an individual who is committed to a mental treatment center will often have fewer facilities, such as exercise areas, open grounds, library, etc., and fewer personal rights than one who is put in prison.

Insanity
Legal classification for a person who has been judged to have a mental disease or defect which renders that person unable to understand inappropriate or illegal conduct.

Insanity is a legal term, not a psychological one. In order to prove insanity, it is necessary to show that the person did not know right from wrong at the time of the crime. Because of the bizarre motives behind John W. Hinckley's assassination attempt on President Reagan, the jury found him not guilty by reason of insanity. Despite the outcome of the case, insanity is very difficult to prove and rarely used as a defense.

The Danger of Labeling

As we have seen, a classification system can be a handy, time-saving device. However, using a label to describe an individual's behavior can also have some rather dire consequences. Suppose you learned that a man living next door to you was classified as "violently antisocial." Chances are that your behavior toward him would change rather dramatically. You would try to avoid meeting him, and if you did run into him, you would find it awkward to talk to him and look him in the eyes. You would probably warn your kids not to play near his house. Everyone else in your neighborhood would react the same way. Naturally he would notice that people were treating him differently. He might react with hurt and anger to the new situation, perhaps seeking confrontations with his formerly friendly neighbors. This would play into people's expectations and further convince them that the "violently antisocial" label was correct. This type of vicious cycle has been labeled the **self-fulfilling prophecy,** a situation in which one's expectations cause to happen what one expects to happen. (See Chapter 16 for a more complete discussion of self-fulfilling prophecy.)

Another potential problem with labels is that observers may interpret behavior to fit the label. In a controversial study, eight people, including a pediatrician, a psychiatrist, and three psychologists, requested permission to enter psychiatric hospitals (Rosenhan, 1973). Each pseudopatient complained, "I hear voices, unclear voices. I think they say 'empty, how-wow, thud.' " The pseudopatients gave false names and occupations to the hospitals but all other background information was true. They were admitted and, in all cases except one, were given the diagnosis of "schizophrenic."

After being admitted, all the pseudopatients stopped faking the symptom of hearing voices and behaved normally. Rosenhan states that "Despite their public 'show' of sanity, the pseudopatients were never detected." They were kept in the hospital from 7 to 52 days, with the average stay being 19 days. At discharge, their records carried the label "schizophrenia in remission," which simply meant that they were not now displaying the symptoms of schizophrenia. The implication was that they were still schizophrenic. This study suggests that labels must be applied with caution because the effect of labels may go far beyond describing symptoms. It was impossible for the pseudopatients to overcome their label.

Identifying the Causes of Maladaptive Behavior

Our concern to this point has been on examining how psychologists have identified and labeled abnormal behavior. We can see that Nancy Spungen engaged in some bizarre behaviors and after careful study we could probably agree on a label for her behavior using DSM III-R. But most of us would also want to take the extra step to explain why she behaved as she did. Throughout history people have been both fascinated and frightened by those who display abnormal behaviors because they couldn't explain why others acted in this way. Explanations are not only important in satisfying curiosity, but they can also help us determine how to treat and/or prevent these maladaptive behaviors. With this in mind, let's briefly review some of the historical and present approaches for understanding maladaptive behavior.

The Mystical Perspective. Some of the earliest explanations for maladaptive behavior focused on spiritual or supernatural forces. The person was believed to be possessed by the forces that took control of his or her behavior. During the Middle Ages people who were believed to be possessed by evil spirits were labeled witches. However, "the force" has

Self-fulfilling prophecy
Expectation that leads one to behave in ways that will cause that expectation to come about.

Early explanations for abnormal behavior focused on supernatural spirits. People possessed by these spirits were labeled as witches and treatment involved driving the spirits from the person.

not always been viewed as evil; in fact in some societies, the individual was viewed as "touched by the gods." You may be surprised to learn that in some communities today, even in highly advanced countries such as the United States, the demonic view of abnormal behavior persists (Golden, 1977).

The Medical Model. Nancy's birth was a traumatic one; she was born five weeks premature, she was a "blue baby" because the umbilical cord was wrapped around her neck cutting off her oxygen at birth, and she had a blood disorder that required a transfusion at birth. At the begin-

It is said that Van Gogh's paintings reflected his quickly changing moods.

ning of her book, Debbie Spungen openly wonders whether Nancy's eventual problems could not be traced to these abnormalities at birth. The idea that abnormal behavior is caused by an organic irregularity originated in ancient Greece. Indeed the term *mental illness* that is used by some people today symbolizes the view that psychological disorders have a medical basis. The medical approach is further evident in the terms often found associated with abnormal behavior: mental hospital, diagnosis, mental patient, cure. These terms imply that we are dealing with a disease that can be explained and treated like a physical illness.

Those who adopt the medical model look for genetic or biological defects that could cause abnormal behavior. As we will see, there is evidence that heredity and physical abnormalities are related to some psychological disorders. Treatment for psychological disorders often includes drugs, and the search for causes centers on biological and physical bases. Indeed, some disorders such as Alzheimer's disease, Down Syndrome, mental retardation, and some types of organically based hyperactivity have clear biological causes. However, the medical model as a broad explanation for maladaptive behavior has come under considerable criticism. In many cases, it has proved impossible to identify an organic or biological cause for disorders. Research has shown that personal and social variables are the root of many disorders and even when there is a biological component, social factors play a large role in determining the onset and symptoms of the disorder.

The Psychoanalytic Model. The psychoanalytic perspective argues that abnormal behavior is the result of unresolved conflicts that occur during infancy and childhood. As we saw in Chapter 13, Sigmund Freud believed that personality is formed in early childhood as an individual attempts to resolve conflicts concerning aggression and sexual behavior. Freud argued that if these conflicts are not successfully resolved during childhood, the person will repress them into the unconscious and not deal with them. Later in life these repressed conflicts will influence the person's behavior because they will try to push their way into consciousness. When this happens, the person experiences anxiety and tries to cope by using defense mechanisms such as rationalization, projection, or reaction formation, as we discussed in Chapter 13. If these efforts are not successful, the anxiety will increase and the individual will develop *neurotic* patterns of behavior. In some cases, the disturbance caused by these unresolved conflicts may become so great that the person can no longer deal with reality; the person then develops his or her own world and behaves in ways that make it difficult to adjust to the real world. This poor contact with reality is called *psychosis*.

As you might imagine, it has proved very difficult to establish clear evidence that specific abnormal behaviors are the result of childhood conflicts. While proof may be difficult, there are many reports in the scientific literature supporting the position that some cases of abnormal behavior may indeed have their roots in early childhood experience.

The Learning/Behavioral Model. Because many maladaptive behaviors are so unusual, we are tempted to look for unusual causes to explain them. Not so, say the learning theorists who argue that maladaptive behavior is learned through the same principles of reinforcement and modeling that shape other behaviors. According to this approach, Nancy's violence, her flights into fantasy, and her drug behavior can be explained by learning principles. If we adopt the learning position, we do not view maladaptive behavior as the symptoms of some underlying medical problem or as a sign of unresolved conflict. Rather, we view the maladaptive behavior as a product of the individual's environment. If we change the environment and/or the reinforcement patterns, we can change the behavior. Some of the professionals who examined Nancy used this learning approach to explain her behavior. Debbie, however, was hurt by this suggestion because

The learning model argues that behavior is a product of the person's environment. Maladaptive behavior is learning through the same principles as is adaptive behavior.

she felt the professionals were telling her that she *caused* Nancy's behavior. This is an oversimplification of the learning model that draws on the wide variety of learning processes we discussed in Chapter 6.

The Cognitive Model. According to the cognitive approach, people's behavior is strongly influenced by their beliefs and attitudes (Beck, 1983). The basis for irrational or bizarre behavior is irrational beliefs or attitudes. Ellis (1987) makes this point clear by stating ". . . people largely disturb themselves by thinking in a self-defeating, illogical, and unrealistic manner . . . (p. 364)." Therefore the way to change behavior is first to change the underlying attitudes. As you can see, the cognitive approach is similar to the learning approach in that both deal with the present and both involve retraining. The difference is that while learning approaches work directly with behavior, the cognitive approach works on teaching the person new attitudes or beliefs in order to change his or her behavior.

The Humanistic Model. As we saw in Chapter 13, the humanists believe that people are basically rational and good. Left to their own devices, people will strive for personal growth and self-actualization. However, problems will arise if people are prevented from satisfying their basic needs or are forced to live up to the expectations of others in their surroundings. When this occurs, people lose sight of their own goals and develop distorted perceptions of themselves. Then they feel threatened and insecure and are unable to accept their own feelings and experiences. It is losing touch with one's feelings, goals, and perceptions that forms the basis of psychological disturbance.

The Systems Model. Thus far we have examined theories that explain abnormal behavior by focusing on the individual and his or her weaknesses. The systems approach, as represented by community psychology, regards the individual as part of a social network made up of family members, friends and acquaintances in the community, and various community organizations. The individual plays a role in relation to each of these people and agencies. For most people, the social network supports and maintains their behavior. However, for some people, the social network is filled with stress and conflicting demands, which play a major role in fostering their abnormal and maladaptive behavior. Thus the community approach suggests that abnormal behavior may be caused as much by a "sick" system as by a "sick" person.

We can illustrate this approach by beginning with the finding that schizophrenia is most prevalent in lower socioeconomic areas. Hollingshead and Redlich (1958) argue that it is the stress associated with the substandard housing, high crime rates, and broken families in these areas that causes the high rate of mental illness. Others, however, dispute this position, arguing instead that more psychological disorders are found in these areas simply because people who suffer behavior disorders often drift downward into the lower classes (Dunham, 1965; Levy & Rowitz, 1973). A resolution of this disagreement has still not been reached but the point of interest here is that the system is being suggested as a possible cause for a psychological disorder.

As we will see, the types of psychological disorders are many and varied, and anyone searching for quick or simple answers in the research and theories may become frustrated. Although medical research on physical illness has a long history, careful research on psychological disorders is relatively recent. Psychologists are still searching for the causes of some disturbances. The present theories serve as guidelines by pointing out ways to examine the disorders. It is unlikely that any single model or approach can explain all disorders. It is more probable that each of the modern perspectives (see Table 14–1) explains certain disorders and that any single maladaptive behavior has many causes. As we examine the disorders, we will give examples of different explanations that have been advanced as the "roots of abnormality."

Table 14–1
Approaches to Psychological Disorders

Approach	Critical Period for Determining Onset of Behavior	Importance Placed on Determining Cause	Major Emphasis of Approach
Medical	Past	Very important	Physiological function
Psychoanalytic	Past	Very important	Childhood conflicts
Learning	Present*	Not important	Present behavior
Cognitive	Present*	Not important	Present behavior and beliefs
Humanistic	Past/present	Mildly important	Conditions preventing person from achieving personal growth
Systems	Present*	Important	Person's role in social network

* Prior learning, reinforcement schedules, and environment also recognized as contributing to condition.

The Medical Student Syndrome

Before examining specific psychological disorders, there is one point we should address. As the symptoms of the various disorders are reviewed, you may find yourself growing increasingly uneasy. Some of these symptoms are depression, difficulty in falling asleep, loss of appetite, headaches, and sexual dysfunction. As you read about them, you may recall that you have periodically felt depressed, suffered headaches, lost your appetite, been unable to sleep, and not functioned sexually according to your expectations. These realizations may cause you to leap to the conclusion, "I've got it!"

In a near panic you may decide that you are schizophrenic, or that you have an affective disorder, or that you suffer from a psychosexual disorder.

The "I've got it" conclusion is often found among medical students as they study physical diseases. They remember times when they felt dizzy and had no appetite, and conclude that they are suffering from cancer; or they recall a time when they had a burning sensation when they urinated, and conclude that they have venereal disease; or they remember when their heart beat wildly and they were short of breath, and decide that they have heart disease. They rush to the emergency room in a state of panic, fearing the worst, only to find out they are in fine physical shape.

It is important to remember that all of us have at some time displayed some of the behaviors associated with the psychological disorders, just as we have had some symptoms of severe medical ailments. However, in most of us, these psychological symptoms are not intense, do not have interfere with our social or occupational functioning for long periods of time, and do not occur with any great frequency. Occasionally experiencing symptoms of this kind is normal and it does not suggest that we are suffering or soon to suffer psychological disorder. The symptoms associated with the psychological disorders are intense and enduring, and they interfere with people's adjustment to their physical and social worlds. With this thought in mind, let us examine some specific psychological disorders.

Our review of disorders will necessarily be selective because the list of possible disorders is long and varied. As you will recall we have already examined some of the disorders in the previous chapters as they related to the topics of those chapters; in Chapter 11 we discussed anorexia and bulimia, in Chapter 9 we examined several childhood disorders (infantile autism, gender identity disorders, childhood schizophrenia, and attention deficit disorders), and in Chapter 10 we covered a number of disorders related to aging (Alzheimer disease, senile dementia).

Anxiety Disorders

We have all experienced anxiety, that diffuse feeling of dread and fear that ties our stomachs in a hard knot. Remember how you felt when you were in your first school play, went out on your first date, or had an important job interview? You probably had trouble falling asleep the night before each of these events. And as the time for the event approached, you probably felt tense and were afraid to open your mouth for fear that the butterflies in your stomach would escape. I recall a close friend who spent an hour before a big football game vomiting and telling everyone he couldn't "go out there"; as you might imagine he went on to have the best game of his life. Like my friend most of us who have these anxiety attacks find ways to control them and are able to complete the task at hand.

Unfortunately, some people experience anxiety that is far out of proportion to the situations they are in, and their responses to these anxiety-arousing situations are exaggerated and interfere with normal daily functioning. These characteristics are common to a group of conditions classified as **anxiety disorders.** It has been estimated that 2 to 4 percent of the population suffers from anxiety disorders. There are a number of behavior patterns classified as anxiety disorders; the common thread, however, is that each is a maladaptive reaction to excessive anxiety. Anxiety disorders were once described as a **neurosis**, but this term proved vague and confusing and it has been dropped in newer classification systems such as DSM III-R. Anxiety and fear are found in many of the disorders we will discuss; indeed, Nancy Spungen experienced high levels of anxiety at many times

Anxiety disorders
Group of conditions in which people feel anxiety that is far out of proportion to the situations they are in; their responses interfere with normal daily functioning.
Neurosis
Broad pattern of psychological disorders characterized by anxiety, fear, and self-defeating behaviors.

Anxiety is a generalized state of dread and worry. While the generalized anxiety disorder slowly creeps up on its victim, panic disorder has a sudden onset and may come and go over time.

during her life. However, keep in mind that in classifying a condition as an anxiety disorder, the anxiety must be a major symptom.

Generalized Anxiety Disorder and Panic Disorder

As can be seen in the case study highlight on p. 535, **general anxiety disorders** keep people in a constant state of agitation and dread. People suffering from this disorder have trouble falling asleep, experience a loss of appetite, feel tense and keyed up, and may have increased heart rate and faintness. They also have trouble concentrating, and consequently their work suffers. People with this disorder worry about what the future holds for them; they worry about what might happen to their friends and their possessions; they worry about almost anything and everything that is happening or might happen. They tend to recall negative information from the past and pay special attention to potentially threatening things in their environment (Mogg, Mathews, & Weinman, 1987).

Whereas generalized anxiety disorder may gradually creep up on a person and consume him or her for a long period of time, the **panic disorder** has a sudden onset and it may come and go over time. Like a giant hand gripping and then releasing the person, the panic disorder is characterized by sudden sweating, dizziness, shortness of breath, chest pains, and feelings of helplessness. As Table 14–2 indicates, panic disorders have more bodily symptoms than generalized anxiety disorders. During a panic attack, the person may fear that he or she is going to die or "go crazy." The most disturbing point of both these disorders is that the victims don't know what is causing their anxiety; like being haunted by an unseen ghost, they don't know what to do or where to hide.

We do not know the reasons why people suffer generalized anxiety disorders or panic disorders. We do know that they are twice as common in females as in males and that they run in families. Research on this last point suggests that people learn to experience these attacks by imitating other family members. On the other hand, psychoanalytic theorists suggest that the cause may be repressed feelings or conflicts that threaten to surface.

Generalized anxiety disorder
Disorder in which people experience overwhelming anxiety, but cannot identify its source.
Panic disorder
Sudden onset of anxiety, overcoming the person with physiological symptoms such as sweating, dizziness, and shortness of breath. This disorder disrupts normal daily functioning.

CASE STUDY OF A GENERALIZED ANXIETY DISORDER

At the time of onset, Miss M. had been doing secretarial work in a large business office, a position in which she took dictation from a number of salesmen and minor executives. Although intellectually competent and physically very attractive, the patient had always been extremely shy in any personal situation involving a man. She led a restricted social life and very seldom went out on dates. She functioned adequately, however, in most business and other group settings. While working for the firm, Miss M. secretly developed a romantic interest in one of the young executives, an interest that she scarcely acknowledged even to herself. She managed to banish it from her (conscious) thoughts entirely when she learned, in casual office conversation, that he was married.

The company offices were on an upper floor of a large downtown office building equipped with automatic elevators. One morning, arriving at work an unaccustomed few minutes late, Miss M. found herself alone in an elevator with the young executive. The man made a complimentary but slightly suggestive remark about the patient's dress. Miss M. blushed and became highly embarrassed, tense, and anxious. By dint of considerable effort, she managed to get through the day's work. The next morning, as she was about to enter the elevator, she experienced an attack of anxiety so severe as to verge upon panic. She left the building, walked about for nearly an hour, and then was able to return. This time she climbed six flights of stairs to the office.

During succeeding days the patient made several efforts to use the elevator, but she invariably found herself becoming too anxious to do so. She continued to use the stairs, and for several months was able to continue work in reasonable comfort, having taken this precaution. Eventually, the use of the stairs became as disturbing as that of the elevator. At this point, the patient was compelled to ask for a leave of absence, and she had not returned to work at the time of consultation.

At no point did the patient consciously associate her attacks of anxiety with the young executive. In fact, as she told the psychiatrist, she "no longer thought of him at all." Miss M. had no doubt that she was ill, but she considered the nature of her illness to be inexplicable.

Source: C. K. Hofling, *Textbook of Psychiatry for Medical Practice*, 1975, p. 326.

Symptom	Panic Disorder*	Generalized Anxiety Disorder*
Sweating, flushing	58.3	22.2
Heart palpitations	89.5	61.1
Chest pain	68.8	11.1
Faintness, light-headedness	52.1	11.1
Blurred vision	31.2	0
Feeling of muscular weakness	47.9	11.1

Table 14–2
Symptoms of Panic Disorder and Generalized Anxiety Disorders

* Percentages of patients reporting particular symptoms (based on Anderson and others, 1984).

Anxiety or panic is experienced when the person feels these unwanted feelings clawing their way into the conscious. Once brought into the conscious, the person will be forced to experience pain and deal with the feelings.

Post-Traumatic Stress Disorder

The years after the Vietnam war have etched the term **post-traumatic stress disorder** into our everyday vocabulary. The evening news reports and newspapers carried the tragic stories of veterans who had terrifying flashbacks of events they experienced during the war, who couldn't adjust to society because of these experiences, and who did everything possible to avoid talking about or thinking about the war. As dramatic as these

Post-Traumatic Stress Disorder
Reexperiencing a stressful event that can occur months or years after the event.

POST-TRAUMATIC STRESS DISORDER

On July 19, 1989, at 3:30 P.M., as United Airlines Flight 232 circled the skies high above Sioux City, Iowa's Gateway Airport, most of the 279 passengers on board and all 11 of the crew members knew that they were in serious trouble. The DC-10 in which they were flying had been crippled by a complete loss of hydraulic power after leaving Denver on its way to Philadelphia. As the pilot circled an inactive runway at the airport, the Sioux City and Woodbury County disaster plan officials were busy arraying fire equipment, ambulances, and medical helicopters in anticipation of what appeared to be an inevitable crash landing. Around 4:00 P.M., after circling for nearly a half hour, the plane approached the runway. Just a few feet from the ground, it pitched sharply to its right, the right wing striking the ground. With this impact, the plane cartwheeled, wing over wing, bursting into flames, disintegrating into many pieces.

Incredibly, 184 passengers and crew members survived this fiery crash. The well-coordinated disaster response plan enacted by Sioux City and Woodbury County delivered the first of the injured passengers to waiting teams of doctors and nurses at local hospitals in just minutes following the crash. This impressively choreographed and flawlessly executed rescue effort was surely responsible for saving the lives of so many of the passengers on Flight 232.

The remarkably quick response at the crash site and the immediate attention given to the medical needs of the survivors of this catastrophe were only part of this disaster plan. Also on hand to administer aid was a team of 16 clinical psychologists from the University of South Dakota. These psychologists were there to provide counseling and psychological support services to the survivors and their families, to the families of those who had died in the crash, and even to the emergency rescue and medical personnel (Jacobs, Quevillin, & Stricherz, 1990). The inclusion of psychologists in the disaster relief plan demonstrates the growing awareness on the part of disaster response planners and community

health officials that people who experience a traumatic event, even though they may have escaped serious physical injury, may have psychological wounds. These psychological wounds, though not always noticeable in the shock and confusion immediately following the traumatic event, nevertheless leave the person at grave risk of developing a serious anxiety disorder known as post-traumatic stress disorder (PTSD).

Although it has only recently been included in the diagnostic manual (DSM-III-R) of the American Psychiatric Association, PTSD is something of an old wine in a new bottle. The symptoms are most readily linked to the emotional trauma of war and, indeed, may be as old as war itself. Nineteenth-century Russian soldiers with the symptoms of PTSD were said to have a "disease of the soul." U.S. soldiers in that same century suffered from "neurasthenia." In World War I the same symptoms described a disorder known as "war neurosis" or "shell shock," while World War II soldiers experienced "combat fatigue." But it was the psychological suffering of a staggering number of Vietnam War veterans that raised the consciousness of the American public regarding the psychological "aftershock" of trauma and added the term "post-traumatic stress disorder" to our vocabulary. (For a review of the unique circumstances of the Vietnam War that contributed to the high incidence of PTSD among Vietnam veterans, see King & King, 1991.)

Although PTSD gained clinical legitimacy as a war-related disorder, it is now being recognized in a broader context. As mental health workers became more familiar with the range of symptoms that can accompany this anxiety disorder and more sophisticated in their understanding of psychological stressors, they realized that events other than war can trigger PTSD. The same symptoms seen in Vietnam War veterans are now being recognized in victims of rape and other violent crimes. Survivors of community disasters such as earthquakes, floods, fires, and airplane crashes like that of United Flight 232 are likewise found to be at risk of suffering PTSD (Slaby, 1989).

The criteria used by the American Psychiatric Association to diagnose PTSD have been revised twice since 1980, most recently in 1987, with another revision scheduled for 1992 (Marcus, 1990). These revisions reflect the broadening sensitivities of mental health workers to trauma-related stress reactions outside the experience of war. The following brief summary of these criteria from the DSM-III-R will be illustrative.

A diagnosis of PTSD can be applied when:

- The person has lived through an event so unusual and so catastrophic that anyone who lived through such an event would likely be distressed. This includes experiences that threatened the person's life, as well as witnessing events in which the person's own life was not threatened, but another person's life was lost or threatened.

- The person continues to relive the traumatic event through obsessive recollections of it, through recurring nightmares about it, or, most dramatically, through hallucinations and flashbacks in which the person actually reexperiences the sights, sounds, and feelings that accompanied the traumatic event.

- The person consistently utilizes a number of defensive strategies designed to avoid circumstances related to the traumatic event. These strategies can include the inability to recall important aspects of the event (psychogenic amnesia), feelings of detachment or estrangement from others, weaker affective (mood-related) responses, and pessimistic expectations about one's future.

- The person behaves in ways that indicate high levels of physiological arousal, as evidenced by difficulty in falling asleep, chronic irritability and a quick temper, hyper-vigilance, and hypersensitivity to loud stimuli. Additionally, the person may show a sympathetic nervous system response to stimuli associated with the event (sweating, pupillary dilation, increased heart rate, etc.).

Many of these symptoms can appear within hours of the traumatic event, but in order to warrant a diagnosis of PTSD, the symptoms must persist for at least one month. When symptoms persist for one month, but abate within six months, the disorder is described as *acute PTSD*. In *chronic PTSD*, the symptoms persist for longer than six months, sometimes for many years. A third category of PTSD is *delayed PTSD*. This classification is made when the symptoms do not surface until at least six months after the trauma. As with chronic PTSD, the symptoms associated with delayed PTSD may linger for many years.

Obviously, the disasters, catastrophes, and random acts of violence that can trigger PTSD cannot be eliminated. But there is something that can be done to help reduce the risk of PTSD following these trauma-inducing events. Communities, like Sioux City, Iowa, that respond in a timely, well-organized fashion to disasters help restore a sense of control to the victims. This, in turn, seems to moderate the psychologically distressing impact of the event, thereby reducing risk of PTSD (Slaby, 1989). The rescue personnel and the mental health professionals who carried out the Sioux City disaster response plan not only saved the lives of many of the passengers on United Flight 232, they may also have saved many of the survivors from the psychological suffering of post-traumatic stress disorder.

accounts are, post-traumatic stress disorders are not confined to the Vietnam war veterans (see Highlight: Post-Traumatic Stress Disorder). Anyone who has suffered a threat to life or integrity, witnessed such a threat to a loved one, seen the sudden destruction of one's home or community, or watched a violent crime or accident may suffer post-traumatic stress disorder.

The disorder involves reexperiencing the event long after it has passed. The event can be relived in recollections or recurrent dreams and nightmares. The individual becomes physically aroused, hyperalert, and has difficulty concentrating on tasks. People suffering from this disorder have difficulty solving interpersonal problems and coping with stress, and these difficulties heighten the intensity of the disorder (Nezu & Carnevale, 1987). Pain, guilt, and fear are common feelings accompanying the disorder. Any event or stimulus (weather, symbol, people, words) associated with the original incident may trigger the disorder.

The term post-traumatic stress disorder became a part of our everyday vocabulary after the Vietnam war. Anyone who has experienced a threat to his or her life or integrity may suffer the disorder which involves reexperiencing the event long after it has passed. Group therapy such as the Vietnam veterans group pictured here is used to help people cope with the disorder.

Table 14–3
Familiar and Rare Phobias

Acrophobia	Fear of heights
Agoraphobia	Fear of open spaces
Haphephobia	Fear of touching or being touched
Hematophobia	Fear of blood
Melanophobia	Fear of bees
Ophidiophobia	Fear of snakes
Panophobia	Fear of everything
Phonophobia	Fear of speaking aloud
Scopophobia	Fear of being stared at

Phobia
An irrational fear of an object or event attached to a specific, identifiable object; phobics can control their anxiety by avoiding that object or situation.

Phobia involves an irrational fear of an event or object. Acrophobia is the fear of heights.

We don't know why some people suffer from this disorder while others who experienced the same event do not. It has been suggested that people who tried to repress their feelings and did not deal with their guilt and fear at the time of the original incident are most likely to suffer post-traumatic stress disorders. The person uses a great deal of energy and concentration to keep from dealing with the event and feelings about it. They live with the ever-present fear that these feelings will emerge, and eventually something serves as the catalyst to bring the event to the surface.

Phobia

Phobia occurs when people have an irrational fear of an object or event. The name is derived from Phobos, who was the Greek god of fear, and most phobias have Greek names (see Table 14–3). Phobics know what causes their fear; it is attached to a specific, identifiable object. They can control their anxiety by avoiding that object or situation. Although this may seem to be a simple solution to anxiety, many phobias can be very disruptive. For example, people suffering from agoraphobia (fear of open or unfamiliar places) may be so overwhelmed by their fear that they will not leave their home. People who suffer a fear of crowds may be unable to go to parties, the movies, the library, class, an office, or other places where crowds may be found. As can be seen from the representative list in Table 14–3 phobias can involve a wide range of objects. In most cases, phobics recognize the irrationality of their fear, but they are powerless to do anything about it. This realization makes the phobia more troublesome.

There are some striking statistics regarding phobias. Women are more likely to suffer from phobias than men. For example, it has been estimated that 95 percent of all zoophobics (people who fear animals) are women (Davison & Neale, 1978). Also, phobics tend to be of average or above-average intelligence, and many of them show few signs of any disorder except the phobia. While phobias occur most often around the age of 50, specific phobias tend to have very distinct age peaks (see Figure 14–1).

Freud was one of the first people to carefully study phobias. He believed that the phobic object is chosen to symbolize the real source of fear or conflict. For example, a woman may harbor a deep resentment and fear of her father. Since these feelings are very threatening to her and make her feel guilty, she may displace them onto some other object, such as an animal, a color, or a situation that can be avoided more easily. The chosen object may be only remotely associated with the real, feared object. However, she can now control the anxiety by avoiding the new, substitute object.

Other theorists believe that phobias, like other behaviors, are learned (e.g., Bandura, 1969). Some phobias may result from classical conditioning (see Chapter 6). For example, a boy wakes up one dark, stormy night fearing that his parents have left him. After a frantic search of the house, he finds his parents, but the trauma of the experience leaves him with a fear of the dark or of lightning. Phobias can also be learned by watching other people showing fear of certain objects or situations, or by hearing people express their fear of objects.

Although the learning approach offers an important explanation for phobias, an interesting question can be raised: Why do phobias focus on some objects and not on others? One suggestion is that human beings are *prepared* to develop aversions to certain objects but not to others (Eysenck, 1979). Those objects that we are prepared (or preprogrammed) to fear are ones that actually represented some danger for us at some time in our history. Thus phobias may focus on heights, snakes, darkness, open spaces, or blood because these objects were once real threats to humans.

On the other hand, phobias will not center on doors, bed sheets, or chairs because these objects historically never represented any danger to people.

Obsessive-Compulsive Disorder

We began our discussion of anxiety disorders with a disorder in which neither the object of anxiety nor reaction to it is specific. We then moved to the phobic disorders in which the object of the anxiety is very clear. We close the section on anxiety by examining disorders where the behavior related to anxiety is very specific; in fact, the behavior itself often increases the person's anxiety and frustration.

In psychological terms, an **obsession** is a recurring, irrational thought that cannot be controlled or banished from one's mind. Some obsessions are quite harmless. For example, you may have had the experience of hearing a catchy tune on the radio that you then hummed for the next few days. No matter where you went or what you did, you couldn't seem to get it out of your mind. While this type of obsession is at worst annoying, other obsessions can cause a great deal of stress. Imagine constantly having thoughts of murdering your brother or being obsessed with the belief that your house is going to burn down. The most common obsessions associated with this disorder involve violence, contamination (e.g., becoming infected by shaking hands), and doubt (American Psychiatric Association, 1987). Not only is the content of these thoughts disturbing, but their constant occurrence keeps you from concentrating on anything else. You might realize that your fears are irrational, but no matter what you do, you cannot control them or block them out. A related problem involves **compulsions,** which are irrational behaviors or rituals that people cannot control. They have a recurring compulsion to perform an act but cannot determine why they feel this desire. Generally, people who have obsessions also suffer compulsions. Shakespeare's Lady Macbeth experienced a hand-washing compulsion; she continually washed her hands in an effort to cleanse the guilt she felt for taking part in a murder. Indeed, there are reported cases of obsessive-compulsives who wash their hands over 500 times a day. Not only does this activity take considerable time, but it leaves the victim's hands painfully raw and cracked. Another common compulsive behavior involves neatness and orderliness; people suffering from this compulsion may spend every day cleaning their room and putting things away. It has also been reported that obsessive-compulsive behaviors are most commonly found in people of high intelligence and socioeconomic status. But, unlike many other anxiety reactions, this disorder occurs about equally in men and women.

Until recently, it was believed that obsessive-compulsive disorders were very rare, occurring in less than .05 percent of the general population. However, more careful studies suggest that the disorder may be 50 to 100 times more prevalent than the original figure (Rasmussen & Eisen, 1990). The average age at onset is late adolescence or early 20s (Swedo, Rappaport, & Leonard, 1989), although onset is generally earlier in males (17.5 years) than in females (20.8). Interestingly, the symptoms often first become evident in women during the latter stages of pregnancy or following childbirth, and their intensity often increases during the menstrual period (Rasmussen & Eisen, 1988).

Some explanations for **obsessive-compulsive disorders** are based on psychoanalytic theory. One view is that people try to keep unwanted thoughts or feelings from entering their consciousness by performing compulsive acts or engaging in obsessive thinking. By constantly engaging in such activities, these people do not allow themselves the chance to focus on threatening thoughts. It has been suggested that guilt underlies obses-

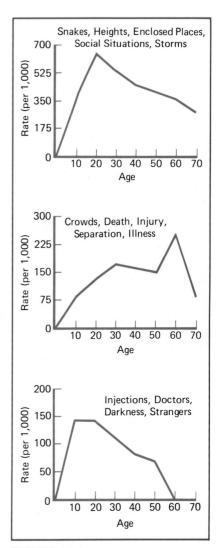

FIGURE 14–1

Specific phobias tend to occur at certain ages.

Obsession
Recurring, irrational thought that cannot be controlled or banished from one's mind. See also *compulsion*, which involves behavior rather than thought.

Compulsion
Irrational behavior or ritual that people cannot control; often they do not know why they need to do this. See also *obsession*, which involves thought rather than behavior.

Obsessive-compulsive disorders
Disorders that occur when the person feels an overwhelming need to think a certain thought (obsession) or perform a certain behavior (compulsion).

CASE STUDY OF AN OBSESSIVE-COMPULSIVE DISORDER

A department store clerk quickly lost her job because of complaints from customers over her slowness in making change and her eccentric behavior. She was obsessed with the number seven. If the number appeared in the cents column, she found herself unable to stop repeating the figure over and over. If the number appeared in the dollars column or in any other circumstance, she felt a strong urge to omit it. She could not take the seventh step on a stairway in stride but always managed to do a little skip. Rather than getting off the elevator on the seventh floor of any building, she preferred the inconvenience of going to a higher or lower floor and walking the rest of the way. She changed her residence several times in order to live in a district where the telephone was given an area code without a seven. When asked about the inconveniences, she commented: "You think it would be easy to stop this thing with numbers altogether; actually it's worse if I don't count. Then I start to feel like something bad is going to happen. And pretty soon I feel this ball inside me, growing like a cancer, a tension that's going to explode . . . and I can't concentrate, until I count my seven's again. Now I'm comfortable again, and I feel safe, really safe."

The patient had been raised by her divorced mother. Throughout her life she heard endless accounts of the cruelties of life and the necessity of being so self-reliant and competent that she would never have to rely on anyone else. Her mother used every waking moment to instruct her daughter by continuously evaluating her performance on trivial as well as important matters. The mother died after an agonizing battle with cancer. She died on the seventh day of July (the seventh month).

Richard M. Suinn. *Fundamentals of Abnormal Psychology.* Nelson-Hall, 1984, p. 141.

sive-compulsive disorders (Rosen, 1975). People may experience guilt over actions they performed or thought about performing; they then adopt an obsession or a compulsive behavior as a form of self-punishment. More recently (Schmeck, 1988; Goodman et al., 1990), investigators have found a physiological link to the disorder; portions of the brain of obsessive-compulsive patients metabolize glucose at a faster rate than do the brains of people not suffering from this disorder. There is still a question of whether this metabolic abnormality is a cause or effect of the disorder.

Cognitive theories have suggested that the irrational anxiety that underlies this disorder may be the result of faulty judgments that people make about objects or situations. They may overestimate and then become obsessed with the danger in a certain situation. Their obsessive thoughts may be warnings they are giving themselves about the possible dangers in the situation, and their compulsive behaviors may be aimed at avoiding these dangers.

Lady Macbeth had a hand-washing compulsion; she continually washed her hands in an effort to wash away her guilt for murder. Obsessive-compulsive disorders can consume one's life and interfere with even the most normal activities.

Anxiety often leads to the bizarre changes in behavior that we discussed in the previous section. Anxiety, however, can also dramatically affect our physical well-being. In fact, this effect can take two forms. In Chapter 13, we discussed psychological factors affecting physical condition in which stress actually causes organic damage to our bodies. For example, an ulcer involves damage to the stomach lining. The second set of physical disorders initiated by stress is the **somatoform disorders** in which the individual shows the physical symptoms of disease or illness but has no organic damage that could cause these symptoms. Somatoform disorders are the dread of every physician because patients believe and act as if they are physically ill, but the physician can find no organic cause for the "illness."

Hypochondriasis is an example of a somatoform disorder; the hypochondriac believes that he or she is seriously ill despite assurances to the contrary by physicians. In fact, he or she often views these assurances as evidence that they have something so terribly bad that "even the doctor is keeping it from me." Every little ache, pain, or cough is interpreted as a sign of serious illness. While hypochondriacs have few specific symptoms, people with *somatization disorder* complain of a number of vague but dramatic symptoms such as headaches, nausea, vomiting, stomach pains, tiredness, and menstrual problems. These people really feel and believe that they are sick, and their belief may cause them to feel depressed and threaten suicide. They may make frequent trips to the doctor and even demand surgery, though the physician can find no organic cause for their complaint.

Conversion Disorder

While the somatization disorder involves a number of vague problems, the **conversion disorder** usually involves one specific symptom (see Figure 14–2). The most common symptoms are paralysis of a limb, loss of sensation in a part of the body, blindness, or deafness (Girdano & Everly, 1987). There are some distinct factors that make conversion disorders rather easy to diagnose. First, there is no organic damage: A patient may be unable to move her left arm, but there is no physical reason for this immobility. Second, the disorder often appears shortly after some stressful event and has a sudden onset; as can be seen in the case study highlighted, Sam's symptoms occurred after the minor traffic accident and after the arguments with his family. Third, the symptoms do not make anatomical sense. For example, people with glove anesthesia report losing sensation in a hand, although they have normal feelings in that arm (see Figure 14–2). Given the connecting system of nerves in the hand and arm, the loss of sensation in a hand is impossible without loss of sensation in parts of that arm as well. Fourth, the symptoms (paralysis, deafness, or blindness) disappear when people are asleep or hypnotized. The fifth factor that distinguishes conversion disorders from real physical problems is that those who have them often show little concern or anxiety about the disabling symptoms. Imagine your own reaction if you suddenly found that your legs were paralyzed. In the highlighted case, we can see that Sam was more interested in the machinery and nurses than in his paralysis.

At this point you may be thinking that people with conversion disorders are simply faking it. This is not true, however. The paralyzed person actually cannot move the affected limb. With people who have lost sensation in a particular area, it is possible to stick pins in that area without getting a response.

Somatoform disorders
Group of disorders in which people feel ill or show other symptoms such as blindness or paralysis, but there is no organic damage.
Hypochondriasis
A somatoform disorder where the person believes that he or she is seriously ill in spite of assurances to the contrary.
Conversion disorder
One of the somatoform disorders, usually involving one specific symptom. The most common symptoms are paralysis of a limb, loss of sensation in a part of the body, blindness, and deafness. There is no organic basis to this disorder.

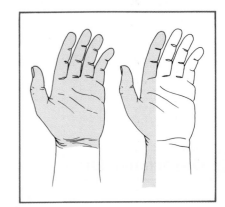

FIGURE 14–2

The symptoms involved in a conversion disorder do not make anatomical sense. On the left is shown the loss of feeling complained of by people with glove anesthesia; on the right is shown the loss of feeling that would occur if there were actual nerve damage.

CASE STUDY OF A CONVERSION DISORDER

Sam B., a college student, was involved in a minor traffic accident on his way home from class. Although he was slightly bruised, medical examination showed no serious physical involvement, and the patient was discharged from the hospital. "I woke up the next morning and couldn't feel my legs, they were numb. . . . I supposed they had gone to sleep on me, but then I tried to move them, and my legs wouldn't move. . . . I couldn't walk anymore." Sam was returned by ambulance to the hospital for extensive neurological and X-ray examinations with negative results. Throughout, he seemed bemused by the procedures, intrigued by the machinery, and taken by the nurses. The diagnosis: conversion disorder.

When Sam was interviewed by a psychologist, the following facts came to light. Just prior to the accident, he had another of many arguments with his family over his education. He wanted to get a job in order to make some money. His parents, both from immigrant backgrounds, had forced him to continue his schooling in spite of constant bickering. He was on an allowance on the condition that he remain in school. Money had always been a problem, since the patient tended to squander it on social activities, girlfriends, and his motorbike:

I was on my bike going home and thinking about the exams coming up the next day. I had the bad luck of having three exams on the same day, and it's tough getting up for them all, you know how it is with teachers, they give you a bundle of stuff to read at the last moment. . . . Anyway, I had to really ace the finals because things hadn't gone so good on the quizzes I took . . . the way grades were determined, if I didn't get three A's on these three finals, I could wind up

with two F's and one D.

So I guess I was distracted going home, I knew there was no way I could cram, I tried that before and look at what it got me. My big worry was the draft, I could be called up if I lost my student deferment. . . . They already took some of my friends.

The accident itself came as a surprise since Sam had always been reasonably cautious on his motorbike. Yet, he had been driving in a carefree and even reckless fashion when the accident occurred. When he was first released from the hospital, he felt "kinda lucky that I wasn't killed, but kinda sorry I wasn't scraped up more than I was." The impression was that a disabling injury would have been painful but useful.

Richard M. Suinn, *Fundamentals of Abnormal Psychology*. Nelson-Hall, 1984, p. 219.

Many theories about the causes of conversion disorders have been proposed. Freud believed that the symptoms were a way of controlling threatening impulses. For example, people who have been taught that masturbation is wrong may develop arm paralysis to control their urges to masturbate. The paralysis solves the problem by making it physically impossible for them to masturbate. Learning theorists argue that conversion disorders are the result of reinforcement patterns. People may find that they can gain attention from others (positive reinforcement) by having these conversion symptoms. Sometimes they receive more direct rewards because of this disorder—for example, they can escape family or job pressures, and get sympathy and attention at the same time.

Dissociative Disorders

Debbie Spungen recalls a particularly disturbing incident that convinced her Nancy needed psychological help. One afternoon she found Nancy holding a brown paper bag over the bannister. Nancy had a strange look on her face. When Debbie asked her what was in the bag, Nancy replied that it was her cat, Aquarius. Nancy planned to drop the bag over the railing to see if Aquarius landed on his feet. Debbie struggled with Nancy to get the bag. After she overpowered her, Nancy blinked and looked around. She innocently asked, "Why are we standing here?" Debbie looked into her daughter's eyes and saw that "she had forgotten why we were at the top of the stairs, forgotten what she'd been about to do" (Spungen, 1983, p. 80). When Debbie told Nancy what had happened, Nancy gently let Aquarius out of the bag and went to her room and cried for an hour.

Dissociative disorders are characterized by "tuning out" or dissociating a part of oneself from the situation at hand. It is almost as if part of the person has split off and taken on its own identity. In Nancy's case it was like there were two independent parts acting out two different scripts; one part planned to hurt Aquarius, and the other part who loved Aquarius was horrified at this plan.

Most people who suffer dissociative disorders do not have control over the onset of the disorder; the symptoms occur after a stressful period or a traumatic event. The most common explanation for dissociative disorders is that they result from repression of unwanted thoughts or urges. People try to control these threatening urges by psychologically separating out the stressed parts of their personality. It is almost as if they tie a number of unwanted thoughts or feelings in a package and store it in one part of their personality. This solution enables them to avoid dealing with these unwanted thoughts or feelings—most of the time. However, the price for this solution is that this "package" of unwanted thoughts may suddenly open up and take control. Or, if the unwanted feelings do not actually take control, they may threaten the individual to such an extent that he or she blocks out *all* thoughts, feelings, or memories. Dissociative disorders are quite rare but let us briefly examine some of them.

Psychogenic Amnesia and Fugue

A classic movie theme involves a character who suddenly forgets who he or she is and spends the rest of the movie trying to recover his or her true identity. **Amnesia** is a selective forgetting of past events. Interestingly enough, the memory loss is often limited to certain events or time periods. For example, a man may forget who he is or where he lives, but remember how to perform acts such as driving an automobile. Some forms of amnesia (organic) are caused by physical injuries, such as a blow to the head. However, the term *psychogenic* indicates that the cause of the memory loss is stress rather than physical injury.

Fugue (from the Latin word meaning "to flee") involves not only the loss of memory, but also physical flight. The person may leave home for a matter of hours or for years. Often the person will suddenly "come to" and remember his or her past. What is interesting is that once the person has "snapped out" of the fugue, he or she will not remember events that occurred during it (Cameron, 1963)—it's like trading one memory loss for another.

Multiple Personality Disorder

The most bizarre of all the dissociative disorders is the **multiple personality disorder.** We open the next chapter with a description of Chris Sizemore, who suffered this disorder. Multiple personality is rare and is most often found in women. The person develops two or more personalities that are displayed at different times; in a sense, she *is* different people at different times. Each personality is self-contained and independent of the other personalities. In fact, some degree of amnesia is generally present, so that while some of the personalities may be aware that the others exist, other personalities remain unaware of the existence or character of the others. The personalities generally show radical differences in attitudes, morals, age, learning ability, and speech patterns. This difference often extends into the physical realm, so that the personalities have different heart rates

Dissociative disorders
Characterized by "tuning out" or dissociating a part of the person from the situation at hand. It is almost as if part of the person has split off and taken on its own identity.
Amnesia
Partial forgetting of past events. Some forms of amnesia are caused by physical injuries, such as a blow to the head. *Psychogenic amnesia* means that the cause of the memory loss is stress rather than physical injury.
Fugue
Involves loss of memory and also physical flight in which the person wanders away from his or her home for a matter of an hour or, in some cases, for years.
Multiple personality disorder
Disorder in which one person assumes two or more personalities. Each personality has its complete set of memories, and one is often "unaware" of the existence of the other.

On September 13, 1980, a park ranger patroling a wooded area in Birch State Park in Florida found a naked, half-starved young woman lying in the brush. The woman could not remember her name or events about her past. She was also unable to remember how she got to the park. Authorities named her "Jane Doe" and an exhaustive search was launched to discover her true identity. With the help of a sedative and hypnosis, Jane Doe began to recall details of her childhood; however she was never able to fully recall her past. The doctors were able to learn that she had wandered away from her home after having some difficulty with her boyfriend.

and blood pressure. In some cases, women with this disorder report that they menstruate much of the month because each personality has a different menstrual cycle (Jen & Evans, 1983). The personalities may differ in physical health, with the dominant personality often being the healthiest. When the personalities are aware of the existence of others, they may go as far as to communicate through letters and notes. In one case, investigators report that one personality wrote the other to give it medical advice (Taylor & Martin, 1944)!

There is an interesting pattern in the way many multiple personality disorders develop. First, between the ages of 4 and 6, the person faces a serious emotional problem; in the case of Chris, the event was the arrival of her twin sisters. The child copes with the problem by creating another personality to deal with the situation. Second, Bliss (1980) reports that people with multiple personality disorders are very adept at inducing self-hypnosis; this ability enables them to form and embrace the new personality. The third step seems to be that the person finds out that retreating into the new personality helps resolve the emotional crisis. This sets the stage for developing new personalities whenever stressful events occur later in life.

Mood Disorders

A few days before I wrote this chapter, a disheveled student shuffled into my office and slowly began a rather bizarre conversation with, "I'm not sure why I came to see you. I know I'm bothering you and that you are very busy." She went on to say that she didn't really like school but didn't know what else to do because she wasn't really good at anything. Her words alone were depressing, but her slow flat manner seemed to darken the room and weigh on both of us. I had been having a rather good day before talking with this student, but our conversation seemed to drag me down for the rest of the day. I was reminded of the book on Nancy Spungen which I had just finished reading. In the book, Nancy's mother, Debbie, who wrote this account of Nancy's troubled life, goes into great detail about Nancy's dramatic mood changes. One moment Nancy would seem happy and the next would find her in the depths of despair. During her times of despair, she would withdraw to her room where she would cry for hours and listen to rock music. Talking to her was like talking to a zombie. At other times, Nancy's mood would suddenly "take the high road"; she seemed pumped up with energy, she couldn't sit still, she was ready to take on the most difficult tasks. Carrying on a conversation with her during these times was like talking to a busy bee. And just as my own mood was changed as a result of my interaction with the student who visited my office, Debbie Spungen's moods were affected by her daughter's moods.

It would clearly take more than one interview to determine whether my student or Nancy Spungen was suffering from a disorder. However, some of the behavior in both of these cases is found in **mood disorders** which involve problems with moods and emotions. Although all of us have periods where we feel down or elated, some people are consumed by their moods, and have trouble functioning because of them. The mood captures the person and takes control of the person's behavior; when in the grip of the mood, the person no longer responds to the environment, but reacts to the mood. Given this general description, let's take a look at some of the specific mood disorders.

Mood disorders
Group of general, nonspecific disturbances that cause high or low feelings and affect a person's ability to function normally.

Depression

Think about the last time you felt depressed. How did you feel and act? For most people, **depression** affects their mood, thoughts, motivation, perceptions, and physical appearance. Looking first at *mood*, we find that depressed people feel sad, irritable, and hopeless; they find little joy in living. They are often consumed by their sadness. Their *thoughts* are filled with self-pity; they see themselves as useless, incompetent, and inferior. They think that their future is hopeless. One of the interesting features of depressives is that they do not seem to be able to distract themselves with happy or positive thoughts (Wagner, 1987). Even when asked to think about positive things, depressives cannot do this. Given these emotions and thoughts, it is little wonder that these depressed people feel little *motivation* to do anything. They often lose their appetite; they lose interest in sex. Even their movements and actions slow down; to an observer, they appear to be moving and talking in slow motion. All of these effects conspire to affect the *physical appearance* of the depressed person (see Table 14–4). Because these people often have trouble sleeping and pay little attention to their physical appearance, they may look gaunt, ragged, almost ghostlike. Finally, people in a state of depression tend to *perceive* their environment in a negative way. They will see a beautiful warm day as posing a threat of severe sunburn or interpret the friendly behavior of a stranger as being manipulative or phony.

Depression not only affects the individual, it also influences those around him or her. Studies with married couples reveal that communication in pairs involving a depressed person focuses on negative topics and is often characterized by misunderstanding (Kowalik & Gotlib, 1987). Another interesting finding is that open aggression is often low in households where there is a depressed mother. On the other hand, when aggression is openly expressed it seems to reduce the degree of depression experienced by the mother (Hops et al., 1987). It seems that the depressed person dampens the expression of emotion by others, and this may create an environment that nurtures and prolongs the depression.

Lest we mislead you, we should understand that depression is a normal reaction to a sad event such as losing a job, the end of a relationship, or the death of a friend or parent. In most cases, depression—even if it is very deep—soon passes and the person begins to cope with the world. However, some people are unable to shake their depression; instead, they sink deeper into it. When the depression lasts an unusually long time and interferes with the person's functioning, it can be considered a disorder. In some cases, it can reach psychotic proportions and hospitalization may be necessary.

Depression is the most common psychological disorder; it has been referred to as the "common cold of mental illness" (Rosenhan & Seligman, 1984). In any single year 15 percent of all adults may suffer from a depression disorder, and at any one time 2 to 4 percent of the population has impaired functioning due to depression (Secunda et al., 1973). Depressive disorders tend to reappear; a person who has had one episode has a 50 percent chance of suffering another one at some time in his or her life. The younger the person is when the first episode occurs, the more likely the person is to have future episodes of depression. At one time it was believed that older people were most likely to have depressive episodes. However, more recent evidence shows that depression is also common among younger people, especially college students. Researchers report that 46 percent of college students still seek professional help for depression during their college years (Beck & Young, 1978). Depression is more common among women than among men; in fact, two-thirds of those who suffer a depression disorder are women. Although the reasons for this

Depression
Disorder in which there is a loss of interest in most activities, including eating or sex, lack of concentration and inability to sleep. May lead to suicide in its extreme forms. See also *bipolar disorder*.

Depressed people find little joy in life. They feel useless and inferior and view life as hopeless.

Table 14–4
Depression Affects Physical Health, Too
There is growing evidence that our psychological state strongly influences our physical well-being. Depression not only influences the chances of developing a physical illness, it also affects the severity of the illness and the recovery process.

Asthma, Depression: A Deadly Combination

Asthmatic youngsters suffering from depression are more likely to die of their illness than their happier, more well-adjusted counterparts, according to researchers.

Recent studies by doctors at the National Jewish Center for Immunology and Respiratory Medicine in Denver indicate that many of their deaths may be preventable.

"One of the things that isn't well-known about asthma is that it is a disease that kills," said Dr. Bruce Miller, who heads the Pediatric Psychophysiologic Treatment Unit at National Jewish, a nationally known treatment and research facility.

Asthma, which affects an estimated 5 percent to 7 percent of the population, doesn't kill very often, but its lethality seems to increase when linked with depression, researchers say.

Miller's message for family doctors is, "stop and consider depression," in asthmatic patients who do not seem to be managing their condition successfully.

Depression, which strikes thousands of American teen-agers and adults, can be treated.

Asthma is a condition marked by attacks that occur when the bronchioles, small airways that deliver oxygen to the lungs, become obstructed due to muscle contractions in the bronchial walls. Allergic reaction is often, although not always, what triggers an attack.

large sex difference are as yet unknown, a recent study (Allgood-Merten, Lewinsohn, & Hops, 1990) suggests that the seeds of adult depression may be found in adolescence. In this study, adolescent females were more likely than their male counterparts to report greater self-consciousness, were less positive about their body image, scored lower on measures of self-esteem, and were more likely to report having experienced a stressful life event. All of these variables have been shown to be related to depressive symptoms in adults. While this study does not tell us why females are more likely to become depressed than males, it does suggest that adolescent females approach adulthood with a psychological makeup that places them at a greater risk than males for depression. While the average length of a depressive episode is 3 to 6 months, many people suffer depression for periods of 2 years or more (Keller, 1981).

Theories of Depression. Because it is such a common and destructive disorder, there have been many attempts to identify the causes of depression.

1. One of the earliest explanations was based on *psychoanalytic theory*. According to this theory, people may suffer the loss of a loved one or the loss of self-esteem during childhood, but instead of expressing their natural feelings of grief and anger, they inhibit them or turn them on the self (Newman & Hirt, 1983). Then, later in life, they may suffer a loss that reminds them of the earlier loss; in other words, the recent loss symbolizes the earlier event and brings up those repressed feelings of guilt and sadness. These people now respond to the current event—which may be the death of a pet or the loss of a job—not only with the feelings aroused by it, but also with the repressed feelings that surrounded the childhood loss. In addition to intense feelings, these people have developed the pattern of turning their anger upon themselves. Turning anger inward results in low self-esteem and, in extreme cases, suicide.

2. *Learning theories* identify reinforcement schedules as the cause of depression. Some investigators argue that people become depressed because they find few positive rewards in their environment (Lewinsohn, 1974; Lewinsohn, Mischel, Chaplin, & Barton, 1980). Life loses its zip and excitement because they feel there is little to be happy about. As a result, they become sad, irritable, and self-pitying. By itself, this depression would certainly make them uncomfortable, but it is only the beginning of a vicious cycle. As they become depressed, other people avoid them; few of us enjoy being around people who are sullen and depressed. As friends retreat, they become even more depressed and develop feelings of worthlessness.

Hammen and Peters (1977) suggest a somewhat different relationship between reinforcement and depression. They argue that the reason that fewer men than women show depressed behavior is that male depression is more negatively reinforced than female depression. That is, a depressed female may receive attention and sympathy, while a depressed male is treated with indifference or a lecture to the effect that it is "unmanly" to be inactive and sulk. Males therefore find other ways to respond to stress and anxiety.

3. *Cognitive theories* take this learning explanation one extra step: They propose that people learn negative views of the world and of themselves, and it is these negative views that lead to depression (Beck, 1983). The negative views that serve as the foundation for depression form a *cognitive triad*—that is, they involve negative thoughts about the self, the world, and the future. Numerous studies have found that depressed people are very pessimistic about the future (Alloy & Ahrens, 1987) and they especially think that bad things will happen to them in the future (Pyszcynski, Holt, & Greenberg, 1987). Coupled with these negative views are illogical interpretations of events. For example, there is a tendency to magnify the importance of minor negative events and minimize the importance of major positive events. Thus a woman may dwell on the fact that she spilled coffee on an old shirt, while dismissing as insignificant a major job promotion. Finally, the cognitive position states that depression-prone people tend to overgeneralize from failures and focus on their negative characteristics. They become overwhelmed with a sense of worthlessness or personal failure and this leads to depression.

4. Other investigators combine learning and cognitive theories to explain depression; this approach uses the **learned helplessness** model (see Chapter 12) to explain depression (Peterson & Seligman, 1984). According to this approach, people must make three choices when explaining uncontrollable bad events that happen to them. First, they must decide whether the event was due to their own actions (internal) or to the situation or circumstances (external). Second, they must determine whether the cause is due to a factor that will persist across time (stable) or one that is momentary and fleeting (unstable). Finally, they must decide whether the cause affects a variety of outcomes (global) or is limited to this single event (specific). As can be seen from Table 14–5, the consequences of these decisions may be very different. The model suggests that believing that one cannot control outcomes or events in the future sets the stage for depression. Explaining bad events as reflections of internal, stable, and global dimensions of the self will initiate a loss of self-esteem and a long-lasting depression. On the flip side of this issue, depressed people tend to see positive events as being caused by external and unstable forces; in other words, they believe that they have little control or influence in creating positive outcomes (Sweeney, Anderson, & Bailey, 1986). Therefore the explanatory style that people develop helps determine whether or not they will become a strong risk to suffer depression.

More recently, some researchers have suggested new ideas about depression that use the learned helplessness model as a starting point (Abramson, Metalsky, & Alloy, 1989). These investigators have proposed a subtype of depression labeled *hopeless depression*. Hopeless depression results when a

Learned helplessness
A response to prolonged stress; the feeling that one's actions do not affect one's environment or what happens to one. Can lead to apathy and depression.

Table 14–5
Examples of Causal Explanations for the Event "My Checking Account Is Overdrawn"

	Explanation	
Style	**Internal**	**External**
Stable		
Global	"I'm incapable of doing any-thing right"	"All institutions chronically make mistakes"
Specific	"I always have trouble figur-ing my balance"	"This bank has always used anti-quated techniques"
Unstable		
Global	"I've had the flu for a few weeks, and I've let every-thing slide"	"Holiday shopping demands that one throw oneself into it"
Specific	"The one time I didn't enter a check is the one time my account gets over-drawn	"I'm surprised—my bank has never made an error before"

Source: Abramson et al., 1978.

negative life event occurs (or a positive life event fails to occur) and the person attributes the cause to stable (enduring) and global (likely to affect many parts of the person's life) causes. This attribution leads to a general feeling of hopelessness and results in apathy, sadness, and "giving up" efforts to exercise control over one's life. This model extends the learned helplessness approach by specifying the causal conditions of this type of depression and by suggesting that a general state of hopelessness leads to "giving up."

5. Another set of theories focuses on the possibility that *physiological conditions* can cause depression. Depression runs in families; people who have a depression disorder are likely to have relatives who have also suffered from depression (Rosenthal, 1970). A number of investigators have uncovered evidence that depression is linked to an unusual structure in the genes (Crow, 1983; Schmeck, 1988b). This structure is inherited and is therefore likely to be found in many members of certain families. The researchers, however, emphasize that this gene abnormality does not cause depression. Rather, it predisposes the person to suffer from a depressive disorder under certain environmental conditions. This finding is exciting because it offers the possibility that doctors can identify and treat depression-prone people before they experience a depressive episode.

It is still somewhat of a mystery how the gene structure can make a person prone to depression. A number of theories have focused on neurotransmitters. In Chapter 2 we discussed how neurons transmit messages. Recall that neurons do not touch one another. Rather, there is a very small gap between the end of one neuron and the beginning of the next. Electrical impulses are passed between this gap by a chemical substance called a neurotransmitter. Many substances serve as neurotransmitters, but the two associated with depression are norepinephrine and serotonin. One biological view is that depression is the result of a lack of these neurotransmitters (Berger, 1978). Another theory argues that depression is the result of too much sodium, which slows the transmission of nerve impulses (Depue & Evans, 1976). It has been found that exercise reduces the level of sodium in the blood, and some clinicians suggest that jogging and other physical exercise may reduce depression.

This is, indeed, a long list of explanations for depression. It might make a neat package if we could conclude by saying that this theory or that one is the "correct" answer. We cannot do this, however, as each theory offers some insight into depression but no single theory holds the

Theory	Cause
Psychoanalytic	Loss of loved one or self-esteem during childhood. Grief and/or anger is repressed. Feelings surface as depression later in life when present event symbolizes earlier loss.
Learning	a) Depression results when few positive rewards are found in present life. Sadness alienates others, leading to fewer rewards and thus increasing depression. b) Depression brings the rewards of sympathy and attention, leading to deeper depression.
Cognition	a) Cognitive triad: depression results from negative thoughts about self, world, and future. Dwell on negative and expect worse in the future. b) Learned helplessness: depression results from uncontrollable bad events. Attribute negative outcomes to stable internal causes that are global. Attribute positive outcomes to external and unstable causes.
Physiological	Abnormality in neurotransmitters. May be abnormally low level of neurotransmitters or too much sodium slowing the transmission of nerve impulses.

Table 14–6
Theories of Depression

key. It may well be that many roads lead to depression. The theories play many key roles; not only do they help us understand the many characteristics of depression, but they also help us plan ways to prevent and treat the disorder. Table 14–6 provides an overview of the various theories.

Mania and Bipolar Disorders

While depressives seem to drag themselves around and have no interest in becoming involved in any project, people in a state of **mania** have the opposite problem. Manics are a fountain of energy who feel ready to take on the world; they have very positive self-images. Unfortunately, they often fail to stay with a project until it is completed, but rather jump from one thing to another. They are easily distracted; they may begin a sentence and fail to finish it because they start another sentence on a new topic. People in a manic state often have an increased sex drive and seem to need less sleep than usual. These manic periods may last for days or even weeks. Pure cases of mania are relatively rare. In most cases, people suffer from a **bipolar disorder,** which means they alternate between manic and depressive states. People with this bipolar disorder generally behave normally in the periods between the extreme affective states. In many of them the extreme mood states appear for only a short time.

Heredity plays a strong role in the cause of bipolar disorders. Evidence has been discovered linking the bipolar disorders to the X chromosome (Cadoret & Winokur, 1975). As we discussed in Chapter 2, females have two X chromosomes and males have only one. This situation would lead us to expect that more females than males have the bipolar disorder and that transmission of the disorder must be from an affected mother. Research has generally supported these predictions. It has, however, proved difficult to pinpoint exactly what is inherited. Bunney and his colleagues (1972)

Mania
Disorder in which people feel full of energy, but find it difficult to stay with any one project for long, are easily distracted, have an increased sex drive, and need less sleep than usual.

Bipolar disorder
Disorder in which the person alternates between manic and depressive stages. Often the extremes of each mood state appear for only a short time and the person generally behaves normally when between states.

CASE STUDY OF A MANIC DISORDER

As seen on the ward the morning after admission, Mrs. L. J., aged 38, presented a striking picture. She had been too excited to eat breakfast, but after gulping a cup of coffee she had taken several daisies from the centerpiece on the table and entwined them in her hair. She paced briskly up and down the hallways singing snatches of popular songs, and she paused briefly from time to time attempting to get other patients and personnel to join in the singing. . . .

Mrs. J. took the initiative in greeting everyone she encountered, patting the women on the back in a familiar manner and putting her arms around the men. It was, however, almost impossible for personnel to maintain a conversation with her. She responded with smiles and laughter to most remarks addressed to her and often talked volubly, but she was too distractible to give attention to any one subject for more than a moment. If an effort was made to detain her or to hold her attention, she would break away with a transient flash of anger.

A brief excerpt from the patient's stream of talk was as follows: "How do I feel? I feel with my hands. How do you feel? No, seriously, everything's wonderful. Couldn't be better. Going 'From Bed to Worse,' Benchley said." (Laughs.) "Really, honey, this is a marvelous place you've got here, mar-ve-lous. 'Marvelous *Vel*.' I really must shampoo my hair.". . .

In the course of the diagnostic evaluation and subsequent treatment of Mrs. J., a full background history was obtained, of which two features may be mentioned here. (1) The present illness had begun about ten days prior to admission upon the patient's having received the information that an ambitious volunteer-service project she chaired had failed to gain the approval of the community agency on which it depended. (2) Her initial response had been one of low spirits and irritability, lasting two or three days and then giving way to a mood of unusual cheerfulness, accompanied by various erratic activities and gaining in intensity until it reached the reckless and irrational gaiety shown on admission. On the previous day, the patient had stopped at a travel agency where, despite her confusion, she had arranged passage for five on a luxury cruise at a cost which was wildly beyond the family's means.

Source: C. K. Hofling, *Textbook of Psychiatry for Medical Practice*, 1975, pp. 351–352.

have suggested that the inherited feature is a condition at the nerve endings that allows for a buildup of norepinephrine. During the buildup phase, little of this neurotransmitter passes between the neurons, causing vulnerability to depression. However, at some point the level of norepinephrine reaches a concentration at which a stressful event causes the neuron to "dump" the neurotransmitter, resulting in a high level of neuron activity and mania.

Suicide

When Debbie and her husband Frank realized they couldn't handle or help Nancy at home, they searched for a residential school designed to deal with the emotionally disturbed. Nancy had a rather checkered history in the residential school and when she was 15 years old she wanted to leave the school and go to college. However, the decision was made to keep her in the school for one more year. Nancy's response to this disappointment was to slash her wrists. She was taken to the hospital, but the wound was not serious. Two weeks later, she again slashed her wrists and nearly died from this suicide attempt. Debbie was convinced that Nancy wanted to kill herself. Debbie even believed that "she (Nancy) egged Sid into stabbing her." In fact, the title of her book on Nancy's life is *And I Don't Want to Live this Life*.

What was behind Nancy's suicidal behavior? Our discussion of depression naturally brings us to the issue of **suicide,** because depression plays a major role in almost 80 percent of suicide attempts. In fact, 15 percent of the people who are clinically depressed will ultimately kill themselves (Murphy, 1983). As you might expect, it is difficult to pinpoint the actual number of suicides. We can clearly label a suicide someone who shoots,

Suicide
The planned taking of one's life.

poisons, or hangs himself. But what of the person who drinks and "accidentally" crashes his or her car into a tree? With this problem in mind, a conservative estimate of the number of successful suicides is between 25,000 and 30,000 each year; there is a suicide attempt every 30 minutes in the United States. And the incidence of suicide is increasing; the rate of suicides has jumped fourfold in the last 30 years. Women attempt suicide three times more frequently than men, but men are three times more likely to be successful in attempts to kill themselves. This sex difference is due in part to the fact that men often use more lethal means (e.g., guns rather than pills) in their suicide attempts. Rates for blacks and American Indians are two to five times higher than suicide rates for whites. Religion does not seem to be a factor in determining who will commit suicide; rates are roughly the same for Catholics, Protestants, Jews, and nonreligious persons. The rate of suicide tends to increase with age, with the highest rates occurring in old age.

However, the last few years have witnessed a dramatic rise in the suicide rates for adolescents and the young adults. Today suicide is the second most frequent cause of death among college students. Most, but not all, adolescents who attempt suicide are socially isolated, come from families where the parents are divorced or separated, and often have parents who are alcoholics. Most adolescents who commit suicide have poor academic records, although they are often of above average intelligence (Rohn, Sartes, Kenny, Reynolds, & Heald, 1977). Table 14–7 features some of the warning signs of the potential for teenage suicide.

Table 14–7
Warning Signs and Preventive Responses to Teenage Suicide

Verbal Comments

Statements such as "I wish I'd never been born," and "You'll be sorry when I'm gone," should be taken just as seriously as the direct threat, "I'm going to kill myself."

Behavior Changes

These cover a wide range and including giving away treasured possessions, taking life threatening risks, and having frequent accidents. Other signs may be complaints of intense loneliness or boredom, a marked increase in agitation or irritability, or getting into trouble with school or the police. There may also be the more customary signs of depression: changes in appetite and sleep habits, suddenly dropping grades, complaints of inability to concentrate, and withdrawal from friends and from favorite activities.

Situational Factors

Inability to communicate with parents, recent problems at school, end of a love relationship, recent involvement with drugs or alcohol all increase the situational risk.

What To Do

Parents and friends should take action by asking questions such as "Are you very unhappy?" "Do you have a plan about taking your life?" "Do you think you really don't want to live anymore?" Asking direct questions about suicide doesn't put ideas into someone's head. Instead it may be a lifesaving measure if the answers are taken seriously. Both parents and friends often don't believe that such statements might be carried out or they may be too frightened to take action. Although friends are sometimes sworn to secrecy about suicidal thoughts, they should contact a parent or responsible adult immediately if they suspect thoughts of suicide and professional help should be obtained at once. If the suicidal threat seems immediate, the nearest suicide prevention center (usually listed under "suicide" or "crisis" in the phone book) should be contacted.

Source: Sarason & Sarason (1987), p. 289.

CASE STUDY OF A SUICIDE

My brother, Bobby Hirsch, shot and killed himself Friday night. Close friends of the family have heard the whole story, but there are others who knew Bobby and might want to understand why he did what he did.

Bobby fought a severe mental illness for many years. Bobby's problems were caused by a chemical imbalance in his brain that caused him to perceive his world in bizarre ways and to make him interpret his perceptions in equally bizarre ways. Gradually, through the use of medication, Bobby was correcting many of these problems. In recent months he had come to understand the truth about his world and himself,

and to understand the cause of his old perceptions and beliefs—and the solutions to his problems.

Bobby was well on the road to recovery with only two obstacles remaining in the way of his becoming a nearly-normal taxpaying citizen. One was controlling the side effects of the medication, which made him very sleepy and lethargic. The other was controlling what he called "panic attacks." Sometimes even medication could not control irrational, nonspecific emotions of fear, horror and dread, which would last a couple of hours and then go away.

It was during a "panic attack" on Friday that Bobby took his life. In that moment he did not understand the

consequences of the sudden impulse. He did not leave a note. Bobby died from his illness in the same way someone with heart disease can die from a heart attack or someone with diabetes can die from an insulin crisis.

Mental illness is not well understood and often carries a social stigma not attached to other illnesses. For years the family has tried to "keep it quiet" to protect Bobby, so that when he was ready to rejoin the world, the world wouldn't be prejudiced against him. But now that Bobby has all his answers, it is better that people know the whole story.

Source: *Bryan-College Station Eagle*, January 28, 1985, p. 6A.

Two major motivations for suicide have been identified (Beck et al., 1978). The main reason (56 percent of suicides) is simply the desire to end life. These individuals are generally depressed, lonely, and feel hopeless. They view suicide as a way to end their problems and stop their suffering. The second motivation is manipulation of others. These people attempt suicide to "teach others a lesson," make them feel guilty, have the final word in an argument, or draw others to them. In many manipulative suicides, the individual intends to remain alive; he or she attempts suicide using less lethal means than do people who are using suicide as a means of ending their problems. Depression is not as evident in manipulative suicides. The manipulative motive was behind at least one of Nancy's suicide attempts; she openly blamed Debbie for the attempt. She was angry at Debbie for going out and said, "If you'd been there I wouldn't have done it."

Hotlines have been set up in many cities to identify people at risk and offer help. These lines are staffed by professionals and paraprofessionals who offer understanding, information, and hope to people contemplating suicide. At one center in Los Angeles, volunteers are provided with a "lethality checklist" to identify the high risk cases, as shown in Table 14–8.

Table 14–8
"Lethality Checklist" for Evaluating Suicide Risk

"Yes" Answers to the Following Questions Indicate a Higher Risk of Suicide:
Does the individual communicate an intent to commit suicide? Is the person highly specific about the details of the suicide plan? (For instance, "I know how many pills it will take for my body weight; my will is folded under the telephone; I will end it at sunset looking out my window; I will be wearing . . .")
Does the person have no family or other social support system?
Is the person facing a concrete life stress?
Is the individual suffering from a serious illness?
Has the person suffered from symptoms such as insomnia, depression, or alcoholism?
Is the individual a male?

Source: Los Angeles Suicide Prevention Center

It is difficult to predict when someone will attempt suicide. Clearly, depression is a warning sign. Another warning is the occurrence of an event in which the person loses a source of social support such as a divorce or the death of a loved one. But the best predictors are past suicide attempts and the threat of a suicide; these threats should be taken seriously because people often threaten or talk about suicide before they carry out the act.

An interesting and controversial debate is currently raging about how clinicians should react to possible suicides. One position is that suicide is the result of a mental disorder and that it is a crime. Therefore, it is the duty of mental health professionals to prevent suicide even if it means placing the potential suicide victim in a hospital or institution until the threat has passed. On the other hand, Thomas Szasz (1986) has argued that suicide is a "fundamental right" *of adults*, and if the person does not want help and actively rejects it ". . . then the mental health professional's duty ought to be to leave him or her alone (or, perhaps, to try to persuade him or her to accept help) (p. 809)." A related question is raised regarding patients who have a terminal disease and whether they should be allowed to commit suicide or refuse treatment that could prolong their life. This is a thorny problem with moral, religious, and legal overtones that has even found its way into our courts. If you examine this question for yourself, you will see why it is likely to be unresolved for many years.

Sexual Disorders

Our discussion of suicide touched on a very interesting issue regarding psychological disorders. In most of the disorders we have discussed, the behaviors involved are, indeed, unusual and, in many cases, disruptive. Suicide has these qualities, but it has an added dimension that treads on moral and ethical ground; it raises the issues of the value of human life and who has the right to take it. When we discuss sexual behavior, we also venture into the realm of morals and may be tempted to label sexual behavior that does not conform to our moral standards as symptomatic of psychological disorders. For example, when Nancy moved to New York City she took a job as a topless go-go dancer at a sleazy bar and also engaged in prostitution. Debbie was repelled by this: "Knowing about it made us feel dirty, ashamed. . . . It hurts me to think about it" (Spungen, 1983, p. 253). While Debbie and others might find Nancy's sexual behavior shocking, was it an indication of a psychological disorder?

Mental health professionals have tried very hard to remove the moral issue from definitions of sexual disorders. For example, homosexuality was identified as maladaptive sexual behavior in DSM-I(1952) and DSM-II(1968). However, it was reclassified as a disorder in DSM-III(1980) and DSM-IIIR(1987) but only when the individual is stressed or expresses concern about sexual preferences. Current efforts at classifying sexual disorders recognize the extraordinary range of people's sexual behavior and apply the label of disorder only to behaviors that cause the person distress or hurt and debase others. Sexual disorders are divided into two general categories. The **paraphilias** are characterized by attraction to deviant objects or acts that interfere with the capacity for reciprocal and affectionate sexual activity. The sexual urges of these disorders involve (1) objects such as undergarments, socks, or shoes, (2) the suffering or humiliation of oneself or one's partner, or (3) children or other nonconsenting people. The second general category is **sexual dysfunctions** which involve inhibitions of sexual desire or psychological impairments that interfere with the normal sexual cycle: desire, excitement, orgasm, and resolution (see Chapter 11). Because the list of sexual disorders is so long and varied, we have space only to examine a few examples from each category.

Paraphilia
Attraction of deviant objects or acts that interferes with the capacity for reciprocal and affectionate sexual activity.
Sexual dysfunction
Inability or impairment of the ability to consistently experience the normal sexual response cycle.

Sadomasochism

For most of us, sexual behavior involves warmth, caring, tender communication, and the desire to please and be pleased. For some people, however, sexual behavior resembles a battleground where pleasure comes from inflicting pain on the partner or experiencing pain. The paraphilia disorder of sadomasochism involves sexual arousal that results from giving or receiving physical pain (Geer, Heiman, & Leittenberg, 1984). Actually, there are two forms of sadomasochism. One is **sadism,** which involves deriving sexual pleasure from inflicting pain on others. The other is **masochism,** which involves becoming sexually aroused from having pain inflicted on oneself. In one survey, slightly less than 5 percent of male and 2 percent of female respondents reported having experienced sexual arousal from receiving or inflicting pain (Hunt, 1974). Of this group, more males reported pleasure from inflicting pain than receiving pain; the reverse relationship was found among females. The likelihood of sadomasochism was greater among young people than old, and much greater among single males than married males.

Physical pain is inflicted through biting, whipping, slapping, or pinching. In addition, psychological humiliation is often inflicted through threatening, belittling, or bullying tactics. These acts do not occur in random ways. Rather, there is often an elaborate script whereby one partner plays the dominant role, such as acting like a master or jailer, while the other person plays the submissive role of a slave or a misbehaving student. Elaborate props such as whips, chains, masks, and leather clothing may be employed to enhance the drama. As you might imagine, the sadist and masochist often seek each other out.

There have been a number of attempts to explain sadomasochistic behavior. One suggests that the pattern results from the effort to relieve guilt over sexual behavior. The masochist may be able to accept sexual experience only by rationalizing that he or she was helpless throughout it. Other explanations suggest that these behaviors may be learned through modeling. Finally, it has been proposed that sadism is the result of a deepseated dislike of the opposite sex or of people in general.

Sexual Dysfunctions

The most common group of sexual disorders falls under the category of sexual dysfunctions. The diagnosis of sexual dysfunction is made only when the problem has a psychological base. For males, these dysfunctions include **erectile dysfunction** (the inability to have an erection or maintain one long enough for ejaculation), **premature ejaculation,** and *retarded ejaculation* (the inability to ejaculate during intercourse). For females, the most common disorders are the *inability to have an orgasm*, **dyspareunia** (the experiencing of pain during intercourse), and **vaginismus** (the involuntary tightening of the vagina so that intercourse is impossible). Most of these dysfunctions are disorders of degree rather than kind. That is, many people have temporary dysfunctions in sexual behavior. For example, it has been estimated that half the male population has experienced periodic **impotence,** and dysfunctions in both sexes may occur during periods of stress, tiredness, or drunkenness (Kaplan, 1974). While these dysfunctions are troublesome, they quickly pass and there is little reason to be overly concerned about them. Some people, however, experience a dysfunction for an extended period of time; their problem is distressing and inhibits normal adjustment. Many of the psychological roots of sexual dysfunction are in childhood experiences or teaching. For example, someone may have been taught that premarital intercourse is evil and morally wrong; this lesson may conflict with present desires and result in impotence. Sexual trauma that occurs in childhood, such as being the victim of rape or molestation, may also interfere with satisfying sexual experiences in adulthood.

Sadism
Deriving sexual pleasure from inflicting pain on others.
Masochism
Becoming sexually aroused by having pain inflicted on oneself.
Erectile dysfunction
Inability to have an erection or maintain one long enough for ejaculation.
Premature ejaculation
Ejaculation which occurs too quickly, according to the definition of the male and the couple.
Dyspareunia
Sexual disorder in which females experience pain during intercourse.
Vaginismus
Sexual disorder in which the involuntary tightening of the vagina makes sexual intercourse impossible.
Impotence
Sexual disorder in which males are unable to have an erection or maintain one long enough for ejaculation.

The disorders we have described so far involve interference with people's basic adjustment to their world. In most cases, people realize they are acting or feeling "abnormally" and are distressed by this realization. They try to deal with reality and the social world in spite of their disorder.

People suffering from **psychosis,** on the other hand, have lost touch with reality. They no longer attempt to adjust to the world as others see it. Instead, they create their own world, different and apart from others, and they respond only to their own reality. Their bizarre behavior and perceptions severely impair their functioning. Most psychotics can no longer care for themselves, and they usually must be hospitalized.

Some investigators believe that psychosis is simply a severe form of the anxiety disorders we discussed earlier in the chapter. Indeed, some of the disorders do have psychotic counterparts. For example, there is a manic-depressive psychotic disorder in which people become so overwhelmed by their moods that they lose touch with reality, cannot function, and must be hospitalized. There are, however, psychotic disorders—including the most common one, schizophrenia—whose symptoms do not resemble those of the less severe anxiety disturbances. Further, many people who suffer from psychosis never show signs of less severe psychological disturbances. These points have led many researchers to conclude that psychosis really is a different type of disorder.

Here we will examine the most common psychosis, schizophrenia. As you read, compare this disorder with the anxiety disorders we discussed earlier in the chapter and determine for yourself whether psychosis is a distinct category of psychological disturbances.

Schizophrenia

Nancy's behavior puzzled many of the specialists who saw her. Her early symptoms included erratic flights of mood, frequent aggressive acts, and a tendency to retreat into her own world when life became rough. When she was 11, a psychologist wrote in his notes that Nancy was "schizophrenic," but he seemed so unsure of his diagnosis that he did not inform her parents. Anyone who has been around many children knows the tremendous variation in their behavior; some seem almost angelic in their behavior while others are monsters in every sense, but most grow out of either extreme and adjust to their world. Thus, it is often difficult to make a clear clinical diagnosis of young children. But unlike most kids, Nancy did not grow out of her symptoms; she took on many others. She had lapses of memory, she became suspicious of people, her moods seemed to fluctuate out of her environment and into her own private world. She was no longer just a difficult child. In desperation, her parents took her to a psychiatrist in New York City. After reviewing Nancy's behavioral history, he stated, ". . . I'd say Nancy's a schizophrenic." Nancy was 15 years old at this time and it was the first time Debbie had heard this diagnosis. We don't know whether Nancy actually was schizophrenic because the psychiatrist's diagnosis was tentative and she was not given a complete examination at this time or any time after. Let us assume, however, that this tentative diagnosis was accurate and use it to examine the disorder known as schizophrenia.

Schizophrenia is actually a group of disorders characterized by disorganization in (1) thoughts, (2) perceptions, (3) communication, (4) emotions, and (5) motor activity. The term **schizophrenia** was first used by the Swiss psychiatrist Evgen Bleuler; literally, it means "split mind." Bleuler used

Psychosis
Disturbance caused by unresolved conflicts that is so great that the person can no longer deal with reality.
Schizophrenia
Group of disorders characterized by disorganization in thoughts, perceptions, communications, emotions, and motor activity.

this term because he observed that in some patients certain mental functions seemed to be separated or split off from others—that is, these patients' thoughts seemed unrelated to their emotions or perceptions. This does not mean, however, that schizophrenics have multiple personalities.

Because schizophrenia involves every aspect of an individual's personality, this disorder is generally considered to be the most devastating of all the mental disorders. While the incidence of schizophrenia is not as high as that of some of the anxiety-based disorders or depression, it is not rare. In the United States, 1 out of every 100 individuals will suffer from schizophrenia, and the number may be increasing (*New York Times*, 1986). The peak period of onset is between the ages of 20 and 35. Men are at highest risk before the age of 25, women after the age of 25.

The severity of this disorder is evidenced by the high percentage of schizophrenics who require hospitalization. Nearly 25 percent of those admitted to psychiatric hospitals are diagnosed as schizophrenic (Sartorious, 1982). And the costs of schizophrenia are enormous. Not only does it disrupt the lives of those in contact with the schizophrenic, but medical treatment and loss of income due to the disorder come to $10 billion to $20 billion a year in the United States (Canero, 1985). The cost of treating the disorder is so high because of its early onset and persistence throughout life in most cases. Psychologists and psychiatrists who work with schizophrenics refer to the "rule of thirds" when discussing the prognosis for someone suffering from this disorder: About one-third of those diagnosed as schizophrenic will get better and never have another encounter with the disorder; another third may get better, but will have recurring schizophrenic episodes all their lives; the final third, the chronic schizophrenics, will never be free of the devastating symptoms. While the factors that determine an individual's prognosis are not clear, it is known that the earlier the onset and the more deviance displayed prior to the appearance of schizophrenia, the less chance of overcoming the disorder (Stoffelmayer, Dillavou, & Hunter, 1983).

People from the lower socioeconomic classes are most frequently diagnosed as schizophrenic (Lindsay & Paul, 1989). We must, however, be cautious in our use of this finding because the symptoms of schizophrenia disrupt a person's life and may cause him or her to "drift" into the lower socioeconomic classes. Unlike some of the psychological disorders we have examined, schizophrenia is not a product of our modern stressful society. There is evidence that it has occurred throughout history, and today it is found in simple primitive societies as well as in modern industrial countries.

Table 14–9 lists the most common subtypes of schizophrenia with their most common symptoms. People may show all or only a few of the symptoms for a type. Whatever the array of symptoms or the subtype of the disorder, schizophrenia is a disabling condition that often requires long periods of hospitalization. Let us briefly examine some of the most common symptoms.

Symptoms of Schizophrenia

Disorganization of Thought. One of the most common symptoms of schizophrenia is **delusions**—irrational beliefs that are held despite the existence of contrary evidence. There are many types of delusions. One is the delusion of grandeur, which is the belief that the person is special or different from other people. For example, a person might believe that he is Jesus or Hitler. Those with delusions of persecution believe that people are "out to get them" and that such people are controlling their thoughts or behaviors. We saw an example of this type of delusion when Nancy loudly accused her cousin's friend of staring at her during Christmas dinner. These delusions form the basis of the disorder known as *paranoid schizophrenia* (see Table 14–9 and Highlight: Case Study of Paranoia).

Delusions
Irrational beliefs that are held in spite of contrary evidence and have no basis in reality. For example, the delusion of grandeur is the belief that the person is special or different from other people (one may think one is Napoleon or Joan of Arc, for instance).

Table 14–9
Major Types of Schizophrenia

Type	Description
1. Disorganized (hebephrenic)	This type is characterized by many delusions, hallucinations, and inappropriate emotions. People may laugh and giggle for no apparent reason. They become childlike, urinate and defecate on the floor, and refuse to wear clothing.
2. Catatonic	The major characteristic of this type is disturbance of motor activity. People may remain in one position for long periods of time without moving, their bodies almost waxy; if someone moves them, they will remain in the new position. In agitated cases, they will show wild, constant movement, often becoming violent and destructive.
3. Paranoid	The major problem in this type is cognitions or thoughts. People believe that others are trying to destroy or control them (delusions of persecution), and they trust no one. They will not let others get close to them for fear that these others will harm them. In some cases, there may be delusions of grandeur in which people believe that they are a famous person or a powerful figure who controls the world. These people may have difficulty functioning because they are concentrating on the "sinister" acts of others.
4. Undifferentiated	This type involves delusions, hallucinations, and disorganized emotions. This is really a "catchall" category for cases that are characterized by extreme disorganization but do not fit any of the other types.

Disorganization of Perception.   When you look at a tree, what do you see? Probably you see some green leaves clinging to some branches and a large trunk supporting this structure. This is the way most of us view a tree. Now imagine looking at that tree in much greater detail. Look at every leaf. Is the leaf dark green or light green? Look at each branch. Is the branch thick or thin, long or short, bent or straight, brown or gray? Now examine the trunk closely. At this point you may be throwing up your hands and exclaiming that this is crazy, that at this rate you could spend the whole afternoon looking at just one tree, and anyway, why examine a tree with such care? You are correct, of course, but this is an example of the perceptual process used by some schizophrenics. They become engrossed in minute details and are unable to block out irrelevant stimuli. They can spend hours looking at a simple object. They may pay this same deep attention to noises. They hear each and every noise in their environment. In each of these cases, the schizophrenic pays attention to the smallest detail of stimuli or events without trying to organize them into larger, meaningful wholes.

Another perceptual phenomenon experienced by some schizophrenics is **hallucination,** which, as we discussed in Chapter 5, involves having a sensory experience without the external stimuli. Hallucinations can involve vision, hearing, taste, touch, or smell. The most common types are auditory: People "hear" voices that are not there. Many times the voices accuse the hearer of doing or thinking bad things. Visual hallucinations can involve seeing people, even those who died many years earlier, or seeing monsters that have come to punish the person.

Clearly, the schizophrenic's perceptions are strange and troubled. But

Hallucination
Involves having a sensory experience without the external stimuli that would have caused it. Hallucinations can involve vision, hearing, taste, touch, and smell, but the most common types involve people "hearing" voices that are not there.

CASE STUDY OF PARANOIA

A prosperous builder aged forty-four was refused a very substantial overdraft from a local bank against the collateral of his firm and property. This was his first serious business reverse in sixteen years of independent building; and he became morose and disturbed about it.

After some months he suddenly expressed the conviction that people were talking about him because the loan had been refused; and that the basis of its refusal was the fact that he had syphilis, and had passed it on to his wife and children. He then went about demanding legal action against the Bank Manager, and various other people, and accusing his General Practitioner of having falsified and then published medical reports about him. He was admitted to the hospital, having refused to see any doctors, after a suicidal attempt in which he had tried to hang himself; leaving a note saying that no one man could stand up to the devilish and calculated campaign of mind reading, calumny, and persecution to which he had been submitted.

During the course of treatment in the hospital he disclosed that his mind was still being read by an electronic machine, in which his thoughts were transcribed into a formula for a new and more terrible atomic bomb. He made a partial remission in response to treatment, and returned to take control of his firm and property; seen for outpatient follow-up and assessment he remains deluded, but can discuss and accept support and reassurance about his general predicament while remaining a competent builder and manager of his business.

Source: From D. Stafford-Clark, & A. C. Smith, *Psychiatry for Students*, 5th ed., 1978, p. 234.

there is an intriguing side to their disorganization. Some investigators have found that people who have a genetic predisposition for schizophrenia tend to display highly creative tendencies (Karlsson, 1972). In fact, a number of the most creative people in music, literature, physics, and art have developed psychological disorders. Hence, hidden deep within the bizarre perceptions of the schizophrenic may lurk the seeds of creativity. However, the other factors associated with the disorder may prevent this creativity from developing or being appreciated.

Disturbances in Communication.   Talking to a schizophrenic is often like communicating with someone who is talking in his or her sleep. The schizophrenic talks in a dreamy tone of voice and does not seem to be paying attention to anything anyone says.

The schizophrenic's speech follows no train of thought. Instead, each sentence follows from an association with a word in the previous sentence. The schizophrenic may also give completely irrelevant replies to questions or may launch into a highly intellectual and complex reply to a very simple question.

Inappropriate Emotions.   Schizophrenics may giggle and laugh when talking about the death of a close friend or relative. On the other hand, they may sob uncontrollably when talking about matter-of-fact issues. Overall, it is difficult to predict what emotions they will show, because their feelings seem to have little connection with the situation or what is happening to them. Another rather common emotional pattern of schizophrenics is apathy.

Unusual Motor Activities.   A wide variety of unusual motor activities is associated with schizophrenia. In some cases, people move in slow motion, as if every movement is achieved only with the greatest effort. They may slowly move their head and stare around the room with an almost vacant glance. In the most extreme instances, they may spend hours without moving. If they move their arms, they let them remain in the new position; they are like molding wax, since they exercise no control over how their body is manipulated. Others may repeat the same motor activity for hours on end. For example, one schizophrenic spent four hours touching first the end of her nose and then her ear. Whatever the particular motor activity, the major characteristic is that it has no connection with the physical reality of the situation and is not aimed at achieving any identifiable goal.

Theories of Schizophrenia

Schizophrenia is one of the most studied of all the psychological disorders. There are at least two reasons for this. The first is the seriousness of the disorder. Second, schizophrenia is very widespread. As we pointed out, schizophrenia is found in almost every culture and is the most common diagnosis for patients hospitalized for a mental disorder. Despite the amount of research, investigators have not reached agreement as to the cause of schizophrenia. There are many theories about its cause; it is likely, in fact, that there are many causes of schizophrenia.

Biological Theories. Some evidence for a biological cause comes from studies of identical twins. Research has found that if one twin has schizophrenia, the other twin has almost a 60 percent chance of developing the disorder (Kendler, 1983; Gottesman & Shields, 1972). While this may be strong evidence that schizophrenia is inherited, it can be argued that besides their identical genetic structure, monozygotic twins also share a very similar childhood environment. Thus learning and other environmental factors could still be responsible for the disorder.

In an effort to counter this environmental argument, investigators examined the development of schizophrenia in people who were born to schizophrenic parents but were adopted as infants by nonschizophrenic parents (Kety, Rosenthal, Wender, & Schulsinger, 1968; Rosenthal, 1973). The researchers found that these people were more likely to develop schizophrenia than adopted children who did not have schizophrenic parents.

The words of the schizophrenic person who did this painting underline the misery caused by this disorder: "The painting really symbolizes a silent scream. . . . [describing], my life or much of it at that time."

These studies, combined with the twin studies, suggest that genetic factors can be one cause of schizophrenia. We must emphasize, however, that genetics can only be one of the causes, because schizophrenia does not always occur in both identical twins when one has the disorder, and not all, or even most, adopted children whose natural parents were schizophrenic became schizophrenic themselves.

Given that schizophrenia can be inherited, our next question concerns how the disorder is passed on. More directly, what does the defective gene do to people that causes them to develop schizophrenia? One study focuses on a neurotransmitter called *dopamine* (Davis, 1974). This research suggests that schizophrenics have too much dopamine and that this dopamine overstimulates their brains, causing schizophrenic behavior (Crow, 1983). Another set of theories focuses on chemicals in the blood. Wagemaker and Cade (1977) treated a schizophrenic woman for a physical disorder by filtering her blood through a dialysis machine. To their surprise, her schizophrenic symptoms almost disappeared after this treatment. When dialysis was tried on three other schizophrenics, their symptoms were also reduced after a short period of time. The investigators argued that the filtering may have removed some substance from the blood that is responsible for schizophrenia.

Another encouraging direction of research has been on brain structure. Images of the brain of schizophrenics have uncovered abnormalities in the frontal lobes (Farkas et al., 1984); as we saw in Chapter 2, the frontal areas are involved in problem solving and mood. These biological studies along with findings that some schizophrenics are helped with drug therapy whereas others are not has led to the belief that there may actually be two types of schizophrenia: one that results from problems with neurotransmitters and the other related to brain structure (Crow, 1985).

Learning Approaches. There are a broad range of approaches suggesting that schizophrenia develops as a result of the individual's attempt to cope with stressful environments. One theory suggests that schizophrenics have learned that retreating into their own world is less stressful than living in the real world. Furthermore the bizarre behavior and the "tuning out" of the real world brings rewards in the form of attention from others. Indeed, Nancy captured the full attention of everyone in her family by her unusual and disruptive behavior. Further support for this learning position comes from the finding that the bizarre behavior of schizophrenic patients decreased when hospital personnel ignored them (Agras, 1967).

Another approach suggests that schizophrenia develops as a means of coping with confusing and difficult family situations. Imagine living in a family where you couldn't predict the behavior of other family members, you couldn't determine how others wanted you to behave, and where communication was vague and often distorted. Your own world where everyone was shut out might seem a very inviting place! In fact investigators have suggested that children in such families are often faced with a special type of conflict known as a **double bind;** this conflicts results when a person receives two mutually contradictory messages. For example consider the plight of the young man in the following example:

> A young man who had fairly well recovered from an acute schizophrenic episode was visited in the hospital by his mother. He was glad to see her and impulsively put his arm around her shoulders, whereupon she stiffened. He withdrew his arm and she asked, "Don't you love me anymore?" He then blushed and she said, "Dear, you must not be so easily embarrassed and afraid of your feelings." The patient was able to stay with her only a few minutes more and following her departure he assaulted an aide. . . . (Bateson, Jackson, Haley, & Weakland, 1956, p. 144)

Double-bind conflict
Results when children receive contradictory messages from their parents, messages that create a "no-win" situation for them—no matter what they do, they are wrong.

Children faced with a double-bind situation will begin to withdraw and cease trying to form close relationships with people. The family situation teaches them that dealing with others is confusing because people's words and actions are often very different.

Finally, other research has examined the characteristics of the parents of schizophrenics (Lewis, Rodnick, & Goldstein, 1981; Shapiro, 1981). The mothers of schizophrenics tend to present a picture of inconsistency and unpredictability. For instance, they may remain aloof and avoid intimacy, yet insist on sharing their child's every activity. The fathers of schizophrenics are often passive, rigid, and detached. While their actions are more consistent than those of the mothers just described, they present poor models of adjustment. In order to deal with this confusing situation, the child makes a hasty retreat into a world of his own. If we carry this explanation to its extreme we might be attempted to agree with R. D. Laing (1964), a humanistic psychologist, who argued that schizophrenics are not crazy: they are simply adjusting to a crazy world!

Cognitive Theories. As we have pointed out, one of the main characteristics of schizophrenics is the way they perceive and think about the world. They often spend large amounts of time focusing on small details and cannot "block out" irrelevant stimuli. One researcher suggests that a cause of schizophrenia may be that people develop faulty ways of perceiving the world; they learn a certain set of expectations that causes them to focus on unimportant parts of their environment (Shakow, 1977). Their adjustment is therefore retarded because they are responding to a world that is different from the one that you and I perceive. Treatment should, therefore, focus on changing the way schizophrenics perceive situations.

Maher (1970) offers another interesting view. He suggests that schizophrenics suffer from a biochemical disturbance that causes them to experience distorted sensations that are different from those experienced by other people. Their seemingly bizarre behavior and beliefs are their efforts to deal with this unusual stimulation. Hence there may be nothing wrong with schizophrenics' reasoning or belief systems. They may be simply using logical processes to deal with the unusual sensory stimulation that they experience.

There are many theories about the causes of schizophrenia. Most likely they all hold some truth in that biological factors may predispose a person toward the disorder, but stressful environments and learning can trigger the disorder.

Personality Disorders

As I read the story about Nancy's life, my first thought was that she was just a mean manipulative kid who did not respond to rewards and punishment. But as I reflected on her life, my view became more complicated. Nancy was bright as was reflected in her score of 134 on the IQ test, but she couldn't seem to stop herself from manipulating and acting aggressively toward others. She loved to get her brother and sister in trouble as evidenced by the time she introduced them to drugs and then reported them to her mother. No matter how many times she was punished or how many friends she lost, she was still manipulative and aggressive.

In Chapter 13 we defined personality as a generalized way of dealing with the environment. However, despite this generalized tendency to respond, most of us are also sensitive to our environments. We change our behavior to meet the demands of the situation. Nancy didn't do this; she seemed stuck on responding in one fashion. Were this the only symptom she showed, we might begin to explore the possibility that she had a personality disorder.

Personality disorders are rigid and maladaptive ways of dealing with the environment. They are characterized not so much by a specific behavior as by a general approach to dealing with events. They usually become evident during adolescence and remain with people throughout their life. Unlike many of the disorders we have discussed, most personality disorders are not characterized by wild or bizarre behaviors. In fact, most people with a personality disorder can function and seldom require hospitalization. However, their behavior is strange enough that other people avoid interacting with them or are distressed by the interactions. The most noticeable characteristic of the personality disorder is that people tend to react to stress in a patterned way. This response is seldom affected by the requirements of the situation. They show little fear of punishment and little concern for the consequences of their behavior, even when their own well-being is at stake (Newman, Patterson & Kosson, 1987). For example, if someone intentionally stepped on your toe, you would most likely shout and make your anger known. But if that someone happened to be a 280-pound, 6'7" male, chances are your shouts would not be so loud. People with an antisocial personality disorder, however, would probably respond to this intimidating person in the same way they would respond to someone of more manageable size.

There are a number of types of personality disorders (see Table 14–10). Here we will examine only one, the antisocial personality. This is the type most commonly found in Western society.

Antisocial Personality

People with **antisocial personality disorders** (often referred to as psychopaths or sociopaths) perform violent and hurtful acts without experiencing the least bit of guilt or remorse. They are incapable of forming close relationships with others, and they are manipulative and insincere. They also seem to be incapable of learning from their mistakes. Many antisocial people

Personality disorders
Rigid and maladaptive ways of dealing with the environment, characterized by a general approach to dealing with events rather than by any one specific behavior. The example discussed in the text is the *antisocial personality disorder*, which is the type of personality disorder most often found in Western society.

Antisocial personality disorder
Disorder in which people perform violent and hurtful acts without the least bit of guilt or regret, are incapable of forming close relationships, and are manipulative and insincere.

Table 14–10
Selective Personality Disorders Identified in DSM-IIIR

Disorder	Symptoms
Paranoid	Pervasive and unwarranted tendency to interpret the actions of others as deliberately demeaning or threatening. Bears grudges, expects to be exploited, distrusts others, and is quick to anger.
Schizoid	Pervasive patterns of indifference to social relationships and restricted range of emotional expression. Chooses solitary activities, indifferent to praise or criticism of others, no close friends.
Histrionic	Pervasive pattern of excessive emotionality and attention seeking. Constantly demands praise and approval, overly concerned about physical attractiveness, is self-centered, displays rapidly shifting and shallow expression of emotions.
Avoidant	Pervasive pattern of social discomfort, fear of negative evaluation, and timidity. Is easily hurt by criticism, fears being embarrassed by blushing or crying, avoids social or occupational activities involving interpersonal contact.
Passive Aggressive	Pervasive pattern of passive resistance to demands for adequate social and occupational performance. Procrastinates, becomes sulky and irritable when asked to do something, works deliberately slowly or does a bad job on unwanted tasks, avoids obligations by claiming to have "forgotten," unreasonably criticizes people in positions of authority.

People with antisocial personality disorder perform violent and hurtful acts without experiencing guilt. Because of their impulsive and destructive behavior, people with this disorder often have lengthy criminal records.

serve prison terms, but once released, they continue with the same kind of behavior that got them into trouble in the first place. One of the more frightening aspects of this disorder is that antisocial people are often very intelligent and use their intelligence to "get away with" their behavior.

Antisocial personality is a relatively common disorder. It has been estimated that 3 percent of American men and 1 percent of American women have this type of personality. In fact, this estimate may be low, since antisocial people seldom seek professional help, and many of the statistics must be based on cases that have come to the attention of law enforcement officials. Clearly, not all people who take part in crimes or antisocial behavior are suffering from antisocial personality disorders. Many criminals carefully plan their crime with a clear reward in mind and they take steps to avoid detection. Although people with antisocial personalities do not lack the capability to reason or plan, their behavior often seems impulsive and lacks prior planning (Sutker & Allair, 1987). Hence the behavior of people with antisocial personality disorders seems irrational and not aimed at personal gain. The disorder can be identified if the person has a long history of antisocial behavior that began by adolescence and continued into adulthood. In addition, people with antisocial personality disorders do not limit their activities to one crime or behavior; rather, they engage in a wide variety of behaviors such as lying, stealing, irresponsible parenting, dealing drugs, and writing bad checks.

What causes people to treat others with such indifference? There is some evidence that an antisocial personality may be inherited. One investigator found that children of antisocial parents who were adopted at birth were more likely to show antisocial behavior than adopted children who did not have antisocial parents (Cadoret, 1978). However, other research has not found a strong link to genetics (Farber, 1981). Another line of research reported that many sociopaths have abnormal brain-wave patterns (Hare, 1983). It has been suggested that these abnormal patterns keep the person from experiencing fear, and hence free him or her to act in antisocial ways. Turning away from biological explanations, some investigators have focused on early childhood conditions. Many people with antisocial personality disorders came from broken homes. It was not the absence of a parent that was associated with the disorder, however. Rather, it was the specific atmosphere surrounding the divorce that was the contributing factor. This included violent arguments, instability, parental neglect, and lack of affection (McCord, 1979).

Substance Use Disorders: Alcohol and Other Drugs

From the age of 13 until she died, Nancy lived a nightmare with drugs as her companion. She began experimenting with drugs when she entered a school for the emotionally disturbed. She confided in her sister, "I get stoned all the time and I've taken acid seven times" (Spungen, 1983, p. 154). The experimentation soon escalated to drug dependence, and she began using heroin. She would do anything to get money to buy drugs; she begged money from her parents and friends, sold drugs, and engaged in prostitution to support her habit. Drugs ruled her life and helped tear her apart, although there were times when she fought to control her habit. She went to a methadone clinic in New York and on her nineteenth birthday she proudly announced that she was completely off drugs. However, some months later she went to England, became involved with the Sex Pistols, and returned to drugs. She tried other clinics, but she could never free herself from the grip of drugs.

Reading the newspaper or watching television shows the extent to which our society is in the grip of alcohol and drug problems. Organizations like MADD (Mothers Against Drunk Driving), SADD (Students Against Drunk Driving), and BADD (Bartenders Against Drunk Driving) provide us with startling reminders of the tragic effects of alcohol. Douglas Ginsburg, a Supreme Court nominee, was forced to withdraw his name from consider-

The destructiveness of substance use disorders has sparked massive campaigns to educate and keep people from becoming dependent on drugs. Much of the effort is aimed at children and adolescents because evidence indicates growing use of drugs and alcohol by children.

ation after he revealed in November 1987 that he had used marijuana in the 1960s and 1970s. Drug use became an issue for the 1988 presidential campaign as candidates rushed forward to deny or confess their use of drugs. Drugs have become the major factor linked to crime in the United States, and the war against drugs has turned areas of our cities into battle-zones (*Newsweek*, March 28, 1988). Campaigns to educate children about the dangers of drug use are found in almost every school and television shows public figures telling the audience to "Just Say No" to drugs. Added urgency is given the effort to control drug use by the finding that AIDS (see Chapter 10) is spread by the sharing of needles by drug users.

Given this background, it is important to put our discussion into a clear perspective. First, we must separate the legal issues from the clinical considerations. For example, Judge Ginsburg broke the law when he used marijuana at a party in the 1970s. But his infrequent social use of the illegal substance would not classify him as having a substance use disorder. As we will see, we become clinically concerned when people cannot control their drug use and/or when drug use impairs their functioning. This distinction may sometimes be difficult for the user to make; I still remember a high school friend who couldn't make it through an hour-long class without smoking, but continued to boast, "I can stop any time I want." A second point is that there are actually two categories of **substance use disorders,** and that use of drugs does not necessarily indicate either of these disorders. The first category is **substance abuse,** which results when (1) there is pathological use of the drug, (2) there is a reduction in social or occupational functioning because of the drug, and (3) there is at least one month's duration of disturbance. Thus a person who has a few drinks at lunch would not be classified as suffering from drug abuse. However, if that person were to feel that he or she had to have a couple of drinks to get through the day, and the drinking resulted in poorer work performance, the classification of substance abuse would be appropriate. In addition to substance abuse, DSM III-R (1987) lists the category **substance dependence** (addiction), which includes the presence of tolerance or withdrawal. **Tolerance** means the need to increase the amount of the drug to achieve the same effects. **Withdrawal** means the presence of physical symptoms such as pain or nausea when use of the substance is discontinued.

Substance use disorders
Disorders including the categories of substance abuse and substance dependence.

Substance abuse
Disorder that results from a pathological use of a drug; a reduction in social or occupational functioning because of the drug; and a duration of disturbance of at least one month.

Substance dependence
Addiction including the presence of tolerance or withdrawal.

Tolerance
Need to increase the amount of the drug to achieve the same effects.

Withdrawal symptoms
Range of physical symptoms, including nausea and pain when a drug-dependent person is deprived of his or her drug of choice.

Alcoholism

As we begin our discussion of alcoholism, the first point to keep in mind is that alcohol is a drug. Addiction to alcohol (alcoholism) is the most common addiction in today's society. There are 12 million alcoholics and the average alcoholic is a man or woman in the middle thirties with "a good job, a good home and a family" (National Council on Alcoholism 1986). Most of us use alcohol on occasion; in fact, two-thirds of adult Americans drink alcohol at times. In low or moderate doses, alcohol may have a relaxing effect, help in sleeping, lower pulse rate, and aid in social interaction. There is evidence that small doses of alcohol may reduce the risk of heart attack, and nursing mothers may be encouraged to drink a glass of beer or wine to help their milk flow (Turner, 1981). In fact, in early colonial America, alcohol enjoyed a very positive reputation (Critchlow, 1986). Colonial Americans drank steadily and consumed large quantities of alcohol on special occasions; The Puritan minister Cotton Mather called alcohol the "good creature of God." By the early 19th century, alcohol began its fall from grace. American society began to emphasize social order and individual responsibility to control one's self-behavior; alcohol was seen as working against self-control.

Because substance abuse involves tolerance and withdrawal, abusers must often be treated in a special program. Elizabeth Taylor went through such a program to deal with her drug dependence.

Large amounts of alcohol lead to impaired judgment, slowed reflexes, nausea, fainting, and possibly death. Extended use of large quantities of alcohol results in liver damage, hypertension, and malnutrition (see Table 14–11). Coleman, Butcher, & Carson (1980) states that alcohol is associated with over half of all deaths and major injuries in automobile accidents, 50 percent of all murders, and 30 percent of all suicides. Nearly one-third of all arrests in the United States are the result of alcohol abuse. Highway accidents in which alcohol is a contributing factor are the greatest cause of death for young people (see Table 14–11). Because of this, most states have raised the legal drinking age from 18 to 21 years old. Another interesting problem related to alcohol involves the expectancies we have about it. Besides impairing many of our functions, most of us believe that alcohol reduces inhibitions. Given these beliefs, we may use being "under the influence" as an excuse for poor performance or behaving in harmful and illegal ways (Critchlow, 1986).

When we talk about alcohol abuse, we are really talking about two categories of people. The larger category is the **problem drinker** or alcohol abuser. This includes people who often drink too much and whose drinking has undesirable effects. Problem drinkers may be people who have learned to deal with stressful situations by drinking, or they may be people who enjoy drinking or getting drunk. A small number of these problem drinkers fall into the category of alcoholic. **Alcoholics** are dependent on alcohol. They have an uncontrollable urge to drink, and because of an increasing tolerance, they must continue to increase the dosage of alcohol. Since they consume such large amounts of alcohol, alcoholics are often in poor physical health and their social relationships suffer.

The number of problem drinkers in the United States is surprisingly high; 10 percent of adult males and 3 percent of adult females are problem drinkers. The rates are even higher among minority groups such as Indians, Hispanics, and blacks (Lex, 1987). Less than half of these problem drinkers are alcoholics. With these large figures, it is surprising to learn that the United States ranks only fifteenth in amount of alcohol consumed; France ranks first. Although today much attention and concern is focused on "hard drugs," the worldwide problem of alcohol abuse is increasing (Helzer, 1987). For example, in England and Wales the number of individuals admitted to hospitals for alcoholism is 20 times greater today than 25 years ago. It has been estimated that alcoholism costs industry $10 billion a year in the United States!

Problem drinkers
People who often drink too much and whose drinking has undesirable effects on their lives or on others. See also *alcoholics*.

Alcoholics
People who are addicted to alcohol; they have an uncontrollable urge to drink, and because of increasing tolerance, must continue to increase their consumption.

Table 14–11
Alcohol Can Kill in Many Ways

Deaths Caused by Alcohol

Nearly 40 percent of all deaths attributed to alcohol were classed as accidental. Violence, including homicide and suicide, accounted for 22 percent of alcohol-related deaths, while physiological damage, such as cirrhosis of the liver, was responsible for another 20 percent.

Alcohol-Related Deaths in the U.S.

In percent of total, based on 1980 figures:	
Accidents (Incl. traffic deaths)	38.9%
Violence (Incl. suicide and homicide)	21.7%
Alcohol as main cause (Incl. cirrhosis of the liver)	20%
Other diseases	11.9%
Alcohol as contributing cause (Incl. stomach cancer)	7.5%
Alcohol-Related Deaths, 1980: 97,528	

Source: U.S. Department of Health and Human Services.

Why do some people become addicted to alcohol and develop an uncontrollable urge to drink when others neither become addicted nor feel a need to drink? As with most other disorders, there are many theories. One view is that alcoholism is inherited. For example, Goodwin (1979) found that sons of alcoholic parents are four times more likely to become alcoholics than sons of nonalcoholic parents. This figure holds true even if the children are not reared by their natural parents. Interestingly enough, daughters of alcoholic parents do not run a greater risk than daughters of nonalcoholic parents of becoming alcoholic. While there is evidence that alcoholism is inherited, we are still unsure of how it works. One recent finding is that sons of alcoholic parents show greater tolerance to low levels of alcohol (i.e., need more alcohol to experience effects) and they have different patterns of brain activity than children of nonalcoholic parents (Schuckit, 1987). It may be that individuals inherit an allergylike response to alcohol. Other theories adopt the position that alcoholism is learned. The individual finds that alcohol reduces stress and therefore "turns to the bottle" whenever stressful situations arise. These two theories represent two sides in an ongoing debate over whether alcoholism is a medical disease or a learned behavior disorder (Koluta, 1988). This debate has recently surfaced in a Supreme Court case in which two veterans are arguing they are due medical benefits because their alcoholism is a disease.

Of course, as with most psychological phenomena, alcoholism is surely not a function solely of heredity or solely of environment. A recent social-cognitive approach to understanding alcohol consumption acknowledges the role of both environmental influences (learning) and physiological reactions (heredity) in shaping the individual's social and behavioral responses to alcohol consumption (Steele & Josephs, 1990). The theorists begin with the observation that people display a variety of different behaviors when they are drinking. Some become loud and boisterous, while others get quiet and withdrawn. Some become aggressive and want to fight, while others get friendly and want to help. Some become excited and "full of themselves," while others become morose and depressed. Furthermore, the same individual can show these varied responses at different times and in different circumstances.

How can such variability be explained? Steele and his colleagues conclude that the wide variety of social and emotional responses is a result of a change in the way people process information when they are under the influence of alcohol. Specifically, they argue that alcohol intoxication causes a sort of cognitive myopia, a short-sightedness in the range of one's perceptions and thoughts. The myopic effects of intoxication interact with both the psychological state of the individual and the situational cues present when the person is drinking to produce a myriad of emotional and behavioral responses.

Although the effects of alcohol consumption vary widely, it is possible, according to Steele, to group them into three classes: (1) drunken excess (extreme or excessive social behavior); (2) drunken self-inflation (ego boosting); and (3) drunken relief (forgetfulness, if only temporary, of troubles and anxieties). According to Steele, drunken excess helps to explain the destructive social behaviors of people who become intoxicated, while the psychologically reinforcing properties of drunken self-inflation and drunken relief may explain, in part, the addictiveness of alcohol.

Drug Addiction

The term *drug* has become a catchword in today's society. Making the statement that Nancy used "drugs" could have many meanings. On the one hand, we might be referring to **narcotics** (morphine, heroin, opium). Narcotics are drugs that in small doses reduce pain, cause drowsiness,

Narcotics
Drugs that in small doses reduce pain, cause drowsiness, and give a feeling of happiness and well-being. Examples are morphine, heroin, and opium.

and give the individual a feeling of happiness and well-being. The term drug might also be used to refer to *amphetamines* (speed and pep pills) or *cocaine*, which are **stimulants** causing the individual to feel excited and full of energy. Another category of drugs is the **hallucinogens** (LSD, STP, mescaline, peyote—see Chapter 5), which cause the individual to feel happy and see visions and illusions. *Barbiturates* and *tranquilizers* are **depressants** that slow the body functions, reduce anxiety, and have a relaxing effect.

The use of drugs seems to be almost as old as civilization itself. There is reference to the use of marijuana in China in 2737 B.C. and to the use of opium in the Middle East before the 8th century B.C. In most cases, the substances that we call "drugs" are used in medical settings in carefully prescribed doses. Narcotics, for example, reduce pain, and marijuana has been used to treat glaucoma (a disease of the eye). However, taken in large doses, most of the drugs that we listed can cause serious physical and psychological impairment and even lead to death.

Although addiction is possible with most of the drugs, it seems to have different characteristics depending on the specific substance being used. For example, the body builds up a tolerance for each of certain drugs. This means that people must increase the dose to get the desired effect from the drug. However, research suggests that while a physical dependence develops for narcotics, amphetamines, barbiturates, and nicotine, there is no physical dependence on hallucinogens. Thus withdrawal from the former set of drugs will be *physically* painful. This finding seems to argue that we need to have little concern about addiction to hallucinogens because withdrawal will not be physically painful. However, closer examination of the issue reveals that there are actually two types of dependence that can develop. The first, *physical dependence*, means the body develops a need for the drug. The second, *psychological dependence*, means that people feel they must have the drug; in other words, the dependence is in the mind. In the latter case, withdrawal may not cause physical pain, but will result in the psychologically painful symptoms of anxiety, depression, and uneasiness. These symptoms are often as difficult to cope with as physical withdrawal symptoms. Psychological dependence develops to each of the drugs we have discussed.

When we discuss drugs, our attention is often drawn to illegal drugs; however, we must not forget that some legal drugs are addictive, dangerous, and easy to obtain.

Today a great deal of controversy surrounds the drug called *cannabis*, which is found in marijuana. Cannabis can be smoked, eaten, or drunk in tea. It generally causes people to feel relaxed and happy, and reduces inhibitions. The majority of research (Stafford-Clark & Smith, 1978) suggests that people do not develop a physical dependence on cannabis. However, psychological dependence can result from prolonged use.

Stimulants
Drugs that excite body functions; examples are caffeine, amphetamines, and cocaine.
Hallucinogens
Drugs such as LSD, STP, mescaline, and peyote, that cause people to see visions and illusions.
Depressants
Drugs that slow body functions or calm nervous excitement; examples are alcohol, nicotine, and heroin.

FIGURE 14–3
Annual Deaths Related to Smoking and Other Causes

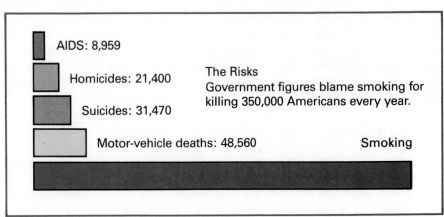

AIDS: 8,959

Homicides: 21,400

Suicides: 31,470

Motor-vehicle deaths: 48,560

The Risks
Government figures blame smoking for killing 350,000 Americans every year.

Smoking

Source: Cowley (April, 1988).

4: Abnormal Psychology

PURE NICOTINE CALLED ADDICTIVE AS COCAINE

When pure nicotine is inhaled, it is as addictive as free-base cocaine, according to the author of a recent University of Toronto study.

"Nicotine is very addictive because you get an immediate effect," said Jo-Ann Lux, a biomedical engineer and pharmacologist. Smokers can experience anything from a sense of well-being and calm to a feeling of agitation depending upon the number of cigarettes consumed, she said. And when nicotine starts to leave the brain, the desire for another cigarette is triggered.

Lux, who completed her research a year ago, said her comparison of nicotine with cocaine is based on the fact that the more quickly a response is felt from a drug, the more addictive it is.

"It takes about five seconds for nicotine to hit the brain once it enters the bloodstream," she said. This addictive quality of nicotine helps to explain why it is so difficult to quit smoking.

"People who are addicted to hard drugs say it is more difficult to get off cigarettes than hard drugs," she said.

"Nicotine is an extremely dangerous drug," she said, because if it is absorbed into the bloodstream in large enough doses, it can cause convulsions and disruption of breathing. In lesser dosages, it significantly increases heartbeat and blood pressure.

Fifteen Toronto men between the ages of 18 and 50 who smoked an average of 25 cigarettes a day participated in the research.

Scripps Howard News Service, *Bryan/College Station Eagle*, Nov. 13, 1987, p. 9A.

Drug addiction has physical, social, and psychological effects. The physical effects include the possibilities of malnutrition, infection, and other physical diseases such as hepatitis. There are two categories of psychological problems. The first concerns the direct effect of the drug. When Nancy Spungen was using drugs, she showed little concern for her own welfare. Her physical appearance deteriorated, she wore the same dirty clothes for long periods of time, and her apartment was a mess. She cared about nothing except getting her high on drugs. Hallucinogens can cause people to experience psychotic episodes in which they lose touch with reality and cannot function. These episodes may last a long time, and later flashbacks can occur in which the symptoms of an earlier episode suddenly return and overwhelm the person without warning and without that person's having taken the drug again. Another issue here involves the long-term effects of drugs. Because concern about many drugs is a fairly recent issue, there is little research aimed at examining how the use of drugs for a period of years may affect people. The issue of long-term effects has become especially important with marijuana; some people have argued that its use should be legalized; others demand stiffer prison sentences for users.

The second category of psychological problems includes the depression and feelings of helplessness that people who are addicted may experience. In essence, their dependence eliminates their freedom to control their lives and makes them a slave to the drug.

The social effects are many also. On the one hand, there is the loss of productivity, high absenteeism, and impaired performance that may be caused by the drug. Social relationships may suffer as people retreat into the world of drugs. There are also legal problems. Because most of these drugs are illegal, the cost of supporting a habit may run well over $200 a day. Most people do not have this amount of spending money and must turn to crime to pay for their drugs. Our jails and prisons have become overcrowded as a result of the large number of people serving time for drug or drug-related offenses.

Drug addiction is widespread in our society and is not confined to individuals in any particular class, race, or sex.

A great deal of research is being conducted to identify factors that determine addiction and the effects of addiction. This research is complicated by the legal, social, and moral issues surrounding drug use. It will probably take many years to completely understand the effects of drugs

Despite massive anti-drug efforts, the drug problem in this country is still growing as newer drugs such as crack and smack are introduced. Dependence on drugs eliminates the person's ability to control his or her life.

A STREET-SIDE PHARMACOPEIA

Over the last two years some drug dealers have abandoned marijuana and heroin to push crack. But others are doing a brisk business in new imports—and some old standbys. A report from the city streets:

Cocaine and crack: A glut has forced the price of a kilogram of cocaine from $65,000 four years ago to $10,000 in some places. In some cities, a vial of crack costs only $3.

Marijuana: Though somewhat harder to find since the crack boom, pot is by far still the nation's most popular illicit drug; 18 million Americans smoke it regularly.

Hallucinogens: A watered-down form of LSD is making a comeback, mostly in the West. Sales of inexpensive liquid PCP are up again on the East Coast.

Mexican heroin: The street price for Black Tar, which is as much as 80 percent pure, can climb to $500 per gram. A bargain brown-powder heroin sells for $120 to $150.

Asian heroin: One form comes from the Golden Crescent (Iran, Afghanistan, Pakistan, India) and another from the Golden Triangle (Burma, Laos, Thailand).

Fentanyl: A potent heroin substitute known as China White, the synthetically produced "designer drug" is mostly a West Coast fad. Street price: $3,200 a gram.

From "The Drug Gangs," *Newsweek*, March 28, 1988, p. 27.

on people. Even with this information, the controversy surrounding the legalization of drugs may continue. This is because the research is unlikely to paint a completely negative or positive picture of these substances. Although some drugs may be shown to be less harmful than others, the exact effects of a substance will be influenced by the characteristics of the person using it. As we have seen, this is the case with alcohol. Overuse has negative consequences for everybody, but even moderate use causes some people to suffer negative effects while others do not.

Summary

1. While there are many ways to define abnormality, most psychologists label a behavior **abnormal** when it causes personal distress and hinders the ability to adapt to the environment. The most commonly used system of classifying psychological disorders today is the **Diagnostic and Statistical Manual Revised (DSM-III-R).**

2. **Insanity** is a legal term used to indicate that a person does not know right from wrong when committing a crime; insanity is not found in psychological classifications. Although a classification system can be a handy, time-saving device; labeling an individual's behavior can be dangerous.

3. Seven approaches for identifying and explaining the causes of maladaptive behavior were discussed in this chapter: the mystical perspective and the medical, psychoanalytic, learning/behavioral, cognitive, humanistic, and systems models.

4. **Anxiety disorders** occur when people experience fear that is out of proportion to the situation they are in, and their responses to anxiety interfere with their ability to perform daily activities. In **generalized anxiety disorders,** the person does not know what is causing the anxiety; he or she simply feels overwhelmed with anxiety. **Panic disorders** involve sudden attacks of extreme anxiety accompanied by a variety of intense symptoms. The **post-traumatic stress disorder** occurs when a person experiences a traumatic event long after it has past; their symptoms are similar to those shown during the original event. **Phobias** are irrational fears of objects or events that not only cause people to psychologically suffer but may also strongly influence their behavior. **Obsessive-compulsive disorders** occur when the person feels an overwhelming need to think a certain thought (obsession) or perform a certain behavior (compulsion).

5. **Somatoform disorders** involve physical symptoms that are caused by stress and have no physiological basis. Included under this category is the **hypochondriac,** who believes that he or she is seriously ill despite assurances to the contrary by physicians. **Conversion disorders** are characterized by one specific and often dramatic symptom. This may be blindness, deafness, or paralysis.

6. In **dissociative disorders,** people separate or dissociate part of their personality from the situation. These disorders include **amnesia, fugue,** and **multiple personalities.** In each of these cases, the

person tries to escape anxiety by removing part of his or her personality from consciousness. The disorder results when the person must deal with the anxiety because it is pushing into the consciousness.

7. **Mood disorders** are disturbances in feelings and emotions. The most common of the mood disorders is **depression.** There are numerous theories about how depression develops, ranging from early childhood experiences to a lack of positive reinforcement in people's present environment. The **learned helplessness** approach combines learning theory and cognitive theory by arguing that depression occurs when people feel that they have no control over their environment. An extension of this model suggests that negative life events that are attributed to stable and global causes lead to hopelessness and this feeling results in sadness, apathy, and "giving up." Finally, there is some evidence that biochemical imbalances either in neurotransmitters or in the blood cause depression.

8. **Bipolar disorders** occur when the person shows wild swings in mood between depression and **mania** (elation). Evidence has been discovered that this disorder is inherited.

9. Depression plays a major role in almost 80 percent of attempted suicides. Suicides are aimed at ending life or manipulating others by making them feel guilty. The best predictors are the threat to commit suicide and past suicide attempts.

10. Sexual disorders are divided into two general categories. **Paraphilias** are characterized by attraction to deviant objects or acts which interfere with the capacity for reciprocal and affectionate sexual activity. **Sadism** and **masochism** are paraphilias which involve inflicting pain or experiencing pain as the means of sexual gratification. **Sexual dysfunctions** (the other major category) are the most common sexual disorders. They involve inhibitions of sexual desire or psychological impairments that interfere with the normal sexual cycle. Included in this group are **impotence** and **premature ejaculation** in males and **dyspareunia** and **vaginismus** in females.

11. **Psychoses** are disorders in which people lose touch with reality and have difficulty functioning in their environment. **Schizophrenia** is the most common psychosis. There are many types of schizophrenia; symptoms include disturbances in thinking, disorganized perceptions, disturbances in communication, inappropriate emotions, and unusual motor activities. Theories of schizophrenia have focused on biological problems, disturbances in learning and cognition and conflict in the family setting.

12. **Personality disorders** involve rigid and maladaptive ways of dealing with the environment. People with this disorder can function, but they often have problems forming close relationships with others. The **antisocial personality** is characterized by the performance of violent or hurtful acts without experiencing guilt or regret.

13. There are two categories of **substance use disorders.** The first is **substance abuse,** which includes pathological use of a drug or drugs and a decrease in functioning for at least one month in duration. The second category is **substance dependence** (addiction), which includes the presence of either tolerance or withdrawal, two different physical reactions to drugs. Alcoholism is the most common addiction in our society.

14. Drug addiction may involve physical and/or psychological dependence. Physical dependence means the body develops a need for the drug. Psychological dependence means that people feel they must have the drug. Psychological symptoms of withdrawal are often as difficult to cope with as physical withdrawal symptoms. Drug addiction has many negative physical, social, and psychological effects. It is widespread in our society and is not confined to one particular class, race, or sex.

Key Terms

abnormal behavior	double-bind conflict	multiple personality disorder	schizophrenia
alcoholics	dyspareunia	narcotics	self-fulfilling prophecy
amnesia	erectile dysfunction	neurosis	sexual dysfunction
antisocial personality disorder	fugue	obsession	somatoform disorders
anxiety disorders	generalized anxiety disorder	obsessive-compulsive disorders	stimulants
bipolar disorder	hallucination	panic disorder	substance abuse
compulsion	hallucinogens	paraphilia	substance dependence
conversion disorder	hypochondriasis	personality disorders	substance use disorders
delusions	impotence	phobia	suicide
depressants	insanity	post-traumatic stress disorder	tolerance
depression	learned helplessness	premature ejaculation	vaginismus
DSM-III-R (Diagnostic and Statistical Manual of Mental Disorders)	mania	problem drinkers	withdrawal symptoms
dissociative disorders	masochism	psychosis	
	mood disorders	sadism	

DELUSION, BENIGN AND BIZARRE, IS RECOGNIZED AS COMMON

BY DANIEL GOLEMAN

Delusions are more common-place than most people assume, a growing number of researchers are concluding. These researchers say the delusions of those with psychiatric disorders are fundamentally no different from, say, a private belief that a color is unlucky or popular beliefs in the existence of flying saucers.

By tracing how delusions develop, researchers hope to find ways to identify people most at risk of mental illness and stop their delusions from developing into full flower even though the disorder is one of the most difficult to treat.

A belief is considered a delusion if a person holds to it no matter how bizarre it is and despite all evidence to the contrary. A belief that flying saucers exist is considered benign, while the belief that a person has been contacted by people on flying saucers is worrisome. Some researchers say most people have minor delusions of one kind or another.

"About four in a hundred people have extremely deviant beliefs," said Loren J. Chapman, a psychologist at the University of Wisconsin, who is conducting a study of how delusions develop. "Some of these people might seem strange to just about anyone, while others are doing very well, with their unusual beliefs limited to isolated topics."

The researchers say people who develop such severe delusions tend to stop searching for alternative explanations far sooner than do most other people.

Hearing Thoughts

Dr. Chapman is testing the hypothesis that those who hold the most deviant beliefs are at risk for mental illness.

One woman studied by Dr. Chapman insisted that people could read her mind from the expression on her face. That belief, and others like it, led Dr. Chapman to predict that the woman, though living a normal life, was at risk for mental illness.

Indeed, when interviewed two years later, she said people heard her thoughts, a delusion that was part of a psychosis she had developed.

In themselves, delusions are benign, the experts say. "The trouble starts when those beliefs gain such intense emotional importance we feel compelled to act on them," said Dr. Hugh Hendrie, chairman of the department of psychiatry at the Indiana University School of Medicine.

Dr. Brendon Maher, a psychologist at Harvard, has put forward the most influential theory about delusions, proposing that they spring from quite ordinary ways of thinking. In his view, delusions are like other beliefs, in that they give order and meaning to what is otherwise a puzzle in life.

"Puzzles demand explanation; the search for an explanation begins and continues until one has been devised," said Dr. Maher.

For instance, a strange sound in the night might be caused by a cat, but a deluded person might assume it was caused by a burglar even if such an explanation was implausible.

"One of the assumptions we make in thinking about delusions is that implausible explanations are rather rare; but I argue they are rather common," said Dr. Maher, who this week became dean of the Graduate School of Arts and Sciences at Harvard.

Self-Confirming Beliefs

"The standard of rational, deductive thinking does not apply to normal thought," Dr. Maher said. "Many or most people privately hold strange beliefs that could be diagnosed as delusional if brought to the attention of a clinician."

Explanatory beliefs tend to be self-confirming in that contradictory data are ignored, while anything that might support the theory is given prominence. That, Dr. Maher says, has been shown to be the case with ordinary beliefs as well as with people who develop delusions.

Dr. Maher's theory is set forth in "Delusional Beliefs" (Wiley), a book he edited with Thomas Oltmanns, a psychiatrist at the University of Arizona.

In evaluating whether a belief is a delusion, clinicians take into account the background of the beliefs in a person's culture, community or peer group.

"If you say someone is controlling your thoughts, that may or may not be an outright delusion," Dr. Chapman said. "For instance, if you think that God is controlling your thoughts—say making you study instead of going out to a movie—and you are a pious person, that belief has cultural support; it's not a deviant belief."

"But if you believe the Devil is making you think bad thoughts, and you do not, for instance, hold to a religion with such a view, then that's a more deviant belief," he said. "And if you believe your uncle in Chicago is making you think evil thoughts, then that's more deviant still."

There are more than 70 different clinical conditions in which delusions can occur, including brain tumors, alcohol intoxication, epilepsy and senility. Delusions are among the prominent symptoms of disorders like manic-depression, schizophrenia and "delusional disorder," which formerly was known as paranoia.

Of these, delusions are the principal symptom only in delusional disorder, in which people are typically coherent and functioning well in other areas of their lives. They will be convinced, for instance, that movie stars are in love with them and sending them covert messages through pointed lines and looks in a film.

Delusions that are symptoms of other problems usually clear up when the underlying mental disorder is treated, Dr. Hendrie said.

"Delusional disorder—where the delusion itself is the problem—is among the most difficult to treat of all psychiatric disorders," Dr. Hendrie said. "You don't want to argue with them about the delusion, but you shouldn't go along with it."

"The trouble is the intensity of their feelings, and that so much of their life revolves around the delusion," he said. "Sometimes the best you can do is let them know they can keep the delusion so long as they don't let it ruin their life."

Scale of Aberration

In trying to understand how delusions come to full flower, Dr. Chapman's study tested thousands of students selected on the basis of psychological surveys given in an introductory psychology course over several years. Researchers found 162 who held extremely unusual beliefs, ideas that while not necessarily delusional could develop into delusions as the years go on. Dr. Chapman has developed a scale that rates people's beliefs in terms of how aberrant they are.

He predicted that even more bizarre beliefs were likely to develop among the people with the most unusual beliefs.

When the students were tested again two years later, three of those considered most at risk, including the woman who thought people could hear her thoughts, had developed a mental illness. But no students who belonged to a comparison group of people holding more normal beliefs had done so.

One of the three who became mentally ill was, on first testing, having no apparent problems in school or adjusting to life. But he maintained that he occasionally heard the voice of an "archangel" offering him moral admonitions. Once, he said, the voice come from the corner of the basement in his parents' home, giving him the counsel that "life is more meaningful than it seems."

Voice of Dead Relative

The man conjectured that the voice might be that of his dead grandfather, whom he had never met. When pressed, he vaguely justified his interpretation by saying the grandfather had "always been involved with the supernatural."

During the intervening two years, he had a psychotic episode in which he heard a picture of Christ in his church speaking to him, telling him to run naked through the snow. He believed that the police who arrested him for public nakedness were devils taking him to Satan to be tortured.

Dr. Chapman also identified nine others whose beliefs became significantly more aberrant and who he concluded were at great risk for becoming mentally ill.

Now, 10 years after the last contact with the students, Dr. Chapman is getting in touch with them once again to see how their delusions have progressed, and if any of those with extremely deviant beliefs became mentally ill.

One source of extreme delusional beliefs, Dr. Maher conjectures, may be a misfunction of a brain circuit that detects when something is odd. "Something in the central nervous system detects discrepancies before you can say exactly what's wrong," he said. "For instance, if you come home and something's been moved, you sense things are out of place before you can tell just what's awry."

"If that circuit misfires, the feeling that something's wrong might occur, causing you to search for an explanation when there is none to be found," Dr. Maher said. "You might be compelled to attach huge significance to a bit of trivia."

The Most Common Delusions

Among people who are otherwise rational, these are the most common persistent false beliefs:

ROMANTIC FIXATIONS. The theme is one of being loved by someone of higher status, such as a celebrity. Fantasies are romantic rather than sexual and often lead to efforts to make contact through calls, letters, stakeouts and the like, a source of harassment to most public figures.

GRANDIOSITY. The person is convinced of having some extraordinary gift, power, insight or prominence that has gone unrecognized. Typical forms are claims of being a relative of someone prominent, of having made startling scientific discoveries or of having a mission.

JEALOUSY. The person is convinced, with no grounds, that a spouse or lover is unfaithful and may seize on trivialities as "proof," confront the partner and try to prevent liaisons by spying or demanding that the partner stay home. There may be violent attacks on the partner, more rarely on the "lover."

PERSECUTION. The most common delusion, its theme is being the object of a plot and being spied on, followed, harassed, etc. The person takes small or imagined slights and setbacks as proof, may be obsessed with correcting some injustice, often by suing, and is typically angry, hostile and violent.

BODILY FIXATIONS. The person is convinced, contrary to all evidence, that there is something terribly wrong with his or her body, such as emitting foul odors, having the skin infested with insects, or being horribly misshapen or injured. Such people often go on a fruitless round of visits to doctors.

Therapy  15

It was with fear and uncertainty that Chris entered Dr. Thigpen's office. According to the country lore on which she had been raised, psychiatrists were doctors for crazy folks; they often locked crazy people in dark padded rooms and let them scream until they exhausted themselves. Was this going to happen to her? Dr. Thigpen sensed Chris's uneasiness and he greeted her with a smile. "Mrs. White, I work a little differently from other doctors. I don't physically examine my patients. I talk to them, and they talk to me. They tell me things about themselves: what is worrying them, what they feel, what they think" (Sizemore & Pitillo, 1977, p. 288).

During the first few sessions Chris talked about her troubles with her husband and her feelings toward her child and her parents. She portrayed herself as a timid woman with little self-confidence who cared little about her appearance. Sometimes she hesitated to discuss a topic or refused to talk. At some of these difficult points Dr. Thigpen would hypnotize her and ask her

questions, often about her childhood.

During the therapy sessions Chris recalled the birth of her twin sisters. She was delighted to have not one but two new sisters. But her delight began to fade as her relatives rushed to admire the matched pair; no one was paying any attention to 6-year-old Chris.

Chris's chance for revenge came one day when she was alone in the house with the twins. She walked to the little bed and peered down at the sleeping girls. She shut her eyes tightly, and when she opened them again, she saw a thin girl standing by the bed. This other girl poked her finger into the twins eyes, grabbed their legs, and fiercely bit their toes. Chris's mother heard the twins shrieking and rushed in to find Chris terrorizing the little girls. Her frantic cries snapped Chris out of her daze. Chris looked around, but the terrible little girl who had tortured her sisters had disappeared. Mrs. Costner yelled at Chris as she wrenched her arm. Chris was astonished; it was not she who had hurt the twins. The other girl had done it.

This was one of a series of bizarre incidents that were to plague Chris throughout much of her life. When stressful events occurred, Chris would suffer a severe headache; then a "different" Chris would appear. One Chris was often unaware of how the other Chris behaved.

Chris's childhood was a nightmare; she never knew which personality would dominate. Oftentimes the "naughty" Chris emerged to commit some mischievous act and then quickly retreated, leaving the little freckled girl to take the blame and to explain behaviors of which she was unaware.

When Chris was 19 she married Ralph White. She soon began having fights with him over his inability to hold a steady job. Then the headaches came. The headaches signaled the coming out of a new personality; one that hated Ralph and cursed him. Chris's confusion increased and her family decided she should see a psychiatrist, at which point she began her sessions with Dr. Thigpen.

One day Chris abruptly

interrupted her therapy session to ask, "Doctor, does hearing voices mean you're going insane?" Dr. Thigpen asked Chris to explain more about the voices. Chris said that she often heard a strange voice coming from inside her head. The next few sessions were spent talking about the voice. Dr. Thigpen was intrigued and his interest sharply increased a few months later when Chris revealed another problem.

On that day the session began with Chris discussing her feelings. Suddenly her face tightened and she began to moan. Dr. Thigpen was about to comfort her when Chris raised her head. Chris sat up in her chair with her eyes glowing; there was an unusual spark of life in this usually drab woman. "Hi, Doc," she chirped as she assumed a sexy slouch in the chair. "Gimme a cigarette," she asked as she winked at Dr. Thigpen. The psychiatrist could hardly contain his surprise as he asked, "Who are you?" As she inched her skirt higher up her leg, Chris answered, "I'm Chris Costner. Chris White is *her*," she said, pointing off into space.

After talking to this new Chris Costner, Dr. Thigpen was convinced that Chris was not faking; she did indeed possess two personalities. One was the dutiful but unhappy Chris White. The other was the sexy Chris Costner, who enjoyed flirting, loved expensive clothes, and who truly believed, "I ain't married to that jerk, *she* is." Dr. Thigpen soon found that he could cause Chris to change personalities simply by calling for either Chris White or Chris Costner. He diagnosed Chris as suffering from the rare psychological disorder called dissociative personality.

Dr. Thigpen continued to question Chris about her childhood in an effort to determine how these personalities had developed. He made Chris White aware of Chris Costner, and he often served as a negotiator between the two personalities. At times he even had the two personalities write notes to each other. Dr. Thigpen structured therapy sessions so that good

The intriguing story of Chris Costner's (l.) battle to unite her diverse personalities became the subject of numerous books and a popular movie (r.) starring Joanne Woodward.

behavior by each of the personalities was rewarded.

However, just when it seemed that the two personalities might be united, Chris began to experience headaches and blackouts again. She had entered into another difficult period in her life. Her marriage had broken up. As Dr. Thigpen's concern for Chris increased, another personality, Jane, emerged as a cultured and self-assured young woman. She was not frivolous like Chris Costner nor weak like Chris White. It was Jane who got a job as a bookkeeper and managed the money. However, even Jane's best-laid plans were sometimes ruined when Chris Costner "came out" to create havoc.

Dr. Thigpen continued to probe Chris to determine how Jane fit in. More tests were given. An EEG (electroencephalogram), which measures brain waves, revealed that Jane was the most relaxed of the personalities and that Chris Costner did show signs of a psychopathic personality (see Chapter 14).

After 14 months of treatment, Chris was significantly improved. She had married Don Sizemore. Both Chris White and Chris Costner faded into obscurity, and only Jane was present. Dr. Thigpen and his associate, Hervey Cleckley, wrote a book called *The Three Faces of Eve*, in which they referred to her

personalities as Eve White, Eve Black, and Jane.

But just as it seemed that Chris would be able to lead a normal life, she suffered a setback; other personalities began to appear. In fact, 12 new personalities "emerged" during the next few years.

Don encouraged Chris to see another psychiatrist near their new home. This psychiatrist suggested that she reveal herself to her friends and explain what she had been going through. Chris began working on a book, *I'm Eve*, in which she described her life. Chris gained confidence and showed tremendous improvement. At the end of her book, Chris stated, "I am in control of my life, I am comfortable in my world" (Sizemore & Pittillo, 1977). And in a newspaper interview, she reported, "You don't know how wonderful it is to go to bed at night and know that it will be you that wakes up the next day" (*New York Post*, September 15, 1975, p. 4). ■

After completing this chapter, you should be able to:

Discuss the historical background of psychotherapy and how it reflects the links between our beliefs concerning the causes of psychological disorders and the way in which we treat those disorders.

Differentiate the various mental health professionals.

Explain the difference between insight therapies and specific therapies.

Describe Freud's theory of psychoanalysis.

Explain the approach of humanistic therapy and differentiate it from Gestalt therapy.

Compare and contrast rational emotive therapy and behavioral therapies while presenting the aims and focuses of each.

Discuss the advantages and disadvantages of group therapies.

Discuss and debate the three major focuses of community psychology.

Describe and give examples of biomedical therapy.

Therapy: Its History and Scope

It was clear at an early age that Chris needed special help and guidance to adjust to her surroundings. Even as a young child, she was unhappy and bewildered by her own actions. She was unable to change her behavior; she did not know what to do to make people like her and she could not stop the "other Chris" from emerging and causing problems for herself and others. Chris needed therapy to help her adjust to her environment and have fulfilling interactions with other people.

There are two broad classifications of therapy that are aimed at dealing with psychological disturbances. One is psychotherapy, which is the use of psychological techniques by a professionally trained individual to help a client change unwanted behavior and adjust to his or her environment. In short, it is the use of language to make positive changes in the life of another. Dr. Thigpen used psychotherapy to treat Chris; he talked to her about her problems, attempted to show her why her different personalities emerged, and discussed methods that she could use to control her behavior. A second type of therapy is **biomedical therapy,** which may be used together with psychotherapy. This therapy includes the use of drugs, surgery, or electric shock to induce behavior change.

As we will see, the concept of therapy covers a wide variety of techniques and processes aimed at dealing with psychological disturbances. In fact, one investigator (Corsini, 1981) identified almost 250 therapeutic techniques. All, however, have three basic goals (Millon, 1969). The first goal of the therapist is to be sure that his or her techniques do not bring harm to or intensify the problems of the client. The second goal of the therapist is to reduce the individual's present discomfort. And finally, the therapist should attempt to aid in the development of a healthier and more adjusted individual. This last goal can present an interesting challenge to the therapist. As we saw in Chapter 13, it may be difficult to clearly define "well-adjusted." Hence, in many situations the therapist and client must work together to identify the specific outcomes they desire from therapy.

Biomedical therapy
Use of drugs, surgery, or electric shock, with or without accompanying psychotherapy, to induce behavior change.

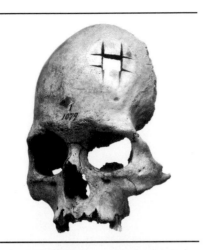

An early view of psychological disorders was that they were caused by demons and evil spirits living inside the person. Treatment focused on getting rid of these spirits. In trephining (top), a hole was chipped in the head to allow the demon to escape. The bottom illustration shows a 16th-century physician's treatment of "fantasy and folly."

Electroconvulsive therapy (ECT)
Technique of biotherapy in which electric shock is administered to the patient's brain, causing epileptic-like convulsions. Has been shown to have short-term benefits for those suffering from depressive disorders.
Prefrontal lobotomy
Surgical technique for treating extreme psychological disorders. Involves cutting connections between the thalamus and the frontal lobes. Seldom used today except when all other methods have failed.

In order to understand the therapy of today, it is useful to turn back to its beginnings. The treatment of psychological disorders is not a modern invention; throughout time people have been intrigued, bewildered, and often afraid of the strange or different behaviors of others. The treatment prescribed for disordered behaviors was generally based on the "theories" people held about the cause of the disorders. As we pointed out in Chapter 14, the ancient view of psychological disorders was that they were caused by demons who inhabited the person. These demons had to be coaxed out of the person and destroyed. Those who were "possessed" were beaten, burned with hot irons, starved, or had holes chipped in their skull (a process called *trephining*) to allow the demon to escape. In 1500 B.C. the Egyptians used magic potions, which included lizard's blood, crocodile dung, and fly specks, to combat the evil spirits. Although Hippocrates and his followers (about the fifth century B.C.) urged a more humane treatment of the mentally ill, the belief in demons persisted throughout the Middle Ages. In many societies large asylums were built to keep the "possessed" from interacting with and contaminating other people. These asylums were really prisons characterized by filthy conditions where the mentally ill were often mistreated.

One of the first major changes in the treatment of people suffering from psychological disorders occurred in the late 1700s and early 1800s. These changes were aimed at reforming the asylums. Philippe Pinel in France and Dorothea Dix in the United States campaigned to improve the treatment of disturbed people in institutions. They criticized the inhumane conditions of the asylums and fought hard to eliminate the corruption and torture present in so many of them. Through their efforts and the efforts of others like them, changes were slowly made. In some institutions patients were given sunny, bright rooms; they were allowed more freedom and exercise; their diets were improved; and they were treated with greater kindness and understanding. As a result of these advances, many patients made dramatic recoveries and were able to return to society.

While some important changes were made in the living conditions of institutionalized patients, there was little advance in therapy techniques until late in the nineteenth century. At this time a young Viennese physician named Sigmund Freud began developing his psychodynamic model (see Chapter 13) of personality. Freud believed that many psychological problems were the result of feelings and emotions that had been repressed during childhood. His position was that treatment of these disorders would be best achieved by helping people recognize and deal with their repressed feelings. Freud's psychoanalytic therapy was characterized by treatment techniques that involved a professional working with one patient at a time in the professional's office.

The early 1900s were also the time of advances in biomedical therapy. The assumption underlying much of the work in biomedical therapies was that mental disorders were diseases much like other physical diseases and should be treated in a similar manner. Since the seat of mental disease was supposedly in the brain, the focus of biological cures was on manipulation of the brain. In 1938 Ugo Cerletti reported therapeutic effects from electric shock therapy. This technique involved administering electric shocks to the patient's brain, causing him or her to experience epilepticlike convulsions. This work was the basis for **electroconvulsive therapy (ECT)** which was widely used during the early 1900s and is still used today. During this same period Egas Moniz, a Portuguese psychiatrist, reported the use of a surgical technique known as **prefrontal lobotomy** to treat psychological disorders.

World War II was responsible for the next chapter in the history of therapy. An alarming number of young men received draft deferments for psychological reasons; further, many soldiers suffered stress disorders

ABUSES IN MENTAL HEALTH TREATMENT ARE NOT ALL IN THE PAST

MOSCOW (AP) — Arbitrary diagnosis, abuse of power and bribery have tainted Soviet psychiatry, and a citizen can be found insane simply for not kowtowing to employers, a Soviet daily said Wednesday in a stunning expose.

"Psychiatric science and practice have long ago been shut off from openness by a high and solid fence," the Komsomolskaya Pravda newspaper said.

"Behind the fence, there is lawlessness," it added.

The paper's six-column article was the longest on psychiatric abuses to appear in the state-run press yet, and was clearly linked to the current campaign for "glasnost," or greater openness on social problems.

Due to the arbitrary way Soviet patients are now diagnosed, the paper said, "the same person can be recognized as a schizophrenic in Moscow, a psychopath in Leningrad and healthy in Kharkov."

Although Komsomolskaya Pravda's article was groundbreaking by Soviet standards, it made no reference to charges by human rights activists and Western groups that psychiatric hospitals are used to warehouse political prisoners.

· · ·

Vladimir Titov, a former political prisoner, was released from a psychiatric hospital last month. He told reporters Oct. 20 that at least a dozen hospitals throughout the country hold people convicted of political offenses.

Prisoners in such hospitals are subjected to heavy medication, poor food and unhealthy living conditions, Titov said.

· · ·

According to Komsomolskaya Pravda, two schools of Soviet psychiatry exist, with the Leningrad school founded by Professor I.F. Sluchevsky giving a narrower definition of schizophrenia than the Moscow school.

In its 1985 "Psychiatrist's Handbook," the Moscow school lists so many symptoms of that illness, including an interest in philosophy, art and religion, that virtually any sane person can be found to have "creeping schizophrenia," the paper said.

It said a young aviator who disagreed with his bosses was subjected to 2½ years of psychiatric care that resulted in various diagnoses, including schizophrenia.

Bribes have been accepted by psychiatrists to send criminals to hospitals, and the problem has reached such a scale that a task force has been set up in the Moscow prosecutor's office to investigate.

From *Bryan-College Station Eagle*, November 12, 1987, pp. 1, 12A.

---

from combat (Sheras & Worchel, 1979). These two facts led to the realization that psychological difficulties were more common than previously believed. Unfortunately, there was a serious shortage of professionals qualified to treat psychological disorders. The shortage led to a reexamination of the field of clinical psychology and a concentration of resources to train more professionals. Group therapy was also developed, in which many individual therapy techniques were adapted for use with groups of people who suffered from similar problems. Not only was there a strong theoretical rationale for this practice, but it also allowed for more economical and widespread use of professional resources.

The World War II era was also a time of significant advances in biotherapy. Doctors working with patients suffering from hypertension and high blood pressure accidentally discovered two drugs that had a calming effect on people suffering from psychological disorders. These drugs are known as **tranquilizers;** their discovery led to the widespread use of drugs to treat both mild and severe psychological disturbances. In fact, **drug therapy** is so popular today that many professionals have voiced concern that this use of drugs has actually become a misuse.

Starting 25 years ago and continuing today, a new and exciting page in the history of therapy is being written. A policy of **deinstitutionalization** is being embraced by many mental health professionals (Shadish, 1984). This policy involves treating people in their local environments rather than placing them in large, isolated state institutions. Treatment of even severely disturbed people in local settings has been made feasible by a number of developments. First, dramatic advances in drug therapy have enabled professionals to help people suffering from a wide range of disturbances achieve a functioning relationship with their environment. People who would once have been hospitalized can now stay in their local settings

Tranquilizers
Depressant drugs that slow the body functions, reduce anxiety, and have a relaxing effect.
Drug therapy
Use of medications to treat both mild and severe psychological disturbances.
Deinstitutionalization
Policy of treating people with psychological problems in their own local environments rather than placing them in large isolated institutions.

Traditional psychotherapy involved a single therapist and client working together to identify, understand, and/or change maladaptive behavior patterns. A variety of techniques including group therapy has developed from this model.

World War II initiated many changes in therapy. One of the most dramatic was the rapid development of group psychotherapy. The number of soldiers who suffered battle stress and other disorders was so great that there were not enough therapists to treat them on a one-to-one basis.

and receive psychotherapy there. A second important development was the passage of the Community Mental Health Centers Act by Congress in 1963; it directed that 600 community-based mental health centers be established. These centers are aimed at supplying outpatient and emergency services. Those working in health centers help people deal with crises and stress before severe and deep-seated disorders develop. A third factor driving community-based treatment is economics; the costs of hospitalizing people are staggering. Finally, there is the realization that in many cases the most effective therapy involves the family and other possible support groups. Removing the individual from the environment in which he or she must learn to function is disruptive and ignores an important element in the adjustment process (Kiesler et al., 1983; Kiesler & Simpkins, 1991).

The emphasis on deinstitutionalization has been accompanied by a focus on *prevention*. As we will see in our discussion of community psychology, efforts are being made to identify people who are considered "at risk" for developing psychological disturbances, and then to make their environments less stressful. The aim is to promote adjustment rather than treat problems after they arise. As we will see later in this chapter, the community psychology movement has had a major impact on the treatment of psychological disorders, and it has been the source of some major controversies.

Another trend has also become the center of heated debate: the proliferation of self-help books. For years many newspapers have carried advice columns such as Dear Ann or Dr. Ruth where people receive advice about problems ranging from pimples to depression. Most of us view these columns as entertaining both in the advice that is given and in the wide variety of problems that are discussed. But there is also a nagging concern that some readers may use these columns to help them "diagnose" their problems and follow the simplistic advice to "treat" their problems. This alarm has increased greatly over the last decade as dozens of books, often authored by respected psychologists and psychiatrists, have appeared, telling readers how to treat shyness, bed wetting, depression, sexual dysfunctions, depression, insomnia, and a host of other problems. At the airport book counter a few months ago, I counted 21 self-help books. Although these books serve the useful purpose of informing readers about certain disorders and giving them the hopeful message that these disorders can be successfully treated, serious concerns have been raised about these do-it-yourself guides (Rosen, 1987). First, as we saw in Chapter 14, the accurate diagnosis and/or identification of behavioral and psychological problems requires careful examination by trained professionals. Readers of self-help books may be seduced into misidentifying their problem. Second, techniques that can be applied by a skillful therapist cannot always be successfully self-administered. Third, self-help efforts may lead to a worsening of a problem. And of greatest concern, there is no provision for monitoring people using these techniques to determine if they are using them correctly and/or if they are helping or hurting themselves. Thus, just as you would be well advised to use caution in treating a persistent stomachache by rushing down to your drugstore and grabbing a new remedy from the shelf, you should use that same caution in embracing a self-help formula suggested in a book you buy at an airport newsstand.

The Therapists

Once Chris and others realized that she needed professional help adjusting to her environment, the next decision concerned who could provide this help. There are a number of professionals who can be consulted for a psychological disorder.

The **psychiatrist** is a medical doctor who has received a degree in medicine and has taken part in a residency program (usually 3 years) for emotional disorders. Psychiatrists may specialize in any of the psychotherapy techniques, and they are the only therapists who can now prescribe drugs or perform psychosurgery. Dr. Thigpen, Chris's first therapist, was a psychiatrist.

The **psychoanalyst** is often a psychiatrist who has been trained in psychoanalytic techniques. As part of this training, psychoanalysts must themselves undergo psychoanalysis, which involves between 200 to 2,000 sessions. We will see that psychoanalytic therapy is very time consuming and involves some very specialized techniques.

The **clinical psychologist** has received a Ph.D. or Psy.D. in clinical psychology. The degree program generally takes from 3 to 6 years after graduating from college. The clinical psychologist receives extensive training in therapy techniques, in methods of testing, and in interpretation of psychological tests. Most clinical psychologists also receive training in conducting research. Most practicing clinical psychologists have interned for a year, during which time they worked with a wide range of clients under the close supervision of other clinical psychologists and psychiatrists. In addition to their training, clinical psychologists who wish to engage in private practice must go through a licensing procedure in most states. This procedure includes taking a written examination and in some cases, an oral examination (*American Psychologist*, 1987). Licensing requirements are determined by each state. Clinical psychologists cannot prescribe drugs, although there is presently much discussion about allowing them to do so (Buie, 1987). Dr. Thigpen consulted a number of clinical psychologists and had them administer psychological tests to Chris in an effort to arrive at a clear identification of her disorder.

A common question from my students is: "What is the difference between a psychiatrist and a clinical psychologist?" As we can see, the most

Psychiatrist
Medical doctor who has received an M.D. degree and has taken part in a residency program in emotional disorders; the only type of therapist who can prescribe drugs or conduct psychosurgery.

Psychoanalyst
Psychiatrist who has had a great deal of training in psychoanalytic techniques and has often undergone psychoanalysis personally.

Clinical psychology
Subfield of psychology dedicated to the diagnosis and treatment of emotional and behavioral disorders.

direct answer concerns the nature of training. Recently, Steven Kingsbury (1987), who was trained both as a clinical psychologist and a psychiatrist, used his personal experience to elaborate on the differences. Psychiatrists are trained to use the medical model approach (see Chapter 14), which stresses diagnosis and specific treatment procedures. Training in medical school is rather formal with the most emphasis placed on "hands-on" treatment of cases. Clinical psychologists, on the other hand, generally receive training in a variety of models for understanding disorders, and the medical model is often deemphasized. Less emphasis is placed on diagnosis and more on research and research procedure: "At best, diagnoses were seen as a useful first part of the picture, a way of grouping research findings in a first attempt to guide understanding" (Kingsbury, 1987, p. 154). Relationships between professor and student are often less formalized and rigid in graduate school than in medical school. The graduate psychology student will generally see fewer cases than the medical student, but the supervision involved in each case is more in-depth. Clearly, there are many similarities between clinical psychologists and psychiatrists, and the training within each field differs widely. The interesting point of Kingsbury's statement is that the nature of training can influence the approach to working with psychological disorders.

The **counseling psychologist** generally has a doctoral degree. Most counseling psychologists take a one-year internship, during which time they work with clients under the direction of a practicing counselor as is the case with clinical psychologists. Most states have licensing procedures for counseling psychologists. Generally, counseling psychologists are trained to deal with adjustment problems rather than with psychological disturbances. For example, the counselor may work with adjustment problems in a school or college setting or work situation. The aim of counseling is to help the person adjust to a situation rather than "treat" a specific disorder (Osipow, 1987).

The **clinical social worker** has a master's degree in social work and often has served an internship. Clinical social workers have their own licensing board, the American College of Social Work, that establishes standards and guidelines for their clinical practice. They may do individual psychotherapy, but more often they practice family therapy. The emphasis on family therapy reflects the clinical social worker's understanding of the importance of social systems in fostering and maintaining psychopathology.

The **psychiatric nurse** is a registered nurse who has received special training in dealing with psychological disorders. Psychiatric nurses are employed by institutions, where they are responsible for a wide variety of activities, including caring for patients and making careful observations of patient behavior.

These are the professionals who administer therapy to over 6 million Americans who seek professional help each year. There is, however, an even larger group of people who are called upon to deal with those who are emotionally disturbed. These people include the police officer who must "defuse" a family conflict or calm a distraught victim of crime; the paraprofessional who receives training to handle crisis calls on a "hot line"; the minister, rabbi, or priest who counsels disturbed individuals or families. Even the neighbor or friend who lends a sympathetic ear so that a distressed individual can "talk out" his or her problems plays a vital role in the effort to deal with psychological disorders. Research suggests that the majority of people with mental health problems do not first go to mental health professionals (Gottlieb, 1983). Instead, they turn first to family members, physicians, neighbors, and members of the clergy for help. In fact, Chris credits her understanding husband, Don, and her cousin Ellen with helping her cope with some of her biggest crises.

Now that we have given a brief history of therapy and reviewed the cast of professionals who practice it, we can turn our attention to some

Counseling and school psychology
Subfield of psychology that helps people with social, educational, and job or career adjustments.
Clinical social worker
Someone who has an M.A. in social work and has served an internship.
Psychiatric nurse
Registered nurse who has received special training in dealing with psychological disorders.

of the specific types of therapy that are in use today. As we will see, each type is based on a theory of the cause of psychological disturbances. For example, person-centered therapy has its roots in humanistic psychology (see Chapter 13), while psychoanalysis grew out of Freud's psychodynamic theory of personality. Although many therapists have favorite types of therapy, few practice only one type. Rather, after carefully evaluating a client, they choose the therapy that they feel will be most effective with that person. The chosen therapy usually involves techniques taken from a number of types of therapies, which we will now examine.

Psychotherapy

During her long battle to deal with her problem, Chris went to a number of psychiatrists and psychologists. These interactions were characterized by discussions between Chris and the therapist. In some cases, the therapist reviewed Chris's background to see what was causing the multiple personalities. In other cases, the aim of the session was for Chris to gain insight into her problem and to give her a chance to vent emotions building up inside her. Still other sessions were devoted to showing Chris how she could change her behavior, and she was rewarded for positive changes. All of these techniques are examples of **psychotherapy,** which involves social interaction between a therapist and client aimed at changing the client's behavior.

There are two major categories of psychotherapy. One—*insight thera-pies*—focuses on the individual as a whole; the aim is to help the person gain insight into his or her problems and life. We include psychoanalysis, humanistic, and Gestalt therapies under this category. Insight therapies deal with the complete personality, often exploring the person's history in order to shed light on his or her present state. Although these therapies deal with the person's symptoms, they view this problem as a sign of a broader disorder. The general view is that once people recognize the causes of their discomfort, they will take the necessary steps to develop more adaptive behaviors. Hence, there is little effort to teach new behaviors or attitudes. The other major category—**specific therapies**—is most concerned with the specific symptoms. Behavior and cognitive therapies are included in this category of psychotherapy. These therapies do not delve deeply into the person's personality or seek insights. Rather, they attempt to change specific problematic behaviors or beliefs. As we have already noted, most therapists do not use one therapy exclusively; thus those who prefer insight therapies do not exclude the presenting problems, and those who prefer specific therapies do not exclude examining the person as a whole when the situation calls for that technique. As you read about the therapies, you may wish to refer back to Chapter 13 to identify the theoretical roots of the technique.

Table 15–2, at the end of the section, summarizes the five types of therapies described here.

Psychoanalysis: An Emphasis on Insight

As we discussed in Chapter 13, Sigmund Freud believed that our personalities are shaped by events in early childhood. According to Freud, all children go through developmental stages. A traumatic event that occurs at any of these stages can have a lasting effect on us. Many of us witness events, have thoughts, or experience emotions that we have been taught are bad and unacceptable. In response to these teachings, we attempt to defend ourselves against these unacceptable thoughts or feelings by forcing them

Psychotherapy
Use of psychological techniques by a professionally trained person to help a client change unwanted behavior and adjust to his or her environment. In short, the use of language to make positive changes in the life of another.
Specific therapy
Therapy aimed at changing a specific behavior or thought pattern.

into our unconscious; in other words, we repress them. These thoughts or emotions fight to enter our consciousness, and we must constantly use energy to keep them locked in the unconscious. Freud believed that anxiety results whenever these unconscious thoughts threaten to break into our consciousness.

To treat these anxiety disorders Freud developed the method of **psychoanalysis.** According to Freud, people can be helped only when they recognize and deal with (work through) their repressed feelings. Hence the aim of therapy is to help people identify these "hidden emotions," bring them into the open, and deal with them. In a sense, therapy is like peeling a banana; its aim is to strip away the outer defenses and uncover repressed feelings that are the cause of unhappiness and maladaptive behavior. This may sound like a difficult task for a therapist; after all, these feelings have been repressed since early childhood. How can they be identified?

When Freud initially developed the psychoanalytic technique, he relied heavily on hypnosis (see Chapter 5). He felt that through hypnosis he could peer into people's unconscious and identify their repressed experiences and feelings. However, it soon became apparent that hypnosis was not effective with everyone. Freud found other gates into the unconscious. As psychoanalysis evolved, he relied on two techniques to unlock the unconscious. One was **free association.** This method involves having clients talk about whatever thoughts come into their mind without worrying about how much sense it makes or its structure. Although this may sound easy, it is often difficult, especially when the thoughts are embarrassing or sensitive. Sometimes clients resist expressing certain thoughts or associations. This *resistance* may be shown by "forgetting" to attend therapy sessions or

Psychoanalysis
Freud's technique of treating anxiety disorders by helping people recognize and deal with their repressed feelings.

Free association
Freud's method of having patients express every thought (no matter how unimportant or irrelevant) that came into their minds during the therapy session.

Free association is one technique used in psychoanalysis. This method involves having clients talk about whatever thoughts come into their mind.

by simply refusing to talk during a session. Freud believed that resistance indicated that the client was close to revealing the repressed emotions and was using a delaying tactic to avoid doing so. The psychoanalyst listens to the client's free associations, observes the resistance, and interprets their meaning.

The second method used to uncover repressed feelings is **dream interpretation.** Freud believed that during sleep our defenses are relaxed and repressed feelings come close to the level of consciousness. However, because our defenses are not completely lifted, the repressed emotions are expressed in a disguised form in dreams. Thus the therapist must look beyond the expressed content (manifest content) to determine the true meaning (latent content) of the dream (as we discussed in Chapter 5). For example, a man might report dreaming that he stands by helplessly as a young boy burns in a fire (manifest content). The therapist might interpret this dream as an expression of the client's resentment of his younger brother (latent content).

The practice of classical psychoanalysis has an almost mystical quality to it. The client is given a comfortable couch to recline upon, and the lights of the therapy room are usually dimmed. The therapist sits in a chair out of the line of sight of the client. These conditions are designed to relax the client and promote the free associations and recall of dreams that are the reflections of repressed thoughts and emotions. The therapist takes a neutral role, becoming involved only to encourage the client to talk or to offer interpretations. The therapist reveals little about himself or herself. He or she becomes a blank screen onto which the client projects all sorts of motives (Nietzel & Bernstein, 1987).

As the psychoanalysis progresses, these projections frequently take the form of intense feelings that the client develops toward the analyst. Since the analyst has taken no active role to encourage a personal relationship with the client, these feelings expressed toward the analyst are considered to be emotions that the client felt at an earlier time in his life toward his mother or father or some other important person in the client's life. Freud referred to this phenomenon as **transference.** When the client acts in a hostile, defiant manner toward the analyst, the transference is said to be negative. When the client is compliant and acquiescent, the transference is said to be positive.

Transference is a very important part of therapy. It gives people the chance to voice emotions that may have been repressed during childhood. According to psychoanalytic theory, these repressed emotions are the cause of anxiety. When they are brought from the unconscious to the conscious and worked through with the therapist, they will no longer cause anxiety attacks. In other words, once the client is able to express these repressed feelings, the therapist can help the client deal with them in a constructive way.

While transference is indeed another window into the unconscious, revealing thoughts and emotions that would otherwise be hidden, transference is not a goal of psychoanalysis, but rather an inevitable side effect. Therefore, it is important for the analyst to acknowledge the transference relationship with the client and to take steps to dissolve it lest the client become too dependent on the analyst.

To summarize, free association, dream analysis, and transference are processes that allow the person to gain *insight* into the foundation of his or her personality and behavior (Gilliland, James, Roberts, & Bowman, 1984). By examining and reexperiencing these early events, the person can see how unresolved conflicts have shaped his or her life. This insight releases the tension and frees the person from the invisible grasp of those long-repressed feelings.

Psychoanalysis is a very expensive endeavor that can cost over $15,000

Dream interpretation
Part of Freud's technique of psychoanalysis; involves helping clients to understand the latent content of their dreams, which represents the repressed feelings that are being expressed.

Transference
Part of Freud's technique of psychoanalysis; occurs when clients transfer to the therapist feelings that were originally aimed at their parents. In this way they are able to work them through on a rational, conscious level.

I gave my psychoanalytic couch away twenty years ago.
Some therapists like to use the couch:
It fosters regression which might be useful.
It might even be used by some therapists
    to avoid a human relationship.
It matters that you remain conscious
    of your sexual and power fantasies.

For some the couch is an icon.
For some it is handy, and for others, dandy
    because it takes the patient out of eye contact.
Personally that is not a problem for me.
If it were, I would use the couch
    because the fewer problems I have,
    the more we can deal with the problems
    that the patient has.

Wilmer (1987), p. 43.

a year. The client may meet with the analyst four or five times a week for a period of time that ranges from one to several years. Because of its cost and its reliance on clients' verbalizations, psychoanalysis tends to attract relatively affluent, well-educated people who express themselves well. Further, this therapy seems to be best suited to treating disorders involving anxiety rather than more severe disorders such as schizophrenia.

While classical psychoanalysis is still practiced today, some therapists have modified the technique. Many psychoanalysts have their patients sit in chairs facing them (see above). There are fewer sessions, so that clients attend therapy only once or twice a week, and the total number of sessions may be reduced to 15 or 20 (DeAngells, 1987). The therapist may also take a more active role, with greater emphasis on interpreting and directing. In addition to these modifications of classical psychoanalytic therapy, numerous therapies have been developed that are based on psychoanalytic theory but represent more radical departures in technique. Some of these therapies are based on positions that place less emphasis on sexual themes and the id, and more emphasis on the social relations and the ego. Other approaches such as intensive short-term psychodynamic therapy (J. Worchel, 1988) replace free association in favor of active confrontation of the client's defenses until unconscious desires and feelings "break through."

In our example at the beginning of the chapter, Dr. Thigpen's approach was basically a psychoanalytic one. He had Chris talk about her childhood and her feelings toward her parents for hours. He attempted to interpret her dreams as they related to her childhood experiences. Through therapy Dr. Thigpen discovered that as a young child, Chris had seen a number of people die in various accidents. She became terrified of death and viewed herself as responsible for the deaths of these people. Was anxiety and guilt about these early deaths responsible for her multiple personalities? While we cannot be sure, it is evident from her book that Chris believed that repressed feelings about death influenced her condition.

Humanistic Therapy: An Emphasis on Self-Acceptance

As we have seen, psychoanalysis focuses on "reconstructing" people's childhood and interpreting their problems in light of those experiences. Carl Rogers (1942, 1951, 1980) and other humanistic psychologists also believe that the root of many disorders is in childhood. However, their approach is very different from that of psychoanalysis. The humanists argue that we naturally strive to reach our potential and lead a fulfilling life. However, as children we often learn that other people have expectations about how we should behave and we learn that the way to get rewards is to live up to others' expectations. If we follow this pattern, however, we may lose

WATCH WHAT YOU SAY AND DO: Someone May Be Interpreting It

I'm often amused at people's reactions when I tell them that I am a psychologist. Suddenly, their whole demeanor changes; they get a bit uncomfortable and self-conscious. Finally, with a nervous giggle they state, "I've got to watch what I say, because I know you'll be interpreting it for a hidden meaning." This view of psychologists peering into our unconscious through our everyday behavior was encouraged by two very interesting works by Freud (*The Psychopathology of Everyday Life*, 1901, and *Jokes and Their Relation to the Unconscious*, 1905). Freud argued that our unconscious wishes, concerns, and fantasies are often revealed through seemingly trivial day-to-day behaviors. One such behavior is the *slip of the tongue*. A colleague of mine recently told me of a conference he had with his daughter's third-grade teacher. The daughter was not doing well and was disrupting the class. The teacher

confided, "You need to help your daughter *strangle* by herself . . . I mean, study by herself." Freud also suggested that our unconscious wishes are revealed through *accidents*. I still remember my favorite cotton shirt that my family hated with a passion; it "accidentally" found its way into a hot dryer that reduced it from size "Large" to a size that wouldn't even fit my 6-year-old daughter. *Forgetting* is not the work of the devil, but of the unconscious, according to Freud. How many times have you forgotten to show up for that unpleasant dentist appointment or arrived late to a boring class? Nietzel and Bernstein (1987) jokingly point out the dilemma of patients in analysis who run the risk of being viewed as dependent if they show up early, resistant if they are late, and compulsive if they arrive exactly on time! Finally, Freud believed that unconscious wishes, especially aggressive ones, are often expressed

in *jokes*. Jokes are relatively safe vehicles because the joker can innocently proclaim that he or she "wasn't serious," and chide the recipient with, "Can't you take a joke?" Earl Butz, a secretary of agriculture under President Reagan, had to resign his office after telling a racially insulting joke that was made public. The resulting furor focused not so much on the joke, but on the speculation that the joke was a sign of Butz's insensitivity to racial issues and his underlying racist attitudes. Certainly there may be accidents, instances of forgetting, and humor that are not designed by our unconscious. But, according to Freud and other psychoanalytic psychologists, these everyday behaviors often offer a road into our unconscious and may be used in therapy to help people gain insight into their behavior.

---

touch with our own desires and feelings. When this happens, we become unhappy and experience anxiety.

According to Rogers, given the proper conditions, people will become more self-aware and happy, and they will strive to meet their own goals. In short, Rogers suggests that people will reduce their own anxiety and mature by their own efforts if they are given the right opportunities. Therefore the aim of therapy is to provide the proper setting for this self-growth and self-exploration to occur. The proper setting is one in which people do not fear social rejection for expressing themselves. In order to achieve this climate, three conditions are necessary. First, the therapist must give clients **unconditional positive regard;** that is, accept and care for them no matter what feelings or behaviors the client reveals in the sessions. Rogers illustrates the importance of positive regard by identifying the "turning point" in a difficult session. The client had been very hard on herself and Rogers responded by saying, "I realize that you don't care about yourself, but I want you to know that I care about you and I care what happens to you" (Baldwin, 1987, p. 45). Second, the therapist must be *genuine* or real. He or she must be open enough to express feelings, whether positive or negative. This may seem to go against the first condition—unconditional positive regard—but it does not. For example, a therapist can show that he or she is very accepting of a client even though certain of the client's behaviors bore or even anger the therapist. It is important for the therapist to express these feelings so that they will not continue to intrude on the client-therapist relationship. Also, the therapist can demonstrate to the client that it is possible to be accepting while still having negative feelings. The final important condition is *empathy* (Rogers, 1977). The therapist comes to sense the feelings and meaning experienced by the client and communicates this understanding to the client. Under these conditions,

Unconditional positive regard
Part of client-centered therapy, in which the therapist tries to create a condition of unconditional positive regard by accepting and caring for clients no matter what feelings or behaviors are revealed in the session.

Carl Rogers, founder of humanistic therapy, believes that the therapist must create an atmosphere of unconditional positive regard during the session. The therapist should be genuine in the expression of feeling and experience empathy for the client.

clients will gain enough confidence to begin the self-exploration process and strive toward personal fulfillment.

The emphasis in **humanistic therapy** is on the person rather than on the therapist. The person determines what will be discussed during therapy. The therapist does not attempt to diagnose or interpret the client's condition. According to the humanists, a diagnosis serves no purpose and only places the client in a dehumanized category. Instead, the therapist responds to the person as a unique individual and attempts to experience the world from the client's perspective. In doing this, the therapist mirrors and rephrases what he or she hears the client saying. Unlike most other therapies, person-centered therapy uses no specific "techniques."

In contrast to psychoanalysis, person-centered therapy focuses on the here-and-now. Although difficulties may have begun in childhood, people must deal with them in the present. The cause of present difficulties is not as important as how the person is responding to these difficulties now. But humanistic therapy does share with psychoanalytic therapy a concern for the global personality. It is not simply aimed at dealing with a single behavior problem. Included in the goals of humanistic therapy are the following:

1. Increased self-awareness

2. Increased self-acceptance

3. Increased comfort with relationships

4. Increased self-reliance

5. Improved functioning (Nietzel & Bernstein, 1987).

If Chris had seen a humanistic therapist, her therapy sessions would have gone very differently. We cannot determine if this type of therapy would have been successful in Chris's case. Unlike Dr. Thigpen, the therapist would have spent little, if any, time discussing her early childhood. Instead, he or she would have supported Chris as she examined her present feelings and attempted to deal with her multiple personalities. The therapist would not have tried to diagnose Chris or probe for a hidden meaning in what she said. He or she would have treated Chris as a unique individual.

There is a mounting body of research (Mitchell, Bozarth, & Krauft, 1977; Truax & Mitchell, 1971) that indicates that therapist characteristics have a strong effect on the progress of therapy: Therapy is most successful when the therapist is perceived as genuine, warm, and caring. Research has also shown that humanistic therapy leads to improvement in the client's self-concept and better interpersonal relationships outside the therapy setting (Rogers & Dymond, 1954; Rubin, 1967).

Gestalt Therapy: An Emphasis on Self-Awareness

Gestalt therapy borrows ideas from both psychoanalytic and humanistic theories. Fritz Perls, a leading figure in Gestalt therapy, argues that our actions are often influenced by emotions and thoughts of which we are unaware. These unconscious forces may lead us to have unsatisfying social interactions. For example, you may become very angry with a waitress who brings you the wrong order. You may believe that your anger is the result of the waitress's incompetent actions (*figure*, in Gestalt terminology). However, your emotion may actually be the result of a fight you had with a friend earlier in the day (*ground*, in Gestalt terms). Thus, Gestalt therapy proposes that in order to improve our adjustment, we must become more aware of ourselves; we must understand both the figure and the

Humanistic therapy
Movement formed by Carl Rogers, Abraham Maslow, and Rollo May which rejects Freudian view of people; argues that people are basically good and worthy of respect; stresses the creative aspect of people in reaching their true potential.

Gestalt therapy
Therapy developed by Fritz Perls, proposing that unconscious thoughts and emotions (background) may lead to behaviors (figure) that are inappropriate to the situation. Encourages people to take responsibility for their actions in the present, while understanding the emotions that are influencing them.

ground that influences our behavior and feeling. Awareness, then, is the central focus of Gestalt therapy.

Although it acknowledges that we are influenced by the past, Gestalt therapy focuses on the present: "The past is no more and the future is not yet. Only the now exists" (Perls, 1970, p. 14). Gestalt therapy uses a number of techniques to facilitate self-awareness in the present. Gestalt therapy sessions generally take place in group settings, and group members encourage each other to deal directly with issues. There is a heavy emphasis on the first-person pronoun. Instead of stating that "It really makes you mad when people don't keep their promises," the person is encouraged to express his or her emotion by saying, "*I* get mad when you (the target of anger) don't keep your promises." Role playing is used to give additional insight into a situation or interaction. For example, a client may play the role of his or her parent in order to better understand the source of a long-standing conflict. There is little research on the effectiveness of Gestalt therapy, but many of the techniques or exercises have been used in other types of therapy (Tyson & Range, 1987).

Cognitive Therapies: An Emphasis on Thoughts, Beliefs, and Attitudes

Had Chris undergone either psychoanalytic or humanistic therapies, strong emphasis would have been placed on exploring and dealing with her feelings. However, if she had gone to a therapist who used a cognitive approach, the course of therapy would have been different. Cognitive therapists (Beck & Emery, 1985; Meichenbaum, 1977) argue that behavior is guided by mental events such as attitudes, beliefs, expectations, and appraisals. Therefore behavior and feelings that are out of touch with reality are signals that the person is operating with faulty attitudes, expectations, or evaluations of situations. The aim of cognitive therapy is to identify and change these faulty thoughts on the presumption that changes in thought will lead to changes in behavior and feelings. In some cases these thoughts or beliefs may involve a specific event or activity; for example, "my classmates won't like me unless I give them gifts." In other cases, the beliefs may be more general and involve our general effectiveness (*efficacy expectations*); for example, "I can't do anything right." Cognitive therapy can be designed to change either the more narrow beliefs or the broader efficacy expectations (Bandura, 1986). There are many cognitive therapies. In order to appreciate how these therapies work, let us focus on one type: rational emotive therapy.

Rational Emotive Therapy (RET). Albert Ellis, the developer of **rational emotive therapy (RET)** (Ellis, 1962; Ellis & Grieger, 1977), believes that our problems are not the result of how we feel; rather, he suggests that how we *think* and *believe* determines how well we will adjust to our environment. In fact, Ellis argues that the way we feel depends on the way we interpret events rather than on the events themselves. For example, imagine that a friend turns down your invitation to go to the movies. According to Ellis, this refusal by itself will not make you too unhappy. However, if you interpret the refusal as a sign that the friend really does not like you and that you are thus an unlikeable person, you will feel very depressed.

There are a number of irrational and destructive attitudes that can lead to depression. Among the most common are:

1. It is necessary that I be loved by every significant person in my environment.

2. It is absolutely necessary that I be completely competent, adequate, and achieve in all areas or I am worthless.

In the "empty chair" exercise, the client places a part of her personality in the empty chair and attempts to explore it and deal with it. For example, a client may feel conflict about being aggressive. "Aggression" is put in one chair and "passiveness" is placed in another chair. The individual alternates sitting in the two chairs and taking the role prescribed for that chair. He or she acts aggressively and talks to the passive part of the personality when sitting in the aggression chair.

Rational Emotive Therapy (RET)
Type of therapy developed by Albert Ellis; focuses on the present and on the client's irrational beliefs. Therapist plays a much more directive and even challenging role than in most other therapies.

He: "Want to go to the movies tonight?"
She: "I'm sorry, I'm afraid I can't make it."

Oh, well, maybe next time.

Gee, what's wrong with me, she must not like me.

Ellis believes that the way we feel depends on the way we interpret events rather than on the events themselves. The man shown here can interpret this event in one of two ways, and it is the way that he interprets it, not the event itself, that will determine how he feels.

3. If something is dangerous, I must be constantly concerned about it.

4. It is a terrible disaster if things do not turn out the way I want them to turn out.

We can see from Chris's report of her childhood that she felt that she was a failure if everyone did not always express approval of her. She was always striving to please others because she feared their rejection.

Since these attitudes are at the root of anxiety, Ellis argues that therapy should be aimed at restructuring the way people think. In order to do this, therapists must take an active and direct teaching role. They must point out people's irrational beliefs and identify more rational attitudes to hold. For example, a therapist might point out to Chris how her irrational fear of rejection makes her adjustment so difficult. The therapist might challenge her belief, asking, "What's so bad about being rejected by others? What's the worst thing that can happen if someone doesn't like you?" The therapist attempts to substitute or replace the person's beliefs that behaviors or events *must* or *should* occur with beliefs that "it would be nice if they did occur, but all will be well even if they do not happen." The therapist who practices RET acts in a directive and challenging manner and is not too concerned about forming a warm, caring relationship with the client. The therapist may also use techniques like role playing to demonstrate the irrationality of many of the client's beliefs. As you can see, RET focuses on the present; although the irrational attitudes may have been learned in the past, the problem (and its solution) is in the present.

RET is widely practiced with people who suffer from anxiety. This form of therapy has the advantage of working faster than therapies that focus on developing insight and warm relationships between therapist and client. Despite this advantage, RET has been criticized on the grounds that too much insensitivity to the client's feelings on the part of the therapist can be destructive in some cases (George & Cristiani, 1981). In responding to this issue, many therapists have combined techniques of RET with those from other therapies in dealing with their clients.

Behavior Therapies: An Emphasis on Behavior

We might refer to the therapies that we have been discussing as "inside" therapies. They are "inside" in that they attempt to change how the person thinks or feels on the assumption that inner processes are responsible for the person's stress and failure to adjust. Changing these inner processes, then, should result in positive changes in behavior. If any of these therapies had been used to treat Chris, many hours would have been spent examining how she felt or thought.

Behavior therapies take a very different approach. These therapies are based on the assumption that maladaptive behavior is learned through the same process by which other behaviors are learned. Assuming that abnormal behavior is learned, it can also be unlearned and a new, more adaptive behavior substituted in its place. According to many behavior therapists, it is a waste of time to focus on internal events like emotions and attitudes. Therapy will be more effective if it concentrates on behavior, an external and observable factor. Behavior therapies can be considered specific therapies because they generally concentrate on changing a clearly identified behavior rather than restructuring the whole personality.

Behavior therapies can be based on any of the theories of learning we discussed in Chapter 6. Those based on classical conditioning associate the problem behavior with either a negative or positive experience. Those based on operant conditioning use rewards or punishment to bring about change. And those therapies rooted in social learning theory involve modeling to create change. Let's review examples of therapies in each of these categories to illustrate the various types.

Classical Conditioning Therapies. In order to illustrate the use of classical conditioning in therapy, let's examine two therapies: aversive conditioning and systematic desensitization.

Aversive Conditioning. From the moment the twin girls were born, Chris felt that people stopped paying attention to her. The little girls received everything, including Chris's bed. However, on the day that the thin, bony-faced girl appeared and hurt the sleeping girls, Chris got attention from her mother. After that, Chris found that others paid attention to her when

Behavior therapies
Therapies based on the assumption that maladpative behavior is learned through the same process as other behaviors and can be unlearned by substituting a more adaptive behavior in its place.

Aversive conditioning involves pairing the target behavior with an unpleasant event so that the target behavior is eventually extinguished. Aversive conditioning has been used to break such undesirable habits as smoking, drinking, and excessive eating.

a different personality emerged. Thus, despite the problems that resulted in her life, there may have been some pleasure associated with the emergence of the different personalities.

According to **aversive conditioning therapy,** the way to handle this type of difficulty is to reverse the process. That is, the person must learn that the presence of a target behavior is associated with an unpleasant event. This technique, therefore, uses classical conditioning as its base for changing behavior.

Aversive conditioning has been used to help people break such undesirable habits as smoking and drinking and to treat sexual deviations. For example, people with a drinking problem may be given a drug that will cause nausea when they drink alcohol. The drug can be taken before the drink (Lemere & Voegtlin, 1950) or mixed with the drink (Nathan, 1976). In this way, drinking alcohol becomes associated with an unpleasant feeling. Your parents may have used a form of aversive conditioning to prevent you from smoking after they found you hiding in a closet taking a few puffs. Their "cure" may have been to force you to smoke the whole cigarette, the result being that you became violently sick. After that, you remembered your "near-death" feeling every time you were tempted to smoke. A similar technique, called *rapid smoking*, has been used to help adults stop smoking (Lichtenstein, Harris, Birchler, Wahl, & Schmahl, 1977). The technique involves having people smoke rapidly until they become sick. Although it has proved useful in some cases, critics argue that rapid smoking may be dangerous, leading to problems such as nicotine poisoning.

A form of aversive conditioning has been developed where people only *imagine* a negative event being associated with a certain behavior (Cautela, 1977). For example, if you wished to stop eating sweets, you might be asked to imagine that candy is actually sugar-coated worms that will invade your stomach when you bite into it.

There has been a lot of controversy about the effectiveness of aversive conditioning. Some therapists report that the technique is very successful. Others argue that it does not produce lasting results; people return to the undesired habits after the therapy is over (Conway, 1977). There has also been some concern that the technique results in overgeneralization, in which the person stops performing many positive behaviors. For example, if you imagined worms in candy, as we just mentioned, you might not

Aversive conditioning
Type of behavior therapy often used to break bad habits such as smoking and drinking; in this type of therapy people receive unpleasant consequences for undesired behavior. This may mean taking a drug (Antibuse) that will make them sick if they drink, or making them smoke so much and so quickly that they become sick.

This woman is in the third phase of systematic desensitization therapy.

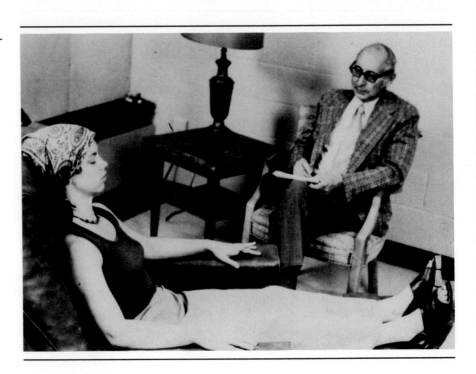

only stop eating candy, you might also give up eating other good foods that remind you of candy. In spite of these criticisms, aversive conditioning is used to help people change undesired behaviors.

Systematic Desensitization.   Two-year-old Chris watched in horror as her father and other men pulled the bloated body of the old man from an irrigation ditch. "It's ole man Williams, I think he's dead." At the word *dead*, Chris gasped and felt her body tremble. From that moment, she developed an irrational fear of death that may have been one of the causes of her multiple personalities.

A number of behavioral techniques have been developed to treat phobias (irrational fears) and other anxiety disorders. One of the techniques is known as **systematic desensitization** (Wolpe, 1958, 1974). This technique is based on the assumption that it is impossible to be relaxed and anxious at the same time. The therapist's aim is to make the client relax in the presence of an object or event that used to cause anxiety. Systematic desensitization involves three steps. First, on the basis of interviews and psychological tests, events or objects that cause stress are identified. These events are arranged in a hierarchy according to the amount of anxiety that they cause. Table 15–1 shows a hierarchy that Wolpe (1958) developed from a client's fear of death; a similar hierarchy might have been created if Chris had been involved in systematic desensitization.

The second step involves teaching the client deep muscle relaxation (Jacobson, 1938). This method calls for clients to focus on and relax different parts of their body. The therapist might first have clients tense and then completely relax the muscles in their arms. Next they may practice relaxing leg or stomach muscles. After about four sessions clients should be able to deeply relax their whole body in practice at home.

The third phase pairs relaxation with the events listed in the hierarchy. The therapy starts with the least stressful event. Clients are told to remain relaxed and calm while vividly imagining the event. If they are successful in doing this, the therapist moves on to the next event in the hierarchy. If they show signs of anxiety or tension, the therapist moves back to the next lower event and begins the relaxation process again. After some time, clients are able to relax even when imagining the most stressful event in the hierarchy.

According to Wolpe and others (Denny & Sullivan, 1976), people who can relax while imagining feared events can also relax when they encounter these events in their everyday lives. Other investigators have changed the procedure to include actual contact with the feared objects or events. For example, Moss and Arend (1977) have used *contact desensitization* to treat clients who have a fear of snakes by having them first relax while holding a rope. Later they practice relaxation while watching a live snake in the room, and in the final sessions they use their relaxation techniques while handling a live snake. As you can see, desensitization involves learning a new response to a stimulus that previously aroused fear and stress. It is evolved from classical conditioning principles (Chapter 6) in that its aim is to condition a new response to an old stimulus. It is also a technique that focuses only on the present situation; there is no attempt to trace the cause of the anxiety. The technique has been used with a wide range of problems, including phobias, alcoholism, test anxiety, and insomnia. In addition, the relaxation method has been combined with cognitive therapies to treat generalized anxiety disorders (Borkovec et al., 1987).

Operant Conditioning Therapies.   Dr. Thigpen used positive reward to reduce the frequency of Chris's multiple personalities. When he wanted to talk with the "Jane" personality, he would reward Chris with kind words and sweets if she would produce this other personality. If one of the other personalities surfaced, Dr. Thigpen would scold Chris and withhold rewards until Jane reemerged. In this way, Dr. Thigpen was able to call up the personalities at will and keep them for a long time.

Table 15–1

Systematic Desensitization Hierarchy

This hierarchy was developed by Wolpe from a client's fear of death. Events that cause stress are identified and arranged according to how much anxiety they cause.

a. Seeing first husband in his coffin
b. Attending a burial
c. Seeing a burial assemblage from afar
d. Reading an obituary notice of a young person dying of heart attack
e. Driving past a cemetery
f. Seeing a funeral
g. Passing a funeral home
h. Reading an obituary notice of an old person
i. Being inside a hospital
j. Seeing a hospital
k. Seeing an ambulance

Source: Wolpe (1958)

Systematic desensitization
Type of behavior therapy based on the assumption that it is impossible to be relaxed and anxious at the same time. Clients are taught deep muscle relaxation; they then pair this with feared or stressful events or objects, with the idea that the relaxation response will overcome the fear reaction. Often used to treat phobias.

The process of rewarding desired behaviors is based on *operant conditioning*, which we discussed in Chapter 6. As you will remember, this type of learning involves rewarding the desired behavior after it has occurred. People soon learn that they can obtain the reward by performing the "right" behavior. As we saw previously, this technique has been used to condition and shape a wide variety of behaviors. In addition to rewarding desired behaviors, *selective* punishment can also be used to extinguish unwanted behaviors. For example, in one case an autistic child was given a mild shock each time he hit himself (Dorsey, Iwata, Ony, & McSween, 1980). When the child learned that a shock followed his hitting behavior the self-destruction ceased.

Because operant conditioning therapy does not require clients to verbalize their conditions or to gain insights into them, the technique can be used with a variety of people and by a variety of therapists. This therapy is suitable for young children (Maher, 1987) as well as older adults; it can be used with the mentally retarded as well as bright people. Operant therapy is used in individual therapy settings, group settings, institutions, and even in communities. Taking this into account, one group of investigators taught the significant others (boyfriend, girlfriend, spouse) of depressed people to administer behavioral therapy at home (Brannon & Nelson, 1987). The significant others were able to reduce the symptoms of the depressives by using this therapy. Operant therapy has been found effective in dealing with a wide array of problems including autism (Chapter 9), hyperactivity (Chapter 9), aggression, phobia, sexual dysfunction, juvenile delinquency, conduct disorder, delusions, and retardation.

In order to explore the technique more closely, let's examine its use in institutions where it is called a **token economy.** The first step in employing this therapy is to develop a contract with the client; the contract identifies the behavior to be changed, the desired change, and the rewards that will follow behavior change.

People taking part in a token economy are given rewards such as poker chips for performing certain behaviors. They can use the tokens to purchase things they want, such as candy or cigarettes. A number of years ago, I conducted research in a juvenile prison that was based on a token economy. When a juvenile entered the prison, he lived first on the top floor, in a room that was bare except for a bed and a sink. He was given plastic tokens for performing such duties as cleaning his room. When he had earned a certain amount of tokens, he could "buy" his way to the next lower floor, which had larger rooms with more attractive furnishings. A new set of behaviors was reinforced with tokens; for example, he might receive tokens for reading books. Once again, when the prescribed amount of tokens was amassed, he could move to a lower floor that had other attractive features such as curtains on the windows and a television. The token economy continued on each floor, with the ground floor being set up so that the boy could obtain his freedom with the proper number of tokens. Other token economies have been used in mental hospitals. For example, Ayllon and Azrin (1968) used a token economy to get schizophrenic patients to perform such behaviors as eating, taking care of their personal hygiene, and doing chores.

Although operant therapy has been used in a variety of settings to treat a variety of disorders, it has been criticized on a number of grounds. First, it invests a great deal of control in the person who gives out the tokens. This person determines the "desired" behaviors and exercises complete control over all others in the economy. Many humanists view this as a negative situation; they feel that it is wrong for one person to have so much control over others. A second criticism is that the desired behavior sometimes stops when the reward is no longer available. In order to increase the probability that the behaviors will occur outside the token economy,

Token economy
Operant conditioning technique in which subjects are given tokens for good performance or behavior which they can exchange for treats or other primary reinforcers.

small rewards or self-rewards are often used (Krasner 1971). These rewards do increase the likelihood that the person will continue performing the desired behavior outside the token economy setting. A third criticism is that the token economy teaches people to perform behaviors only for rewards; because of this, they may fail to appreciate or value the behavior in its own right. For example, if you are given a reward each time you read a book, you may read simply to obtain the reward and never develop pleasure in reading.

Despite all the criticisms of operant conditioning therapies, it is clear that such therapies can bring about behavioral change. In some cases, this technique may be the only way to change someone's behavior. A therapist who uses it, however, must take into account the ethical and methodological considerations that we have discussed.

Modeling Therapies. As you will recall from Chapter 6, a third learning theory is social learning theory. This theory argues that we learn new behaviors by watching others and **modeling** their behavior. We then exhibit those behaviors when we are rewarded for doing so. Imitation plays a major role in our lives and in therapeutic settings. My brother, who is a psychiatrist, observed that sometimes the patients he placed in institutions would actually increase the number of bizarre behaviors they exhibited soon after commitment. At first he was puzzled, but he soon

Modeling
Used as a therapeutic technique to teach new behaviors or strengthen existing ones. Also used to reduce a number of phobias by showing the model interacting with the feared object.

BIOFEEDBACK: Using Operant Conditioning to Change Physiological Activity

When we think of behavior, we think of observable actions like walking, interacting with others, or working on the job. Most of us are not aware that our internal mechanisms or behavior, such as heartbeat, breathing, and the neuron firings in our brain influence our basic functioning. As we saw in Chapter 12, these internal activities are related to stress and anxiety and they underlie psychosomatic disorders such as hypertension and ulcers. It might then follow that if we could control our internal behaviors, we might be able to reduce or eliminate the stress and anxiety-related disorders. If operant therapies can be used to change external behavior, perhaps they can be used to modify and control our internal body activities.

One of the problems with teaching us how to control our bodies is that most of us are not good at monitoring physiological messages such as our heart rate or muscle tension. For example, it is unlikely that you are aware of how fast your heart beats at different times during the day. **Biofeedback** techniques are designed to help people control their physiological functions without the use of drugs. The technique is based on operant principles of learning (see Chapter 6). People are given information about the behavior (physiological response) that they wish to change, and positive reinforcement when they make the desired response. In practice, these goals involve connecting the person to a device that will measure the desired physiological response; this may be heart rate, muscle tension, skin temperature, blood pressure, or

Biofeedback is based on principles of learning theories. People are given information about their physiological responses such as heart rate or breathing, and they are given feedback when their responses change.

even brain waves. These devices not only monitor the response, they also give the person information about the state of the response. Sometimes the feedback is in the form of a tone. As the physiological condition changes, the tone changes. The reinforcement for the desired change is that the person hears the tone change in the desired direction.

Biofeedback has been used to treat a wide range of problems including high blood pressure, migrane headaches, asthma, tension, peptic ulcers, and even epilepsy (Girdano & Iverly, 1987).

More recently, however, some important questions have been raised (Miller, 1983). For one thing, some of the earlier claims, such as self-

conditioning of brain waves, have not been replicated in later research. A second question concerns the process by which biofeedback works. Specifically, investigators wondered if it was the physiological response itself that was being conditioned, or if people were learning to indirectly control their physiological response by tensing and relaxing various skeletal muscles or through cognitive processes such as imagination. While the answer to this question is not necessarily important to the therapeutic effectiveness of biofeedback, it does raise the issue of whether other less elaborate and expensive techniques could be used to achieve the same ends.

Biofeedback therapy
Type of therapy designed to help people control their physiologocal functions without the use of drugs or other biotherapy techniques. Helps people reduce tension and stress, reduce phobic reactions, and control headaches. Has also been combined with other psychotherapies. See also *biofeedback*.

realized that the patients were imitating the behaviors of other patients in the institution. Although we can learn maladaptive behaviors by watching others, modeling can also be used effectively to teach adaptive behaviors.

Albert Bandura and his associates have used the modeling technique to reduce a wide range of phobic behaviors, such as fear of dogs and snakes (Bandura, 1968; Rosenthal & Bandura, 1978). The procedure generally involves showing clients a series of pictures of a model interacting with the feared object. For example, people who are afraid of snakes may first see the model watching a snake from a distance. In the next picture, the model may move closer to the snake. As the sequence progresses, the

Table 15–2   Summary of Theory-Based Therapies

Type	Scope	Time Focus	Relationship with Therapist	Goal	Role of Therapist
Psychoanalytic	insight	emphasis on childhood	minor importance	provide insight	interpret
Client-centered	insight	present	major importance	promote self-acceptance	provides accepting environment
Gestalt	insight	present	moderate importance	promote self-awareness	focus client on feelings and behavior
Cognitive	specific (thoughts, feelings, and attributions)	present	minor importance	change thoughts, feelings, and attributions	identify faulty cognitions and suggest more adaptable ones
Behavior therapies	specific (behavior)	present	minor importance	change specific behavior	develop contingencies or associations so client will learn new behaviors

model will touch the snake and finally handle it. Watching these models over a period of time does reduce the severity of clients' phobias.

The modeling technique can also be used to get clients involved by asking them to perform the behavior that is modeled by the therapist or other model. In our snake example, after people watch the model handle the snake, they will be asked to handle a live snake themselves. This participant modeling is effective in reducing fears and teaching new behaviors (Bandura, 1977). Further research has found that modeling is most effective when the model is similar to the client. For example, Kornhaber and Schroeder (1975) found that children were more likely to handle a snake after watching a child model this behavior than after seeing an adult handle the snake.

Modeling offers a number of exciting therapeutic possibilities because the technique is relatively easy to use and almost any behavior can be modeled. There are, however, still many questions about why the technique is effective (Sherman, 1979). Does the model teach a new behavior? Does watching the model allow the viewer to imagine performing the behavior? Does the model show the observer that no negative consequences will follow the feared behavior? And under what condition and with what types of disorders will modeling be most effective? These questions need to be answered by research so that the most effective modeling techniques can be identified.

Table 15–2 summarizes the types of psychotherapies described in this section.

Group Therapies: An Emphasis on Communication and Relationships

If we examine Chris's life, we find that many of her problems resulted from her attempts to interact with other people. She longed for attention and often felt neglected. Her multiple personality problem began at a time when she felt most neglected. As a school-aged youngster, she had difficulties making friends and interacting with her schoolmates. Still later in life, Chris had difficulties interacting with her husband. This stress caused a new personality to emerge. Chris entered psychotherapy with Dr. Thigpen in the late 1940s. Dr. Thigpen used the individual, or one-on-one, therapy method that was widely practiced at that time.

The late 1940s and early 1950s saw the emergence of a different style of therapy, called **group therapy.** This type of therapy generally involves one therapist and a group of clients (usually 6 to 12). The clients discuss their problems in the group and receive feedback from other group members as well as from the therapist. Unlike the other therapies we have discussed, group therapy is a setting, not a theory of therapy. In fact, almost all of the therapies we have discussed in this chapter have been used in a group setting (Phares, 1988).

Although the aim of both individual and group therapy is to bring about positive change and facilitate adjustment, there are some important differences between the two settings that influence the therapy process. In individual therapy the relationship is between the therapist and the client. In group therapy we have the additional client-client relationship. Thus, the therapist must be concerned with creating a good group climate in which members can change and grow. Group members look to the therapist to define the basic rules of therapy. The therapist must teach by setting examples for other members to follow; in a sense, the therapist must play two roles—that of therapist and that of group member. The relationship of the therapist to group members is important, but so are the relationships among group members. Because of these many demands, some groups are run by two therapists.

The therapist works on developing a trusting and cohesive relationship within the group. Members of cohesive groups are more open in their feelings, more committed to group goals, and more likely to attend therapy regularly. One patient recalled, "The most important thing in it [group therapy] was just having a group there, people that I could talk to, that wouldn't walk out on me. There was so much caring and hating and loving in the group and I was part of it" (Yalom, 1975, p. 48).

Group therapy offers a number of advantages over individual therapy (Yalom, 1975). First, as we pointed out earlier, it is more economical. One therapist can work with a number of clients at the same time. Second, since many of the clients' problems involve interpersonal relationships, the group setting is the best place to examine these problems and "practice"

Group therapy
Involves 1 (sometimes 2) therapists and from 6 to 12 clients; clients receive feedback from others in the group as well as from the therapist. Many different therapeutic techniques may be used.

Group therapy is not only more economical than one-to-one counseling, but it can be especially helpful in problems arising from social interactions. Since the root of much stress involves interacting with other people, the group is the natural place to deal with these problems.

interpersonal behaviors. Third, Yalom points out that other group members often serve as a source of hope and encouragement for individual members. Group members encourage one another to deal with their problems and offer hope for improvement. Fourth, the other group members show each individual member that he or she is not the only one to have problems and that others have similar problems. People who suffer psychological disorders often fall into the trap of thinking they are the only ones who ever had this problem. Finally, other group members can identify problems and give helpful feedback. The group members and the therapist can also serve as models of positive social skills.

After this long list of advantages, you might naturally ask why all therapy is not practiced in groups. Despite the many positive characteristics of group therapy, it has some important limitations. Researchers point out that many clients may need individual therapy before they can function well in a group setting (Shertzer & Stone, 1974). These clients may be too insecure to interact with others. Some people find it difficult to develop trust in a group interaction, and lacking this trust, they are unwilling to discuss their problems and feelings openly. Related to the trust issue is the issue of confidentiality; members must trust each other not to disclose information learned in the group to people outside the group. In some groups the therapist's attention may be spread too thin to give each client the help that he or she needs. Finally, the pressure to conform to group rules may limit the therapy process.

Family Therapy.   Before closing our discussion of group therapy, let's take a brief look at a group therapy that is becoming increasingly popular. As its name implies, **family therapy** involves working with the family as a unit. Often the family includes parents and children, and it is often the preferred method for dealing with child adjustment problems (Kaslow, 1991). In other cases (couples therapy), the family is two adults who may be working on their relationship. The family or systems approach views the family as a unique organization having roles, rules of behavior, and identifiable communication patterns. Although family members may be unaware of the family structure in which they operate, a trained therapist

Family therapy
Type of psychotherapy that involves the whole family, rather than just one member of it, since it is often the family system as a whole that can create stress and contribute to the development of psychological disorders. Couples working on a relationship also participate in family therapy.

Family therapy involves the therapist working with the family as a unit. The aim is to make the family a more effective group and help family members see the roles and communication patterns that have developed.

can often identify it by watching family members interact in a therapy setting. The family therapist believes that the family system can create stress and contribute to the development of psychological disorders. While one member of the family may be presenting particular problem behavior, this behavior may simply be a symptom of a problem within the family unit (Garvin, 1987). In other words, the family, as well as individuals, needs to be treated. In addition to causing psychological disorders, some family structures maintain maladaptive behavior in family members. For example, when Chris began suffering her multiple personalities, she took on the role of "problem child" in her family. Her mother became the "protector" who cared for Chris and tried to explain her behavior to others. Her father took on the role of "concerned parent" who worried about Chris and talked about her problem to other family members. Chris's sisters became "helpers" who had to aid in the daily chores because Chris's problems took up much of their parents' time and energy. While the system was designed to help Chris, it could also have contributed to maintaining her behavior by labeling her the "problem child." Further, if therapy was to change Chris's behavior, all the other members of her family would have to change their roles, too. There would no longer be a need for a "protector" or "concerned parent" or "helper" sisters. The point here is that it makes little sense to create change in one individual and then return that person to a family setting that encourages the old maladaptive behavior.

With these considerations in mind, the family therapist attempts to work with the whole family. The therapist sees all the members of the family together and observes their behavior. He or she attempts to identify the family role structure and communication patterns. In "treating" the family, the therapist will take an active role, requesting family members to behave in certain ways (Haley, 1980). He or she will have the members work on open communication and encourage the expression of repressed emotions. The "rules" of the family will be identified and openly stated. These unwritten rules will then be examined, and the therapist will point out how many of them have outlived their usefulness and exist now only through habit. Through this process, the family system is changed to encourage more adaptive behavior from its members. The beauty of this approach is that the therapist sets change in motion and observes during the therapy sessions how well this change is working to increase the "health" of the family.

Community Psychology:
An Emphasis on Early Identification and Prevention

In the late 1950s and early 1960s, attitudes about the treatment of psychological disturbances began to change in this country. As we pointed out earlier, it was realized that hospitalization was not the best means of treatment for many people, and besides, it was very expensive. It also became clear that traditional individual and small-group therapy efforts would not be sufficient; the demand was outstripping the resources, and traditional therapy was often unavailable to the people who needed it the most, such as the poor and the culturally deprived. Finally, mental health care providers agreed that after-the-fact treatment of problems should not be the only way of dealing with mental health problems; steps should be taken to prevent many problems from developing in the first place.

These attitudes gave rise to a policy of deinstitutionalization (Shadish, 1984) and to the development of **community psychology.** There were two cornerstones of community psychology. One was the decision to give attention to the *prevention* as well as to the treatment side of mental health problems. In fact, it was thought that prevention should be given priority

Community psychology
Subfield of psychology dedicated to promoting mental health at the community level; seeks to prevent and treat psychological problems by working to evaluate and to improve community organizations.

Community psychology involves developing community-based centers to prevent or give early attention to emotional, social, and behavioral problems. One program in this effort is the shelter for battered and abused women where women can receive guidance and a safe haven in their own community.

over treatment (Iscoe, 1982). The second was that mental health programs should be *community based*; that is, training, education, prevention, and treatment programs should be available in local communities where they would be near the people who needed them. In support of this policy, Congress passed the Community Mental Health Centers Act in 1963. The act stated that one mental health center should be developed for every 50,000 people. The centers would be set up in local communities, where they could offer a wide variety of services in a convenient and nondisruptive manner. For example, a person could walk into the center during a lunch break or after work and receive psychotherapy on an outpatient basis. If the person required hospitalization, he or she could be accommodated in the local center, where frequent visits by family members would be possible. Many of the centers would operate "hot lines" so that people suffering a crisis could talk with a professional or trained paraprofessional on the phone. Over 600 of these centers have been established to date.

The concept of prevention is broadly defined by community psychologists. There are, in fact, three levels of prevention.

Primary Prevention. Efforts of primary prevention are aimed at eliminating the cause of mental health problems. In the case of Chris Sizemore, we might ask whether or not steps could have been taken to prevent her from developing multiple personalities. A major thrust of primary prevention programs is education. A National Mental Health Association commission emphasized this function and called for programs in the schools to prevent unwanted pregnancies and help people anticipate and manage life stresses (Long, 1986). Other programs offer new parents child-rearing classes to prepare them to care for their children and anticipate problems that might arise when the new baby is taken home. It is possible that if Chris's parents had received such a program, they may have been able to take steps to lessen Chris's anxiety when they brought home the twins. Another part of primary prevention involves identifying groups of people who are likely candidates to experience mental health problems. These "at risk" groups may be people of certain ages (adolescents or the elderly) or socioeconomic positions (poor), or those undergoing particular work stress (workers on strike). Vietnam combat veterans have been added to this list and special programs are available to prevent or reduce the

Hot lines, part of secondary prevention programs, allow people in crisis to talk with trained professionals. Hot lines have been set up to aid people contemplating suicide, runaways, battered women, and people with drug and alcohol problems.

severity of post-traumatic stress disorders (Fairbank & Nicholson, 1987). Once these groups are identified, efforts are made to take facilities and educational programs to them, rather than simply waiting for them to come to a center. In this sense, prevention efforts are mobile, reaching out to the people who may be in need of them.

Secondary Prevention. Primary prevention efforts are like medical inoculations; their aim is to prevent people from developing the problem. If this goal cannot be accomplished, the next best alternative is *secondary prevention*, which aims to identify and treat problems early in order to reduce their severity and duration and the suffering associated with them. Many secondary prevention efforts try to develop an "early-warning network" by training people in the community to identify psychological problems and help troubled people get in contact with the treatment facilities they need. In addition, hotlines have been set up, giving troubled people access to a trained paraprofessional. The trained people who staff these lines counsel people contemplating suicide, alcoholics, runaways, and battered women about where they can receive further help.

Tertiary Prevention. The third level of prevention is rehabilitation and follow-up treatment of people who have been hospitalized or have been in long-term treatment. The aim here is to help these people reenter society and lead productive lives. Educational activities include job training, family counseling, and social skills training. In addition, there are **halfway houses** where people with common problems can live together after they have been discharged from hospitals. They receive training and counseling on everday issues, from how to shop in a grocery store to how to write out a check. They may also receive psychotherapy. Research (Fairweather, Sanders, Maynard, Cresler, & Bleck, 1969) has found that people who have spent time in halfway houses are less likely to require rehospitalization than people who are thrust immediately into their old environment. Halfway houses have also been set up for alcoholics, drug addicts, and ex-prisoners.

Community mental health centers also offer a wide range of counseling and consulting services on a sliding-fee scale so that they are affordable to all. Thus they offer counseling to many people who would normally be unable to afford it. The centers have also made people more aware of the value of counseling and therapy.

Halfway house
Homes where peole live after they have been discharged from an institutionalized setting and before they can live independently.

The mental health centers' role in prevention is indeed a valuable one. Nevertheless, there have been a number of criticisms of these centers. Often they do not have a large enough staff to meet the problems of the community. Goals may not be clearly stated, so that people are confused about the purpose and types of service offered by a center.

The policy of deinstitutionalization has been linked to the growing problem of the homeless (Mathews, 1988). Critics argue that people who should be in mental health institutions are being dumped onto the streets. They are unable to hold jobs or provide adequate care for themselves, and become part of the rapidly growing sea of people living on the streets of our cities. Although getting people out of institutions is a positive goal, placing them in community environments where they are unprepared to function creates a terrible strain on both the individuals and the community. The problem of the homeless has reached such importance that it became a major issue in the 1988 presidential campaign. The solution to the problem still proves to be elusive.

The dilemma of the homeless pits two important issues against each other: the responsibility of the community to take care of its citizens and the rights and freedom of the individual to determine the type of care he or she will accept. These basic values also clash in the recent controversy over involuntary outpatient commitment (Mulvey, Geller, & Roth, 1987). The policy of involuntary commitment allows an individual to be placed on outpatient treatment in the community against his or her wishes if specified criteria of dangerousness, inability to care for self, or need for treatment have been met. On the positive side, this policy allows the individual to remain in the community and ensures that he or she will receive treatment. Critics, however, argue that people should have the right to determine whether or not they want treatment and that forcing people into treatment undermines the trust necessary in a therapeutic relationship. Another concern is that this policy forces the dual role on community mental health centers of being both healers and jailers.

Biomedical Therapy

Now that we have sampled a number of psychotherapy techniques, let's turn our attention to the second major category of therapies: biomedical therapy. Ancient history is filled with examples of attempts to treat psychological disorders with physical methods. These early methods were based on the assumption that the disorder was caused by some physical or supernatural invader in the individual's body. As medical science developed, the uselessness of these methods was recognized. However, the desire to treat psychological disorders using physical methods remained. In some cases, this desire was based on the medical model, which viewed all psychological disorders as diseases or illnesses whose causes were due to a malfunction of the body. In other cases, the desire for a physical treatment was based on the belief that even problems of a psychological nature could be treated quickly and effectively with drugs.

The quest to find medical cures for psychological disorders, however, did not lead to a careful, concentrated effort to develop these cures. Rather, until recently, the story of biomedical therapy has been one of *serendipity*, or accidental, lucky discoveries. A procedure or drug being used to treat one type of medical illness was accidentally discovered to have therapeutic effects on a psychological disorder. In most of these cases, the discoverers had no idea why the procedure was effective; they only knew that it seemed to work. As we will see, even with the improved techniques and methods of study used today, scientists are still unsure why many drugs are effective.

PROMOTING MENTAL HEALTH THROUGH PERSONAL GROWTH GROUPS

Our discussion of therapy has dealt with the "treatment" of behavioral and/or emotional problems. We've pointed out which therapies are best suited for different disorders. There is, however, another important side to the mental health issue that doesn't involve treatment or even prevention of disorders. Rather its aims are to help people learn more about themselves, to explore and expand their awareness, and to experiment with new behaviors and ways to relate to other people. In short, this side of the mental health issue is concerned with personal growth and awareness. Personal growth techniques are not forms of psychotherapy; the aim is not to treat people with psychological disturbances. Most people in growth groups have adjusted to their physical and social environments but feel that something is missing in their "normal" lives. They may be dissatisfied with their relationships or feel unfulfilled in their work.

Many different techniques have been developed to help people in their quest for personal growth. Some are based on theory and careful research, while others have a dubious grounding. Many in the field are professionals who have received extensive training. Unfortunately, there are others whose training is inadequate. Because of the disparity in qualifications, it is important to be careful when choosing a personal growth technique and leader.

Transpersonal psychology is one personal growth approach. It attempts to increase people's awareness of themselves, to expand their experiences, and teach them how to become completely absorbed in experiences. This approach combines psychological theory, religion (including the teachings of Buddha, Lao Tzu, and the Dali Lamas of Tibet), and modern philosophy. Transpersonal psychologists attempt to develop all parts of the person, including the physical, emotional, mental, intuitive, psychic, and mystical aspects of personality (McWaters, 1975). Transpersonal psychology operates on the assumption that physical, emotional, intellectual, and spiritual growth are interrelated. The movement argues that intuition, imagination, and altered states of consciousness (dreams, meditation, and drug-related experiences) are all part of human experience and should be examined.

T-groups, also called sensitivity training groups, have a different goal. The emphasis of these groups is on allowing people to experience how groups develop and to receive feedback about their effectiveness as a group member. These groups are generally made up of 8 to 15 members and 1 or 2 trainers. These trainers make observations about the process of the group, focusing on such issues as how decisions are made, how group roles and norms form, and how individual members contribute to the process. The group itself begins with no structure and no assigned task. Thus, individual members are forced to develop a structure and define the group's goals. This process not only gives the members additional insight into how groups operate, but also gives them information about how they as individuals help or hinder the group process. T-groups have been widely used in industrial and educational settings to aid group performance (Heller & Monahan, 1977).

Whereas the aim of the T-group is to help members examine the group process, the aim of the **encounter group** or **sensitivity group** is to expand personal awareness and growth (Brammer & Shostrom, 1977; Shapiro, 1978). Encounter groups provide intense, personal interactions in a setting where self-expression is encouraged. In a sense, encounter groups attempt to rid people of their interpersonal "hang-ups." There are numerous exercises emphasizing nonverbal expression and touching. It is from such exercises that encounter groups have gotten the label "touchy-feely" groups. The variations on the encounter group are almost unlimited. In the marathon group, members interact and live together for 2 or 3 days. It is believed that this increases the intensity of interaction and removes many inhibitions about interpersonal communication.

Many people profit from encounter groups by becoming freer in their expression and more sensitive to their own feelings (Dies & Greenburg, 1976; Golembiewski & Blumburg, 1973). However, during the 1960s the encounter group became something of a fad; groups were led by unqualified leaders and variations were tried simply because they were unusual. Because of the intensity of interaction, there were "casualties," people who suffered negative effects from the group experience. Sometimes these negative effects caused long-term suffering. It has been estimated that from 9 to 33 percent of the participants in encounter groups had negative experiences (Lieberman, Yalom, & Miks, 1973; Yalom & Lieberman 1971). Some of these casualties resulted because participants had not been properly selected for the group.

Transpersonal psychology
Tries to increase people's self-awareness through a mixture of psychological theory, religion, and modern philosophy. Its aim is to increase personal growth in many different ways and on different levels.

T-group
Training technique to help people learn about group process and development.

Biomedical therapy includes a wide range of techniques that involve some type of physical treatment. Most of these treatments must be administered under the direction of a psychiatrist or other medical doctor. Most individuals who receive biomedical therapy are also given some type of psychotherapy. For example, one group of therapists recently reported effectively treating obsessive-compulsives and depressives using a combination of chemotherapy and behavior therapy (Christensen, Hadiz-Pavlovic, Andrews, & Mattick, 1987). The drugs allowed the patients to focus their attention on the therapy and concentrate on the reward contingencies.

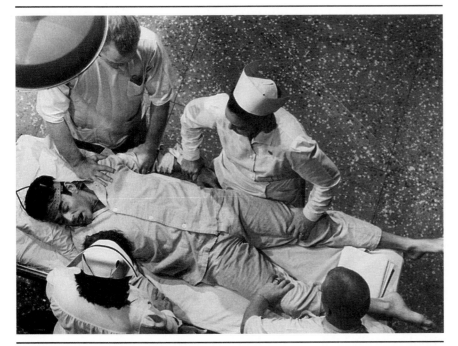

Electroconvulsive Therapy

When Chris first visited Dr. Thigpen, she was very depressed and had considered suicide. After talking to Chris for several sessions, Dr. Thigpen suggested that she undergo electric shock treatment. Chris recoiled in fear—she had visions of jerking in pain on a cold steel table while electric shocks were sent through her head. Because of her extreme fear of the treatment and because she began to recover from her depression, Dr. Thigpen decided against shock therapy in Chris's case.

Chris's fears were somewhat exaggerated. *Electroconvulsive therapy (ECT)* has been developed to the point where it does not cause the patient great discomfort. However, the preparation for the procedure can frighten some patients. Before receiving ECT, patients are given a sedative and a muscle relaxant to reduce the risk of injury. They are then placed on a well-padded mattress, and electrodes are attached to the head. In order to reduce the risk of injury, the electric current is applied to only one side of the head. The current of 70 to 130 volts is given for a period of .1 to .5 second. The shock causes the patient to go into convulsions similar to those suffered in an epileptic seizure. Following the convulsions, most patients remain unconscious for 5 to 30 minutes. ECT generally involves 8 to 20 treatments at the rate of 3 per week. All this may sound terrible, more like something from a horror movie than a humane treatment for psychological disorders! However, people generally awake feeling only a little hazy; they have no memory of the procedure.

Although most patients are not harmed by the procedure, that alone is not sufficient reason to use it. The crucial question is: Does it relieve their psychological suffering? Research suggests that electroconvulsive therapy does provide short-term benefits for those suffering from depressive disorders (Scovern & Kilmann, 1980). In fact, 60 to 90 percent of those who receive this therapy show rapid signs of improvement, whereas there is only a 40 to 50 percent recovery rate found in those who are not treated (Fink, 1978).

Although the research is encouraging, it also points out the limits of electroconvulsive therapy. First, the procedure has little effect on disorders other than depression. Second, there are few *long-term* benefits from the

Encounter group (also called sensitivity group)
Aims at expanding personal awareness and growth rather than treating emotional disorders. Such groups try to rid people of their interpersonal "hang-ups." Variations include marathon groups and nude encounter groups.

procedure. In fact, people who receive ECT for depression suffer a relapse (become depressed again) more frequently than those who recover without therapy (Millon, 1969). Finally, some people experience considerable stress and uncomfortable side effects such as headaches, nausea, and memory loss that can last for days or longer. There has also been some evidence suggesting that ECT may destroy some brain cells.

Clearly, there are pros and cons to electroconvulsive therapy. After reviewing both sides of the issue, the American Psychiatric Association (1987) concluded that this therapy should be regarded as a useful procedure under the right circumstances. Electroconvulsive therapy is given to over 100,000 Americans each year. Often these people are suffering from severe depression, have not responded to drug treatment, and the therapist has concluded that they may attempt suicide if not relieved of their depression. In many cases, patients are placed on drug therapy after ECT, and studies have shown this combination of treatments can be effective (Dietz, 1985).

Psychosurgery

For many decades it has been known that certain parts of the brain control different functions (see Chapter 2). In the early 1930s, Egas Moniz, a Portuguese pyschiatrist, reasoned that people suffering from emotional disorders might be helped by destroying the connections from the parts of the brain that control emotions. He developed a surgical technique known as the *prefrontal lobotomy*, which involved cutting the connections between the thalamus (emotional center) and the frontal lobes (thought center). Moniz reported that this procedure calmed patients and helped many recover from severe psychological disturbances. Psychosurgery was hailed as a major breakthrough in the treatment of emotional disorders, and Moniz was awarded a Nobel Prize for his work. Thousands of prefrontal lobotomy operations were performed during the 1940s and 1950s.

However, it was not long before research began to cast doubt on the effectiveness of psychosurgery. It seems that psychosurgery does succeed in reducing the intensity of people's emotions. As such, it can help those suffering from high levels of anxiety or agitated emotions. But the research also showed that many people became zombie-like after the operation; they went through the motions of life without showing any emotional reaction to their environment or expressing any ambition or hopes. This aspect of psychosurgery has received attention in the movies made from

Movies such as *One Flew Over the Cuckoo's Nest* dramatize the concerns surrounding psychosurgery. The effects of the surgery cannot be undone so misuses of the procedure or an incorrect diagnosis are particularly tragic.

the novel *One Flew Over the Cuckoo's Nest* (Kesey, 1962) and the tragic true-life story of Frances Farmer, a well-known actress during the 1940s.

Given the overwhelmingly negative reaction to lobotomies, you may be surprised to learn that psychosurgery is still being performed. The psychosurgical procedure performed today on some patients, mainly those suffering from severe depression or obsessive-compulsive disorder, is known as *cingulotomy*. The cingulum is a bundle of nerve fibers that provides a connection between the emotion-related structures of the limbic system (amygdala, septum, hypothalamus, etc.) and the frontal lobe cortex where thought originates. Cingulotomy involves severing these nerve fibers to disrupt the flow of information from the limbic system to the cortex.

Dr. H. Thomas Ballantine, a neurosurgeon at Massachusetts General Hospital who has performed hundreds of cingulotomies, reports that nearly three-fourths of the patients who received this treatment showed improvements in their symptoms (*Newsweek*, 1990). Further, independent studies of these patients done by researchers at MIT reveal that cingulotomy does not interfere with intellectual functioning nor does it seem to change the patient's personality, as lobotomies did.

Still, it seems unlikely that psychosurgery will ever be widely used. Most mental health practitioners view psychosurgical procedures as barbaric, pointing to the fact that brain tissue, once destroyed, can never be replaced. Instead, advances in biomedical treatments of mental disorders will most likely be seen in the area of chemotherapy.

Chemotherapy

Drug therapy, **chemotherapy,** began in 1952 in a very accidental way. Indian doctors had used reserpine, an extract of *Rauwolfia serpentina* (snakeroot plant), as a general medicine since 1920. As the use of the drug became more widespread, physicians noticed that reserpine had a calming effect on patients. More importantly, this calming effect occurred without making the patient drowsy or reducing alertness. In 1952 reserpine and another drug (chlorpromazine), which had also been used for medical purposes, were introduced as *tranquilizers*, medication for the treatment of emotional disturbances. Chemotherapy was readily embraced by the medical and psychological world as a major advance because it seemed to be a quick and inexpensive way to treat psychological disturbances. The discovery of tranquilizers launched the field of **psychopharmacology,** which is the study of drugs to treat psychological disorders.

Drugs are currently divided into three categories. **Antianxiety drugs** (minor tranquilizers) reduce anxiety and tension without causing drowsiness or a loss of mental alertness. The most popular antianxiety drugs are Valium, Librium, and Miltown. Since almost everyone suffers attacks of anxiety and tension at some time, antianxiety drugs have become the most widely used prescription drugs in the United States; in fact, almost 23 million prescriptions were written for Valium alone in 1985 (U.S. Food and Drug Administration, 1986). Dr. Thigpen, for example, gave Chris tranquilizers to calm her during her fits of anxiety. These minor tranquilizers are not only prescribed by psychiatrists for people suffering from diagnosed disorders; family physicians and other doctors tend to prescribe them to help people cope with stressful situations. The wide use of tranquilizers has been viewed with alarm. There is a fine line that separates wise use from abuse, and people must be careful not to rely on these drugs to solve all their problems. This warning is particularly important because scientists have not yet discovered exactly how these drugs work. There has been some information suggesting that prolonged use can lead to dependence (Baker, 1983). Further, people may use the drugs to treat

Chemotherapy
Treatment of disorders through the use of drugs; a form of biotherapy.
Psychopharmacology
Study of drugs to treat psychological disorders.
Antianxiety drugs
Minor tranquilizers that reduce anxiety and tension without causing drowsiness or a loss of mental alertness. Most popular are Valium, Librium, and Miltown.

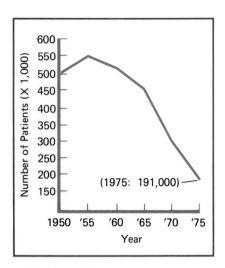

FIGURE 15–1

Reduction of schizophrenic patients hospitalized for mental disorders, 1950–1975.

the symptoms of stress without trying to uncover and deal with the causes of their tension.

A second category of drugs is made up of **antipsychotic drugs.** These drugs, which include Thorazine and Stelazine, are used to calm and relieve the delusions of schizophrenics so that the person can be helped or reached by psychotherapy. Further, these drugs reduce the symptoms of some schizophrenics to such a degree that they can leave the hospital and live in a home environment while receiving other treatment (see Figure 15–1). Antipsychotic drugs are so effective that nearly 87 percent of all patients hospitalized for psychological disorders receive some form of such medication (MacDonald & Tobais, 1976).

In spite of the value of the antipsychotic drugs, they have been criticized. The side effects include headaches, nausea, blurred vision, drooling, stiff muscles, and fainting. There is even some evidence that prolonged use of the drugs can cause permanent brain damage (MacDonald, Lidsky, & Kern, 1979). Another criticism is that drugs are often used to control patients rather than to treat their disorders. Patients taking antipsychotic drugs become docile and are easily controlled by hospital staff. Thus there is a strong temptation to prescribe drugs when a patient is acting in a disruptive manner. Despite these criticisms, many clinicians agree that the careful use of antipsychotic drugs along with psychotherapy can have very positive effects. Research efforts are now being aimed at developing drugs that do not bring about undesired side effects and at determining exactly how these antipsychotic drugs work.

Tranquilizers are drugs that bring people "down" from highly anxious or agitated states. **Antidepressant drugs,** such as Tofranil and Elavil, work by lifting the person's spirits and increasing his or her activity level. Generally, the antidepressant drugs are given to people who are suffering from deep states of depression. It is interesting that the antidepressant drugs do not work equally well with all depressed individuals; in some cases, they are very effective, while in others, they have almost no effect (Gelenberg, 1979). Factors such as the person's age, specific symptom pattern, personality, and emotional state influence the effect that the drug will have. Hence there is a certain degree of unpredictability in using these drugs. Unfortunately, there are also a number of unpleasant side effects associated with antidepressant drugs; these include nausea, restlessness, and insomnia.

Another drug, *lithium carbonate*, has been introduced in the last decade. Lithium is used to treat people suffering from bipolar disorders (see Chapter 14), which are characterized by wide swings in mood. If used in the proper dosage, the drug is effective in keeping people from becoming too elated or too depressed. However, lithium is a dangerous drug that can cause death if its concentration in the blood becomes too high. Thus people who receive lithium treatment must take regular blood tests.

The advances in chemotherapy have both exciting and frightening implications. On the positive side, drugs offer the possibility that people suffering from psychological disorders can be treated quickly, efficiently, and inexpensively. Further, there is evidence that drugs can be used to treat people who suffer disorders, such as schizophrenia, which are difficult to treat with psychotherapy. However, some issues must be considered before adopting chemotherapy. First, drugs generally reduce only the symptoms of the disorder and not its cause. Because patients are relieved quickly of unpleasant symptoms, they may be tempted to avoid dealing with the underlying problem. If they take this position, they will lose control over their lives; they will become dependent on drugs to make them feel good. A second problem related to chemotherapy is that the drugs can be used simply to control people's behavior rather than to treat their problems. People who work on wards in mental health institutions are often faced with

Antipsychotic drugs
Major tranquilizers that are used to calm and relieve the delusions of schizophrenics. Two most commonly used are Thorzaine and Stlezine.

Antidepressant drugs
Drugs that work by lifting the person's spirits and increasing his or her activity level. Two examples are Tofranil and Elavil.

the simultaneous demands of a number of patients. Because they cannot help all of them immediately, they may resort to drugs to quiet disruptive patients and bring peace to the wards. This is clearly a misuse of drugs.

Does Therapy Work?

We have traveled through the complex and sometimes confusing world of therapy. As we have seen, there are long-term and short-term therapies, insight and specific therapies, therapies that focus on the client's emotions and therapies that focus on changing behaviors, therapies that use drugs and therapies that use words. Regardless of the type of therapy, the aim is the same: to help people deal with psychological disorders and change maladaptive behaviors. Now we must ask the basic question: Is therapy effective in treating psychological disturbances?

At first glance, this seems a simple question to answer. All we need to do is give therapy to one group of people suffering from a disorder and withhold it from another group of people suffering the same disorder. At the end of a certain period of time, we can check to see which group has improved the most.

This solution seems so simple that it is hard to believe that there is still so much controversy as to the effectiveness of therapy. However, as is so often the case in scientific investigations, the simple here turns out to be very complex. The first question that is raised deals with the issue of improvement. What does it mean to say someone is improved? For example, after many sessions with Dr. Thigpen, Chris understood her problem of multiple personalities and felt better about herself. However, she continued to suffer the emergence of different personalities. Would we say that Chris was improved because she felt better, or would we say that she showed no improvement because the multiple personalities still existed? It seems possible to make strong argument for either position. A second issue involves the duration of improvement (Meltzoff & Kornreich, 1970). How are we to compare the effectiveness of a therapy that results in a quick but temporary change in the person's behavior with the effectiveness of a therapy that takes a long time but results in a more permanent change? A third issue concerns who is to determine the success of therapy. The therapist's opinion may be biased because he or she has a strong interest in believing that the therapy is successful. The client's opinion may also be influenced by the expectation and desire to see the therapy as successful. Objective criteria such as test scores or behavioral measures may be the most unbiased, but they are difficult to use on a long-term basis.

A related issue is why therapy works. If we can determine that psychotherapy is successful, we would also like to know why this is so. Does the success of therapy depend on characteristics of the client, characteristics of the therapist, the specific techniques used in therapy, or simply the expectations of those involved? You can see now why the "simple" question: Does it work? is very complicated.

Given this complexity, it is easier to understand why there are no clear-cut answers about the effectiveness of therapies. In 1952 Hans Eysenck created a furor when he concluded that people receiving psychotherapy showed no more improvement than those receiving no treatment. Eysenck based his conclusion on a review of 24 studies of people suffering moderate psychological disturbances (neuroses). His shocking conclusion led a number of investigators to review his data and to conduct additional research. These more recent reviews of a larger body of research suggest that psy-

THE PLACEBO EFFECT: The Importance of Belief

Throughout history, the physician has been highly respected. Stories of miracles worked by physicians are commonplace in every age. But when we look at the history of medicine, it seems amazing that even the hardiest patient could have survived, let alone improved, under early medical techniques. Patients ingested almost every known organic and inorganic material, including crocodile dung, teeth of swine, powder of precious stones, furs, feathers, human perspiration, oil of ants, blood, and earthworms. They were purged, poisoned, punctured, cut, blistered, bled, leached, heated, frozen, and sweated (Shapiro, 1971). Today we know that most of these treatments had no medical value. Yet there are carefully documented stories of patients improving. How could this have happened?

A number of investigators have suggested that these miraculous recoveries are examples of the placebo effect (Honigfield, 1964; Shapiro, 1971). Simply put, the **placebo effect** describes the situation in which a treatment that has no curative value of its own has a healing effect on the patient because of the patient's belief in its effectiveness. Although the placebo effect has been most frequently applied in medicine, some clinicians (Wilkens, 1973) have suggested that it may be one of the reasons that psychotherapy works. According to this position, almost any method of psychotherapy should show positive results if the client believes it will be effective. If this is the case, it is clear that the therapist must convey to the client that the method being used will be successful.

There are a number of possible reasons for the placebo effect. One of the most common explanations focuses on the "self-fulfilling prophecy," which we discussed in Chapter 14. According to this position, people are motivated to interpret events to support their expectancies. In order to illustrate this, let us suppose that we have two people, Bob and Mary, who are in group therapy to overcome shyness. Mary strongly believes that the therapy will be effective, whereas Bob does not. After two sessions of therapy, Mary and Bob meet a stranger on the bus and strike up a short conversation. For Mary, this becomes a sign that the therapy is working; even though she still found it hard, she would never have been able to talk to a stranger at all before therapy. Her new confidence motivates her to talk to other people. Bob, on the other hand, focuses on the fact that he felt uncomfortable talking to the stranger. For Bob, this is a sign that reinforces his belief that the therapy has not been helping him. His trust in the therapy decreases even further, and he eventually drops out of the group. In this example we can see that the expectancy not only influenced the way Mary and Bob interpreted their behaviors, but it also had future consequences for their efforts in therapy.

A second reason for the placebo effect involves the feelings of control. In Chapter 12 we discussed how a lack of control can cause stress. Many people enter therapy because they believe that they have no control over their feelings or behaviors. Gatchel (1980) suggests that the expectancy that therapy will be effective gives people a feeling of control over their lives. This perceived control reduces their stress and anxiety.

A third explanation for the placebo effect focuses on effort justification. As we will see in Chapter 16, research on cognitive dissonance theory has found that people are motivated to justify their effort; the more effort they choose to expend, the greater their need to justify it. One way to justify effort is to change one's attitudes to believe that the effortful behavior was a positive and valuable experience. Cooper and Axsom (1982) point out that therapy frequently involves a great deal of effort on the part of clients. Not only is it often difficult to talk about one's problems, but clients must also sacrifice their time and money. It would be even more difficult to continue making these sacrifices if they believed that the therapy wasn't helping them. Therefore, in order to justify their sacrifices and efforts, clients may become motivated to believe in the effectiveness of the therapy.

At first glance, it may seem that the placebo effect suggests that therapy is simply a process of self-deception. This is not the case. Rather, both physicians and therapists have known for a long time that a patient's attitudes and beliefs are very important in determining the effectiveness of treatment. Any treatment will be more effective if the patient believes in it and is willing to use it in the proper manner. Research on the placebo effect suggests that the way in which the treatment is presented to the patient or client is one major factor in determining the effectiveness of that treatment.

Placebo effect
Situation in which a treatment that has no curative value of its own has a healing effect because of the patient's belief in its effectiveness.

chotherapy does have positive effects, although it does not work for everyone (Shapiro & Shapiro, 1983). An examination of a larger number of studies on the outcome of psychotherapy led investigators to conclude that a person receiving psychotherapy is generally better off than 75 percent of those people who receive no treatment (Smith, Glass, & Miller, 1980; Glass & Kliegl, 1983). A similar review of research on therapy with children and adolescents concluded that ". . . the average treated youngster was better adjusted after treatment than 79% of those not treated" (Weisz et al., 1987, p. 542). Although this is encouraging, there is also an indication that psychotherapy may actually leave a small percentage of clients worse off than they would have been had they received no treatment (Bergin & Lambert, 1978).

Results such as these raise an additional interesting question: What factors determine the effects of psychotherapy? The answers are characteristics of the client, characteristics of the therapist, the nature of the problem, and the type of therapy.

Looking first at *client characteristics*, it has been shown that people who are physically healthy, highly motivated to improve, and of relatively high intelligence are most likely to make rapid progress in therapy. On the other hand, people who have a low tolerance for anxiety, low motivation to improve, and feel that they have been forced into psychotherapy may actually get worse from therapy.

Numerous studies have found that empathy, warmth, and genuineness are important *therapist characteristics* (Rogers & Truax, 1967; Gurman, 1977). Regardless of the type of therapy, an open, trusting relationship between client and therapist is vital to the success of the treatment. Therapists who show empathy, warmth, and genuineness are much more able to establish this type of relationship than are cold, distant therapists. This position was supported in a study that found that male college students suffering from neurotic disorders showed equal improvement when treated by either an experienced therapist or a college professor who was chosen for personal characteristics of warmth and understanding (Strupp & Hadley, 1979).

The *nature of the problem* also influences the success of therapy. Psychotherapy as the sole method of treatment has not proved particularly effective in treating serious disorders such as schizophrenia, alcoholism, certain types of affective disorders, or drug abuse. However, psychotherapy can play an important role in these cases when biological methods such as chemotherapy or ECT are used. On the other hand, high rates of success for psychotherapy have been found for anxiety and psychosexual disorders.

The final factor concerns the *type of therapy*. Is one type of therapy more effective than another? This may be the most difficult nut to crack of all, for a number of reasons! First, the goal of the therapies differ widely. Chemotherapy is designed to increase the person's immediate functioning; behavior therapy aims to change specific behaviors; psychodynamic therapy attempts to increase insight and make changes in one's personality. How can we compare effectiveness if the goals of the therapies are different? Second, some therapies are useful for a very specific type of client whereas others have broader application. As we saw, psychoanalytic, client-centered, Gestalt, and RET therapies require clients who can verbalize their feelings and communicate with the therapist. Behavioral and biomedical therapies are not restricted to verbal clients. Finally, the various therapies are suited for different disorders, and effectiveness will be determined by the match between disorder and therapy. Chemotherapy is one of the most effective treatments for schizophrenia. Other research has found behavioral and cognitive therapies most effective for treating phobias, conduct disorders, somatoform disorders, and sexual disorders (Andrews & Harvey, 1981; Shapiro & Shapiro, 1982).

As you can see, we started out with a seemingly simple question and ended up with a very complex answer. It does seem that therapy can be very useful for treating many psychological disorders, but everyone will not be helped by therapy. Further, no single type of therapy will be effective for treating all disorders. Hence it is important that therapists screen potential clients in order to choose those who are most likely to benefit from their therapy. In addition, more therapists are taking an **eclectic approach** which avoids becoming locked into one type of therapy, but, instead, bases the choice of technique on the demands of each individual case (Nietzel & Bernstein, 1987).

Eclectic approach
Therapy where the choice of techniques differs depending on the needs of the client.

Summary

1. Many methods of therapy have been developed for dealing with psychological disturbances. These methods may be broadly divided into psychotherapy and biomedical therapy. **Psychotherapies** involve a trained professional who uses verbal interactions to bring about behavior change and positive adjustment in an individual or group. **Biomedical therapy** involves some type of physical treatment, including the use of drugs, surgery, and electric shock to induce behavior change. It is often used together with psychotherapy.

2. The treatment of psychological disorders is not new. The treatment methods used during any particular time were based upon the "theories" held by the people of the time about the causes of disorders. Historically, many treatment methods have been quite inhumane. The first major reforms in treating the mentally disturbed came in the late 1700s and early 1800s. The American Dorothea Dix and the Frenchman Phillipe Pinel brought about improvements by criticizing the deplorable conditions of the asylums and the mistreatment of the mentally ill.

3. In the early 1900s significant advancements were made in the treatment of psychological disorders by advances in the biomedical therapies and mental disorders started to be treated as a physical disease would be. World War II signaled the need for new ways to offer therapy to large numbers, which led to the development of group therapy. World War II also led to the use of drug therapy for psychological disorders. Today, deinstitutionalization is being made possible through the use of drug therapy, even with severely disturbed patients. This emphasis on deinstitutionalization is accompanied by a focus on prevention. Critics say that drug therapy is being overused and that deinstitutionalization is adding to the growing problem of the homeless.

4. Mental health professionals include psychiatrists, psychoanalysts, clinical psychologists, counseling psychologists, clinical social workers, and psychiatric nurses. Most people with psychological problems turn first to family members, neighbors, friends, physicians, or clergy before going to mental health professionals.

5. Many types of psychotherapy were discussed in this chapter. **Psychoanalysis,** developed by Sigmund Freud, is based on the notion that events in early childhood are important determinants of one's personality. Feelings or events associated with early childhood may be **repressed,** leading to anxiety later on. Freud believed that these repressed feelings enter the person's **unconscious** and can be released through the use of **free association** or **dream interpretation.**

6. Carl Rogers and other humanistic psychologists propose that **humanistic therapy** will help people through a process of self-growth. Humanistic therapy involves creating an atmosphere of **unconditional positive regard** in which the therapist relays warmth and concern for the client. In this setting the client is able to gain the confidence necessary for self-exploration and personal growth.

7. **Gestalt therapy,** developed mainly by Fritz Perls, proposes that unconscious thoughts and emotions (background) may lead to behaviors (figure) that are inappropriate to the situation. In Gestalt therapy people are helped to take responsibility for their actions, while understanding the emotions that are influencing their behaviors.

8. According to **rational emotive therapy (RET),** irrational thoughts are responsible for the way we feel about ourselves and others. RET therapists are concerned only with the present, and use a challenging, directive approach to help clients discover their anxiety-producing irrational thoughts.

9. **Behavior therapies** assume that abnormal behaviors are learned, and thus can be unlearned by changing the events that reinforce maladaptive behaviors. Behavior therapists may use a variety of techniques to change behaviors. **Aversive conditioning** may be used to break undesirable habits. **Systematic desensitization** is used to help overcome phobias. With **operant conditioning,** positive rewards are used to motivate people to perform desirable behaviors. These rewards often take the form of **token economies. Biofeedback** is a method that teaches people to control their physiological functions by giving them feedback about these functions. Another method of changing behaviors involves **modeling.** With this type of behavior therapy, the client watches someone else engage in the desired behavior and imitates them.

10. In psychotherapy, a therapist may see only a single client at a time, or may work with a group of clients. In **group therapy,** clients not only receive feedback from the therapist, but also from group members. **Family therapy** involves seeing a family as a whole during the therapy session. Family therapy assumes that the family system can create stress and contribute to the development of psychological disorders.

11. **Community psychology** attempts to prevent stress by changing the environment. When environmental change is not possible, community psychologists strive to help those people suffering from mild disorders before their disturbances become severe. These goals are often met through the use of self-help groups of community mental health centers.

12. There are a number of techniques used to help people achieve greater personal growth. These methods are not therapies, since they are not aimed at treating a specific disorder. Included in this category are **transpersonal psychology, T-groups,** and **encounter (sensitivity) groups.**

13. There is a wide variety of biomedical therapies. **Electroconvulsive therapy (ECT)** involves electric shock; it is used most often with severely depressed patients. **Psychosurgery** involves cutting connections between different parts of the brain; the **prefrontal lobotomy** is the best-known type. **Chemotherapy** is the use of drugs (antianxiety, antipsychotic, and antidepressant) to treat psychological disorders.

14. Determining if therapy works is a difficult task. The broadest answer is that it is helpful to most people with psychological disorders. The factors that determine therapy effectiveness are client type therapist's characteristics, the nature of the disorder, and therapy type. Some therapies are more effective with some types of disorders and with clients than with others. Because of this, many therapists adopt the **eclectic approach** which bases the choice of therapy technique on the demands of the individual case.

Key Terms

antianxiety drugs
antidepressant drugs
antipsychotic drugs
aversive conditioning
behavior therapies
biofeedback therapy
biomedical therapy
chemotherapy
clinical psychology
clinical social worker
community psychology
counseling and school psychology
deinstitutionalization
dream interpretation

drug therapy
eclectic approach
electroconvulsive therapy
encounter (sensitivity) group
family therapy
free association
Gestalt therapy
group therapy
halfway house
humanistic psychology
modeling
placebo effect
prefrontal lobotomy
psychiatric nurse

psychiatrist
psychoanalysis
psychoanalyst
psychotherapy
psychopharmacology
rational emotive therapy (RET)
specific therapy
systematic desensitization
T-group
token economy
tranquilizers
transference
transpersonal psychology
unconditional positive regard

THE SELF: FROM TOKYO TO TOPEKA, IT CHANGES

BY DANIEL GOLEMAN

While Western psychology assumes that human nature is the same everywhere, there are profound psychological differences from culture to culture, according to a growing body of evidence.

Of course, in many ways people are the same around the world, but psychotherapists are increasingly aware that in concentrating on similarities they have ignored many crucial differences.

Although psychotherapists have acknowledged the influence of ethnicity on therapy, they are now realizing just how drastically the psychological world of people growing up in Nairobi, Tokyo or Calcutta differs from that portrayed by Western theories.

Differences in child-rearing, family dynamics and social structure have psychological ramifications that may explain why some emotional problems occur in parts of the world but not in others. For example, agoraphobia, in which people are afraid to leave their homes, and anorexia, an obsessive desire to lose weight, occur only in Western countries.

And although some disorders, like schizophrenia, are found around the world, the symptoms are quite different in various cultures.

"I find our view of so-called common humanity to be overwhelmingly Western-centered," said Alan Roland, a psychoanalyst in New York City who has treated people in India and Japan. "The prevailing psychological maps we assume in the West to be universal simply do not apply to people in much of the world."

The movement to broaden the theories of Western psychology has gained momentum in recent years as more and more immigrants to the United States have come into psychotherapy.

"You just can't do psychotherapy with a person from Vietnam or El Salvador as you would with a Boston housewife," said Arthur Kleinman, a professor of anthropology and psychiatry at Harvard Medical School. "The ethnocentric arrogance of

Western psychotherapy is being challenged head on by the growing recognition of the problems in treating non-Western immigrants."

To remedy the fact that the training of psychotherapists rarely takes into account the importance of cultural differences, many universities have begun advanced courses for professionals on the topic.

One of the most extensive criticisms of Western psychology has been made by Dr. Roland in his book, "In Search of Self in India and Japan," published last year by Princeton University Press. Dr. Roland's analysis of patterns in India and Japan led him to conclude that many fundamental differences hinge on the Western emphasis on raising children to be independent, in contrast to the Eastern focus on cultivating an intense emotional closeness and sense of dependency.

During the first four or five years of life in many Asian cultures, for instance, children sleep with their mothers, are always in the company of a nurturing family member and are largely indulged in their whims. By contrast, American children are typically put in their own bedrooms and encouraged to establish autonomy—by going off to day care, for example.

"In India or Japan, the idea of making a young child sleep alone would be seen as a punishment," Dr. Roland said.

Around the age of 5, though, there is a "crackdown" on children in which they are no longer indulged, but are held to strict standards of behavior. "The crackdown is the central trauma of childhood," Dr. Roland said. "Children are scolded, shamed, physically punished, to make sure they fit themselves into the strict hierarchy of the culture."

"Compared to Americans, there's much less of a sense of an individual self among Asians," he added. "They experience themselves as far more embedded in a net of extremely close emotional relationships. They have what might be called a familial self, one that includes their close relationships in their own sense of who they are. This kind of self simply does not exist in the West to nearly the same degree."

The child's "family self" promotes the feeling that what shames the child shames the family, and so exerts a force toward instilling good behavior, Dr. Roland said.

The lack of privacy that typifies crowded Asian households is balanced by an inner preserve of unshared feelings, Dr. Roland said. "Along with this emotional enmeshment, people develop a private self, a strong inner boundary behind which all kinds of secret feelings and fantasies are kept," he added.

Personal relationships in such Asian countries tend to be both more subtle and more complex than those Westerners are used to.

"You expect others to sense what's going on in you without your having to say anything directly," Dr. Roland said. Because relationships such as marriage and work in these traditional cultures are typically for life, without the escape clause that Western social mobility offers, people expect a high degree of sensitivity from each other.

One way feelings of anger and hurt are handled in Asian cultures is by the development of a "spiritual self," Dr. Roland said, a dimension that is nurtured in India through ritual and meditation and in Japan largely through aesthetic pursuits like flower arranging and the tea ceremony.

The more fixed social hierarchies of Asian countries foster a complicated set of standards that often confuses Americans, Dr. Roland said. In contrast to the West, where people strive for an inner consistency, in Asia people are more comfortable with selves that vary according to the particular relationship.

"This may be the biggest area of East-West misunderstanding," he said. "In Asia, people may say entirely different things on the same subject to different people, depending on their relationship. To a Westerner, it seems hypocrisy, while to the Asian it is only proper behavior."

Maladies like agoraphobia and anorexia are found almost exclusively in the West or among Westernized people, but therapists can only speculate on what it is in Western culture that causes them.

Similarly researchers are puzzled about what it is in the cultures of

Misunderstandings Hinder Treatment

Many recent immigrants, particularly people from troubled areas of Southeast Asia and Central America, have severe psychological problems that American therapists may have trouble treating because of cultural differences, experts say.

For example, in a study of members of the Hmong tribe who fled Laos for the United States, Joseph Westermeyer, a psychiatrist and anthropologist at the University of Wisconsin, found that 43 percent suffered serious psychiatric disorders, more than twice the rate found among the general population in America.

Equally high rates of psychiatric problems have been found in other immigrant groups who have fled repression and civil wars in their countries, particularly in Southeast Asia and Central America.

But cultural misunderstandings can complicate treatment for these patients. For one thing, the concept of psychotherapy is foreign to most people from non-Western cultures. Many of these people do not understand why talking about their problems would be helpful.

Asians in America tend not to seek psychotherapy or to drop out sooner than others if they do, said Stanley Sue, a psychologist and director of the Center on Asian-American Mental Health at the University of California at Los Angeles.

"One major reason is the stigma in Asian cultures of having mental problems," Dr. Sue said. "It's a loss of face that reflects on your whole family."

Sometimes therapists confuse simple cultural differences with signs of problems. In some Hispanic cultures, for instance, people do not leave home until they are married, even if they are in their 30's, said Melvin Delgado, a professor at the Boston University School of Social Work. Therapists applying American cultural expectations might consider it a sign of "pathological dependence."

"If an Asian patient complains that his parents are demanding and restrictive, an American therapist might try making the patient more assertive, suggesting he talk back to his parents," Dr. Sue said. "It won't work. Therapists have to be careful about proposing solutions that clients from other cultures can't abide."

One technique Dr. Sue suggests is altering the first session, which typically is largely diagnostic, to offer patients a concrete experience that calms the patient's anxiety or clarifies confusion.

"That helps the client believe that talking about problems can help," Dr. Sue said.

Eastern Asia that promote the practice of "koro," in which men or women become panicked by the fear that their penis or nipples will retract into their body and kill them.

"There are some psychiatric disorders, like depression and schizophrenia, that are universal," Dr. Kleinman said. "But even among them, the power of culture to radically shape symptoms is profound."

"Take schizophrenia," he said. "The most interesting cross-cultural finding, other than the fact that it occurs everywhere, is that the patients in the poorest non-Western societies have the best outcomes. It may be because people in those societies have more tolerant attitudes, or stronger social ties that make people more supportive."

One major difference in depression, Dr. Kleinman said, is that people who do not live in Western countries report mostly physical symptoms, like backaches or loss of appetite, rather than emotional angst. That, too, bodes well for treatment. "In societies where there is little preoccupation with the emotional symptoms of depression, there are fewer complications in its course," Dr. Kleinman said.

The New York Times, March 7, 1989. Copyright © 1989 by the New York Times. Reprinted by permission.

Interpersonal Relations

16

The old saying "Here today, gone tomorrow" may have been written to describe rock singers. How many of the performers who were popular five or ten years ago are still around today? There is, however, one notable exception; in 1983, Mick Jagger and the Rolling Stones released their album *Undercover*, marking the group's twentieth year together. For a rock group to enjoy twenty years of popularity is a feat in itself, and it becomes even more amazing when you think about the scandalous life led by Jagger and the Rolling Stones!

The group had an innocent enough beginning. Michael Phillip Jagger grew up in a middle-class home in Kent, England. He was a bright kid whose only distinction was that he idolized American blues singers, especially Muddy Waters, Little Richard, Howlin' Wolf, and Chuck Berry. Although he did not have a great deal of musical talent, Mick, as he was known to his friends, formed a small band, Little Boy Blue and the Blue Boys, with some neighborhood kids.

In 1961, at the age of 18, Mick enrolled in the London School of Economics. One day, he sat down on the commuter train next to a tall quiet fellow who was on his way to Sudcup Art College. The boy, Keith Richards, noticed that Mick was carrying a stack of American blues records, and asked if Mick "liked that kind of music, too." The boys spent the trip talking about their common interests in music, and as a result, Mick invited Keith to join the Blue Boys. The heart of the Rolling Stones was formed.

Although England was not ready for the rhythm and blues sound, small "underground" R&B clubs were being established. While performing at one of these clubs the Blue Boys met Brian Jones. After joining the Blue Boys, Brian's first contribution was to suggest the group change its name to *Rolling Stones*, after a popular Muddy Waters's song. The Rolling Stones played in small clubs for the first couple of years, with limited success. During this time, a new group with the unlikely name *The Beatles* was making its impact felt throughout England.

Mick wanted to build on The Beatle's image but felt the Stones needed a manager to accomplish this. Most reputable managers turned Mick down because they felt that the group's style of music would not be accepted by the public. Finally, a fast-talking young Dutchman, Andrew Loog Oldham, persuaded the group to hire him even though he had almost no experience as a manager. What Oldham lacked in experience he made up for in motivation and dreams. Oldham saw his job as changing the musical tastes of the world.

Oldham's first task was to get the Stones a record contract. He approached Decca Records, which was reeling from its ill-fated decision a year earlier to turn down The Beatles. It wasn't hard for Oldham to persuade Decca Records to take a chance with the Stones, because as a former Decca employee stated, "Things got so bad [after turning down the Beatles] that if a boy with a guitar had just walked along Albert Embankment past our office, the whole A&R staff would have rushed out to sign him up (Norman, 1984,

p. 94). In June 1963 the Stones were ready to release their first record.

In order to ride the wave begun by The Beatles, the Stones gave up their crew cuts and sports jackets in favor of long hair and an odd assortment of clothing. Along with this change in appearance came a complete change in the image of the group. Brian Jones's background and stories of drugs and wild sex parties contributed to the Stones "bad guys" image. To make matters worse, many of the Stones' concerts ended in riots with people injured and property damaged.

One lingering question is whether or not Mick Jagger contributed willingly to these events. He incited concert crowds by refusing to start on time: The audience became frustrated waiting to see their idol, and their level of excitement became almost frantic. He adopted many of the sensual and suggestive moves of the popular black R&B singers James Brown and Chuck Berry, and used these to "turn on his audience." Jagger chose songs for the group to record. Their first big hit, (I Can't Get No) Satisfaction, dripped with sexual and drug overtones. Their music taunted and ridiculed societal norms. And, Jagger was busted for possessing drugs.

There was, however, another side to Mick, one that was not visible to the public. Mick tried to look after the other members of the Stones. For one, he was concerned about Brian Jones's growing drug habit. In one rather funny incident, Mick went to speak with Brian about seeking help for his drug habit. During his talk, Brian jumped up shouting, "I'll kill myself," and jumped from the window into a moat that surrounded the house. Mick, thinking Brian would drown, leapt into the moat to save him, only to find that the water was just four feet deep! As Brian laughed uncontrollably, Mick's good will turned to anger because he had ruined one of his best pairs of velvet pants. Eventually, it was Brian's drug habit that led Mick to drop him from the group in 1969.

As Mick's star began to rise, he was confronted with a number of difficult and tragic events. To begin, Marianne Faithful, his girlfriend, lost a baby in her seventh month of pregnancy. Both Mick and Marianne began using drugs, and Mick was busted for drug possession when police raided a party he attended. Brian Jones, who was dropped from the Stones, was found one morning lying in the bottom of his swimming pool. There is still a question whether his death was an accident, a suicide, or murder. The events surrounding these tragedies only fueled the hostility that people, especially Americans, felt toward the Stones. Speaking about their tour in the United States, Keith Richards stated, "I've never been hated by so many people I've never met as in Nebraska in the mid-sixties. Everyone looked at you with a look that could kill. You could tell they just wanted to beat the——out of you" (Norman, 1984, p. 125).

Even when Mick tried to change people's attitudes, his efforts backfired. At the end of one of their U.S. tours, Mick decided to give a free concert to show his appreciation to his fans. He was somehow persuaded to hire the Hell's Angels as security guards. During the performance, people in the audience began to strip and throw themselves at the stage, only to be forced back by the Angels. It was bedlam. The violence climaxed when one of the Angels stabbed a young man to death right in front of Mick Jagger. No one tried to help, and as the boy died the Stones played on. The newspapers had a field day accusing Mick Jagger and the Stones of callousness and insensitivity.

Life for Mick Jagger continued on its roller coaster run. He broke up with Marianne Faithful and married Bianca Pérez. Bianca never fit in with the Stones and the marriage ended in divorce. Stories of drugs and sex orgies still stalked the Stones. In 1990 Mick married Jerry Hall; he and Jerry have two children, a girl and a boy.

In 1989, the Rolling Stones toured the United States, extending their career into a third decade. The legend of the Rolling Stones lives on.

Mick Jagger and the Rolling Stones have been making headlines and music for over two decades. The public's response to Jagger has been influenced by stories of Jagger's attitudes, social relationships, and his life-style.

After completing this chapter, you should be able to:

Define and describe the domains of social psychology.

Describe our biases for attributing people's actions to internal or external causes and discuss the biases that can come into play when we make attributions.

Describe the potential influence of self-fulfilling prophecy and provide an example.

Discuss how we make attributions about ourselves and compare this process with that used in person perception.

Understand the influence of culture on self and other attributions.

Discuss the components of attitudes and the influences that help us to develop particular attitudes.

Discuss the difficulty in changing attitudes and describe the ways in which attitudes are changed.

Describe and provide an example of cognitive dissonance.

Discuss the elements of attraction.

Elaborate about the decision to help or not to help in various situations.

The Scope and History of Social Psychology

Whether we see Mick Jagger as a villain or a hero, it is easy to separate his life from our own. He lives in the "fast lane" with lots of money, exotic vacations, and famous friends. He seems so different from us; yet is he really that different? Like each of us, he must decide what to eat for breakfast, what type of automobile to buy, and what to wear to a party. Like each of us, he thinks about what people around him are "really like." And like each of us, he makes friends and develops interpersonal relationships. In the end, Mick Jagger, like each of us, is a unique individual, and like each of us he shares much in common with other people. Thus we can focus either on his uniqueness or on how he is much like other people.

This difference in focus helps us illustrate the differences between the approach taken by personality psychology (Chapter 13) and social psychology. As we already know, personality psychology focuses on individual differences between people. It centers on the single individual, attempts to explain how that person is unique, and predicts that person's behavior in a variety of situations. If we used the personality approach to understand Mick Jagger, we would examine his behavior across settings and time.

Social psychology, on the other hand, focuses more on the common ground that exists between people. It would argue that all of us develop attitudes, form impressions of others, love, hate, and belong to groups. We are social beings and as a result much of our behavior is influenced by other people. Thus, instead of studying a single individual across time, social psychology studies how a variety of people act in a particular situation. Summing up, we can define **social psychology** as the area of psychology that uses scientific methods to "understand and explain how the thought, feeling, and behavior of individuals are influenced by the actual, imagined, or implied presence of others" (Allport, 1985, p. 3).

Social psychology
Scientific study of the ways in which the thoughts, feelings, and behavior of individuals are influenced by the actual, imagined, or implied presence of others; the scientific study of the way most people act most of the time.

619

The Field of Social Psychology

Social psychology is a relatively young branch of psychology. In fact, it was once estimated that 90 percent of all social psychologists who ever lived were alive in 1974 (Cartwright, 1979). Until recently, social psychology was largely confined to the United States, although in the last 20 years there has been explosive growth in the field, especially in Europe, South America, and Japan (Jones, 1985; Graumann, 1988). As you will see, social psychology, probably more than other fields in psychology, has been dramatically influenced by social concerns and world events; many of its topics of study have been determined by "issues of the day" (Parker, 1989). For this reason, it is difficult to tie a neat bow around the field and say "This is what social psychologists study." In fact, one investigator referred to social psychology as "a large circus tent, where a lot of acts are going on simultaneously, and the acts occasionally cross, intermingle, and overlap" (Aronson, 1989).

Although we can trace the first social psychology experiment to 1897, the field as we know it today was not established until the 1930s. Kurt Lewin, who emigrated to the United States from Hitler's Germany in 1933, was fascinated by the influence that people have on each other. He felt that almost every human behavior, from our beliefs to what we like to eat, is in some way influenced by other people. With World War II raging, Lewin was given the opportunity not only to test his views but to put them to use in the war effort. He conducted a number of experiments showing how people were influenced by others. In one he demonstrated that what housewives served their families for dinner could be influenced by the groups to which they belonged (Lewin, 1943). In another he showed that a democratic style of leadership created a better work climate than an autocratic style. During this period another group of social psychologists, who were also interested in influence, assembled at Yale University. Using a national concern about propaganda as their starting point, this group carefully analyzed communications that were effective in changing people's attitudes. They identified three parts of the communication process (communicator, message, audience) and studied the role of each. Their work established social psychology's interest in the area of attitude change.

In the mid 1950s, Leon Festinger captured the interest of social psychologists by introducing his theory of *cognitive dissonance*. Festinger was interested in the general issue of how people use social situations to learn about themselves. As we will see later in this chapter, dissonance theory focuses on the relationship between behavior and attitudes; Festinger argues that our behavior affects our attitudes.

Spurred on by national concerns with civil rights and the Vietnam War, social psychologists placed greater emphasis on studying the relationships between people and groups in the 1960s and 1970s. The field expanded as exciting new research was conducted in such areas as interpersonal relationships (attraction, aggression, love, conflict), group dynamics (Chapter 17), intergroup relations (Chapter 17), helping, and impression formation. The research and theories of this period also set the groundwork for social psychology in the 1980s and 1990s. Psychologists realized that we are not simply manipulated by the environment and then automatically respond to events and other people. Instead, we process, interpret, and add our own explanation to events, and our behavior is as much affected by our interpretation as it is by the event itself. For example, let's assume that you and a friend attend a Rolling Stones concert. You are interested in the influence that the blues performers had on today's rock stars while your friend is very concerned with the increased use of drugs in today's society. Although you and your friend see the same concert, each of you has a different set of reactions to and interpretations of Mick Jagger's

Kurt Lewin is generally recognized as the founder of modern social psychology. He urged the development of theory, the use of experimental methods to test hypotheses, and the combination of applied and theoretical social psychology.

Leon Festinger developed cognitive dissonance theory which captured the interest of social psychologists during the 1950s and 1960s. Festinger's work anticipated the present-day focus on cognitive social psychology.

wild behavior. Today's emphasis on *cognitive social psychology* (Rowe, 1987) examines how people process information and how this processing affects their behavior in social situations.

Since its inception, social psychology has been concerned with both developing theories about human behavior and applying these theories to better understand and deal with social issues. Social psychology has applications in areas such as prejudice, international relations, terrorism and brainwashing, women's issues, the legal process, business and industry, advertising, the environment, and sports, to name a few. In this chapter we will examine how social psychology can help us to better understand our relationships with other people: how we determine what other people are like, how we are influenced by them, and why we are attracted to and offer help to some people in some situations. In Chapter 17, our attention will be more focused on our interaction with others in groups.

Perceiving and Evaluating Others

As we wrote this chapter, we kept asking ourselves, "What is Mick Jagger really like?" Both of us have been to Rolling Stones concerts, read newspaper stories about Jagger, seen him in television interviews, and read books about the Stones. As we discussed Jagger, our views of him often changed. At times we decided that Jagger really cared only about himself, used others for his advantage, and tried to cash in on the music craze begun by the Beatles. Other times, we saw Jagger as a sensitive person who was easily hurt by others and who played a "wild" role as a form of self-protection; we felt that he was dedicated to introducing a new music form to the world. In yet a third impression we saw Mick Jagger as a pawn who was used by managers, and had little direction of his own.

The rules that people follow and the mistakes they make in forming impressions constitute a fascinating area of study. Understanding these rules and biases not only helps us see how we get to know others, but also shows how people decide what we are like.

In attempting to bring the work on impression formation together, we should keep in mind two models of the way people process information about their world. One model (attribution theories) views people as scientists who take observable events and attempt to determine the causes behind them. The second model (social cognition) sees people as having preconceived notions and expectations that they attempt to support. Let us examine the attribution process and the biases associated with it before we turn to the social cognition model.

The Attribution Process

The **attribution model** suggests that we act like scientists in our everyday world. We observe behaviors and attempt to determine whether they are caused by the actor or the environment. If we decide that the actor was responsible, we ask what the behavior tells us about that actor. In taking this step we often attribute specific traits or characteristics to the actor. In other words, attribution involves determining the causes of behavior and then deciding what the behavior tells us about the actor.

Situations versus Personal Traits. One of the first objectives in getting to know people is to figure out what causes their actions. Did they act because of some inner need, attitude, or ability (a *disposition*)? Or did outside events or *situations* cause their behavior? If we think there is

Attribution
Process of inferring characterisitcs of people from their observable behavior; a way of explaining the behavior of others.

A favorite ploy of many children is to convince their parents that their naughty behavior was caused by external events: "It wasn't my fault." Parents, on the other hand, use information about distinctiveness, consistency, and the response of others to make attributions about their children.

an internal (dispositional) cause, then we learn something about that particular person. However, if we decide that there is an external (situational) cause, then we learn about the situation the person is in, but not about the person's characteristics.

Harold Kelley (1967) uses the example of seeing a woman, Mary, laugh while watching a movie. We have two choices in deciding what caused Mary's laughter: (1) it could be caused by Mary herself (she has a good sense of humor; she laughs at anything and everything); or (2) it could result from the situation Mary is in (the movie is so funny that anyone who saw it would laugh).

According to Kelley, we base our decision on three elements: *distinctiveness*, *consensus* and *consistency*.

1. How *distinctive* is the behavior? Does Mary respond this way to all such situations (all movies) or only to this particular situation (this movie)? If Mary laughs only at this movie, it is a funny movie. If Mary laughs at most movies, however, we are more likely to decide that the behavior is caused by a personal characteristic of Mary's.

2. How do *other people respond* to the same situation (consensus)? If everyone responds in the same way to an event, we assume that the behavior is caused by the event. But if Mary is the only person responding this way to this particular event, we assume her behavior is caused by something in her.

3. How *consistent* is the person's behavior? Does Mary laugh every time she sees this movie? If there is no consistency in her behavior, then we can't really infer anything about her from this behavior.

Assigning Traits to Individuals. Mick Jagger felt that Brian Jones's drug habit was destroying the group. After giving the situation a great deal of thought, Mick told Brian that he could no longer perform with the Stones. Not long afterward, Brian was found dead at the bottom of his swimming pool. Some people suggested that Mick had driven Brian to commit suicide; that Mick was a cruel and heartless person. Others argued that Jagger's primary concern was for Brian's health. Perhaps Mick hoped that not letting Brian play with the Stones would shock him into seeking help for his drug problem.

Both explanations assign traits to Mick. Both explanations are based on the same behavior (Mick firing Brian), and both agree that Mick was indeed responsible for firing Brian (dispositionally caused behavior). Yet the explanations assign different traits to Mick as a result of his actions. This example raises the question of how we move from observing behaviors to assigning specific traits to people.

According to Jones and Davis (1965), people first ask themselves if the actor knew what the effects of his or her actions would be. Did Mick know that Brian Jones might die as the result of being fired from the Rolling Stones? The next question people ask is whether the actor had the ability to bring about the outcome. In this case, we might agree that Mick had the ability to fire Brian, but did he have the ability to drive Brian further into drugs and possible suicide? Next, we must ask what effects the actor intended to result from his or her action. Did Mick intend for his actions to result in Brian's death or did he want his actions to result in Brian getting treatment?

Before making the attribution, we take one more step: We attempt to determine if there are other possible reasons for the behavior. For example, did the situation play a role? Specifically in the case of Mick's firing of Brian, did the flagging popularity of the Rolling Stones cause Mick's actions? If so, we discount or subtract the influence of the situation and moderate out attributions (Trope, Cohen, & Moza, 1988).

In this scene, the group of girls is ignoring the outsider. Before we decide that the group members are rude, we must determine that they knew the effects of their behavior, had the ability to exclude the outsider, and intended to exclude her and hurt her feelings.

Based on the information we have gathered about the *knowledge*, *ability*, and *intention* of the actor, we then assign an underlying trait or disposition. In this case, if we decide that Mick was a cruel person, we could then expect him to act uncaringly in other situations. If we believe, however, that Mick did not intend for harm to come to Brian, we will withhold assigning any trait to him as a result of Brian's death. Our expectations might lead us to interpret his future behavior as fitting our view of him. Although this seems like a complicated process, we make attributions automatically and we are generally unaware of the steps we use to assign traits.

As we pointed out, the ultimate aim of the attribution process is to explain other people's behavior. Once we can do this, we can better predict their future actions. Therefore, assigning a trait to a person not only explains his or her present behavior but also predicts future behavior.

Tendencies and Biases in Attribution

The attribution model is very rational. If we were to build a robot to make attributions, we would program it to follow exactly these principles. But although the result might be a machine that spits out very logical inferences, it would not duplicate the attributions made by people. And though we might like to consider ourselves as rational, logical human beings, we know that we are not always completely rational and unemotional. Just as our feelings and biases affect how we act, they also influence how we make attributions about other people. Since these biases are very interesting and revealing, let us quickly examine how some of them affect our attributions.

Hedonic Relevance. Consider this situation: You see a young man break into the front of a long line of people waiting to purchase the few remaining tickets to a Rolling Stones concert. If you were merely passing by, you might see this action as somewhat rude, but you might also try to explain it by saying that other people in the line were "saving his place." However, if you were one of the people in line, your attribution would probably not be so kind; you would probably see this man as terribly rude and uncaring. The difference in the two cases is that in the first situation the behavior did not directly affect you, whereas in the second situation it did. **Hedonic relevance** refers to the degree to which an actor's behavior is rewarding or costly to the observer.

Hedonic relevance influences attributions in two ways. First, it increases the likelihood that a person's behavior will be seen as representing an underlying trait or disposition. In our example this means that the person waiting in line would be more likely to attribute a trait to the line-breaker than would the passerby. The second consequence of hedonic relevance is that it increases the extremity of the evaluation. Although the passerby may see the line-breaker as somewhat rude, the person waiting in line would see this same man as very rude. The important point to remember in this example is that the behavior of the person is exactly the same in both cases. Therefore, a completely rational attribution should not take into account whether or not the observer was affected by it.

Overemphasizing Behavior/Underemphasizing Context. Suppose that your professor assigns you to argue in a debate the position that the tuition in your school should be raised so high that only the rich can afford it. You want to do well in the course so you comply with the assignment. Later on you may be surprised to find that a number of your classmates believe that you truly feel that higher education should be available only to the rich. In this case, your classmates are attributing an attitude to you solely on the basis of your behavior; they have failed to give sufficient weight to the situation in which your behavior occurred. A truly accurate attributor would carefully review both the behavior and the context in which it took place. Because the tendency to base attributions solely on behavior without considering the situation is so common, it is often referred to as the **fundamental attribution error** (Ross, 1977). Unfortunately, the tendency to overemphasize behavior and underemphasize context occurs in a wide variety of situations. We are especially likely to make the fundamental attribution error when we are busy (Gilbert, Pelham, & Krull, 1988) or distracted (Baumeister, Hutton, & Tice, 1989). Finally, it has been suggested that one reason we ignore situational factors is that such factors are so blatant (Jones, 1990). Like a detective trying to solve a mystery, we often become so preoccupied with uncovering the complex reasons that we ignore the obvious. "As it stands, the question of how naive attributors perceive situational constraint is one of the most important but least understood aspects of interpersonal perception" (Jones, 1990, p. 130).

Looking Out or Looking in: Actor-Observer Differences. Jones and Nisbett (1972) report that there is a general tendency for people to view the behavior of others as being caused by internal traits, while they see their own behavior as being determined by the situation they are in. Two possible reasons have been suggested to explain this bias. One reason is that people have more information about themselves than they do about others (Monson & Snyder, 1977). In other words, we know that we tend to behave differently in different situations. However, when we do not know the history of other people, we may assume that their behavior is less varied than our own and therefore caused by their personal traits.

Another reason has to do with the *salience* of information. (What is salient in a situation would be what is outstanding or what we focus on.) When we observe other people acting, our attention is focused on them and they become the most central piece of information. However, when we act, our attention is focused on the environment. There is a great deal of evidence that we base our attributions on the most salient information in a setting. In one study, for example, experimenters told subjects to focus their attention on one member of a pair during a conversation (Taylor

Hedonic relevance
Refers to the degree to which an actor's behavior is rewarding or costly to the observer.

Fundamental attribution error
The tendency to base attributions solely on behavior without considering the possible influence of the situation.

& Fiske, 1975). Subjects rated the member on whom they had focused as being the person who directed the flow of conversation.

Another interesting effect has been recently uncovered (Gilbert et al., 1987). These investigators examined people who either interacted with the target person or who passively observed that person's behavior. They found that the passive perceivers attributed behavior to the actor's dispositions, such as we discussed earlier. However, the perceivers who were involved in the interaction felt that they were the cause of many of the actor's behaviors. It seems, therefore, that we have two goals in making attributions: to explain the actor's actions and to enhance our power in social situations. If we simply observe behavior, we focus our attention on the actor and see his or her behavior as resulting from traits or dispositions. However, if we are involved in the behavior, we inflate our influence by believing that we had some responsibility for the behavior of others.

Order Effects: When We Know Affects What We Know

Writing the opening story for this chapter proved an interesting experience for us. Both of us read Philip Norman's book on Mick Jagger and the Rolling Stones. Yet when we began to write the chapter opening, we each had a very different view of Mick Jagger. When we discussed our differing views, we found that one of us had read the book's prologue while the other had begun the book with the first chapter. The prologue describes how at the Stones' Philadelphia concert in 1981 Jagger purposefully kept the audience waiting for four hours to increase excitement. It also mentions the drug problems and wild life lived by the Stones. The first chapter describes Mick's childhood as a bright promising student at Wentworth Count Primary School. One of his teachers is quoted as saying, "If I remember him at all, it's running in from the playground with both knees grazed and a great big smile on his face" (Norman, 1984, p. 41). So although both of us eventually read the same information about Mick Jagger, the order in which we read this information was different. Could this have affected the final picture that each of us formed of Mick Jagger?

If we followed strictly logical rules in making attributions, the order in which we receive information would make no difference in our final impression. However, the research suggests that we do not follow the rules of logic when making attributions. In general, the first information we receive has greater influence than later information; in other words, there is a **primacy effect** influencing our attributions. In order to demonstrate this effect, consider the following two descriptions:

Person A	Person B
intelligent	envious
industrious	stubborn
impulsive	critical
critical	impulsive
stubborn	industrious
envious	intelligent

What is the general impression you get of these two people? Solomon Asch (1946) gave the descriptions to subjects and asked them to give their impression of the person described. Despite the fact that the information is the same in both lists, people gave Person A a more positive rating than Person B. As you can see, the only difference in the two lists is that the positive traits come first in Person A's description, while they come last in the list for Person B.

Primacy effect
In impression formation, the fact that people tend to base their impressions on what they hear first.

First impressions are important because they often set the direction for future interactions. First impressions guide our behavior and we often interpret later behavior to fit our first impressions.

In general, primacy effects are strongest when we are judging stable characteristics such as personality or intelligence. Clearly the message here is that if you want someone to form a good impression of you, it is most important that your first encounter be the best. The first information people receive about you will have the strongest (but not the only) influence on their overall impression.

There are a number of explanations for the primacy effect (Asch & Zukier, 1984). One suggests that we form an impression on the basis of the first information we receive and then interpret later information to fit this impression. For example, if we decide that a person is intelligent, we may interpret "critical" as meaning thoughtful or thorough. However, if we decide the person is envious, we may interpret "critical" to mean nasty or negative. Looking at performance, if a person does well on an early test and we decide he or she is intelligent, we may explain away later poor performance as being due to the person's temporary state (a sleepless night before the test) or to the environment (the testing room was hot and noisy). Similarly, if we decide that a person is unintelligent on the basis of early performance, later good performance can be explained away as luck. In each of these cases, we can maintain our first impressions by the way we interpret later information.

The Social Cognition Model: The Influence of Self on Attributions

As we have seen, the attribution model presents a picture of people carefully sifting through information (although often using biased rules) before arriving at a position (attribution). The **social cognition model** argues that people have **schemas,** or preconceived notions about how their social world works (Fiske & Taylor, 1984). We have schemas about individuals (such as Mick Jagger), groups (such as rock stars), and events (such as rock concerts). Our schemas affect (1) what we pay attention to, (2) what we remember, and (3) what we retrieve from our memories. Once a schema is formed, we tend to process information in a way that supports that schema. We interpret events to fit our schema, and we are more likely to remember information that supports our schema than to remember information that refutes it (Holtgraves, Srull, & Socall, 1989). For example, if you have a schema that rock stars are drug abusers, you will be more likely to remember that Mick Jagger used drugs than that he was the one who set up the rule that Stones members would be fired if they used drugs. According to the social cognition position, this process is automatic. That is, we don't recall a schema and then intentionally try to support it. Rather, schemas are always present in our minds, guiding the way we deal with our world.

In order to show how schemas influence our interpretation of events and people, investigators showed students a photograph of "Kurt Walden" and asked them to rate his facial expression (Rothbart & Birrell, 1977). Some students were told that Walden was a Nazi Gestapo leader who carried out cruel experiments during World War II. Others were told he was a leader of the anti-Nazi underground movement and that he saved thousands of Jews. Subjects who believed Walden was a Nazi rated his facial expression as hard, cruel, and frowning, whereas students who believed he had saved lives rated his face as warm and kindly. Thus students' preconceived notions about a Nazi leader and an anti-Nazi leader affected how they viewed his photograph.

The attribution and social cognition models suggest two of the ways in which we process information and form impressions of others. Both

Social cognition model
Belief that people have schemata, or preconceived notions about how their social world works; these schemata influence the way people interpret events and even the information they remember; once formed, information is processed in a way that tends to support the schema.
Schema (plural, **schemata**)
Term used by Piaget to refer to a mental structure that organizes responses to experiences.

models are useful in helping us to understand this complex process and both identify some interesting biases and tendencies in the way we perceive our world. The models raise some points that are important to remember. First, we do not intentionally misrepresent our world or the people in it. We call it as we see it, but the way we see it may not be completely accurate. Second, we generally believe that our perceptions reflect reality. We rarely take into account a possible bias in our own perceptions, though we have little trouble believing that people whose perceptions do not agree with ours are biased. Third, there is a **false consensus effect** underlying our perceptions; we tend to overestimate the number of people who make the same inferences and hold the same opinions as we do (Goethals, 1986). Finally, despite the problems associated with these processes, they are necessary if we are to function in our world. We are bombarded with too much information every day to remember and store it all. We must organize it and choose what is important. The assignment of traits or dispositions and the development of schemas help us in this necessary task.

Getting What We Expect:
The Self-Fulfilling Prophecy

One of the saddest incidents associated with the Rolling Stones was the drug addiction and eventual downfall of Marianne Faithful. A picture of innocence when she first met Mick Jagger, Marianne presented to the public an image of "A convent girl singing sweetly and shyly, with high walls and no sex" (Norman, 1984, p. 135). However, when she began spending time with Mick Jagger, people changed their views of her. They believed she was a swinger and a drug addict: "People always assumed I was already a drug addict when I was with Mick—but I wasn't" (p. 309). These assumptions led some people to treat Marianne as if she were a drug addict; police and customs officials routinely searched her belongings for drugs and raided parties she attended. As her romance with Mick began to break up, Marianne adopted the role many had prepared for her: She became a heroin addict and attempted suicide. We can only wonder what role people's expectations played in setting the eventual course of Marianne's life.

Research, does present a convincing case that our expectations about people and events may indeed set the stage for having these expectations fulfilled. Rosenthal and Jacobson (1968b) offered a dramatic example of how the self-fulfilling prophecy may intrude into the classroom. These investigators told elementary-school teachers that tests had indicated that some of their students could be expected to outperform other students. These "high achievers" were clearly identified to the teachers. In fact, no tests had been given; these "high achievers" had simply been chosen at random. At the end of the school year, the students' IQs were measured. As can be seen from Figure 16–1, the "high achievers" outperformed the other students in the classroom—despite the fact that there were no real differences in the students' abilities. The only difference was the expectations of the teachers.

A review of 135 studies showing the **self-fulfilling prophecy** gives a picture of how the process occurs (Harris & Rosenthal, 1985). Our expectations lead us to create a climate that encourages the expected behavior; studies revealed that teachers acted warmly (verbally and nonverbally) toward the high-expectancy students and they offered these students extra encouragement. We give positive feedback when our expectations are fulfilled; thus, teachers gave more specific and informative feedback to the high-expectancy students. We manage our input to create conditions sup-

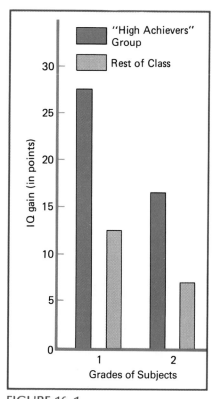

FIGURE 16–1

In this study, the teacher's expectations about students' ability created a self-fulfilling prophecy and led to the "high achievers" performing better.

False consensus effect
The tendency to overestimate the number of people who make the same inferences and hold the same opinions as we do.
Self-fulfilling prophecy
Expectation that leads one to behave in ways that will cause that expectation to come about.

portive of our expectations; thus the teachers gave the high-expectancy students more material and more challenging tasks to perform. Finally, we control the *output* situations so that our expectations will be fulfilled; in the classroom, the teachers provided the high-expectancy students with more opportunities to respond. We also learned from this research that we are unaware of the lengths to which we go to set the stage for the self-fulfilling prophecy. We believe that we are merely observing the behavior of the target, when, in fact, we are carefully guiding that behavior (Jones, 1990).

For the most part, when we speak of the self-fulfilling prophecy, we are referring to a situation where the observer's expectations influence the actor's *behaviors,* rather than simply biasing the observer's *perceptions* (Jussim, 1991).

The self-fulfilling prophecy is found in a variety of situations outside the classroom (Miller & Turnbull, 1986). Negotiators who expect their opponent to be aggressive and difficult direct their own behavior to bring out the expected tendencies in the opponent. Even students who expect their professor to be cold and difficult set the stage to have their worst fears (and expectations) realized. Most disturbing of all is that fact that nations may ignite the sparks of war because they expect another nation to be hostile and aggressive. Numerous writers (e.g., Markey, 1985) have argued that our expectation that the Russians will start a nuclear war leads us to increase our stockpile of nuclear weapons. Seeing us increase our arms leads the Russians to build more weapons. This arms race, fueled by the expectations of each side, draws us closer to the self-fulfilling prophecy of a nuclear war.

Knowing Ourselves

Our previous discussion focused on how we determine what other people are like. We saw some of the cognition work that we might go through to develop an image of Mick Jagger. Now let us briefly ask how we learn about ourselves—how we know our attitudes, abilities, likes, and dislikes. We examined the process that we go through in identifying our emotions in Chapter 12. Here we will expand on that discussion.

Stop for a minute and ask yourself how you know what your attitudes or abilities are. It might surprise you to learn that we often apply the same attribution process to understanding ourselves that we use to learn about others. Investigators suggest that we determine our own attitudes by reviewing our behavior and the situation in which that behavior occurred (Bem 1972; Goethals, Messick, & Allison, 1990). For example, if you are asked your opinion of Saddam Hussein, you might review your past behavior regarding Hussein. You might recall the times you made angry comments about him and questioned his sanity. In making this review, you will also notice that no one was forcing you to take these positions. On the basis of your actions and the situations under which these actions occurred, you will conclude that you don't care much for Hussein. Likewise, if you are asked how well you play tennis, you will review the folks you beat (and those who beat you) and then attribute an ability to yourself.

Just as your attributions about others are tinged with preset biases, your attributions about yourself are also often biased. One such bias is known as **egocentricity.** We tend to exaggerate the importance of our contributions in shaping events. One interesting study found that both husbands and wives estimated that they did about 70 percent of the household chores (Ross & Sicoly, 1979). Because of this bias, we often make more extreme attributions about ourselves than the situation warrants. A

Egocentricity
The tendency to exaggerate the role of one's personal contributions in shaping events.

CULTURE: The Unseen Hand Guiding Our Perceptions of Self and Others

Early in this chapter, we pointed out that social psychology is largely a product of the United States. Therefore, many of the theories and results of studies must be examined with this point in mind. Without conducting research in many cultures and in many lands, we cannot know whether our research is teaching us about people in general or about Americans. Fortunately, social psychologists are sensitive to this issue, so cross-cultural research (studies examining similar issues in different cultures) is becoming increasingly common (Brislin, 1990; Bond, 1988; Triandis, 1989). The culture in which we live has a profound influence on a wide range of our behaviors. One of the more interesting influences involves our self-image and perceptions of others.

According to a number of investigators, people in Western cultures such as the United States tend to view the individual as "independent, self-contained, and autonomous" (Markus & Kitayama, 1991). They see the individual's behavior as being guided by internal attributes such as traits, abilities, motives, and values. The focus of Western cultures is on individualism (Triandis, 1989, 1990). People desire to be individually recognized for their achievements and contributions.

This view greatly contrasts with that held by people in Eastern cultures such as China, Japan, and Thailand. The Eastern viewpoint is that the self is *interdependent* with the surrounding context. Therefore, the individual can only be conceived of as he or she relates to others, such as friends and family, and to the environment, such as the village.

Individuals in Eastern societies take a collectivistic view. Their desire is to belong, to fit in. They stress group goals and group actions, and they shrink from any individual recognition that separates them from their family or group.

These different approaches have wide-ranging implications for individual and interpersonal perceptions. Taking the matter of the self first, the Western focus on an independent self motivates people to strive for internal consistency (Miller, 1984). For example, Westerners strongly desire to act consistently over time and to ensure that their attitudes match their personal behavior. Individuals strive for "self-expression" and reaching their "full potential" (Sampson, 1988, 1989). The Eastern view gives rise to very different self behavior. Since Easterners wish to remain in harmony with their surroundings, they put less stress on internal consistency; rather, their focus is on acting as the situation dictates. Because situations change, they feel no discomfort in acting one way (for example, friendly) under one set of conditions and the opposite way (unfriendly) under a different set of conditions. Where Westerners strive for harmony with the self, Easterners strive for harmony with the situation.

These cultural views have a distinct influence on the attributions one makes about the behavior of others. People in Western cultures attempt to discount or eliminate the influence of situational factors on behavior. They are prone to making the fundamental attribution error, which is deciding that the observed behavior is the result of underlying traits, while

ignoring or diminishing the role of situational factors as the cause of the behavior. People in Eastern cultures are less prone to assign traits to others and more likely to describe others by their behavior: "He acts friendly when he meets people he likes" rather than "He is a friendly person" (Zebrowitz-McArthur, 1988). Because of this focus, people in Eastern cultures are less likely to make the fundamental attribution error (Markus & Kitayama, 1991). In an interesting study, Indian Hindus and North Americans were asked to explain deviant behaviors that occurred in several incidents that were described to them (Miller, 1984). One of the incidents involved a motorcycle accident in which the passenger was badly hurt. The driver, an attorney, took the injured passenger to the hospital and left him in the waiting room, then hurried off to court without consulting a physician. The passenger later died. In explaining the incident, 36 percent of the responses from North Americans involved traits of the attorney (irresponsible, success-oriented) and 17 percent referred to situational factors (need to deal with important court case). In contrast, only 15 percent of the explanations from the Indian subjects referenced traits, while 32 percent cited situational factors.

Clearly, our culture influences how we view ourselves and the attributions we make about other people. This point should be kept in mind when you consider any research involving human behavior. You may also want to remember this point when you read about behaviors of people in other cultures that appear irrational or illogical to you.

---

second bias is that we desire to develop the best possible image of ourselves. In order to do this, we tend to overestimate our role in creating good or successful outcomes, and underestimate our contribution to bad events. For example, women taking part in a study were asked to teach mathematics to 9-year-old boys. Some of the pupils did very well, while others did poorly. When asked to explain their pupils' behavior, the women tended to believe that they were good teachers when a boy did well, but they blamed a poor performance on the student himself (Johnson, Feigenbaum, & Weiby, 1964).

Finally, once we make attributions about ourselves, those attributions are very resistant to change. We "protect" our self-image by interacting with people who will confirm that image and by engaging in behaviors that confirm that image. For example, subjects who stated in public that they were exercisers tended to bolster this image by associating with other exercisers, recalling information about their own exercise activities, and actually exercising more than subjects who were not told to state their self-image (Kendzierski, 1990).

The points to remember here are that we do make attributions about ourselves by examining our past behavior and the situations under which that behavior occurred, and, as when making attributions about others, our self-attributions are often biased by predetermined tendencies (see Highlight, Culture: The Unseen Hand Guiding Our Perceptions of Self and Others).

Our Beliefs and Attitudes

One cannot talk about Mick Jagger and the Rolling Stones without also talking about drugs. The Stones' rise to fame occurred about the same time that the recreational use of hard drugs became recognized as a world-wide problem. The Stones were often linked to drugs; various members of the group, including Mick, were busted and jailed for drug possession. The irony of this situation was that Mick Jagger held very negative attitudes about drugs: "Anyone who knew Jagger knew that his attitude toward drugs was as coy and cautious as to women, hairdressers, clothes, and the color of his cars . . . (Norman, 1984, p. 196)." Yet despite this attitude, Mick did at times use drugs.

Whether we discuss Mick Jagger and drugs or a friend's particular views on politics, abortion, or television preachers, our discussion will certainly include a reference to attitudes and beliefs. Although we "know" what we mean when we talk about attitudes, we might be hard pressed to put into words what we mean by the concept **attitude**. Most investigators, however, view attitudes as *learned, relatively enduring feelings about objects, events, or issues* (McGuire, 1985). It is generally agreed that attitudes have three components.

1. The first is *evaluation*; that is, attitudes place a positive or negative meaning on the object or event in question. For example, your opinion about drug use probably includes a good or bad component.

2. Attitudes have a *belief* component. Beliefs are statements that express a relationship between events or objects. For example, you might believe that drug use leads to violence or crime.

3. The third component is *action*. Attitudes often describe how people should act toward an object or event. If you hold a negative attitude toward drug use, you might well avoid people who use drugs or support severe punishment of drug users and pushers.

Recently, some researchers have suggested that there may also be a physiological component to our attitudes (Cacioppo, Martzke, Petty, & Tassinary 1988; Cacioppo & Petty, 1986). They point out that portions of our face show greater neural activity when happy, and other portions show increased activity when we are sad. As we discussed in Chapter 2,

Attitudes
Learned, relatively enduring feelings about objects, events, or issues.

our neurons receive electrical impulses and these impulses can be measured. These investigators have reported some success in determining people's attitudes toward objects and events by measuring neural activity in facial muscles. Imagine the diabolical possibilities should this technique prove accurate; you could determine what your friends and enemies truly believed by measuring the neural activity in their facial muscles!

The Development of Attitudes

Where do attitudes come from? Clearly we are not born with attitudes. And just as clearly, we all have attitudes toward people and events with which we have had no experience. For example, most of us have attitudes toward the Russians; but few of us have been to Russia or met a single Russian. Where, then, do our attitudes come from?

One approach to answering this question has been to focus on the type of information we base our attitudes on (Zanna & Rempel, 1988). According to this view, attitudes can be based on factual information, information about our emotions or "gut reactions" to issues and objects, or information about our past behavior. A second way to answer this question is to examine the sources that help form our attitudes. Before we examine this approach, note that because our attitudes are influenced by multiple sources, we often hold attitudes that are different from—and in some cases, even conflict with—each other (Olson & Zanna, 1991). And as we will see, we often expend considerable psychological energy attempting to make our attitudes more internally consistent.

Parents. Parents influence their children's attitudes in two ways (Worchel, Cooper, & Goethals, 1991). First, they use rewards and punishments. Children who voice the "right" attitudes are likely to get praise and smiles, whereas children who express the "wrong" attitudes are likely to be greeted with frowns and scolding. Parents are especially powerful

Parents strongly influence their children's attitudes because parents control rewards and punishments, and children view their parents as being powerful and correct. Parents also control the situations and information that will be available to their children.

sources of influence for young children because they have almost total control over the rewards and punishments in their children's world. Second, parents are able to control the information that reaches their children. Many parents decide which television programs and books their children will watch and read.

Parental influence on attitudes is strong and lasting. There are several reasons for this. One is that children tend to believe their parents; they see them as the best and smartest people in the world. A second reason is that it's much easier to create new attitudes than it is to change old ones. Parents in this sense are in at the start; because they help their children form attitudes to begin with, they don't have to change their preexisting ones. Finally, attitudes formed in one's early years tend to persist because people tend to seek out information that supports their attitudes and ignore information that conflicts with them. (Recall our discussion of the self-fulfilling prophecy.)

Peers. When children start school, they begin to spend more time with peers in the classroom, on the playground, and in other formal and informal groups. These peers supply the child with new information and present different ways to look at issues. This in itself would influence the child's attitudes. There is, however, another way that peers shape attitudes, and that is with the threat of rejection. Children quickly learn that the way to be accepted by other children is to act and believe as they do. Both children and adults often adopt the attitudes of their peers because they fear rejection if they do not (see Chapter 17). Not only are our attitudes affected by the groups to which we belong, our attitudes also affect the groups in which we seek membership (Bodenhausen, Gaclick, & Wyer, 1987). We choose groups that express attitudes similar to our own.

Personal Experience. We hold many attitudes based on personal experiences. In fact, many of our most strongly held and most difficult to change attitudes result from our personal experiences (Olson & Zanna, 1983). The reason is that we tend to trust knowledge from personal experience more than that gathered from other people. There is, however, a danger in this tendency. Because we are so prone to trust our own experiences, we may be tempted to overgeneralize from them without careful consideration. For example, you might have had a particularly bad experience on your first visit to New York City. You may therefore conclude that New York is a terrible city and that New Yorkers are an unfriendly lot. With this attitude firmly entrenched, it is unlikely that you will visit the city again or question whether your experience was truly representative of that city or its people.

The Media. Before most people saw or heard the Rolling Stones, they had read stories about them in the newspaper. One newspaper, *News of the World,* constantly ran stories about the drug use and wild sex life of the Stones. Thus, by the time people saw the Stones, many had developed strong attitudes about them.

One reason for the power of the media is their ability to reach so many people. For example, ninety-seven percent of American homes contain at least one television set. This is a higher percentage than the number of homes that have indoor plumbing! By the age of 12, most children in the United States have spent more time watching television than attending school (Gerbner & Gross, 1976).

A second reason for media power is that the media are often the only source of information we have about events. For example, most of us base our attitudes about Saddam Hussein and the Iraqis on information

By age 12, most children have spent more time watching television than going to school. Because the media reach so many people and are often the only source of information on topics, they play a major role in attitude formation.

we receive from the media. We have no direct experience with any of these events or people, nor do we know anyone who has.

Although it is generally accepted that the media do influence us, there has been some disagreement over which media has the greatest influence. Our first response to this question might be that television has the greatest effect because it allows us to both see and hear the communicator. However, a review of the research has failed to find that one medium is always more persuasive than every other medium (Taylor & Thompson, 1982). Rather, it seems that a medium's effectiveness depends on such factors as the audience, the type of message, and the communicator.

Attitude Change

Up to this point, we have focused on the agents that influence the development of new attitudes. In a sense, we can view these agents as the pioneers of our attitudes; they tread on new territory, trying to get us to accept new information about issues that are often unfamiliar to us.

The focus changes when people are older. Then we are frequently no longer dealing with the formation of new attitudes, but rather with the effort to bring about an **attitude change.** The task facing those who wish to change our attitudes is somewhat different and more difficult than that faced by those aiming to get us to develop new attitudes. When we change an attitude, we are not only accepting a new position or new information, we are also giving up an old position. We may be reluctant to do this because our existing attitude is part of an interlocking or balanced system (Heider, 1946). If we change it, there is often pressure to change other attitudes.

Given that attitudes become so entrenched, how can we ever hope to influence others to change their opinions? This question has been examined by social psychologists since World War II when studies were conducted to change ·the food that Americans ate (Lewin, 1943) and to determine the best way to construct and deliver messages regarding the war effort

Attitude change
Accepting a new position or new information while giving up an old position.

(Hovland, Lumsdaine, & Sheffield, 1949). Recently, there has been an attempt to develop a general model that explains how attitudes are changed (Petty & Cacioppo, 1986, 1990). The model, called **Elaboration Likelihood Model (ELM)** argues that there are two routes to persuasion. The *central route* involves scrutinizing and evaluating the arguments that are presented in the message. How reliable are the facts? How consistent is the argument? Convincing people via the central route involves focusing their attention on the content of the message and presenting a clear, well-reasoned position. The *peripheral route* consists of issues outside the content of the message, such as the communicator's characteristics or our own mood. Do we like the communicator? Is he or she credible and trustworthy? Are we in a good or bad mood when we hear the message?

Either route can result in attitude change. The task for the communicator is to determine whether the message is strong and well reasoned. If it is, then the communicator will want to focus the audience's attention on the communication. However, if the support for the desired position is weak, the communicator should direct efforts toward creating a mood in the audience and having them focus on the communicator, rather than the message. With this model in mind, let us examine how the communicator, the message, and the audience influence whether or not we will change our attitudes.

The Communicator. Characteristics of the communicator are most important when the message is not a strong one and the peripheral route is persuasion is being used. *Who* says something is often as, if not more, important than what is said. There are several factors that determine the effect of a communicator. One is *credibility*—how believable the communicator is. For example, Hovland and Weiss (1952) found that an audience was more likely to believe an eminent scientist than the Communist newspaper *Pravda* on the subject of building nuclear submarines. Credible sources have the strongest effect on our attitudes immediately after we hear the message; the effect of credibility, however, may diminish over time (Pratkanis, Greenwald, Leippe, & Baumgardner, 1988). Similarly, we are more readily persuaded if we see the communicators as *trustworthy* (see Cooper & Croyle, 1984).

Another factor that affects the persuasiveness of a communicator is *similarity* to the audience. Imagine that you are interested in repainting your apartment. You walk into a paint store and choose your paint, and while waiting for the cashier you meet a salesman who recently completed a painting job much like the one you're about to undertake. He notices the brand of paint you have chosen, and he tells you that he used another brand and was very happy with it. He suggests that you switch brands. Now imagine yourself in a similar situation, but this time you are met by a paint salesman who informs you that he recently completed a painting job that was not only very different from the one you're planning but also took a lot more paint. He, too, notices the brand of paint you selected and suggests that you change to another brand. In which case would you be more likely to buy the brand being pushed by the salesman? Brock (1965) conducted this study in a paint store and found that the salesman who said he had used the different brand of paint for a job similar to the one the customer was planning was more persuasive. Other research has found that similar communicators are more effective when the issue involves evaluations—what is good or bad—rather than facts (Goethals & Nelson, 1973). Thus, someone similar to you may be more successful in convincing you that Rolling Stones music is good than that Mick Jagger does not use drugs.

Elaboration Likelihood Model (ELM)
Model which argues that there are two routes to persuasion: the central route that evaluates the arguments as presented in the message, and the peripheral route where the message is evaluated on situational factors, such as the characteristics of the communicator.

CENSORSHIP: What We Don't Know Can Influence Us

As war raged in the Persian Gulf, most of us sat glued to our television sets, anxiously trying to learn "how things were going." It seemed that this would be one war in which the people at home would get a live, accurate, up-to-the-minute account of events that were taking place. Early reports led to much optimism that this would be a short war, maybe a matter of weeks, with few casualties. But many of the news reports were accompanied by a statement to the effect that the information had been censored, and only "approved" information was being given. Debates began about the wisdom of such censorship. On the one hand, it was argued that the public had a right to know about events, and there should be no "editing" of the information. On the other hand, there was the equally strong argument that the disclosure of certain kinds of information might aid the enemy and reduce the morale of people at home.

The debate about censorship is not new. In fact, we can trace it back to Plato, who wanted to censor poets because their work impaired people's "rational ability to know what is real and good" (Davenport, 1991). More recently, the United States Congress was the scene of heated exchanges about censorship during debates on federal support of the arts (Hyde, 1990).

While much concern with censorship deals with whether it is right or wrong, we will consider a different issue here: What is the effect of censorship on the potential audience? It seems that one of the reasons behind the censorship of negative information during the Persian Gulf war was the belief that if people did not get negative information, they would not form negative attitudes toward the war. However, some research suggests just the opposite. A number of investigators have found that when people are told they cannot have access to a communication, they often change their attitude *toward* the position supported by the censored document (Ashmore, Ramchandra, & Jones, 1971; Worchel & Arnold, 1973). In other words, the attitude change results without hearing the communication. Interestingly, censorship leads to this attitude change even when the censor is seen as attractive and/or as an expert. Going a step further, it was found that even when subjects agreed that the agent may have had good reasons for keeping the communication from them, they changed their attitudes toward the position of the unavailable communication anyway.

These effects are quite dramatic and suggest that censorship may have results that are the opposite of those intended by the censor. How can we explain this? One explanation is based on *reactance theory* (Brehm & Brehm, 1981). The theory states that each of us has a set of free behaviors—behaviors that we feel free to engage in at a time of our choosing. When our freedom is threatened or eliminated, we become motivated to restore that freedom. During this process, the threatened freedoms become more important and attractive to us. In the case of censorship, the censor threatens our freedom to have access to a communication *and* indirectly threatens our freedom to hold the position advocated by the censored communication. We restore our freedom by changing our attitude and by attempting to gain access to the censored item.

We have shown evidence for attitude change in the face of censorship. The research also found that subjects expressed a greater desire to hear a censored communication than one that had not been censored. Support for this reactance theory position comes from another line of research. This research shows that as the supply of an item such as an automobile or even a cookie diminishes, people tend to place greater value on that item and to express a greater desire to have it (Worchel, Lee, & Adewole, 1975; Verhallen, 1982). According to our reasoning, as the item becomes scarce, there is greater threat to the person's freedom to have that item.

The message in this discussion is that we often want what is denied us. Censorship denies us access to information, and may therefore lead to an increased desire to have that information. And when it is clear that the censored message supports a particular position, people may change their attitudes to bring them more into line with the censored position. Therefore, censorship often backfires on the censor.

Reading between the lines here tells you that one way to convince people to adopt a particular position when you have weak support for that position is to inform your audience that they cannot have access to your full message. What people can't hear may have a powerful influence on their opinions!

The Message.   Presentation of the message can be accomplished using either central or peripheral route processing. If we want the audience to focus on and understand the message, we use the central processing route. It has been found that people who already agree with our position are most persuaded by an argument that presents only information supporting the desired position. However, people who disagree with us see the communication as fair and can be persuaded by a message that presents arguments on both sides of the issue (Hovland et al., 1949). If we do

Table 16–1
Opinion Change Determined by the Kind of Presentation and Message of Difficulty

	Simple Message	Complex Message
Written	2.94	4.73
Audiotape	3.75	2.32
Videotape	4.78	3.02

Note: Higher numbers indicate greater opinion change.
Source: Adapted from Chaiken and Eagly (1976).

present both sides, we are best advised to first present the information that supports the desired position and then give the nonsupporting information. The medium through which we present the message also determines our eventual success in being persuasive. If the message is a complicated or complex one, it is most effective when presented in written form such as a newspaper. In this way readers can study and learn about the points being made. However, a simpler message is more persuasive when presented over television (Chaiken & Eagly, 1976, Table 16–1).

Some messages are more effectively presented using the peripheral route model. For example, if we want to influence people's attitudes about using drugs, we can present a message that arouses fear; we might show pictures of people who died from drug overdoses or people in jail as a result of being busted for drug possession. On the other hand, we could tone down our message and appeal to reason rather than fear. Research (Leventhal & Niles, 1965) indicates that a relatively high degree of fear is effective in changing attitudes if the message also includes information about how people can take appropriate steps to avoid the fear-arousing consequences (e.g., where to go for drug addiction treatment). On the other side of the picture, it has also been found that messages that put people in a good mood can change attitudes (Biggers & Pryor, 1982). For example, communications that pair information with soothing music or pleasant pictures may be very persuasive. These "add ons" divert people's attention from the content of the message and focus them on their emotions.

Thus, the way we construct and present our message determines not only whether people will be persuaded by it or not, but the route by which this persuasion will result.

The Audience. Research on the audience is much less conclusive than that on the communicator and the message. Few personal characteristics that make people vulnerable for attempts at persuasion have been identified. We might expect people of lower intelligence to be more easily influenced than more intelligent people. However, people of lower intelligence may have difficulty understanding the message and therefore be less affected by it. Overall, it seems that personal characteristics of the audience influence the type of message that will be most persuasive. For example, people who hold a position opposite to that advocated by the communication will be most influenced by a message that is two-sided and draws specific conclusions (Linder & Worchel, 1970). On the other hand, an audience that already agrees with the message's position may be more influenced by a one-sided argument that does not explicitly draw conclusions. It has also been found that people in a good mood are more likely to be persuaded, unless the message is a complex one that requires considerable attention and thought to understand (Bless et al., 1990).

The Relationship between Attitudes and Behavior

There is a real temptation to leave this section on attitudes; we've developed a relatively neat package on how attitudes are formed and changed. But the account of Mick Jagger's life and a host of events in 1987 and 1988 suggest that this is not the end of the story. Looking first at Jagger, we find a man who had strong antidrug attitudes, but was busted for possessing drugs. Jagger is hardly a unique example of inconsistency between attitudes and behavior. We find that President Ronald Reagan, who stated publicly that negotiating with terrorists is wrong, was involved with attempts to trade weapons to the Iranians for the release of hostages. And we find a bizarre series of extramarital incidents involving popular television preachers (James Bakker and Jimmy Swaggert) who vigorously denounced sex outside of marriage. Despite these tirades, both men admitted that they were involved in extramarital sexual relationships. Were these people simply deceiving us about their attitudes? This may be possible, but it is probably not the case. If this is not the answer, what, then, is the relationship between attitudes and behavior?

The answer to this question is that there are a number of things to consider when predicting behavior, in addition to attitudes (see Figure 16–2). One is the *situation*. If someone is pointing a gun at you and asking you to contribute to the Save the Sharks campaign, you are not likely to refuse even if you do not believe this to be a worthy cause. Another important consideration is *feelings of efficacy* (the belief about how effective action will be). One study found that even if people believed nuclear war was a real possibility, they took no action (e.g., demonstrating against nuclear weapons, stocking a shelter) unless they believed their behavior would affect the likelihood of war (Fiske, 1987). Another study found that speeches aimed at getting women to perform breast self-examinations were most

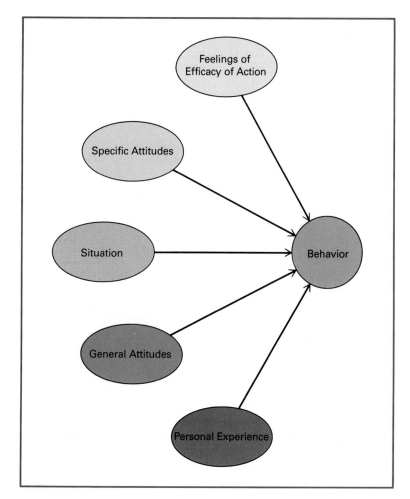

FIGURE 16–2

Relation Between Attitudes and Behavior

General attitudes are not good predictors of behavior. Attitudes dealing with the specific situation, personal experience, feelings of efficacy, and the nature of the situation play a larger role in influencing our behavior.

persuasive in eliciting this behavior if they helped women feel confident about performing the exams and dealing with the situation should they find a lump (Meyerowitz & Chaiken, 1987). Still a third issue concerns the *attitude* itself. The more specific the attitude the more likely it will guide behavior. In order to predict whether Mick Jagger would use drugs at a party, we would need to know his attitude on this specific topic (his own use of drugs at social events), not simply his attitude about drug use, in general. Finally, attitudes that evolve from *personal experience* are the best predictors of behavior. An antidrug attitude that you developed because of a personal experience is more likely to guide your behavior than one you developed by listening to television messages. Further, attitudes formed through direct experience are more difficult to change than those not based on experience.

When Behaving Is Believing

We have seen that attitudes can guide our behavior under some circumstances. There is, however, a flip side to this relationship that has been recognized by social psychologists for years. That is, our behavior may also drive our attitudes. For example, you may decide that you like the Rolling Stones because you paid $30 to hear their concert and nearly lost your life in the stampede that occurred at the concert!

A Theory of Cognitive Dissonance

One of the first investigators to recognize this behavior-attitude relationship was Leon Festinger. Festinger's theory (1957) was actually rather simple, but it gave rise to a large number of unique predictions and studies. He argued that people strive to have their attitudes, beliefs, and behaviors support one another. When these components come into conflict, a person will become uncomfortable and experience a state of **cognitive dissonance.** In order to relieve the dissonance, the person will try to change the cognitions so that they will once again be in agreement.

Cognitive dissonance theory became the central theory in social psychology for at least two decades, stimulating hundreds of studies and changing the way we viewed the relationship between attitudes and behavior (Zukier, 1989).

The most interesting cases of cognitive dissonance involve the relationship between attitudes and behaviors (Wicklund & Brehm, 1976). We desire consistency between our attitudes and behaviors, and if we cannot justify our behavior by external factors, we change our attitudes to justify the behavior. When we believe that we have *freely chosen* to perform a particular act, we will become motivated to realign our attitudes to justify that behavior.

Let us now examine two interesting predictions that are based on this theory. In each of these cases, notice that the final attitude is a function of the behavior.

Effort Justification. According to dissonance theory, we love those things for which we suffer **(effort justification).** In other words, suffering leads to liking. As we can see, it would be dissonant to hold the two cognitions that (1) I worked hard for X and (2) X is worthless. Since I cannot change

Cognitive dissonance
State that occurs when a person's attitudes, beliefs, and behaviors are in conflict. In order to relieve the dissonance, the person will try to change the cognitions so that they will again be in agreement. (Festinger used the term cognition because these are the person's mental representations of attitudes and behaviors.)

the fact that I have worked hard for X, I can reduce my dissonance by changing my attitude about X; I can come to believe that X is valuable. In one of the early dissonance experiments investigators had subjects perform either a very difficult task, an easy task, or no task at all to get into a group (Aronson & Mills, 1959). The subjects then heard their group discuss a very boring topic. Although all the subjects heard the same discussion, those who had performed the difficult task to gain admission to the group rated the discussion as more interesting than did the other subjects. More recent research found that we are especially likely to justify our actions when we perform an unpleasant task for an unpleasant person (Rosenfeld, Giacalone, & Tedeschi, 1984)!

Just-Barely-Sufficient Threat.   Imagine that John, a young child, is told by his mother she will be very upset if he takes a cookie from the cookie jar. The mother leaves the room and the hungry child longingly eyes the scrumptious cookies, but he does not take one. John now has the dissonant cognitions that (1) I am not taking a cookie and (2) the cookie looks wonderfully delicious. How does he resolve this dissonance? If his mother's threat had been severe or drastic ("I'll cut your hands off if you take a cookie!"), John could justify his actions by believing that he did not take the cookie because of his mother's severe threat. However, he knows that as his mother's threats go, this one was rather mild, so it does not justify his behavior. John can, however, justify his behavior by derogating the cookies: "They're probably stale and taste awful." Adopting this attitude, the child now has the cognitions that (1) he did not choose to eat (2) a terrible-tasting cookie. These cognitions fit nicely together. Thus dissonance theory suggests that we will derogate attractive objects or activities that we chose to forgo without strong external constraints **(just-barely-sufficient threats).** This effect was demonstrated in a study in which children received either a mild or severe warning not to play with a toy robot (Aronson & Carlsmith, 1963). Those children who did not play with the robot rated it lower in attractiveness in the mild-warning case than in the severe-warning case.

According to cognitive dissonance theory, we come to value the things for which we suffer, and the more we suffer the more we value. We might conclude that avid joggers enjoy running because they run. Further, the more difficult the conditions under which they run, the more they will like running.

Getting People to Behave

Dissonance theory teaches us that when people choose to behave in a way that is inconsistent with their attitudes, they will change their behavior to support the behavior. But how do we get people to behave in this inconsistent way? To answer this question, imagine that you are a magazine salesperson. After the first week of no sales, you are ready to quit. Bud, the sales manager, takes you aside and gives you one simple rule: "The trick to selling is to get people to let you inside their home. No matter how you do it, get them to invite you inside." Your sales would probably show a dramatic increase if you followed Bud's advice. It has been supported by research.

Foot-in-the-Door.   The phenomenon known as the **foot-in-the-door** suggests that people will be more likely to perform a large, difficult, or costly act (buying magazines) if they first agree to perform a small or easy task (invite the salesperson into their home). By committing themselves to the small task, they feel involved in the larger effort and view themselves as people who get involved or support causes. This new self-image makes it more difficult for them to refuse later requests (Eisenberg, Cialdini,

Effort justification
Attempt to make something we have to work hard for more valuable in order to make the effort worthwhile.
Just-barely-sufficient threat
Aspect of dissonance theory that suggests that we will derogate attractive objects or activities that we choose to forgo without strong external constraints.
Foot-in-the-door approach
Persuasive technique that gets people to agree first to a small request and then later be more willing to agree to a second request.

Salespeople often use the foot-in-the-door technique to close a sale. The technique involves first getting the target to commit to a small act (letting the salesperson into the house) before being asked to make a larger commitment (buy the product).

McCreath, & Shell, 1987). For example, one group of investigators (Freedman & Fraser, 1966) found that residents were most likely to allow a billboard in their yard advertising safe driving if they had earlier signed a safe-driving petition or had agreed to display a small safe-driving card in their window.

After reviewing the research on the foot-in-the-door, one psychologist commented, "It scares me enough that I am rarely willing to sign a petition anymore, even for a position I support (Cialdini, 1984, p. 80)."

Door-in-the-Face.   The opposite approach, the **door-in-the-face** technique, also works. Researchers have found that people who at first refuse a large request will be more likely to go along with a smaller request than those not given the chance to refuse the large request (Cialdini, 1975). This effect may occur because people feel guilty about turning down the first request; they therefore go along the second time in order to reduce their guilt. It is also possible that, compared to the large first request, the second request seems quite reasonable.

Liking: Positive Attitudes about People

In our previous discussion, we were concerned with general attitudes; these attitudes could have involved rock concerts, nuclear war, or mountain climbing. Let's shift our discussion from the individual (and his or her general attitudes) to the relationship between individuals. In doing so, we focus on a specific attitude: attraction.

One of the more interesting attitudes that we form concerns our **attraction** for other people; we can, in fact, define attraction as a positive attitude we have about others. Because friendship is such a central part of our lives, let's take some time to see how attraction develops.

Door-in-the-face approach
Persuasive technique based on the fact that people who at first refuse a large request will be more likely after that to comply with a smaller request.
Attraction
A positive attitude about another person.

Of all the people you meet, why do you form friendships with some, but not with others? If we had answers to these questions, we could spend our time constructing the perfect world! Although we do not have *the* formula for attraction, we can draw upon the vast research in the areas of rewards, reciprocity, similarity, proximity, and physical attractiveness to better understand why people are attracted to each other.

Rewards: Receiving and Giving

Mick met Keith when the Blue Boys were just forming. The group needed a good lead guitarist so they could begin to perform in public. Mick learned that Keith was a superb guitar player who "had managed to master nearly all of Chuck Berry's introductions and solos"; he was just what Mick needed to back him up. It is certainly possible that Mick was attracted to Keith for what Keith could do for him.

One of the major findings research on attraction is that we like people who reward us. In fact, a number of investigators have suggested that we view our relationships as economic transactions (Homans, 1974; Lindskold, 1982). We weigh the rewards and costs and are attracted to those people who provide the greatest profit for us. The rewards and costs include many things, such as emotions, materials, power of security. We are attracted to people who reward us. The greater the reward, the more we like the provider.

There have been many interesting extensions of the reward hypothesis. One extension is that we like not only the people who directly reward us but also those who are around us when good things happen to us—even if they had nothing to do with the positive event. For example, Veitch and Griffitt (1976) found that a stranger who appeared in a room after a subject heard good news was liked better than one who appeared after the subject heard bad news. According to this position, the success of the Rolling Stones may have enhanced the attraction between Mick and Keith.

Before rushing off to take stock of what you can do to reward others around you, there is another finding that you should consider. People report that their most satisfying relationships are those where both parties reward each other (Rook, 1987). Always being the recipient of rewards and favors may lead us to feel that we have nothing to contribute. We can bolster our esteem by doing things for others. Thus, we will be attracted to others who both reward and help us and allow us to reward and help them. In fact, there is considerable evidence that we are most comfortable with relationships that we consider equitable—that is, in which the rewards each person receives are proportional to what he or she contributes (Brehm, 1988; Simpson, 1990). In other words, we like people with whom we have interactions that we consider fair and just.

Similarity: Birds of a Feather

One of the first things Keith noticed about Mick when he first met him was that Mick was carrying a stack of blues records. As they discussed music, Mick and Keith learned that they had similar tastes. Further discussion showed that the two had smiliar backgrounds and aspirations. Could these similarities have set the stage for their friendship?

Indeed, there has been a great deal of research showing that similarity is one of the strongest predictors of attraction (Byrne, 1971). The similarity can be on almost any dimension, including attitudes, ability, intelligence, economic condition, race, height, physical attractiveness, and sometimes personality. On the other side of the coin, we are also repelled by people with whom we have little in common (Rosenbaum, 1986). As with most rules, there are also some exceptions to the similarity-attraction relationship. It seems that we are not attracted to people who have a characteristic that we do not admire in ourselves (Goldman & Olczak, 1976). For example, if you are unhappy with the fact that you weigh 345 pounds, you will not necessarily be attracted to another person who weighs 345 pounds. There is also evidence that having certain opposite personal needs and motives may lead to attraction. If you have a strong need to be dominant, for example, you may be attracted to a submissive person. In this kind of relationship your needs will not be in conflict with your partner's needs.

There are several possible reasons for this similarity-attraction effect. First, similar others validate our own opinions and actions, and this validation is rewarding. For example, if you have just purchased a new jeep, it is gratifying to find someone else who has just bought a jeep. Seeing that others have done the same thing makes you feel that your own action was not unusual or incorrect. A second reason for the similarity-attraction relationship is that we often expect to have a positive interaction with similar others. For example, if you were raised on a farm, you would have a great deal to discuss with another person raised on a farm. You might have a somewhat more difficult time engaging in conversation with someone who was raised in a large city and has very different opinions and interests. A third reason is that we expect similar others to like us. Since we enjoy being liked, we are attracted to those similar others. Thus there are a number of reasons why "birds of a feather flock together" (and like each other).

Proximity: To Be Near You

After their meeting in 1961, Mick and Keith were constantly together. When their band got started, they lived together. Interestingly, when Mick married Bianca and began spending a great deal of time with her, the relationship between Mick and Keith became strained. As illustrated by this example, we are often attracted to those people who are with us a great deal.

As far back as 1932, Bossard noticed a relationship between physical closeness (**proximity**) and attraction. In examining the application for marriage licenses in Philadelphia, he found that an overwhelming number of the engaged people tended to live close to their partners-to-be. Clearly these results could occur for two reasons: It is possible that people who like each other choose to live close together. Or it is possible that simply being close together leads people to like each other.

In order to test the latter possibility, Leon Festinger, Stanley Schachter, and Kurt Back (1950) studied friendships in a married-student housing project. Couples in this project were randomly assigned to apartments so that there was no chance that previous attraction would influence where they lived. During the course of the year the residents were asked to indicate whom they were most friendly with. The results showed that 44 percent of the couples were most friendly with their next-door neighbor, while only 10 percent were most friendly with people who lived down the hall. The fact that proximity leads to liking has been found in dormitories, intercity housing projects, and surveys of residential neighborhoods.

There are many reasons why proximity leads to liking. Simple familiarity is one. There is a great deal of research showing that the more we are

Proximity
Physical closeness.

exposed to a person, name, or song, the more we come to like it (Moreland & Zajonc, 1982; Zajonc, 1970). This may be one of the reasons politicians are so determined to get the most media coverage possible. They will often go to great lengths just to be seen by the public. Another reason for the proximity effect is that people who are physically close are more likely to reward each other than people who are physically distant. Finally, since it is a fact that people must interact with those who are physically close to them, it is certainly more comfortable to like these people than to dislike them (Berscheid & Walster, 1978).

Proximity does not always lead to liking, however. FBI statistics show that muggings, murders, robberies, and assaults are most likely to be committed by people in the victims' family or neighborhood (Berscheid & Walster, 1978). Indeed, physical proximity helped lead to a bitter conflict between Keith and Brian Jones. Brian became very jealous of Keith when he saw his girlfriend flirting with Keith. Because they were always together, Brian watched every painful moment of the flirtations, and it was not long before Brian and Keith were bitter enemies. We might, therefore, conclude from this that proximity intensifies the existing feelings in relationships.

Physical Attractiveness:
The Way You Look

The three women who played the biggest role in Mick's life were Marianne Faithful, Bianca Macias, and Jerry Hall. The three women had little in common with the exception that they were all beautiful. Although most of us would like to think we do not base friendship on something as frivolous as physical attractiveness, research suggests that this is not the case; beauty does lead to friendship in many cases. This holds for both males and females, and children as well as adults (Hatfield & Sprecher, 1986).

The influence of physical attractiveness is greater than simply guiding attraction. The research shows that we see attractive people as being more intelligent than unattractive people, even when the behavior of the two is the same. Attractive people are seen as less guilty and given a lighter

All of Mick Jagger's wives were beautiful, as can be seen from these photos (Marianne Faithful, left; Bianca Macias, middle; Jerry Hall, right). Do you find yourself making any attributions about their personalities or behavior on the basis of their attractiveness?

Table 16–2
Gateways to Friendship

We like people who
1. reward us
2. like us
3. are similar to us
4. live close to us
5. are physically attractive
6. are around us when good things happen
7. like the same people and things we like
8. satisfy our needs

Although we may desire the most attractive person around, we are most likely to become romantically involved with someone of comparable attractiveness to ourselves.

sentence than unattractive people, even when the facts of the crime were the same for both defendants. Going one step further, the friends of an attractive same-sex pair were rated more positively than the friends of an unattractive person (Kernis & Wheeler, 1981)!

All this seems rather absurd and shallow. Why does physical attractiveness have such a strong effect? One possibility is that we like physically attractive people for the status they can bring to us. Second, research suggests that we see ourselves as being more similar to attractive people than to unattractive people (Marks, Miller, & Maruyama, 1981). As we have seen, similarity leads to attraction. A third reason is that there may be truth in our evaluations; attractive people often have more pleasing personalities and a higher sense of well-being than unattractive people (Umberson & Hughes, 1984). This difference may result because attractive people have more frequent and more varied social interactions than unattractive people. Perhaps we can conclude that physical attractiveness does not cause the more pleasing personality, but it opens up the opportunities where this personality can develop.

If all this is true, are unattractive people doomed to a life of unhappiness and loneliness? Obviously not. Although we might want attractive friends and partners, research suggests that we often end up with partners who are about as attractive as we are (Kalick & Hamilton, 1987). This occurs because friendship is a two-way street; we like people who are going to be attracted to us. Further, we are often more comfortable with people who are as attractive as we are.

LOOKING GOOD: The Rest of the Story

Our discussion of physical attractiveness suggests that beauty is one basis for friendship. Not only does research support this point of view, but the billions of dollars that men and women spend each year on beauty aids suggests that many of us certainly believe it. But let's look a little deeper to better understand the importance of looking good.

In doing this, the first point we discover is that physical attractiveness is not valued the same by everyone. A careful review of the research suggests that men value physical attractiveness in women more than women value an attractive appearance in men (Feingold, 1990a). For example, men were more likely than women to state that physical attractiveness is an important determinant for mate selection. And men were also more likely to advertise for a "physically attractive" partner in personal ads than women were. But this is not the end of the story. When it comes to behavior (how attracted people are to a partner when they actually interact), the differences between the ratings of men and women are smaller. And when we examine same-sex popularity, it seems that while physical attractiveness is related to

men's attraction to male friends, there is no such relationship in female-female friendships (Feingold, 1990b).

We generally expect attractive people to be happier and better adjusted than unattractive people. But there is another side to this issue. Attractive people often feel tremendous pressure to live up to others' expectations (Worchel, Cooper, & Goethals, 1991). They feel they *should* be happier and perform better than others, and are extremely disturbed when they are not and do not. And attractive people may have difficulty determining the basis for the positive feedback they receive from others. Are the compliments due to their performance or their appearance? Illustrating this point, one study had people write an essay, either under conditions where the evaluator could see them or where the evaluator could not observe them (Major, Carrington, & Carnevale, 1984). The subjects then received a very positive evaluation of their work. Attractive men and women later reported being less convinced that they had done good work when they knew the judge had seen them than when the judge had not seen them. Those who knew the judge had seen them could not determine whether

the evaluation was based solely on their work or was contaminated by their physical attractiveness.

Finally, we pointed out that there can be value in having attractive friends. We are often rated more positively by others if we have attractive friends than if we do not. Yet there is a risk of being associated with attractive people, especially if we are not particularly attractive ourselves. Investigators showed subjects pictures of either beautiful or unattractive models (Kenrick, Gutierres, & Goldberg, 1989). The subjects were then shown average-looking models. Those who had seen the attractive models rated the average models as less attractive than subjects who had seen the less attractive models. The male subjects in a subsequent study reported loving their current mate less when they had been exposed to attractive models than when they had seen more plain-looking models. It seems that in these studies the subjects compared (and contrasted) the average-looking person with the model. The average-looking person was viewed as less attractive by comparison, while he or she seemed more attractive when compared with the unattractive model.

Helping Behavior

Our discussion on attraction focused on liking our fellow human beings and moving toward them. A seemingly logical extension of this focus is that we are willing to help and aid others. But as we will see, although we are social animals who are attracted to others and desire to be attractive to others, we are not necessarily helpful social animals. This point was reinforced by the sad and bizarre incident that occurred during the Stones' appreciation concert outside San Francisco in December 1969. A crowd of 300,000 danced, drank, and "did drugs" as the Stones performed. The Hell's Angels had been hired as security guards to protect the band and keep order. As Jagger and the Stones played, a young black man came running down an aisle toward the stage. As he approached the stage, a Hell's Angel plunged a knife into the man's chest. Jagger watched the scene in disbelief. However, even more unbelievable was that few people in the crowd tried to help the bleeding man. After calling for a doctor, the Stones continued to play, even playing their popular song "Street Fighting Man" as the young man died.

Would you stop to help this person? Research suggests that the decision to help involves a complex series of decisions and is influenced by the anticipation of rewards and your mood.

We might be tempted to pass this incident off as the result of a bunch of doped-up hippies who were too stoned to know what was happening around them. Unfortunately, there are too many like incidents for us to hide behind such flippant explanations. We can to some extent counter these stories with ones in which people helped, but we are still left with the question of why (*and under what conditions*) people help others and why they do not. In closing, our chapter on interpersonal relations, let us briefly address this question.

Why Do People Help . . . Or Not Help?

We begin our discussion of helping by asking the seemingly simple question: Why do people help? What appears to be a simple question turns out to have a complex answer.

One approach to answering this question argues that we must first identify the underlying motivation behind the behavior. Helping, it is argued, results from one of two motivations (Batson, 1990; Batson & Weeks, 1991). The first is **altruism,** a motivational state with the ultimate goal of increasing the other's welfare. When altruism motivates your behavior, you are acting mainly to help the other person. The second motive for helping is **egoism,** whose ultimate goal is increasing one's own welfare. When egoism guides your behavior, you help in order to make yourself feel better or to gain rewards. To understand this distinction, assume that you watched the young man being stabbed at the Stones' concert. If you rushed to his aid because you felt that he needed you and you wanted to relieve his pain, your behavior would be described as altruistic. However, if you helped because you felt bad and knew that helping would reduce your bad feelings, or if you helped because you thought of the press coverage your action might receive, your helping would be termed egotistic.

To the recipients of help, this distinction might not be important. But the distinction does have some important implications. For example, a person guided by an egotistical motive should be less likely to help when it is easy to justify not helping, when the costs of helping are high, or when it is easy to ignore the victim's need for help (Batson & Flory, 1990). None of these situations is likely to deter helping when the motive is altruistic. With this discussion in mind, let's quickly examine some of the factors that have been shown to influence when people help . . . or do not help.

Rewards. It would be nice to believe that people are basically good and that they help others out of the goodness of their hearts. Not so, argue many scholars who have studied helping behavior (Bar-Tal, 1984; Blau, 1964). They suggest that people make decisions about helping in the same way they decide about many of their other behaviors; that is, they consider the cost of the behavior and the rewards that will follow. If the reward is greater than the cost, they help. However, if the cost exceeds the reward they do not help. (Recall our discussion about attraction and how we view our relationship as economic transactions.)

Mood and Empathy. A number of studies have shown that we are more likely to help people when we feel good (Berkowitz, 1987). It seems to make little difference what brought on this good feeling. Helping increases after we hear good news, listen to soothing music, or have a stroke of good fortune.

The exact reason why mood affects helping is the center of some debate. Some investigators argue that seeing others in distress causes us to feel empathy for them; in a sense, we feel the emotions of the distressed person. Knowing how they feel, we help them so that they will feel better (Batson, 1984). Other investigators, however, take a less complimentary view of helping. They suggest that we help to make ourselves feel better (Cialdini

Altruism
A motivational state with the ultimate aim of increasing the other's welfare.
Egoism
A motivational state with the ultimate aim of increasing one's own welfare.

et al., 1987). We help when we are in a good mood in order to preserve our good mood, and we help when we are uncomfortable in order to reduce our discomfort. In support of this position, these investigators showed that even when subjects felt empathy for a victim, they were most likely to help when they believed that by helping they would reduce their own feelings of sadness. This reasoning recalls our earlier discussion of altruism and egoism.

Although we may debate whether we help in order to help ourselves or to help others, it is clear that our mood does affect if and when we help.

Norms.   **Norms** are general rules of behavior that apply to everyone (see Chapter 17). There are, in fact, many norms that guide our helping behavior. For example, the *norm of social responsibility* states that we should help people in need without concern for future exchanges (Berkowitz, 1972; Schwartz & Howard, 1984). In support of these norms, research has found that people are more willing to help others who are dependent on them than people who are not (Berkowitz & Connor, 1966).

However, we also live by a norm that dictates that we should respect other people's privacy; in other words, "mind your own business." This norm may make us reluctant to become involved with people for fear of invading their privacy.

The Decision to Help

Up to this point, we have been talking about helping as if it involved a simple decision: to help or not to help. A closer look, however, reveals that there is a lot more involved than a simple help/no help decision. Some investigators have suggested that the process of helping (or not helping) be viewed as a series of steps or a decision tree (Latané & Darley, 1970, see Figure 16–3). A quick examination of these steps should not only help us better understand Mick Jagger's behavior at the San Francisco concert but it may also come in handy when we are in an emergency situation. In developing their decision tree, these investigators focused on a particular type of helping, **bystander intervention.** This act involves offering aid in an emergency situation, such as an accident, acute illness, or assault.

1. *Noticing the Victim.* This is a rather obvious point; people are unlikely to offer help unless they notice the individual in need. What may not be so obvious is the lengths that people will go to in order *not* to "notice" the victim. In a study on a subway, Piliavin and her colleagues (1969) observed that riders who did not offer help often moved away from a victim and refused to look at him. Our first question about the Stones concert, then, is whether or not Jagger noticed the stabbing incident.

2. *Interpreting the Situation As an Emergency.* After we see the victim, we must decide whether he or she needs help. Accounts of the stabbing suggest that Jagger was aware of the commotion, but he wasn't sure what was really happening. If we want to be helped we must do everything possible to let others know that we need help. In order to demonstrate this, researchers set up a situation in which a woman was attacked by a man (Shotland & Straw, 1976). In one condition, she yelled, "I don't know you," in the middle of the fight; in the other, she made no reference to her relationship to the attacker. In the first case, 65 percent of the male bystanders intervened to help, whereas in the latter case, only 19 percent helped. When the assailant was unknown to the woman, it was clear that this was not a "lovers' quarrel" and that she needed help.

Investigators attempted to identify the types of situations people inter-

Norms
Rules that govern specific behavior and apply to all members of the group.
Bystander intervention
Offering aid in an emergency situation.

FIGURE 16–3

The Decision to Help

Helping actually involves a series of decisions. A negative decision at any stage ensures that helping will not result.

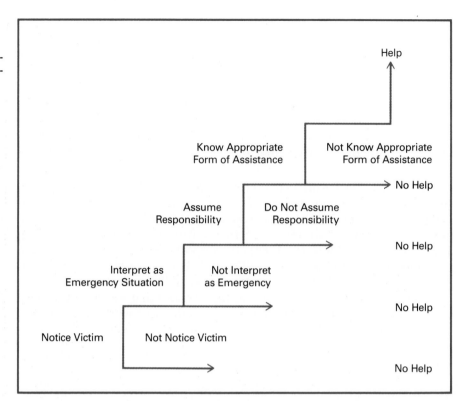

preted as emergencies by having them rate a large number of theoretical situations (Shotland & Huston, 1979). People generally agreed that emergencies were accidents where harm to the victim was evident or very likely. Least likely to be seen as an emergency were everyday problems where no harm to the victim was likely.

3. *Assuming Responsibility: Is There Safety in Numbers?* Assume you knew that at 3 P.M. on a given day you were going to faint and that you would need the help of others to revive you. As the time approached, would you rush to a busy street corner where there were many passersby, or would you choose a less popular side street where fewer people passed? Most of us would probably choose the busy street, thinking that in a crowd there would be at least one person who would stop to help us. Research, however, indicates that this choice may not be a wise one (Bar-Tal, 1976; Latané & Darley, 1970). In fact, indications are that when there are fewer people present, there is a greater chance of an individual receiving help.

In order to illustrate this phenomenon, Darley and Latané (1968) asked college students to participate in a discussion about their problems in adjusting to college life. When the subject arrived, he or she was told that in order to prevent embarrassment, subjects would communicate with each other from private booths over a sound system. There would be no face-to-face interaction. The subject was then led into a booth. In some cases, the subject believed that there would be only two people in the group. In other cases, the subject thought that there would be three people in the group. In the third condition, the subject believed that six people would participate in the discussion. Actually, there was only one subject in the study. The voices of other discussants were tape-recorded.

In the discussion, one tape-recorded voice, designated as the "future victim" spoke first. He talked about some of his difficulties and then mentioned that he was prone to seizures in times of stress. After the other subjects spoke, the "victim" began to speak again. Suddenly he seemed to be having a seizure and said, "I-er-um-I think I-I need-er-if-if-could-er somebody er-er-er-er-er-er give me a little-er give me a little-er give me a little help here because I-er-I'm . . ." (chokes, then quiet) (Darley & Latané,

1968, p. 379). The experimenter, sitting outside the booth, recorded the time it took the subject to search for help. As can be seen from Figure 16–4, the larger the group, the less likely the subjects were to help. In fact, 85 percent of the subjects helped if they believed that no one else knew of the victim's plight, whereas only 31 percent helped if they felt that four others (in the six-person group) knew of the victim's need.

How can we explain such an effect? One possible explanation is based on the notion of responsibility. When the subjects believed that they were the only ones who knew of the problem, they were more likely to feel responsible for helping the victim than when there were other people present. It was easy for the subject to think that "others must be doing something." Another possible reason for the effect involves the interpretation of the problem. In the large group the subject may have felt that the victim did not really need help because he or she did not hear anyone else making an effort to aid the victim. In this case, the subject used the response of the others to determine the extent of the emergency. Alone with the victim however, the subject has to make a decision about the urgency of the situation based solely on a personal interpretation of the victim's plight.

Thus simply having a number of people present does not increase the likelihood of helping behavior. In such cases, bystanders may *diffuse* responsibility for helping.

Another aspect of assuming responsibility involves determining the cause of the emergency. One investigator suggests that when people view a person as the victim of uncontrollable circumstances, they are more likely to feel pity, and help, than when they feel the person was responsible or could have controlled the emergency (Betancourt, 1990).

4. *Knowing How to Help*. Imagine finding an unconscious woman on the sidewalk who is bleeding from the mouth and ears. You can see clearly that she needs help and that no one else is available. What do you do in this case? For most of us, this would be a very threatening situation. We have heard that it is dangerous to move an unconscious person. But do we leave the woman lying on the sidewalk and go search for medical help? Or do we stay with her, hoping someone else will come along? This type of dilemma may cause people to feel so helpless that they take no action (Bar-Tal, 1976). In order to be of assistance, people must decide that they can take some action that will help the victim. Since many people do not have specific training in how to help in emergencies, they may decide that there is nothing they can do. Even if Jagger had reached this point in the decision process, he may have failed to act because he knew nothing about how to help a stabbing victim.

5. *Taking Action*. Even after going through all the earlier steps, the bystander must finally decide to take action. There are a number of variables that determine whether or not a person will actually decide to help. One involves the person's belief as to whether the victim deserves to be helped. In one study that was mentioned earlier, subway riders were more likely to help a victim if they thought that person was ill than if they thought the person was drunk (Piliavin et al., 1969). Presumably they felt that the ill person was deserving of help, whereas the drunk person was responsible for his plight and therefore did not deserve help. Another factor involves the costs of helping.

We are unlikely to offer help if we view the costs as high and/or the rewards as low. In the case of the stabbing at the Stones concert, the potential costs were clearly very high. Tensions were running high in the crowd and had Mick Jagger gone into the crowd to help the victim, he, too, may have become a victim of violence.

As we can see, the act of helping is really a complex process. What can be done to increase the chances that people will make positive decisions at each step on the route to helping others?

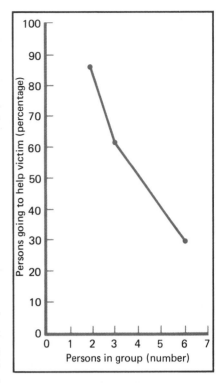

FIGURE 16–4

The research shows that the more people that are present in an emergency, the less likely it is that an observer will offer help.

Summary

1. As social beings, much of our behavior is influenced by other people. **Social psychology,** a relatively recent branch of psychology, is the scientific study of the way in which people are affected by social situations and social relationships. It is concerned with applying the theories it has developed to better understand and deal with social issues.

2. **Attribution** involves inferring personal characteristics from observable behavior. Based upon the information we gather about the knowledge, ability, and intention of an actor, we often assign an underlying trait or disposition. The ultimate aim of the attribution process is to understand and predict people's behavior.

3. There are many biases in the attribution process. People make stronger attributions when the behavior affects them; there is also a bias toward giving more weight to the behavior than to the situational context it occurred in.

4. According to the **social cognition model,** people make attributions guided by schemas of perceived notions about the world. These schemas influence our interpretations of events and people; they even influence how we recall past information.

5. As part of the attribution process, first impressions are difficult to change because they set in motion the **self-fulfilling prophecy.** Our expectations lead us to create a climate that encourages the expected behavior.

6. **Attitudes** are learned, relatively enduring feelings about objects, events, or issues. They have at least three components: evaluation, belief, and action. There may also be a physiological component. Parents, peers personal experience, and the media all play a role in the development of attitudes.

7. Attitude change involves substituting new attitudes for old ones. A general model which explains how attitudes are changed is called **Elaboration Likelihood Model (ELM).** It argues that there are two routes to persuasion. The central route involves scrutinizing and evaluating the message content. The peripheral route consists of outside issues such as the communicator's characteristics or our mood. Either route can result in attitude change. Research in this area continues to focus on the communicator, the message, and the audience.

8. The relationship between attitudes and behavior can be affected by the situation, the feelings of efficacy, and/or the attitude itself.

9. **Cognitive dissonance** theory is based on the assumption that people strive to have their attitudes, beliefs, and behaviors support one another. Dissonance theory suggests that changing behavior often causes people to change their attitudes. Both **foot-in-the-door** and **door-in-the-face approach** have been found to change attitudes. These approaches may change the way people feel about themselves.

10. We have an **attraction** for people who reward us directly or who are present when good things happen to us. We like people who are physically close to us, although **proximity** can also lead to disliking. Whereas we may be most attracted to physically attractive others, we often choose to become romantically involved with people whose physical attractiveness is about equal to our own.

11. Helping depends upon such things as rewards, mood, empathy and certain expected norms. Research on bystander intervention shows that the decision to help in emergency situations is the end result in a complex chain of events. Before helping will occur, people need to notice the person in distress, interpret the situation as an emergency, feel responsible to help, know the appropriate way to help, and decide to offer aid. A negative decision at any stage assures no helping. Research has shown that an individual is less likely to help in a group situation because responsibility is diffused.

Key Terms

altruism	effort justification	just-barely-sufficient threat
attitude change	egocentricity	norms
attitude	egoism	primacy effect
attraction	Elaboration Likelihood Model (ELM)	proximity
attribution	false consensus effect	schema
bystander intervention	foot-in-the-door approach	self-fulfilling prophecy
cognitive dissonance	fundamental attribution error	social cognition model
door-in-the-face approach	hedonic relevance	social psychology

GREAT ALTRUISTS: SCIENCE PONDERS SOUL OF GOODNESS

It was still dark that morning in 1942 when the Gestapo rousted from bed the Jews of Bobawa, a Polish village. In the confusion, twelve-year-old Samuel Oliner slipped away and hid on a roof, still in his pajamas. The next afternoon, when he dared to look around, the ghetto was silent. The Jews of Bobawa, murdered that day, by then were lying in a mass grave in the nearby countryside.

Samuel found some clothes in an empty house and, skirting German patrols and Polish looters, fled to the country. There, after walking for two days, he found his way to the farmhouse of Balwina Piecuch, a peasant woman who had been friendly with his family. Mrs. Piecuch knew, when Samuel knocked at the door, that she would be shot if the Germans found her harboring a Jew. Without hesitating, she took Samuel in.

Balwina Piecuch taught Samuel the rituals of Polish Catholic life—how to go to confession, how to pray, catechism. With her help, Samuel posed as an impoverished Polish stable boy in search of work and a place to live. Thus Samuel survived the war.

Exemplars of Human Goodness

By some estimates, there were as many as 200,000 Jews who, like Samuel Oliner, were saved from the Nazis by non-Jewish rescuers. In Berlin 5,000 Jews survived through the combined efforts of tens of thousands of Germans, many of whom fooled the Gestapo by moving Jews from hiding place to hiding place.

Now, in a remarkable project, researchers are reaching into the caldron of good and evil that was World War II to retrieve for study those exemplars of human goodness, the non-Jews who, like Mrs. Piecuch, risked their lives to help Jews survive the Nazis.

The director of the project is Samuel Oliner, now a sociologist at Humboldt State University in Arcata, California.

"We want to find the common threads among those few who helped, and the differences between the rescuers and those others who might have helped but chose to look the other way," Dr. Oliner said in an interview. He heads the Altruistic Personality Project, in which researchers working in the United States, Canada, Europe and Israel will conduct, if funds allow, detailed interviews with 400 people who rescued Jews during the war.

Strong Sense of Self-Worth

Dr. Oliner and his associates, who have already interviewed 140 rescuers, believe they are racing the clock to reach the rest before they die. On the basis of the interviews he has conducted already, however, he has reached some preliminary conclusions about the characteristics of the rescuers.

In broad strokes, his findings are in accord with the views of such humanistic psychologists as Abraham Maslow and Erich Fromm, who saw a strong sense of self-worth and security as the psychological base from which people could reach out to help others.

To be sure, there is no single, all encompassing explanation for the rescuers' acts. Indeed, some saved Jews for selfish reasons, they were paid or bribed. Most sheltered people they knew or with whom they had ties. But many rescued complete strangers.

Dr. Oliner's research project is part of a broad search under way to understand what leads an individual to help when others turn their backs on a person in need. While that question is one that theologians and philosophers have sought to answer for thousands of years, psychologists of late have made intensive efforts to provide their own insights.

Spurred by Murder of Kitty Genovese

Ironically, the current research on altruism was spurred, in large part, by a tragic instance of its absence, the 1964 murder of Kitty Genovese as thirty-eight neighbors in Kew Gardens, Queens, looked on without calling the police for help. The incident galvanized psychologists, who realized that they had no ready explanation for why these neighbors refused to help, or for contrasting acts of human kindness.

Psychoanalysts have proposed several psychological motives for altruism. One view, for example, holds that those who help others to their own detriment are masochistic. Another sees altruism as an effort to expiate unconscious guilt or shame. For example, Erik Erikson attributed Mohandas Gandhi's humanitarianism, in part, to such guilt.

Behaviorists, on the other hand, have explained altruism in terms of the reinforcement people get from making themselves feel good by doing good. Behavior geneticists have studied twins to see if there is an inherited temperament that predisposes some toward acts of kindness.

Sociobiologists offer an entirely different analysis of altruism, noting that it is seen, too, in animals. For example, in several species of primates, members of one troop will raise an orphaned youngster from another troop. Some sociobiologists argue that altruism is a survival strategy in evolution, since helping others who share one's genes is a form of reproductive success. But such theories, in Dr. Oliner's view, do little to explain what impelled the rescuers he is studying to risk their lives—and often their families' lives, too.

What can be said, for example, of the motives of the S.S. officer who concealed a Jewish couple until the end of the war in his living quarters directly above the S.S. Center in Berlin? Or, for that matter, what drove the Belgian countess who not only hid 100 women and children on her estate, but also cooked kosher food for them?

Of most interest to the researchers is the contrast between these rescuers and the vast majority of non-Jews who also could have saved Jews, but did not. Dr. Oliner has so far interviewed twenty non-rescuers, and plans to talk to 180 more.

The preliminary findings from his project, and results from a variety of other studies, converge on the formative experiences people have in childhood, which seem to make them, many years later, more predisposed than others to come to the aid of the distressed.

On the basis of this preliminary data, Dr. Oliner has identified a key cluster of the factors that seem to be at play in the rescuers as a group. There were, in his view, three elements that combined to lead the rescuers to their acts of kindness and heroism.

Foremost among them was having compassionate values. In most cases, these values seem to have come from someone in the person's childhood who embodied them. Perry London, a psychologist at Harvard University who studied a group of rescuers now living in Israel, concluded that "almost all the rescuers" had a strong identification with a parent who was a "very strong moralist."

But, Dr. Oliner points out, espousing such values was in itself not enough. The rescuers were also distinguished by a sense of competence. They saw themselves as in control of their lives. Moreover, they also seemed inclined to take calculated risks.

And, finally, the rescuers had to have at their disposal the wherewithal to put their values and sense of competence into action. For some that meant a special expertise, such as being an expert skier who could escort Jews across the snow-covered Alps to Switzerland; for others, it simply meant having a home large enough to have a hiding place and having family and friends who supported the rescue effort.

Though Dr. Oliner cautions that these findings are preliminary, they dovetail with results from several other diverse studies of altruists.

In an approach similar to that taken by Dr. Oliner, Nancy McWilliams, a psychoanalyst, has conducted intensive clinical interviews with five people who have dedicated their lives to helping others. Although exploratory, Dr. McWilliams's research is instructive because her subjects represent an extreme of altruism; they include a woman who cares for the children of lepers in the Far East, and a man who runs an international adoption agency for crippled or otherwise unwanted children.

She began her study because she was dissatisfied with the psychoanalytic theories of altruism that saw it as pathological. "These are the kind of people who don't show up in psychotherapists' offices," she said. "They're not neurotic or depressed, they have good relationships and a sense of humor about themselves."

She found a common pattern in the early development of those she studied. Most had suffered the loss in early childhood of a warm and nurturant caretaker, such as the death of a mother. And in every case there was a "rescue" by someone in their lives who they felt saved them by replacing the lost person. For some it was a housekeeper; for others an older sibling or their father.

"As children, they idealized that person," Dr. McWilliams said. "He or she became their model for altruism. Moreover, most grew up in families with strong religious values. Many of them feel a sense of 'doing God's work,' as one put it, though none is observant now."

One of the most detailed theories of the roots of altruism is that proposed by Ervin Staub, a psychologist at the University of Massachusetts. Writing in *The Biological and Social Origins of Altruism and Aggression,* a collection of articles by several experts published in 1985 by Cambridge University Press, Dr. Staub reports evidence that altruism requires more than just compassionate values and the psychological and practical competence to put them into effect.

"Goodness, like evil, often begins in small steps," Dr. Staub said in an interview. "Heroes evolve; they aren't born. Very often the rescuers made only a small commitment at the start— to hide someone for a day or two. But once they had taken that step, they began to see themselves differently, as someone who helps. What starts as mere willingness becomes intense involvement."

Dr. Staub cites the example of Raoul Wallenberg, the Swedish diplomat who used his status to save hundreds of Hungarian Jews. "The first person Wallenberg rescued was a business partner who was a Hungarian Jew. Soon, though, Wallenberg was manufacturing passes that made Jews candidates for Swedish citizenship, and so protected them from the Germans. As his involvement grew, it got to the point that he was exposing himself to great risks by giving out the passes to Jews waiting in line for Nazi deportation trains."

But there is a special kind of person who is more likely than most to take that first step to help, and to stay with the effort to the end, the altruist.

"There is a pattern of child-rearing that seems to encourage altruism in later years," said Dr. Staub, who is studying the roots of altruism in childhood. "A warm and nurturant relationship between parent and child is essential, but not enough in itself. The same holds for having parents who espouse altruistic values—it's important, but not sufficient."

From his own research and that of others Dr. Staub has identified a particular style of disciplining children which seems essential for children to learn the lessons of altruism.

"The parents who transmit altruism most effectively," he said, "exert a firm control over their children. Although they are nurturant, they are not permissive. They use a combination of firmness, warmth and reasoning. They point out to children the consequences to others of misbehavior—and good behavior. And they actively guide the child to do good, to share, to be helpful."

Children who have been coached to be helpful, or who engaged in altruistic projects such as making toys for poor, hospitalized children, Dr. Staub has found, are later more altruistic when a spontaneous situation in which they can help others arises.

There may be quite specific interactions between parents and children that cultivate such altruism, according to results from a major series of studies by Carolyn Zahn-Waxler and her colleagues at the National Institute of Mental Health.

The beginnings of altruism, her research shows, can be seen in toddlers as young as two years. At that age altruism typically takes such forms as trying to make an upset playmate stop crying by offering toys or food, or otherwise consoling him.

Whether a child displays altruism seems tied to how the mother or other caretakers treat the child in key moments, particularly times when another person is in distress. For example, according to Dr. Zahn-Waxler, children who were more often altruistic had mothers who tended to explain to them the consequences of hurting other children, and to do so with great feeling, with an admonition such as,

"I don't like to be with you when you act like that."

When the mothers gave a calm, unemotional admonition, it did not seem to lead the children to be altruistic. Nor were the children of mothers who frequently handled the child's transgressions by simply telling them, "No! Stop!" without explaining why.

Some mothers Dr. Zahn-Waxler studied, particularly those who blamed their children for mistreating playmates, induced a guilt-ridden altruism in their young children. These children often feel they have caused hurts that were not their doing.

On the other hand, the young children of chronically depressed mothers seem to be particularly sensitive to the distress of other children, Dr. Zahn-Waxler finds. While they are not overly guilty about the distress, they are preoccupied by it.

A healthier kind of altruism, she believes, is that produced by "the nurturant but moralizing parent who arouses the child to concerned action."

The Individual in Groups

17

As the bus rolled south, Josh Gibson reflected on the events that had taken place over the last few weeks. Despite the fact that he was just 20 years old, he had already earned a reputation as one of the most powerful long-ball hitters in the Negro National League. His success was noticed by Gus Greenlee, who offered him a contract to play on his team.

Greenlee was a newcomer to baseball, and his money was much needed in the Negro National League, which was struggling to stay alive during the Great Depression. This was an era when blacks were barred from playing on white major league teams. As a result, two leagues existed in the United States—one for white players and one for black players. The white league had the superior organization and facilities, and stars such as Babe Ruth. Greenlee, however, promised to bring new life to black baseball. Thus when he made his offer, Josh Gibson eagerly signed the contract. Josh was now headed for spring

training with the newly formed Pittsburgh Crawford Giants.

Spring training began in mid-February. Josh needed this time to work himself back into shape and regain his fluid swing and sharp hitting eye. Spring training offered such an opportunity, since the players were isolated from the demanding crowds of spectators and there were no long bus rides to interfere with their training. Josh, like many of the players, spent a great deal of time alone and concentrated on improving his batting and his fielding.

On March 25 the season began in Monroe, Louisiana. The fans marveled as the Crawfords rolled into town in their new bus and took the field dressed in brand-new uniforms. Black baseball had not witnessed such extravagance since its beginning in the early 1920s.

Josh was proud of his team and he enjoyed the company of the players on and off the field. As the season wore on, they became a close-knit group. In the early part of the season the games were played

in the South. Here, although the weather was good, the social climate was not always welcoming. In some small towns the Craws would have to leave town immediately after the game because there was no hotel that accepted blacks. At some parks they were allowed to play on the field but could not use the locker rooms for showering or changing clothes because they were for "Whites Only."

After the games Josh and a number of his teammates would go out on the town. Even off the field it was not hard to tell that the players belonged together. The dress fad of the time was sport caps and "plus fours" (long baggy knickers). When the players went out after the games, they wore this town uniform. At first Josh had been reluctant to dress in plus fours. Baggy pants on his huge frame made him look like an out-of-control sailboat. However, after a great deal of good-natured pressure from his teammates, Josh wore them.

By the end of the season the Craws had not only developed a style of baseball, they had also adopted a clearly identifiable structure as a group. Satchel Paige, who was by far the best-known player on the team, was something of an outsider (Brashler, 1978). He was the player who most often "played to the fans," both on and off the field, and he rarely spent his free time with his teammates. Josh, who had become a star in his own right, became one of the leaders of the team. On the field and off, he associated with the team members—in fact, he was rarely seen without them. The players looked up to Josh, and by the end of the 1932 season he was being billed in black newspapers as the "Black Babe Ruth."

The long season finally ended, with the Craws having compiled a 99–36 record. Many of the players looked forward to going home to be with their families. However, the end of baseball season in the United States marked the beginning of winter baseball in the Latin American countries. Scouts from the Latin teams followed both the black and the white leagues, and many of the Craws, including Josh, were offered contracts.

When these offers came, the Craws gathered together to discuss the winter leagues. There were many advantages to playing on the Latin teams. First was the money; in many cases, the salaries were better than those they received in the United States. The second advantage was that there was no color barrier in the Latin countries; black and white Americans and Latins played on the same teams. This offered the black players an opportunity to directly compare themselves with white major league players. There were also many drawbacks to the winter leagues. The ball players would be away from their families for many months. It also meant continued travel and living in hotels.

Josh and his teammates discussed the pros and cons of winter baseball and decided to give it a try. Josh delighted the fans with his booming homeruns. He continued to play in the United States in the summer and in Latin America during the winter. He stayed with the Crawfords until they began to break up in 1937. The Crawfords, however, had become a close-knit group, and even though the players eventually all played for other teams, they kept in contact with one another.

The color barrier was finally broken in 1945 when Branch Rickey signed Jackie Robinson to play with the Brooklyn Dodgers. Unfortunately for the Craws, this action came too late for them to have their shot at the big leagues. Only Satchel Paige was given a chance to play with the major league teams. The breaking of the color barrier was too late to affect the career of Josh Gibson, who died in 1947 at the age of 35. ▬

The biggest job facing the Craws coach, Oscar Charleston (standing), was to get the individual players to work as a group. Gibson (third from left) was a team player and as the catcher, he was the player who had the best view of the team.

After completing this chapter, you should be able to:

List and explain the five reasons that people belong to groups.

Explain roles and norms and their advantages and disadvantages to a group.

Discuss the factors that can lead people to conform to group norms.

Compare the behavior of men and women in groups.

Compare and contrast the theories of leadership.

Discuss the advantages and disadvantages of group decision making.

Describe the factors that can influence a person's performance in a group.

Identify and discuss the roots of prejudice and other forms of intergroup conflict.

Discuss the ways to reduce prejudice and intergroup conflict.

Studying Individuals in Groups: History and Scope

There are many outstanding aspects in the story of Josh Gibson. One of the clearest is the important role the Craws played in his life. This group was the center of his life during his adult years. He worked and played with members of this group; his attitudes, behavior, and even his dress were influenced by the group members. Moving closer to home, examine your own daily life to see how important groups are. At any one time, you probably belong to five or six groups (social, religious, school, sports), and each of these groups affects your life.

For almost a century, social scientists have recognized the important role that groups play in our lives. In 1896, the sociologist LeBon was struck by the violent and often irrational behavior of crowds. He reasoned that people lose their individuality in crowds and become guided by the group mind. LeBon argued that crowds are driven by emotion and instinct and are, therefore, free of the restraints of civilized life and reason (Turner, 1987). At about this same time, the social psychologist Norman Triplett (1898) observed cyclists racing in head-to-head competition and racing alone—to "beat the clock." He noticed that the cyclists had faster times when they raced in head-to-head competition. He followed up on this observation by developing an experiment in which children wound string on a fishing reel either alone or in competition with another child. He found that the children worked harder when in the presence of another child than when alone. These early efforts suggested that being in groups influenced people in a variety of ways and that groups should be the object of further study.

This viewpoint was questioned by Floyd Allport (1924), who argued that groups were no more than the sum of their parts. He observed that "no one ever tripped over a group" and concluded that we should not study groups, and should concentrate instead on examining individuals.

Allport's view, in turn, was countered by Solomon Asch (1952), who said that trying to understand human social behavior by examining individuals alone was like trying to learn about water (H_2O) by examining hydrogen and oxygen in isolation. Asch argued that groups are more than simply the sum of their parts; there is something unique about the combination of people that cannot be understood by studying only individuals.

An even stronger force in the study of groups was Kurt Lewin, who founded modern social psychology (see Chapter 16). He demonstrated how people influenced each other in groups; in doing this, he conducted a number of fascinating studies on leadership, individual performance in groups, and the effect of public commitment on attitudes and behavior. Lewin helped found **organizational psychology,** the branch of psychology that studies how organizational structure and dynamics affect people's functioning in business and industrial settings. Lewin and his colleagues developed the T-group (or training group) method. This technique helps managers and other group leaders learn about group process and experiment with different group behaviors (see Chapter 15).

During the period in which Lewin was working, Carolyn and Muzafir Sherif were developing another approach to studying groups. Although their initial research focused on the development of group norms (or rules), these investigators soon turned their attention to examining the relationship between groups (intergroup relations). They were interested in the hostility that developed between different groups and how this hostility could be reduced.

From these beginnings, the study of groups has expanded to include many areas of psychology, a host of group behaviors, and a wide variety of applied issues. Developmental psychologists are concerned with such groups as the family, play groups, and classroom groups; clinical psychologists have interests in group and couple therapy; organizational psychologists focus on work groups; sports psychologists examine teams. Other research on groups has focused on juries, combat units, and even terrorist groups.

Before examining some of the specific research in the group area, let's quickly address one issue that is often raised by students. As we've seen, the study of groups has deep roots in both psychology and **sociology.** Although there is a great deal of overlap between the two fields, there are also some important differences in the emphasis of each.

Psychology tends to focus on the individual and how he or she reacts to social stimuli. Psychologists are concerned with how the individual's actions, attitudes, and perceptions are affected by being in a group. Using this approach, we might examine how Josh Gibson's hitting was affected by being on the Craws, or how his teammates influenced Josh to play in the Latin League. On the other hand, sociology would focus on the group as an entity (Oskamp, 1984). Sociologists would be interested in the structure of the group, and how the group fit into broader social developments such as social class or industrialization.

With this review in mind, let's move to examining groups and their influence on us.

Organizational psychology
Branch of psychology that studies how organizational structures and dynamics affect people's behavior in business and industrial settings.
Sociology
Study of the functioning and organization of human society and human behavior.

Why Belong to a Group?

Take a few minutes to list the groups you belong to. What can you learn from this list? First, you belong to a number of groups. Second, the groups you belong to vary in size, function, and types of members. Some are small, others are large. The functions of the groups you belong to are probably very different; on your list you probably included your family, work groups, social groups, study groups, and religious groups. Given that so many of our activities are performed in groups, it is important to ask why people join groups.

Rewards

Most groups offer their members a wide range of rewards. In Josh's case, he joined the Craws because of the attractive salary. In your own case, it's likely that you have joined some groups for the material rewards they offer. For example, one study revealed that workers joined unions because membership offered them higher wages and job security (Rose, 1952). However, in addition to material rewards, there are a number of other benefits that come from group membership. Prestige and recognition are two such rewards. Josh enjoyed prestige as a member of the Craws. People would often point him out as a member of the famous Craws team, and fans flocked to get his autograph.

Social Support

The social support we get from groups is similar to a reward, but the feeling is somewhat different. Just being in a group often gives us a sense of well-being and comfort. It may be hard to describe exactly where this feeling comes from, but a number of investigators have identified it as resulting from social or emotional support (Hill, 1987). This support means that we have others who listen to our problems and comfort us. Knowing that the group is behind us enhances our feeling of mastery and frees us to try new things. As we saw in Chapter 12, social support enhances mental health and reduces stress. In fact, one study found that Israeli soldiers in the 1982 Israel-Lebanon war were less likely to develop combat stress reactions if they viewed their platoon as a source of social support (Solomon, Mikulincer, & Hobfoll, 1986). In the same study, the investigators found that the lack of social support led to increased feelings of loneliness and combat stress. This study supported the advice of the Greek general Anasander in the first century A.D. that fighting units should be formed by placing "brothers in rank beside brothers, friends beside friends, and lovers beside their favorites."

Groups such as Weight Watchers offer members social support as well as information on how to lose weight. Members suffer and triumph together and give encouragement and hope that the goals can be accomplished.

Information and Evaluation

Groups are often a valuable source of information for us. During registration and before final examinations, college campuses often become alive with small groups of students busily exchanging information about the best professor to take Math 301 with and hints about how to study for the Econ 227 final. People join garden clubs, investment groups, and travel clubs to get information they cannot get on their own.

In addition to this type of information, we also join groups to get information about ourselves. Though we don't often think about this sort of information, it plays a central role in our lives. For example, Josh Gibson was driven by the desire to find out how good a baseball player he was. Practicing with his father had shown him that he could hit and throw a baseball. But was he really good? In order to answer this question, he needed to compare his abilities with others. Playing for the Craws showed him that he was as good as, and in most cases better than, other black players. Still, Josh wanted to know whether he was as good as the white major leaguers who got so much publicity. This desire for comparison with white players was one reason he joined the Latin American teams during the winter season.

In some cases, tangible reality will give us the answer to a question. For example, Josh Gibson could measure how far he could throw or hit a ball (physical reality), but this would not tell him how good a player he was. Similarly, it is difficult to think of a tangible reality that would tell us whether our religious beliefs are "correct" or how attractive we are.

In order to find these answers we must turn to **social reality:** the beliefs, attitudes, and behaviors of others. **Social comparison** theory suggests that we often learn about ourselves by comparing our performance with that of other people (Festinger, 1957; Suls & Wills, 1990). Josh determined his ability by comparing it with the ability of other players. We decide whether our attitudes are reasonable by finding out what others believe. We even evaluate our physical characteristics by comparing them with other people's characteristics.

Going a step further, we not only want to *evaluate* our attitudes, attributes, and abilities, we also want to *validate* them; in other words, we

Social reality
Beliefs, attitudes, and behaviors of other people.

Social comparison
Using social reality to evaluate oneself—comparing oneself against the beliefs, attitudes, and behaviors of other people.

One of the ways we learn about ourselves is to compare with other people. In many activities, such as gymnastics, social comparison allows us to determine how good we are at an activity.

want to know that our abilities are good and that we hold correct attitudes (Tesser, Millar, & Moore, 1988). In order to satisfy the need for evaluation and validation we tend to join groups whose members are similar to us. For example, if you are an intermediate level tennis player, you won't want to join a group of beginners. Beating beginners won't tell you much about your game. On the other hand, you also avoid joining a group of advanced players; being thrashed by them won't tell you much about your game either. Most likely, you will be attracted to other intermediate players who can both give you information about how well you are playing and allow you to see whether you have made progress.

Achieving Goals

Another reason people join groups is to achieve certain goals. In some cases, these goals cannot be achieved without belonging to a group. Josh Gibson could not have played baseball without belonging to a team. A mountain climber needs a team to reach the summit of a cliff. In other cases, people join groups because membership makes achieving the goal easier. Thus many people join Weight Watchers because they find it easier to stick to a diet if others are also doing it. It's not impossible to diet on your own, but it's easier if you're part of a group.

Establishing Self-Identity

There is an old dieter's saying: "You are what you eat." Research on groups modifies that saying to read: "You are the groups to which you belong." If someone were to ask you to tell about yourself, you would probably give them information about your interests, goals, and experiences, and the groups to which you belong (your family, your university, your social club). If you look around your own home, you might find mementos of groups to which your family members belonged; pictures of an old softball team, a cheerleading squad, a school class, or a pennant from a university. These examples illustrate another reason for joining groups: We achieve a large part of our self-identity from the groups to which we belong. Groups help us identify who we are and allow us to demonstrate this identity to others and to ourselves. For example, Brown and Lohr (1987) interviewed seventh and twelfth graders and found that students who belonged to groups had higher self-esteem than those who did not belong. Further, a student's self-esteem was directly related to the status of the position he or she occupied in the group. As we will see later in this chapter, because our self-identity is so closely tied to our groups, we tend to elevate the status of our own groups and depreciate that of outgroups. This process may well be one of the foundations for prejudice and discrimination.

There is another interesting way in which groups affect our self-identity. Many of us, whether children or adults, evaluate ourselves on the basis of appraisals that we think others have made of us (Felson, 1989). For example, before responding to the question of whether or not you are attractive, you might ask yourself how your friends would describe you. When you do this, your self-image becomes a **reflected appraisal,** mirroring the image you believe others have of you. In this way the group becomes a resource for learning how others evaluate you, and this information, in turn, influences your self-image.

Clearly, then, there are a number of reasons for joining groups. It is unlikely that any one group will satisfy all of our motives. For this reason we seek membership in a wide variety of groups. But no matter how many different groups we belong to, they all share a somewhat similar structure, which we will look at next.

Reflected appraisal
Basing self-image on the image we believe others have of us.

Whether we talk about a baseball team such as the Craws or a family, there are certain similarities that exist in all groups. A **group** consists of two or more people interacting in such a manner that each person influences others and is, in turn, influenced by other group members. Groups have boundaries so that people know who is a member and who is not a member (Forsyth, 1990). In a similar fashion, group members often go through a cycle in which their behavior changes. There are also similarities in the structure of most groups. In almost every group there are norms and roles that guide the behavior of members and contribute to the smooth functioning of the group.

Norms

In general, the Craws were a loosely run team in which a great deal of individual freedom was allowed. However, there were certain rules that applied to everyone. All team members were expected to be in uniform and at the ball park some hours before the game. All team members were expected to be at the bus with their bags packed at a certain time. We find that other groups also have general rules. Families, for example, often have agreements about what time everyone will eat meals. Social clubs such as fraternities and sororities may have rules about acceptable dress or behavior. Professional societies generally have rules of ethics that guide the conduct of all members.

Rules that govern specific behavior and apply to all members of the group are called **norms.** Norms may be written, as are the bylaws of many groups, or they may be unwritten but clearly understood codes. Whatever their form, norms "specify what must, or must not, be done when" (Steiner, 1972, p. 171).

In an interesting experiment on norms, Roethlisberger and Dickson (1939) observed work groups on a production line. They found that these

Group
Two or more persons who are interacting with one another in such a manner that each person influences and is influenced by each other person.

Norms
Rules that govern specific behavior and apply to all members of the group.

Norms are rules that govern specific behavior and apply to all members of the group. Workers often develop norms regarding how hard members should work, and enforce these norms through such means as "binging."

groups developed unwritten rules about how much each worker should produce. These norms allowed the men to work at a comfortable rate. Any worker who produced too much or too little was treated to a *binging* ritual that was designed to force him to produce in conformity with the group norm. Binging involved the other workers joking about the man's work and then playfully but forcefully hitting him on the shoulder. The "bing" was not strong enough to severely hurt him, but it was strong enough to give him the message to change his work habits. Going a step further, in an experiment by Milgram and his colleagues (1986), they had a confederate cut into lines at railroad ticket counters, betting parlors, and other locations in New York. As Figure 17–1 shows, they found that the people who were most affected by the norm violation (cutting into lines) were most likely to enforce the norm (object to the line breaker).

Roles

In addition to norms that apply to everyone, groups have rules that apply only to people in certain positions. These are called **roles,** and they define the obligations and expectations of that specific position. For example, on a baseball team there is the role of catcher. The rules applying to where and how this position is played are different from those applying to the pitcher or the first baseman. The formal roles on a baseball team are easily learned from a rule book. In addition to these formal roles, groups also have informal roles. For example, as one of the biggest men on the team, Josh was expected to come to the aid of team members if they got into scuffles on or off the field.

Roles
Group rules that apply only to people in certain positions; roles define the obligations and expectations of that specific position.

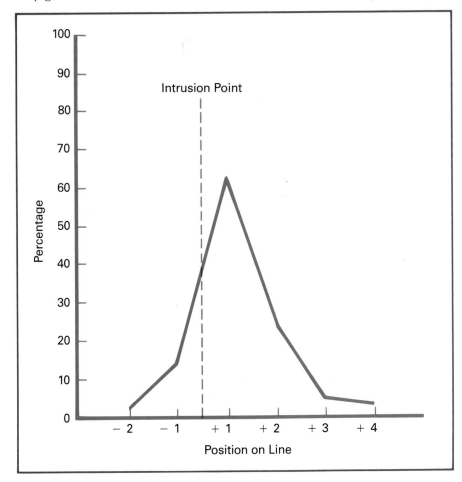

FIGURE 17–1
Percentage of persons objecting according to position in line.

Roles not only affect group member's behaviors and expectations; they also influence how observers interpret behavior. For example, in one study 14-year-old subjects saw a videotape in which one girl was assigned the role of "questioner" and the other girl the role of "contestant" in a quiz show game. As it happened the contestant missed a number of the questions. The observers subsequently rated the questioner as more intelligent and as having more ability than the contestant. These results occurred even though the roles were randomly assigned and subjects never saw the questioner answer any questions (Block & Funder, 1986).

Together, roles and norms give the group stucture, let members know what is expected of them, and influence how members will be perceived. This knowledge also helps group members predict the behavior of other group members.

Although norms and roles can help the group run smoothly, they can also prove disruptive and troublesome when they outlive their usefulness. For example, when smallpox was a real threat to children in the United States, most school systems adopted a written norm that students must have a smallpox vaccination before they could attend school. Partly because of the vaccination program, the threat of smallpox was virtually eliminated in the United States. However, many school systems continue to require students to have the vaccine despite the fact that it has possible negative side effects and smallpox is almost nonexistent in the United States. A second problem with norms and roles is that people belong to many groups and the demands of one group may conflict with those of another. For example, a woman who is a professor, mother, lead singer in a band, and member of the school board may find that the demands of one role make it difficult, if not impossible, for her to meet the demands of the other roles. This **role conflict** will result in considerable stress and require her to make adjustments in her various roles. Finally, roles may severely limit the freedom of group members and force them to take positions they are not suited for and do not enjoy. For example, a friend of ours in the Forest Service was recently promoted to an administrative position in Washington, D.C. She loved working in the national park but hated being confined in an office, although her salary and responsibilities were greater in her new role.

Social Dilemmas:
Groups versus Individuals

Josh Gibson knew that if he were to gain recognition, he would do it as a power hitter. Therefore, each time he got up to bat, he wanted to hit a home run. However, there were times when the team needed Josh to bunt the ball so that a base runner could advance. These situations pitted Josh's individual needs against the needs of the group. This is an example of a classic group problem that has been named the **social dilemma** (Samuelson & Messick, 1986). We find social dilemmas in many situations. For example, old New England towns were often built around a pasture or commons. The commons served everyone's needs as long as no one farmer put too many cows on the pasture and overgrazed it. The situation, however, posed a personal dilemma for the farmer; if he added an extra cow or two, his profit would increase, but if all the farmers did this the commons would be ruined. All too often the farmers chose to satisfy their individual needs, resulting in the Tragedy of the Commons, the destruction of the pasture (Hardin, 1968).

Looking at the situation, we can understand why individuals in groups often act out of self-interest. First, if you were the farmer, you might think that adding an extra cow or two really wouldn't hurt. The problem

Role Conflict
Situation that exists when the demands of roles the individual holds require conflicting behaviors.

Social dilemma
Situation where individual needs are in conflict with group needs.

arises when all the farmers think this way. Second, even if you foresaw the ultimate disaster, you might not trust your neighbor to act for the good of the group. You are not going to let that so-and-so profit by your good will, so you add cows to get what you can before the commons are ruined for everyone.

Social dilemmas occur when environmental concerns are at the heart of the issue, for example, energy use, pollution control, or physical space. The situation is always the same: short-term individual goals versus long-term group goals.

Social dilemmas are notoriously difficult to resolve. Groups attempt to control a member's behavior by establishing norms to punish members acting only in their self-interest (Sato, 1987) and by increasing the member's identification with and concern for the group (Lynn & Oldenquist, 1986). In the latter case, the state of Texas attempted to reduce traffic accidents and inconsiderate driving habits with a campaign that emphasized that Texans "Drive Friendly." The campaign appealed to residents' pride in their state and emphasized that the name Texas was derived from the word friendship. There even were bumper stickers with the slogan "Drive Friendly" written across the state flag. The social dilemma is seen as a major conflict between groups and their members; the task for the group is how to fulfill individual needs and at the same time have members contribute to the group and follow group norms.

Group Change and Development

When you read the story of the Crawford Giants' 1932 season, an important point unfolds. The Craws were a very different group when they met for spring training than they were during the middle of the season, and they were a different team at the end of the season than they were in the middle. For example, at the beginning of the season, the Craws were very interested in getting to know one another, so they spent a great deal of their free time together. However, later in the season, the team members spent more time in small cliques, and some of the players were more concerned about gaining individual recognition than about the team's performance. If you review any group to which you belong, you will find that groups are not cast in stone. Rather, they are dynamic units that are constantly changing and developing, and these changes have profound effects on the group members.

The issue of group development has long been of interest to psychologists. In reviewing observations of small laboratory groups and therapy groups, Tuckman (1965) found that groups went through predictable stages of development: forming, storming, norming, performing, and adjourning. For example, during the first stage, forming, group members focus their attention on defining their group boundaries and determining who will be a group member. During the middle stage, norming, group members often discuss and decide upon the norms, or rules, that will guide the members' behavior. They might, for instance, examine whether decisions will be made by majority vote or group consensus (everyone agreeing).

More recently, other investigators have expanded the research to a broader range of groups, including political parties, fraternities, political action groups, social movements, and religious groups (McGrath, 1988; Worchel, Coutant-Sassic, & Grossman, 1991). This research also found that groups develop through predictable stages and that group members' behavior changes from stage to stage. For example, when a group is newly forming, group members are often concerned with establishing the group's identity and building its morale. During this early stage, groups often demand conformity and punish deviants, strong leaders emerge, and the

Table 17–1
Life Cycle of a Group Member

Stage	Behavior
Prospective member	Reconnaissance (learning about the group)
New member	Assimilation (fitting in)
Full member	Role negotiation
Marginal member	Resocialization (independence)
Ex-member	Reminiscence (remembering activities in the group)

Source: After Moreland, R. L., & Levine, S. M. 1982.

group avoids cooperating with other groups (Worchel et al., 1991). However, later in the group's life, members focus on identifying group goals and on group performance. At this point there is less demand for conformity, the opinions of individual members will be accepted if the other members feel they will help group performance, and group members become increasingly concerned with personal reward and recognition.

The point of this discussion is to remind you that groups are forever changing and that these changes strongly affect the behaviors that are most likely to occur. Before leaving this issue, let us complicate it a bit more. Just as the group changes over time, so does the group membership. Individuals are constantly moving into and out of the group, and each of these individuals goes through stages of development (Moreland & Levine, 1982, 1988). As can be seen in Table 17–1, as a prospective member, you will be most concerned with learning about the group and the costs and benefits of membership in it. After you have been a group member for some time, you may enter the marginal stage where you attempt to gain some independence from the group. Therefore, we might view a group as a moving highway filled with vehicles (group members) that are each moving at different speeds, some entering the highway and some leaving it. With this dynamic view of groups in mind, let's examine some of the specific behaviors that take place within the group setting.

Conformity: Dancing to the Group's Tune

For any group to function, group members must adhere to norms. The Craws could never have gotten to the ballpark, much less played a game, if each team member did exactly what he wanted to do. Some players might make it to the game on time wearing their uniform, while others might arrive 2 hours later wearing bathing suits. But uniformity of behavior among the Craws went far beyond following clear team rules. Recall the opening description where we discussed how Josh Gibson came to wear baggy "plus fours" even though he hated this outfit. If we think of our own behavior in groups, we will acknowledge that we have often acted to meet group expectations, even when we were uncomfortable doing so.

Conformity is behavior that occurs when we change our actions or attitudes as a result of real or imagined group pressures, despite personal feelings to the contrary. In the case of Josh's dress, it would not be conformity if he started wearing "plus fours" simply because he liked them, and then found his friends also wearing similar outfits. Josh's behavior was a clear case of conformity because (1) he would not have chosen this style of

Conformity
The behavior that occurs when a person changes his or her actions or attitudes as a result of real or imagined group pressures, despite personal feelings to the contrary.

dress had he been on his own, and (2) he wore "plus fours" because he was pressured to do so by his friends.

Clearly some degree of conformity is necessary if we are to function in groups. And much conforming behavior that is not necessary for group functioning involves harmless acts or attitudes. For example, every kid in Ms. Anderson's third-grade class thinks that New Kids on the Block is the greatest music group to ever live. But conformity can also lead to dangerous actions such as using drugs because "everyone else is doing it" or adopting prejudiced attitudes in order to be accepted. And because the basis for conformity is real or imagined group pressure, individuals may act without considering the implications of their behavior or assuming responsibility for it. Because of the central role that conformity plays in our lives, it is important that we understand it and identify the reasons why people conform.

Why We Conform

In order to understand why we change our behavior to match that of other group members, we must recall our discussion of the reasons people join groups. One major reason is that groups serve as a source of information for us. Consider, for example, your attitude toward nuclear power. Most of us know very little about the topic; to really understand the details involved, we would have to take many courses in physics, engineering, and economics. How, then, can we form an attitude on this issue and make decisions about it? One way is to find out what other people believe. Even as children we learn to seek information from groups, and we generally find that if many people tell us the same thing, it is true. Groups then develop power to influence our attitudes and behavior because of their informational value. This type of influence has been labeled **informational pressure,** and it is the basis of much conforming behavior (Kelley, 1952).

We also suggested that people gain identity, security, and an opportunity to achieve important goals by belonging to groups. Therefore being part of a group and being accepted by others are important to our well-being

Informational pressure
A type of influence a group has, based on the group's value as a source of information.

Conformity involves changing behavior or attitudes to make oneself more similar and acceptable to a group. In order to determine whether conformity is influencing behavior, we must know that a person would have acted differently without group pressure.

and self-esteem. As we grow up and become members of many groups, we learn an important lesson about the "personality" of groups. Groups accept members as long as those members conform to the group norms and standards. People who do not conform are often ridiculed, rejected, and in some cases quickly made ex-members of the group. The moral of this story is that conformity leads to acceptance. Because belonging to groups is so important in everyone's life and because rejection and ridicule by the group are often painful, the group possesses **normative social pressure** to influence the behavior of its members. Returning to the Josh Gibson example, it is clear that his conversion to "plus fours" was largely due to normative pressure: His friends teased him and poked fun at him until he adopted the style. His behavior was aimed at keeping his membership in the group.

Before leaving this discussion of why we conform, some additional points need to be made. First, in most cases, groups use both informational and normative pressures to get their members to conform. One type of pressure may be more effective at times than the other, but both types are generally employed. Second, the two types of pressure cause different types of conformity. People who react to normative pressure are acting on the fear that the group will reject them; they conform only as a means of being accepted by the group. In these cases, the normative pressure leads only to *simple compliance*—a change in public behavior but no change in private attitudes. An example of simple compliance is prisoners of war openly criticizing their own country while in the hands of their captors. Once they are free, however, they no longer voice these opinions. On the other hand, when a person uses the group as a source of information to decide the correct course of action or belief, *private acceptance* is more likely to result. This involves a change in both public behavior and private attitudes.

Normative social pressure
Type of group pressure based on the desire to belong to the group.

Factors Influencing Conformity

Understanding the pressures that motivate us to conform gives us only part of the picture of conformity. For example, Josh Gibson and Satchel Paige played on the same team and experienced many of the same pressures to conform. Yet Josh generally went along with the group, while Satchel marched to his own drummer, often angering the others. What determines whether or not a person will follow or resist group pressure?

In order to study the effects of group pressure, Solomon Asch (1951) developed a technique in which all group members except the unsuspecting subject were confederates of the experimenters. After all group members were seated, the experimenter asked each group member in turn to respond to a simple question (Figure 17–2). The subject was always toward the end of the group. In some cases, all the confederates gave an obviously incorrect response. Asch considered the subject to be conforming when he also gave the incorrect answer, even though he knew the correct answer. Asch expected that given the ease of the task and the obvious incorrect group answer there would be a few examples of conformity. Instead he found that about 35 percent of the subjects' responses reflected conformity. Asch's method was used by various other researchers (Moscovici, 1985) to study the conditions that affect conformity. We can consider these findings under the broad headings of individual, group, and task effects.

The Individual. One of the simplest explanations for the differences between Josh and Satchel could be personality: Josh might have had a personality that disposed him to conform whereas Satchel did not. However, despite a great deal of research, investigators have not found particular personalities that push people to conform. On the other hand, it does seem that people's position in their group affects whether they comply

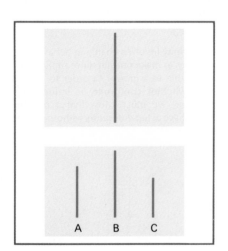

FIGURE 17–2

Subjects were asked which line on the bottom card was most nearly the same length as the single line on the top card. The obvious answer is "B" but the naïve subject, upon hearing the confederates give "C" as the answer, might be influenced by his or her cohorts. The correct answer is obvious, but subjects are influenced by the group to give an incorrect response.

with norms. In general, conformity will be greatest among people who (1) expect future interaction with group members (Lewis, Langan, & Hollander, 1972); (2) are strongly attracted to the group (Sakurai, 1975); (3) do not feel accepted by the group (Dittes & Kelley, 1956) and (4) are not completely confident about their ability (Geller, Endler, & Wiesenthal, 1973).

Looking at another individual characteristic, controversy was sparked by research on gender differences and conformity. Early studies (Gerard, Wilhelmy, & Connelly, 1968) found that women conformed more than men. At first glance, these results would seem to support the unflattering stereotype of women as easily influenced. However, more recent work has found that women conform more only on tasks that are male-oriented (requiring mathematical or mechanical ability), and these differences are most likely to occur when women know their behavior is being observed (Eagly, Wood, & Fishbaugh, 1981). Further, it has been suggested that women's conformity in many cases is not an example of blind following; rather their behavior is motivated by their concern for the group and their desire to keep group conflict at a minimum (Wood, 1987). As we saw in our discussion of social dilemmas, the group can be disrupted by a member who decides to satisfy personal needs.

The Group. One of the first questions researchers asked about the group regarded size: Does conformity increase as the size of the group increases? The answer seems to be that conformity increases until the group reaches a certain size; from then on, the addition of more people does not affect conformity. Early research suggested that the magic number was four; that is, conformity reached its maximum when the group numbered four, but did not then increase with additional people (Asch, 1951). However, Leon Mann (1977) had two, four, six and eight persons line up at a bus stop in Jerusalem. He then observed how other people would respond to these lines of different lengths. He found that only 17 percent of those who first arrived joined lines of two or four persons. However, 58 percent and 83 percent of the first arrivers took their place in the six- and eight-person lines, respectively. Therefore it seems that the maximum number of people producing the maximum conformity will be a function of the setting and other task and group variables.

Another important characteristic of group influence is whether or not the group is unanimous in its opinion. In order to demonstrate this effect, Asch (1956) had subjects judge the line-comparison task under three conditions. In one condition, the group of confederates unanimously chose the same incorrect line on 12 of the 18 trials. In the second condition, one of the confederates always gave the correct answer even when the remainder of the group responded incorrectly. In the third condition, one confederate gave an incorrect answer that differed from the incorrect answer given by the other confederates. The results were dramatic. When subjects were confronted with a unanimous majority, the conformity rate was the same as it was in the earlier studies, about 35 percent. However, when there was one other nonconformer in the group, conformity dropped to about 9 percent. This drop occurred even when the other confederate gave an incorrect response that was different from the incorrect answer given by the other confederates.

A final but very interesting characteristic concerns whether or not the people who are the source of pressure can be categorized into units. One investigator suggests that we respond to categories of people as a single unit rather than as individuals (Wilder, 1977). For example, if nine members of a baseball team separately asked you to contribute to a charity, they would be able to exert less pressure on you than nine unrelated individuals would. This is because you would view the players as a unit and respond to them as a unit rather than as separate individuals.

The Task.   As might be expected, conformity is greater when the task is difficult or ambiguous. This, however, does not mean that there isn't considerable conformity on simple tests that have clearly correct answers. We saw an example of the latter type of conformity in the original Asch study. Interestingly, it seems that for simple tasks, increasing the group size yields greater conformity, while for difficult tasks, group size makes less of a difference (Campbell & Fairey, 1989). In other words, when you are being pressured to do something you know is incorrect, it matters how many people are pressuring you.

Obedience: "I Was Only Following Orders"

As we discussed conformity, another type of behavior might have come to your mind. **Obedience** is following the direct orders of someone in a position of higher authority. This is very different from conformity, where it may be unclear what others want or expect and where those others often have no clear authority. For example, when Oscar Charleston, the Craws' coach, told the players when they must be in their hotel rooms on nights before the game, both his authority to make rules and the rule itself were clear. The players' behavior in response to the orders of their strict and demanding coach was clearly a case of obedience.

When we think of the sinister side of obedience, we are inevitably reminded of World War II, when over 6 million innocent people were tortured and killed by Nazis who claimed that they were only following the orders of their superiors. Some of us may also recall the murder of innocent Vietnamese villagers at My Lai by soldiers of Charlie Company who "were only following orders." And most of us will recall Lt. Colonel Oliver North's proud explanation for his illegal acts in the Iran-Contra affair. He, too, was acting on the orders of his superiors.

These and many other such cases are dramatic reminders of the terrible consequences that can follow blind obedience. But since the situations mentioned involved people under stress obeying superiors with enormous power, we might be tempted to soothe our troubled minds by reasoning that "normal people" do not blindly follow orders in most situations, especially if doing so would mean hurting other people. Or, closer to home, we might assure ourselves, "I certainly wouldn't follow orders that I felt were wrong or could injure others."

This reasoning might make you feel better, but the evidence is against you. Stanley Milgram (1963, 1965) found that "normal" people in "normal" times will often follow orders to hurt innocent people. Milgram recruited subjects from New Haven and Bridgeport, Connecticut, through newspaper advertisements. The male subjects were between 20 and 50 years old and came from a variety of backgrounds and occupations. They represented the "average" type of person you would find in these cities. When subjects arrived at the experimental setting, they were told they were to teach another subject by the use of electric shock. They met the other subject, a nice middle-aged man, who was led away and "hooked up" to electrodes in another room. The subjects were told that each time the "learner" made an incorrect response, they were to increase the level of shock they administered. As the experiment continued and the learner made more mistakes, the subjects would hear him scream in pain when they shocked him. (Actually, no shocks were delivered to the "learner," who was a confederate of the experimenters.) At one point he begged them to stop the experiment. When the subjects hesitated or asked about the learner's welfare, the experimenter ordered them to continue administering the shock. The subjects could clearly see the level of shock they were administering; the different levels were labeled "very strong shock," "extreme-intensity shock," and "danger—severe shock."

Obedience
The following of direct and explicit orders of a person in a position of authority.

How many of these people do you think continued following the experimenter's orders until they reached the top-level shock labeled "XXX"? Two-thirds of Milgram's subjects dutifully followed the orders, despite their belief that they might be injuring their victim. Most of us would claim that we would never do such a thing. In fact, Milgram asked a group of senior psychology students at Yale University and a group of psychiatrists to predict how many subjects would follow orders to inflict the maximum level of pain. They predicted that less than 2 percent would obey the order to give the 450-volt shock. Yet 65 percent of the people tested did indeed follow orders till the end!

In a very different setting, Hofling and his colleagues (1966) studied whether nurses in a hospital would follow orders to violate hospital rules and deliver a potentially harmful dosage of a drug to a patient. Nurses on duty received a phone call from a doctor they did not know. He ordered them to administer 20 milligrams of a drug for which the maximum stated dosage was 10 milligrams a day. This order not only was higher than the maximum safe dosage, but it violated hospital policy that no nurse was to give a patient drugs without the doctor being physically present. Despite these violations, 21 of the 22 nurses who were telephoned followed the doctor's orders.

These and other studies suggest that obedience results because people do not feel responsible for actions they perform under orders from an authority figure. They feel that the person giving the orders has taken the responsibility for the results of their actions. This sentiment was clearly echoed at the Nüremburg trials after World War II when many of the Nazi war criminals stated that they believed their actions were wrong but did not feel responsible for them, because they were merely following orders. Findings such as these should cause us to pause and question our actions. How often do we justify our behavior by convincing ourselves that we are not responsible because we are only doing what we are told to do?

But the feeling of not being responsible is insufficient to explain why people so readily follow orders, especially in cases where the behavior far exceeds the scope of the order. For example, the cruelty and savagery of the men in Charlie Company was clearly not demanded in their orders to "pacify" My Lai village. In a careful examination of many "crimes of obedience"—criminal activity that was later justified as following orders—Herbert Kelman and Lee Hamilton (1989) identified some other factors that underlie the willingness to follow orders. One is *ideological zeal,* the belief that the required actions are right or in support of a good cause. Another is that people get *personal gratification* from such actions—they feel powerful and free carrying out the orders. A third reason is that individuals believe they will reap *material gain* or *personal advancement* by following the specified orders.

Still another factor that influences whether or not we follow orders is the *role* we are filling. Roles often include rules that we follow the orders of certain others. In the Milgram study, people were in the role of "subject"; it is expected that someone in this role will follow the commands of the experimenter. In the Hofling study, the role of "nurse" includes following the orders of doctors. Other roles that include following orders are soldier, child, employee, and (even) student. As you can see, there are many forces pushing us to be obedient.

A Question of Ethics.   The research on obedience is eye opening for a number of reasons. Not only are the results quite startling, but the methods used to obtain them also give us reason for reflection. Was it fair and ethical to place unsuspecting people in such an uncomfortable position? Subjects in the Milgram study suffered a great deal of psychological stress. Even though they continued to give the ordered shocks, Milgram reported that many of his subjects sweated profusely, fidgeted incessantly,

GENDER DIFFERENCES IN GROUP BEHAVIOR: Exploding Some Myths

Watching events unfold in the Persian Gulf war was both sad and unreal. We saw the war "live and in color" on television. The television coverage brought home the horrors of war. In addition to the roller-coaster feelings of revulsion, sorrow, and hope, another feeling lurked in the back of our minds. Something was wrong with those pictures of soldiers preparing for battle. It took a while to identify what that "something" was, but Dan Rather, the CBS anchorman, put his finger on the issue 48 hours after the first bombs had been dropped on Iraq. Most of us expect war to be the domain of men. Even the term *soldier* brings to mind a rugged *man* dressed for battle. Yet many of the pictures of the troops preparing for war showed women dressed in battle fatigues and close to the fighting. In fact, 6 percent of the American soliders sent to the Persian Gulf were women. The television coverage of women in the war zone was a vivid reminder of the increasing presence of women in all types of groups, often in leadership roles.

Research comparing men and women in groups has become increasingly common over the past few decades, and the results are important and sometimes surprising. The early studies tended to present a rather unflattering picture of women in groups, suggesting that they were more likely to conform to majority opinion than men were (Gerard, Wilhelmy, & Conolley, 1968). Some studies suggested that women were less likely than men to join in group discussions (James, 1959) or to emerge as leaders (Craig & Sherif, 1986). Concern about women's ability to act in groups seemed to be present in the legal system as well. Although women were guaranteed the right to vote in 1920, it was not until 1957 that they were given the right to serve on federal juries, and only in 1975 did the Supreme Court rule that they could not be excluded from serving on a jury simply because of their gender!

More recent and careful research has revealed a rather different picture of the role of women in groups. The group behavior of women resembles that of men much more than originally thought (Deaux, 1976), although some interesting differences have been uncovered. While men join more groups than women, women spend more time in groups than men (Booth, 1972), and women's groups tend to be more unified than men's groups (Winstead, 1986). Second, men tend to be more task-oriented in groups than women, who tend to be more concerned about ensuring that the group will function smoothly (Wood, 1987). Along these lines, men tend to be more concerned about maximizing their payoffs than women (Miller & Crandall, 1980). Supporting this position is the finding that women are less likely to take advantage of the weakness of others. It has also been suggested that the small gender differences in the rate of conformity results because women view conformity as a way of facilitating group functioning, while men are more concerned with projecting an image of independence (Wood, 1987). Interestingly, both men and women adopt more positive, socially oriented behavior when interacting with a woman than when interacting with a man (Carli, 1989). Finally, although there may be only a slight difference in emergence into leadership roles, men and women display different styles of leadership. Men tend to be more directive and task-oriented, while women adopt a more democratic style (Hollander, 1985).

Recently, there has been a great deal of speculation that the gender differences that have been observed are not due to gender, but result from other factors. For example, males tend to conform less and perform better than females when the group task is masculine in nature, such as solving math or engineering problems. However, the gender difference reverses when the group problem is one in which females are expected to excel (Sistrunk & McDavid, 1971). Another explanation for gender differences concerns socialization. Males receive early training to show independence and be concerned with task issues, while women are socialized to be more concerned about social issues (Eccles, 1991). Status may also play an important role because men often hold higher status in groups than women do. It is interesting that as our society has given men and women more equal status and the differences in socialization patterns have diminished, research has found more similarity in the group behaviors of men and women (Forsyth, 1990). Finally, women often labor under unfair and biased expectations from others. We tend to expect men to perform better and assume leadership positions, and we are less willing to accept excellence from women at face value. One interesting study at West Point found that while women leaders performed as well as men and their groups had equally good morale, their success was explained as being due to luck or to having a good group to begin with. However, observers explained the success of male leaders as resulting from their own ability and efforts (Rice, Bender, & Vitters, 1980).

This discussion suggests that there may not be as big a difference in behavior between men and women in groups as once suspected, and that what differences do exist may not be due solely to gender.

---

fell into uncontrollable fits of nervous giggling, and showed other signs of discomfort and stress. They left the experiment with the unpleasant realization that they had given shocks in the belief that they were hurting the learner. Most of us can comfort ourselves by saying that we would not hurt another person simply because we were ordered to do so. The subjects in the Milgram studies could not protect their self-image with such thoughts, for they had just learned that they would do exactly this.

Although there are a number of reasons to question the procedures used in the obedience studies, there were some positive outcomes. In a follow-up questionnaire sent to subjects who had been in the Milgram study, 84 percent reported that they were glad they had participated. Also, the results obtained from the studies on obedience have furthered our understanding of human behavior. We now know the power of orders and we have a greater comprehension of why people act as they do. The impact of the results would have been considerably less if Milgram and others had used a less powerful task, such as ordering subjects to write down random numbers or compose uncomplimentary stories about another person.

The issue of ethics is difficult to address in regard to designs such as those used in the obedience studies. On one hand, psychologists need to use designs that have a strong impact on subjects if they wish to obtain valid results. On the other hand, they need to constantly keep in mind their responsibility as researchers to protect the rights and welfare of subjects. Today most psychologists submit the design of their studies to ethics committees for review to ensure that subjects' rights are protected. Committees suggest different procedures if they think greater protection is necessary. Guidelines for the ethical conduct of research have been devised by the American Psychological Association, and there are now federal and state laws protecting human experimental subjects. The effort to guarantee the rights and safety of human subjects is a continuing one, and, with the wholehearted cooperation of researchers, experimental designs that are sensitive to the subjects' welfare (both human and other animals) have become the rule, as we discussed in Chapter 1.

Leadership

The discussion of obedience demonstrated how readily people will follow the orders of leaders. Because leaders can have such a strong influence on group members' behaviors, it is important to understand how someone becomes a group leader and what factors play a part in making a person an effective leader.

A **leader** can be defined as the person who has the greatest influence on the activities of the group (Shaw, 1981). The use of this definition has given rise to two interesting observations. As far back as 1904, Terman pointed out that each member of a society is both a leader and a follower. It is unusual to find a group where the same person is always the leader; different people at different times are able to influence the group's activities. Some people may lead more often than others, but, depending on the time and circumstances, we are all leaders and we are all followers.

A second point is that at any one time there are often two leaders in a group. One of these leaders (the *task specialist*) is generally concerned with solving the tasks facing the group; he or she is most involved with getting the job done and presenting the group with guidance on solving problems. The other person who has a strong influence on the group is concerned with person-oriented activities. This *socioemotional* leader may be the clown in the group, since he or she often reduces group tension, diffuses interpersonal conflicts, encourages other members to contribute, and influences the emotional tone of the group.

It is interesting to find that the Craws' pattern of leadership fit this scheme. Oscar Charleston, the player-manager, was clearly the task specialist. He was older and more experienced than the other players, and even had he not held the title of manager, his main concern would have been

Leader
The person in a group who has the most amount of influence.

to get the Craws to play a good "brand" of baseball. But Charleston, because of his age and focus, was not the person who set the emotional tone of the team. Players like Josh and Jimmie Crutchfield were the social/emotional leaders. They kept the team members from becoming too depressed when they were playing badly, and they thought up jokes to reduce tensions when personal conflicts threatened the team spirit. These two types of leadership helped the team function more smoothly.

Theories of Leadership

As you might expect, there is a great deal of interest in determining why some people emerge as successful leaders. Discovering a formula for successful leadership would allow organizations such as businesses, the military, a baseball team, or even your own groups to ensure that they had the best leadership possible. Unfortunately the search for such a formula has proved as elusive as the search of the early Spanish explorers for the fountain of eternal youth. However, unlike that earlier search, social and organizational psychologists have made headway in identifying some of the factors that affect leadership (Gilmore, 1988).

Early efforts were guided by the belief that successful leaders would possess certain traits such as intelligence and need for achievement that would equip them for their leadership position (Terman, 1904). However, after hundreds of studies aimed at identifying the magic traits, investigators have largely abandoned this *great person approach to leadership*. There are no traits or set of traits that ensure that a person will be a successful leader (Forsyth, 1990).

If it isn't the person's traits that determine his or her success, maybe the characteristics of the situation hold the key. The *situational approach to leadership* argues that situational variables such as the needs and structure of the group and the presence of an outside threat determine who emerges as leader. Hence, being in the right place at the right time is the critical

The situational theory of leadership states that conditions rather than personal traits determine who will emerge as the leader. Research has shown that the person seated at the head of a table often becomes the group leader.

FOCUS ON POWER AND ITS ABUSE

No discussion of influence would be complete without mentioning **power,** for power is the capacity to influence other people. Take a moment to consider the people who have power over you. Where does their power come from? Social psychologists (French & Raven, 1959; Madden, 1987; Boulding, 1989) have identified at least six roots of power.

1. *Coercive* power relies on threats and punishment in order to "influence." Because it is easy to use this type of power and it achieves quick results, coercive power is used frequently. However, it has two critical drawbacks. First, the low-power person dislikes the high-power person and is motivated to sever the relationship as soon as that becomes possible. Second, the use of coercive power requires that the low-power person be watched so that he or she does not try to deceive or avoid the "grip" of the high-power person; people obey the coercive leader only because they fear him or her and not because they believe it is the right course of action. Only coercive power, because it is a punishment situation, requires that the low-power person be watched.

2. *Reward* power relies upon positive reinforcement as a means of "influence." In this case, the low-power person is motivated to stay in the relationship and surveillance is not generally necessary. However, reward power is costly to the high-power individual because lower-power people are influenced only as long

as the high-power person continues to possess rewards.

3. *Legitimate* power comes when the person has a specific role (for example, president, captain, boss). One cannot "use up" legitimate power, but this power is limited to specific domains; for example, a boss can only influence behavior at work.

4. *Expert* power is based on the person being seen as an expert in a certain area; Josh Gibson was an expert hitter. Like legitimate power, the domain of expert power is limited. The use of expert power does not require that the low-power person be watched.

5. *Referent* power comes when a person is liked and admired. We want to be similar to those we admire; thus we change our behavior to be like theirs. Referent power does not weaken when it is used nor does it require surveillance.

6. *Information* power is based on having information that someone needs or wants. For example, an eyewitness can influence a jury because of the information he or she has. This type of power is very limited and evaporates once others have the information.

Lord Acton once remarked that "Power tends to corrupt, and absolute power tends to corrupt absolutely." All too often we witness support for Lord Acton's observation: Richard Nixon and Watergate, Ronald Reagan's staff and arms sales to Iran, Jim and Tammy Bakker and The PTL ministry. Power does seem to "go to the head" of the power holder. If we examine the use of power carefully, we can understand some of the

reasons why this occurs.

Power holders see themselves as influencing others. This leads them to belittle the powerless and devalue their contributions; the power holder believes that he or she is different from (better than) the powerless person and, thus, should be able to operate under a different set of rules. Also the power holder often views others as trying to get his or her power and, as a result, he or she mistrusts others and tries to set himself or herself apart from them. Further, having power makes one the center of attention. Praise is directed to the powerful and they are generally a focal point for communication. As a result, the powerful person often develops an inflated sense of self-worth. Finally, power is like a new toy; one is tempted to use it. This may, indeed, be a protective reaction because research (Michner & Lyons, 1972) has shown that powerful people who do not use their power are taken advantage of.

As we see, there are a number of forces that invite people to take advantage of their power. It is interesting to note that George Washington argued strongly that American presidents should be allowed to serve only a limited time in office. The founding fathers also set up the various branches of government to check and balance the power of each other. Laws such as the open disclosure law have more recently been instituted to further curb abuse of power. Even in interpersonal relationships, people often attempt to develop elaborate sets of norms to reduce the misuse of power. However, even with these safeguards, we still see many examples of abuse of power.

variable. For example, research has shown that the person seated at the head of a table often becomes the group's leader because he or she can maintain eye contact with the other group members (Howells & Becker, 1962).

Although it is true that the situation can affect who emerges as leader, this is only part of the story. As a result, most recent approaches to leadership take an *interaction approach.* This approach argues that the emergence of a successful leader is determined by a combination of leader traits, the needs of the group, and the situation (Chemers, 1987; Hollander, 1985). This approach also argues that people with different traits will be successful leaders at different times. For example, Fred Fiedler (1978) found that

Power
Capacity to influence other people.

leaders whose main aim is to complete a task are effective in groups that have either a high degree of structure or very little structure. On the other hand, leaders whose main concern is the satisfaction and happiness of group members are most effective in groups with a moderate degree of structure and in situations where the requirements of the task are not completely clear. Taking all this into account, the bottom line is that in order to have effective leaders, we must match the leader's characteristics to those of the group and the situation.

Resisting Influence

Based on our review of the research on conformity and the discussion of groups, you may find it hard to believe that our world is not filled with robots waiting to be guided. Clearly this is not the case. We do not always conform nor do we always do what others tell us. For example, research has found that fewer than 50 percent of patients comply with their doctor's orders to take their medication (Leventhall et al. (1984). Therefore let us briefly ask what factors lead us to resist pressures from other individuals and groups.

Some of the factors that aid in resisting influence are obvious. For example, people of high status or those who have been in a group for a long period of time can often get away with being deviate. It seems that these people build up credits that give them some freedom to be different. Other people deviate from norms in order to be noticed or to project an image of independence (Schlenker, 1985). In addition to these factors, there are some other, less obvious, forces that lead us to resist influence and deviate from group norms.

Restoring Our Freedom

On their long bus trips between games, the Craws would often pass the time playing jokes on one another. All the players were eventually the target of these antics, but on one trip Tincan Kincannon decided he had had enough. To punctuate his position, he placed a gun in his lap and ordered the others to keep their distance. Although this might seem like

Deviating from the group is one way to establish independence and become the focus of attention.

an airtight strategy to ensure peace and quiet, it had the exact opposite effect. During the whole trip the players schemed to make Tincan the butt of their jokes. When Tincan finally fell asleep, the players stole his fried chicken and tied the bones around his neck.

This example demonstrates an important point about social pressure. Pressure aimed at making us act or think in a certain way often creates a counterpressure within us to take the opposite course of action. It has been argued that all of us feel that we have the freedom to engage in a wide range of behaviors or hold a variety of attitudes (Brehm & Brehm, 1981). Pressure to adopt a particular position threatens our freedom. When this happens, we experience a psychological state called **reactance** that motivates us to resist the pressure and regain our freedom. One way we resist the pressure is to adopt an attitudinal position opposite that demanded of us or to engage in a behavior that has been forbidden. For example, Tincan's threat to shoot anyone who made him the butt of a joke threatened the freedom of the players to carry out their pranks. Although there was clearly pressure (the loaded gun) to leave Tincan alone, there was also the opposite pressure to regain freedom. Researchers have found that threats to freedom lead to an increase in the attractiveness of the threatened freedom and a stronger desire to engage in the threatened behavior.

Lack of Identifiability

When he was on the field or in a town where people recognized him, Josh felt that he had to live up to his image and act the way people expected him to. In these situations, if he made a mistake or did something wrong, people would know about it. However, he reported feeling free when he played his first season in Puerto Rico. There he was just another face in the crowd; people didn't know him and he didn't have to be so careful about how he acted.

As far back as 1898, the sociologist Le Bon realized that groups often change people into "primitive beings," causing them to do things they would not think of doing on their own. A number of years later, Philip Zimbardo (1970) examined the reasons why groups have such an effect on people. He suggested that in some groups people tend to lose their personal identity and assume the identity of the group; in more psychological terms this is referred to as **deindividuation.** Because they no longer seem to have a personal identity, group members lose the feeling of responsibility for their own actions, and they no longer feel the same restraints against socially disapproved behavior. People's behavior in such a situation is generally emotional, impulsive, and intense. Deindividuated people show little concern for the results of their actions because they feel that they cannot be personally identified and that the group will assume responsibility for whatever they do. Further, people in the deindividuation condition are less aware of their feelings and behavior and less concerned about social evaluation.

A number of factors are likely to make people in groups feel deindividuated. The first is anonymity: When people feel they cannot be personally identified, they are most likely to feel deindividuated. Anonymity can often be achieved by having everyone in a group dress alike so that no one person stands out. A second factor is group size: The larger the group, the more likely it is that people will feel deindividuated. Mullen (1987) found that the violence perpetrated by lynch mobs became more horrifying as the size of the mob increased. A third factor is emotional: Deindividuation is more likely to result when people are aroused and in a new or unstructured situation.

The feeling of not being responsible for one's behavior can have many effects on people. For our present purposes, we will focus on one study

Reactance
Psychological state that motivates us to regain our freedom by resisting group pressure.
Deindividuation
Occurs in groups when people lose their personal identities and assume the identity of the group.

(Singer, Brush, & Lublin, 1965). It found that deindividuated subjects were less likely to conform to group opinions than were subjects who were more identifiable. It seems that the reduced concern about social evaluation freed people to express their own opinions rather than conform to group pressure. Sometimes people find being deindividuated an exhilarating experience that frees them to act more spontaneously. For example, we often find the meekest person screaming and shouting during a football or basketball game where he or she is an anonymous face in the crowd. This person would never dream of behaving in this way when alone or in a small group. In some cases, then, deindividuation can be fun and have positive results.

However, there is a darker side to deindividuation. People who live in large cities often feel deindividuated. As a result, they interact in an impersonal way, and this type of interaction can lead them to feel lonely and alienated. Since they are uncomfortable with the loss of personal identity associated with deindividuation, many people will try to regain their uniqueness by wearing clothing that separates them from the crowd, by putting their name on their automobile license plate, or by decorating their home in an unusual way.

Group Decision Making

In previous sections we focused on the general structure of groups and the types of pressures they can place on individuals. The points we raised apply to any group, regardless of the purpose they have for coming together. Let us now narrow our focus a bit and look at specific activities in our own groups. We will be able to identify two rather common activities. One is decision making: Group decisions range from solving problems to deciding who will lead the group. The study of decision making takes on additional importance when we realize that people's feelings about their groups are often determined as much by how decisions are made as by how much each person benefits from the decisions. For example, in one study subjects played the role of an employee who received a low payment for a job (Greenberg, 1987). The low payment upset subjects and turned them against their "employer" only when they felt the procedure for deciding on payment was unfair. The other common activity of groups is to perform tasks that range from playing baseball to building a house. In this section we will examine the decision-making process, and in the next we will focus on task performance.

To begin our study of decision making, let's look once again at the Craws. An important dilemma faced by many of the Craws at the end of the 1932 season was whether or not to play winter baseball in Latin America. Josh didn't know what to do. He loved playing baseball and he needed extra money. On the other hand, he had heard stories about the political unrest in many Latin American countries and about the rowdy fans whose wild enthusiasm sometimes resulted in serious injury to the players. Many of the other players felt the same way, so they came together to discuss the situation and made a decision about their future. Given the diversity of opinions, it was somewhat surprising that after a discussion of the risks, Josh's circle of friends decided to play winter baseball. This example raises a number of important questions. How are group decisions made? What factors in a group influence the decisions it will make? Do groups generally make wiser decisions than individuals acting alone?

Group Polarization

One of the interesting aspects of the Craws' decision to play winter ball was its rather drastic nature. The players knew little about Latin America, the league, or the conditions under which they would be playing. They were altering their lives on the basis of very little information.

This decision seems odd, especially in view of early theories about groups that held that people are less bold in groups than when acting alone. William Whyte (1956) speculated that people in organizations and business bureaucracies were less creative and less risk-oriented because they feared being ridiculed for taking extreme positions. A graduate student in the School of Industrial Management at MIT decided to show the conservative effect of groups. He wrote up some cases about people facing problems or dilemmas and asked groups to suggest possible solutions to these cases (Stoner, 1961). To his surprise, he found that the group solutions were more risky and extreme than the solutions that individuals suggested when working on their own. The host of research that followed Stoner's study also made the point that when the subjects made subsequent individual decisions, their solutions were more risky than the individual solutions they made before the group discussion. Thus, not only did the groups make riskier decisions, but participating in group discussions made the subjects take more risks when they later acted on their own.

For a number of years, investigators believed that groups influenced their members to make riskier decisions, and this area of research was referred to as the "risky shift." However, later research found that people do not always become more risk-oriented when placed in groups. This research showed that group discussions tend to polarize people and move them to believe more strongly in the position they initially held (Moscovici & Zavalloni, 1969). For example, if someone is inclined to make a risky decision on a particular issue, discussing the issue in a group will probably push him or her to take an even riskier position. However, if the person prefers a conservative position, the group discussion will push him or her to take an even more conservative position. Further, the research showed that the **group polarization effect** occurs in a wide range of areas, including attitudes, interpersonal impressions, and judgments about the importance of values. Given this new evidence, we can argue that the team discussion resulted in a decision for the Craws to play baseball in Latin America because most of the individual members were already leaning in this direction. If most of the players had had serious reservations, the group discussion would have strengthened these reservations and the players would have decided not to go to Latin America.

There are a number of possible reasons for this polarization effect. One explanation suggests that because the group rather than the individual will be held responsible for the decision—the diffusion of responsibility theory—people feel more free to adopt extreme opinions as group members. For example, if winter baseball had turned out to be a disaster, no single Craws player could be held responsible for getting the others to go to Latin America. A second explanation suggests that individual group members compare their viewpoints to the positions held by others in the group. When we find that our position is not as extreme as that of some other members, we change our position to be more extreme. We want to be at least as extreme as others in our group. By being as extreme as other group members, we present a positive self-image. Martin Kaplan (1987) suggests the concern about self-image is most strong when the group decision involves judgment or value-laden issues where factual information is not important. According to this *social comparison approach*, the positions held by the other group members is the most important information influencing the decision making of an individual group member.

Group polarization effect
Groups tend to polarize people and move them to believe more strongly in the position that they first held.

However, a third approach takes a rather different view (Burnstein, 1984). The *persuasive argument hypothesis* argues that it is the information about *why* people hold certain positions that is most important. People examine the arguments that others use to support their positions, and they change their position in the direction of the most persuasive arguments. This hypothesis may be most often supported when the group is faced with a decision about an intellectual or factual issue such as agreeing how far away Venus is from Earth.

A recent "sign of the times" study offered support for the persuasive arguments position. The investigators recognized that in today's world, groups often do not meet face-to-face; rather, members communicate with each other over computer terminals. In doing so, people may not be able to give as complete and complex arguments in favor of their position. Therefore, if the persuasive arguments position is correct, there should be less polarization in computer-mediated groups than in face-to-face groups. A study compared decisions in these two types of groups and found less polarization in the computer-mediated groups (McGuire, Kiesler, & Siegel, 1987). This study is not only relevant to the theory, but it may be of practical use to you if you are interested in getting a group to make a particular decision! Further, we may wonder whether or not Josh Gibson would have ever played winter ball in Latin America if the Craws had been communicating over computer terminals!

Groupthink

We have seen that groups often make more extreme decisions than people acting on their own. This finding leads us to ask another question regarding such decision making: Are the decisions made by groups of better or worse *quality* than those made by one person? Offhand, we might expect to find that groups make better decisions than individuals. The people in a group may bring a variety of information to it and may present different ways of looking at a problem. This seemed to happen when the Craws considered the possibility of playing winter baseball in Latin America. Each of the players had heard different stories about the pros and cons of baseball "south of the border," and through an exchange of information the players were able to make a decision.

Unfortunately, groups do not always make the best use of the information available to them. The results of an unfortunate group decision were seen on April 17, 1961. On that date 1,400 Cuban exiles landed at the Bay of Pigs in Cuba. They planned to set up a beachhead there, and unite with Cuban rebels in the Escambray Mountains to overthrow Premier Fidel Castro. They felt that their plan could not possibly fail. Their mission had been devised by one of the best intelligence organizations in the world, the United States Central Intelligence Agency (CIA), and the plan had been approved by President John F. Kennedy and his personal advisers.

However, the impossible happened. Nothing went as planned; instead of being greeted by friendly rebels, the exiles were met by a well-prepared Cuban Army that was quickly victorious over the exiles. The United States suffered a severe political setback, and the world wondered how such a respected group of men as Kennedy and his advisers could have decided on such a foolish plan.

Irving Janis (1982) carefully analyzed the Bay of Pigs fiasco and concluded that the decision-making process was responsible for the poor decision. Janis suggested that the Kennedy group, like many other decision-making groups, was a victim of groupthink. **Groupthink** occurs when group members become so concerned with reaching agreement among all mem-

Groupthink
Occurs when group members become so concerned with reaching agreement of all members of the group that they fail to critically evaluate their ideas.

Groupthink occurred in Kennedy's group of advisors who planned the Bay of Pigs invasion. The group had a strong leader in President Kennedy, and many members were afraid of voicing disagreement.

bers of the group that they fail to critically evaluate their ideas. Because they are so worried about keeping a positive group atmosphere, they fail to make good use of the information available to them. Groupthink is most likely to occur in close-knit groups in which group members like one another and are proud to belong to the group. Thus, an illusion of agreement exists in the group; because no one is openly expressing disagreement, group members feel that everyone must be feeling the same way. The group also develops the illusion that it can do no wrong. A strong and respected leader reinforces groupthink, since group members are unwilling to "buck" his or her authority and have a false confidence that their leader cannot be wrong.

Can groupthink be avoided? Janis says yes. He cites many examples, including one involving Kennedy and his advisers, where groupthink did not occur. Just over a year after the Bay of Pigs incident, Kennedy learned that the Russians were positioning nuclear missiles with atomic warheads in Cuba. He called a series of meetings with his advisers, many of whom had been involved in the Bay of Pigs decision. However, Kennedy was determined to avoid the pitfalls of that earlier decision so this time he encouraged his advisers to consider numerous alternative plans and to critically evaluate each one. Persons outside the group were called in to give advice. Kennedy himself did not take an early stand and even stayed away from several meetings. As a result of these actions, groupthink was avoided and the advisers settled on an effective and successful plan of action.

How can groupthink be avoided? Janis has the following suggestions:

1. Group members should be encouraged to carefully consider each alternative and to play the role of devil's advocate.

2. The leader should refrain from stating a preference and should encourage group discussion.

3. Outsiders should be invited to give their opinions on the issues.

4. Several meetings should be called to reassess new information and review the most preferred decision.

5. From time to time the group can be subdivided into smaller groups, each to consider the problem independently.

Who Influences the Decision?

If we knew that seven of the Craws players wanted to play winter baseball and two did not, we would not be surprised to find that the decision of the team was to play winter baseball. Both our own experience and research results show that the majority opinion generally rules the group's decision. And group members view decisions made by the majority as more fair than those issued by a dictator or pushed through by a minority group (Miller, Jackson, Mueller, & Scherching, 1987).

Much of the research on group decision making has been conducted on juries or mock juries. This research has found that the majority opinion is the one most often adopted by the jury. Juries deliberating under the unanimous-decision rule generally reach the same decision as do juries allowed to adopt the two-thirds-decision rule, but the unanimous-decision juries take longer to reach a decision and they discuss a broader range of information while doing so (Davis, Bray, & Holt, 1977). Interestingly, juries spend relatively little time (15 percent on average) discussing the testimony and much time (50 percent on average) talking about their personal experiences (James, 1959). And individual jurors often yield to majority pressure without really being convinced that the majority is correct (Wrightsman, 1991). For example, in the trial of Juan Corona, a man charged with murdering twenty-five drifters, a holdout juror is reported to have stated, "Please, I'll change my vote. Just don't hate me. I'll change my vote so you can go home to your wife" (Villasenor, 1977, p. 213). One more point in the majority's favor is that groups generally spend their time discussing information known by the majority of members and avoid information that is known by only a few (Stasser, Taylor, & Hanna, 1989).

But the majority does not always win the day. Sometimes the minority can be very influential. In an early study of bomber aircraft crews, it was found that the crew was more likely to adopt the position of the high-status crew member (the pilot) than of the low-status member (the gunner), even when both members had the correct answer (Torrance, 1954). Even apart from the issue of status, there is increasing evidence that the minority can play a very influential role in groups. In a series of studies using mock injuries and problem-solving groups, investigators examined the steps

Although majorities usually rule in groups, people in the minority can be effective if they take a clear, consistent stand and show their confidence in the position.

that minorities can take to maximize their influence (Moscovici & Personnaz, 1980; Nemeth, 1985).

Minorities are effective to the extent that they *become visible* and create conflict and tension in the group (Mucchi-Faina, 1989). The most important feature of minority influence is *consistency*. The minority member(s) must stay with the position they adopt and not appear willing to compromise or give in to the pressures of the majority. Second, the minority position must be *clear*; the other group members must be able to identify the minority's stand on the issue. Finally, the minority must appear *self-confident* and certain of their position. They will be less effective if they look hesitant and unsure of themselves.

It is rather easy to understand the power of the majority. As we pointed out, the majority often has the power to eject members from the group if they deviate from the norms. Thus, in addition to informational pressure, the majority exerts its influence through normative social pressure. The minority, on the other hand, has no normative power. They must rely on informational pressure. By adopting a consistent and confident stand even in the face of group pressures, the minority may cause other group members to question the majority position.

A number of investigators have carefully analyzed the minority influence process and arrived at some interesting conclusions. First, because minorities force people to consider information, minority influence often results in private acceptance (Nemeth & Staw, 1989). Majority influence, on the other hand, often begets simple compliance without changing private attitudes. A related point is that minority influence creates more long-lasting change than does majority influence. Second, compared to majorities, minorities stimulate people to develop novel and creative solutions (Nemeth, 1991). An unyielding minority may cause other group members to search for new information and additional solutions to the problems that face the group. In a sense, hearing the minority position frees you to think about the issues involved in the problem. Hearing the majority position leads you to focus on the few issues being discussed *and* on group issues, such as whether or not you will be accepted if you do not conform (Maass & Volpato, 1989). Third, it generally takes longer for the minority to influence the group than it does for the majority. This is one reason why it is important for the minority to remain steadfast in their position.

Before rushing out to trumpet minority positions in groups, we must recall two points. First, in most cases, the majority determines group decisions. Second, being in the minority can be a lonely and difficult position. The group often does not like the minority, and sometimes ejects it from the group (Moscovici, 1976). Interestingly, groups are more likely to reject minorities early in the group's development than later (Worchel, Grossman, & Coutant-Sassic, 1991).

Group Performance

We now turn our attention to task performance in groups. There are a number of interesting questions concerning the work of groups. One of the oldest is whether groups are more effective than individuals. In other words, if you have a job to do, should you do it on your own or enlist the aid of other group members? At first glance the answer may seem simple. Certainly groups should be more effective because the more people you can enlist, the greater the variety of talents you will have to draw on. Also, group members bring different backgrounds and perspectives to a problem, and groups also permit the division of tasks so that individuals

According to social facilitation theory, performance of well-learned behaviors is enhanced by an audience. Josh hit his longest homeruns when he was in front of large crowds of screaming fans.

have a chance to become experts in a single area. All these factors argue in favor of working in groups, and clearly there are certain tasks that can only be performed by a group. However, before embracing the group as the ideal solution to all situations, we must consider other issues.

There is an age-old warning: If you want something done right, do it yourself. Anyone who has sat through seemingly endless committee meetings knows painfully well that groups can get sidetracked on unimportant issues as different members press for influence and control. Investigators have identified two general types of problems that can plague groups and reduce their effectiveness (Steiner, 1976). The first is *coordination loss*; groups lose effectiveness to the extent that they cannot identify and coordinate the talents of their members. For example, a baseball team may have players with tremendous ability, but the team will only function well if these talents are identified and the players are assigned to the appropriate positions.

A second potential problem for groups is *motivation loss*, which takes place when members do not utilize their talents or give their maximum effort to the task. This loss often occurs when group members become discouraged because they feel their efforts are going unrecognized. In professional sports one sign of loss of motivation is when players demand to be traded because they are not being recognized or given enough playing time.

There is no simple answer to the question of whether groups are better at task performance than individuals acting alone. The answer depends on the type of task, the talents of the group's members, and how well the group can solve the problems of coordination and motivation loss.

Thus far we have been comparing individual to group performance. There is an equally interesting comparison to be made between the performance of individuals working alone and the performance of people working in or in front of groups. In other words, how does the group affect individual performance?

Social Facilitation: Lending a Helping Hand

Whether we are athletes or students in a class, some of our most agonizing moments come when we are called on to perform in front of other people. All eyes are riveted on us as our moment of reckoning arrives. Is the audience friend or foe? Does audience presence help us perform better or destroy our best-laid plans? A related question is how can we best prepare for these times. If we know we will be performing in front of an audience, should we practice under similar conditions or should we seek isolation to prepare? Questions such as these have intrigued psychologists for decades, and the answers they have discovered have stimulated some interesting theories.

In order to place these questions in a clearer light, we begin by examining the approach of the Craws. Like many other athletes, the Craws players felt that they could best prepare if they were not distracted by their attentive fans. Each year they gathered in Hot Springs, Arkansas, for spring training. Here the players could practice their hitting and fielding without the hordes of fans that would be present during their regular games. Josh Gibson enjoyed spring training, but he was always anxious for the season to start. He usually hit his longest homeruns and made his best defensive plays when he was in front of large crowds of screaming fans.

A number of early studies showed that people work faster when in the presence of others than when alone (Allport, 1924; Travis, 1925; recall our discussion of Triplett, 1898). Investigators found that this effect even transcends human beings. Chen (1937) studied ants digging tunnels and building nests. In some cases, he had the ants work alone, while in other cases, the subject ant worked with one or two other ants. Chen examined the balls of dirt excavated by the ant to determine the speed of work. He found that the ant worked harder (removed more dirt balls) when other ants were present. In addition to supplying such practical information as to how to get lazy ants to work, these early studies suggested that working in the presence of others increased individual performance.

Other studies, however, show that sometimes groups are bad for people's performance. For example, Pessin (1933) found that the presence of an audience inhibited the learning of a maze task and a nonsense-syllable task. However, Pessin made another interesting discovery: After subjects had learned the tasks on their own, their performance increased when they were placed in front of a group.

Robert Zajonc (1965) attempted to make sense out of these contradictory results. He suggested that the presence of others tends to arouse and excite people. The arousal is further increased when the audience causes people to worry about the impression they are making (Cottrell, 1972). This arousal creates an additional pool of energy that aids the performance of well-learned behaviors. We call this **social facilitation.** However, this additional arousal hinders the learning of new and complex responses. We call this social inhibition. Thus the presence of others leads to social facilitation of well-learned responses, but leads to social inhibition for learning new and complex behaviors.

Although Zajonc's reasoning explains some of the social facilitation, other investigators have developed other explanations for the effect (Geen & Bushman, 1987). One possibility is that when we are aroused, we narrow the range of our attention; we pay closer attention to fewer items. This change in the focus of attention may help in the performance of simple tasks but hurt the performance of more complex tasks. Still a third explanation suggests that audiences are distracting (Sanders, 1981). The conflict between paying attention to the audience and concentrating on the task at hand increases the performer's arousal. This, in turn, energizes the performance of simple and well-learned tasks, but inhibits the performance of new tasks. Regardless of the reason, however, the implication of the research on social facilitation is that people should learn new responses while they are alone and then perform these responses in front of a group.

Whatever the reason for the effect, audiences can either help or hurt our performance depending on the nature of the task and how well we have learned it.

Social Loafing: A Place to Hide

In most of the research on social facilitation, subjects work on a task where their individual performance is visible and measurable. This is similar to the situation faced by a baseball player; although he is a member of a team, people can easily determine how well he is playing. The research shows that in situations like these the group often has a positive effect on the person's performance. However, what happens when the person performs in a group where his or her contribution is not easily observable? In this type of situation the group has a very different effect.

In one experiment groups of one to eight people were instructed to pull on a rope, and then the total force was measured (Ringelmann, as reported in Moede, 1927). When Ringelmann looked at the average force exerted by each member, he found that as the group size increased, the force supplied by each individual member decreased. More than 50 years later Latané, Williams, and Harkins (1979) had individuals cheer as loudly as they could. Sometime after this the cheerers were placed in groups ranging in size from two to six members. They were then asked to cheer

Social facilitation
Occurs because the presence of other people tends to arouse people; this arousal creates an additional pool of energy that aids the performance of well-learned behaviors.

There are many explanations for the social facilitation effect. One suggests that audiences increase the person's concern with being evaluated.

as loudly as they could. Again, the results showed that although more noise was produced by groups, each individual cheered less loudly in the groups than when alone. The larger the group, the less loudly each person cheered.

These findings seem to contradict those we reported in support of social facilitation; in fact, we are arguing that the presence of others may result in **social loafing.** How can we reconcile these two bodies of research? If we carefully examine the situations, we can develop an answer. In the social facilitation studies, the individual's output was clearly identifiable and the individual could be evaluated as a result of his or her output. However, in the social loafing situations where the presence of others reduced output, the individual's output was pooled with that of other group members. Therefore, the output could not be linked with the specific person and that person could not be evaluated. Steve Harkins and his associates (Harkins, 1987; Harkins & Szymanski, 1989) have demonstrated that identifiability and the opportunity for evaluation determine whether group members will exhibit social facilitation or social loafing. Another interesting explanation (Mullen & Baumeister, 1987) centers on the focus of attention. In the social facilitation settings, performers know that others are watching them, and their own attention becomes focused on themselves. You are probably aware of this effect if you have ever asked a question in a large class; suddenly everyone is looking at you, and you become very concerned with doing a good job (asking a brilliant question). However, in situations that have produced social loafing, no one person is the center of attention, and people pay less attention to themselves or their own productivity. A final speculation concerns the group itself. Social loafing is most likely to occur when people care little about the group or do not feel an important part of the group. Research has shown that when the group is important to the individual, social loafing is reduced or eliminated (Brickner, Harkins, & Ostrom, 1986; Worchel, Hart, & Buttermeyer, 1987). In summary, it seems that we are most likely to loaf when we cannot be evaluated by our individual output, when our attention is not focused on ourselves, and when the group is not important to us. However, when the situation is reversed (evaluation possible, attention focused on self, and group is important), social facilitation will result from the presence of others, at least on simple or well-learned activities.

Social loafing
Peoples' motivation to work decreases when they are in groups where their individual performance cannot be observed; the larger the group, the easier to reduce effort without being detected.

Intergroup Relations, Prejudice, and Discrimination

As we have seen, groups are wondrously complex and affect our lives in many ways. On the positive side, they help us establish our identity; they enhance order in our world; they offer us protection and comfort; and they can increase our performance on tasks. These advantages are, however, achieved at a price. Being in a group often means that we must conform to group rules, and in doing so, we may lose a bit of our uniqueness. But this cost is minor compared to another effect that often accompanies being in a group; that cost is prejudice and discrimination.

Josh Gibson was well acquainted with prejudice and discrimination; his life was greatly influenced by these social phenomena. Because of the racial prejudice that existed during his lifetime, he could only play baseball on black teams in the United States. Racial prejudice determined the restaurants where Josh could eat, the dressing rooms where he could change his clothes, and the hotels where he could sleep. Racial prejudice meant that Josh had to fear for his life and safety in the same towns where he entertained baseball fans.

BUILDING GROUPS THAT WORK

Almost every discussion of business and industry at some point makes reference to Japanese practices. There is general agreement that the Japanese not only produce high-quality products, but also do it very efficiently—that is, they get the most out of the individual worker. When we examine how the Japanese get the most out of the individual, we find that they rely strongly on the group.

The Japanese develop strong worker loyalty and a willingness to sacrifice for the company by recruiting friends from the same school and putting them on the same work team (Zander, 1982). In order to reduce competition between people, promotions and bonuses are given to groups rather than to individuals. The company provides for a variety of worker needs, including health care, housing, clubs for social and leisure activity, and stores where items can be purchased at discounted prices. As a result, it is common for a Japanese worker to spend his or her entire life with one company.

Another group-based technique pioneered by Japanese industry and recently adopted by such American industrial giants as Ford, AT&T, and General Electric is the quality circle (QC). The quality circle is a small group (usually fewer than twelve members) of volunteers who meet regularly to discuss their work and to develop solutions to problems relating to job quality and working conditions (Munchus, 1983). QCs may deal with such issues as how to reduce vandalism, distribute bonuses, improve communication and job training, and create more comfortable working environments. The members of the QC can come from any job level, and an organization may have several QCs operating at the same time. For QCs to be effective, both labor and management must cooperate in developing the quality circle program and agree to use the suggestions coming from QCs. Experience with quality circles has shown that they can—at least on a short-term basis—improve job satisfaction and increase productivity and company profitability (Griffin, 1988).

Indeed, groups can be very valuable to business and industry, but good groups do not happen by accident. A major focus of psychologists who study human behavior in work settings (industrial/organizational psychology) is developing effective groups. Research in this area has identified a number of steps that will help develop effective working groups (Hackman, 1987, 1990; Zander, 1982). The first step, called *prework*, involves determining whether a group is really necessary to perform the work at hand. In this first stage, managers decide what work needs to be done, what skills will be necessary in the group, what authority the group should have, and what goals will be set for the group. The second stage involves *creating the conditions necessary for performance*. In this stage, managers identify the necessary material and human resources the group will need. It is also important at this stage to examine the physical work setting and ensure that group members will have such things as adequate space, comfortable temperatures, and easy communication.

The third stage involves *forming the team*. At this point, it is important to define who will be in the group and who will not—in other words, the boundaries of the group must be clear. This goal may be facilitated by giving group members distinctive uniforms and/or names. During this stage, members must understand and accept the tasks they are to perform; the group must agree on the division of labor within it. Finally, managers must *clarify the expected behaviors*. Employees need to know how their work will be evaluated, how their work activities will be planned, and in the case of multiple groups working on tasks, how group efforts will be coordinated. In the final stage, managers must *provide ongoing assistance*. This means supplying feedback to the group about how their work is progressing, as well as ensuring that the group's resources are replenished when necessary. Managers should monitor group activity, identifying problems and offering constructive solutions. They should be a source of continuing information, letting the group know about new techniques or new materials that may help in their work effort. They must walk a fine line between facilitating group performance and hindering group development by being too directive or too disruptive.

This discussion confirms what we all know: Working in groups can be very satisfying and enjoyable, or it can be frustrating and inhibiting. Being a good group member requires patience, knowledge, and understanding. Developing a successful work group demands the same characteristics.

Before examining prejudice more closely, there are a few points that must be made. Although the terms *prejudice* and *discrimination* are often used interchangeably, this usage is incorrect. **Prejudice** is an unjustified negative *attitude* toward an individual based solely on that person's membership in a group (Brewer & Kramer, 1985). Our prejudices are generally supported by *stereotypes* about the group in question. **Stereotypes** are oversimplified generalizations about the characteristics of a group. Stereotyping, then, involves placing people into categories with each category having its own set of characteristics (Hamilton & Troiler, 1986). They influence our memory and interpretation of events surrounding members of the

Prejudice
Unjustified negative attitude toward an individual based soley on that person's membership in a group.

Stereotypes
Oversimplified generalizations about the characteristics of a group.

Discrimination is often practiced even when it hurts the person practicing it. Employers may hire a less qualified white male even when they have applications from more qualified blacks or females.

group. For example, research suggests that we interpret ambiguous events to fit our stereotypes (Wilder, 1985). Further, we are less likely to distinguish between members of a stereotyped group than we are to make distinctions between members of our own group (Brigham, 1985). **Discrimination,** on the other hand, is negative, often aggressive *behavior* aimed at the target of prejudice. Exclusion from social clubs, neighborhoods, or jobs are examples of discrimination. Although everyone who holds prejudicial attitudes does not practice discrimination, such attitudes do make discrimination more likely.

Prejudice and discrimination have a number of characteristics that make them more difficult to understand than many other attitudes and behaviors. First, prejudice is baseless. These attitudes are not formed from facts or personal experience—it is not unusual to find someone who is racially prejudiced despite having limited interaction with minorities. Second, discrimination is often practiced even when it hurts the person practicing it. For example, an employer may hire a less qualified white male even when there are applications from more qualified minorities or women. Finally, the person who is the target of prejudice often takes on these prejudicial attitudes. For example, Goldberg (1968) asked female students to evaluate a manuscript. Half the students were told that the article was written by a man and half were told that it was written by a women. Despite the fact that the articles were the same, even women rated the manuscript higher if they thought it was written by a man.

Discrimination
(2) Negative, often aggressive, behavior aimed at the target of prejudice.

The Roots of Prejudice and Intergroup Conflict

How do people develop prejudicial attitudes? There are a number of theories about the roots of prejudice. Some of the earlier theories tried to lay the blame for prejudice on the individual's personality (Adorno et al., 1950). These investigators had some success in identifying certain personality traits that made people more likely to develop prejudicial attitudes. However, all people with these traits do not hold prejudicial attitudes, and many people without these traits are prejudiced. Thus we cannot blame prejudice on personal characteristics. As a result, most theories of prejudice are aimed at identifying situational causes of prejudice.

Group Categorization. Early in this chapter we pointed out that the groups to which we belong help establish our self-identity. Belonging to good, successful groups helps us and others see ourselves as good, and being in unsuccessful groups hurts our self-image. At first glance, we might believe that people are motivated to join "good" groups and avoid "bad" groups. This certainly happens, but so does something else.

In our effort to be associated with the best groups, we are tempted *to perceive* our own groups (ingroups) as being good and outgroups as being bad (Tajfel & Turner, 1985). Likewise, we do everything we possibly can to widen the differences between our group and the outgroups. This occurs even when people are randomly assigned to groups, and when they have never before met the members of their own group or of the outgroup. For example, Tajfel (1970) assigned subjects to two groups on the basis of their judgment of some paintings. He then gave the subjects the opportunity to award money to members of their own group and members of the outgroup. He found that subjects gave more money to ingroup members than to outgroup members. This effect occurred even when subjects did not anticipate meeting members of either group (Turner, 1981).

Because we belong to many groups at one time, we cannot constantly be separating all of our ingroups from all of our outgroups. Thus, outgroup discrimination is most likely to occur when a certain category or group characteristic is salient, or important for us (Brewer & Miller, 1984). For example, Josh Gibson was a member of the Craws, a black, and a male. During a baseball game, the category of "Craws" was most important; as a result, we can suspect he did everything possible to see his team as better than other teams. After the games, when he had to make his way through a small Southern town, the category of *black* was probably most salient (likely to occupy his attention); under these conditions we could expect him to make distinctions on the basis of skin color. Finally, distinctions on the basis of sex might have occurred if Josh had been engaged in a debate about whether or not women should play on the same professional baseball teams as men. Thus, simply being a member of a group leads us to enhance the position of our salient ingroups and depreciate salient outgroups. But, the effect of belonging to a group does not stop there.

Researchers found that group formation affects the way people perceive members of their own group as well as of the outgroup (Linville, Salovey, & Fischer, 1986). In a series of studies these investigators found that people tend to see outgroup members as being relatively similar, while they see greater variability in members of their own group. In other words, people tend to believe that their own group is made up of people with many different traits, whereas members of the outgroup are all the same. Believing that all members of the outgroup are similar has an effect on our behavior; namely, we feel that we only need meet a few members of the outgroup to know what all outgroup members are like. In other words, "met one, know them all." This belief leads us to reduce our contact with outgroup members and makes it difficult to change our beliefs about the outgroup (Quattrone, 1985; Judd & Park, 1988). You can imagine how unfair this effect is if you consider that an outsider visiting your university might conclude that he or she "knows" what all the students are like after meeting only two or three.

As if all this were not bad enough, Miles Hewstone (1988) reports another effect of ingroup-outgroup categorization. He found that people tend to attribute positive behavior by outgroup members as being the result of the situation or luck. However, they view negative behavior by outgroup members as due to enduring dispositions or traits. Quite the reverse happens for the ingroup behaviors; positive ones are viewed as resulting from stable traits whereas negative ones are seen as being due to the situation.

As you might imagine, these activities not only initiate prejudice, they sustain these attitudes by reducing contact between ingroup and outgroup members.

Competition.   True competition occurs when two or more parties are attempting to reach a goal so that if one party attains the goal, the other party does not. For example, a baseball game where only one team can win is an example of competition. It is rather easy to understand how competition can lead groups to dislike each other. In fact, competition often feeds upon itself and spreads because neither group wants to "give up" or back down (Brockner & Rubin, 1985).

Once groups perceive themselves to be in competition, conflict and hatred often escalate. Neither group is willing to make concessions because to do so may make them look weak. The issue then becomes one of *saving face*. The groups move further apart, and to justify this division, each group develops the belief that the outgroup is a threat (Bar-Tal, 1990). The more strongly a group member identifies with the ingroup, the more likely that individual is to develop negative attitudes about the outgroup (Struch & Schwartz, 1989). The hatred increases when the group resorts to threats of violence in an effort to force the outgroup to yield and demonstrate that the ingroup is strong (Deutsch & Krauss, 1960). The result is that the groups move still further apart because they now have "evidence" that the outgroup is bad and bent on a course of violence.

A terrible example of the destructive role of conflict and prejudice was recently played out in the Persian Gulf. Iraq's invasion of Kuwait shocked the world, and the United Nations responded by setting a deadline for Iraq to withdraw, threatening an armed response if Iraq did not comply. Iraq felt that it would lose face and show weakness if it withdrew, so it hardened its position and threatened to attack Israel if it were attacked by UN forces. The UN forces felt that *they* would show weakness if they did not respond with force to Iraq's threat. So war broke out, with each side viewing the other as the aggressor. Hatred and negative attitudes between the two sides increased, and these feelings would persist long after the last shot had been fired on the battlefield.

Learning.   In Chapter 15 we examined how parents influence their children's attitudes through control of rewards and information. Just as parents can teach attitudes to their children, so, too, can they teach them to be prejudiced against specific groups. The child who hears his or her parents criticize a particular group of people may mimic this position. In some cases, parents even directly reward their children for expressing prejudicial attitudes, but more often the prejudice is transmitted less directly. The strong influence of parents is seen in the fact that prejudicial attitudes are observable in many children as young as 3 years old (Milner, 1981).

Prejudicial attitudes are also reinforced by the media, which present certain groups in a negative way (Devine, 1989). Some years ago the news media habitually reported the race of a criminal if he or she was black, but made no mention of race when the criminal was white. Newspaper readers might easily have gotten the impression that most criminals were black.

The prejudicial attitude is very difficult to change if it is further supported by peer groups. For instance, children who see that most of their friends have a negative attitude toward blacks or Hispanics will express similar attitudes. In doing this, they are accepted by their group; to do otherwise would lead to rejection. It will be extremely difficult to change their prejudice so long as they continue to associate with that peer group.

Scapegoat Theory. Aronson (1976) relates an interesting story about the origin of the term **scapegoat.** During the Jewish days of atonement in ancient times, a rabbi would place his hands on the head of a goat while reciting the sins of his congregation. The intent was to symbolically transfer the sins from the people to the goat. The goat was then chased into the wilderness, taking the sins of the congregation with him. This animal became known as the scapegoat.

One of the earliest theories of prejudice suggested that prejudice and discrimination are the result of scapegoating (Dollard et al., 1939). In Chapter 11 we discussed frustration-aggression theory—the view that frustration motivates aggression. Once frustrated, people will aggress *unless* the cause of the frustration is beyond reach or too powerful to attack. In these cases, the frustrated person may displace his or her aggression onto a safer target, even if this target is not directly responsible for the frustration. According to this theory, then, a minority group may be singled out as the target or scapegoat for aggression and hostility because it is safe to attack and it often has highly visible characteristics (color, accent, name, etc.) that separate it from the more powerful majority (Konečni, 1979).

Researchers have found some support for this scapegoat theory. For example, Miller and Bugelski (1948) frustrated white workers at a civilian work camp by not allowing them to attend a movie. They then measured the workers' attitudes toward Mexicans and Japanese and found them more hostile toward these minority groups after being frustrated than before. It seems that the workers displaced their anger onto these minority groups. It is interesting to note that the greatest violence against the Jews in Russia occurred during times of economic hardship.

One way to reduce prejudice is to have people work for a common goal with those they may be prejudiced against.

Reducing Prejudice and Discrimination

It is one thing to know what causes prejudice and quite another to know how to reduce or combat it. This point is painfully clear from the history of the United States. Although many theories exposed the roots of prejudice before 1950, significant steps toward reducing racial discrimination were not taken until the late 1950s, after the Supreme Court ruled that "separate but equal" schools for blacks and whites were inherently unequal and unfair. It took the passage of the Voting Rights Act in 1965 to ensure equal access to one of the basic freedoms (voting) in the United States. And even today statistics demonstrate that discrimination still exists in the work world, and social research indicates that antiblack attitudes and behavior are still with us (Dovidio & Gaertner, 1986). These points demonstrate the importance of developing an understanding of how prejudice can be reduced.

Equal-Status Contact. One of the earliest suggestions on how to reduce prejudice was to increase contact between the members of different groups (Allport, 1954). Supposedly contact would allow members of the different groups to learn about each other and see that their stereotypes were invalid. Arguments such as this played a role in the Supreme Court's decision to mandate integration of public schools. Despite enthusiastic predictions that desegregation would reduce prejudice, the results of research have been disappointing (Amir & Sharan, 1984; Stephan, 1985). Studies showed that an *increase* in prejudice often followed desegregation. Further,

Scapegoating
Singling out a person or a minority group as the target (scapegoat) for aggression and hostility when the real target is too powerful to be attacked.

the self-esteem of black children did not increase, and in some cases actually decreased, when they entered integrated schools. The only bright spot in this largely dismal picture was that achievement by black children tended to increase in the integrated setting.

These results may seem surprising and discouraging. However, to put them in proper perspective, imagine that tomorrow you were suddenly enrolled in a fourth-year medical school anatomy class. Obviously you would not be on an equal footing with the other students. At first you would probably be perceived by the other students as rather dumb and your self-esteem would suffer as you compared yourself to them. Over time, however, your performance probably would improve and your self-image would be restored.

This example makes two points about the value of personal contact. First, contact in itself will not necessarily reduce prejudice. In order to be effective, the contact must be between people of equal status so that neither party is inherently disadvantaged by the situation. Equal-status contact has been found to reduce prejudice and intergroup stereotypes (Brewer & Miller, 1984). In a recent study (Ben-Ari & Amir, 1988) on changing Israelis' attitudes toward Egyptians, it was found that the influence of contact was enhanced if Israelis had positive information about Egyptians before the contact occurred. This information helped the Israelis see the Egyptians as equals. Second, we must distinguish between the immediate and long-term effects of the contact. Although equal-status contact may not immediately reduce prejudice, the longer-term effects may well be positive.

Cooperation. The integration of baseball could have taken place in two ways. One method would have been to have the black and white teams play each other. Or integration could have been (and was) achieved by having whites and blacks play together on the same team. Which method would we expect to be more successful?

The research strongly suggests that the latter method would be the more successful method of integration by far because it would bring people from the two racial groups together to work toward a common goal (winning) rather than competing against each other.

In a classic study, Muzafer Sherif, and his colleagues created hostility between two groups of children at a summer camp (Sherif et al., 1961). The groups competed against each other on a series of tasks and soon they were openly fighting against each other. Sherif then decided to find out if simple contact between the two groups would reduce intergroup hostility. Accordingly, the two groups were brought together in a number of situations that did not involve competition: for example, eating together in the dining hall. This did not, however, lead to less hostility—it just gave them an additional chance to fight, and insults as well as food were hurled between them.

The researchers then had the two groups come together in situations where their combined efforts were needed to solve problems whose solution would benefit both groups. For example, the groups went on a camping trip together, and the truck bringing their food became stuck. In order to move the truck, members from both groups had to push together. After a series of such events where the groups had to work on a common problem, the hostility between the two groups decreased markedly. Further research found that cooperative efforts aimed at a common goal reduce intergroup hostility only when those efforts succeed in obtaining the goal (Worchel, et al., 1978).

This research suggests that prejudice can be reduced if people can be placed in situations where they must work with the people or groups they are prejudiced against. This reasoning served as the basis for the *jigsaw method* that has been successfully used to reduce prejudice in the classroom (Aronson & Bridgeman, 1979). Students are divided into ethnically mixed groups and given a problem to solve. Each member of the group receives only one part of the answer; in order for the group to solve the problem, all members have to contribute their part. A weak group member will hurt the whole group. Thus group members must help one another in order for their group to be successful.

It has been suggested that intergroup cooperation works because it causes people to redefine their groups (Worchel, 1985). In such situations it is no longer blacks against whites; the group contains both white and black members. In this way the salience of racial distinction is reduced.

Experiencing Prejudice. Young, white, middle-class individuals in the United States rarely, if ever, experience what it is like to be the object of prejudice. They don't know what it is like to be told they cannot play on a team because of their skin color or be refused a job because they are "too old." In a fascinating demonstration a third-grade schoolteacher in Riceville, Iowa, decided to turn the tables (Elliot, 1971). One day she announced to her class that "The blue-eyed people are smarter than the brown-eyed people. . . . Blue-eyed people are cleaner than brown-eyed people. They are more civilized." She let the blue-eyed students sit in front of the room and forced the brown-eyed children to sit in the back. The blue-eyed children were also given extra privileges. Almost immediately the blue-eyed children adopted this prejudice and began to tease and ridicule the brown-eyed students. They refused to associate with them and a fight even broke out because one boy called another "Brown-eyes." The next morning the teacher told the class that she had lied and that the brown-eyed children were actually the better and brighter group. With the situation reversed, the brown-eyed children began to tease and taunt the blue-eyed children.

On the third day the teacher and children talked about the experience and how it felt to be the object of prejudice and discrimination. The teacher pointed out that they had only had this experience for one day, but that some children have to face prejudice every day of their lives. The children talked about how bad prejudice was and decided they didn't like themselves when they discriminated against others.

This method has been used by other investigators in school settings (Weiner & Wright, 1973). They have found that children who personally experienced prejudice and discrimination were less likely to adopt these attitudes and behaviors toward others.

Summary

1. The study of groups dates back to the turn of the century. Sociologists are most interested in examining group structure, whereas psychologists focus on the effects of the group on the individual.

2. People belong to **groups** for many reasons. In some cases, they get rewards such as money, prestige, and security. Groups can also be a source of social support. Sometimes, people join groups in order to evaluate and validate their attitudes, values, and abilities. Another reason is that groups may be necessary for a person to obtain his or her goals. The groups to which people belong become part of their self-identity.

3. Almost all groups develop **norms,** which are rules that apply to all members. Norms define what must be done and when. **Roles** are norms that apply only to people occupying a specific position in the group. Roles define the obligations and expectations of that position. Although norms and roles can help a group run smoothly by making the behavior of members predictable, they can sometimes be harmful.

4. **Social dilemmas** result when there is conflict between the actions that satisfy the individual's short-run needs and the behavior that fulfills the longer-range needs of the group. Groups use norms and appeals to group loyalty to encourage members to act in the interest of the group. They also establish norms to punish members acting only in their own self interest.

5. Groups are constantly changing. Observations suggest that groups develop through stages, and

the focus of the group is different in each stage. Group members also go through stages that affect their behavior.

6. **Conformity** occurs when people change their attitudes or behaviors as a result of real or imagined group pressure, despite personal feelings to the contrary. Conformity may involve only a change in behavior, or it may include changing both public behavior and private attitudes.

7. **Obedience** involves following the direct and explicit orders of a leader. Research conducted by Stanley Milgram showed that a surprising number of people would follow the orders of an authority figure even when they were ordered to hurt someone. Ideological zeal, personal gratification, and material gain, as well as a lack of responsibility, are some of the reasons people are willing to follow orders.

8. The **leader** is the person who has the greatest amount of influence in the group. The most current view is that who emerges as leader is affected by characteristics of the leader, followers, and situation. No single style of leadership is always effective. Different styles are effective in different situations.

9. **Reactance** occurs when we feel our freedom being threatened. Reactance leads us to resist influence that threatens our freedom.

10. **Deindividuation** occurs when the person becomes submerged in the group and loses his or her individual identity. Deindividuation is most likely to result in large groups where uniforms are worn and members are anonymous. As a result of deindividuation, people may not feel responsible for their behavior.

11. People's feelings about the group are often determined by how the group decision is made as by how much each person benefits from the decision. In most cases, the group adopts the position held by the majority of its members. However, the minority can be influential if it adopts a clear, unyielding position. Even when not influencing the final group position, minorities often stimulate members to think creatively.

12. In a group people tend to take stronger stands on issues than they would outside the group. This effect has been referred to as **group polarization.** It has been argued that this effect occurs because information is exchanged in group discussion and because people in groups do not feel personally responsible for their attitudes or behaviors. It also seems that people in groups compare their attitudes and behaviors, and since no one wants to be seen as the most undecided, each group member tries to adopt a position that is at least as strong as that of the other group members.

13. **Groupthink** results when people are more concerned about arriving at a group consensus than in making the best decision. In order to avoid groupthink, group members must be encouraged to express their opinions even if they disagree with the position of the other group members. The group also needs to seek outside information and opinions.

14. A person's performance is also influenced by the group. Research has shown that although people can learn new and complex tasks better if they are alone, the presence of others leads to the **social facilitation** of well-learned responses. However, **social loafing,** or less than full effort, may result if people perform tasks as part of a group effort and if their individual input on the task is not identifiable.

15. **Prejudice** is an unjustified negative *attitude* toward an individual based solely on that person's membership in a group. **Discrimination** is negative, often aggressive, *behavior* aimed at the target of prejudice. There are a number of theories about why prejudice and discrimination develop: one places the blame on the formation of a group; another suggests that people learn how to be prejudiced and against whom they should direct their prejudice; a third argues that prejudice and discrimination are the result of displaced aggression.

16. It is very difficult to change prejudice. In order to change biased attitudes, it is important to have people work together to achieve common goals. The effects of cooperation are most positive when the combined effort is successful.

Key Terms

conformity	leader	reactance	social facilitation
discrimination	normative social pressure	reflected appraisal	social loafing
deindividuation	norms	role conflict	social reality
group	obedience	roles	sociology
group polarization effect	organizational psychology	scapegoating	stereotypes
groupthink	power	social comparison	
informational pressure	prejudice	social dilemma	

AS BIAS CRIME SEEMS TO RISE, SCIENTISTS STUDY ROOTS OF RACISM

DANIEL GOLEMAN

As racial and ethnic violence erupts throughout the world, psychologists are striving to understand what impels people to acts of hatred, particularly when they act in groups.

Researchers are focusing on who commits such crimes, what motivates them and exactly why people who would not commit violent acts on their own express their hatred so freely in groups.

Scientists studying hate crimes have made these findings:

¶They are far more lethal than other kinds of attacks, resulting in the hospitalization of their victims four times more often than is true for other assaults.

¶They are crimes of youth: most of those who perpetrate them are in their teens or 20's. But they are not crimes of youthful rebellion: those who carry them out are venting feelings shared by their families, friends and community, researchers say.

¶The large majority are committed by people in groups of four or more. And the more people in the group, the more vicious the crime.

¶They reflect the primal emotions aroused by the love of one's own group; these deep feelings of group identity are particularly vivid in times of economic and political uncertainty and among people who suffered emotional neglect as children.

These factors are at play, experts say, as racial, religious and ethnic incidents erupt around the world, in riots between Azerbaijanis and Armenians, anti-Semitism in Russia, the racial killing in Bensonhurst, Brooklyn, and the tensions in the borough between blacks and Koreans.

"Everyone who collects data reports a steady increase in hate crimes in the last year or two," said Howard Ehrlich, director of the National Institute Against Prejudice and Violence in Baltimore.

The Federal Bureau of Investigation, for instance, reported that last year its civil rights unit had a record number of cases. "These crimes are certainly on the increase," said Mike Kortan, a bureau spokesman.

Although the figures may reflect increased reporting rather than an actual increase in crime, rates for what the police call "bias crimes"—acts of violence inspired by racism and other prejudice—are also rising. The Boston Police Department, which had recorded about 150 bias crimes each year from 1986 to 1988, had 202 cases in 1989.

In New York City, such crimes were up 14 percent for the first four months of 1990 compared with the same time last year, said Inspector Paul Sanderson of the Bias Incident Investigation Unit.

For 1989 the Anti-Defamation League of B'nai B'rith monitored a 12 percent increase in anti-Semitic incidents from the previous year, including harassment, assaults, desecration and vandalism. "It's the highest number we've recorded in 11 years," said Gail Gans, who works in the league's research office.

Particularly troubling to Ms. Gans and others who track such statistics is the activity on college campuses. In 1989 racial or ethnic incidents were reported on 115 American campuses. "What's most distressing is that it's spreading," said Dr. Ehrlich. "Of the 115 campuses, 52 were places where there hadn't been such trouble before."

Bias crimes vary widely, from a swastika daubed on a synagogue to the beating of a white youth waiting for a bus in a black neighborhood. Certain patterns are particularly common.

"Most hate crimes are matters of turf; the most frequent is an attack on someone who is just passing through a neighborhood where he's seen as out of place," said Jack McDevitt, a sociologist at Northeastern University.

Dr. McDevitt has analyzed 452 cases of bias crime that occurred in Boston from 1983 to 1987. He reported his findings last year at a conference of the American Society of Criminology in Reno, Nevada.

Of all bias crimes, Dr. McDevitt found, 57 percent involved issues of turf; they were attacks on someone walking, driving through or working in a neighborhood, or on a family moving into the area or not wanted there.

Typical of those, he said, was what happened to an Asian family that moved into an all-white neighborhood in Boston. On the first night someone broke several windows with rocks; on the second night the walls were spray-painted with racist slurs. On the third night the family moved back to its old neighborhood, leaving an older son to guard its possessions. A mob of 20 youths taunted the son until he came out, then beat him.

Another common pattern is an attack on someone who has wandered into a neighborhood not realizing he or she is "out of place." In one such incident, Dr. McDevitt said, a 12-year-old black girl took a shortcut from her school to a new convenience store nearby. As she was walking there, a group of white youths drove alongside and asked what she was doing in "their" neighborhood. They started taunting her, got out, pushed her down and kicked her, breaking a rib.

In Dr. McDevitt's study, most of the perpetrators of racist incidents were young white men, just under two-thirds; one-third were black. Of the total sample, two-thirds were 29 or younger. Virtually none of the perpetrators were women, but women accounted for 20 percent of the victims.

And while most of the crimes by blacks were against whites, Dr. McDevitt said that "whites attack everybody: blacks, Hispanics, gays, Asians." He added that in Boston bias crimes by Asian-Americans and Hispanic Americans were rare, though Vietnamese were the third most frequently victimized group.

Patterns vary, of course, in other cities. In Miami, for instance, tensions are greatest between Hispanic residents and blacks, said Dr. McDevitt.

The Ugly Crowd: Viciousness In Numbers

The viciousness of bias incidents is among Dr. McDevitt's most startling findings. Half involved assaults. Of these, the victims were injured in 74 percent of the cases; the national average for injury to an assault victim is 29 percent.

More telling, at least one victim required hospitalization in 30 percent of the prejudice-based assaults, while for other assaults the average rate of injuries that severe is 7 percent.

The usual number of perpetrators in such crimes, Dr. McDevitt found, is four or more. The most common number of victims is one.

"It's a coward's crime," said Detective Brian Flynn, who investigates such incidents for the Boston police. "It takes just 10 seconds to break a window in the dead of night, but they have to get together in numbers to get their guts up."

Sheer numbers encourage viciousness, new research shows. For instance, Brian Mullen, a psychologist at Syracuse University has analyzed newspaper accounts of 60 lynchings in the United States earlier in this century.

"The larger the mob, the more atrocious and savage the lynching, and the more likely to include burning or mutilating the victim," said Dr. Mullen.

One reason crowds draw out a viciousness that the individuals would not display on their own, psychologists say, is that there is a diffusion of responsibility. Being one among many means that no one person need take the blame for what happens.

Anonymity is also a force in unleashing the crowd's viciousness. The hoods and night meetings of the Ku Klux Klan have long taken advantage of this, said Dr. Steven Salmony, a psychologist at the University of North Carolina who has studied the dynamics of Klan violence by observing Klan rallies and by interviewing members, including one who shared secret documents.

But most bias crimes are anonymous in a larger sense: the crowd itself offers anonymity and, in most cases, its members do not know their victim. More than 85 percent of the crimes he analyzed were committed by strangers, Dr. McDevitt found.

Dr. Mullen said, "The tragedy is that when people in the mob look back afterward, they almost always say they can't believe they did those things. It's like it was someone else doing it."

That fact is telling, according to Dr. Mullen. "In the moment that people get carried away by a crowd, they literally forget themselves," he said. "They forget their own sense of what's

right and wrong, of the normal limits to what they will do."

In many cases, those who commit bias crimes have been primed for racist actions by the values expressed by family members. "When they're sitting around the dinner table at home they hear this racist garbage from their mom and dad," said Detective Flynn, "It makes them feel they have their family's approval."

The Emotional Roots: Primal Feelings Turned Loose

Psychoanalysts see primal feelings at play when prejudice leads to acts of hatred. "The excitement of a group encourages people to regress to the psychological level of early childhood," said Dr. Salmony.

Early childhood, Dr. Salmony said, is a time where the emotional world is split into sharp dichotomies of good and bad, love and hate. "In adulthood, for some people that becomes an emotional split with intense love for your own group and an intense hatred for another group," he said.

That emotional dynamic means that the underside of pride in one's own group is dislike of another.

Most people harbor such feelings lightly, if at all, and can keep the impulse to act on them under control. While these attitudes are revealed, for instance, in ethnic jokes and slurs, they rarely lead to overt acts of bias in most people, Dr. Salmony said.

In fact, psychologists say, ethnic jokes can offer a kind of safety valve for hostilities.

"The racist remarks of stand-up comedians just reflect the fact that ethnic and racial mistrust always exists in the folk culture, and shows up in humor," said Dr. Vamik Volkan, a psychiatrist at the University of Virginia. "But its not bad: if you can laugh about it, you're not likely to act on it."

Such humor can even form a positive bond to the ridiculed group. "If you make the same kind of degrading remarks about yourself, your family and your own group, as many comedians do, then it forms an emotional link to the groups you attack," Dr. Volkan said.

But, he said, "when a comedian's humor is only derisive of the other group, and the comedian is hate-filled, then it adds to the hatred," said Dr. Volkan.

Such hostility carries the most emotional intensity, Dr. Salmony said, in people whose parents ignored their basic emotional needs as children.

For such people, said Dr. Salmony, "being in a crowd where hostile feelings toward a group are being expressed triggers a regression to a primitive level of mental activity. They fall prey to an emotional contagion where they see their own group as the source of all that is good, and those in an opposing group as equally bad. It intensifies their hatred toward those seen as outsiders."

At that moment, striking out against the hated group has a paradoxical effect: it makes the one who hates feel good about himself. "The aggression enhances their own sense of identity with a group they love," said Dr. Salmony. "It's a malignant kind of narcissism that fills them with a heightened feeling of their own value."

Economic Factors: Shifting Blame in Troubled Times

The ethnic tensions that are shattering Eastern Europe and the Soviet Union have a similar basis, said Ervin Staub, a psychologist at the University of Massachusetts who is the author of "The Roots of Evil" (Cambridge University Press). Of course, the removal of political repression has allowed long-smoldering ethnic resentments to surface. But they have erupted with such intensity for other reasons, Dr. Staub said.

"In times of great economic insecurity and political turmoil, people need to affirm a sense of their own value," he said. "These things shake your identity. You need to recreate a positive view of yourself and the group you are rooted in. But the very definition of yourself as a member of one group includes enmity towards another group."

Dr. Volkan said: "Who you are implies, at an emotional level, who you are not, and stress makes you cling all the more stubbornly to your ethnic identity."

Dr. Staub, who is from Hungary, added, "In Romania it was the Romanians against the Hungarians, in Czechoslovakia it was the Czechs against the Slovaks, and everyone was against the Jews."

"These enmities are ancient, but they surface whenever life is in turmoil," Dr. Staub said. "Devaluing the other elevates the self: this feeling that I am good is all the more important when you feel your world is out of control."

Hatred of another group "shifts responsibility for your problems to someone else and gives the appearance that life can be controlled if you just can do away with this enemy," Dr. Staub said. "A shared enemy strengthens the group."

That is why the protection of territory, whether a neighborhood or a province, is so common in ethnic tensions, said Dr. Volkan, who has studied ethnic tensions between Greeks and Turks on his native Cyprus, as well as similar friction in other parts of the world.

"The group's boundaries make each person inside the group feel closer," said Dr. Volkan. "An outsider who pierces that boundary attacks the identity it defines."

The recent increase in bias incidents in America, social scientists say, is spurred by economic worries. The last such increase, according to many of those interviewed, was during the recession of the late 1970s. However no one has precise figures from the period; widespread tracking of bias crimes began only in the mid-1980s.

Nevertheless, those who study hate crimes say shaky economic periods heighten intergroup tensions. "The last rise in hate crimes in America was during the last economic recession," said Ivan Light, a sociologist at University of California at Los Angeles. "The roots of intergroup conflict are as much in economic competition as it is in negative stereotypes."

Dr. Salmony said: "Economic and political uncertainties lead to personal insecurities. For the most vulnerable people, it's a short step to ethnic violence."

A case in point is the tension between blacks and Koreans, currently so prominent in New York City. According to Dr. Light, who has been studying relations between blacks and Koreans in Los Angeles since 1980, there is an economic undertone to the friction.

"Many blacks see non-black merchants in their communities in a way that heightens tensions," said Dr. Light. "Their theory is that if you spend money with a Korean grocer on the corner, then your money leaves the black community. And that merchant's store blocks the upward mobility of some black who might have had a store of his own there."

The same economic worries are fueling other intergroup tensions, said Detective Flynn of the Boston police. As part of his duties with the unit that investigates bias crimes, he lectures to high school students. Most of those who commit the crimes are from working-class backgrounds.

"You talk to white kids who feel they can't get any jobs because there's a quota that favors minorities," said Detective Flynn. "You find it just fuels their prejudice and resentment. Then you talk to black kids who feel they're left out of the job market because of their race and you find they have the same animosity toward whites."

Dr. Light added, "People get along fine when they have money in their pocket and can pay the rent."

Statistical Methods

M. ELIZABETH WETMORE

OBJECTIVES

After completing this chapter, you should be able to:

Define and differentiate between descriptive and inferential statistics.

Know the difference between a frequency histogram and frequency polygon and draw one of each.

Explain the difference between a mean, a mode and a median.

Define standard deviation and explain how it is used in a normal distribution.

Explain the uses of a standard score.

Explain and provide an example of correlation.

Students often complain that multiple-choice tests do not fairly measure their knowledge. They feel that these and similar tests, like the college entrance exams, always seem to ask about things the students don't know, while not asking about what they do know. An alternative is an open-ended test. A teacher might, for instance, ask students to write down everything that they remember about a particular lesson. How would students respond to such open-ended questions? Would performance on multiple-choice entrance exams be similar to performance on open-ended questions? Psychologists are now investigating these and other questions about open-ended exams. In doing so, they take advantage of **statistics,** a branch of mathematics used to describe data and to draw conclusions based on data. You don't have to be an expert in math to understand statistics, but you do have to learn a special vocabulary. To make statistics and their use more interesting and understandable, we will analyze data from an actual experiment on open-ended exams.

Twenty-five students from introductory psychology courses at the University of Virginia took part in an experiment investigating how students learn from textbooks (Wetmore, 1982). The students were asked to read a selection from an introductory biology textbook. This selection contained

Statistics
Branch of mathematics used by psychologists to describe data and to draw conclusions based on data.

699

54 ideas. The students were told to read the selection at whatever speed they felt comfortable and to do whatever they normally do when reading a homework assignment for the first time. After they were through reading, they were asked to recall in their own words everything they could remember from what they had just read. These lists were then analyzed to see how many of the 54 ideas each student recalled. Table A–1 shows the number of ideas recalled by each student. Statistics can help us understand this data. We will use one branch of statistics to describe the data and then another branch to draw conclusions.

Descriptive Statistics

Descriptive statistics
Tools for summarizing data taken of a group of objects, people, or events.
Frequency distribution
Tells how many scores fall into each of the intervals chosen to describe the data.
Frequency histogram
Way to show frequency distribution in graph form; intervals are placed along the horizontal axis, frequencies along the vertical axis.
Frequency polygon
Way to show frequency distribution in graph form; line graph connects a series of points representing the frequency of scores in each interval.

Descriptive statistics are tools for summarizing numerical data so that the numbers can be more easily understood. The data may be any set of measurements taken of a group of objects, people, or events.

Frequency Distributions

A **frequency distribution** is one way of summarizing data; it reduces individual scores into groups of scores. To do this, we simply select a set of ranges (or intervals) and count how many scores fall into each one.

We can make a frequency distribution for the data presented in Table A–1 in two steps: (1) arrange (or rank order) the scores from lowest to highest as shown in Table A–2; (2) using an interval of 5, list the number of scores in each interval. These two steps produce the frequency distribution shown in Table A–3.

Such a frequency distribution can often be better understood if shown on a graph rather than in a table. The two most commonly used graphs are the *frequency histogram* and the *frequency polygon*.

Once a frequency distribution has been made, most of the work of making both a **frequency histogram** and a **frequency polygon** has been done. Histograms are made by placing the intervals along the horizontal axis and marking the frequencies along the vertical axis. Histograms are also known as bar graphs. A histogram for the data presented in Table A–3 can be seen in Figure A–1.

Another way of showing frequency distributions in graph form is to use a frequency polygon. Polygons are made by connecting a series of points representing the frequency of scores in each interval. A polygon for the data presented in Table A–3 can be seen in Figure A–2.

Table A–1

Subject Number	Number of Ideas Recalled
1	37
2	31
3	33
4	36
5	28
6	44
7	43
8	20
9	21
10	37
11	36
12	32
13	35
14	31
15	31
16	40
17	41
18	27
19	25
20	30
21	38
22	30
23	30
24	30
25	41

Table A–2

Rank Order of Raw Scores			
20	30	35	40
21	30	36	41
25	31	36	41
27	31	37	43
28	31	37	44
30	32	38	
30	33		

The frequency distribution, histogram, and polygon for the data presented in Table A–1 show at a glance that the scores were well below the highest possible score of 54. They ranged from the low 20s to the mid 40s, with the most frequent scores in the low 30s. Students apparently had trouble recalling all the ideas. But let's look more closely before drawing conclusions.

Measures of Central Tendency

Frequency distributions, histograms, and polygons all summarize whole distributions. Sometimes, however, single numbers are easier to compare. Statisticians therefore summarize properties of distributions with single numbers. An interesting property is a **measure of central tendency,** a score value that represents the mathematical center of a group of scores, or, to put it another way, a score that represents in some sense the "typical" score. Three different statistics are used to describe the central tendency of a distribution: the mean, the median, and the mode.

The **mean** is the most widely used measure of central tendency. It is commonly called the average and is determined by adding all the scores in the sample and dividing by the total number of scores in the sample. The mean number of ideas recalled in Table A–1 is 33.08. It was determined by adding all the students' scores to get 827 and dividing by 25 (the number of students in the sample).

The **median** is the score that divides a distribution in half. Look back at the rank ordering of scores in Table A–2. In this case the median is 32, because there are as many scores ranked above it as ranked below it.

Table A–3

Frequency Distribution for Scores in Table A–1

Class Interval	Number of Scores in Each Interval
20–24	2
25–29	3
30–34	9
35–39	6
40–44	5

Measure of central tendency
Score value that represents the mathematical center of a group of scores.
Mean
Often called the average; determined by adding all the scores in a sample and dividing by the total number of scores in the sample.
Median
Score that divides a distribution in half—there are as many scores ranked above it as below it.

FIGURE A–1

A frequency histogram for data in Table A–3. The numbers under each bar indicate an interval of exam scores. The height of the bar indicates the number of scores (frequency in each interval).

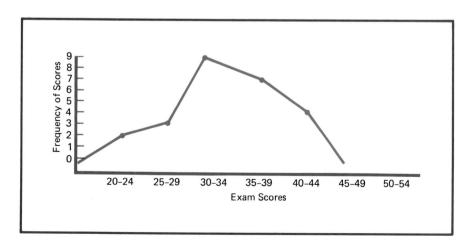

FIGURE A–2

A frequency polygon for data in Table A–3. The points represent the number of scores in each interval.

| | Subset 1 | | Subset 2 | | Subset 3 |
Subject Number	Number of Ideas Recalled	Subject Number	Number of Ideas Recalled	Subject Number	Number of Ideas Recalled
1	37	6	44	11	36
2	31	7	43	12	32
3	33	8	20	13	35
4	36	9	21	14	31
5	28	10	37	15	31
Mean	33.00		33.00		33.00
Range	9.00		24.00		5.00
Variance	10.80		110.00		4.40
Standard Deviation	3.29		10.50		2.10

Mode
Often called the most typical scores, it is the score that occurs most often in a sample.
Range
A measure of variation, the difference between the largest and smallest number in the distribution.
Variance
Measure of variation, the average squared difference of each number in a sample from the mean of all numbers in the sample.
Standard deviation
Measure of variation. The square root of the *variance* is often used to express how far any given score is from the mean of a set of scores.

Table A–5

d (Difference from Mean)	d (Difference squared)
37–33	4	16
31–33	−2	4
33–33	0	0
36–33	3	9
28–33	−5	25
44–33	11	121
40–33	7	49
36–33	3	9
41–33	8	64
37–33	4	16
35–33	2	4
27–33	−6	36
25–33	−8	64
31–33	−2	4
30–33	−3	9
38–33	5	25
31–33	−2	4
30–33	−3	9
43–33	10	100
20–33	−13	169
30–33	−3	9
30–33	−3	9
32–33	−1	1
21–33	−12	144
41–33	8	64
		964

$$\frac{964}{25} = 38.56$$

In other words, 50 percent of the scores fall above 32 and 50 percent fall below.

The **mode** is commonly called the most typical score. It is simply the score that occurs most often in a sample. You can see in Table A–2 that 30 is the most frequent score for number of ideas recalled. Therefore, 30 is the mode of this data.

Measures of Variation

Measures of central tendency do not always tell us all we need to know about a distribution. They do not tell us, for example, how different the scores are from one another; that is, they do not show variation in scores. Several distributions could have the same mean, but differ in their variation. Table A–4 shows examples for three subsets of data taken from Table A–1.

All three of these subsets have a mean of 33, but they differ greatly in their variation. The subjects in subset 3 have scores that are relatively close to one another, the subjects in subset 1 have scores that are slightly farther from one another, and the subjects in subset 2 have scores that are quite different from one another. The histograms in Figure A–3 show this more clearly. Three statistics are used most often to describe variation. These are called the range, the variance, and the standard deviation.

The simplest measure of variation is the **range,** the difference between the largest and smallest number in the distribution. The range for the data presented in Table A–1 is 24 (44 − 20 = 24).

The range uses only extreme scores. A more common measure, the **variance,** uses every score to compute a single number to summarize the variation. It is the average squared difference of each number in the sample from the mean of all numbers in the sample. To compute the variance for the data in Table A–1, we first subtract the mean of 33 from each score and square the difference. We then find the average or mean of these squared differences; this is the sum of the squared differences divided by the number of squared differences. In this case, variance of the number of ideas recalled $= \frac{964}{25} = 38.56$.

The **standard deviation** is simply the square root of the variance. Therefore, the standard deviation for the number of ideas recalled (Table A–5) is $\sqrt{38.56} = 6.21$. The standard deviation is often used to express how far any given score is from the mean of a set of scores. For example, in

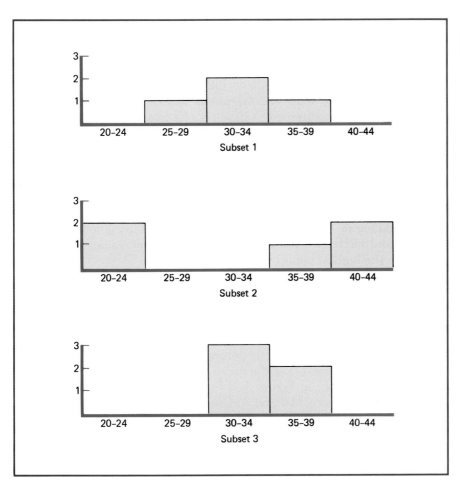

Table A–1, subjects 8 and 9, with respective scores of 20 and 21, are more than one standard deviation below the mean. Subjects 6 and 7, with respective scores of 44 and 43, are more than one standard deviation above the mean.

Inferential Statistics

Statistics can be used to organize and describe data, but they have another very important use. Psychologists often make educated guesses, or hypotheses, about their data. They use **inferential statistics** to test those hypotheses. We might, for example, try to form an hypothesis to explain why most scores in the present data were well below the total possible score of 54. One hypothesis is that the experiment used poor students. The experiment used a sample of college students, which is a subset of all college students. The hypothesis is that the sample does not represent enough good students from the population of all college students. Table A–6 provides data that allow us to test this hypothesis. The table shows SAT verbal scores for the sample of students who gave the original data in Table A–1. We can compare this sample to the national population by using a special distribution that is discussed in the next section.

Inferential statistics
Used to test hypotheses made by psychologists.

Normal Distribution

Subject Number	SAT Verbal Score
1	530
2	620
3	580
4	640
5	380
6	530
7	760
8	560
9	580
10	690
11	720
12	560
13	660
14	560
15	610
16	690
17	650
18	590
19	560
20	560
21	710
22	780
23	580
24	630
25	630

Mean = 614.4
Standard Deviation = 83.19

Normal distribution
Represents the assumption that most measurements taken will be close to average, some will be a small distance from average, and few will be very far from average. People's height, weight, and IQs show this distribution.

Normal curve
Symmetrical, bell-shaped curve that occurs when a normal distribution is plotted as a frequency polygon.

When we take a large number of measurements of almost any characteristic or event, we come up with a **normal distribution,** which represents the assumption that most measurements taken of a characteristic or event will be close to average, some measurements will be a small distance from average, and few measurements will be very far from average. For example, people's heights are approximately normally distributed; most people have a height close to average, some people have a height slightly above or below average, and very few people have a height greatly above or below average. This is also true of people's weights, their IQs, and many of the behaviors studied by psychologists.

The normal distribution can be plotted as a frequency polygon called the **normal curve,** which is symmetrical and shaped like a bell. The mean, median, and mode of a normal curve have the same value, which corresponds to the highest point on the curve.

We can make a normal curve if we know the mean and standard deviation of a set of scores. The national mean for college-bound students taking the SAT verbal subtest is 424, and the standard deviation is 110. Figure A–4 shows the normal curve for the SAT verbal subtest on the College Boards Entrance Examination.

It has been established that 68 percent of all measurements are between one standard deviation below the mean and one standard deviation above the mean. We can see in Figure A–4 that 68 percent of all college-bound students score between 314 and 534 on the SAT verbal subtest. A more detailed listing of areas under portions of the normal curve can be found in Table A–7.

Now let's compare the scores in Table A–6 with the national scores. The mean score in Table A–6 is 614. We can see in Figure A–4 that this mean is a little over 1.5 standard deviations *above* the national mean score of 424. Table A–7 shows that only 0.67 of the area under the normal curve lies to the right of 1.5 standard deviations above the mean. This indicates that only 6.7 percent of college-bound students score higher than 1.5 standard deviations above the mean. The results are therefore contrary to our hypothesis. The sample was *not* made up of only poor students. In fact, the students were very good compared to the national population. The high quality of the students is further shown in the next section, which describes a way to compare each individual with the population.

FIGURE A–4

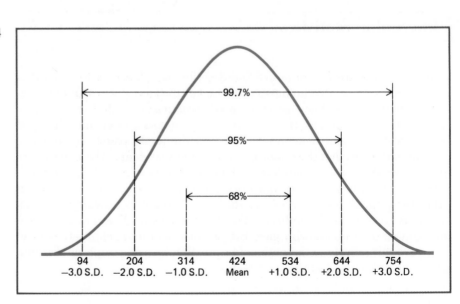

	Area Under Normal Curve as Proportion of Total Area		
Standard Deviation	Area to the Left of This Value Indicates the Proportion of People Who Score *Lower* Than This Score	Area to the Right of This Value Indicates the Proportion of People Who Score *Higher* Than This Score	Area Between This Value and the Mean Indicates the Proportion of People Whose Scores Fell between This Score and the Mean
−3.0	.001	.999	.499
−2.5	.006	.994	.494
−2.0	.023	.977	.477
−1.5	.067	.933	.433
−1.0	.159	.841	.341
−.50	.309	.691	.191
0.0	.500	.500	.000
+.05	.691	.309	.191
+1.0	.841	1.590	.341
+1.5	.933	.067	.433
+2.0	.977	.023	.477
+2.5	.994	.006	.494
+3.0	.999	.001	.499

Standard Scores

Often we want to know how a particular person scores in relation to other people. For example, you may have taken the SAT verbal subtest yourself and may want to know how you performed relative to the average college-bound student. To do this, you could compute your standard score and, using Table A–7, see what percentage of students scored lower and higher than you.

A **standard score** is a single number that expresses where a score lies relative to a population. For example, subject number 17 in Table A–6 got a score of 650 on the SAT verbal subtest. To compute his or her standard score, you simply subtract the mean from his or her score and divide by the standard deviation. (Recall that the national mean was 424 and the standard deviation was 110.)

Standard score for score of 650:

$$= \frac{650 - 424}{110}$$

$$= \frac{226}{110} = 2.05 \text{ standard deviation units from the mean}$$

$$= 2.05 \text{ standard score}$$

Using column one of Table A–7, we see that subject number 17 scored higher than 97.7 percent of all college-bound students. Column two indicates that only 2.3 percent scored higher, and column three indicates that 43 percent of the national population received a score falling between this subject's score and the national mean score.

Standard score
Single number that expresses where a score lies relative to a population. Expresses the value of a score relative to the mean and the standard deviation of its distribution.

Table A–8

Data from Experimental Group

Subject Number	Number of Ideas Recalled
26	32
27	41
28	40
29	43
30	35
31	39
32	34
33	36
34	28
35	40
36	37
37	41
38	44
39	37
40	41
41	25
42	30
43	47
44	42
45	39
46	25
47	31
48	27
49	26
50	42

Mean = 36.08
Standard deviation = 6.33

By contrast, subject number 5 received a score of 380:

$$= \frac{380 - 424}{110}$$

$$= \frac{-44}{110} = -.4 \text{ standard deviations}$$

$$= -.4 \text{ standard score}$$

Using Table A–7 again, we see that subject number 5 scored higher than only 30.9 percent, 69 percent scored higher, and 19 percent of the national population received a score between this score and the national mean score.

You can use standard scores to compare each individual in Table A–6 with the national population. These comparisons will show clearly that we have no basis for saying that good students were underrepresented.

Statistical Significance

Perhaps students scored low because they did not study enough. From this we could form the hypothesis that extra study will improve performance. Table A–8 provides data for testing this hypothesis. The students who gave the data in Table A–8 read the passage, rated the importance of each idea in the passage, and then read it again before they tried to recall it. Let's call this the *experimental group*. The students who gave the data in Table A–1 read the passage once and then tried to recall it. We will call this group of students the *control group*. Students had an equal chance of being assigned to the experimental group or to the control group, and both groups were treated identically except for the different amounts of study. We can test our hypothesis about studying by comparing the data from the two groups.

One of the descriptive statistics that we discussed earlier provides a good comparison. The mean number of ideas recalled for the experimental group was 36 ideas. The mean for the control group was 33 ideas. It appears that having students study more improves comprehension and memory of ideas. But we cannot accept this without first performing a test of **statistical significance,** which determines whether the difference in the mean performance of these two groups reflects a true difference between the groups or is simply a result of sampling error. The difference would be due to **sampling error** if by chance we happened to get better readers in the experimental group than in the control group, or if we happened to get more students in the experimental group who knew a great deal about biology.

A test of statistical significance gives us a precise way to evaluate an obtained difference between sample means. To test statistical significance, we compute a test statistic that takes into account both the size of the difference in the means and the variation of the means being compared. To compute this statistic we must know not only the difference between the means, but the variation of the mean scores as well.

Standard Error of the Mean.   If we draw several samples from the same population and compute the mean of each sample on some characteristic, the means of these samples will be different. Random samples drawn from a population vary simply due to chance. The **standard error of the mean** indicates the variation of a sample mean and tells how likely it is that the sample mean represents the population mean.

To determine the standard error of the mean, we simply divide the standard deviation of a sample by the square root of the number of subjects

Statistical significance
Means that a difference in scores is a true difference, not a result of sampling error.
Sampling error
Failure to represent important subject characteristics equally in all conditions of an experiment. As a result, the conditions differ because the sample of subjects is different.
Standard error of the mean
Shows the variation of a sample mean and tells how likely it is that the sample mean represents the population mean.

in the sample. The standard error of the mean for the data in Table A–1 is

$$\frac{6.21}{\sqrt{25}} = \frac{6.21}{5} = 1.24$$

The standard error of the mean for the data in Table A–8 is

$$\frac{6.33}{\sqrt{25}} = \frac{6.33}{5} = 1.27$$

The standard error of the mean will decrease with an increase in sample size. Thus, the mean of a large sample is more likely to be representative of the population mean.

From the standard error of the means, we can compute a **standard error of the difference between two means.** It is computed by finding the square root of the sum of the standard errors. The standard error of the difference between the means in the present experiment is

$$\sqrt{1.24 + 1.27} = \sqrt{2.5} = 1.58$$

Once we know the standard error of the difference between two means, we can compute the test statistic, the ratio of the difference between the means to the standard error of the difference between the means.

$$\text{test statistic} = \frac{\text{difference between means}}{\substack{\text{standard error of the} \\ \text{difference between the means}}}$$

A ratio of 2.0 or more generally indicates a statistically significant difference between means, or a true difference between groups, not simply a sampling error.

A test statistic of 2.0 is selected because a value that large or larger can occur by chance less than 5 in 100 times. We treat the test statistic as a standard score. Looking at column two in Table A–7, we can see that the probability of obtaining a standard score two deviations above the mean is .023, and the chance of obtaining a standard score two standard deviations below the mean is also .023. The total probability, therefore, is .046. This means that, if we get a test statistic of 2.0, we are likely to say there is a difference between the population means (when there really isn't one) only 5 out of 100 times; 95 percent of the time we will be correct.

Recall our hypothesis that having students study more will improve their recall. This hypothesis appears to be correct. The mean of the experimental group was 36 and the mean of the control group was 33. Now, using a test statistic, let's see if this difference is statistically significant.

$$\text{test statistic} = \frac{\text{difference between means}}{\substack{\text{standard error of the} \\ \text{difference between the means}}}$$

$$= \frac{36 - 33}{1.58} = \frac{3}{1.58} = 1.90$$

Since this value is less than 2.0, we must conclude that the difference between the means is not statistically significant. We *cannot* say with 95 percent certainty that having college students study the passage more improves their comprehension and recall of those ideas.

A nonsignificant test statistic means that we must withhold conclusion.

Standard error of the difference between two means
Computed by finding the square root of the sum of the standard errors of the means.

It means that we must design more sensitive tests if we are still interested in the original hypothesis. For example, we might have another experimental group study even harder. However, in the present comparison, considerably more studying produced only three more ideas on the average. Therefore, it may be better to consider other hypotheses.

One alternative is that scores were low because students left out unimportant ideas. Deese (1980) supported this hypothesis to some extent, but he also showed that students omitted many important ideas. In fact, the data available at the present time suggest that students do not respond extremely well to open-ended questions about lessons. Apparently, they need more structure than that provided by open-ended tests.

Another question that one can ask about open-ended tests is how they relate to multiple-choice tests. We will take up this question in the next section.

Correlation

Correlation is a procedure for describing the relationship between two sets of paired scores. The sets are said to be positively correlated if high scores in one set are paired with high scores in the other set, while low scores are paired with low scores. Height and weight, for example, are positively correlated; tall people tend to weigh more, and short people tend to weigh less. The sets are said to be negatively correlated if high scores in one set are paired with low scores in the other. Reading ability and reading time, for example, are negatively correlated; more able readers require less time to read a passage. The two sets are said to be independent or uncorrelated if there is no such relationship. The number of letters in a person's last name and his or her IQ, for example, are uncorrelated; there is no relationship between these two sets of data.

We can quickly determine if two sets of scores are correlated by drawing a **scatter plot.** We place one variable (height) on the horizontal axis of a graph, and the other (weight) on the vertical axis. Then we plot a person's score on one variable along the horizontal axis and his or her score on the second variable along the vertical axis. We draw a dot where the two scores intersect. Figure A–5 shows a scatter plot of two variables that have a perfect positive correlation. Figure A–6 shows a scatter plot of two variables that have a perfect negative correlation. Figure A–7 shows a scatter plot of two variables that are totally uncorrelated.

Let's examine a scatter plot of the present data to compare SAT scores, which are based upon multiple-choice test results, with open-ended test scores. There is obviously not a perfect correlation between these two variables, but there does appear to be a slight positive correlation. Those students

Correlation
A measure of the extent to which variables change together. If two variables increase and decrease at the same time, they are positively correlated; if one increases while the other decreases, they are negatively correlated. This does not necessarily indicate a cause-and-effect relationship between the variables, however.

Scatter plot
Graph formed by marking the intersection of a person's score on one variable, which is indicated on one axis of the graph, with that person's score on another variable, which is indicated on the axis of the graph.

FIGURE A–5

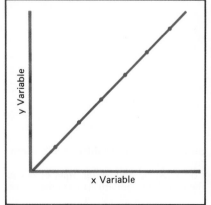

FIGURE A–6

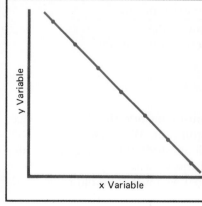

FIGURE A–7

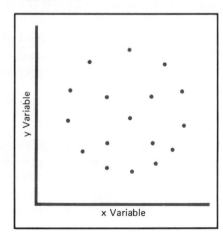

who recalled a larger number of ideas also tend to be those students who received a higher SAT verbal subtest score, and those students who recalled fewer ideas tend to be those students who received a lower SAT verbal subtest score.

To more precisely describe the relationship between two sets of scores, we use a **correlation coefficient,** which ranges from $+1.0$ to -1.0. A perfect positive correlation receives a $+1.0$, whereas a perfect negative correlation receives a -1.0. Most correlation coefficients, however, fall between $+1.0$ and -1.0 because few things are perfectly correlated. If two sets of scores are uncorrelated, the correlation coefficient will equal 0.

The Product-Moment Correlation. The most widely used index of correlation is called the **product-moment correlation** coefficient. We can compute this coefficient in five steps. Let's compute the coefficient for the present data to see if there is a relationship between number of ideas recalled in a textbook selection and SAT verbal subtest scores (Tables A–1 and A–6). First we must determine the differences in all the scores in each set from their respective means (see Table A–9). Remember that the mean number of ideas recalled was 33 and the mean SAT verbal subtest score was 614. Second, we must determine the sum of the products of the differences. See Table A–10. Third, we compute the standard deviations for both sets of scores. In this case, we have already computed them. Remember that the standard deviation for the number of ideas recalled was 6.21, and the standard deviation for the SAT verbal subtest scores was 83.19. Fourth, we multiply the product of the two standard deviations by the number of subjects in the sample.

$$25(6.21 \times 83.19) =$$
$$25(516.61) = 12915.15$$

Fifth, we divide this number into the sum of the products of the differences.

$$\frac{5152}{12915} = .399$$

Correlation coefficient
Tells whether or not one can predict one measure knowing another, but does not indicate that one variable *causes* another.
Product-moment correlation
Measure of the extent to which changes in two variables are related to each other.

Table A–9

Subject Number	Number of Ideas Recalled	Difference from Mean	SAT Verbal Subtest Score	Difference from Mean
1	37	4	530	−84
2	31	−2	620	6
3	33	0	580	−34
4	36	3	640	26
5	28	−5	380	−234
6	44	11	530	−84
7	43	10	760	146
8	20	−13	560	−54
9	21	−12	580	−34
10	37	4	690	76
11	36	3	720	106
12	32	−1	560	−54
13	35	2	660	46
14	31	−2	560	−54
15	31	−2	610	−4
16	40	7	690	76
17	41	8	650	36
18	27	−6	590	−24
19	25	−8	560	−54
20	30	−3	560	−54
21	38	5	710	96
22	30	−3	780	166
23	30	−3	580	−34
24	30	−3	630	16
25	41	8	630	16

Table A–10

Subject Number	Product of the Differences			
1	4 ×	−84 =	−336
2	−2 ×	6 =	−12
3	0 ×	−34 =	0
4	3 ×	26 =	78
5	−5 ×	−234 =	1170
6	11 ×	−84 =	−924
7	10 ×	146 =	1460
8	−13 ×	−54 =	702
9	−12 ×	−34 =	408
10	4 ×	76 =	304
11	3 ×	106 =	318
12	−1 ×	−54 =	54
13	2 ×	46 =	92
14	−2 ×	−54 =	108
15	−2 ×	−4 =	8
16	7 ×	76 =	532
17	8 ×	36 =	288
18	−6 ×	−24 =	144
19	−8 ×	−54 =	432
20	−3 ×	−54 =	162
21	5 ×	96 =	480
22	−3 ×	166 =	−498
23	−3 ×	−34 =	102
24	−3 ×	16 =	−48
25	8 ×	16 =	128
			5152

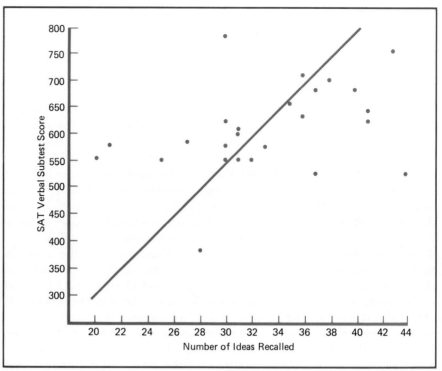

FIGURE A–8

As we predicted from the scatter plot in Figure A–8, this is not a perfect correlation, but it is a moderate positive correlation. For the number of subjects in this sample, it is statistically significant at the .05 level. This means that performance on the SAT verbal subtest score does appear to be similar to performance on open-ended tests, and we are 95 percent certain that this correlation did not occur simply due to sampling error or chance.

Statistics go hand in hand with research designs. Chapter 1, for example, discusses the use of correlations with specific designs, and it goes over the logic of drawing conclusions from correlations. The more you learn about experimental designs, the more you will understand statistics. And the more you learn about statistics, the more you will understand research designs. You will do well, therefore, to refer back to this appendix when you read Chapter 1 and other chapters that take up specific research designs.

In summary, students question the accuracy of highly structured multiple-choice exams. The research reviewed here suggests, however, that going to the opposite extreme of open-ended tests is not the answer. The research suggests further that scores on very structured and very unstructured exams are correlated. Teachers are as eager as students to improve exams—if you have some ideas, speak up. Your ideas could become the basis for future experiments.

Summary

1. **Statistics** is a branch of mathematics used by psychologists to describe data and to draw conclusions based on data.

2. **Descriptive statistics** are tools for summarizing data taken on a group of objects, people, or events.

3. A **frequency distribution** is a useful way of summarizing data. It tells how many scores fall into each of the intervals chosen to describe the data.

4. A **measure of central tendency** is a score value that represents the center of a group of scores.

The **mean,** the **median,** and the **mode** are used to describe the central tendency of a distribution.

5. **Measures of variation** tell us how different the scores in a distribution are from one another. The **range,** the **variance,** and the **standard deviation** are used to describe the variation of a distribution.

6. **Inferential statistics** are used to test hypotheses made by psychologists.

7. The **normal distribution** represents the assumption that most measurements taken on a characteristic or event will be close to average, some measurements will be a small distance from average, and few measurements will be very far from average.

8. **Standard scores** are used when we want to know how a particular person scores in relation to other persons on some characteristic or event. They express the value of a score relative to the mean and the standard deviation of its distribution.

9. A **test of statistical significance** is performed to determine if the difference in the mean performance of two groups reflects a true difference between groups or is simply a result of sampling error.

10. **Correlation** is a procedure for describing the linear relationship between two sets of paired scores. A correlation coefficient tells us whether or not we can predict one measure knowing another, but does not indicate that one variable causes another.

Key Terms

correlation
correlation coefficient
descriptive statistics
frequency distribution
frequency histogram
frequency polygon
inferential statistics
mean
measure of central tendency

median
mode
normal curve
normal distribution
product-moment correlation
range
sampling error
scatter plot
standard deviation

standard error of the difference
   between two means
standard error of the mean
standard score
statistical significance
statistics
variance

Glossary

Abnormal behavior Behavior may be so labeled when it is unusual, causes distress to others, and makes it difficult for a person to adjust to his or her environment.

Absolute refractory period Period after a cell has fired, during which it will not fire again. Usually lasts for about 1 millisecond.

Absolute threshold Least amount of a certain stimulus energy that can be detected.

Accommodation (1) Changes in the shape of the lens to focus objects at different distances. (2) Term used by Piaget to refer to the process of adjusting one's schema to fit environmental demands. Compare with *assimilation*.

Acetylcholine (ACh) Chemical transmitter in neurons that tends to transmit fast-acting, excitatory messages.

Achievement motive (nAch) Motive to do things as rapidly and/or as well as possible.

Achievement tests Designed to measure a person's current knowledge and skills and reflect what has been learned in the past.

Active synthesizing processes Mental operations that impose organization on sensory information.

Addiction Physical dependence on a substance so that the body builds up a tolerance for a dose of the drug and needs ever-increasing amounts. If the drug is not taken, people experience painful symptoms of withdrawal, which may include headaches, cramps, nausea, uncontrollable trembling, and restlessness.

Adolescence Passage of time from childhood to adulthood that extends from about age 12 to the late teens.

Affective disorders Group of disorders involving problems with emotions and mood. People are said to be suffering from an affective disorder when their moods, such as depression, take over and they have trouble functioning.

Affiliation motive Motive or desire to associate with and be around other people.

Afterimage Visual experience that continues after the stimulus has ceased; occurs because some activity continues in the retina after seeing the stimulus. Consists of the opposite color of what was seen in the original stimulus: blue for yellow, red for green, black for white.

Aggression cues Any stimuli that an individual has learned to associate with aggressive behavior.

Aggression motive Motive, whether innate or learned, to attack objects or other organisms.

Air pollution syndrome (APS) Physical reactions to pollution characterized by headache, insomnia, gastrointestinal problems, irritated eyes, and depression.

Alcoholics People who are addicted to al-

cohol; they have an uncontrollable urge to drink, and because of increasing tolerance, must continue to increase their consumption.

Algorithm Step-by-step procedure, that, if used properly, guarantees a correct response to a specific problem.

Allele A single gene may occur in one of several different forms called alleles; alleles may be dominant or recessive.

Alternate states of consciousness Differing mental states as measured by a specific pattern of physiological and subjective responses.

Altruism A motivational state with the ultimate aim of increasing the other's welfare.

Alzheimer's disease Condition caused by degeneration of the neurons that produce the neurotransmitter acetylcholine. Most common in people over age 60.

Amnesia Partial forgetting of past events. Some forms of amnesia are caused by physical injuries, such as a blow to the head. *Psychogenic amnesia* means that the cause of the memory loss is stress rather than physical injury.

Amniocentesis Process in which fluid is taken from a mother's womb to test for Down syndrome and other genetic disorders.

Amplitude Distance between the top and bottom of a sound wave; amplitude increases as sounds get louder.

Anal stage During the second and third years of life, the main focus of pleasure shifts from the mouth to the anal area. A major battle between child and parents occurs during this stage over the issue of toilet training.

Analytic introspection Method used in structuralism; a way of isolating the elementary sensations of which experiences are made.

Analytical psychology Jung's complex, almost mystical theory of personality; includes his belief that the libido was a force resulting from the desire to be creative.

Androgens Male hormones secreted by the testes that increase male sex drive and influence the development of secondary sex characteristics.

Anorexia nervosa Condition in which a person loses his or her appetite, eats little, and slowly begins to starve.

Antianxiety drugs Minor tranquilizers that reduce anxiety and tension without causing drowsiness or a loss of mental alertness. Most popular are Valium, Librium, and Miltown.

Antidepressant drugs Drugs that work by lifting the person's spirits and increasing his or her activity level. Two examples are Tofranil and Elavil.

Antipsychotic drugs Major tranquilizers

that are used to calm and relieve the delusions of schizophrenics. Two most commonly used are Thorzaine and Stlezine.

Antisocial personality disorder Disorder in which people perform violent and hurtful acts without the least bit of guilt or regret, are incapable of forming close relationships, and are manipulative and insincere.

Antrograde amnesia Difficulty in remembering events that happen after an injury.

Anvil One of three small bones in the middle ear, it transmits sounds from the eardrum to the inner ear.

Anxiety disorders Group of conditions in which people feel anxiety that is far out of proportion to the situations they are in; their responses interfere with normal daily functioning.

Apgar scoring system Scale used to assess the condition of newborns; low scores show possible neurological damage.

Appraisal theory Automatic evaluation of a situation as threatening or nonthreatening. Appraisal influences both arousal (emotions) and behavior (response).

Aptitude tests Tests used to predict capacity for future performance.

Aqueous humor Clear fluid that carries nourishment to the cornea of the eye.

Articulation Process of altering the shape of the pharynx, oral cavity, and nasal cavity in order to change speech sounds.

Artificial intelligence (AI) Field where computers are programmed to simulate human thought processes and to act intelligently.

Ascending nerves Nerves that carry sensory information up the spinal cord to specific areas of the brain.

Assimilation Term used by Piaget to refer to the process of interpreting events in a way that fits existing ideas (or schema). Compare with *accommodation*.

Attachment Tendency of youngsters to seek closeness to certain people.

Attention Focusing on important stimuli and ignoring irrelevant ones; a selective process in memory.

Attention deficit disorder Inability of a child to concentrate on a task for the same length of time as another child of the same age.

Attitude change Accepting a new position or new information while giving up an old position.

Attitudes Learned, relatively enduring feelings about objects, events, or issues.

Attraction A positive attitude about another person.

Attribution Process of inferring characteristics of people from their observable behavior; a way of explaining the behavior of others.

Autokinetic effect Tendency for a stationary light viewed against darkness to look as if it is moving; the light seems to glide, jerk, and swoop through space.

Autonomic nervous system Functional subdivision of the nervous system; regulates glands and organs. Divided into sympathetic and parasympathetic divisions.

Availability heuristic Assessment of the probability of an event by how many similar events can be recalled easily.

Aversive conditioning Type of behavior therapy often used to break bad habits such as smoking and drinking; in this type of therapy people receive unpleasant consequences for undesired behavior. This may mean taking a drug (Antibuse) that will make them sick if they drink, or making them smoke so much and so quickly that they become sick.

Avoidance training Occurs when a subject learns to make a response to avoid a negative reinforcer.

Axon Long fiber carrying neural impulses away from the cell body to the terminal branches to be passed on to other neurons.

Axon terminal Tiny knob at the end of an axon's terminal branch.

Backward masking Ability of a stimulus to wipe out the sensory memory of a preceding stimulus.

Barbiturates Depressant drugs that slow the body functions, reduce anxiety, and have a relaxing effect.

Basal ganglia Four masses of gray matter in the brain that control background muscle tone and large, general muscle movements—part of the motor system.

Basilar membrane Located inside the cochlea in the inner ear, it is attached to the oval window at one end and the tip of the cochlea at the other end. Vibrations in the oval window cause hair cells on the basilar membrane to move. When these hair cells are bent, they send nerve impulses to the brain that are experienced as sound.

Behavior therapies Therapies based on the assumption that maladaptive behavior is learned through the same process as other behaviors and can be unlearned by substituting a more adaptive behavior in its place.

Behavioral assessment Assessment that consists of examining a person's present behavior to predict future actions. Can also be used to assign traits to people.

Behavioral medicine New field in medicine; focus is on the effects of stress and better ways of dealing with it.

Behavioral neuroscientists and biopsychologists Study the biological underpinnings of behavior.

Behavioral sinks Develop as a result of overcrowding; they aggravate all forms of pathology that can be found within a group.

Behaviorism Approach to psychology based on the premise that human behavior can be described by focusing only on the observable stimulus and response.

Binocular cues Cues to depth perception that we use when we are looking with both eyes.

Binocular disparity Experience of seeing a different view from each of our eyes;

two views are fused by the brain and produce depth perception.

Biofeedback Technique that provides people with feedback on their physiological functions (such as heart rate and blood pressure) so that they can learn to control these functions and achieve a more relaxed state.

Biofeedback therapy Type of therapy designed to help people control their physiological functions without the use of drugs or other biotherapy techniques. Helps people reduce tension and stress, reduce phobic reactions, and control headaches. Has also been combined with other psychotherapies. See also *biofeedback*.

Biomedical therapy Use of drugs, surgery, or electric shock, with or without accompanying psychotherapy, to induce behavior change.

Bipolar cells Cells in the retina, connected to rods and cones, that actively participate in the process of coding or interpreting the information contained in light. One-to-one connections to cones; one-to-many connections to rods.

Bipolar disorder Disorder in which the person alternates between manic and depressive stages. Often the extremes of each mood state appear for only a short time and the person generally behaves normally when between states.

Blind spot Area in the retina that is blind because it is where the optic nerve exits from the retina.

Body language Communication through body movement.

Boilermaker's deafness Partial hearing loss caused by spending long periods of time around loud noises (above 85 decibels).

Bone conduction Another way that sound is transmitted; when a person speaks, the jaw bones conduct vibrations to the cochlea. We hear our own voice through bone-conducted and air-conducted sounds; we hear others' voices only through air-conducted sounds.

Brainstem Midbrain and hindbrain combined.

Broca's aphasia Speech that is slow, labored, and slightly distorted; caused by injury to Broca's area in the cortex.

Bulimia Eating disorder in which the individual goes through cycles of dieting for a period of time and then gorging with food (binging). After binging, the person will purge the food by vomiting or using laxatives.

Burnout Job-related emotional exhaustion that includes a depersonalized feeling and a reduced sense of accomplishment.

Bystander intervention Offering aid in an emergency situation.

Calories Units of energy produced when food is oxidized or burned by the body.

Case history Method used in psychology that looks in depth at a few individuals or at the effects of a single event.

Cataracts Widespread disease affecting vision that is characterized by cloudy lenses and can result in blindness if lenses are not removed surgically.

Catecholamines Chemical transmitters in

neurons that tend to transmit slow-acting, inhibitory messages.

Catharsis Release of tension through aggression.

Central nervous system Nerve tissue in the brain and spinal cord.

Cerebellum Part of the hindbrain; made up of two wrinkled hemispheres. Coordinates the force, range, and rate of body movements.

Cerebral cortex (cerebrum) Two wrinkled hemispheres that are part of the forebrain; governs our most advanced human capabilities, including abstract reasoning and speech.

Chemical transmitters (neurotransmitters) Chemicals that carry messages between neurons; some are excitatory, some inhibitory.

Chemotherapy Treatment of disorders through the use of drugs; a form of biotherapy.

Chromosomes Threadlike chains of genes; humans have 23 pairs.

Chronological age A person's age in years and months.

Chunking Process of grouping elements such as letters or words into units (or chunks) that function as wholes. Memory span consists of 7 ± 2 chunks.

Circadian rhythms Internal biological clock that regulates the need for sleep or food on a 24-hour cycle.

Clairvoyance Perception of an object, action, or event by means of ESP.

Classical conditioning The process whereby an originally neutral stimulus comes to elicit a response that was originally given to another stimulus. It takes place when the neutral stimulus is repeatedly paired with the other stimulus.

Clinical psychology Subfield of psychology dedicated to the diagnosis and treatment of emotional and behavioral disorders.

Clinical social worker Someone who has an M.A. in social work and has served an internship.

Cochlea Part of the inner ear; a tube coiled in on itself about three turns, like a spiral around a central core. Contains the basilar membrane inside it.

Cognitive dissonance State that occurs when a person's attitudes, beliefs, and behaviors are in conflict. In order to relieve the dissonance, the person will try to change the cognitions so that they will again be in agreement.

Cognitive learning theory Attempts to explain the function of thought processes in learning.

Cognitive map A mental picture of an area or territory.

Cognitive overload An inability to respond to stimuli because there are too many events occurring in the environment.

Cognitive psychology Subfield of psychology concerned with the mental events that intervene between stimuli and responses.

Cohabitation Relationship between two unmarried people who live together.

Cold spots Areas of the skin where only cold is felt, even if stimulated by a warm object (when this occurs it is called *para-doxical cold*).

Color blindness Inability to see or distinguish between colors. There are several types of color blindness: red-green, blue-yellow, and total color blindness.

Community psychology Subfield of psychology dedicated to promoting mental health at the community level; seeks to prevent and treat psychological problems by working to evaluate and to improve community organizations.

Complex tones Sounds containing many frequencies.

Compulsion Irrational behavior or ritual that people cannot control; often they do not know why they need to do this. See also *obsession*, which involves thought rather than behavior.

Concepts Mental or cognitive groups of similar objects, events, states, or ideas.

Concrete operational stage One of Piaget's stages of cognitive development; lasts from 7 years to 12 years of age. Main theme is extending mental operations from concrete objects to purely symbolic terms.

Conditioned response (CR) Learned response to a conditioned stimulus (CS). Usually a less strong response than an unconditioned response (UR).

Conditioned stimulus (CS) Stimulus to which a subject learns to respond through repeated pairings with an unconditioned stimulus (US).

Cones Light receptors in the eye; located mostly in the fovea, are best for seeing details, and are responsible for color vision.

Confirmation bias Tendency in hypothesis testing to avoid observations that might be disconfirming in favor of those that offer confirmation.

Conflict State that occurs when a person is motivated to choose between two or more mutually exclusive goals or courses of action.

Conformity The behavior that occurs when a person changes his or her actions or attitudes as a result of real or imagined group pressures, despite personal feelings to the contrary.

"Connectionist" parallel distributed processing Term given to a model that is patterned after brain processes that perform many operations simultaneously to connect information that is distributed throughout the brain.

Conscious mind According to Freud, this includes whatever the person is perceiving or thinking at the moment.

Consciousness The perception of what passes in a person's own mind (Locke's definition).

Constancies Aspects of perception such as apparent size or shape that remain constant when visual information changes.

Continuous reinforcement schedule Subject receives a reinforcer for every correct response.

Control group The group of subjects in an experiment that is treated exactly the same as the experimental group(s) except that the control group is not exposed to the independent variable and thus serves as the basis for comparison.

Conversion disorder One of the somatoform disorders, usually involving one specific symptom. The most common symptoms are paralysis of a limb, loss of sensation in a part of the body, blindness, and deafness. There is no organic basis to this disorder.

Cornea Transparent part of the eye that is shaped like a crystal ball.

Corpus callosum Large cable of nerve fibers that connects the two cerebral hemispheres.

Correlation A measure of the extent to which variables change together. If two variables increase and decrease at the same time, they are positively correlated; if one increases while the other decreases, they are negatively correlated. This does not necessarily indicate a cause-and-effect relationship between the variables, however.

Correlation coefficient Tells whether or not one can predict one measure knowing another, but does not indicate that one variable *causes* another.

Counseling and school psychology Subfield of psychology that helps people with social, educational, and job or career adjustments.

Creative thinking Capacity to think up new and useful ways of solving problems.

Critical period Stage of development during which the organism must have certain experiences or it will not develop normally.

Cross-sectional research Research in which people of all different ages are tested in various ways; compare with *longitudinal research*, in which one group is tested continually over a period of time, at different ages.

Crowding Feeling or psychological state that often, but not always, accompanies high density.

Crystallized intelligence Specific mental skills, such as one's vocabulary.

Cycle The distance between wave crests in a sound wave.

Dancing reflex Causes infants to prance with their legs in a "tip-toe" stepping motion when they are held upright with feet touching a surface.

Dark adaptation Downward adjustment of sensitivity to light; occurs in the rods when one enters a dark room, for example.

Date rape Coercive sex that occurs in dating relationships.

Daydreams Thoughts that divert attention away from an immediately demanding task.

Decibel Unit for measuring loudness; each tenfold increase in sound level adds 10 decibels.

Defense mechanisms Ways of coping with anxiety; an unconscious distortion of reality in order to defend against anxiety. See *displacement*; *projection*; *rationalization*; *reaction formation*; *repression*; *sublimation*; and *suppression*.

Deindividuation Occurs in groups when people lose their personal identities and assume the identity of the group.

Deinstitutionalization Policy of treating people with psychological problems in their own local environments rather than placing them in large isolated institutions.

Delusions Irrational beliefs that are held in spite of contrary evidence and have no basis in reality. For example, the delusion of grandeur is the belief that the person is special or different from other people (one may think one is Napoleon or Joan of Arc, for instance).

Demand characteristics Elements in a questionnaire or experiment that communicate what behavior is expected from the subjects.

Dendrites Short fibers extending from the body of a neuron, receiving impulses from other neurons and carrying them to the cell body.

Density Measure of the number of people in a given area. Not to be confused with crowding, which is a psychological state rather than a physical measure.

Deoxyribonucleic acid (DNA) Controls the way in which protein chains are built, and, thus, contains the basic blueprints for life; genes are made up of DNA.

Dependent variable The variable that is measured in an experiment.

Depolarization Occurs when a neuron is sending or receiving a neural impulse.

Depressants Drugs that slow body functions or calm nervous excitement; examples are alcohol, nicotine, and heroin.

Depression Disorder in which there is a loss of interest in most activities, including eating or sex, lack of concentration and inability to sleep. May lead to suicide in its extreme forms. See also *bipolar disorder*.

Descending nerves Carry commands down the spinal cord to move muscles.

Descriptive statistics Tools for summarizing data taken of a group of objects, people, or events.

Development Process whereby the genes that an organism inherits from its parents come to be expressed as specific physical and behavioral characterisitcs.

Developmental psychology Subfield of psychology that examines the function of age on behavior. Examines the age at which people should be performing certain behaviors and how events that occur at various ages affect behavior.

Dichotic listening The subject hears different messages in each ear and is asked to repeat only one of them.

Difference threshold Smallest difference in intensity that can be noticed between two stimuli.

Discrimination (1) Occurs when subjects learn to respond only to certain stimuli, but not to other, similar stimuli.

Discrimination (2) Negative, often aggressive, behavior aimed at the target of prejudice.

Displaced aggression Taking out one's anger and/or frustration on someone or something other than the actual cause of one's anger.

Displacement Defense mechanism that involves redirecting an emotion from the person who caused it to another, safer or more available, target.

Dissociative disorders Characterized by "tuning out" or dissociating a part of the person from the situation at hand. It is almost as if part of the person has split off and taken on its own identity.

Door-in-the-face approach Persuasive technique based on the fact that people who at first refuse a large request will be more likely after that to comply with a smaller request.

Doppler shift Occurs as cars zoom by on a racetrack; as they go by, the engine sound drops sharply to a lower pitch. Sound waves bunch up as cars approach on a racetrack and spread out as cars speed away. The bunched-up waves have a shorter distance between their wave crests (higher frequency); the spread-out waves have a longer distance between their wave crests (lower frequency).

Double-bind conflict Results when children receive contradictory messages from their parents, messages that create a "no-win" situation for them—no matter what they do, they are wrong.

Double-blind control Procedure used in an experiment in which neither subject nor experimenter is aware of how the independent variable is being manipulated.

Double helix Model of the structure of DNA molecules, similar to a spiral staircase, the steps of which contain a genetic code.

Down syndrome Disorder characterized by mental retardation and altered physical appearance; caused by a genetic mutation that adds an extra chromosome to the twenty-first pair, giving the child 47 chromosomes.

Dream interpretation Part of Freud's technique of psychoanalysis; involves helping clients to understand the latent content of their dreams, which represents the repressed feelings that are being expressed.

Dreams Series of images, thoughts, and emotions that occur during sleep.

Drive Tension or state that results when a need is not met; it compels the organism to satisfy the need.

Drug therapy Use of medications to treat both mild and severe psychological disturbances.

DSM-R III Stands for Diagnostic and Statistical Manual, revised third edition, which was published in 1987. It is one of the most commonly used systems for classifying abnormal behavior, and was developed by the American Psychiatric Association.

Dualism Theory that the mind and brain are separate entities. See also *monism*.

Dyspareunia Sexual disorder in which females experience pain during intercourse.

Ear canal Tube-like passage that funnels sound to the eardrum.

Eardrum Fine membrane stretched over the inner end of the ear canal; vibrates when sound waves strike it.

Eclectic approach Therapy where the choice of techniques differs depending on the needs of the client.

Ecological theory Size constancy occurs because we see some aspect of the visual scene that remains unchanged when distance changes.

Effort justification Attempt to make something we have to work hard for more valuable in order to make the effort worthwhile.

Ego According to Freud, a second dimension of personality that works to control the impulses of the id; tries to satisfy the desires of the id by dealing with the environment.

Egocentricity The tendency to exaggerate the role of one's personal contributions in shaping events.

Egoism A motivational state with the ultimate aim of increasing one's own welfare.

Elaboration Likelihood Model (ELM) Model which argues that there are two routes to persuasion: the central route that evaluates the arguments as presented in the message, and the peripheral route where the message is evaluated on situational factors, such as the characteristics of the communicator.

Electra complex During the phallic stage, according to Freud, girls discover that they are biologically inferior to boys because they lack a penis. They envy their father's penis and become attracted to him, fantasizing about having a male baby by their father.

Electroconvulsive therapy (ECT) Technique of biotherapy in which electric shock is administered to the patient's brain, causing epileptic-like convulsions. Has been shown to have short-term benefits for those suffering from depressive disorders.

Electromagnetic spectrum Forms the entire range of wavelengths of electromagnetic radiation; wavelengths corresponding to visible colors cover only a small part of this spectrum.

Embryo Term for a human organism from the third week through the eighth week in the uterus.

Emotions Affective stages or feelings accompanied by physiological changes that often influence behavior.

Empty chair technique Therapeutic technique in which clients place different parts of their personality in chairs and act each of the parts.

Encode To select and represent information in a specific form (verbally or visually) in memory.

Encounter group (also called **sensitivity group**) Aims at expanding personal awareness and growth rather than treating emotional disorders. Such groups try to rid people of their interpersonal "hang-ups." Variations include marathon groups and nude encounter groups.

Endocrine system Major coordinating system that regulates body chemistry.

Endorphin and enkephalin Neural transmitters with chemical structures similar to opium and its derivatives, morphine and heroin.

Engineering psychology Subfield of psychology that is concerned with making human contact with tools and machines as comfortable and as error-free as possible.

Engram Name assigned by Karl Lashley to the elusive physical representation of learning and memory in the brain.

Environmental psychology Subfield of psychology that analyzes how behavior is influenced by environmental factors such as architecture, weather, space, crowding, noise, and pollution.

Episodic memory A person's memories about events, including the time and place they occurred.

Equilibrium Sense of overall body orientation (for example, the difference between standing upright or tilting backward).

Erectile dysfunction Inability to have an erection or maintain one long enough for ejaculation.

Escape training Through the use of negative reinforcement a subject learns to make a response to remove a stimulus (such as a shock).

Estrogen Female sex hormone. The level of estrogen is at its highest during the period of ovulation, and determines the onset of menstruation and the period of fertility. Estrogen also influences the development of secondary sex characteristics.

Ethologists Scientists who study animal behavior in natural settings.

Experiment Investigation in which a researcher directly manipulates one variable while measuring the effects on some other variable.

Experimental psychology Subfield of psychology that examines the behaviors and cognitions (thoughts) that are related to learning, memory, perception, motivation, and emotion.

Experimenter bias Expectations on the part of the person running an experiment that subjects will behave in a certain way—these behaviors can affect the subjects as well as the perceptions of the experimenter.

Extinction In classical conditioning, the gradual falling off or decrease in a response when the conditioned stimulus (CS) is repeatedly presented alone without the unconditioned stimulus (US). In operant conditioning, a falling off of a response when it is no longer followed by a reinforcer.

Extrasensory perception (ESP) Reception of information by means other than our usual senses of hearing, sight, taste, touch, and smell.

Extrinsic motivation Motivated behavior that results from external factors, such as a promotion or other type of reward.

False consensus effect The tendency to overestimate the number of people who make the same inferences and hold the same opinions we do.

Family-resemblance concepts Categories where members share more attribute values with members of their own group than they do with members of other groups and no particular attributes define a category.

Family therapy Type of psychotherapy that involves the whole family, rather than just one member of it, since it is often the family system as a whole that can create stress and contribute to the development of psychological disorders. Couples working on a relationship also participate in family therapy.

Farsightedness Occurs when an eye is flattened in shape like a vertical egg; far-sighted people see far objects well, but see near objects poorly.

Fear Reaction to a specific danger in the environment.

Fetal alcohol syndrome Postnatal birth

complications caused by a mother drinking heavily during pregnancy. The condition is identified by low birth weight and developmental abnormalities.

Fetus Human organism from the third month through to the time of birth.

Field experiment Experiment performed in a natural setting rather than in the controlled setting of the laboratory.

Fight-or-flight response Response of the sympathetic division of the autonomic nervous system that involves increased oxygen consumption, respiratory heart rate, blood pressure, and muscle tension.

Figure Object standing out against a background or against its surroundings.

Figure-ground reversal (or **multistable perception**) Occurs when figure and ground in a picture suddenly reverse; what was seen as figure is seen as background, and vice versa.

Fissure of Rolando (central fissure) One of three fissures of the cerebral cortex.

Fissure of Sylvius (lateral fissure) One of three fissures in the cerebral cortex.

Fixed-interval schedule Reinforces the first response made after a certain time interval (e.g., after 5 minutes or 2 weeks). Produces a slow rate of responding immediately after a reinforcer is received, building up to a high rate of response as the end of the time interval is reached.

Fixed-ratio schedule Schedule that reinforces the first response after a certain number of responses have been made. Produces a fast, steady rate of responding.

Fluid intelligence General mental skills, such as the ability to make inferences or deductive reasoning.

Focal colors Eleven colors that are seen as being more distinct than other colors.

Foot-in-the-door approach Persuasive technique that gets people to agree first to a small request and then later be more willing to agree to a second request.

Forebrain The part of the brain that develops from the top core of the embryo brain; contains the hypothalamus, thalamus, and the cerebrum.

Forensic psychology Subfield of psychology concerned with behaviors that relate to our legal system. Forensic psychologists work with judges and lawyers who are trying to improve the reliability of witnesses and jury decisions and are also consulted on the mental competency of accused people.

Forgetting Inability to remember or retrieve information from memory.

Formal operational stage One of Piaget's stages of cognitive development; lasts from about 13 years of age through adulthood. Main theme is the ability to consider many possible solutions to a problem and the ability to systematically test those possibilities.

Fovea Center area of the retina where vision is best; contains most of the cones on the retina.

Free association Freud's method of having patients express every thought (no matter how unimportant or irrelevant) that came into their minds during the therapy session.

Free association test Procedure in which a person looks at or listens to, a target word, and then reports other words that come to mind.

Frequency Number of wave crests that occur in a second; measured in cycles per second.

Frequency distribution Tells how many scores fall into each of the intervals chosen to describe the data.

Frequency histogram Way to show frequency distribution in graph form; intervals are placed along the horizontal axis, frequencies along the vertical axis.

Frequency of sound waves Number of wave crests that occur in a second. Changes in pitch correspond to changes in frequency.

Frequency polygon Way to show frequency distribution in graph form; line graph connects a series of points representing the frequency of scores in each interval.

Frontal lobe One of four lobes in the cerebral cortex; receives sensory impulses after they have been processed by other lobes and sends out commands to muscles to make voluntary movements.

Frostbite Result of ice forming in the skin cells; these frozen cells die, and if the affected area is large enough, a finger, toe, or large patch of skin may literally die.

Frustration Basically, the result of being blocked from getting what you want when you want it.

Frustration-aggression theory Theory that aggression is always a consequence of frustration and that frustration always leads to some form of aggression.

Fugue Involves loss of memory and also physical flight in which the person wanders away from his or her home for a matter of an hour or, in some cases, for years.

Functional fixedness Tendency of people to see an object only in terms of its most familiar use.

Functionalism Approach to psychology that emphasizes the function of thought; led to important applications in education and the founding of educational psychology, a subfield of psychology.

Fundamental attribution error The tendency to base attributions solely on behavior without considering the possible influence of the situation.

Galvanic skin response (GSR) Resistance of the skin to electrical current.

Gametes Sex cells; female gamete is an ovum, male gamete is a sperm. Each gamete has 23 chromosomes; ovum and sperm combine to form a zygote.

Gender identity disorder Disorder that can occur in childhood, when a child rigidly adopts the role and outlook of the opposite sex.

Gender roles Society's approved ways for men and women to behave.

General adaptation syndrome Stress response noted by Hans Selye; occurs in three phases—alarm reaction, stage of resistance, and stage of exhaustion.

Generalization See *response generalization*; *stimulus generalization*.

Generalized anxiety disorder Disorder in which people experience overwhelming anxiety, but cannot identify its source.

Genes Basic units of heredity. Located on the chromosomes.

Genetics The study of how traits are inherited

Genital stage Begins at puberty with the start of sexual tension. Basic goals are to marry, raise a family, and become involed in a life's work.

Genotype Unique set of genes that we inherit from our parents.

Gestalt laws of organization Describe how we group stimulus elements according to their characteristics.

Gestalt psychology German school of psychology based on the premise that we experience wholes, or gestalts, rather than separate sensations.

Gestalt therapy Therapy developed by Fritz Perls, proposing that unconscious thoughts and emotions (background) may lead to behaviors (figure) that are inappropriate to the situation. Encourages people to take responsibility for their actions in the present, while understanding the emotions that are influencing them.

Glaucoma Eye disease that causes pressure to build up inside the eye; most common cause of blindness.

Global therapies Therapies that focus on the individual as a whole and aim to help the person gain insight into his or her problems and life.

Glove anesthesia People with this symptom report losing all sensation in a hand, although they have normal sensation in the arm. This is physically impossible given the system of nerves in the hand and arm; glove anesthesia is a conversion disorder.

Glucoreceptors Cells in the hypothalamus that monitor the glucose content of the blood. If the blood is low in glucose, the glucoreceptors send out signals that cause hunger and motivate us to eat.

Gonads Reproductive organs that secrete sex hormones. Called ovaries in females, testes in males. Sex hormones control ovulation, pregnancy, and the menstrual cycle in females, and the production of sperm in males, as well as regulating secondary sex characteristics in both sexes.

Grammar Set of rules for combining language symbols to form sentences.

Grasp reflex Causes infants to close their fingers tightly around an object that touches the palm.

Ground Background or surroundings against which an object stands out.

Group Two or more persons who are interacting with one another in such a manner that each person influences and is influenced by each other person.

Group polarization effect Groups tend to polarize people and move them to believe more strongly in the position that they first held.

Group therapy Involves 1 (sometimes 2) therapists and from 6 to 12 clients; clients receive feedback from others in the group as well as from the therapist. Many different therapeutic techniques may be used.

Groupthink Occurs when group members become so concerned with reaching agreement of all members of the group that they fail to critically evaluate their ideas.

Halfway house Homes where people live after they have been discharged from an institutionalized setting and before they can live independently.

Hallucination   Involves having a sensory experience without the external stimuli that would have caused it. Hallucinations can involve vision, hearing, taste, touch, and smell, but the most common types involve people "hearing" voices that are not there.

Hallucinogens   Drugs such as LSD, STP, mescaline, and peyote, that cause people to see visions and illusions.

Hammer   One of three small bones in the middle ear, transmits sounds from the eardrum to the inner ear.

Hassles   Minor, but daily annoying events.

Health psychology   Branch of psychology that examines the relationship between psychological factors and illness, including intervention to reduce illness and policy formation.

Heat exhaustion   Reaction to heat which involves fainting, nausea, vomiting, and headaches.

Heatstroke   Serious disorder that results when the body's sweating mechanism completely breaks down; it is accompanied by headache, staggering, coma, and possibly death.

Hedonic relevance   Refers to the degree to which an actor's behavior is rewarding or costly to the observer.

Helping behavior   Coming to the aid of another person.

Hertz   One cycle per second of a sound wave.

Heuristic   Rule-of-thumb strategy that is used because it has been successful in the past. Sometimes used when solving a problem backward—from the goal to the beginning.

Hierarchy   An organization that arranges information into levels of categories and subordinate categories.

Hindbrain   Part of the brain that develops from the bottom core in the embryonic neural tube; contains the medulla, pons, and cerebellum.

Holonomic brain theory   Theory proposed by Karl Pribram that learning alters information that is lawfully distributed throughout the brain.

Holophrastic speech   Use of single words to express phrases. For example, "out" might mean "I want to go out."

Homeostasis   Attempt by the body to maintain a constant internal state.

Homosexuality   Sexual desire for those of the same sex as oneself.

Hormones   Chemical messengers released by the glands into the bloodstream. Either directly change their target tissue or cause it to release other hormones that change tissues elsewhere in the body.

Human development   Process by which the genes inherited from parents come to be expressed as specific physical and behavioral characteristics.

Human language   Systematic means of communicating verbally, with the written word, or with a sign language.

Humanistic   psychology   Movement formed by Carl Rogers, Abraham Maslow, and Rollo May which rejects Freudian view of people; argues that people are basically good and worthy of respect;

stresses the creative aspect of people in reaching their true potential.

Hypermnesia   Increased recall that can result from hypnosis.

Hypnagogic images   Hallucinations that occur during the drowsy interval before sleep.

Hypnosis   State of consciousness induced by the words and actions of a hypnotist whose suggestions are readily accepted by the subject

Hypnotic susceptibility tests   Tests that are used to predict the extent to which people are willing to yield to hypnotic suggestions.

Hypochondriasis   A somataform disorder where the person believes that he or she is seriously ill in spite of assurances to the contrary.

Hypothalamus   Part of the forebrain; controls body temperature and the rate at which we burn fat and carbohydrates, among other functions.

Hypothermia   Occurs when the internal body temperature drops below a normal level; heart rate and blood pressure increase dramatically and death due to heart attack can result if temperature does not increase.

Hypothesis   Idea that is tested experimentally; an assumption that is based on theory.

Iconic memory   A momentary visual image that remains apparent after a stimulus is withdrawn.

Id   According to Freud, part of the personality made up of instinctual drives that serve as the basic motivation for all our behavior.

Identification   Process of acquiring personality and social behaviors by taking on characteristics of others.

Identity crisis   Term used by Erikson to describe the search for an identity during adolescence that involves trying out and testing different roles.

Illusions   Perceptual distortions.

Imaginal thought   The conscious or unconscious manipulation of "mental images."

Imitation   Acquisition of knowledge and behavior by watching other people act and then doing the same thing ourselves.

Impotence   Sexual disorder in which males are unable to have an erection or maintain one long enough for ejaculation.

Imprinting   Process whereby a young fowl or bird attaches itself to the first object it sees.

Incentive   External stimulus that has the capacity to motivate behavior even if a drive is not apparently present.

Indefensible spaces   Areas in an apartment complex that are not open to observation, such as enclosed stairways and alleys; such areas invite intruders and breed crime.

Independent variable   The variable that is manipulated in an experiment.

Individual psychology   Adler's approach to personality development, based on his belief that each person is unique and adjusts differently to social influences.

Industrial-organizational psychology   Subfield of psychology concerned with selecting, training, and managing employees.

Infantile autism   Infants who from a very early age are withdrawn, do not react to others, and become attached to inanimate objects rather than to people.

Inferential statistics   Used to test hypotheses made by psychologists.

Informational pressure   A type of influence a group has, based on the group's value as a source of information.

Insanity   Legal classification for a person who has been judged to have a mental disease or defect which renders that person unable to understand inappropriate or illegal conduct.

Insight   Discovery of relationships that lead to the solution of a problem. Insight learning is the sudden and irreversible learning of a solution to a problem.

Instincts   Innate or inborn predispositions to act in specific ways.

Intelligence   The capacity to learn and use information.

Intelligence quotient (IQ)   Mental age divided by chronological age and multiplied by 100.

Interaction distance   Amount of space between people in various situations; differs with the relationship between people and the kind of interaction they're engaged in.

Interference theory   Theory that we forget information because other information gets in the way. See also *proactive inhibition*; *retroactive inhibition*.

Internalization   Process of bringing behavior under the control of inner, personal standards that make people obey rules even if there are no external restraints.

Interview   Assessment technique that involves direct questioning of a person. Unstructured interview consists of planned questions to start, but interviewer is free to develop the conversation as he or she wishes. Structured interview consists of a set of specific questions asked according to a set plan.

Intrinsic motivation   Motivated behavior that derives from the enjoyment of performing the task rather than from an expected reward.

Iris   Flat doughnut-shaped network of muscles behind the aqueous humor of the eye.

Just-barely-sufficient threat   Aspect of dissonance theory that suggests that we will derogate attractive objects or activities that we choose to forgo without strong external constraints.

Key-word method   Mnemonic system of using imagery to learn foreign vocabulary; consists of forming an image that will act as a link between the key word and the other word we want to remember.

Kinesis   Study of body language, or communication through body movement.

Kinetic depth effect   Detection of depth through movement.

Korsakoff's   syndrome   Brain damage caused by severe thiamine deficiency. Usually caused by alcoholism.

Laboratory experiment   Experiment performed in a controlled environment created for the experiment.

Latency period   Lasts from sixth year to puberty. Children lose interest in sex-related activities and focus energy on schoolwork and hobbies, among other things.

Latent content of dreams Hidden content determined by unconscious impulses. Freud said the latent content of dreams often involves an unacceptable desire that would create pain or anxiety if it were expressed directly, so it is disguised in a dream.

Latent learning Refers to learning that does not show itself immediately in performance.

Law and psychology Examines factors that influence jury verdicts, the way in which people determine what is just, and how procedural aspects of a trial affect its outcome.

Law of brightness constancy Law stating that we see an object's brightness as constant when the amount of light striking it changes.

Law of connectedness We group connected elements.

Law of effect The law that animals tend to repeat behaviors that are followed by "good effects," and they tend to stop behaviors that are not followed by desirable results.

Law of enclosure We group elements in the same perceived enclosed region.

Law of nearness or proximity One of the Gestalt laws of organization; states that we group elements that are close together.

Law of shape constancy Law stating that we see an object's shape as constant when the object's slant changes, or when we view it from a different angle.

Law of similarity One of the Gestalt laws of organization; states that we group elements that are similar or look alike.

Law of size constancy Law stating that we see an object's size as constant even if the object's distance from us changes.

Leader The person in a group who has the most amount of influence.

Learned helplessness A response to prolonged stress; the feeling that one's actions do not affect one's environment or what happens to one. Can lead to apathy and depression.

Learning Process by which experience or practice results in a relatively permanent change in what one is capable of doing.

Learning set Occurs when one's previous experience makes one ready to solve a particular problem.

Lens Part of the eye that is located directly behind the pupil; helps the cornea focus light onto the back of the eye.

Lesbians Female homosexuals.

Letters The smallest meaningful units of written language.

Libido Energy force that propels people to satisfy the drive for survival (includes eating, drinking, and sexual activity).

Life-span development approach Concerned with the description and explanation of changes in behavior within an individual and differences between individuals from conception to death.

Light adaptation Upward adjustment in sensitivity to light; occurs in the cones when one suddenly goes from a dark room into bright sunlight, for example.

Linear perspective Monocular cue to depth; artists use it to create the impression of depth in their paintings.

Linguistic relativity Sapir-Whorf's hypothesis that language influences the way we perceive things and the way we think.

Locus of control According to Rotter, people learn general expectancies about whether the source of control of what happens to them is outside or inside them. Internals believe they control their own fate; externals believe luck and chance control their fate.

Longitudinal fissure One of three fissures in the cerebral cortex; separates the two cerebral hemispheres.

Longitudinal research Research in which the same person or group of people is tested over a period of time. An example would be studying the same group of people from their birth until they were in their twenties. Compare with *cross-sectional research*, in which a number of people of different ages are tested at one time.

Long-term memory Holds information that is transferred from short-term memory; it can last a lifetime.

Loudness Measurement of sound based on the amplitude of sound waves.

Lungs Organs of respiration lying within the chest cavity. Supply the blood with oxygen and are the source of energy for the production of speech sounds.

Major life events Stressful occurrences that involve some change in a person's life.

Mania Disorder in which people feel full of energy, but find it difficult to stay with any one project for long, are easily distracted, have an increased sex drive, and need less sleep than usual. See also *bipolar disorder*.

Manifest content of dreams Portion of the dream that the person remembers. Contrast with *latent content of dreams*, which is the hidden element determined by impulses of which the person is unaware.

Mantra Secret word, sound, or phrase used in Transcendental Meditation.

Masochism Becoming sexually aroused by having pain inflicted on oneself.

Masturbation Self-manipulation of one's genitals.

Maturation Unfolding of genetically determined abilities.

Mean Often called the average; determined by adding all the scores in a sample and dividing by the total number of scores in the sample.

Measure of central tendency Score value that represents the mathematical center of a group of scores.

Median Score that divides a distribution in half—there are as many scores ranked above it as below it.

Meditation State of consciousness similar to hypnosis, except that the hypnotist's authority is transferred to the meditators themselves.

Medulla Lowest part of the hindbrain; slender tube housing nerve centers that control breathing, heartbeat, and posture.

Membrane potential An electric tension that exists in a neuron between the cell's inside and outside environment. Also called *polarization*.

Memory System that allows people to retain information over time.

Memory span The number of items that we can read through at one time and then recall in sequence with no mistakes.

Memory trace Change that occurs as a result of memorizing.

Menarche Beginning of menstruation, which marks the onset of puberty for girls.

Menopause Cessation of menstruation, marking the end of a woman's ability to bear children; accompanied by physical and hormonal changes.

Mental age Average performance of children at a specific chronological age.

Mental sets Readiness to view a problem in a particular way and see certain relationships.

Mentally retarded Significant subaverage intellectual functioning; specifically an IQ of 70 or lower.

Metabolic rate Rate at which food is transformed by the body into energy.

Midbrain Part of the brain that develops from the middle core of the embryo brain; contains the reticular formation.

Minnesota Multiphasic Personality Inventory (MMPI) One of the most popular personality questionnaires used by clinicians. Designed to identify specific psychological disorders. Consists of 550 statements to which people can respond true, false, or cannot say. Aimed at identifying 10 different disorders.

Mnemonic systems Systems created to aid memory; examples are the key-word method and verbal mediation.

Mode Often called the most typical scores, it is the score that occurs most often in a sample.

Modeling Used as a therapeutic technique to teach new behaviors or strengthen existing ones. Also used to reduce a number of phobias by showing the model interacting with the feared object.

Monism Theory that the mind and brain are one organic whole. See also *dualism*.

Monocular cues Cues to depth perception that operate even when only one eye is used.

Mood General diffuse feeling states that are often long-lasting and low-intensity.

Mood disorders Group of general, nonspecific disturbances that cause high or low feelings and affect a person's ability to function normally.

Moro reflex (also called the **startle reflex**) Causes a motor reaction of infant's arms, legs, and trunk in response to a sudden loud noise or loss of support.

Morphemes Smallest sounds that can change the meaning of words.

Motion parallax Apparent motion seen when an observer moves past objects.

Motivation Why an organism acts in a certain way at a certain time.

Motive Condition that energizes and directs the behavior of an organism.

Motor cortex Part of the cerebral cortex; located in front of the central fissure. Controls motor responses of the body.

Motor system Functional subdivision of the nervous system; includes basal ganglia, cerebellum, and the motor cortex. Controls voluntary muscle movements.

Multiple personality disorder Disorder in

which one person assumes two or more personalities. Each personality has its complete set of memories, and one is often "unaware" of the existence of the other.

Multistable perceptions (also called **figure-ground reversal**) Occurs when a picture shows alternating appearances; what was seen as figure becomes the background, and vice versa.

Mutation Abnormal chromosome structure, responsible for such diseases as Down syndrome.

Myelin sheath Fatty covering of some axons that allows neural impulses to be conducted faster.

Myelinization Development of myelin sheaths during infancy, childhood, and adolescence.

Mysticism View that alternate state experiences are a response to an external reality that exists beyond the visible and understandable universe.

Narcotics Drugs that in small doses reduce pain, cause drowsiness, and give a feeling of happiness and well-being. Examples are morphine, heroin, and opium.

Nasal cavity Open space inside the nose.

Natural observation Research method that involves studying people's reactions to naturally occurring events in natural settings.

Near point of accommodation Nearest point at which print can be read distinctly.

Nearsightedness Occurs when an eye is elongated like a horizontal egg; near-sighted people see near objects well, but see far objects poorly.

Need Internal or homeostatic imbalance that must be satisfied in order to keep the body performing at a consistent level.

Negative reinforcement Occurs when a stimulus is taken away or stopped.

Negative set Mental set that reduces the chance of learning a new relationship.

Nervous system Pervasive communication system in the body that monitors the outside world and manages the brain and behavior.

Neurons Cells in the nervous system that receive and send impulses.

Neurosis Broad pattern of psychological disorders characterized by anxiety, fear, and self-defeating behaviors.

Neurotic behaviors Attempts to cope with anxiety.

Noise Psychological concept; unwanted sound, sound that is unpleasant, bothersome, or actually physiologically harmful.

Nonverbal communication Communication through facial expression, gesture, body movement, etc.

Nonverbal leakage Betrayal through nonverbal cues of emotions people are attempting to hide.

Normal curve Symmetrical, bell-shaped curve that occurs when a normal distribution is plotted as a frequency polygon.

Normal distribution Represents the assumption that most measurements taken will be close to average, some will be a small distance from average, and few will be very far from average. People's height, weight, and IQs show this distribution.

Normative social pressure Type of group pressure based on the desire to belong to the group.

Norms Rules that govern specific behavior and apply to all members of the group.

Obedience The following of direct and explicit orders of a person in a position of authority.

Obesity In humans, being more than 15 percent over the "ideal" weight, given the person's height and overall body build.

Object permanence Knowledge that objects continue to exist even when they can no longer be experienced.

Observational learning Learning by watching other people and observing the consequences of their actions. This type of learning occurs without external reinforcement or without even performing the behavior.

Obsession Recurring, irrational thought that cannot be controlled or banished from one's mind. See also *compulsion*, which involves behavior rather than thought.

Obsessive-compulsive disorders Disorders that occur when the person feels an overwhelming need to think a certain thought (obsession) or perform a certain behavior (compulsion).

Occipital lobe One of four lobes in the cerebral cortex; receives visual impulses from the eyes.

Oedipus complex According to Freud, boy desires sexual relationship with mother, but is afraid father will find out and castrate him as punishment. In order to get rid of these fears, boy identifies with and tries to be like father. Identification with father helps form the superego because boy internalizes the father's values.

Olfactory cells Odor-sensitive cells contained in the passageway between the nose and the throat.

Open-office design Office space or area that has no real closure rather than a traditional concept of an office with floor-to-ceiling walls and a door.

Operant conditioning Type of learning that occurs when desired responses are rewarded or reinforced and undesired responses are ignored or punished.

Ophthalmoscope Uses mirrors or prisms to direct light through the pupil so that eye doctors can examine the eye's internal structures.

Opponent-process theory of emotion Theory suggesting that each emotion or state that we experience triggers an opposite emotion or state.

Optic nerve Bundle of nerve fibers that carry neural signals to the brain.

Oral cavity Open space inside the mouth.

Oral stage Infant is born with general desire for physical pleasure, which is focused in the mouth region; these impulses are satisfied by eating, sucking, and biting. This is a stage of total dependency on the parents.

Organizational psychology Branch of psychology that studies how organizational structures and dynamics affect people's behavior in business and industrial settings.

Orthographic rules Law that specifies legal and illegal letter combinations in a word.

Oscilloscope Device for converting sound waves to visible waves.

Osmometric thirst Thirst motivated by osmoreceptors in the hypothalamus that detect the depletion of intracellular water cells.

Osmoreceptors Cells in the hypothalamus that are sensitive to intracellular water levels; they send "thirst" signals to other areas of the brain when they detect that water is being depleted from the cells.

Osteoporosis Condition of aging where the loss of bone calcium causes bones to become thinner and weaker. After menopause, the rate of loss is greater for women than for men.

Otolith structures Organs that signal head orientation with respect to gravity.

Oval window Membrane stretched over the opening of the inner ear.

Ovaries Female reproductive glands that secrete estrogen into the bloodstream.

Ovulation In women, the time when the egg is available to be fertilized and secretion of estrogen is at its highest; occurs once a month.

Ovum Mature female sex cell which after fertilization develops into an offspring. The first two-week period of development after fertilization is called the period of the ovum.

Pancreas Large gland located behind the stomach; as part of the endocrine system, it controls the level of sugar in the blood by secreting insulin and glucagon.

Panic disorder Sudden onset of anxiety, overcoming the person with physiological symptoms such as sweating, dizziness, and shortness of breath. This disorder disrupts normal daily functioning.

Papillae Small elevations on the tongue; contain our taste sensors, called taste buds.

Paradoxical cold Occurs when a warm object stimulates a cold spot on the skin—cold is felt.

Paradoxical warmth Occurs when a cold object stimulates a warm spot on the skin—warmth is felt.

Paranoid People suffering from delusions of persecution are called paranoid; they believe that people are "out to get" them and interpret others' actions as plots against them.

Paraphilia Attraction to deviant objects or acts that interferes with the capacity for reciprocal and affectionate sexual activity.

Parapsychologists Those who study ESP and PK.

Parasympathetic division Part of the autonomic nervous system; functional subdivision of the nervous system; controls the relaxation responses.

Parathyroid glands Four pea-shaped glands next to the thyroid in the throat; part of the endocrine system. Produce a hormone that causes lethargy when its level is too high, and muscle spasms when its level is too low.

Parietal lobe One of four lobes in the cerebral cortex; responds to touch, pain, and temperature.

Partial reinforcement schedule Subject is reinforced every few responses or every once in awhile, but not for every response.

Peak experiences Fleeting moments in people's lives where they feel truly spontaneous and unconcerned with time or other physical constraints. A feeling of being totally absorbed in the situation, in the moment, without cares from the past or concern for the future.

Perception Process of interpreting stimuli taken in from the environment.

Perceptual release theory This theory holds that dreams and hallucinations are caused by actions and reactions in the brain.

Peripheral nervous system All nerve tissue that is not in the brain and spinal cord.

Peripheral vision Using the sides of one's eyes (and thus depending on the rods rather than the cones) to see something—usually occurs at night or in dim light.

Personal space The area around the body that people feel "belongs" to them. When interacting with others, people maintain a distance to protect their personal space.

Personality Unique set of enduring characteristics and patterns of behavior (including thoughts and emotions) that influence the way a person adjusts to his or her environment.

Personality assessment Description and measurement of individual characteristics.

Personality disorders Rigid and maladaptive ways of dealing with the environment, characterized by a general approach to dealing with events rather than by any one specific behavior. The example discussed in the text is the *antisocial personality disorder*, which is the type of personality disorder most often found in Western society.

Personality psychology Subfield of psychology that focuses on individual differences and on explaining and predicting the unique ways that people respond to their environment.

Person-centered therapy Theory created by Carl Rogers aimed at providing the proper setting for the self-growth of the person. Since the person (rather than the therapist) determines what will be discussed during therapy, it is referred to as person-centered therapy.

Person-environment fit The physical and social conditions that best suit our living needs.

Phallic stage According to psychoanalytic theory begins at the age of four; focus of pleasure is the genital organs. Trauma at this stage is called Oedipus complex for boys, Electra complex for girls.

Pharynx Open space inside the throat.

Phenotype The way one's genotype (genetic inheritance) is expressed in observable characteristics.

Pheromones Odorous chemicals released by one animal that directly affect the arousal of another animal.

Phobia An irrational fear of an object or event attached to a specific, identifiable object; phobics can control their anxiety by avoiding that object or situation.

Phonemes Smallest meaningful unit of speech sound.

Phonological rule Rule that specifies legal and illegal phoneme combinations.

Phosphenes Visual sensations arising from spontaneous discharges of light-sensitive neurons in the eyes.

Phrenology Determination of an individual's personality type by the examination of the bumps and contours of his or her head.

Physiological psychology Subfield of psychology that examines the areas of learning, memory, perception, motivation, and emotion by studying the neurobiological events that underlie them.

Pinna Outer flap of the ear.

Pitch Difference between low and high notes. Changes in pitch correspond to changes in frequency of sound waves.

Pituitary gland Small gland that lies in a recess at the base of the brain and is connected to the hypothalamus, which controls it. Part of the endocrine system, it is often called the master gland because it has such wide-ranging effects. Secretes many different types of hormones, which control growth and sexual reproduction, among other things.

Placebo In drug studies, a drug substitute made from inactive materials that is given to the control group in drug research.

Placebo effect Situation in which a treatment that has no curative value of its own has a healing effect because of the patient's belief in its effectiveness.

Placenta Special filter used to exchange food and wastes between an embryo and his or her mother.

Pleasure principle Immediate satisfaction of drives without regard to reality, logic, or manners; guides the id.

Polarization Electric tension that exists in a neuron between the cell's inside and outside environment. Also called *membrane potential*.

Polygenic traits Traits that are determined by the action of more than one gene pair. Most human traits are polygenic.

Polygraph Also called a lie detector. Machine that records changes in heart rate, blood pressure, respiration, and galvanic skin response. Lies are identified when there is a change from baseline responses to neutral questions to a heightened response to questions about critical events.

Pons Part of the hindbrain; a tube formed by a massive cable of nerve fibers. Connects the medulla to the midbrain.

Positive reinforcement Occurs when a positive stimulus is added to the environment.

Positron emission tomography (PET scan) Computer-generated representation of brain activity.

Posthypnotic amnesia Inability of a hypnotized subject to recall certain experiences until an appropriate cue is given.

Posthypnotic suggestions Suggestions made to a subject while hypnotized which are to be carried out after hypnosis has ended.

Post-Traumatic Stress Disorder Reexperiencing a stressful event that can occur months or years after the event.

Power Capacity to influence other people.

Precognition Perception of future thoughts, events, or actions.

Preconscious mind According to Freud, the preconscious is essentially one's memory, including thoughts that people may not be aware of but that they can retrieve from memory.

Prefrontal lobotomy Surgical technique for treating extreme psychological disorders. Involves cutting connections between the thalamus and the frontal lobes. Seldom used today except when all other methods have failed.

Prejudice Unjustified negative attitude toward an individual based solely on that person's membership in a group.

Premature ejaculation Ejaculation which occurs too quickly, according to the definition of the male and the couple.

Preoperational stage One of Piaget's stages of cognitive development; lasts from 2 to 7 years of age. Main theme is discovering mental operations, which are plans, strategies, and rules for solving problems and for classifying.

Preparedness Idea that animals are more prepared to make certain responses than others, and may find other responses more difficult to make.

Primacy effect In impression formation, the fact that people tend to base their impressions on what they hear first.

Primary motives Motives such as hunger, thirst, and the need for air and rest. These motives are usually unlearned, common to all animals, and vital for the survival of the organism or the species.

Primary reinforcers Events or objects that are reinforcing in and of themselves (such as food).

Primary sexual characteristics Traits directly concerned with sexual reproduction; the production of live ovum by girls and live sperm by boys.

Primary territories Owned and controlled by people; these territories are central to their lives.

Privacy Freedom to decide what we will communicate about ourselves to a person or group and when that communication will occur.

Proactive inhibition Interference of previous learning with memory for new learning.

Problem drinkers People who often drink too much and whose drinking has undesirable effects on their lives or on others. See also *alcoholics*.

Problem solving Thinking aimed at overcoming obstacles that stand in the way of a goal.

Product-moment correlation Measure of the extent to which changes in two variables are related to each other.

Projection Defense mechanism that involves seeing our own shortcomings or undesirable traits in other people rather than in ourselves.

Projective tests Based on Freud's theory that people will project unconscious desires onto ambiguous and nonthreatening stimuli. The stimuli can be an incomplete sentence or a picture. People's responses are analyzed to see what they tell about them.

Propositional thought Conscious or unconscious manipulation of symbols that can be true or false.

Proprioception The sense of where our body parts are; determined by sense organs in joints, muscles, and tendons, which connect muscles with bones.

Prototype Typical, or standard, example.

Proxemics Study of personal space.

Proximity Physical closeness.

Psychiatric nurse Registered nurse who

has received special training in dealing with psychological disorders.

Psychiatrist Medical doctor who has received an M.D. degree and has taken part in a residency program in emotional disorders; the only type of therapist who can prescribe drugs or conduct psychosurgery.

Psychoactive drugs Drugs that produce subjective effects: depressants, stimulants, and hallucinogens.

Psychoanalysis Freud's technique of treating anxiety disorders by helping people recognize and deal with their repressed feelings.

Psychoanalyst Psychiatrist who has had a great deal of training in psychoanalytic techniques and has often undergone psychoanalysis personally.

Psychokinesis (PK) Direct mental influence over physical objects or processes.

Psychological test Test designed to identify individual differences among people; tests have been developed to measure attitudes, abilities, achievement, and personality traits.

Psychology Scientific study of behavior and the applications gained from that knowledge.

Psychology of minorities Subfield of psychology that examines behavior of people in minority groups, including women who are minorities in some contexts.

Psychopharmacology Study of drugs to treat psychological disorders.

Psychophysical function The relationship between physical energies and psychological experiences over a wide range of physical magnitudes.

Psychophysics Studies the relationship between physical energies and psychological experiences.

Psychophysiological disorder Often referred to as psychosomatic illness; an actual physical illness in which stress is a contributing factor. An example is a peptic ulcer.

Psychosis Disturbance caused by unresolved conflicts that is so great that the person can no longer deal with reality.

Psychosurgery Various techniques of biotherapy involving surgery to the brain. The best known is the *prefrontal lobotomy*, in which connections are cut between the thalamus and the frontal lobes. Seldom used today, except when all other methods have failed.

Psychotherapy Use of psychological techniques by a professionally trained person to help a client change unwanted behavior and adjust to his or her environment. In short, the use of language to make positive changes in the life of another.

Puberty The time in adolescence when sexual reproduction becomes possible.

Public territories Territories that do not improve feelings of ownership, but people feel that they control them while they are occupying them; an example is a table at a restaurant.

Punishment Stimulus that decreases the likelihood of a response when it is added to an environment. Compare with *reinforcement*.

Pupil Opening in the iris of the eye; looks like a black spot in the center of the iris.

Pure tones Sounds containing a single frequency.

Pyramidal cells Giant cells of the motor cortex that send a long axon through the brain down to neurons in the spinal cord. Control precise physical movements and speech.

Questionnaire Standard set of questions used to assess behavior that can be given to many people at one time and usually can be scored quickly.

Randomization Procedure used in an experiment whereby subjects are randomly assigned to either the control group or the experimental group(s). It ensures that each person has an equal chance of being assigned to each group, thus making it highly probable that subject differences will be equally distributed between groups.

Range A measure of variation, the difference between the largest and smallest number in the distribution.

Rape Coercive sexual assault on an individual.

Rational Emotive Therapy (RET) Type of therapy developed by Albert Ellis; focuses on the present and on the client's irrational beliefs. Therapist plays a much more directive and even challenging role than in most other therapies.

Rationalization Defense mechanism that involves justifying one's behavior by finding logical or desirable reasons for it.

Reactance Psychological state that motivates us to regain our freedom by resisting group pressure.

Reaction formation Defense mechanism that conceals unacceptable impulses by expressing instead the opposite impulse.

Real difference A difference that could occur by chance less than 5 percent of the time.

Reality anxiety Response to a specific danger in the environment.

Reality principle This is what guides the ego; it tries to satisfy the desires of the id by taking into account the possibilities of reward and punishment that exist in the situation.

Recall tests Measure a person's ability to reproduce material. *Cued recall* is when part of the material is provided as a cue for the rest; *free recall* is when no cues are provided and any order of recall is allowed.

Receptor sites Areas on the dendrite that receive the chemical transmitter.

Recognition tests Measure a person's ability to pick the correct answer when several answers are given; often occur in the form of multiple-choice questions on tests.

Reconstruction Organization and recoding (often done unconsciously) of memory over time; may lead to distortions of memory.

Reflected appraisal Basing self-image on the image we believe others have of us.

Reflex Automatic action that requires no conscious effort.

Rehearsal Process of repeating information in order to retain it in short-term memory or transfer it to long-term memory.

Reinforcement Event whose occurrence just after a response increases the likelihood that the response will be repeated.

See *positive, negative reinforcement*; compare with *punishment*.

Relative refractory period Period during which a cell will only fire in response to an extra-strong impulse; lasts for a few milliseconds.

Relaxation response Phrase used by Benson to refer to the physiological patterns observed during meditation; a decrease in oxygen consumption, respiratory rate, heart rate, blood pressure, and muscle tension.

Releasing stimulus In animals, an event that causes a predetermined response. For example, some female mammals release pheromones, a chemical substance signaling the male that the female is sexually receptive.

Reliability of a test Means that you get the same results on the test every time you administer it.

REM rebound Sharp increase of REM sleep after going through a period of sleep deprivation.

REM sleep Stage of sleep marked by rapid eye movements (REMs) and dreams.

Representativeness heuristic Strategy whereby we estimate the probability that an event or object belongs to a category because of its similarity to that category.

Repression Defense mechanism that involves blocking or keeping unpleasant thoughts or memories from conscious awareness. Differs from suppression in that it is an unconscious process whereas suppression is a conscious process.

Response generalization Means giving different, but similar, responses to the same stimulus.

Resting state Occurs whenever a neuron is not sending or receiving neural impulses.

Retention Process of holding information in memory.

Reticular activating system (RAS) Functional subdivision of the nervous system; activates all regions of the brain for incoming sensory impulses, plays an important part in alertness and selective attention.

Retina Tissue covering most of the eye's interior wall; contains rods and cones.

Retinal image The image that the object projects on to the back wall of the eye.

Retrieval Process of getting information out of memory.

Retrieval cues Aids to retrieval that are often encoded with the information to be remembered; an example would be category names.

Retroactive inhibition Interference of new learning with memory for previous learning.

Retrograde amnesia Partial loss of memory for events that occurred before an injury.

Ribonucleic acid (RNA) Messenger molecules sent out by DNA to control how specific kinds of protein chains are made.

Rods Light receptors located on the periphery or sides of the retina; they are best for seeing in dim light.

Role conflict Situation that exists when the demands of roles the individual holds require conflicting behaviors.

Roles Group rules that apply only to people in certain positions; roles define the

obligations and expectations of that specific position.

Rooting reflex Causes infants to turn their head toward anything that touches their cheek.

Rorschach inkblot test Projective test that measures personality by having subjects describe what they see in ten different inkblots.

Saccades Eye movements from one fixation point to the next as we read.

Sadism Deriving sexual pleasure from inflicting pain on others.

Sampling error Failure to represent important subject characteristics equally in all conditions of an experiment. As a result, the conditions differ because the sample of subjects is different.

Savings Difference between one's original learning time and the relearning time; measured by a savings test.

Savings tests Measure people's ability to take advantage of what they have learned before in order to relearn material faster.

Scapegoating Singling out a person or a minority group as the target (scapegoat) for aggression and hostility when the real target is too powerful to be attacked.

Scatter plot Graph formed by marking the intersection of a person's score on one variable, which is indicated on one axis of the graph, with that person's score on another variable, which is indicated on the axis of the graph.

Schema Term used by Piaget to refer to a mental structure that organizes responses to experiences.

Schizophrenia Group of disorders characterized by disorganization in thoughts, perceptions, communications, emotions, and motor activity.

Secondary reinforcers Events or objects that are reinforcing only after they have been paired with other primary reinforcers. Money is a good example of a secondary reinforcer.

Secondary sexual characteristics Traits typical of a sex, but not directly concerned with reproduction; for girls, the development of breasts and pubic hair; for boys, growth of the scrotum, pubic hair, and a beard.

Secondary territories Not "owned by people," and not as central to their lives; examples are the neighborhood street, the social or country club, or even a regular seat in a classroom.

Self-actualization Process whereby a person strives to learn, create, and work to the best of his or her ability.

Self-concept Consists of our judgments and attitudes about our behavior, abilities, and even our appearance; it is our answer to the question, "Who am I?"

Self-efficacy belief Belief that the individual can cope well with stress and change, based on personal abilities and available resources.

Self-fulfilling prophecy Expectation that leads one to behave in ways that will cause that expectation to come about.

Self-hypnosis Procedure in which people learn to hypnotize themselves so that they can more readily follow their own suggestions.

Semantic memory A person's general background knowledge about words, symbols, concepts, and rules.

Semicircular canals Three arching structures in the inner ear that detect changes in head position.

Sensation-seeking motive A motive for arousal.

Sensorimotor stage One of Piaget's stages of cognitive development, extends from birth to about 2 years of age. Main theme is discovering relationships between sensations and motor behavior.

Sensory deprivation Absence of almost all sensory stimulation.

Sensory memory Holds sensations briefly so that they can be identified; lasts from 1 to 2 seconds.

Set-point theory Suggests that the number of fat cells in the body is established during early childhood and does not change later in the life span.

Sex-linked traits Occur when the gene for a trait is located on the chromosome that determines one's sex (in humans, on the X chromosome in pair 23). Examples are color blindness and hemophilia.

Sexual dysfunction Inability or impairment of the ability to consistently experience the normal sexual response cycle.

Sexually transmitted disease (STD) Any infectious disease transmitted by sexual intercourse.

Shaping Procedure used in operant conditioning in which each part of a behavior is reinforced that eventually leads to the whole behavior that is desired.

Short-term memory Holds information that has been transferred out of sensory memory; lasts about 30 seconds unless information is repeated or rehearsed.

Signal-detection theory Attempts to explain people's perceptual judgments by analyzing their sensitivity to sensory stimuli in addition to the criteria they use to make decisions.

Single-gene traits Some genes determine specific traits all on their own, rather than in combination with other genes. An example is eye color.

Sleep Period of rest for the body and mind during which bodily functions are partially suspended and sensitivity to external stimuli is diminished, but readily or easily regained.

Sleeper effect The fact that over time, the credibility of a communicator makes no difference in people's attitudes; seems to occur because people tend to separate the source from the message as time passes.

Sleep spindles Medium-voltage, medium-frequency brain waves characteristic of stage-2 sleep.

Social cognition model Belief that people have schemata, or preconceived notions about how their social world works; these schemata influence the way people interpret events and even the information they remember; once formed, information is processed in a way that tends to support the schema.

Social comparison Using social reality to evaluate oneself—comparing oneself against the beliefs, attitudes, and behaviors of other people.

Social dilemma Situation where individual needs are in conflict with group needs.

Social facilitation Occurs because the presence of other people tends to arouse people; this arousal creates an additional pool of energy that aids the performance of well-learned behaviors.

Social-learning theory Learning by imitation.

Social loafing People's motivation to work decreases when they are in groups where their individual performance cannot be observed; the larger the group, the easier to reduce effort without being detected.

Social motives Motives that come from learning and social interaction rather than based on biological needs (see *primary motives*). These motives include affiliation, aggression, and achievement.

Social psychology Scientific study of the ways in which the thoughts, feelings, and behavior of individuals are influenced by the actual, imagined, or implied presence of others; the scientific study of the way most people act most of the time.

Social reality Beliefs, attitudes, and behaviors of other people.

Social skill training Aimed at teaching people to exercise control over their social environment and thus avoid a state of learned helplessness.

Social support Network of people upon whom you can rely in time of crisis.

Sociology Study of the functioning and organization of human society and human behavior.

Somatoform disorders Group of disorders in which people feel ill or show other symptoms such as blindness or paralysis, but there is no organic damage.

Somatosensory cortex Part of the cerebral cortex; located behind the central fissure. Controls sensory responses of the body.

Somatotype A person's body build. Sheldon characterized people as either endomorphic (soft, round, fat), mesomorphic (muscular, hard, rectangular), or ectomorphic (tall, thin, fragile).

Sound Physical property caused by changes in air pressure; measured in decibels (db.). Contrast with *noise*, which is a psychological concept.

Sound spectrograms Visible representation of speech.

Specific therapy Therapy aimed at changing a specific behavior or thought pattern.

Spinal cord Cable of long nerve fibers running from the brainstem down through the backbone to the lower back, through which ascending nerves carry sensory information up to the brain and descending nerves carry commands down from the brain to move muscles.

Spontaneous recovery Occurs when a response reappears without any retraining after having been extinguished.

Standard deviation Measure of variation. The square root of the *variance* is often used to express how far any given score is from the mean of a set of scores.

Standard error of the difference between two means Computed by finding the square root of the sum of the standard errors of the means.

Standard error of the mean Shows the variation of a sample mean and tells how likely it is that the sample mean represents the population mean.

Standard score Single number that expresses where a score lies relative to a population. Expresses the value of a score relative to the mean and the standard deviation of its distribution.

Standardized tests Tests that have been given to many people so that one person's score can be evaluated with respect to a large population.

Statistical significance Means that a difference in scores is a true difference, not a result of sampling error.

Statistics Branch of mathematics used by psychologists to describe data and to draw conclusions based on data.

Stereotypes Oversimplified generalizations about the characteristics of a group.

Stimulants Drugs that excite body functions; examples are caffeine, amphetamines, and cocaine.

Stimulus discrimination Making different responses to different stimuli.

Stimulus generalization Occurs when responses are made to stimuli that are similar to, but not the same as, the original conditioned stimulus (CS).

Stimulus-seeking motive Motive to explore and manipulate new objects to increase stimulation and arousal.

Stirrup One of three small bones in the middle ear; transmits sounds from the eardrum to the inner ear.

Stress Process by which the individual responds to events that disrupt or threaten to disrupt his or her equilibrium.

Stressor The event that gives rise to stress.

Structuralism Approach to psychology based on identifying the elements of human experience and finding out how those elements are combined into thoughts and feelings.

Sublimation Defense mechanism that involves rechanneling the energy associated with one emotion or event into a seemingly unrelated activity.

Substance abuse Disorder that results from a pathological use of a drug; a reduction in social or occupational functioning because of the drug; and a duration of disturbance of at least one month.

Substance dependence Addiction including the presence of tolerance or withdrawal.

Substance use disorders Disorders including the categories of substance abuse and substance dependence.

Sucking reflex Causing sucking in infants when anything touches the lips.

Suicide The planned taking of one's life.

Superego According to Freud, the superego represents our conscience, including the moral values of right and wrong instilled in us by our parents.

Suppression Defense mechanism that involves consciously blocking or avoiding unpleasant thoughts. Differs from repression in that it is a conscious process and repression is unconscious.

Survey Method used in psychology; uses questionnaires that are given to large samples of people.

Sympathetic division Part of the autonomic nervous system; functional subdivision of the nervous system; controls the fight-or-flight responses.

Synapse Junction between two neurons.

Synaptic space Very small gap between the axon terminal of one cell and the dendrite of the next cell.

Synaptic transmission Occurs as a neural impulse; moves from one neuron to another.

Synaptic vesicles Tiny oval sacs on the axon terminal filled with a chemical transmitter substance.

Systematic desensitization Type of behavior therapy based on the assumption that it is impossible to be relaxed and anxious at the same time. Clients are taught deep muscle relaxation; they then pair this with feared or stressful events or objects, with the idea that the relaxation response will overcome the fear reaction. Often used to treat phobias.

Taste buds Taste sensors contained in papillae on the tongue.

Telepathy Perception of another's mental state or emotion by means of ESP.

Temporal lobe One of four lobes in the cerebral cortex; receives sound and smell impulses and has centers that control speech.

Teratogens Drugs taken by the mother during pregnancy that cause abnormal fetal development.

Territoriality The claiming of control or ownership of areas or objects.

Testes Male reproductive glands, which secrete androgens into the bloodstream.

Testosterone Male sex hormone.

Test statistic Ratio of the difference between the means to the standard error of the difference between means.

Texture gradient Monocular cue to depth. As we look at something with texture, the nearer elements are spaced farther apart than the more distant elements.

Thalamus Two egg-shaped structures that are part of the forebrain. Often called a relay station because sensory pathways from all over the body pass through it.

Thematic Apperception Test (TAT) Projective test that measures personality by showing the subject an ambiguous scene and asking him or her to tell a story about it.

Theory Explanation about why behavior occurs; theories generate hypotheses that can be tested experimentally.

Theta waves Low-voltage, low-frequency brain waves characteristic of stage-1 sleep.

Thought Mental activity of manipulating symbols.

Thyroid glands Large, butterfly-shaped glands in the front and sides of the throat; part of the endocrine system. Produce thyroxin, a hormone that determines the rate at which food is transformed in the body into energy.

Thyroxin Hormone produced by the thyroid glands; determines the rate at which food is transformed in the body into energy.

Tinnitus A disorder in which one constantly hears noises when there's no external noise.

Tip-of-the-tongue (TOT) phenomenon State of being on the verge of recalling something; often subjects say that the word or whatever they are trying to record is "on the tip of the tongue."

Token economy Operant conditioning technique in which subjects are given tokens for good performance or behavior which they can exchange for treats or other primary reinforcers.

Tolerance Need to increase the amount of the drug to achieve the same effects.

Tonic neck reflex Causes infants who are on their back to move their arms and legs into a "fencing" position when the head is turned to one side.

Trace decay theory Memory traces fade away in time if their strength is not maintained through use.

Traits Fairly permanent qualities that cause people to respond similarly across a variety of situations.

Tranquilizers Depressant drugs that slow the body functions, reduce anxiety, and have a relaxing effect.

Transcendental Meditation (TM) A simplified yoga technique that allows people to meditate after a short training course.

Transference Part of Freud's technique of psychoanalysis; occurs when clients transfer to the therapist feelings that were originally aimed at their parents. In this way they are able to work them through on a rational, conscious level.

Transpersonal psychology Tries to increase people's self-awareness through a mixture of psychological theory, religion, and modern philosophy. Its aim is to increase personal growth in many different ways and on different levels.

Transsexual Person who has undergone a sex-change operation that changes the anatomical features to be like those of the opposite sex.

Trial and error Approach to problem solving that involves trying different possibilities until something works.

Two-point threshold The least distance between two stimuli that can be perceived as separate on the skin.

Type A behavior Coronary-prone behavior pattern; a response to stress that involves becoming more active, more competitive, more "driven."

Unconditional positive regard Part of client-centered therapy, in which the therapist tries to create a condition of unconditional positive regard by accepting and caring for clients no matter what feelings or behaviors are revealed in the session.

Unconditioned response (UR) Automatic or reflexive reaction to a stimulus.

Unconditioned stimulus (US) Something that automatically or reflexively causes a response.

Unconscious According to Freud, a storehouse of unacceptable images, including past events, current impulses, and desires of which one is not aware.

Unconscious inference theory Size constancy occurs because we unconsciously make accurate inferences about object size when we have accurate information about retinal image size and object distance.

Uterus (womb) Hollow, muscular organ in which a mother carries a fetus in the 9 months before birth.

Vaginismus Sexual disorder in which the involuntary tightening of the vagina makes sexual intercourse impossible.

Validity of a test Means that the test actually measures what you say it measures; best way to tell this is to see if the results of the test successfully predict the type of behavior in which you are interested.

Variable Factor that is allowed to vary in a scientific study.

Variable-interval schedule Reinforces the first response made after varying time intervals (the first interval might be 5 minutes, then 9 minutes, then 1 minute, etc.). Produces a slow, steady rate of response.

Variable-ratio schedule Reinforces the first response made after a varying number of responses (the tenth response; the fourth response after that; the twelfth response after the previous response, etc.). Produces a rapid, steady rate of responding.

Variance Measure of variation, the average squared difference of each number in a sample from the mean of all numbers in the sample.

Verbal mediation Mnemonic system in which one relates new material to verbal mediators, which are words that are easy to remember.

Vestibular system Inner-ear structure that detects body orientation and changes in body orientation.

Visual angle Angle between lines formed by the top and bottom of an object one is looking at. The visual angle gets smaller as an object moves farther away, which means that the retinal image of the object also gets smaller.

Visual cliff Apparatus used to test depth perception in infants.

Vitreous humor Semiliquid gel that fills the eye's main chamber and gives it a spherical shape.

Vocal cords Membranes in the throat that vibrate to make sounds during speaking.

Voice stress analyzer Records amount of voice tremor, which may be affected by stress. A decrease in voice tremor indicates tension, and, presumably, the fact that the person is lying.

Volumetric thirst Thirst motivated by a drop in blood pressure caused by a depletion of extracellular fluid.

Warm spots Areas on the skin where only hot is felt, even if stimulated by a cold object (when this occurs it is called *paradoxical warmth*).

Waveform Shape of a sound wave; changes in waveform allow us to distinguish between the sound of a piano and a violin, for instance.

Weber's Law Law stating that a just-noticeable change in a stimulus is proportional to the original stimulus magnitude.

Wernicke's aphasia Speech that includes wrong words, nonsense words, and shifting from topic to topic. Caused by injury to Wernicke's area in the cortex.

Withdrawal symptoms Range of physical symptoms, including nausea and pain when a drug-dependent person is deprived of his or her drug of choice.

Yerkes-Dodson principle Theory that the most effective level of arousal for performance depends on the difficulty of the task.

Zener cards Special cards used to test for ESP.

Zygote Cell formed by the union of an ovum and a sperm.

References

ABRAMSON, L., SELIGMAN, M., & TEASDALE, J. (1978). Learned helplessness in humans. Critique and reformation. *Journal of Abnormal Psychology, 87*, 49–74.

ABRAMSON, L. Y., METALSKY, G., & ALLOY, L. (1989). Hopelessness depression: A theory-based subtype of depression. *Psychological Review, 96*, 358–372.

ABRAMSON, P., PERRY, L., ROTHBLATT, A., SEELEY, T., & SEELEY, D. (1981). Negative attitudes toward masturbation and pelvic vasocongestion: The thermographic analysis. *Journal of Research in Personality, 15*, 497–509.

ABRAVANEL, E., & SIGAFOOS, A. P. (1984). Exploring the presence of irritation during early infancy. *Child Development, 55*, 381–392.

ACOSTA, S. (1990). Auditory hallucinations and delusional thinking: A review and critique of outcome studies. *Behavioral Residential Treatment, 5*, 189–206.

ADAMS, G. (1928, December). The decline of psychology in America. *American Mercury*, 450–454.

ADAMS, G. (1934, January). The rise and fall of psychology. *Atlantic Monthly*, 82–92.

ADAMS, G., & HUSTON, T. (1975). Social perception of middle-aged persons varying in physical attractiveness. *Developmental Psychology, 11*, 657–658.

ADAMS, J., VORHEES, C. V., & MIDDAUGH, L. D. (1990). Developmental neurotoxicity of anticonvulsants: Human and animal evidence on phenytoin. Special Issue: Qualitative and quantitative comparability of human and animal developmental neurotoxicity. *Neurotoxicology and Teratology, 12*, 203–214.

ADAMS, J. L. (1976). *Conceptual blockbusting: A pleasurable guide to better problem solving.* San Francisco: San Francisco Book Co.

ADLER, A. (1927). *The practice and theory of individual psychology.* New York: Harcourt, Brace & World.

ADLER, A. (1939). *Social interest.* New York: Putnam.

ADORNO, T. W., FENKEL-BRUNSWICK, E., LEVINSON, D. J., & SANFORD, R. N. (1950). *The authoritarian personality.* New York: Harper & Row.

AGMON, E. (1990). Music theory as cognitive science: Some conceptual and methodological issues. *Music Perception, 7*, 285–308.

AGRAS, S., SYLVESTER, D., & OLIVEAU, D. (1969). The epidemiology of common fears and phobias. *Comprehensive Psychiatry, 10*, 151–156.

AGRAS, W. S. (1967). Behavior therapy in management of chronic schizophrenia. *American Journal of Psychiatry, 124*, 240–243.

AGUILAR, S., GOMAZ, J., & JUAN, C. (1989). A neurobiological model for near death experiences. *Journal of Near Death Studies, 7*, 205–222.

AIELLO, J. R., & AIELLO, T. (1974). The development of personal space: Proxemic behavior of children 6 through 16. *Human Ecology, 2*(3), 177–189.

AINSLIE, R. C., & SOLYOM, A. E. (1986). The replacement of the fantasied oedipal child: A disruptive effect of sibling loss on the mother-infant relationship. *Psychoanalytic Psychology, 3*, 257–268.

AINSWORTH, M. D. (1963). The development of infant-mother interactions among the Ganda. In D. M. Foss (Ed.), *Determinants of infant behavior* (Vol. 2). New York: Wiley.

AINSWORTH, M. D. (1973). The development of infant-mother attachment. In B. Caldwell & H. Ricciuti (Eds.), *Review of child development research* (Vol. 3). Chicago: University of Chicago Press.

AINSWORTH, M. D., SALTER, D., & WITTIG, B. A. (1967). Attachment and exploratory behavior of one-year-olds in a strange situation. In B. M. Foss (Ed.), *Determinants of infant behavior* (Vol. 4). New York: Wiley.

AINSWORTH, M. S. (1979). Infant-mother attachment. *American Psychologist, 34*, 932–937.

AJZEN, I., & FISHBEIN, M. (1977). Attitude-behavior relations: A theoretical analysis and review of empirical research. *Psychological Bulletin, 84*, 888–918.

AKISKAL, H. S., & McKINNEY, W. T., JR. (1975). Overview of recent research in depression. *Archives of General Psychiatry, 32*, 285–305.

ALBERT, S. A., & MOSS, B. M. (1988). *Geriatric neuropsychology.* New York: Guilford.

ALCOCK, J. E. (1986). Chronic pain and the injured worker. *Canadian Psychology, 27*, 196–203.

ALDERFER, C. (1972). *Existence, relatedness and growth.* New York: Free Press.

ALKON, D. L. (1983). Learning in a marine snail. *Scientific American, 249*, 70–84.

ALLARD, F., & BENNETT, N. (1985). Skill in sport. *Canadian Journal of Psychology, 39*, 294–312.

ALLEN, V., & GREENBERGER, D. (1980). Destruction and perceived control. In A. Baum & J. Singer (Eds.), *Advances in environmental psychology* (Vol. 2). Hillsdale, NJ: Erlbaum.

ALLGOOD-MERTEN, B., LEWINSOHN, P., & HOPS, H. (1990). Sex differences and adolescent depression. *Journal of Abnormal Psychology, 99*, 55–63.

ALLOY, L. B., & AHRENS, A. H. (1987). Depression and pessimism for the future: Biased use of statistically relevant information in predictions for self versus others. *Journal of Personality and Social Psychology, 52*, 366–378.

ALLPORT, F. H. (1924). *Social psychology.* Cambridge, MA: Riverside.

ALLPORT, G. W. (1937). *Personality: A psychological interpretation.* New York: Holt, Rinehart and Winston.

ALLPORT, G. W. (1954). *The nature of prejudice.* Reading, MA: Addison Wesley.

ALLPORT, G. W. (1985). The historical background of social psychology, In G. Lindzey & E. Aronson (Eds.), *Handbook of Social Psychology*, Vol. 1 (3rd ed). New York: Random House.

ALLPORT, G. W., & ODBERT, H. S. (1936). Trait names: A psycholexical study. *Psychological Monographs, 47* (1, Whole No. 211).

ALSTERMARK, B., ISA, T., LUNDBERG, A., & PETERSON, L. G. (1989). The effect of low pyramidal lesions on forelimb movements in the cat. *Neuroscience Research, 7*, 71–75.

ALTMAN, I. (1975). *The environment and social behavior.* Monterey, CA: Brooks/Cole.

ALTMAN, I. (1987). Centripetal and centrifugal trends in psychology, *American Psychologists, 42*, 1058–1069.

ALTMAN, I., & CHEMERS, M. (1980). *Culture and environment.* Monterey, CA: Brooks/Cole.

ALTMAN, I., LEVINE, M., & NADIEN, J. (1970). Unpublished results cited in S. Milgram, "The experience of living in cities." *Science, 167*, 1461–1468.

ALTMAN, I., & VINSEL, A. (1977). Personal space: An analysis of E. T. Hall's proxemics framework. In I. Altman & J. Wehwill (Eds.), *Human behavior and environment: Advances in theory and research* (Vol. 1). New York: Plenum.

ALTMAN, I., VINSEL, A., & BROWN, B. (1981). Dialectic conceptions in social psychology: An application to social penetration and privacy regulation. In L. Berkowitz (Ed.), *Advances in experimental social psychology* (Vol. 14). New York: Academic.

ALTUS, W. D. (1959). Birth order, intelligence and adjustment. *Psychological Reports, 5*, 502.

ALTUS, W. D. (1966). Birth order and its sequelae. *Science, 151*, 44–49.

AMERICAN OSTEOPATHIC ACADEMY OF SPORTS MEDICINE (1989). Anabolic-androgenic steroids and substance abuse in sport: Policy statement and position paper. *AOASM*: Middleton, WI.

AMERICAN PSYCHIATRIC ASSOCIATION. (1987). *Diagnostic and statistical manual of mental disorders* (3rd ed, rev.: DSM III-R). Washington, DC: American Psychiatric Association.

AMERICAN PSYCHOLOGICAL ASSOCIATION (1990). Ethical principles of psychologists (amended June 2, 1989). *American Psychologist, 45*, 390–395.

AMERICAN PSYCHOLOGICAL ASSOCIATION (1991a). *1989 doctorate employment survey.* Washington, DC: APA Press.

AMERICAN PSYCHOLOGICAL ASSOCIATION (1991b). *1988–89 characteristics of graduate departments of psychology.* Washington, DC: APA Press.

AMERICAN PSYCHOLOGICAL ASSOCIATION COMMITTEE ON EMPLOYMENT AND HUMAN RESOURCES (1986). The changing face of American psychology. *American Psychologist, 41*, 1311–1327.

AMERICAN PSYCHOLOGIST. (1987). Model act for state license of psychologists. *American Psychologist, 42*, 696–703.

AMIR, Y., & SHARAN, S. (1984). *School desegregation: Cross-cultural perspectives.* Hillsdale, NJ: Erlbaum.

AMSEL, A., & LASHOTTE, M. E. (1984). *Mechanisms of adaptive behavior.* New York: Columbia University Press.

ANCH, A. M., MITLER, M. M., WALSH, J. K., & BROWMAN, C. (1988). *Sleep: A scientific perspective.* Englewood Cliffs, NJ: Prentice Hall.

ANDERSON, C. (1987). Temperature and aggression: Effects on quarterly, yearly, and city rates of violent and nonviolent crime. *Journal of Personality and Social Psychology, 52*, 1161–1173.

ANDERSON, C. A., & ANDERSON, D. C. (1984). Ambient temperature and violent crime: Tests of the linear and curvilinear hypothesis. *Journal of Personality and Social Psychology, 46*, 91–97.

ANDERSON, J. R., & BOWER, G. H. (1973). *Human associative memory.* Washington, DC: Winston.

ANDERSON, J. R., & KOSSLYN, S. M. (Eds.). (1984). *Tutorials in learning and memory: Essays in honor of Gordon Bower.* San Francisco: Freeman.

ANDERSON, W. F., & DIACOMAKOS, E. G. (1981). Genetic engineering in mammalian cells. *Scientific American, 245,* 106–121.

ANDERSSON, B., & LARSSON, S. (1961). Influence of local temperature changes in the preoptic area and rostral hypothalamus on the regulation of food and water intake. *Acta Physiologica Scandinavica,* 15–89.

ANDERSSON, B., & LARSSON, S. (1961). Physiological and pharmacological aspects of the control of hunger and thirst. *Acta Physiologica Scandinavica,* 188–201.

ANDERSSON, T., & MAGNUSSON, D. (1990). Biological maturation in adolescence and the development of drinking habits and alcohol abuse among young males: A prospective longitudinal study. *Journal of Youth and Adolescence, 19,* 33–41.

ANDO, Y., & HATTORI, H. (1973). Statistical studies in the effects of intense noise during human fetal life. *Journal of Sound and Vibration, 27,* 101–110.

ANDREW A. K. (1989). Meeting the needs of young deaf-blind children and their parents: I. *Child Care, Health and Development, 15,* 195–206.

ANDREW, A. K. (1989). Meeting the needs of young deaf-blind children and their parents: II. *Child Care, Health and Development, 15,* 251–264.

ANDREW, J. D. W. (1967). The achievement motive and advancement in two types of organizations. *Journal of Personality and Social Psychology, 6,* 163–168.

ANDREWS, G., & HARVEY R. (1981). Does psychotherapy benefit neurotic patients? *Archives of General Psychiatry, 38,* 1203–1208.

ANDRUCCI, G. L., ARCHER, R. P., & PANCOAST, D. L. (1989). The relationship of MMPI and sensation seeking scales to adolescent drug use. *Journal of Personality Assessment, 53,* 253–266.

ANDRYKOWSKI, M. A., & REDD, W. H. (1987). Longitudinal analysis of the development of anticipatory nausea. *Journal of Consulting and Clinical Psychology, 55,* 36–41.

ANSPACHER, C. (1972, January 26). Rock really does deafen. *San Francisco Chronicle,* p. 1.

ANSTIS, S. (1986). Recovering motion information from luminance. *Vision Research, 26,* 147–159.

ANTONOVSKY, A., & SAGY, S. (1990). Confronting developmental tasks in the retirement transition. *Gerontologist, 30,* 362–368.

APGAR, V. A. (1953). A proposal for a new method of evaluation of the newborn infant. *Current Researches in Anesthesia and Analgesia, 32,* 260–267.

APPLEYARD, D., & LINTELL, M. (1972). The environmental quality of city streets: The residents' point of view. In W. Mitchell (Ed.), *Environmental design: Research and practice.* Los Angeles: University of California/EDRA.

ARENBERG, D. (1967). Regression analyses of verbal learning on adult age at two anticipation intervals. *Journal of Gerontology, 22,* 411–414.

ARGYLE, M. (1967). *The psychology of interpersonal behavior.* Baltimore: Penguin.

ARGYLE, M., & DEAN, J. (1965). Eye-contact, distance and affiliation. *Sociometry, 28,* 289–304.

ARGYLE, M., & McHENRY, R. (1971). Do spectacles really affect judgments of intelligence? *British Journal of Social and Clinical Psychology, 10,* 27–29.

ARMBRUSTER, B. B., & ANDERSON, T. H. (1981). *Content Area Textbooks,* Reading Education Report N. 23 (Center for the Study of Reading), University of Illinois at Urbana-Champaign, Urbana, IL.

ARMBRUSTER, B. B., & ANDERSON, T. H. (1984). Structures of explanation in his-

tory textbooks or so what if Governor Stanford missed the spike and hit the rail? *Journal of Curriculum Studies, 16,* 181–194.

ARMSTRONG, G. B., & GREENBERG, B. S. (1990). Background television as an inhibitor of cognitive processing. *Human Communication Research, 16,* 355–386.

ARNOLD, M. B. (1960). *Emotion and personality* (2 vols.). New York: Columbia University Press.

ARONOFF, J., BARCLAY, A., & STEVENSON, L. (1988). The recognition of threatening facial stimuli. *Journal of Personality and Social Psychology, 54,* 647–655.

ARONSON, E. (1976). *The social animal* (2nd ed.). San Francisco: Freeman.

ARONSON, E. (1989). Analysis, synthesis, and the treasuring of the old. *Personality and Social Psychology Bulletin, 15,* 493–507.

ARONSON, E., & BRIDGEMAN, D. (1979). Jigsaw groups and the desegregated classroom: In pursuit of common goals. *Personality and Social Psychology Bulletin, 5,* 438–446.

ARONSON, E., & CARLSMITH, J. M. (1963). The effect of the severity of threat on the devaluation of forbidden behavior. *Journal of Abnormal and Social Psychology, 66,* 584–588.

ARONSON, E., & LINDER, D. E. (1965). Gain and loss of esteem as determinants of interpersonal attractiveness. *Journal of Experimental Social Psychology, 1,* 156–171.

ARONSON, E., & MILLS, J. (1959). The effect of severity of initiation on liking for a group. *Journal of Abnormal and Social Psychology, 59,* 177–181.

ARONSON, E., WILLERMAN, B., & FLOYD, J. (1966). The effect of a pratfall on increasing interpersonal attractiveness. *Psychonomic Science, 4,* 227–228.

ASCH, S. (1946). Forming impressions of personality. *Journal of Abnormal and Social Psychology, 41,* 258–290.

ASCH, S. (1951). Effects of group pressure upon the modification and distortion of judgment. In H. Guetzkow (Ed.), *Groups, leadership and men.* Pittsburgh: Carnegie.

ASCH, S. (1952). *Social psychology.* Englewood Cliffs, NJ: Prentice Hall.

ASCH, S. (1956). Studies of independence and conformity: I. A minority of one against a unanimous majority. *Psychological Monographs, 70,* No. 9.

ASCH, S. E., & ZUKIER, H. (1984). Thinking about persons. *Journal of Personality and Social Psychology, 46,* 1230–1240.

ASHMORE, R., RAMCHANDRA, V., & JONES, R. (1971, April). *Censorship as an attitude change induction.* Paper presented at Eastern Psychological Association Convention, New York.

ASIN, K. E., & WIRTSHAFTER, D. (1990). Evidence for dopamine involvement in reinforcement obtained using a latent extinction paradigm. *Pharmacology, Biochemistry and Behavior, 36,* 117–120.

ASSOCIATION OF AMERICAN PUBLISHERS. (1983). *How to prepare for and take examinations.* New York.

ASTIN, A. W., GREEN, K. C., & KORN, W. S. (1987). *The American freshman: Twenty year trends.* American Council on Education and University of California, Los Angeles.

ASTLEY, S. J., & LITTLE, R. E. (1990). Maternal marijuana use during lactation and infant development at one year. *Neurotoxicity and Teratology, 12,* 161–168.

ATKINSON, J., & BIRCH, D. (1978). *An introduction to motivation.* New York: Van Nostrand.

ATKINSON, R. (1957). Motivational determinants of risk-taking behavior. *Psychological Review, 64,* 359–372.

ATKINSON, R. C. (1975). Mnemontechnics

in second-language learning. *American Psychologist, 30,* 821–828.

ATKINSON, R. C., & SHIFFRIN, R. M. (1971). The control of short-term memory. *Scientific American, 224,* 82–90.

ATKINSON, R. C., & SHIFFRIN, R. M. (1977). Human memory: A proposed system and its control processes. In G. H. Bower (Ed.), *Human memory: Basic processes.* New York: Academic.

ATTNEAVE, F. (1976). Multistability in perception. In R. Held & W. Richards (Eds.), *Recent progress in perception.* San Francisco: Freeman.

AU, T. K. (1983). Chinese and English counterfactuals: The Sapir-Whorf hypothesis revisited. *Cognition, 15,* 155–187.

AUSTIN, W. T. (1982). Portrait of a courtroom: Social and ecological impressions of the adversing process. *Criminal Justice and Behavior, 9,* 286–302.

AYLLON, T., & AZRIN, N. H. (1968). *The token economy: A motivational system for therapy and rehabilitation.* New York: Appleton-Century-Crofts.

BACH, G., & WYDEN, P. (1968). *The intimate enemy: How to fight fair in love and marriage.* New York: Avon.

BACHRACH, A. J., ERWIN, W., & MOHR, J. P. (1965). The control of eating behavior in an anorexic by operant conditioning techniques. In L. P. Ullman & L. Krasner (Eds.), *Case studies in behavior modification.* New York: Holt, Rinehart and Winston.

BACH-Y-RITA, P. (1972). *Brain mechanisms in sensory substitution.* New York: Academic.

BACH-Y-RITA, P. (1982). Sensory substitution in rehabilitation. In L. Illis, M. Sedwick, & H. Granville (Eds.), *Rehabilitation of the neurological patient.* Oxford: Blackwell Press.

BACH-Y-RITA, P., & HUGHES, B. (1985). Tactile vision substitution: Some instrumentation and perceptual considerations. In D. Warren & E. Strelow (Eds.), *Electronic spatial sensing for the blind.* The Hague: Martinus-Nijhoff.

BACKLUND, E. D., GRANBERG, P. O., HAMBERGER, B., SEDVAU, G., SEIGER, A., & OLSON, L. (1985). Transplantation of adrenal medullary tissue to striatum in Parkinsonism. In A. Bjorklund & U. Stemevi (Eds.), *Neural grafting in the mammalian CNS.* Amsterdam: Elsevier.

BADIAJ, P., CULBERTSON, S., & HARSH, J. (1973). Choice of longer or stronger signalled shock over short or weaker signalled shock. *Journal of the Experimental Analysis of Behavior, 19,* 25–32.

BAILEY, I. L. (1984). *Low vision: Principles and practice.* Berkeley: University of California, School of Optometry.

BAILLARGEON, R. (1987). Object permanence in 3 1/12- and 4 1/2-month-old infants. *Developmental Psychology, 23,* 655–664.

BAKER, C. (1983). *Physicians desk reference.* Oradell, NJ: Medical Economics.

BAKER, J. G., & BUTLER, P. (1987). Issues in psychotherapy with chronically ill adolescents. *Journal of Child and Adolescent Psychology, 4,* 186–191.

BAKWIN, H. (1949). Psychologic aspects of pediatrics. *Journal of Pediatrics, 35,* 512–521.

BALAY, J., & SHEVRIN, H. (1988). The subliminal psychodynamic activation method: A critical review. *American Psychologist, 43,* 161–174.

BALDWIN, M. (1987). Interview with Carl Rogers on the use of self in therapy. *Journal of Psychotherapy and the Family, 3,* 45–53.

BALES, J. (1987). House bill outlaws worker polygraphs. *APA Monitor, 18,* 17.

BALES, R. F., & SLATER, P. (1955). Role differentiation in small decision-making groups. In T. Parson & R. F. Bales (Eds.), *Family socialization and interaction processes.* Glencoe, IL: Free Press.

BALL, K., & SEKULER, R. (1986). Improving visual perception in older observers. *Journal of Gerontology, 41,* 176–182.

BANCROFT, J. (1984). Hormones and human sexual behavior. *Journal of Sex and Marital Therapy, 10,* 3–21.

BANDURA, A. (1962). Social learning through imitation. In M. R. Jones (Ed.), *Nebraska symposium on motivation.* Lincoln, NE: University of Nebraska Press.

BANDURA, A. (1965). Behavior modification through modeling procedures. In L. Krosner & L. P. Ullman (Eds.), *Research in behavior modification.* New York: Holt, Rinehart, and Winston.

BANDURA, A. (1965). Influence of models' reinforcement contingencies on the acquisition of imitative responses. *Journal of Personality and Social Psychology, 1,* 589–595.

BANDURA, A. (1968). Social learning interpretation of psychological dysfunctions. In P. London & D. Rosenhan (Eds.), *Foundations of abnormal psychology.* New York: Holt, Rinehart and Winston.

BANDURA, A. (1969). Social-learning theory of identificatory processes. In D. A. Goslin (Ed.), *Handbook of socialization theory and research.* Chicago: Rand McNally.

BANDURA, A. (1973). *Aggression: A social learning analysis.* New York: Holt, Rinehart and Winston.

BANDURA, A. (1977). *A social learning theory.* Englewood Cliffs, NJ: Prentice-Hall.

BANDURA, A. (1982). Self-efficacy mechanism in human agency. *American Psychologist, 37,* 122–147.

BANDURA, A. (1986). *Social foundations of thought and action: A social cognition theory.* Englewood Cliffs, NJ: Prentice-Hall.

BANDURA, A., & MENLOVE, F. L. (1968). Factors determining vicarious extinction of avoidance through symbolic modeling. *Journal of Personality and Social Psychology, 8,* 99–108.

BANDURA, A., REESE, L., & ADAMS, N. (1982). Microanalysis of action and fear arousal as a function of differential levels of perceived self-efficiency. *Journal of Personality and Social Psychology, 66,* 3–11.

BANDURA, A., ROSS, D., & ROSS, S. A. (1961). Transmission of aggression through imitation of aggressive models. *Journal of Abnormal and Social Psychology, 63,* 575–582.

BANDURA, A., ROSS, D., & ROSS, S. A. (1963a). Imitation of film-mediated aggressive models. *Journal of Abnormal and Social Psychology, 66,* 3–11.

BANDURA, A., ROSS, D., & ROSS, S. A. (1963b). Vicarious reinforcement and imitative learning. *Journal of Abnormal and Social Psychology, 67,* 601–607.

BANDURA, A. & WALTERS, R. H. (1963). *Social learning and personality development.* New York: Rinehart & Winston.

BANKS, W., & MCQUATER, G. (1976). Achievement motivation and black children. *IRCD Bulletin, 11,* 1–8.

BANKS, W., MCQUATER, G., & HUBBARD, J. (1977). Task-liking and intrinsic-extrinsic achievement orientations in black adolescents. *Journal of Black Psychology, 3,* 61–71.

BARABASZ, A. F., & BARABASZ, M. (1989). Effects of restricted environmental stimulation: Enhancement of hypnotizability for experimental and chronic pain control. *International Journal of Clinical and Experimental Hypnosis, 37,* 217–231.

BARBER, T. X. (1961). Antisocial and criminal acts induced by hypnosis: A review of experimental and clinical findings. *Archives of General Psychiatry, 5,* 301–312.

BARBER, T. X. (1970). *LSD, marihuana, yoga and hypnosis.* Chicago: Aldine.

BARBER, T. X., & GLASS, L. B. (1962). Significant factors in hypnotic behavior. *Journal of Abnormal and Social Psychology, 64,* 222–228.

BARBIZET, J. (1970). *Human memory and its pathology.* San Francisco: Freeman.

BARD, P. (1938). Studies in the cortical representation of somatic sensibility. *Harvey Lectures, 33,* 143–169.

BARDWICK, C. (1971). *The psychology of women: A study of bio-cultural conflicts.* New York: Harper & Row.

BARKER, M. (1976). Planning for environmental indices: Observer appraisals of air quality. In K. Craik & E. Zube (Eds.), *Perceiving environmental quality.* New York: Plenum.

BARKER, R. G., & WRIGHT, H. (1955). *Midwest and its children.* New York: Row and Peterson.

BARON, R. A., & BELL, P. A. (1976a). Aggression and heat: The influence of ambient temperature, negative affect, and a cooling drink on physical aggression. *Journal of Personality and Social Psychology, 33,* 245–255.

BARON, R. A., & BELL, P. A. (1976b). Physical distance and helping: Some unexpected benefits of "crowding in" on others. *Journal of Applied Social Psychology, 6,* 95–104.

BARON, R. A., & BYRNE, D. (1987). *Social psychology of human interaction,* 5th ed. Boston: Allyn & Bacon.

BARON, R. A., & LAWTON, S. F. (1972). Environmental influences of model effects by high ambient temperatures. *Psychonomic Science, 26,* 180–182.

BARON, R. M., MANDEL, D., ADAMS, C., & GAFFEN, L. (1976). Effects of social density in University residential environments. *Journal of Personality and Social Psychology, 34,* 434–446.

BARON, R. P. (1987). Effects of negative ions on interpersonal attraction: Evidence for intensification. *Journal of Personality and Social Psychology, 52,* 547–553.

BARON, R. S. (1984). Group dynamics. In I. A. Kohn (Ed.), *Social psychology.* Dubuque, IA: W. C. Brown.

BARON, R. S., CUTRONA, C. E., HICKLIN, D., RUSSELL, D., & LUBAROFF, D. (1990). Social support and immune function among spouses of cancer patients. *Journal of Personality and Social Psychology, 59,* 344–352.

BARRET, D. E., RADKE-YARROW, M., & KLEIN, R. E. (1982). Chronic malnutrition and child behavior: Effects of early caloric supplementation on social and emotional functioning at school age. *Developmental Psychology, 18,* 541–556.

BAR-TAL, D. (1976). *Prosocial behavior: Theory and research.* Washington, DC: Hemisphere.

BAR-TAL, D. (1984). American study of helping behavior: What? Why? and Where? In E. Staub, D. Bar-Tal, J. Karylowski, & J. Reykowski (Eds.), *Development and maintenance of prosocial behavior.* New York: Plenum.

BAR-TAL, D. (1990). *Group beliefs: A conception for analyzing group structure, process, and behavior.* New York: Springer-Verlag.

BAR-TAL, D., & SAXE, L. (1976). Perceptions of similarly and dissimilarly attractive couples and individuals. *Journal of Personality and Social Psychology, 33,* 772–781.

BARUCH, B., BARNETT, R., & RIVERS, C. (1983). *Lifeprints.* New York: McGraw-Hill.

BARUCH, G. K., & BARNETT, R. C. (1980). On the well-being of adult women. In L. A. Bond & J. C. Rosen (Eds.), *Competence and coping during adulthood.* Hanover, NH: University Press of New England.

BARUCH, G. K., BIENER, L., & BARNETT, R. C. (1987). Women and gender in research on work and family stress. *American Psychologist, 42,* 130–136.

BATES, E., MACWHINNEY, B., CASELLI, C., DEVESCOVI, A., NATALE, F., & VENZA, V. (1984). A cross-linguistic study of the development of sentence interpretation strategies. *Child Development, 55,* 341–354.

BATESON, G., JACKSON, D. D., HALEY, J., & WEAKLAND, J. (1956). Toward a theory of schizophrenia. *Behavioral Science, 1,* 251–264.

BATSON, C. D. (1984). *A theory of altruistic motivation.* Unpublished manuscript, University of Kansas, Lawrence.

BATSON, C. D. (1990a). Good samaritans—or priests and levites? *Personality and Social Psychology Bulletin, 16,* 758–768.

BATSON, C. D. (1990b). How social an animal? The human capacity for caring. *American Psychologist, 45,* 494–503.

BATSON, C. D., & FLORY, J. D. (1990). Goal-relevant cognitions associated with helping by individuals high on intrinsic, end religion. *Journal for the Scientific Study of Religion, 29,* 310–346.

BATSON, C. D., & WEEKS, J. (1991). Helping. In R. Baron & W. Graziano (Eds.), *Social psychology.* New York: Holt, Rinehart & Winston.

BAUM, A., FISHER, J., & SOLOMON, S. (1981). Type of information, familiarity, and the reduction of crowding stress. *Journal of Personality and Social Psychology, 40,* 11–23.

BAUM, A., & GREENBERG, C. (1975). Waiting for a crowd: The behavioral and perceptual effects of anticipated crowding. *Journal of Personality and Social Psychology, 32,* 667–671.

BAUM, A., SINGER, J., & BAUM, C. (1981). Stress and the environment. *Journal of Social Issues, 37,* 4–35.

BAUM, A., & VALINS, S. (1977). *Architecture and social behavior: Psychological studies in social density.* Hillsdale, NJ: Erlbaum.

BAUMANN, J. F. (1986). Effects of rewritten content textbook passages on middle grade students' comprehension of main ideas: Making the inconsiderate considerate. *Journal of Reading Behavior, 18,* 1–21.

BAUMEISTER, R. E. (1985, April). The championship choke. *Psychology Today,* pp. 48–53.

BAUMEISTER, R. F. (1987). How the self became a problem: A psychological review of historical research. *Journal of Personality and Social Psychology, 52,* 163–176.

BAUMEISTER, R., & COOPER, J. (1981). Can the public expectation of emotion cause that emotion? *Journal of Personality, 49,* 49–59.

BAUMEISTER, R. F., HUTTON, D. G., & TICE, D. M. (1989). Cognitive processes during deliberate self-presentation: How self-presenters alter and misinterpret the behavior of their interaction partners. *Journal of Experimental Social Psychology, 25,* 59–78.

BAUMEISTER, R., & STEINHIBER, A. (1984). Paradoxical effects of supportive audiences on performance under pressure: The home field disadvantage in sports championships. *Journal of Personality and Social Psychology, 47,* 85–93.

BAUMEISTER, R. F. & TICE, D. M. (1986). How adolescence became the struggle for self: A historical transformation of psychological development. In J. Suls & A. F. Freenwald (Eds.), *Psychological perspectives on the self* (Vol. 3). Hillsdale, NJ: Erlbaum.

BAUMRIND, D. (1968). Authoritarian vs. authoritative control. *Adolescence, 3,* 255–272.

BAUMRIND, D. (1971). Current patterns of parental authority. *Developmental Psychology Monograms, 1,* 1–103.

BAUMRIND, D. (1982). Reciprocal rights and

responsibilities in parent-child relations. In J. Rubinstein & B. D. Brent (Eds.), *Taking sides: Clashing views on controversial psychological issues.* Guilford, CT: Dushkin.

BAYLOR, G. W., & DESLAURIERS, D. (1988). Dreams as problem solving: A method of study: II. The oral defense dream. *Imagination, Cognition and Personality, 7,* 23–45.

BEAL, A. L. (1985). The skill of recognizing musical structures. *Memory and Cognition, 13,* 405–412.

BEAHRS, J. O. (1989). Spontaneous hypnosis in the forensic context. Annual Scientific Meeting of the American Academy of Psychiatry and the Law, *Bulletin of the American Academy of Psychiatry and the Law, 17,* 171–181.

BECK, A. T. (1967). *Depression: Clinical, experimental and theoretical aspects.* New York: Harper & Row.

BECK, A. T. (1976). *Cognitive therapy and emotional disorders.* New York: International University Press.

BECK, A. T. (1983). Negative cognitions. In E. Levitt, B. Lubin, & J. Brooks (Eds.), *Depression: Concepts, controversies, and some new facts* (2nd ed.). Hillsdale, NJ: Erlbaum.

BECK, A. T., & EMERY, G. (1985). *Anxiety disorders and phobias: A cognitive perspective.* New York: Basic.

BECK, A. T., RUSH, J. A., SHAW, B. R., & EMERY, G. (1978). *Cognitive therapy of depression: A treatment manual.* Copyright A. T. Beck, M.D.

BECK, A. T., & YOUNG, J. E. (1978). College blues. *Psychology Today, 12,* 80–92.

BECK, R. C. (1978). *Motivation: Theories and principles.* Englewood Cliffs, NJ: Prentice-Hall.

BECK, R. C. (1990). *Motivation: Theories and principles,* 3rd ed. Englewood Cliffs, NJ: Prentice Hall.

BECKER, L., & SELIGMAN, C. (1981). Welcome to the energy crisis. *Journal of Social Issues, 37,* 1–7.

BECKER, M., WARR-LEEPER, G. A., & LEEPER, H. A. (1990). Fetal alcohol syndrome: A description of oral motor, articulatory, short-term memory, grammatical, and semantic abilities. *Journal of Communication Disorders, 23,* 97–124.

BECKETT, P. A. (1990). Similar processing of real and subjective contour Poggendorff figures by men and women. *Perceptual and Motor Skills, 70,* 51–56.

BEER, T. A. (1986). The process of retirement: A review and recommendation for future investigation. *Personnel Psychology, 39,* 31–55.

BEKERIAN, D. A., & BOWERS, J. M. (1983). Eyewitness testimony: Were we mislead? *Journal of Experimental Psychology: Learning, Memory, and Cognition, 9,* 139–145.

BELL, A. P., & WEINBERG, M. S. (1978). *Homosexualities.* New York: Simon & Schuster.

BELL, P. (1981). Physiological, comfort, performance and social effects of heat. *Journal of Social Issues, 37,* 71–94.

BELL, P. A. (1978). Effects of noise and heat stress on primary and subsidiary task performance. *Human Factors, 20,* 749–752.

BELLEZZA, F. S. (1983). Mnemonic-device instruction with adults. In G. M. Pressley & J. R. Levin (Eds.), *Cognitive strategy research: Psychological foundation.* New York: Springer-Verlag.

BELSKY, J. (1985). Two waves of day-care research: Developmental effects and conditions of quality. In R. Ainslie (Ed.), *The child and the day-care setting.* New York: Praeger.

BELSKY, J., & ROVINE, M. J. (1988). Nonmaternal care in the first year of life and the security of infant-parent attachment. *Child Development, 59,* 157–167.

BELSKY, J., ROVINE, M., & TAYLOR, D. G. (1984). The Pennsylvania infant and family development project, III: The origins of individual differences in infant-mother attachment: maternal and infant contributions. *Child Development, 55,* 718–728.

BEM, D. (1972). Self-perception theory. In L. Berkowitz (Ed.), *Advances in experimental social psychology* (Vol. 6). New York: Academic Press.

BEM, D. J., & ALLEN, A. (1974). On predicting some of the people some of the time: The search for cross-situational consistencies in behavior. *Psychological Review, 81,* 506–520.

BEM, S. L. (1987). Masculinity and femininity exist only in the mind of the perceiver. In J. M. Reinisch, L. A. Rosenbaum, & S. A. Sanders (Eds.), *Masculinity/feminity: Basic perspectives.* New York: Oxford University Press.

BEN-ARI, R., & AMIR, Y. (1988). Intergroup contact, cultural information, and change in ethnic attitudes. In W. Stroebe et al. (Eds.), *The social psychology of intergroup conflicts.* New York: Springer-Verlag.

BENBOW, C. P. (1988). Sex differences in mathematical reasoning in intellectually talented preadolescents. Their nature, effects, and possible causes. *Behavior and Brain Sciences, 11,* 169–232.

BENDERLY, B. L. (1987). *The myth of two minds: What gender means and doesn't mean.* New York: Doubleday.

BENJAMIN, L. T. (1986). Why don't they understand us? A history of psychology's public image. *American Psychologist, 41,* 941–946.

BENJAMIN, L. T., JR. (1988). *A history of psychology: Original sources and contemporary research.* New York: McGraw-Hill.

BENSON, G., & ZIEMON, G. (1981). The relationship of weather to children's behavior problems. Unpublished manuscript, Colorado State University. Cited in J. D. Fisher, P. Bell, & A. Baum, *Environmental psychology* (2nd ed.), 1984.

BENSON, H. (1975). *The relaxation response.* New York: Morrow.

BENSON, H., & PROCTOR, W. (1984). *Beyond the relaxation response: How to harness the healing power of your personal beliefs.* New York: Times Books.

BENTLER, P., & PRINCE, C. (1970). Psychiatric symptomology in transvestites. *Journal of Clinical Psychology, 26,* 434–435.

BERCEL, N. A. (1960). A study of the influence of schizophrenic serum on the behavior of the spider: Zilla-X-notata. In D. D. Jackson (Ed.), *The etiology of schizophrenia.* New York: Basic.

BERGER, P. A. (1978). Medical treatment of mental illness. *Science, 200,* 974–981.

BERGIN, A., & LAMBERT, M. (1978). The evaluation of therapeutic outcomes. In S. Garfield & A. Bergin (Eds.), *Handbook of psychotherapy and behavior change* (2nd ed.). New York: Wiley.

Berkeley Wellness Letter (1990). Vol. 6, Issue 6, p. 7. University of California.

Berkeley Wellness Letter (1990). Heading off headaches. Vol. 7, Issue 2, pp. 4–5. University of California.

BERKOWITZ, L. (1962). *Aggression: A social psychology analysis.* New York: McGraw-Hill.

BERKOWITZ, L. (1965). The concept of aggressive drive: Some additional considerations. In L. Berkowitz (Ed.), *Advances in experimental social psychology* (Vol. 2). New York: Academic.

BERKOWITZ, L. (1987). Mood, self-awareness, and willingness to help. *Journal of Personality and Social Psychology, 52,* 721, 729.

BERKOWITZ, L. (1990). On the formation and regulation of anger and aggression: A cognitive-neuroassociationistic analysis. *American Psychologist, 45,* 494–503.

BERKOWITZ, L. (1972). Social norms, feelings, and other factors affecting helping and altruism. In L. Berkowitz (Ed.), *Advances in experimental social psychology* (Vol. 6). New York: Academic.

BERKOWITZ, L., & CONNOR, W. H. (1966). Success, failure, and social responsibility. *Journal of Personality and Social Psychology, 4,* 664–669.

BERLIN, B., & KAY, P. (1969). *Basic color terms: Their universality and evolution.* Berkeley: University of California Press.

BERLYNE, D. E. (1957). Perceptual curiosity, exploratory behavior, and maze learning. *Journal of Comparative and Physiological Psychology, 50,* 228–232.

BERLYNE, D. E. (1958). The influence of complexity and novelty in visual figures on orienting responses. *Journal of Experimental Psychology, 55,* 289–296.

BERLYNE, D. E. (1960). *Conflict, arousal and curiosity.* New York: McGraw Hill.

BERLYNE, D. E. (1969). *The justifiability of the concept of curiosity.* Paper delivered at the XIX International Congress of London.

BERNARD, P. (1924). *Instinct.* New York: Holt, Rinehart and Winston.

BERRERA, M., SANDLER, I., & RAMSAY, T. (1981). Preliminary development of a scale of social support: Studies on college students. *American Journal of Community Psychology, 9,* 435–447.

BERSCHEID, E. (1982). Attraction and emotion in interpersonal relationships. In M. Clark & S. Fiske (Eds.), *Affect and cognition.* Hillsdale, NJ: Erlbaum.

BERSCHEID, E. (1983). Emotion. In H. Kelley et al. (Eds.), *Close relationships.* San Francisco: Freeman.

BERSCHEID, E., & WALSTER, E. (1978). *Interpersonal attraction.* Reading, MA: Addison-Wesley.

BERSH, P. J., WHITEHOUSE, W. G., BLUSTEIN, J. E., & ALLOY, L. B. (1986). Interactions of Pavlovian conditioning with zero operant contingency: Chronic exposure to signaled inescapable shock maintains learned helplessness effects. *Journal of Experimental Psychology Animal Behavior Processes, 12,* 277–290.

BERTENTHAL, B. I., & BAI, D. L. (1989). Infant's sensitivity to optical flow for controlling posture. *Developmental Psychology, 25,* 936–945.

BERTENTHAL, B. I., & CAMPOS, J. J. (1990). A systems approach to the organizing effects of self-produced locomotion during infancy. *Advances in Infancy Research, 6,* 1–60.

BESSON, J., & CHAOUCH, A. (1987). Peripheral and spinal mechanisms of naciception. *Physiological Reviews, 11,* 67–186.

BEST, P. J., & RANCK, J. B., JR. (1982). The reliability of the relationship between hippocampal unit activity and sensory-behavioral events in the rat. *Experimental Neurology, 75,* 652–664.

BEST, P. J., & THOMPSON, L. T. (1989). Persistence, reticence, and opportunism of place-field activity in hippocampal neurons. Meeting of the Society for Neuroscience. *Psychobiology, 17,* 230–235.

BETANCOURT, H. (1990). An attribution-empathy model of helping behavior: Behavioral intentions and judgments of help-giving. *Personality and Social Psychology Bulletin, 16,* 573–591.

BETTELHEIM, B. (1960). *The informed heart.* New York: Harper & Row.

BEUMONT, P. J., ABRAHAM, S., & TURTLE, J. (1980). Paradoxical prolactin response to goradotropin-releasing hormone during weight gain in patients with anorexia nervosa. *Journal of Clinical Endocrinology and Metabolism, 51,* 1283–1285.

BEVAN, W. (1991). Contemporary psychology: A tour inside the onion. *American Psychologist, 46,* 475–483.

BICKMAN, L., TEGER, A., GABRIELE, T., MCLAUGHLIN, C., BERGER, M., & SUNADAY, E. (1973). Dormitory density and helping behavior. *Environment and Behavior, 5,* 465–490.

BIEBER, I. A. (1976). A discussion of "Homosexuality": The ethical challenge. *Journal of Consulting and Clinical Psychology, 44,* 163–166.

BIGGERS, T., & PRYOR, B. (1982). Attitude change: A function of emotion-relating qualities of environment. *Personality and Social Psychology Bulletin, 8,* 94–99.

BINDRIM, P. (1968). A report on a nude marathon. The effect of physical nudity upon the practice interaction in the marathon group. *Psychotherapy: Theory, Research and Practice, 5,* 180–188.

BINET, A., & SIMON, T. (1905). New methods for the diagnosis of the intellectual levels of subnormals. *Annals of Psychology, 11,* 191.

BIRCH, J. (1985). A practical guide for colour-vision examination: Report of the standardization committee of the international research group on colour-vision deficiencies. *Ophthalmic and Physiological Optics, 5,* 265–285.

BIRDWHISTELL, R. L. (1967). Some body motion elements accompanying spoken American English. In L. Thayer (Ed.), *Communication: Concepts and perspectives.* Washington, DC: Spartan.

BISHOP, G. (1987). Lay conceptions of physical symptoms. *Journal of Applied Social Psychology, 17,* 127–146.

BJORKSTEN, J. (1968). The cross-linkage theory of aging. *Journal of the American Geriatrics Society, 16,* 408–427.

BJÖRNTORP, P. (1972). Disturbances in the regulation of food intake. *Advances in Psychosomatic Medicine, 7,* 116–127.

BLACK, J. B. (1984). Understanding and remembering stories. In J. R. Anderson & S. M. Kosslyn (Eds.), *Tutorials in reading and memory.* San Francisco: Freeman.

BLACKMAN, J. A. (1989). The relationship of inadequate oxygenation of the brain at birth and developmental outcome. *Topics in Early Childhood Special Education, 9,* 1–13.

BLACKWELL, B. (1981). Biofeedback in a comprehensive behavioral medicine program. *Biofeedback and Self-Regulation, 6,* 445–472.

BLAIR, S. M. (1973). Psychiatric diagnosis [Letter to the editor]. *Science, 180,* 363.

BLASKOVITCH, J., GINSBURG, G. P., & HOWE, R. C. (1975). Blackjack and the risky shift: II. Monetary stakes. *Journal of Experimental Social Psychology, 11,* 224–232.

BLATT, S., & BERMAN, W. (1984). A methodology for the use of the Rorschach in clinical research. *Journal of Personality Assessment, 48,* 226–239.

BLAU, F. D. (1975). Women in the labor force: An overview. In J. Freeman (Ed.), *Women: A feminist perspective.* Palo Alto, CA: Mayfield.

BLAU, P. M. (1964). *Exchange and power in social life.* New York: Wiley.

BLEHAR, M. C., LIEBERMAN, A. F., & AINSWORTH, M. D. (1977). Early face-to-face interaction and its relation to later infant-mother attachment. *Child Development, 48,* 182–194.

BLENKER, M. (1965). Social work and family relationships in later life with some thoughts on filial maturity. In E. Shanas & G. Streif (Eds.), *Social structure and the family.* Englewood Cliffs, NJ: Prentice-Hall.

BLESS, H., BOHNER, G., SCHWARZ, F., & STRACK, F. (1990). Happy and mindless? Moods and the processing of persuasion communications. *Personality and Social Psychology Bulletin, 16,* 331–340.

BLESS, H., BOHNER, G., SCHWARZ, N., & STRACK, F. (1990). Mood and persuasion: A cognitive response analysis. *Personality and Social Psychology Bulletin, 16,* 331–345.

BLISS, E. (1980). Multiple personalities: Report of fourteen cases with implications for schizophrenia and hysteria. *Archives of General Psychiatry, 37,* 1388–1397.

BLOCK, J., & FUNDER, D. C. (1986). Social roles and social perception: Individual differences in attribution and error. *Journal of Personality and Social Psychology, 51,* 1200–1207.

BLOOM, A. H. (1981). *The linguistic shaping of thought: A study in the impact of language on thinking in China and the West.* New Jersey: Erlbaum.

BLOOM, B. L. (1988). *Health psychology: A psychosocial perspective.* Englewood Cliffs, NJ: Prentice Hall.

BLOOM, F. E., LAZERSON, A., & HOFSTADTER, L. (1985). *Brain, mind, and behavior.* New York: Freeman.

BLOOM, L. M., HOOD, L., & LIGHTBROWN, P. (1974). Imitation in language development: If, when and why. *Cognitive Psychology, 6,* 380–420.

BLOUGH, D. S. (1982). Pigeon perception of letters of the alphabet. *Science, 218,* 397–398.

BLUEN, S., BARLING, J., & BURNS, W. (1990). Predicting goals performance, job satisfaction, and digression by using the achievement strivings and impatience-irritability dimensions of Type A behavior. *Journal of Applied Psychology, 75,* 212–216.

BLUM, B. (1953). *Psychoanalytic theories of personality.* New York: McGraw-Hill.

BLYTH, D., HILL, J., & THEIL, K. (1982). Early adolescent's significant others: Grade and gender differences in perceived relationships with familial and non-familial adults and young people. *Journal of Youth and Adolescence, 11,* 425–450.

BOCHNER, S., & INSKO, C. A. (1966). Communicator discrepancy, source credibility, and opinion change. *Journal of Personality and Social Psychology, 4,* 614–621.

BODENHEUSEN, G., GACLICK, L., & WYER, R. S. (1987). Affective and cognitive factors in intragroup communication. *Review of Personality and Social Psychology, 9,* 137–166.

BOHANNON, J. N. III. (1988). Flashbulb memories for the space shuttle disaster: A tale of two theories. *Cognition, 29,* 179–196.

BOLDIZAR, J., PERRY, D., & PERRY, L. (1989). Outcome values and aggression. *Child Development, 60,* 571–579.

BOLTON, P. J. (1983). Drugs of abuse. In D. F. Hawkins (Ed.), *Drugs and pregnancy: Human teratogenesis and related problems.* London: Churchill Livingston.

BONANNO, G. A. (1990). Remembering and psychotherapy. *Psychotherapy, 27,* 175–186.

BOND, M. H. (1988). *The cross-cultural challenge to social psychology.* Newbury Park, CA: Sage.

BONDFORD, L., GIFF, T., & BENNE, K. (Eds.), (1964). *T-group theory: Laboratory method.* New York: Wiley.

BONTHIUS, D. J., & WEST, J. R. (1990). Alcohol-induced neuronal loss in developing rats: Increased brain damage with binge exposure. *Alcoholism Clinical and Experimental Research, 14,* 107–119.

BOOTH, A. (1972). Sex and social participation. *American Sociological Review, 37,* 183–193.

BOOTH, A., SCHELLEY, G., MAZUR, A., THARP, G., & KITTOK, R. (1989). Testosterone and winning and losing in human competition. *Hormones and Behavior, 23,* 555–576.

BOOTH, W. (1988). CDC paints a picture of HIV infection in the U.S. *Science, 239,* 253–254.

BOOTZIN, R. R., & MAX, D. (1981). Learning and behavioral theories of anxiety and stress. In I. L. Kutash & L. B. Schlesinger (Eds.), *Pressure point: Perspectives on stress and anxiety.* San Francisco: Jossey-Bass.

BORCHARDT, D. H., & FRANCIS, R. D. (1984). *How to find out in psychology: A guide to the literature and methods of research.* New York: Pergamon.

BORKOVEC, T., MATHEWS, A., CHAMBERS, A., EBRAHIMI, S., LYTLE, R., & NELSON, R. (1987). The effects of relation training with cognitive or nondirective therapy and the role of relaxation-induced anxiety in the treatment of generalized anxiety. *Journal of Consulting and Clinical Psychology, 55,* 683–688.

BORNSTEIN, M. H., KESSEN, W., & WEISKOPF, S. (1976). Color vision and categorization in young human infants. *Journal of Experimental Psychology: Human Perception and Performance, 2,* 115–129.

BOSSARD, J. (1932). Residential propinquity as a factor in marriage selection. *American Journal of Sociology, 38,* 219–224.

BOSZORMENY-NAGY, I., & ULRICH, D. (1981). Contextual family therapy. In A. Gorman & A. Kniskern (Eds.), *Handbook of family therapy.* New York: Brunner/Mazel.

BOTWINICK, J. (1977). Intellectual abilities. In J. E. Birren & K. W. Schaie (Eds.), *Handbook of the psychology of aging.* New York: Van Nostrand.

BOUCHARD, C. (1990). Genetic factors in obesity. *Medical Clinics of North America, 73,* 67–81.

BOUCHARD, T. J. & MCGUE, M. (1981). Familial studies of intelligence: a review. *Science, 212,* 1055–1059.

BOUCHER, J. D., & EKMAN, P. (1975). Facial areas and emotional information. *Journal of Communication, 25,* 21–29.

BOULDING, K. E. (1989). *Three faces of power.* Newbury Park, CA: Sage.

BOUMA, H. (1973). Visual interference in the parafoveal recognition of initial and final letters of words. *Vision Research, 13,* 767–782.

BOURNE, L. E., & RESTLE, F. (1959). A mathematical theory of concept identification. *Psychological Review, 66,* 278–296.

BOWER, G., & COHEN, P. (1982). Emotional influences in memory and thinking: Data and theory. In M. Clark & S. Fisher (Eds.), *Emotions and affect.* Hillsdale, NJ: Erlbaum.

BOWER, G. H. (1981, June). Mood and memory. *Psychology Today.*

BOWER, G. H., & CLARK, M. C. (1969). Narrative stories as mediators for serial learning. *Psychonomic Science, 14,* 181–182.

BOWER, G. H., CLARK, M., WINZENZ, D., & LESGOLD, A. (1969). Hierarchical retrieval schemes in recall of categorized word lists. *Journal of Verbal Learning and Verbal Behavior, 8,* 323–343.

BOWER, G. H., & KARLIN, M. B. (1974). Depth of processing pictures of faces and recognition memory. *Journal of Experimental Psychology, 103,* 751–757.

BOWER, G. H., & TRABASSO, T. (1964). Concept identification. In R. C. Atkinson (Ed.), *Studies in mathematical psychology.* Stanford, CA: Stanford University Press.

BOWER, T. (1977, February). Blind babies see with their ears. *New Scientist,* pp. 255–257.

BOWLBY, J. (1973). *Attachment and loss: Vol. 2. Separation, anxiety and anger.* New York: Basic.

BOZZI, B. (1987, July). Sexist sales. *Psychology Today,* p. 11.

BRACKBILL, Y. (1958). Extinction of the

smile response in infants as a function of reinforcement schedule. *Child Development, 29,* 115–124.

BRADLEY-JOHNSON, S., JOHNSON, C. M., SHANAGAN, R. H., RICKERT, V. L., & TARDONA, D. R. (1984). Effects of token reinforcement on WISC-R performance of black and white, low socioeconomic second graders. *Behavioral Assessment, 6,* 365–373.

BRADY, J. V., PORTER, R. W., CONRAD, D. G., & MASON, J. W. (1958). Avoidance behavior and the development of gastroduodenal ulcers. *Journal of the Experimental Analysis of Behavior, 11,* 69–73.

BRAFF, D. L. (1989). Sensory input deficits and negative symptoms in schizophrenic patients. *American Journal of Psychiatry, 146,* 1006–1011.

BRAMEL, D., JAUB, B., & BLUM, B. (1968). An observer's reaction to the suffering of his enemy. *Journal of Personality and Social Psychology, 8,* 384–392.

BRAMMER, L. M., & SHOSTROM, E. L. (1977). *Therapeutic psychology: Fundamentals of counseling and psychotherapy* (3rd ed.). Englewood Cliffs. NJ: Prentice-Hall.

BRANNON, S. E., & NELSON, R. O. (1987). Contingency management treatment of outpatient unipolar depression: A comparison of reinforcement and extension. *Journal of Consulting and Clinical Psychology, 55,* 3–9.

BRASHLER, W. (1978). *Josh Gibson: A life in the Negro Leagues.* New York: Harper & Row.

BRASS, D. A., MYER, E. C., & DEWEY, W. L. (1989). Possible hyperendorphinergic pathophysiology of the Rett syndrome. *Life Sciences, 15,* 366–369.

BRAUNSTEIN, M. L., & ANDERSON, G. J. (1981). Velocity gradients and relative depth perception. *Perception & Psychophysics, 29,* 145–155.

BRAUNSTEIN, M. L., & ANDERSON, G. J. (1984) Shape and depth perception from parallel projections of three-dimensional motion. *Journal of Experimental Psychology: Human Perception and Performance, 10,* 749–760.

BRAY, D. W., & HOWARD, A. (1980). Career success and life satisfaction of middle-aged managers. In L. A. Bond & J. C. Rosen (Eds.), *Competence and coping during adulthood.* Hanover, NH: University Press of New England.

BRAZELTON, T. B. (1987, August). *Opportunities for intervention with infants at risk.* Paper presented a meeting of the American Psychological Association, New York.

BRECHNER, K., & LINDER, D. (1981). A social trap analysis of energy distribution systems. In A. Baum & J. Singer (Eds.), *Advances in environmental psychology* (Vol. 3). Hillsdale, NJ: Erlbaum.

BREHM, J., & CROCKER, J. (1962). An experiment on hunger. In J. Brehm & A. Cohen (Eds.), *Explorations in cognitive dissonance.* New York: Wiley.

BREHM, J., & SELF, E. (1989). The intensity of motivation. *Annual Review of Psychology, 40,* 109–132.

BREHM, J. W., & BREHM, S. (1981). *Psychological reactance: A theory of freedom and control.* New York: Academic.

BREHM, S. S. (1988). *Intimate relationships.* New York: Random House.

BREHM, S. S., & BREHM, J. W. (1981). *Psychological reactance: A theory of freedom and control.* New York: Academic.

BRENNEN, T., BAGULEY, T., BRIGHT, J., & BRUCE, V. (1990). Resolving semantically induced tip-of-the-tongue states for proper nouns. *Memory and Cognition, 18,* 339–347.

BRESLOW, S., & BUELL, P. (1960). Mortality from coronary heart disease and physical

activity of work in California. *Journal of Chronic Disease, 11,* 615–626.

BREWER, M., & KRAMER, R. (1985). The psychology of intergroup attitudes and behavior. In *Annual Review of Psychology.* New York: Annual Reviews Inc.

BREWER, M., & MILLER, N. (1984). Beyond the contact hypothesis: Theoretical perspectives on desegregation. In M. Brewer & N. Miller (Eds.), *Groups in contact: The psychology of desegregation.* New York: Academic.

BRICKMAN, P. (1987). *Commitment, conflict, and caring.* Englewood Cliffs, NJ: Prentice Hall.

BRICKNER, M. A., HARKINS, S., & OSTROM, T. (1986). The effect of personal involvement: Thought-provoking implications for social loafing. *Journal of Personality and Social Psychology, 51,* 763–769.

BRIER, E. G. (1974, October). Nonverbal communication: How we send emotional messages. *Psychology Today,* pp. 53–56.

BRIGHAM, J. C. (1985). Race and eyewitness identifications. In S. Worchel & W. Austin, *The psychology of intergroup relations.* Chicago: Nelson Hall.

BRIGGS, R. M. (1990). Reducing direct-care staff absenteeism: Effects of a combined reinforcement and punishment procedure. *Mental Retardation, 28,* 163–168.

BRIM, O. G., JR. (1976). Theories of male mid-life crisis. *Counseling Psychologist, 6,* 2–9.

BRISLIN, R. W. (1990). *Applied cross-cultural psychology.* Newbury Park, CA: Sage.

BROADBECK, J. (1957). Neural control of hunger, appetite and satiety. *Yale Journal of Biological Medicine, 29,* 565–574.

BROADBENT, D. (1971). *Decision and stress.* New York: Academic.

BROADBENT, D., & LITTLE, E. (1960). Effects of noise reduction in the work situation. *Occupational Psychology, 34,* 133–140.

BROCK, S. B., & YERIAN, J. M. (1986). Integrating career planning into the academic fabric: A model project. *Journal of College Student Personnel, 27,* 176–177.

BROCK, T. (1965). Communicator-recipient similarity and decision change. *Journal of Personality and Social Psychology, 1,* 650–654.

BROCKNER, J., & RUBIN, J. Z. (1985). *Entrapment in escalating conflicts.* New York: Springer-Verlag.

BROOKS, L. (1974). *Law, psychiatry and the mental health system.* Boston: Little, Brown.

BROOKS, L. W., & DANSEREAU, D. F. (1983). Effects of structural schema training and text organization on expository prose processing. *Journal of Educational Psychology, 75,* 811–820.

BROVERMAN, J. K., VOGEL, S. R., BROVERMAN, D. M., CLARKSON, F. G., & ROSENKANTZ, P. S. (1972). Sex-role stereotypes: A current appraisal. *Journal of Social Issues, 28,* 59–78.

BROWER, K. J., BLOW, F. C., ELIOPULOS, G. A., & BERESFORD, T. P. (1989). Anabolic androgenic steroids and suicide. *American Journal of Psychiatry, 146,* 1075.

BROWER, K. J., ELIOPULOS, G. A., FREDERIC, C., & CATLIN, D. H. (1990). Evidence for physical and psychological dependence on anabolic androgenic steroids in eight weight lifters. *American Journal of Psychiatry, 147,* 510–512.

BROWER, S., DOCKETT, K., & TAYLOR, R. (1983). Residents' perceptions of territorial features and perceived local threat. *Environment and Behavior, 15,* 419–437.

BROWN, B. (1987). Territoriality. In D. Stokols & I. Altman (Eds.) *Handbook of environmental psychology, Vol. 1.* New York: Wiley Interscience.

BROWN, B. B. (1979, August). Territoriality and residential burglary. Paper presented

at the American Psychology Association, New York.

BROWN, B. B., & LOHR, M. J. (1987). Peer-group affiliation and adolescent self-esteem: An integration of ego-identity and symbolic-interaction theories. *Journal of Personality and Social Psychology, 52,* 47–55.

BROWN, G. W., HARRIS, T., & COPELAND, J. R. (1977). Depression and loss. *British Journal of Psychiatry, 130,* 1–18.

BROWN, J. E., & FRANK, J. S. (1987). Influence of event anticipation on postural actions accompanying voluntary movement. *Experimental Brain Research, 67,* 645–650.

BROWN, P. K., & WALD, G. (1964). Visual pigments in single rods and cones of the human retina. *Science, 144,* 45–52.

BROWN, R. (1958). *Words and things.* New York: Free Press.

BROWN, R. (1965). *Social psychology.* New York: Free Press.

BROWN, R., CAZDEN, C. B., & BELLUGI, U. (1969). The child's grammar from I to III. In J. P. Hill (Ed.), *Minnesota symposium on child psychology* (Vol. 2). Minneapolis: University of Minnesota Press.

BROWN, R. W., & MCNEILL, D. (1966). The "tip-of-the-tongue" phenomenon. *Journal of Verbal Learning and Verbal Behavior, 5,* 325–337.

BROWNELL, K. D. (1982). Obesity: Understanding and treating a serious prevalent and refractory disorder. *Journal of Consulting and Clinical Psychology, 50,* 820–840.

BROWNELL, K., & VENDITTI, B. (1983). The etiology and treatment of obesity. In W. Fann et al. (Eds.), *Phenomenology and the treatment of psychophysiologic disorders.* New York: Spectrum.

BROWNELL, K. D., KELMAN, M. S., & STUNKARD, A. J. (1983). Treatment of obese children with and without their mothers: Changes in weight and blood pressure. *Pediatrics, 71,* 515–523.

BROWNELL, K. D., STUNKARD, A. J., & MCKEON, P. E. (1985). Weight reduction at the worksite: A promise partially fulfilled. *American Journal of Psychiatry, 142,* 47–52.

BRUNER, J. S., GOODNOW, J. J., & AUSTIN, G. A. (1956). *A study of thinking.* New York: Wiley.

BRUNER, J. S., & KOSLOWSKI, B. (1972). Visually preadapted constituents of manipulatory action. *Perception, 1,* 1–122.

BRUNSWICK, E. (1943). Organismic achievement and environmental probability. *Psychological Review, 50,* 255–272.

BRY, A. (1976). *60 hours that transform your life: est.* New York: Avon.

BRYAN, A. I., & BORING, E. G. (1946). Women in American psychology: Statistics from the OPP Questionaire. *American Psychologist, 1,* 71–79.

BRYANT, J. (1985). *Testimony on the effects of pornography: Research findings.* Paper presented at the U.S. Justice Department Hearings, Houston.

BUCK, R. (1980). Nonverbal behavior and the theory of emotions: The facial feedback hypothesis. *Journal of Personality and Social Psychology, 38,* 811–824.

BUCK, R. (1985). Prime theory: An integrated view of motivation and emotion. *Psychological Review, 92,* 389–413.

BUCK, R. (1990). William James, the native of knowledge, and current issues in emotion, cognition, and communication. *Personality and Social Psychology Bulletin, 16,* 612–625.

BUCKHOLTZ, N. S., ZHOU, D., FREEDMAN, D. X., & Potter, W. Z. (1990). Lysergic acid diethylamide (LSD) administration selectively downregulates serotonin-sub-2 receptors in rat brain. *Neuropsychopharmacology, 3,* 148–173.

BUCKOUT, R. (1986). Personal values and expert testimony. [Special Issue: The ethics of expert testimony], *Law and Human Behavior, 10*, 127–144.

BUGLIOSI, V., & GENTRY, C. (1974). *Helter skelter: The true story of the Manson murders.* New York: Norton.

BUIE, J. (1987, November). Prescription privilege points, counter-points debated at convention. *The APA Monitor,* p. 6.

BUNNEY, W. E., JR., GOODWIN, F. K., MURPHY, D. L., & BORGE, G. F. (1972). The "switch process" in manic-depressive illness: I and II. *Archives of General Psychiatry, 27*, 295–302.

BUREAU OF LABOR STATISTICS (1981). *Employment and earnings,* January.

BUREAU OF THE CENSUS (1987). *Statistical abstract of the U.S.* Washington, DC: Superintendent of Documents, U.S. Government Printing Office.

BURGER, J. (1990). Behavioral effects of early postnatal lead exposure in herring gull (*Lanus angentatus*) chicks. *Pharmacology, Biochemistry and Behavior, 35*, 7–13.

BURGESS, E., & WALLIN, P. (1953). *Engagement and marriage.* Philadelphia: Lippincott.

BURISH, T. G., CAREY, M. P., KROZELY, M. G., & GRECO, A. F. (1987). Conditioned side effects induced by cancer chemotherapy: Prevention through behavioral treatment. *Journal of Consulting and Clinical Psychology, 55*, 42–48.

BURKHARDT, D. A., GOTTESMANN, J., KERSTEN, D., & LEGGE, G. E. (1984). Symmetry and constancy in the perception of negative and positive luminance contrast. *Journal of the Optical Society of America, 1*, 309–316.

BURNAM, M. A., PENNEBAKER, J. W., & GLASS, D. C. (1975). Time consciousness, achievement striving, and the type A coronary-prone behavior pattern. *Journal of Abnormal Psychology, 84*, 76–79.

BURNSTEIN, E., VINOKUR, E., & TROPE, Y. (1973). Interpersonal comparison versus persuasive argumentation: A more direct test of alternative explanations for group-induced shifts in individual choice. *Journal of Experimental Social Psychology, 9*, 236–245.

BURNSTEIN, S. (1984). Persuasion as argument processing. In M. Brandstatter, J. Davis, & G. Stocker-Kreichgaver (Eds.), *Group decision process.* London: Academic.

BURROWS, G. D., & DENNERSTEIN, L. (Eds.). (1980). *Handbook of hypnosis and psychosomatic medicine.* Amsterdam: Elsevier/North Holland.

BURT, C. (1966). The genetic determination of differences in intelligence: A study of monozygotic twins reared together and apart. *British Journal of Psychology, 57*, 137–153.

BUSS, A. H. (1980). *Self-consciousness and social anxiety.* San Francisco: Freeman.

BUSS, A. H., & FINN, S. E. (1987). Classification of personality traits. *Journal of Personality and Social Psychology, 52*, 432–444.

BUTCHER, J., & OWEN, P. (1978). Objective personality inventories: Recent research and some contemporary issues. In B. B. Wolman (Ed.), *Clinical diagnosis of mental disorders: A handbook.* New York: Plenum.

BUTLER, R., & ALEXANDER, H. (1955). Daily patterns of visual exploratory behavior in the monkeys. *Journal of Comparative and Physiological Psychology, 48*, 249–257.

BUTLER, R. N., & LEWIS, M. I. (1982). *Aging and mental health* (3rd ed.). St. Louis: Mosby.

BYRNE, D. (1971). *The attraction paradigm.* New York: Academic.

BYRNE, D., BASKETT, C. D., & HODGES, L. (1971). Behavioral indicators of interpersonal attraction. *Journal of Abnormal and Social Psychology, 1*, 137–149.

BYRNE, D., & KELLEY, K. (1981). *An introduction to personality* (3rd ed.). Englewood Cliffs, NJ: Prentice-Hall.

CACIOPPO, J. T., MARTZKE, J., PETTY, R., & TASSINARY, L. (1988). Specific forms of facial EMG response index emotions during an interview: From Darwin to the continuous flow hypothesis of affect-laden information processing. *Journal of Personality and Social Psychology, 54*, 592–604.

CACIOPPO, J. T., & PETTY, R. E. (1986). Stalking rudimentary processes of social influence: A psychological approach. In M. Zanna, J. Olson, & C. Herman (Eds.), *Social influence: The Ontario Symposium.* Hillsdale, NJ: Erlbaum.

CADORET, R. J. (1978). Psychopathology in adopted-away off-spring of biological parents and antisocial behavior. *Archives of General Psychiatry, 35*, 176–184.

CADORET, R. J., & WINOKUR, G. (1975). X-linkage in manic-depressive illness. *Annual Review of Medicine, 26*, 21–25.

CALDER, B., & STAW, B. (1975). Self-perception of intrinsic and extrinsic motivation. *Journal of Personality and Social Psychology, 31*, 599–605.

CALHOUN, J. (1962). Population density and social pathology. *Scientific American, 206*, 139–148.

CAMERON, N. (1963). *Personality development and psychopathology.* Boston: Houghton-Mifflin.

CAMPBELL, F. W. (1974). The transmission of spatial information through the visual system. In F. O. Schmitt & F. G. Worden (Eds.), *The neurosciences: Third study program.* Cambridge, MA: MIT Press.

CAMPBELL, J. D., & FAIREY, P. J. (1989). Information and normative routes to conformity: The effect of faction size as a function of norm extremity and attention to the stimulus. *Journal of Personality and Social Psychology, 57*, 457–468.

CAMPBELL, S. S., & TOBLER, I. (1984). Animal sleep: A review of sleep duration across phylogeny. *Neuroscience & Biobehavioral Reviews, 8*, 269–300.

CAMPFIELD, L. A. & SMITH, F. J. (1986). *Transient declines in blood glucose and meal initiation: Evidence for functional role of peripheral glucoreceptors.* International Conference on The Physiology of Food and Fluid Intake, Seattle, Washington, July 7–11.

CAMPOS, J. L., LANGER, A., & KROWITZ, A. (1970). Cardiac responses on the visual cliff in prelocomotor human infants. *Science, 170*, 196–197.

CANDLAND, D. K. (1968). *Psychology: The experimental approach.* New York: McGraw-Hill.

CANERO, R. (1985). Schizophrenic disorders. In H. Kaplan & B. Sadock (Eds.), *Comprehensive textbook of psychiatry* (4th ed.). (Vol. 1). Baltimore: Williams & Wilkins.

CANESTRARI, R. E. (1963). Paced and self-paced learning in young and elderly adults. *Journal of Gerontology, 18*, 165–168.

CANNON, D. S., & BAKER, T. B. (1981). Emetic and electric shock alcohol aversion therapy. *Journal of Consulting and Clinical Psychology, 49*, 20–33.

CANNON, W. B. (1914). The emergency function of the adrenal medulla in pain and the major emotions. *American Journal of Physiology, 33*, 356–372.

CANNON, W. B. (1929). *Bodily changes in pain, hunger, fear and rage.* New York: Appleton-Century-Crofts.

CANNON, W. B., & WASHBURN, A. (1912). An explanation of hunger. *American Journal of Physiology, 29*, 441–454.

CANTRELL, D. P. (1983). *Psychology: Strategies for success.* Tempe, AZ: Amoleside Publishers.

CANTRIL, H. (1965). *The pattern of human concerns.* New Brunswick, NJ: Rutgers University Press.

CAPLAN, N., WHITEMORE, J., BUI, Q., & TRAUPMANN, M. (1985). *Scholastic achievement among the children of Southeast Asian refugees.* Ann Arbor, MI: University of Michigan Institute for Social Research.

CAPPON, D. (1971). Mental health in the high rise. *Canadian Journal of Public Health, 62*, 426–431.

CARIGLIA-BULL, T., & PRESSLEY, M. (1990). Short-term memory differences between children predict imagery effects when sentences are read. *Journal of Experimental Child Psychology, 49*, 381–398.

CARINS, R. (1987). An evolutionary and developmental perspective on aggressive patterns. In Zahn-Waxler C. Cummings, E. M. & Iannotti, R. (Eds.) *Altruism and aggression.* Cambridge: Cambridge University Press.

CARLI, L. (1989). Are women more social and men more task oriented? A meta-analytic review of sex differences in group interaction, coalition formation, and cooperation in prisoner's dilemma games. Unpublished manuscript, University of Massachusetts.

CARLSMITH, J. M., & ANDERSON, C. (1979). Ambient temperature and the occurrence of collective violence: A new analysis. *Journal of Personality and Social Psychology, 37*, 337–344.

CARLSMITH, J. M., ELLSWORTH, P. C., & ARONSON, E. (1976). *Methods of research in social psychology.* Reading, MA: Addison-Wesley.

CARLSON, M., HUBEL, D. H., & WIESEL, T. N. (1986). Effects of monocular exposure to oriented lines on monkey striate cortex. *Developmental Brain Research, 25*, 71–81.

CARLSON, M., MARCUS-NEWHALL, A., & MILLER, N. (1990). Effects of situational aggression cue: A quantitative review. *Journal of Personality and Social Psychology, 58*, 622–633.

CARLSON, N. R. (1991). *Physiology of behavior,* 4th ed. Boston: Allyn & Bacon.

CARLSON, V. R. (1977). Instructions and perceptual constancy judgments. In W. Epstein (Ed.), *Stability and constancy in visual perception: Mechanics and processes.* New York: Wiley.

CARPENTER, F. (1974). *The Skinner primer.* New York: Free Press.

CARPENTER, G. C. (1974). Visual regard of moving and stationary faces in early infancy. *Merrill-Palmer Quarterly, 20*, 181–194.

CARTWRIGHT, D. (1979). Contemporary social psychology in historical perspective. *Social Psychology Quarterly, 42*, 82–93.

CARVER, C. S., COLEMAN, A., & GLASS, D. (1977). The coronary-prone behavior pattern and the suppression of fatigue on a treadmill test. *Journal of Personality and Social Psychology, 33*, 460–466.

CARVER, C., & GLASS, D. (1978). Coronary-prone behavior pattern and interpersonal aggression. *Journal of Personality and Social Psychology, 36*, 361–366.

CARVER, C., & SCHEIER, M. F. (1981). *Attention and self-regulation.* New York: Springer-Verlag.

CARVER, R. P. (1985). How good are some of the world's best readers? *Reading Research Quarterly, 20*, 389–419.

CASPER, R. C., & DAVIS, J. M. (1977). On the course of anorexia nervosa. *American Journal of Psychiatry, 134*, 974–978.

CASPI, A., BOLGER, N., & ECKENRODE, J. (1987). Linking person and context in the daily stress process. *Journal of Personality and Social Psychology, 52*, 184–195.

CASTANEDA, C. (1972). *Journey to Ixtlan: The lessons of Don Juan.* New York: Simon & Schuster.

CASTILLO, M., & BUTTERWORTH, G. (1981). Neonatal localization of a sound in visual space. *Perception, 10,* 331–338.

CATTELL, J. M. (ED.) (1906). *American men of science: A biographical directory.* New York: Science.

CATTELL, R. B. (1949). *The culture-free intelligence-test.* Champaign, IL: Institute for Personality and Ability Testing.

CATTELL, R. B. (1965). *The scientific analysis of personality.* Harmondsworth, England: Penguin.

CATTELL, R. B. (1973). *Personality and mood by questionnaire.* San Francisco: Jossey-Bass.

CAUTELA, J. R. (1977). Covert conditioning: Assumptions and procedures. *Journal of Mental Imagery, 1,* 53–64.

CAVAN, S. (1966). *Liquor license.* Chicago: Aldine.

CECI, S. J., ROSS, D. F., & TOGLIA, M. P. (1987). Suggestibility of children's memory: Psycholegal implications. *Journal of Experimental Psychology General, 116,* 38–49.

CERELLA, J. (1979). Visual classes and natural categories in the pigeon. *Journal of Experimental Psychology: Human Perception and Performance, 5,* 68–77.

CERELLA, J. (1982). Mechanisms of concept formation in the pigeon. In D. J. Ingle et al. (Eds.), *Analysis of visual behavior.* Cambridge, MA: MIT Press.

CERNEY, M. S. (1990). The Rorschach and traumatic loss: Can the presence of traumatic loss be detected from the Rorschach? *Journal of Personality Assessment, 54*(3 and 4), 781–789.

CHAIKA, E. (1984). The force of linguistic structures on cultural values: Some distinctions, as exemplified by the "Big Dan" rape case. *Interface, 11,* 68–74.

CHAIKEN, S., & EAGLY, A. (1976). Communication modality as a determinant of message persuasiveness and message comprehensibility. *Journal of Personality and Social Psychology, 34,* 605–614.

CHAIKEN, S., & PILINER, P. (1986). Women, but not men are what they eat. *Personality and Social Psychology Bulletin, 13,* 166–176.

CHAPOUTHIER, G. (1989). The search for a biochemistry of memory. Symposium: Memory and aging. *Archives of Gerontology and Geriatrics; 1989 Suppl. 1,* 7–19.

CHASE, W. G., & SIMON, H. A. (1973) Perception in chess. *Cognitive Psychology, 4,* 55–81.

CHEMERS, M. (1983). Leadership theory and research: A systems-process integration. In P. Paulus (Ed.), *Basic group processes.* New York: Springer-Verlag.

CHEMERS, M. (1987). Leadership processes: Intrapersonal, interpersonal, and societal influences. *Review of Personality and Social Psychology, 8,* 252–277.

CHEN, S. C. (1937). Social modifications of the activity of ants in next building. *Physiological Zoology, 10,* 420–437.

CHERNISS, C. (1989). Career stability in public service professionals: A longitudinal investigation based on biographical interviews. *American Journal of Community Psychology, 17,* 399–422.

CHESS, S. (1971). Autism in children with congenital rubella. *Journal of Autism and Childhood Schizophrenia, 1,* 33–47.

CHIDESTER, T. R (1990). Trends and individual differences in response to short-haul flight operations. *Aviation, Space, and Environmental Medicine, 61,* 132–138.

CHOMSKY, N. (1975). *Reflections on language.* New York: Pantheon.

CHRISTENSEN, H., HADIZ-PAVLOVIC, D., ANDREWS, G., & MATTICK, R. (1987). Behavior therapy and tricyclic medication in the treatment of obsessive-compulsive disorder: A quantitative review. *Journal of Clinical and Consulting Psychology, 55,* 701–711.

CHRISTENSEN, J. M., & TALBOT, J. M. (1986). A review of psychological aspects of space flights. *Aviation, Space, and Environmental Medicine, 57,* 203–212.

CHRISTENSEN, L., KRIETSCH, K., WHITE, B. & STAGNER, B. (1985). Impact of dietary change on emotional distress. *Journal of Abnormal Psychology, 94,* 565–579.

CHUGANI, H. T., & PHELPS, M. E. (1986). Maturational changes in cerebral function in infants determined by IDG position emission tomography. *Science, 231,* 840–843.

CHUMLEA, W. C. (1982). Physical growth in adolescence. In B. B. Wolman (Ed.), *Handbook of developmental psychology.* Englewood Cliffs, NJ: Prentice-Hall.

CHURCHLAND, P. M. (1984). *Matter and consciousness: A contemporary introduction to the philosophy of mind.* Cambridge, MA: MIT Press.

CIALDINI, R. B. (1975). Reciprocal concessions procedure for inducing compliance: The door-in-the-face technique. *Journal of Personality and Social Psychology, 31,* 206–215.

CIALDINI, R. B. (1984). *Influence: How and why people agree to things.* New York: Morrow.

CIALDINI, R. B., SCHULLER, M., HOLLIHAN, D., ARPS, K., FULTZ, J., & BEAMAN, A. (1987). Empathy-based helping: Is it selflessly or selfishly motivated. *Journal of Personality and Social Psychology, 52,* 749–758.

CICIRELLI, V. G. (1982). Sibling influence throughout the life span. In M. E. Lamb & B. Sutton-Smith (Eds.), *Sibling relationships: Their nature and significance across the life span.* Hillsdale, NJ: Erlbaum.

CLAPTON, W. (1973). Personality and career change. *Industrial Gerontology, 17,* 9–17.

CLARK, C. R., GEFFEN, G. M., & GEFFEN, L. B. (1989). Catecholamines and the covert orientation of attention in humans. *Neuropsychologia, 27,* 131–139.

CLARK, F. I., GRIGG, P., & CHAPIN, J. W. (1989). The contribution of articular receptors to proprioception with the fingers in humans. *Journal of Neurophysiology, 61,* 186–193.

CLARK, F. J., BURGESS, R. C., CHAPIN, J. W., & LIPSCOMB, W. T. (1985). Role of intramuscular receptors in the awareness of limb position. *Journal of Neurophysiology, 54,* 1529–1540.

CLARK, K. B., & CLARK, M. P. (1947). Racial identification and preferences in Negro children. In T. M. Newcomb & E. L. Hartley (Eds.), *Readings in social psychology.* New York: Holt, Rinehart and Winston.

CLARK, M. (1982). A role for arousal in the link between feeling states, judgements, and behavior. In M. Clark & S. Fisher, *Emotions and affect.* Hillsdale, NJ: Erlbaum.

CLARKE, A. (1952). An examination of the operation of residual propinquity as a factor of mate selection. *American Sociological Review, 27,* 17–22.

CLAUSEN, J. (1986, August 30). *Early adult choices and the life course.* Paper presented at the 81st annual meeting of the American Sociological Association, New York.

CLECKLEY, H. (1976). *The mask of sanity* (5th ed.). St. Louis, MO: Mosby.

CLEMMER, E. J. (1986). Not so anomalous observations question ESP in dreams. [Special Issue: Psychological Science Education], *American Psychologist, 41,* 1173–1174.

CLIFFORD, M., & WALSTER, E. (1973). The effect of physical attractiveness on teacher expectation. *Sociology of Education, 46,* 248.

CLORE, G., & ORTONY, A. (1991). What more is there to emotion concepts than prototypes? *Journal of Personality and Social Psychology, 60,* 48–50.

COATES, D. L., & LEWIS, M. (1984). Early mother-infant interaction and infant cognitive status as predictors of school performance and cognitive behavior in six-year-olds. *Child Development, 55,* 1219–1230.

COCHISE, C. N., & GRIFFITH, A. (1971). *The first 100 years of Nino Cochise.* New York: Abelard-Schuman.

COE, W. C. (1977). The problem of relevance versus ethics in researching hypnosis and antisocial conduct. *Annals of the New York Academy of Sciences, 296,* 90–104.

COFER, C. (1974). *Motivation and emotion.* Glenview, IL: Scott, Foresman.

COFER & APLEY (1964). *Motivation: Theory and research.* New York: Wiley.

COHEN, A. (1959). Communication discrepancy and attitude change: A dissonance theory. *Journal of Personality, 27,* 386–396.

COHEN D. (1976). *Dreams, visions, and drugs: A search for other realities.* New York: Franklin Watts.

COHEN, D., & SHAYWITZ, B. (1982). Preface to the special issue on neurobiological research on autism. *Journal of Autism and Developmental Disorders, 12,* 103–107.

COHEN, L. D., KIPNES, D., KUNKLE, E. G., & KUBZANSKY, P. E. (1955). Observations of a person with congenital insensitivity to pain. *Journal of Abnormal and Social Psychology, 51,* 333–338.

COHEN, S. (1977). Environmental load and the allocation of attention. In A. Baum & S. Valins (Eds.), *Advances in environmental research.* Hillsdale, NJ: Erlbaum.

COHEN, S. (1981). Sensory changes in the elderly. *American Journal of Nursing, 81,* 1851–1880.

COHEN, S., EVANS, G., KRANTZ, D., STOKOLS, D., & KELLY, S. (1981). Aircraft noise and children: Longitudinal and cross-sectional evidence of adaptation to noise and the effectiveness of noise abatement. *Journal of Personality and Social Psychology, 40,* 331–345.

COHEN, S., GLASS, D. C., & SINGER, J. E. (1973). Apartment noise, auditory discrimination, and reading ability in children. *Journal of Experimental Social Psychology, 9,* 407–422.

COHEN, S., & WEINSTEIN, W. (1981). Nonauditory effects of noise on behavior and health. *Journal of Social Issues, 37,* 36–40.

COHEN-TANNOUDJI, J., LOCATELLI, A., & SIGNORET, J. P. (1986). Non-pheromonal stimulation by the male of LH release in the anostrous ewe. *Physiology and Behavior, 36,* 921–924.

COHN, S. A., EMMERICH, D. S. & CARLSON, E. A. (1989). Differences in the responses of heterozygous carriers of colorblindness and normal controls to briefly presented stimuli. *Vision Research, 29,* 255–262.

COK, F. (1990). Body image and satisfaction in Turkish adolescence. *Adolescence, 25,* 409–413.

COLE, C. S., & COYNE, J. C. (1977). Situational specificity of laboratory-induced learned helplessness. *Journal of Abnormal Psychology, 86,* 615–623.

COLE, D. (1987, November). Dismantling gender myths. *Psychology Today.*

COLE, R. A. (1973). Listening for mispronunciations: a measure of what we hear during speech. *Perception and Psychophysics, 13,* 153–156.

COLEMAN, J. C., BUTCHER, J. N., & CARSON, R. C. (1980). *Abnormal psychology in modern life* (6th ed.). Glenview, IL: Scott, Foresman.

COLLINS, A. M., & QUILLIAN, M. R. (1969). Retrieval time from semantic memory. *Journal of Verbal Learning and Verbal Behavior, 8,* 240–247.

COLLINS, B. (1973). *Public and private conformity: Competing explanations by improvisation, cognitive dissonance, and attribution the-*

ories. Andover, MA: Warner Modular Publications.

COLT, E. W., WARDLAW, S. L., & FRANTZ, A. G. (1981). The effect of running on plasma beta-endorphin. *Life Sciences, 28,* 1637–1640.

COMMITTEE OF VETERANS AFFAIRS (1981). *Legacies of Vietnam: Comparative adjustment of veterans and their peers.* Washington, DC: U.S. Government Printing Office.

COMSTOCK, G., CHAFFE, S., KATZMAN, N., McCOMBS, M., & ROBERTS, D. (1979). *Television and human behavior.* New York: Columbia University Press.

CONDUS, M. M., MARSHALL, K. J., & MILLER, S. R. (1986). Effects of the key-word mnemonic strategy on vocabulary acquisition and maintenance by learning disabled children. *Journal of Learning Disabilities, 19,* 609–613.

CONE, J., & HAYES, S. (1980). *Environmental problems and behavioral solutions.* Monterey, CA: Brooks/Cole.

CONLEY, J. J. (1984). Relation of temporal stability and cross-situational consistency in personality: Comment on the Michel-Epstein debate. *Psychological Review, 91,* 491–496.

CONRAD, R. (1964). Acoustic confusions in immediate memory. *British Journal of Psychology, 55,* 75–84.

CONROY, J., & SUNDSTROM, E. (1977). Territorial dominance in dyadic conversation as a function of similarity of opinion. *Journal of Personality and Social Psychology, 39,* 570–576.

CONTERAS, P. C. (1990). D-serine antagonized phencyclidine and MK 801 induced stereotyped behavior and ataxia. *Neuropharmacology, 29,* 291–293.

CONWAY, J. (1977). Behavioral self-control of smoking through aversive conditioning and self-management. *Journal of Consulting and Clinical Psychology, 45,* 348–357.

COOK, S. W. (1978). Interpersonal and attitudinal outcomes in cooperating interracial groups. *Journal of Research and Development in Education, 12,* 97–113.

COOK, E. W., HODES, R. L., & LANG, P. J. (1986). Preparedness and phobia: Effects of stimulus content on human visceral conditioning. *Journal of Abnormal Psychology, 95,* 195–207.

COOPER, H. (1979). Statistics combining independent studies: A meta-analysis of sex differences in conformity research. *Journal of Personality and Social Psychology, 37,* 131–146.

COOPER, J., & AXSON, D. (1982). Effort justification in psychotherapy. In G. Weary & H. Mirels (Eds.), *Integrations of clinical and social psychology.* New York: Oxford University Press.

COOPER, J., & CROYLE, R. T. (1984). Attitudes and attitude change. *Annual Review of Psychology, 35,* 395–426.

COOPER, J., DARLEY, J. M., & HENDERSON, J. T. (1974). On the effectiveness of deviant and conventionally appearing communicators. A field experiment. *Journal of Personality and Social Psychology, 29,* 752–757.

COOPER, J., & FAZIO, R. (1979). The formation and persistence of attitudes that support intergroup conflict. In W. Austin & S. Worchel (Eds.), *The social psychology of intergroup relations.* Monterey, CA: Brooks/Cole.

COOPER, J., & MACKIE, D. (1986). Video games and aggression in children. *Journal of Applied Social Psychology, 16,* 726–744.

COOPER, J., & WORCHEL, S. (1970). Role of undesired consequences in arousing cognitive dissonance. *Journal of Personality and Social Psychology, 16,* 199–206.

COOPER, L. A., & SHEPARD, R. N. (1973). Chronometric studies of the rotation of mental images. In W. G. Chase (Ed.), *Visual information processing.* New York: Academic.

COOPER, L. A., & SHEPARD, R. N. (1984). Turning something over in the mind. *Scientific American, 25,* 106–114.

COOPER, R., & ZUBEK, J. (1958). Effects of enriched and restricted early environments on the learning ability of bright and dull rats. *Canadian Journal of Psychology, 12,* 159–164.

COOPER, S. H., & HARTMANN, E. (1986). Hostility levels of lifetime nightmare sufferers: A test of a clinical hypothesis. *Psychoanalytic Psychology, 3,* 373–377.

COOPER, S., & HODGES, W. (1983). *The mental health consultation field.* New York: Human Sciences.

COREN, S. (1986). An efferent component in the visual perception of direction and extent. *Psychological Review, 93,* 391–410.

COREN, S., & GIRGUS, J. S. (1978). *Seeing is deceiving.* Hillsdale, NJ: Erlbaum.

COREY, G., & COREY, M. S. (1977). *Groups: Process and practice.* Monterey, CA: Brooks/Cole.

CORNELIUS, R. (1991). Gregorio Maranon's two-factor theory of emotion. *Personality and Social Psychology Bulletin, 17,* 65–69.

CORNILLEAU-PÉRES, V., & DROULEZ, J. (1989). Visual perception of surface curvature: Psychophysics of curvature detection induced by motion parallax. *Perception and Psychophysics, 16,* 351–364.

CORNSWEET, T. N. (1970). *Visual perception.* New York: Academic.

CORSINI, R. J. (Ed.). (1981). *Handbook of innovative psychotherapies.* New York: Wiley.

COSTA, P., & McCRAE, R. R. (1988). Personality in adulthood: A six-year longitudinal study of self-reports and spouse ratings on the NEO personality inventory. *Journal of Personality and Social Psychology, 54,* 853–963.

COSTA, P. T., JR., & McCRAE, R. R. (1980). Still stable after all these years: Personality as a key to some issues in aging. In P. B. Baltes & O. G. Brim, Jr. (Eds.), *Lifespan development and behavior* (Vol. 3). New York: Academic.

COSTANTINO, G., MALGADY, R. G., & ROGLER, L. G. (1988). *Tell-Me-A-Story (TEMAS) Manual.* Los Angeles: Western Psychological Services.

COTMAN, C. W., & McGAUGH, J. L. (1980). *Behavioral neuroscience.* New York: Academic.

COTTRELL, N. (1972). Social facilitation. In C. McClintock (Ed.), *Experimental social psychology.* New York: Holt, Rinehart & Winston.

COUNCIL ON SCIENTIFIC AFFAIRS. (1986). Scientific status of refreshing recollection by the use of hypnosis. *International Journal of Clinical and Experimental Hypnosis, 34,* 1–11.

COWART, B. J. (1988). Age related changes in taste and smell. *Pride Institute Journal of Long Term Home Health Care, 7,* 23–27.

COWLEY, G. (1988, April). Science and the cigarette. *Newsweek,* p. 67.

COWLEY, G. (1988, May 23). The wisdom of animals. *Newsweek,* 52–59.

COX, F. D. (1974). *Youth, marriage and the seductive society.* Dubuque, IA: William C. Brown.

COX, R. M., & RISBERG, D. M. (1986). Comparison of in-the-ear and over-the-ear hearing aid fittings. *Journal of Speech and Hearing Disorders, 5,* 362–369.

COYNE, J. (1976). Depression and the response of others. *Journal of Abnormal Psychology, 85,* 186–193.

COYNE, J. (1976). Toward an interactional description of depression. *Psychiatry, 39,* 14–27.

COYNE, J., & LAZARUS, R. (1981). Cognition, stress, and coping: A transactional perspective. In I. Kutash & L. Schlesinger (Eds.), *Pressure point: Perspective on stress and anxiety.* San Francisco: Jossey-Bass.

CRAIG, C., & McCANN, J. (1980). Developing strategies for influencing residential consumption of electricity. *Journal of Environmental Systems, 9,* 175–188.

CRAIG, J. M., & SHERIF, C. W. (1986). The effectiveness of men and women in problem-solving groups as a function of group gender composition. *Sex Roles, 14,* 453–466.

CRAIK, F. I. M., & LOCKHART, R. S. (1972). Levels of processing: a framework for memory research. *Journal of Verbal Learning and Verbal Behavior, 11,* 671–684.

CRANDALL, V. (1973). Achievement. In H. Stevenson (Ed.), *Child psychology.* Chicago, IL: University of Chicago Press.

CRANO, W. D. (1987). Aggression: The focus of a recent conference in Spain. *European Science Notes, U. S. Office of Naval Research,* London, pp. 467–473.

CRANO, W., & MELLON, P. (1978). Causal inference of teachers' expectations across logged panel analysis. *Journal of Educational Psychology, 70,* 39–49.

CRASILNECK, H. D. (1990). Hypnotic techniques for smoking control and psychogenic impotence. *American Journal of Clinical Hypnosis, 32,* 147–153.

CREASEY, H., RUMSEY, J. M., SCHWARTZ, M., DUARA, R., ET AL. (1986). Brain morphometry in autistic men as measured by volumetric computed tomography. *Archives of Neurology, 43,* 669–672.

CRISMORE, A. (1984). The rhetoric of textbooks: Metadiscourse. *Journal of Curriculum Studies, 16,* 279–296.

CRISP, A. H., PALMER, R. L., & KALUCY, R. S. (1976). How common is anorexia nervosa? A prevalence study. *British Journal of Psychiatry, 128,* 549–554.

CRITCHLOW, B. (1986). The powers of John Barleycorn: Beliefs about the effects of alcohol on social behavior. *American Psychologist, 41,* 751–764.

CROCKENBURG, S. B. (1972). Creativity tests: A boon or boon-doggle for education? *Review of Educational Research, 42,* 27–45.

CRONBACK, L. J., & SNOW, R. E. (1977). *Aptitudes and instructional methods.* New York: Irvington.

CRONSHAW, S. F. (1986). The status of employment testing in Canada: A review and evaluation of theory and practice. *Canadian Psychology, 27,* 183–195.

CROSBY, F., BROMLEY, S., & SAXE, L. (1980). Recent unobtrusive studies of black and white discrimination and prejudices: A literature review. *Psychological Bulletin, 87,* 546–563.

CROW, T. (1983). *Disorders of neuronumoural transmission.* New York: Academic.

CROW, T. J. (1985). The two syndrome concept: Origins and current status. *Schizophrenia Bulletin, 11,* 471–486.

CRUTCHFIELD, R. S. (1955). Conformity and character. *American Psychologist, 10,* 191–198.

CRYSTAL, S. (1982). *America's old age crisis: Public policy and the two worlds of aging.* New York: Basic.

CSIKSZENTMIHALYI, M. (1974). Flow: Studies of enjoyment (Report No. RO1 HM22-883-02). Washington, DC: U.S. Public Health Service.

CUNNINGHAM, S. (1983, June). Animal activists rally in streets, urge Congress to tighten laws. *APA Monitor,* pp. 1–27.

CURTISS, S. (1977). *Genie: A psycholinguistic study of a modern-day "wild child."* New York: Academic.

CUTRONA, C. E. (1990). Stress and social support—in search of optimal matching. *Journal of Social and Clinical Psychology, 9,* 3–14.

CUTRONA, C. E., & RUSSELL, D. (1990). Type of social support and specific stress: Toward a theory of optimal matching. In I. Sarason, B. Sarason, & G. Pierce (Eds.), *Social support: An international view.* New York: Wiley.

CUTTING, J. E., & PROFFITT, D. R. (1981). Gait perception as an example of how we may perceive events. In R. D. Walk & H. L. Pick, Jr. (Eds.), *Intersensory perception and sensory integration.* New York: Plenum.

DABBS, J., & MORRIS, R. (1990). Testosterone, social class, and antisocial behavior in a sample of 4,462 men. *Psychological Science, 1,* 209–211.

DAGENBACH, D., HORST, S., & CARR, T. H. (1990). Adding new information to semantic memory: How much learning is enough to produce automatic priming? *Journal of Experimental Psychology, Learning, Memory, and Cognition, 16,* 581–591.

DAHLQUIST, L. M. (1990). The treatment of persistent vomiting through shaping and contingency management. *Journal of Behavior Therapy and Experimental Psychiatry, 21,* 77–80.

DAMOS, D. L., & SLOEM, K. A. (1985). Type A behavior pattern, multiple task performance, and subjective estimation of mental workload. *Bulletin of the Psychonomic Society, 23,* 53–56.

DANA, R. H. (1986). The Thematic Apperception Test used with adolescents. In A. I. Rabin (Eds.), *Projective techniques for adolescents and children.* New York: Springer.

DANE, A. (1991). Report from Charlie Battery. *Popular Mechanics, 168,* 23–28, 126.

DANIELS, J. (1950). *The man of independence.* Philadelphia: Lippincott.

DARLEY, J. M., & COOPER, J. (1972). The "Clean for Gene" phenomenon: Deciding to vote for or against a candidate on the basis of the physical appearance of his supporters. *Journal of Applied Social Psychology, 2,* 24–33.

DARLEY, J. M., & LATANE, B. (1968). Bystander intervention in emergencies: Diffusion of responsibility. *Journal of Personality and Social Psychology, 8,* 377–383.

DARWIN, C. (1859). *The origin of species.* London.

DARWIN, C. (1872). *The expression of emotion in man and animals.* London: Murrary (Reprinted in 1965 by University of Chicago Press).

DAVENPORT, M. (1991). *The origins of the censorship of art.* Presentation at Texas A&M philosophy series on Ethics, College Station, TX (January 22, 1991).

DAVENPORT, Y. B., ADLAND, M. L., GOLD, P. W., & GOODWYN, F. K. (1979). Manic-depressive illness: Psycho-dynamic features of multigenerational families. *American Journal of Orthopsychiatry, 49,* 24–35.

DAVIDSON, P. (1987). Hypnosis and migraine headache: Reporting a clinical series. *Australian Journal of Clinical and Experimental Hypnosis, 15,* 111–118.

DAVIDSON, W. S., II (1974). Studies of aversive conditioning for alcoholics: A critical review of theory and research methodology. *Psychological Bulletin, 81,* 571–581.

DAVIS, C. M. (1928). Self-selection of diet by newly weaned infants. *American Journal of Diseases of Children, 36,* 651–679.

DAVIS, E. T. (1990). Modeling shifts in perceived spatial frequency between the fovea and the periphery. *Journal of the Optical Society of America, 7,* 286–296.

DAVIS, J. A. (1974). A two-factor theory of schizophrenia. *Journal of Psychiatric Research, 11,* 25–29.

DAVIS, J. H. (1980). Group decision and procedural justice. In M. Fishbein (Ed.), *Progress in social psychology* (Vol. 1). Hillsdale, NJ: Erlbaum.

DAVIS, K. E. (1985, February). Near and dear: Friendship and love compared. *Psychology Today,* pp. 22–32.

DAVIS, J., BRAY, R., & HOLT, R. (1977). The empirical study of decision processes in juries. In J. Tapp & F. Levine (Eds.), *Law, justice and the individual in society: Psychological and legal issues.* New York: Holt, Rinehart, & Winston.

DAVIS, J., CAMPBELL, C., GALLAGHER, R., & ZUKRAKOV, M. (1971). Disappearance of a humoral satiety factor during food deprivation. *Journal of Comparative and Physiological Psychology, 75,* 476–482.

DAVIS, J., GALLAGHER, R., & LADOVE, R. (1967). Food intake controlled by a blood factor. *Science, 156,* 1247–1248.

DAVIS, J., & LAMBERTH, J. (1974). Affective arousal and energization properties of positive and negative stimuli. *Journal of Experimental Psychology, 103,* 196–200.

DAVIS, J., TINDALE, R., NAGAO, D., HINSZ, V., & ROBERTSON, B. (1984). Order effects in multiple decisions by groups: A demonstration with mock juries and trial procedures. *Journal of Personality and Social Psychology, 47,* 1003–1012.

DAVISON, G. C., & NEALE, J. M. (1978). *Abnormal psychology* (2nd ed.). New York: Wiley.

DAY, R. H., & WEBSTER, W. R. (1989). Negative afterimages and the McCollough effect. *Perception and Psychophysics, 46,* 419–424.

DEAN, L., PUGH, W., & GUNDERSON, E. (1978). The behavioral effects of crowding. *Environment and Behavior, 10,* 419–431.

DE ANGELLS, T. (1987, August). Short-term therapy is "magical" choice for many patients. *The APA Monitor,* p. 34.

DEAUX, K. (1976a). Sex: A perspective on the attribution process. In H. Harvey, W. J. Ickes, & R. F. Kidd (Eds.), *New directions in attribution research.* Hillsdale, NJ: Erlbaum.

DEAUX, K. (1976b). *The behavior of women and men.* Belmont, CA: Brooks/Cole.

DECI, E. (1971). Effects of externally mediated rewards on intrinsic motivation. *Journal of Personality and Social Psychology, 18,* 105–115.

DECI, E. (1972). Intrinsic motivation extrinsic reinforcement and equity. *Journal of Personality and Social Psychology, 22,* 113–120.

DECKEL, A. W., MORAN, T. H., COYLE, J. T., SANBERG, P. R., & ROBINSON, R. G. (1986). Anatomical predictors of behavioral recovery following fetal striatal transplants. *Brain Research, 365,* 249–258.

DEESE, J. (1959). Influence of inter-item associative strength upon immediate free recall. *Psychological Reports, 5,* 305–312.

DEESE, J. (1965). *The structure of associations in language and thought.* Baltimore, MD: Johns Hopkins University Press.

DEESE, J. (1980). Text structure, strategies, and comprehension in learning from textbooks. In J. Robinson (Ed.), *Research in science education: New questions, new directions.* Boulder, CO: BSCS.

DEESE, J. (1984). *Thought into speech.* Englewood Cliffs, NJ: Prentice-Hall.

DE GROOT, A. D. (1966). Perception and memory versus thought: some old ideas and recent findings. In B. Kleinmuntz (Ed.), *Problem solving: research, method, and theory.* New York: Wiley.

DEINER, E. (1977). Deindividuation: Causes and consequences. *Social Behavior and Personality, 5,* 143–155.

DEINER, E., FRASER, S. C., BEAMAN, A. L., & KELEM, R. T. (1976). Effects of deindividuation variables on stealing among Halloween trick-or-treaters. *Journal of Personality and Social Psychology, 33,* 178–183.

DELAMATER, A. R., LOLORDO, V. M., & BERRIDGE, K. C. (1986). Control of fluid palatability by exeroceptive Pavlovian signals. *Journal of Experimental Psychology Animal Behavior Processes, 12,* 143–152.

DELGADO, J. M. R. (1960). Emotional behavior in animals and humans. *Psychiatric Research Reports, 12,* 259–266.

DELMONTE, M. M. (1985a). The effect of meditation on drug use: A literature review. *Gedrag Tijdschrift voor Psychologie, 13,* 36–48.

DELMONTE, M. M. (1985b). Meditation and anxiety reduction: A literature review. *Clinical Psychology Review, 5,* 91–102.

DELOACHE, J. S. (1987). Rapid change in the symbolic functioning of very young children. *Science, 238,* 1556–1557.

DELUCA, R. V., & HOLBORN, S. W. (1990). Effects of fixed-internal and fixed-ration schedules of token reinforcement on exercise with obese and nonobese boys. *Psychological Record, 40,* 67–82.

DEMARE, D., BRIER, J., & LIPS, H. M. (1988). Violent pornography and self-reported likelihood of sexual aggression. *Journal of Research in Personality, 22,* 140–153.

DEMBER, W. (1965). A new look in motivation. *American Scientist, 53,* 409–427.

DEMENT, W. C. (1974). *Some must watch while some must sleep.* New York: Norton.

DEMEYER, M. K. (1976). The nature of the neuropsychological disability in autistic children. In E. Shopler & R. J. Reichler (Eds.), *Psychopathology and child development.* New York: Plenum.

DE MILLE, A. (1982). *Reprieve: A memoir.* Garden City, NY: Doubleday.

DENING, T. R., & BERRIOS, G. E. (1989). Wilson's disease: A prospective study of psychopathology in 31 cases. *British Journal of Psychiatry, 155,* 206–213.

DENMARK, F. L. (1989). Back to the future in the education and training of psychologists. *American Psychologist, 44,* 725–730.

DENNEY, N. W. (1974). Classification abilities in the elderly. *Journal of Gerontology, 29,* 309–314.

DENNIS, W. (1940). Does culture appreciably affect patterns of infant behavior? *Journal of Social Psychology, 12,* 305–317.

DENNIS, W. (1973). *Children of the creche.* Englewood Cliffs, NJ: Prentice-Hall.

DENNY, D., & SULLIVAN, B. (1976). Desensitization and modeling treatments of spider fear using two types of scenes. *Journal of Consulting and Clinical Psychology, 44,* 573–579.

DEPUE, R. A., & EVANS, R. (1976). The psychobiology of depressive disorders. In B. H. Maher (Ed.), *Progress in experimental personality research* (Vol. 8). New York: Academic.

DER-KARABETRAN, A., & SMITH, A. (1977). Sex-role stereotyping in the United States: Is it changing? *Sex Roles, 3,* 193–198.

DE SCHAMPHELEIRE, D. (1990). MMPI characteristics of professional prostitutes: A cross-cultural replication. *Journal of Personality Assessment, 54*(1 and 2), 343–350.

DESOR, T. (1972). Toward a psychological theory of crowding. *Journal of Personality and Social Psychology, 21,* 79–83.

DEUTSCH, J. A. (1983). *The psychological basis of memory.* New York: Academic.

DEUTSCH, M., & KRAUSS, R. M. (1960). The effect of threat upon interpersonal bargaining. *Journal of Abnormal and Social Psychology, 61,* 181–189.

DEVINE, P. G. (1989). Stereotypes and prejudice: Their automatic and controlled components. *Journal of Personality and Social Psychology, 56,* 5–18.

DE VRIES, H. A. (1970). Physiological effects

of an exercise training regimen upon men aged 52 to 88. *Journal of Gerontology, 25,* 325–336.

DE VRIES, H. A. (1975). Physiology of exercise and aging. In D. S. Woodruff & J. E. Birren (Eds.), *Aging: Scientific perspectives and social issues.* New York: Van Nostrand.

DEWIED, O, & VON RES, J. M. (1989). Neuropeptides; Animal behavior and human psychopathology. *European Archives of Psychiatry and Neurological Science, 238,* 323–331.

DEWSBURY, D. (1990). Early interactions between animal psychologists and animal activists and the founding of the APA Committee on Precautions in Animal Experimentation. *American Psychologist, 45,* 315–327.

DIACONIS, P. (1978). Statistical problems in ESP research. *Science, 201,* 131–136.

DICK, M. B., KEAN, M. L., & SANDS, D. (1989). Memory for action events in Alzheimer-type dementia: Further evidence of an encoding failure. *Brain and Cognition, 9,* 71–87.

DIEHL, J. A., & MCKEEVER, W. F. (1987). Absence of exposure time influence on lateralized face recognition and object naming latency tasks. *Brain and Cognition, 6,* 347–359.

DIES, R., & GREENBURG, B. (1976). Effects of physical contact in an encounter group context. *Journal of Consulting and Clinical Psychology, 44,* 400–405.

DIETZ, J. (1985, February 10). Electroshock therapy is making a comeback. *Boston Globe.* (Citing research from National Institute of Mental Health).

DIMENTO, J. (1981). Making usable information on environmental stressors: Opportunities for the research and policy communities. *Journal of Social Issues, 37,* 172–205.

DIPPEL, B., LAUER, C., RIEMANN, D., MAJER-TRENDEL, K. (1987). Sleep and dreams in eating disorders, Ninth World Congress of the International College of Psychosomatic Medicine. *Psychotherapy and Psychosomatics, 48,* 165–169.

DITTES, J., & KELLEY, H. H. (1956). Effects on different conditions of acceptance upon conformity to group norms. *Journal of Abnormal and Social Psychology, 53,* 100–107.

DOBELLE, W. H. (1977). Current status of research on providing sight to the blind by electrical stimulation of the brain. *Journal of Visual Impairment and Blindness, 71,* 290–297.

DODGE, K., & CRICK, N. (1990). Social information-processing of aggressive behavior in children. *Personality and Social Psychology Bulletin, 16,* 8–22.

DODWELL, P. C. & HUMPHREY, G. K. (1990). A functional theory of the McCollough effect. *Psychological Review, 97,* 78–89.

DOERNER, W. R. (1985, July 8). To America with skills. *Time,* pp. 42, 44.

DOLLARD, J., DOOB, L., MILLER, N., MOWRER, O., & SEARS, R. (1939). *Frustration and aggression.* New Haven, CT: Yale University Press.

DONDERI, D. C., & MURPHY, S. B. (1983). Predicting activity and satisfaction following cataract surgery. *Journal of Behavioral Medicine, 6,* 313–328.

DONNERSTEIN, E., & LINZ, D. G. (1986, December). The question of pornography: It is not sex, but violence, that is an obscenity in our society. *Psychology Today,* pp. 56–59.

DONNERSTEIN, E., & WILSON, D. W. (1976). Effects of noise and perceived control on ongoing and subsequent aggressive behavior. *Journal of Personality and Social Psychology, 34,* 774–781.

DORFMAN, L. I. (1989). Retirement preparation and retirement satisfaction in the rural elderly. *Journal of Applied Gerontology, 8,* 432–450.

DORSEY, M. F., IWATA, B. A., ONY, P., & MCSWEEN, T. (1980). Treatment of self-injurious behavior using a water mist: Initial response suppression and generalization. *Journal of Applied Behavior Analysis, 13,* 343–353.

DOSEY, M. A., & MEISELS, M. (1969). Personal space and self-protection. *Journal of Personality and Social Psychology, 11,* 93–97.

DOTY, R. L. (1975). Changes in the intensity and pleasantness of human vaginal odors during the menstrual cycle. *Science, 190,* 1316–1318.

DOVIDIO, J. F., & GAERTNER, S. (1986). *Prejudice, discrimination, and racism.* Orlando, FL: Academic.

DRAIK, F. I. M., & LOCKHART, R. S. (1972). Levels of processing: A framework for memory research. *Journal of Verbal Learning and Verbal Behavior, 11,* 671–684.

DRISCOLL, C. D. STREISSGUTH, A. P., & RILEY, E. P. (1990). Prenatal alcohol exposure: Comparability of effects in humans and animal developmental neurotoxicity. *Neurotoxicity and Teratology, 12,* 231–237.

DRUG ABUSE COUNCIL, (1980). *The facts about "drug abuse."* New York: Free Press.

DUBRIS, A. J. (1982). *Contemporary applied management.* Plano, TX: Business Publications.

DUCHEK, J. M., & HEELY, J. H. (1989). A dissociative word-frequency: Levels of processing interaction in episodic recognition and lexical decision tasks. *Memory and Cognition, 17,* 148–162.

DUGOVIC, C., WAUQUIER, A., LEYSEN, J. E., & MARRANNES, R. (1989). Functional role of 5-HT-sub-2 receptors in the regulation of sleep and wakefulness in the rat. *Psychopharmacology, 97,* 436–442.

DUNCAN, M. G. (1987). Only the Marlboro man: A psychological study of a political agitator. *Political Psychology, 8,* 165–190.

DUNHAM, H. W. (1965). *Community and schizophrenia: An epidemiological analysis.* Detroit: Wayne State University Press.

DUNKE, K. (1945). On problem solving. *Psychological Monographs, 58,* 5 (Whole No. 270).

DUNKER, K. (1945). On problem solving. *Psychological Monographs, 58* (5, Whole No. 270).

DUNN, J., & KENDRICK, C. (1982). *Siblings: Love, envy, and understanding.* Cambridge, MA: Harvard University Press.

DUNPHY, D. C. (1963). The social structure of urban adolescent peer groups. *Sociometry, 26,* 230–246.

DURLAK, J. (1979). Comparative effectiveness of paraprofessional and professional helpers. *Psychological Bulletin, 86,* 80–92.

DUSTIN, R., & GEORGE, R. (1977). *Action counseling for behavior change* (2nd ed.). Cranston, RI: Carroll.

DUTTON, D. G., & ARON, A. P. (1974). Some evidence for heightened sexual attraction under conditions of high anxiety. *Journal of Personality and Social Psychology, 30,* 510–517.

DUVAL, S., & HENSLEY, V. (1976). Extensions of objective self-awareness theory: The focus of attention causal attribution hypothesis. In J. H. Harvey, W. J. Ickes, & R. F. Kidd (Eds.), *New directions in attribution research* (Vol. 1). Hillsdale, NJ: Erlbaum.

DUVAL, S., & WICKLUND, R. A. (1972). *A theory of objective self-awareness.* New York: Academic.

DWECK, C. S. (1986). Motivational processes affecting learning. *American Psychologist, 41,* 1040–1048.

EAGLY, A., WOOD, W., & FISHBAUGH, L. (1981). Sex differences in conformity: Surveillance by the group as a determinant of male conformity. *Journal of Personality and Social Psychology, 40,* 384–394.

EBBINGHAUS, H. (1885). *Memory: A contribution to experimental psychology* (H. A. Ruger & C. E. Bussenius, Trans.). New York: Teachers College.

EBENHOLTZ, S. M., & SHEBILSKE, W. L. (1975). The doll reflex: Ocular counterrolling with head-body tilt in median plane. *Vision Research, 15,* 713–717.

EBENHOLTZ, S. M. (1981). Hysteresis effects in the vergence control system: Perceptual implications. In D. F. Fisher, R. A. Monty, & J. W. Senders (Eds.). *Eye movements: Cognition and visual perception.* Hillsdale, NJ: Erlbaum.

ECCLES, J. (1991). Gender role socialization. In R. M. Baron & W. G. Graziano (Eds.), *Social psychology.* New York: Holt, Rinehart & Winston.

ECCLES, J. C. (1973). *The understanding of the brain.* New York: McGraw-Hill.

ECCLES, J. C. (1983). Attributional processes as mediators of sex differences in achievement. *Journal of Educational Equality and Leadership, 3,* 19–27.

EDELMAN, M. W. (1981). Who is for the children? *American Psychologist, 36,* 109–116.

EDNEY, J. J. (1975). Territoriality and control: A field experiment. *Journal of Personality and Social Psychology, 31,* 1108–1115.

EFRAN, M. G. (1974). The effect of physical appearance on the judgement of guilt, interpersonal attraction, and severity of recommended punishment in a simulated jury task. *Journal of Research in Personality, 8,* 45–54.

EHRET, C., & SCRANTON, W. (1983). *Overcoming jet lag.* New York: Benton.

EHRLICH, P. (1968). *The population bomb.* New York: Ballantine.

EIBL-EIBESFELDT, I. (1970). *Ethology: The biology of behavior* (E. Klinghammer, Trans.). New York: Holt, Rinehart and Winston.

EISDORFER, C. (1968). Arousal and performance: Experiments in verbal learning and a tentative theory. In G. A. Talland (Ed.), *Human aging and behavior.* New York: Academic.

EKMAN, P., & FRIESEN, W. V. (1971). Constants across cultures in the face and emotion. *Journal of Personality and Social Psychology, 17,* 124–129.

EKMAN, P., FRIESEN, W., & ANCOLI, S. (1980). Facial signs of emotional experience. *Journal of Personality and Social Psychology, 17,* 1125–1134.

EKMAN, P., FRIESEN, W., & O'SULLIVAN, M. (1988). Smiling when lying. *Journal of Personality and Social Psychology, 564,* 414–420.

EKMAN, P., SORENSON, E. R., & FRIESEN, W. V. (1969). Pancultural elements in facial displays of emotion. *Science, 164,* 86–88.

ELIOPOULOS, C. (1987). *A guide to the nursing of the aging.* Baltimore, MD: Williams and Wilkins.

ELKIND, D. (1979, February). Growing up faster. *Psychology Today,* pp. 38–45.

ELKIND, D. (1984). *All grown up and no place to go.* Reading, MA: Addison-Wesley.

ELLIOT, J. L., & GENTILE, J. R. (1986). The efficacy of a mnemonic technique for learning disabled and nondisabled adolescents. *Journal of Learning Disabilities, 19,* 237–241.

ELLIS, A. (1987). The impossibility of achieving consistently good mental health. *American Psychologist, 42,* 364–375.

ELLIS, A. (1962). *Reason and emotion in psychotherapy.* New York: Lyle Stuart.

ELLIS, A., & GRIEGER, R. (1977). *RET: Handbook of rational-emotive therapy.* New York: Springer.

ELLIS, H. (1902). Mescal: A study of a divine

plant. *Popular Science Monthly, 41*, 52–71.

ELLSWORTH, P., & TOURANGEAU, R. (1981). Our failure to disconfirm what nobody ever said. *Journal of Personality and Social Psychology, 40*, 363–369.

ELWORTH, C. L., LARRY, C., & MALSTROM, F. V. (1986). Age, degraded viewing environments, and the speed of accommodation. *Aviation, Space, and Environmental Medicine, 57*, 54–58.

ENGEN, T. (1980, May). Why the aroma lingers on. *Psychology Today*, p. 138.

ENNS, M. P., & HORNUNG, D. E. (1988). Comparisons of the estimates of smell, taste and overall intensity in young and elderly people. *Chemical Senses, 13*, 131–139.

EPSTEIN, N., & JACKSON, E. (1978). An outcome study of short-term communication training with married couples. *Journal of Consulting and Clinical Psychology, 46*, 207–212.

EPSTEIN, N., & VLOK, L. (1981). Research on the results of psychotherapy: A summary of evidence. *American Journal of Psychiatry, 138*, 1027–1035.

EPSTEIN, S. (1979). The stability of behavior: I. On predicting most people much of the time. *Journal of Personality and Social Psychology, 37*, 1097–1126.

EPSTEIN, S. (1983). The stability of confusion: A reply to Mischel and Peake. *Psychological Review, 90*, 179–184.

EPSTEIN, W. (1973). The process of "taking into account" in visual perception. *Perception, 2*, 267–285.

EPSTEIN, Y. (1981). Crowding, stress and human behavior. *Journal of Social Issues, 37*, 126–145.

EPSTEIN, Y., & KARLIN, R. (1975). Effects of acute experimental crowding. *Journal of Applied Social Psychology, 5*, 34–53.

ERDNER, R. A., & GUY, R. R. (1990). Career identification and women's attitudes toward retirement. *International Journal of Aging and Human Development, 30*, 129–139.

ERICKSON, M. H. (1980). The hypnotic induction of hallucinatory color vision followed by pseudonegative after-images. In E. L. Rossi (Ed.), *The nature of hypnosis and suggestion*. New York: Irvington.

ERIKSON, E. H. (1959). Identity and the life cycle: Selected papers. *Psychological Issues, 1*, 50–100.

ERIKSON, E. H. (1963). *Childhood and society*. New York: Norton.

ERLENMEYER-KIMLING, L., & JARVIK, L. F. (1963). Genetics and intelligence: A review. *Science, 142*, 1477–1479.

ERON, L. (1980). Presumption for reduction of aggression. *American Psychologist, 35*, 244–252.

ERON, L. (1982). Parent-child interaction, television violence, and aggression of children. *American Psychologist, 37*, 197–211.

ERON, L. (1987). The development of aggressive behavior from the perspective of developing behaviorism. *American Psychologist, 42*, 435–442.

ESTES, T. H., & SHEBILSKE, W. L. (1980). Comprehension: Of what the reader sees of what the author says. In M. L. Kamil & S. J. Moe (Eds.), *Twenty-ninth yearbook of the national reading conference*.

ESTES, T. H., & VAUGHAN, J. L., JR. (1985). *Reading and learning in the content classroom: Diagnosis and instructional strategies* (3rd ed.). Boston: Allyn & Bacon.

ESTROFF, T. W., SCHWARTZ, R. H., & HOFFMAN, N. G. (1989). Adolescent cocaine abuse: Addictive potential, behavioral and psychiatric effects. *Clinical Pediatrics, 28*, 550–555.

EVANS, G. W. (1979). Behavioral and physiological consequences of crowding in humans. *Journal of Applied Social Psychology, 9*, 27–46.

EVANS, G. W., & HOWARD, R. B. (1973). Personal space. *Psychological Bulletin, 80*, 334–344.

EVANS, G. W., & JACOBS, S. (1981). Air pollution and human behavior. *Journal of Social Issues*, 95–125.

EXNER, J. (1974). *The Rorschach: A comprehensive system*. New York: Wiley.

EXNER, J. (1986a). *The Rorschach: A comprehensive system* (2nd ed.), Vol. 1. New York: Wiley.

EXNER, J. (1986b). Some Rorschach data comparing schizophrenics with borderline and schizotypal personality disorders. *Journal of Personality Assessment, 50*(3), 455–471.

EXNER, J. (1990). *A Rorschach workbook for the comprehensive system*. Asheville, NC: Rorschach Workshops.

EXNER, J., THOMAS, E., & MASON, B. (1985). Children's Rorschachs: Description and prediction. *Journal of Personality Assessment, 49*(1), 13–21.

EYSENCK, H. J. (1952). The effects of psychotherapy: An evaluation. *Journal of Consulting Psychology, 16*, 319–324.

EYSENCK, H. J. (1971). *The IQ argument: Race, intelligence, and education*. La Salle, IL: Open Court.

EYSENCK, H. J. (1979). The conditioning model of neurosis. *Communications in Behavioral Biology, 2*, 155–199.

EYSENCK, H. J. (1981). *A model for personality*. New York: Springer.

EYSENCK, H. J. (1986). Personality and social behavior. In A. Furnham (Ed.), *Social behavior in context*. Newton, MA: Allyn & Bacon.

FABBRI, A., JANNINI, E. A., GNESSI, L., & MORETTI, C. (1989). Endorphins in male impotence for naltrexone stimulation of erectile activity in patient therapy. *Psychoneuroendocrinology, 14*, 103–111.

FAIRBANK, J. A., & NICHOLSON, R. A. (1987). Theoretical and empirical issues in the treatment of post-traumatic stress disorder in Vietnam veterans. *Journal of Clinical Psychology, 43*, 44–55.

FAIRBORN, C., & COOPER, P. (1982). Self-induced vomiting and bulimia nervosa: An undetected problem. *British Medical Journal, 284*, 1153–1155.

FAIRWEATHER, G., SANDERS, D., MAYNARD, H., CRESLER, D., & BLECK, D. (1969). *Community life for the mentally ill: An alternative to institutional care*. Chicago: Aldine.

FANTZ, R. L. (1963). Patterns of vision in newborn infants. *Science, 140*, 296–297.

FARBER, S. (1981). *Identical twins reared apart: A reanalysis*. New York: Basic.

FARINA, A., GHLIA, D., BOUDREAU, L. A., ALLEN, J. G., & SHERMAN, M. (1971). Mental illness and the impact of believing others know about it. *Journal of Abnormal Psychology, 77*, 1–5.

FARIS, R. E. L., & DUNHAM, H. W. (1939). *Mental disorders in urban areas: An ecological study of schizophrenia and other psychoses*. Chicago: University of Chicago Press.

FARKAS, T., WOLF, A. P., JAEGER, S., BRODIE, J. D., Christman, D. R., & Fowler, J. S. (1984). Regional brain glucose metabolism in chronic schizophrenia: A position emission transaxial tomographic study. *Archives of General Psychiatry, 41*, 293–300.

FARRAN, D. C., & RAMEY, C. T. (1977). Infant day care and attachment behaviors toward mothers and teachers. *Child Development, 48*, 1112–1116.

FAZIO, R., & ZANNA, M. (1981). Direct experience and attitude-behavior consistency. In L. Berkowitz, *Advances in Experimental Social Psychology* (Vol. 14). New York: Academic.

FEAGIN, J. R. (1984). *Racial and ethnic relations* (2nd ed.). Englewood Cliffs, NJ: Prentice-Hall.

FEATHER, N. T. (1975). Reactions to male and female success and failure in sex-linked occupations: Impressions of personality, causal attributions, and perceived likelihood of different consequences. *Journal of Personality and Social Psychology, 31*, 20–31.

FEDERAL BUREAU OF INVESTIGATION. (1983). *Uniform crime reports*. Washington, DC: U.S. Government Printing Office.

FEINGOLD, A. (1990a). Gender differences in effects of physical attractiveness on romantic attraction: A comparison across five research paradigms. *Journal of Personality and Social Psychology, 59*, 981–993.

FEINGOLD, A. (1990b). Good looking people are not what we think. Unpublished manuscript. Yale University, New Haven, CT.

FELDMAN, J. A., & BALLARD, D. H. (1982). Connectionist models and their properties. *Cognitive Psychology, 6*, 205–254.

FELDMAN, M. W., & LEWONTIN, R. C. (1975). The heritability hang-up. *Science, 190*, 1163–1168.

FELSON, R. B. (1989). Parents and the reflected appraisal process. A longitudinal analysis. *Journal of Personality and Social Psychology, 57*, 965–971.

FENIGSTEIN, A. (1984). Self-consciousness and the overperception of self as a target. *Journal of Personality and Social Psychology, 47*, 860–870.

FENIGSTEIN, A., SCHERER, M., & BUSS, A. H. (1975). Public and private self-consciousness: Assessment and theory. *Journal of Consulting and Clinical Psychology, 43*, 522–524.

FERGUSON, M. (1973). *The brain revolution: The frontiers of mind research*. New York: Taplinger.

FERRELL, R. (1980). *Off the record*. New York: Harper & Row.

FERRERO, G. (1911). *Criminal man according to the classification of Cesare Lombroso*. New York: Putnam's.

FESTINGER, L. (1954). A theory of social comparison processes. *Human Relations, 7*, 117–140.

FESTINGER, L. (1957). *A theory of cognitive dissonance*. Stanford, CA: Stanford University Press.

FESTINGER, L., & CARLSMITH, M. (1959). Cognitive consequences of forced compliance. *Journal of Abnormal and Social Psychology, 58*, 203–210.

FESTINGER, L., SCHACHTER, S., & BACK, K. (1950). *Social pressures in informal groups: A study of a housing community*. Stanford, CA: Stanford University Press.

FIEDLER, F. E. (1971). *Leadership*. New York: General Learning Press.

FIEDLER, F. E. (1973). The trouble with leadership training is that it doesn't train leaders. *Psychology Today, 21*, 23–30.

FIEDLER, F. E. (1978). The contingency model and the dynamics of the leadership process. In L. Berkowitz (Ed.), *Advances in experimental social psychology* (Vol. 2). New York: Academic.

FINK, M. (1978). Myths of "shock therapy" *American Journal of Psychiatry, 134*, 991–996.

FINKE, R. A. (1989). *Principles of mental imagery*. Cambridge, MA: M.I.T. Press.

FINUCCI, J. M., & CHILDS, B. (1981). Are there really more dyslexic boys than girls? In A. Ansara, N. Geschwind, A. Galabuda, M. Albert, & N. Gartrell (Eds.), *Sex differences in dyslexia*. Townson, MD: The Orton Dyslexia Society.

FISHBEIN, M. (1974). Attitudes towards objects as predictions of single and multiple behavioral criteria. *Psychological Review, 81*, 59–74.

FISHBEIN, M., & AZJEN, I. (1975). *Belief, attitude, intention, and behavior: An introduction to theory and research*. Reading, MA: Addison-Wesley.

FISHER, A. E. (1962). Effects of stimulus variation on sexual satiation in the male rat. *Journal of Comparative and Physiological Psychology, 55,* 614–620.

FISHER, D. F., & PETERS, C. W. (1981). Comprehension and the competent reader. New York: Praeger.

FISHER, J., & BYRNE, D. (1975). Too close for comfort: Sex differences in response to invasions of personal space. *Journal of Personality and Social Psychology, 32,* 15–21.

FISHER, J., NADLER, A., & WHITCHER, S. (1980). *Recipient reactions to aid: A conceptual review and a new theoretical framework.* Unpublished manuscript, University of Connecticut, Storrs.

FISHER, J. D., BELL, P., & BAUM, A. (1984). *Environmental psychology* (2nd ed.). New York: Holt, Rinehart, and Winston.

FISKE, S. (1987). People's reaction to nuclear war: Implications for psychologists. *American Psychologist, 42,* 207–217.

FISKE, S., & TAYLOR, S. (1984). *Social cognition.* Reading, MA: Addison-Wesley.

FITZSIMONS, J. (1973). Some historical perspectives in the physiology of thirst. In A. Epstein et al. (Eds.), *The neuropsychology of thirst.* Washington, DC: V. H. Winston.

FLAHERTY, C. F. (1982). Incentive contrast; A review of behavioral changes following shifts in reward. *Animal Learning and Behavior, 10,* 404–440.

FLEMING, I., BAUM, A., & WEISS, L. (1987). Social density and perceived control as mediators of crowding stress in high-density residential neighborhoods. *Journal of Personality and Social Psychology, 52,* 899–906.

FLOWERS, M. L. (1977). A lab test of some implications of Janis' groupthink hypothesis. *Journal of Personality and Social Psychology, 35,* 888–897.

FOLKARD, S., HUME, K. I., MINORS, D. S., WATERHOUSE, J. M., & WATSON, F. L. (1985). Independence of the circadian rhythm in alertness from the sleep/wake cycle. *Nature, 313,* 678–679.

FORGAS, J., BURNHAM, D., & TRIMBOLI, C. (1988). Mood, memory and social judgements in children. *Journal of Personality and Social Psychology, 54,* 697–703.

FORSYTH, D. (1990). *An introduction to group dynamics,* 2nd ed. Pacific Grove, CA: Brooks/Cole.

FORSYTH, D. R. (1983). *An introduction to group dynamics.* Monterey, CA: Brooks/Cole.

FORSYTHE, J. (1986, July). Stolen moments. *Psychology Today,* pp. 16–17.

FOWLER, R. D. (1990). Psychology: The core discipline. *American Psychologist, 45,* 1–6.

FOX, S. G., & WALTERS, H. A. (1986). The impact of general versus specific expert testimony and eyewitness confidence upon mock juror judgment. *Law and Human Behavior, 10,* 215–228.

FOX, W. F. (1967). Human performance in the cold. *Human Factors, 9,* 203–220.

FOZARD, J. L., WOLF, E., BELL, B., McFARLAND, R. A., & PODOLSKY, S. (1977). Visual perception and communication. In J. E. Birren & K. W. Schaie (Eds.), *Handbook of the psychology of aging.* New York: Van Nostrand.

FRAIBERG, S. (Ed.). (1980). *Clinical studies in infant mental health.* New York: Basic.

FRALEY, L. E., & VARGAS, E. A. (1986). Separate disciplines: The study of behavior and the study of the psyche. *Behavior Analyst, 9,* 47–59.

FRANK, R. G., UMLAUF, R. L., WONDERLICH, S. A., & ASHKANAZI, G. S. (1986). Hypnosis and behavioral treatment in a worksite smoking cessation program. *Addictive Behaviors, 11,* 59–62.

FRANKE, K. J., & DURLAK, J. A. (1990). Impact of life factors on attitudes toward

death. *Omega Journal of Death and Dying, 21,* 41–49.

FRANKEL, A. J. (1984). *Four therapies integrated: A behavioral analysis of Gestalt, T. A., and ego psychology.* Englewood Cliffs, NJ: Prentice-Hall.

FRANKENBURG, W. K., & DODDS, J. B. (1967). The Denver developmental screening test. *Journal of Pediatrics, 71,* 181–191.

FRANKLIN, R. (1982). *Human motivation.* Monterey, CA: Brooks/Cole.

FRASER, S., GOUGE, C., & BILLIG, M. (1971). Risky shifts, cautious shifts and group polarization. *European Journal of Social Psychology, 1,* 7–29.

FRAWLEY, P. J., & SMITH, J. W. (1990). Chemical aversion therapy in the treatment of cocaine dependence as part of a multimodal treatment program: Treatment outcome. *Journal of Substance Abuse Treatment, 7,* 21–29.

FREDERICK, C. J. (1978). Current trends in suicidal behavior in the United States. *American Journal of Psychotherapy, 32(2),* 172–200.

FREDERIKSEN, C. H. (1975). Effects of context-induced processing operations on semantic information acquired from discourse. *Cognitive Psychology, 1,* 139–166.

FREDERIKSEN, C. H. (1975). Representing logical and semantic structures of knowledge acquired from discourse. *Cognitive Psychology, 1,* 371–458.

FREEDMAN, D. X. (1986). Hallucinogenic drug research—if so, so what? *Pharmacology, Biochemistry, and Behavior, 24,* 407–415.

FREEDMAN, J., & FRASER, S. (1966). Compliance without pressure: The foot-in-the-door technique. *Journal of Personality and Social Psychology, 4,* 195–202.

FREEDMAN, J., HESHKA, S., & LEVY, A. (1975). Population density and pathology: Is there a relationship? *Journal of Experimental Social Psychology, 11,* 539–552.

FREEDMAN, J., KLEVANSKY, S., & EHRLICH, P. (1971). The effect of crowding on human task performance. *Journal of Applied Social Psychology, 1,* 7–25.

FREEDMAN, J. L., & DOOB, A. N. (1968). *Deviancy.* New York: Academic.

FREMER, J. J., DIAMOND, E. E., & CAMARA, W. J. (1989). Developing a code of fair testing practices in education. *American Psychologist, 44,* 1062–1067.

FRENCH, E. G. (1958). Effects of interaction of motivation and feedback on task performance. In J. W. Atkinson (Ed.), *Motives in fantasy, action, and society.* New York: Van Nostrand.

FRENCH, J. R., & RAVEN, B. H. (1959). The basis of social power. In D. Cartright (Ed.), *Studies in social power.* Ann Arbor: University of Michigan Press.

FREUD, S. (1900). *The interpretation of dreams,* Vols. IV, V. London: Hogarth Press (standard edition, 1953).

FREUD, S. (1933). *New introductory lectures on psycho-analysis.* New York: Norton.

FREUD, S. (1955). *Beyond the pleasure principle.* The standard edition (Vol. 18). London: Hogarth. (Originally published in 1920.)

FREY, D., IRLE, M., & HOCHGURTEL, G. (1979). Performance of an unpleasant task: Effects of over- vs. under-payment on perception of adequacy of rewards and task attractiveness. *Journal of Experimental Social Psychology, 15,* 275–284.

FRIED, P. A., & WATKINSON, B. (1990). 36- and 48-month neurobehavioral follow-up of children prenatally exposed to marijuana, cigarettes, and alcohol. *Journal of Development and Behavioral Pediatrics, 11,* 49–58.

FRIEDMAN, H. S., & BOOTH-KEWLEY, S. (1987). The "disease-prone personality": A meta-analytic view of the construct. *American Psychologist, 42,* 539–555.

FRIEDMAN, L. (1981). How affiliation affects stress in fear and anxiety situations. *Journal of Personality and Social Psychology, 40,* 1102–1117.

FRIEDMAN, M., & ROSENMAN, R. H. (1974). *Type A behavior and your heart.* New York: Knopf.

FRIER, R. C. (1989). PCP: A relook at the chemistry, intoxication, psychosis, and treatment. *Psychiatric Forum, 14,* 52–57.

FRIEZE, I., PARSONS, J. E., JOHNSON, P. B., RUBLE, D. N., & ZELLMAN, G. L. (1978). *Women and sex roles: A social psychological perspective.* New York: Norton.

FRIMAN, P. C., & LEIBOWITZ, J. M. (1990). An effective and acceptable treatment alternative for chronic thumb- and finger-sucking. *Journal of Pediatric Psychology, 15,* 57–65.

FROMM, E. (1955). *Man for himself.* New York: Holt, Rinehart, and Winston.

FROMM, E. (1956). *The art of loving.* New York: Harper & Row.

FRONE, M., & McFARLIN, D. (1989). Chronic occupational stressors, self-focused attention, and well-being: Testing a cybernetic model of stress. *Journal of Applied Psychology, 74,* 876–883.

FUCCI, D., ELLIS, L., & PETROSINA, L. (1990). Speech clarity/intelligibility: Test-retest reliability of magnitude estimation scaling. *Perceptual and Motor Skills, 70,* 232–234.

FUERST, M. (1991, May). An STD primer. *American Health: Fitness of Body and Mind,* 45–46.

FURUMOTO, L. (1980). Mary Whiton Calkins (1863–1930). *Psychologist Women Quarterly, 5,* 55–68.

FURUMOTO, L., & SCARBOROUGH, E. (1986). Placing women in the history of psychology: The first American women psychologists. *American Psychologist, 41,* 35–42.

GADDIS, T. E. (1955). *Birdman of Alcatraz.* New York: Random.

GALANTER, E. (1962). Contemporary psychophysics. In R. Brown et al. (Eds.), *New directions in psychology.* New York: Holt, Rinehart and Winston.

GALIZIO, M., & HENDRICK, C. (1972). Effect of musical accompaniment on attitude: The guitar as a prop for persuasion. *Journal of Applied Social Psychology, 2,* 350–359.

GALLUP, G. G., JR. (1982). *Adventures in immortality.* New York: McGraw-Hill.

GALTON, F. (1879). Psychometric experiments. *Brain, 2,* 149–162.

GANELLEN, R., & BLANEY, P. (1984). Hardiness and social support as moderators of the effects of life stress. *Journal of Personality and Social Psychology, 47,* 156–163.

GANGULI, H. C. (1985). Meditation subculture and drug use. *Human Relations, 38,* 953–962.

GARCIA, J., & KOELLING, R. A. (1966). Relation of cues to consequences in avoidance learning. *Psychonomic Science, 4,* 123–124.

GARCIA, P., & MIGUEL, A. (1989). Visual inhomogeneity and eye movements in multistable perception. *Perception and Psychophysics, 16,* 397–400.

GARDNER, B. T., & GARDNER, R. A. (1975). Evidence for sentence constituents in the early utterances of child and chimpanzee. *Journal of Experimental Psychology: General, 104,* 244–267.

GARDNER, H. (1983). *Frames of mind: The theory of multiple intelligences.* New York: Basic Books.

GARDNER, R. A., & GARDNER, B. T. (1969). Teaching sign language to a chimpanzee. *Science, 165,* 664–672.

GARFIELD, S. L., & BERGIN, A. E. (Eds.). (1978). *Handbook of psychotherapy and behavior change* (2nd ed.). New York: Wiley.

GARNER, W. (1970). Good patterns have few alternatives. *American Scientist, 58,* 34–42.

GARRO, L. C. (1986). Language, memory,

and focality: A reexamination. *American Anthropologist, 88*, 128–136.

GARVIN, C. (1987). *Contemporary group work* (2nd ed.). Englewood Cliffs, NJ: Prentice Hall.

GASH, D. M., COLLIER, T. J., & SLADEK, J. R., Jr. (1985). Neural transplantation: A review of recent developments and potential applications to the aged brain. *Neurobiology of Aging, 6*, 131–150.

GATCHEL, R. (1980). Perceived control: A review and evaluation of therapeutic implications. In A. Baum & J. Singer (Eds.), *Advances in environmental psychology*. Hillsdale, NJ: Erlbaum.

GATCHEL, R., & BAUM, A. (1983). *Introduction to health psychology*. Reading, MA: Addison-Wesley.

GEBHARD, A. (1972). Incidence of overt homosexuality in the United States and Western Europe. In J. M. Livingood (Ed.), *National Institute of Mental Health task force on homosexuality: Final report and background papers*. Rockville, MD: National Institute of Mental Health.

GEEN, R. (1987). Exposure to explicit sexual material and sexual assault: A review of behavioral and social science research. In M. Walsh (Ed.). *The psychology of women: Ongoing debates*. New Haven, CT: Yale University Press.

GEEN, R. (1990). *Human aggression*. Monterey, CA: Brooks/Cole

GEEN, R. (1991). Social motivation. *Annual Review of Psychology, 42*, 377–400.

GEEN, R. G., BEATTY, W., & ARKIN, R. (1984). *Human motivation: Physiological, behavioral, and social approaches*. Boston: Allyn & Bacon.

GEEN, R. G., & BUSHMAN, B. J. (1987). Drive theory: Effects of socially engendered arousal. In B. Mullen & G. R. Goethals (Eds.), *Theories of groups behavior*. New York: Springer-Verlag.

GEEN, R. G., & QUANTY, M. (1977). The catharsis of aggression: An evaluation of a hypothesis. In L. Berkowitz (Ed.), *Advances in experimental social psychology* (Vol. 10). New York: Academic.

GEER, J., & BROUSSARD, D. (1990). Scaling heterosexual behavior and arousal: Consistency and sex differences. *Journal of Personality and Social Psychology, 58*, 664–671.

GEER, J., HEIMAN, J., & LEITTENBERG, H. (1984). *Human sexuality*. Englewood Cliffs, NJ: Prentice-Hall.

GEHRINGER, W. L., & ENGEL, E. (1986). Effect of ecological viewing conditions on the Ames' distorted room illusion. *Journal of Experimental Psychology: Human Perception and Performance, 12*, 181–185.

GEISELMAN, E. R., FISHER, R. P., MacKINNON, D. P., & HOLLAND, H. L. (1985). Eyewitness memory enhancement in the police interview: Cognitive retrieval mnemonics versus hypnosis. *Journal of Applied Psychology, 70*, 410–412.

GELDARD, F. A. (1972). *The human senses*. New York: Wiley.

GELENBERG, A. J. (1979). The rational use of psychotropic drugs: Prescribing antidepressants. *Drug Therapy, 9*, 95–112.

GELLER, S. H., ENDLER, N. S., & WIESENTHAL, D. L. (1973). Conformity as a function of task generalization and relative competence. *European Journal of Social Psychology, 3*, 53–62.

GEOFFROY, M., SCHEEL-KRUGER, J, & CHRISTENSEN, A. V. (1990). Effect of imipramine in the "learned helplessness" model of depression in rats is not mimicked by combinations of specific uptake inhibitors and scopolamine. *Psychopharmacology, 101*, 371–375.

GEORGE, R., & CHRISTIANI, T. (1981). *Theory, methods, and process of counseling and psychology*. Englewood Cliffs, NJ: Prentice-Hall.

GERARD, H. B., WILHELMY, R. A., & CONNELLY, E. S. (1968). Conformity and group size. *Journal of Personality and Social Psychology, 8*, 79–82.

GERBNER, G., & GROSS, L. (1976). The scary world of TV's heavy viewer. *Psychology Today, 24*, 41–45.

GERGEN, A. E. (1971). The evaluation of therapeutic outcomes. In A. E. Bergin & S. L. Garfield (Eds.), *Handbook of psychotherapy and behavior change: An empirical analysis*. New York: Wiley.

GERGEN, K. (1971). *The concept of self*. New York: Holt, Rinehart, and Winston.

GERGEN, K., & GERGEN, M. (1971). International assistance from a psychological perspective. *Yearbook of world affairs* (Vol. 25). London: Institute of World Affairs.

GERSON, K. (1986, November). Briefcase, baby or both. *Psychology Today*, pp. 30–36.

GESCHEIDER, G. A., BOLANOWSKI, S. J., VERRILLA, R. T., & ARPAJIAN, D. J. (1990). Vibrotactile intensity discrimination measured by three methods. *Journal of the Acoustical Society of America, 87*, 330–338.

GESCHWIND, N. (1979). Specializations of the human brain. *Scientific American, 241*, 180–199.

GEWIRTZ, J. L. (1965). The course of infant smiling in four child-rearing environments in Israel. In B. M. Foss (Ed.), *Determinants of infant behavior* (Vol. 3). London: Methuen.

GEWIRTZ, J. L., & BAER, D. M. (1958). The effect of brief social deprivation on behaviors for a social reinforcer. *Journal of Abnormal Social Psychology*, 165–172.

GIANOULAKIS, C., BELIVEAU, D., ANGELOGIANNI, P., & MEANEY, M. (1989). Different pituitary b-endorphin and adrenal cortisol response to ethanol in individuals with high and low risk for future development of alcoholism. *Life Sciences, 45*, 1097–1109.

GIBBS, M. (1982). Identification and classification of child psychopathology. In J. Lachenmeger & M. Gibbs (Eds.), *Psychopathology in childhood*. New York: Gardner.

GIBSON, J. J. (1957). Optical motions and transformation as stimuli for visual perception. *Psychological Review, 64*, 288–295.

GIBSON, J. J. (1979). *The ecological approach to visual perception*. Boston: Houghton Mifflin.

GIFFORD, R. (1987). *Environmental psychology: Principles and practice*. Boston: Allyn & Bacon.

GILBERT, D. T., & JONES, E. E. (1988). Perceiver-induced constraint: Interpretations of self-generated reality. *Journal of Personality and Social Psychology, 50*, 269–280.

GILBERT, D. T., JONES, E. E., & PELHAM, B. (1987). Influence and interference: What the active perceiver overlooks. *Journal of Personality and Social Psychology, 52*, 861–870.

GILBERT, L. C. (1986). Chessplayers: Gender, myth and psychological research. Paper presented to the American Psychological Association-convention.

GILBERT, W., & VILLA-KOMAROFF, L. (1980). Useful proteins from recombinant bacteria. *Scientific American, 242*, 74–94.

GILCHRIST, A. (1975). *Perceived achromatic color as a function of ratios within phenomenal planes*. Unpublished doctoral dissertation. Rutgers University.

GILCHRIST, A. L. (1988). Lightness contrast and failures of constancy: A common explanation. *Perception and Psychophysics, 43*, 415–421.

GILCHRIST, A. L., & JACOBSEN, A. (1989). Qualitative relationships are decisive. *Perception and Psychophysics, 15*, 92–94.

GILLAM, B. (1980). Geometrical illusions. *Scientific American, 242*, 102–111.

GILLBERG, C., TERENIUS, L., & LONNERHOLM, G. (1985). Endorphin activity in childhood psychosis: Spinal fluid levels in 24 cases. *Archives of General Psychiatry, 42*, 780–783.

GILLIGAN, J. (1976). Beyond morality: Psychoanalytic reflections on shame, guilt, and love. In T. Pickona (Ed.), *Moral development and behavior theory, research, and social issues*. New York: Holt, Rinehart and Winston.

GILLILAND, B., JAMES, R., ROBERTS, G., & BOWMAN, J. (1984). *Theories and strategies in counseling and psychotherapy*. Englewood Cliffs, NJ: Prentice-Hall.

GILLIN, J. C., & BYERLEY, W. F. (1990). The diagnosis and management of insomnia. *New England Journal of Medicine, 322*, 239–248.

GILLIN, J. D., KAPLAN, J., STILLMAN, R., & WYATT, R. J. (1976). The psychedelic model of schizophrenia: The case of N,N-dimethyltryptamine. *American Journal of Psychiatry, 133*, 203–208.

GILMORE, T. N. (1988). *Making a leadership change*. San Francisco: Jossey Bass.

GINSBERG, H., POLLMAN, V., WAUSM, M., & HOPE, M. (1977). Variation of aggressive interaction among male elementary school children as a function of changes in social density. *Environmental Psychology and Nonverbal Behavior, 2*, 67–75.

GINTER, G., & LINDSKOLD, S. (1975). Rate of participation and expertise as factors influencing leader choice. *Journal of Personality and Social Psychology, 32*, 1085–1089.

GIRDANO, D., & IVERLY, G. (1987). *Controlling stress and tension* (2nd ed.). Englewood Cliffs, NJ: Prentice Hall.

GLASS, A. L. (1984). Effect of memory set in reaction time. In J. L. Anderson & S. M. Kosslyn (Eds.), *Tutorials in reading and memory*. San Francisco: Freeman.

GLASS, D. C. (1977). *Behavior patterns, stress, and coronary disease*. Hillsdale, NJ: Erlbaum.

GLASS, D. C., & SINGER, J. (1972). *Urban stress: Experiments on noise and social stressors*. New York: Academic.

GLASS, D. C., SINGER, J. E., & PENNEBAKER, J. (1977). Behavioral and physiological effects of uncontrollable environmental events. In D. Stokols (Ed.), *Perspectives on Environment and Behavior, 5*, 131–149.

GLASS, D. C., SNYDER, M. L., & HOLLIS, J. F. (1974). Time urgency and the type A coronary-prone behavior pattern. *Journal of Applied Social Psychology, 4*, 125–140.

GLASS, G., & KLIEGL, R. (1983). An apology for research integration in the study of psychotherapy. *Journal of Counseling and Clinical Psychology, 51*, 28–41.

GLASS, J. C., & TRENT, C. (1981, March/April). Changing students' attitudes toward older persons. *The Social Studies*, pp. 72–76.

GLASS, L. KIRSCH, M., & PARRIS, F. (1977). Psychiatric disturbance associated with Erhard Seminars Training: I. A report of cases. *American Journal of Psychiatry, 134*, 245–247.

GLASSMAN, E. (1974). Macromolecules and behavior: A commentary. In F. O. Schmitt & F. G. Worden (Eds.), *The neurosciences: Third study program*. Cambridge, MA: MIT Press.

GLENN, M. D. (1975). Psychological well-being in the post-parental stage: Some evidence from national surveys. *Journal of Marriage and the Family, 32*, 105–110.

GLICK, I. O., WEISS, R. S., & PARKES, C. M. (1974). *The first year of bereavement*. New York: Wiley.

GLUCKSBERG, S., & WEISBERG, R. W. (1966). Verbal behavior and problem solving: Some effects of labelling in a functional fixedness problem. *Journal of Experimental Psychology, 71,* 659–664.

GOETHELS, G. R. (1984, August). *Social comparison theory: Psychology from the lost found.* Presented at the American Psychology Association, Toronto.

GOETHELS, G. R. (1986). Fabricating and ignoring social reality: Self-serving estimates of consensus. In J. Olson, C. Herman, & M. Zanna (Eds.), *Relative deprivation and social comparison: The Ontario Symposium* (Vol. 4). Hillsdale, NJ: Erlbaum.

GOETHALS, G. R., & DARLEY, J. M. (1977). Social comparison theory: An attributional approach. In J. M. Suls & R. L. Miller (Eds.), *Social comparison processes: Theoretical and empirical perspectives.* Washington, DC: Hemisphere/Halsted.

GOETHALS, G. R., MESSICK, D. M., & ALLISON, S. T. (1990). The uniqueness bias: Studies of constructive social comparison. In J. Suls & T. A. Wills (Eds.), *Social comparison: Contemporary theory and research.* Hillsdale, NJ: Erlbaum.

GOETHALS, G. R., & NELSON, R. (1973). Similarity in the influence process: The belief-value distinction. *Journal of Personality and Social Psychology, 25,* 117–122.

GOETHALS, G. R., & WORCHEL, S. (1981). *Adjustment and human relations.* New York: Knopf.

GOETHALS, G., & ZANNA, M. (1979). The role of social comparison in choice shifts. *Journal of Personality and Social Psychology, 37,* 1469–1476.

GOLD, J., RYCKMAN, R., & MOSKY, N. (1984). Romantic mood induction and attraction to a dissimilar other: Is love blind? *Personality and Social Psychology Bulletin, 10,* 358–368.

GOLD, P. E., & MCGAUGH, J. L. (1975). A single-trace, two-process view of memory storage processes. In P. Deutsch & J. A. Deutsch (Eds.), *Short-term memory.* New York: Academic.

GOLD, P. E., & MCGAUGH, J. L. (1977). Hormones and memory. In L. H. Miller, C. A. Sandman, & A. J. Kastin (Eds.), *Neuropeptide influences on the brain and behavior.* New York: Raven.

GOLDBAND, S. (1980). Stimulus specificity of physiological response to stress and the Type A coronary-prone behavior pattern. *Journal of Personality and Social Psychology, 39,* 670–679.

GOLDBERG, P. A. (1968). Are women prejudiced against women? *Trans-action, 5,* 28–30.

GOLDEN, K. M. (1977). Voodoo in Africa and the United States. *American Journal of Psychiatry, 134,* 1425–1427.

GOLDENSOHN, S. S. (1986). Psychoanalytic economics in the coming generation. *Journal of the American Academy of Psychoanalysis, 14,* 433–458.

GOLDFIELD, E. C. (1989). Transition from rocking to crawling: Postural constraints on infant movement. *Developmental Psychology, 25,* 913–919.

GOLDFRIED, M. R., & DAVISON, G. C. (1976). *Clinical behavior therapy.* New York: Holt, Rinehart and Winston.

GOLDMAN, J., & OLCZAK, P. (1976). Psychosocial maturity and interpersonal attraction. *Journal of Research in Personality, 10,* 146–154.

GOLDMAN, R., JAFFA, M., & SCHACHTER, S. (1968). Yom Kippur, Air France, dormitory food, and the eating behavior of obese and normal persons. *Journal of Personality and Social Psychology, 10,* 117–123.

GOLDSTEIN, J., & BASKIN, D. (1988). Sex differences in daydreaming behavior. *Journal of Mental Imagery, 12,* 83–90.

GOLDSTEIN, M. J. (1959). The relationship between coping and avoiding behavior and response to fear-arousing propaganda. *Journal of Abnormal and Social Psychology, 58,* 247–252.

GOLEMBIEWSKI, R., & BLUMBURG, A. (1973). *Sensitivity training and the laboratory approach.* Itasca, IL: Peacock.

GOLLEDGE, R. G. (1987). Environmental cognition. In D. Stokols & I. Altman (Eds.) *Handbook of environmental psychology, Vol 1.* New York: Wiley Interscience.

GOMEZ, J., & DALLY, P. (1980). Psychometric ratings in assessment of progress in anorexia nervosa. *British Journal of Psychiatry, 136,* 290–296.

GOODMAN, G. S., & REED, R. S. (1986). Age differences in eyewitness testimony. *Law and Human Behavior, 10,* 317–332.

GOODWIN, D. W. (1979). Alcoholism and heredity. *Archives of General Psychiatry, 36,* 57–61.

GOODMAN, W. K., ET AL. (1990). Specificity of serotonin reuptake inhibitors in the treatment of obsessive-compulsive disorders. *Archives of General Psychiatry, 47,* 577–585.

GORDON, S., & SCALES, P. (1977). The myth of the normal sexual outlet. *Journal of Pediatric Psychology, 2,* 101–103.

GORDON-SALANT, S. (1986). Effects of aging on response criteria in speech-recognition tasks. *Journal of Speech and Hearing Research, 29,* 155–162.

GORENSTEIN, E. (1982). Frontal lobe functions in psychopaths. *Journal of Abnormal Psychology, 91,* 368–379.

GORELICK, D. A., & WILKINS, J. N. (1989). Inpatient treatment of PCP abusers and users. *American Journal of Drug and Alcohol Abuse, 15,* 1–12.

GOTTESMAN, I. I., & SHIELDS, J. (1972). *Schizophrenia and genetics: A twin study vantage point.* New York: Academic.

GOTTLIEB, B. H. (1983). Social support as a focus for integrative research in psychology. *American Psychologist, 38,* 278–288.

GOUZOULES, S., GOUZOULES, H., & MARLES, P. (1984). Rhesus monkey (Macaca mulatta) screams: Representational signalling in the recruitment of agonistic aid. *Animal Behavior, 32,* 182–193.

GRAEN, G., ALVARES, K., ORRIS, J., & MARTELLA, J. (1970). Contingency model of leadership effectiveness: Antecedent and evidential results. *Psychology Bulletin, 74,* 284–296.

GRAFMAN, J., SALAZAR, A., WEINGARTNER, H., VANCE, S., & AMIN, D. (1986). The relationship of brain-tissue loss volume and lesion location to cognitive deficit. *Journal of Neuroscience, 6,* 301–307.

GRAHAM, E. S., & KABACY, R. E. (1990). Expert testimony by psychologists: Novel scientific evidence. *Law and Psychology Review, 14,* 71–85.

GRAHAM, K. G., & ROBINSON, H. A. (1984). *Study skills handbook: A guide for all teachers.* ERIC Clearinghouse on Reading and Communication Skill. Urbana, IL: International Reading Association.

GRAHAM, S. (1974). The sociological approach to epidemiology. *American Journal of Public Health, 64,* 1046–1049.

GRASSIAN, S., & FRIEDMAN, N. (1986). Effects of sensory deprivation in psychiatric seclusion and solitary confinement. *International Journal of Law and Psychiatry, 8,* 49–65.

GRAUMANN, C. F. (1988). Introduction to a history of social psychology. In M. Hewstone, W. Stroebe, J. Codol, & G. M. Stephenson (Eds.), *Introduction to social psychology,* Oxford, England: Basil Blackwell.

GRAY, J. (1971). *The psychology of fear and stress.* New York: McGraw-Hill.

GREEN, D., MILLER, N., & GERARD, V. (1975). Personality traits and adjustment. In H. Gerard & N. Miller (Eds.), *School desegregation: A long-range study.* New York: Plenum.

GREEN, D. M., & SWETS, J. A. (1966). *Signal detection theory and psychophysics.* New York: John Wiley.

GREENE, E., WILSON, L., & LOFTUS, E. F. (1989). Impact of hypnotic testimony on the jury. *Law and Human Behavior, 13,* 61–78.

GREENBERG, D. J., & O'DONNELL, W. J. (1972). Infancy and the optional level of stimulation. *Child Development, 43,* 639–645.

GREENBERG, M. A. (1980). A theory of indebtedness. In K. Gergen, M. Greenberg, & R. Willis (Eds.), *Social exchange: Advances in theory and research.* New York: Plenum.

GREENOUGH, W. T. (1984). Structural correlates of information storage in the mammalian brain: A review and hypothesis. *Trends in Neurosciences, 7,* 229–233.

GREGG, C., CLIFTON, R. K., & HAITH, M. M. (1976). A possible explanation for the frequent failure to find cardiac orienting in the newborn infant. *Developmental Psychology, 12,* 75–76.

GREYSON, B., & FLYNN, C. P. (Eds.). (1984). *The near-death experience.* Springfield, IL: Chas. C Thomas.

GRICE, H. P. (1975). Logic and conversation. In G. Harman & D. Davidson (Eds.), *The logic of grammar.* Encino, CA: Dickinson.

GRIFFIN, R. W. (1988). Consequences of quality in an industrial setting: A longitudinal assessment. *Academy of Management Journal, 31,* 338–358.

GRIFFITH, W. (1970). Environmental effects on interpersonal affective behavior: Ambient effective temperature and attraction. *Journal of Personality and Social Psychology, 15,* 240–244.

GRIFFITH, W., & VEITCH, R. (1971). Hot and crowded: Influence of population density and temperature on interpersonal affective behavior. *Journal of Personality and Social Psychology, 17,* 92–98.

GRIM, R., KOHLBERG, L., & WHITE, S. (1968). Some relationships between conscience and attentional processes. *Journal of Personality and Social Psychology, 8,* 239–253.

GRIMES, J. D., & SWISHER, J. D. (1989). Educational factors influencing adolescent decision making regarding use of alcohol and drugs. *Journal of Alcohol and Drug Education, 35,* 1–15.

GRIMES, J. F. (1972). *The thread of discourse.* The Hague: Mouton.

GRINKER, J. (1982). Physiological and behavioral basis of human obesity. In D. Pfaff (Ed.), *The physiological mechanisms of motivation.* New York: Springer-Verlag.

GROOME, D. (1986). Cognitive science and behaviorism. *Bulletin of the British Psychological Society, 39,* 18.

GROSSBERG, S., & LEVINE, D. S. (1987). Neural dynamics of attentionally modulated Pavlovian conditioning: Blocking, inter-stimulus interval and secondary reinforcement. *Applied Optics.*

GROTH, A. N., & BIRNBAUM, H. J. (1979). *Men who rape: The psychology of the offender.* New York: Plenum Press.

GROTH-MARNAT, G., & SCHUMAKER, J. F. (1990). Hypnotizability, attitudes toward eating, and concern with body size in a female college population. *American Journal of Clinical Hypnosis, 32,* 194–200.

GRUDER, C. L., COOK, T., HENNIGAN, K., FLAY, B., ALLESI, C., & HALAMAJ, J. (1978). Empirical tests of the absolute sleeper effect predicted from the discounting cue hypothesis. *Journal of Personality and Social Psychology, 36,* 1061–1074.

GRUEN, G. E., OFFENBACH, S. I., & KEANE, T. (1986). Hypothesis testing on a proportional reasoning task by children at different Piagetian stage levels. *International Journal of Behavioral Development, 9,* 91–104.

GUENTHER, R. (1982, August 4). Ways are

found to minimize pollutants in airtight houses. *Wall Street Journal*, p. 25.

GUEST, L. (1948). The public's attitude toward psychologists. *American Psychologist, 3*, 135–139.

GUILFORD, J. P. (1967). *The nature of human intelligence.* New York: McGraw-Hill.

GUILLEMINAULT, C., & DEMENT, W. C. (1977). Amnesia and disorders of excessive daytime sleepiness. In R. R. Drucher-Colin & J. L. McGaugh (Eds.), *Neurobiology of sleep and memory.* New York: Academic.

GUPTA, R, STRINGER, B., & MEAKIN, A. (1990). A study to access the effectiveness of Home-Based Reinforcement in a secondary school: Some preliminary findings. Special Issue: Disruption and discipline in schools. *Educational Psychology in Practice, 5*, 197–200.

GURMAN, A. S. (1977). Therapist and patient factors influencing the patient's perception of facilitative therapeutic conditions. *Psychiatry, 40*, 218–231.

GUSTAVSON, C. R., GARCIA, J., HANKINS, W. G., & RUSINIAK, K. W. (1974). Coyote predation control by aversive conditioning. *Science, 184*, 581–583.

GYNTHER, M., & GREEN, S. (1980). Accuracy may make a difference, but does difference make for accuracy? A response to Prichard and Rosenblatt. *Journal of Consulting and Clinical Psychology, 48*, 268–272.

HABER, E. A. & SHORT-DeGRAFF, M. A. (1990). Intergenerational programming for an increasingly age-segregated society. *Activities, Adoption, and Aging, 14*, 35–49.

HABER, R. N. (1969). Eidetic images. *Scientific American, 220*, 36–55.

HACKMAN, J. R. (1987). The design of work teams. In J. W. Lorsch (Ed.), *Handbook of organization behavior* (pp. 315–342). Englewood Cliffs, NJ: Prentice Hall.

HACKMAN, J. R. (1990). Work teams in organizations: An orienting framework. In J. R. Hackman (Ed.), *Groups that work (and those that don't).* San Francisco: Jossey Bass.

HAGESTAD, G. O. (1980). *Role change and socialization in adulthood: The transition to the empty nest.* Unpublished manuscript, The Pennsylvania State University.

HAITH, M. M., & CAMPOS, J. J. (1977). Human infancy. *Annual Review of Psychology, 28*, 251–293.

HAITH, M. M. & McCARTY, M. E. (1990). Stability of visual expectations at 3.0 months of age. *Developmental Psychology, 26*, 68–74.

HALBERSTADT, A. (1986). Family, socialization of emotional expression and nonverbal communication styles and skills. *Journal of Personality and Social Psychology, 51*, 827–836.

HALEY, J. (1980). *Leaving home: The therapy of disturbed young people.* New York: McGraw-Hill.

HALFORD, G. S., & BOYLE, F. M. (1985). Do young children understand conservation of number? *Child Development, 56*, 165–176.

HALL, C. (1966). *The meaning of dreams.* New York: McGraw-Hill.

HALL, C., & LINDZEY, G. (1978). *Theories of personality* (3rd ed.). New York: Wiley.

HALL, E. T. (1959). *The silent language.* New York: Fawcett.

HALL, E. T. (1966). *The hidden dimension.* New York: Doubleday.

HALL, J. A. (1982). The use of dreams and dream interpretation. In M. Stein (Ed.), *Jungian analysis.* LaSalle, IL: Open Court.

HALL, J. F. (1983). Recall versus recognition: A methodological note. *Journal of Experimental Psychology: Learning, Memory, and Cognition, 9*, 346–349.

HALLAGAN, J. B., HALLAGAN, L. F., & SNY-

DER, M. B. (1989). Anabolic-androgenic steroid use by athletes. *New England Journal of Medicine, 321*, 1042–1045.

HALLIDAY, M. A. K. (1973). *Explorations in the functions of language.* London: Edward Arnold.

HALPERN, D. F. (1986). *Sex differences in cognitive abilities.* Hillsdale, NJ: Erlbaum.

HALPERN, D. L., BLAKE, R., & HILLENBRAND, J. (1986). Psychoacoustics of a chilling sound. *Perception & Psychophysics, 39*, 77–80.

HAMBURG, D., ELLIOTT, G., & PARRON, D. (EDS.). (1982). *Health and behavior: Frontiers of research in the biomedical sciences.* Washington, DC: National Academy Press.

HAMILTON, D., & TROILER, T. (1986). Stereotypes and stereotyping: An overview of the cognitive approach. In J. Dovidio & S. Gaertner (Eds.), *Prejudice, discrimination, and racism.* New York: Academic.

HAMILTON, J. O. (1974). Motivation and risk-taking behavior: A test of Atkinson's theory. *Journal of Personality and Social Psychology, 29*, 856–864.

HAMILTON, S. (1981). Adolescents in community settings: What is to be learned? *Theory and Research in Social Education, 9*, 23–38.

HAMMEN, C. L., & PETERS, S. D. (1977). Differential responses to male and female depressive reactions. *Journal of Consulting and Clinical Psychology, 45*, 994–1001.

HANES, B., PRAWAT, R. S., & GRISSOM, S. (1979). Sex-role perceptions during adolescence. *Journal of Educational Psychology, 71*, 850–855.

HANSEL, C. E. M. (1980). *ESP and parapsychology: A critical re-evaluation.* New York: Prometheus.

HARDIN, G. (1969). The tragedy of the commons. *Science, 162*, 1243–1248.

HARE, R. (1978). Electrodermal and cardiovascular correlates of sociopathy. In R. Hare & D. Schalling (Eds.), *Psychopathic behavior: Approaches to research.* New York: Wiley.

HARE, R. D. (1983). Diagnosis of antisocial personality disorder in two prison populations. *American Journal of Psychiatry, 140*, 887–890.

HARKINS, S. (1987). Social loafing and social facilitation. *Journal of Experimental Social Psychology, 23*, 1–18.

HARKINS, S., & PETTY, R. E. (1981). Effects of source magnification of cognitive effort in attitudes: An information-processing view. *Journal of Personality and Social Psychology, 40*, 401–413.

HARKINS, S., & SZYMANSKI, (1987). Social loafing and social facilitation: New wine in old bottles. *Review of Personality and Social Psychology, 9*, 167–188.

HARLOW, H. F. (1971). *Learning to love.* San Francisco: Albion.

HARKINS, S. G. & SZYMANSKI, K. (1989). Social loafing and group evolution. *Journal of Personality and Social Psychology, 56*, 934–941.

HARLOW, H. F., HARLOW, M. K., & MEYER, D. R. (1950). Learning motivated by a manipulation drive. *Journal of Experimental Psychology, 40*, 228–234.

HARLOW, H. F., & SUOMI, S. J. (1970). Nature of love simplified. *American Psychologist, 25*, 161–168.

HARLOW, H. F., & ZIMMERMAN, R. R. (1959). Affectional responses in the infant monkey. *Science, 130*, 421–432.

HARMON, L. D. (1973, November). The recognition of faces. *Scientific American*, pp. 32–38.

HARRELL, G. (1986). *Consumer behavior.* Orlando, FL: Harcourt Brace Jovanovich.

HARRIMAN, A. (1955). The effect of preoperative preference for sugar over salt upon

compensatory salt selection by adrenalectomized rats. *Journal of Nutrition, 57*, 271–276.

HARRINGTON, D. M., BLOCK, J. H., & BLOCK, J. (1987). Testing aspects of Carl Rogers's theory of creative environments: Child-rearing antecedents of creative potential in young adolescents. *Journal of Personality and Social Psychology, 52*, 851–856.

HARRIS, D. B. (1957). Problems in formulating a scientific concept of development. In D. B. Harris (Ed.), *The concept of development.* Minneapolis: University of Minnesota Press.

HARRIS, M. J., & ROSENTHAL, R. (1985). Mediation of interpersonal expectancy effects: 31 metanalyses. *Psychological Bulletin, 97*, 363–386.

HART, R. (1970). The concept of APS: Air Pollution Syndrome(s). *Journal of South Carolina Medical Association, 66*, 71–73.

HARTSHORNE, H., & MAY, M. A. (1928). *Studies in the nature of character* (Vol. 1). *Studies in deceit.* New York: Macmillan.

HASDORF, A. H., OSGOOD, D. E., & ONO, Y. (1966). The semantics of facial expressions and the prediction of the meanings of stereoscopically fused facial expressions. *Scandinavian Journal of Psychology, 7*, 179–188.

HASHIM, S. A., & VAN ITALLIE, T. B. (1965). Studies in normal and obese subjects with a monitored food dispensary device. *Annals of the New York Academy of Science, 131*, 654–661.

HASTIE, R. (1986). Notes on the psychologist expert witness. [Special Issue: The ethics of expert testimony], *Law and Human Behavior, 10*, 79–82.

HATCH, O. G. (1982, September). Psychology, society, and politics. *American Psychologist*, pp. 1031–1037.

HATFIELD, E., & SPRECHER, S. (1986). *Mirror, mirror . . . the importance of looks in everyday life.* Albany, NY: State University of New York Press.

HATHAWAY, S. R., & McKINLEY, J. (1942). A multiphasic personality schedule (Minnesota): III. The measurement of symptomatic depression. *Journal of Psychology, 14*, 73–84.

HATHAWAY, S. R., & McKINLEY, J. C. (1943). *MMPI Manual.* New York: Psychological Corporation.

HAWKINS, R. D., & KANDEL, E. R. (1984). Is there a cell-biological alphabet for simple forms of learning? *Psychological Review, 91*, 375–391.

HAY, D. F., MURRAY, P., CECIRE, S., & NASH, A. (1985). Social learning of social behavior in early life. *Child Development, 56*, 43–57.

HAYS, L. R., LITTLETON, S., & STILLNER V. (1990). Anabolic steroid dependence. *American Journal of Psychiatry, 147*, 122.

HAYDUK, L. (1983). Personal space: Where we now stand. *Psychological Bulletin, 94*, 293–335.

HAYES, C., & HAYES, K. (1951). *The ape in our house.* New York: Harper & Row.

HAZAN, C., & SHAVER, P. (1987). Romantic love conceptualized as an attachment process. *Journal of Personality and Social Psychology, 52*, 511–524.

HEATHERTON, T., HERMAN, P., & POLIVY, J. (1991). Effects of physical threat and ego threat on eating behavior. *Journal of Personality and Social Psychology, 60*, 138–143.

HEBB, D. O. (1955). Drives and the C. N. S. (conceptual nervous system). *Psychological Review, 62*, 243–254.

HEBERLEIN, T. A., & BLACK, J. S. (1976). Attitudinal specificity and the prediction of behavior in a field setting. *Journal of Personality and Social Psychology, 33*, 474–479.

HECKEL, R. V., & HIERS, J. M. (1977). Social

distance and locus of control. *Journal of Clinical Psychology, 33,* 469–471.

HEDL, J. J., & BARTLETT, J. C. (1989). Test anxiety, sentence comprehension, and recognition memory. *Anxiety Research, 1,* 269–278.

HEIDER, F. (1946). Attitudes and cognitive organization. *Journal of Personality, 21,* 107–112.

HEILBRUN, K. (1990). Response style, situation, third-party information, and competency to stand trial: Research issues in practice. *Law and Human Behavior, 14,* 193–196.

HEILMAN, M., & STOPECK, M. (1985). Being attractive, advantage or disadvantage? Performance-based evaluations and recommended personal actions as a fraction of appearance, sex, and job type. *Organizational Behavior and Human Decision Processes, 35,* 202–215.

HEINEMANN, E. G. (1989). Brightness contrast, brightness constancy, and the ratio principle. *Perception and Psychophysics, 15,* 89–91.

HELLER, J., GOFF, B., & SOLOMON, S. (1977). Toward an understanding of sounding: The role of physical instruction. *Journal of Personality and Social Psychology, 35,* 183–190.

HELLER, K., & MONAHAN, J. (1977). *Psychology and community change.* Homewood, IL: Dorsey.

HELLER, J. I., & GREENE, J. G. (1979). Information processing analysis of mathematical problem solving. Paper presented at the Applied Problem Solving Conference, Evanston, IL.

HELMREICH, R., SPENCE, J., & PRED, R. (1988). Making it without losing it: Type A, achievement motivation and scientific attainment revisited. *Personality and Social Psychology Bulletin, 14,* 495–504.

HELMS, D. B., & TURNER, J. S. (1981). *Exploring child behavior.* New York: Holt, Rinehart and Winston.

HELZER, J. E. (1987). Epidemiology of alcoholism. *Journal of Consulting and Clinical Psychology, 55,* 284–292.

HENDRICK, C., & HENDRICK, S. (1983). *Liking, loving and relating.* Monterey, CA: Brooks/Cole.

HENNING, M., & JARDIN, A. (1976). *The managerial woman.* New York: Doubleday.

HERBERT, W. (1983). Remembrance of things partly. *Science News, 124,* 378–381.

HEREK, G. M. (1986). The instrumentality of attitudes: Towards a neofunctional theory. *Journal of Social Issues, 428,* 99–104.

HERGENHAN, B. (1980). *An introduction to theories of personality.* Englewood Cliffs, NJ: Prentice-Hall.

HERING, E., *Zur lehre vom lichtsinne,* 1878.

HERMAN, B. H., HAMMOCK, M. K., ARTHUR-SMITH, A., EGAN, J., CHATOOR, I., ZELNICK, N., CARRADINE, K., APPELGATE, K., BOECKS, & SHARP, S. D. (1986, November). Role of opioid peptides in autism: Effects of acute administration of naltrexone. *Society for Neuroscience Abstracts.*

HERMAN, L. M., RICHARDS, D. G., & WOLZ, J. P. (1984). Comprehension of sentences by bottlenosed dolphins. *Cognition, 16,* 129–219.

HERON, W. (1961). Cognitive and physiological effects of perceptual isolation. In P. Solomon et al. (Eds.), *Sensory deprivation.* Cambridge, MA: Harvard University Press.

HERRNSTEIN, R. J. (1973). *IQ in the meritocracy.* Boston: Atlantic Monthly Press.

HERRNSTEIN, R. J. (1979). Acquisition, generalization, and discrimination reversal of a natural concept. *Journal of Experimental Psychology: Animal Behavior Processes, 5,* 116–129.

HERRNSTEIN, R. J. (1984). Objects, categories, and discriminative stimuli. In H. L.

Roitblat, T. G. Bever, & H. S. Terrace (Eds.), *Animal cognition.* Hillsdale, NJ: Erlbaum.

HERRNSTEIN, R. J., & DEVILLIERS, P. A. (1980). Fish as a natural category for people and pigeons. In G. H. Bower (Ed.), *The psychology of learning and motivation* (Vol. 14). New York: Academic.

HERSCH, P. (1991, May). Teen epidemic. *American Health: Fitness of Body and Mind,* 42–45.

HERSKOVIC, J. E., KIETZMAN, M. L., & SUTTON, S. (1986). Visual flocker in depression: Response criteria, confidence ratings and response times. *Psychological Medicine, 16,* 187–197.

HERTZMAN, M., REBA, R. C., & KOTLYAROV, E. V. (1990). Single photon emission computed tomography in phencyclidine and related drug abuse. *American Journal of Psychiatry, 147,* 255–256.

HERZOG, D. (1982). Bulimia: The secretive syndrome. *Psychosomatics, 23,* 481–483.

HESS, E. H. (1958). "Imprinting" in animals. *Scientific American, 286,* 81–90.

HESS, E. H. (1965). Attitude and pupil size. *Scientific American, 212,* 46–54.

HETHERINGTON, A., & RANSON, S. (1939). Experimental hypothalamohypapyseal obesity in the rat. *Proceedings for the Society of Experimental Biology and Medicine, 41,* 465–466.

HETHERINGTON, E. M., COX, M., & COX, R. (1978). The aftermath of divorce. In J. H. Stevens, Jr. & M. Matthew (Eds.), *Mother-child, father-child relations.* Washington, DC: National Association for the Education of Young Children.

HEWSTONE, M. (1988). Attributional bases of intergroup conflict. In W. Stroebe, A. Kruglanski, D. Bar-Tal, & M. Hewstone (Eds.), *The social psychology of intergroup conflict.* New York: Springer-Verlag.

HIGHGATE, M. S., & NEUFIELD, R. W. (1986). Schizophrenic memory-search performance involving nonverbal stimulus properties. *Journal of Abnormal Psychology, 95,* 67–73.

HILAND, D. N., & DZIESZKOWSKI, M. A. (1984). Hypnosis in the investigation of aviation accidents. *Aviation, Space, and Environmental Medicine, 55,* 1136–1142.

HILGARD, E. R. (1965). *Hypnotic susceptibility.* New York: Harcourt, Brace and World.

HILGARD, E. R. (1967). A quantitative study of pain and its reduction through hypnotic suggestion. *Proceedings of the National Academy of Sciences, 57,* 1581–1586.

HILGARD, E. R. (1967). Individual differences in hypnotizability. In J. E. Gordon (Ed.), *Handbook of clinical and experimental hypnosis.* New York: Macmillan.

HILGARD, E. R. (1969a). Experimental psychology and hypnosis. In L. Chertok (Ed.), *Psychophysiological mechanisms of hypnosis.* Berlin: Springer-Verlag.

HILGARD, E. R. (1969b). Pain as a puzzle for psychology and physiology. *American Psychologist, 24,* 103–113.

HILGARD, E. R., & HILGARD, J. R. (1975). *Hypnosis in the relief of pain.* Los Altos, CA: William Kaufman.

HILL, A. L. (1978). Savants: Mentally retarded individuals with specific skills. In N. R. Ellis (Ed.), *International review of research in mental retardation* (Vol. 9). New York: Academic Press.

HILL, C. (1987). Affiliation motivation: People who need people . . . but in different ways. *Journal of Personality and Social Psychology, 52,* 1008–1018.

HINTON, G. E., & ANDERSON, J. A. (1981). *Parallel models of associative memory.* Hillsdale, NJ: Erlbaum.

HIRAI, T. (1978). *Zen and the mind: A scientific approach to Zen practice.* Scranton, PA: Japan Publications, Inc., c/o Harper & Row.

HIROTO, D. S. (1974). Locus of control and

learned helplessness. *Journal of Experimental Psychology, 102,* 187–193.

HIRSCH, E. D. (1977). *The philosophy of composition.* Chicago: University of Chicago Press.

HITE, S. (1976). *The Hite report.* New York: Macmillan.

HITE, S. (1981). *The Hite report on male sexuality.* New York: Knopf.

HITE, S. (1988). *Women and love. A cultural revolution in progress.* New York: Alfred Knopf.

HOBFOLL, S. E., & LIEBERMAN, J. R. (1987). Personality and social resources in immediate and continued stress resistance among women. *Journal of Personality and Social Psychology, 52,* 18–26.

HOBSON, J. A., & MCCARLEY, R. W. (1977). The brain as a dream state generator: An activation-synthesis hypothesis of the dream process. *American Journal of Psychiatry, 134,* 1335–1348.

HOBSON, J. A., & SCHMAJUK, N. A. (1988). Brain state and plasticity: An integration of the reciprocal interaction model of sleep cycle oscillation with attentional models of hippocampal function. *Archives Iteliennes de Biologie, 126,* 209–224.

HOBSON, J. A., HOFFMAN, S. A., HELFAND, R., & KOSTNER, D. (1987). Dream bizarreness and the activation synthesis hypothesis. *Human Neurobiology, 6,* 157–164.

HOCHBERG, J. (1970). Components of literacy: Speculations and exploration research. In H. Levin & J. P. Williams (Eds.), *Basic studies on reading.* New York: Basic.

HOCHBERG, J. E. (1978). *Perception.* Englewood Cliffs, NJ: Prentice-Hall.

HOCHREICH, D. J., & ROTTER, J. B. (1970). Have college students become less trusting? *Journal of Personality and Social Psychology, 15,* 211–214.

HOCK, E., & DEMEIS, D. (1990). Depression in mothers of infants: The role of maternal employment. *Developmental Psychology, 86,* 285–291.

HODGKINS, J. (1962). Influence of age on the speed of reaction and movement in females. *Journal of Gerontology, 17,* 385–389.

HOEBEL, B. G., & TEITELBAUM, P. (1962). Hypothalamic control of feeding and self-stimulation. *Science, 61,* 189–193.

HOFFERTH, S. L., & PHILLIPS, D. A. (1987). Child care in the United States, 1970–1995. *Journal of Marriage and the Family, 49,* 559–571.

HOFFMAN, L. W. (1984). Maternal employment and the young child. In M. Perlmutter (Ed.), *Parent-child interaction and parent-child relations in child development. Minnesota Symposia on Child Psychology, Vol. 17.* Hillsdale, NJ: Erlbaum.

HOFFMAN, L. W., & NYE, F. I. (1974). *Working mothers.* San Francisco: Jossey-Bass.

HOFFMAN, M. L. (1979, May/June). Empathy, guilt and social cognition. Paper presented at the Ninth Annual Symposium of the Jean Piaget Society, Philadelphia.

HOFFMAN, M. L. (1980). Moral development in adolescence. In J. Adelson (Ed.), *Handbook of adolescent psychology.* New York: Wiley.

HOFFMAN, M. L. (1984). Parent discipline, moral internalization and development of prosocial motivation. In E. Staub et al. (Eds.). *Development and maintenance of prosocial behavior.* New York: Plenum.

HOFLING, C. K. (1975). *Textbook of psychiatry for medical practice* (3rd ed.). Philadelphia: Lippincott.

HOFLING, C. K., BROTZMAN, E., DALRYMPLE, S., GRAVES, N., & PIERCE, C. M. (1966). An experimental study in nurse-physician relationships. *The Journal of Nervous and Mental Disease, 143*(2), 171–180.

HOGAN, R., & SCHROEDER, D. (1981, July).

Seven biases in psychology. *Psychology Today*, pp. 8–14.

HOGAN, T. P., & HENDRICKSON, E. (1984). The study habits of adult college students. *Lifelong Learning, 8*, 7–10.

HOKANSON, J. E., & SHELTERS, S. (1961). The effect of overt aggression on physiological arousal level. *Journal of Abnormal and Social Psychology, 63*, 446–448.

HOKANSON, J. E., BURGESS, M., & COHEN, M. (1963). Effect of displaced aggression on systolic blood pressure. *Journal of Abnormal and Social Psychology, 67*, 214–218.

HOLAHAN, C. J. (1980). Action research in the guilt environment. In R. Price & P. Politser (Eds.), *Evolution and action in the social environment.* New York: Academic.

HOLAHAN, C. J. (1982). *Environmental psychology.* New York: Random.

HOLDEN, C. (1972). Nader on mental health centers: A movement that got bogged down. *Science, 177*, 413–415.

HOLDEN, C. (1975). Lie detectors: PSE gains audience despite critics' doubt. *Science, 190*, 359–362.

HOLDEN, C. (1989). Street-wise research. *Science, 246*, 1376–1381.

HOLLANDER, E. P. (1958). Conformity status and idiosyncrasy credit. *Psychological Review, 65*, 117–127.

HOLLANDER, E. P. (1978). *Leadership dynamics.* New York: Free Press.

HOLLANDER, E. P. (1985). Leadership and power. In G. Lindzey & E. Aronson (Eds.), *Handbook of social psychology* (3rd ed.), Vol. 2. New York: Random House.

HOLLANDER, E. P., & JULIAN, J. W. (1978). A further look at leader legitimacy, influence, and innovation. In L. Berkowitz (Ed.), *Group process.* New York: Academic.

HOLLINGSHEAD, A. B., & REDLICH, F. C. (1958). *Social class and mental illness, a community study.* New York: Wiley.

HOLMES, D. S. (1974). Investigations of repression: Differential recall of material experimentally or naturally associated with ego threat. *Psychological Bulletin, 81*, 632–653.

HOLMES, D., FROST, R., & LUTZ, D. (1981). Multiple sessions of systolic blood pressure biofeedback: Its effects on ability to control systolic pressure during training, after training, and its effects on pulse rate. *Journal of Research in Personality, 15*, 30–44.

HOLMES, T., & MASUDA, M. (1974). Life change and illness susceptibility. In B. Dohrenwend & B. Dohrenwend (Eds.), *Stressful life events: Their nature and effects.* New York: Wiley.

HOLMES, T. H., & RAHE, R. H. (1967). The social readjustment rating scale. *Journal of Psychosomatic Research, 11*, 213–218.

HOLROYD, K. A., HOLM, J. E., HURSEY, K. G., PENZIEN, D. B., CORDINGLEY, G. E., THEOFANOUS, A. G., RICHARDSON, S. C., & TOBIN, D. L. (1988). Treatment of recurrent vascular headache: A comparison of a home-based behavioral treatment with an abortive pharmacological intervention. *Journal of Consulting and Clinical Psychology, 56*, 218–223.

HOLROYD, K. A., HOLM, J. E., PENZIEN, D. B., CORDINGLEY, G. E., HURSEY, K. G., THEOFANOUS, A. G., & MARTIN, N. (1989). Long-term maintenance of improvements achieved with (abortive) pharmacological and nonpharmacological treatments for migraine: Preliminary findings. *Biofeedback and Self-Regulation, 14*, 301–308.

HOLT, A. (1931). *Animal drive and the learning process, an essay toward radical empiricism* (Vol. I). New York: Holt.

HOLT, R. R. (1986). Clinical and statistical prediction: A retrospective and would-be integrative perspective. *Journal of Personality Assessment, 50*, 376–386.

HOLTGRAVES, T., SRULL, T. K., & SOCALL, D. (1989). Conversation memory: The effects of speaker status on memory for the assertiveness of conversation remarks. *Journal of Personality and Social Psychology, 56*, 149–160.

HOLTZMAN, W. (1975). New developments in Holtzman inkblot techniques. In P. McReynolds (Ed.), *Advances in Psychological assessment* (Vol. 3). San Francisco: Jossey-Bass.

HOMANS, G. (1974). *Social behavior in its elementary forms* (rev. ed.). New York: Harcourt Brace Jovanovich.

HONIGFELD, G. (1964). Non-specific factors in treatment. I. Review of placebo reactions and placebo reactors. *Diseases of the Nervous System, 25*, 145–156.

HOOK, E. B. (1973). Behavioral implications of the human XYY genotype. *Science, 179*, 131–150.

HOPS, H., BIGLAN, A., SHERMAN, L., ARTHUR, J., FRIEDMAN, L., & OSTEEN, V. (1987). Home observations of family interactions of depressed women. *Journal of Consulting and Clinical Psychology, 55*, 341–346.

HORN, J. L. (1978). Human ability systems. In P. B. Baltes (Ed.), *Life-span development and behavior* (Vol. 1). New York: Academic.

HORN, J. L., & DONALDSON, G. (1980). Cognitive development II: Adulthood development of human abilities. In O. G. Brim, Jr. & J. Kagan (Eds.), *Constancy and change in human development: A volume of review essays.* Cambridge, MA: Harvard University Press.

HORN, J. M., LOEHLIN, J. C., & WILLERMAN, L. (1979). Intellectual resemblance among adoptive and biological relatives: The Texas adoption project. *Behavior Genetics, 9*, 177–208.

HORNE, J. A., & MINARD, A. (1985). Sleep and sleepiness following a behaviorally active day. *Ergonomics, 28*, 567–575.

HORNER, M. S. (1968). *Sex differences in achievement motivation in competitive and non-competitive situations.* Unpublished doctoral dissertation, University of Michigan.

HORNER, M. S. (1970). *Feminine personality and conflict.* Monterey, CA: Brooks/Cole.

HORNESTEIN, H. A., & MOSLEY, J. L. (1987). Iconic memory deficit of mildly mentally retarded individuals. *American Journal of Mental Deficiency, 91*, 415–421.

HORNEY, K. (1937). *The neurotic personality of our time.* New York: Norton.

HOROWITZ, M. J., DUFF, D. F., & STRATTON, L. O. (1964, December). *Archives of general psychiatry* (Vol. II). Washington, DC: American Medical Association.

HORTON, D. L., & TURNAGE, T. W. (1976). *Human learning.* Englewood Cliffs, NJ: Prentice-Hall.

HORTON, R. W. (1973). An empirical investigation of variation in students' premarital sex standards and behavior. *Dissertation Abstracts International, 34*, 1385–1386.

HOVDA, D. A., & VILLEBLENCE, J. R. (1989). Depth perception in cats after cerebral hemispherectomy: Comparisons between neonatal and adult lesioned animals. *Behavioral Brain Research, 32*, 231–240.

HOVEY, S. R., & BERKRAM, G. M. (1990). Needs and research related to the grieving spouse. *Pastoral Psychology, 38*, 213–217.

HOVIS, J. K., & GUTH, S. L. (1989). Changes in luminance affect dichotic unique yellow. Annual Meeting of the Association for Research in Vision and Ophthalmology. *Journal of the Optical Society of America, 6*, 1297–1301.

HOVLAND, C. I., LUMSDAINE, A., & SHEFFIELD, F. (1949). *Experiments on mass communication.* Princeton, NJ: Princeton University Press.

HOVLAND, C. I., & WEISS, W. (1952). The influence of source credibility on communication effectiveness. *The Public Opinion Quarterly, 15*, 635–650.

HOWARD, D. (1972). *Territory in bird life.* New York: Dutton.

HOWARD, G. S. (1991). Culture tales: A narrative approach to thinking, cross-cultural psychology, and psychotherapy. *American Psychologist, 46*, 187–197.

HOWELLS, L., & BECKER, S. (1962). Seating arrangement and leadership emergence. *Journal of Abnormal and Social Psychology, 64*, 148–150.

HOYENGA, K. B., & HOYENGA, R. T. (1988). *Psychobiology: The neuron and behavior.* Pacific Grove, CA: Brooks/Cole.

HUBA, G. J., NEWCOMB, M. D., BENTLER, P. M. (1986). Adverse drug experiences and drug use behaviors: A one-year longitudinal study of adolescents. *Journal of Pediatric Psychology, 11*, 203–219.

HUBEL, D. H. (1982). Explorations of the primary visual cortex. *Nature, 229*, 515–524.

HUBEL, D. H., & WIESEL, T. N. (1965). Receptive fields and functional architecture in two nonstriate visual areas (18 and 19) of the cat. *Journal of Neurophysiology, 28*, 229–289.

HUBEL, D. H., & WIESEL, T. N. (1970). The period of susceptibility to the physiological effects of unilateral eye closure in kittens. *Journal of Physiology, 206*, 419–436.

HUBER, R., & GIBSON, J. W. (1990). New evidence for anticipatory grief. *Hospice Journal, 6*, 49–67.

HUBER, V. L. (1986). The interplay of goals and promises of pay-for-performance on individual and group performance: An operant interpretation. *Journal of Organizational Behavior Management, 7*, 45–64.

HUDLOW, H. (1984, March). Fatigue and long-distance flying. *Business and Commercial Aviation*, 19–21.

HUGHES, J. (1975). Isolation of an endogenous compound from the brain with pharmacological properties similar to morphine. *Brain Research, 88*, 295–308.

HUGHES, J. N., & BAER, D. B. (1991). *The clinical child interview.* New York: Guildford Press.

HUGHES, J., SMITH, T. W., KOSTERLITZ, H. W., FOTHERGILL, L. A., MORGAN, B. A., & MORRIS, H. R. (1975). Identification of two related pentapeptides from the brain with potent opiate agonist activity. *Nature, 258*, 577–579.

HULICKA, I. M., & GROSSMAN, J. L. (1967). Age-group comparisons for the use of mediators in paired associate learning. *Journal of Gerontology, 22*, 46–51.

HULL, C. L. (1943). *Principles of behavior: An introduction to behavior theory.* New York: Appleton-Century-Crofts.

HULL, C. L. (1951). *Essentials of behavior.* New Haven, CT: Yale University Press.

HULTSCH, D. F. (1971). Adult age differences in free classification and free recall. *Developmental Psychology, 4*, 338–342.

HULTSCH, D. F., & DEUTSCH, F. (1981). *Adult development and aging.* New York: McGraw-Hill.

HUMPHREY, G. K., DODWELL, P. C., MUIR, D. W., & HUMPHREY, D. E. (1988). Can blind infants and children use sonar sensory aids? Special Issue: Child development: When things go wrong. *Canadian Journal of Psychology, 42*, 84–119.

HUNT, M. (1974). *Sexual behavior in the 1970s.* Chicago: Playboy Press.

HUNT, M. (1982). *The universe within.* New York: Simon & Schuster.

HUNTER, F., & ASH, P. (1973). The accuracy and consistency of polygraph examiner's diagnoses. *Journal of Police Science and Administration, 1*, 370–375.

HUNTER, F., & YOUNISS, J. (1982). Changes

in functions of three relationships during adolescence. *Developmental Psychology, 18,* 806–811.

HURT, H. (1975). The hottest place in the whole U.S.A. *Texans Monthly, 3,* 50ff.

HURVICH, L. M., & JAMESON, D. (1974). Opponent processes as a model of neural organization. *American Psychologist, 29,* 88–102.

HUSBAND, R. W. (1940). Cooperation versus solitary problem solution. *Journal of Social Psychology, 11,* 405–409.

HUTCHINGS, D. E. (1990). Issues of risk assessment: Lessons from the use and abuse of drugs during pregnancy. Special Issue: Qualitative and quantitative comparability of human and animal developmental neurotoxicity. *Neurotoxicology and Teratology, 12,* 183–189.

HUXLEY, A. D. (1952). *The doors of perception.* New York: Harper & Row.

HYDE, C. (1986). Ethics, religion, and sexuality. In J. S. Hyde, (Ed.), *Understanding human sexuality.* New York: McGraw-Hill.

HYDE, H. J. (1990, April 30). The culture war. *National Review,* p. 27.

HYDE, J. S. (1986). *Understanding human sexuality* (3rd ed.). New York: McGraw-Hill.

HYDE, J. S., & LINN, M. C. (1988). Gender differences in verbal ability: A meta-analysis. *Psychological Bulletin, 104,* 53–69.

HYGGE, S., & ÖHMAN, S. (1978). Modeling processes in the acquisition of fears: Vicarious electrodermal conditioning to fear-relevant stimuli. *Journal of Personality and Social Psychology, 36,* 271–279.

HYMAN, R. (1977). The case against parapsychology. *The Humanist, 37,* 47–49.

INGRAM, J. A. (1984–1985). Differential diagnosis: The schizophrenic disorders and the hallucinogens. *Psychiatric Forum, 13,* 47–56.

ISAACSON, R. L. (1970, March). When brains are damaged. *Psychology Today,* pp. 38–42.

ISCOE, I. (1982). Toward a viable community health psychology: Caveats from the experiences of the community mental health movement. *American Psychologist, 37,* 961–965.

ISEN, A. (1970). Success, failure, attention, and reaction to others: The warm glow of success. *Journal of Personality and Social Psychology, 15,* 294–301.

ISEN, A., DAUBMAN, K., & NOWICKI, G. (1987). Position affect facilitates creative problem solving. *Journal of Personality and Social Psychology, 52,* 112–113.

ISING, H., & MELCHERT, H. (1980). Endocrine and cardiovascular effects of noise. *Proceedings of the Third International Congress. ASHA Report No. 10.*

ITTLESON, W. H., PROSHANSKY, H. M., RIVLIN, L. G., & WINKEL, G. (1974). An introduction to environmental psychology. New York: Holt, Rinehart and Winston.

IVERSON, I. H. (1986). Time allocation, sequential, and kinematic analyses of behaviors controlled by aperiodic reinforcement schedule. *Psychological Record, 36,* 239–255.

IVEY, A., & SIMEK-DOWNING, L. (1980). *Counseling and psychology.* Englewood Cliffs, NJ: Prentice-Hall.

IZARD, C. (1990). The substrate and function of emotion feeling: William James and current theory. *Personality and Social Psychology Bulletin, 16,* 625–635.

IZARD, C. E. (1977). *Human emotions.* New York: Plenum.

IZARD, C. E. (1981). Differential emotions theory and the facial feedback hypothesis of emotion activation: Comments in Tourajeau and Ellsworth's "The role of facial response in the experience of emotion." *Journal of Personality and Social Psychology, 40,* 350–354.

IZARD, C. E. (1982). Comments on emotion and cognition: Can there be a working relationship? In M. Clark & S. Fiske (Eds.), *Emotions and cognition.* Hillsdale, NJ: Erlbaum.

JACKSON, M. D., & MCCLELLAND, J. L. (1979). Processing determinants of reading speed. *Journal of Experimental Psychology, 108,* 151–158.

JACOBS, A. M., NAZIR, T. A., & KELLER, O. (1988). Perception of lowercase letters in peripheral vision: A discrimination matrix based on saccade latencies. *Perception and Psychophysics, 46,* 95–102.

JACOBS, G. A., QUEVILLIN, R. P., & STRICHERZ, M. (1990). Lessons from the aftermath of Flight 232: Practical considerations for mental health professions' response to air disasters. *American Psychologist, 45,* 1329–1335.

JACOBS, S., & KIM, K. (1990). Psychiatric complications of bereavement. *Psychiatric Annals, 20,* 314–317.

JACOBSEN, F. M. (1990). Waking in a lighted room. *Biological Psychiatry, 27,* 372–374.

JACOBSON, E. (1938). *Progressive relaxation,* (2nd ed.) Chicago: University of Chicago Press.

JACOBSON, J. L., & WILLE, D. E. (1986). The influence of attachment patterns on developmental changes in peer interaction from the toddler to the preschool period. *Child Development, 57,* 338–347.

JAFFE, J., PATTERSON, R., & HODGSON, R. (1980). Addictions, issues and answers. Holland: Multimedia Publications.

JAGACINSKI, C. M. (1991). Personal decision-making: The impact of missing information. *Journal of Applied Psychology, 76,* 19–30.

JAMES, R. (1959). Status and competence of jurors. *American Journal of Sociology, 64,* 563–570.

JAMES, W. (1884). What is emotion? *Mind, 19,* 188–205.

JAMES, W. (1890). *The principles of psychology.* New York: Holt.

JAMES, W. (1967). *The varieties of religious experience.* New York: Modern Library. (Originally published 1902).

JANAL, M. N., COLT, E. W., CLARK, W. C., & GLUSMAN, M. (1984). Pain sensitivity, mood and plasma endocrine levels in man following long-distance running—effects of naloxone. *Pain, 19,* 13–25.

JANIS, I. L. (1971). Groupthink. *Psychology Today, 5*(6), 43–46ff.

JANIS, I. L. (1972). *Victims of groupthink: A psychological study of foreign policy decisions and fiascoes.* Boston: Houghton Mifflin.

JANIS, I. L. (1982). *Groupthink: Psychological studies of policy decisions and fiascoes* (2nd ed.). Boston: Houghton Mifflin.

JANIS, I. L., & FESHBACH, S. (1953). Effects of fear-arousing communication. *Journal of Abnormal and Social Psychology, 48,* 78–92.

JANIS, I. L., KAYE, D., & KIRSCHNER, P. (1965). Facilitating effects of "eating-while-reading" on responsiveness to persuasive communications. *Journal of Personality and Social Psychology, 1,* 181–186.

JANOWITZ, H. D. (1967). Role of gastrointestinal tract in the regulation of food intake. In C. F. Code (Ed.), *Handbook of physiology: Alimentary canal, I.* Washington, DC: American Physiological Society, pp. 219–224.

JANOWITZ, H. D., & GROSSMAN, M. (1949). Some factors affecting the food intake of normal dogs and dogs with esophagostomy and gastric fistula. *American Journal of Physiology, 159,* 143–148.

JECKER, J., & LANDY, D. (1969). Liking a person as a function of doing him a favor. *Human Relations, 22,* 371–378.

JEFFREY, D., & KATZ, R. (1977). *Take it off and keep it off.* Englewood Cliffs, NJ: Prentice-Hall.

JELLISON, J. M., & GREEN, J. (1981). A self-presentational approach to the fundamental attribution error: The horn of internality. *Journal of Personality and Social Psychology, 40,* 643–649.

JENKINS, C. D. (1976). Recent evidence supporting psychologic and social risk factors for coronary disease. *New England Journal of Medicine, 294,* 987–994.

JENS, K., & EVANS, H. (1983). *The diagnosis and treatment of multiple personality clients.* Snowbird, UT: Rocky Mountain Psychological Association.

JENSEN, A. R. (1969). How much can we boost IQ and scholastic achievement? *Harvard Educational Review, 39,* 1–23.

JENSEN, A. R. (1973). *Educability and group differences.* New York: Harper & Row.

JEROME, E. A. (1959). Age and learning—experimental studies. In J. E. Birren (Ed.), *Handbook of aging and the individual.* Chicago: University of Chicago Press.

JERSILD, A. T., & HOLMES, F. B. (1935). Children's fears. *Child development monograph* No. 20. New York: Teacher's College, Columbia University.

JOBE, J. B., SAMPSON, J. B., ROBERTS, D. E., & KELLY, J. A. (1986). Comparison of behavioral treatments of Raynaud's disease. *Journal of Behavioral Medicine, 9,* 89–96.

JOHANSSON, G. (1976). Visual motion perception. In R. Held & W. Richards (Eds.), *Recent progress in perception.* San Francisco: Freeman.

JOHN, E. R., TANG, Y., BRILL, A. B., YOUNG, R., & ONO, K. (1986). Double-labeled metabolic maps of memory. *Science, 233,* 1167–1175.

Johns Hopkins Medical Letter (1989). Of Mice and Men, *Health After 50, 1,* 1.

Johns Hopkins Medical Letter (1990). *Health After 50, 1,* 8.

Johns Hopkins Medical Letter (1990). *Health After 50, 2,* 2.

Johns Hopkins Medical Letter (1990). Headway on migraines. *Health After 50, 2,* 1.

Johns Hopkins Medical Letter (1990). Heading off migraines. *Health After 50, 2,* 1.

JOHNSON, R. J., FEIGENBAUM, R., & WEIBY, M. (1964). Some determinants and consequences of the teacher's perception of causation. *Journal of Educational Psychology, 55,* 237–246.

JONES, A., & CRANDALL, R. (EDS.). (1991). Handbook of self-actualization [Special Issue of *Journal of Social Behavior and Personality, 6,* 5, whole issue].

JONES, E. (1957). *The life and work of Sigmund Freud* (Vol. 3). New York: Basic.

JONES, E., ROCK, L., SHAVER, K. G., GOETHALS, G. R., & WARD, L. M. (1968). Pattern of performance and ability attribution: An unexpected primacy effect. *Journal of Personality and Social Psychology, 10,* 317–340.

JONES, E., WOOD, G., & QUATTRONE, G. (1981). Perceived variability of personal characteristics in in-groups and out-groups: The role of knowledge and evaluation. *Personality and Social Psychology Bulletin, 7,* 523–528.

JONES, E., & WORTMAN, C. (1973). *Ingratiation: An attributional approach.* Morristown, NJ: General Learning Press.

JONES, E. E. (1964). *Ingratiation.* New York: Appleton-Century-Crofts.

JONES, E. E. (1985). Major developments in social psychology during the past five decades. In G. Lindzey & E. Aronson (Eds.), *Handbook of social psychology,* 3rd ed. (Vol. 1, pp. 1–46). New York: Random House.

JONES, E. E. (1990). *Interpersonal perception.* New York: W. H. Preeman.

JONES, E. E., & DAVIS, K. (1965). From acts to dispositions: The attribution process in person perception. In L. Berkowitz (Ed.), *Advances in experimental social psychology* (Vol. 2). New York: Academic.

JONES, E. E., & HARRIS, V. A. (1967). The attribution of attitudes. *Journal of Experimental Psychology, 3*, 1–24.

JONES, E. E., & McGILLIS, D. (1976). Correspondent interferences and the attribution cube: A comparative reappraisal. In J. H. Harvey, W. J. Ickes, & R. F. Kidd (Eds.), *New directions in attribution research* (Vol. 1). Hillsdale, NJ: Erlbaum.

JONES, E. E., & NISBETT, R. (1972). The actor and the observer: Divergent perceptions of the causes of behavior. In E. E. Jones, D. Kanouse, H. H. Kelley, R. E. Nisbett, S. Valins, & B. Weiner (Eds.), *Attribution: Perceiving the causes of behavior.* Morristown, NJ: General Learning Press, 79–94.

JONES, E. E., WORCHEL, S., GOETHALS, G. R., & GRUMET, J. F. (1971). Prior expectancy and behavioral extremity as determinants of attitude attribution. *Journal of Experimental Social Psychology, 7*, 59–80.

JONES, E. E., & WORTMAN, C. (1973). *Ingratiation: An attribution approach.* Morristown, NJ: General Learning Press.

JONES, H. E., & CONRAD, H. S. (1933). The growth and decline of intelligence: A study of a homogeneous group between the ages of ten and sixty. *Genetic Psychology Monographs, 13*, 223–298.

JONES, R. A., & BREHM, J. W. (1970). Persuasiveness of one and two-sided communications as a function of awareness there are two sides. *Journal of Experimental Social Psychology, 6*, 47–56.

JONES, T., & DAVEY, G. C. (1990). The effects of cued UCS rehearsal on the retention of differential "fear" conditioning: An experimental analogue of the "worry" process. *Behaviour, Research, and Therapy, 28*, 159–164.

JULESZ, B. (1971). *Foundations of cyclopean perception.* Chicago: University of Chicago Press.

JULIAN, J. W., REGULO, C. R., & HOLLANDER, E. P. (1968). Effects of prior agreement from others on task confidence and conformity. *Journal of Personality and Social Psychology, 9*, 171–178.

JUNG, C. G. (1928). *Contributions to analytical psychology.* New York: Harcourt Brace.

JUNG, J. (1969). Current practices and problems in the use of college students in psychological research. *The Canadian Psychologist, 9*, 59–66.

JUSSIM, L. (1991). Social perception and social reality: A reflection-construction model. *Psychological Review, 98*, 54–70.

KAGAN, J. (1973). What is intelligence? *Social Policy,* 88–94.

KAGAN, J. (1986). Rates of change in psychological process. *Journal of Applied Developmental Psychology, 7*, 125–130.

KAGAN, J., & FREEMAN, M. (1963). Relation of childhood intelligence, maternal behaviors, and social class to behavior during adolescence. *Child Development, 34*, 899–911.

KAGAN, J., & MOSS, H. (1962). *Birth to maturity.* New York: Wiley.

KAGAN, J., KEARSLEY, R. B., & ZELANZO, P. R. (1977). The effects of infant day care on psychological development. *Educational Quarterly, 1*, 109–142.

KAHANA, B., & KAHANA, E. (1971). Theoretical and research perspectives on grandparenthood. *Aging and Human Development, 2*, 261–268.

KAHNEMEN, D., & TVERSKY, A. (1972). Subjective probability: A judgment of representativeness. *Cognitive Psychology, 3*, 430–454.

KAHNEMAN, D., & TVERSKY, A. (1973). On the psychology of prediction. *Psychological Review, 80*, 237–251.

KALAT, J. W. (1988). *Biological psychology* (3rd ed.). Belmont, CA: Wadsworth.

KALICK, S. M., & HAMILTON, T. E. (1987). The matching hypothesis reexamined. *Journal of Personality and Social Psychology, 51*, 673–682.

KALISH, R. A., & REYNOLDS, D. K. (1976). *Death and ethnicity: A psychocultural study.* Los Angeles: University of Southern California Press.

KALLSON, F. (1946). The genetic theory of schizophrenia. *American Journal of Psychiatry, 103*, 309–322.

KALLMAN, H. J., BECKSTEAD, J. W., & CAMERON, P. A. (1988). Ipsilateral and contralateral masking of duration. *Perception and Psychophysics, 43*, 31–37.

KAMIN, L. J. (1973). Heredity, intelligence, politics and society. Invited address, Eastern Psychological Association, Washington, DC.

KAMIN, L. J. (1976). Heredity, intelligence, politics, and psychology. In N. J. Block & G. Dworkin (Eds.), *The IQ controversy.* New York: Pantheon.

KAMIN, L. J. (1979). Psychology as social science: The Jensen affair, ten years after. Presidential address, Eastern Psychological Association, Philadelphia.

KANDEL, E. R., & SCHWARTZ, J. H. (1982). Molecular biology of learning: Modulation of transmitter release. *Science, 218*, 433–443.

KANDELL, J. (1977, August 7). French rank crime high on their list of major worries. *The New York Times,* p. 13.

KANGELARI, S., ABRAMOVICH-POLYAKOV, D., & RUDENKO, V. (1966). The effects of noise and vibration on morbidity rates (Russia). *Gigiena Truda: Professional 'Nye Zabolevaniy, 6*, 47–49.

KANTOR, R. N. (1983). How inconsiderate are children's textbooks? *Journal of Curriculum Studies, 15*, 61–72.

KAPLAN, C. A., & SIMON, H. A. (1990). In search of insight. *Cognitive Psychology, 22*, 371–419.

KAPLAN, H. S. (1974). *The new sexual therapy: Actives treatment of sexual dysfunctions.* New York: Brunner-Mazel.

KAPLAN, M. (1987). The influencing process in group decision making. *Review of Personality and Social Psychology, 8*, 189–212.

KAPOULA, Z, OPTICAN, L. M., & ROBINSON, D. A. (1989). Visually induced plasticity of postsaccadic ocular drift in normal humans. *Journal of Neurophysiology, 61*, 879–891.

KARLINS, M., COFFMAN, J., & WALTERS, G. (1969). On the fading of social stereotypes: Studies in three generations of college students. *Journal of Personality and Social Psychology, 13*, 1–16.

KARLSSON, J. (1972). An Icelandic family study of schizophrenia. In A. Kaplan (Ed.), *Genetic factors in schizophrenia.* Springfield, IL: Chas. C Thomas.

KARP, D. A. (1989). The social construction of retirement among professionals 50–60 years old. *Gerontologist, 29*, 750–760.

KASHKIN, K. B., & KLEBER, H. D. (1989). Hooked on hormones? An anabolic steroid addiction hypothesis. *Journal of the American Medical Association, 262*, 3166–3170.

KASLOW, F. W. (1991). The art and science of family psychology: Retrospective and perspective. *American Psychologist, 46*, 621–626.

KATCHADOURIAN, H. A. (1977). *The biology of adolescence.* San Francisco: Freeman.

KATKOFF, L (Ed.). (1984). *Primary prevention in the work place.* New York: Haworth.

KATZ, I. (1967). The socialization of academic motivation in minority group children. In D. Levine (Ed.), *Nebraska symposium on motivation* (Vol. 15). Lincoln, NE:

University of Nebraska Press, pp. 133–191.

KATZMAN, R. (1976). The prevalence and malignancy of Alzheimer disease. *Archives of Neurology, 33*, 217–218.

KAUFMAN, B. N. (1982). *A miracle to believe in.* New York: Fawcett.

KAUFMAN, B. N. (1984). *A sense of warning.* New York: Dell.

KAY, L. (1982). *Spatial perception through an acoustic sensor.* Christchurch, New Zealand: University of Canterbury.

KAYE, K., ELKIND, L. GOLDBERG, D., & TYTUN, A. (1989). Birth outcomes for infants of drug abusing mothers. *New York State Journal of Medicine, 89*, 256–261.

KAZDIN, A. E. (1976). The rich rewards of rewards. *Psychology Today, 10*(6), 98, 101–102, 105, 114.

KEELE, S. W., & ELLS, J. G. (1972). Memory characteristics of kinesthetic information. *Journal of Motor Behavior, 4*, 127–134.

KEESEY, R., BOYLE, P., KEMNITZ, J., & MITCHELL, J. (1976). The rule of the lateral hypothalamus in determining the body weight set point. In D. Novin et al. (Eds.), *Hunger: Basic mechanisms and clinical implications.* New York: Raven.

KEESEY, R. E., & POWLEY, T. L. (1975). Hypothalamic regulation of body weight. *American Scientist, 63*, 558–565.

KEHOE, J. E., FEYER, A. M., & MOSES, J. L. (1981). Second-order conditioning of the rabbits' nictitating membrane response as a function of the CS2-CS1 and CS-1-VS intervals. *Animal Learning and Behavior, 9*, 304–315.

KEIL, W., VON STRALENDORFF, F., & HUDSON, R. (1990). A behavioral bioassay for analysis of rabbit nipple-search pheromone. *Physiology on Behavior, 47*, 526–529.

KEISER, R. E., & PRATHER, E. N. (1990). What is the TAT? A review of ten years of research. *Journal of Personality Assessment, 54*(3 and 4), 800–803.

KELLER, H. (1954). *The story of my life.* New York: Doubleday.

KELLER, M. (1981, December 2). Treatment for depression varies. In a series by Dava Sobel. *The New York Times.*

KELLEY, H. H. (1952). Two functions of reference groups. In G. E. Swanson, T. M. Newcomb, & E. L. Hartley (Eds.), *Readings in social psychology* (2nd ed.). New York: Holt.

KELLEY, H. H. (1967). Attribution theory in social psychology. In D. Levine (Ed.), *Nebraska Symposium on Motivation, 15*, 192–238.

KELLEY, H. H. (1971). *Attribution in social interaction.* Morristown, NJ: General Learning Press.

KELLEY, H. H. (1983). Love and commitment. In H. Kelley, E. Berscheid, A. Christensen, J. Harvey, T. Huston, G. Levinger, E. McClintock, L. Peplau, & D. Peterson (Eds.), *Close relationships.* New York: Freeman.

KELLOGG, T. H. (1902). The histrionic element of mental disease. *New York Medical Journal, LXXVI*, 107–110.

KELLY, D. D. (1981a). Physiology of sleep and dreaming. In E. R. Kendal & J. H. Schwartz (Eds.), *Principles of neural science.* New York: Elsevier/North Holland.

KELLY, D. D. (1981b). Disorders of sleep and consciousness. In E. R. Kendal & J. H. Schwartz (Eds.), *Principles of neural science.* New York: Elsevier/North Holland.

KELLY, E. (1954). *Clown.* Englewood Cliffs, NJ: Prentice-Hall.

KELMAN, H. C., & HAMILTON, V. L. (1989). *Crimes of obedience.* New Haven, CT: Yale University Press.

KELMAN, H. C., & HOVLAND, C. I. (1953). "Reinstatement" of the communicator in delayed measurement of opinion change.

Journal of Abnormal and Social Psychology, 48, 326–335.

KEMLER NELSON, D. G. (1984). The effect of intention on what concepts are acquired. *Journal of Verbal Learning & Verbal Behavior*, 23, 734–759.

KEMLER NELSON, D. G. (1988). When category learning is holistic: a reply to Ward & Scott. *Memory & Cognition*, 16, 79–84.

KENDLER, H. H. (1987). *Historical foundations of modern psychology*. Chicago: Dorsey.

KENDLER, K. S. (1983). Overview: A current perspective on twin studies in schizophrenia. *American Journal of Psychiatry*, 140, 1413–1425.

KENDZIERSKI, D. (1990). Exercise self-schemata: Cognitive and behavioral correlates. *Health Psychology*, 9, 69–82.

KENNY, W. R., & GROTELUESCHEN, A. D. (1984). Making the case for case study. *Journal of Curriculum Studies*, 16, 37–51.

KENRICK, D., & CIALDINI, R. (1977). Romantic attraction: Misattribution versus reinforcement explanations. *Journal of Personality and Social Psychology*, 35, 381–391.

KENRICK, D. T., GUTIERRES, S. E., & GOLDBERG, L. L. (1989). Influence of popular erotica on judgments of strangers and mates. *Journal of Experimental Social Psychology*, 25, 159–167.

KENSITON, K. (1969). The uncommitted: Alienated youth in American society. *Youth and Society*, 1, 110–127.

KENT, R., & FOSTER, S. (1977). Direct observational procedure. Methodological issues in naturalistic settings. In A. Ciminero, K. Calhoun, & H. Adams (Eds.), *Handbook of behavioral assessment*. New York: Wiley.

KERMOIAN, R., & LEIDERMAN, P. H. (1986). Infant attachment to mother and child caretaker in an East African community. [Special Issue: Cross-cultural human development.] *International Journal of Behavioral Development*, 9, 455–469.

KERNIS, M., & WHEELER, L. (1981). Beautiful friends and ugly stranger: Radiation and contrast effects in perception of same-sex pairs. *Personality and Social Psychology Bulletin*, 7, 224–231.

KERR, N., & BRUUN, S. (1981). Ringelmann revisited: Alternative explanations for the social loafing effect. *Personality and Social Psychology Bulletin*, 7, 224–231.

KESEY, K. (1962). *One flew over the cuckoo's nest*. New York: Viking.

KESSEN, W. (1965). *The child*. New York: Wiley.

KESSLER, J. W. (1988). *Psychopathology of childhood* (2nd ed.). Englewood Cliffs, NJ: Prentice Hall.

KETY, S. S., ROSENTHAL, D., WENDER, P., & SCHULSINGER, F. (1968). The type and prevalence of mental illness in the biological and adoptive families of adopted schizophrenics. In D. Rosenthal & S. S. Kety (Eds.), *The transmission of schizophrenia*. New York: Pergamon.

KEYES, R. (1980). *The height of your life*. Boston: Little, Brown.

KIESLER, C. A., & KIESLER, S. B. (1969). Group pressure and conformity. In J. Mills (Ed.), *Experimental and social psychology*. New York: Macmillan.

KIESLER, C. A., McGUIRE, T., MECHANIC, D., MOSHER, L. R., NELSON, S., NEWMAN, F., RICH, R., & SCHULBERG, H. (1983). Federal mental health policymaking: An assessment of deinstitutionalization. *American Psychologist*, 38, 1292–1297.

KIESLER, C. A., & SIMPKINS, C. (1991). The de facto national system of psychiatric inpatient care: Piecing together the national puzzle. *American Psychologist*, 46, 579–584.

KIEWRA, K. A. (1983). The process of review: A levels of processing approach. *Contemporary Educational Psychology*, 8, 366–374.

KILHAM, W., & MANN, L. (1974). Level of destructive obedience as a function of transmitter and executant roles in the Milgram obedience paradigm. *Journal of Personality and Social Psychology*, 29, 696–702.

KIMMEL, M. S. (1988, May). Ms. Scoutmaster. *Psychology Today*, pp. 64–65.

KING, D. W., & KING, L. A. (1991). Validity issues in research on Vietnam veteran adjustment. *Psychological Bulletin*, 109, 107–124.

KINGSBURG, S. J. (1987). Cognition differences between clinical psychologists and psychiatrists. *American Psychologists*, 43, 152–156.

KINSEY, A. C., POMEROY, W. B., & MARTIN, C. E. (1948). *Sexual behavior in the human male*. Philadelphia: Saunders.

KINSEY, A. C., POMEROY, W. B., MARTIN, C. E., & GEBHARD, P. H. (1953). *Sexual behavior in the human female*. Philadelphia: Saunders.

KINTSCH, W. (1974). *The representation of meaning in memory*. New York: Wiley.

KINTSCH, W., MANDEL, T. S., & KOZMINSKY, E. (1977). Summarizing scrambled stories. *Memory and Cognition*, 5, 547–552.

KINTSCH, W., & VAN DIJK, T. A. (1978). Toward a model of text comprehension and production. *Psychological Review*, 85, 363–394.

KINZEL, A. S. (1970). Body buffer zone in violent prisoners. *American Journal of Psychiatry*, 10, 263–270.

KISER, L. J., BATES, J. E., MASLIN, C. A., & BAYLES, K. (1986). Mother-infant play at six months as a predictor of attachment security at thirteen months. *Journal of the American Academy of Child Psychiatry*, 25, 68–75.

KISSILEFF, H. R. (1969). Food-associated drinking in the rat. *Journal of Comparative and Physiological Psychology*, 67, 284–300.

KITE, M. E., DEAUX, K., & MIELE, R. (1991). Stereotypes of young and old: Does age outweigh gender? *Psychology and Aging*, 6, 19–27.

KLATT, D. H., & KLATT, L. C. (1990). Analysis, synthesis, and perception of voice quality variations among female and male talkers. *Journal of the Acoustical Society of America*, 87, 820–857.

KLECK, R. E., & RUBENSTEIN, C. (1975). Physical attractiveness, perceived attitude similarity, and interpersonal attraction in an opposite-sex encounter. *Journal of Personality and Social Psychology*, 31, 107–114.

KLEINKE, C., & WALTON, J. (1982). Influence of reinforced smiling on affective responses in an interview. *Journal of Personality and Social Psychology*, 42, 557–565.

KLEINMUNTZ, B., & SZUCKO, J. (1984a). A field study of the fallibility of polygraph lie detection. *Nature*, 308, 449–450.

KLEINMUNTZ, B., & SZUCKO, J. (1984b). Lie detection in ancient and modern times. *American Psychologist*, 39, 766–776.

KLEITMAN, N. (1963). *Sleep and wakefulness*. Chicago, IL: University of Chicago Press.

KLINE, P. (1972). *Fact and Fantasy in Freudian theory*. London: Methuen.

KLINGER, E. (1987, October). The power of daydreams. *Psychology Today*, pp. 37–44.

KNITTLE, J. L. (1975). Early influences on development of adipose tissue. In G. A. Bray (Ed.), *Obesity in perspective*. Washington, DC: U.S. Government Printing Office.

KNIVETON, B. H. (1986). Peer models and classroom violence: An experimental study. *Educational Research*, 28, 111–116.

KNOWLES, E. (1982). From individuals to group members: A dialectic for the social sciences. In W. Ickes & E. Knowles (Eds.), *Personality, roles and social behavior*. New York: Springer-Verlag.

KNOWLES, E. (1983). Social physics and the effects of others: Tests of the effects of audience size and distance on social judgments and behavior. *Journal of Personality and Social Psychology*, 45, 1263–1271.

KNOX, V. J., CRUTCHFIELD, L., & HILGARD, E. R. (1975). The nature of task interference in hypnotic dissociation: An investigation of hypnotic behavior. *International Journal of Clinical and Experimental Hypnosis*, 23, 305–323.

KNOX, V. J., MORGAN, A. H., & HILGARD, E. R. (1974). Pain and suffering in ischemia: The paradox of hypnotically suggested anesthesia as contradicted by reports from the "hidden observer." *Archives of General Psychiatry*, 30, 840–847.

KOBASA, S. (1979). Stressful life events, personality, and health: An inquiry into hardiness. *Journal of Personality and Social Psychology*, 37, 1–11.

KOBASA, S. (1982). Commitment and coping in stress resistance among lawyers. *Journal of Personality and Social Psychology*, 42, 707–717.

KOBASA, S., MADDI, S., & KAHN, S. (1982). Hardiness and health: A prospective study. *Journal of Personality and Social Psychology*, 42, 168–177.

KOE, G. G. (1989). Hypnotic treatment of sleep terror disorder: A case report. *American Journal of Clinical Hypnosis*, 32, 36–40.

KOENDERINK, J. J. (1986). Optic flow. *Vision Research*, 26, 161–179.

KOHLBERG, L. (1963). The development of children's orientations toward a moral order. I. Sequence in the development of moral thought. *Vita Humana*, 6, 11–33.

KOHLBERG, L. (1978). Revisions in the theory and practice of moral development. *New Directions for Child Development*, 2, 83–88.

KOHLBERG, L., COLBY, A., GIBBS, J., & SPEICHER-DUBIN, B. (1978). *Standard form scoring manual*. Cambridge, MA: Center for Moral Education.

KOHLER, W. (1925). *The mentality of apes*. New York: Harcourt Brace Jovanovich.

KOHN, A. (1988, April). You know what they say: Are proverbs nuggets of truth or fool's gold? *Psychology Today*, pp. 36–41.

KOHN, I., FRANCK, K., & FOX, A. (1975). Defensible space modifications in row-house communities. *National Science Foundation Report*.

KOHN, M. L. (1972). Class, family, and schizophrenia: A reformulation. *Social Forces*, 50, 295–313.

KOKMEN, E. (1984). Dementia—Alzheimer's type. *Mayo Clinic Proceedings*, 59, 35–42.

KOLATA, G. (1988, May). Alcoholic genes or misbehavior? *Psychology Today*, pp. 34–37.

KOLB, L., & BRODY, H. K. H. (1982). *Modern clinical psychiatry*. Philadelphia: Saunders.

KOLODNY, R., MASTERS, W., HENDRYX, J., & TORO, G. (1971). Plasma testosterone levels and semen analysis in male homosexuals. *New England Journal of Medicine*, 285, 1170–1174.

KONEČNI, V. J. (1975). Annoyance, type, and duration of post-annoyance activity and aggression: The "catharsis effect." *Journal of Experimental Psychology: General*, 104, 76–102.

KONEČNI, V. J. (1979). The role of aversive events in the development of intergroup conflict. In W. Austin & S. Worchel (Eds.). *The social psychology of intergroup behavior*. Monterey, CA: Brooks/Cole.

KONEČNI, V. J., & DOOB, A. N. (1972). Catharsis through displacement of aggression. *Journal of Personality and Social Psychology*, 23, 379–387.

KONEČNI, V. J., & EBBESEN, E. B. (1986). Courtroom testimony by psychologists on eyewitness identification issues: Critical notes and reflections [Special Issue: The ethics of expert testimony], *Law and Human Behavior, 10,* 117–126.

KONEČNI, V. J., LIBAUSER, L., MORTON, H., & EBBESEN, E. B. (1975). Effects of a violation of personal space on escape and helping responses. *Journal of Experimental Social Psychology, 11,* 288–299.

KORCHIN, S. (1976). *Modern clinical psychology.* New York: Basic.

KORCHIN, S., & SHULDBERG, D. (1981). The future of clinical assessment. *American Psychologist, 36,* 1147–1158.

KORNHABER, R., & SCHROEDER, H. (1975). Importance of model similarity on extinction of avoidance behavior in children. *Journal of Consulting and Clinical Psychology, 43,* 601–607.

KOSLOWSKI, M. R., & MARSHALL, J. F. (1981). Plasticity of neostriatal metabolic activity and behavioral recovery from vibrostriatal injury. *Experimental Neurology, 74,* 318–321.

KOSSLYN, S. M. (1980). *Image and mind.* Cambridge, MA: Harvard University Press.

KOSSLYN, S. M. (1981). The medium and the message in mental imagery: A theory. *Psychological Review, 88,* 46–66.

KOSSLYN, S. M. (1983). *Ghosts in the mind's machine.* New York: Norton.

KOSSLYN, S. M. (1984). Mental representations. In J. R. Anderson & S. M. Kosslyn (Eds.), *Tutorials in reading and memory.* San Francisco: Freeman.

KOSSLYN, S. M., BALL, T. M., & REISER, B. J. (1978). Visual images preserve spatial information: Evidence from studies of image scanning. *Journal of Experimental Psychology: Human Perception and Performance, 4,* 47–60.

KOSTEN, T. R. (1990). Neurobiology of abused drugs: Opioids and stimulants. *Journal of Nervous and Mental Disease, 178,* 217–227.

KOWALIK, D. L., & GOTLIB, I. H. (1987). Depression and marital interaction: Concordance between intent and perception of communication. *Journal of Abnormal Psychology, 96,* 127–134.

KRAEMER, H. C., BECKER, H. B., BRODIE, H. X. H., DOERING, C. H., MOOS, R. H., & HAMBURG, D. (1976). Orgasmic frequency and plasma testosterone levels in normal human males. *Archives of Sexual Behavior, 5,* 125–132.

KRAFT, C. L., & ELWORTH, C. L. (1969). Measurement of aircrew performance: The flight deck workload and its relation to pilot performance. (NTIS70–19779/AD699934-DTIC).

KRAL, K. (1962). Senescent forgetfulness: Benign and malignant. *Canadian Medical Association Journal, 86,* 257–260.

KRALY, E. S. (1984). Physiology of drinking by eating. *Psychological Review, 91,* 478–490.

KRALY, E. S., MILLER, L., & HECHT, E. (1983). Histaminergic mechanisms for drinking by insulin in the rat. *Physiology and Behavior, 31,* 233–236.

KRAMER, F. M., JEFFERY, R. W., FORSTER, J. L., and Snell, M. K. (1989). Long-term follow-up of behavioral treatment for obesity: Patterns of weight regain among men and women. *International Journal of Obesity, 13,* 123–136.

KRAMER, M. (1977). *Psychiatric services and the changing institution scene, 1952–1985.* National Institute of Mental Health (DHEW publication #Adm. 77–433).

KRAMER, R. L. (1989). The treatment of childhood night terrors through the use of hypnosis: A case study. *International Journal of Clinical and Experimental Hypnosis, 37,* 283–284.

KRASNER, L. (1971). The operant approach in behavior therapy. In A. Bergin & S. Garfield (Eds.), *Handbook of psychotherapy*

and behavior change, New York: Wiley.

KRECH, D., CRUTCHFIELD, R., & BALLACHEY, E. (1962). *Individual in society: A textbook of social psychology.* New York: McGraw-Hill.

KRENZ, E. W. (1986). Hypnosis versus autogenic training: A comparison. *American Journal of Clinical Hypnosis, 28,* 209–213.

KREPS, J. M. (Ed.). (1976). *Women and the American economy.* Englewood Cliffs, NJ: Prentice-Hall.

KROGER, W. S., & DOUCE, R. G. (1980). Forensic uses of hypnosis. *American Journal of Clinical Hypnosis, 23,* 86–93.

KRUPAT, E. (1982). *Psychology is social* (2nd ed.). Glenview, IL: Scott, Foresman.

KRUPAT, E. (1985). *People in cities: The urban environment and its effects.* Cambridge, England: Cambridge University Press.

KÜBLER-ROSS, E. (1969). *On death and dying.* New York: Macmillan.

KÜBLER-ROSS, E. (1974). *Questions and answers on death and dying.* New York: Macmillan.

KUHN, M., & McPHARTLAND, T. (1954). An empirical investigation of self-attitudes. *American Social Review, 19,* 68–76.

KURDEK, L. A. (1989). Relationship quality in gay and lesbian cohabiting couples: A 1-year follow-up study. *Journal of Social and Personal Relationships, 5* 39–59.

KURTINES, W., & GRIEF, E. B. (1974). The development of moral thought: Review and evaluation of Kohlberg's approach. *Psychological Bulletin, 81,* 453–470.

LACKEY, E., & NASS, G. A. A. (1969). A comparison of sexual attitudes and behavior in an international sample. *Journal of Marriage and the Family, 31,* 364–379.

LACROIX, A., & HAYNES, S. (1987). Gender differences: The health effects of workplace roles. In R. Barrett, L. Beiner, & G. Baruch (Eds.), *Gender and stress,* New York: The Free Press.

LAFORGE, J., & HENDERSON, P. (1990). Counselor competency in the courtroom. *Journal of Counseling and Development, 68,* 156–159.

LAGERLOF, O. (1982). Tricyclic psychopharmaca and color vision. *Documenta Ophthalmologica Proceedings Series, 33,* 487–491.

LAGONE, J. (1981, March). Healing the hostages. *Discover.* New York: Time, Inc.

LAING, R. D. (1964). Is schizophrenia a disease? *International Journal of Social Psychiatry, 10,* 184–193.

LAIRD, J. (1974). Self-attribution of emotion: The effects of expressive behavior on the quality of emotional experience. *Journal of Personality and Social Psychology, 29,* 475–486.

LAIRD, J., & BRESLER, C. (1990). William James and the mechanisms of emotional experience. *Personality and Social Psychology Bulletin, 16,* 636–651.

LAMB, H. R., & ZUSMAN, J. (1979). Primary prevention in perspective. *American Journal of Psychiatry, 136,* 12–17.

LAMB, M. E. (1987). Predictive implications of individual differences in attachment. *Journal of Consulting and Clinical Psychology, 55,* 817–824.

LAMBERT, N. M. (1988). Adolescent outcomes of hyperactive children. *American Psychologist, 43,* 786–799.

LAMM, H., & MYERS, D. (1978). Group-induced polarization of attitudes and behavior. In L. Berkowitz (Ed.), *Advances in Experimental Social Psychology* (Vol. 11). New York: Academic.

LANDESMAN-DWYER, S., KELLER, S. L., & STREISSGUTH, A. P. (1977). Naturalistic observations of newborns: Effects of maternal alcohol intake. Paper presented at the American Psychological Association Annual Meeting, San Francisco.

LANDFIELD, P. W. (1976). Synchronous EEG

rhythms: Their nature and their possible functions in memory, information, transmission, and behavior. In W. H. Gispen (Ed.), *Molecular and functional neurobiology.* Amsterdam: Elsevier.

LANGER, E. (1978). Rethinking the role of thought in social interaction. In J. H. Harvey, W. Ickes, & R. Kidd (Eds.), *New direction in attribution* (Vol. 2). Hillsdale, NJ: Erlbaum.

LANGER, E., JANIS, I., & WOLFER, J. (1975). Reduction of psychological stress in surgical patients. *Journal of Experimental Social Psychology, 11,* 155–165.

LANGER, E. J., & RODIN, J. (1976). The effects of choice and enhanced personal responsibility for the aged: A field experiment in an institutional setting. *Journal of Personality and Social Psychology, 34,* 191–198.

LANGMAN, L., ABRAMSON, P., & FOOTE, D. (1981, February 16). The latchkey children. *Newsweek,* pp. 96–97.

LANZETTA, J. T., BIERNAT, J., & KLECK, R. (1982). Self-focused attention, behavior, autonomic arousal and the experience of emotion. *Motivation and Emotion, 6,* 49–63.

LANZETTA, J. T., & ORR, R. (1986). Excitatory strength of expressive faces: Effects of happy and fear expressions and context on the extension of conditioned fear response. *Journal of Personality and Social Psychology, 50,* 190–194.

LAPIERE, R. T. (1934). Attitudes vs. actions. *Social Forces, 13,* 230–237.

LARKIN, J. H., & REIF, F. (1979). Understanding and teaching problem solving in physics. *European Journal of Science Education, 1,* 191–203.

LASH, J. P. (1980). *Helen and teacher: The story of Helen Keller and Anne Sullivan Macy.* New York: Dell.

LASHLEY, K. S. (1929). *Brain mechanisms and intelligence.* Chicago: University of Chicago Press.

LASHLEY, K. S. (1950). In search of the engram. *Symposia of the Society for Experimental Biology, 4,* 454–482.

LASKA, S. B., & MICKLIN, M. (1979). The knowledge dimension of occupational socialization: Role models and their social influences. *Youth and Society, 10,* 360–378.

LASSWELL, H. D. (1948). The structure and function of communication in society. In L. Bryson (Ed.), *Communication of ideas.* New York: Harper & Row.

LATANÉ, B., & DARLEY, J. M. (1970). *The unresponsive bystander: Why doesn't he help?* New York: Appleton-Century-Crofts.

LATANÉ, B., WILLIAMS, K., & HARKINS, S. (1979). Many hands make light the work: The causes and consequences of social-loafing. *Journal of Personality and Social Psychology, 37,* 822–832.

LAUDERDAL, P., SMITH-CUNNICA, P., PARKER, J., & INVERARITY, J. (1984). External threat and the definition of deviance. *Journal of Personality and Social Psychology, 46,* 1058–1068.

LAURENCE, J. R., & PERRY, C. (1983). Hypnotically created memory among highly hypnotizable subjects. *Science, 222,* 523–524.

LAVENKA, N. M. (1989). The measurement of intrinsic and extrinsic product quality: A magnitude estimation approach. *Journal of the Market Research Society, 31,* 213–224.

LAVIE, P., & HOBSON, J. A. (1986). Origin of dreams: Anticipation of modern theories in the philosophy and physiology of the eighteenth and nineteenth centuries. *Psychological Bulletin, 100,* 229–240.

LAWSON, E. (1971). Hair color, personality, and the observer. *Psychological Reports, 28,* 311–322.

LAZARSFELD, P. F., BERELSON, B., & GAUDET,

H. J. (1948). *The people's choice* (2nd ed.). New York: Columbia University Press.

LAZARUS, R. (1981). A cognitivist's reply to Zajonc on emotion and cognition. *American Psychology, 36,* 222–223.

LAZARUS, R. (1981, July). Little hassles can be hazardous to health. *Psychology Today,* pp. 58–52.

LAZARUS, R. (1982). Thoughts on the reduction between emotion and cognition. *American Psychology, 37,* 1019–1024.

LAZARUS, R., COYNE, J., & FOLKMAN, S. (1982). Cognition, emotion, and motivation. The doctoring of Humpty Dumpty. In R. Newfeld (Ed.), *Psychological stress and psychopathology.* New York: McGraw-Hill.

LAZARUS, R., & DELONGIS, A. (1983). Psychological stress and coping in aging. *American Psychology, 38,* 245–254.

LAZARUS, R., & LAUNIER, R. (1978). Stress-related transactions between person and environment. In L. Pervin & M. Lewis (Eds.), *Perspectives in interactional psychology.* New York: Plenum.

LAZARUS, R. S. (1968). Emotions and adaptation: Conceptual and empirical relations. In W. J. Arnold (Ed.), *Nebraska symposium on motivation.* Lincoln, NE: University of Nebraska Press.

LAZARUS, R. S., & FOLKMAN, S. (1987). Coping and adaptation. In W. D. Gentry (Ed.), *The handbook of behavioral medicine.* New York: Guilford.

LAZELL, E. W., & PRINCE, L. H. (1929). A study of the causative factors of dementia praecox. *U. S. Veterans Bureau Medical Bulletin, 114,* 241–248.

LEAHEY, T. H. (1987). *A history of psychology: Main currents in psychological thought.* Englewood Cliffs, NJ: Prentice Hall.

LEBON, G. (1903). *The crowd* (trans.). London: Allen & Unwin.

LECUYER, R. (1975). Space dimensions, the climate of discussion and group decisions. *European Journal of Social Psychology, 5,* 509–514.

LECUYER, R. (1976). Social organization and spatial organization. *Human Relations, 19,* 1045–1060.

LEE, T. (1970). Perceived distance as a function of direction in the city. *Environment and Behavior, 2,* 40–51.

LEFEVRE, C. (1972). The mature woman as a graduate student. *School Review, 80,* 281–297.

LEIBERMAN, A. F. (1977). Preschooler's competence with a peer. Relations with attachment and peer experience. *Child Development, 48,* 1277–1287.

LEITENBERG, H., & SLAVIN, L. (1983). Comparison of attitudes toward transsexuality and homosexuality. *Archives of Sexual Behavior, 12,* 337–346.

LEMERE, F., & VOEGTLIN, W. L. (1950). An evaluation of the aversion treatment of alcoholism. *Quarterly Journal of Studies on Alcohol, 11,* 199–204.

LENNEBERG, E. H. (1967). *Biological foundations of language.* New York: Wiley.

LEON, G., & ROTH, L. (1977). Obesity: Psychological causes, conditions, and speculations. *Psychology Bulletin, 84,* 117–139.

LEPPER, M., & GREENE, D. (1978). *The hidden costs of reward: New perspectives in the psychology of motivation.* Hillsdale, NJ: Erlbaum.

LERNER, I. M., & LIBBY, W. L. (1976). *Heredity, evolution, and society.* San Francisco: Freeman.

LERNER, J. V., & GALAMBOS, N. L. (1986). Child development and family change: The influences of maternal employment on infants and toddlers. *Advances in Infancy Research, 4,* 39–86.

LEVENTHAL, H. (1982). The integration of emotion and cognition: A view from the perceptual monitor theory of emotion. In

M. Clark & S. Feske (Eds.), *Affect and emotion.* Hillsdale, NJ: Erlbaum.

LEVENTHAL ET AL. (1984). Compliance: A self-regulation perspective. In D. Gentry (Ed.), *Handbook of behavioral medicine.* New York: Alfred Press.

LEVENTHAL, H., & NILES, P. (1965). Persistence of influence for varying duration of exposure to threat stimuli. *Psychology Reports, 16,* 223–233.

LEVENTHAL, H., SINGER, R., & JONES, S. (1965). The effects of fear and specificity of recommendation upon attitudes and behavior. *Journal of Personality and Social Psychology, 2,* 20–29.

LEVINE, J., & RUSSO, E. (1987). Majority and minority influence. *Review of Personality and Social Psychology, 8,* 13–54.

LEVINE, M. (1975). *A cognitive theory of learning.* Hillsdale, NJ: Erlbaum.

LEVINSON, D. J. (1978). *The seasons of a man's life.* New York: Knopf.

LEVINSON, D. J. (1984). A conception of adult development. *American Psychologist, 4,* 3–13.

LEVINSON, P., & FLYNN, J. (1965). The objects attacked by cats during stimulation of the hypothalamus. *Animal Behavior, 13,* 217–220.

LEVIN, H. S. (1990). Memory deficit after closed-head injury. *Journal of Clinical and Experimental Neuropsychology, 12,* 129–153.

LEVITT, E. E. A reversal of hypnotically "refreshed" testimony: A brief communication. *International Journal of Clinical and Experimental Hypnosis, 38,* 6–9.

LEVY, L., & ROWITZ, L. (1973). *The ecology of mental disorder.* New York: Behavioral Publications.

LEVY-LEBOYER, C. (1988). Success and failure in applying psychology. *American Psychologist, 43,* 779–785.

LEWIN, K. (1931). Environmental forces in child behavior and development. in C. Murchison (Ed.), *A handbook of child psychology.* Worcester, MA: Clark University Press.

LEWIN, K. (1943). Forces behind food habits and methods of change. *Bulletin of the National Resource Council, 108,* 35–65.

LEWIN, K. (1943). Defining the field at a given time. *Psychological Review, 50,* 292–310.

LEWIN, K., LIPPITT, R., & WHITE, R. (1939). Patterns of aggressive behavior in experimentally created social climates. *Journal of Psychology, 10,* 271–299.

LEWINE, R. (1981). Sex differences in schizophrenia: Timing or subtypes. *Psychological Bulletin, 90,* 432–444.

LEWINSOHN, P. H. (1974). A behavioral approach to depression. In R. J. Friedman & M. M. Katz (Eds.), *The psychology of depression: Contemporary theory and research.* Washington, DC: Winston-Wiley.

LEWINSOHN, P. M., MISCHEL, W., CHAPLIN, W., & BARTON, R. (1980). Social competence and depression: The role of illusory self-perceptions. *Journal of Abnormal Psychology, 89,* 203–212.

LEWIS, J., BADDELEY, A. D., BONHAM, K. G., & LOVETT, D. (1970). Traffic pollution and mental efficiency. *Nature, 225,* 96.

LEWIS, R., RODNICK, E., & GOLDSTEIN, M. (1981). Interfamilial interactive behavior, parental communciation deviance, and risk of schizophrenia. *Journal of Abnormal Psychology, 90,* 448–457.

LEWIS, S., LANGAN, C., & HOLLANDER, E. P. (1972). Expectations of future interaction and the choice of less desirable alternatives in conformity. *Sociometry, 35,* 440–447.

LEX, B. W. (1987). Review of alcohol problems in ethnic minority groups. *Journal of Consulting and Clinical Psychology, 55,* 293–300.

LEY, D., & CYBRIWSKY, R. (1974). Urban

graffiti as territorial markers. *Annals of the Association of American Geographers, 64,* 491–505.

LEY, R. (1977). Encoding specificity and associates in cued recall. *Memory and Cognition, 5,* 523–525.

LI, E. C., & WILLIAMS, S. E. (1990). Repetition deficits in three aphasic syndromes. *Journal of Communication Disorders, 23,* 77–88.

LICHTENSTEIN, E., HARRIS, D., BIRCHLER, G., WAHL, J., & SCHMAHL, D. (1973). Comparison of rapid smoking, warm, smoky air, and attention placebo in modification of smoking behavior. *Journal of Consulting and Clinical Psychology, 40,* 92–98.

LIDZ, T. (1968). The family language and the transmission of schizophrenia. In D. Rosenthal & S. Kety (Eds.), *The transmission of schizophrenia.* New York: Pergamon.

LIEBER, A., & SHERIN, C. (1972). Homicides and the lunar cycle: Toward a theory of lunar influence on human emotional disturbance. *American Journal of Psychiatry, 129,* 69–74.

LIEBERMAN, M. A., YALOM, I. D., & MILES, M. B. (1973). *Encounter groups: First facts.* New York: Basic.

LIEBERT, R. M., & BARON, R. A. (1972). Some immediate effects of televised violence on children's behavior. *Developmental Psychology, 6,* 469–475.

LIEBERT, R. M., NEALE, J. M., & DAVIDSON, E. S. (1973). *The early window: Effects of television on children and youth.* Elmsford, NY: Pergamon.

LIEM, J., & LIEM, R. (1976). Life events, social supports, and physical and psychological well-being. Paper presented at American Psychological Association meeting, Washington, DC.

LILLY, J. C. (1956). Mental effects of reduction of ordinary levels of physical stimuli on intact healthy persons. *Psychiatric Research Reports, 5,* 1–9.

LIMBER, J. (1973). The genesis of complex sentences. In T. E. Moore (Ed.), *Cognitive development and the acquisition of language.* New York: Academic.

LIMBER, J. (1977). Language in child and chimp? *American Psychologist, 32,* 280–295.

LINDER, D. E., & WORCHEL, S. (1970). Opinion change as a result of effortly drawing a counter-attitudinal conclusion. *Journal of Experimental Social Psychology, 6,* 432–448.

LINDSAY, K. P., & PAUL, G. L. (1989). Involuntary commitments to public mental institutions: Issues involving the over representation of blacks and assessment of relevant functioning. *Psychological Bulletin, 106,* 171–183.

LINDSAY, R. C. (1986). Confidence and accuracy of eyewitness identification from lineups. *Law and Human Behavior, 10,* 229–239.

LINDSKOLD, S. (1982). *You and me.* Chicago: Nelson Hall.

LINEVILLE, P., SALOVEY, P., & FISCHER, G. (1986). Stereotyping and perceived distributions of social characteristics: An application to ingroup-outgroup perception.

LINZ, D., DONNERSTEIN, E., & ADAMS, S. M. (1989). Physiological desensitization and judgments about female victims. *Human Communication Research, 15,* 509–522.

LIPKIN, R. (1988). Making machines in mind's image. *Insight, 4*(7), 8–12.

LIPKIN, R. (1988a). The great society of mind. *Insight, 4*(7), 16–17.

LIPSCOMB, D. M. (1969). Ear damage from exposure to rock and roll music. *Archives of Otolaryngology, 90,* 545–555.

LISLE, L. (1980). *Portrait of an artist: A biography of Georgia O'Keeffe.* New York: Washington Square Press.

LITT, M. D. (1988). Self-efficacy and perceived control: Cognitive mediators of pain tolerance. *Journal of Personality and Social Psychology, 54,* 149–160.

LITTLE, K. B. (1965). Personal space. *Journal of Experimental Social Psychology, 1,* 237–347.

LIVSON, N., & PESKIN, H. (1980). Perspectives on adolescence from longitudinal research. In J. Aselson (Ed.), *Handbook of adolescent psychology.* New York: Wiley.

LOCKE, J. (1964). An essay concerning human understanding (Vol. 1). New York: Meridian. (Originally published 1690)

LOCKMAN, J. J. (1986). Perceptumotor coordination in sighted infants: Implications for visually impaired children. *Topics in Early Childhood Special Education, 6,* 23–36.

LOEHLIN, J. C., & NICHOLS, R. (1976). *Heredity, environment and personality: A study of 850 sets of twins.* Austin, TX: University of Texas Press.

LOFTUS, E. F. (1975). Leading questions and the eyewitness. *Cognitive Psychology, 1,* 560–572.

LOFTUS, E. F. (1981). *Eyewitness testimony.* Cambridge, MA: Harvard University Press.

LOFTUS, E. F. (1984, February). Eyewitnesses: Essential but unreliable. *Psychology Today,* pp. 22–26.

LOFTUS, E. F. (1986). Ten years in the life of an expert witness. *Law and Human Behavior, 10,* 241–263.

LOFTUS, E. F., & PALMER, J. (1974). Reconstruction of automobile destruction: An example of interaction between language and memory. *Journal of Verbal Learning and Verbal Behavior, 13,* 585–589.

LOGAN, R. D. (1986). A reconceptualization of Erikson's theory: The repetition of existential and instrumental themes. *Human Development, 29,* 125–136.

LOMBARD, L. S., KAHN, S. P., & FROMM, E. (1990). The role of imagery in self-hypnosis: Its relationship to personality characteristics and gender. *International Journal of Clinical and Experimental Hypnosis, 38,* 25–38.

LONG, B. B. (1986). The prevention of mental-emotional disabilities. *American psychologist, 41,* 825–829.

LONGSTRETH, L. E., LONGSTRETH, G. V., RAMIREZ, C., & FERNANDEZ, G. (1975). The ubiquity of Big Brother. *Child Development, 46,* 769–772.

LONGUET-HIGGINS, H. C. (1986). Visual motion ambiguity. *Vision Research, 26,* 181–183.

LOO, C. (1972). The effects of special density in the social behavior of children. *Journal of Applied Social Psychology, 4,* 372–381.

LOPATA, H. Z. (1973a). Self-identity in marriage and widowhood. *Sociological Quarterly, 14,* 407–418.

LOPATA, H. Z. (1973b). *Widowhood in an American city.* Cambridge, MA: Schenkman.

LOPICCOLO, J. (1978). The professionalization of sex therapy: Issues and problems. In J. LoPiccolo & L. LoPiccolo, *Handbook of sex therapy.* New York: Plenum.

LOPICCOLO, J., & HEIMAN, J. (1977). The role of cultural value in the prevention and treatment of sexual problems. In C. Quills, V. Wincze, & D. Barlow (Eds.), *The prevention of sexual disorders.* New York: Plenum.

LOPICCOLO, J., & LOBITZ, W. (1972). The role of masturbation in the treatment of orgasmic dysfunctions. *Archives of Sexual Behavior, 2,* 163–172.

LORAYNE, H., & LUCAS, J. (1974). *The memory book.* New York: Ballantine.

LORENZ, K. (1966). On aggression. New York: Harcourt Brace Jovanovich.

LOTTER, V. (1974). Factors related to outcome in autistic children. *Journal of Autism and Childhood Schizophrenia, 4,* 263–277.

LOVAAS, O. I. (1977). *The autistic child.* New York: Halsted.

LOVAAS, O. I. (1987). Behavioral treatment and normal educational and intellectual functioning in young autistic children. *Journal of Consulting and Clinical Psychology, 55,* 3–9.

LOWE, C. A., & KASSIN, S. M. (1948). Biased attributions for political messages. The role of involvement. Paper presented at Eastern Psychological Association meeting.

LOWENTHAL, M. F. (1972). Some potentialities of a life-cycle approach to the study of retirement. In F. M. Carp (Ed.), *Retirement.* New York: Behavioral Publications.

LOWENTHAL, M. F. (1977). Toward a sociopsychological theory of change in adulthood and old age. In J. E. Birren & K. W. Schaie (Eds.), *Handbook of the psychology of aging.* New York: Van Nostrand.

LOWENTHAL, M. F., & CHIRIBOGA, D. (1973). Social stress and adaptation: Toward a life-course perspective. In C. Eisdorfer & M. P. Lawton (Eds.), *The psychology of adult development and aging.* Washington, DC: American Psychological Association.

LOWREY, G. H. (1978). *Growth and development of children.* Chicago: Year Book Med. Pub., Inc.

LUBIN, B., LARSEN, R. M., & MATARAZZO, I. D. (1984). Patterns of psychological test usage in the United States: 1932–1982. *American Psychologist, 39,* 451–453.

LUBORSKY, L, & SPENCE, D. P. (1978). Quantitative research on psychoanalytic therapy. In S. L. Garfield & A. E. Bergin (Eds.), *Handbook of psychotherapy and behavior change: An empirical analysis* (2nd ed.). New York: Wiley.

LUCAS, O. N. (1975). The use of hypnosis in hemophilia dental care. *Annals of the New York Academy of Science, 240,* 263–266.

LUNDE, D. (1975). *Murder and madness.* Stanford: Stanford Alumni Association.

LUNN, R., & BANKS, W. P. (1986). Visual fatigue and spatial frequency adaptation to video displays of text. *Human Factors, 28,* 457–464.

LURIA, A. R. (1968). *The mind of a mnemonist: A little book about a vast memory* (L. Solotaroff, trans.). New York: Basic.

LYKKEN, D. T. (1959). The GSR in the detection of guilt. *Journal of Applied Psychology, 43,* 385–388.

LYKKEN, D. T. (1975, March). Guilty knowledge test: The right way to use a lie detector. *Psychology Today,* pp. 56–60.

LYKKEN, D. T. (1981). *A tremor in the blood: Uses and abuses of the lie detector.* New York: McGraw-Hill.

LYNCH, K. (1960). *The image of the city.* Cambridge, MA: MIT Press.

LYNN, M. & OLDENQUIST, A. (1986). Egoistic and nonegoistic motives in social dilemmas. *American Psychologist, 41,* 529–534.

LYNN, S. J., RHUE, J. W., & WEEKES, J. R. (1990). Hypnotic involuntariness: A social cognitive analysis. *Psychological Review, 97,* 169–184.

MAAS, A., & VOLPATO, C. (1989, June). Theoretical perspectives on minority influence: Conversion vs. divergence. Paper presented at the third Workshop on Minority Influence, Perugia, Italy.

MAAS, A., WEST, S., & CIALDINI, R. (1987). Minority influence and conversion. *Review of Personality and Social Psychology, 8,* 55–79.

MCADAMS, D. P., & LOSOFF, M. (1984). Friendship motivation in fourth and sixth graders: A thematic analysis. *Journal of Social and Personal Relationships, 1,* 11–27.

MCARTHUR, L. A. (1976). The lesser influence of consensus than distinctiveness information on causal attributions: A test of the person-thing hypothesis. *Journal of Personality and Social Psychology, 33,* 733–742.

MCBRIDE, G., KING, M. G., & JAMES, J. W. (1965). Social proximity effects on galvanic skin responses in adult humans. *Journal of Psychology, 61,* 153–157.

MCBURNEY, D. H., & COLLINGS, V. B. (1977). *Introduction to sensation/perception.* Englewood Cliffs, NJ: Prentice-Hall.

MCCAIN, G., COX, V., PAULUS, P., LUKE, A., & ABADZI, H. (1985). The reduction of crowding in a school environment. *Journal of Applied Social Psychology, 45,* 1263–1271.

MCCALL, R. B. (1986). Effects of hallucinogenic drugs on serotonergic neural systems. *Pharmacology, Biochemistry, and Behavior, 24,* 359–363.

MCCALL, R. B. (1988). Science and the press: Like oil and water? *American Psychologist, 43,* 87–94.

MCCARTNEY, K., SCARR, S., PHILLIPS, D., & GRAJEK, S. (1985). Day care as intervention: Comparison of varying quality programs. *Journal of Applied Developmental Psychology, 6,* 247–260.

MCCARTHY, D., & SAEGERT, S. (1979). Residential density, social overload and social withdrawal. *Human Ecology, 6,* 253–272.

MCCAULEY, C. R., & SEGAL, M. (1987). Social psychology of terrorist groups. *Review of Personality and Social Psychology, 9,* 231–256.

MACCOBY, E. E., & JACKLIN, C. N. (1974). *The psychology of sex differences.* Stanford, CA: Stanford University Press.

MACCOBY, E. E., & JACKLIN, C. N. (1980). Sex differences in aggression: a rejoinder and reprise. *Child Development, 51,* 964–980.

MCCLELLAND, D. C. (1955). Some social consequences of achievement motivation. In M. R. Jones, (Ed.), *Nebraska symposium on motivation.* Lincoln, NE: University of Nebraska Press.

MCCLELLAND, D. C., ATKINSON, J. W., CLARK, R. A., & LOWELL, E. I. (1953). *The achievement motive.* New York: Appleton-Century-Crofts.

MCCLELLAND, L. A. (1974). *Crowding and social stress.* Unpublished doctoral dissertation, University of Michigan.

MCCLELLAND, L. A., & COOK, S. (1980). Promoting energy conservation in master-metered apartments through group financial incentives. *Journal of Applied Social Psychology, 10,* 20–31.

MCCLOSKEY, M., & SANTEE, J. (1981). Are semantic memory and episodic memory distinct systems? *Journal of Experimental Psychology: Human Learning and Memory, 7,* 66–71.

MCCLOSKEY, M., WIBLE, C. G. & COHEN, N. J. (1988). Is there a special flashbulb-memory mechanism? *Journal of Experimental Psychology: General, 117,* 171–181.

MCCONKIE, G. W. (1978, November). *Where do we read?* Paper presented at the annual meeting of the Psychonomic Society, San Antonio, TX.

MCCORD, J. (1979). Some child-rearing antecedents of criminal behavior in adult men. *Journal of Personality and Social Psychology, 37,* 1477–1486.

MCCORMACK, J. K., PATTERSON, T. W., OHLDE, C. D., GARFIELD, N. J., & CHAUER, A. H. (1990). MMPI configural interpretation as applied to Posttraumatic Stress Disorder in Vietnam veterans. *Journal of Personality Assessment, 54*(3 and 4), 628–638.

MCCRAE, R., & COSTA, P. T. (1987). Validation of the five-factor model of personality across instruments and observers. *Journal of Personality and Social Psychology, 52,* 81–90.

MACDONALD, M. L., LIDSKY, T. I., & KERN, J. M. (1979). Drug-instigated affects. In A. P. Goldstein & F. H. Kanfer (Eds.),

Maximizing treatment gains: Transfer enhancement in psychotherapy. New York: Academic.

MacDonald, M. L., & Tobias, L. L. (1976). Withdrawal causes relapse? Our response. *Psychological Bulletin, 83,* 448–451.

McDougall, W. (1908). *An introduction to social psychology.* London: Methuen.

MacDuffee, E. J., Shupert, C. L., & Leibowitz, H. W. (1988). The influence of peripheral stimuli on the amount and direction of autokinesis. *Perception and Psychophysics, 13,* 395–400.

McElhose, P. (1988). The "other" STDs as dangerous as ever. *RN,* June, 53–58.

McEntee, W. J., & Crook, T. H. (1990). Age associated memory impairment: A role for catecholamines. *Neurology, 40,* 526–530.

McFadden, S. A., & Wild, J. M. (1986). Binocular and depth perception in the pigeon. *Journal of Experimental Analysis of Behavior, 45,* 149–160.

McGovern, T., & Hawks, B. (1988). The liberating science and art of undergraduate psychology. *American psychologist, 43,* 108–114.

McGrath, J. (1984). *Groups: Interaction and performance.* Englewood Cliffs, NJ: Prentice-Hall.

McGrath, J. E. (Ed.). (1988). *The social psychology of time.* Newbury Park, CA: Sage.

McGrath, J. J. (1963). Irrelevant stimulation and vigilance performance. In D. Buckner & J. J. McGrath (Eds.), *Vigilance: A symposium.* New York: McGraw-Hill.

McGrew, P. L. (1970). Social and spatial density effects on spacing behavior in preschool children. *Journal of Child Psychology and Psychiatry, 11,* 197–205.

McGrother, C. W., & Marshall, B. (1990). Recent trends in incidence, morbidity and survival in Down's syndrome. *Journal of Mental Deficiency Research, 49,* 19–57.

McGuire, T. W., Kiesler, S., & Siegel, J. (1987). Group and computer-mediated discussion effects in risk decision making. *Journal of Personality and Social Psychology, 52,* 917–930.

McGuire, W. (1961). The effectiveness of supportive and refutational defenses in immunization and restoring beliefs against persuasion. *Sociometry, 24,* 184–197.

McGuire, W. (1984). The search for self: Going beyond self-esteem and the reactive self. In R. A. Zucker, J. Arnoff, & A. I. Robin, (Eds.), *Personality and the prediction of behavior.* New York: Academic.

McGuire, W. J. (1985). Attitudes and attitude change. In G. Linzey & E. Aronson (Eds.), *Handbook of Social Psychology,* Vol. 2 (3rd ed.). New York: Random House.

McKenzie-Mohr, D., & Zanna, M. (1990). Treating women as sexual objects: Look to the (gender schematic) male who has viewed pornography. *Personality and Social Psychology Bulletin, 16,* 296–308.

McKenna, R. J. (1972). Some effects of anxiety level and food cues on the eating behavior of obese and normal subjects. *Journal of Personality and Social Psychology, 22,* 311–319.

Mackintosh, N. J. (1983). *Conditioning and associative learning.* New York: MIT Press.

Mackworth, N. (1961). Researches on the measurement of human performance. In H. Sinaiko (Ed.), *Selected papers on human factors in the design and use of control systems.* New York: Dover.

MacLeod, C. M. (1988). Forgotten but not gone: Savings for pictures and words in long-term memory. *Journal of Experimental Psychology, Learning, Memory, and Cognition, 14,* 195–212.

MacLeod, M. D., & Ellis, H. D. (1986). Modes of presentation in eyewitness testimony research. *Human Learning Journal*

of Practical Research and Applications, 5, 39–44.

McMullen, S., & Rosen, R. (1979). The use of self-administered masturbation training in the treatment of primary dysfunction. *Journal of Consulting and Clinical Psychology, 47,* 912–918.

McNally, R. J. (1986). Pavlovian conditioning and preparedness: Effects of initial fear level. *Behavior Research and Therapy, 24,* 27–33.

McNeill, J. W., & Todd, F. J. (1986). The operant treatment of excessive verbal ruminations and negative emotional arousal in a case of child molestation. *Child and Family Behavior Therapy, 8,* 61–69.

MacNichol, E. F. (1964). Three-pigment color vision. *Scientific American, 211,* 48–56.

McPherson, B., & Guppy, N. (1979). Preretirement life-style and the degree of planning for retirement. *Journal of Gerontology, 34,* 254–263.

McTeer, W. (1972). *The scope of motivation.* Monterey, CA: Brooks/Cole.

McWaters, B. (1975). An outline of transpersonal psychology: Its meaning and relevance for education. In T. Roberts (Ed.), *Four psychologies applied to education.* New York: Schenkman.

Madden, J. (1986). The effects of schemes on children's drawings of the results of transformations. *Child Development, 57,* 924–933.

Madden, M. E. (1987) Perceived control and power in marriage: Marital decision making and task performance. *Personality and Social Bulletin, 13.* 73–82.

Maher, B. (1966). *Principles of psychopathology.* New York: McGraw-Hill.

Maher, B. A. (1970). Delusional thinking and cognitive disorder. Paper presented at annual meeting of the American Psychological Association.

Maher, C. A. (1987). Involving behaviorally disordered adolescents in instructional planning: Effectiveness of GOAL procedure. *Journal of Child and Adolescent Psychotherapy, 4,* 205–210.

Maier, N. R. F. (1931). Reasoning in humans. II: The solution of a problem and its appearance in consciousness. *Journal of Comparative Psychology, 12,* 181–194.

Maier, R. (1984). *Human sexuality in perspective.* Chicago: Nelson-Hall.

Maier, S., & Seligman, M. (1976). Learned helplessness: Theory and evidence. *Journal of Experimental Psychology: General, 105,* 3–46.

Maier, S. F., Seligman, M. E. P., & Solomon, R. L. (1969). Pavlovian fear conditioning and learned helplessness. In B. A. Campbell & R. M. Church (Eds.), *Punishment and aversive behavior.* New York: Appleton-Century-Crofts.

Major, B., Carrington, P. I., & Carnevale, P. J. D. (1984). Physical attractiveness and self-esteem. Attributions for praise from an other-sex evaluator. *Personality and Social Psychology Bulletin, 10,* 43–50.

Major, B., Cozzarelli, C., Sciacchitano, A., Cooper, M., Testa, M., & Mueller, P. (1990). Perceived social supports, self-efficacy, and adjustment to abortion. *Journal of Personality and Social Psychology, 59,*452–463.

Malamud, W. (1944). The psychoneuroses. In J. McV. Hunt (Ed.), *Personality and the behavior disorders* (Vol. 2). New York: Ronald Press.

Malamuth, N. (1984). Aggression against women: Cultural and individual causes. In N. Malamuth & E. Donnerstein (Eds.), *Pornography and Sexual Aggression.* Orlando, FL: Academic Press.

Malamuth, N. (1987). Do sexually violent media indirectly contribute to aggression behavior? In M. Walsh (Ed.), *The psychol-*

ogy of women: Ongoing debates. New Haven, CT: Yale University Press.

Malamuth, N., Haber, S., & Feshbach, S. (1980). Testing hypotheses regarding rape: Exposure to sexual violence, sex differences, and the "normality" of rapists. *Journal of Research in Personality, 14,* 121–127.

Malcolm X, & Arthur Haley (1973). *The autobiography of Malcolm X.* New York: Ballantine.

Malgady, R., Rogler, L., & Constantino, G. (1987). Ethnocultural and linguistic bias in mental health evaluation of Hispanics. *American Psychologist, 42,* 228–234.

Malinowski, B. (1927). *Sex and repression in savage society.* New York: Meridian.

Mandler, G. (1982). The structure of value: Accounting for trade. In M. Clark & S. Fiske (Eds.), *Affect and cognition.* Hillsdale NJ: Erlbaum.

Mandler, G. (1984). *Mind and body: Psychology of emotion and stress.* New York: Norton.

Mann, L. (1977). The effect of stimulus queues on queue-joining behavior. *Journal of Personality and Social Psychology, 35,* 337–342.

Mann, L., Newton, J., & Innes, J. (1982). A test between deindividuation and emergent norm theories of crowd aggression. *Journal of Personality and Social Psychology, 42,* 260–272.

Manucia, G. K., Bauman, D., & Cialdini, R. B. (1984). Mood influences on helping: Direct effects or side effects. *Journal of Personality and Social Psychology, 46,* 357–364.

Manz, W., & Lueck, H. (1968). Influence of wearing glasses on personality ratings: Cross-cultural validation of an old experiment. *Perceptual and Motor Skills, 27,* 704.

Maranto, G. (1984). Aging: Can we slow the inevitable? *Discover, 5,* 17–21.

Marcia, J. E. (1980). Identity in adolescence. In J. Adelson (Ed.), *Handbook of adolescent psychology.* New York: Wiley.

Margolis, A. (1971). The black student in political strife. *Proceedings of the 79th Annual Convention of the American Psychological Association, 6,* 395–396.

Markey, E. J. (1985). The politics of arms control: A matter of perception. *American Psychologist, 40,* 557–560.

Markiewicz, B. Kucharski, D., Spear, N. E. (1986). Comparison of memory for Pavlovian conditioned aversions to temperature, vibration, odor, or brightness. *Developmental Psychobiology, 19,* 139–154.

Marks, G., Miller, N., & Maruyama, G. (1981). Effect of targets' physical attractiveness on assumptions of similarity. *Journal of Personality and Social Psychology, 41,* 198–206.

Marks, W. B., Dobelle, W. H., & MacNichol, E. F., Jr. (1964). Visual pigments of single primate cones. *Science, 143,* 1181–1183.

Markus, H. R., & Kitayama, S. (1991). Culture and the self: Implications for cognition, emotion, and motivation. *Psychological Review, 98,* 224–253.

Marriott, J. A. (1986). Self-hypnosis and the healing process. *Australian Journal of Clinical Hypnotherapy and Hypnosis, 7,* 9–16.

Marshall, J. (1969). *Law and psychology in conflict.* New York: Doubleday.

Marshall, J. F. (1985). Neural plasticity and recovery of function after brain injury. *International Review of Neurobiology, 26,* 201–247.

Martens, R., & Landers, P. (1972). Evaluation potential as a determinant of coaction effects. *Journal of Experimental Social Psychology, 8,* 347–359.

Martin, B. (1981). *Abnormal Psychology: Clinical and scientific perspectives* (2nd ed.). New York: Holt.

MARTIN, E. A. (1986). An investigation regarding the use of a dynamic seat-pan display for training and as a device for communicating roll-axis motion information. Third Symposium on Aviation Psychology. *Aviation, Space, and Environmental Medicine, 57,* 1189–1193.

MARTIN, I., & LEVEY, A. B. (1989). Propositional knowledge and mere responding. *Biological Psychology, 28,* 149–155.

MARTIN, P., BENINGER, R. J., HAMON, M., & PUECH, A. J. (1990). Antidepressant-like action of 8-OH-DPAT, a 5-HT-sub(1A) agonist, in the learned helplessness paradigm: Evidence for a postsynaptic mechanism. *Behavioural Brain Research, 38,* 135–144.

MARTIN, P., MASSOL, J., & PUECH, A. J. (1990). Captopril as an antidepressant? Effects on the learned helplessness paradigm in rats. *Biological Psychiatry, 27,* 968–974.

MARTIN, W. R., & SLOAN, J. W. (1986). Relationship of CNS tryptaminergic processes and the action of LSD-like hallucinogens. *Pharmacology, Biochemistry, and Behavior, 24,* 393–399.

MARTINDALE, D. (1976, April). Torment in the tower. *Chicago,* pp. 96–101.

MARTINDALE, D. A. (1971). Territorial dominance behavior in dyadic verbal interactions. *Proceedings of the American Psychological Association, 79th Annual Convention, 6,* 305–306.

MARTINI, F. (1989). *Fundamentals of anatomy and physiology.* Englewood Cliffs, NJ: Prentice Hall.

MASLACH, C. (1979). Negative emotional biasing of unexplained arousal. In C. Izard (Ed.), *Emotion, personality and psychopathology.* New York: Plenum.

MASLOW, A. H. (1954). *Motivation and personality.* New York: Harper & Row.

MASLOW, A. H. (1968). *Toward a psychology of being* (2nd ed.). New York: Van Nostrand.

MASLOW, A. H. (1970). *Motivation and personality* (2nd ed.). New York: Harper & Row.

MASSARO, D. W. (1970). Perceptual auditory images. *Journal of Experimental Psychology, 85,* 411–417.

MASSARO, D. W., & COHEN, M. M. (1990). Perception of synthesized audible and visible speech. *Psychological Science, 1,* 55–63.

MASSON, M. E. J., & McDANIEL, M. A. (1981). The role of organizational processes in long-term retention. *Journal of Experimental Psychology: Human Learning and Memory, 7,* 100–110.

MASTERS, J. C., & YORKIN-LEVIN, K. (Eds.) (1984). *Boundary areas in social and developmental psychology.* New York: Academic.

MASTERS, W. H., & JOHNSON, V. E. (1966). *Human sexual response.* Boston: Little, Brown.

MASTERS, W. H., & JOHNSON, V. E. (1975). *The pleasure bond.* Boston: Little, Brown.

MASTERS, W. H., & JOHNSON, V. E. (1970). *Human sexual inadequacy.* Boston: Little, Brown.

MASTERS, W. H., & JOHNSON, V. E. (1979). *Homosexuality in perspective.* Boston: Little, Brown.

MASTERS, W. H., & JOHNSON, V., & KOLODNY, R. (1988). *CRISIS: Heterosexual behavior in the age of AIDS.* New York: Grove Press.

MATARAZZO, J. (1980). Behavioral health and behavioral medicine: Frontiers for a new health psychology. *American Psychology, 35,* 807–817.

MATHENY, K., AYCOCK, D., PUSH, J., CURLETTE, W., & SILVA-CANNELLA, K. (1986). Stress coping: A qualitative and quantitative synthesis with implications for treatment. *Counseling Psychologist, 14,* 499–549.

MATHER, J. A., & LACKNER, J. R. (1981). Adaptation to visual displacement: Contribution of proprioceptive, visual, and attentional factors. *Perception, 10,* 367–374.

MATHIEU, J. (1990). A test of subordinates' achievement and affiliation needs as moderators of leader path-goal relationships. *Basic and Applied Social Psychology, 11,* 179–190.

MATIN, L. (1981). Visual location and eye movements. In W. A. Wagenaar, A. H. Wertheim, & H. W. Leibowitz (Eds.), *Symposium on the study of motion perception.* New York: Plenum.

MATIN, L., & MacKINNON, E. G. (1964). Autokinetic movement: Selective manipulation of directional components by image stabilization. *Science, 143,* 147–148.

MATTHEWS, K., & CARRA, J. (1982). Suppression of menstrual distress symptoms: A study of type A behavior. *Personality and Social Psychology Bulletin, 8,* 146–151.

MATTHEWS, K., HELMREICH, R., BEANE, W., & LUCKER, G. (1980). Pattern A, achievement striving, and scientific merit: Does pattern A help or hinder? *Journal of Personality and Social Psychology, 39,* 962–967.

MATHEWS, K. E., & CANNON, L. K. (1975). Environmental noise level as a determinant of helping behavior. *Journal of Personality and Social Psychology, 24,* 323–350.

MATHEWS, T. (1988, March 7). Homeless in America: What can be done? *Newsweek,* pp. 57–58.

MAYER, J. (1955). Regulation of energy intake and body weight: The glucostatic theory and liostatic hypothesis. *Annals of the New York Academy of Sciences, 63,* 15–43.

MAYER, J., SALOVEY, P., GOMBERG-KAUFMAN, S., & BLAINEY, K. (1991). A broader conception of mood experience. *Journal of Personality and Social Psychology, 60,* 100–111.

MAYER, L. A. (1975, June). That confounding enemy of sleep. *Fortune.*

MAYES, A. R. (1986). Learning and memory disorders and their assessment. [Special Issue: Methods in neuropsychology], *Neuropsychologica, 24,* 25–39.

MEAD, M. (1928). *Coming of age in Samoa.* Chicago: University of Chicago Press.

MEAD, M. (1935). *Sex and temperament in three primitive societies.* New York: Morrow.

MEDRICH, E., ROIZEN, J., RUBIN, V., & BUCKLEY, S. (1982). *The serious business of growing up.* Berkeley: University of California Press.

MEDVEDEV, Z. A. (1975). Aging and longevity: New approaches and new perspectives. *The Gerontologist, 15,* 196–201.

MEE, C. L. (1978). *Seizure.* New York: Jove.

MEHRABIAN, A. (1971). Nonverbal communication. In M. R. Jones (Ed.), *Nebraska symposium on motivation.* Lincoln, NE: University of Nebraska Press.

MEHRABIAN, A., & STRAUBINGER, T. (1989). Patterns of drug use among young adults. *Addictive Behaviors, 14,* 99–104.

MEICHENBAUM, D. (1977). *Cognitive behavior modification: An integrative approach.* New York: Plenum.

MEINDL, J., & LERNER, M. (1984). Exacerbation of extreme responses to an outgroup. *Journal of Personality and Social Psychology, 47,* 71–84.

MELENDY, M. R. (1901). *Maiden, wife and mother: How to attain health, beauty, and happiness.* Chicago: American Literary Association.

MELTZOFF, J., & KORNREICH, M. (1970). *Research in psychotherapy.* New York: Atherton.

MENDEL, G. (1955). Letter to Carl Nagele (1867). In M. Gabriel & S. Fogel (Eds.), *Great experiments in biology.* Englewood Cliffs, NJ: Prentice-Hall.

MENDELSHON, R., & ORCUTT, G. (1979). An empirical analysis of air pollution-does-response curves. *Journal of Environmental Economics and Management, 6,* 85–106.

MERCKELBACH, H., & VAN DEN HOUT, M. A. (1988). Electrodermal and cardiovascular responses to phobia-relevant stimuli in a trace conditioning paradigm: Effects of instructions. *Journal of Psychophysiology, 2,* 181–193.

MERZENICH, M. M., NELSON, R. J., STRYKER, M. P., CYNADER, M. S., SCHOPPMAN, A., & ZOOK, J. M. (1984). Somatosensory cortical map changes following digit amputation in adult monkeys. *Journal of Comparative Neurology, 224,* 591–605.

MESSER, W. S., & GRIGGS, R. A. (1989). Student belief and involvement in the paranormal and performance in introductory psychology. *Teaching of Psychology, 16,* 187–191.

METCALFE, J. (1986). Feeling of knowing in memory and problem solving. *Journal of Experimental Psychology: Human Perception and Performance, 6,* 58–66.

MEYEROWITZ, B., & CHAIKEN, S. (1987). The effect of message training on breast self-examination attitudes, intentions, and behavior. *Journal of Personality and Social Psychology, 52,* 500–510.

MICHNER, H. A., & LYONS, M. (1972). Perceived support and upward mobility as determinants of revolutionary coalition behavior. *Journal of Experimental Social Psychology, 8,* 180–195.

MIDDELWEEND, M. J., FESTEN, J. M., & PLOMP, R. (1990). Difficulties with speech intelligibility in noise in spite of a normal pure-tone audiogram. *Audiology, 29,* 1–7.

MIDDLEMIST, R. D., KNOWLES, E. S., & MATTER, C. F. (1976). Personal space invasions in the lavatory: Suggestive evidence for arousal. *Journal of Personality and Social Psychology, 33,* 541–546.

MIDDLETON, H., ZOLLINGER, J., & KEENE, R. (1986). Popular peers as change agents for the socially neglected child in the classroom. *Journal of School Psychology, 24,* 343–350.

MILGRAM, S. (1963). Behavioral study of obedience. *Journal of Abnormal and Social Psychology, 67,* 376.

MILGRAM, S. (1965). Liberating effects of group pressure. *Journal of Personality and Social Psychology, 1,* 127–134.

MILGRAM, S. (1970). The experience of living in cities. *Science, 167,* 1461–1468.

MILGRAM, S. (1977). *The individual in a social world.* Reading, MA: Addison-Wesley.

MILGRAM, S., LIBERTY, H., TOLEDO, R., & WACKENHUT, J. (1986). Response to intrusion in waiting lines. *Journal of Personality and Social Psychology, 51,* 683–689.

MILLER, A. G. (1977). Actor and observer perceptions of the learning of a task. *Journal of Experimental Social Psychology, 11,* 95–111.

MILLER, A. G. (1982). Historical and contemporary perspectives on stereotypes. In A. G. Miller (Ed.), *In the eye of the beholder: Contemporary issues in stereotyping.* New York: Praeger.

MILLER, B. C. (1976). A multivariate developmental model of marital satisfaction. *Journal of Marriage and the Family, 38,* 643–657.

MILLER, C. E., & CRANDALL, R. (1980). Experimental research on the social psychology of bargaining and coalition formation. In P. B. Paulus (Ed.), *Psychology of group influence* (pp. 333–374). Hillsdale, NJ: Erlbaum.

MILLER, C. F., JACKSON, P., MUELLER, J., & SCHERSCHING, C. (1987). Some social psychological effects of group decision rules. *Journal of Personality and Social Psychology, 52,* 325–332.

MILLER, D., & TURNBULL, W. (1986). Expectations and interpersonal processes. *Annual Review of Psychology, 37,* 233–256.

MILLER, G. A. (1956). The magical number seven plus or minus two: Some limits on our capacity for processing information. *Psychological Review, 62,* 81–97.

MILLER, G. A., GALANTER, E., & PRIBRAM, K. H. (1960). *Plans and the structure of behavior.* New York: Holt.

MILLER, J. A. (1984, April 21). Looking out for animal research. *Science News,* p. 247.

MILLER, J. G. (1984). Culture and the development of everyday social explanation. *Journal of Personality and Social Psychology, 46,* 961–978.

MILLER, M. (1973). *Plain speaking.* New York: Berkeley.

MILLER, M. (1982). In J. Roloff, Occupational noise—the subtle pollutant. *Science News, 121,* 347–350.

MILLER, M. M., & POTTER-EFRON, R. T. (1989). Aggression and violence associated with substance abuse. Special Issue: Aggression, family violence and chemical dependency. *Journal of Chemical Dependency Treatment, 3,* 1–36.

MILLER, N. E. (1944). Experimental studies of conflict. In J. McV. Hunt (Ed.), *Personality and the behavior disorders.* (Vol. 1). New York: Ronald Press.

MILLER, N. E. (1978). Biofeedback and visceral learning. *Annual Review of Psychology, 29,* 373–404.

MILLER, N. E. (1983). Behavioral medicine: Symbiosis between laboratory and clinic. In M. R. Rosenzweig & L. W. Porter (Eds.), *Annual review of psychology.* Palo Alto, CA: Annual Reviews.

MILLER, N. E., & BUGELSKI, R. (1948). Minor studies of aggression: II: The influence of frustrations imposed by the in-group on attitudes expressed toward the out-group. *Journal of Psychology, 25,* 437–453.

MILLER, N. E., & DICARA, L. (1967). Instrumental learning of heart-rate changes in curarized rats: Shaping and specificity to discriminative stimulus. *Journal of Comparative and Physiological Psychology, 63,* 12–19.

MILLON, T. (1969). *Modern psychopathology.* Philadelphia: Saunders.

MILLS, P. J., SCHNEIDER, R. H., HILL, D., & WALTON, K. G. (1990). Beta-adrenergic receptor sensitivity in subjects practicing Transcendental Meditation. *Journal of Psychosomatic Research, 34,* 29–33.

MILNER, B. (1970). Memory and the medial temporal regions of the brain. In K. H. Pribram & D. E. Broadbent (Eds.), *Biology of memory.* New York: Academic.

MILNER, D. (1981). Racial prejudice. In J. Turner & H. Giles (Eds.), *Intergroup behavior.* Chicago: University of Chicago Press.

MINSHEW, N. J., PAYTON, J. B., & SCLABASSI, R. J. (1986). Cortical neurophysiologic abnormalities in autism. *Neurology, 36,* (Suppl. 1),

MINTZ, N. C. (1956). Effects of aesthetic surroundings: II. Prolonged and repeated experience in a "beautiful" and an "ugly" room. *Journal of Psychology, 41,* 459–466.

MINUCHIN, S., ROSMAN, B. L., & BAKER, L. (1978). *Psychosomatic families.* Cambridge, MA: Harvard University Press.

MISCHEL, W. (1986). *Personality and assessment.* New York: Wiley.

MISCHEL, W. (1973). Toward a cognitive social learning reconceptualization of personality. *Psychological Review, 80,* 252–283.

MISCHEL, W. (1976). *Introduction to personality* (2nd ed.). New York: Holt.

MISCHEL, W. (1977). On the future of personality measurement. *American Psychologist, 32,* 246–254.

MISCHEL, W. (1981). *Introduction to personality* (3rd ed.). New York: Holt.

MISCHEL, W. (1986). *Introduction to personal-*

ity (4th ed.). New York: Holt, Rinehart & Winston.

MISCHEL, W., & PEAKE, P. K. (1982). Beyond déjà vu in the search for cross-situational consistency. *Psychological Review, 89,* 730–755.

MITCHELL, K. M., BOZARTH, J. D., & KRAUFT, C. C. (1977). A reappraisal of the therapeutic effectiveness of accurate empathy, nonpossessive warmth, and genuineness. In A. S. Gurman & A. M. Razin (Eds.), *Effective psychotherapy: A handbook of research.* New York: Pergamon.

MIYAUCHI, S., TAKINO, R., FUKUDA, H., & HIDEKI, S. (1987). Electrophysiological evidence for dreaming: Human cerebral potentials associated with rapid eye movement during REM sleep. *Electroencephalography and Clinical Neurophysiology, 66,* 383–390.

MOEDE, W. (1927). Die Richtlinien der Leisturgs-Psychologie. *Industrielle Psychotechnik, 4,* 193–207.

MOEN, P., DOWNEY, G., & BOLGER, N. (1990). Labor-force reentry among U.S. homemakers in midlife: A life-course analysis. *Gender and Society, 4,* 230–243.

MOGG, K., MATHEWS, A., & WEINMAN, J. (1987). Memory bias in clinical anxiety. *Journal of Abnormal Psychology, 96,* 94–98.

MONAHAM, L., KUHN, D., & SHUBER, P. (1979). Intrapsychic versus cultural explorative of the "fear of success" motive. *Journal of Personality and Social Psychology, 29,* 60–64.

MONAHAN, J., & LOFTUS, E. (1982). The psychology of law. *Annual Review of Psychology, 33,* 441–475.

MONSON, T., & SNYDER, M. (1977). Actors observers, and the attribution process: Toward a reconceptualization. *Journal of Experimental Social Psychology, 13,* 89–111.

MONTPLAISIR, J., POIRIER, G., & DEMONTIGNY, C. (1990). HLA antigens in depression and hypersomnia. *Biological Psychiatry, 27,* 664–666.

MOODY, R. (1975). *Life after life.* New York: Bantam.

MOOK, D. G. (1987). *Motivation: The organization of action.* New York: Norton.

MOORE-EDE, M. C., CZEISLER, C. A., & RICHARDSON, G. S. (1983a). Circadian timekeeping in health and disease. *New England Journal of Medicine, 309,* 469–476.

MOORE, M. L. (1978). *Realities in childbearing.* Philadelphia: Saunders.

MOORE, T. (1975). Training for what? Alternative emphasis? *AEP—Association of Educational Psychologists Journal, 3,* 21–24.

MORAY, N. (1959). Attention in dichotic listening. Affective cues and the influence of instructions. *Quarterly Journal of Experimental Psychology, 11,* 56–60.

MORELAND, R. & ZAJONC, R. (1982). Exposure effects in person perception: Familiarity, similarity and attraction. *Journal of Experimental Social Psychology, 18,* 395–415.

MORELAND, R. L., & LEVINE, J. M. (1988). Group dynamics over time: Development and socialization in small groups. In J. E. McGrath (Ed.), *The social psychology of time* (pp. 151–181). Newbury Park, CA: Sage.

MORENO, C. R., BOROD, J. C., WELKOWITZ, J., & ALPERT, M. (1990). Lateralization for the expression and perception of facial emotion as a function of age. *Neuropsychologia, 28,* 199–209.

MORENO, F. J. (1977). *Between faith and reason.* New York: New York University Press.

MORGAN, C. D., & MURRAY, H. A. (1935). A method for investigating phantasies: The Thematic Apperception Test. *Archives of Neurology and Psychiatry, 34,* 289–306.

MORGAN, M. J. (1989). Vision of solid objects. *Nature, 339,* 101–103.

MORGAN, M. J., FITCH, M. D., HOLMAN, J. G., & LEA, S. E. G. (1976). Pigeons learn the concept of an "A." *Perception, 5,* 57–66.

MORRELL, E. M., & HOLLANDWORTH, J. G. (1986). Norepinephrine alterations under stress conditions following the regular practice of meditation. *Psychosomatic Medicine, 48,* 270–277.

MORRIS, W. N. (1987). *Mood.* New York: Springer-Verlag.

MORRIS, W. N., WORCHEL, S., BOIS, J. L., PEARSON, J. A., ROUNTREE, C. A., SAMAHA, G. M., WACHTLER, J., & WRIGHT, S. L. (1976) Collective coping with stress: Group reactions to fear, anxiety, and ambiguity. *Journal of Personality and Social Psychology, 33,* 674–679.

MORRISON, A. M., WHITE, R. P., & VAN VELSOR, E. (1987, August). Executive women: Substance plus style. *Psychology Today,* pp. 18–26.

MORRISON, F. J., & LORD, C. (Eds.). (1984). *Applied developmental psychology.* New York: Academic.

MORSE, M. L., VENECIA, D., & MILATAIN, J. (1989). Near death experiences: A neurophysiological explanatory model. *Journal of Near Death Studies, 10,* 45–53.

MORTENSEN, C. (1972). *Communication: The study of human interaction.* New York: McGraw-Hill.

MORTIMER, J. A. (1983). Alzheimer's disease and senile dementia: Prevalence and incidence. In B. Reisberg (Ed.), *Alzheimer's disease* (pp. 141–148). New York: The Free Press.

MOSCOVICI, S. (1976). *Social influence and social changes.* London: Academic Press.

MOSCOVICI, S. (1985). Social influence and conformity. In G. Lindzey & E. Aronson (Eds.), *The handbook of social psychology* (3rd ed.). New York: Random House.

MOSCOVICI, S., & PERSONNAZ, B. (1980). Studies in social influences. Minority influence and conversion behavior in a perceptual look. *Journal of Experimental Social Psychology, 16,* 270–283.

MOSCOVICI, S., & ZAVALLONI, M. (1969). The group as a polarizer of attitudes. *Journal of Personality and Social Psychology, 12,* 125–135.

MOSLEY, J. L. (1985). High-speed memory-scanning task performance of mildly mentally retarded and nonretarded individuals. *American Journal of Mental Deficiency, 90,* 81–91.

MOSS, M., & AREND, R. (1977). Self-directed contact desensitization. *Journal of Consulting and Clinical Psychology, 45,* 730–738.

MOTT, T. (1986). Current status of hypnosis is the treatment of phobias. *American Journal of Clinical Hypnosis, 28,* 135–137.

MOWAT, F. (1963). *Never cry wolf.* Boston: Atlantic Monthly Press, Little, Brown.

MOYER, K. (1976). *The psychology of aggression.* New York: Harper & Row.

MOYER, K. E. (1983). *The psychology of aggression.* New York: Harper & Row.

MOYER, K. W. (1968). Kinds of aggression and their physiological basis. *Communications in Behavioral Biology, 2,* 65–87.

MUCCHI-FAINA, A. (1989, JUNE). *Minority influence processes: Assimilation, reactive differentiation, active differentiation.* Paper presented at the Third Workshop on Minority Influence, Perugia, Italy.

MUEHLENHARD, C., LINTON, M., FELTS, A., & ANDREWS, S. (1985 June). *Men's attitudes toward the justifiability of date rape: Intervening variables and possible solutions.* Paper presented at the Society for the Scientific Study of Sex.

MUELLER, C., & DONNERSTEIN, E. (1977). The effects of humor-induced arousal upon aggressive behavior. *Journal of Research in Personality, 11,* 73–82.

MUHELMAN, J. T., BRUKER, C., & INGRAM, C. M. (1976). The generosity shift. *Journal of Personality and Social Psychology, 34,* 344–351.

MULLEN, B. (1987). Self-attention theory: The effects of group composition on the individual. In B. Mullen & G. R. Goethals (Eds.), *Theory of group behavior.* New York: Springer-Verlag.

MULLEN, B., & BAUMEISTER, R. F. (1987). Group effects on self-attention and performance: Social loafing, social facilitation and social impairment. *Review of Personality and Social Psychology, 9,* 189–228.

MULLER, E. E. (1987). Neural control of somatotropic function. *Physiological Reviews, 10,* 962–1053.

MULVEY, E. P., GELLER, J., & ROTH, L. H. (1987). The promise and peril of involuntary outpatient commitment. *American Psychologist, 42,* 571–584.

MUNCHUS, G. (1983). Employer-employee based quality circles in Japan: Human resource implications for American farms. *Academy of Management Review, 8,* 255–261.

MUNSTERBERG, H. (1915). *Psychology and industrial efficiency.* Boston: Houghton Mifflin.

MURPHY, G. E. (1983). The problems in studying suicide. *Psychiatric Developments, 4,* 339–350.

MURRAY, H. (1938). *Explorations in personality.* New York: Oxford University Press.

MURRAY, J. R., POWERS, E. A., & HAVIGHURST, R. J. (1971). Personal and situational factors producing flexible careers. *The Gerontologist, 11,* 4–12.

MURSTEIN, B. I. (1972). Physical attractiveness and marital choice. *Journal of Personality and Social Psychology, 22,* 8–12.

MUSANTE, L., MacDOUGALL, J., & DEMBROSKI, T. (1984). The type A behavior pattern and attributions for success and failure. *Personality and Social Psychology Bulletin, 10,* 544–553.

MUSCHINSKY, P. (1987). *Psychology applied to work* (2nd ed.). Chicago: Dorsey.

MUSSEN, P. H., & JONES, M. C. (1957). Self-conceptions, motivations, and interpersonal attitudes of late and early maturing boys. *Child Development, 28,* 243–256.

MUZIKA, E. G. (1990). Evolution, emptiness and the fantasy self. *Journal of Humanistic Psychology, 30,* 89–100.

MYERS, D. G. (1982). Polarizing effect of social interaction. In J. Davis & G. Stocker-Kreidgaver (Eds.), *Group decision making.* New York: Academic.

NADLER, A., SHAPIRA, R., & BEN-ITZHAK, S. (1982). Good looks may help: Effects of helpers' physical attractiveness and sex of helper in males' and females' help-seeking behavior. *Journal of Personality and Social Psychology, 42,* 90–99.

NAGELMAN, D. B., HALE, S. L., & WARE, S. (1983). Prevalence of eating disorders in college women. Paper presented at the American Psychology Association, Anaheim.

NAHEMOW, L., & LAWTON, M. P. (1975). Similarity and propinquity in friendship formation. *Journal of Personality and Social Psychology, 32,* 205–213.

NAIL, P., LEVY, L., RUSSIN, R., & CRANDELL, R. (1981). Time estimation and obesity. *Personality and Social Psychology Bulletin, 7,* 139–146.

NANEZ, J. E. (1989). Perception of impending collision in 3- to 6-week-old human infants. *Infant Behavior and Development, 11,* 447–463.

NAPIER, R., & GERSHENFELD, M. (1981). *Groups: Theory and experience.* Boston: Houghton Mifflin.

NASH, R. (1967). *Wilderness and the American mind.* New Haven, CT: Yale University Press.

NATHAN, P. E. (1976). Alcoholism. In H. Leitenberg (Ed.). *Handbook of behavior modification and behavior therapy.* Englewood Cliffs, NJ: Prentice-Hall, Inc.

NATIONAL COMMISSION ON YOUTH. (1980). *The transition of youth to adulthood: A bridge too long.* Boulder, CO: Westview.

NATIONAL COUNCIL ON ALCOHOLISM (1986). *Alcoholics are sick people who can be helped.*

NATIONAL INSTITUTES OF HEALTH. (1984). Osteoporosis. *Consensus Development Conference Statement, 5*(3). Bethesda, MD: U.S. Government Printing Office.

NATIONAL RESEARCH COUNCIL. (1986). *Electronic travel aids: New directions for research.* Washington, DC: National Academy Press.

NEDELMAN, D., & SULZBACHER, S. (1972). Dicky at thirteen years of age: A long-term success following early applications of operant conditioning procedures. In G. Semb (Ed.), *Behavioral analysis and education.* Lawrence, KA: Follow-through Project.

NEDLER, A., & FISHER, J. (1984). Effects of donor-recipient relationships on recipients' reactions to aid. In E. Staub et al. (Eds.), *Development and maintenance of prosocial behavior.* New York: Plenum.

NEISSER, U. (1982). *Memory observed.* San Francisco: Freeman.

NEISSER, U. (1986). Remembering Pearl Harbor: Reply to Thompson and Cowan, *Cognition, 23,* 285–286.

NELSON, L. P., & NELSON, V. (1973). Religion and death anxiety. Paper presented at Society for the Scientific Study of Religion and Religious Research Association, San Franciso.

NEMETH, C. (1986). Intergroup relations between majority and minority. In S. Worchel & W. Austin (Eds.), *Psychology of intergroup relations.* Chicago: Nelson Hall.

NEMETH, C. (1991). Minority dissent as a stimulant to group performance. In S. Worchel, W. Wood, & J. Simpson (Eds.), *Group process and productivity.* Newbury Park, CA: Sage.

NEMETH, C., & STAW, B. M. (1989). The tradeoffs of social control and innovation in groups and organizations. In L. Berkowitz (Ed.), *Advances in experimental social psychology* (Vol. 23, pp. 175–210). Orlando, FL: Academic Press.

NEUGARTEN, B. L. (1968). The awareness of middle age. In B. L. Neugarten (Ed.), *Middle age and aging.* Chicago: University of Chicago Press.

NEUGARTEN, B. L. (1970). Dynamics of transition of middle age to old age. *Journal of Geriatric Psychiatry, 4,* 71–87.

NEUGARTEN, B. L., & HAGESTAD, G. O. (1976). Age and the life course. In R. H. Binstock & E. Shanas (Eds.), *Handbook of aging and the social sciences.* New York: Van Nostrand.

NEUGARTEN, B. L., & WEINSTEIN, K. K. (1964). The changing American grandparent. *Journal of Marriage and the Family, 26,* 199–204.

NEVID, J. S., LAVI, B., & PRIMAVERA, L. H. (1986). Cluster analysis of training orientations in clincial psychology. *Professional Psychology Research and Practice, 17,* 367–370.

NEWCOMER, J. (1977). Sonicguide: Its use with public school blind children. *Journal of Visual Impairment and Blindness, 71,* 268–271.

NEWELL, A., SHAW, J. C., & SIMON, H. A. (1958). Elements of a theory of human problem solving. *Psychological Review, 65,* 151–166.

NEWELL, A., & SIMON, H. A. (1972). *Human problem solving.* Englewood Cliffs, NJ: Prentice-Hall, Inc.

NEWMAN, J. P., PATTERSON, C. M., & KASSON, D. S. (1987). Response perseveration in psychopaths. *Journal of Abnormal Psychology, 96,* 145–148.

NEWMAN, L., & HIRT, J. (1983). The psychoanalytic theory of depression symptoms as a function of aggressive wishes and level of field articulation. *Journal of Abnormal Psychology, 92,* 42–48.

NEWMAN, O. (1972). *Defensible space.* New York: Macmillan.

NEWMAN, O. (1975). *Design guidelines for creating defensible space.* Washington, DC: U.S. Government Printing Office.

NEWSWEEK. (March 28, 1988). The drug gangs. Pp. 20–29.

NEW YORK TIMES (March 17, 1986). *Advancing on Schizophrenia.* Section I, p. 1.

NEW YORK TIMES NEWS SERVICE. (1981, November 29). Depression linked to specific gene. *The New York Times.*

NEZU, A., NEZU, C., & BLISSETT, S. (1988). Sense of humor as a moderator of the relation between stressful events and psychological distress: A prospective analysis. *Journal of Personality and Social Psychology, 54,* 520–525.

NEZU, A. M., & CARNEVALE, G. J. (1987). Interpersonal problem solving and coping reactions of Vietnam veterans with posttraumatic stress disorder. *Journal of Abnormal Psychology, 96,* 155–157.

NICHOLLS, J. G. (1986). Varieties of interpretation achievement motivation: A reply to Kukla. *Psychological Review, 93,* 381–382.

NIELSEN, A. C. *National audience demographics, 1988. Psychological Review, 93,* 381–382.

NIETZEL, M. T., & BERNSTEIN, P. A. (1987). *Introduction to clinical psychology* (2nd ed.). Englewood Cliffs, NJ: Prentice Hall.

NIJIMA, A. (1969). Afferent impulse charges from glucoreceptors in the liver of the guinea pig. *Annals of the New York Academy of Sciences, 157*(2) 690–700.

NIMH (1982). *Television and behavior: Ten years of scientific progress and implications for the eighties.* Washington, DC: U.S. Government Printing Office.

NISBETT, R., & ROSS, L. (1980). *Human inference: Strategies and shortcomings of social judgment.* Englewood Cliffs, NJ: Prentice-Hall.

NISBETT, R. E. (1968). Taste, deprivation, and weight determinants of eating behavior. *Journal of Personality and Social Psychology, 10,* 107–116.

NISBETT, R. E. (1972). Hunger, obesity, and the ventromedial hypothalamus. *Psychological Review, 79,* 433–453.

NISBETT, R. E., & BORGIDA, E. (1975). Attribution and the psychology of prediction. *Journal of Personality and Social Psychology, 32*(5), 932–943.

NOESJIRWAN, J. (1977). Contrasting cultural patterns of interpersonal closeness in doctors' waiting rooms in Sydney and Jakarta. *Journal of Cross-Cultural Psychology, 8,* 359–368.

NORMAN, D. A. (1973). Memory, knowledge, and the answering of questions. In R. L. Solso (Ed.), *Contemporary issues in cognitive psychology.* Washington, DC: Winston.

NORMAN, D. A., & RUMELKART, D. E. (1975) *Exploration in cognition.* San Francisco: Freeman.

NORMAN, P. (1984). *Symphony for the devil: The Rolling Stones story.* New York: Dell.

NORMAN, W. T. (1963). Toward an adequate taxonomy of personality attributes. Replicated factor structure in peer nomination personality ratings. *Journal of Abnormal and Social Psychology, 66,* 574–583.

NORMOYLE, J., & LAVROKES, P. (1984). Fear of crime in elderly women: Perceptions of control, predictability, and territory. *Personality and Social Psychology Bulletin, 10,* 191–202.

NORRIS, M. P., & WEST, R. L. (1990). Adult age differences in activity memory: Cue and strategy utilization. In T. M. Hess (Ed.), *Aging and cognition: Knowledge, organization and utilization adult development and aging* (pp. 1–31). Amsterdam: Elsevier.

NOTTLEMAN, E., & SUSMAN, E. (1985). *Passage through puberty.* Paper presented at the annual meeting of the American Association for the Advancement of Science.

NUCKOLLS, K., CAASEL, J., & KAPLAN, B. (1972). Psychosocial assets, life crisis and the prognosis of pregnancy. *American Journal of Epidemiology, 95,* 431–441.

NUSSBAUM, M. P., BLETHEN, S. L., CHASALOW, F. I., & JACOBSON, M. S. (1990). Blunted growth hormone responses to clonidine in adolescent girls with early anorexia nervosa: Evidence for an early hypothalamic defect. *Journal of Adolescent Health Care, 11,* 145–148.

NYDEGGER, C., & MITTENESS, L. (1979). Transitions in fatherhood. *Generations, 4,* 14–15.

OADES, R. D. (1985). The role of noradrenaline in tuning and dopamine in switching between signals in the CNS. *Neuroscience & Biobehavioral Reviews, 9,* 261–282.

OAKNIN, S., RODRIGUEZ DEL CASTILLO, A., GUERRA, M., BATTANER, E., & MAS, M. (1989). Change in forebrain Na, K-ATPase activity and serum hormone levels during sexual behavior in male rats. *Physiology and Behavior, 45,* 407–410.

O'BOYLE, M. W., & BEWNBOW C. P. (1990). Enhanced right hemisphere involvement during cognitive processing may relate to intellectual precocity. *Neuropsychologia, 28,* 211–216.

O'BRYANT, S. L., & MORGAN, L. A. (1990). Recent widows' kin support and orientation to self-sufficiency. *Gerontologist, 30,* 391–398.

O'CONNELL, A., & RUSSO, M. (Eds.). (1990). *Women in psychology: A bibliographic sourcebook.* Westport, CN: Greenwood Press.

ODEGAARD, C. E. (1987). An historical perspective on the dilemmas confronting psychology. *American Psychologist, 42,* 1048–1051.

OGLOFF, J. R. (1990). The admissibility of expert testimony regarding malingering and deception. Special Issue: Malingering and deception: An update. *Behavioral Sciences and the Law, 8,* 27–43.

OLDS, J. (1973). Brain mechanisms of reinforcement learning. In L. D. E. Berlyne & K. B. Masden (Eds.), *Pleasure, reward, preference: Their nature, determinants, and role in behavior.* New York: Academic.

OLSEN, K. M. (1969). Social class and age-group differences in the timing of family status changes: A study of age norms in American society. Unpublished doctoral dissertation, University of Chicago.

OLSEN, Y. D., BRUHN, P., & OBERG, R. G. E. (1986). Cortical hyperprofusion as a possible cause of subcortical aphasia. *Brain, 109,* 393–410.

OLSON, J., & ZANNA, M. (1991). Attitudes and beliefs. In R. Baron & W. Graziano (Eds.), *Social psychology.* New York: Holt, Rinehart & Winston.

O'LEARY, J., & WRIGHT, F. (1986). Shame and gender issues in pathological narcissism. *Psychoanalytic Psychology, 3,* 327–339.

O'LEARY, K. D., & WILSON, G. T. (1987). *Behavior therapy: Application and outcome* (2nd ed.). Englewood Cliffs, NJ: Prentice Hall.

OLSHAN, N. H. (1980). *Power over your pain without drugs.* New York: Rawson, Wade.

OLSON, I. M., & ZANNA, M. P. (1983). Attitudes and beliefs. In D. Perlman & P. C. Cozby (Eds.), *Social psychology.* New York: Holt.

OLSZEWSKI, D. A., ROTTON, J., & SOLER, E. (1976). Conversation, conglomerate noise, and behavioral after-effects. Paper presented at Midwest Psychology Association meeting, Chicago.

OLTON, D. S., BECKER, J. T., & HANDELMANN, G. E. (1980). Hippocampal function: Working memory or cognitive mapping. *Physiological Psychology, 8,* 239–246.

OLWEUS, D., MATTESSON, A., SCHIALLENG, D., & LOW, H. (1988). Circulating testosterone levels and aggression in adolescent males: A casual analysis. *Psychosomatic Medicine, 50,* 261–272.

O'NEAL, E., BRUNAULT, M., CARIFIO, M., TRAUTWINE, R., & EPSTEIN, J. (1980). Effect of insult upon personal space. *Journal of Nonverbal Behavior, 5,* 56–62.

OPTIONS FOR HEALTH. (1987). *Police woman offers suggestions for preventing sexual assault.* Temple, TX: Scott and White Hospital.

ORNE, M. T. (1962). On the social psychology of the psychological experiment: With particular reference to demand characteristics and their implications. *American Psychologist, 17,* 776–783.

ORNE, M. T. (1965). Social control in the psychological experiment: Antisocial behavior and hypnosis. *Journal of Personality and Social Psychology, 1,* 189–200.

ORNE, M. T. (1972). On the simulating subject as a quasi-control group in hypnosis research: What, why, and how. In E. Fromm & R. E. Shor (Eds.), *Hypnosis: Research development and perspectives.* Chicago: Aldine.

ORNE, M. T. (1980). In G. D. Burrows & L. Dennerstein (Eds.), *Handbook of hypnosis and psychosomatic medicine.* Amsterdam: Elsevier/North Holland, pp. 29–51.

ORNITZ, E. M. (1976). The modulation of sensory input and motor output in autistic children. In E. Scholpler & R. J. Reichler (Eds.), *Psychopathology and child development.* New York: Plenum.

ORNSTEIN, R. E. (1977). *The psychology of consciousness* (2nd ed.). New York: Harcourt Brace Jovanovich.

ORNSTEIN, S., & ISABELLA, L. A. (1990). Age vs. stage models of career attitudes of women: A partial replication and extension. *Journal of Vocational Behavior, 36,* 1–19.

ORR, S. P., & LANZETTA, J. T. (1984). Extinction of an emotional response in the presence of facial expressions of emotion. *Motivation and Emotion, 8,* 55–66.

ORTONY, A., & TURNER, T. (1990). What's basic about basic emotion? *Psychology Review, 97,* 315–331.

OSGOOD, C. E. (1966). Dimensionality of the semantic space for communication via facial expressions. *Scandinavian Journal of Psychology, 7,* 1–30.

OSIPOW, S. H. (1987). Counseling psychology: Theory, research, and practice in career counseling. In M. R. Rozenzweig & L. W. Porter (Eds.), *Annual Review of Psychology,* Vol. 38. Palo Alto, CA: Annual Review.

OSKAMP, S. (1988). *Television as a social issue.* Newbury Park, CA: Sage Publications.

OSKAMP, S. (1984). Introduction: Social and organizational psychology. In S. Oscamp (Ed.), *Applied social psychology annual,* Vol. 5. Beverly Hills, CA: Sage.

OTT, D., & ECKMILLER, R. (1989). Dynamic adaptation of the blind pointing characteristic to stepwise lateral tilts of body, head, and trunk. *Behavioral Brain Research, 30,* 99–110.

OVERTON, S., & FORREST, L. (1986). Career planning of undergraduates: The Career Assistance Project. *Journal of College Student Personnel, 27,* 275–276.

OWEN, D. R. (1972). The 47, XYY male: A review. *Psychological Review, 78,* 209–233.

PAAP, K. R., & ROSKE-HOFSTRAND, R. J. (1986). The optimal number of menu options per panel. *Human Factors, 28,* 377–385.

PACHELLA, R. G. (1986). Personal values and the value of expert testimony. [Special Issue: The ethics of expert testimony], *Law and Human Behavior, 10,* 145–150.

PAGE, H. A., ELFNER, L. B., & JARNISON, N. (1966). Autokinetic effect as a function of intermittency of the light source. *Psychological Record, 16,* 189–192.

PALUDI, M. (1984). Psychomatic properties and underlying assumptions of four objective measures of fear of success. *Sex Roles, 10,* 765–781.

PANIAGUA, F. A. (1986). Synthetic behaviorism: Remarks on function and structure. *Psychological Record, 36,* 179–184.

PAPATHOMAS, T. V., & JULESZ, B. (1989). Stereoscopic illusion based on the proximity principle. *Perception, 18,* 589–594.

PARASURAMAN, S., GREENHAUS, J. H., RABINOWITZ, S. & BEDEIAN, A. G. (1989). Work and family variables as mediators of the relationship between wives' employment and husbands' well-being. *Academy of Management Journal, 32,* 185–201.

PARKE, D., BERKOWITZ, D., LEYENS, J. P., WEST, S. G., & SEBASTIAN, J. R. (1977). Some effects of violent and nonviolent movies on the behavior of juvenile delinquents. *Advances in Experimental Social Psychology, 10,* 139–169.

PARKER, I. (1989). *The crisis in modern social psychology—and how it ended.* London: Routledge Kegan Paul.

PARKES, C. M., & BROWN, R. (1972). Health after bereavement: A controlled study of young Boston widows and widowers. *Psychosomatic Medicine, 34,* 449–461.

PARROTT, W., & SABINI, J. (1990). Mood and memory under natural conditions: Evidence for mood incongruent recall. *Journal of Personality and Social Psychology, 59,* 321–336.

PASAMANICK, B., & LILIENFELD, A. (1955). Association of maternal and fetal factors with the development of mental deficiency: I. Abnormalities in the prenatal and perinatal periods. *Journal of the American Medical Association, 159,* 155–160.

PATTERSON, B. C. (1979). *Hondo, my father.* Austin, TX: Shoal Creek Publishers.

PATTERSON, F. G. (1978). The gestures of a gorilla: Language acquisition in another pongid. *Brain and Language, 5,* 72–97.

PATTERSON, G. R. (1979). A performance theory for coercive family interaction. In R. B. Cairns (Ed.). *Social interaction: Analysis and illustrations.* Hillsdale, NJ: Erlbaum.

PATTERSON, M. (1977). Interpersonal distance affect and equilibrium theory. *Journal of Social Psychology, 101,* 205–214.

PAUL, S. M. (1977). Movement and madness: Toward a biological model of schizophrenia. In J. D. Master & M. E. P. Seligman (Eds.), *Psychopathology: Experimental models.* San Francisco: Freeman.

PAULUS, D. L., & MARTIN, C. L. (1987). The structure of personality capabilities. *Journal of Personality and Social Psychology, 52,* 354–365.

PAULUS, P., McCAIN, G., & COX, V. (1978). Death rates, psychiatric commitments, blood pressure and perceived crowding as a function of institutional crowding. *Environmental Psychology and Nonverbal Behavior, 3,* 107–116.

PAULUS, P., & McCAIN, G. (1983). Crowding in jails. *Basic and applied social psychology, 4,* 89–107.

PAVIO, A. (1978). Comparisons of mental clocks. *Journal of Experimental Psychology: Human Perception and Performance, 4,* 61–71.

PAVIO, A. (1986). *Mental representations: A dual coding approach.* New York: Oxford.

PAVLOV, I. P. (1927). *Conditioned reflexes.* New York: Oxford University Press.

PAYNE, P. A., & FRIEDMAN, G. H. (1986). Group applications of hypnosis for college students. *Journal of College Student Personnel, 27,* 154–160.

PEABODY, D. (1987). Selecting representative trait adjectives. *Journal of Personality and Social Psychology, 52,* 81–90.

PEAKE, P., & MISCHEL, W. (1984). Getting lost in the search for large coefficients: Reply to Conley. *Psychological Review, 91,* 497–501.

PEARCE, J. M. (1987). A model for stimulus generalization in Pavlovian conditioning. *Psychological Review, 94,* 61–73.

PEARLIN, L. I. (1980). Life strains and psychological distress among adults. In M. J. Smelser & E. H. Erikson (Eds.), *Themes of work and love in adulthood.* Cambridge, MA: Harvard University Press.

PEARSON, J. L., HUNTER, A. G., ENSMINGER, M. E., & KELLAM, S. G. (1990). Black grandmothers in multigenerational households: Diversity in family structuring and parenting involvement in the Woodlawn community. Special Issue: Minority children. *Child Development, 61,* 434–442.

PEDERSON, F. A., CAIN, R., ZASLOW, M., & ANDERSON, B. (1983). Variations in infant experience associated with alternative family role organization. In L. Laesa & I. Siegel (Eds.), *Families as learning environments for children.* New York: Plenum.

PEKALA, R. J., & FORBES, E. J. (1990). Subjective effects of several stress management strategies: With reference to attention. *Behavioral Medicine, 16,* 13–39.

PELLEGRINI, R. (1973). Impressions of male personality as a function of beardedness. *Psychology, 10,* 29.

PELLEGRINO, J. W. (1985, October). Anatomy of analogy. *Psychology Today,* pp. 49–54.

PENFIELD, W. (1975). *The mastery of the mind: A critical study of consciousness and the human brain.* Princeton, NJ: Princeton University Press.

PENFIELD, W., & RASMUSSEN, T. (1950). *The cerebral cortex of man.* New York: Macmillan.

PENICK, S. B., SMITH, G. P., WIENEKE, K., JR., & HINKLE, L. E. (1963). An experimental evaluation of the relationship between hunger and gastric motility. *American Journal of Physiology, 205,* 421–426.

PENNEBAKER, J. W. (1980). Perceptual and environmental determinants of coughing. *Basic and Applied Social Psychology, 1,* 83–91, 94.

PENNEBAKER, J. W. (1982). *The psychology of physical symptoms.* New York: Springer-Verlag.

PENNEBAKER, J. W., & SKELTON, A. (1981). Selective monitoring of physical sensations. *Journal of Personality and Social Psychology, 41,* 213–223.

PEPLER, R. (1963). Performance and well-being in heat. In J. Hardy (Ed.), *Temperature: Its measurement and control in science and industry, 3,* Part 3. New York: Van Nostrand.

PEREZ, J. (1979). *Family counseling.* New York: Van Nostrand.

PERLS, F. S. (1969). *Ego, hunger and aggression: The beginning of Gestalt therapy.* New York: Random House.

PERLS, F. S. (1969). *Gestalt therapy verbatim.* Lafayette, CA: Real People Press.

PERLS, F. S. (1970). Four lectures. In J. Fagan & I. L. Sheperd (Eds.), *Gestalt therapy now.* Palo Alto, CA: Science and Behavior Books.

PEROVE, D. R., & SPIELBERGER, C. D. (1966). Anxiety and the perception of punishment. *Mental Hygiene, 50,* 390–397.

PERRONE, J. A. (1986). Anisotropic responses to motion toward and away from the eye. *Perception & Psychophysics, 39,* 1–8.

PERRY, D. G., WHITE, A. J., & PERRY, L. C. (1984). Does early sextyping result from children's attempts to match their behavior to sex role stereotypes? *Child Development, 55,* 2114–2121.

PERSINGER, M. A., & KRIPPNER, S. (1989). Dream ESP experiments and geomagnetic activity. *Journal of the American Society for Psychical Research, 83,* 101–110.

PERVIN, L. A. (1963). Performance and satisfaction as a function of individual-environment fit. *Psychological Bulletin, 69,* 56–68.

PESSIN, J. (1933). The comparative effects of social and mechanical stimulation on memorizing. *American Journal of Psychology, 45,* 263–270.

PETERSON, C., & SELIGMAN, M. (1984). Causal explanations as a risk factor for depression: Theory and evidence. *Psychological Review, 91,* 347–375.

PETERSON, C. C., & MURPHY, L. (1990). Adolescents' thoughts and feelings about AIDS in relation to cognitive maturity. *Journal of Adolescence, 13,* 185–187.

PETERSON, J. A., & PAYNE, B. (1975). *Love in the later years.* New York: Associated Press.

PETERSON, L. R., & PETERSON, M. J. (1959). Short-term retention of individual items. *Journal of Experimental Psychology, 58,* 193–198.

PETERSON, S. A., & GREIL, A. L. (1990). Death experience and religion. *Omega Journal of Death and Dying, 21,* 75–82.

PETRI, H. L. (1991). *Motivation: Theory, research, and applications,* 3rd ed. Belmont, CA: Wadsworth.

PETTY, H., & CACIOPPO, J. T. (1988). The elaboration likelihood model of persuasion. In L. Berkowitz (Ed.), *Advances in experimental social psychology,* Vol. 19.

PETTY, R., & CACIOPPO, J. (1990). Involvement and persuasion: Tradition versus integration. *Psychological Bulletin, 107,* 367–374.

PHARES, E. J. (1976). *Locus of control in personality.* Morristown, NJ: General Learning Press.

PHARES, E. J. (1984). *Introduction to personality.* Columbus, OH: Merrill.

PHARES, E. J. (1988). *Clinical psychology: Concepts, methods, and professions* (3rd ed.). Chicago: Dorsey.

PHARES, E. J. (1988). *Introduction to personality* (2nd ed.). Glenview, IL: Scott Foresman.

PHINNEY, V., JENSEN, L., OLSEN, J., & CUNDICK, B. (1990). The relationship between early development and psychosexual behaviors in adolescent females. *Adolescence, 25,* 321–332.

PIAGET, J. (1932). *The moral judgement of the child.* New York: Harcourt Brace Jovanovich.

PIAGET, J. (1960). *The child's conception of the world.* London: Routledge.

PILIAVIN, I., RODIN, J., & PILIAVIN, J. (1969). Good Samaritanism: An underground phenomenon? *Journal of Personality and Social Psychology, 13,* 289–299.

PILLAI, M., & JAMES, D. (1990). Are the behavioral states of the newborn comparable to those of the fetus? *Early Human Development, 22,* 39–49.

PION, G. M. (1987). Preliminary report: 1985 doctorate employment survey. Washington, D.C.: American Psychological Association.

PITTMAN, T. S., & HELLER, J. F. (1987). *Social motivation. Annual review of psychology.* Palo Alto, CA: Annual Review, Inc.

PLANNED PARENTHOOD. (1976). 11 million teenagers: What can be done about the epidemic of adolescent pregnancies in the United States? New York: PPFA.

PLINER, P., CHAIKEN, S., & FLETT, G. (1990). Gender differences in concern with body weight and physical appearance over the life span. *Personality and Social Psychology Bulletin, 16,* 263–273.

PLOMIN, R., & DEFRIES, J. C. (1980). Genetics and intelligence: Recent data. *Intelligence, 4,* 15–24.

PLOMIN, R., DEFRIES, J. C., & McCLEARN, G. E. (1980). *Behavioral genetics: A primer.* San Francisco: Freeman.

PLUTCHIK, R. (1980). *Emotion: A psychoevolutionary analysis.* New York: Harper & Row.

PODD, M. H. (1972). Ego identity status and morality: The relationship between two developmental constructs. *Developmental Psychology, 6,* 497–507.

POLLEN, D. A., & RONNER, S. F. (1982). Spatial computation performed by simple and complex cells in the visual cortex of the cat. *Vision Research, 22,* 101–118.

POON, L. W. (1980). *Aging in the 1980's.* Washington, DC: American Psychological Association.

POPE, H. G., & KATZ, D. L. (1990). Homicide and near-homicide by anabolic steroid users. *Journal of Clinical Psychiatry, 51,* 28–31.

POPE, K. (1990). Ethical and malpractice issues in hospital practice. *American Psychologist, 45,* 1066–1070.

POPLIN, D. (1978). *Social problems.* Glenview, IL: Scott, Foresman.

POPULATION REFERENCE BUREAU, 1977. (1977) *World population data sheet.* Washington, DC: Population Reference Bureau.

PORTEOUS, J. D. (1977). *Environment and behavior.* Reading, MA: Addison-Wesley.

PORTUGES, S. H., & FESHBACH, N. D. (1972). The influence of sex and social class upon imitations of teachers by elementary school children. *Child development, 43,* 981–989.

POTTER, R. K., KOPP, G. A., & KOPP, H. G. (1966). *Visible speech.* New York: Dover.

POULTON, E. C. (1970). *Environment and human efficiency.* Springfield, IL: Chas. C Thomas.

POULTON, E. C. (1978). A new look at the effects of noise: A rejoinder. *Psychological Bulletin, 85,* 1068–1079.

POULTON, E. C. (1979). Composite model for human performance in continuous noise. *Psychological Review, 86,* 361–375.

POWER, T. G., & PARKE, R. D. (1986). Patterns of early socialization: Mother- and father-infant interaction in the home. *International Journal of Behavioral Development, 9,* 331–341.

POWLEY, T., & KEESEY, R. (1970). Relationship of body weight to the lateral hypothalamic feeding syndrome. *Journal of Comparative and Physiological Psychology, 70,* 25–36.

PRATKANIS, A., GREENWOLD, A., LEIPPE, M., & BAUMGARDNER, M. (1988). In search of reliable persuasion effects: III. The sleeper effect is dead. Long live the sleeper effect. *Journal of Personality and Social Psychology, 54,* 203–218.

PREMACK, A. J., & PREMACK, D. (1972, November). Teaching language to an ape. *Scientific American, 227,* 25–36.

PREMACK, D. (1976). *Intelligence in ape and man.* Hillsdale, NJ: Erlbaum.

PRENTICE-DUNN, S., & ROGERS, R. (1980). Effects of deindividuating situational cues and aggressive models on subjective deindividuation and aggression. *Journal of Personality and Social Psychology, 39,* 104–113.

PRESIDENT'S COMMISSION ON MENTAL HEALTH, 1978. REPORT TO THE PRESIDENT (1978). Washington, DC: U.S. Government Printing Office.

PRESIDENT'S COUNCIL ON ENVIRONMENTAL QUALITY. (1978). Environmental Protection Agency, Washington, DC: U.S. Government Printing Office.

PRESSER, H. B. (1977). Social consequences of teenage childbearing. In W. Petersen & L. Day (Eds.), *Social demography: The state of the art*. Cambridge, MA: Harvard University Press.

PRESSMAN, M. R. (1986). Sleep and sleep disorders: An Introduction. [Special Issue: Sleep disorders], *Clinical Psychology Review, 6*, 1–9.

PRIBRAM, K. (1977). Some observations on the organization of studies of mind, brain, and behavior. In N. E. Zinberg (Ed.), *Alternate states of consciousness: Multiple perspectives on the study of consciousness*. New York: Free Press.

PRIBRAM, K. H. (1988). A holonomic brain theory: Cooperativity and reciprocity in processing the configural and cognitive aspects of perception. Hillsdale, NJ: Erlbaum.

PRITCHARD, R. D. (1990). *Measuring and improving organizational productivity: A practical guide*. New York: Praeger.

PROFFITT, D. R., & CUTTING, J. E. (1980). An invariant for wheel-generated motions and the logic of its determination. *Perception, 9*, 435–449.

PYSZCYNSKI, T., HOLT, K., & GREENBERG, J. (1987). Depression, self-focused attention, and expectancies for positive and negative future life events for self and others. *Journal of Personality and Social Psychology, 52*, 994–1001.

QUATTRONE, G. (1985). On the perception of a group's variability. In S. Worchel & W. Austin (Eds.), *Psychology of intergroup relations*, Chicago: Nelson-Hall.

QUATTRONE, G., & JONES, E. (1980). The perception of variability with in-groups and out-groups: Implications for the law of small numbers. *Journal of Personality and Social Research, 38*, 141–152.

QUAY, H. C., ROUTH, D. K., & SHAPIRO, S. K. (1987). Psychopathology of childhood from description to validation. In M. Rosenzweig & L. Porter (Eds.), *Annual review of psychology*. Palo Alto, CA: Annual Review Inc.

QUIMBY, S. L. (1989). The near death experience as an event in consciousness. *Journal of Humanistic Psychology, 20*, 87–100.

RAAIJMAKERS, J. G. W., & SHIFFRIN, R. M. (1981). Search of associative memory. *Psychological Review, 88*, 93–134.

RACHMAN, S., & HODYSON, R. (1980). *Obsessions and compulsions*. Englewood Cliffs, NJ: Prentice-Hall.

RAPOPORT, R., & RAPOPORT, R. N. (1971). *Dual career families*. Baltimore: Penguin.

RASMUSSEN, S., & EISEN, J. (1988). Clinical and epidemiologic findings of significance to neuropharmacologic trials in OCD. *Psychopharmacology Bulletin, 24*, 466–470.

RASMUSSEN, S., & EISEN, J. (1990). Epidemiology of obsessive-compulsive disorder. *Journal of Clinical Psychiatry, 51*, 10–13.

RAVEN, J. C. (1947). *Progressive matrices*. London: Lewis.

RAY, O. S., & KSIR, C. (1987). *Drugs, society, and human behavior* (4th ed.). St. Louis, MO: Times Mirror/Mosby College Publishing.

RAYNER, K. (Ed.). (1983). *Eye movements in reading: Perceptual and language processes*. New York: Academic.

RAYNOR, J. O. (1970). Relationships between achievement-related motives, future orientation, and academic performance. *Journal of Personality and Social Psychology, 15*, 28–33.

READ, P. P. (1974). *Alive: The story of the Andes survivors*. Philadelphia: Lippincott.

REDDING, G. M., & WALLACE, B. (1988). Head posture effects in prism adaptation during hallway exposure. *Perception and Psychophysics, 44*, 69–75.

REDFERN, P. H. (1989). "Jet-lag": Strategies for prevention and cure. *Human Psychopharmacology: Clinical and Experimental, 4*, 159–169.

REED, S. K. (1988). *Cognition: Theory and application*. Pacific Grove, CA: Brooks/Cole, 63.

REGAN, D. (1986). Visual processing of four kinds of relative motion. *Vision Research, 26*, 127–145.

REGAN, D. T., WILLIAMS, M., & SPARLING, S. (1972). Voluntary expiation of guilt: A field experiment. *Journal of Personality and Social Psychology, 24*, 42–45.

REICHEL, D., & GELLER, E. (1981). Applications of behavioral analysis for conserving transportation energy. In A. Baum & J. Singer (Eds.), *Advances in environmental psychology* (Vol. 3). Hillsdale, NJ: Erlbaum.

REISER, M. (1980). *Handbook of investigative hypnosis*. Los Angeles: LEHI Publishing Co.

REISER, M. (1982). Erickson and law enforcement: Investigative hypnosis. In J. K. Zeig (Ed.), *Ericksonian approach to hypnosis and psychotherapy*. New York: Brunner/Mazel.

REISER, M. (1986). Admission of hypnosis-induced recollections into memory. *American Journal of Forensic Psychology, 4*, 19–28.

REISER, M., & NIELSON, M. (1980). Investigative hypnosis: A developing specialty. *American Journal of Clinical Hypnosis, 23*, 75–77.

RESCORLA, R. A., & HOLLAND, P. C. (1982). Behavioral studies of associative learning in animals. *Annual Review of Psychology, 33*, 265–308.

RESTAK, R. (1979). *The brain: The last frontier*. Garden City, NY: Doubleday.

RESTAK, R. (1984). *The brain*. New York: Bantam.

RESTLE, F. (1962). The selection of strategies in cue learning. *Psychological Review, 69*, 329–343.

RHODEWALT, F. (1984). Self-involvement, self-attribution and the Type A coronary-prone behavior pattern. *Journal of Personality and Social Psychology, 47*, 662–670.

RHOLES, W. S., RISKIN, J., & LANE, J. (1987). Emotional states and memory biases: Effects of cognition priming and mood. *Journal of Personality and Social Psychology, 52*, 91–99.

RICE, B. (1974). Rattlesnakes, French fries, and pupillometric oversell. *Psychology Today, 7*, 55–59.

RICE, B. (1978). The new truth machine. *Psychology Today, 12*, 61–78.

RICE, R., GENTILE, D., & MCFARLIN, D. (1991). Facet importance and job satisfaction. *Journal of Applied Psychology, 76*, 31–39.

RICE, R. W., BENDER, L. R., & VITTERS, A. G. (1980). Leader sex, follower attitudes toward women, and leadership effectiveness: A laboratory study. *Organizational Behavior and Human Performance, 25*, 46–78.

RICHARDSON, G. A., & DAY, N. L. (1986). Alcohol use during pregnancy and neonatal outcome. *Infant Behavior and Development, 9*. [Special Issue: Abstracts of papers presented at the fifth international conference of infant studies.]

RILEY, M. W., JOHNSON, M. E., & FONER, A. (1972). *Aging and society: A sociology of age stratification*. New York: Russell Sage Foundation.

RIMLAND, B. (1964). *Infantile autism: The syndrome and its implications for a neural theory of behavior*. New York: Appleton-Century-Crofts.

RIMM, D. C., & MASTERS, J. C. (1979). *Behavior therapy: Techniques and empirical findings*. New York: Academic.

RING, K. (1980). *Life at death: A scientific investigation of the near-death experience*. New York: Cowark, McCann, & Geoghegan.

RINGNESS, T. A. (1975). *The affective domain in education*. Boston: Little, Brown.

RINGWALT, C. L., & PALMER, J. H. (1989). Cocaine and crack users compared. *Adolescence, 24*, 851–859.

RINN, W. E. (1988). Mental decline in normal aging: A review. *Journal of Geriatric Psychiatry and Neurology, 1*, 144–158.

RITCHIE, G. G. (WITH ELIZABETH SHERRILL). (1978). *Return from tomorrow*. Waco, TX: Chosen Books.

RITTLE, R. M. (1981). Changes in helping behavior: Self versus situational perceptions as mediators of foot-in-the-door effect. *Personality and Social Psychology Bulletin, 7*, 431–437.

RITZER, G. (1977). *Working: Conflict and change* (2nd ed.). Englewood Cliffs, NJ: Prentice-Hall.

ROBERTSON, J. F. (1976). Significance of grandparents: Perception of young adult grandchildren. *The Gerontologist, 16*, 137–140.

ROBINSON, F. P. (1941). *Effective behavior*. New York: Harper & Row.

ROCK, I. (1977). In defense of unconscious inference. In W. Epstein (Ed.), *Stability and constancy in visual perception: Mechanisms and processes*. New York: Wiley.

ROCK, I., & HARRIS, C. S. (1967). Vision and touch. *Scientific American, 216*, 96–104.

ROCK, I., & PALMER, S. (1990, December). The legacy of Gestalt psychology. *Scientific American*, pp. 84–90.

RODIN, J. (1975). Causes and consequences of time perception differences in overweight and normal weight people. *Journal of Personality and Social Psychology, 31*, 808–910.

RODIN, J. (1977). The effects of stimulus-bound behavior on biological self-regulation: Feeding, obesity and external control. In G. Schwartz & D. Shapiro (Eds.), *Consciousness and self-regulation*. New York: Plenum.

RODIN, J. (1981). Understanding obesity: Defining the samples. *Personality and Social Psychology Bulletin, 7*, 147–151.

RODIN, J., & BAUM, A. (1978). Crowding and helplessness: Potential consequences of density and loss of control. In A. Baum & Y. Epstein (Eds.), *Human response to crowding*. New York: Halsted.

RODIN, J., & ICKOVICS, J. (1990). Women's health: Review and research agenda as we approach the 21st century. *American Psychology, 45*, 1018–1034.

RODIN, J., & LANGER, E. (1977). Long-term effects of a control-relevant intervention with the institutionalized aged. *Journal of Personality and Social Psychology, 35*, 891–902.

RODIN, J., & SALOVEY, P. (1989). Health psychology. *Annual Review of Psychology*, Palo Alto, CA: Annual Reviewer.

RODIN, J., SLOCHOWER, J., & FLEMING, B. (1977). Effect on degree of obesity, age of onset, and weight loss on responsiveness to sensory and external stimuli. *Journal of Comparative and Physiological Psychology, 36*, 988–999.

RODIN, J., SLOCHOWER, J., & FLEMING, B. (1977). The effects of degree of obesity, age of onset and energy deficit on external responsiveness. *Journal of Comparative and Physiological Psychology, 91*, 586–597.

RODIN, J., SOLOMON, S., & METCALF, J. (1978). Role of control in mediating perceptions of density. *Journal of Personality and Social Psychology, 36*, 988–999.

RODNING, C., BECKWITH, L., & HOWARD, J. (1989). Characteristics of attachment organization and play organization in prenatally drug-exposed toddlers. *Development and Psychopathology, 4*, 277–289.

ROETHLISBERGER, F., & DICKSON, W. (1939).

Management and the worker. Cambridge, MA: Harvard University Press.

ROFE, Y. (1984). Stress and affiliation: A utility theory. *Psychological Review, 91,* 251–268.

ROFE, Y., & LEWIN, I. (1983). Affiliation among individuals suffering from severe diseases. Bar-Ilan University, Israel, unpublished manuscript.

ROGERS, B. J., & COLLETT, T. S. (1989). The appearance of surfaces specified by motion parallax and binocular disparity. *Quarterly Journal of Experimental Psychology: Human Experimental Psychology, 41,* 697–717.

ROGERS, C. (1942). *Counseling and psychotherapy: Newer concepts in practice.* Boston: Houghton Mifflin.

ROGERS, C. (1951). *Client-centered therapy.* Boston: Houghton Mifflin.

ROGERS, C. (1970). *On becoming a person: A therapist's view of psychotherapy.* Boston: Houghton Mifflin.

ROGERS, C. R. (1977). Carl Rogers on personal power: Inner strength and its revolutionary impact. New York: Delacorte.

ROGERS, C. R. (1980). *A way of being.* Boston: Houghton Mifflin.

ROGERS, C., & DYMOND, A. (1954). *Psychotherapy and personality change.* Chicago: University of Chicago.

ROGERS, C. R., & TRUAX, C. B. (1967). The therapeutic conditions antecedent to change: A theoretical view. In C. R. Rogers (Ed.), *The therapeutic relationship and its impact: A study of psychotherapy with schizophrenics.* Madison, WI: University of Wisconsin Press.

ROGERS, R. (1987). APA's position on the insanity defense: Empiricism versus emotionalism. *American Psychologist, 42,* 840–848.

ROGERS, R., & DECKER, C. (1975). Effects of fear appeals and physiological arousal upon emotion, attitudes, and cigarette smoking. *Journal of Personality and Social Psychology, 32,* 222–230.

ROGERS, R. L., MEYER, J. S., & MORTEL, K. H. (1990). After reaching retirement age physical activity sustains cerebral perfusion and cognition. *Journal of the American Geriatrics Society, 38,* 123–128.

ROHN, R. D., SARTES, R. M., KENNY, T., REYNOLDS, B., & HEALD, F. P. (1977). Adolescents who attempt suicide. *Journal of Pediatrics, 90,* 636–638.

ROITBLAT, H. L., BEVER, T. G., & TERRANCE, H. S. (1984). *Animal cognition.* Hillsdale, NJ: Erlbaum.

ROLLS, B. J. (1985). Experimental analysis of the effects of variety in a meal on human feeding. *American Journal of Clinical Nutrition, 42* (suppl. 5), 932–939.

ROLLS, B. J., VON DUIJENVOORDE, P. M., & ROLLS, E. T. (1984). Pleasantness changes and food intake in a varied four-course meal. *Appetite, 5,* 337–348.

ROOK, K. S. (1987). Social support versus companionship: Effects of life stress, loneliness, and evaluations by others. *Journal of Personality and Social Psychology, 52,* 1132–1147.

ROOS, P. (1968). Jurisdiction: An ecological concept. *Human Relations,* 75–84.

ROSCH, E. (1974). Linguistic relativity. In A. Silverstein (Ed.), *Human communication: Theoretical perspectives.* New York: Halstead.

ROSCH, E., & LLOYD, B. B. (Eds.). (1978). *Cognition and categorization.* Hillsdale, NJ: Erlbaum.

ROSCH, E. H., & MERVIS, C. B. (1975). Family resemblance: Studies in the internal structure of categories. *Cognitive Psychology, 7,* 573–605.

ROSE, A. (1952). *Union solidarity.* Minneapolis: University of Minnesota Press.

ROSE, S. (1973). *The conscious brain.* New York: Knopf.

ROSEMAN, I., SPINDEL, M., & JOSE, P. (1990). Appraisals of emotion-elevating events: Testing a theory of discrete emotions. *Journal of Personality and Social Psychology, 59,* 899–915.

ROSEN, G. (1987). Self-help treatment books and the commercialization of psychotherapy. *American Psychologist, 42,* 46–51.

ROSEN, M. A. (1975). A dual model of obsessional neurosis. *Journal of Consulting and Clinical Psychology, 43,* 453–459.

ROSEN, R., & ROSEN, L. (1981). *Human sexuality.* New York: Knopf.

ROSEN, S. (1984). Some paradoxical status implications of helping and being helped. In E. Staub et al. (Eds.), *Development and maintenance of prosocial behavior.* New York: Plenum.

ROSEN, S., BERGMAN, M., PLESTOR, D., EL-MOFTY, A., & SATTI, M. (1962). Presbycosis study of a relatively noise-free population in the Sudan. *Annals of Otology, Rhinology and Laryngology, 71,* 727–743.

ROSENBAUM, M. E. (1986). The repulsion hypothesis: On the nondevelopment of relationships. *Journal of Personality and Social Psychology, 51,* 1156–1166.

ROSENBERG, R. (1982). *Beyond separate spheres: Intellectual roots of modern feminism.* New Haven, CT: Yale University.

ROSENBLATT, P. C., & BUDD, L. B. (1977). Territoriality and privacy in married and unmarried couples. *Journal of Social Psychology, 31,* 240–242.

ROSENFELD, A. H. (1986, October). A farewell to jet lag? *Psychology Today,* p. 10.

ROSENFELD, P., GIACALONE, R., & TEDESCHI, J. (1984). Cognitive dissonance and impression management explanations for effort justification. *Personality and Social Psychology Bulletin, 10,* 394–401.

ROSENFIELD, S. (1989). The effects of woman's employment: Personal control and sex differences in mental health. *Journal of Health and Social Behavior, 30,* 77–99.

ROSENHAN, D. L. (1973). On being sane in insane places. *Science, 179,* 250–258.

ROSENHAN, D. L. (1975). The contextual nature of psychiatric diagnosis. *Journal of Abnormal Psychology, 84,* 462–474.

ROSENHAN, D. L., & SELIGMAN, M. (1984). *Abnormal psychology.* New York: Norton.

ROSENTHAL, D. (1970). *Genetic theory and abnormal behavior.* New York: McGraw-Hill.

ROSENTHAL, R. (1966). *Experimenter effects in behavioral research.* New York: Appleton-Century-Crofts.

ROSENTHAL, R. (1973). The Pygmalion effect lives. *Psychology Today,* 56–63.

ROSENTHAL, R., & JACOBSON, L. V. (1968a). Teacher expectations for the disadvantaged. *Scientific American, 4,* 19–23.

ROSENTHAL, R., & JACOBSON, L. V. (1968b). *Pygmalion in the classroom: Teacher expectation and pupils' intellectual development.* New York: Holt.

ROSENTHAL, T., & BANDURA, A. (1978). Psychological modeling: Theory and practice. In S. L. Garfield & A. E. Bergin (Eds.), *Handbook of psychotherapy and behavior change: An empirical analysis* (2nd ed.). New York: Wiley.

ROSENZWEIG, M. L. (1984). U.S. psychology and world psychology. *American Psychologist, 39,* 877–884.

ROSENZWEIG, M. R. (1966). Environmental complexity, cerebral change and behavior. *American Psychologist, 21,* 321–332.

ROSS, A. O. (1987). *Personality: The scientific study of complex human behavior.* New York: Holt.

ROSS, L. (1977). The intuitive psychologist and his short-comings: Distortions in the attribution process. In L. Berkowitz (Ed.), *Advances in experimental social psychology* (Vol. 10). New York: Academic.

ROSS, L., BIERBRAUER, G., & HOFFMAN, S. (1976). The role of attribution processes in conformity and dissent: Revisiting the Asch situation. *American Psychologist, 31,* 148–157.

ROSS, L. D. (1981). The "intuitive scientist" formulation and its developmental implications. In J. H. Harell & L. Ross (Eds.), *Social cognitive development: Frontiers and possible futures.* Cambridge, England: Cambridge University Press.

ROSS, L. D., LEPPER, M., STRACK, F., & STEINMETZ, J. (1977). Social explanation and social expectation: Effects of real and hypothetical explanations on subjective likelihood. *Journal of Personality and Social Psychology, 35,* 817–829.

ROSS, M., & SICOLY, F. (1979). Egocentric biases in availability and attribution. *Journal of Personality and Social Psychology, 37,* 322–336.

ROSS, N. (1984, November 24). Researchers debate use of animals in studies. Began, TX: Eagle. (Syndicated story—Knight-Ruler News Service.)

ROTHBART, M. K. (1971). Birth order and mother-child interaction in an achievement situation. *Journal of Personality and Social Psychology, 17,* 113–120.

ROTHBART, M., & BIRRELL, P. (1977). Attitude and the perception of faces. *Journal of Research in Personality, 11,* 209–215.

ROTTER, J. (1954). *Social learning and clinical psychology.* Englewood Cliffs, NJ: Prentice-Hall.

ROTTER, J. B. (1966). Generalized expectancies for internal vs. external control of reinforcement. *Psychological Monographs, 80* (whole No. 609).

ROTTER, J. B. (1975). Some problems and misconceptions related to the construct of internal versus external control of reinforcement. *Journal of Consulting and Clinical Psychology, 43,* 56–67.

ROTTER, J. B. (1978). Generalized expectancies for problem solving and psychotherapy. *Cognitive Therapy and Research, 2,* 1–10.

ROTTER, J. B. (1982). *The development and application of social learning theory.* New York: Praeger.

ROTTER, J. B., & HOCHREICH, D. J. (1975). *Personality.* Glenview, IL: Scott, Foresman.

ROTTON, J., BARRY, T., FREY, J., & SOLER, E. (1978). Air pollution and interpersonal attraction. *Journal of Applied Social Psychology, 8,* 57–71.

ROTTON, J., FREY, J., BARRY, T., MILLIGAN, M., & FITZPATRICK, M. (1979). The air pollution experience and interpersonal aggression. *Journal of Applied Social Psychology, 9,* 397–412.

ROUTTENBERG, A. (1968). The two-arousal hypothesis: Reticular formation and limbic system. *Psychological Review, 75,* 51–80.

ROWE, D. C. (1987). Resolving the person-situation debate: Invitation to interdisciplinary dialogue. *American Psychologist, 42,* 218–227.

ROYCE, J. R., STAYTON, W. R., & KINKADE, R. G. (1962). Experimental reduction of autokinetic movement. *American Journal of Psychology, 75,* 221–231.

ROZIN, P., & KALAT, J. W. (1971). Specific hungers and poison avoidance as adaptive specializations of learning. *Psychological Review, 78,* 459–486.

RUBIN, A. (1973). *Liking and loving: An invitation to social psychology.* New York: Holt.

RUBIN, I. (1966). Sex after forty and after seventy. In R. Brecher & E. Brecher (Eds.), *An analysis of human sexual response.* New York: Signet.

RUBIN, J. (1967). Increased self-acceptance: A means of reducing prejudice. *Journal of Personality and Social Psychology, 5,* 233–238.

RUBIN, J. A., PROVENZANO, F. J., & LURIA, A. (1974). The eye of the beholder: Parents' views on sex of newborns. *American Journal of Orthopsychiatry, 44,* 512–519.

RUBIN, L. B. (1979). *Woman of a certain age.* New York: Harper Colophon.

RUBIN, Z., PEPLAU, L. A., & HILL, C. T. (1978). Loving and learning: Sex differences in romantic attachments. Unpublished manuscript, Brandeis University.

RUFF, H. A., & BIRCH, H. G. (1974). Infant visual fixation: The effect of concentricity, curvilinearity, and the number of directions. *Journal of Experimental Child Psychology, 17,* 460–473.

RUMBAUGH, D. M. (Ed.). (1977). *Language learning by a chimpanzee: The Lana project.* New York: Academic.

RUMELHART, D. E., & McCLELLAND, J. L. (Eds.). (1986). *Parallel distributed processing, I and II.* Cambridge, MA: MIT Press.

RUSH, J. H. (1989). Imich essay contest paper: How the scientific establishment's acceptance of ESP and PK would influence contemporary society. *Journal of the American Society for Psychical Research, 83,* 241–249.

RUSHTON, J. P., BAINERD, C., & PRESSLEY, M. (1983). Behavioral development and construct validity: The principle of aggregation. *Psychological Bulletin, 94,* 18–38.

RUSSEK, M. (1971). Hepatic receptors and the neurophysiological mechanisms controlling feeding behavior. In S. Ehrenpreis (Ed.), *Neurosciences research* (Vol. 4). New York: Academic.

RUSSELL, D. (1984). Sexual exploitation: Rape, child abuse, and workplace harassment. Beverly Hills, CA: Sage.

RUSSELL, F. (1982). *Tragedy in Dedham.* New York: McGraw-Hill.

RUSSELL, J. (1991). In defense of a prototype approach to emotion concepts. *Journal of Personality and Social Psychology, 60,* 37–47.

RUSSO, N. F., & DENMARK, F. L. (1987). Contributions of women to psychology. *Annual Review of Psychology, 38,* 279–298.

RUTTER, M. (1974). The development of infantile autism. *Psychological Medicine, 4,* 147–163.

RUX, J. M. (1976). Widows and widowers: Instrumental skills, socioeconomic status, and life satisfaction. Unpublished doctoral dissertation, Pennsylvania State University.

RUYS, T. (1971). Windowless offices. *Man-Environment Systems, 1,* 549.

RYKMAN, R. M. (1979). *Theories of personality.* New York: Van Nostrand.

SAARILUOMA, P. (1985). Chess players' intake of task-relevant cues. *Memory and Cognition, 13,* 385–391.

SABEL, B. A., SLAVIN, M. D., & STEIN, D. G. (1984). GMI ganglioside treatment facilitates behavioral recovery from bilateral brain damage. *Science, 225,* 340–342.

SACERDOTI, E. D. (1974). Planning in a hierarchy of abstraction spaces. *Artificial Intelligence, 5,* 115–135.

SACERDOTI, E. D. (1977). *A structure for plans and behavior.* Amsterdam: Elsevier.

SACHS, J. S. S. (1967). Recognition memory for syntactic and semantic aspects of connected discourse. *Perception and Psychophysics, 2,* 437–442.

SACK, R. L., LEWY, A. J., WHITE, D. M., & SINGER, C. M. (1990). Morning vs. evening light treatment for winter depression: Evidence that the therapeutic effects of light are mediated by circadian phase shifts. *Archives of General Psychiatry, 47,* 343–351.

SAFER, M., THARPS, Q., JACKSON, T., & LEVENTHAL, H. (1979). Determinants of three stages of delay in seeking care at a

medical center. *Medical Care, 17,* 11–29.

SAGHIR, M. I., & ROBINS, E. (1973). *Male and female homosexuality: A comprehensive investigation.* Baltimore: Williams and Wilkins.

ST. GEORGE-HYSLOP, P. H., TANZI, R. E., POLINSKY, R. J., HAINES, J. L., NEE, L., WATKINS, P. C., MYERS, R. H., FELDMAN, R. G., POLLEN, O., DRACHMAN, O., GROWDON, J., BRUNI, A., FONCIN, J. F., SALMON, O., FROMMETH, P., AMADUCCI, L., SORBI, S., PIACENTINI, S., STEWART, G. D., HOBBS, W. J., CONNEALLY, M., & GUSELLA, J. F. (1987). The genetic defect causing familial Alzheimer's disease maps on chromosome 21. *Science, 235,* 885–890.

SAKURAI, M. M. (1975). Small group cohesiveness and detrimental conformity. *Sociometry, 38,* 340–357.

SAMEROFF, A. J., & CHANDLER, M. J. (1975). Reproductive risk and the continuum of caretaking casualty. In F. D. Horowitz (Ed.), E. M. Hetherington, S. Scarr-Salapatek, & G. M. Siegel (Assoc. Eds.), *Review of child development research,* Vol. 4. Chicago: University of Chicago Press.

SAMPAIO, E. (1989). Is there a critical age for using the Sonicguide with blind infants? *Journal of Visual Impairment and Blindness, 83,* 105–108.

SAMPSON, E. E. (1988). The debate on individualism: Indigenous psychologies of the individual and their role in personal and societal functioning. *American Psychology, 43,* 15–22.

SAMPSON, E. E. (1989). The challenge of social change for psychology: Globalization and psychology's theory of the person. *American Psychology, 44,* 914–921.

SAMUEL, A. G., & RESSLER, W. H. (1986). Attention within auditory word perception: Insights from the phonemic restoration illusion. *Journal of Experimental Psychology: Human Perception and Performance, 12,* 70–79.

SAMUELSON, C., & MESSICK, D. (1986). Inequities in access to and use of shared resources in social dilemmas. *Journal of Personality and Social Psychology, 51,* 962–967.

SANDERS, E. (1974, November). Charlie and the devil. *Esquire,* pp. 105–111.

SANDERS, G. (1981). Driven by distinction: An integrative review of social facilitation theory and research. *Journal of Experimental Social Psychology, 17,* 227–251.

SANTEE, R., & MASLACH, C. (1982). To agree or not to agree: Personal dissent amid social pressure to confirm. *Journal of Personality and Social Psychology, 42,* 690–701.

SAPIR, E. (1949). In D. G. Mandelbaum (Ed.), *Selected writings of Edward Sapir.* Berkeley and Los Angeles: University of California Press.

SARASON, I. G. (1975). Test anxiety and the self-disclosing coping model. *Journal of Consulting and Clinical Psychology, 43,* 148–153.

SARASON, I. G. (1981). Test anxiety, stress and social support. *Journal of Personality, 49,* 101–114.

SARASON, I. G., & SARASON, B. R. (1987). *Abnormal psychology: The problems of maladaptive behavior* (5th ed.). Englewood Cliffs, NJ: Prentice Hall.

SARNOFF, I., & ZIMBARDO, P. G. (1961). Anxiety, fear and social affiliation. *Journal of Abnormal and Social Psychology, 62,* 356–363.

SARTORIOUS, N. (1982). Epidemiology and mental health policy. In M. O. Wagenfeld, P. V. Lemkau, & B. Justice (Eds.), *Public mental health: Perspectives and prospects.* Beverly Hills, CA: Sage.

SATO, K. (1987). Distribution of the cost of maintaining common resources. *Journal of Experimental Social Psychology, 23,* 19–31.

SAVAGE-RUMBAUGH, E. S. (1986). *Ape language: From conditioned responses to symbols.* New York: Columbia University Press.

SAVAGE-RUMGAUH, E. S., McDONALD, K., SEVCIK, R. A., & HOPKINS, W. D. (1986). Spontaneous symbol acquisition and communicative use by Pygmy Chimpanzees (Pan paniscus). *Journal of Experimental Psychology: General, 115,* 211–235.

SAVINAR, J. (1975). The effect of ceiling height on personal space. *Non-Environmental Systems, 5,* 321–324.

SCALA, J. (1978). Weight control and the food industry. In G. Bray (Ed.), *Recent advances in obesity research* (Vol. 2). London: Newman.

SCARR, S. (1984). Day care as language intervention. *First-Language, 5,* 75–77.

SCARR, S. (1986). *Mother care/other care.* New York: Basic Books.

SCARR, S., & MacCARTNEY, K. (1983). How people make their own environments: A theory of genotype-environment effects. *Child Development, 54,* 424–435.

SCARR, S., & WEINBERG, R. A. (1977). Intellectual similarities within families of both adopted and biological children. *Intelligence, 1,* 187–191.

SCARR-SALAPATEK, S. (1971). Race, social class, and IQ. *Science, 174,* 1285.

SCARR-SALAPATEK, S. (1975). Genetics and the development of intelligence. In F. Horowitz (Ed.), *Review of child development research* (Vol. 4). Chicago: University of Chicago Press.

SCHACHT, T., & NATHAN, P. (1977). But is it good for psychologists? Appraisal and status of DSM-III. *American Psychologist, 32,* 1017–1025.

SCHACHTER, D. L. (1976). The hypnagogic state: A critical review of the literature. *Psychological Bulletin, 83,* 452–481.

SCHACHTER, D. L. (1983). Amnesia observed: Remembering and forgetting in a natural environment. *Journal of Abnormal Psychology, 92,* 236–242.

SCHACHTER, S. (1951). Deviation, rejection and communication. *Journal of Abnormal and Social Psychology, 46,* 190–207.

SCHACHTER, S. (1959). *The psychology of affiliation.* Stanford, CA: Stanford University Press.

SCHACHTER, S. (1971). *Emotion, obesity, and crime.* New York: Academic.

SCHACHTER, S. (1971). Some extraordinary facts about obese humans and rats. *American Psychologist,* 129–144.

SCHACHTER, S., & FRIEDMAN, L. N. (1974). The effects of work and cue prominence on eating behavior. In S. Schachter & J. Rodin (Eds.), *Obese humans and rats.* Hillsdale, NJ: Erlbaum.

SCHACHTER, S., & GROSS, L. P. (1968). Manipulated time and eating behavior. *Journal of Personality and Social Psychology, 10,* 98–106.

SCHACHTER, S., & LATANE, B. (1964). Crime cognition and the autonomic nervous system. In D. Levine (Ed.), *Nebraska Symposium on Motivation,* 221–273.

SCHACHTER, S., & SINGER, J. F. (1962). Cognitive, social and physiological determinants of emotional state. *Psychological Review, 69, 337,* 379–399.

SCHACHTER, S., & WHEELER, L. (1962). Epinephrine, chlorpromazine and amusement. *Journal of Applied Social Psychology, 65,* 121–128.

SCHAFFER, H. R., & EMERSON, P. E. (1964). The development of social attachments in infancy. *Monographs of the Society for Research in Child Development, 29* (3, Serial No. 94).

SCHAIE, K. W. (1982). Longitudinal data sets: Evidence for ontogenetic development or chronicles of cultural change. *Journal of Social Issues, 38,* 65–72.

SCHAIE, K. W. (Ed.). (1983). *Longitudinal*

studies of adult psychological development. New York: Guilford.

SCHAIE, K. W., & LABOUVIE-VIER, G. (1974). Generational and ontogenetic components of change in adult cognitive behavior. A fourteen-year cross-sequential study. Journal of Developmental Psychology, 10, 305–320.

SCHALLER, M. (1975). Chromatic vision in human infants: Conditioned operant fixation to "hues" of varying intensity. Bulletin of the Psychonomic Society, 6, 39–42.

SCHANK, R. (1973). Identification of conceptualizations underlying natural language. In R. Schank & R. Colby (Eds.), Computer models of thought and language. San Francisco: Freeman.

SCHANK, R., & ABELSON, R. P. (1977). Scripts, plans, goals, and understanding: An inquiry into human knowledge structures. New York: Halsted.

SCHARF, M. B., & BROWN, L. (1986). Hypnotic drugs: Use and abuse. [Special Issue: Sleep disorders], Clinical Psychology Review, 6, 39–50.

SCHEERER, M. (1963). Problem solving. Scientific American, 208, 118–128.

SCHEIN, E. H. (1975). How "career anchors" hold executives to their career paths. Personnel, 52, 11–24.

SCHERER, S. S. (1986). Reinnervation of the ectraocular muscles in goldfish in nonselective. Journal of Neuroscience, 6, 764–773.

SCHILLER, P., & WIENER, M. (1962). Binocular and stereoscopic viewing of geometric illusions. Perceptual and Motor Skills, 15, 739–747.

SCHLENKER, B. R. (1985). The self and social life. New York: McGraw-Hill.

SCHLESIER-STROPP, B. (1984). Bulimia: A review of the literature. Psychological Bulletin, 95, 247–257.

SCHLESINGER, A. (1965). A thousand days. Boston: Houghton Mifflin.

SCHLESINGER, B., & SCHLESINGER, R. (1989). Postponed parenthood: Trends and issues. Journal of Comparative Family Studies, 20, 355–363.

SCHLINGER, H., BLAKELY, E., & KAOZOR, T. (1990). Pausing under variable-ratio schedules: Interaction of reinforcer magnitude, variable-ration size, and lowest ratio. Journal of the Experimental Analysis of Behavior, 53, 133–139.

SCHLOSSBERG, H. (1954). Three dimensions of emotion. Psychological Review, 61, 81–88.

SCHMECK, H. M. (1988a, March 8). Region in brain is limited to obsessive disorder. New York Times, pp. C1–3.

SCHMECK, H. M. (1988b, February 16). Depression: Studies bring new drugs and insights. New York Times, pp. C1–3.

SCHNAPER, N. (1980). Comments germane to the paper entitled "The reality of death experience" by Ernst Rodin. Journal of Nervous and Mental Disease, 168, 268–270.

SCHOMMER, N. (1985, August). Beating jet lag. Savvy, pp. 26–29.

SCHOR, C. M., CARSON, M., PETERSON, G., & SUZUKI, J. (1989). Effects of interocular blur suppression ability on monovision task performance. Special Issue: 32nd annual contact lens issue. Journal of the American Optometric Association, 60, 188–192.

SCHROEDER, D., & COSTA, P. (1984). Influence of life event stress on physical illness: Substantive effects or methodological flaws? Journal of Personality and Social Psychology, 46, 853–863.

SCHUCK, J. R., & LEE, R. G. (1989). Backward masking, information processing, and schizophrenia. Schizophrenia Bulletin, 15, 491–500.

SCHUCKIT, M. A. (1987). Biological vulnerability to alcoholism. Journal of Consulting and Clinical Psychology, 55, 301–309.

SCHULL, W. J., NORTON, S. & JENSH, R. P. (1990). Ionizing radiation and the developing brain. Special Issue: Qualitative and quantitative comparability of human and animal developmental neurotoxicity. Neurotoxicology and Teratology, 12, 249–260.

SCHULZ, R. (1984). Human sexuality (2nd ed.). Englewood Cliffs, NJ: Prentice-Hall.

SCHUSTERMAN, R. J., & KRIEGER, K. (1984). California sea lions are capable of semantic comprehension. Psychological Record, 34, 3–23.

SCHUSTERMAN, R. J., & KRIEGER, K. (1986). Artificial language comprehension and size transposition by a California sea lion (Zalophus californianus). Journal of Comparative Psychology, 100, 348–355.

SCHWAB, M. E.. & THOENEN, H. (1985). Dissociated neurons regenerate into sciatic but not optic nerve explants in culture irrespective of neurotropic factors. Journal of Neuroscience, 5, 2415–2423.

SCHWARTZ, D., & BARSKY, S. (1977). The home court advantage. Social Forces, 55, 641–661.

SCHWARTZ, G. E. (1975). Biofeedback, self-regulation, and the patterning of physiological processes. American Scientist, 63, 314–324.

SCHWARTZ, J. (1984, March). The human side. Office Administration and Automation, p. 97.

SCHWARTZ, J. C., STRICKLAND, R. G., KROLICK, G. (1974). Infant day care: behavioral effects at preschool age. Developmental Psychology, 10, 502–506.

SCHWARTZ, S. H. (1970). Elicitation of moral obligation and self-sacrificing behavior: An experimental study of volunteering to be a bone marrow donor. Journal of Personality and Social Psychology, 15, 283–293.

SCHWARTZ, S. H., & HOWARD, J. A. (1984). Internalized values as motivators of helping behavior. In E. Staub et al. (Eds.), Development and maintenance of prosocial behavior. New York: Plenum.

SCLAFANI, A., & NISSENBAUM, J. W. (1988). Robust conditioned flavor preference produced by intragastric starch infusions in rats. American Journal of Physiology, 255, R672–R675.

SCMID, R. E. (1987, June 12). America's marriages setting records high and low. Lawrence Journal-World, p. 8D.

SCOVERN, A. W., & KILMANN, P. R. (1980). Status of electroconvulsive therapy: Review of the outcome literature. Psychological Bulletin, 87, 260–303.

SEARS, P. S., & BARBEE, A. H. (1977). Career and life satisfactions among Terman's gifted women. In J. C. Stanley, W. C. George, & C. H. Solano (Eds.), The gifted and the creative: Fifty-year perspective. Baltimore: Johns Hopkins University Press.

SEARS, R. R. (1977). Sources of life satisfactions of the Terman gifted man. American Psychologist, 32, 119–128.

SEARS, R. R., WHITING, J. W. M., NOWLIS, J., & SEARS, P. W. (1953). Child-rearing antecedents of aggression and dependency in young children. Genetic Psychology Monographs, 47, 135–234.

SECUNDA, S. K., KATZ, M. M., FRIEDMAN, R. J., & SCHUYLER, D. (1973). Special report 1973: The depressive disorders. Washington, DC: U.S. Government Printing Office (DHEW Publication No. 739157).

SEEMAN, M., & EVANS, J. W. (1962). Alienation and learning in a hospital setting. American Sociological Review, 27, 772–783.

SEGAL, B. (1989). Drug-taking behavior among school-aged youth: The Alaska experience and comparisons with lower 48 states. Drugs and Society, 4, 174.

SEGAL, M. W. (1974). Alphabet and attraction: An unobtrusive measure of the effect of propinquity in a field study. Journal

of Personality and Social Psychology, 30, 654–657.

SEGHERS, C. (1948). Color in the office. The Management Review, 37, 452–453.

SEITZ, P. F., McCORMICK, M. M., & WATSON, I. M. (1990). Relational spectral features for place of articulation in nasal consonants. Journal of the Acoustical Society of America, 87, 351–358.

SEKULER, R., & BLAKE, R. (1987). Sensory underload. Psychology Today, 21, 48–51.

SEKULER, R., KLINE, D., & DISMUKES, K. (1982). Aging and human visual function. New York: Alan R. Liss.

SELFE, L. (1977). Nadia: A case of extraordinary drawing ability in an autistic child. New York: Academic Press.

SELIGMAN, C., & DARLEY, J. (1977). Feedback as a means of decreasing residential energy consumption. Journal of Applied Psychology, 62, 363–368.

SELIGMAN, C., & HUTTON, R. (1981). Evaluating energy conservation programs. Journal of Social Issues, 37, 51–72.

SELIGMAN, C., KRISS, M., DARLEY, J., FAZIO, R., BECKER, L., & PRYOR, J. (1979). Predicting residential energy consumption from homeowners' attitudes. Journal of Applied Social Psychology, 9, 70–90.

SELIGMAN, M. E. P. (1974). Depression and learned helplessness. In R. J. Friedman & M. M. Katz (Eds.), The psychology of depression: Contemporary theory and research. Washington, DC: Winston-Wiley.

SELIGMAN, M. E. P. (1975). Helplessness: On depression development and death. San Francisco: Freeman.

SELIGMAN, M. E. P. (1991). Learned optimism. New York: Knopf.

SELIGMAN, M. E. P., MALER, S. F., & GEER, J. (1968). The alleviation of learned helplessness in the dog. Journal of Abnormal Psychology, 78, 256–262.

SELYE, H. (1976). The stress of life (rev. ed.). New York: McGraw-Hill.

SETTLE, R. G. (1986). Chemosensory properties of sour tastants. Physiology and Behavior, 36, 619–623.

SEYFARTH, R. M., CHENEY, D. L., & MARLER, P. (1980). Vervet monkey alarm calls: semantic communication in a free-ranging primate. Animal Behavior, 28, 1070–1094.

SEYLER, L., CANALIS, E., SPARE, S., & REICHLIN, S. (1978). Abnormal gonadotropin secretory responses to LRH in transsexual women after diethylstibestrol priming. Journal of Clinical Endocrinology Metabolism, 47, 176–183.

SHADISH, W. R. (1984). Policy research: Lessons from the implementation of deinstitutionalization. American Psychologist, 39, 725–738.

SHAKOW, D. (1977). Segmental set: The adaptive process in schizophrenia. American Psychologist, 32, 129–139.

SHAPIRO, A. (1971). Placebo effects in medicine, psychotherapy, and psychoanalysis. In A. Bergin & S. Garfield (Eds.), Handbook of psychotherapy and behavior change. New York: Wiley.

SHAPIRO, D. (1977). A biofeedback strategy in the study of consciousness. In N. E. Zinberg (Ed.), Alternate states of consciousness: Multiple perspectives on the study of consciousness. New York: Free Press.

SHAPIRO, D., & SHAPIRO, D. (1982). Meta-analysis of comparative therapy outcome studies: A replication. Psychological Bulletin, 92, 581–604.

SHAPIRO, D., & SHAPIRO, D. (1983). Comparative therapy outcome research: Methodological implications of meta-analysis. Journal of Counseling and Clinical Psychology, 51, 54–64.

SHAPIRO, J. (1978). Methods of group psychotherapy and encounter. Itasca, IL: Peacock Press.

Shapiro, S. (1981). *Contemporary theories of schizophrenia*. New York: McGraw-Hill.

Shashoua, V. E. (1967). Identification of specific changes in the pattern of brain protein synthesis after training. *Science, 193*, 1264–1266.

Shaver, P., Schwartz, J., Kirson, D., & O'Connor, C. (1987). Emotion Knowledge: Further exploration of a prototype approach. *Journal of Personality and Social Psychology, 52*, 1061.

Shaw, M. (1981). *Group dynamics: The psychology of small group behavior* (3rd ed.). New York: McGraw-Hill.

Shaw, M. E. (1955). A comparison of two types of leadership in various communication nets. *Journal of Abnormal and Social Psychology, 50*, 127–134.

Shebilske, W. L. (1975). Reading eye movements from an information processing point of view. In D. W. Massaro (Ed.), *Understanding Language; an information processing analysis of speech perception, reading, and psycholinguistics*. New York: Academic Press.

Shebilske, W. L. (1977). Visuomotor coordination in visual direction and position constancies. In W. Epstein (Ed.), *Stability and constancy in visual perception: Mechanisms and processes*. New York: Wiley.

Shebilske, W. L. (1980). Structuring an internal representation of text: A basis for literacy. In P. A. Kolers, M. E. Wrolstad, & H. Bouma (Eds.), *Processing of visible language* (Vol. 2). New York: Plenum.

Shebilske, W. L. (1981). Visual direction illusions in everyday situations: Implications for sensorimotor and ecological theories. In D. F. Fisher, R. A. Monty, & J. W. Senders (Eds.), *Eye movements: Cognition and visual perception*. Hillsdale, NJ: Erlbaum.

Shebilske, W. L. (1984). Context effects and efferent factors in perception and cognition. In W. Prinz & A. F. Sanders (Eds.), *Cognition and motor processes*. New York: Springer-Verlag.

Shebilske, W. L., & Ebenholtz, S. M. (1971). Ebbinghaus derived-list experiments reconsidered. *Psychological Review, 78*, 553–555.

Shebilske, W. L., & Reid, L. S. (1979). Reading eye movements, macro-structure and comprehension processes. In P. A. Kolers, M. E. Wrolstad, & H. Bouma (Eds.), *Processing visible language* (Vol. 1). New York: Plenum.

Shebilske, W. L., & Rotondo, J. H. (1981). Typographical and spatial cues that facilitate learning from textbooks. *Visible Language, 15*, 41–54.

Sheeby, J. B., & Wilkinson, M. (1989). Depth perception after prolonged usage of night vision goggles. *Aviation, Space, and Environmental Medicine, 60*, 573–579.

Sheldon, W. H. (1942). *The varieties of temperament: A psychology of constitutional differences*. New York: Harper & Row.

Sheldon, W. Hart, E., & McDermott, E. (1949). *Varieties of delinquent youth: An introduction to constitutional psychiatry*. New York: Harper & Row.

Shepard, R. N., & Cooper, L. A. (1982). *Mental images and their transformations*. Cambridge, MA: MIT Press.

Shepard, R. N., & Farrell, J. E. (1985). Representation of the orientation of shapes. [Special Issue: Seeing and knowing], *Acta Psychologica, 59*, 103–121.

Shepard, R. N. & Metzler, J. (1971). Mental rotation of three-dimensional objects. *Science, 171*, 701–703.

Sheppard, J. J., & Mysak, E. D. (1984). Ontogeny of infantile oral reflexes and emerging chewing. *Child Development, 55*, 831–843.

Sheras, P., & Worchel, S. (1979). *Clinical Psychology: A social psychological approach*. New York: Van Nostrand.

Sherif, M. (1936). *The psychology of social norms*. New York: Harper & Row.

Sherif, M., Harvey, O., White, B., Hood, W., & Sherif, C. (1961). *Intergroup conflict and cooperation: The Robber's Cove experiment*. Norman, OK: Institute of Group Relations, University of Oklahoma.

Sherman, A. R. (1979). In vivo therapies for phobic reactions, instrumental behavior problems, and interpersonal and communication problems. In A. P. Goldstein & F. H. Kanfer (Eds.), *Maximizing treatment gains: Transfer enhancement in psychotherapy*. New York: Academic.

Sherrod, D. (1974). Crowding, perceived control and behavioral aftereffects. *Journal of Applied Social Psychology, 4*, 171–196.

Shertzer, B., & Stone, S. C. (1974). *Fundamentals of counseling* (2nd ed.). Boston: Houghton Mifflin.

Shields, J. (1962). *Monozygotic twins brought up apart and brought up together*. London: Oxford University Press.

Shiller, V. A., Izard, C. E., & Hembree, E. A. (1986). Patterns of emotion expression during separation in the strange-situation procedure. *Developmental Psychology, 22*, 378–382.

Shiromani, P. J., Siegel, J. M., Tomaszewski, K. S., & McGinty, D. J. (1986). Alterations in blood pressure and REM sleep after pontine carbachol microinfusion. *Experimental Neurology, 91*, 285–292.

Shockley, W. (1972). Dysgenics, geneticity, and raceology: A challenge to the intellectual responsibility of educators. *Phi Delta Kappa, 53*, 297–307.

Shor, R. E., & Orne, E. C. (1962). *The Harvard group scale of hypnotic susceptibility: Form A*. Palo Alto, CA: Consulting Psychologists Press.

Shotland, R. L., & Huston, T. L. (1979). Emergencies: What are they and do they influence bystanders to intervene? *Journal of Personality and Social Psychology, 37*, 1822–1834.

Shotland, R. L., & Straw, M. K. (1976). Bystander response to an assault: When a man attacks a woman. *Journal of Personality and Social Psychology, 34*, 990–999.

Shurley, J. (1963). *Proceedings of the third world congress of psychiatry* (Vol. 3). Toronto, Ontario: University of Toronto Press.

Shyne-Athwal, S., Riccio, R. V., Chakraborty, G., & Ingoflia, N. A. (1986). Protein modification by amino acid addition is increased in crushed sciatic but not optic nerves. *Science, 231*, 603–605.

Siassi, I. (1984). Psychiatric interview and mental status examination. In G. Goldstein & M. Hersen (Eds.), *Handbook of psychological assessment*. New York: Pergamon.

Sicherman, B. & Green, C. H., with Kantrov, I. & Walker, H. (Eds.). (1980). *Notable American women: The modern period*. Cambridge, MA: Belknap.

Sieber, J. E., & Saks, M. (1989). The census of subject pool characteristics and policies. *American Psychologist, 44*, 1053–1061.

Siegel, J. (1990). Stressful life events and use of physician service among the elderly: The motivating role of pet ownership. *Journal of Personality and Social Psychology, 58*, 1081–1086.

Siegel, R. K. (1977). Hallucinations. *Scientific American, 237*, 132–139.

Siegelman, M. (1974). Parental background of male homosexuals and heterosexuals. *Archives of Sexual Behavior, 3*, 3–18.

Sigall, H., & Ostrove, N. (1975). Beautiful but dangerous: Effects of offender attractiveness and nature of crime on juridic judgments. *Journal of Personality and Social Psychology, 31*, 410–414.

Silver, E. A. (1981). Recall of mathematical problem information: Solving related problems. *Journal for Research in Mathematics Education, 12*, 54–64.

Silverman, L. H. (1976). Psychoanalytic theory: "The reports of my death are greatly exaggerated." *American Psychologist, 31*, 621–637.

Silvern, S. B., & Williamson, P. A. (1987). The effects of video game play on young children's aggression, fantasy, and prosocial behavior. *Journal of Applied Developmental Psychology, 8*, 453–462.

Simmermon, R., & Schwartz, K. M. (1986). Adult development and psychotherapy: Bridging the gap between theory and practice. *Psychotherapy, 23*, 405–410.

Simmons, R., Blyth, D., & McKinney, K. (1983). The social and psychological effects of puberty on white females. In J. Brooksgunn & A. Petersen (Eds.), *Girls at puberty*. New York: Plenum.

Simon, H. A., & Newell, A. (1971). Human problem solving: The state of the theory in 1970. *American Psychologist, 26*, 145–159.

Simpson, E. (1974). Moral development research. A case study of scientific cultural bias. *Human Development, 17*, 81–105.

Simpson, J. (1990). Influence of attachment styles on romantic relationships. *Journal of Personality and Social Psychology, 59*, 971–980.

Simpson, M. L. (1984). The status of study strategy instruction: Implications for classroom teachers. *Journal of Reading, 28*, 136–143.

Sinex, F. M. (1974). The mutation theory of aging. In M. Rickstein (Ed.), *Theoretical aspects of aging*. New York: Academic.

Singer, J. K., & Kolligan, J. (1987). Personality: Developments in the study of private experience. In M. Rosenzweig & L. Porter (Eds.), *Annual Review of Psychology*, Vol. 38. Palo Alto, CA: California Annual Review.

Singer, J. L. (1975). *The inner world of daydreaming*. New York: Harper & Row.

Singer, J. L. (1984). *The human personality*. New York: Harcourt Brace Jovanovich.

Singer, J. L. (1985). Transference and the human condition: A cognitive-affective perspective. *Psychoanalytic Psychology, 2*, 189–219.

Singer, J. L., Brush, C., & Lublin, S. (1965). Some aspects of deindividuation: Identification and conformity. *Journal of Experimental Social Psychology, 1*, 356–378.

Singer, J. E., Lundberg, V., & Frankenhauser, M. (1978). Stress on the train: A study of urban commuting. In A. Baum, J. Singer, & S. Valins (Eds.), *Advances in environmental psychology* (Vol. 1). Hillsdale, NJ: Erlbaum.

Singh, R. (1989). Single-session treatment of refractory headache: Evaluation with three patients. *Australian Journal of Clinical and Experimental Hypnosis, 17*, 9–105.

Singh, S. N., & Churchill, G. A. (1986). Using the theory of signal detection to improve ad recognition testing. *Journal of Marketing Research, 23*, 327–336.

Sistrunk, F., & McDavid, J. W. (1971). Sex variable in conforming behavior. *Journal of Personality and Social Psychology, 17*, 200–207.

Sizemore, C., & Pittillo, E. (1977). *I'm Eve*. Garden City, NY: Doubleday.

Skayholt, T. M., Morgan, J. I., & Negron-Cunningham, H. (1989). Mental imagery in career counseling and life planning: A review of research and intervention methods. *Journal of Counseling and Development, 67*, 287–292.

Skinner, B. F. (1948). *Walden two*. New York: Macmillan.

SKINNER, B. F. (1953). *Science and human behavior*. New York: Macmillan.

SKINNER, B. F. (1957). *Verbal behavior*. New York: Appleton-Century-Crofts.

SKINNER, B. F. (1960). Pigeons in a pelican. *American Psychologist, 15*, 28–37.

SKINNER, B. F. (1938, 1966). *The behavior of organisms*. Englewood Cliffs, NJ: Prentice-Hall.

SKINNER, B. F. (1974). *About behaviorism*. New York: Knopf.

SKINNER, B. F. (1978). The ethics of helping people. In L. Wispe (Ed.), *Sympathy, altruism, and helping behavior*. New York: Academic.

SKINNER, B. F. (1986). Some thoughts about the future. *Journal of the Experimental Analysis of Behavior, 45*, 229–235.

SKINNER, B. F. (1987). *Upon further reflection*. Englewood Cliffs, NJ: Prentice Hall.

SKINNER, B. F. (1990). Can psychology be a science of mind? *American Psychologist, 45*, 1206–1210.

SKLAR, L., & ANISMAN, H. (1981). Stress and cancer. *Psychological Bulletin, 89*, 369–406.

SKOLNICK, A. S. (1986). *The psychology of human development*. New York: Harcourt Brace Jovanovich.

SLABY, A. E. (1989). *After-shock: Surviving the delayed effects of trauma, crises, and loss*. New York: Fair Oaks Press.

SLADE, A. (1987). Quality of attachment and early symbolic play. *Developmental Psychology, 23*, 78–85.

SLOBIN, D. I. (1971). *Psycholinguistics*. Chicago: Scott, Foresman.

SMETANA, J. G. (1985). Preschool children's conceptions of transgressions: Effects of varying moral and conventional domain-related attributes. *Developmental Psychology, 21*, 18–29.

SMITH, A. D. (1977). Adult age differences in cued recall. *Developmental Psychology, 13*, 326–331.

SMITH, C. A., & ELLSWORTH, P. C. (1987). Patterns of appraisal and emotion related to taking an exam. *Journal of Personality and Social Psychology, 52*, 475–488.

SMITH, C. P., RYAN, E. R., & DIGGINS, D. R. (1972). Moral decision making: Cheating on examinations. *Journal of Personality, 40*, 640–660.

SMITH, D. (1976). The social content of pornography. *Journal of Communication, 26*, 16–33.

SMITH, E. E., & MEDIN, D. L. (1981). Categories and concepts. Cambridge, MA: Harvard University Press.

SMITH, M., GLASS, G., & MILLER, T. (1980). *The benefits of psychotherapy*. Baltimore: Johns Hopkins University Press.

SMITH, P., KENDELL, L., & HULIA, C. (1969). *The measurement of satisfaction in worth and retirement*. Chicago: Rand McNally.

SMITH, S. M. (1988). Environmental context-dependent memory. In G. Davies & D. Thomson (Eds.), *Memory in context: Context in memory*. New York: Wiley.

SMITH, T., & BREHM, S. (1981). Person perception and the type A coronary-prone behavior pattern. *Journal of Personality and Social Psychology, 40*, 1137–1149.

SNOWDEN, C. (1969). Motivation, regulation, and the control of meal parameters with oral and intragastric feeding. *Journal of Comparative and Physiological Psychology, 69*, 91–100.

SNYDER, M. (1987). *Public appearances: Private realities*. New York: Freeman.

SOBEL, E. F. (1980, April). Countertransference issues with the later life patient. *Contemporary Psychoanalysis, 16* (2), 211–222.

SOKOLOV, E. N. (1987). Physiology of higher nervous activity: Prospects of its development. *Neuroscience and Behavior, 17*, 1–11.

SOLANTO, M. V. (1984). Neuropharmacological basis of stimulant drug action in attention deficit disorder with hyperactivity. A review and synthesis. *Psychological Bulletin, 95*, 387–409.

SOLOMON, H., & CORBIT, J. (1974). An opponent process theory of motivation. I. The temporal dynamics of affect. *Psychological Review, 81*, 119–145.

SOLOMON, Z., MIKULINCER, M., & HOBFOLL, S. (1986). Effects of social support and battle intensity on loneliness and breakdown during combat. *Journal of Personality and Social Psychology, 51*, 1269–1276.

SOLSO, R. L. (1988). *Cognitive psychology*. Boston: Allyn & Bacon.

SOMMER, R. (1959). *Personal space: The behavioral basis of design*. Englewood Cliffs, NJ: Prentice-Hall.

SOMMER, R., & ROSS, H. (1958). Social interaction on a geriatric ward. *International Journal of Social Psychiatry, 4*, 128–133.

SOMMERSSCHIELD, H., & REYHER, J. (1973). Posthypnotic conflict, repression, and psychopathology. *Journal of Abnormal Psychology, 82*, 278–290.

SOPHIAN, C. (Ed.). (1984). *Origins of cognitive skills: The eighteenth annual Carnegie symposium on cognition*. Hillsdale, NJ: Erlbaum.

SORENSEN, R. C. (1973). *Adolescent sexuality in contemporary America*. New York: World.

SORRENTINO, R. M., & BOUTILLIER, R. G. (1956). The effect of quantity and quality of verbal interaction on ratings of leadership ability. *Journal of Experimental Social Psychology, 52*, 296–305.

SPANOS, N. P., D'EON, J. L., PAWLAK, A. E., & MAH, C. D. (1989–1990). A multivariate study of hypnotic susceptibility. *Imagination, Cognition and Personality, 9*, 33–48.

SPANOS, N. P., JAMES, B., & DE-GROOT, H. P. (1990). Detection of simulated hypnotic amnesia. *Journal of Abnormal Psychology, 99*, 179–182.

SPARK, G. M., & BRODY, E. M. (1970). The aged are family members. *Family Process, 9*, 195–210.

SPEARMAN, C. (1927). *The abilities of man*. New York: Macmillan.

SPECTOR, P., DWYER, D., & JEX, S. (1988). Relation of job stress to affective health and performance outcomes: A comparison of multi-date sources. *Journal of Applied Psychology, 73*, 11–19.

SPEISMAN, J. C., LAZARUS, R. S., MORDKOFF, A. M., & DAVIDSON, L. A. (1964). The experimental reduction of stress based on ego-defense theory. *Journal of Abnormal and Social Psychology, 68*, 367–380.

SPENCE, J., HELMREICH, R., & PRED, R. (1987). Impatience versus achievement striving Type A pattern: Differential effect on students' health and academic achievement. *Journal of Applied Psychology, 72*, 522–528.

SPENCE, J., PRED, R., & HELMREICH, R. (1989). Achievement strivings, scholastic aptitude, and academic performance: A follow-up to "Impatience versus achievement strivings in Type A pattern." *Journal of Applied Psychology, 74*, 176–178.

SPERLING, G. (1960). The information available in brief visual presentations. *Psychological Monographs, 74* (11, Whole No. 498).

SPERRY, R. W. (1970). Perception in the absence of neocortical commissures. In *Perception and its disorders* (Res. Publ. A. R. N. M. D., Vol. 48). New York: The Association for Research in Nervous and Mental Disease.

SPINHOVEN, P. (1988). Similarities and dissimilarities in hypnotic and nonhypnotic procedures for headache control: A review. *American Journal of Clinical Hypnosis, 30*, 183–194.

SPITZER, R. L. (1975). On pseudoscience in science, logic in remission, and psychiatric diagnosis: A critique of D. L. Rosenhan's "On being sane in insane places," *Journal of Abnormal Psychology, 84*, 442–452.

SPITZER, R. L. (1976). More on pseudoscience in science and the case for psychiatric diagnosis: A critique of D. L. Rosenhan's "On being sane in insane places," and "The contextual nature of psychiatric diagnosis." *Archives of General Psychiatry, 33*, 459–470.

SPORACINO, S. ET AL. (1981). Type A behavior and well-being among municipal employees. Paper presented at 89th annual meeting of American Psychological Association, Los Angeles.

SPRING, B., CHIODO, J., & BOWEN, D. (1987). Carbohydrates, tryptophan and behavior: A methodological review. *Psychological Bulletin, 102*, 234–256.

SPRINGER, S. P., & DEUTSCH, G. (1985). *Left brain, right brain* (rev. ed.). New York: Freeman.

SPUNGEN, D. (1983). *And I don't want to live this life*. New York: Fawcett.

SROUFE, L. A. (1985). Attachment classification from the perspective of infant-care-giver relationships and infant temperament. *Child Development, 56*, 1–14.

SROUFE, L. A. (1986). Appraisal: Bowlby's contribution to psychoanalytic theory and developmental psychology—attachment, separation, loss. [Special Issue: 30th anniversary of the Association of Child Psychology and Psychiatry and Applied Disciplines], *Journal of Child Psychology and Psychiatry and Applied Disciplines, 841–849*.

SROUFE, L. W. (1978). Emotional development in infancy. In J. Osofsky (Ed.), *Handbook of infancy*. New York: Wiley.

SROUFE, L., & WATERS, E. (1976). The ontogenesis of smiling and laughter. A perspective on the organization of development in infants. *Psychological Review, 83*, 173–189.

STACK, D. M., & MUIR, D. W. (1990). Tactile stimulation as a component of social interchange: New interpretations for the still-face effect. *British Journal of Developmental Psychology, 8*, 131–145.

STAFFORD, R., BACKMAN, E., & DIBONA, P. (1977). The division of labor among cohabiting and married couples. *Journal of Marriage and the Family, 39*, 43–58.

STAFFORD-CLARK, D., & SMITH, A. C. (1978). *Psychiatry for students* (5th ed.). London: Allen & Unwin.

STAHL, P. W. (1985). The hallucinogenic basis of early Valdivia phase ceramic bowl iconography. *Journal of Psychoactive Drugs, 17*, 105–123.

STARK, E. (1986). Young, innocent and pregnant. *Psychology Today, 20*, 28–35.

STARK, E. (1987a, August). The making of a manager. *Psychology Today*, pp. 28–32.

STARK, E. (1987b, June). Motherhood and science do mix. *Psychology Today*, p. 14.

STASSER, G., TAYLOR, L. A., & HANNA, C. (1989). Information sampling in structured and unstructured discussions in three- and six-person groups. *Journal of Personality and Social Psychology, 57*, 67–78.

STECK, L., LEVITAN, D., MCLANE, D., & KELLEY, H. (1982). Care, need, and conceptions of love. *Journal of Personality and Social Psychology, 43*, 481–491.

STEELE, C. M., & JOSEPHS, R. A. (1990). Alcohol myopia: Its prized and dangerous effects. *American Psychologist, 45*, 921–933.

STEIN, A. (1974). *Lovers, friends, slaves*. New York: Berkley.

STEIN, M. (1982). *Jungian analysis*. La Salle, IL: Open Court.

STEINER, I. D. (1972). *Group process and productivity*. New York: Academic.

STEINER, I. (1976). Task performing groups. In J. Thibaut, J. Spence, & R. Carson (Eds.), *Contemporary trends in social psychol-*

ogy. Morristown, NJ: General Learning Press.

STEISSGUTH, A. P., BARR, H. M., & MARTIN, D. C. (1983). Maternal alcohol use and neonatal habituation assessed with the Brazelton scale. *Child Development, 54,* 1109–1118.

STENDLER, C. B. (1952). Critical periods in socialization and overdependency. *Child Development, 23,* 1–2.

STEPHAN, W. G. (1978). School desegregation: An evaluation of predictions made in *Brown* vs. *Board of Education. Psychology Bulletin, 85,* 217–238.

STEPHAN, W. G. (1985). Intergroup relations. In G. Lindzey & E. Aronson (Eds.), *Handbook of social psychology* (3rd ed.), Vol. 2. New York: Random House.

STERN, P. C., & ARONSON, E. (1984). *Energy use: The human dimension.* New York: Freeman.

STERN, Y., MAYEUX, R., HERMANN, A., & ROSEN, J. (1988). Prism adaptation in Parkinson's disease. *Journal of Neurology, Neurosurgery, and Psychiatry, 51,* 1584–1587.

STERNBERG, R. (1988). Triangulating lore. In R. Sternberg & M. Barnes (Eds.), *The psychology of love.* New Haven, CT: Yale University Press.

STERNBERG, R. J. (1982). Reasoning, problem solving, and intelligence. In R. J. Sternberg (Ed.), *Handbook of human intelligence.* Cambridge, England: Cambridge University Press.

STERNBERG, R. J. (1984). Toward a triarchical theory of human intelligence. *Brain and Behavior Sciences, 7,* 269–315.

STERNBERG, R. J. (1985). *Beyond IQ: A triarchical theory of human intelligence.* New York: Cambridge University Press.

STERNBERG, R. J. (1986). A triangular theory of love. *Psychology Review, 93,* 119–135.

STERNBERG, R. J. (1986). *Intelligence applied.* New York: Harcourt Brace Jovanovich.

STERNBERG, R. J., & DAVIDSON, J. E. (Eds.) (1986). *Conceptions of giftedness.* New York: Cambridge University Press.

STERNBERG, R. J., & GARDNER, M. K. (1983). Unities in inductive reasoning. *Journal of Experimental Psychology: General, 112;* 80–116.

STERNBERG, R. J., & WAGNER, R. K. (Eds.) (1986). *Practical intelligence: Nature and origins of competence in the everyday world.* New York: Cambridge University Press.

STERNBERG, S. (1966). High-speed scanning in human memory. *Science, 153,* 652–654.

STEVENS, G., & GARDNER, S. (1982). *The women of psychology* (Vols. 1 & 2). Cambridge, MA: Schenkman.

STEVENS, J. C., & CAIN, W. S. (1987). Old-age deficits in the sense of smell as gauged by thresholds, magnitude matching, and odor identification. *Psychology and Aging, 2,* 36–42.

STEVENS, S. S., & GALANTER, E. H. (1957). Ratio scales and category scales for a dozen perceptual continua. *Journal of Experimental Psychology, 54,* 377–411.

STEVENS-LONG, J., & COBB, N. J. (1983). *Adolescence and early adulthood.* Palo Alto, CA: Mayfield.

STEVENSON, H. W. (1983). *Making the grade: School achievement in Japan, Taiwan, and the United States.* Stanford, CA: Center for Advanced Studies in Behavioral Studies.

STEVENSON, H. W. (1988). Culture and schooling: Influences on cognitive development. In E. M. Hetherington, R. Lerner, & M. Perlmutter (Eds.), *Child development and a life-span perspective.* Hillsdale, NJ: Erlbaum.

STEVENSON, I., COOK, E. W., & McCLEAN, R. N. (1990). Are persons reporting "near death experiences" really near death? A study of medical records. *Omega Journal of Death and Dying, 20,* 46–54.

STEVENSON, S. B., CORMACK, L. K., & SCHOR, C. M. (1989). Hyperacuity, superresolution and gap resolution in human stereopsis. *Vision Research, 28,* 1597–1605.

STEWART, A., & SALT, P. (1981). Life stress, life-styles, depression and illness in adult women. *Journal of Personality and Social Psychology, 40,* 1063–1069.

STIFTER, C., & FOX, N. (1986). Preschool children and ability to identify and label emotions. *Journal of Nonverbal Behavior, 10,* 255–266.

STINNINN, N., CARTER, L. M., & MONTGOMERY, J. E. (1972). Older persons' perceptions of their marriages. *Journal of Marriage and the Family, 34,* 665–670.

STINNETT, N., & WALTERS, J. (1977). *Relationships in marriage and family.* New York: Macmillan.

STIPP, D. (August 16, 1988). Firms have a bright idea to cure the winter blues. *Wall Street Journal,* p. 25.

STOFFELMAYER, B. E., DILLAVOU, D., & HUNTER, J. E. (1983). Premorbid functioning and outcome of schizophrenia: A cumulative analysis. *Journal of Consulting and Clinical Psychology, 51,* 338–352.

STOKOLS, D. (1972). On the distinction between density and crowding: Some implications for future research. *Psychological Review, 79,* 275–278.

STONE, A., & NEALE, J. (1984). New measures of daily coping: Development and preliminary results. *Journal of Personality and Social Psychology, 46,* 892–906.

STONE, J., COHEN, F., & ADLER, N. (1979). *Health psychology.* San Francisco: Jossey-Bass.

STONER, J. (1961). A comparison of individual and group decisions, including risk. Unpublished master's thesis, School of Industrial Management, M. I. T.

STRANG, J., GRIFFITHS, P., & GOSSOP, M. (1990). Crack and cocaine use in South London drug addicts. *British Journal of Addiction, 85,* 193–196.

STREIF, G. F., & SHNEIDER, G. J. (1971). *Retirement in American society: Impact and process.* Ithaca, NY: Cornell University Press.

STRELOW, E. R., KAY, N., & KAY, K. (1978). Binaural sensory aid: Case studies of its use by two children. *Journal of Visual Impairment and Blindness, 72,* 1–9.

STREUFERT, S., & STREUFERT, S. C. (1969). Effects of conceptual structure, failure and success: An attribution of causality and interpersonal attitudes. *Journal of Personality and Social Psychology, 11,* 138–147.

STRICKLAND, B. (1958). Sex-related differences: Health and illness. *Psychology of Women Quarterly, 12,* 381–399.

STRODBECK, F., & MANN, R. (1956). Sex-role differentiation in jury deliberations. *Sociometry, 19,* 3–11.

STROEBE, M., & STROEBE, W. (1983). Who suffers more? Sex differences in health risks of the widowed. *Psychological Bulletin, 93,* 279–301.

STROM, R., & STROM, S. (1990). Grandparent education. *Journal of Instructional Psychology, 17,* 85–91.

STRONGMAN, K. T. (1973). *The psychology of emotion.* New York: Wiley.

STRUBE, M. J., TURNER, C., CEIRO, D., STEVENS, J., & HINCHEG, F. (1984). Interpersonal aggression and the Type A coronary-prone behavior pattern: A theoretical distinction and practical implications. *Journal of Personality and Social Psychology, 47,* 839–847.

STRUCH, N., & SCHWARTZ, S. H. (1989). Intergroup aggression: Its predictors and distinctness from in-group bias. *Journal of Personality and Social Psychology, 56,* 364–373.

STRUPP, H. H., & HADLEY, S. W. (1979). Specific versus nonspecific factors in psychotherapy: A controlled study of outcome. *Archives of General Psychiatry, 36* (10), 1125–1136.

STUART, P., TAYLOR, A., & GAMMON, C. B. (1975). Effects of type and dose of alcohol on human physical aggression. *Journal of Personality and Social Psychology, 32,* 169–175.

STUNKARD, A. J. (1979). Behavioral medicine and beyond: The example of obesity. In O. Pomerleau & J. Brady (Eds.), *Behavioral medicine: Theory and practice.* Baltimore: Williams & Wilkens.

SUEDFELD, P. (1975, January–February). The benefits of boredom: Sensory deprivation reconsidered. *American Scientist.*

SUEDFELD, P. (1981). Aloneness as a healing experience. In L. A. Peplau & D. Perlman (Eds.), *Loneliness: A sourcebook of current theory, research, and therapy.* New York: Wiley-Interscience.

SUEDFELD, P., & COREN, S. (1989). Perceptual isolation, sensory deprivation, and rest: Moving introductory psychology texts out of the 1950s. *Canadian Psychology, 30,* 17–29.

SUGARMAN, A., QUINLAN, D., & DEVENIS, L. (1981). Anorexia nervosa as a defense against anaclitic depression. *The International Journal of Eating Disorders,* D. Van Nostrand, Autumn, Vol. 1.

SUGARMAN, S. (1983). *Children's early thought: Developments in classification.* New York: Cambridge University Press.

SUINN, R. M. (1984). *Fundamentals of abnormal psychology.* Chicago: Nelson-Hall.

SULS, J., & WILLS, T. A. (Eds.) (1990). *Social comparison: Contemporary theory and research.* Hillsdale, NJ: Erlbaum.

SUNDSTROM, E. (1978). Crowding as a sequential process: Review of research on the effects of population density on humans. In A. Baum & Y. Epstein (Eds.), *Human response to crowding.* Hillsdale, NJ: Erlbaum.

SUNDSTROM, E. (1986). *Work places.* Cambridge, England: Cambridge University Press.

SUOMI, S. J. (1977). Peers, play, and primary prevention in primates. In *Proceedings of the third Vermont conference on the primary prevention of psychopathology: Promoting social competence and coping in children.* Hanover, NH: University Press of New England.

SUOMI, S. J., & HARLOW, H. F. (1976). The facts and functions of fear. In M. Zuckermann & C. D. Spielberger (Eds.), *Emotions and anxiety: New concepts, methods, and applications.* Hillsdale, NJ: Erlbaum.

SUSSMAN, M. B., & BURCHINAL, L. (1962). Kin family network: Unheralded structure in current conceptualization of family functioning. *Marriage and Family Living, 24,* 231–240.

SUTKER, P. B., & ALLAIN, A. W. (1987). Cognitive abstraction, shifting, and control: Clinical sample comparison of psychopaths and nonpsychopaths. *Journal of Abnormal Psychology, 96,* 73–75.

SUZUKI, S. (1986). Evaluating methods for teaching orientation and mobility with Sonicguide. *Journal of Visual Impairment and Blindness, 80,* 537–538.

SWAIN, D. (1981). The fantasy-reality distinction in televised violence: Modifying influences on children's aggression. *Journal of Research in Personality, 15,* 323–330.

SWEDO, S., RAPPAPORT, J., & LEONARD, H. (1989). Obsessive-compulsive disorders in children and adolescents. *Archives of General Psychiatry, 46,* 335–345.

SWEENEY, P. D., ANDERSON, K., & BAILEY, S. (1986). Attributional style in depression: A meta-analytic review. *Journal of Personality and Social Psychology, 50,* 974–991.

SWEET, M. J., & JOHNSON, C. G. (1990). Enhancing empathy: The interpersonal implications of a Buddhist meditation technique. Special Issue: Psychotherapy and religion. *Psychotherapy, 27,* 19–29.

SWENSON, R. (1973). *Interpersonal relations.* Glenwood, IL: Scott, Foresman.

SWETS, J. A. (1964). *Signal detection and recognition by human observers.* New York: Wiley.

SZASZ, T. S. (1961). *The myth of mental illness: Foundations of a theory of personal conduct.* New York: Harper & Row.

SZASZ, T. S. (1970). *Ideology and insanity: Essays on the psychiatric dehumanization of a man.* Garden City, NY: Anchor Books.

SZASZ, T. S. (1986). The case against suicide prevention. *American Psychologist, 41,* 806–812.

TAJFEL, H. (1970). Experiments in intergroup discrimination. *Scientific American, 223,* 96–102.

TAJFEL, H. (1981). Social stereotypes and social groups. In J. Turner & H. Giles (Eds.), *Intergroup behavior.* Chicago: University of Chicago Press.

TAJFEL, H., & TURNER, J. (1985). The social identity theory of intergroup behavior. In S. Worchel & W. Austin (Eds.), *Psychology of intergroup relations* (2nd ed.). Chicago: Nelson-Hall.

TAKAHASHI, K. (1986). Examining the strange-situation procedure with Japanese mothers and 12-month-old infants. *Developmental Psychology, 34,* 265–270.

TANFORD, S., & PENROD, S. (1982). Biases in trials involving defendants charged with multiple offenses. *Journal of Applied Social Psychology, 12,* 453–480.

TANNER, J. (1972). Sequence, tempo, and individual variation in growth and development of boys and girls aged twelve to sixteen. In J. Kagan & R. Coles (Eds.), *Twelve to sixteen: Early adolescence.* New York: Norton.

TANNER, J. M. (1978). *Foetus into man: Physical growth from conception to maturity.* Cambridge, MA: Harvard University Press.

TARLER-BENLOLO, L. (1978). The role of relaxation in biofeedback training. *Psychological Bulletin, 85,* 727–755.

TARRIS, D., & OFFIR, C. (1977). *The longest war: Sex differences in perspective.* New York: Harcourt Brace Jovanovich.

TART, C. T. (1977). Putting the pieces together: A conceptual framework for understanding discrete states of consciousness. In N. E. Zinberg (Ed.), *Alternate states of consciousness: Multiple perspectives on the study of consciousness.* New York: Free Press.

TARTTER, V. C., & KNOWLTON, K. C. (1981). Perception of sign language from an array of 27 moving spots. *Nature, 289,* 676–678.

TAVRIS, C. (1986). How to publicize science: A case study. In J. H. Goldstein (Ed.), *Reporting science: The case of aggression.* Hillsdale, NJ: Erlbaum.

TAYLOR, J. A. (1951). The relationship of anxiety to the conditioned eyelid response. *Journal of Experimental Psychology, 41,* 81–92.

TAYLOR, R. E. (1981). Hinckley case might revive insanity issue. *Wall Street Journal,* April 28, p. 33.

TAYLOR, S. (1981, July 27). The plea of insanity and its use in criminal cases. *The New York Times.*

TAYLOR, S. E. (1986). *Health psychology.* New York: Random House.

TAYLOR, S. E. (1990). Health psychology: The science and the field. *American Psychology, 45,* 40–50.

TAYLOR, S., LICHMAN, R., & WOOD, J. (1984). Attribution, beliefs about control and adjustment to breast cancer. *Journal of Personality and Social Psychology, 46,* 489–502.

TAYLOR, S. E., & FISKE, S. T. (1975). Point of view and perceptions of causality. *Journal of Personality and Social Psychology, 32,* 439–445.

TAYLOR, S., & THOMPSON, S. (1982). Stalking the elusive "vividness" effect. *Psychological Review, 89,* 155–181.

TAYLOR, S. P., VARDARIS, R. M., RAWITCH, A. B., GAMMON, C. B., & CRANSTON, J. W. (1976). The effects of alcohol and delta p-tetrahydrocannibol on human physical aggression. *Aggressive Behavior, 2,* 153–162.

TAYLOR, W., & MARTIN, M. (1944). Multiple personality. *Journal of Abnormal and Social Psychology, 39,* 281–300.

TAYLOR, W. N. (1985). *Hormonal manipulation: A new era of monstrous athletes.* Jefferson, NC: McFarland.

TAYLOR, W. N. (1987). Synthetic anabolic androgenic steroids: A plea for controlled substance status. *Physician and Sports Medicine, 15,* 140–150.

TEEVAN, R. C., & McGHEE, P. E. (1972). Childhood development of fear of failure motivation. *Journal of Personality and Social Psychology, 21,* 345–348.

TEGER, A. (1980). *Too much invested to quit.* New York: Pergamon.

TEGHTSOONIAN, R. (1971). On the exponent in Steven's law and the constant in Ekman's law. *Psychological Review, 18,* 71–80.

TEICHMAN, M., BARNES, Z., & RAVAV, G. (1989). Personality and substance use among adolescents: A longitudinal study. *British Journal of Addiction, 84,* 181–190.

TEMPLAR, D. I. (1972). Death anxiety in very religiously involved persons. *Psychological Reports, 31,* 361–362.

TERMAN, L. A. (1904). A preliminary study in the psychology and pedagogy of leadership. *Pedagogical Seminary, 4,* 413–451.

TERMAN, L. M. (1916). *The measurement of intelligence.* Boston: Houghton Mifflin.

TERMAN, L. M., & MERRILL, M. A. (1937). *Measuring intelligence.* Boston, MA: Houghton Mifflin.

TERRANCE, H. S., PETITTO, L. A., SANDERS, R. J., & BEVER, T. G. (1979). Can an ape create a sentence? *Science, 206,* 891–901.

TESSER, A., MILLAR, M., & MOORE, J. (1988). Some affective consequences of social comparison and reflection process: The pain and pleasure of being close. *Journal of Personality and Social Psychology, 54,* 49–61.

TEYLER, T. J., & DiSCENNA, P. (1986). The hippocampal memory indexing theory. *Behavioral Neuroscience, 100,* 147–154.

THIGPEN, C. H., & CLECKLEY, H. M. (1974). *The three faces of Eve.* New York: Popular Library.

THOMAN, E. B., LIEDERMAN, P. H., & OLSON, J. P. (1972). Neonate-mother interaction during breast feeding. *Developmental Psychology, 6,* 110–118.

THOMAS, J. L. (1989). Gender and perception of grandparenthood. *International Journal of Aging and Human Development, 29,* 269–282.

THOMAS, M. H., HORTON, R. W., LIPPINCOTT, E. C., & DRABMAN, R. S. (1977). Desensitization to portrayals of real-life aggression as a function of exposure to television violence. *Journal of Personality and Social Psychology, 35,* 450–458.

THOMPSON, C. P., & OAWAN, T. (1986). Flashbulb memories: A nicer selection of a Neisser recollection. *Cognition, 22,* 102–109.

THOMPSON, D. (1983). Psychological classics: Older works in developmental psychology frequently cited today. *Journal of Genetic Psychology, 143,* 169–174.

THOMPSON, H. B. (1903). *The mental traits of sex.* Chicago: University of Chicago Press.

THOMPSON, J. (1941). Development of facial expression of emotion in blind and seeing children. *Archives of Psychology, 37,* No. 264.

THOMPSON, L. T., & BEST, P. J. (1990). Long-term stability of the place field activity of single units recorded from the dorsal hippocampus of freely behaving rats. *Brain-Research, 509,* 299–308.

THOMPSON, R. F. (1986). The neurobiology of learning and memory. *Science, 233,* 941–947.

THOMPSON, R. F., & WOODRUFF-PAK, D. S. (1987). A model system approach to age and the neuronal bases of learning and memory. In M. W. Riley, J. D. Matarazzo, & A. Baum (Eds.), *The aging dimension.* Hillsdale, NJ: Erlbaum.

THORKILDSEN, T. A. (1989). Justice in the classroom: The student's view. *Child Development, 60,* 323–334.

THORNDIKE, E. L. (1911). *Animal intelligence.* New York: Macmillan.

THORNDIKE, E. L. (1913). *The psychology of learning.* New York: Teachers College.

THORNDIKE, E. L. (1932). *The fundamentals of learning.* New York: Teachers College.

THORNDIKE, P. W. (1977). Cognitive structures in comprehension and memory of narrative discourse. *Cognitive Psychology, 9,* 77–110.

THORNDIKE, P. W. (1984). Applications of schema theory in cognitive research. In J. L. Anderson & S. M. Kosslyn (Eds.), *Tutorials in learning and memory.* San Francisco: Freeman.

THURSTONE, L. L. (1946). Theories of intelligence. *Science Monthly, 62,* 101–112.

TIGHE, T. J. (1982). *Modern learning theory: Foundations and fundamental issues.* New York: Oxford University Press.

TIMBERLAKE, W., WAHL, G., & KING, D. (1982). Stimulus and response contingencies in the misbehavior of rats. *Journal of Experimental Psychology: Animal Behavior Processes, 8,* 62–85.

TIME. (1978, December 25). Parental line: Same old birds and bees, p. 60.

TIMMER, S. G., ECCLES, J., & O'BRIEN, K. (1985–1986, Winter). How families use time. *ISR Newletter* (University of Michigan), 3–4.

TINBERGEN, N. (1951). *The study of instinct.* New York: Oxford University Press.

TOLMAN, E. C., & HONZIK, C. H. (1930). Introduction and removal of reward and maze performance in rats. *University of California Publications in Psychology, 4,* 257–275.

TOMASALLO, M., & FARRAR, M. J. (1986). Object permanence and relational words: A lexical training study. *Journal of Child Language, 13,* 495–505.

TOMKINS, S. (1981). The role of facial response in the experience of emotion: A reply to Tourangeau and Ellsworth. *Journal of Personality and Social Psychology, 40,* 355–357.

TORDOFF, M. G. (1988). How do non-nutritive sweeners increase food intake? *Appetite, 11,* 5–11.

TORDOFF, M. G., & FRIEDMAN, M. I. (1986). Hepatic portal glucose infusions decrease food intake and increase food preference. *American Journal of Physiology, 251,* R192-R196.

TORDOFF, M. G., & FRIEDMAN, M. I. (1988). Hepatic control of feeding: Effect of glucose, fructose, and mannitol. *American Journal of Physiology, 254,* R969–976.

TORRANCE, E. P. (1954). The behavior of small groups under the stress of conditions of survival. *American Sociological Review, 19,* 751–755.

TOUFEXIS, A. (1989, January 30). Shortcut to the Rambo look: 97-1b. weaklings no more, teens take steroids to bulk up. *Time,* p. 78.

TOYNBEE, A. (1965). *A study of history* (Vol. 1). New York: Oxford University Press.

TRAVIS, L. (1925). The effect of a small audience upon eye-hand coordination. *Journal* of Abnormal and Social Psychology, 20, 142–146.

TRIANDIS, H. (1989). Cross-cultural studies of individualism and collectivism. Nebraska Symposium on Motivation. Lincoln: University of Nebraska Press.

TRIANDIS, H. (1990). Theoretical concepts that are applicable to the analysis of ethnocentrism. In R. W. Brislin, (Ed.), Applied -Cross-Cultural Psychology. Newbury Park, CA: Sage.

TRIANDIS, H. C. (1980). Preface in H. C. Triandis & W. Lambert (Eds.), Handbook of cross-cultural psychology (Vol. 1). Boston: Allyn & Bacon.

TREIMAN, D. J., & HARTMAN, H. I. (1981). Women, work, and wages: Equal pay for jobs of equal value. Washington, DC: National Academy Press.

TREISMAN, A. M. (1960). Contextual cues in selective listening. Quarterly Journal of Experimental Psychology, 12, 242–248.

TRIBICH, D., & MESSER, S. (1974). Psychoanalytic character type and status of authority as determiners of suggestibility. Journal of Consulting and Clinical Psychology, 42, 842–848.

TRICKER, R., O'NEILL, M. R., & COOK, D. (1989). The incidence of anabolic steroid use among competitive bodybuilders. Journal of Drug Education, 19, 313–325.

TRIPLETT, N. (1898). The dynamogenic factors in pace-making and competition. American Journal of Psychology, 9, 507–533.

TRIPP, C. (1975). The homosexual matrix. New York: McGraw-Hill.

TROLL, L. E. (1971). The family of later life: A decade review. Journal of Marriage and the Family, 33, 263–290.

TROLL, L. E. (1982). Early and middle adulthood (2nd ed.). Belmont, CA: Wadsworth.

TROLL, L. E. (1983). Grandparents: The family watchdogs. In T. H. Brubaker (Ed.), Family relationships in later life. Beverly Hills, CA: Sage.

TROPE, Y., COHEN, O., & MOZA, Y. (1988). The perceptual and inferential effects of situational inducements on dispositional attribution. Journal of Personality and Social Psychology, 55, 165–177.

TROTTER, R. J. (1987). Three heads are better than one. Psychology Today, 20, 56–62.

TRUAX, C. B., & MITCHELL, A. (1971). Research on certain therapist interpersonal skills in relation to process and outcome. In A. E. Bergin & S. L. Garfield (Eds.), Handbook of psychotherapy and behavior change. New York: Wiley.

TRUSS, T. J. (ED.). (1981). Child health and human development: An evaluation and assessment of the state of the science. NIH publication No. 82–2304.

TRYON, R. C. (1940). Genetic differences in maze-learning abilities in rats. In 39th Yearbook, Part 1. National Society for the Study of Education. Chicago: University of Chicago Press.

TSANG, R. C. (1938). Hunger motivation in gastrectomized rats. Journal of Comparative Psychology, 1–17.

TSUJIMOTO, T., YAMADA, N., SHIMODA, K., & HANADA, K. (1990a). Circadian rhythms in depression: I. Monitoring of the circadian body temperature rhythm. Journal of Affective Disorders, 18, 193–197.

TSUJIMOTO, T., YAMADA, N., SHIMODA, K., & HANADA, K. (1990b). Circadian rhythms in depression: II. Circadian rhythms in inpatients with various mental disorders. Journal of Affective Disorders, 18, 199–210.

TUBER, S. (1983). Children's Rorschach scores as predictors of later adjustment. Journal of Consulting and Clinical Psychology, 51(3), 379–385.

TUCKMAN, B. W. (1965). Developmental sequence in small groups. Psychological Bulletin, 63, 384–399.

TULVING, E. (1972). Episodic and semantic memory. In E. Tulving & W. Donaldson (Eds.), Organization of memory. New York: Academic.

TULVING, E. (1983). Elements of episodic memory. New York: Oxford University Press.

TULVING, E., & PEARLSTONE, Z. (1966). Availability versus accessibility of information in memory for words. Journal of Verbal Learning and Verbal Behavior, 5, 381–391.

TURIEL, E. (1978). The development of concepts of social structure. In J. Glick & A. Clark-Steward (Eds.), The development of social understanding. New York: Gardner.

TURNER, C. W., & BERKOWITZ, L. (1972). Identification with film aggressor (overt role taking) and reactions to film violence. Journal of Personality and Social Psychology, 21, 256–264.

TURNER, J. (1981). The experimental social psychology of intergroup behavior. In J. Turner & H. Giles (Eds.), Intergroup behavior. Chicago: University of Chicago Press.

TURNER, J. C. (1987). Rediscovering the social group. Oxford: Basil Blackwell.

TURNER, R. M. (1986). Maintaining sleep (DIMS). [Special Issue: Sleep disorders], Clinical Psychology Review, 6, 27–38.

TURNER, T. A drink a day keeps the doctor away. In Family Weekly. New York: Family Weekly, 23.

TURVEY, M. T., & CARELLO, C. (1985). The ecological approach to perceiving-acting: A pictorial essay. Paper presented at a conference on sensorimotor interactions in space perception and action. February 1985, at the Center for Interdisciplinary Research, Bielefeld, West Germany.

TYSON, G., & RANGE, L. M. (1987). Gestalt dialogues as a treatment for mild depression: Time works just as well. Journal of Clinical Psychology, 43, 227–230.

UBELL, E. (1984, November 25). How to prepare for old age. Parade Magazine, pp. 13–15.

UDOLF, R. (1981). Handbook of hypnosis for professionals. New York: Van Nostrand.

UHLENBERG, P. (1980). Death and the family. Journal of Family History, 5, 313–320.

UMAKANTHA, A. (1989). Hypnotically enhanced testimony: Its role and admissibility in the legal process. Law and Psychology Review, 13, 131–144.

UMBERSON, D., & HUGHES, M. (1984). The importance of physical attractiveness on psychological achievement and well-being. Paper presented at the meeting of the American Society and Association, San Antonio, TX.

UNDERWOOD, B. J. (1982). Studies in learning and memory. New York: Praeger.

UNDERWOOD, B., BERENSON, J., BERESON, R., CHERGET, K., WILSON, D., KULIK, J., MOORE, B., & WENZEL, G. (1977). Attention, negative affect, and altruism: An ecological validation. Personality and Social Psychology Bulletin, 3, 54–58.

UNDERWOOD, G., CLEWS, S., & EVERETT, J. (1990). How do readers know where to look next? Local information distributions influence eye fixations. Quarterly Journal of Experimental Psychology: Human Experimental Psychology, 42, 38–65.

U.S. DEPARTMENT OF HEALTH & HUMAN Services. (1988). Understanding AIDS. Rockville, MD: HHS Publication No. (CDC) HHS-88–8404.

U.S. ENVIRONMENTAL PROTECTION AGENCY, OFFICE OF NOISE ABATEMENT AND CONTROL. (1978, August). Noise: A health problem.

U.S. FOOD AND DRUG ADMINISTRATION, NATIONAL CENTER FOR DRUGS AND BIOLOGICS, "Drug Utilization in the United States—1985." Issued December 1986.

U.S. RIOT COMMISSION. (1968). Report of the national advisory commission on civil disorders. New York: Bantam.

VAILLANT, G. E. (1977). Adaptation to life. Boston: Little, Brown.

VALINS, S. (1966). Cognitive effects of false heart rate feedback. Journal of Personality and Social Psychology, 4, 400–408.

VALINS, S. (1972). Persistent effects of information about internal reactions: Ineffectiveness of debriefing. In H. London & R. Nisbett (Eds.), The cognitive alteration of feeling states. Chicago: Aldine.

VALLACHER, R., & WEGNER, D. (1987). What do people think they're doing? Action identification and human behavior. Psychological Review, 94, 3–15.

VAN BUSKIRK, S. S. (1977). A two-phase perspective on the treatment of anorexia nervosa. Psychological Bulletin, 84, 529–538.

VANCE, E., & WAGNER, N. (1976). Written descriptions of orgasm: A study of sex differences. Archives of Sexual Behavior, 5, 87.

VAN DEUSEN, J., & KIERNAT, J. (1986). An exploration of the rocking chair as a means of relaxation. Physical and Occupational Therapy in Geriatrics, 4, 31–38.

VAN ROSSUM, E. J., & SCHENK, S. M. (1984). The relationship between learning conception, study strategy, and learning outcome. British Journal of Educational Psychology, 54, 73–83.

VEIT, D. T., SCRUGGS, T. E., & MASTROPIERI, M. A. (1986). Extended mnemonic instruction with learning disabled students. Journal of Educational Psychology, 78, 300–308.

VEITCH, R., & GRIFFITT, W. (1976). Good news, bad news: Affective and interpersonal effects. Journal of Applied Social Psychology, 6, 69–75.

VENER, K. J., SZABO, S., & MOORE, J. G. (1989). The effect of shift work on gastrointestinal (GI) function: A review. Chronobiologia, 18, 421–439.

VENN, J. (1987). The Stanford Hypnotic Clinical Scale and a group of obstetrical patients. American Journal of Clinical Hypnosis, 30, 66–70.

VERBRUGGE, L. (1989). Role responsibilities, role burdens and physical health. Journal of Community Psychology, 30, 282–304.

VERHALLEN, T. (1982). Scarcity and consumer choice behavior. Journal of Economic Psychology, 2, 299–322.

VERINIS, J., & ROLL, S. (1970). Primary and secondary male characteristics: The hairiness and large penis stereotypes. Psychological Reports, 26, 123–126.

VERTES, R. P. (1984). Brainstem control of the events of REM sleep. Progress in Neurobiology, 22, 241–288.

VILLASENOR, V. (1977). Jury: The people vs. Juan Corona. Boston: Little, Brown.

VOLK, S., SCHULZ, H., & YASSOURIDIS, A. (1990). The influence of two behavioral regimens on the distribution of sleep and wakefulness in narcoleptic patients. Sleep, 13, 136–142.

VON FRISCH, K. (1974). Decoding the language of the bee. Science, 185, 663–668.

WADDEN, T. A., STUNKARD, A. J., & BROWNELL, K. D. (1983). Very low calorie diets: Their efficacy, safety, and future. Annals of Internal Medicine, 99, 675–684.

WAGEMAKER, H., JR., & CADE, R. (1977). The use of hemodialysis in chronic schizophrenia. American Journal of Psychiatry, 134, 684–685.

WAHBA, M., & BIRDWELL, L. (1976). Maslow reconsidered: A review of research on the response hierarchy. Organizational Behavior and Human Performance, 15, 212–240.

WAIN, H. J. (1980). Pain control through use of hypnosis. ASCH, 23, 41–46.

WALD, B. K., ARCHER, R. P., & WINSTEAD, B. A. (1990). Rorschach characteristics of mothers of incest victims. Journal of Personality Assessment, 55(3 and 4), 417–425.

WALDRON, I., & JACOBS, J. (1989). Effects of multiple roles on women's health: New evidence from a longitudinal study. *Journal of Occupation Medicine, 30*, 977–983.

WALK, R. D., & GIBSON, E. J. (1961). A comparative and analytical study of visual depth perception. *Psychological Monographs, 75.*

WALKER, J. (1986). Methods and optics of perceiving color in a black and white grating. *Scientific American, 254*, 112–118.

WALKER, M. B., & TRIBOLI, C. (1984). The role of nonverbal signals in coordinating speaking turns. *Journal of Language and Social Psychology, 3*, 257–272.

WALLACE, B. (1979). *Applied hypnosis: An overview.* Chicago: Nelson-Hall.

WALLACE, R. (1970). Physiological effects of transcendental meditation. *Science, 167*, 1751–1754.

WALLACE, W. H., TURNER, S. H., & PERKINS, C. C. (1957). *Preliminary studies of human information storage,* Signal Corps Project No. 132C, Institute for Cooperative Research, University of Pennsylvania, December.

WALLACH, H. (1948). Brightness constancy and the nature of achromatic colors. *Journal of Experimental Psychology, 38*, 310–324.

WALLACH, H., & O'CONNELL, D. N. (1953). The kinetic depth effect. *Journal of Experimental Psychology, 45*, 205–217.

WALLACH, M., KOGAN, N., & BEM, D. (1962). Group influence on individual risk taking. *Journal of Abnormal and Social Psychology, 65*, 75–86.

WALLIN, B. G., & FAGIUS, J. (1986). The sympathetic nervous system in man: Aspects derived from microelectrode recordings. *Trends in Neuroscience, 9*, 63–66.

WALLIN, P. (1953). A Guttman scale for measuring women's neighborliness. *American Journal of Sociology, 59*, 243–246.

WALLIN, P., & VOLLMER, H. M. (1953). Marital happiness of parents and their children's attitudes to them. *American Sociological Review, 18*, 424–431.

WALSH, M. R. (1987). *The psychology of women: Ongoing debates.* New Haven, CT: Yale University Press.

WALSTER, E., ARONSON, E., ABRAHAMS, D., & ROTTMAN, L. (1966). Importance of physical attractiveness in dating behavior.

WALSTER, E., ARONSON, E., & ABRAHAMS, D. (1966). On increasing the persuasiveness of a low prestige communicator. *Journal of Experimental Social Psychology, 2*, 325–342.

WALTER, G. H., & ASHTON, P. (1980). The relationship of teacher-offered empathy, genuineness, and respect to pupil classroom behavior. Paper presented at the American Educational Research Association, Boston.

WARD, T. B. (1988). When is category learning holistic? A reply to Kemler Nelson. *Memory & Cognition, 16*, 85–89.

WARD, T. B., & SCOTT, J. (1987). Analytic and holistic modes of learning family-resemblance concepts. *Memory & Cognition, 15*, 42–54.

WARE, R. (1988). Seasonal depression. *All things considered.* National Public Radio (January 21).

WARREN, D. H., & STRELOW, E. R. (Eds.). (1985). *Electronic spatial sensing for the blind: Contributions from perception, rehabilitation, and computer vision.* The Hague: Martinus-Nijhoff.

WARREN, W. H., BLACKWELL, A. W., & MORRIS, M. W. (1989). Age differences in perceiving the direction of self-motion from optical flow. *Journal of Gerontology, 44*, 147–153.

WASHBURN, M. F. (1916). *Movements and mental imagery: Outlines of a motor theory of the complexer mental processes.* Boston: Houghton Mifflin.

WATERHOUSE, L., & FEIN, D. (1984). Developmental trends in cognitive skills for children diagnosed as autistic and schizophrenic. *Child Development, 55*, 236–248.

WATERS, H. F., & MALAMUD, P. (1975, March 10). Drop that gun, Captain Video. *Newsweek, 85*, 81–82.

WATKINS, J. G. (1989). Hypnotic hyperamnesia and forensic hypnosis: A cross examination. *American Journal of Clinical Hypnosis, 32*, 71–83.

WATSON, J. B. (1913). "Psychology as the behaviorist views it. *Psychological Review, 20*, 158–177.

WATSON, J. B., & RAYNER, R. (1920). Conditioned emotional reactions. *Journal of Experimental Psychology, 3*, 1–14.

WATSON, J. D. (1968). *The double helix.* New York: Cambridge University Press.

WATSON, J. D., & CRICK, F. H. C. (1953). Molecular structure of nucleic acid: A structure for deoxyribose nucleic acid. *Nature, 171*, 737–783.

WATSON, P. C., & JOHNSON-LAIRD, P. N. (1972). *Psychology of reasoning: Structure and content.* Cambridge, MA: Harvard University Press.

WATSON, R. I. (1973). Investigation into deindividuation using a cross-cultural survey technique. *Journal of Personality and Social Psychology, 25*, 342–345.

WATSON, R. I. (1974). *Eminent contributions to psychology: A bibliography of primary references* (Vol. I). New York: Springer.

WAUGH, N. C., & NORMAN, P. A. (1965). Primary memory. *Psychological Review, 72*, 89–104.

WEBB, L., DELANEY, J. J., & YOUNG, L. R. (1989). Age, interpersonal attraction, and social interaction: A review and assessment. *Research on Aging, 11*, 107–123.

WEBB, W. B. (Ed.). (1973). *Sleep: An active process.* Glenview, IL: Scott, Foresman.

WEBB, W. B. (1974). Sleep as an adaptive response. *Perceptual and Motor Skills, 38*, 1023–1027.

WEBB, W. M., & WORCHEL, P. (1986). Trust and distrust. In S. Worchel & W. Austin (Eds.), *The psychology of intergroup relations.* Chicago: Nelson Hall.

WECHSLER, D. (1958). *The measurement and appraisal of adult intelligence.* Baltimore: Williams & Wilkins.

WEGNER, D. (1987, October). *Thought patterns of depressives.* Paper presented at the meeting of the Society of Experimental Social Psychologists, Charlottesville, VA.

WEGNER, D. M., & VALLICHER, R. R. (1981). *The self in social psychology.* New York: Oxford University Press.

WEINER, M. J., & WRIGHT, F. E. (1973). Effects of undergoing arbitrary discrimination upon subsequent attitudes toward a minority group. *Journal of Applied Social Psychology, 3*, 94–102.

WEINGARTNER, H., GRAFMAN, J., BOUTELLE, W., KAYE, W., & MARTIN, P. R. (1983). *Forms of memory failure, 221*, 380–382.

WEINTRAUB, W. (1987). Personality profiles of American presidents as revealed in their public statements. The presidential news conferences of Jimmy Carter and Ronald Reagan. *Political Psychology, 7*, 285–296.

WEISS, B. (1982). Food additives and environmental chemicals as sources of childhood behavior disorders. *Journal of the American Academy of Child Psychiatry, 21*, 144–152.

WEISS, C. H. (1985, March/April). Media report card for social science. *Society*, pp. 37–47.

WEISS, J. M. (1972, June). Psychological factors in stress and disease. *Scientific American.*

WEISS, J. M., GOODMAN, P. A., LOSITO, B. G., CORRIGAN, S., CHARRY, J. M., & BAILEY, W. H. (1981). Behavioral depression produced by an uncontrollable stressor: Relationships to norepinephrine, dopamine, and serotonin levels in various regions of rat brain. *Brain Research Reviews, 3*, 167–205.

WEITZENHOFFER, A. M., & HILGARD, E. R. (1962). *Stanford hypnotic susceptibility scales, form C.* Palo Alto, CA: Consulting Psychologists Press.

WELCH, R. B. (1978). *Perceptual modification.* New York: Academic.

WELFORD, A. I. (1989). Recall, recognition and serial learning: A signal detection measurement. *Perceptual and Motor Skills, 69*, 115–118.

WELLS, A. (1975). *Mass media and society* (2nd ed.). Palo Alto, Ca: Mayfield.

WELLS, G. L. (1986). Expert psychological testimony: Empirical and conceptual analyses of effect. [Special Issue: The ethics of expert testimony], *Law and Human Behavior, 10*, 83–95.

WELSH, B. (1979). Extra-auditory health effects of industrial noise: Survey of foreign literature. Aerospace Medical Research Laboratory, Aerospace Medical Division, Air Force Systems Command, Wright-Patterson, June.

WERNER, O. R. (1986). Long-term endocrinologic changes in subjects practicing the Transcendental Meditation and TM-Sishi program. *Psychosomatic Medicine, 48*, 59–66.

WEST, D. (1967). *The young offender.* Harmondsworth, England: Penguin.

WESTALL, C. A., & ASLIN, R. N. (1984). Fixational eye movements and autokinesis in amblyopes. *Ophthalmic and Physiological Optics, 4*, 333–337.

WETMORE, M. E. (1982). The relationship between perceived text structure, familiarity of content, and recall of expository text. Unpublished doctoral dissertation, University of Virginia.

WHEELER, L., DECI, E., REIS, H., & ZUCKERMAN, B. (1978). *Interpersonal influence.* Boston: Allyn & Bacon.

WHITE, C. Unpublished doctoral dissertation. Catholic University, Washington, DC.

WHITE, M. (1975). Interpersonal distance as affected by room size, status, and sex. *Journal of Social Psychology, 95*, 241–249.

WHITE, R. W. (1975). *Lives in progress: A study of the national growth of personality* (3rd ed.). New York: Holt.

WHITLEY, B. (1990). The relationship of heterosexuals' attributions for the causes of homosexuality to attitudes toward lesbians and gay men. *Personality and Social Psychology Bulletin, 16*, 369–377.

WHORF, B. L. (1956). *Language, thought, and reality.* New York: Wiley.

WHYTE, W. (1956). *The organization man.* New York: Simon & Schuster.

WICKELGREN, W. A. (1977). *Learning and memory.* Englewood Cliffs, NJ: Prentice-Hall.

WICKELGREN, W. A. (1979). *Cognitive psychology.* Englewood Cliffs, NJ: Prentice-Hall.

WICKER, A. (1979). *An introduction to ecological psychology.* Monterey, CA: Brooks/Cole.

WICKER, F. W., PAYNE, G. C., ROBERSON, K. E., & GARCIA-FALCON, R. (1985). Participant differentiation on nonclinical fear and anxiety. *Motivation & Emotion, 9*, 53–70.

WICKLUND, R. A., & BREHM, J. W. (1976). Perspectives on cognitive dissonance. Hillsdale, NJ: Erlbaum.

WICKS-NELSON, R., & ISRAEL, A. (1984). *Behavior disorders of children.* Englewood Cliffs, NJ: Prentice-Hall.

WIDOM, C. S. (1978). A methodology for

studying noninstitutionalized psychopaths. In R. R. Hare & D. Schalling (Eds.), *Psychopathic behavior: Approaches to research.* Chichester, England: Wiley.

WIEL, A. T. (1977). The marriage of the sun and moon. In N. E. Zinberg (Ed.), *Alternate states of consciousness: Multiple perspectives on the study of consciousness.* New York: Free Press.

WIGGAM, A. E. (1928). *Exploring your mind with the psychologists.* New York: Bobbs-Merrill.

WILCOX, J. (1986). Psychotherapy and narcolepsy. *Neuropsychobiology, 14,* 170–172.

WILDER, D. A. (1977). Perception of groups, size of opposition, and social influence. *Journal of Experimental Social Psychology, 13,* 253–268.

WILDER, D. A. (1985). Cognitive factors affecting success of intergroup contact. In S. Worchel & W. Austin (Eds.), *Psychology of intergroup relations.* Chicago: Nelson-Hall.

WILDER, D. A., & ALLEN, V. L. (1973, May). The effect of absent social support on conformity. Paper presented at the meeting of the Midwestern Psychological Association, Chicago.

WILDER, L. (1975). Articulatory and acoustic characteristics of speech sounds. In D. W. Massaro (Ed.), *Understanding language: An information-processing analysis of speech perception, reading, and psycholinguistics.* New York: Academic Press.

WILKINS, W. (1973). Expectancy of therapeutic gain: An empirical and conceptual critique. *Journal of Consulting and Clinical Psychology, 40,* 69–77.

WILLERMAN, B., & SWANSON, L. (1953). Group prestige in voluntary organizations. *Human Relations, 6,* 57–77.

WILLIAMS, K. W., & DURSO, F. T. (1986). Judging category frequency: Automaticity or availability? *Journal of Experimental Psychology: Learning, Memory, and Cognition, 12,* 387–396.

WILLIAMS, R. L. (1972). Themes concerning blacks. St. Louis, MO: Williams.

WILLINGS, D., & BRUCE, C. (1984). Meeting the creative mood halfway. *Gifted Education International, 2,* 111–113.

WILMER, H. (1987). *Practical Jung: Nuts and bolts of Jungian psychotherapy.* Wilmette, IL: Chiron.

WILSON, A. (1986). Archaic transference and anaclitic depression: Psychoanalytic perspectives on the treatment of severely disturbed patients. *Psychoanalytic Psychology, 3,* 237–256.

WILSON, G. (1966). Arousal properties of red versus green. *Perceptual and Motor Skills, 23,* 947–949.

WILSON, J. D. (1988). Androgen abuse by athletes. *Endocrine Review, 9,* 181–199.

WINDHOLZ, G. (1990). Pavlov and the Pavlovians in the laboratory. *Journal of the History of the Behavioral Sciences, 26,* 64–74.

WINDHOLZ, G., & LAMAL, P. A. (1986). Pavlov and the concept of association. *Pavlovian Journal of Biological Science, 21,* 12–15.

WINSTEAD, B. (1986). Sex differences in same sex friendships. In V. J. Derlega & B. Winstead (Eds.), *Friendship and social interaction.* New York: Springer-Verlag.

WINSTON, W. W. (1986). The role of facial responses in self-reports of emotion. A critique of Laird. *Journal of Personality and Social Psychology, 50,* 808–812.

WINTERBOTTOM, M. R. (1953). The relationship of childhood training in independence to achievement motivation. Unpublished doctoral dissertation, University of Michigan.

WIRTENBURG, T., & NAKAMURA, C. (1976). Education: Barrier or boon to changing occupational roles of women. *Journal of Social Issues, 32,* 165–179.

WIRTZ, P. W., & HARRELL, A. V. (1987). Effects of postassault exposure to attack-similar stimuli on long-term recovery of victims. *Journal of Consulting and Clinical Psychology, 55,* 10–16.

WOLFE, J. M. (1986). Stereopsis and binocular rivalry. *Psychological Review, 93,* 269–282.

WOLFE, L. (1980, September). The sexual profile of that Cosmopolitan Girl. *Cosmopolitan,* 254–265.

WOLLMAN, M. C., & ANTROBUS, J. S. (1987). Cortical arousal and mentation in sleeping and waking subjects. *Brain and Cognition, 6,* 334–346.

WOLMAN, B. B., DALE, L. A., SCHMEIDLER, G. R., & ULLMAN, M. (Eds.). (1985). *Handbook of parapsychology.* New York: Van Nostrand Reinhold.

WOLPE, J. (1958). *Psychotherapy by reciprocal inhibition.* Stanford, CA: Stanford University Press.

WOLPE, J. (1962). The experimental foundations of some new psychotherapeutic methods. In A. J. Bachrach (Ed.), *Experimental foundations of clinical psychology.* New York: Basic.

WOLPE, J. (1974). *The practice of behavior therapy.* New York: Pergamon.

WONG, E., & WEISSTEIN, N. (1985). A new visual illusion: Flickering fields are located in a depth plane behind nonflickering fields. *Perception, 14,* 13–17.

WOOCHER, F. D. (1986). Legal principles governing expert testimony by experimental psychologists. [Special Issue: The ethics of expert testimony], *Law and Human Behavior, 10,* 47–61.

WOOD, W. (1987). Meta-analytic review of sex differences in group performance. *Psychological Bulletin, 102,* 53–71.

WOOD, W., & EAGLY, A. (1981). Stages in the analysis of persuasive messages: The role of causal attributions and message comprehension. *Journal of Personality and Social Psychology, 40,* 246–259.

WOOD, W., JONES, M., & BENJAMIN, L. T. (1986). Surveying psychology's public image. *American Psychologist, 41,* 947–953.

WOODRUFF, D. S. (1977). *Can you live to be 100?* New York: Chatham Square Press.

WOODS, P. J. (Ed.) (1979). *The psychology major.* American Psychological Association: Washington, D.C.

WOODS, S. J. (1986). Hypnosis as a means of achieving cognitive modification in the treatment of academic anxiety: II. *Australian Journal of Clinical Hypnotherapy and Hypnosis, 7,* 23–40.

WOODWORTH, R. S. (1938). *Experimental psychology.* New York: Holt.

WOOLFOLK, R. L., & RICHARDSON, F. C. (1984). Behavior therapy and the ideology of modernity. *American Psychologist, 39,* 777–786.

WOOLLEY, H. T. (1910). Psychological literature: A review of the recent literature on the psychology of sex. *Psychological Bulletin, 7,* 335–342.

WORCHEL, F. (1988). Personality assessment. In C. Reynolds & T. Gutkin (Eds.), *The handbook of school psychology.* New York: Wiley.

WORCHEL, F. F., & DUPREE, J. L. (in press). Projective storytelling techniques. In C. Reynolds & R. Kamphous (Eds.).

WORCHEL, F. F., AARON, L. L., YATES, D. F. (1990). Gender bias on the Thematic Apperception Test. *Journal of Personality Assessment, 54*(3 and 4), 593–602.

WORCHEL, J. (In press.) Brief short-term psychodynamic psychotherapy. In R. A. Wells & V. J. Giannetti (Eds.), *Handbook of Brief Psychotherapy.* New York: Plenum Press.

WORCHEL, P. (1979). Trust and distrust. In W. Austin & S. Worchel (Eds.), *The social psychology of intergroup relations.* Monterey, CA: Brooks/Cole.

WORCHEL, S. (1984). The darker side of helping: The social dynamics of helping and cooperation. In E. Staub et al. (Eds.), *Development and maintenance of prosocial behavior.* New York: Plenum.

WORCHEL, S. (1985). Cooperation and the reduction of intergroup conflict: Some determining factors. In S. Worchel & W. Austin (Eds.), *Psychology of intergroup relations.* Chicago: Nelson-Hall.

WORCHEL, S. (1987). *The process of group formation and identity.* Paper presented at Office of Naval Research Conference on Small Groups, London, England (July).

WORCHEL, S. (1988). *The road to intergroup attraction: Cooperation or helping?* Paper presented at Conference on Social Justice, Leiden, Netherlands (August).

WORCHEL, S., & ANDREOLI, V. (1978). Facilitation of social interaction through deindividuation of the target. *Journal of Personality and Social Psychology, 36,* 549–557.

WORCHEL, S., ANDREOLI, V., & FOLGER, R. (1977). Intergroup cooperation and intergroup attraction: The effect of previous interaction and outcome of combined effort. *Journal of Experimental Social Psychology, 13,* 131–140.

WORCHEL, S., & ARNOLD, S. (1973). The effects of censorship and attractiveness of the censor on attitude change. *Journal of Experimental Social Psychology, 9,* 365–377.

WORCHEL, S., AXSOM, D., FERRIS, F., SAMAHA, G., & SCHWEITZER, S. (1978). Determinants of the effects of intergroup cooperation on intergroup attraction. *Journal of Conflict Resolution, xxii,* 429–439.

WORCHEL, S., & BROWN, E. (1984). The role of plausibility in influencing environmental attractions. *Journal of Experimental Social Psychology, 20,* 86–96.

WORCHEL, S., & BURNHAM, C. A. (1967). Reduction of autokinesis with information about the registration of eye position. *American Journal of Psychology, 80,* 434–437.

WORCHEL, S., COOPER, J., & GOETHALS, G. R. (1988). *Understanding social psychology* (4th ed.). Homewood, IL: Dorsey.

WORCHEL, S., COOPER, J., & GOETHALS, G. (1991). *Understanding social psychology,* 5th ed. Pacific Grove: Brooks/Cole.

WORCHEL, S., COUTANT-SASSIC, D., & GROSSMAN, M. (1991). A model of group development and independence. In S. Worchel, W. Wood, & J. Simpson (Eds.), *Group process and productivity.* Newbury Park, CA: Sage.

WORCHEL, S., & GOETHALS, G. R. (1988). *Personal adjustment: Pathways to personal growth* (2nd ed.). Englewood Cliffs, NJ: Prentice Hall.

WORCHEL, S., & GOETHALS, G. R. (1989). *Adjustment: Pathways to personal growth.* Englewood Cliffs, NJ: Prentice Hall.

WORCHEL, S., GROSSMAN, M., & COUTANT-SASSIC, D. (In press.) Minority influence in the group context: How group factors affect when the minority will be influential. In A. Mucci-Faina & S. Moscovici (Eds.), *Minority influence.* Chicago: Nelson-Hall.

WORCHEL, S., HART, D., & BUTTEMEYER, J. (1987). *Is social loafing a group phenomenon?* Paper presented at Southwestern Psychological Association. New Orleans.

WORCHEL, S., LEE, J., & ADEWOLE, A. (1975). Effects of supply and demand on ratings of object value. *Journal of Personality and Social Psychology, 32,* 906–914.

WORCHEL, S., & LOLLIS, M. (1982). Reactions to territorial contamination as a function of culture. *Personality and Social Psychology Bulletin, 8,* 370–375.

WORCHEL, S., & TEDDLIE, C. (1976). The experience of crowding: A two-factor theory. *Journal of Personality and Social Psychology, 34,* 30–40.

WORCHEL, S., & YOHAI, S. M. L. (1979). The role of attribution in the experience of crowding. *Journal of Experimental Social Psychology, 15,* 91–104.

WRIGHT, H. F. (1967). *Recording and analyzing child behavior.* New York: Harper & Row.

WRIGHT, J. D. (1978). Are working women really more satisfied? Evidence from several national surveys. *Journal of Marriage and the Family, 40,* 301–313.

WRIGHTSMAN, L. (1991). *Psychology and the legal system.* Pacific Grove, CA: Brooks/Cole.

WURTELE, S. K. (1988). Increasing women's calcium intake: The role of health beliefs, intentions, and health values. *Journal of Applied Social Psychology, 18,* 627–639.

WYDEN, B. (1971, December). Growth: 45 crucial months. *Life,* pp. 93–95.

WYER, R., HENNINGER, M., & HINKLE, R. (1977). An informational analysis of actors' and observers' belief attributions in a role-playing situation. *Journal of Experimental Social Psychology, 13,* 199–217.

YALOM, I. D. (1975). *The theory and practice of group psychotherapy* (2nd ed.). New York: Basic.

YALOM, I. D., & LIEBERMAN, A. (1971). A study of encounter group casualties. *Archives of General Psychiatry, 25,* 16–30.

YARMEY, D. A. (1986). Ethical responsibilities governing the statements experimental psychologists make in expert testimony. [Special Issue: The ethics of expert testimony], *Law and Human Behavior, 10,* 101–115.

YATES, F. A. (1966). *The art of memory.* Chicago: University of Chicago Press.

YEKOVICH, F. R., & THORNDYKE, P. W. (1981). An evaluation of alternative functional models of narrative schemata. *Journal of Verbal Learning and Verbal Behavior, 20,* 454–469.

YESALIS, C. E., STREIT, A. L., VICARY, J. R., & FRIEDL, K. E. (1989). Anabolic steroid use: Indications of habituation among adolescents. *Journal of Drug Education, 19,* 103–116.

YONAS, A., GRANDUD, C. E., ARTERBERRY, M. E., & HANSON, B. L. (1986). Infants' distance perception from linear perspective and texture gradients. *Infant Behavior and Development, 9,* 247–256.

YUILLE, J. C., & CUTSHALL, J. L. (1986). A case study of the eyewitness memory of a crime. *Journal of Applied Psychology, 7,* 291–301.

ZAFIROPOULOU, M., & MCPHERSON, F. M. (1986). "Preparedness" and the severity and outcome of clinical phobias. *Behavioral Research and Therapy, 24,* 221–222.

ZAGER, L., & MEGARGEE, E. (1981). Seven MMPI alcohol and drug abuse scales: An empirical investigation of their interrelationships, convergent and discriminant validity, and degree of racial bias. *Journal of Personality and Social Psychology, 40,* 532–544.

ZAHORIK, D. M., HOUPT, K. A., & SWARTZMAN-ANDERT, J. (1990). Taste-aversion learning in three species of ruminants.

Applied Animal Behaviour Science, 26, 27–39.

ZAIDEN, J. (1982). Psychodynamic therapy: Clinical applications. In A. Rush (Ed.), *Short-term psychotherapies for depression.* New York: Guilford.

ZAJONC, R. (1970). Brainwash: Familiarity breeds comfort. *Psychology Today, 13,* 32–35.

ZAJONC, R. B. (1965). Social facilitation. *Science, 149,* 269–274.

ZAJONC, R. B. (1968). Attitudinal effects of mere exposure. *Journal of Personality and Social Psychology, 9,* 1–27.

ZAJONC, R. B. (1976). Family configuration and intelligence. *Science, 192,* 227–236.

ZAJONC, R. B. (1980). Feeling and thinking. Preferences need no interferences. *American Psychologist, 35,* 151–175.

ZAMETKIN, A. J., & RAPOPORT, J. L. (1987). Neurobiology of attention deficit disorder with hyperactivity: Where have we come in 50 years? *Journal of the American Academy of Child and Adolescent Psychiatry, 26,* 676–686.

ZAMETKIN, A., RAPOPORT, J. L.. MURPHY, D. L., LINNOILA, M., & ISMOND, D. (1985). Treatment of hyperactive children with monoamine oxidase inhibitors. I. Clinical efficacy. *Archives of General Psychiatry, 42,* 962–966.

ZANDER, A. (1982). *Making groups effective.* San Francisco: Jossey-Bass.

ZANNA, M., & REMPEL, J. (1988). Attitudes: A new look at an old concept. In D. Bartal & A. Kruglanski (Eds.), *The social psychology of knowledge.* New York: Cambridge University Press.

ZEBROWITZ-MCARTHUR, L. (1988). Person perception in cross-cultural perspective. In M. H. Bond (Ed.), *The cross-cultural challenge to social psychology,* Newbury Park, CA: Sage.

ZEIG, J. K. (Ed.). (1982). *Ericksonian approach to hypnosis and psychotherapy.* New York: Brunner/Mazel.

ZIEGLER, H., & KARTEN, H. (1974). Central trigeminal structures and the lateral hypothalamus syndrome in the rat. *Science, 186,* 636–637.

ZEINER, A. R., STANITIS, T., SPURGEON, M., & NICHOLS, N. (1985). Treatment of alcoholism and concomitant drugs of abuse. *Alcohol, 2,* 555–559.

ZELLNER, D. A., STEWART, W. F., ROZIN, P., & BROWN, J. M. (1988). Effect of temperature and expectations on liking for beverages. *Physiology and Behavior, 44,* 61–68.

ZIGMOND, M. J., & STRICKER, E. M. (1973). Recovery of feeding and drinking by rats after intraventricular 6-hydroxydopamine or lateral hypothalamic lesions. *Science, 182,* 717–719.

ZILBOORG, G., & HENRY, G. W. (1941). *A history of medical psychology.* New York: Norton.

ZILLMAN, D. (1971). Excitation transfer in communication-mediated aggressive behavior. *Journal of Experimental Social Psychology, 7,* 419–434.

ZILLMAN, D. (1979). *Hostility and aggression.* Hillsdale, NJ: Erlbaum.

ZILLMAN, D. (1983). Arousal and aggression. In R. Green & E. Donnerstein (Eds.), *Ag-

gression: Theoretical and empirical reviews.* New York: Academic.

ZILLMAN, D., JOHNSON, R. C., & DAY, K. D. (1974). Attribution of apparent arousal and proficiency of recovery from sympathetic activation affecting excitation transfer to aggressive behavior. *Journal of Experimental Social Psychology, 10,* 503–515.

ZIMBARDO, P. (1970). The human choice: Individuation, reason and order versus individuation, impulse and chaos. In W. J. Arnold & D. Levine (Eds.), *Nebraska symposium on motivation.* Lincoln, NE: University of Nebraska Press.

ZIMBARDO, P. (1971). The psychological power and pathology of imprisonment. Statement prepared for the U.S. House of Representatives Committee on the Judiciary (Subcommittee No. 3, Robert Kastemeyer, Chairman, hearings on prison reform). Unpublished paper, Stanford University.

ZIMBARDO, P., & EBBESEN, E. (1970). *Influencing attitudes and changing behavior.* Reading, MA: Addison-Wesley.

ZINBERG, N. E. (1977). The study of consciousness states: Problems and progress. In N. E. Zinberg (Ed.), *Alternate states of consciousness: Multiple perspectives on the study of consciousness.* New York: Free Press.

ZOLA-MORGAN, S., SQUIRE, L. R., & AMARAI, D. G. (1986). Human anmesia and the medial temporal region: Enduring memory impairment following a bilateral lesion limited to field CAI of the hippocampus. *Journal of Neuroscience, 6,* 2950–2967.

ZUBEK, J. P. L., BAYER, A., & SHEPARD, J. M. (1969). Relative effects of prolonged social isolation and confinement: Behavioral and EEG changes. *Journal of Abnormal Psychology, 74,* 625–631.

ZUCKER, S. H., & ALTMAN, R. (1973). An on-the-job training program for adolescent trainable retardates. *Training School Bulletin, 79,* 106–110.

ZUCKERMAN, M. (1969). Variables affecting deprivation results. In J. P. L. Zubek (Ed.), *Sensory deprivation: Fifteen years of research.* New York: Appleton-Century-Crofts.

ZUCKERMAN, M. (1986). On the meaning and implications of facial prominence. *Journal of Nonverbal Behavior, 10,* 215–229.

ZUCKERMAN, M., PERSKY, H., LINK, K., & BASU, G. (1968). Experimental and subject factors determining responses to sensory deprivation, social isolation and confinement. *Journal of Abnormal Psychology, 73,* 183–194.

ZUKIER, H. (1982). The role of the correlation and the dispersion of predictor variables in the use of nondiagnostic information. *Journal of Personality and Social Psychology, 43,* 1163–1175.

ZUKIER, H. (1989). Introduction. In S. Schachter & M. Gazzaniga (Eds.), *Extending psychological frontiers: Selected works of Leon Festinger.* New York: Russell Sage Foundation.

ZURCHER, L. (1977). *The mutable self: A self-concept for social change.* Beverly Hills, CA: Sage.

Acknowledgments

Fig. 2-10 Adapted from Carol Wald. © 1987 Discover Magazine.

Tb. 3-2 Teghtsoonian, R. (1971). On the exponent in Steven's law and the constant in Ekman's law. *Psychological Review*, *18*, 71–80. Copyright © 1971 by the American Psychological Association. Reprinted by permission of the publisher and author. **Fig 3-7** Spatially Quantized Images by Ed Manning, c/o Blocpix Images, 972 E. Broadway, Stratford, CT 06497. **Fig. 3-8** Photo © Douglas Faulker/Photo Researchers, Inc. Color chips courtesy of Scientific Publishing Co. **Fig. 3-10** Fritz Goro, Time, Inc. From *Seeing: Illusion, brain, and mind* by J. P. Frisby. Published by Oxford University Press, New York, 1980. **Figs. 2-3, 2-5, 2-6, 3-13, 3-17, 3-18** Morris, C. *Psychology: An Introduction*, 6th ed. Copyright © 1988. By permission of Prentice-Hall, Inc, Englewood Cliffs, New Jersey.

Fig. 4-1 Dr. Joseph Campos, University of Illinois. **Fig. 4-9** NASA

Fig. 5-1 Ken Lax/Medichrome **Fig. 5-3** Reproduced from *Some must watch while some must sleep* by William E. Dement, M. D., which was originally published as a volume in The Portable Stanford series of the Stanford Alumni Association. Used with permission. **Fig. 5-4** From *Biological psychology*, 3rd ed., by James W. Kalat. Copyright © 1988, 1984, 1981 by Wadsworth, Inc. Reprinted by permission of the publisher. **Fig. 5-6** Courtesy Ronald K. Siegel. **Figs. 5-7, 5-8, 5-9** *Scientific American*, 1977, *237*, No. 4, p. 134. **Fig. 5-10** Heron, W. (1961). Cognitive and psychological effects of perceptual isolation. In P. Solomon et al., (Eds.), *Sensory deprivation*. Cambridge, MA: Harvard University Press. Reprinted by permission.

Fig. 6-5 Sepp Sitz/Woodfin Camp **Fig. 6-6** Maier, S. F., Seligman, M. E. P., & Solomon, R. L. Pavlovian fear conditioning and learned helplessness. In *Punishment and aversive behavior*, B. A. Campbell & R. M. Church (Eds.), p. 321 © 1969. Adapted by permission of Prentice-Hall, Inc., Englewood Cliffs, NJ. **Fig. 6-10** Darley, J. M., Glucksberg, S., & Kinchla, R. A. (1991). *Psychology*, 5th ed., p. 192. Copyright © 1991. Used by permission of Prentice-Hall, Inc., Englewood Cliffs, NJ.

Fig. 7-5 Reed, S. K. (1988). *Cognition: Theory and application*. Reprinted by permission of John Wiley & Sons, Inc. **Fig. 7-6** Collins, A. M., & Quillian, M. R. (1969). Retrieval time from semantic memory. *Journal of Verbal Learning and Verbal Behavior*, *8*, 240–247.

Tb. 8-1 The Psychological Corporation. **Fig. 8-4** Art Resource **Fig. 8-8** (*left*) Bill Dyer/Photo Researchers; (*center*) Gail Rugin/Photo Researchers; (*right*) Robert W. Hernandez/Photo Researchers **Fig. 8-9** Copyright © 1988 by the New York Times Company; reprinted by permission **Fig. 8-10** Ford Motor Company **Figs 8-17 and 8-18** Horn, J. L., & Donaldson, G. (1980).

Cognitive development II: Adulthood development of human abilities. In O. G. Brim, Jr., and J. Kagan (Eds.), *Constancy and change in human development: A volume of review essays*. Cambridge, MA: Harvard University Press. **Fig. 8-20** Selfe, L. (1979). *Nadia*. New York: Academic Press.

Fig. 9-1 Schaie, K. W., & Strother, C. R. (1968). A cross-sequential study of age changes in cognitive behavior. *Psychological Bulletin*, *70*, 671–680. Copyright © 1968 by the American Psychological Association. Reprinted by permission. **Tb. p. 323** Reprinted with permission from the International Anesthesia Research Society from A proposal for a new method of evaluation of the newborn infant, by V. A. Apgar, *Anesthesia and Analgesia*, *32*, 260–267. **Fig. 9-2** Frankenburg, W. K., & Dodds, J. B. (1967). The Denver development screening test. *Journal of Pediatrics*, *71*, 181–191. **Fig. 9-3** Wright, H. F. (1967). *Recording and analyzing child behavior*. New York: Harper & Row.

Fig. 10-1 Tanner, J. M. (1978). *Foetus into man: Growth from conception to maturity*. Cambridge, MA: Harvard University Press. Reprinted by permission. **Tb. 10-2** Erikson, E. H. (1963). *Childhood and society*. New York: Norton. Reprinted by permission of Hogarth Press. **Fig. 10-2** Hunter, F., & Youniss, J. (1982). Changes in functions of three relationships during adolescence. *Developmental Psychology*, *18*, 806–811. Copyright 1982 by the American Psychological Association. Reprinted by permission of the publisher and author. **Fig. 10-3** Mark L. Fuerst. An STD primer, *American Health: Fitness of Body and Mind*, May 1991, p. 46. **Fig. 10-4** Olsen, K. M. (1969). Social class and age-group differences in the timing of family status changes: A study of age norms in American society. Unpublished doctoral dissertation, University of Chicago.

Pp. 381–382 Excerpts from *Alive: The story of the Andes survivors* by Paul Piers Read. Copyright © 1974 by Paul Piers Read. Reprinted by permission of HarperCollins Publishers. **Tb. 11-1** Reproduced by special permission of *Playboy* from Sexual behavior in the 1970's by Morton Hunt. Copyright © 1974 by Morton Hunt. **Fig. 11-2** Kinsey, A. C., Pomeroy, W. B., Martin, C. E., & Gebhard. P. H. (1953). *Sexual behavior in the human male*. Reprinted by permission of the Kinsey Institute for Research in Sex, Gender, and Reproduction, Inc. **Fig. 11-4** Albert Bandura.

Figs 12-1 and 12-9 Shaver, P., Schwartz, J., Kirson, D., & O'Connor, C. (1987). Emotion knowledge. *Journal of Personality and Social Psychology*, *52*, 1061. Copyright © 1987 by the American Psychological Association. Reprinted by permission of the publisher and author. **P. 437, Fig. B** Holden, C. (1975). Lie detectors: PSE gains audience despite critics' doubt. *Science*, *190*, 359–362. Copyright © 1975 by the American Association for the Advancement of Science. **Fig. 12-8** Dr. Paul Ekman, Univeristy of California.

Tb. 13-1 Mischel, W. (1986). *Introduction to personality: A new look*, 4th ed. Copyright © 1986 by

Holt, Rinehart and Winston, Inc. Reprinted by permission of the publisher. **Tb. 13-2** Summary of the characteristics of self-actualizing people from *Motivation and personality*, 2nd ed. by Abraham Maslow. Copyright 1954 by Harper & Row, Publishers, Inc. Copyright © 1970 by Abraham H. Maslow. Reprinted by permission of Harper & Row, Publishers, Inc. **Tb. 13-3** Harrington, D. M., Block, J. H., & Block, J. (1987). Testing aspects of Carl Rogers's theory of creative environments: Child-rearing antecedents of creative potential in young adolescents. *Journal of Personality and Social Psychology*, *52*, 851–856. Copyright © 1987 by the American Psychological Association. Reprinted by permission of the publisher and author. **Tb. 13-4** Rotter, J. B. (1966). Generalized expectancies for internal vs. external control of reinforcement. *Psychological Monographs*, *80* (whole No. 609). Copyright © 1966 by the American Psychological Association. Reprinted by permission of the publisher and author. **Tb. 13-5** Buss, A. H., & Finn, S. E. (1988). Model of higher order and control limits. *Journal of Personality and Social Psychology*, *54*. Copyright © 1988 by the American Psychological Association. Reprinted by permission of the publisher and author. **Tb. 13-7** O'Leary, K. Daniel, & Wilson, G. Terence, *Behavior therapy: Application and outcome*, 2nd ed., p. 27. © 1987, Reprinted by permission of Prentice-Hall, Inc., Englewood Cliffs, NJ.

Tb. 14-5 Abramson, L., Seligman, M., & Teasdale, J. (1978). Learned helplessness in humans: Critique and reformation. *Journal of Abnormal Psychology*, *87*, 49–74. Copyright © 1978 by the American Psychological Association. Reprinted by permission **Tb. 14-7** Sarason, Irwin G. & Sarason, Barbara R., (1987). *Abnormal psychology: The problem of maladaptive behavior*, 5th ed., p. 289. Reprinted by permission of Prentice-Hall, Inc., Englewood Cliffs, NJ. **Fig. 14-3** Cowley, G. (1988). *Newsweek*, April 11, 1988.

P. 586 (top) Wilmer, H. (1987). Rule of thumb: Using a couch in therapy. *In practical Jung: Nuts and bolts of Jungian psychotherapy*. Wilmette, IL: Chiron.

Tb. 16-1 Chaiken, S., & Eagly, A. (1976). Communication modality as a determinant of message persuasiveness and message comprehensibility. *Journal of Personality and Social Psychology*, *34*, 605–614. Copyright © 1976 by the American Psychological Association. Reprinted by permission of the publisher and author.

Fig. 17-1 Milgram, S., Liberty, H., Toledo, & Wachenhut, J. (1986). Response to intrusion in waiting lines. In *Journal of Personality and Social Psychology*, *51*, 686–689. Copyright © 1986 by the American Psychological Association. Adapted by permission of the publisher and author. **Tb. 17-1** Moreland, R. L., & Levine, S. M. (1982). Socialization in small groups: Temporal changes in individual-group relations. In L. Berkowitz (Ed.), *Advances in experimental social psychology*. New York: Academic Press.

Photographs

Chapter 1: xvi George Mars Cassidy/Tony Stone/Worldwide. **2** Chris Regas. **5** Peter Turnley/Black Star. **9** (*top*) UPI/Bettmann Newsphotos. **9** (*bottom*) Courtesy B.F. Skinner. **12** The Bettmann Archive. **15** Hank Morgan/Photo Researchers. **16** James Wilson/Woodfin Camp & Associates. **18** Laimute E. Druskis. **19** Mark Antman/The Image Works. **25** Ken Karp. **27** Mimi Forsyth/Monkmeyer Press. **28** Anthony Jalandoni/Monkmeyer Press. **31** Louis Fernandez/Black Star. **33** Barbara Alper/Stock, Boston.

Chapter 2: 38 Ted Horowitz/The Stock Market. **40** Diana Walker/Gamma Liaison. **51** Lester V. Bergman & Associates. **60** (*top*) CNRI/Photo Researchers. **60** (*bottom*) NIH/Photo Researchers. **63** (*left*) Sylvia Martin/Photo Researchers. **63** (*right*) UPI/Bettmann Newsphotos. **65** Tony Duffy/Allsport. **69** Richard Hutchings/Photo Researchers. **74** UPI/Bettmann Newsphotos.

Chapter 3: 80 Steve Niedorf/The Image Bank. **82** (*top*) AP/Wide World Photos. **82** (*bottom*) Wolfgang Bayer/Bruce Coleman, Inc. **83** (*top*) Courtesy Chevrolet. **83** (*bottom*) Rodale Press. **87** Bohdan Hrynewych/Southern Light. **104** Michel Legrand/Sygma. **107** (*top*) Terry G. Murphy/Animals Animals. **107** (*bottom*) Vandystadt/Allsport. **109** A.I. Parnes/Photo Researchers. **111** George and Judy Manna/Photo Researchers. **112** (*left and right*) Sensory Aids Corp. of Bensenville. **113** Sensory Aids Corp. of Bensenville. **114** Courtesy Singer Link Corp.

Chapter 4: 120 Christina Rose Mufson/Comstock. **122** (*left and right*) NASA. **125** (*top*) Barbara Kirk/The Stock Market. **125** (*bottom*) Alex Goff/Monkmeyer Press. **126** David Linton, *Scientific American.* **129** M. Elizabeth Wetmore. **130** Baron Wolman/Woodfin Camp & Associates. **131** (*left*) Louis Goldman/Photo Researchers. **131** (*right*) Guy Gillette/Photo Researchers. **133** The Bettman Archive. **134** (*top left*) Karen R. Preuss/Taurus Photos. **134** (*top center*) Beth Maynor/Photo Researchers. **134** (*top right*) Kees Van Den Berg/Photo Researchers. **134** (*bottom left and right*) Courtesy Albert Yonas, University of Michigan.

Chapter 5: 148 Howard Sochurek/The Stock Market. **150** Jack Jeffers. **152** Scala/Art Resource. **155** Courtesy Professor Ernest Hilgard, Stanford University. **157** Bruce Roberts/Photo Researchers. **162** Courtesy Stanford University. **163** Phototake. **166** Mike Mazzaschi/Stock, Boston. **169** (*top left*) Helen Marcus/Photo Researchers. **169** (*top right*) Martin Rogers/Stock, Boston. **169** (*bottom right*) Van Bucher/Photo Researchers. **170** Charles Gatewood. **175** The Bettmann Archive. **178** Arlene Collins/Monkmeyer Press.

Chapter 6: 190 Ronnie Kaufman/The Stock Market. **195** Courtesy of Professor Benjamin Harris. **204** (*left*) Breck P. Kent/Animals Animals. **204** (*right*) Stock, Boston. **206** Billy E. Barnes/Southern Light. **208** Springer/Bettmann Film Archive. **209** Zig Lesczynski/Animals Animals. **210** Teri Stratford/Photo Researchers. **215** Lilo Hess/Three Lions, Inc. **218** Agence France-Presse International Newspictures.

Chapter 7: 226 Christopher Morris/Black Star. **228** UPI/Bettmann Newsphotos. **229** Hugh Rogers/Monkmeyer Press. **230** National Library of Medicine. **237** Leonard Freed/Magnum. **238** David Woo/Stock, Boston. **242** Sandy Roessler/FPG International. **244** UPI/Bettmann Newsphotos. **246** Barbara R. Lewis/Monkmeyer Press. **250** AP/Wide World Photos. **254** Manfred Kage/

Peter Arnold, Inc. **255** (*left and right*) NINCDS/Science Source/Photo Researchers. **257** Hugh Rogers/Monkmeyer Press. **261** (*top, bottom, and right*) AP/Wide World Photos. **262** Irene Springer.

Chapter 8: 266 Joe Bator/The Stock Market. **268** (*top*) Francis Leroy, Biocosmos/Photo Researchers. **268** (*bottom*) A.C. Barrington Brown; from J.D. Watson, *The Double Helix* (New York: Atheneum, 1968), p. 215. **270** Suzanne Szasz/Photo Researchers. **275** (*top*) B.G. Murray, Jr./Animals Animals. **275** (*bottom*) Courtesy New York Stock Exchange. **279** (*left*) James D. Wilson/Woodfin Camp & Associates. **279** (*right*) Enrico Ferorelli/DOT. **295** (*top*) Courtesy of Martin Marietta Corp. **295** (*bottom*) NASA. **299** (*top and bottom*) Suzanna Szasz/Photo Researchers.

Chapter 9: 308 Jo Browne/Mick Smee/Tony Stone/Worldwide. **310** By permission of Harper & Row, Publishers Inc. **313** Joan Teasdale/Stock Market. **315** (*left*) Courtesy Gesell Institute. **315** (*right*) Wayne Behling. **316** Earl Dotter/Archive Pictures. **319** (*top left*) D.W. Fawcett/D. Phillips/Photo Researchers. **319** (*top right and middle left*) Petit Format/Nestlé/Science Source/Photo Researchers. **319** (*middle right*) Martin M. Rotker/Taurus Photos. **319** (*bottom*) Petit Format/Nestlé/Science Source/Photo Researchers. **323** Lew Merrim/Monkmeyer Press. **324** (*top left*) Mimi Forsyth/Monkmeyer Press. **324** (*top right*) Suzanne Szasz/Photo Researchers. **324** (*bottom*) George S. Zimbel/Monkmeyer Press. **327** (*left and right*) Doug Goodman/Monkmeyer Press. **329** Mimi Forsyth/Monkmeyer Press. **330** W. Zehr/Alpha/FPG. **331** Thomas McAvoy, Time-Life Picture Agency, © Time Inc. **332** Harry F. Harlow, University of Wisconsin Primate Laboratory. **334** Alan Mercer/Stock, Boston. **335** Leonore Weber/Taurus Photos. **339** Arthur Tress/Photo Researchers.

Chapter 10: 344 Erika Stone. **346** Dennis Brack/Black Star. **349** (*top*) Strix Pix/Monkmeyer Press. **349** (*bottom*) Richard Hutchings/Photo Researchers. **354** Charles Gupton/Stock, Boston. **361** Paul Conklin/Monkmeyer Press. **365** John Isaac/United Nations Photo. **366-367** Courtesy of Joyce Turner. **371** UPI/Bettmann Newsphotos. **372** M. Philippot/Sygma. **374** (*top*) Bob Daemmrich/Stock, Boston. **374** (*bottom*) Tim Davis/Photo Researchers. **378** Laima Druskis.

Chapter 11: 380 Michael K. Daly/The Stock Market. **372** Jean-Pierre Laffont/Sygma. **384** G. Planchenault/Allsport/Vandystadt. **386** Georg Gerster/Photo Researchers. **387** Richard Pasley/Stock, Boston. **389** Dr. Neal E. Miller. **390** Mimi Forsyth/Monkmeyer Press. **391** (*left*) L.L.T. Rhodes/Taurus Photos. **391** (*right*) Ethan Hoffman/Archives Pictures. **392** Robert Goldstein/Photo Researchers. **393** Jan Lukas/Photo Researchers. **394** (*top*) Jeff Jacobsen/Archive Pictures. **394** (*bottom*) Teri Stratford. **396** Susan Rosenberg/Photo Researchers. **398** Robert Gerhart/Rodale Press. **400** Stefan Meyers/Animals Animals. **404** Alex Webb/Magnum. **412** Charles Harbutt/Archive Pictures. **420** AP/Wide World Photos. **422** NASA.

Chapter 12: 428 Paul Fusco/Magnum Photos. **430** Robert Isear/Photo Researchers. **434** Walter Chandoa. **436** Bohdan Hrynewych/Southern Light. **441** (*top*) Bonnie Freer/Photo Researchers. **441** (*bottom left*) AP/Wide World Photos. **441** (*bottom right*) Richard J. Quartaert/Taurus Photos. **444** Erich Hartmann/Magnum Photos. **446** AP/Wide World Photos. **449** Blumebild/FPG International **451** Ken Karp. **453** (*left*) John Lawlor/The Stock Market. **453** (*center*) Pete Saloutos/The Stock Market. **453** (*right*) Beth Ull-

mann/Taurus Photos. **455** Historical Pictures Service. **456** Owen Franken/Stock, Boston. **459** Richard Hutchings/Photo Researchers. **461** Phil Huber/Black Star. **462** Baron Wolman/Woodfin Camp & Associates. **464** Ian Berry/Magnum Photos. **467** James Steinbert/Photo Researchers. **468** Jim Pickerell/FPG International.

Chapter 13: 474 Jim Weiner/Photo Researchers. **476** Library of Congress. **478** Mary Evans Picture Library/Sigmund Freud copyright Ltd. **483** Corroon & Co./Monkmeyer Press. **484** Brownie Harris/The Stock Market. **487** (*top*) The Bettmann Archive. **487** (*left*) Scala/Art Resource. **487** (*right*) Douglas Mazonowicz/Art Resource. **489** (*left and right*) AP/Wide World Photos. **490** J.M. Mejuto/FPG International. **495** Jeffry W. Myers/FPG International. **497** Kagan/Monkmeyer Press. **507** Culver Pictures. **510** Eric Kahan/Leo de Wys Inc. **512** Peter Steiner/The Stock Market.

Chapter 14: 520 Allen Lee Page/The Stock Market. **522** Ebet Roberts. **524** (*left*) Culver Pictures. **524** (*right*) F. Richard-Artdia/Allsport. **525** (*left*) Danielle Pellegrini/Photo Researchers. **525** (*right*) Bill Anderson/Monkmeyer Press. **527** Wide World Photos. **529** (*top*) Culver Pictures. **529** (*bottom*) Art Resource. **531** Tony O'Brien/Picture Group. **534** Whitney Museum of American Art. **537** J.P. Laffont/Sygma. **538** Photofest. **540** Culver Pictures. **543** UPI/Bettmann Newsphotos. **545** Henryk Kaiser/Leo deWys Inc. **559** Kathy Stimson. **563** Lester Glassner Collection. **564** Courtesy the Ad Council. **565** Ralph Merlino/Shooting Star. **569** A. Tannenbaum/Sygma.

Chapter 15: 574 Stacy Pick/Stock, Boston. **576** (*top*) C. Sizemore and E. Petillo, *I'm Eve* (Garden City, NY: Doubleday, 1977). **576** (*center*) Movie Star News. **578** (*top*) The American Museum of Natural History. **578** (*bottom*) The Bettmann Archive. **580** (*top*) Bob Capece/Monkmeyer Press. **580** (*bottom*) UPI/Bettmann Newsphotos. **584** Susan Rosenberg. **588** The Bettmann Archive. **589** Susan Rosenberg. **591** John Chiasson/Gamma Liaison. **592** Courtesy Dr. Joseph Wolpe. **595** David Gonzales, Camarillo State Hospital. **596** Susan McCartney/Photo Researchers. **598** Bohdan Hrynewych/Stock, Boston. **599** Ann Chwatsky/Leo deWys Inc. **601** Ann Chwatsky/Leo deWys Inc. **602** Paul Fortin/Stock, Boston. **605** Photofest. **606** Culver Pictures.

Chapter 16: 616 Gabe Palmer/The Stock Market. **618** Ken Regan/Camera 5. **620** (*top*) Archives of the History of American Psychology, University of Akron. **620** (*bottom*) Karen Zebulon; courtesy Dr. Leon Festinger. **622** Tom Abbott/Leo deWys Inc. **623** Renate Hiller/Monkmeyer Press. **625** Charles Feil/Stock, Boston. **631** Van Bucher/Photo Researchers. **633** Arlene Collins/Monkmeyer Press. **639** Rafael Macia/Photo Researchers. **640** Rhoda Sidney/Leo deWys, Inc. **643** (*left*) Deborah Feingold/Outline Press. **643** (*center*) Outline Press. **643** (*right*) Fabian/Sygma. **644** Mimi Forsyth/Monkmeyer Press. **646** Gabe Palmer/The Stock Market.

Chapter 17: 654 Bob Daemmrich/Stock, Boston. **656** Courtesy of James "Cool Papa" Bell. **659** Arlene Collins/Monkmeyer Press. **660** Patrick Ward/Stock, Boston. **662** Jan Halaska/Photo Researchers. **667** Bob Daemmrich/Stock, Boston. **674** Walker Research, Inc. **676** Ellis Herwig/Stock, Boston. **681** UPI/Bettmann Newsphotos. **682** Joseph Nettis/Photo Researchers. **684** Courtesy of Bill Yancy. **685** William Edward Smith/The Stock Market. **688** Louis Fernandez. **691** Frank Siteman/Stock, Boston.

Name Index

Birchler, B., 592
Birdwell, L., 423
Birdwhistell, R.L., 444
Birnbaum, H., 406
Birrell, P., 626
Bishop, G., 460
Black, J.B., 276
Blackman, J.A., 322–23
Blainey, P., 432
Blake, R., 99, 105
Blakely, E., 206
Blanck P., 472
Blau, P.M., 367, 646
Bleck, D., 602
Blenker, M., 365
Bless, H., 448, 636
Blethen, S.L., 66
Bleuler, E., 555
Bliss, E., 544
Block, J., 493
Block, J.H., 493, 664
Bloom, A.H., 281–82
Bloom, B.L., 464
Bloom, L.M., 272
Blough, D.S., 287
Bluen, S., 466
Blumberg, A., 604
Blutt, 515
Blyth, D., 353, 355
Bodenhausen, G., 632
Bohannon, J.N. III, 261
Bohner, G., 448
Bolanowski, S.J., 90
Boldizar, J., 413
Bolger, N., 367
Bolger, N., 459
Bonanno, G.A., 231
Bond, M.H., 629
Bonthius, D.J., 322
Booth, A., 411, 672
Booth, W., 405
Boring, E.G., 10
Borkovec, T., 593
Bornstein, M.H., 281
Borod, J.C., 56
Bossard, J., 642
Botwinick, J., 318, 371, 374
Bouchard, C., 395
Bouchard, T.J., 300
Boucher, J.D., 443–44
Boulding, K.E., 675
Bourne, L.E., 283
Boutelle, W., 254
Bowen, D., 391
Bower, 220
Bower, G.H., 238, 245, 259, 286
Bower, T., 112
Bowers, J.M., 246
Bowlby, J., 315, 332
Bowles, B., 228
Bowman, J., 585
Boyle, F.M., 329
Bozarth, J.D., 588
Bozzi, B., 363
Brackbill, Y., 331
Bradley-Johnson, S., 84
Braff, D.L., 236
Brammer, 604,
Brannon, S.E., 594
Brashler, W., 656
Brass, D.A., 48
Braunstein, M.L., 135
Bray, D.W., 366
Bray, R., 682
Brazelton, T.B., 323
Brehm, J., 387
Brehm, J.W. 635, 638, 677
Brehm, S.S., 635, 641, 677

Brennen, T., 249
Bresler, C., 439
Breslow, S., 464
Brewer, M., 687, 689, 692
Brickman, P., 452
Brickner, M.A., 686
Bridgeman, D., 692
Brier, E.G., 407
Briggs, R.M., 210
Bright, J., 249
Brill, A.B., 222
Brislin, R.W., 629
Brock, S.B., 22
Brock, T., 634
Brockner, J., 690
Brody, E.M., 365, 372
Brody, H.K.H., 174
Brody, J., 518–19
Broughton, R., 188
Broussard, D., 401
Brown, 445
Brown, B.B., 354, 661
Brown, J.E., 63
Brown, J.M., 109
Brown, L., 74
Brown, P.K., 98
Brown, R., 261, 273, 274, 375
Brown, R.W., 248–49
Browne, M., 118–19
Brownell, K.D., 395
Bruce, C., 166
Bruce, V., 249
Bruner, J.S., 124–25, 285
Brush, C., 678
Bryan, A.I., 10
Buck, R., 431, 437
Buckholtz, N.S., 174
Buckhout, R., 250, 251
Buckley, 65
Buell, P., 464
Bugelski, R., 691
Bui, Q., 300
Buie, J., 581
Bunney, W.E., Jr., 549–50
Burchinal, M., 365
Burger, W., 124, 527
Burish, T.G., 198
Burkhardt, D.A., 132
Burnham, C.A., 137
Burnham, D., 448–49
Burns, W., 466
Burnstein, S., 680
Burt, C., 299
Bushman, B.J., 685
Buss, A.H., 502
Butcher, J., 512
Butcher, J.N., 566
Butler, P., 525
Butler, R,N., 376
Buttermeyer, J., 686
Butterworth, G., 108
Byerley, W.F., 163
Byrne, D., 480, 641

Cacioppo, J.T., 448, 630, 634
Cade, R., 560
Cadoret, R.J., 549, 563
Cain, R.,336
Cain, W.S., 109
Calder, B., 419
Calkins, M.W., 10
Camara, 31
Cameron, N., 543
Cameron, P.A., 235
Campbell, F.W., 94
Campbell, J.D., 670
Campbell, S., 188
Campbell, S.S., 161

Campfield, L. A., 389
Campos, J.J., 326
Campos, J.L., 126
Candland, D.K.,110
Canero, R., 556
Canestrari, R.E., 371
Cannon, W.B., 179, 388, 397, 435, 437
Cantrell, D.P., 21
Caplan, N., 300
Carey, M.P., 198
Cariglia-Bull, T., 236
Carins, R., 386
Carli, L., 672
Carlsmith, J.M., 445, 639
Carlson, M., 94, 417
Carlson, N.R., 388, 390, 398, 401, 406
Carlson, V.R., 400
Carlsonmille, E.A., 97
Carnevale, G.J., 536, 645
Carpenter, G.C., 126
Carr, T.H., 245
Carra, J., 466
Carrington, P.I., 645
Carson, M., 91
Carson, R.C., 566
Carter, L.M., 373
Cartwright, D., 620
Carver, R.P., 6
Casper, R.C., 396
Caspi, A., 459
Castaneda, C., 154
Castillo, M., 108
Cattell, R.B., 10, 299, 502, 503
Cautela, J.R., 592
Cazden, C.B., 273
Ceci, S.J., 250
Cerella, J., 287
Cerletti, U., 578
Cerny, 515
Chaika, E., 282
Chaiken, S., 397, 636, 638
Chandler, M.J., 323
Chapin, J.W., 115
Chaplin, W., 547
Chapman, L.J., 572, 573
Chapouthier, G., 48
Charcot, J., 478
Chase, W.G., 242
Chaslow, F.I., 66
Chasuck, A., 48
Chatney, V., 314–15
Chemers, M., 675
Chen, S.C., 684–85
Cheney, D.L., 278
Cherniss, C., 361, 362, 363
Chess, S., 339
Chidester, T.R., 164
Childs, B., 300
Chiodo, J., 391
Chollar, S., 391
Chomsky, N., 273
Christensen, A.V., 204
Christensen, J.M., 136
Christensen, L., 392
Chumlea, W.C., 348
Churchill, G.A., 88
Cialdini, R.B., 455, 639, 640, 646
Cicirelli, V.G., 365
Clapton, W., 365
Clark, C.R., 48
Clark, F.I., 115
Clark, M., 245, 448
Clark, M.C., 259
Clausen, J., 363
Cleckley, H., 576
Clemmer, E.J., 184
Clews, S., 142
Clifton, R.K., 126

Jacobs, G.A., 538
Jacobs, J., 461
Jacobs, S., 376
Jacobsen, A., 132
Jacobsen, F.M., 163
Jacobson, 593
Jacobson, J.L., 333
Jacobson, L., 627
Jacobson, M.S., 66
Jagger, M.P., 617–18
James, B., 176
James, D., 320
James, R., 585, 672, 682
James, W., 8, 10, 313, 384–85, 435, 437, 442
Jameson, D., 98
Janis, I., 680–81
Janowitz, H.D., 388, 390
Jardin, A., 362
Jarnison, N., 137
Jarvik, L.F., 300
Jeffrey, D., 392, 395
Jens, K., 544
Jensen, A.R., 301
Jensen, L., 353
Jensh, R.P., 322
Jerome, E.A., 370–71
Jex, S., 464
Jobe, J.B., 198
Joffrey, R., 40
Johansson, G., 128
John, E.R., 222
Johnson, C.G., 180
Johnson, M.E., 365
Johnson, R.J., 629
Johnson, V., 401, 403
Johnson-Laird, P.N., 291
Jones, 496
Jones, 504
Jones, B., 617
Jones, E.E., 620, 622, 624
Jones, H.E., 296
Jones, M., 23
Jones, M.C., 353
Jones, R., 635
Jones, T., 197, 624, 628
Jose, P., 439
Josephs, R.A., 567
Juan, C., 186
Judd, 689
Julesz, B., 133
Jung, C., 486, 487–88
Jung, J., 30
Jussim, L., 628

Kabacy, R.E., 250
Kagan, J., 301–2, 336, 518
Kahana, B., 372
Kahana, E., 373
Kahn, S.P., 176
Kahneman, D., 292
Kaiser, 516
Kakule, A., 160
Kalat, J.W., 256, 341, 391
Kalick, S.M., 644
Kalish, R.A., 375, 376
Kallman, H.J., 235
Kamin, L.J., 217, 218, 299, 301–2
Kandel, E., 222
Kanner, L., 338
Kant, I., 311
Kanter, 357
Kantor, R.N., 6
Kaozor, T., 206
Kapaula, Z., 115
Kaplan, C.A., 215
Kaplan H.S., 554
Kaplan, M., (87), 679

Karlin, M.B., 238
Karmer, 159
Kashkin, K.B., 65
Kaslow, F.W., 599
Kasson, D.S., 562
Katz, I., 392
Katzman, R., 264, 373
Kaufman, B., 309–10
Kaufman, R.K., 309–10
Kaufman, S., 309–10
Kay, K., 112
Kay, L., 112
Kay, N., 112
Kay, P., 281
Kaye, K., 254, 322
Keane, T., 329
Kearsley, R.B., 336
Keele, S.W., 237
Keene, R., 354
Keesey, R., 390
Kehoe, J.E., 201
Keil, W., 110
Keith, J., 489
Kellam, S.G., 372
Keller, M., 546
Keller, O., 142
Kelley, H.H., 669
Kelley, K., 480
Kelley, H., 622
Kelly, E., 429–30
Kelly, J.A., 198
Kelman, H., 395, 671
Kemler-Nelson, D.G., 287
Kendler, H.H., 4
Kendler, K.S., 559
Kendrick, C., 337
Kendzierski, D., 630
Kenny, T., 551
Kenrick, D., 455
Kenrick, D.T., 645
Kent, J., 274
Kent, R., 510
Kermoian, R., 331
Kern, J.M., 608
Kernis, M., 644
Kersten, D., 132
Kesey, K., 607
Kessen, W., 281, 316
Kety, S.S., 559
Khorana, G., 74
Kiernat, J., 180
Kiesler, C.A., 580
Kiesler, S., 680
Kietzman, M.L., 88
Kilmann, P.R., 604
Kim, K., 376
Kimmel, M.S., 363
King, D., 213
King, D.W., 538
King, L.A., 538
Kingsbury, S., 582
Kinkade, R.G., 137
Kinsey, A., 402, 404, 405
Kintsch, W., 276
Kipnes, D., 110
Kirchner, 247
Kirson, D., 432, 450, 452
Kiser, L.J., 332
Kissileff, H.R., 399
Kitayama, S., 629
Kite, M.E., 363
Klatt. D.H., 141
Klatt, L.C., 141
Kleber, H.D., 65
Klein, R.E., 322
Kleinke, C., 442
Kleinman, A., 614, 615
Kleinmuntz, B., 436

Kleitman, N., 157
Kliegl, R., 610
Kline, D., 364
Kline, P., 486
Klotzky, 247
Kniveton, B.H., 31
Knox, V.J., 176
Koe, G.G., 159
Koenderink, J.J., 128
Koffka, K., 9
Kohlberg, L., 350–51, 359
Kohler, W., 9, 214–15
Kokmen, E., 371
Kolata, G., 567
Kolb, L., 174
Kolligan, J., 494
Kolodny, R., 403, 405
Konecni, V.J., 250, 412, 691
Korchin, S., 512
Kornhaber, R., 597
Kornreich, M. 609
Koslowski, B., 124–25
Kosslyn, S.M., 240–41, 283
Kosten, T.R., 169
Kotlyarov, E.V., 174
Kowalik, D.L., 545
Koziminsky, E., 276
Kraepelin, E., 525
Kraft, C., 136
Kral, K., 373
Kraly, E.S., 399
Kramer, F.M., 395
Kramer, M.B., 119
Kramer, R., 687
Krasner, L., 595
Krauft, C.C., 588
Krauss, R.M., 690
Krenz, E.W., 177
Krieger, K., 280
Krippner, S., 183
Kroger, W.S., 176, 177
Krolick, G., 336
Krozely, M., 198
Krull, 624
Ksir, C., 173
Kubler-Ross, E., 376
Kubzansky, P.E., 110
Kucharski, D., 213
Kulick, J., 261
Kunkel, E.G., 110
Kurdek, L.A., 359
Kurtines, W., 351

La Forge, J., 251
Labouvie-Vier, G., 296
LaCroix, A., 461
Ladd-Franklin, C., 10
Lagerlof, O., 97
Laing, R.D., 561
Laird, J., 439
Lamal, P.A., 194
Lamb, M.E., 333
Lambert, N.M., 340
Landfield, P.W., 254
Lane, J., 449
Langan, C., 669
Lange, C., 435
Langer, E., 468
Langer, E.J., 462
Langway, 355
Lanzetta, J.T., 442
Larkin, J.H., 290
Larsen, R.M., 516
Lash, J.P., 192, 208
Lashley, K.S., 221
Latane, B., 647, 648–49, 685–86
Laurence, J.R., 177
Lavenka, N.M., 89

Subject Index

Continuous reinforcement schedule, 205
Control, aggression and desire for, 415
Control group, 28
Conversion disorder, 541–42
Cornea, 90
Coronary-prone behavior pattern, 465–66
Corpus callosum, 52
Correlation, 27, 708–10
  product-moment, 709–10
Correlation coefficient, 709
Coughing reflex, 323
Counseling psychologists, 582
Counseling psychology, 17–18
Crack, 570
Creative thinking, 288–89
Cretinism, 67
Critical periods, 330–31
Critical value, 44
Cross-modality matching, 89
Cross-sectional research, 317–18
  intelligence and, 296
Crowds, 354
Crystallized intelligence, 297
Cues
  external, 393
  monocular, 133–35
  retrieval, 248, 248
  silent, 343
Culture fairness, I.Q. testing and, 299
Current clinical syndromes, in *DSM*, 526
Cycle, 103

Dancing reflex, 324
Dark adaptation, 94
Date rape, 406
Day care, childhood development and, 336
Daydreams, 166–67
Deafness, boilermaker's, 105
Deception, research ethics and, 32
Decibel, 105
Decision criterion, 86
Defense mechanisms, 480–82
Deindividuation, 677
Deinstitutionalization, 579
Delta waves, 157
Delusions, 556, 572–73
Demand characteristics, 26
Dementia, 373
Dendrites, 42, 47
Denial
  defense mechanism of, 481
  stage of dying, 376
Deoxyribonucleic acid (DNA), 68
Dependent variables, 28
Depolarization, 44
Depressants, 168–69, 568
Depression, 545–49
  dying and, 376
  preparatory, 376
  reactive, 376
  theories of, 546–49
    cognitive, 547
    learned helplessness, 547
    learning, 546–47
    physiological, 548
    psychoanalytic, 546
Depth of processing, memory and, 233,
    237–38, 260
Depth perception, 132–36
  of infants, 124, 134–35
Descending nerve cells, 56
Descriptive statistics, 700–703
  frequency distributions, 700–701
  measures of central tendency, 701–2
  measures of variation, 702–3
Determinism, 384
Development
  from birth to 1 year, 321, 323–26

cognitive, 326–31
continuity/discontinuity of, 312
early/later experiences and, 312
methods of studying, 315, 317–18
motor, 323–25
personality/social, 331–37
prenatal, 318–20, 322–23
study of, history/scope, 311–18
unidirectional pressures/reciprocal inter-
    actions, 312
Developmental psychology, 16
Diabetes, 67
Diagnostic and Statistical Manual of Mental
    Disorders (DSM), 406, 526
Dichotic listening, 239
Difference threshold, 84
Discrimination
  between stimuli, 201
  stimulus, 212–13
Disorders, psychological
  childhood, 338–40
  classification, 525–27
    DSM III-R axes of, 526
  psychoanalytic psychology and, 12
  See also Abnormal psychology
Displaced aggression, 412
Displacement, 481
Dissociative disorders, 542–44
  fugue, 543
  multiple personality disorder, 543–44
  psychogenic amnesia, 543
DNA, 68
  structure of, 267–68
Dominant alleles, 70
Door-in-the-face technique, 640
Dopamine, 560
Doppler shift, 107
Double approach-avoidance conflict, 463,
    464
Double bind conflict, 560
Double-blind control, 29–30
Down syndrome, 69–70, 256
Dream interpretation, 585
Dreams
  manifest/latent content of, 157, 480
  scientific study of, 157
  subjective patterns during, 159–62
Drive, 385
Drive theories of motivation, 385–86
Drug Abuse Council, 168
Drug addiction, 567–70
Drugs
  addiction to, 567–70
  antianxiety, 607–8
  antidepressant, 608
  antipsychotic, 608
  psychoactive, 167
Drug therapy, 579
Duodenum, 389
Dying, stages of adjustment to, 375–77
Dyspareunia, 554

Ear canal, 100
Eardrum, 100–101
Eating. *See* Hunger/eating
Eclectic approach to psychotherapy, 611
Ecological theory, 131
Effect, law of, 194–95
Efficacy
  expectations, 589
  feelings of, 637
  self-, belief in, 468
Effort justification, 638
Ego, 482–83
Egocentricity, 628–29
Egocentrism, childhood, 328–29

Ego ideal, 483
Egoism, 646
Elaboration Likelihood Model (ELM)
  audience, 636
  communicator, 634
  message, 635–36
Elavil, 608
Electra complex, 485
Electroconvulsive therapy (ECT), 578,
    605–6
Electromagnetic spectrum, 97
Embryo, 320
Emotions
  appraisal of situation and, 439–40
  inappropriate, 558
  influence of, 448–49
  lie detection and, 436–37
  moods and, 432
  nonverbal communication of, 443–48
  study of, history/scope, 431–34
  theories of, 434–43
    Cannon-Bard, 435–437
    James-Lange, 435
    opponent-process, 442
    Schacter-Singer, 437–39
    somatic, 440–42
Empathy, 587
  helping behavior and, 646–47
"Empty chair" exercise, 589
Enclosure, law of, 127, 128
Encoding, 238–41
  efficient, 257–59
  in long-term memory, 241
  in short-term memory, 238–41
  strategies, 500
Endocrine system, 42, 50, 64–67
  function, 66–67
  structure, 64
Endorphins, 48
Engineering psychology, 18–19
Engrams, 221
Enkaphalin, 48
Environment, development and, 311–12
Environmental psychology, 19
Episodic memory, 243
Equilibrium, 113, 114
Erectile dysfunction, 554
Eros, 482
Escape training, 203
Estrogen, 66
Estrogen, 400
Ethics
  obedience research and, 671–73
  in research, 31–34
Ethological/organismic approach to devel-
    opment, 312, 314–15
Excitement phase of sexual response, 401
Exhaustion stage, of general adaptation syn-
    drome, 456
Expectancies, 500
Experiment(s)
  field, 31
  laboratory, 31
  "looking box", 126
  memory, 230
  reaching, 124–25
  visual cliff, 124
Experimental psychology, 10–12
Experimenter bias, 29–30
Expert power, 675
External ear, 100
Externals (personality type), 498
Extinction
  of classically conditioned response, 199–
    200
  of operant behaviors, 209–11
Extrasensory perception (ESP), 183–84
Extrinsic motivation, 418, 419

Media
  attitude development and, 632
  violence and, 414–15
Median, 701
Medical model of maladaptive behavior, 529–30
Medical student syndrome, 532–33
Meditation, 178–80
Medulla, 49
Membrane potential, 43
Memory, 227–65
  aging and, 264–65
  encoding, 238–41
  experiments, 230
  forgetting and, 251–53
  improving, 256–62
  influence of emotions on, 448–49
  neurobiological basis of, 253–56
  study of, 229–33
  testing of, 231–33
  types of, 233–38
    long-term, 233, 237–38, 241, 243–46, 248–51
    sensory, 233, 234–36
    short-term, 233, 236–37
Memory Book, The (Lorayne & Lucas), 257, 262
Memory span, 242
Memory traces, 254–55
Menarche, 348
Menopause, 403–4
Menstruation, 348
Mental age, 271
Mental illness, 530
Mental images, 282–83
Mental set, 292
Mental Status Exam, 511
Mentally retarded, 298
Mescaline, 170
Message, attitude change and presentation of, 635–36
Metabolic rate, 67
Method of adjustment, 85
Method of constant stimuli, 85–86
Method of limits, 85
Midbrain, 51
Middle adulthood, 362–67
  developmental sequence in, 362–64
  family commitments in, 365
  occupational commitments in, 365–67
  periods of, 362–63
  physical changes in, 364
Middle ear, 102
Midlife transition, 362
Miltown, 607
Minnesota Multiphasic Personality Inventory (MMPI), 513
Minorities, psychology of, 20
Mnemonic systems, 259
Mode, 702
Modeling, operant conditioning and, 207
Modeling therapies, 595–97
Monocular cues, 133–35
Mood disorders, 544–53
  depression, 545–49
    suicide and, 550–53
  mania/bipolar disorders, 549–50
Moods, 432
  helping behavior and, 646–47
Moral commitments, 359
Moral development in adolescence, 349–51
Moral reasoning, 350–51
Moro reflex, 324–25
Morphemes, 276
Mother Care/Other Care (Scarr), 336
Mothers Against Drunk Driving (MADD), 564

Motion, depth perception and, 135–36
Motion parallax, 135, 136
Motivation, 383–427
  achievement, 418–22
  extrinsic, 418, 419
  increasing, operant conditioning and, 207
  intrinsic, 418, 419
  sensation-seeking, 408–9
  social, 409–17
  stimulus-seeking, 408–9
  hunger/eating, 387–97
  sexual behavior and, 399–407
  study of, history/scope, 383–87
    cognitive theories, 386–87
    drive theories, 385–86
    incentive theories, 386
    instinct theories, 384–85
  thirst, 397–99
  unconscious, 479–80
Motive(s), 384
  hierarchy of, 422–23
Motor activities, unusual, 558–59
Motor cortex, 52, 53
Motor development of infant, 323–26
Motor system, 63
Movement and Mental Imagery (Washburn), 10
Moving patterns, organization of, 128–29
Muller-Lyer illusion, 136
Multiple component theories of intelligence, 302–4
Multiple memory theory, 233
  short-term memory and, 236–37
Multiple personality disorder, 543–44
Multistable perception, 128
Mutation, 69
Mutator genes, 70
Myelin sheaths, 42, 321
Myelinization, 321
Mystical approach to maladaptive behavior, 528–29

Naps, 188–89
Narcolepsy, 163
Narcotics, 567–68
Nasal cavity, 141
National Commission on the Causes and Prevention of Violence, 415
Nativism, 311
Naturalistic observation, 26–27, 510
Nature/nurture controversy, 299–301
Near point of accommodation, 91
Near-death experiences, 184–86
Nearness, law of, 127, 128
Nearsightedness, 91–92
Needs, 385
Negative reinforcement, 202–3
Nerve(s)
  ascending/descending, 56
Nervous system
  anatomy, 49–54
    brain, 49–56
    spinal cord, 56–58
  basic units, 42–49
  central, 56
  functional subdivisions, 58–64
    autonomic nervous system, 61–62
    language control, 63–64
    limbic system, 58–61
    reticular activating system, 58
    skeletal muscle control, 62–63
  peripheral, 56
Neural impulses, 43–45
Neurobiological correlates of memory, 253–56
Neurons, 42–49
  axonal transmission and, 43–45
  synaptic transmission and, 45–49

Neuroscience, behavioral, 41–42
Neurosis, 533
Neurotransmitters, 47–49
Nicotine, 168, 569
Nielsen, A.C., 30
Night terrors, 159
Noise, research on effects of, 118–19
Nonsense syllables, memory experiments and, 230
Nonverbal communication of emotions, 443–48
  body language and, 444–45
  facial expressions and, 443–44
  fear/anxiety, 450–52
  learned vs. innate, 445–48
  love, 452–56
Nonverbal leakage, 445
Normal curve, 704–5
Normal distribution, 704
Normative social pressure, 667
Norms, 662–63
  of social responsibility, 647

Obedience, 670–71
Obesity, 392–94
  arousal and, 394
  external cues and, 393
  set-point theory and, 393
Object permanence, 327–28
Observational learning, 497
Obsession(s), 537, 539
Obsessive-compulsive disorder, 537–40, 541
Occipital lobe, 52
Occupational commitments
  in late adulthood, 374–75
  in middle adulthood, 365–67
  in young adulthood, 361–62
Oedipus complex, 484–85
Olfactory cells, 109–10
On Death and Dying (Kubler-Ross), 376
One Flew Over the Cuckoo's Nest (Kesey), 607
Operant behavior(s)
  acquisition of, 201–9
  extinction of, 209–12
Operant conditioning, 195, 201–14
  acquiring operant behaviors, 201–7
  discrimination, 212–13
  encouraging first response, 207–8
  extinction of operant behaviors, 209–11
  generalization, 212
  implications for learning, 211–12
  language development and, 273
  preparedness, 213–14
Operant conditioning therapies, 593–95
Ophthalmoscope, 91
Opponent-process theory of emotions, 98, 442
Optic nerve, 92
Oral cavity, 141
Oral stage, 483
Organ inferiorities, 488, 489
Organization
  in long-term memory, 243–45, 248
  in perception, 127–29
Organizational psychology, 658
Orgasm, 401
  inability to have, 554
Origin of Species (Darwin), 314
Orthographic rules, 275
Oscilloscope, 102
Osmometric thirst, 398
Osmoreceptors, 398
Osteoporosis, 369
Otolith structures, 114–15
Oval window, 102
Ovaries, 66, 400
Overtone frequencies, 105